INTRODUCTION TO
DIGITAL COMMUNICATION

Rodger E. Ziemer
Department of Electrical and Computer Engineering
University of Colorado at Colorado Springs

Roger L. Peterson
Motorola Labs
Schaumburg, Illinois

Prentice Hall
Upper Saddle River, New Jersey 07458
http://www.prenhall.com

Library of Congress Cataloging-in-Publication Data

Ziemer, Rodger E.
  Introduction to digital communication/Rodger E. Ziemer, Roger L. Peterson.—2nd ed.
    p. cm.
  Includes bibliographical references and index.
  ISBN 0-13-890481-5
    1. Digital communications. I. Title: Digital communication. II. Peterson Roger L. III.
  Title.
  TK5103.7.Z55 2000
  621.382—dc21

                                                                    00-036316
                                                                    CIP

Vice president and editorial director: *Marcia Horton*
Publisher: *Tom Robbins*
Associate editor: *Alice Dworkin*
Editorial assistant: *Jessica Power*
Marketing manager: *Danny Hoyt*
Production editor: *Pine Tree Composition*
Executive managing editor: *Vince O'Brien*
Managing editor: *David A. George*
Art director: *Jayne Conte*
Cover design: *Bruce Kenselaar*
Art editor: *Adam Velthaus*
Manufacturing manager: *Trudy Pisciotti*
Manufacturing buyer: *Dawn Murrin*
Assistant vice president of production and manufacturing: *David W. Riccardi*

 © 2001, 1992 by Prentice-Hall, Inc.
Upper Saddle River, New Jersey

The author and publisher of this book have used their best efforts in preparing this book. These efforts include the development, research, and testing of theories to determine their effectiveness.

Printed in the United States of America
10 9 8 7 6 5 4 3 2

ISBN 0-13-896481-5

Prentice-Hall International (UK) Limited, *London*
Prentice-Hall of Australia Pty. Limited, *Sydney*
Prentice-Hall Canada Inc., *Toronto*
Prentice-Hall Hispanoamericana, S. A., *Mexico*
Prentice-Hall of India Private Limited, *New Delhi*
Prentice-Hall of Japan, Inc., *Tokyo*
Pearson Education Asia Pte. Ltd., *Singapore*
Editora Prentice-Hall do Brasil, Lda., *Rio de Janeiro*

Contents

Contents

Preface

The philosophy of this book remains the same as that of the first edition, in particular to provide an introduction to the essentials of digital communications based on sound mathematical underpinnings and anchored in the literature of the various topics considered. After providing a treatment of the basic theory of digital modulation and coding in the first eight chapters, the three additional specialized areas of spread spectrum, cellular, and satellite communications are given one-chapter overviews. The intent is to not only provide firm foundation in the basic theory of digital communications, but to give an introduction to three areas that have provided the basis of a number of applications in recent years and show avenues of research that are currently receiving much attention. For example, spread-spectrum communications includes the subareas of code families with good correlation properties, multiuser detection, and ultra wideband communications for resolving multipath channels. Cellular radio provides a host of research areas, such as capacity optimization of multiuser communication systems and means for accommodating mixed-rate traffic. Satellite communications has enjoyed a resurgence of interest with the proposed (with one realized) low-earth orbit mobile voice communication systems, satellite navigational systems, and small aperture antenna system applications. With this philosophy, we feel that both the needs of the practicing engineer in the communications industry and the senior/beginning graduate student are met. The former is provided with a means to review or self-study a topic of importance on the job, and the latter is provided background in basic theory with an introduction to possible topics for further research.

Virtually all electrical engineering programs include a course on linear systems in the junior year, and this book is written under that assumption. However, since the content of these linear systems courses varies from program to program, an overview of linear systems is included in Chapter 2. An additional reason for providing this information is to set notation and define special signals used throughout the book.

Another assumption of the authors is that the typical student taking a course using this book will have had a junior-level course on probability. Often such courses contain additional topics from statistics and random processes. However, since coverage of these topics varies from program to program, the necessary material on random processes for this book is included in Chapter 2. For those students that may not have had a prior course on probability, our recommendation is that one be taken before a course taught using this book is taken. However, for very diligent students who may not wish to do this, or whose probability course was taken in the distant past, Appendix A of this book provides a brief overview of the necessary topics from probability. This material may be reviewed in conjunction with Chapter 1 and will not be needed until the latter part of Chapter 2, where random processes are covered.

After an introduction to the general features of digital communication systems, Chapter 1 includes an overview of channel characteristics and an introduction to link power calculations. The latter subject is returned to in Chapters 10 and 11 in conjunction with a consideration of cellular radio and satellite communication links, respectively. The introduction of this subject in Chapter 1 provides a link between performance requirements of communication systems in terms of signal-to-noise ratio at the receiver input and the requirements of transmitter power implied by the performance desired and the channel attenuation characteristics.

As already mentioned, Chapter 2 is a review of signal and system theory, analog modulation, and random processes. In addition to providing definitions of basic signals and setting notation, a very simple simulation of noise through a linear system (Butterworth digital filter) is illustrated by an example. This sets the context for simulation of a simple digital communication system illustrated by example in Chapter 3. The student is then encouraged to do his or her own simulations in several problems of Chapter 3.

In Chapter 3, the subject of digital data transmission is introduced. The receiver structure assumed is that of a linear filter followed by a threshold detector. Optimization of the receiver filter through maximization of peak signal-to-root-mean-square noise ratio at its output leads to the concept of the classic matched filter receiver. The data transmission schemes considered are binary. Although the channel is initially considered to be of infinite bandwidth, optimum systems for the strictly bandlimited case are eventually considered. Equalization methods for compensating for intersymbol interference introduced by bandlimiting in the channel are next considered. The chapter ends with a brief consideration of signal design for bandlimited channels and noise effect in pulse-code modulation systems.

The purpose of Chapter 4 is to provide a sound theoretical basis for the digital modulation systems introduced in Chapter 3, as well as to extend the results in several directions. The approach used is that of Bayes's detection couched in the language of signal space. The background noise is assumed to be additive and white, which allows the use of any orthogonal basis function set that spans the signal space, giving a very clear geometric picture of the digital signal reception process. As an extension of Chapter 3, Chapter 4 considers M-ary digital data transmission and the explicit treatment of modulation schemes suitable for practical channels. The concepts of equivalent bit error probability and bandwidth efficiency in terms of bits per second per hertz of bandwidth are introduced in order to provide a basis of comparison of M-ary systems. The chapter ends with several example design problems and a basic introduction to orthogonal frequency division multiplexing.

Building on the ideal systems covered in Chapter 4, Chapter 5 takes up several topics that can be considered degradation sources for those ideal systems. Synchronization methods at various levels (i.e., carrier, bit, and frame) are discussed, and the degradation imposed by imperfect carrier synchronization is characterized. Fading channel effects are characterized and diversity transmission for combating them is discussed. The chapter ends by discussing envelope plots, eye diagrams, and phasor plots as means to characterize communication system performance and their generation by computer simulation is illustrated.

Chapters 6 through 8 take up the subject of coding, with the elements of information theory and block coding considered in Chapter 6 and the elements of convolutional coding is considered in Chapter 7. Theoretical foundations are provided, but the major underlying objective of Chapters 6 and 7 is always one of system applications. All coding techniques considered in Chapters 6 and 7 are characterized in terms of their ability to lower the signal-to-noise ratio required to achieve a desired probability of bit error (power efficiency) and the bits per second that can be supported per hertz of bandwidth (bandwidth efficiency). Chapter 8 provides a brief treatment of another error control scheme called automatic repeat request (ARQ), which utilizes a feedback channel.

Chapter 9 contains an overview of spread-spectrum communications. The important concept of multiuser detection is considered where, when signals from multiple users are being received, the detection process takes into account their statistical characteristics and the improvement of detector performance over what could be obtained if the other-user signals were treated as noise.

Chapter 10 deals with cellular radio communications. The cellular concept is introduced along with the major degradations experienced in such systems including other-user interference and multipath fading. First- and second-generation cellular systems are discussed and provide an excellent example of a case where the move has been made from analog to digital transmission for several reasons.

Chapter 11 treats satellite communications as an example where digital communications concepts and applications have come into extensive use over the years. The concepts are illustrated with several design examples. Characteristics of several low-earth orbit satellite communication systems for mobile phone communications are summarized.

The first edition of this book has been used successfully to teach courses on digital communications to ambitious undergraduates and first-year graduate students for several years. Typically, after the introduction provided in Chapter 1 is covered, basic digital modulation theory and coding (Chapters 3–7) are covered after spending some time on signal, system, and random process review. The use of computer simulation is emphasized from the start, with the assignment at about mid-semester of a computer simulation project to be worked on throughout the semester. Weekly problem sets are assigned and graded. An in-class closed-book midterm examination is given to encourage students to become intimately familiar with basic random process, modulation and digital detection principles (usually, this occurs at the end of Chapter 3). Depending on the scope of the computer project and the initiative shown by the class, a final examination may or may not be given.

We wish to thank the many persons who have contributed either directly or indirectly to this book. These include our colleagues at various locations throughout the world. We specifically thank David Kisak of SAIC for his careful review and constructive criticism of Chapters 6 through 8, Nick Alexandru for his corrections of several examples in the first edition, Jerry Brand of Harris Corporation and John Haug of Motorola for their reading and constructive criticism of Chapter 10. The Office of Naval Research is acknowledged as indirectly supporting the writing of this book through research grants to Rodger Ziemer, as well as the National Science Foundation, which provided research and development time while he was a program officer there during the production of the second edition. We also thank the reviewers of the book for their helpful comments and suggestions, a majority of which have been incorporated. In particular, we acknowledge the input of Professor Vijay K. Jain, University of South Florida; Professor Peter Mathys, University of Colorado at Boulder; Professor Laurence B. Milstein, University of California at San Diego; Professor Peyton Z. Peebles, Jr., University of Florida; and Professor William Tranter, Virginia Tech for the first edition. And we would also like to acknowledge the input of Mohammad Maqusi, Texas Tech University, and Richard J. Kozick, Bucknell University for this second edition.

Any errors or shortcomings that remain are the responsibility of the authors.

Most importantly, we thank our wives, Sandy Ziemer and Ann Clark, for their patience during the writing of both the first and second editions of the book, and the second author thanks his daughter Diane Peterson for love and support during this project. The first author wishes to specifically mention his children, Amy and Mark Ziemer, who apparently paid more attention to his writing activities than he thought—both are now published authors themselves!

Rodger Ziemer
Roger Peterson
January 17, 2000

1

Introduction to Digital Data Transmission

1.1 INTRODUCTION

This book is concerned with the transmission of information by electrical means using *digital communication techniques.* Information may be transmitted from one point to another using either digital or analog communication systems. In a digital communication system, the information is processed so that it can be represented by a sequence of discrete messages as shown in Figure 1–1. The digital source in Figure 1–1 may be the result of sampling and quantizing an analog source such as speech, or it may represent a naturally digital source such as an electronic mail file. In either case, each message is one of a finite set containing q messages. If $q = 2$, the source is referred to as a *binary source*, and the two possible digit values are called *bits*, a contraction for *binary digits.* Note also that source outputs, whether discrete or analog, are inherently random. If they were not, there would be no need for a communication system.

For example, expanding on the case where the digital information results from an analog source, consider a sensor whose output voltage at any given time instant may assume a continuum of values. This waveform may be processed by sampling at appropriately spaced time instants, quantizing these samples, and converting each quantized sample to a binary number (i.e., an analog-to-digital converter). Each sample value is therefore represented by a sequence of 1s and 0s, and the communication system associates the message 1 with a transmitted signal $s_1(t)$ and the message 0 with a transmitted signal $s_0(t)$. During each signaling interval either the message 0 or 1 is transmitted with no other possibilities. In practice, the transmitted signals $s_0(t)$ and $s_1(t)$ may be conveyed by the following means (other representations are possible):

1. By two different amplitudes of a sinusoidal signal, say, A_0 and A_1
2. By two different phases of a sinusoidal signal, say, $\pi/2$ and $-\pi/2$ radians
3. By two different frequencies of a sinusoidal signal, say, f_0 and f_1 hertz

In an analog communication system, on the other hand, the sensor output would be used directly to modify some characteristic of the transmitted signal, such as amplitude, phase, or frequency, with the chosen parameter varying over a continuum of values.

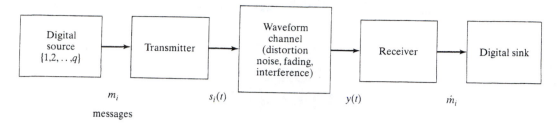

FIGURE 1-1   Simplified block diagram for a digital communication system.

Interestingly, digital transmission of information actually preceded that of analog transmission, having been used for signaling for military purposes since antiquity through the use of signal fires, semaphores, and reflected sunlight. The invention of the telegraph, a device for digital data transmission, preceded the invention of the telephone, an analog communications instrument, by more than thirty-five years.[1]

Following the invention of the telephone, it appeared that analog transmission would become the dominant form of electrical communications. Indeed, this was true for almost a century until today, when digital transmission is replacing even traditionally analog transmission areas. Several reasons may be given for the move toward digital communications:

1. In the late 1940s it was recognized that *regenerative repeaters* could be used to reconstruct the digital signal essentially *error free* at appropriately spaced intervals.[2] That is, the effects of noise and channel-induced distortions in a digital communications link can be almost completely removed, whereas a repeater in an *analog* system (i.e., an amplifier) regenerates the noise and distortion together with the signal.

2. A second advantage of digital representation of information is the flexibility inherent in the processing of digital signals.[3] That is, a digital signal can be processed independently of whether it represents a discrete data source or a digitized analog source. This means that an essentially unlimited range of signal conditioning and processing options is available to the designer. Depending on the origination and intended destination of the information being conveyed, these might include *source coding, compression, encryption, pulse shaping for spectral control, forward error correction (FEC) coding,* special modulation

---

[1]The telegraph was invented by Samuel F. B. Morse in the United States and by Sir Charles Wheatstone in Great Britain in 1837, and the first public telegram was sent in 1844. Alexander Graham Bell invented the telephone in 1876.

[2]See [1] in the references at the end of the chapter.

[3]An excellent overview of terminology, ideas, and mathematical descriptions of digital communications is provided in an article by Ristenbatt [2].

to *spread* the signal spectrum, and *equalization* to compensate for channel distortion. These terms and others will be defined and discussed throughout the book.

3. The third major reason for the increasing popularity of digital data transmission is that it can be used to exploit the cost effectiveness of digital integrated circuits. Special-purpose digital signal-processing functions have been realized as large-scale integrated circuits for several years, and more and more modem[4] functions are being implemented in ever smaller packages (e.g., the modem card in a laptop computer). The development of the microcomputer and of special-purpose programmable digital signal processors mean that data transmission systems can now be implemented as *software*.[5] This is advantageous in that a particular design is not "frozen" as hardware but can be altered or replaced with the advent of improved designs or changed requirements.

4. A fourth reason that digital transmission of information is the format of choice in a majority of applications nowadays is that information represented digitally can be treated the same regardless of its origin, as already pointed out, but more importantly easily intermixed in the process of transmission. An example is the Internet, which initially was used to convey packets or files of information or relatively short text messages. As its popularity exploded in the early 1990s and as transmission speeds dramatically increased, it was discovered that it could be used to convey traditionally analog forms of information, such as audio and video, along with the more traditional forms of packetized information.

In the remainder of this chapter, some of the systems aspects of digital communications are discussed. The simplified block diagram of a digital communications system shown in Figure 1–1 indicates that any communications system consists of a *transmitter,* a *channel* or transmission medium, and a *receiver*.[6]

To illustrate the effect of the channel on the transmitted signal, we return to the binary source case considered earlier. The two possible messages can be represented by the set {0, 1} where the 0s and 1s are called bits (for binary digit) as mentioned previously. If a 0 or a 1 is emitted from the source every T seconds, a 1 might be represented by a voltage pulse of A volts T seconds in duration and a 0 by a voltage pulse of $-A$ volts T seconds in duration. The transmitted waveform appears as shown in Figure 1–2a. Assume that noise is added to this waveform by the channel that results in the waveform of Figure 1–2b. The receiver consists of a filter to remove some of the noise followed by a sampler. The filtered output is shown in Figure 1–2c and the samples are shown in Figure 1–2d. If a sample is greater than 0, it is decided that A was sent; if it is less than 0 the decision is

---

[4]A contraction of modulator/demodulator. *See* J. Sevenhans, B. Verstraeten, and S. Taraborrelli, "Trends in Silicon Radio Large Scale Integration," IEEE Commun. Mag., Vol. 38, pp. 142–147, Jan. 2000 for progress in IC realization of radio functions.

[5]See the *IEEE Communications Magazine* special issue on software radios [3].

[6]This block diagram suggests a *single link* communications system. It is often the case that communication systems are *many-to-one, one-to-many,* or *many-to-many* in terms of transmitters (sources) and receivers (sinks).

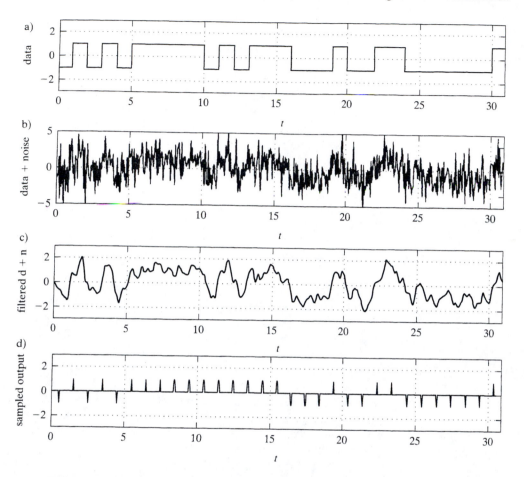

FIGURE 1–2 Typical waveforms in a simple digital communication system that uses a filter/sampler/thresholder for a detector: (a) undistorted digital signal; (b) noise plus signal; (c) filtered noisy signal; (d) hard-limited samples of filtered noisy signal—decision = 1 if sample > 0 and –1 if sample < 0. Note the errors resulting from the fairly high noise level.

that a $-A$ was sent. Because of the noise added in the channel, errors may be made in this decision process. Several are evident in Figure 1–2 upon comparing the top waveform with the samples in the bottom plot. The synchronization required to sample at the proper instant is no small problem, but will be considered to be carried out ideally in this example.

In the next section, we consider a more detailed block diagram than Figure 1–1 and explain the different operations that may be encountered in a digital communications system.

1.2   COMPONENTS OF A DIGITAL COMMUNICATIONS SYSTEM

The mechanization and performance considerations for digital communications systems will now be discussed in more detail. Figure 1–3 shows a system block diagram that is more detailed than that of Figure 1–1. The functions of all the blocks of Figure 1–3 are discussed in this section.

1.2.1   General Considerations

In most communication system designs, a general objective is to use the resources of bandwidth and transmitted power as efficiently as possible. In many applications, one of these resources is scarcer than the other, which results in the classification of most channels as either bandwidth limited or power limited. Thus we are interested in both a transmission scheme's *bandwidth efficiency,* defined as the ratio of data rate to signal bandwidth, and its *power efficiency,* characterized by the probability of making a reception error as a function of signal-to-noise ratio. We give a preliminary discussion of this power-bandwidth efficiency trade-off in Section 1.2.3. Often, secondary restrictions may be imposed in choosing a transmission method, for example, the waveform at the output of the data modulator may be required to have certain properties in order to accommodate nonlinear amplifiers such as a traveling-wave tube amplifier (TWTA).

1.2.2   Subsystems in a Typical Communication System

We now briefly consider each set of blocks in Figure 1–3, one at the transmitting end and its partner at the receiving end. Consider first the source and sink blocks. As previously discussed, the discrete information source can be the result of desiring to transmit a natu-

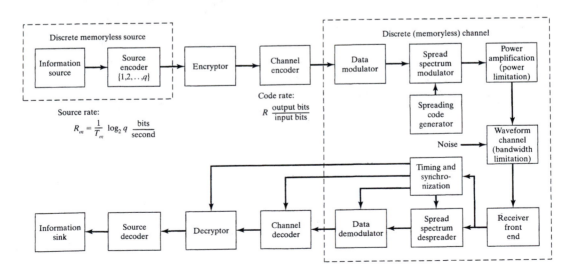

FIGURE 1–3   Block diagram of a typical digital communication system.

rally discrete alphabet of characters or the desire to transmit the output of an analog source. If the latter is the case, the analog source, assumed lowpass of bandwidth W hertz in this discussion, is sampled and each sample quantized. In order to recover the signal from its samples, according to the sampling theorem (Chapter 2), the sampling rate f_s must obey the Nyquist criterion, which is[7]

$$f_s \geq 2W \text{ samples/second} \qquad (1\text{-}1)$$

Furthermore, if each sample is quantized into q levels, then $\log_2 q$ bits are required to represent each sample value and the minimum source rate in this case is

$$R_m = (f_s)_{\min} \log_2 q = 2W \log_2 q \text{ bits/second} \qquad (1\text{-}2)$$

Consider next the source encoder and decoder blocks in Figure 1–3. Most sources possess *redundancy*, manifested by dependencies between successive symbols or by the probabilities of occurrence of these symbols not being equal, in their outputs. It is therefore possible to represent a string of symbols, each one being selected from an alphabet of q symbols, from the output of a redundant source by fewer than $\log_2 q$ bits per symbol *on the average*. Means for doing so will be discussed in Chapter 6. Thus the function of the source encoder and decoder blocks in Figure 1–3 is to remove redundancy before transmission and decode the reduced-redundancy symbols at the receiver, respectively.

It is often desirable to make the transmissions *secure* from unwanted interceptors. This is the function of the encryptor and decryptor blocks shown in Figure 1–3. This is true not only in military applications, but many civilian applications as well (consider the undesirability, for example, of a competitor learning the details of a competing bid for a construction project that is being sent to a potential customer by means of a public carrier transmission system). Although much of the literature on this subject is classified, [5] provides an excellent overview.

In many communications systems, it might not be possible to achieve the level of transmission reliability desired with the transmitter and receiver parameters available (e.g., power, bandwidth, receiver sensitivity, and modulation[8] technique). A way to improve performance in many cases is to encode the transmitted data sequence by adding redundant symbols and using this redundancy to detect and correct errors at the receiver output. This is the function of the channel encoder/decoder blocks shown in Figure 1–3. It may seem strange that redundancy is now added after removing redundancy with the source encoder. This is reasonable, however, since the channel encoder *adds controlled redundancy*, which the channel decoder makes use of to correct errors, whereas the redundancy removed by the source encoder is uncontrolled and is difficult to make use of in

---

[7]To emphasize that communication theory stands on the shoulders of many pioneers, historical references are given in this chapter from time to time; [4] is the one pertaining to Nyquist's development of sampling theory.

[8]Modulation and demodulation denote the imposing of the information-bearing signal on a carrier at the transmitter and the recovery of it at the receiver, respectively. There are several reasons for modulation, among which are ease of radiation by an antenna, the imposition of a specific band of frequencies to a given user by a regulatory body, the sharing of a common frequency resource by many users, and combatting perturbations imposed by the channel.

error correction. It is therefore difficult to use it in improving the level of system transmission reliability.[9]

The data modulator produces a continuous-time waveform suitable for transmission through the channel, while the data demodulator's function is to extract the data from the received signal, now possibly distorted and noisy. The basic idea involving data detection from a distorted, noisy received signal was illustrated by the discussion given in connection with Figure 1–2. Since it is one of the main functions of this book to characterize the performances of various digital modulation schemes, we will dispense with further discussion here.

The next set of blocks, the spread-spectrum modulator and demodulator, suggests an additional level of modulation beyond the data modulation. Spread-spectrum modulation is not always employed, but there are important reasons for doing so in some cases which will be given shortly. In spread-spectrum communication system design, bandwidth efficiency is not of primary concern (an exception to this statement is when spread spectrum is being used to provide access for multiple users to the same spectrum allocation; in this case the designer wants to accommodate as many users as possible). The term *spread spectrum* refers to any modulation scheme that produces a spectrum for the transmitted signal much wider than and *independent* of the bandwidth of the information to be transmitted. There are many schemes for doing this, and some of them will be discussed in Chapter 9. Why would such a scheme be employed? Among the reasons for doing so are

1. To provide some degree of resistance to interference and jamming (i.e., intentional disruption of communications by an enemy) [referred to as *jam resistance (JR)*].
2. To provide a means for masking the transmitted signal in background noise in order to lower the probability of intercept by an adversary [referred to as *low probability of intercept (LPI)*].[10] It is important to point out that JR and LPI are not achieved simultaneously, for the former implies that one uses the maximum transmitted power available, whereas the latter implies that the power level is *just sufficient* to carry out the communication.
3. To provide resistance to signal interference from multiple transmission paths [commonly referred to as *multipath*].
4. To permit the access of a common communication channel by more than one user [referred to as *multiple access*].
5. To provide a means for measuring range or distance between two points.

---

[9]Both source and channel encoding are important and comprehensive subject areas with considerable research being done in both. We consider channel coding in Chapters 6 and 7. Source coding is particularly germane to vocoder design, a device that is essential in second and third generation cellular systems. References [6] and [7] provide comprehensive treatments of the subject.

[10]Two levels of security are used in secure communications: (1) *transec* refers to *transmission security* and is the type provided by spread spectrum; (2) *comsec* stands for *communications security* and is the type provided by encripting the message before transmission.

Final operations, such as power amplification and filtering to restrict the spectrum of the transmitted signal, are performed before transmission in many communications systems. Likewise, there are several preliminary operations performed in any receiver, such as amplification, mixing, and filtering. The power amplification and receiver front-end blocks shown in Figure 1–3 incorporate these functions.

The channel can be of many different types. Possibilities include twisted wire pairs, waveguides, free space, optical fiber, and so on. Further discussion of some of these will be given shortly.

1.2.3   Capacity of a Communications Link

It is useful at this point to explore briefly the concept of the *capacity* of a digital communication link. Suppose that the communications system designer is asked to design a digital communication link that transmits no more than P watts and such that the majority of the transmitted power is contained in a bandwidth W. Assume that the only effect of the channel is to add thermal noise (see Appendix B for a short discussion about thermal noise) to the transmitted signal and that the bandwidth of this noise is very wide relative to the signal bandwidth, W. The statistics of this noise are assumed Gaussian; the channel is called the *additive white Gaussian noise (AWGN)* channel. Given these constraints, there exists a maximum rate at which information can be transmitted over the link with arbitrarily high reliability. This rate is called the *error-free capacity* of a communication system. The pioneering work of Claude Shannon [8] in the late 1940s proves that signaling schemes exist such that error-free transmission can be achieved at any rate lower than capacity. Shannon showed that the normalized error-free capacity is given by

$$\frac{C}{W} = \log_2\left(1 + \frac{P}{N_0 W}\right) = \log_2\left(1 + \frac{E_b}{N_0}\frac{R}{W}\right) \text{ bits} \tag{1–3}$$

where

C = channel capacity, bits/s

W = transmission bandwidth, hertz

P = $E_b R$ = signal power, watts

N_0 = single-sided noise power spectral density, watts/hertz

E_b = energy per bit of the received signal, joules

R = data rate in bits/s (not to be confused with the *code rate* to be defined in Chapter 6)

More will be said later about these parameters. For now, an intuitive understanding will be sufficient. For example, the capacity, C, is the maximum rate at which *information* can be put through the channel with arbitrarily high reliability if the source is suitably matched to the channel. Its full significance requires a definition of information content of a message and how the source is to be matched to the channel; both of these topics are addressed in Chapter 6. The rate of information transfer may be conveniently expressed in bits per second (bits/s), which is the number of binary symbols that must be transmitted per second to represent a digital data sequence or to represent an analog signal with a given fidelity. These units are discussed further in Chapter 6.

An ideal communication system can be defined as one in which data is transmitted at the maximum rate $R = C$ bits/s. Thus, setting $R = C$ on the right-hand side of (1–3), we have for the ideal system that

$$\frac{C}{W} = \log_2 \left[1 + \frac{E_b}{N_0} \left(\frac{C}{W} \right) \right] \tag{1–4}$$

Solving for E_b/N_0, we obtain an explicit relation between E_b/N_0 and $C/W = R/W$:

$$\frac{E_b}{N_0} = \frac{2^{C/W} - 1}{C/W} \tag{1–5}$$

The graph of this equation is shown in Figure 1–4.

If the information rate, R, at the channel input is less than C, Shannon proved that it is theoretically possible through coding to achieve error-free transmission through the

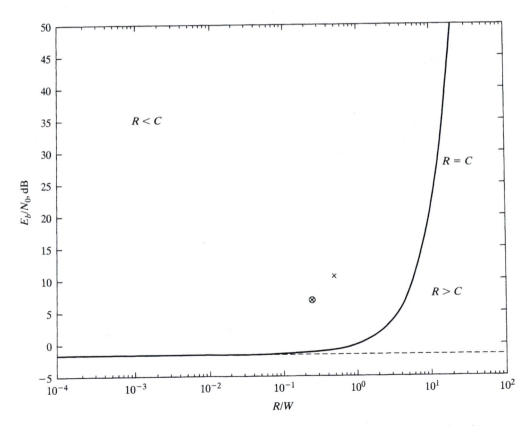

FIGURE 1–4 Power-bandwidth tradeoff for error-free transmission through noisy, bandwidth-limited channels.

channel. This result, sometimes referred to as *Shannon's second theorem,* does not provide a constructive means for finding codes that will achieve error-free transmission, but does provide a yardstick by which the performance of practical communication schemes may be measured. At points below and to the right of the curve shown in Figure 1–4, no amount of coding or complexity will achieve totally reliable transmission. At points above and to the left of the curve, error-free transmission is possible, although perhaps at a very high price in terms of bandwidth, complexity, or transmission delay. Note that data transmission is possible at all points in the plane of Figure 1–4, but some errors are unavoidable at rates above capacity.

This plot can be separated into a *bandwidth-limited region,* where $R/W > 1$, and a *power-limited region,* where $R/W < 1$. That is, if the number of bits/s/Hz is greater than unity, the scheme is efficient in terms of utilizing bandwidth. If the number of bits/s/Hz is less than unity, the scheme is efficient in terms of power utilization. For power limited operation, an interesting behavior is noted: As $R/W \to 0$ (i.e., infinite bandwidth) the limiting signal-to-noise ratio, E_b/N_0, approaches ln(2) or about −1.6 dB.[11] At any E_b/N_0 greater than −1.6 dB zero probability of making a transmission error is possible at the expense of infinite transmission bandwidth. Even more important to note, however, is that this is simply one point on the graph; *for any given rate-to-bandwidth ratio,* a *signal-to-noise ratio exists above which error-free transmission is possible and below which it is not.* Quite often, practical communication schemes are compared with this ideal by choosing some suitable probability of error, say, 10^{-6}, and finding the signal-to-noise ratio necessary to achieve it. This signal-to-noise ratio is then plotted versus R/W for the system, where W is found according to some suitable definition of bandwidth. Example 1–1 illustrates the concepts just presented.

EXAMPLE 1–1 _____

A certain binary digital communications system can achieve an error probability of $P_E = 10^{-6}$ at an E_b/N_0 of 10.6 dB (power efficiency). Its rate-to-bandwidth ratio is approximately $R/W = 1/2$ bits/s/Hz (bandwidth efficiency).

(a) Assuming that $P_E = 10^{-6}$ can be viewed as error free, locate the operating point of this system on the plot of Figure 1–4.

(b) Error correction coding is now imposed on the system of part (a). For the coding scheme used, two encoded bits are sent for each source bit. The coding scheme reduces the required E_b/N_0 to achieve $P_E = 10^{-6}$ by 3.6 dB over the uncoded system. Locate the operating point for the coded scheme on Figure 1–4.

(c) Is transmission operation in the bandwidth-limited or power-limited regime?

Solution: (a) The point $E_b/N_0 = 10.6$ dB and $R/W = 1/2$ bits/s/Hz is shown as the × in Figure 1–4.

---

[11]As discussed in Section 1.4.1, a decibel (dB) is 10 times the logarithm to the base 10 of a power ratio. Although E_b/N_0 is the ratio of energy to power per hertz of bandwidth, it is dimensionally equivalent to a ratio of powers.

   (b)   For this part, we may subtract 3.6 dB from the value of E_b/N_0 used in part (a) to give
             7 dB. However, because of the two encoded bits for each source bit, we now have
             $R/W = 1/4$ bits/s/Hz (the rate at which *information bits* are sent through the channel is
             kept constant). This point is shown as the $\otimes$ in Figure 1–4.

   (c)   Both schemes operate in the power-limited region. Note that plenty of room is left for
             improvement in either case.

1.3   COMMUNICATIONS CHANNEL MODELING

1.3.1   Introduction

The *channel* is defined as a single path for transmitting signals either in one direction only
or in both directions. If a single direction only, the channel is called half duplex; if transmission can take place simultaneously in both directions, it is referred to as full duplex.
The physical means by which the transmission is effected could make use of electromagnetic energy or acoustical energy, for example. If electromagnetic, the type of transmission could be further categorized as taking place in what is normally referred to as the
radio spectrum (300 to 3×10^{11} Hz) or in the infrared, visible, or ultraviolet regions. Furthermore, the type of propagation can be guided or free space. Table 1–1 gives a listing of
various electromagnetic spectrum bands along with typical applications.
    With all these possibilities, it is difficult to say anything of a generally applicable
nature that applies to all modes of transmission. Indeed, the mode of transmission employed determines, to a large degree, the perturbations that the transmitted signal experiences in passing through the channel.

1.3.2   Specific Examples of Communication Channels

   1.3.2.1 Propagation Channels [9].   Perhaps the type of channel that comes to
mind first when discussing communication systems is what will be referred to as the
propagation channel. It is worthwhile to point out a few characteristics and current uses.
Noise in propagation channels varies in nature and intensity with frequency. At low
frequencies, the normal thermal noise of the electronic devices used in the
communication subsystems is enhanced by environmental and human-made noise
intercepted by the antenna, such as atmospheric noise, or spherics, from lightning
discharges, power line corona, and commutator noise [10]. At higher frequencies,
depending on the gain characteristics and pointing of the antenna, the communication
subsystem thermal noise is often accompanied by galactic noise from our solar system
and others. In addition, rain will enhance the noisiness of a communication system
through the scattering of the electromagnetic waves from the raindrops, particularly at
very high frequencies, where rain greatly attenuates the propagating signal as well.
    Radio systems have found a myriad of applications over the 100-plus years that
they have been in existence. Three relatively recent application areas are mentioned here.
The most obvious one is perhaps that of *cellular mobile radio,* or its more inclusive and

TABLE 1–1 Frequency Bands and Communications Applications

Frequency	Wavelength	Band Designation	Typical Applications
3–30 Hz	10^4–10^5 km	ELF	Survivable communications (military)
30–300 Hz	10^3–10^4 km	SLF	Survivable communications (military)
300–3000 Hz	10^2–10^3 km	ULF	Survivable communications (military)
3–30 kHz	10–100 km	VLF	Survivable communications (military) Sonar (acoustic) Omega navigation (10–14 kHz)
30–300 kHz	1–10 km	LF	Loran C navigation (100 kHz) Amateur radio
300–3000 kHz	0.1–1 km	MF	Commercial AM radio (0.54 – 1.6 MHz)
3–30 MHz	10–100 m	HF	Commercial communications Over-the-horizon radar Citizens band radio Amateur radio
30–300 MHz	1–10 m	VHF	Citizens band radio Television (54–88 MHz, Ch. 2–6; 174–216 MHz, Ch. 7–13) Commercial FM (88–108 MHz) Navigational aids: VOR/ILS Military radio: SINCGARS; HAVE QUICK Phased-array radars Air-ground communications
300–3000 MHz	0.1–1 m	UHF	Air-ground communications Television (420–890 MHz, Ch. 14–83) Navigational aids Cellular radio Tactical air surveillance and control Global positioning systems IFF/TACAN/JTIDS Common carrier microwave
3–30 GHz	1–10 cm	SHF	Common carrier microwave Radio navigation Satellite television Precision approach radar Advanced Communication Technology Satellite Airborne fire control and navigation radar
30–300 GHz	0.1–1 cm	EHF	Millimeter wave seeker/sensor Navy auto carrier landing Artillery location radar Strategic satellite communications
300 GHz–3 THz	0.1–1 mm		Experimental
	7–3 μm	Mid IR	Far infrared at upper end
	3–0.7 μm	Near IR	Laser communications
	0.7–0.4 μm	Visible light	Laser communications
	0.4–0.1 μm	Ultraviolet	

Key: E = extremely; S = super; U = ultra; V = very; L = low; M = medium; H = high; μm = micron = 10^{-6} meters; k = kilo = $\times 10^3$; M = mega = $\times 10^6$; G = giga = $\times 10^9$; T = tera = $\times 10^{12}$.

more recent cousin, *personal communications systems*. Such systems are the topic of Chapter 10.

A by now familiar type of propagation channel is the satellite communications channel. Satellite communications is the subject of Chapter 11. In the mid-1970s, it was thought that all of the exciting applications of communication satellites had been thought of and, hence, further research on satellite communications was unnecessary. This was thought to be even more the case once optical fibers had been extensively laid under the oceans, since the major commercial application of satellite communication systems up to that time had been for long-haul communications. With the installation of the very wide-band and low-cost (relative to satellite systems) optical fibers, therefore, it was argued that the need for long-haul satellite communications was essentially dead, except for a few remote and/or low population regions of the earth. However, with the advent of cellular mobile radio systems, it was thought by many research groups that the next logical development in the quest for communications anywhere, anytime should be *satellite mobile personal communications systems*. Several industrial concerns are actively developing these systems, which involve constellations of several satellites (a few tens to hundreds) in low- or medium-earth orbits capable of relaying conversations (and later perhaps video and data) between two arbitrary points on the earth's surface using hand-held devices (i.e., telephones, computers, personal digital assistants or PDAs, etc.). The exact means for accomplishing this vary widely depending on the system being developed. For example, some depend on the use of the terrestrial telephone system and some do not.

Yet another relatively recent development in satellite communications is that of very small aperture earth terminals. These are characterized by the small dishes mounted on the sides of dwellings for television delivery. The advantages of this development for television access are economy (after the initial investment), much greater programming variety, and not having to put up with unsightly large dishes as in the past. Also appearing on the horizon are satellite systems for providing Internet connections for hard-to-access locations.

1.3.2.2 Land Line [11, 12].   Following the propagation channel the most obvious communication medium, perhaps, is land line. The most geographically pervasive example of this is the telephone system. A few years ago, we could have referred to it as wire line, but more and more of the telephone plant is being replaced by optical fibers, which have tremendously more bandwidth than the original wire-line form of this system. While the original form of the telephone system used analog transmission, the move now is to digital transmission for reasons already cited. The installation of more fiber communication paths means that a broader range of services is available, with perhaps the most obvious of these being the Internet. While fiber was not a requisite for development of the Internet, it is definitely more supportive of its wide geographical dispersion and the range of media becoming available over it.

Another example of a land line system, not quite so geographically pervasive as the telephone system, is cable television. The coaxial cable has wider bandwidth than the wireline twisted pair telephone system. The cable was originally intended as a single direction (simplex) connection although future developments may make much of the plant two-way (duplex) to give two-way wideband connections to homes and businesses. Cable television networks have a tree structure. When modified so that signals can be sent in the reverse direction (down the tree, so to speak), it is found that the medium is much noisier because every branch on the tree acts as a noise sensor and funnels noise back to the cable plant (toward the tree trunk). This noise ingress can be controlled by careful plant maintenance to make sure sources for it (bad connections and openings in the cable) are minimized. As with the telephone plant, more and more television cable is being replaced by fiber, although the connections between the backbone and home or business are typically coaxial cable.

1.3.2.3 Compact Disc (CD) Channels [13]. As one final example, we summarize the characteristics of a medium that perhaps, at first, one would not consider a communications medium at all. Yet, no one can deny that the CD, and its derivative, the compact disc-read only memory, or CD-ROM, have taken a leading position in storage and reproduction of software and data as well as delivery of audio and video works for entertainment. The CD was developed in the 1970s by Sony of Japan and Phillips of the Netherlands. The information is stored digitally on the disc material by etching a series of pits along a spiral path (the region between two adjacent pits is called a land) and reading from the disc by illumination with a laser beam. In read-write CDs, the recording process is accomplished by means of moderate laser beam illumination, called *write power*, that provides sufficient heat to allow modification of a layer on the disc such that, when the illuminated spot cools, crystals are formed. When illuminated again with a stronger beam at *erase power*, the material forms an amorphous layer and is then ready to be rerecorded. Reading the data on the disc is accomplished with a laser beam illumination that is weaker than either the write or read powers.[12]

For the communications engineer, the truly amazing accomplishment in development of the CD for information storage is not in the recording/playback process, however. Rather, it is in the coding and decoding done to provide for the reliable reading of data from the disc. The recording process utilizes a process called *eight-to-fourteen modulation,* which takes 8-bit bytes (a byte is eight bits) and converts them to 14-bit blocks for recording in such a manner that there are no 1s in succession. This allows a closer packing of bits in the recording process, wherein 1s are represented by the transition from a land to a pit and vice versa; 0s are then represented by the distances between intensity changes of the radiation detected when the disc is illuminated by the laser beam. The bits recorded on the disc are the code symbols of a two-step encoding process interposed between the data (or sampled audio or video) and the recording process, or between the reading process and the final data destination. Both encoding steps utilize Reed-Solomon block codes (to be considered in Chapter 6). The reason for two encoders (only one could be used with correction capabilities equivalent to the two separate ones) is to allow encoding of symbols *along and across* the recording paths, with scrambling of symbols between these two

---

[12]Older "Write Once Read Many" recording media employed a magnetic layer whose direction of magnetization could be modified once heated by a laser beam.

steps. The net result of this record/playback encoding process is an extremely high toler-ance for errors that may be caused by imperfections in the recording medium, either through the manufacturing process or by accident, such a scratches or smudges on the medium. It is rather ironic that the development of the CD provided the most widespread application (in terms of users and units sold) of coding pioneered by Claude Shannon [14], although this was not at all clear when the CD first appeared on the market.

1.3.3 Approaches to Communication Channel Modeling

In a digital communication system, the channel can be modeled using one of two ap-proaches, which will be referred to as (1) the *discrete channel approach* and (2) the *con-tinuous waveform representation*. In this section, we concentrate on the second approach. The first approach will be dealt with in more detail in Chapter 6.

1.3.3.1 Discrete Channel Approach. In the discrete memoryless model of a channel, attention is focused on discrete input symbols and discrete output symbols and the set of conditional probabilities relating them.[13] The channel is memoryless if successive channel uses are independent. In this example, we assume binary input and output symbol sets. The probability relationship between these two sets can be expressed by the matrix equation

$$\begin{bmatrix} P(Y = 0) \\ P(Y = 1) \end{bmatrix} = \begin{bmatrix} P(Y = 0 \,|\, X = 0) & P(Y = 0 \,|\, X = 1) \\ P(Y = 1 \,|\, X = 0) & P(Y = 1 \,|\, X = 1) \end{bmatrix} \begin{bmatrix} P(X = 0) \\ P(X = 1) \end{bmatrix} \tag{1-6}$$

where Y is a binary-valued random variable referring to the output and X is a binary-valued random variable referring to the input. The probabilities on the left-hand side of (1-6) are called output probabilities, the ones in the square matrix are called *transition probabilities*, and the ones in the column matrix on the right-hand side are called input probabilities. Written out, the matrix equation (1-6) is equivalent to

$$\begin{aligned} \beta_1 &= p_{11}\alpha_1 + p_{12}\alpha_2 \\ \beta_2 &= p_{21}\alpha_1 + p_{22}\alpha_2 \end{aligned} \tag{1-7}$$

where

$$\begin{aligned} \beta_1 &= P(Y = 0) = 1 - \beta_2 = 1 - P(Y = 1) \\ \alpha_1 &= P(X = 0) = 1 - \alpha_2 = 1 - P(X = 1) \\ p_{11} &= P(Y = 0 \,|\, X = 0) \\ p_{12} &= P(Y = 0 \,|\, X = 1) \\ p_{21} &= P(Y = 1 \,|\, X = 0) = 1 - p_{11} \\ p_{22} &= P(Y = 1 \,|\, X = 1) = 1 - p_{12} \end{aligned}$$

---

[13] A model that includes memory could involve probabilities for the source symbols that are conditioned on one or more previous symbols or channel transition probabilities that are conditioned on previously transmitted sym-bols or both.

The last four probabilities are known as *channel transition probabilities* and can be found by knowing the channel characteristics and the receiver structure.

EXAMPLE 1–2

In this example, suppose $\alpha_1 = 0.6$ and $\alpha_2 = 0.4$. Also, let $p_{11} = p_{22} = 0.9$ and $p_{12} = p_{21} = 0.1$. A channel with equal crossover probabilities, p_{12} and p_{21}, is known as a binary symmetric channel (BSC).

(a) Find the probabilities, β_1 and β_2, of a 0 and a 1, respectively, at the output of the channel.

(b) Given that a 0 was received, what is the probability that this resulted from a 0 being sent?

Solution: **(a)** From (1–7),

$$\beta_1 = (0.9)(0.6) + (0.1)(0.4) = 0.58$$

$$\beta_2 = (0.1)(0.6) + (0.9)(0.4) = 0.42$$

(b) Using Bayes' rule (see Appendix A),

$$P(X = 0 \mid Y = 0) = \frac{P(Y = 0 \mid X = 0)\, P(X = 0)}{P(Y = 0)}$$

$$= \frac{(0.9)\,(0.6)}{0.58} = 0.93$$

where $P(Y = 0) = 0.58$ was obtained from part (a).

1.3.3.2 Waveform Description of Communication Channels. The block diagram for a simplified description of a channel at the waveform level is shown in Figure 1–5. Although not all possible perturbations on the input signal are shown, several

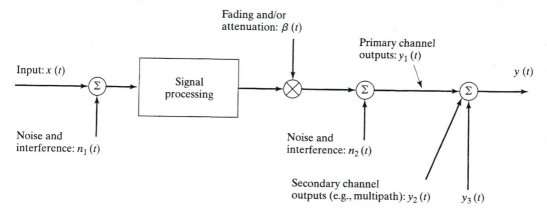

FIGURE 1–5   Channel model at the waveform level showing various perturbations.

representative ones are shown in order to discuss typical conditions that may prevail. The block diagram of Figure 1–5 is suggestive of a propagation channel, although it might be applicable to other types of channels as well.

1.3.4   Interference and Distortion in Communication Channels

There are several types of signal interferences and distortions that may arise in practical channels, as illustrated in Figure 1–5. These are enumerated here for convenience in later discussions.

1. Additive noise, which usually denotes a random waveform due to the chaotic motion of charge carriers.
2. Interference, typically denoting random waveforms due to other communication sources or human-made noise such as power line corona discharge at the channel input.
3. Deterministic signal processing, which may include linear filtering, frequency translation, and so on.
4. Multiplication by an attenuation factor, $\beta(t)$, which may be a function of time that is independent of the signal (often referred to as fading).
5. Additive noise or interference at the channel output.
6. Addition of other channel outputs that are secondary in nature (examples are multipath signals and signals from other sources that may or may not be intentional).

Note that all the perturbations shown in Figure 1–5 result in a *linear* channel as far as the input signal is concerned. That is, noise and interference terms are additive or, if multiplicative, are independent of the signal. Furthermore, the signal processing is assumed to be a linear operation.[14] Although channels that introduce nonlinear perturbations on the transmitted signal are important, the analysis of the effect of such perturbations is difficult, and many practical channels may be modeled as linear. Consequently, linear channel models are focused on in this book. Two specific types of channels will now be discussed to illustrate the applications of the general model shown in Figure 1–5.

EXAMPLE 1–3

As a first example of the application of the channel model shown in Figure 1–5, consider the block diagram of Figure 1–6, which illustrates a satellite relay link. Transmission up to the satellite is effected by a carrier of frequency f_1, and the noise $n_1(t)$ represents noise added in this portion of the transmission, which is usually due primarily to the input stages of the satellite retransmission system. The function of the satellite retransmission, or relay, is to amplify the received signal and translate it in frequency to a new spectral location suitable for

---

[14]A system is linear if superposition holds; i.e., if x_1 and x_2 are inputs to a system, denoted as $\mathcal{H}(\cdot)$, producing the outputs $y_1 = \mathcal{H}(x_1)$ and $y_2 = \mathcal{H}(x_2)$, superposition holds if the input $\alpha_1 x_1 + \alpha_2 x_2$ produces the output $y = \mathcal{H}(a_1 x_1 + a_2 x_2) = a_1 y_1 + a_2 y_2$.

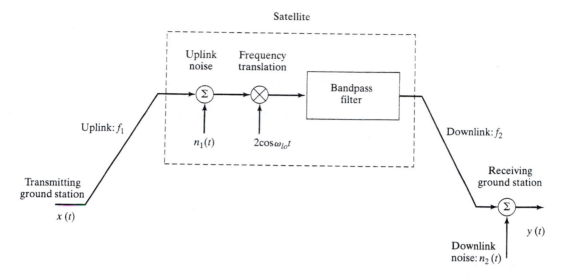

FIGURE 1–6 Model for a satellite communications link.

transmission to the destination earth station. Noise is also added in the downlink of the transmission system and is represented as $n_2(t)$. Other channel perturbations could be included, such as interference due to adjacent channels and/or signals from adjacent satellites in the same orbit. To illustrate the function of the multiplication by $2\cos\omega_{lo}t$, where the subscript *lo* stands for local oscillator, assume that the input is $x(t) = m(t)\cos 2\pi f_1 t = m(t)\cos\omega_1 t$, where $m(t)$ is a slowly varying modulating signal, then, ignoring the noise for now, the input to the bandpass filter onboard the satellite is

$$z(t) = 2m(t)\cos\omega_{lo}t\cos\omega_1 t = m(t)\cos(\omega_1 - \omega_{lo})t + m(t)\cos(\omega_1 + \omega_{lo})t$$

Depending on whether $f_2 > f_1$ or $f_2 < f_1$ is desired, the bandpass filter is centered in frequency to pass the first term or the last term. Usually, for reasons to be discussed in Chapter 11, the downlink frequency is chosen to be lower than the uplink frequency so that the downlink signal without noise is $y(t) = m(t)\cos(\omega_1 - \omega_{lo})t$; i.e., $f_2 = (\omega_1 - \omega_{lo})/2\pi$.

The additive noise and interference mentioned in Example 1–3 can fall into two possible categories: externally generated noise and noise generated internally to the communication system. Examples of the former include solar and galactic noise due to electromagnetic wave emissions from stars, including our sun, and other heavenly bodies; atmospheric noise that results primarily from electromagnetic waves generated by natural electrical discharges within the atmosphere; and human-made noise such as corona discharge from power lines. The modeling of this noise is, in general, difficult and imprecise due to its highly variable nature.

Internally generated noise is due primarily to the random motion and random production and annihilation of charge carriers within electrical components making up a

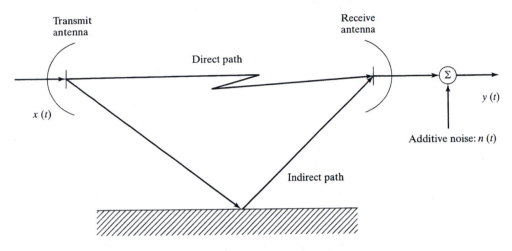

FIGURE 1–7   Model for a line-of-sight microwave relay link.

communication system. There are several treatises on the physical description and characterization of such noise (see, e.g., [10]). A short summary of its statistical description in terms of noise figure and noise temperature is given in Appendix B.

EXAMPLE 1–4

Figure 1–7 illustrates a suitable model for certain types of terrestrial microwave communications links. In addition to additive noise, which is represented by $n(t)$ in the figure, an indirect transmission path, commonly referred to as *multipath*, exists. Thus the equation relating channel input to output is

$$y(t) = a_1 x(t - T_1) + a_2 x(t - T_2) + n(t) \tag{1–8}$$

where a_1 and a_2 are constants referred to as the attenuations of the direct and indirect transmission paths, respectively, and T_1 and T_2 are their respective delays. This channel model is an extremely simple one and yet, by virtue of the multipath term, results in two signal perturbations, known as *intersymbol interference (ISI)* and *fading*, either one of which can introduce severe performance degradations.

To illustrate the idea of ISI, consider Figure 1–8, which illustrates received binary data signals from the direct and indirect paths after demodulation. The differential delay $\tau = T_1 - T_2$ is assumed to be less than one bit period although it could be several bit periods in duration. Actually, it would be impossible to observe these separate signals because they are received together at the antenna.[15] However, they are shown separately to illustrate that some bits destructively interfere and others reinforce each other. Unfortunately, those that destructively interfere dominate the probability of error (the average of 10^{-5}, which is a typical bit

---

[15]The addition of direct and multipath signals takes place at radio frequency but is shown here at baseband for simplicity.

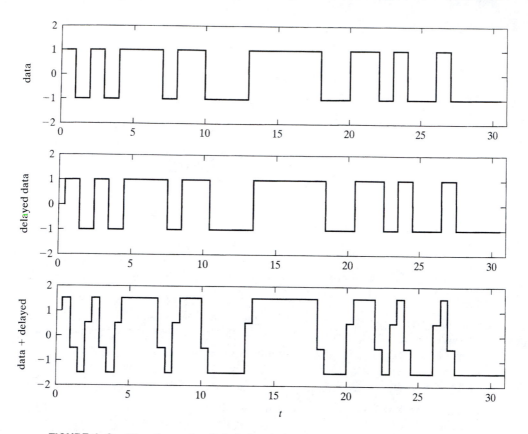

FIGURE 1–8 Waveforms for digital signal showing the effect of intersymbol interference. The undelayed bit stream is shown in the top figure and the delayed bit stream is shown in the middle figure. The delay, τ, is one-half bit. The received waveform (bottom figure) is the sum of the undelayed and one-half of the delayed bit stream.

error probability for a reinforcing situation, and of 10^{-2}, which might be typical for an interfering case, is very nearly 10^{-2}).

The phenomenon of fading is similar to that of ISI except that the destructive and constructive interference takes place with the high-frequency carrier. To illustrate the phenomenon of fading, consider a pure cosinusoidal input to the channel, which is representative of an unmodulated carrier. The output of the channel, ignoring the noise term, is

$$y(t) = A[a_1 \cos 2\pi f_0 t + a_2 \cos 2\pi f_0 (t - \tau)] \qquad (1\text{–}9)$$

where the amplitude A is the amplitude of the input and where, for convenience, the time reference has been chosen such that the delay of the direct component is 0. Using suitable trigonometric identities, (1–9) can be put into the form

$$y(t) = AB(\tau) \cos[2\pi f_0 t + \theta(\tau)] \qquad (1\text{--}10)$$

where

$$B(f_0; \tau) = \sqrt{a_1^2 + 2a_1 a_2 \cos 2\pi f_0 \tau + a_2^2} \qquad (1\text{--}11)$$

and

$$\theta(f_0; \tau) = -\tan^{-1} \left(\frac{a_2 \sin 2\pi f_0 \tau}{a_1 + a_2 \cos 2\pi f_0 \tau} \right) \qquad (1\text{--}12)$$

Equation (1–11) shows that as the differential delay τ changes by an integer multiple of a half-carrier period, the received signal changes from a minimum amplitude of

$$AB_{\min} = |a_1 - a_2|A \qquad (1\text{--}13)$$

to a maximum amplitude of

$$AB_{\max} = |a_1 + a_2|A \qquad (1\text{--}14)$$

The carrier frequency in a line-of-sight terrestrial microwave link can be of the order of 10^{10} Hz = 10 GHz or higher. The wavelength at 10 GHz is

$$\lambda = \frac{c}{f_0} = 3 \text{ cm}$$

where f_0 is the carrier frequency in hertz and $c = 3 \times 10^8$ m/s is the free space speed of propagation for electromagnetic waves. Thus a change in differential path length of only 1.5 cm at a carrier frequency of 10 GHz means that conditions change from reinforcement to cancellation for the received carrier. This can impose severe system degradation. Because of this frequency dependence, such channels are referred to as *frequency selective fading*.

A plot of $B(\tau; f_0)$ as given by (1–11) as a function of f_0 better illustrates the frequency-dependent nature of the channel. Figure 1–9 shows that the transmitted signal will have "notches" placed in its spectrum each τ^{-1} hertz of bandwidth. The bandlimited nature of the channel is therefore apparent. Any modulated signal with bandwidth of the order of or greater than τ^{-1} hertz will suffer distortion as it propagates through the channel because of this notching effect. The differential delay between the main and secondary paths therefore imposes an upper limit on the bandwidth of the signals that the channel can support unless compensation for the notches is accomplished somehow (such compensation can be achieved partially by an *equalizer*).

Another possibility for minimizing degradation is to lengthen the signal duration so that it is much longer than the multipath delay differential. For binary signaling, this of course implies a lower data rate. There are ways to lengthen the symbol duration without accepting a lower data rate, however. In Chapter 4, one such technique, referred to as orthogonal frequency division multiplexing (OFDM), will be discussed.

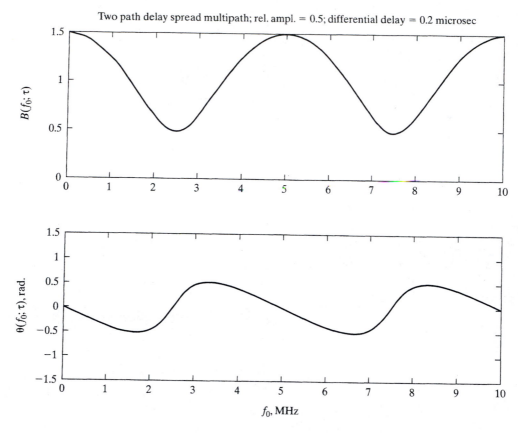

FIGURE 1–9 Received signal amplitude and phase shift versus frequency for a two-path channel.

The dual of the situation where two signals arrive at the receiver with different delays is the situation where they arrive with different Doppler shifted frequencies (in general, such a channel is called *Doppler spread*). To investigate this case, consider

$$y_{\text{dopp}}(t) = A[a_1 \cos 2\pi f_0 t + a_2 \cos 2\pi(f_0 - f_d)t] \tag{1–15}$$

$$= AC(t) \cos[2\pi f_0 t + \phi(t)]$$

where it follows from appropriate algebra and trigonometry that

$$C(t) = A\sqrt{a_1^2 + 2a_1 a_2 \cos 2\pi f_d t + a_2^2} \tag{1–16}$$

and

$$\phi(t) = -\tan^{-1}\left(\frac{a_2 \sin 2\pi f_d t}{a_1 + a_2 \cos 2\pi f_d t}\right) \tag{1–17}$$

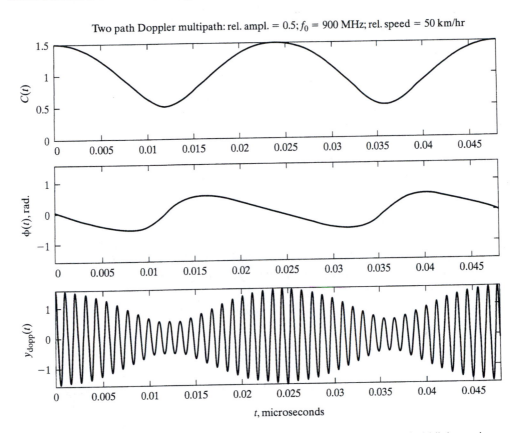

FIGURE 1–10 Time-varying envelope (top), time-varying phase (middle), and composite signal (bottom) for a two-ray Doppler spread channel.

In contrast to the case of the two sinusoidal components being received with different delays, which resulted in a frequency-dependent attenuation and phase shift of the composite signal, the received signal in this case has a time-varying envelope and phase shift as illustrated in Figure 1–10. Because of the time-varying envelope and phase of the received signal, such channels are also referred to as *time selective*.

A word is in order about the physical mechanisms that may give rise to multipath. The model illustrated in Figure 1–7 for the two-path case is, of course, an oversimplified view of the physical channel, as are all models. A two-path multipath channel would arise under conditions where the propagation path is highly stratified due to a temperature inversion or where stray reflections take place off an object, such as a building or airplane. Such multipath is referred to as *specular* because the indirect path results in a component that is essentially a mirror-like reflection, or specular, version of the direct component. When several indirect paths combine to produce a noise-like multipath component, the resulting multipath is referred to as *diffuse*. In the specular case, alleviation of the adverse effects of the multipath can be combated by employing a filter at the receiver, referred to as an equalizer, that has a frequency response function that is approximately the inverse of the frequency response of the channel. In the case of diffuse multipath, the indirect-path signal power essentially acts as a signal-dependent noise.

If destructive interference of the carrier, known as fading, is the predominant channel-induced perturbation, an obvious solution is to change carrier frequency so that reinforcement results from the multipath component. Since the exact path differential is unknown or may change slowly with time, a solution is to transmit on several frequencies simultaneously, called *frequency diversity*. Other types of diversity are also possible, such as *space diversity,* wherein several different transmission paths are used; *polarization diversity*, wherein horizontally or vertically (or counter rotating) polarized carrier waves are used, and *time diversity,* wherein the transmission of a symbol is spread out over time. Channel coding, to be discussed in Chapters 6 and 7, is a form of time diversity.

1.3.5   External Channel Propagation Considerations

When dealing with radio-wave propagation channels, several considerations pertain to conditions within the propagating medium. Often, the earth's atmosphere is involved for a portion or the entire propagation path, and its effects can be very important in design of a communication system. Several of these radio-wave propagation factors are discussed here:

1. *Attenuation* (absorption) caused by atmospheric gases. The principal gaseous constituents of the earth's atmosphere that produce significant absorption are oxygen and water vapor. The first three absorption bands are centered at frequencies of 22.2 GHz (H_2O), 60 GHz (O_2), and 118.8 GHz (O_2) [10].[16] The frequency dependence of the absorption has been found to depend on an empirical line-width constant, which is a function of temperature, pressure, and humidity of the atmosphere. Details of an empirical model to predict attenuation due to atmospheric absorption are presented in Appendix C.

2. *Attenuation* (scattering and absorption) by hydrometeors (rain, hail, wet snow, clouds, etc.). The relationship between rain rate, R (in mm/h measured at the earth's surface), and specific attenuation can be approximated by

$$\alpha = aR^b \text{ dB/km} \tag{1-18}$$

   where a and b are frequency- and temperature-dependent constants [15–17]. An empirically based method for obtaining a and b is discussed in Appendix C.

3. *Depolarization* by hydrometeors, multipath, and Faraday rotation. It is often desirable to use polarization of the transmitted electromagnetic wave as a means to separate two transmitted signals at the same carrier frequency. This is the case, for example, when diversity transmission is used to combat fading—for each carrier frequency or spatial path used it is possible to add another path through

---

[16]A plot of the attenuation versus frequency due to absorption reveals that these peaks are fairly broad so that significant signal attenuation takes place well on either side of these resonant frequencies.

the use of two perpendicularly polarized waves. When the propagation is through rain or ice crystals, it is possible for a small portion of an electromagnetic wave that is, say, horizontally polarized to be converted to vertical polarization, thereby creating crosstalk between the two transmissions. This effect is generally small at frequencies below 10 to 20 GHz. For further discussion of this effect, see [18].

4. *Noise emission* due to gaseous absorption and hydrometeors. The gaseous constituents of the earth's atmosphere, and clouds or precipitation when present, all act as an absorbing medium to electromagnetic waves; therefore, they are also radiation sources of thermal noise.

5. *Scintillation* (rapid variations) of amplitude and phase caused by turbulence or refractive index irregularities. Scintillation on a radio-wave path describes the phenomenon of rapid fluctuations of the amplitude, phase, or angle of arrival of the wave passing through a medium with small-scale refractive index irregularities that cause changes in the transmission path with time. Scintillation effects, often referred to as *atmospheric multipath fading,* can be produced in both the troposphere and the ionosphere.

6. *Antenna gain degradations* due to phase decorrelation across the antenna aperture. The antenna gain in a communications system is generally defined in terms of the antenna's behavior when illuminated by a uniform plane wave. Amplitude and phase fluctuations induced by the atmosphere can produce perturbations across the physical antenna aperture resulting in a reduction of total power available at the feed. The resulting effect on the antenna will look to the system like a loss of antenna gain, or a gain degradation. This gain degradation increases as the electrical receiving aperture size increases; hence the problem becomes more significant as operating frequency and/or physical aperture size increases.

7. *Bandwidth limitations* of the channel due to multipath have been illustrated by Example 1–4. The effects of such bandwidth limitations and possible cures for them will be discussed further in Chapter 3 where equalization is discussed.

1.4   COMMUNICATION LINK POWER CALCULATIONS

In this section, we look at the computation of power levels in a radio-frequency communications link. We first review the meaning of the decibel unit because of its convenience in such calculations.

1.4.1   Decibels in Communication System Performance Calculations

It is often convenient in calculations involving communications systems to use a decibel (dB) scale because of the tremendous ranges of some variables and parameters encountered. Recall that a decibel is defined as 10 times the logarithm to the base 10 of a ratio of two powers. That is,

$$R_{db} = 10 \log_{10} \left(\frac{P}{P_{ref}} \right) \qquad (1\text{–}19)$$

where P and P_{ref} are two powers having the same units (e.g., watts, milliwatts, etc.). Since power is proportional to the magnitude of a voltage phasor squared, we can also write

$$R_{dB} = 10 \log_{10} \left(\frac{|V|^2}{|V_{ref}|^2} \right) = 20 \log_{10} \left(\frac{|V|}{|V_{ref}|} \right) \qquad (1\text{–}20)$$

In (1–19), suppose that P_{ref} is a reference level of 1 watt. Then, a power level of P referenced to 1 watt, termed P dBW, is defined by (1–19) with P_{ref} set equal to 1 watt:

$$P_{dBW} = 10 \log_{10} P \qquad (1\text{–}21)$$

Sometimes the reference level of 1 milliwatt is used. The resulting power level is then in units of dBm (decibels referenced to one milliwatt). It follows that

$$P_{dBm} = P_{dBW} + 30 \qquad (1\text{–}22)$$

since 1 watt = 10^3 milliwatts and $10 \log_{10}(10^3) = 30$.

It is also sometimes convenient to express bandwidth, temperature, or other quantities with dimensions in terms of decibels. If this is done, the dimension of the referenced quantity is simply attached to the decibel. For example, a 1 MHz bandwidth can be expressed as

$$B_{dB\text{-}Hz} = 10 \log_{10} \left(\frac{1 \times 10^6 \text{ Hz}}{1 \text{ Hz}} \right) = 60 \text{ dB-Hz}$$

and a temperature of 300 kelvins can be expressed as

$$T_{dB\text{-}K} = 10 \log_{10} \left(\frac{300 \text{ K}}{1 \text{ K}} \right) = 24.77 \text{ dB-K}$$

Although this might seem somewhat strange, it will turn out to be very convenient in the future when we consider calculation of powers in communication systems.

1.4.2 Calculation of Power Levels in Communication Systems; Link Budgets

We now assume the scenario of Figure 1–11. A transmitter in a communication system is transmitting at an average power level of P_T watts. We wish to find the level of the received power at the output terminals of a receiving antenna located a distance d meters away from the transmitter. We attack this problem by first considering the power density provided by a transmitter that isotropically radiates the power. The approach used here is applicable to communications between platforms, which can be viewed as far removed from the earth's surface so that inverse square law propagation is valid. Since a sphere of radius d has surface area $4\pi d^2$, it follows that the *power density* at the receiver is

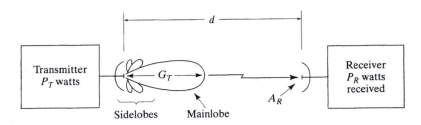

FIGURE 1–11 Hypothetical communications link for computing received signal power.

$$p_R = \frac{P_T}{4\pi d^2} \ \text{watts/m}^2 \tag{1–23}$$

However, some transmitters are equipped with directional antennas that radiate more power in a given direction. This directivity, shown schematically in Figure 1–11, is described by a power gain factor, G_T, so that the power density at the receiver site is G_T times (1–23). The amount of power captured by the receiver is p_R times the aperture area, A_R, of the receiving antenna. The aperture area is related to the maximum antenna gain by

$$G_R = \frac{4\pi A_R}{\lambda^2} \tag{1–24}$$

where $\lambda = c/f$ is the wavelength of the radiation. For a parabolic antenna the aperture area A_R in (1–24) is the *effective* area, which is less than the physical area by an efficiency factor ρ_R. Typical values for ρ_R range from 60% to 80%. Putting (1–23) and (1–24) together with the transmitting antenna directivity factor, G_T, yields the result

$$P_R = \frac{P_T G_T G_R \lambda^2}{(4\pi d)^2} \tag{1–25}$$

Equation (1–25) includes only the power loss due to spreading of the transmitted wave. If other losses are also present, such as atmospheric absorption, or ohmic, losses in the waveguides leading to the antennas, (1–25) is modified to

$$P_R = \left(\frac{\lambda}{4\pi d}\right)^2 \frac{P_T G_T G_R}{L_0} \tag{1–26}$$

where L_0 is the loss factor for the additional losses. When expressed in terms of decibels, (1–26) becomes

$$P_{R,\text{dBW}} = 20 \log_{10}\left(\frac{\lambda}{4\pi d}\right) + 10 \log_{10}(P_T G_T) + G_{R,\text{dB}} - L_{0,\text{dB}} \tag{1–27}$$

The product $P_T G_T$ is referred to as the equivalent isotropic radiated power (EIRP), and the term $-20 \log_{10}(\lambda/4\pi d)$ is called the *free-space loss* in decibels (the minus sign is because a *loss* is a positive quantity).

EXAMPLE 1–5 _____

Consider a satellite at an altitude of 800 km transmitting to a mobile receiver. The following parameters relate to this satellite-mobile link:

Satellite EIRP (G_T = 30 dB; P_T = 100 W): 50 dBW

Transmit frequency: 1500 MHz = 1.5 GHz (λ = 0.2 m)

Mobile receiver antenna gain: 3 dB

Total system losses: 6 dB

Find the received signal power at the mobile receiver antenna terminals.

Solution: The free-space *loss* in dB is

$$L_{\text{free space}} = -20 \log_{10}\left(\frac{\lambda}{4\pi d}\right) = -20 \log_{10}\left[\frac{0.2}{4\pi(800,000)}\right] = 154.03 \text{ dB}$$

From (1–27), the received power in dBW is

$$P_{R,\text{dBW}} = -154.03 + 50 + 3 - 6 = -107.03 \text{ dBW} = -77.03 \text{ dBm} = 1.98 \times 10^{-8} \text{ mW}$$

Note that increasing the frequency by a factor of 10 to 15 GHz would increase the free space loss by 20 dB. However, for a constant aperture transmitting antenna, G_T would be increased by 20 dB since $G_T = 4\pi A_T/\lambda^2$. This even tradeoff is optimistic, however, for two reasons. First, losses increase with increasing frequency, particularly atmospheric absorption and absorption due to hydrometeors. Second, antenna efficiency is lower at higher frequencies, and the 20 dB increase in free-space loss is not exactly compensated by a 20 dB increase in transmit antenna gain.

_____

We continue our consideration of communication link power budgets by considering the noise power. A receiver can be characterized by its noise figure, F, or by its effective noise temperature, T_e, as shown in Appendix B. The two are related by

$$T_e = T_0(F - 1) \tag{1–28}$$

where T_0 = 290 K is standard ("room") temperature. The average noise power generated internally to the receiver, referenced to the receiver input, is

$$P_{n,\text{int}} = kT_eB \tag{1–29}$$

where $k = 1.38 \times 10^{-23}$ J/K is Boltzmann's constant and B is the bandwidth of interest. To include the effect of noise seen by the antenna, we add the temperature of the antenna, T_{ant}, to T_e to get

$$P_n = k(T_{ant} + T_e)B = kTB \tag{1-30}$$

where $T = T_{ant} + T_e$.

The antenna temperature is not a physical temperature, but depends on where the antenna is pointed and the frequency band of the received signal. If the antenna is on board a satellite and pointed toward the earth, a reasonable value for T_{ant} is 300 K. If the receive antenna is mounted on the ground and pointed at the sky between 10 and 90 degrees with respect to the horizontal and the signal frequency is between 1 and 20 GHz, $T_{ant} \approx 50$ K. Moderate rainfall rates (≈ 10 mm/h) affect this very little, but severe rainstorms may cause an increase of 10 to 50 K due to scattering of sky background noise into the antenna by the raindrops (see item 4 under Section 1.3.5). If the antenna is pointed at the sun, the antenna temperature becomes very high, and this condition is to be avoided.

Putting (1–30) together with (1–25), the received signal-to-noise (SNR) power ratio in the bandwidth B is

$$\frac{P_R}{P_n} = \left(\frac{\lambda}{4\pi d}\right)^2 \frac{P_T G_T G_R}{L_0 kTB} \tag{1-31}$$

Note that this expression holds at the receiver input or the receiver output (assuming the bandwidth B remains the same), since signal and noise powers are multiplied by the same gain factor for the receiver. The ratio G_R/T serves as a figure of merit for the receiver in that the larger this ratio, the greater the SNR. We will use (1–31) in Chapters 3, 4, and 11 to carry out design examples for communication systems.

EXAMPLE 1–6

Consider the satellite communications link of Example 1–5 with the following additional parameters:

Receiver noise figure: $F = 5$ dB $= 3.162$ ratio

Receiver antenna temperature: $T_{ant} = 50$ K

Receiver bandwidth: $B = 1$ MHz

Find the received SNR.

Solution: From (1–28),

$$T_e = (3.162 - 1)(290) = 627.1 \text{ K}$$

From (1–30) we find the receiver noise power to be

$$P_n = (1.38 \times 10^{-23})(50 + 627.1) \times 10^6 = 9.343 \times 10^{-15} \text{ watts} = -140.3 \text{ dBW}$$

Using the result of Example 1–5, we find the SNR to be

$$\frac{P_R}{P_n} = -107.03 - (-140.3) = 33.27$$

The free-space loss term in (1–25) resulted from considering ideal propagation in free space. It is a result of the wave spreading in spherical wave fronts. For terrestrial propagation (i.e., propagation along the surface of the earth), the attenuation with distance from the source will not usually obey an inverse square law with distance for a number of reasons. The first, and most obvious, reason is that the wave does not propagate as spherical wave fronts. A second reason is that other losses are present, such as attenuation of a wave front propagating with the ground as one limiting surface, which introduces attenuation losses due to the finite conductivity of the ground. A third reason, and this is most pertinent to cellular radio, is that the propagating wave is the superposition of many waves due to refraction, reflection, and scattering. In view of this, we generalize (1–27) by replacing the free-space loss term with

$$L_{\text{prop}} = L(d_0) + 10n \log_{10}\left(\frac{d}{d_0}\right) = L_0 + 10n \log_{10} d \text{ dB } (d_0 = 1 \text{ m}) \qquad (1\text{--}32)$$

where L_0 and n are constants that depend on carrier frequency, antenna height and type, terrain type, and so on. These constants may be determined for a particular situation analytically in simple environments, empirically, or a combination of the two.

A commonly used model for propagation in cellular systems is the *Hata* model [9], which is empirically derived (i.e., an analytical model was fit to extensive measurements of power levels in terrestrial radio wave propagation in Tokyo). This model will be discussed more fully in Chapter 10.

EXAMPLE 1–7

The following parameters apply to a certain cellular radio system:

Frequency	= 900 MHz
Base station antenna height	= 30 m
Mobile antenna height	= 2 m

For these parameter values, application of the Hata model for urban propagation gives $L_0 = 19.53$ dB and $n = 3.52$. Application in a suburban area gives $L_0 = 9.59$ dB and $n = 3.52$. Find the loss at 10 km for both the urban and suburban situations.

Solution: For the urban case,

$$L = 19.53 + 35.2 \log_{10} d$$

For $d = 10,000$ m, we obtain $L = 19.53 + (35.2)(4) = 160.33$ dB.

For the suburban case, we have

$$L = 9.59 + 35.2 \log_{10} d$$

For $d = 10,000$ m, the loss is now $L = 150.39$ dB.

1.5   DRIVING FORCES IN COMMUNICATIONS

Citizens of nations with ready access to information technology seem to demand ever increasing information transfer rates. It is sometimes difficult to ascertain true demand versus apparent demand stimulated by advertising by manufacturers of equipment and suppliers of services. It appears that one result of this "more begets more" mentality will be wideband communications to the home at affordable cost [19–21] in the near future. Just how this delivery will take place is not clear. Indeed, in the United States, the demarcation lines once sharply defined by government regulation between telephone services, broadcast, and entertainment media have all but disappeared. Furthermore, the mode of delivery depends on such factors as location (e.g., mountainous terrain, city streets, etc.) and population density (e.g., higher population density makes wideband delivery more economically feasible, lower population density means that services must be scaled back or government subsidies are necessary).

It is true in the United States, at least, that the invention and development of many modern communication techniques and systems were hastened by the expenditure of large amounts of government research and development funds. Yet, during peacetime, production of commercial communications gear far outstrips the military in terms of units produced and consumed. This is partly due to a larger per unit cost resulting from the necessary ruggedization of military gear and the relatively small numbers produced (unless in time of war). Commercial development and sales, however, are of necessity of affordable cost per unit with far more units produced. In the competitive societies of the developed nations, this not only means a tremendous value to the consumer, but also continually more efficient and better performing units as production of a given product continues. Examples are many—CD players, televisions, video cameras and players, and so on. Consider, for example, the development of cellular telephone systems. When first developed in the 1970s, it was thought that the number of subscribers would number a few 10,000s and the price of a hand-held telephone unit exceeded $1,000. Present-day numbers far exceed this initial estimate, with there being in excess of 75 million United States subscribers of cellular telephones alone (June 1999 statistics); correspondingly, the price of a hand-held unit has dropped below $100 or is even free with the subscription service.

Another example is the development and acceptance of the Internet—predicted by several experts to be the technological advance of the twentieth century that will have the biggest impact on the way we live and work within the next twenty-five years.[17] As an interesting comparison of adoption of specific technologies by the public, consider the following time periods for reaching 50 million users in the United States:

Internet—3 years
Television—13 years
Personal computer—16 years
Radio—38 years

Granted, the U.S. population is far larger now than when the radio was first introduced to the general public, but the rate of acceptance of the Internet has indeed been astounding. References [20–24] provide some very interesting reading on what can be expected of communication trends in the future.

1.6 COMPUTER USE IN COMMUNICATION SYSTEM ANALYSIS AND DESIGN

Generally, analysis and design of any device or system nowadays makes extensive use of computers. In the case of communication systems, computer use can take two forms—computational procedures (with suitable plotting capability) and simulation. The latter makes use of sampling theory and random number generation to represent the signals and noise within a communication systems. Signal processing operations are implemented in terms of suitably designed algorithms. Very complete system simulations are possible with only portable and desktop computers.

Within the past few years, several convenient and powerful computer simulation tools for communication systems have appeared on the market. Some of these are very expensive and comprehensive while others much more affordable but, generally, with less capability than the more expensive ones. Examples of the more expensive variety are MIL3's OPNET for radio channel and network modeling and CACI's COMNET III for network simulation.[18] Examples of the less expensive types are MATLAB's Communications Toolbox [25], Visual Solution's VisSim/Comm, and Elanix's SystemView [26].[19] All of these programs are block-diagram based: The user constructs a block diagram of the system to be simulated from a palette of blocks, which is then implemented in terms of computer software by the mathematical functions represented by the blocks. In this book, we will use MATLAB exclusively for analysis and simulation. Furthermore, we will construct our own MATLAB programs rather than use the Communications Toolbox. This will be done for two reasons. The first is that we want to use the least expensive option possible, and

---

[17]L. Geppert and W. Sweet, issue editors, "Technology 2000 Analysis and Forecast," *IEEE Spectrum*, Jan. 2000.
[18]http://www.mil3.com/ and http://www.caciasl.com/, respectively.
[19]http://www.mathworks.com/, http://www.vissim.com/, and http://www.elanix.com/, respectively.

MATLAB's Student version [27, 28] can be obtained for $100.[20] Second, we feel that in a learning environment, such as a course for which this book would be used, should encourage understanding of how and why a particular software program is implemented rather than to simply use the canned capability of one of the simulation packages. A less important reason is that the more complex simulation programs involve a fairly extensive learning time in order to get reasonably proficient with them. It is a toss up whether this learning time is longer or shorter than the time required to write one's own program but, with the latter approach, one achieves the understanding required to design the simulation program. We begin writing simulation programs at the end of Chapter 2.

General papers on computer simulation and modeling of communication systems can be found in several archival publications [29].

1.7   PREVIEW OF THE BOOK

In this chapter, we have attempted to set the context of digital communications. The remainder of the book enlarges upon the theory of digital communications with many design examples used as illustrations.

Chapter 2 is a review of signal and system theory. It is assumed that the student has had a prior course on signals and systems before taking this course. However, very ambitious students can fill a void in this regard with diligent study of Chapter 2. Another purpose of Chapter 2 is to introduce notation that will be used throughout the book. It has been similarly assumed that the student has had a prior course on probability. Those persons that are a little rusty in regard to probability will find a short review of the essentials of this subject in Appendix A. In many undergraduate probability courses, random signals are not studied, or very little time is spent on them. Accordingly, a section on random signals has been included in Chapter 2.

In Chapter 3, the subject of digital data transmission is introduced. The treatment is simplified in that perfect synchronization of the receiver is assumed and the noise is taken as additive and white. In addition, a particular type of receiver structure is assumed, namely, a linear filter followed by a threshold detector. The receiver filter is optimized to maximize peak signal-to-rms (root-mean-square) noise ratio at its output, and the result is the classic matched filter receiver. The data transmission schemes considered are binary. Although the channel is initially considered to be of infinite bandwidth, this is eventually relaxed by considering optimum systems for the strictly bandlimited case. Next in the chapter is a consideration of equalization methods—that is, means for undoing the inter-symbol interference introduced by bandlimiting in the channel. The chapter ends with a brief consideration of signal design for bandlimited channels and noise effects in pulse-code modulation systems. This chapter includes all the essentials of the digital data transmission process and can be used in an abbreviated course as the sole consideration of standard digital data modulation systems.

---

[20]As of Dec. 1999, MathWorks has made student versions of MATLAB and SIMULINK directly available from The MathWorks, Inc., 24 Prime Park Way, Natick, MA 01760, Tel. (508) 647–7632 for $100. There are no limitations on array sizes and other MathWorks products, such as the Communications Toolbox, can be added on.

The purpose of Chapter 4 is to provide a sound theoretical basis for the digital modulation systems introduced in Chapter 3, as well as to extend the results in several directions. The approach used is that of Bayes' detection couched in the language of signal space. The background noise is still considered to be additive, Gaussian, and white, which allows the use of any orthogonal basis function set that spans the signal space. This is a considerable simplification and one that gives a very clear geometric picture of the digital signal reception process. The main generalization of Chapter 4 over Chapter 3, in addition to putting the signal reception and detection problem on a sound theoretical basis, is to consider *M*-ary digital data transmission and the explicit treatment of modulation schemes suitable for practical channels. In order to compare *M*-ary systems on an equivalent basis, the concepts of equivalent bit error probability and bandwidth efficiency in terms of bits per second per hertz of bandwidth are introduced. This chapter ends with several example design problems and a basic introduction to orthogonal frequency division multiplexing.

Chapter 5 takes up several topics that can be considered to be degradation sources for the ideal systems considered in Chapter 4. Synchronization methods at various levels (i.e., carrier, bit, and frame) are discussed, and the degradation imposed by imperfect carrier synchronization is characterized. The detrimental effects of fading channels are characterized, and a means to combat them, namely diversity transmission, is discussed. The chapter ends by considering several gross means of characterizing practical digital communication system performance, including envelope plots, eye diagrams, and phasor plots.

Chapters 6 through 8 take up the subject of coding, with the elements of information theory and block coding considered in Chapter 6, and the elements of convolutional coding covered in Chapter 7.

Coding is a very broad subject, and over the years a rich theory has grown up around it. Wherever possible, the theoretical foundations are provided, but the underlying objective of Chapters 6 and 7 is always one of system applications. Accordingly, the student is reminded again and again of the two fundamental characteristics of any application of digital communications, whether coding is employed or not. These are the concepts of power and bandwidth efficiency as introduced in Chapter 1. Thus all coding techniques considered in Chapters 6 and 7 are characterized in terms of their ability to lower the signal-to-noise ratio required to achieve a desired probability of bit error (power efficiency) and the bits per second that can be supported per hertz of bandwidth (bandwidth efficiency). Chapter 8 provides a brief treatment of another error control scheme called automatic repeat request (ARQ), which utilizes a feedback channel.

Chapter 9 contains an overview of spread-spectrum communications. There is much that can be said of this fascinating subject and entire textbooks have been written on it. Only the high points are given here to introduce the student to the basic ideas. The important concept of multiuser detection is considered where, when signals from multiple users are being received, the detection process takes into account their statistical characteristics and improves the detector performance over what could be obtained if the other-user signals were treated as noise.

Chapter 10 deals with cellular radio communications. Both fading channel models and the analysis of terrestrial communications links under fading conditions are treated in some depth, although several entire books exist on the subject. Although first-generation cellular systems were analog, second-generation systems use digital techniques even though they are limited primarily to voice. With the advent of third-generation systems in the early 2000s, the use of digital modulation techniques is mandatory because such systems must handle voice, video, and data. Only with digital transmission will such mixed types of traffic be accommodated. These ideas are discussed after an introduction to the basics of cellular radio.

Chapter 11 treats satellite communications as an example where digital communications concepts and applications have come into extensive use over the years. The concepts are illustrated with several design examples.

REFERENCES

[1] B. Oliver, J. Pierce, and C. Shannon, "Philosophy of PCM," *Proc. IRE*, Vol. 36, pp. 1324–1331, Nov. 1948.

[2] M. Ristenbatt, "Alternatives in Digital Communications," *Proc. IEEE*, Vol. 61, pp. 703–721, June 1973.

[3] Special Issue on Software Radios, *IEEE Commun. Mag.*, Vol. 33, May 1995.

[4] H. Nyquist, "Certain Topics in Telegraph Transmission Theory," *Trans. AIEE*, Vol. 47, pp. 617–644, April 1928.

[5] W. Diffie and M. Hellman, "New Directions in Cryptography," *IEEE Trans. Inf. Theory*, Vol. IT-22, pp. 644–654, Nov. 1976.

[6] N. Jayant and P. Noll, *Digital Coding of Waveforms: Principles and Applications to Speech and Video* (Upper Saddle River, NJ: Prentice-Hall, 1984).

[7] G. Held, *Data Compression*, 2nd ed. (New York: John Wiley, 1987).

[8] C. Shannon, "A Mathematical Theory of Communications," *Bell Syst. Tech. J.*, Vol. 27, pp. 379–423, July 1948, and pp. 623–656, Oct. 1948.

[9] T. S. Rappaport, R. Muhamed, and V. Kapoor, "Propagation Models," in *The Communications Handbook*, J. D. Gibson (ed.) (Boca Raton, FL: CRC Press, 1997)

[10] A. van der Ziel, *Noise in Measurements* (New York: Wiley-Interscience, 1976).

[11] P. E. Green, Jr., *Fiber Optic Networks* (Upper Saddle River, NJ: Prentice Hall, 1993)

[12] R. C. Bray and D. M. Baney, "Optical Networks: Backbones for Universal Connectivity," *Hewlett-Packard Journal*, Vol. 48, pp.19–31, Dec. 1997

[13] I. Lebow, *Understanding Digital Transmission and Recording* (Piscataway, NJ: IEEE Press, 1998)

[14] N. Sloane and A. Wyner (eds.), *Claude Elwood Shannon Collected Papers* (Piscataway, NJ: IEEE Press, 1993)

[15] R. Olsen, et al., "The aR^b Relation in the Calculation of Rain Attenuation," *IEEE Trans. Antenn. Propag.*, Vol. AP-26, pp. 318–329, Mar. 1978.

[16] R. Crane, "Prediction of Attenuation by Rain," *IEEE Trans. Commun.*, Vol. COM-28, pp. 1717–1733, Sept. 1980.

[17] D. Hogg and T. Chu, "The Role of Rain Attenuation in Satellite Communications," *Proc. IEEE*, pp. 1308–1331, Sept. 1975.

[18] L. Ippolito, *Radio Propagation in Satellite Communications* (New York: Van Nostrand Reinhold, 1986).

[19] I. Lebow, *Information Highways and Byways* (Piscataway, NJ: IEEE Press, 1995).

[20] Special Issue on Communications in the 21st Century, *Proc. IEEE*, Vol. 85, Oct. 1997.

[21] Special Issue on The Global Information Infrastructure, *Proc. IEEE*, Vol. 85, Dec. 1997.

[22] V. Li, "Personal Information Service (PIS)—An Application of Wide-Band Communications, 2012 A.D.," *Proc. IEEE*, Vol. 86, pp. 737–740, April 1998.

[23] U. Black, *Mobile and Wireless Networks* (Upper Saddle River, NJ: Prentice Hall, 1996).

[24] E. Wesel, *Wireless Multimedia Networks* (Reading, MA: Addison-Wesley, 1997).

[25] User's Guide for "Communications Toolbox," Natick, MA: The Math Works, Inc., 1996.

[26] Elanix, Inc., Westlake Village, CA 91362.

[27] *MATLAB*® *student version, Version 5.3 User's Guide* (Natick, MA: The MathWorks, Inc., 1999).

[28] *SIMULINK student version, User's Guide,* version 3.0 (Natick, MA: The MathWorks, Inc., 1999).

[29] Special Issues on Computer Modeling of Communication Systems, *IEEE Journ. on Selected Areas in Commun.,* Jan. 1984, Jan. 1988, and May 1997.

PROBLEMS

1–1. An analog source has a bandwidth of 4 kHz. Plot the minimum source rate in bits per second versus the logarithm to the base 2 of the number of levels to which each sample is quantized for the following cases: 2 levels, 4 levels, 8 levels, 16 levels, 32 levels, 64 levels, 128 levels, 256 levels.

1–2. In a digital telephone system, it is determined that the voice spectrum has significant frequency content up to 3 kHz. The channel can accommodate 18 kilobits per second. What is the maximum number of quantization levels to which each sample can be quantized?

1–3. **(a)** Show the steps in deriving (1–5) from (1–4).

    (b) Plot your own curve like Figure 1–4 on a piece of graph paper.

    (c) An error correction code is used in conjunction with a digital modulation scheme that employs bits of duration T_b and requires a bandwidth of $W = T_b^{-1}$ hertz. The code imposes a bandwidth expansion factor of 2, that is, each information bit requires 2 code bits. Therefore, the rate out of the encoder must be twice the bit rate into the encoder, necessitating twice the bandwidth. The code provides a bit error probability of 10^{-5} at a signal-to-noise ratio, E_b/N_0, of 6 dB, which is considered error-free for all practical purposes. Accounting for the code bandwidth expansion, plot the performance of this system on your graph constructed in part (b).

1–4. A customer desires a communication system that is capable of conveying 60 kilobits per second through a channel of bandwidth 10 kHz. The customer can achieve a received signal power of 1 picowatt. The channel noise is 10^{-19} watts per hertz of bandwidth. Should your company submit a bid to build the communication system?

1–5. A *Gray* code is sometimes used to represent symbols in a digital communication system. If $b_1 b_2 b_3 \ldots b_n$ denotes a binary number representation, the Gray encoded number is found using the rules

$$g_1 = b_1$$
$$g_n = b_n \oplus b_{n-1}$$

where ($\oplus$ denotes modulo-2 addition without carry) and the Gray encoded number is represented by $g_1g_2g_3 \ldots g_n$. Construct a table giving the binary code along with the corresponding Gray code representations for the decimal digits 0–7.

1–6. Referring to (1–6), consider a communication system with the following values for the different probabilities:

$$P(Y = 0|X = 0) = 0.7 \quad P(Y = 0|X = 1) = 0.1$$
$$P(Y = 1|X = 0) = 0.3 \quad P(Y = 1|X = 1) = 0.9$$
$$P(X = 0) = 0.4; P(X = 1) = 0.6$$

(a) Find the probabilities $P(Y = 0)$ and $P(Y = 1)$ at the channel output.

(b) Find the probability that a 1 was sent given that a 1 was received.

(c) What is the probability that a 0 was sent given that a 1 was received?

1.7. (a) Derive the relations (1–11) and (1–12). Show that

$$B_{max} = A|a_1 + a_2|$$
$$\text{and } B_{min} = A|a_1 - a_2|$$

(b) Plot a figure like the ones shown in Figure 1–9 for $a_1 = 1$, $a_2 = 0.2$, and $\tau = 10^{-6}$ seconds. Assume $A = 1$.

(c) Comment on the distortion introduced by such a channel to a digital signal of bandwidth 10 kHz, 100 kHz, 1 MHz, and 10 MHz. You can use descriptors like "negligible," "moderate," and "extreme."

1–8. (a) Consider Figure 1–8c with the delay of the second bit stream, $\tau = 0$. A modulation scheme is employed for which the probability of bit error is $P_b = 1/2 \exp(-E_b/N_0)$, where E_b is the energy per bit and N_0 is the noise power spectral density. It follows from Figure 1–8c that $E_b = (a_1 + a_2)^2 T_b$ for $\tau = 0$. Assume that $a_2 = 0.5a_1$. Find the constant k, defined as $k = a_1^2 T_b/N_0$ such that $P_b = 10^{-5}$. This part of the problem is that of calibration.

(b) Now let $\tau = 0.5T$ and $a_2 = 0.5a_1$. Find P_b for each bit in Figure 1–8c using the constant k obtained in part (a). Find the average P_b over the first ten bits shown in Figure 1–8c (i.e., the sequence 1, –1, 1, –1, 1, 1, 1, –1, 1, 1).

(c) Obtain P_b averaged over the 10-bit sequence as a function of τ for $0 \le \tau \le T_b$ assuming the amplitude values of part (b). Plot versus τ. This is fairly easy once one deduces the energies of an "interfered" bit and a "reinforced bit".

Note: The calculations in this problem illustrate the use of a "typical data sequence" to evaluate the degradation due to memory effects in digital communications systems. Normally, the computation would be carried out over a much longer sequence with the aid of a computer.

1–9. Doppler frequency shift is given by $f_d = v/\lambda = vf_c/c$ where v is the velocity of the receiver relative to the transmitter or reflecting object, λ is the wavelength of the transmitter radiation, f_c is the frequency of the radiated signal (usually the carrier frequency in the case of a modulated signal) and $c = 3 \times 10^8$ m/s is the speed of electromagnetic propagation.

a) A sinusoidal signal is radiated from a cellular radio base station to a moving automobile traveling at a speed of 75 km/hr directly away from the base station. There is both a direct propagation path to the automobile and a reflected path from an object some distance in front of it. Accounting for the distance difference and reflection, the relative amplitudes of the direct and reflected waves is 1:0.2. The carrier frequency is 900 MHz. The antenna on the automobile is omnidirectional. Write down expressions and plot the envelope and phase functions given in (1–16) and (1–17) for this situation.

b) If the periods of the functions $C(t)$ and $\phi(t)$ are appreciable fractions of a bit period in a digital communication system, Doppler spread will impose nonnegligible degradation on the system. Consider the following bit rates for a digital communication system communicating with the automobile: 1 kbps; 10 kbps; 50 kbps. Label the degradations for each of these with the descriptors "negligible," "moderate," and "extreme."

1–10. Coefficients for the aR^b relationship for rain attenuation are given in the following table for various frequencies:

Frequency GHz	a	b
12	0.0215	1.136
15	0.0368	1.118
20	0.0719	1.097
30	0.1860	1.043
40	0.3620	0.972

Compute the rain attenuation per kilometer for the following combinations of rain rate and carrier frequency:
(a) $f = 12$ GHz; $R = 1$ mm/h (light rain)
(b) $f = 40$ GHz; $R = 1$ mm/h
(c) $f = 12$ GHz; $R = 25$ mm/h (heavy rain)
(d) $f = 40$ GHz; $R = 25$ mm/h
(e) $f = 20$ GHz; $R\ 10$ mm/h (moderate rain)

1–11. The available noise power per hertz from a resistive source is $P_{avail} = kT$ watts where $k = 1.38 \times 10^{-23}$ J/K is Boltzmann's constant and T is the temperature in kelvins. Compute the available noise power spectral density (the power per hertz) from a resistor at room temperature ($T = 290$ K) in dBm/Hz and dBW/Hz.

1–12. Consider a geostationary-orbit satellite at an altitude of 35,784 km above the earth's equator (such a satellite has a period equal to one day and appears stationary relative to the earth if it is in an equatorial orbit). The transmit frequency is 12 GHz. The transmit and receive antennas have a 1 m^2 aperture with an aperture efficiency of 70%. The transmit power is 100 watts. Assume total system losses of 6 dB. Find the signal power at the receive antenna terminals in dBW, dBm, and microwatts.

1–13. **(a)** Consider a geostationary satellite (see Problem 1–12 for an explanation of this term) where the transmit frequency is 20 GHz. Transmit and receive antenna apertures of 2 m^2 are used and the aperture efficiency is 75%. Assume 2 dB of hardware losses and 0.4 dB of attenuation due to atmospheric absorption. Also, allow for attenuation due to a moderate rain storm of 10 mm/h, which is 2 km in extent over the transmission path (see Problem 1–10 for the computation of this loss). Find the required transmit power in watts to provide a receive power at the antenna terminals of one picowatt.

(b) Redo part (a) for a frequency of 15 GHz. Assume the aperture efficiency stays the same, but scale the atmospheric absorption inversely proportional to frequency squared. You can recompute the rain attenuation given the information in Problem 1–10.

1–14. Consider a geostationary ground-satellite-ground link with the following parameters:

Uplink frequency:	12 GHz
Downlink frequency:	10 GHz
Slant range:	40,000 km
Atmospheric absorption:	0.2 dB
System losses:	3 dB (uplink and downlink)
Rain attenuation:	Negligible
Antenna aperture (satellite and ground):	1.5 m²
Antenna aperture efficiency:	70%
Receiver noise figure (satellite and ground):	4.5 dB
Satellite receiver antenna temperature:	300 K
Ground receiver antenna temperature:	50 K
Bandwidth (uplink and downlink):	100 kHz

Find the ground and satellite transmitter powers to provide a 20 dB signal-to-noise power ratio in both uplink and downlink. Assume that the same antennas are used for transmit and receive. Assume the effect of noise on the uplink is negligible on the downlink.

1–15. Equation (1–24) gives an expression for one important attribute of an antenna, the maximum gain, or simply gain. Another important parameter is the 3 dB mainlobe beamwidth, which is the angle bounded by the points on the mainlobe gain pattern (see Figure 1–11) where the gain falls to one-half of the maximum value. A useful approximation to this 3 dB beamwidth for an antenna with a circular aperture of diameter d is

$$\phi_{3\text{ dB}} = \frac{\lambda}{d\sqrt{\rho}} \text{ radians}$$

where ρ is the aperture efficiency and λ is the wavelength.

(a) Show that (1–24) in the case of a circular aperture antenna of diameter d and efficiency ρ, becomes

$$G = \rho \left(\frac{\pi d}{\lambda} \right)^2$$

(b) Compute the maximum gain and 3 dB beamwidth for a circular-aperture antenna of diameter 1 meter and efficiency 75% for the following frequencies: 10 GHz, 15 GHz, 20 GHz, 30 GHz.

1–16. It is desired to have a circular-aperture antenna with a gain of 30 dB operating at a frequency of 1.5 GHz. The aperture efficiency is 75%. What should the diameter be? What is the 3 dB beamwidth? (Refer to Problem 1–15.)

1–17. (a) For a satellite transmitter operating at 20 GHz, a circular-aperture antenna with a two-degree beamwidth is desired. The aperture efficiency is 65%. What should the antenna diameter be to achieve this beamwidth? What is the corresponding gain? (Refer to Problem 1–15.)

(b) Find the diameter of an antenna that will provide a 150-mile diameter spot at the equator within the 3 dB beamwidth if the platform on which the antenna is mounted is a geostationary-orbit satellite. Assume the operating frequency and efficiency of part (a). What is the gain of the antenna? (Geostationary altitude is 35,784 km above the earth's equator.)

2

Signals, Systems, Modulation, and Noise: Overview

2.1 REVIEW OF SIGNAL AND LINEAR SYSTEM THEORY

2.1.1 Introduction

In the study of communication systems one is interested in how signals are transmitted through systems. Several concepts in this chapter should already be familiar from earlier courses on signal and system theory. The purposes of this review are to collect in one place several definitions, theorems, and formulas that will be used throughout the book as well as to establish notation that will be convenient to use later. More details are provided in books on linear system theory [1].

2.1.2 Classification of Signals

Signals are functions of time that represent any physical quantity of interest. In a communication system context, signals usually represent voltages or currents, but they could also represent other physical quantities, such as light waves. In this book, we will be concerned primarily with *continuous-time*, or *analog*, *signals* that can be modeled as functions of a continuous-time *variable*.[1] *Discrete-time signals*, which are specified only at discrete values of the independent variable, or time, are of secondary interest.

A second way that signals may be categorized are as *deterministic* or *random*. A brief definition of this categorization is that a deterministic signal has a completely specified value for each value of time, t, whereas the value of a random signal is not precisely known for each t, but can be specified only in terms of a probability distribution. Both types of signals will be used in this book. Random signals and noise are described probabilistically in Section 2.7. This categorization is exhaustive in that a signal is either deterministic or random.

Yet a third classification often used for signals is that of *finite energy* or *finite power*. The energy of a signal $x(t)$, assumed to be defined over the entire t-axis, is given by

---

[1]Continuous-time signals will be used to represent digital messages. Such signals are sometimes referred to as digital signals.

$$E = \lim_{T \to \infty} \int_{-T}^{T} |x(t)|^2 \, dt \tag{2-1}$$

The average power (assuming a one-ohm load) of a signal is defined as

$$P = \lim_{T \to \infty} \frac{1}{2T} \int_{-T}^{T} |x(t)|^2 \, dt \tag{2-2}$$

An energy signal is one for which $0 < E < \infty$, while a power signal is one for which $0 < P < \infty$. For a power signal, $E = \infty$, and for an energy signal, $P = 0$. This categorization is not exhaustive; one can contrive examples of signals that are neither energy nor power signals.

A final useful classification for signals is *periodic* and *aperiodic*. A signal $x(t)$ is periodic with *fundamental period* T_0 if

$$x(t) = x(t + T_0), \quad \text{all } t \tag{2-3}$$

where T_0 is the smallest constant that satisfies (2–3). Often, T_0 is referred to simply as the period. All signals not satisfying (2–3) are called *aperiodic*. If $x(t)$ is periodic with period T_0, it is easy to show that

$$P = \frac{1}{T_0} \int_{T_0} |x(t)|^2 \, dt \tag{2-4}$$

where integration is over any period.

Several signals that will be used often in this book are summarized in Table 2–1.

2.1.3 Fundamental Properties of Systems

A *system* is mathematically represented as a transformation of one signal (or set of signals) into another signal (or set of signals). Symbolically, such a transformation is written as

$$y(t) = \mathcal{H}[x(t)] \tag{2-5}$$

for the case of a single input $x(t)$ and a single output $y(t)$, defined over some suitable interval of time. Without further specifications or restrictions one cannot proceed further with analysis of the effect of $\mathcal{H}[\cdot]$ on $x(t)$.

One such restriction is that of linearity. A system is linear if superposition holds. That is, if $y_1(t)$ is the response of $\mathcal{H}[\cdot]$ to $x_1(t)$ and $y_2(t)$ is its response to $x_2(t)$, its response to the arbitrary, linear combination, $a_1 x_1(t) + a_2 x_2(t)$, of these two inputs is

$$
\begin{aligned}
y(t) &= \mathcal{H}[a_1 x_1(t) + a_2 x_2(t)] \\
&= a_1 \mathcal{H}[x_1(t)] + a_2 \mathcal{H}[x_2(t)] \\
&= a_1 y_1(t) + a_2 y_2(t)
\end{aligned}
\tag{2-6}
$$

where a_1 and a_2 are arbitrary constants. The superposition property is of fundamental importance in linear system analysis. Of course, many communication systems are not linear, but (2–6) is nevertheless a convenient starting point in many instances.

TABLE 2–1   Definitions of Several Useful Signals

Graph	Name	Definition
	1. Unit step function	$u(t) = \begin{cases} 1, t \geq 0 \\ 0, t < 0 \end{cases}$
	2. Unit impulse function, $\delta(t)$	$\int_{-\infty}^{\infty} \delta(t)x(t)dt = x(0), x(t)$ continuous at $t = 0$
	3. Signum, or sign, function	$\mathrm{sgn}\,(t) = \begin{cases} 1, t > 0 \\ 0, t = 0 \\ -1, t < 0 \end{cases}$
	4. Symmetrical unit rectangular pulse	$\Pi(t) = \begin{cases} 1, |t| \leq 1/2 \\ 0, \text{ otherwise} \end{cases}$
	5. Pulse function	$P_T(t) = \begin{cases} 1, 0 \leq t \leq T \\ 0, \text{ otherwise} \end{cases} = \Pi\left(\dfrac{t - T/2}{T}\right)$
	6. Symmetrical unit triangular pulse	$\Lambda(t) = \begin{cases} 1 - |t|, |t| \leq 1 \\ 0, \text{ otherwise} \end{cases}$
	7. sinc function	$\mathrm{sinc}\,(t) = \dfrac{\sin \pi t}{\pi t}$ (zero crossings at integer t-values)

Other properties often invoked on a system are *time invariance (fixed)* and *causality*. The former is mathematically expressed as

$$\mathcal{H}[x(t - t_0)] = y(t - t_0) \tag{2–7}$$

That is, for a time-invariant linear system the response to $x(t)$ delayed by t_0 is the response $y(t)$ delayed by t_0 or $y(t - t_0)$. Causality refers to a system that does not anticipate its input or, mathematically, as one where

$$x(t) = 0, \quad \text{for } t \leq t_0 \tag{2–8}$$

implies that

$$y(t) = 0, \quad \text{for } t \leq t_0 \tag{2–9}$$

A causal system is sometimes referred to as a *realizable system* since it states that no physically realizable system can respond before its input is applied. Somewhat surprisingly, noncausal system models are often used in communication system analysis.

The mathematical representation of a linear system is conveniently accomplished in terms of the *superposition integral*, which is

$$y(t) = \int_{-\infty}^{\infty} \tilde{h}(t, \lambda) x(\lambda) d\lambda \tag{2-10}$$

where $\tilde{h}(t, \lambda)$ is the system response at time t to a unit impulse applied at time $t = \lambda$. If the system is also time invariant, (2–10) simplifies to

$$y(t) = \int_{-\infty}^{\infty} h(t - \lambda) x(\lambda) d\lambda \triangleq h(t) * x(t) \tag{2-11}$$

or, by a change of variables, the equivalent form

$$y(t) = \int_{-\infty}^{\infty} x(t - \lambda) h(\lambda) d\lambda \triangleq x(t) * h(t) \tag{2-12}$$

where $h(t)$ is the response of the system to a unit impulse applied at time $t = 0$ and the asterisk denotes the convolution operation. The name *superposition* results by considering the input signal, $x(t)$, as being resolved into a sum of delayed impulses weighted by the signal values at these instants and obtaining the response of the system to this resolution of the input signal by invoking the superposition property (2–6). The resulting response is the integral (2–11), with (2–12) following by a simple change of variables. The operation represented by (2–11) and (2–12) is called *convolution* when not specifically applied to system analysis.

A second way to represent a restricted class of systems is in terms of an ordinary, integro-differential equation relating output to input. If the system is linear and time invariant, this differential equation is linear with constant coefficients.

2.1.4 Complex Exponentials as Eigenfunctions for Fixed, Linear Systems; Frequency Response Function

The mathematical convenience of representing sinusoidal signals as the real (or imaginary) part of a complex exponential signal is well appreciated from circuit analysis courses. This idea will be extended later in regard to narrowband signals. The reason complex exponentials are convenient for linear system analysis will be considered briefly here by making use of the superposition integral (2–12). Assume that the input to a fixed linear system is $x(t) = \exp(j\omega t)$. When t is replaced by $t - \lambda$ and the result substituted into (2–12), it follows that

$$y(t) = \int_{-\infty}^{\infty} h(\lambda)\exp[j\omega(t-\lambda)]d\lambda$$

$$= \left[\int_{-\infty}^{\infty} h(\lambda)\exp(-j\omega\lambda)d\lambda\right]\exp(j\omega t)$$

$$= \tilde{H}(\omega)\exp(j\omega t) \qquad (2\text{--}13)$$

The complex function of frequency, $\tilde{H}(j\omega)$, referred to as the *frequency response function* of the system, can be expressed as a function of $\omega = 2\pi f$ in radians/s, where f is in hertz. Equation (2–13) can be written as

$$\tilde{H}(\omega) = \tilde{H}(2\pi f) = |H(f)|\exp[j\underline{/H(f)}] \qquad (2\text{--}14)$$

where $|H(f)|$ is called the *amplitude response* function and $\underline{/H(f)}$ is referred to as the *phase response* function of the system. The frequency response function is also the *Fourier transform* of the impulse response, which is defined by (2–13). Fourier transforms are discussed in more detail later.

Since the system output is the same form as the input when the input is a complex exponential, $\exp(j\omega t)$, this particular input is called an *eigenfunction* of the system. Using this property of a linear system, together with the superposition property, means that the *response of the system to any input that can be resolved into a summation of complex exponentials* can easily be found. Next discussed, therefore, will be a review of Fourier series and Fourier transform representations for signals. It will be approached from the standpoint of generalized vector spaces, a concept that will be developed further in regard to the detection of signals in noise.

2.1.5   Orthogonal Function Series

Consider the representation of a finite-energy signal, $x(t)$, defined on a T-second interval $(t_0, t_0 + T)$ in terms of a set of preselected time functions, $\{\phi_1(t), \phi_2(t), \dots, \phi_N(t)\}$. It is convenient to choose these functions with properties analogous to the mutually perpendicular, unit vectors of three-dimensional vector space. The mutually perpendicular property, referred to as *orthogonality*, is expressed as

$$\int_{t_0}^{t_0+T} \phi_m(t)\phi_n^*(t)dt = 0, \quad m \neq n \qquad (2\text{--}15)$$

where the conjugate suggests that complex-valued $\phi_n(t)$s may be convenient in some cases. Further assume that the $\phi_n(t)$s have been chosen such that

$$\int_{t_0}^{t_0+T_0} |\phi_m(t)|^2 dt = 1 \qquad (2\text{--}16)$$

In view of (2–16), the $\phi_n(t)$s are said to be *normalized*. This normalization will simplify future equations.

It is desired to approximate $x(t)$ as accurately as possible by a series of the form

$$y(t) = \sum_{n=1}^{N} d_n \, \phi_n \, (t) \tag{2-17}$$

Because of the orthogonality of the $\phi_n \, (t)$s, one may think of the sum (2–17) representing a point in an N-dimensional, generalized vector space with coordinates defined by the basis functions $\{\phi_1(t), \phi_2(t), \ldots, \phi_N(t)\}$.

The d_ns are constants to be chosen such that $y(t)$ represents $x(t)$ as closely as possible according to some criterion. It is convenient to measure the error in the integral-square sense, which is defined as[2]

$$\text{Integral-squared error} = \varepsilon_N = \int_{t_0}^{t_0+T} |x(t) - y(t)|^2 \, dt \tag{2-18}$$

To find $d_1, d_2, \ldots, d_N$ such that ε_N as expressed by (2–18) is a minimum, (2–17) is substituted into (2–18) to give

$$\varepsilon_N = \int_T \left[x(t) - \sum_{n=1}^{N} d_n \phi_n \, (t) \right]\left[x^*(t) - \sum_{n=1}^{N} d_n^* \, \phi_n^* \, (t) \right] dt \tag{2-19}$$

where

$$\int_T (\cdot)dt = \int_{t_0}^{t_0+T} (\cdot) \, dt$$

This can be expanded as

$$\varepsilon_N = \int_T |x(t)|^2 \, dt - \sum_{n=1}^{N} \left[d_n^* \int_T x(t)\phi_n^*(t)dt + d_n \int_T x^*(t)\phi_n(t)dt \right] + \sum_{n=1}^{N} |d_n|^2 \tag{2-20}$$

which was obtained by making use of (2–15) through (2–17) after interchanging the orders of summation and integration. It is convenient to add and subtract the quantity

$$\sum_{n=1}^{N} \left| \int_T x(t)\phi_n^* \, (t) \right|^2 dt$$

to (2–20), which, after rearrangement of terms, yields

$$\varepsilon_N = \int_T |x(t)|^2 \, dt - \sum_{n=1}^{N} \left| \int_T x(t)\phi_n^* \, (t) \, dt \right|^2 + \sum_{n=1}^{N} \left| d_n - \int_T x(t)\phi_n^*(t)dt \right|^2 \tag{2-21}$$

To show the equivalence of (2–20) and (2–21), it is easiest to work backwards from (2–21).

Now the first two terms on the right-hand side of (2–21) are independent of the coefficients d_n. The last summation of terms on the right-hand side is nonnegative and is

---

[2]If the d_ns are chosen to minimize the integral-square error between $x(t)$ and $y(t)$, the right-hand side of (2–17) is a generalized truncated Fourier series.

added to the first two terms. Therefore, to minimize ε_N through choice of the d_ns, the best that can be done is make each term of the last sum zero. That is, choose the nth coefficient d_n, such that

$$d_n = \int_{t_0}^{t_0+T} x(t)\phi_n^*(t)dt, \quad n = 1,2,\cdots,N \qquad (2\text{-}22)$$

This choice for $d_1, d_2, \ldots, d_N$ minimizes the integral-square error, ε_N. The resulting coefficients are called the *generalized Fourier coefficients*.

The minimum value for ε_N is

$$\varepsilon_{N,\min} = \int_T |x(t)|^2\, dt - \sum_{n=1}^{N}\left|\int_T x(t)\phi_n^*(t)\right|^2 \qquad (2\text{-}23)$$

It is natural to inquire as to the possibility of $\lim_{N\to\infty} \varepsilon_{N,\min}$ being zero. For special choices of the set of functions $\phi_1(t), \phi_2(t), \ldots, \phi_N(t), \ldots$, referred to as *complete sets* in the space of all integrable-square (finite energy) signals, it will be true that

$$\lim_{N\to\infty} \varepsilon_{N,\min} = 0 \qquad (2\text{-}24)$$

In the sense that the integral-square error is zero, one may then write

$$x(t) = \sum_{n=1}^{\infty} d_n\phi_n(t) \qquad (2\text{-}25)$$

For a complete set of orthonormal functions, $\phi_1(t), \phi_2(t), \ldots, \phi_N(t), \ldots$, it follows from (2-22) that

$$\int_{t_0}^{t_0+T} |x(t)|^2\, dt = \sum_{n=1}^{\infty} |d_n|^2 \qquad (2\text{-}26)$$

This formula, referred to as *Parseval's theorem*, states that the energy in $x(t)$ can be obtained by summing the energies associated with each $\phi_n(t)$.

2.1.6   Complex Exponential Fourier Series

Recalling that complex exponentials are eigenfunctions for fixed, linear systems, one is naturally led to a consideration of their use for the orthogonal functions in the orthogonal function series expansion of a signal. Let

$$\phi_n(t) = \exp(j2\pi n f_0 t) = \exp(jn\omega_0 t), \quad n = 0, \pm 1, \pm 2, \ldots \qquad (2\text{-}27)$$

where the interval under consideration is $(t_0, t_0 + T_0)$ and[3]

$$\omega_0 = 2\pi f_0 = 2\pi/T_0$$

---

[3] f_0 and ω_0 will be used as convenient.

The functions (2–27) are not normalized but have the integral-square value T_0. Instead of normalizing them, a factor of $1/T_0$ will be inserted in (2–22). Thus the orthogonal function series which results from using the complex exponentials (2–27) in (2–25) is

$$x(t) = \sum_{n=-\infty}^{\infty} X_n \exp(jn\omega_0 t), \quad t_0 \leq t \leq t_0 + T_0 \tag{2–28}$$

where

$$X_n = \frac{1}{T_0} \int_{T_0} x(t) \exp(-jn\omega_0 t) dt, \quad n = \cdots -2, -1, 0, 1, 2, \cdots \tag{2–29}$$

Equation (2–28) is referred to as the *complex exponential Fourier series of x(t)* and (2–29) gives the *expansion coefficients*. Since $\exp(j\omega_0 t)$ is periodic with period, T_0, so is the sum on the right-hand side of (2–28). Thus, if $x(t)$ is not periodic, (2–28) represents it only in the interval $(t_0, t_0 + T_0)$. If $x(t)$ is periodic with period T_0, (2–28) represents it for *all t*.

Using Euler's theorem $\exp(\pm jx) = \cos x \pm j \sin x$ in (2–28), we obtain the trigonometric sine-cosine form of the Fourier series:

$$x(t) = a_0 + \sum_{n=1}^{\infty} a_n \cos n\omega_0 t + \sum_{n=1}^{\infty} b_n \sin n\omega_0 t \tag{2–30}$$

where it can be shown that

$$a_0 = X_0$$
$$a_n = X_n + X_{-n} \tag{2–31}$$
$$b_n = j(X_n - X_{-n})$$

Yet a third form of the Fourier series can be obtained by using the identity

$$a_n \cos n\omega_0 t + b_n \sin n\omega_0 t = A_n \cos(n\omega_0 t + \theta_n) \tag{2–32}$$

where

$$A_n = \sqrt{a_n^2 + b_n^2}$$
$$\text{and} \quad \theta_n = -\tan^{-1} \frac{b_n}{a_n} \tag{2–33}$$

in (2–30). This results in the Fourier cosine series given by

$$x(t) = A_0 + \sum_{n=1}^{\infty} A_n \cos(n\omega_0 t + \theta_n) \tag{2–34}$$

where $A_0 = a_0$.

Table 2–2 summarizes these three forms of the Fourier series together with the implications of symmetry properties of the waveform on the series coefficients, and Table 2–3 gives results for the complex exponential series of several commonly occurring signals.

TABLE 2–2 Summary of Fourier Series Properties[4]

Series	Coefficients[5]	Symmetry Properties
1. Trigonometric sine-cosine $$x(t) = a_0 + \sum_{n=1}^{\infty} (a_n \cos n\omega_0 t + b_n \sin n\omega_0 t)$$ $$\omega_0 = 2\pi/T_0 = 2\pi f_0$$	$$a_0 = \frac{1}{T_0} \int_{T_0} x(t)\, dt$$ $$a_n = \frac{2}{T_0} \int_{T_0} x(t) \cos n\omega_0 t\, dt$$ $$b_n = \frac{2}{T_0} \int_{T_0} x(t) \sin n\omega_0 t\, dt$$	a_0 = average value of $x(t)$ $a_n = 0$ for $x(t)$ odd $b_n = 0$ for $x(t)$ even $a_n, b_n = 0$, n even, for $x(t)$ odd half-wave symmetrical
2. Trigonometric cosine $$x(t) = A_0 + \sum_{n=1}^{\infty} A_n \cos(n\omega_0 t + \theta_n)$$	$$A_0 = a_0; A_n = \sqrt{a_n^2 + b_n^2}$$ $$\theta_n = -\tan^{-1} \frac{b_n}{a_n}$$	A_0 = average value of $x(t)$ $A_n = 0$, n even, for $x(t)$ odd half-wave symmetrical
3. Complex exponential $$x(t) = \sum_{n=-\infty}^{\infty} X_n \exp(jn\omega_0 t)$$	$$X_n = \frac{1}{T_0} \int_{T_0} x(t) \exp(-jn\omega_0 t)\, dt$$ $$X_n = \begin{cases} (a_n - jb_n)/2, n > 0 \\ (a_{-n} + jb_{-n})/2, n < 0 \end{cases}$$	X_0 = average value of $x(t)$ X_n is real for $x(t)$ real and even X_n is imaginary for $x(t)$ real and odd $X_n = 0$, n even, for $x(t)$ odd, half-wave symmetrical $X_n = X_{-n}^*$ for $x(t)$ real

Recalling the derivation of the orthogonal function series, it is seen that partial sums of exponential (and trigonometric) Fourier series minimize the integral-square error between the series and the signal under consideration.

Parseval's theorem (2–26) specializes for a complex exponential Fourier series to

$$\frac{1}{T_0} \int_{T_0} |x(t)|^2\, dt = \sum_{n=-\infty}^{\infty} |X_n|^2 \tag{2–35}$$

which states that the power in a periodic signal $x(t)$ is the sum of the powers in its phasor components (which is what the Fourier series expansion coefficients are).

If $x(t)$ is real, then $X_n = X_{-n}^*$ for its Fourier series. Therefore, representing X_n as $X_n = A_n \exp(j\theta_n)$, it follows that $A_n = A_{-n}$ and $\theta_n = -\theta_{-n}$ for the Fourier coefficients of a real signal.

---

[4] $x(t)$ even means that $x(t) = x(-t)$; $x(t)$ odd means that $x(t) = -x(-t)$; half-wave odd symmetry means that $x(t) = -x(t \pm T_0/2)$.

[5] $\int_{T_0} (\cdot)\, dt$ means integration over any period T_0 of $x(t)$.

TABLE 2–3 Coefficients for the Complex Exponential Fourier Series of Several Signals

Name of Waveform	Graph of Waveform	Waveform (one period)	Complex Exponential Fourier Series Coefficients
1. Half-rectified sine wave ($A = 1$ for all figures)		$x(t) = \begin{cases} A \sin 2\pi f_0 t, & 0 \le t \le T_0/2 \\ 0, & \text{otherwise} \end{cases}$ $f_0 = T_0^{-1}$	$X_n = \begin{cases} A/[\pi(1 - n^2)], & n = 0, \pm 2, \pm 4, \cdots \\ 0, & n \text{ odd and } \ne 1 \\ -jnA/4, & n = \pm 1 \end{cases}$
2. Full-rectified sine wave *		$x(t) = A|\sin 2\pi f_0 t|$	$X_n = \begin{cases} \dfrac{2A}{\pi(1 - n^2)}, & n \text{ even} \\ 0, & n \text{ odd} \end{cases}$
3. Pulse-train signal ($\tau = 0.5$, $t_0 = 0.1$ and $T_0 = 1$ shown)		$x(t) = A \Pi\left(\dfrac{t - t_0}{\tau}\right)$	$X_n = \dfrac{A\tau}{T_0} \operatorname{sinc}(n f_0 \tau) \exp(-j2\pi n f_0 t_0)$, $f_0 = T_0^{-1}$
4. Square wave ($T_0 = 1$ shown)		$x(t) = \begin{cases} A, & |t| \le T_0/4 \\ -A, & T_0/4 < |t| \le T_0/2 \end{cases}$	$X_n = \begin{cases} 2A/(|n|\pi), & n = \pm 1, \pm 5, \cdots \\ -2A/(|n|\pi), & n = \pm 3, \pm 7, \cdots \\ 0, & n \text{ even} \end{cases}$
5. Triangular wave ($T_0 = 2$ shown)		$x(t) = A(1 - 4|t|/T_0)$, $|t| \le T_0/2$	$X_n = \begin{cases} \dfrac{4A}{\pi^2 n^2}, & n \text{ odd} \\ 0, & n \text{ even} \end{cases}$

*Note that $T_0/2$ is the period of the full-rectified sine wave.

2.1.7 The Fourier Transform

The Fourier transform of a signal, $x(t)$, is defined as

$$X(f) = \int_{-\infty}^{\infty} x(t) \exp(-j2\pi ft)\, dt \qquad (2\text{--}36)$$

and the inverse Fourier transform of $X(f)$ is

$$x(t) = \int_{-\infty}^{\infty} X(f) \exp(j2\pi ft)\, df \qquad (2\text{--}37)$$

Except for the difference in sign in the exponent, these are identical relationships. The notation $x(t) \leftrightarrow X(f)$ is often used to denote a Fourier transform pair. Since $|\exp(-j2\pi ft)| = 1$, it follows that (2–36) exists if (1) $\int_{-\infty}^{\infty} |x(t)| dt < \infty$ (absolutely integrable) and (2) $x(t)$ has finite discontinuities, if any. At a discontinuity of $x(t)$, the inversion integral (2–37) converges to $[x(t_0^+) + x(t_0^-)]/2$ where $x(t_0)$ is discontinuous; otherwise, it converges to $x(t)$.

The conditions for existence of the Fourier transform of $x(t)$, being sufficient conditions, mean that there are signals that violate either one or both conditions and yet possess a Fourier transform. An example is $\text{sinc}(t)$, which is not absolutely integrable. We may include signals that do not have Fourier transforms in the ordinary sense by generalization to transforms in the limit. For example, to obtain the Fourier transform of a constant, we consider $x(t) = A\Pi(t/\tau)$ and let $\tau \to \infty$ after obtaining its Fourier transform.

The derivation of a catalog of Fourier transforms is facilitated by means of Fourier transform theorems. Several useful theorems are listed in Table 2–4. Proofs may be found in books on system theory. Useful Fourier transform pairs are given in Appendix F, Table F–7.

A useful Fourier transform pair for spectral analysis among other applications is obtained by applying pair 17 of Table F–7 by observing that $\delta(t - t_0) * p(t) = p(t - t_0)$ where the asterisk denotes convolution. If $p(t)$ represents one period of a periodic signal, it follows that the signal can be written as $y_s(t) * p(t)$, where $y_s(t) = \sum_{n=-\infty}^{\infty} \delta(t - nT_0)$ is called the ideal sampling waveform. The Fourier transform of the convolution of the ideal sampling waveform with $p(t)$ is

$$x(t) = y_s(t) * p(t) \leftrightarrow Y_s(f)P(f) \qquad (2\text{--}38)$$

where $Y_s(f)$ and $P(f)$ are the Fourier transforms of $y_s(t)$ and $p(t)$, respectively. That is, the Fourier transform of the periodic signal[6]

$$x(t) = \sum_{m=-\infty}^{\infty} p(t - mT_0) \qquad (2\text{--}39)$$

---

[6]The only condition on $p(t)$ is that its Fourier transform exist.

TABLE 2–4   Fourier Transform Theorems

Name of Theorem	Signal	Transform
1. Superposition *	$a_1 x_1(t) + a_2 x_2(t)$	$a_1 X_1(f) + a_2 X_2(f)$
2. Time delay	$x(t - t_0)$	$X(f) \exp(-j2\pi f t_0)$
3. (a) Scale change	$x(at)$	$\dfrac{1}{\lvert a \rvert} X\left(\dfrac{f}{a}\right)$
(b) Time reversal#	$x(-t)$	$X(-f) = X^*(f)$
4. Duality	$X(t)$	$x(-f)$
5. (a) Frequency translation	$x(t) \exp(j2\pi f_0 t)$	$X(f - f_0)$
(b) Modulation	$x(t) \cos(2\pi f_0 t)$	$\dfrac{1}{2}[X(f - f_0) + X(f + f_0)]$
6. Differentiation	$\dfrac{d^n x(t)}{dt^n}$	$(j2\pi f)^n X(f)$
7. Integration	$\displaystyle\int_{-\infty}^{t} x(\lambda)\,d\lambda$	$\dfrac{1}{j2\pi f} X(f) + \dfrac{1}{2} X(0)\delta(f)$
8. Convolution	$\displaystyle\int_{-\infty}^{\infty} x_1(t - \lambda) x_2(\lambda)\,d\lambda =$	$X_1(f) X_2(f)$
	$\displaystyle\int_{-\infty}^{\infty} x_1(\lambda) x_2(t - \lambda)\,d\lambda$	
9. Multiplication	$x_1(t) x_2(t)$	$\displaystyle\int_{-\infty}^{\infty} X_1(f - \lambda) X_2(\lambda)\,d\lambda =$
		$\displaystyle\int_{-\infty}^{\infty} X_1(\lambda) X_2(f - \lambda)\,d\lambda$

* a_1 and a_2 are arbitrary constants.

$x(t)$ is assumed to be real in 3b.

is

$$X(f) = f_0 \sum_{n=-\infty}^{\infty} \delta(f - nf_0)\, P(f)$$

$$= f_0 \sum_{n=-\infty}^{\infty} P(nf_0)\, \delta(f - nf_0)$$

(2–40)

which follows since $\delta(f - f_0) P(f) = \delta(f - f_0) P(f_0)$. The Poisson sum formula results by inverse Fourier transforming (2–40) to yield

$$\sum_{m=-\infty}^{\infty} p(t - mT_0) = f_0 \sum_{n=-\infty}^{\infty} P(nf_0)\exp(j2\pi nf_0 t) \qquad (2\text{–}41)$$

EXAMPLE 2–1

Find the Fourier transform of the periodic triangular signal

$$x(t) = 5 \sum_{n=-\infty}^{\infty} \Lambda\left(\frac{t - 5n}{2}\right) \qquad (2\text{–}42)$$

Solution: Matching this with (2–41), we have $p(t) = 5\Lambda(t / 2)$ with $T_0 = 5$ and $f_0 = 1/5$. From Table F–7, pair 3, we obtain

$$P(f) = (5)(2)\,\text{sinc}^2(2f) = 10\,\text{sinc}^2(2f)$$

From the Poisson sum formula (2–41), we see that

$$\sum_{n=-\infty}^{\infty} 5\Lambda\left(\frac{t - 5n}{2}\right) = \sum_{n=-\infty}^{\infty} 2\text{sinc}^2(2n/5)\exp\left(j\frac{2\pi nt}{5}\right)$$

which is the Fourier series of the given $x(t)$. The waveform, $x(t)$, given by (2–42), is plotted in the top figure of Figure 2–1 and partial sum approximations of its Fourier series given above is plotted in the bottom two figures for the sum running from –5 to 5 and –10 to 10.

2.1.8   Signal Spectra

The Fourier transform $X(f)$ of a signal $x(t)$ is, in general, complex. A graphical representation of a signal's Fourier transform, or spectrum, therefore requires two plots. These usually are its magnitude $|X(f)|$, referred to as the *amplitude spectrum*, and its phase $\underline{/X(f)}$, referred to as the *phase spectrum*. With the result (2–40) for the Fourier representation of periodic signals, we can conveniently make spectral plots for periodic or aperiodic signals. The former consist of impulses weighted by the value of the signal (amplitude or phase) spectrum at intervals of the fundamental frequency, f_0, while for aperiodic signals the plots are continuous functions of frequency.

2.1.9   Energy Relationships

Parseval's theorem for Fourier transforms is

$$\int_{-\infty}^{\infty} x(t)y^*(t)dt = \int_{-\infty}^{\infty} X(f)Y^*(f)\, df \qquad (2\text{–}43)$$

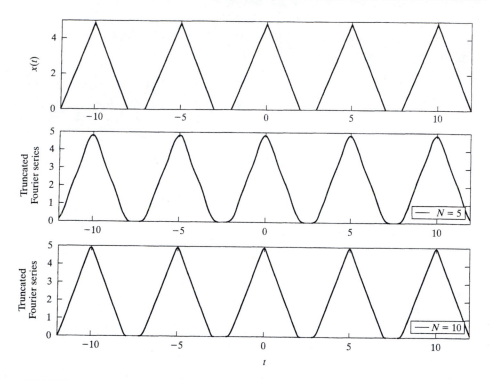

FIGURE 2–1 Periodic triangular waveform and partial-sum Fourier series approximations.

where $x(t) \leftrightarrow X(f)$ and $y(t) \leftrightarrow Y(f)$ are assumed to have finite energy. A special case of (2–43) is obtained by letting $y(t) = x(t)$, which yields

$$\int_{-\infty}^{\infty} |x(t)|^2 \, dt = \int_{-\infty}^{\infty} |X(f)|^2 \, df \qquad (2\text{–}44)$$

Thus the energy in a signal may be found in the time domain or the frequency domain.

The function

$$G(f) = |X(f)|^2 \qquad (2\text{–}45)$$

is referred to as the *energy spectrum* or *energy spectral density of $x(t)$*. Equation (2–45) is convenient for analyzing the distribution of energy of a signal with frequency. For example, the fraction of total energy above a certain frequency W, referred to as out-of-band energy, contained in a lowpass signal $x(t)$ is

$$\Delta E = \frac{\displaystyle\int_{W}^{\infty} G(f)\,df}{\displaystyle\int_{0}^{\infty} G(f)\,df} \qquad (2\text{–}46)$$

where the fact that $G(f)$ is even [it is the magnitude squared of $X(f)$] has been used.

2.1.10 System Analysis

Recalling the superposition integrals (2–11) and (2–12), which relate the output to input of a fixed, linear system through the impulse response, theorem 8 of Table F–6 can be applied to obtain

$$Y(f) = H(f) \, X(f) \tag{2–47}$$

where $X(f)$, $Y(f)$, and $H(f)$ are the Fourier transforms of $x(t)$, $y(t)$, and $h(t)$, respectively. Comparison of the definition of the Fourier transform integral (2–36) with (2–13) shows that $H(f) = \mathcal{F}[h(t)]$ is the same as the system frequency response function considered earlier. Indeed, from the inverse Fourier transform integral for $y(t)$, the output signal can be written as

$$y(t) = \int_{-\infty}^{\infty} H(f) \, X(f) \exp(j2\pi \, ft) df \tag{2–48}$$

which can be thought of as a superposition of elemental responses of the system of the form $H(f) \, X(f) \, df$ to the complex exponential inputs $\exp(j2\pi ft)$ as f varies from $-\infty$ to ∞.
    By rewriting (2–47) as

$$H(f) = \frac{Y(f)}{X(f)} \tag{2–49}$$

a third way of obtaining the transfer function of a system results. The three methods are:

1. $\tilde{H}(\omega) = \tilde{H}(2\pi f)$ is the multiplier of the resulting response, $\tilde{H}(\omega) \exp(j\omega t)$, when the system input is $\exp(j\omega t)$.
2. $H(f)$ is the Fourier transform of $h(t)$.
3. $H(f)$ is the ratio of the Fourier transform of the output to the Fourier transform of the input of a system.

Ordinarily, $h(t)$ is considered to be real, although it is convenient to use complex impulse responses in the analysis of narrowband systems to be considered shortly. If $h(t)$ is real, the magnitude of its Fourier transform, or the system's amplitude response, is an even function of frequency and its phase is odd.
    A system that passes some spectral components of an input signal while heavily attenuating, or ideally rejecting, other parts of its spectral components is called a *filter*. A filter can be classified as *lowpass*, *bandpass*, or *highpass* depending on whether it passes low-frequency spectral components, a band of spectral components, or the high-frequency spectral components of an input signal, respectively. Ideal filters and practical approximations to ideal filters will be discussed shortly.

2.2 BASIC ANALOG MODULATION TECHNIQUES [2]

In Section 2.1.10 the convolution theorem of Fourier transforms was applied in carrying out the analysis of fixed linear systems. In this section, applications of the Fourier transform to modulation theory are considered.

In these considerations it will be convenient to refer to a signal, $x(t)$, as *lowpass, bandpass,* or *highpass* according to whether its amplitude spectrum, $|X(f)|$, has significant values for $|f| < W$, $|f \pm f_0| < W / 2$, or $|f| > W$, respectively, where W is the bandwidth of $x(t)$ (or cutoff frequency for the highpass case) and f_0 is the center frequency of the bandpass spectrum. For consistency, we refer to the nonzero extent of the signal for positive frequencies only as its bandwidth.

2.2.1 Double-Sideband Modulation

The modulation theorem of Fourier transforms states that if the Fourier transform of $m(t)$ is $M(f)$, then the Fourier transform of

$$x(t) = A\, m(t)\cos 2\pi f_0 t \qquad (2\text{–}50)$$

is

$$X(f) = \frac{A}{2}\left[M(f - f_0) + M(f + f_0)\right] \qquad (2\text{–}51)$$

If $m(t)$, usually referred to as the *message signal*, is lowpass with bandwidth W, then $X(f)$ is a bandpass signal of bandwidth $2W$. This is referred to as *double-sideband (DSB)* modulation, which is seen to consist of multplication of $m(t)$ by the carrier $\cos 2\pi f_0 t$. A representative waveform and spectrum for DSB is shown in Figure 2–2a.

If $m(t)$ in (2–50) is replaced by

$$p(t) = 1 + a\, m(t) \qquad (2\text{–}52)$$

where a is referred to as the *modulation index*, the result is double-sideband with carrier, commonly referred to as *amplitude modulation (AM)*. The function $A\,[1 + a\,m(t)]$ defines the *envelope* of the AM-modulated signal, or the variation of the peaks of the positive (or negative) carrier half cycles. They vary from a maximum of $A\,[1 + a\max m(t)]$ to a minimum of $A\,[1 + a\min m(t)]$. Usually, it is assumed that $|\min m(t)| = 1$, $\min m(t) < 0$. In this case, if $a = 1$, the minimum of the envelope is zero. Assuming that $|\min m(t)| = 1$, the percent of modulation is $a \times 100\%$; for example, if $a = 0.5$, the percent modulation is 50%.

Use of the modulation theorem (pair 5b in Table 2–4), the Fourier transform of 1 (pair 8 of Table F-7), and superposition (pair 1 of Table 2–4) gives the spectrum of an AM-modulated signal as

$$X(f) = \frac{A}{2}\left[\delta\,(f - f_0) + \delta\,(f + f_0) + aM\,(f - f_0) + aM\,(f + f_0)\right] \qquad (2\text{–}53)$$

where the delta functions reflect the presence of finite power at the carrier frequency f_0. A typical waveform and spectrum for AM are illustrated in Figure 2–2b.

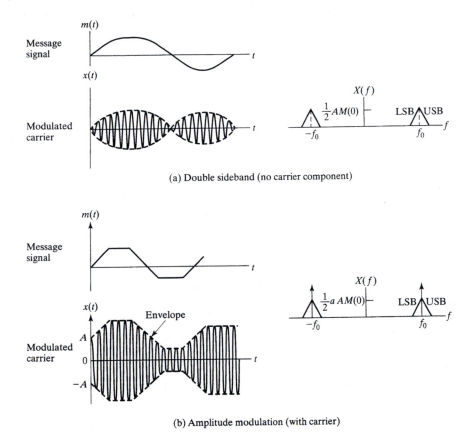

FIGURE 2–2   Waveforms and spectra for AM and DSB modulation.

The demodulation of DSB and AM can be accomplished with a coherent demodulator (analyzed in Problem 2–14) as indicated in Figure 2–3 for DSB. This requires the generation of a carrier reference that is phase coherent with the received carrier (no carrier component is present in the case of DSB) at the receiver, which can be accomplished by squaring of the received signal, filtering out the resulting component at $2f_0$, and dividing the frequency by two. An alternative nonlinear structure that can be used to demodulate DSB is a *Costas loop*, to be discussed in reference to digital modulation in Chapter 5. Since a carrier component is present in AM, the demodulation process can be accomplished in a simpler manner by using an *envelope detector*.

2.2.2   The Hilbert Transform; Single-Sideband Modulation

A Hilbert transform consists of a $-\pi/2$-rad phase shift in the frequency domain. For any linear system, $\underline{/H(f)}$ must be odd. Therefore, the transfer function of a Hilbert transformer is

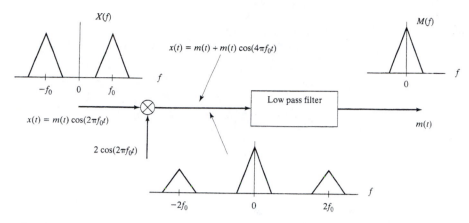

FIGURE 2–3 Block diagram, signals, and spectra for a coherent demodulator with DSB.

$$H(f) = -j\,\text{sgn}\,(f) = \begin{cases} \exp(-j\pi/2), f > 0 \\ \exp(j\pi/2), f < 0 \end{cases} \tag{2-54}$$

where $\text{sgn}\,(f) = 2u(f)-1 = \begin{cases} 1, f > 0 \\ -1, f < 0 \end{cases}$ is the signum function.

The impulse response of a Hilbert transformer can be obtained as an inverse Fourier transform in the limit of a suitably chosen function that approaches $-j\text{sgn}(f)$ as a parameter approaches zero. An example is

$$H_a(f) = -j[\exp(-af)u(f) - \exp(af)u(-f)] \to -j\text{sgn}(f) \text{ as } a \to 0 \tag{2-55}$$

which has the inverse Fourier transform

$$h_a(t) = \frac{4\pi t}{a^2 + (2\pi t)^2} \tag{2-56}$$

The impulse response of a Hilbert transformer, therefore, is

$$h(t) = \lim_{a \to 0} h_a(t) = \frac{1}{\pi t} \quad \text{(Table F–7, pair 15)} \tag{2-57}$$

Thus, using the superposition integral, the output of a Hilbert transform filter for an arbitrary input, $x(t)$, may be written as

$$\hat{x}(t) = \frac{1}{\pi} \int_{-\infty}^{\infty} \frac{x(\lambda)}{t - \lambda} d\lambda \tag{2-58}$$

Note that the Fourier transform of (2–58) is

$$\mathscr{F}[\hat{x}(t)] = -j\text{sgn}\,(f)\,X\,(f) \tag{2-59}$$

The applications of the Hilbert transform of most interest in this book are to modulation theory. Consider a complex signal

$$z_p(t) = x(t) + j\hat{x}(t) \tag{2–60}$$

with Fourier transform, $Z_p(f)$. It follows from (2–59) that $Z_p(f)$ can be written as

$$Z_p(f) = X(f) + j[-j\text{sgn}(f)X(f)] = [1 + \text{sgn}(f)]X(f) \tag{2–61}$$

where $X(f)$ is the Fourier transform of $x(t)$. Note that $1 + \text{sgn}(f) = \begin{cases} 2, f > 0 \\ 0, f < 0 \end{cases}$. On the other hand, we write the spectrum of a signal with nonzero spectrum only for negative frequencies as

$$Z_n(f) = [1 - \text{sgn}(f)]X(f) \tag{2–62}$$

Note that $1 - \text{sgn}(f) = \begin{cases} 0, f > 0 \\ 2, f < 0 \end{cases}$. The corresponding signal is

$$z_n(t) = x(t) - j\hat{x}(t) \tag{2–63}$$

That is, this is the signal whose spectrum is identically zero for $f > 0$.

The signals expressed by (2–60) and (2–63) are referred to as *analytic signals*; that is, they are complex-valued signals whose spectra are nonzero only for $f > 0$ or $f < 0$, respectively.

Now consider the signal

$$x(t) = \text{Re}\left[\frac{A}{2} z(t)\exp(j2\pi f_0 t)\right] \tag{2–64}$$

where $z(t)$ is an analytic signal of the form $z(t) = m(t) \mp j\hat{m}(t)$. Expanding (2–64) and taking the real part, it follows that

$$x(t) = \frac{A}{4}[m(t)\cos 2\pi f_0 t \pm \hat{m}(t)\sin 2\pi f_0 t] \tag{2–65}$$

where $m(t)$ represents a message signal and $\hat{m}(t)$ is its Hilbert transform. Recalling that for any complex quantity $\text{Re}(A) = (A + A^*)/2$, we may write (2–64) as

$$x(t) = \frac{A}{4}[z(t)\exp(j2\pi f_0 t) + z^*(t)\exp(-j2\pi f_0 t)] \tag{2–66}$$

where $z(t) = m(t) \mp j\hat{m}(t)$. Using the frequency translation theorem and assuming $M(f) = \mathcal{F}[m(t)]$ to be lowpass [i.e., $M(f) = 0$, $|f| > W$], it follows that

$$X(f) = \begin{cases} M(f - f_0), & f_0 - W \le f \le f_0 \\ M(f + f_0), & -f_0 \le f \le -f_0 + W \\ 0, & \text{otherwise} \end{cases} \tag{2–67}$$

if the plus sign is chosen in (2–65), and

$$X(f) = \begin{cases} M(f - f_0), & f_0 \leq f \leq f_0 + W \\ M(f + f_0), & -f_0 - W \leq f \leq -f_0 \\ 0, & \text{otherwise} \end{cases} \tag{2–68}$$

if the minus sign is chosen in (2–65). The former is referred to as single-sideband, lower-sideband (SSBL) transmitted and the latter as single-sideband, upper-sideband (SSBU) transmitted modulation. As in the case of AM and DSB, a coherent demodulator can be used to demodulate SSB (see Problem 2–14). The bandwidth of SSB is half that of AM or DSB.

The modulation types just considered are referred to as *linear analog modulations* because a linear operation is performed on the message to produce them.

2.2.3 Angle Modulation

Angle modulation is a nonlinear modulation scheme and does not lend itself easily to Fourier analysis. Consequently, special cases must be considered. In this section, the spectrum for sinusoidally modulated angle modulation is developed.

Two common types of analog angle modulation are phase modulation (PM) and frequency modulation (FM). The former has the general form

$$x_{PM}(t) = A\cos[2\pi f_0 t + k_p m(t)] \tag{2–69}$$

where A is the carrier amplitude, $m(t)$ is the message signal, and k_p is the phase deviation constant. An FM-modulated signal has the general form

$$x_{FM}(t) = A\cos\left[2\pi f_0 t + 2\pi f_d \int^t m(\alpha)\, d\alpha\right] \tag{2–70}$$

where f_d is called the frequency deviation constant.

For $m(t) = A_m \cos(2\pi f_m t)$, both PM- and FM-modulated waveforms can be written in terms of a parameter called the modulation index, β, as

$$x_{PM}(t) = A\cos(2\pi f_0 t + \beta_{PM} \cos 2\pi f_m t) \tag{2–71}$$

$$\text{and } x_{FM}(t) = A\cos(2\pi f_0 t + \beta_{FM} \sin 2\pi f_m t)$$

where

$$\beta_{PM} = A_m k_p \text{ for PM}$$

$$\beta_{FM} = \frac{A_m f_d}{f_m} \text{ for FM} \tag{2–72}$$

The result for PM is obvious; the result for FM is obtained by letting $m(t) = A_m \cos(2\pi f_m t)$ in (2–70) and noting that $2\pi f_d \int^t m(\alpha)\, d\alpha$ integrates to $2\pi f_d \int^t A_m \cos 2\pi f_m \alpha\, d\alpha = (A_m f_d)/f_m \sin 2\pi f_m t$. Typical waveforms for both cases are shown in Figure 2–4.

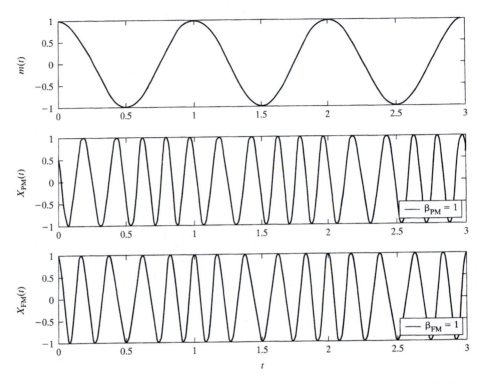

FIGURE 2–4   FM and PM waveforms for a sinusoidal message signal; $f_m = 1$ Hz
and $A_m = 1$.

To express $x(t)$ for FM or PM in a trigonometric series, we proceed as follows.
Write $x(t)$ as

$$x(t) = \text{Re}[A \exp(j2\pi f_0 t)\exp(j\beta \sin 2\pi f_m t)] \qquad (2\text{–}73)$$

This is not normally a periodic signal (it is only if f_m and f_0 are harmonically related).
However, $\exp[j\beta \sin(2\pi f_m t)]$ is periodic and can therefore be expressed as a Fourier series as

$$\exp[j\beta \sin (2\pi f_m t)] = \sum_{n=-\infty}^{\infty} B_n \exp(j2\pi n f_m t) \qquad (2\text{–}74)$$

where

$$B_n = \frac{1}{2\pi} \int_0^{2\pi} \exp[j(\beta \sin u - nu)]du \triangleq J_n(\beta)$$

with $J_n(\beta)$ the Bessel function of order n and argument β. Thus, the sinusoidally angle-
modulated waveform can be written as

TABLE 2–5 An Abbreviated Table of Bessel Function Values

β	$J_0(\beta)$	$J_1(\beta)$
0.1	0.997	0.050
0.2	0.990	0.100
0.5	0.938	0.242
1.0	0.765	0.440
2.0	0.224	0.577
5.0	−0.178	−0.328
8.0	0.172	0.235
10.0	−0.246	0.043

$$x(t) = \text{Re}\left\{A \exp(j2\pi f_0 t) \sum_{n=-\infty}^{\infty} J_n(\beta) \exp(j2\pi n f_m t)\right\}$$

$$= A \sum_{n=-\infty}^{\infty} J_n(\beta) \cos 2\pi(f_0 + n f_m)t \tag{2–75}$$

This is a trigonometric series representation that can be used to plot spectra of the sinusoidally modulated signal for given values of β, f_0, and f_m. Handy relationships involving Bessel functions useful in calculating the spectra are

$$J_n(\beta) = (-1)^n J_{-n}(\beta) \text{ and } J_{n+1}(\beta) = \frac{2n}{\beta} J_n(\beta) - J_{n-1}(\beta) \tag{2–76}$$

Values of $J_0(\beta)$ and $J_1(\beta)$ useful for computing J_n-values for $n > 1$ are given in Table 2–5.

EXAMPLE 2–2

(a) Plot the amplitude spectrum for a unit-amplitude FM-modulated signal where the modulating signal is $m(t) = A_m \cos(2\pi f_m t)$ with $A_m = 4$, $f_m = 10$, and the carrier frequency $f_0 = 500$ Hz. The frequency deviation constant is $f_d = 5$ Hz/volt.

(b) The frequency deviation constant is increased to 20 Hz/volt. All other parameters remain the same. Plot the amplitude spectrum for this case.

(c) The same frequency constant as was used in part (b) is employed, but the modulation frequency is changed to $f_0 = 40$ Hz. Plot the amplitude spectrum for this case.

Solution: (a) From (2–72), the modulation index is

$$\beta = 4(5)/10 = 2$$

so that the modulated signal is

$$x(t) = \cos[1000\pi t + 2\sin(20\pi t)] = \sum_{n=-\infty}^{\infty} J_n(2)\cos[2\pi(500 + 10n)t]$$

The Bessel function values required can be computed from (2–76) with $J_0(2) = 0.224$ and $J_1(2) = 0.557$ (see Table 2–5). The results are given below:

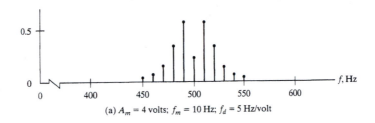

(a) $A_m = 4$ volts; $f_m = 10$ Hz; $f_d = 5$ Hz/volt

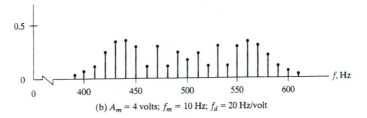

(b) $A_m = 4$ volts; $f_m = 10$ Hz; $f_d = 20$ Hz/volt

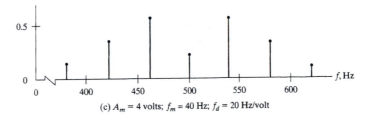

(c) $A_m = 4$ volts; $f_m = 40$ Hz; $f_d = 20$ Hz/volt

FIGURE 2–5 Amplitude spectra for sinusoidally modulated FM signals.

n:	0	1	2	3	4	5	6
$J_n(2)$:	0.224	0.577	0.353	0.129	0.034	0.007	0.001

The amplitude spectrum is plotted in Figure 2–5a.

(b) Now the modulation index is

$$\beta = 4(20)/10 = 8$$

We again use (2–76) to compute the required values for $J_n(8)$. The results are:

n	$J_n(8)$	n	$J_n(8)$
0	0.172	6	0.338
1	0.235	7	0.321
2	−0.113	8	0.224
3	−0.292	9	0.126
4	−0.105	10	0.061
5	0.186	11	0.025

The amplitude spectrum for this case is shown in Figure 2–5b.

(c)   For this case

$$\beta = 4(20)/40 = 2$$

The values for $J_n(\beta)$ are the same as for part (a), but the spectral lines are spaced by 40 Hz rather than 10 Hz. The plot of the amplitude spectrum is provided in Figure 2–5c.

From the example, it is noted that the magnitudes of the spectral lines become small as they fall sufficiently far from the carrier frequency. A guideline that can be used is that $\beta + 1$ spectral lines on either side of the carrier are significant. Thus, the required transmission bandwidth for a sinusoidally modulated FM carrier is given by

$$B_T = 2(\beta + 1)f_m \text{ hertz} \tag{2–77}$$

This is called Carson's rule. For nonsinusoidally modulated FM signals, a deviation constant is defined as

$$D = \frac{f_d}{W} \max|m(t)| \tag{2–78}$$

where W is the lowpass bandwidth of the message. This is used in place of β in (2–77) to yield

$$B_T = 2(D + 1)W \text{ hertz} \tag{2–79}$$

where the message bandwidth W corresponds to f_m. Note that $B_T > W$, the message bandwidth.

One advantage of an angle-modulated signal is that its power is independent of the modulated signal level. If $f_0 \gg B_T$, it can be shown that the power in the modulated signal is

$$P_{\text{FM,PM}} = 0.5A^2 \tag{2–80}$$

The demodulation of FM can be accomplished by means of a phase-locked loop in which the loop bandwidth is of the order of the message bandwidth. The demodulated message signal is available at the input to the voltage-controlled oscillator. (See Appendix D for an overview of phase-lock loop theory.) If this is the case, the output of the demodulator (input to the VCO of the phase-locked loop) is proportional to the derivative of the argument of (2–70). Other types of circuits can be designed to approximate this operation and are collectively referred to as *discriminators*. A lowpass filter normally follows the discriminator operation with a bandwidth equal to, or slightly greater than, the message bandwidth in order to filter out any noise that has frequency components with frequencies above the message bandwidth.

2.3   COMPLEX ENVELOPE REPRESENTATION OF BANDPASS SIGNALS AND SYSTEMS

2.3.1   Bandpass Signals

Analytic signals and their spectra were defined by (2–60) through (2–63). Let $x(t)$ be a real signal with a bandpass spectrum $X(f)$ around frequency f_0 as illustrated in Figure 2–6a. It then follows that $X_p(f) = [1 + \text{sgn}(f)] X(f)$ is just twice the positive frequency portion of $X(f)$, as illustrated in Figure 2–6b and, from (2–60), $x_p(t) = x(t) + j\hat{x}(t)$ where $\hat{x}(t)$ is the Hilbert transform of $x(t)$. By the frequency translation theorem (Table F–7), it follows that $x_p(t)$ can be written as

$$x_p(t) = \tilde{x}(t)\exp(j2\pi f_0 t) \tag{2-81}$$

where $\tilde{x}(t)$ is a complex-valued lowpass signal with the spectrum as illustrated in Figure 2–6c, referred to as the *complex envelope of* $x(t)$. For example, the complex envelope of $A\cos(2\pi f_0 t + \theta)$ is $A\exp(j\theta)$.

The complex envelope of a signal can be found in two ways. First, we can find the analytic signal $x_p(t) = x(t) + j\hat{x}(t)$ and then solve (2–81) for $\tilde{x}(t)$. Second, we can take the positive frequency portion of $X(f)$ multiplied by a factor of 2 to give $X_p(f)$, translate it to baseband, and inverse Fourier transform this translated spectrum to get $\tilde{x}(t)$. Since $x_p(t) = x(t) + j\hat{x}(t)$, where $x(t)$ and $\hat{x}(t)$ are the real and imaginary parts, respectively, of $x_p(t)$, it follows from (2–81) that

$$x(t) = \text{Re}[\tilde{x}(t)\exp(j2\pi f_0 t)] \tag{2-82}$$

and

$$\hat{x}(t) = \text{Im}[\tilde{x}(t)\exp(j2\pi f_0 t)] \tag{2-83}$$

Therefore, from (2–82), the real signal $x(t)$ can be expressed in terms of its complex envelope as

$$x(t) = x_R(t)\cos(2\pi f_0 t) - x_I(t)\sin(2\pi f_0 t) \tag{2-84}$$

where $\tilde{x}(t) = x_R(t) + jx_I(t)$ or

$$x_R(t) = \text{Re}[\tilde{x}(t)] \text{ and } x_I(t) = \text{Im}[\tilde{x}(t)] \tag{2-85}$$

The signals $x_R(t)$ and $x_I(t)$ are known as the *inphase and quadrature* components, respectively, of $x(t)$. Equation (2–84) can, of course, be written in the equivalent *envelope-phase* form

$$x(t) = r(t)\cos[2\pi f_0 t + \phi(t)] \tag{2-86}$$

where

$$r(t) = \sqrt{x_R^2(t) + x_I^2(t)}$$

$$\phi(t) = \tan^{-1}\left[\frac{x_I(t)}{x_R(t)}\right] \tag{2-87}$$

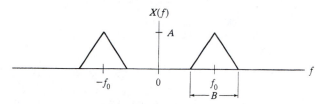

(a) A bandpass signal spectrum.

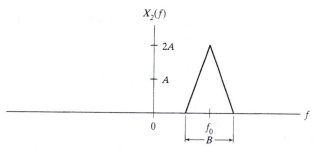

(b) Twice the positive frequency portion of $X(f)$, corresponding to $\mathcal{F}[x(t) + j\hat{x}(t)]$.

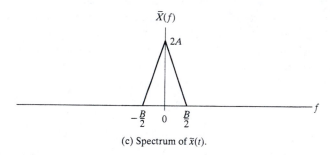

(c) Spectrum of $\tilde{x}(t)$.

FIGURE 2–6 Signal spectra relating to representation of bandpass signals in terms of complex envelopes.

EXAMPLE 2–3

Find the complex envelope of the signal

$$x(t) = \exp(-\alpha t)\cos[2\pi(f_0 + \Delta f)t]u(t) \qquad (2\text{–}88)$$

Solution: Using the transform pair

$$\exp(-\alpha t)u(t) \longleftrightarrow \frac{1}{\alpha + j2\pi f}$$

and the modulation theorem, we find the Fourier transform of $x(t)$ to be

$$X(f) = \frac{0.5}{\alpha + j2\pi(f - \Delta f - f_0)} + \frac{0.5}{\alpha + j2\pi(f + \Delta f + f_0)} \qquad (2\text{–}89)$$

Taking the positive-frequency part of (2–89), shifting it to the left by f_0 Hz, and doubling it, we find the Fourier transform of the complex envelope to be

$$\tilde{X}(f) = \frac{1}{\alpha + j2\pi(f - \Delta f)} \tag{2–90}$$

Taking the inverse Fourier transform of (2–90), with the aid of the transform pair given above and the frequency translation theorem, the complex envelope is found as

$$\tilde{x}(t) = \exp[-(\alpha - j2\pi\Delta f)\,t]\,u(t) \tag{2–91}$$

Note that in this simple case, the complex envelope could have been found more directly by writing (2–88) as

$$x(t) = \text{Re}\{\exp[-(\alpha - j2\pi\Delta f)t]\,\exp(j2\pi f_0 t)\,u(t)\} \tag{2–92}$$

and simply identifying the complex envelope with the first exponential.

2.3.2   Bandpass Systems

A bandpass system is one whose frequency response function is limited to a passband of frequencies around a center frequency f_0. From (2–82) with a change of notation, its impulse response can be represented in terms of a complex envelope $\tilde{h}(t)$ as

$$h(t) = \text{Re}[\tilde{h}(t)\exp(j2\pi f_0 t)] \tag{2–93}$$

where $\tilde{h}(t) = h_R(t) + jh_I(t)$. If the input is bandpass, also with representation (2–82), the output is

$$y(t) = x(t) * h(t) = \int_{-\infty}^{\infty} h(\lambda)x(t - \lambda)\,d\lambda \tag{2–94}$$

$$= \int_{-\infty}^{\infty} \text{Re}[\tilde{h}(\lambda)\exp(j2\pi f_0\lambda)]\text{Re}\{\tilde{x}(t - \lambda)\exp[j2\pi f_0(t - \lambda)]\}d\lambda$$

It is convenient to represent $h(t)$ and $x(t)$ in (2–94) in the form

$$h(t) = \frac{1}{2}\tilde{h}(t)\exp(j2\pi f_0 t) + \text{c.c.} \tag{2–95}$$

and

$$x(t) = \frac{1}{2}\tilde{x}(t)\exp(j2\pi f_0 t) + \text{c.c.} \tag{2–96}$$

where c.c. stands for the complex conjugate of the immediately preceding term. The system output can be expressed in terms of these expressions as

$$y(t) = \int_{-\infty}^{\infty} \left\{\frac{1}{2}\tilde{h}(\lambda)\exp(j2\pi f_0\lambda) + \text{c.c.}\right\} \left\{\frac{1}{2}\tilde{x}(t-\lambda)\exp[j2\pi f_0(t-\lambda)] + \text{c.c.}\right\}d\lambda$$

$$= \frac{1}{4}\int_{-\infty}^{\infty} \tilde{h}(\lambda)\tilde{x}(t-\lambda)d\lambda\exp(j2\pi f_0 t) + \text{c.c.} \tag{2-97}$$

$$+ \frac{1}{4}\int_{-\infty}^{\infty} \tilde{h}(\lambda)\tilde{x}^*(t-\lambda)\exp(j4\pi f_0\lambda)d\lambda \exp(-j2\pi f_0 t) + \text{c.c.}$$

The second pair of terms is approximately 0 by virtue of the factor $\exp(j4\pi f_0\lambda)$ in the integrand since $h(\lambda)$ and $\tilde{x}(t-\lambda)$ are slowly varying (they are lowpass with bandwidth much less than f_0) with respect to this complex exponential factor and, thus, the integrand cancels half cycle by half cycle. Thus (2-97) can be written as

$$y(t) = \frac{1}{2}\text{Re}\{[\tilde{h}(t)*\tilde{x}(t)]\exp(j2\pi f_0 t)\} = \frac{1}{2}\text{Re}[\tilde{y}(t)\exp(j2\pi f_0 t)] \tag{2-98}$$

where

$$\tilde{y}(t) = \tilde{h}(t)*\tilde{x}(t) = \mathcal{F}^{-1}[\tilde{H}(f)\tilde{X}(f)] \tag{2-99}$$

in which $\tilde{H}(f)$ and $\tilde{X}(f)$ are the Fourier transforms of $\tilde{h}(t)$ and $\tilde{x}(t)$, respectively.

EXAMPLE 2–4

Consider the system described by the differential equation

$$\frac{d^2y(t)}{dt^2} + \frac{1}{Q}\frac{dy(t)}{dt} + 2\pi f_0 y(t) = \frac{1}{Q}\frac{dx(t)}{dt} \tag{2-100}$$

with input given by (2–88). Taking the Fourier transform of both sides of (2–100), we find the system transfer function to be

$$H(f) = \frac{1}{1 + jQ(f/f_0 - f_0/f)} \tag{2-101}$$

For $Q \gg 1$, it can be shown by plotting, that the frequency response of the filter is appreciable only in the neighborhood of f_0. Assuming that $\Delta f \ll f_0$, where Δf is defined in (2–88), we can use the bandpass analysis technique derived above to find the output.

To proceed, note that for $Q \gg 1$, $H(f)$ can be approximated as

$$H(f) = \frac{1}{1 + j2Q(f - f_0)/f_0} + \frac{1}{1 + j2Q(f + f_0)/f_0} \tag{2-102}$$

which results from the approximation

$$\frac{f}{f_0} - \frac{f_0}{f} \approx 2\frac{f \pm f_0}{f_0}, \text{ if } f \approx \mp f_0 \qquad (2\text{--}103)$$

Taking the positive frequency half of (2–102), shifting it to the left by f_0, and doubling it results in the lowpass equivalent transfer function, which is

$$\tilde{H}(f) = \frac{2}{1 + j2Qf/f_0} \qquad (2\text{--}104)$$

We use (2–99) to find the envelope of the output and thence the real output (it is easiest in this case to carry out the convolution rather than multiplying the Fourier transforms together and inverse Fourier transforming). Inverse Fourier transformation of (2–104) gives

$$\tilde{h}(t) = 2\gamma\exp(-\gamma t)u(t) \qquad (2\text{--}105)$$

where

$$\gamma = \frac{\pi f_0}{Q} \qquad (2\text{--}106)$$

Substitution of (2–91) and (2–105) into (2–99) and carrying out the convolution results in

$$\tilde{y}(t) = \begin{cases} 0, & t < 0 \\ \dfrac{\gamma}{\gamma - \beta}[\exp(-\beta t) - \exp(-\gamma t)], & t \geq 0, \gamma \neq \beta \\ \gamma t \exp(-\gamma t), & t \geq 0, \gamma = \beta \end{cases} \qquad (2\text{--}107)$$

For $\gamma \neq \beta$ the real output is

$$y(t) = \text{Re}[\tilde{y}(t)\exp(j2\pi f_0 t)] \qquad (2\text{--}108)$$

$$= A(\Delta f)\{\exp(-\alpha t)\cos[2\pi(f_0 + \Delta f)t + \phi(\Delta f)] - \exp(-\pi f_0 t/Q)\cos[2\pi f_0 t + \phi(\Delta f)]\}$$

where

$$A(\Delta f) = \frac{\pi f_0/Q}{\sqrt{(\pi f_0/Q - \alpha)^2 + (2\pi\Delta f)^2}} \qquad (2\text{--}109)$$

and

$$\phi(\Delta f) = \tan^{-1}\left[\frac{2\pi\Delta f}{\pi f_0/Q - \alpha}\right] \qquad (2\text{--}110)$$

Direct application of the superposition integral to the real signals would have involved considerably more labor.

2.4 SIGNAL DISTORTION AND FILTERING

In this section the description of the effect of a system on signal transmission is considered. The concept of a distortionless system is first defined together with the artifice of ideal filters. Following this, the characterization of a filter in terms of group and phase delay is introduced and used to describe the effect of nonideal filters on signal transmission. Next, several types of practical filter designs and characteristics are summarized. The section closes with a summary of zero-memory nonlinear system characteristics and techniques for the analysis of zero-memory nonlinear systems.

2.4.1 Distortionless Transmission and Ideal Filters

In many signal transmission systems, the goal is to obtain an output signal that resembles the input signal or some function of it.[7] If the output of a system is a scaled, delayed version of its input, the system is said to be *distortionless*. Thus the input-output relationship for a fixed, linear, distortionless system in the time domain is

$$y(t) = H_0 x(t - t_0) \qquad (2\text{--}111)$$

where $x(t)$ is the input, $y(t)$ is the output, and H_0 and t_0 are constants referred to as the system's gain (or attenuation) and delay, respectively. Using the delay theorem of Fourier transforms (pair 2, Table F–7), the transfer function of a fixed, linear, distortionless system is

$$H(f) = H_0 \exp(-j2\pi f t_0) \qquad (2\text{--}112)$$

That is, the amplitude response of a distortionless system is a constant and its phase response is a linear function of frequency. If the input signal is bandlimited, these conditions need hold only for the frequency range over which the input signal has significant spectral content. Depending on whether a signal is lowpass, bandpass, or highpass, three types of ideal signal transmission system characteristics can be defined as shown in Figure 2–7. Such systems are referred to as *ideal filters,* a term that is in one sense a misnomer in that their impulse responses exist for $t < 0$. Thus ideal filters are noncausal, as illustrated in Figure 2–8, which shows the impulse responses of ideal lowpass, bandpass, and highpass filters, respectively (see Problem 2–20).

Filters for which the amplitude response is not constant over the bandwidth of the input signal are said to introduce *amplitude distortion*; those with nonlinear phase responses introduce *phase distortion.*

2.4.2 Group and Phase Delay

Given a filter with transfer function $H(f)$ written in complex exponential form as

---

[7] In some cases, such as the matched filter to be discussed later, output signal fidelity is not the primary consideration, but rather, the maximization of the output signal-to-noise ratio at time t_0.

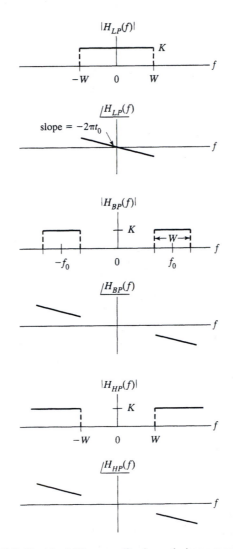

FIGURE 2–7   Ideal filter amplitude and phase responses.

$$H(f) = A(f)\exp[j\theta(f)] \tag{2–113}$$

where $A(f)$ is its amplitude response and $\theta(f)$ its phase response, the *group delay* of the filter is defined as

$$t_g(f) = -\frac{1}{2\pi}\frac{d\theta(f)}{df} \tag{2–114}$$

and its *phase delay* is defined as

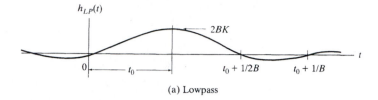

(a) Lowpass

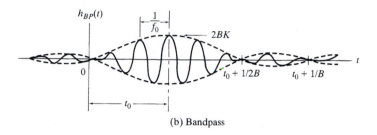

(b) Bandpass

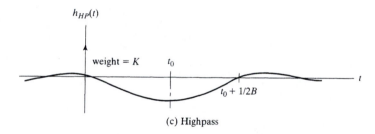

(c) Highpass

FIGURE 2–8 Impulse responses for ideal filters.

$$t_p(f) = -\frac{1}{2\pi}\frac{\theta(f)}{f} \tag{2–115}$$

Figure 2–9 illustrates these concepts, where it is shown that the group delay is the magnitude of the slope of the phase response curve of the system when plotted as a function of $2\pi f$. The phase delay is the magnitude of the slope of a line from the origin to an arbitrary point $2\pi f$ on the same curve. The physical significance of the group and phase delay functions is the following:

1. Group delay gives the delay experienced by a signal in passing through a system assuming the system's amplitude response is constant and its phase is linear over the signal bandwidth.
2. The phase delay of a system at frequency f gives the delay imposed by the system on a steady-state sinusoidal input of frequency f.

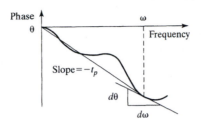

$$\text{Group delay; } t_g = -\frac{d\theta}{d\omega}, \quad \begin{matrix} \theta & \text{in radians} \\ \omega & \text{in radians/s} \end{matrix}$$

$$= -\frac{1}{2\pi}\frac{d\theta}{df}, \quad \begin{matrix} \theta & \text{in radians} \\ f & \text{in hertz} \end{matrix}$$

FIGURE 2–9   Illustration of group and phase delays.

From (2–112) and Figure 2–9 it is seen that signal distortion results if the group delay is not equal to the phase delay for all frequencies (i.e., a constant). Thus, group delay is an important measure of *phase*, or *delay*, *distortion* for a system. Example plots of group delay versus frequency are given in the following subsection, where practical filter types are discussed.

To examine further the effect of a system with nonideal amplitude and phase responses on a signal, consider Figure 2–10. These nonideal responses may be expressed as

$$A(f) = A_0 + \Delta A(f) \tag{2–116}$$

and

$$\theta(f) = -2\pi t_0 f + \Delta\theta(f) \tag{2–117}$$

where $\Delta A(f)$ and $\Delta\theta(f)$ are deviations from the ideal characteristics. The output of the filter due to an input signal $x(t)$ with Fourier transform $X(f)$ is

$$y(t) = \mathcal{F}^{-1}\{X(f)A(f)\exp[j\theta(f)]\} \tag{2–118}$$

For $\Delta A(f)$ and $\Delta\theta(f)$ small over the passband of the signal, the filter transfer function is well approximated by

$$A(f)\exp[j\theta(f)] \approx [A_0 + \Delta A(f) + jA_0\Delta\theta(f)]\exp(-j2\pi ft_0) \tag{2–119}$$

where (2–116) and (2–117) have been substituted, $\exp(j\Delta\theta)$ was expanded in a power series, and all terms above first order dropped.

Two cases can be considered for $\Delta A(f)$ and $\Delta\theta(f)$, a lowpass system and a bandpass system. Consider the case of a lowpass system first. For a lowpass system it must be true that $A(f)$ is even and $\theta(f)$ is odd. Since $\Delta A(f)$ and $\Delta\theta(f)$ are small perturbations on the ideal responses A_0 and $-2\pi t_0 f$, they may be expanded in power series as

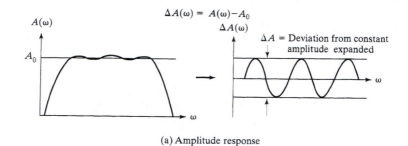

(a) Amplitude response

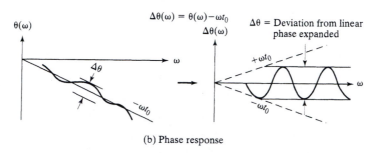

(b) Phase response

FIGURE 2–10 Nonideal amplitude and phase response functions for a filter.

$$\Delta A(f) = a_2 f^2 + a_4 f^4 + \cdots \tag{2–120}$$

and

$$\Delta\theta(f) = b_3 f^3 + b_5 f^5 + \cdots \tag{2–121}$$

respectively, where the even and odd symmetry conditions just mentioned have been imposed. Use of (2–120) and (2–121) in (2–119), and substitution of the resulting equation into (2–118), gives the expression

$$y(t) = \mathscr{F}^{-1}\{[A_0 + a_2 f^2 + jA_0 b_3 f^3 + a_4 f^4 + jA_0 b_5 f^5 + \cdots]X(f)\exp(-j2\pi t_0 f)\} \tag{2–122}$$

By the time delay and differentiation theorems of Fourier transforms, (2–122) can be inverse transformed to give the series

$$y(t) = A_0 x(t - t_0) + A_2 x^{(2)}(t - t_0) + B_3 x^{(3)}(t - t_0) + A_4 x^{(4)}(t - t_0) + B_5 x^{(5)}(t - t_0) + \cdots \tag{2–123}$$

where

$$\begin{aligned} A_2 &= -a_2/(2\pi)^2, \quad B_3 = -A_0 b_3/(2\pi)^3 \\ A_4 &= a_4/(2\pi)^4, \quad B_5 = A_0 b_5/(2\pi)^5 \end{aligned} \tag{2–124}$$

and $x^{(n)}(t)$ denotes the nth derivative of $x(t)$.

EXAMPLE 2–5

Consider the lowpass input signal

$$x(t) = B \exp\left(-\frac{t^2}{2\tau^2}\right)$$

where B and τ are constants, to a filter with amplitude and phase responses approximated by

$$A(f) = A_0 + a_2 f^2$$

and

$$\theta(f) = b_3 f^3$$

respectively (the delay $t_0 = 0$ for simplicity). In this case (2–123) becomes

$$y(t) = A_0 x(t) + A_2 x^{(2)}(t) + B_3 x^{(3)}(t)$$

where A_2 and B_3 were defined previously. Taking derivatives of $x(t)$ and substituting into the expression for $y(t)$, one obtains

$$y(t) = A_0 B \exp\left(-\frac{t^2}{2\tau^2}\right) - \frac{A_2 B}{\tau^2}\left(1 - \frac{t^2}{\tau^2}\right)\exp\left(-\frac{t^2}{2\tau^2}\right) + \frac{B_3 B}{\tau^3}\left(\frac{3t}{\tau} - \frac{t^3}{\tau^3}\right)\exp\left(-\frac{t^2}{2\tau^2}\right)$$

$$(2\text{–}125)$$

The first term corresponds to the undistorted output signal, the second term represents amplitude distortion, and the third term represents phase distortion. Undistorted and distorted waveforms are compared in Figure 2–11 for a Gaussian pulse of amplitude $A_0 = B = 1$.

Consider next the bandpass case. Use of the theory developed in Section 2.2 allows (2–118) to be rewritten as

$$\tilde{y}(t) = \mathcal{F}^{-1}\{\tilde{X}(f)\tilde{A}(f)\exp[j\tilde{\theta}(f)]\} \qquad (2\text{–}126)$$

where the tildes denote complex envelopes. Since $\tilde{Y}(f) = \tilde{X}(f)\,\tilde{A}(f)\,\exp[j\,\tilde{\theta}(f)]$ is the Fourier transform of a complex-envelope quantity, it is no longer true that $\tilde{A}(f)$ must be an even function of frequency and that $\tilde{\theta}(f)$ must be odd. Therefore, $\Delta A(f)$ and $\Delta \theta(f)$ in (2–116) and (2–117) are expanded as

$$\Delta A(f) = a_1 f + a_2 f^2 + a_3 f^3 + \cdots \qquad (2\text{–}127)$$

and

$$\Delta \theta(f) = b_0 + b_2 f^2 + b_3 f^3 + \cdots \qquad (2\text{–}128)$$

where $\tilde{A}(f) = A_0 + \Delta A(f)$ and $\tilde{\theta}(f) = -2\pi t_0 f + \Delta \theta(f)$. Expansion of (2–126) to second-order terms in $\Delta A(f)$ and $\Delta \theta(f)$ and substitution of the power series (2–127) and (2–128) gives

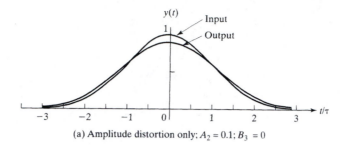

(a) Amplitude distortion only; $A_2 = 0.1; B_3 = 0$

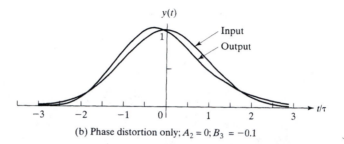

(b) Phase distortion only; $A_2 = 0; B_3 = -0.1$

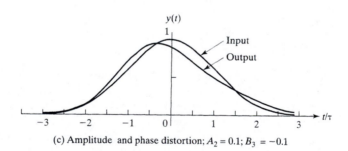

(c) Amplitude and phase distortion; $A_2 = 0.1; B_3 = -0.1$

FIGURE 2–11   Example showing the effect of amplitude and phase response perturbations on system response.

$$\tilde{y}(t) = A_0\left(1 + jb_0 - \frac{1}{2}b_0^2\right)\tilde{x}(t - t_0) + jA_1\tilde{x}^{(1)}(t - t_0) + (A_2 + jB_2)\tilde{x}^{(2)}(t - t_0) + \cdots \quad (2\text{–}129)$$

where

$$A_1 = -\frac{a_1\left(1 + jb_0 - \frac{1}{2}b_0^2\right)}{2\pi}, \quad A_2 = -\frac{a_2\left(1 - \frac{1}{2}b_0^2\right) - A_0b_0b_2}{(2\pi)^2} \quad (2\text{–}130)$$

$$B_2 = -\frac{(A_0b_2 + a_2b_0)}{(2\pi)^2}$$

Thus, for an input signal of the form

$$x(t) = \text{Re}[\tilde{x}(t)\exp(j2\pi f_0 t)] \tag{2-131}$$

the output

$$y(t) = \text{Re}[\tilde{y}(t)\exp(j2\pi f_0 t)] \tag{2-132}$$

is obtained where $\tilde{y}(t)$ is given in terms of $\tilde{x}(t)$ by (2–129). The term $A_0\tilde{x}(t - t_0)$ represents the undistorted output and all other terms are distortion

EXAMPLE 2–6

Consider the amplitude-modulated input signal

$$x(t) = \text{Re}[(1 + a\cos 2\pi f_m t)\exp(j2\pi f_0 t)]$$

to a system with $b_0 = 0$; A_1, A_2, and B_2 are, for the moment, unspecified. It is also assumed that $t_0 = 0$ for simplicity. It follows that

$$\tilde{x}(t) = 1 + a\cos 2\pi f_m t$$

$$\tilde{x}^{(1)}(t) = -2\pi f_m a\sin 2\pi f_m t$$

$$\tilde{x}^{(2)}(t) = -(2\pi f_m)^2 a\cos 2\pi f_m t$$

Therefore, the complex envelope of the output is

$$\tilde{y}(t) = A_0(1 + a\cos2\pi f_m t) - jA_1(2\pi f_m)a\sin2\pi f_m t - (A_2 + jB_2)(2\pi f_m)^2 a\cos 2\pi f_m t$$

The real output is obtained as $y(t) = \text{Re}[\tilde{y}(t)\exp(j2\pi f_0 t)]$. The result is

$$y(t) = A_0[1 + a\cos(2\pi f_m t)]\cos(2\pi f_0 t) + A_1(2\pi f_m)a\sin(2\pi f_m t)\sin(2\pi f_0 t)$$

$$- A_2(2\pi f_m)^2 a\cos(2\pi f_m t)\cos(2\pi f_0 t) + B_2(2\pi f_m)^2 a\cos(2\pi f_m t)\sin(2\pi f_0 t)$$

The first term is the undistorted output signal and the other terms represent various types of distortion. Each of these distortion terms will now be considered separately.

1. $A_1 = B_2 = 0$, $A_2 \neq 0$. In this case, the output signal becomes

$$y(t) = A_0[1 + a(1 - 4\pi^2 f_m^2 A_2/A_0)\cos(2\pi f_m t)]\cos(2\pi f_0 t).$$

As a result of the deviation of the amplitude response from A_0, distortion is introduced into the amplitude modulation in that the modulation index, a, is changed.

2. $A_2 = B_2 = 0$, $A_1 \neq 0$. The output signal for this case can be written

$$y(t) = A_0[1 + a\cos(2\pi f_m t)]\cos2\pi f_0 t + 2\pi f_m A_1 a\sin(2\pi f_m t)\sin(2\pi f_0 t)$$

Because of the second term, which is in phase quadrature to the amplitude-modulated first term, phase modulation is introduced and a slightly distorted envelope results (*harmonic distortion,* or distortion at frequency of f_m hertz, is introduced into the envelope). Such distortion is referred to as *modulation conversion* or *AM-to-PM conversion.*

3. $A_1 = A_2 = 0$, $B_2 \neq 0$. Again, as in case 2, a distortion term is introduced that is in phase quadrature to the modulated input carrier. In the present case, however, the distortion arises because of the departure of the filter's phase response characteristic from the ideal linear response $-2\pi t_0 f$.

EXAMPLE 2–7

Consider the phase-modulated signal

$$x(t) = \text{Re}\{\exp[j(2\pi f_0 t + a \cos(2\pi f_m t))]\} = \cos[2\pi f_0 t + a \cos(2\pi f_m t)]$$

with the corresponding complex envelope

$$\tilde{x}(t) = \exp[\,ja \cos(2\pi f_m t)]$$

Its derivatives are

$$\tilde{x}^{(1)}(t) = -j2\pi f_m a \sin(2\pi f_m t)\exp[\,ja \cos(2\pi f_m t)]$$

$$\tilde{x}^{(2)}(t) = -j(2\pi f_m)^2 a[\cos(2\pi f_m t) - ja \sin^2(2\pi f_m t)]\exp[ja \cos(2\pi f_m t)]$$

As in Example 2–6, assume that $A_3 = B_3 = 0$. If $t_0 = b_0 = 0$, the output complex envelope is

$$\tilde{y}(t) = [A_0 + 2\pi f_m A_1 a \sin 2\pi f_m t$$

$$+ (B_2 - jA_2)(2\pi f_m)^2 a(\cos 2\pi f_m t - ja \sin^2 2\pi f_m t)]\exp(ja \cos 2\pi f_m t)$$

The real output signal is found as $y(t) = \text{Re}[\tilde{y}(t) \exp(j2\pi f_0 t)]$. The result is

$$y(t) = [A_0 + 2\pi f_m A_1 a \sin 2\pi f_m t$$

$$+ (2\pi f_m)^2 a(B_2 \cos 2\pi f_m t + A_2 a \sin^2 2\pi f_m t)]\cos(2\pi f_0 t + a \cos 2\pi f_m t)$$

$$+ (2\pi f_m)^2 a(A_2 \cos 2\pi f_m t + B_2 a \sin^2 2\pi f_m t)\sin(2\pi f_0 t + a \cos 2\pi f_m t)$$

As was done in Example 2–6, two special cases will be considered.

1. If $A_2 = B_2 = 0$ and A_1 is not zero, the phase-modulated input signal produces an output signal that has the same phase modulation as the input signal but has an additional amplitude modulation. That is, *PM-to-AM conversion* has taken place. From the expression for $y(t)$, it is seen that PM-to-AM conversion results from a linear deviation of the amplitude response ($A_1 \neq 0$) from the ideal constant-amplitude response.

2. If A_2 and B_2 are not both zero, a term that is in phase quadrature to the phase-modulated input signal is produced. This results in both a nonconstant envelope as well as distortion of the phase modulation on the input signal.

In this section it has been shown how nonideal amplitude and phase characteristics for linear, time-invariant systems distort signals. In the case of modulated signals, these nonideal characteristics may modify the original modulating signal by converting it from one type of modulation to another, or they may modify the modulating signal itself by introducing distortion. This distortion may involve the production of new frequencies. Another way new frequencies may be produced is through the presence of nonlinearities, either intentional or unintentional, in the system. We consider this topic next.

2.4.3   Nonlinear Systems and Nonlinear Distortion

It is indeed fortunate that linear system models have such broad applicability. However, there are many instances in communication system analysis and design that require the modeling of nonlinear systems. For purposes of modeling, a time-invariant system can be classified as having either *zero memory* or *nonzero memory*. For *zero-memory systems*, the input-output relationship is of the form

$$y(t) = G[x(t)] \tag{2-133}$$

where $G[\cdot]$ is a single-valued function of its argument. That is, the output of the system at time t depends only on the input to the system at the same instant of time, not on past or future values. For a *nonzero memory system*, however, the output depends on past values of the input as well as the input at the present time if the system is causal, and on future values also if the system is noncausal (not physically possible, but nevertheless mathematically convenient in some cases).

Consider a zero-memory, fixed, nonlinear system with transfer characteristic given as

$$\begin{aligned} y(t) &= a_0 + a_1 x(t) + a_2 x^2(t) + a_3 x^3(t) + \cdots \\ &\equiv y_0(t) + y_1(t) + y_2(t) + y_3(t) + \cdots \end{aligned} \tag{2-134}$$

Models such as this have several uses. For example, (2–134) could represent an amplifier driven slightly nonlinear; the first term represents a dc bias, the second term the desired output, and the remaining terms undesired terms due to nonlinearities.

Let the input in (2–134) be the sum of two sinusoidal components at frequencies f_1 and f_2:

$$x(t) = A_1 \cos 2\pi f_1 t + A_2 \cos 2\pi f_2 t \tag{2-135}$$

The output components are

$$y_0(t) = a_0$$

$$y_1(t) = a_1 A_1 \cos 2\pi f_1 t + a_1 A_2 \cos 2\pi f_2 t$$

$$\begin{aligned} y_2(t) = a_2 \Bigg[&\frac{A_1^2}{2} + \frac{A_2^2}{2} + \frac{A_1^2}{2} \cos 4\pi f_1 t + \frac{A_2^2}{2} \cos 4\pi f_2 t \\ &+ A_1 A_2 \cos 2\pi (f_1 + f_2)t + A_1 A_2 \cos 2\pi (f_1 - f_2)t \Bigg] \end{aligned} \tag{2-136}$$

$$\begin{aligned} y_3(t) = &\frac{a_3 A_1^3}{4} (3 \cos 2\pi f_1 t + \cos 6\pi f_1 t) \\ &+ \frac{3 a_3 A_1^2 A_2}{2} \left[\cos 2\pi f_2 t + \frac{1}{2} \cos 2\pi (2f_1 + f_2)t + \frac{1}{2} \cos 2\pi (2f_1 - f_2)t \right] \end{aligned}$$

$$+ \frac{3a_3A_2^2 A_1}{2} \left[\cos 2\pi f_1 t + \frac{1}{2} \cos 2\pi (2f_2 + f_1)t + \frac{1}{2} \cos 2\pi (2f_2 - f_1)t \right]$$

$$+ \frac{a_3A_2^3}{4} (3 \cos 2\pi f_2 t + \cos 6\pi f_2 t)$$

and so on.

The total output is the sum of y_0, y_1, y_2, y_3, and so on. Note that the following frequencies are present in the output:

1. dc
2. The original frequencies, f_1 and f_2
3. Harmonics of f_1 and f_2 (i.e., frequencies at $2f_1$, $2f_2$, $3f_1$, etc.)
4. Sums and differences of harmonics of f_1 and f_2 (i.e., frequencies at $f_1 + f_2$, $f_1 - f_2$, etc.)

If (2–134) represents an amplifier driven slightly into its nonlinear region of operation, the third set of frequencies mentioned represents *harmonic distortion* and the fourth set represents *intermodulation distortion* components of the output.

EXAMPLE 2–8

Suppose that a nonlinear device represented by the transfer characteristic (2–134) is to be used as a *mixer*. The input is the sum of three terms, a local oscillator signal,

$$x_{LO}(t) = L \cos 2\pi f_{LO} t$$

and two desired sinusoidal signals,

$$x_A(t) = A \cos 2\pi f_A t$$

$$x_B(t) = B \cos 2\pi f_B t$$

The first two terms in (2–134) give outputs at dc and feedthrough outputs,

$$a_1 x(t) = a_1 (L \cos 2\pi f_{LO} t + A \cos 2\pi f_A t + B \cos 2\pi f_B t)$$

The third term in (2–134), $a_2 x^2(t)$, results in the following outputs:

$$a_2 x_{LO}^2(t) = \frac{a_2 L^2}{2} (1 + \cos 4\pi f_{LO} t)$$

$$a_2 x_A^2(t) = \frac{a_2 A^2}{2} (1 + \cos 4\pi f_A t)$$

$$a_2 x_B^2(t) = \frac{a_2 B^2}{2} (1 + \cos 4\pi f_B t)$$

$$2a_2 x_A(t) x_B(t) = a_2 AB[\cos 2\pi (f_A - f_B) t + \cos 2\pi (f_A + f_B)t]$$

$$2a_2 x_{LO}(t) x_A(t) = a_2 AL[\cos 2\pi (f_{LO} - f_A)t + \cos 2\pi (f_{LO} + f_A)t]$$

$$2a_2 x_{LO}(t) x_B(t) = a_2 LB[\cos 2\pi (f_{LO} - f_B)t + \cos 2\pi (f_{LO} + f_B)t]$$

Of these seven output components, all except the last two represent undesired output terms. In the last two terms, either the frequencies $f_{LO} - f_A$ and $f_{LO} - f_B$ or $f_{LO} + f_A$ and $f_{LO} + f_B$ would be selected at the output. The former are referred to as the *low-side frequencies* from the mixer, and the latter are referred to as *high-side frequencies*. It is important that no undesired output frequencies are close to the desired frequencies at the output. A typical spectral plot for the output is provided in Figure 2–12. If one considers the frequencies at the output resulting from the term $a_3 x^3(t)$, numerous such terms are obtained. The terms of primary interest are $3x^2_A(t)x_B(t)$ and $3x_A(t)x^2_B(t)$, which can be expanded to give *third-order intermodulation products*. That is, they contain frequencies at $2f_A \pm f_B$ and $2f_B \pm f_A$. The amplitudes of these components are proportional to the amplitude of one signal multiplied by the square of the amplitude of the other signal. Because of this, these products change amplitude three times faster than $x_A(t)$ and $x_B(t)$ if both A and B change simultaneously. If these signals fall within the passband of the system following the mixer, where they cannot be eliminated by filtering, they contribute to the interference at the mixer output.

Several terms are used when referring to mixer performance. These are (1) conversion loss, (2) compression, (3) isolation, (4) harmonic distortion (second order), (5) intermodulation distortion (third order), and (6) noise figure. These are briefly described below.

Conversion loss: This is the ratio of power in the desired output signal to power in the input signal. In general, conversion loss decreases with increasing local oscillator frequency and increasing power of the local oscillator signal. Since two output sidebands are generated for a single input frequency, and only one is desired, the conversion loss of a passive mixer must be at least 3 dB. Typical values range from 5 to 8 dB.

Compression: The 1 dB compression point of a mixer is defined as the input signal power level that causes a 1 dB increase in conversion loss. It is weakly dependent on the local oscillator power level.

Isolation: The ratio of local oscillator signal power at the output (IF) port to the local oscillator signal power at the local oscillator port is referred to as the *LO-to-IF isola-*

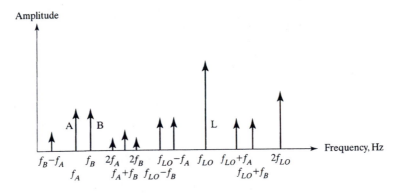

Amplitude

Frequency, Hz

$f_B - f_A$ f_B $2f_A$ $2f_B$ $f_{LO} - f_A$ f_{LO} $f_{LO} + f_A$ $2f_{LO}$

f_A $f_A + f_B$ $f_{LO} - f_B$ $f_{LO} + f_B$

A   B   L

FIGURE 2–12   Typical spectral representation of a mixer output.

tion. It typically is maximized for double balanced mixers. The ratio of radio-frequency (RF) signal power at the IF port to RF signal power at the RF port is referred to as *RF-to-IF isolation.* RF-to-IF isolation typically decreases with increasing frequency. Isolation values for typical double-balanced mixers can be 50 dB or more.

Harmonic distortion: The primary harmonic distortion component at a mixer output is second order distortion, and it refers to the power in second harmonic component of the IF signal due to the mixer (care must be taken to exclude second harmonic due to feedthrough of the RF or LO signal sources). Second harmonic distortion, in general, decreases with increasing LO signal power and increases with increasing input signal power.

Intermodulation distortion: These components consist of sums and differences of harmonics of frequencies present at the mixer inputs, the primary ones being the third-order differences at the frequencies $2f_A - f_B$ and $2f_B - f_A$, where f_A and f_B are the frequencies of input signals *A* and *B*. A figure of merit used to describe the intermodulation performance of a mixer is the *third-order intercept,* which is defined as the *theoretical* intersection of the graphs (assumed linear) of powers expressed in dBm or dBW, of the desired and intermodulation output powers versus input signal power. Recall from Example 2–8 that the latter graph has a slope three times greater than that of the former as a function of input power. This concept is illustrated in Figure 2–13. The higher the intercept point, the better the suppression of third-order products. The third-order intercept point of a physical mixer varies with input signal power level and LO power, although theoretically no dependence on these parameters is predicted.

Noise figure: This is the ratio of output port signal-to-noise ratio to input port signal-to-noise ratio. It is, in general, frequency dependent, although average values are sometimes used. Since the noise figure of an ideal attenuator at room temperature is theoretically equal to the attenuation factor of the device, it is not a bad approximation to use the conversion loss of a mixer as an estimate for its noise figure. (See Appendix B for the definition of noise figure for a general device.)

2.5 PRACTICAL FILTER TYPES AND CHARACTERISTICS [1]

2.5.1 General Terminology

In this section several practical lumped-element filter types are summarized together with their frequency response characteristics.[8] These include Butterworth, Chebyshev, and Bessel (or linear phase). All filter frequency response characteristics considered are low-pass and, with the exception of Chebyshev, are assumed to have 3 dB frequencies normalized to 1 rad/s. There is no loss in generality in doing so, for frequency scaling and

---

[8]Details on realization of these filters in both lumped-element and transmission-line (stripline) form can be found in a number of references. For lumped-element realizations, see [4].

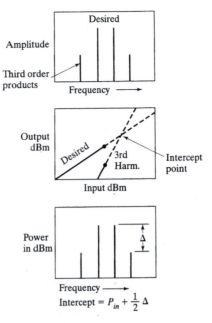

FIGURE 2–13 Plot of intermodulation distortion power and primary component output power versus input power for a mixer, which illustrates the concept of third-order intercept.

transformations can be used to obtain other filter types. For example, consider a filter transfer function written as a function of the Laplace transform variable s in the form

$$H(s) = \frac{N(s)}{D(s)} \tag{2-137}$$

where

$$N(s) = \sum_{k=0}^{m} a_k s^k = (s - z_1)(s - z_2) \cdots (s - z_m) \tag{2-138}$$

and

$$D(s) = \sum_{k=0}^{n} b_k s^k = (s - p_1)(s - p_2) \cdots (s - p_n) \tag{2-139}$$

are numerator and denominator polynomials in s of degrees m and n, respectively. The roots of $N(s)$, $z_1, z_2 \ldots, z_m$, are the *zeros* of $H(s)$ and the roots of $D(s)$, $p_1, p_2, \ldots, p_n$, are the *poles* of $H(s)$. If a 3 dB cutoff frequency other than 1 rad/s is desired, s is replaced in (2–137) to (2–139) by

$$s' = \frac{s}{\omega_c} \tag{2-140}$$

where ω_c is the new 3 dB cutoff frequency.

If a *bandpass* filter is desired, s in (2–137) to (2–139) is replaced by

$$s' = \frac{s^2 + \omega_c^2}{s\omega_b} \tag{2-141}$$

The upper and lower band edge frequencies are given by

$$\omega_u = \frac{1}{2}\omega_b + \frac{1}{2}\sqrt{\omega_b^2 + 4\omega_c^2} \tag{2-142}$$

$$\omega_l = -\frac{1}{2}\omega_b + \frac{1}{2}\sqrt{\omega_b^2 + 4\omega_c^2}$$

The differences of these two equations results in the filter bandwidth in radians per second, or

$$\omega_b = \omega_u - \omega_l \tag{2-143}$$

and their product gives

$$\omega_u\omega_l = \omega_c^2 \tag{2-144}$$

Thus ω_c is the geometric center frequency of the bandpass filters. If $\omega_c \gg \omega_b$, it follows from (2–142) that

$$\omega_c = \frac{1}{2}(\omega_u + \omega_l) \tag{2-145}$$

A *highpass* transfer function can be obtained from (2–137) to (2–139) by replacing s by

$$s' = \frac{1}{s} \tag{2-146}$$

and following this transformation with a frequency scaling to obtain the desired 3 dB low cutoff frequency.

If a wideband bandpass filter is desired, an alternative to using (2–141) is to cascade lowpass and highpass sections. This is not satisfactory for the narrowband case because of the excess attenuation introduced at band center.

A band reject filter can be obtained by putting a highpass and lowpass filter in parallel. The combined transfer function is then

$$H_{BR}(s) = H_{LP}(s) + H_{HP}(s) \tag{2-147}$$

and it is assumed that where the magnitude of $H_{LP}(j\omega)$ is small for $s = j\omega$, the magnitude of $H_{HP}(j\omega)$ is not, and vice versa, except in the reject band where both are small. In other words, the cutoff frequency of the lowpass arm, $H_{LP}(s)$, is below that of the highpass arm, $H_{HP}(s)$. Alternatively, a band reject transformation, given by

TABLE 2–6   Coefficients for the Denominator Polynomial
of Butterworth Filters of Orders 1–5 (Unity 3 dB Frequency)

Order	b_0	b_1	b_2	b_3	b_4	b_5
1	1	1				
2	1	1.414	1			
3	1	2	2	1		
4	1	2.613	3.414	2.613	1	
5	1	3.236	5.236	5.236	3.236	1

$$s' = \frac{s\omega_b}{s^2 + \omega_c^2} \tag{2-148}$$

can be used in (2–137) to produce a notch filter. Note that this is the inverse of (2–141).

The Butterworth, Chebyshev, and Bessel filters mentioned previously will now be considered.

2.5.2   Butterworth Filters (Maximally Flat[9])

The Butterworth design is an all-pole configuration with

$$N(s) = 1 \tag{2-149}$$

and $D(s)$ has the coefficients given in Table 2–6. The pole positions of a filter with cutoff frequency of 1 rad/s all lie on a unit circle and may be computed from

$$p_k = -\sin\frac{(2k-1)\pi}{2n} + j\cos\frac{(2k-1)\pi}{2n}, \; k = 1, 2, \cdots, n \tag{2-150}$$

The amplitude and phase responses are found by using (2–150) in (2–137) through (2–139). The general form of the amplitude response for a 1 rad/s cutoff frequency is[10]

$$A(\Omega) = -10\log_{10}\left(1 + \Omega^{2n}\right) \text{ dB} \tag{2-151}$$

where Ω denotes a normalized frequency variable for the 1 rad/s cutoff frequency. The group delay is found by obtaining the phase response and differentiating with respect to Ω.

EXAMPLE 2–9

The transfer function of a third-order Butterworth filter, from Table 2–6, is

$$H(s) = \frac{1}{s^3 + 2s^2 + 2s + 1}$$

[9]By maximally flat it is meant that the Butterworth filter transfer function has $(2n - 1)$ derivatives equal to zero at $\omega = 0$.

[10]Ω is used for the frequency in rad/s when the filter cutoff frequency is 1 rad/s; ω is used for arbitrary cutoff.

Letting $s = j\Omega$ results in

$$H(j\Omega) = \frac{1}{1 - 2\Omega^2 + j(2\Omega - \Omega^3)} = \frac{1}{D(\Omega)}$$

from which

$$A(\Omega) = 20 \log_{10} |H(\Omega)| = -10 \log_{10}(1 + \Omega^6)$$

$$\theta(\Omega) = -\tan^{-1} \frac{\text{Im } D(\Omega)}{\text{Re } D(\Omega)} = -\tan^{-1}\left(\frac{2\Omega - \Omega^3}{1 - 2\Omega^2}\right)$$

The group delay in terms of normalized frequency is

$$t_g(\Omega) = -\frac{d\theta(\Omega)}{d\Omega} = \frac{2 + \Omega^2 + 2\Omega^4}{1 + \Omega^6}$$

Results for any cutoff frequency, say, ω_c, can be obtained by letting $\Omega = \omega/\omega_c$. The expressions for the attenuation, phase delay, and group delay are plotted in Figure 2–14.

2.5.3 Chebyshev Filters (Equal Ripple)

The Chebyshev approximation to an ideal filter gives much faster rolloff in the transition region than a Butterworth filter of the same order. This is achieved by allowing ripples in the passband. The poles of a normalized Chebyshev filter transfer function are obtained by moving the poles of a normalized Butterworth transfer function to the right by a factor

$$R_c = \tanh A \tag{2-152}$$

where

$$A = \frac{1}{n} \cosh^{-1}(1/\varepsilon) \tag{2-153}$$

in which

$$\varepsilon = \sqrt{10^{R/10} - 1} \tag{2-154}$$

and R is the passband ripple in decibels. This construction results in the poles of the Chebyshev filter lying on an ellipse with semi-major and semi-minor axes

$$b, a = \frac{1}{2}\left[(\sqrt{\varepsilon^{-2} + 1} + \varepsilon^{-1})^{1/n} \pm (\sqrt{\varepsilon^{-2} + 1} + \varepsilon^{-1})^{-1/n}\right] \tag{2-155}$$

The amplitude response function of a Chebyshev filter can be expressed as

$$A(\Omega) = -10 \log_{10}[1 + \varepsilon^2 C_n^2(\Omega)] \text{ dB} \tag{2-156}$$

where $C_n(\Omega)$ is a Chebyshev polynomial of order n. Chebyshev polynomials of order 5 and less are tabulated in Table 2–7. A recursion relation for obtaining $C_n(\Omega)$ is

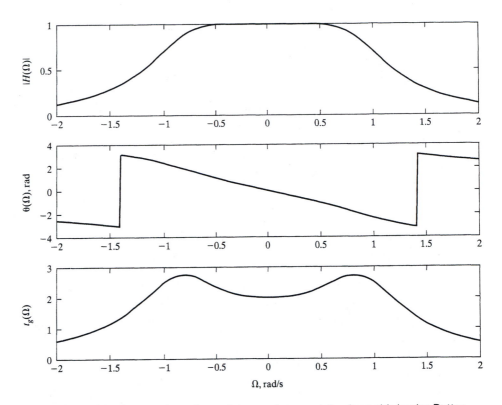

FIGURE 2–14 Attenuation, phase delay, and group delay for a third-order Butterworth filter.

$$C_n(\Omega) = 2\Omega C_{n-1}(\Omega) - C_{n-2}(\Omega), \ n = 2, 3, \cdots \qquad (2\text{–}157)$$

where $C_0(\Omega) = 1$.

At $\Omega = 1$, Chebyshev polynomials have a value of unity, which means that the attenuation as defined by (2–156) would have a value equal to the ripple in decibels. The 3 dB cutoff is slightly greater than 1 rad/s and, in fact, is equal to cosh A, where A is given by (2–153). In order to obtain an amplitude response function 3 dB down at $\Omega = 1$, Ω in (2–156) should be replaced by Ω cosh A.

TABLE 2–7 Chebyshev Polynomials

Order	Chebyshev Polynomial
1	Ω
2	$2\Omega^2 - 1$
3	$4\Omega^3 - 3\Omega$
4	$8\Omega^4 - 8\Omega^2 + 1$
5	$16\Omega^5 - 20\Omega^3 + 5\Omega$

The Chebyshev filter design just discussed is often referred to as a Chebyshev I design to differentiate it from the case where the stop band is designed to have a specified ripple. The latter is referred to as a Chebyshev II design.

MATLAB has filter design M-files included in its Signal Processing Toolbox. The Student Edition of MATLAB, Version 5.3 [3], includes many filter design functions for both analog and digital filters. Included are Butterworth (butter), Chebyshev I (chebyl), and Chebyshev II (cheby2) for lowpass, bandpass, band reject, or high pass designs. To find out the usage of these design aids, do a help _____ in the MATLAB Command Window, where the blank is the name of the filter desired [3].

2.5.4 Bessel (Maximally Flat Delay) Filters

The Bessel filter design is optimized to give an approximately linear phase or maximally flat group delay. The low pass approximation to constant delay results from the general transfer function

$$H(s) = \frac{1}{\sinh s + \cosh s} \qquad (2\text{--}158)$$

by expressing the hyperbolic functions as continued fraction expansions and truncating at different lengths. The resulting transfer functions are referred to as *Bessel*. As the order of a Bessel filter is increased, the region of flat delay is extended further into the stop band, but the steepness of the rolloff in attenuation in the transition region does not improve significantly. Therefore, Bessel filters are used in applications where transient properties, not rejection of undesired signals, are of main concern. The transfer function of a Bessel filter can be written in the form

$$H(s) = \frac{k_n}{B_n(s)} \qquad (2\text{--}159)$$

where $B_n(s)$ is a Bessel polynomial of order n defined recursively by

$$B_n(s) = (2n - 1)B_{n-1}(s) + s^2 B_{n-2}(s) \qquad (2\text{--}160)$$

with

$$B_0(s) = 1 \text{ and } B_1(s) = s + 1$$

and k_n is a constant chosen to give an amplitude response normalized to unity at $\Omega = 0$. It should be noted that application of (2–159) does not automatically result in a filter with a 3 dB cutoff frequency of 1 rad/s. Further details on filter design are provided in [4].

2.6 SAMPLING THEORY

The representation of signals in terms of periodically taken sample values is important in any communications system for several reasons:

1. Analog messages can be sampled, quantized, and sent in digital format.
2. A knowledge of sampling theory makes it possible to represent analog signals and systems digitally and thereby simulate communications systems on a digital computer for analysis and design purposes.
3. High-speed digital signal processors are now available that make possible digital implementation of many communications system functions that were previously implemented by analog circuitry.

In this section we give a derivation of the sampling theorem and discuss its use for representation of lowpass and bandpass signals.

2.6.1   The Lowpass Sampling Theorem

The lowpass sampling theorem states that *any signal with no frequency components above W Hz can be represented by samples taken at a minimum rate of $f_s = 2W$ samples per second, where it is assumed that there are no singularities in the spectrum of the sampled signal at $f = W$.*

To recover an undistorted version of the original signal, the sample values can be passed through an ideal lowpass filter of bandwidth f_3 Hz where $W \leq f_3 \leq f_s - W$. In practicality, no signal is ideally bandlimited, and no filter is ideal. Consequences of these nonideal properties of signals and filters on the sampling process will be discussed later.

To prove the sampling theorem, consider $x(t)$ with Fourier transform $X(f)$, where $|X(f)| = 0$ for $|f| \geq W$, as shown in Figure 2–15a. To carry out the sampling process, $x(t)$ is multiplied by the pulse train

$$p(t) = \sum_{n=-\infty}^{\infty} \frac{1}{\tau} \Pi \left(\frac{t - nT_s}{\tau} \right) \tag{2–161}$$

producing the sampled signal, $x_s(t)$, given by

$$x_s(t) = \sum_{n=-\infty}^{\infty} \frac{1}{\tau} \Pi \left(\frac{t - nT_s}{\tau} \right) x(t) \tag{2–162}$$

This sampled signal is shown in Figure 2–15b, and the sampling process is known as "natural" sampling. To simplify the derivation of the sampling theorem, we replace the "practical" pulse train $p(t)$ by the ideal impulse sampling waveform

$$\delta_s(t) = \sum_{n=-\infty}^{\infty} \delta(t - nT_s) \tag{2–163}$$

The practical pulse train, $p(t)$, can be obtained from (2–163) by convolving (2–163) with $(1/\tau)\Pi(t/\tau)$. The effect of practical sampling will be examined later. [Note that $(1/\tau)\Pi(t/\tau) \rightarrow \delta(t)$ as $\tau \rightarrow 0$.]

From the multiplication theorem of Fourier transforms, it follows that the spectrum of the ideal sampled waveform is

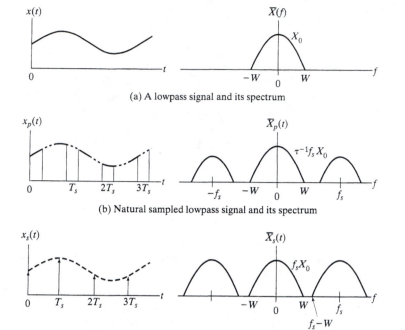

(a) A lowpass signal and its spectrum

(b) Natural sampled lowpass signal and its spectrum

(c) Ideal sampled waveform and its spectrum

(d) Recovered sampled signal

FIGURE 2–15   Steps in the sampling process.

$$X_s(f) = \mathcal{F}\left[\sum_{n=-\infty}^{\infty} \delta(t - nT_s)\right] * X(f) \tag{2–164}$$

Substituting the Fourier transform of the bracketed sum in (2–164) from Table F–7 (item 17), we find the sampled signal spectrum to be

$$X_s(f) = \left[f_s \sum_{n=-\infty}^{\infty} \delta(f - nf_s)\right] * X(f)$$

$$= f_s \sum_{n=-\infty}^{\infty} X(f - nf_s), \; f_s = T_s^{-1} \tag{2–165}$$

where the operations of convolution and summation have been interchanged in the first expression, and it is noted that the convolution of a delta function with another function simply moves the latter to the location of the delta function.

Assuming that $f_s \geq 2W$ and that $|X_s(f)| = 0$ for $|f| \geq W$, it follows that the separate terms in the sum (2–165) do not overlap. This is illustrated in Figure 2–15c. Thus an ideal lowpass filter can be used to separate the lowpass part of $X_s(f)$ from all remaining terms. Let this ideal lowpass filter have transfer function

$$H(f) = H_0 \Pi\left(\frac{f}{2B}\right) \exp(-j2\pi t_0 f), \quad W < B < f_s - W \qquad (2\text{–}166)$$

where H_0 is a gain constant and B is the filter bandwidth. The output of the filter is then

$$y(t) = \mathcal{F}^{-1}[X_s(f)\, H(f)] = f_s H_0 x(t - t_0) \qquad (2\text{–}167)$$

which follows by invoking the time delay theorem and the fact that $\Pi(f/2B) = 1$ within the lowpass part of $X_s(f)$ and is 0 for the remaining terms of $X_s(f)$. This lowpass filter recovery of a distortionless version (i.e., a scaled, time-delayed replica) of $x(t)$ is illustrated in Figure 2–15d.

Returning to (2–162), we investigate the effect of natural sampling. With natural sampling, (2–164) is replaced by

$$X_p(f) = \mathcal{F}\left[\frac{1}{\tau} \Pi\left(\frac{t}{\tau}\right) * \sum_{n=-\infty}^{\infty} \delta(t - nT_s)\right] * X(f)$$

$$= \left\{\mathcal{F}\left[\frac{1}{\tau} \Pi\left(\frac{t}{\tau}\right)\right] \mathcal{F}\left[\sum_{n=-\infty}^{\infty} \delta(t - nT_s)\right]\right\} * X(f)$$

$$\qquad\qquad (2\text{–}168)$$

$$= \left\{\mathrm{sinc}(f\tau)\left[f_s \sum_{n=-\infty}^{\infty} \delta(f - nf_s)\right]\right\} * X(f)$$

$$= f_s \sum_{n=-\infty}^{\infty} \mathrm{sinc}(nf_s\tau)\, X(f - nf_s)$$

It is seen that the spectrum of a natural sampled signal differs from that of an ideal sampled signal by the envelope factor $\mathrm{sinc}(nf_s\tau)$. This is illustrated in Figure 2–15b. Indeed, as $\tau \to 0$, $\mathrm{sinc}(nf_s\tau) \to 1$, and the two spectra are identical.

The consequences of $f_s < 2W$ will be the overlap of the separate terms in (2–165). This is referred to as aliasing and is illustrated by the following example.

EXAMPLE 2–10 _____

Consider the signal $x(t) = 2\cos(20\pi t)$, which is sampled at the following rates: **(a)** 30 samples per second; **(b)** 15 samples per second. Recovery is accomplished in both cases by an ideal lowpass filter with $H(f) = \Pi(f/30)$. Describe the output in both cases.

Solution: **(a)** Since $X(f) = \delta(f - 10) + \delta(f + 10)$, the spectrum of the sampled signal is

$$X_{sa}(f) = 30 \sum_{n=-\infty}^{\infty} [\delta(f - 10 - 30n) + \delta(f + 10 - 30n)]$$

The spectrum of the signal at the output of the lowpass recovery filter is

$$Y_a(f) = 30[\delta(f - 10) + \delta(f + 10)]$$

This corresponds to an output of

$$y_a(t) = 60 \cos(20\pi t)$$

which is proportional to the original signal.

(b)   The spectrum of the sampled signal now is

$$X_{sb}(f) = 15 \sum_{n=-\infty}^{\infty} [\delta(f - 10 - 15n) + \delta(f + 10 - 15n)]$$

and the spectrum of the output signal is

$$Y_b(f) = 15[\delta(f - 10) + \delta(f + 10) + \delta(f - 5) + \delta(f + 5)]$$

which results in the time domain output

$$y_b(t) = 30 \cos(20\pi t) + 30 \cos(10\pi t)$$

Because of the low sampling rate, we now have a component $30 \cos(10\pi t)$ from undersampling, which "impersonates" an actual signal component.

2.6.2   Nonideal Effects in Sampling

If the requirements of ideal band-limited signals and an ideal recovery filter are not met, the results of the sampling process will be less than ideal. We have already seen the effects of sampling at too low a rate (undersampling) in Example 2–10. The effects of a nonband-limited spectrum for the sampled signal and a nonideal recovery filter are illustrated in Figures 2–16a and 2–16b, respectively.

The effects of a nonideal spectrum are the same as the effects of undersampling—frequencies from frequency-translated versions of $X(f)$ appear in the output spectrum. The effects of a nonideal recovery filter are similar in that unwanted frequencies appear in the output spectrum. However, in contrast to sampling and recovery of a nonband-limited spectrum where the unwanted frequencies appear back *in band*, the unwanted spectral components here are at *out-of-band* frequencies.

From Figure 2–16, it should be clear that either of these nonideal effects can be combated by using a higher sampling frequency. In addition, aliasing due to sampling nonband-limited spectra can be combated by passing the signal to be sampled through a *prefilter* that attenuates the out-of-band components.

2.6.3   Sampling of Bandpass Signals

Of great interest in communications systems is how to sample bandpass signals. This sampling can be accomplished in a straightforward fashion using an inphase and quadrature mixing process as illustrated in Figure 2–17. Both sets of samples (inphase and quad-

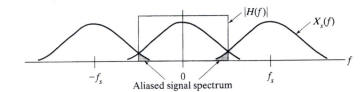

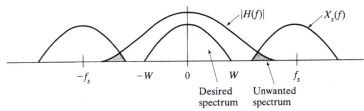

(a) Illustration of the effect of sampling a nonband-limited signal

(b) Illustration of the effect of a nonideal recovery filter

FIGURE 2–16 Nonideal effects in sampling.

rature) are necessary to completely represent the bandpass signal. This follows directly from (2–84), where a bandpass signal $x(t)$ was represented in terms of its inphase and quadrature components. If the bandwidth of $x(t)$ is originally W hertz, then both $x_R(t)$ and $x_I(t)$ are $W/2$ hertz in bandwidth (single-sided bandwidths assumed). Consequently, both must be sampled at a rate of $f_s = W$ samples per second for an overall sampling rate of $x(t)$ of $2W$ samples per second. Once the inphase and quadrature sample sequences are processed, and the analog inphase and quadrature signals recovered, the bandpass signal can be regenerated, if desired, by multiplying these respective signals by $\cos(\omega_0 t)$ and $\sin(\omega_0 t)$ and summing the result.

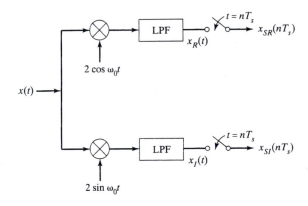

FIGURE 2–17 Illustration of the use of quadrature sampling for bandpass signals.

2.6.4   Oversampling and Down Sampling to Ease Filter Requirements [5]

In the derivation of the sampling theorem, it is assumed that the signal being sampled is ideally band limited. To make this approximately so, the sampling operation is usually preceded by an anti-aliasing filter to ensure that the analog signal being sampled has no spectral components above the half-sampling rate (called the Nyquist rate). To relax the design requirements of this anti-aliasing filter, oversampling can be used as illustrated in Figure 2–18a. The rigid filtering requirements to eliminate out-of-band spectral components are then passed to a digital filter, operating at the oversample rate, whose output is downsampled as shown. An analogous set of operations can be used to recover the sampled signal from the samples as shown in Figure 2–18b.

2.6.5   Pulse Code Modulation [6]

We have seen how a lowpass signal of bandwidth W can be represented by its sample values spaced by $T_s \le 1/2W$. If these samples are quantized, each quantized sample represented by a binary number, and these binary numbers represented by ON-OFF pulse sequences (in Chapter 4, we consider the case of digital carrier modulation), we have what is referred to as pulse code modulation (PCM). Figure 2–19 shows a PCM system and typical signals at each point in the block diagram. Note that a sample-and-hold operation (i.e., the samples are taken and held for an interval of time) is used rather than multiplication of $x(t)$ by a pulse train so that the quantizer and binary code modulator have a constant input value over the sample duration. For example, the first sample at $t = 0$ has value 2 decimal or 010 binary, the second sample at $t = T_s$ has value 4 decimal or 100 binary, and so on. The first sample, 010, is sent through the system as a zero-amplitude

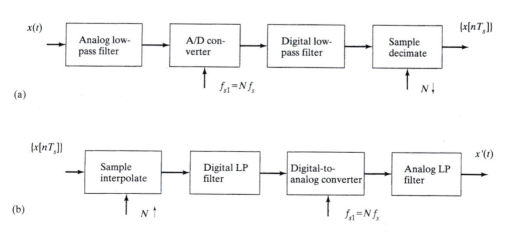

FIGURE 2–18   The use of oversampling in A/D (a) and D/A (b) conversion to relax analog filter requirements.

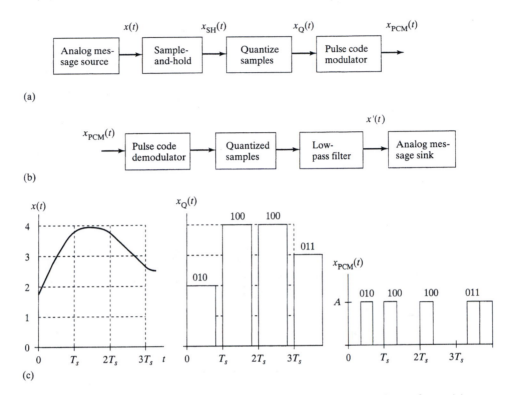

FIGURE 2–19 A pulse code modulator (a), demodulator (b), and waveforms (c).

pulse followed by a pulse of amplitude A and then followed by another zero-amplitude pulse. The same procedure is followed for the next sample, in this case a pulse of amplitude A followed by two zero-amplitude pulses, and so on.

At the reception end, the samples are demodulated by essentially the reverse set of operations used at the transmitter. The reconstructed signal is filtered by a lowpass filter to eliminate sampling harmonics. Note that this reconstruction cannot be perfect, however, due to the effects of the quantization. The difference between the reconstructed signal and the ideal signal is called *quantizing noise*. Quantizing noise is most serious when the signal is small and covers only a few of the lower quantizing intervals. For this reason, a quantizer is sometimes preceded by a signal compressor, which is a zero memory nonlinear device with the input–output characteristic as shown in Figure 2–20a. From this characteristic, it is noted that small-amplitude signals are enhanced and large amplitude signals are compressed. After digital-to-analog conversion and smoothing, an expander, with the characteristic shown in Figure 2–20b, is used so that the net result on the signal is as though nothing were done save for the effects of quantizing noise. The combination of compression and expansion is called *companding*.

The μ-law compressor is commonly used in the United States and is defined by

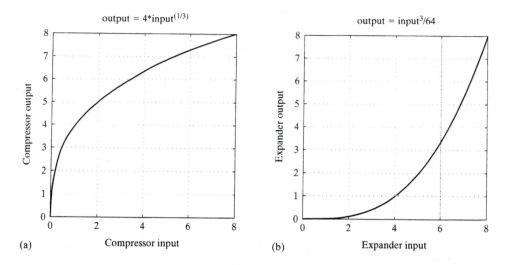

FIGURE 2–20 Input-output characteristics of a signal compressor (a) and expander (b) (first quadrant portion only shown).

$$|y(t)| = \frac{\ln\left[1 + \mu|x(t)|\right]}{\ln(1 + \mu)} \tag{2–169}$$

where μ is a positive constant and it is assumed that $|x(t)| \leq 1$. In telephone companies in the United States, Canada, and Japan, $\mu = 255$ is used. Another compressor law used in Europe is the A-law, which is defined by

$$|y(t)| = \begin{cases} \dfrac{A|x(t)|}{1 + \ln A}, & 0 \leq |x(t)| \leq 1/A \\ \dfrac{1 + \ln[A|x(t)|]}{1 + \ln A}, & 1/A \leq |x(t)| \leq 1 \end{cases} \tag{2–170}$$

where A is a positive constant typically of the order of 90.

EXAMPLE 2–11

Consider the signals

$$x_1(t) = 8\cos(20\pi t)$$

and

$$x_2(t) = \cos(20\pi t)$$

sampled at the rate 51 samples per second. We quantize each sample by rounding it to 4 bits to obtain the following sample values:

Sample Number	$x_1(n)$	$Q(x_1)$	$x_2(n)$	$Q(x_2)$
0	8.00	8	1.00	1
1	2.66	3	0.33	0
2	-6.23	-6	-0.78	-1
3	-6.80	-7	-0.85	-1
4	1.71	2	0.21	0
5	7.94	8	0.99	1

The normalized root-mean-square (rms) error averaged over one cycle is

$$\Delta_i = \frac{1}{N} \left\{ \sum_{n=0}^{N-1} \left(\frac{x_i(n) - Q[x_i(n)]}{x_{i,\max}} \right)^2 \right\}^{1/2}, i = 1,2 \qquad (2\text{--}171)$$

where N is the number of samples in one cycle of the signal. The results are

$$\Delta_1 = 0.011$$

and

$$\Delta_2 = 0.079$$

for $x_1(n)$ and $x_2(n)$, respectively.

We now put both signals through the companding operation

$$y_i(n) = 4x_i^{1/3}(n), i = 1,2$$

and

$$z_i(n) = \frac{1}{64} \{Q[y_i(n)]\}^3, i = 1,2$$

which has been chosen for convenience. Note that without quantization,

$$z_i(n) = \frac{1}{64} [4x_i^{1/3}(n)]^3 = x_i(n), i = 1,2$$

The results of the companding-quantizing operation are given in the following table:

Sample Number	$y_1(n)$	$Q[y_1(n)]$	$z_1(n)$	$y_2(n)$	$Q[y_2(n)]$	$z_2(n)$
0	8.00	8	8.00	4.00	4	1.00
1	5.54	6	3.38	2.76	3	0.42
2	-7.36	-7	-5.36	-3.68	-4	-1.00
3	-7.58	-8	-8.00	-3.79	-4	-1.00
4	4.78	5	1.95	2.38	2	0.13
5	7.98	8	8.00	3.99	4	1.00

The normalized rms error now is

$$\Delta_{1,\text{companded}} = 0.035$$

and

$$\Delta_{2,\text{companded}} = 0.049$$

It is seen that the rms error for $x_1(n)$ is more with companding than without, while it is less for $x_2(n)$. The reason is that the small sample values for $x_2(n)$ were expanded before quantizing so that greater resolution was available in the quantization process.

2.6.6 Differential Pulse Code Modulation

Differential pulse code modulation (DPCM) makes use of the memory that exists between samples when analog sources are sampled. For example, speech signals will have considerable memory between samples taken at a high sampling rate. Because of this memory, the value of a future sample may be predicted from the current sample. The prediction for a given sample is then subtracted from the actual signal sample value and the quantized and encoded error is transmitted through the channel. At the receiver, the encoded error samples are decoded and added to the predicted sample values constructed at the receiver. These samples are then lowpass filtered to reproduce an approximation to the analog signal that was originally sampled at the source. In this manner, fewer bits per second can be used to transmit the information through the channel. This pulse modulation technique will not be considered further in this book. The reader is referred to [5] for more details.

2.7 RANDOM PROCESSES [2]

In the first part of this chapter, techniques for describing and analyzing deterministic signals and the effects of systems on such signals were considered. In this section, signal and system analysis procedures for *random signals* or random processes will be described. These analysis techniques require the use of probabilistic concepts.

As discussed in Chapter 1, the requirement for representing waveforms in communication systems in terms of random processes arises due to two considerations. First, noise is, by its very nature, unpredictable and must be represented probabilistically. Second, by the nature of information itself, the signals in a communication system are random.

In addition to signals and noise in communication systems, examples of random processes are the pressure fluctuations at some point on the surface of an airplane wing, the height of ocean waves in the ocean, and the power delivered to its customers by an electric power plant. The mathematical description of such processes is given in the next section.

2.7.1 Mathematical Description of Random Processes

It is convenient to assign numerical values to the outcomes of a chance experiment. This assignment, together with the underlying probability assignment, is referred to as a random variable. Imagine now a chance experiment where functions of time are assigned to each possible outcome of the experiment. An example is the spinning of a pivoted pointer and the measurement of the angle that the pointer makes with respect to some reference position measured when it stops. Let this angle be represented by the random variable Θ. Suppose that the probability density function (pdf) of Θ, either through measurement or physical considerations, is hypothesized to be uniform over the interval $[0, 2\pi)$. For a given realization of Θ, say θ, the time function

$$X(t) = A \cos(\omega_0 t + \theta), \quad -\infty < t < \infty \tag{2-172}$$

is assigned, where A and ω_0 are constants and t is time. The collection of all possible such waveforms together with the underlying probability assignment is called a *random process*. Each realization of a particular waveform is referred to as a *sample function*. Several possible sample functions are sketched in Figure 2–21. Several other examples of random processes will be given shortly.

A random process is completely described by the joint probability density function (pdf) of its values at an arbitrary number, N, of time instants. Let these time instants be $t_1 < t_2 < \ldots < t_N$ and let the sample values of the random process at these time instants be denoted by $X_1 = X(t_1)$, $X_2 = X(t_2)$, $\ldots$, $X_N = X(t_N)$. Then the joint probability density function

$$f_X(x_1,t_1;x_2,t_2;\cdots;x_N,t_N) \tag{2-173}$$

conveys all the information about the random process that can practically be known. Note that if the joint density function at $N-1$ instants is desired, it can be obtained by integrating over the undesired variable. In some cases, this description would be enormously difficult to give. In other cases, such as the example given by (2–172), it is relatively simple, for knowledge of the waveform at two instants in time (not separated by a period of the sinusoidal waveform) means that it is known at all other instants, provided ω_0 and A are known.

Although the N-fold joint density (or distribution) function constitutes a complete statistical description of a random process, it may not be possible to obtain in some cases. Also, one may not be interested in a complete statistical description of the random process. Often, the knowledge of only the first-order density function or perhaps only certain moments of the random process is required. Moments of primary interest are the mean and the variance. These, in general, are functions of time. The mean at time $t = t_1$ is

$$E[X(t_1)] = \overline{X(t_1)} = \int_{-\infty}^{\infty} x f_X(x,t_1)dx = m(t_1) \tag{2-174}$$

where $E[\cdot]$ is the expectation operator. The second moment at time $t = t_1$ is

$$E[X^2(t_1)] = \overline{X^2(t_1)} = \int_{-\infty}^{\infty} x^2 f_X(x,t_1)dx \tag{2-175}$$

In terms of these moments, the variance is

$$\sigma_X^2(t_1) = E\{[X(t_1) - m(t_1)]^2\} = E[X^2(t_1)] - \{E[X(t_1)]\}^2 \tag{2-176}$$

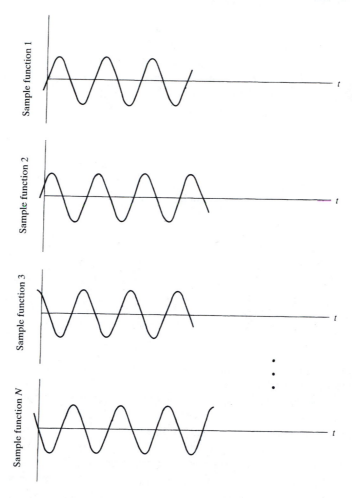

FIGURE 2–21 Several sample functions of the random process $\{A\cos(\omega_0 t + \Theta)\}$ where Θ is a random variable in $[0, 2\pi)$.

These averages provide a partial description of the process at a single time instant. Another average, which gives a partial description of how the process at one time instant depends statistically on the process at a second time instant, is provided by the *autocorrelation function*, $R_X(t_1, t_2)$, defined by

$$R_X(t_1, t_2) \triangleq E[X(t_1) X(t_2)]$$

$$= \int_{-\infty}^{\infty} \int_{-\infty}^{\infty} x_1 x_2 f_{X,X}(x_1, t_1; x_2, t_2) \, dx_1 dx_2 \tag{2–177}$$

where $f_{X_1 X_2}(x_1, t_1; x_2, t_2)$ is the joint pdf of the random process at two time instants. The autocorrelation function is, in general, a function of the two time instants t_1 and t_2. The *auto-*

covariance function is obtained by subtracting the mean at time t_1 from $X(t_1)$ and the mean at time t_2 from $X(t_2)$ before finding the average of their product. The autocovariance function, $C_X(t_1, t_2)$, and autocorrelation function are related by

$$C_X(t_1, t_2) = R_X(t_1, t_2) - m(t_1)\, m(t_2) \tag{2-178}$$

Note that the variance at time t_1 is equal to $C_X(t_1, t_1)$.

While the mean and variance of an arbitrary random process are, in general, functions of the time instant chosen to compute the average, and the autocorrelation function is a function of two time instants, there is a class of random processes, referred to as *stationary*, for which the mean and variance are time independent and $R_X(t_1, t_2)$ is a function only of the time difference $t_2 - t_1$.

A *strictly stationary* process is one for which the N-fold joint pdf is not dependent on the time origin chosen for the sampling instants. In particular, it is a function only of the *time differences* $t_2 - t_1, t_3 - t_1, \ldots, t_N - t_1$. Strict-sense stationarity implies that the mean and variance are independent of time and that the autocorrelation function is a function only of the time difference $t_2 - t_1$. For an even larger class of random processes, referred to as *wide-sense stationary*, the mean and variance are time independent and the autocorrelation function is dependent only on the time difference $t_2 - t_1$, but the N-fold probability density is not necessarily independent of the choice of time origin. Quite often, wide-sense stationarity, or stationarity of second order, is all that is required in a given situation.

EXAMPLE 2–12

Consider the random-phase sinusoidal process with sample functions given by (2–172). Using the definition of the average of a function of a random variable, the mean and mean square are

$$E[X(t)] = \int_0^{2\pi} A\cos(\omega_0 t + \theta)\, \frac{d\theta}{2\pi} = 0$$

$$E[X^2(t)] = \int_0^{2\pi} A^2 \cos^2(\omega_0 t + \theta)\, \frac{d\theta}{2\pi}$$

$$= \int_0^{2\pi} \frac{A^2}{2}\, \frac{d\theta}{2\pi} + \int_0^{2\pi} \frac{A^2}{2} \cos(2\omega_0 t + 2\theta)\, \frac{d\theta}{2\pi}$$

$$= \frac{A^2}{2} = \sigma_X^2$$

respectively. (Recall that the density function of Θ is $1/2\pi$ in the interval 0 to 2π and 0 otherwise.) Because the mean is zero, the variance and the mean-square value are equal. The autocorrelation function is

$$R_X(t, t + \tau) = E[X(t)\, X(t + \tau)]$$

$$= \int_0^{2\pi} A^2 \cos(\omega_0 t + \theta) \cos[\omega_0(t + \tau) + \theta]\, \frac{d\theta}{2\pi}$$

$$= \frac{A^2}{2} \cos \omega_0 \tau$$

where $t_1 = t$ and $t_2 = t + \tau$. The autocorrelation function is seen to be function only of the time difference $t_2 - t_1 = \tau$, and the mean and variance are independent of time. This process is therefore wide-sense stationary.

Several properties of the autocorrelation function of a stationary random process are illustrated by Example 2–12. First, it is evident that

$$E\left[X^2(t)\right] = R_X(0) \tag{2-179}$$

which follows by setting $\tau = 0$ in the definition of $R_X(\tau) = E[X(t) X(t + \tau)]$. Second, by considering

$$E\left\{[X(t + \tau) \pm X(t)]^2\right\} \geq 0 \tag{2-180}$$

which, being the expectation of a nonnegative quantity is itself nonnegative, it follows that

$$|R_X(\tau)| \leq R_X(0) \tag{2-181}$$

Third, since $X(t)$ is assumed stationary, it follows that

$$R_X(\tau) = E[X(t) X(t + \tau)] = E[X(t' - \tau) X(t')] = R_X(-\tau) \tag{2-182}$$

where the substitution $t' = t + \tau$ has been used. Finally, it will be shown in the next section that the Fourier transform of $R_X(\tau)$ is nonnegative; that is,

$$S_X(f) \triangleq \int_{-\infty}^{\infty} R_X(\tau)\exp(-j2\pi f\tau)d\tau \geq 0 \tag{2-183}$$

The function $S_X(f)$ is called the *power spectral density* of the random process $X(t)$.

It is useful to talk about the joint statistics of two random processes, say, $X(t)$ and $Y(t)$. For example, $X(t)$ could represent the input to a system and $Y(t)$ could represent its output. Complete statistical characterization of the joint chance experiment giving rise to the processes then requires the specification of not only the density functions of $X(t)$ and $Y(t)$ at N time instants, but also the joint density function of both processes at an arbitrarily selected set of time instants. If, for all values of N and $t_1, t_2, \ldots, t_N$, this joint density function factors into the product of the density functions of the separate processes, $X(t)$ and $Y(t)$, the random processes are said to be *statistically independent*. If the joint density function of $X(t)$ and $Y(t)$ is independent of time origin, the processes are said to be *jointly stationary*.

One final property of many random processes is that of *ergodicity*. For ergodic random processes, statistical averages may be found as a corresponding time average. The mean, mean square, and autocorrelation function as time averages, for example, are given by

$$\langle X(t) \rangle = \lim_{T \to \infty} \frac{1}{2T} \int_{-T}^{T} X(t)\, dt \tag{2-184}$$

$$\langle X^2(t) \rangle = \lim_{T \to \infty} \frac{1}{2T} \int_{-T}^{T} X^2(t)dt \tag{2-185}$$

and

$$\langle X(t) X(t + \tau) \rangle = \lim_{T \to \infty} \frac{1}{2T} \int_{-T}^{T} X(t) X(t + \tau) dt \qquad (2\text{--}186)$$

respectively, where the angular brackets signify a time average. For an ergodic process, it is true that

$$E[X(t)] = \langle X(t) \rangle,$$

$$E[X^2(t)] = \langle X^2(t) \rangle, \qquad (2\text{--}187)$$

and $\quad E[X(t) X(t + \tau)] = \langle X(t) X(t + \tau) \rangle$

with similar statements holding for all other possible averages. From (2–187) it is seen that an ergodic process must be at least wide-sense stationary and, in fact, strict-sense stationary because all time averages are interchangeable with the corresponding statistical averages. For a process to be ergodic, it is apparent that each sample function must be statistically representative of the entire collection of all possible sample functions. Ergodicity is a necessity in almost any experiment involving the measurement of the statistics of a random process, such as the measurement of average power, for the measurement is by necessity made on a single sample function.

EXAMPLE 2–13 _____

The measurement of the autocorrelation function of an ergodic (and therefore stationary) random process can be approximated by the system shown in Figure 2–22. A sample function (realization) of the random process is delayed by an amount τ, multiplied by an undelayed version, and the product averaged by a lowpass filter with impulse response $h(t)$. Assume that this filter is an ideal integrator with impulse response

$$h(t) = \frac{1}{T}[u(t) - u(t - T)]$$

where T is the integration time. The output of the integrator, by the superposition integral, is

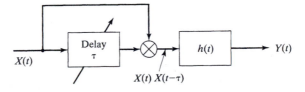

FIGURE 2–22   System for the measurement of the autocorrelation function of a random process.

$$Y(t) = \int_{-\infty}^{\infty} h(\lambda) X(t - \lambda) X(t - \lambda - \tau) d\lambda$$

$$= \frac{1}{T} \int_{0}^{T} X(t - \lambda) X(t - \lambda - \tau) d\lambda$$

Measures of goodness of the estimate $Y(t)$ are its mean and variance. The mean is

$$E[Y(t)] = \frac{1}{T} \int_{0}^{T} E[X(t - \lambda) X(t - \lambda - \tau)] d\lambda$$

where the expectation can be taken inside the integral because both integrals exist (the expectation is really an integral of the random quantity times its pdf) and form an iterated double integral. The expectation is recognized as the autocorrelation function of $X(t)$, $R_X(\tau)$. Therefore,

$$E[Y(t)] = \frac{1}{T} \int_{0}^{T} R_X(\tau) d\lambda = R_X(\tau)$$

Any estimate whose expectation is equal to the quantity being estimated is called *unbiased*. Therefore, the system of Figure 2–22 produces an unbiased estimate of the autocorrelation function.

The variance of $Y(t)$ can be found by first computing its mean-square value, which is

$$E[Y^2(t)] = \frac{1}{T^2} E\left\{ \left[\int_{0}^{T} X(t - \lambda) X(t - \lambda - \tau) d\lambda \right]^2 \right\}$$

$$= \frac{1}{T^2} \int_{0}^{T} \int_{0}^{T} E[X(t - \lambda) X(t - \alpha) X(t - \lambda - \tau) X(t - \alpha - \tau)] d\lambda \, d\alpha$$

where the double integral follows by writing the squared integral as an iterated integral. Without further assumptions this result for $E[Y^2(t)]$ cannot be simplified further. If $X(t)$ is Gaussian and zero mean, however, the expectation in the integrand can be simplified. It can be shown that $E[Y^2(t)]$ simplifies to[11]

$$E[Y^2(t)] = R_X^2(\tau) + \frac{1}{T} \int_{-T}^{T} \left(1 - \frac{|u|}{T} \right) R_X^2(u) du + \frac{1}{T} \int_{-T}^{T} \left(1 - \frac{|u|}{T} \right) R_X(u - \tau) R_X(u + \tau) du$$

where the evenness property of $R_X(\tau)$ has been used. Subtracting the mean of $Y(t)$ squared, which is $R_X^2(\tau)$, results in the variance. The result is

$$\sigma_Y^2 = \frac{1}{T} \int_{-T}^{T} \left(1 - \frac{|u|}{T} \right) [R_X^2(u) + R_X(u - \tau) R_X(u + \tau)] du$$

In the limit as $T \to \infty$, $\sigma_Y^2 \to 0$ if the integral

---

[11]For purposes of simplification, the following result for the expectation of the product of four zero-mean Gaussian random variables is useful:

$$E[X_1 X_2 X_3 X_4] = E[X_1 X_2] E[X_3 X_4] + E[X_1 X_3] E[X_2 X_4] + E[X_1 X_4] E[X_2 X_3]$$

$$\int_{-\infty}^{\infty} [R_X^2(u) + R_X(u - \tau) R_X(u + \tau)] \, du$$

is bounded. This is indeed the case for many autocorrelation functions of interest, as will be shown in the problems. An unbiased estimate whose variance approaches zero as the interval of data from which the estimate is made approaches infinity is said to be *consistent*. This estimate for the autocorrelation function is therefore consistent.

2.7.2 Input-Output Relationships for Fixed Linear Systems with Random Inputs; Power Spectral Density

2.7.2.1 Partial Descriptions. Consider a fixed linear system as shown in Figure 2–23, with an input, $X(t)$, assumed present since $t = -\infty$, assumed to be a sample function of a stationary random process. The system's output, $Y(t)$, is given in terms of $X(t)$ by the superposition integral:

$$Y(t) = \int_{-\infty}^{\infty} h(\alpha) X(t - \alpha) \, d\alpha \qquad (2-188)$$

Because of the presence of the input since $t = -\infty$, any system transients have long since died out and the output is stationary also. A partial description of the output is provided by its mean and autocorrelation function. From (2–188) the mean is

$$m_Y = E[Y(t)] = E\left[\int_{-\infty}^{\infty} h(\alpha) X(t - \alpha) \, d\alpha \right]$$

$$= \int_{-\infty}^{\infty} h(\alpha) E[X(t - \alpha)] \, d\alpha \qquad (2-189)$$

$$= m_X \int_{-\infty}^{\infty} h(\alpha) \, d\alpha$$

which follows because m_X is time independent for a stationary process.
The autocorrelation function of the output can be shown to be

$$R_Y(\tau) = \int_{-\infty}^{\infty} \int_{-\infty}^{\infty} h(\alpha) h(\beta) R_X(\tau - \beta + \alpha) \, d\alpha \, d\beta \qquad (2-190)$$

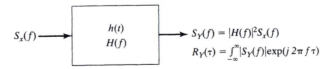

FIGURE 2–23 Fixed, linear system with a sample function of a random process as an input.

The double integral in this equation appears difficult to evaluate even for simple autocorrelation functions. Because of its similarity to a convolution, it appears that it might be advantageous to express it in terms of frequency domain quantities. Accordingly, let $H(f)$ be the Fourier transform of the impulse response, or frequency response function of the system, and let $S_X(f)$ be the Fourier transform of $R_X(\tau)$, later to be justified as being called the power spectral density of $X(t)$:

$$S_X(f) = \int_{-\infty}^{\infty} R_X(\tau)\exp(-j2\pi f\tau)d\tau \tag{2-191}$$

From the evenness of $R_X(\tau)$ it follows that $S_X(f)$ is real and even.

From the inverse Fourier transform integral, it follows that

$$R_X(0) = E[X^2(t)] = \int_{-\infty}^{\infty} S_X(f)df \tag{2-192}$$

That is, the integral of $S_X(f)$ is the mean-square value, or average power, of the input. The function $S_X(f)$ is called the power spectral density of the process $X(t)$. It is a function that describes the distribution of power with frequency of a random process. This interpretation will be given more justification shortly.

If $R_X(\tau - \beta + \alpha)$ in (2–190) is represented in terms of the inverse Fourier transform of $S_X(f)$, the resulting triple integral can be reduced to

$$R_Y(\tau) = \int_{-\infty}^{\infty} H(f)H^*(f)S_X(f)\exp(j2\pi f\tau)df \tag{2-193}$$

which is recognized as the inverse Fourier transform of $|H(f)|^2 S_X(f)$. That is,

$$\mathscr{F}[R_Y(\tau)] = S_Y(f) = |H(f)|^2 S_X(f) \tag{2-194}$$

or the power spectral density of the output is the magnitude squared of the frequency response function times the power spectral density of the input. This extremely useful result, which is illustrated in Figure 2–24, can be used in the analysis of linear systems with random inputs that have been present so long that the transients have died out.

That $S_X(f)$ physically represents the density of power of $X(t)$ versus frequency can be seen by considering the output of an ideal bandpass filter of bandwidth $\Delta W \ll 1$ centered at frequency f_0 with passband gain of unity. According to (2–193) with $\tau = 0$, the power in $X(t)$ in bandwidth ΔW is

$$R_Y(0) = E[Y^2(t)] = 2\int_{f_0-\Delta W/2}^{f_0+\Delta W/2} S_X(f)df \tag{2-195}$$

$$\approx 2S_X(f_0)\Delta W$$

which follows by the evenness of $S_X(f)$ and the definition of an integral. Since both $R_Y(0)$ and ΔW are positive, it follows that

$$S_X(f_0) = \frac{R_Y(0)}{2\Delta W} > 0 \tag{2-196}$$

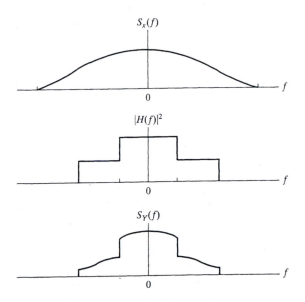

FIGURE 2–24   Obtaining the output spectrum of a fixed linear system with a stationary random process at its input.

which represents the power density in a very small bandwidth ΔW centered at frequency f_0. Since f_0 is arbitrary and power is nonnegative, it follows that the power spectral density function is a nonnegative function of frequency.

The fact that $S_X(f)$, which represents a power density with frequency of the process $X(t)$, is the Fourier transform of the autocorrelation function is referred to as the *Wiener-Khintchine theorem*. Its proof proceeds by considering the time average of the energy density of a time-truncated version of the random process. The reader may consult other references for the proof of the Wiener-Khintchine theorem [2].

EXAMPLE 2–14 _____

A useful mathematical artifice is white noise, which has a constant power spectral density for all frequencies and therefore infinite power. Let the power spectral density of a white-noise process be

$$S_W(f) = \frac{N_0}{2}, \quad -\infty < f < \infty \tag{2–197}$$

where N_0 is the single-sided (positive frequencies only) spectral density. By the Wiener-Khintchine theorem,

$$R_W(\tau) = \mathscr{F}^{-1}\left(\frac{N_0}{2}\right) = \frac{N_0}{2}\delta(\tau) \tag{2–198}$$

Now consider a filter with transfer function $H(f)$ with white noise at its input. What is the bandwidth of an equivalent ideal filter with the same maximum gain, say, H_0, that passes the same power as the original filter? From (2–194) the power out of the original filter is

$$\sigma_Y^2 = N_0 \int_0^\infty |H(f)|^2 \, df$$

and from the equivalent filter, it is

$$\sigma_Y^2 = N_0 H_0^2 B_N$$

where B_N is its bandwidth (to be found). Setting these two powers equal results in

$$B_N = \frac{1}{H_0^2} \int_0^\infty |H(f)|^2 \, df \tag{2–199}$$

which is referred to as the *noise equivalent bandwidth* of the filter. Table 2–8 gives the ratio of noise equivalent bandwidth to 3 dB bandwidth for several filters.

2.7.2.2 Output Statistics of Linear Systems. Given a linear system with transfer function $H(f)$ and impulse response $h(t)$ with a random input waveform $X(t)$, what can be said about the pdf of the output at a single time instant t if one knows the pdf of the input? *This problem has no general solution. However, if the input is Gaussian* at a single time instant, *the output is Gaussian also.* If the input has zero mean, so does the output. The variance of the output is then given by

$$\sigma_Y^2 = R_Y(0) = \int_{-\infty}^\infty |H(f)|^2 S_X(f) \, df \tag{2–200}$$

and one may immediately write down the first-order density function of the output.[12] This procedure will be used extensively in the analysis of digital communication systems.

EXAMPLE 2–15 _____

Consider the system shown in Figure 2–25. The inputs to the first-order lowpass filters are assumed to be independent white Gaussian noise processes with two-sided power spectral densities $N_1/2$ and $N_2/2$, respectively. The filter transfer functions of the filters are

$$H_1(f) = \frac{1}{1 + j(f/f_1)}$$

and

$$H_2(f) = \frac{1}{1 + j(f/f_2)}$$

---

[12]A first-order Gaussian pdf has the form

$$f_Y(y) = \frac{\exp[-(y - m_Y)^2/2\sigma_Y^2]}{\sqrt{2\pi\sigma_Y^2}}$$

where m_Y is the mean of the random variable Y and σ_Y^2 is its variance.

TABLE 2–8   Ratio of Noise Bandwidth to 3 dB Bandwidth of Various Filters

Filter Type	Order	B_N/B_3
Butterworth - Exact result: $\dfrac{B_N}{B_3} = \dfrac{\pi/2n}{\sin(\pi/2n)}$	1	$\pi/2 = 1.57$
	2	1.11
	3	1.04
	4	1.03
	5	1.02
	6	1.01
Bessel:	1	1.57
	2	1.16
	3	1.08
	4	1.04
	5	1.04
	6	1.04
Chebyshev I (1/2 dB ripple)	1	1.57
	2	1.15
	3	1.00
	4	1.08
	5	0.96
	6	1.07
Chebyshev I (1 dB ripple)	1	1.57
	2	1.21
	3	0.96
	4	1.15
	5	0.92
	6	1.13
Chebyshev I (2 dB ripple)	1	1.57
	2	1.33
	3	0.86
	4	1.28
	5	0.82
	6	1.27
Chebyshev I (3 dB ripple)	1	1.57
	2	1.48
	3	0.78
	4	1.43
	5	0.73
	6	1.41

Reproduced from [7] with permission.

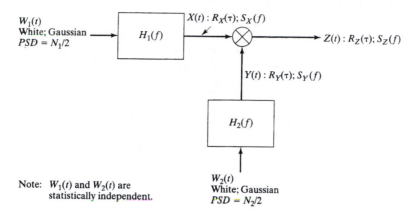

FIGURE 2–25   System analyzed in Example 2–15.

respectively, where f_1 and f_2 are their 3 dB frequencies.

The following will be found: (1) the autocorrelation functions, $R_X(\tau)$ and $R_Y(\tau)$, of the signals at the outputs of the two filters; (2) the power spectral densities, $S_X(f)$ and $S_Y(f)$, of the two signals at the outputs of the two filters; and (3) the autocorrelation function, $R_Z(\tau)$, and the power spectral density, $S_Z(f)$, at the output of the multiplier.

Solution: Using (2–194), the power spectral densities at the filter outputs are found to be

$$S_X(f) = |H_1(f)|^2 \frac{N_1}{2} = \frac{N_1/2}{1 + (f/f_1)^2}$$

and

$$S_Y(f) = |H_2(f)|^2 \frac{N_2}{2} = \frac{N_2/2}{1 + (f/f_2)^2}$$

Using the Fourier transform pair

$$A \exp(-\alpha|\tau|) \leftrightarrow \frac{2\alpha A}{\alpha^2 + (2\pi f)^2}$$

we find that the inverse Fourier transforms of $S_X(f)$ and $S_Y(f)$, which are the autocorrelation functions $R_X(\tau)$ and $R_Y(\tau)$, are

$$R_X(\tau) = N_1 \left(\frac{\pi f_1}{2} \right) \exp(-2\pi f_1|\tau|)$$

and

$$R_Y(\tau) = N_2 \left(\frac{\pi f_2}{2} \right) \exp(-2\pi f_2|\tau|)$$

respectively. The variances of $X(t)$ and $Y(t)$ are

$$\sigma_X^2 = R_X(0) = N_1 \left(\frac{\pi f_1}{2} \right)$$

and

$$\sigma_Y^2 = R_Y(0) = N_2\left(\frac{\pi f_2}{2}\right)$$

respectively. Note that $\pi f_1/2$ and $\pi f_2/2$ are the equivalent noise bandwidths (in hertz) of the two filters with transfer functions $H_1(f)$ and $H_2(f)$, respectively.

Since the multiplier inputs are statistically independent, the autocorrelation function of the multiplier output is

$$R_Z(\tau) = E[Z(t)Z(t+\tau)]$$

$$= E[X(t)\,X(t+\tau)\,Y(t)\,Y(t+\tau)]$$

$$= E[X(t)\,X(t+\tau)]\,E[Y(t)\,Y(t+\tau)]$$

$$= R_X(\tau)\,R_Y(\tau)$$

Again using the Fourier transform pair given on the previous page, we find the Fourier transform of $R_Z(\tau)$, which gives $S_Z(f)$, to be

$$S_Z(f) = \mathscr{F}\left\{\left[N_1\left(\frac{\pi f_1}{2}\right)\exp(-2\pi f_1|\tau|)\right]\left[N_2\left(\frac{\pi f_2}{2}\right)\exp(-2\pi f_2|\tau|)\right]\right\}$$

$$= \mathscr{F}\left\{N_1 N_2\left(\frac{\pi f_1}{2}\right)\left(\frac{\pi f_2}{2}\right)\exp[-2\pi(f_1+f_2)|\tau|]\right\}$$

$$= \frac{\pi N_1 N_2[f_1 f_2/4(f_1+f_2)]}{1+[f/(f_1+f_2)]^2}$$

The fact that the inputs to the filters are Gaussian has not yet been used. Using the fact that a linear transformation of a Gaussian process results in a Gaussian process, one could use the variances calculated here and means (they are zero; why?) of $X(t)$ and $Y(t)$ to write down their marginal pdfs according to (A-17) which gives the pdf of a Gaussian random variable. The result for the pdf of $Z(t)$ does not follow immediately, however, but requires a transformation of random variables. Suppose that $X(t) = Y(t)$ so that $N_1 = N_2$ and $f_1 = f_2$. Then

$$\sigma^2 = \sigma_X^2 = \sigma_Y^2 = N_1\left(\frac{\pi f_1}{2}\right) = N_2\left(\frac{\pi f_2}{2}\right)$$

and

$$E[X(t)] = E[Y(t)] = 0$$

It is then well known that $Z(t)$, which is the square of a Gaussian random process, is then exponentially distributed with probability density function $f_Z(z) = \exp(-z^2/2\sigma^2)/2\sigma^2$, $z \geq 0$.

2.7.2.3 The Central and Noncentral Chi-Square Distributions. Useful probability distributions result from sums of squares of independent Gaussian random variables of the form

$$Z = \sum_{i=1}^{n} X_i^2 \tag{2-201}$$

where n is the degrees of freedom. If $E(X_i) = 0$ and $\mathrm{var}(X_i) = \sigma^2$, the resultant pdf is known as *central chi-square*, or simply chi-square, which has the form

$$f_Z(z) = \frac{1}{\sigma^n 2^{n/2} \Gamma(n/2)} z^{n/2-1} \exp(-z/2\sigma^2), z \geq 0 \tag{2-202}$$

where $\Gamma(x)$ is the gamma function defined as $\Gamma(x) = \int_0^\infty t^{x-1} \exp(-t)dt$, $x > 0$ with the properties that $\Gamma(n) = (n-1)!$ if n is an integer and $\Gamma(1/2) = \sqrt{\pi}$, $\Gamma(3/2) = \sqrt{\pi}/2$. Note that for the central chi-square distribution of two degrees of freedom, an exponential pdf results.

If $m_i = E(X_i)$, the resulting pdf has the form

$$f_Z(z) = \frac{1}{2\sigma^2} \left(\frac{z}{s^2}\right)^{(n-2)/4} \exp[-(z+s^2)/2\sigma^2] \, I_{n/2-1}\left(\frac{s\sqrt{z}}{\sigma^2}\right), z \geq 0 \tag{2-203}$$

where $s^2 = \sum_{i=1}^{n} m_i^2$ and $I_m(x) = \sum_{k=0}^{\infty} \frac{(x/2)^{m+2k}}{k!\Gamma(m+k+1)}$, $x \geq 0$, is the mth-order modified Bessel function of the first kind (a transcendental function like cos x). This is called a *noncentral chi-square pdf.*

2.7.3 Examples of Random Processes

In this section two examples of random processes are investigated in terms of their pdfs, means, and autocorrelation functions. It is not the intent to exhaustively catalog a large number of random processes, but to provide intuitive insight into the properties of various random waveforms through the consideration of several examples. Also introduced will be the concept of a cyclostationary process, which is a process exhibiting periodicity in its mean and autocorrelation function.

EXAMPLE 2–16 _____

Consider a random process whose sample functions are constant functions of time, but random variables, for $-\infty < t < \infty$. That is, the sample functions are of the form

$$X(t) = A, \ -\infty < t < \infty$$

where A is a random variable with density function $f_A(a)$. The mean of this random process is

$$E[X(t)] = \int_{-\infty}^{\infty} a f_A(a)da = E[A]$$

while its autocorrelation function is

$$R_X(t_1, t_2) = E[X(t_1) X(t_2)] = \int_{-\infty}^{\infty} a^2 f_A(a) da = E[A^2]$$

Both are independent of the particular time instants chosen for evaluation. Because the sample functions are time independent (constants, but random variables), the marginal pdf at any arbitrarily selected time $t = t_1$ is simply $f_A(a)$. The joint density function at two arbitrarily selected times, t_1 and t_2, can be written as

$$f_X(x_1, t_1; x_2, t_2) = f_X(x_2, t_2 \mid x_1, t_1) f_A(x_1)$$

where $f_X(x_2, t_2 \mid x_1, t_1)$ is the conditional density function at time t_2, given the value of x_1 at time t_1. Because the sample functions are time independent, knowledge of the value of the random process at time t_1 completely specifies its value at time t_2. In particular, since the sample functions are time independent, it follows that

$$f_X(x_2, t_2 \mid x_1, t_1) = \delta(x_2 - x_1)$$

which is a mathematical statement that the value $X(t)$ at time t_2 is equal to the value at time t_1. Consequently, the joint density function is

$$f_X(x_1, t_1; x_2, t_2) = \delta(x_2 - x_1) f_A(x_1)$$

and the autocorrelation function can be computed according to

$$R_X(t_1, t_2) = \int_{-\infty}^{\infty} \int_{-\infty}^{\infty} x_1 x_2 \delta(x_2 - x_1) f_A(x_1) \, dx_1 dx_2$$

$$= \int_{-\infty}^{\infty} x_1^2 f_A(x_1) dx_1 = E[A^2]$$

as before.

This random process, although relatively simple, is useful for demonstrating the computation of various statistical characterizing functions. It is also an example of a random process that is stationary in the strict sense but is not ergodic.

EXAMPLE 2–17

The next random process to be considered is characterized by sample functions of the form

$$X(t) = A\cos(\omega_0 t + \Theta)$$

Initially, ω_0 and Θ will be taken as constants and A will be modeled as a random variable with pdf $f_A(a)$. The mean is

$$E[X(t)] = \int_{-\infty}^{\infty} a \cos(\omega_0 t + \Theta) f_A(a) da$$

$$= E[A]\cos(\omega_0 t + \Theta)$$

which is a periodic function of time. The autocorrelation function is calculated as

$$R_X(t_1, t_2) = E[X(t_1) X(t_2)]$$

$$= \int_{-\infty}^{\infty} a^2 \cos(\omega_0 t_1 + \Theta)\cos(\omega_0 t_2 + \Theta) f_A(a)\, da$$

$$= \frac{1}{2} E[A^2]\{\cos[\omega_0(t_2 - t_1)] + \cos[\omega_0(t_2 + t_1) + 2\Theta]\}$$

which has the property that

$$R_X(t_1 + T, t_2 + T) = R_X(t_1, t_2) \tag{2-204}$$

where $T = 2\pi/\omega_0$. This periodicity property, together with the mean being a periodic function of period $T = 2\pi/\omega_0$, defines a nonstationary class of random processes referred to as *cyclostationary* in the wide sense.

A way to remove the nonstationary character of the random process is through *phase randomizing*. For example, if Θ is a uniformly distributed random variable in the interval $[0, 2\pi)$, then

$$E[X(t)] = 0 \text{ and } R_X(t_1, t_2) = \frac{1}{2} E[A^2]\cos \omega_0(t_2 - t_1)$$

In other words, the process is now wide-sense stationary.

While phase randomizing removes the nonstationary character, it is important to consider whether the model is a good description of the physical process. If, for example, the random process is being observed with a total lack of knowledge of the time origin, phase randomizing is probably a good model of the physical process. If, on the other hand, a model is desired for the generation of a phase reference for the observed sinusoid, phase randomization should not be performed since it implies total lack of knowledge of the phase of the observed process.

2.7.4 Narrowband Noise Representation[13]

Given a stationary random process $\{n(t)\}$ with power spectral density $S_n(f)$, it is often convenient to represent its sample functions in the form

$$n(t) = n_c(t) \cos(2\pi f_0 t) - n_s(t) \sin(2\pi f_0 t) \tag{2-205}$$

or, alternatively, as

$$n(t) = r(t) \cos[2\pi f_0 t + \theta(t)] \tag{2-206}$$

where

$$r(t) = \sqrt{n_c^2(t) + n_s^2(t)} \text{ and } \theta(t) = \tan^{-1}\left[\frac{n_s(t)}{n_c(t)}\right] \tag{2-207}$$

---

[13]Lower case letters will be used for the noise waveforms considered in this section even though the convention used until now has been to represent random variables with upper case letters.

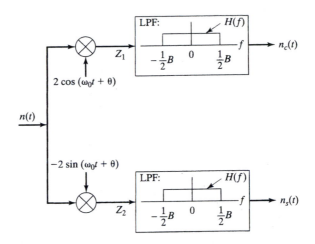

FIGURE 2–26 Block diagram of a system for determining narrowband noise spectra.

In (2–205), $n_c(t)$ and $n_s(t)$ are referred to as the *inphase and quadrature components*, or simply, the quadrature components, and are lowpass random processes whose power spectral densities will be given shortly. The random processes $r(t)$ and $\theta(t)$ are referred to as the *envelope and phase*, and are also lowpass, or slowly varying with respect to $n(t)$. If $\{n(t)\}$ is narrowband in the sense that its bandwidth is less than $f_0/2$, then $n_c(t)$ and $n_s(t)$ can be found by the operations depicted in Figure 2–26. Since these operations are linear, the quadrature components are Gaussian if $\{n(t)\}$ is Gaussian.

The spectra of $\{n_c(t)\}$ and $\{n_s(t)\}$ are identical and can be found from the operation[14]

$$S_{n_c}(f) = S_{n_s}(f) = \text{Lp}[S_n(f - f_0) + S_n(f + f_0)] \qquad (2\text{–}208)$$

where $\text{Lp}(\cdot)$ denotes the lowpass part of the spectrum in the argument. The Fourier transform of the cross-correlation function between $\{n_c(t)\}$ and $\{n_s(t)\}$, referred to as the *cross spectrum*, is given by

$$S_{n_c n_s}(f) = j\text{Lp}[S_n(f - f_0) - S_n(f + f_0)] \qquad (2\text{–}209)$$

From (2–209) it follows that if the power spectral density of $n(t)$ is symmetrical about $f = f_0$ for $f > 0$ (or $f < 0$ since the power spectrum of a signal is even), the cross spectrum is zero and the processes $\{n_c(t)\}$ and $\{n_s(t)\}$ are uncorrelated. If they are also Gaussian, then they are independent since uncorrelated Gaussian processes are statistically independent. This holds for any time separation of the two processes. However, it is also true that $\{n_c(t)\}$ and $\{n_s(t)\}$ are independent *at the same time instant* even if the power spectrum of $\{n(t)\}$ is not symmetrical about $f = f_0$ for $f > 0$. An example will illustrate the procedure for obtaining the spectra pertaining to $\{n_c(t)\}$ and $\{n_s(t)\}$.

---

[14]For proofs of these relationships, see [2, 8].

EXAMPLE 2–18

Consider the narrowband noise spectrum shown in Figure 2–27. Two choices will be made for f_0, the first of which gives uncorrelated quadrature components and the second of which does not.

  Case 1: $f_0 = 4$ Hz. In this case, $S_n(f)$ is symmetrical about $f = f_0$ for $f > 0$ and the quadrature components are uncorrelated. Construction of the spectrum for this choice of f_0 is illustrated in Figure 2–27b.

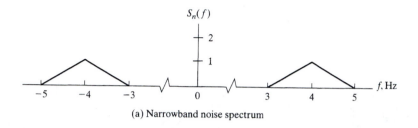

(a) Narrowband noise spectrum

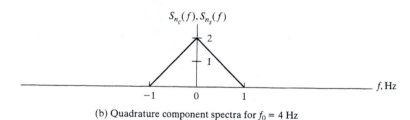

(b) Quadrature component spectra for $f_0 = 4$ Hz

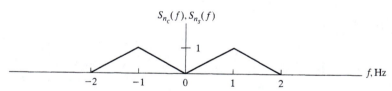

(c) Quadrature component spectra for $f_0 = 3$ Hz

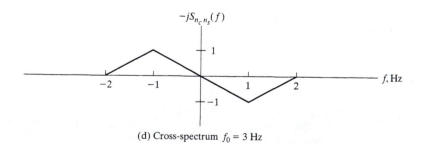

(d) Cross-spectrum $f_0 = 3$ Hz

FIGURE 2–27 Narrowband noise spectra.

Case 2: $f_0 = 3$ Hz. The spectra for this case are shown in Figure 2–27c and d. In this case, the quadrature components are correlated (i.e., their correlation function is not zero for all delays). In fact, the cross-correlation function of $\{n_c(t)\}$ and $\{n_s(t)\}$ is

$$R_{n_c n_s}(\tau) = \mathcal{F}^{-1}\{j[\Lambda(f+1) - \Lambda(f-1)]\}$$

$$= j[-\text{sinc}^2(\tau)\exp(j2\pi\tau) + \text{sinc}^2(\tau)\exp(-j2\pi\tau)]$$

$$= 2\text{sinc}^2(\tau)\sin(2\pi\tau)$$

Although $R_{n_c n_s}(\tau) = 0$ for $\tau = 0$ it is not zero for all τ and the quadrature components are therefore correlated.

As stated previously, the random processes $\{n_c(t)\}$ and $\{n_s(t)\}$ are Gaussian if the random process $\{n_s(t)\}$ is Gaussian because the operations that produce them are linear (i.e., superposition holds). Figure 2–27d illustrates this fact. However, it also illustrates that the correlation of $\{n_c(t)\}$ and $\{n_s(t)\}$ *at the same instant* is zero. Thus, at the same instant, it is true that $\{n_c(t)\}$ and $\{n_s(t)\}$ are statistically independent, no matter if the symmetry conditions given previously hold or not. It follows, therefore, by transformation of random variables that the *envelope* of $n(t)$ has a Rayleigh pdf, which is given by

$$f_R(\alpha) = \frac{\alpha}{\sigma^2}\exp\left(-\frac{\alpha^2}{2\sigma^2}\right), \quad \alpha \geq 0 \qquad (2\text{–}210)$$

where α is an arbitrary independent variable (r has been used to denote the random process itself), and σ^2 is the mean-square value of $n(t)$, which is also the variance since $E[n(t)] = 0$.

2.7.5 Distributions of Envelopes of Narrowband Gaussian Processes

As given above, a Rayleigh random variable is the square root of the sum of the squares of two independent, zero mean, equal variance, independent Gaussian random variables—that is, it is the pdf of the *envelope* at time t of the signal (2–205), which we rewrite in other notation as

$$s_1(t) = x(t)\cos(2\pi f_0 t) - y(t)\sin(2\pi f_0 t) \qquad (2\text{–}211)$$

where $x(t)$ and $y(t)$ are independent, zero-mean Gaussian random processes with variance σ^2.

On the other hand, the pdf of the envelope at time t of the signal

$$s_2(t) = A\cos(2\pi f_0 t + \theta) + x(t)\cos(2\pi f_0 t) - y(t)\sin(2\pi f_0 t) \qquad (2\text{–}212)$$

where $x(t)$ and $y(t)$ are defined as before, A is a constant amplitude, and θ is a random variable uniformly distributed in $[0, 2\pi)$ and known as Ricean. The first term is often referred to as the specular component and the latter two terms make up the diffuse component. This is in keeping with the idea that (2–212) results from transmitting an unmodulated sinusoidal signal through a dispersive channel, with the specular component being a direct-ray reception of that signal while the diffuse component is the resultant of multiple independent reflections of the transmitted signal (the central limit theorem of probability can be invoked to justify that the quadrature components of this diffuse part are Gaussian random processes). Note that the Rayleigh model (2–210) is a special case of the Ricean model with $A = 0$.

It is instructive at this point to derive the Ricean pdf. The derivation proceeds by expanding the first term of (2–212) using the trigonometric identity for the cosine of the sum of two angles to rewrite it as

$$
\begin{aligned}
s_2(t) &= A\cos\theta \cos(2\pi f_0 t) - A\sin\theta \sin(2\pi f_0 t) \\
&\quad + x(t)\cos(2\pi f_0 t) - y(t)\sin(2\pi f_0 t) \\
&= [A\cos\theta + x(t)]\cos(2\pi f_0 t) - [A\sin\theta + y(t)]\sin(2\pi f_0 t) \\
&= X(t)\cos(2\pi f_0 t) - Y(t)\sin(2\pi f_0 t)
\end{aligned}
$$
(2–213)

where

$$
X(t) = A\cos\theta + x(t)
$$
(2–214)

and

$$
Y(t) = A\sin\theta + y(t)
$$
(2–215)

These random processes, given θ, are independent Gaussian random processes with variance σ^2. Their means are $E[X(t)] = A\cos\theta$ and $E[Y(t)] = A\sin\theta$, respectively. The goal is to find the pdf of

$$
R(t) = \sqrt{X^2(t) + Y^2(t)}
$$
(2–216)

Given θ, we may write down the joint pdf of $X(t)$ and $Y(t)$ as

$$
\begin{aligned}
f_{XY}(x,y|\theta) &= \frac{\exp[-(x - A\cos\theta)^2/2\sigma^2]}{\sqrt{2\pi\sigma^2}}\frac{\exp[-(y - A\sin\theta)^2/2\sigma^2]}{\sqrt{2\pi\sigma^2}} \\
&= \frac{\exp\{-[x^2 + y^2 - 2A(x\cos\theta + y\sin\theta) + A^2]/2\sigma^2\}}{2\pi\sigma^2}
\end{aligned}
$$
(2–217)

Now make the change of variables

$$
\left.\begin{aligned}
x &= r\cos\phi \\
y &= r\sin\phi
\end{aligned}\right\}, r \geq 0 \text{ and } 0 \leq \phi < 2\pi
$$
(2–218)

We recall that the transformation of a joint pdf requires multiplication by the Jacobian of the transformation, which in this case is just r. Thus

$$
\begin{aligned}
f_{R\phi}(r, \phi|\theta) &= \frac{\exp\{-[r^2 + A^2 - 2rA(\cos\theta\cos\phi + \sin\theta\sin\phi)]/2\sigma^2\}}{2\pi\sigma^2} \\
&= \frac{\exp\{-[r^2 + A^2 - 2rA\cos(\theta - \phi)]/2\sigma^2\}}{2\pi\sigma^2}
\end{aligned}
$$
(2–219)

The pdf over R alone may be obtained by integrating over θ with the aid of the definition

$$I_0(u) = \frac{1}{2\pi} \int_0^{2\pi} \exp(u \cos \alpha) d\alpha \qquad (2\text{-}220)$$

where $I_0(u)$ is referred to as the modified Bessel function of order zero. Since the integrand is periodic with period 2π, the integral can be over any 2π range. The result of the integration of (2–219) produces

$$f_R(r) = \frac{r}{\sigma^2} \exp[-(r^2 + A^2)/2\sigma^2] I_0\left(\frac{Ar}{\sigma^2}\right), \qquad r \geq 0 \qquad (2\text{-}221)$$

Since the result is independent of θ, this is the marginal pdf of R alone. It is referred to as a Ricean density function after S. O. Rice who first derived it.[15]

From (2–220), it may be seen that $I_0(0) = 1$ so that (2–221) reduces to the Rayleigh pdf (2–210) for $A = 0$, as it should.

2.8   COMPUTER GENERATION OF RANDOM VARIABLES

2.8.1   Introduction

It is usually desirable to model the essential features of a communication system so that a theoretical analysis can be carried out. Such an analysis allows a range of parametric trade-offs to be done. However, it is not always possible to do so, especially if nonlinearities are present, or if the interference is non-Gaussian, or if memory is introduced into the transmitted symbol sequence by the channel or receiver front end. In cases such as these it may be desirable, and even necessary, to perform a digital computer simulation of the communication system, or a subsystem thereof. There are several general-purpose digital-computer simulation programs that are useful in instances demanding a simulation approach [9]. Even with such general purpose simulation programs, it is necessary to understand the principles involved in a simulation so that they are not misused. Furthermore, it is sometimes preferable to do a special-purpose simulation for a specific problem. The purpose of this section, therefore, is to introduce some of the ingredients necessary for digital computer simulation of a system. In particular, generation of pseudo-random digital sequences, called PN (for pseudo-noise) sequences, and simulation of Gaussian noise having a desired power spectral density will be described.

Before describing the generation of PN sequences and random noise, it is worthwhile to give a short overview of the methods that can be used in doing a simulation. The most general way is to represent the signals and noise as sample data sequences and to perform the filtering and other signal processing functions on this sample data. Certain

[15]See S. O. Rice, "Mathematical Analysis of Random Noise," *Bell System Technical Journal*, Vols. 23 and 24, pp. 282–332 and 46–156, 1944 and 1945. Reprinted in N. Wax, *Selected Papers on Noise and Stochastic Processes*, New York: Dover Publications, 1954.

statistics of the output of the simulated communication system can then be computed to characterize its performance. This approach, which is referred to as the Monte Carlo approach, is very time consuming because the simulation is carried out sample by sample where the spacing of the time samples is dictated by the sampling theorem. Sometimes it is possible to decrease the simulation time by using important sampling techniques. Such techniques essentially bias the noise probability distribution functions to make low-probability events more probable. After the simulation is completed, the results are unbiased in accordance with the bias put in originally.

Another technique is to use a typical data sequence, or hybrid, approach. This approach was illustrated in Problem 1–8. In this approach, the effect of the communication system on the signal alone is simulated using a typical data sequence. A particularly appropriate signal for simulating binary data is a PN sequence, mentioned above and to be discussed briefly in Section 2.8.4 and in detail in Chapter 9. After the effects of the system on the signal are determined through simulation, the effects of the noise are included by using an analytical expression to compute the desired statistic, usually a probability of symbol error, on a symbol-by-symbol basis. These probabilities (or whatever other statistics are desired) are then averaged over the pdf used for the data to obtain the performance averaged over a typical data sequence. In this manner, system memory can be included in a straightforward fashion. This approach is much less time consuming than the Monte Carlo approach. Generally speaking, however, it can be used only for the case where the communication system is linear from the point that the noise enters it to the output where the statistic of interest is computed. Furthermore, the noise must be Gaussian. These assumptions are necessary because the output statistics of a linear system with a Gaussian input are Gaussian. Thus, they make it possible to carry out the analysis required to obtain the desired statistic, say a probability of symbol error. While this discussion may not be entirely clear now, it is hoped that it will become clear in succeeding chapters where performance characteristics of communication systems are obtained.

2.8.2 Generation of Random Variables Having a Specific Distribution

The simulation of noise involves two ideas: the first is the generation of a time series of random variables, and the second is shaping the spectrum of the time series to produce the desired correlation properties.

Consider the first problem—that of generating time series, or sequences, of random variables. We assume that all random variables in a given sequence are identically distributed and that they are independent of each other. Such sequences are referred to as iid (for *independent, identically distributed*). Therefore, for an iid sequence denoted by $\{V_n\}$, we assume that each random number is drawn independently from a population having a pdf $f_V(v)$. Now random number generators that generate uniformly distributed numbers are available in most high-level computer languages. Let U be a uniform random variable in the interval $[0, 1)$, and let

$$V = g(U) \tag{2–222}$$

where $g(U)$ is an invertible transformation. Then the pdf of V is related to that of U by

$$f_V(v) = f_U(u) \left| \frac{du}{dv} \right|_{u=g^{-1}(v)} \tag{2-223}$$

$$= \begin{cases} \left| \dfrac{du}{dv} \right|, & 0 \le u \le 1 \\ 0, & \text{otherwise} \end{cases}$$

since $f_U(u) = 1$, $0 \le u \le 1$, and is zero otherwise. If $du/dv \triangleq dg^{-1}(v)/dv > 0$, then $|du/dv| = du/dv = dg^{-1}(v)/dv$. On the other hand, if $du/dv \triangleq dg^{-1}(v)/dv < 0$ then $|du/dv| = -du/dv = -dg^{-1}(v)/dv$. Thus,

$$f_V(v) = \begin{cases} \dfrac{dg^{-1}(v)}{dv}, & \dfrac{dg^{-1}(v)}{dv} > 0 \\ -\dfrac{dg^{-1}(v)}{dv}, & \dfrac{dg^{-1}(v)}{dv} < 0 \end{cases} \quad 0 \le u \le 1 \tag{2-224}$$

Therefore, integration yields

$$g^{-1}(v) = \begin{cases} \displaystyle\int_{-\infty}^{v} f_V(\lambda)d\lambda, & \dfrac{dg^{-1}(v)}{dv} > 0 \\ -\displaystyle\int_{-\infty}^{v} f_V(\lambda)d\lambda, & \dfrac{dg^{-1}(v)}{dv} < 0 \end{cases} \tag{2-225}$$

Thus, a uniform random number generator can be used to generate a random variable of arbitrary pdf provided an invertible transformation, $g(v)$, can be found via (2–225). Note that the integral of $f_V(v)$ in (2–225) is simply the cumulative distribution function of V.

EXAMPLE 2–19

Find the required transformation to generate a Rayleigh distributed random variable with pdf

$$f_V(v) = \begin{cases} v \exp(-v^2/2), & v \ge 0 \\ 0, & v < 0 \end{cases}$$

Solution: From the desired $f_V(v)$, we have

$$\int_{-\infty}^{v} f_V(\lambda)\, d\lambda = \begin{cases} 0, & v < 0 \\ 1 - \exp(-v^2/2), & v \ge 0 \end{cases}$$

Therefore,

$$u = g^{-1}(v) = 1 - \exp(-v^2/2) \text{ if } v \ge 0 \text{ and } v = -\sqrt{-2 \ln(1 - u)}, 0 \le u \le 1$$

In summary, if U is a random variable uniformly distributed in $[0, 1)$, then

$$V = \sqrt{-2 \ln(1 - U)} \quad \text{or} \quad V = \sqrt{-2 \ln U}$$

is Rayleigh distributed, where the last expression holds because if U is uniformly distributed in [0, 1) then so is $1 - U$.

Note that generation of a Gaussian random variable by this method is not practical because to obtain the inverse transformation it is necessary to invert the transcendental Q-function. We therefore look for some other transformation to generate Gaussian random variables.[16] To do so, we use the fact that if two zero-mean Gaussian random variables, X_1 and X_2, having the same variance are transformed to polar coordinates via the transformation

$$X_1 = R\cos\Theta \text{ and } X_2 = R\sin\Theta \qquad (2\text{--}226)$$

then R is Rayleigh and Θ is uniform in the interval [0, 2π), and R and Θ are independent. Therefore, if we generate R and Θ, we can generate X_1 and X_2 by virtue of (2–226); R is generated according to Example 2–19 and Θ is $2\pi V$ where V is uniform in [0, 1).

2.8.3 Spectrum of a Simulated White Noise Process

Now consider the spectral characteristics of a time series of iid random variables. Figure 2–28a shows such a time series of random variables, where each has zero mean. The sampling interval is T_s. To a system with this iid sequence as input, the sample values appear as a stair-step process shown in Figure 2–28b. The power spectral density of a random process is [2]

$$S(f) = \lim_{T\to\infty}\left(\frac{1}{T}E\left\{\left|\mathscr{F}\left[X_T(t)\right]\right|^2\right\}\right) \qquad (2\text{--}227)$$

where T is a truncation interval such that

$$X_T(t) = \begin{cases} X(t), & |t| \le T/2 \\ 0, & \text{otherwise} \end{cases} \qquad (2\text{--}228)$$

That is, the power spectrum is obtained by finding the magnitude squared of the Fourier transform of the truncated signal, $X_T(t)$, taking the expectation of this, dividing by the truncation interval, and taking the limit as the truncation interval goes to infinity (the last two operations amount to time averaging, of course).

The process $X(t)$ in this case is

$$X(t) = \sum_{n=-\infty}^{\infty} X_n P_{T_s}(t - nT_s) \qquad (2\text{--}229)$$

---

[16]Note that most numerical computation packages, such as MATLAB, have Gaussian random number generators in addition to uniform random number generators.

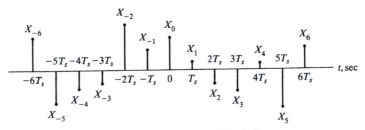

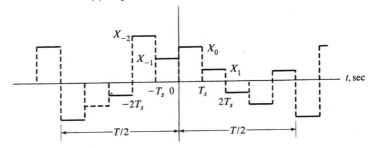

(a) A squence of *iid* random variables in time

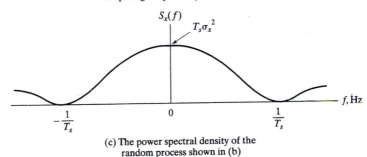

(b) A stairstep equivalent to (a) for purposes of
computing the power spectrum

(c) The power spectral density of the
random process shown in (b)

FIGURE 2–28 Waveforms and power spectrum relating to the simulation of random waveforms.

where $P_{T_s}(t) = 1, 0 \leq t \leq T_s$, and is 0 otherwise, is defined in Table 2–1. Assume that truncation to $-T/2 \leq t \leq T/2$ corresponds to $-N \leq n \leq N$. Then $T = 2NT_s$, and (2–227) becomes[17]

$$S(f) = \lim_{N \to \infty} \left(\frac{1}{(2N+1)T_s} E\left\{ \left| \mathscr{F}\left[\sum_{n=-N}^{N} X_n P_{T_s}(t - nT_s) \right] \right|^2 \right\} \right) \qquad (2\text{–}230)$$

[17]Note that $T \doteq (2N+1)T_s + 2\Delta t$, in general, but Δt will be of no consequence in the limit at $T \to \infty$.

Now

$$\mathcal{F}\left[\sum_{n=-N}^{N} X_n P_{T_s}(t - nT_s)\right] = \sum_{n=-N}^{N} X_n \mathcal{F}[P_{T_s}(t - nT_s)] \qquad (2\text{–}231)$$

$$= \sum_{n=-N}^{N} X_n T_s \operatorname{sinc}(T_s f) \exp(-j2\pi nT_s f)$$

Now write the magnitude squared of this sum as a double sum and interchange the order of summation and expectation to obtain

$$E\left\{\left|\mathcal{F}\left[\sum_{n=-N}^{N} X_n P_{T_s}(t - nT_s)\right]\right|^2\right\} = \sum_m \sum_n E(X_m X_n) T_s^2 \operatorname{sinc}^2(T_s f)$$

$$\times \exp[-j2\pi (n - m) T_s f] \qquad (2\text{–}232)$$

$$= \sum_{n=-N}^{N} E(X_n^2) T_s^2 \operatorname{sinc}^2(T_s f) = (2N + 1) E(X_n^2) T_s^2 \operatorname{sinc}^2(T_s f)$$

which follows because X_m and X_n, $m \neq n$, are independent and have zero means. Hence (2–230 gives)

$$S(f) = T_s E(X_n^2) \operatorname{sinc}^2(T_s f) \qquad (2\text{–}233)$$

which is plotted in Figure 2–28c. This plot shows that if T_s^{-1} is much greater than the bandwidth of any system that the time series is driving, then the input to the system will appear like white noise. Furthermore, the two-sided power spectral density of this process at $f = 0$ is

$$N_0/2 = T_s E(X_n^2) \qquad (2\text{–}234)$$

so that the mean-square value (also the variance since their means are zero) of the random variables X_n should be chosen as

$$E(X_n^2) = \frac{N_0}{2T_s} \qquad (2\text{–}235)$$

Further spectral shaping of this process, if required, can be accomplished by digital filtering.

EXAMPLE 2–20

As an example in generating noise waveforms, the MATLAB program below generates filtered white noise and compares the output noise sample variance with the theoretical value.

```
% Program simulates a white noise waveform, filters it with a Butterworth filter
% and compares the sample variance of the filtered noise with theoretical value
clf
n_order = input(' Enter number of poles of filter ');
N0 = input(' Enter single-sided noise power spectral density ');
```

```
n_samp = input(' Enter total number of samples in noise waveform ');
for B = .5:.5:4      % Do several bandwidth values
  fs = 10*B;          % Set sample rate high so generated noise looks "white"
  BN = (pi/(2*n_order))/sin(pi/(2*n_order))*B; % Noise equivalent BW of filter
  var_filt_out = BN*N0;   % Theoretical variance of output noise from filter
  var_samples = N0*fs/2;  % Variance of generated samples according to (2-235)
  N_in = [];
  N_out = [];
  N_out_ss = [];
  N_in = sqrt(var_samples)*randn(1, n_samp); % "White" input noise vector
  Lt = length(N_in);
  t = [0:1/fs:(Lt-1)/fs];  % Vector of time values for plotting purposes
  [num,den] = butter(n_order,2*B*pi,'s');% Generate BW filter poles and zeros
  N_out = (lsim(num,den,N_in,t))';        % Output noise vector from filter
  n_samp_excl = fix(100/B);               % Exclude beginning samples for
  N_out_ss(1:Lt-n_samp_excl)=N_out(n_samp_excl+1:Lt); %computing sample variance
  samp_var_out = sum(N_out_ss.^2)/(n_samp-n_samp_excl);%Output sample variance
  disp('Bandwidth; Theoretical variance; Sample variance:')
  var_out = [B var_filt_out samp_var_out];
  disp(var_out)
end
subplot(2,1,1),plot(t,N_in), ylabel('White noise'),xlabel('t'), . . .
  title(['Filtered white noise; ',num2str(n_order),'rd-order Butterworth filter;
  bandwidth = ',num2str(B),' Hz'])
  subplot(2,1,2),plot(t,N_out),ylabel('Filtered noise'),xlabel('t')
```

Some typical variance results for a third-order Butterworth filter with 5000 samples and $N_0 = 1$ W/Hz are given below:

Bandwidth, Hz	Theoretical variance	Variance - simulation
0.5	0.524	0.537
1.0	1.047	1.065
1.5	1.571	1.562
2.0	2.094	2.022
2.5	2.618	2.646
3.0	3.665	3.489

Figure 2–29 shows typical waveforms for the input and output noise waveforms from the filter.

2.8.4   Generation of Pseudo-Noise Sequences [8]

Maximum-length pseudonoise (PN) sequences, also called m-sequences, are binary-valued sequences that approximate a sequence of coin tossings for which a 1 represents a head and a 0 represents a tail. They have several advantageous features:

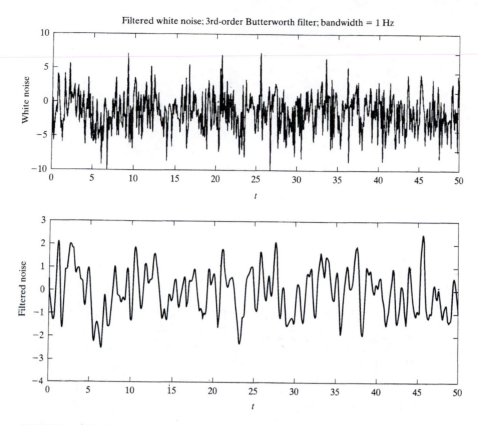

FIGURE 2-29 Input and output sample functions from a filter driven by simulated white noise.

1. They are easily generated by feedback shift register structures.
2. They have autocorrelation functions that are highly peaked for zero delay and are nearly 0 for nonzero delays. In this sense, they approximate the properties of white noise.
3. As pointed out, they approximate the randomness properties of a coin toss sequence in that the number of 1s and 0s differ by one (by necessity, the length of a PN sequence is odd as will be seen shortly).

Figure 2–30a illustrates a feedback structure for generating a 7-bit sequence. At each clock pulse, the contents of the shift-register shift to the right by one register. The output is taken from the right-most register, and the input is derived by modulo-2 adding without carrying the contents of stages 2 and 3. This is a *proper* feedback connection in that the maximum-length sequence for a shift register with three stages is generated—in particular, $2^3 - 1 = 7$. That the maximum length is 7 can be reasoned as follows. There are

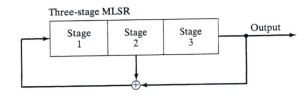

(a) Maximal-length feedback shift register
for a 7-bit pn sequence

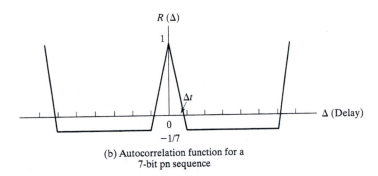

(b) Autocorrelation function for a
7-bit pn sequence

FIGURE 2–30   Shift-register configuration and autocorrelation function for a 7-bit
PN sequence.

8 possible loadings, or states, of the shift register because each register can assume one of two possible values, and there are three registers ($2^3 = 8$). However, one of these states is 000, and if it appears, the shift register never can leave this state (a 0 will always be fed back). Thus, for a three-stage generator, 7 is the maximum number of possible states, and this corresponds to the maximum length that can be generated by the feedback shift register before the sequence repeats. The sequence may be shorter than 7 if an improper feedback connection is used; the one in Figure 2–30 is proper.

We assume that the feedback shift register runs continuously, and therefore its output is periodic. The autocorrelation function of this periodic signal, viewed as now taking on values of 1 or − 1 for T_c-second intervals can be found as a time average over one period of the sequence times itself delayed. For zero delay, it is clear that this average is one; for nonzero delays equal to integer values of 1 bit (but not a multiple of the sequence length), it is easy to see that the correlation is −1 divided by the sequence length. The correlation values for noninteger delays must be straight lines connecting the integer-delay correlation values since the averaging process is a sum of integrals of either 1 or −1 over portions of the T_c-second intervals in one period of the sequence. Therefore, the autocorrelation function for the 7-bit PN sequence generated by the feedback shift register of Figure 2–30a is that shown in Figure 2–30b. A table of proper connections for shift-register lengths 2 through 5 is given below.

Shift-Register Length	Sequence Length	Sequence (initial state is all 1s)	Feedback Digit
2	3	110	$x_1 \oplus x_2$
3	7	1110010	$x_2 \oplus x_3$
4	15	111100010011010	$x_3 \oplus x_4$
5	31	111110011010010	$x_2 \oplus x_5$
		0001010111011000	

EXAMPLE 2–21

The MATLAB M-file given below is a function that will generate PN sequences of lengths $2^m - 1$, where $m = 5, 6, 7, 9, 10, 11,$ and 15.

```
%       function output = pngen(m,k,shift_reg0): PN generator with 2
%       feedback connections. The length is 2^m - 1. The initial
%       load is the array shift_reg0, which is length m; if empty,
%       initial load is all 0s with a 1 in right-most position. The
%       right-end tap is exclusive-ORed with a second tap where k specifies
%       the other tap fed back. The PN generator is of the Fibonacci form.
%       See Ex. 3-13 of Peterson, Ziemer, and Borth for the procedure to
%       determine the feedback connection from the primitive polynomial
%       entry in Table 3-5. Combinations that work are m=5, k=3;
%       m=6, k=2; m=7, k=4; m=9, k=5; m=10, k=4; m=11, k=3; m=15, k=2.
%
function output = pngen(m,k,shift_reg0)
no_rep = 2^m-1;
output = zeros(1,no_rep);
if isempty(shift_reg0) == 1
   shift_reg = zeros(1, m);
   shift_reg(m) = 1;
else
   shift_reg = shift_reg0;
end
for i = 1:no_rep
      feedback = xor2(shift_reg(1),shift_reg(k));
      shift_reg(1:m-1) = shift_reg(2:m);
      shift_reg(m) = feedback;
      output(i) = shift_reg(m);
end

function Q = xor2(X,Y)
% XOR2      Exclusive "or" (2-input)
%
%    Q = xor2(X,Y)      The two inputs will result in the logical
%                       output of 1 or 0.
Q = (X&~Y) + (~X&Y);
```

A 31-bit PN sequence with the initial load [0 0 1 0 0] is generated as shown below:

» PN = pngen(5, 3, [0 0 1 0 0])

PN =

Columns 1 through 12

0 0 1 0 1 0 1 1 1 0 1 1

Columns 13 through 24

0 0 0 1 1 1 1 1 0 0 1 1

Columns 25 through 31

0 1 0 0 1 0 0

2.9 SUMMARY

1. Signals can be classified as deterministic or random. For the former, each value of the signal is specified by a known equation. For the latter, each value must be specified in terms of a probability of occurrence.
2. Signals can also be classified as energy, power, or neither. The energy of a signal $x(t)$ is defined as

$$E = \lim_{T \to \infty} \int_{-T}^{T} |x(t)|^2 \, dt$$

and the power of a signal is defined as

$$P = \lim_{T \to \infty} \frac{1}{2T} \int_{-T}^{T} |x(t)|^2 \, dt$$

For energy signals $0 < E < \infty$, while for power signals $0 < P < \infty$.

3. Yet a third classification of signals is periodic and aperiodic. For a periodic signal

$$x(t + T_0) = x(t), \quad -\infty < t < \infty$$

where the smallest T_0 satisfying this relation is called the (fundamental) period. Signals not satisfying this relation are called aperiodic.

4. A class of systems of great interest are fixed (time-invariant), linear systems. A system is linear if superposition holds. A system is fixed or time invariant if the only effect on the output, if the input is shifted in time, is that the output is time shifted the same amount as the input. For fixed linear systems, the superposition integral can be used to find the output. That is, the impulse response (i.e., the response of the system to a unit impulse applied at time zero) is convolved with the input to give the output.

5. It can be shown that for a fixed, linear system, $\exp(j\omega t)$ is an *eigenfunction*. That is, the output is proportional to $\exp(j\omega t)$, where the constant of proportionality is the *frequency response function* of the system, defined as

$$\tilde{H}(j\omega) = \int_{-\infty}^{\infty} h(t)\exp(-j\omega t)\, dt$$

where $h(t)$ is the impulse response of the system. The magnitude of the complex function $H(f) = \tilde{H}(j2\pi f)$ is called the *amplitude response* of the system, and its argument is called the *phase response*.

6. Because of the property of a fixed, linear system mentioned in point 5 and because of the superposition property of a linear system, it is useful to approximate inputs by sums of complex exponentials of the form $\exp(j2\pi n f_0 t)$. If the period of a periodic function, $x(t)$, is $T_0 = 1/f_0$ then the doubly infinite series

$$x(t) = \sum_{n=-\infty}^{\infty} X_n \exp(j2\pi n f_0 t)$$

where

$$X_n = \frac{1}{T_0} \int_{-\infty}^{\infty} x(t)\exp(-j2\pi n f_0 t)\, dt$$

represents $x(t)$ exactly except at points of discontinuity. This is known as the *complex exponential Fourier series* and the coefficients X_n are called *Fourier coefficients*. For a linear system, the eigenfunction property says that the nth Fourier coefficient of the output is equal to the nth Fourier coefficient of the input times the frequency response function of the system evaluated at the frequency nf_0.

7. While the Fourier series is good for periodic signals, a useful complex exponential representation for aperiodic energy signals is the *Fourier transform* and its inverse, defined by the relations

$$X(f) = \int_{-\infty}^{\infty} x(t)\exp(-j2\pi ft)\, dt$$

and

$$x(t) = \int_{-\infty}^{\infty} X(f)\exp(j2\pi ft)\, df$$

Now the eigenfunction property for a fixed, linear system states that

$$Y(f) = H(f)X(f)$$

where $X(f)$ and $Y(f)$ are the Fourier transforms of input and output, respectively, and $H(f)$ is the frequency response function.

8. Signal spectra can be plotted with the aid of the Fourier transform. The amplitude spectrum of a signal is a plot of the magnitude of the Fourier transform of the signal versus frequency, and the phase spectrum is a plot of the argument of the Fourier transform versus frequency. For periodic signals, the Fourier transform can still be used, but the amplitude spectrum consists of weighted impulses at the frequencies of the spectral components.

9. Parseval's theorem states that for two signals $x(t)$ and $y(t)$ with Fourier transforms $X(f)$ and $Y(f)$, respectively,

$$\int_{-\infty}^{\infty} x(t)y^*(t)dt = \int_{-\infty}^{\infty} X(f)Y^*(f)df$$

If $x(t) = y(t)$, then the energy of $x(t)$ is

$$E = \int_{-\infty}^{\infty} |x(t)|^2 \, dt = \int_{-\infty}^{\infty} |X(f)|^2 \, df$$

Energy within a bandwidth W can be computed by means of the last integral by carrying out the integration from $-W$ to W.

10. Another useful application of the Fourier transform is to analog modulation theory. Using the modulation theorem of Fourier transforms allows one to easily find spectra for double-sideband and amplitude (with carrier) modulation. The definition of the Hilbert transform, which amounts to a -90 degree phase shifter, allows one to write the time domain waveform for single-sideband modulation. These modulation examples are referred to as linear because superposition holds with respect to the modulating signal. Angle modulation is nonlinear and, as a result, its spectrum can be found only for special cases. One such case is that of sinusoidal message signals, which results in a trigonometric series with Bessel function coefficients for the time domain waveform.

11. Another useful application of the Hilbert transform is to define the complex envelope of a bandpass signal as $\tilde{x}(t)$ in the equation

$$x_p(t) = \tilde{x}(t) \exp(j2\pi f_0 t)$$

where $x_p(t)$ is the inverse Fourier transform of twice the positive frequency half of the bandpass signal. A bandpass system can also have its impulse response represented by a complex envelope by a similar equation. These concepts are useful in that the complex envelope of the output of a linear system is the convolution of the complex envelopes of the input and the impulse response. This considerably simplifies the analysis of bandpass systems with bandpass inputs.

12. A distortionless system is one that produces an output that is a scaled, delayed replica of the input. Such a system has an amplitude response that is constant and a phase response that is linear over the band of frequencies occupied by the input. If the amplitude response is not constant over the passband of the input, amplitude distortion results, while if the phase response is not a linear function of frequency over the pass-

band of the input, phase, or delay distortion, results. Practical fixed, linear systems may introduce a combination of these two distortions or either one alone. The group delay of a filter is minus the derivative of its phase response with respect to the radian frequency, ω. A filter that does not introduce delay distortion has a constant group delay over the passband of the input signal.

13. Ideal filters have amplitude responses that are constant and phase responses that are linear over the passband of any input. Outside of their passbands, ideal filters have zero amplitude response. Ideal filters can be lowpass, bandpass, or highpass. They are unrealizable, but can be approximated by realizable filters. Three examples of practical, realizable filters were introduced: Butterworth, Chebyshev, and Bessel.

14. Nonlinear systems can perform useful functions in a communication system, or they can introduce unwanted distortion. A mixer is an example of a useful nonlinear system. An amplifier with nonlinearities is an example of a nonlinear system that introduces unwanted distortion into any signal passing through it. A nonlinear system can introduce frequencies into the output that weren't present in the input. These can be categorized as harmonic distortion (a term in the output with a frequency that is an integer multiple of an input frequency) or intermodulation distortion (a term in the output with a frequency that is the difference of two input frequencies or their harmonics).

15. The lowpass sampling theorem states that samples taken at twice the bandwidth, W, of a lowpass signal, or greater, will allow recovery of the original signal by ideal lowpass filtering, with the lowpass filter bandwidth obeying $W < B < f_s - W$, where f_s is the sampling frequency. Quadrature sampling allows lowpass sampling to be extended to bandpass sampling. That quadrature sampling works is a direct consequence of the concept of a complex envelope for a bandpass signal and its representation in terms of inphase and quadrature components. For a bandpass signal of bandwidth W, quadrature sampling allows the signal to be represented by a minimum of $2W$ samples per second, or W samples per second for each quadrature component.

16. Representation of a signal in terms of periodically taken samples and quantization of these samples to a finite number of levels allows an analog signal to be transmitted through a digital communication system. Representation of each quantized sample by a binary number and transmission of these binary values through a communication channel by means of some type of binary modulation system is referred to as pulse code modulation. In order to decrease the effect of the quantization, an amplitude compressor is sometimes used at the output of the analog message source before quantization. An expander, which undoes what the compressor did at the source, is then used at the channel output. The combination of both operations is called *companding*.

17. Random signals were the next topic considered in this chapter. As mentioned in point 1 of this summary, they must be described in terms of a probability distribution at each time instant of interest. The most general description of a random signal would be an N-fold pdf referring to the amplitudes of the random signal at N time

instants. Other, less comprehensive statistical descriptions of random processes are commonly used, such as the mean, mean-square, and autocorrelation function, which is the average of the product of the random signal amplitude at two different time instants.

For stationary processes, the autocorrelation function is a function only of the difference of these two time instants. This time difference is referred to as the delay variable. The Fourier transform of the autocorrelation function of a stationary random signal with respect to the delay variable gives the power spectral density of the signal. The power spectral density gives the distribution of power with frequency for the signal; its integral over all frequency gives the average power of the signal. For a linear system with frequency response function $H(f)$, the power spectrum of the output, $S_y(f)$, equals the power spectrum of the input, $S_x(f)$, times $|H(f)|^2$.

In general, it is difficult to obtain the output statistics of any system being driven by an arbitrary random signal. Two exceptions are zero-memory invertible nonlinear devices, where the pdf of the output at a single time instant, $f_Y(y)$, can be related to that of the input, $f_X(x)$, by

$$f_Y(y) = \left| \frac{dg^{-1}(y)}{dy} \right| f_X(x)|_{x=g^{-1}(y)}$$

where $Y = g(X)$ is the transformation relating output to input. The other exception is the case of a fixed, linear system being driven by a stationary Gaussian signal, in which case the output is also known to be Gaussian and stationary. Since a Gaussian pdf can be specified completely once the mean, variance, and autocorrelation function (or power spectral density) are known, one can readily determine the output statistics in this situation.

18. The last topic taken up in this chapter was that of digital computer simulation of signals and noise necessary for computer simulation of communication systems. This entails the implementation of random number generators as computer algorithms, the approximation of random signals by time sequences of random numbers, and the implementation of digital filters.

REFERENCES

[1] R. E. Ziemer, W. H. Tranter, and D. R. Fannin, *Signals and Systems: Continuous and Discrete,* 4th ed. (Upper Saddle River, NJ: Prentice Hall, 1998).

[2] R. E. Ziemer and W. H. Tranter, *Principles of Communications: Systems, Modulation, and Noise,* 4th ed. (New York: John Wiley, 1995.)

[3] *The Student Edition of MATLAB, Version 5.3 User's Guide* (Natick, MA: The MathWorks, Inc., 1999.).

[4] A. I. Zubrev, *Handbook of Filter Synthesis* (New York: John Wiley, 1967).

[5] K. Shenoi, *Digital Signal Processing in Telecommunications* (Upper Saddle River, NJ: Prentice Hall, 1995).

[6] M. D. Floyd and G. D. Hillman, "Pulse-Code Modulation Codec-Filters," Chapter 27 in J. D. Gibson, ed., *The Communications Handbook* (Boca Raton, FL: CRC Press, 1997).

[7] R. D. Shelton and A. F. Adkins, "Noise Bandwidth of Common Filters," *IEEE Trans. on Commun.*, Vol. 28, pp. 828–830, Dec. 1970.

[8] R. L. Peterson, R. E. Ziemer, and D. E. Borth, *Introduction to Spread Spectrum Communications*, Chapter 3 (Upper Saddle River, NJ: Prentice Hall, 1995).

[9] Special Issues on Computer Modeling of Communication Systems, *IEEE Journ. on Selected Areas in Commun.*, Jan. 1984, Jan. 1988, and May 1997.

PROBLEMS

2–1. Classify the following signals as to (1) finite power or finite energy, (2) periodic or aperiodic. What are the periods of those that are periodic and the energies or powers, as the case may be, for case (1)?

   (a) $\cos 20\pi t + \sin 26\pi t$

   (b) $\exp(-10|t|)$

   (c) $\Pi(t + 1/2) - \Pi(t - 1/2)$

   (d) $\dfrac{1}{\sqrt{t^2 + 1}}$

   (e) $\cos 120\pi t + \cos 377t$

2–2. Classify the following systems as to (1) linear or nonlinear; (2) fixed or time varying; (3) causal or noncausal. The notation used is as follows: $x(t)$ represents the input, $y(t)$ represents the output, and $h(t)$ represents the system's impulse response.

   (a) $h(t) = \dfrac{1 - \cos 20\pi t}{(20\pi t)^2}$

   (b) $\dfrac{dy(t)}{dt} + 10y(t) = x^2(t)$

   (c) $\dfrac{dy(t)}{dt} + t\,y(t) = x(t)$

   (d) $\dfrac{dy(t)}{dt} + y(t) = x(t + 1)$

   (e) $\dfrac{dy(t)}{dt} + y^2(t) = x(t)$

2–3. Find the response of a system with impulse response $h(t) = 10\exp(-10t)u(t)$ to the following inputs:

   (a) $x(t) = u(t)$

   (b) $x(t) = \Pi\left(\dfrac{t}{2}\right)$

   (c) $x(t) = \exp(-3t)\,u(t)$

   (d) $x(t) = \exp(j6\pi t)\,u(t)$

   (e) $x(t) = \cos(6\pi t)\,u(t)$

2–4. (a) Show that the following set of functions is orthonormal on the interval $0 \le t \le 4$:

$$\phi_1(t) = \Pi(t - 0.5), \phi_2(t) = \Pi(t - 1.5)$$

$$\phi_3(t) = \Pi(t - 2.5), \phi_4(t) = \Pi(t - 3.5)$$

(b) Expand the signal

$$x(t) = \exp\left(-\frac{t}{2}\right)u(t)$$

as an orthogonal function series on the interval $0 \le t \le 4$ using the set of functions above.
(c) Find the integral squared error for the expansion found in part (b).

2–5. Derive the relationships (2–31) between the exponential Fourier series coefficients and the sine-cosine Fourier series.

2–6. Carry out the derivation of the cosine form of the Fourier series given by (2–34) starting with the exponential Fourier series. Express A_0, A_n, and θ_n in terms of X_0 and X_n.

2–7. Derive Parseval's theorem given by (2–35).

2–8. Derive the Fourier series given in Table 2–3.

2–9. Use (2–41) to obtain Fourier transforms for the periodic signals shown in Figure P2–9.

2–10. Use pair 17 of Table F–7 and the multiplication theorem of Fourier transforms to derive the spectrum of an impulse sampled signal.

2–11. Use appropriate Fourier transform theorems to obtain the amplitude and phase spectra for the signal $\Pi\,[(t - 2)/4]\exp[\,j2\pi(t - 2)]$.

2–12. Given a message signal with the spectrum

$$M(f) = \Pi\left(\frac{f}{20}\right)$$

and a carrier signal

$$c(t) = \cos 200\pi t$$

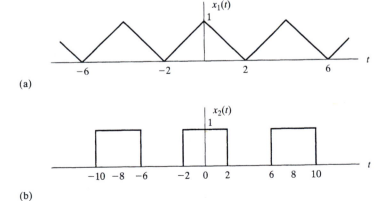

(a)

(b)

FIGURE P2–9

sketch the spectra of the following modulated signals:
(a) Double sideband.
(b) AM with modulation index 0.5.
(c) Single sideband, upper sideband transmitted.
(d) Single sideband, lower sideband transmitted.

2–13. Derive and sketch modulated time-domain waveforms for the cases listed in Problem 2–12 (a) and (b).

2–14. Show that the coherent demodulator shown in Figure P2–14 can be used to demodulate AM, DSB, and SSB. The ideal LPF bandwidth is $B \geq W$, where W is the bandwidth of $m(t)$. What is the theoretical maximum value that B can assume and still have the demodulator function properly?

2–15. An FM modulator operates with frequency deviation constant $f_d = 10$ Hz/V, carrier amplitude $A = 1$ volt, and carrier frequency $f_0 = 1,000$ Hz. The input message is $m(t) = A_m \cos(2\pi f_m t)$. Plot the amplitude spectrum of the modulator output for the following cases:
(a) $A_m = 2$ V and $f_m = 200$ Hz
(b) $A_m = 2$ V and $f_m = 20$ Hz
(c) $A_m = 2$ V and $f_m = 4$ Hz
(d) $A_m = 10$ V and $f_m = 20$ Hz

2–16. **(a)** Show that the power for a DSB-modulated signal of the form (2–50) is

$$P_{\text{DSB}} = \frac{1}{2} A^2 \overline{m^2(t)} = \frac{1}{2} A^2 P_m$$

where P_m is the power in $m(t)$.

(b) Show that the power in an AM-modulated signal of the form

$$x_c(t) = A[1 + am(t)] \cos 2\pi f_0 t$$

is

$$P_{\text{AM}} = \frac{1}{2} A^2 (1 + a^2 P_m)$$

where P_m is as defined in (a) and the average value of $m(t)$ is 0.

(c) Using the fact that the powers of a signal and its Hilbert transform are equal, show that the power in a SSB signal of the form (2–64) is

$$P_{\text{SSB}} = \frac{A^2}{2} P_m$$

(d) Prove the power relationship for the angle modulated signal given by (2–78).

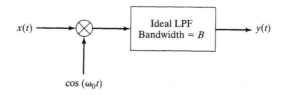

FIGURE P2–14

2–17. (a) Derive the Hilbert transform of the signal $m(t) = \Pi(t/2)$.

    (b) Use the result obtained in part (a) to obtain the analytic signal corresponding to the $m(t)$ given there.

    (c) Sketch the amplitude spectrum of the analytic signal found in part (b).

2–18. (a) Obtain the complex envelope of the narrowband signal

$$x(t) = \exp(-|t|) \cos 1000\pi t$$

    where $f_0 = 500$ Hz.

    (b) Obtain the time-domain response of a filter with transfer function given by (2–102) to the input signal given in part (a) for $Q = 100$ and $f_0 = 500$ Hz.

2.19. Given a filter with transfer function

$$H(f) = \left[H\left(\frac{f}{10}\right) + H\left(\frac{f}{20}\right) \right] \exp(-j 20\pi f)$$

From a sketch of the amplitude and phase response, determine what type of distortion, if any, is imposed on the following inputs:

(a) $x_1(t) = \cos 5\pi t + \cos 15\pi t$

(b) $x_2(t) = \cos 12\pi t + \cos 18\pi t$

(c) $x_3(t) = \cos 18\pi t + \cos 30\pi t$

2–20. Analytically obtain the impulse response for the filters with transfer functions shown in Figure 2–7.

2–21. Derive the group and phase-delay functions for the following filters: (a) first order Butterworth, (b) second-order Bessel, (c) second-order Chebyshev.

2–22. Derive the response of a filter with amplitude response

$$A(f) = (1 + 0.1 f^2)\Pi(f/10)$$

and phase response

$$\theta(f) = -0.2\pi f + 0.05 f^2$$

to the input $x(t) = \cos 2\pi t$.

2–23. Derive (2–129).

2–24. Derive the AM-to-PM conversion term (see Example 2–6) for a filter with

$$\Delta A(f) = -0.1f + 0.1 f^2$$

$$\Delta \theta (f) = 0.1 f^2$$

and the input

$$x(t) = (1 + 0.2 \cos 20\pi t) \cos 100\pi t$$

Let $t_0 = 0$ and $A_0 = 1$. Assume that the filter passband is centered at the carrier frequency and bandwidth wide enough to pass the modulated signal.

2–25. Obtain the response of the filter of Problem 2–24 to the phase-modulated signal

$$x(t) = \cos (100\pi t + 0.1 \cos 10\pi t)$$

2–26. Consider the signal

$$x(t) = 4 \cos 30\pi t$$

(a) If the signal is sampled by an impulse train, sketch its spectrum for the following sampling rates:
   (i) 35 samples per second
   (ii) 15 samples per second
   (iii) 10 samples per second
(b) Suppose each of the sampled signals of part (a) is passed through a lowpass reconstruction filter with transfer function

$$H(f) = \Pi\left(\frac{f}{32}\right)$$

Find the output in each case. In the cases where there is aliasing, indicate which terms in the output are aliases and which are desired components.

2–27. The signal

$$x(t) = 2 \cos 190\pi + 3 \cos 210\pi t$$

is viewed as a bandpass signal of bandwidth 10 Hz centered around $f_0 = 100$ Hz. Design a quadrature sampler to yield the sample values, $x_{SI}(t)$ and $x_{SR}(t)$, in Figure 2–18. Draw a circuit involving parallel arms with lowpass filters, multiplication by $\sin 2\pi f_0 t$ and $\cos 2\pi f_0 t$, and a summing device to reconstruct $x(t)$. Draw spectra to justify the operation of the quadrature sampler and the reconstruction filter.

2–28. Plot the μ-law compressor characteristic given by (2–169) for $|x(t)| \le 1$ for $\mu = 10, 100, 255,$ and 1000.

2–29. Plot the A-law compressor characteristic given by (2–170) for $A = 10, 75, 100, 200,$ and 1000.

2–30. Verify the numbers in both tables of Example 2–11 and obtain the normalized rms error values for both the noncompanding and the companding cases.

2–31. A random process is defined as in (2–172) but with Θ having the density

$$f_\Theta(\theta) = \begin{cases} \dfrac{2}{\pi}, & 0 \le \theta \le \dfrac{\pi}{2} \\ 0, & \text{otherwise} \end{cases}$$

(a) Find the mean and variance of this random process.
(b) Obtain its autocorrelation function.
(c) Is the process stationary? Cyclostationary?

2–32. Which of the following functions are suitable for autocorrelation functions? If a function is not suitable, tell why it isn't ($A > 0$).
(a) $A \exp(-\alpha|\tau|)$, $\alpha > 0$
(b) $A \sin \omega_0 \tau$
(c) $A \exp(-\beta|\tau|)u(\tau)$, $\beta > 0$
(d) $A \Pi(\tau/\tau_0)$
(e) $A \operatorname{sinc}(2W\tau)$

(f) $A \exp[-(\tau/2\,\tau_0)^2]$

(g) $A\,\tau^2 \exp(-\alpha|\tau|)$

2-33. Show that the time average mean and variance of the process defined by (2–172) with Θ uniform in $[0, 2\pi)$ are equal to the statistical average mean and variance.

2-34. Derive the expression for the variance of the output of the system shown in Figure 2–22 assuming that the input is a stationary Gaussian random process.

2-35. Obtain the autocorrelation functions and power spectral densities of the outputs of the following systems having the input autocorrelation functions or power spectral densities as the case may be.

(a) $\begin{cases} H(f) = \Pi\,(f/2B) \\ R_X(\tau) = \dfrac{N_0}{2}\,\delta(\tau) \end{cases}$

B and N_0 are positive constants.

(b) $\begin{cases} h(t) = A \exp(-\alpha t)u(t) \\ S_X(f) = \dfrac{B}{1 + (2\pi\beta f)^2} \end{cases}$

A, B, β, and α are positive constants.

2-36. (a) Derive the general result for the ratio of equivalent noise to 3 dB bandwidths of an nth-order Butterworth filter given in Table 2–8.

(b) Numerically verify the results given for Butterworth filters of order 1 through 6.

2-37. The two statistically independent inputs to a multiplier have autocorrelation functions

$$R_X(\tau) = A \cos \omega_0 \tau$$

$$R_Y(\tau) = B \operatorname{sinc}(2W\tau)$$

Obtain and plot the power spectrum of the multiplier output.

2-38. Suppose that the inputs to a multiplier are independent random processes with power spectral densities $S_X(f) = 5\Pi(f/10)$ and $S_Y(f) = 2\Pi(f/6)$. Compute and sketch the power spectral density of the output of the multiplier.

2-39. The input to a lowpass filter with impulse response

$$h(t) = \exp(-10t)u(t)$$

is white, Gaussian noise with single-sided power spectral density 1 W/Hz. Obtain the following:

(a) The mean of the output.

(b) The autocovariance function of the output.

(c) The pdf of the output at a single time instant, t_1.

(d) The joint pdf of the output at time instants t_1 and $t_1 + 0.1$ s.

2-40. Referring to Example 2–15, obtain the pdf of $Z(t)$ at an arbitrary time t if $N_1 = N_2 = N_0$ and $f_1 = f_2 = f_0$. Assume that both inputs are stationary Gaussian processes with zero means.

2–41. **(a)** Find the transformation $V = g(U)$ from a uniform random variable U in $[0, 1]$ to give an exponentially distributed random variable with pdf

$$f_V(v) = \begin{cases} \alpha \exp(-\alpha v), & v \geq 0 \\ 0, & \text{otherwise} \end{cases}$$

where α is a positive constant.

(b) Verify this result by performing a Monte Carlo simulation in MATLAB.

2–42. **(a)** Write a MATLAB program to generate jointly Gaussian random variables with zero mean and unity variance in accordance with (2–226). Verify to your satisfaction that they are closely Gaussian by generating a long sequence and plotting their histograms, using the function hist( ) in MATLAB. Compare the generation time for this Gaussian generator with that furnished in MATLAB, randn( ), by using the timing feature of MATLAB.

(b) Check the independence (uncorrelatedness) of the two sets of random variables, $\{X_1\}$ and $\{X_2\}$, by computing the sample correlation coefficient defined as

$$\rho = \frac{1}{N-1} \frac{\sum\limits_{i=1}^{N}(X_{1i} - \hat{m}_1)(X_{2i} - \hat{m}_2)}{\hat{\sigma}_1 \hat{\sigma}_2}$$

where N is the total number of random variables generated, and $\hat{m}_j$ and $\hat{\sigma}_j$ are the sample mean and variance, respectively, of random variable set $\{X_j\}$, $j = 1, 2$. They are defined by the equations

$$\hat{m}_j = \frac{1}{N} \sum_{i=1}^{N} X_{ji}$$

and

$$\hat{\sigma}_j^2 = \frac{1}{N-1} \sum_{i=1}^{N} (X_{ji} - \hat{m}_j)^2, \quad j = 1,2$$

(ideally $\hat{m}_i$ should be zero in this case).

3

Basic Digital
Communication Systems

3.1 INTRODUCTION

The simplest type of digital communication problem is considered in this chapter, namely, binary digital communication systems operating in additive white Gaussian noise (AWGN) backgrounds. By binary, we mean that only one of two possible signals may be transmitted during each signaling interval of T_b seconds in duration. Digital communication systems where more than two possible signals may be transmitted during each signaling interval are considered in Chapter 4.

We also assume for simplicity in this chapter that the signal shapes are completely known at the receiver and that their starting and ending times are known exactly. Variations from this perfect state of affairs will be analyzed in Chapters 4 and 5.

The reasons for considering the simplest case in this chapter is to become familiar with analysis techniques for digital communications systems and to consider some simple examples.

3.2 THE BINARY DIGITAL COMMUNICATIONS PROBLEM

3.2.1 Binary Signal Detection in AWGN

The general binary detection problem to be considered in this section is illustrated in Figure 3–1. During a given signaling interval of T_b seconds duration, one of two possible signals, denoted by $s_1(t)$ and $s_2(t)$, is present together with additive noise, $n(t)$. The energies of $s_1(t)$ and $s_2(t)$ in a T_b-second interval, which are assumed to be finite, are denoted as E_1 and E_2, respectively. The noise is assumed to be Gaussian and white with double-sided power spectral density $N_0/2$. A decision as to which signal is present is to be made each T_b-second interval based only on the information received during that interval.

The receiver consists of a linear, time-invariant filter followed by a sampler and threshold comparator. The initial conditions of the filter are set to 0 just prior to the arrival of each new signal. If the sample taken at the end of a particular T_b-second interval is greater than the threshold, V_T, the decision is made that $s_2(t)$ was present; if the sample

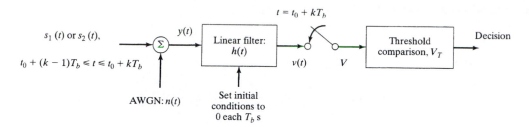

FIGURE 3–1   Receiver structure for detecting binary signals in white Gaussian noise.

value is less than V_T, the decision that $s_1(t)$ was present is made.[1] Without loss of generality, consider the first signaling interval and let t_0 account for any delays in the system.[2] Denoting the sample value taken at time $t = t_0 + T_b$ by V, the decision strategy just described is expressed mathematically as

$$\text{If } V > V_T, \text{ decide that } s_2(t) \text{ was sent}$$
$$\text{If } V < V_T, \text{ decide that } s_1(t) \text{ was sent} \tag{3–1}$$

Because the filter is linear and time invariant, its output at time T_b can be expressed in terms of its impulse response, $h(t)$, as

$$V = v(t_0 + T_b) = \int_{t_0}^{t_0 + T_b} y(\lambda) \, h(t_0 + T_b - \lambda) d\lambda \tag{3–2}$$

where $y(t) = s_1(t) + n(t)$ if $s_1(t)$ is present and $y(t) = s_2(t) + n(t)$ if $s_2(t)$ is present. The question now is: How should $h(t)$ and V_T be chosen to optimize receiver performance? Before answering this question, the criterion to be used to decide on optimality of performance must be chosen. The usual criterion employed is minimum average probability, P_E, of making a decision error. To carry out the optimization, the probability of error is expressed in terms of $h(t)$ and V_T, which are then chosen so that P_E is minimized for given $s_1(t)$, $s_2(t)$, and N_0.

Given $s_1(t)$ is present at the filter input, its output at $t = t_o + T_b$ is

$$V = S_1 + N, \ s_1(t) \text{ present} \tag{3–3}$$

where S_1 is the output signal component at time $t = t_o + T_b$ for the input $s_1(t)$, and N is the output-noise component. Similarly, given $s_2(t)$ is present at the input, the output can be expressed as

$$V = S_2 + N, \ s_2(t) \text{ present} \tag{3–4}$$

[1]The optimality of this procedure is discussed in Chapter 4.

[2]The determination of t_0 is called symbol synchronization and is no small matter. Synchronization methods are discussed in Chapter 5.

where the notation is similar to that used for (3–3).

Both signal and noise components may be expressed in terms of superposition integrals. For the present, however, use is made of the fact that N is a Gaussian random variable (the superposition integral is a linear transformation) and only its mean and variance are required in order to determine its probability density function (pdf). Since $n(t)$ has zero mean (implied by its constant power spectrum), so does N. Its variance is, therefore, the same as its mean-square value, which may be expressed by (2–200) as

$$\sigma_N^2 = \int_{-\infty}^{\infty} |H(f)|^2 \frac{N_0}{2} \, df = N_0 \int_0^{\infty} |H(f)|^2 \, df \qquad (3\text{–}5)$$

where $H(f)$ is the frequency response function of the filter. Since (3–3) and (3–4) are linear transformations of Gaussian random variables, they are also Gaussian but with nonzero means. Given that $s_1(t)$ is present at the receiver input, the probability density function of V is

$$f_V(v|S_1) = \frac{\exp[-(v - S_1)^2/2\sigma_N^2]}{\sqrt{2\pi\sigma_N^2}} \qquad (3\text{–}6)$$

which is a Gaussian pdf with mean S_1 and variance σ_N^2. Similarly, the conditional pdf of V given that $s_2(t)$ is present at the receiver input is

$$f_V(v|S_2) = \frac{\exp[-(v - S_2)^2/2\sigma_N^2]}{\sqrt{2\pi\sigma_N^2}} \qquad (3\text{–}7)$$

Recall that S_1 and S_2 are the filter outputs at time $t = t_0 + T_b$ with $s_1(t)$ and $s_2(t)$ present, respectively, at its input. These two conditional density functions are sketched in Figure 3–2 assuming that $S_1 < V_T < S_2$. Note that there is no loss in generality in this assumption. If $S_2 < S_1$, the roles of $s_1(t)$ and $s_2(t)$ are simply reversed.

Figure 3–2 shows the two ways that an error can be made: in particular, if $s_1(t)$ was sent and $V > V_T$ or if $s_2(t)$ was sent and $V < V_T$. The corresponding probabilities of error are shown as the crosshatched areas in Figure 3–2. From Figure 3–2 it follows that the probability of error given $s_1(t)$ present is

$$P(\varepsilon|S_1) = \int_{V_T}^{\infty} f_V(v|S_1)\,dv \qquad (3\text{–}8)$$

and if $s_2(t)$ is present it is

$$P(\varepsilon|S_2) = \int_{-\infty}^{V_T} f_V(v|S_2)\,dv \qquad (3\text{–}9)$$

If the a priori probability that $s_1(t)$ was sent is p, and the a priori probability that $s_2(t)$ was sent is $q = 1 - p$, the average probability of error is

$$P_E = pP(\varepsilon|S_1) + qP(\varepsilon|S_2) \qquad (3\text{–}10)$$

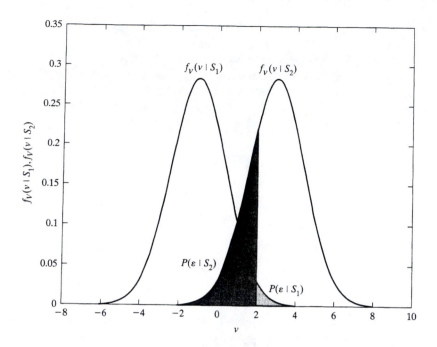

FIGURE 3–2 Conditional probability density functions of the filter output at time $t = t_o + T_b$ ($\sigma_N^2 = 2$, $S_1 = -1$, $S_2 = 3$, and $V_T = 2$. Note that $V_T \neq V_{T,\text{opt}}$ in this case).

If (3–8) and (3–9) are substituted into (3–10), the result differentiated with respect to V_T, and the derivative set equal to 0, the optimum choice for the threshold in terms of minimizing P_E is

$$V_{T,\text{opt}} = \frac{\sigma_N^2}{S_2 - S_1} \ln\left(\frac{p}{q}\right) + \frac{S_1 + S_2}{2} \tag{3–11}$$

or, if $p = q$,

$$V_{T,\text{opt}} = \frac{S_1 + S_2}{2} \tag{3–12}$$

If $p = q$ and $V_T = V_{T,\text{opt}}$, the average probability of error may be expressed as

$$P_E = \frac{1}{2} \text{erfc}\left(\frac{S_2 - S_1}{2\sqrt{2}\sigma_N}\right) = Q\left(\frac{S_2 - S_1}{2\sigma_N}\right) \tag{3–13}$$

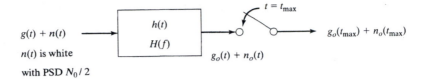

FIGURE 3–3   Block diagram of the system pertinent to the matched filter derivation.

where erfc(u) = 1 − erf(u) is the complementary error function and $Q(u)$ is the Gaussian integral, sometimes referred to as the Q-function.[3]

3.2.2   The Matched Filter

In order to find the filter that gives the minimum probability of error, as expressed by (3–13), what may appear to be an unrelated detour will be taken. Consider the situation depicted in Figure 3–3. A linear, time-invariant filter with a known signal $g(t)$ plus white noise at its input is followed by a sampler that samples the filter output at time $t = t_{max}$, at which time the peak signal-to-rms noise ratio at the filter output is desired to be a maximum. At time t_{max}, the sample value consists of a signal-related component, $g_o(t_{max})$, and a noise component, $n_o(t_{max})$. Let the variance of this noise component be σ^2. The frequency response function, $H_o(f)$, for the filter that provides the maximum (peak) signal-(squared)-to-(mean-squared)-noise ratio at its output at time t_{max} is desired, where the signal-to-noise ratio is defined as

$$\zeta^2 = \frac{g_o^2(t_{max})}{\sigma^2} \tag{3–14}$$

To proceed, $g_o(t_{max})$ and σ^2 are expressed in terms of $H(f)$, where $H(f)$ is the frequency response function of the filter. If the double-sided power spectral density of the input noise is $N_0/2$, σ^2 may be expressed as

$$\sigma^2 = \frac{N_0}{2} \int_{-\infty}^{\infty} |H(f)|^2 \, df \tag{3–15}$$

which is the same as (3–5). Using the inverse Fourier transform, the signal component at the filter's output is

[3]See Appendix E for rational approximations and tables for $Q(x)$. Recall that
$$Q(x) = \int_x^\infty \frac{1}{\sqrt{2\pi}} \exp(-u^2/2)\,du = \frac{1}{2} \text{erfc}(x/\sqrt{2}).$$ A finite-integral representation is [1]
$$Q(x) = \frac{1}{\pi} \int_0^{\pi/2} \exp\left(-\frac{x^2}{2\sin^2\phi}\right)d\phi.$$ For large arguments, $Q(x) \cong \frac{\exp(-x^2/2)}{(x\sqrt{2\pi})}, x \gg 1.$

$$g_o(t) = \int_{-\infty}^{\infty} G(f)H(f)\exp(j2\pi ft)\,df \tag{3-16}$$

where $G(f)$ is the Fourier transform of the input. Setting $t = t_{max}$ and taking the ratio of (3–16) squared to (3–15), an expression for ζ^2, the signal-to-noise ratio to be maximized, is obtained in terms of $H(f)$:

$$\zeta^2 = \frac{\left| \int_{-\infty}^{\infty} G(f)\,H(f)\exp(j2\pi ft_{max})\,df \right|^2}{\dfrac{N_0}{2}\int_{-\infty}^{\infty} |H(f)|^2\,df} \tag{3-17}$$

It will be verified shortly that the maximum value for (3–17) is achieved if, and only if,

$$H(f) = H_o(f) = kG^*(f)\exp(-j2\pi ft_{max}) \tag{3-18}$$

where k is an arbitrary constant. For this $H_o(f)$, it can be verified by direct substitution into (3–17) that the maximum value for ζ^2 is

$$\zeta^2_{max} = \frac{2E_g}{N_0} \tag{3-19}$$

where

$$E_g = \int_{-\infty}^{\infty} |G(f)|^2\,df = \int_{-\infty}^{\infty} |g(t)|^2\,dt \tag{3-20}$$

is the total energy contained in $g(t)$.

To show that $H_o(f)$ given by (3–18) does indeed provide the maximum value for ζ^2 given by (3–19), Schwarz's inequality will be applied. Schwarz's inequality is a generalization of the inequality involving the dot product of two vectors **A** and **B**, which is

$$|\mathbf{A}\cdot\mathbf{B}| = |\mathbf{A}||\mathbf{B}||\cos\theta| \le |\mathbf{A}||\mathbf{B}| \tag{3-21}$$

where θ is the angle between them and $|\mathbf{A}|$ denotes the magnitude of **A**, and so on. That (3–21) holds is obvious, since $|\cos\theta| \le 1$. Furthermore, since $|\cos\theta| = 1$ if, and only if, $\theta = n\pi$, where n is an integer, it follows that equality holds in (3–21) if, and only if, $\mathbf{A} = k\mathbf{B}$, where k is a constant (i.e., if **A** and **B** are collinear).

The generalization of (3–21), which is one form of Schwarz's inequality, occurs if **A** is replaced by $X(f)$, **B** is replaced by $Y(f)$, and the dot product is replaced by $\int_{-\infty}^{\infty} X(f)Y^*(f)\,df$, where the asterisk denotes a complex conjugate [both $X(f)$ and $Y(f)$ may be complex functions]. Then the inequality analogous to the square of (3–21) is (an equivalent maximization since the magnitude of the inner product is being maximized)

$$\left| \int_{-\infty}^{\infty} X(f)Y^*(f)\,df \right|^2 \le \int_{-\infty}^{\infty} |X(f)|^2\,df \int_{-\infty}^{\infty} |Y(f)|^2\,df \tag{3-22}$$

with equality if, and only if, $X(f) = kY(f)$, where k is a constant.[4]

To maximize (3–17), let $G(f) = X(f)$, $H(f) \exp(j2\pi f\, t_{max}) = Y^*(f)$, and replace the numerator of (3–17) by the right-hand side of (3–22) to obtain the inequality

$$\zeta^2 \le \frac{\displaystyle\int_{-\infty}^{\infty} |G(f)|^2\, df \int_{-\infty}^{\infty} |H(f)|^2\, df}{\dfrac{N_0}{2} \displaystyle\int_{-\infty}^{\infty} |H(f)|^2\, df} = \frac{2}{N_0} \int_{-\infty}^{\infty} |G(f)|^2\, df = \frac{2E_g}{N_0} \qquad (3\text{–}23)$$

Equality holds if, and only if, $X(f) = kY(f)$ or, in other words, if (3–18) holds. Thus, (3–23) shows that the maximum for ζ^2 is indeed given by (3–19) and that this maximum is achieved if, and only if, (3–18) holds.

The frequency response function of the optimum filter is given by (3–18), where k can be set equal to 1 since it is arbitrary. The impulse response of the optimum filter is the inverse Fourier transform of $H_o(f)$, which is

$$h_0(t) = \mathscr{F}^{-1}[H_o(f)]$$

$$= \int_{-\infty}^{\infty} G^*(f) \exp\left[j2\pi(t - t_{max})f\right] df \qquad (3\text{–}24)$$

$$= \left[\int_{-\infty}^{\infty} G(f) \exp\left[j2\pi(t_{max} - t)f\right] df\right]^*$$

$$= g^*(t_{max} - t)$$

In other words, the impulse response of the optimum filter for a real signal is the time reverse of the input signal. For this reason, the filter is said to be *matched* to the input signal and it is referred to as a *matched filter*. A matched filter, according to (3–23), *maximizes the filter output signal squared at time t_{max} divided by the output noise variance.* This maximum value for the signal-to-noise ratio, according to (3–19), is *twice the energy of the input signal divided by the single-sided input-noise spectral density,* regardless of the input signal shape.

The output signal component from a matched filter can be found by applying the superposition integral. Using (3–24), the output is found to be

$$g_o(t) = \int_{-\infty}^{\infty} g(\lambda)\, h_o(t - \lambda)\, d\lambda$$

$$= \int_{-\infty}^{\infty} g(\lambda)\, g^*(t_{max} - t + \lambda)\, d\lambda \qquad (3\text{–}25)$$

This is essentially the autocorrelation function of the input signal. If $t = t_{max}$, (3–25) becomes

---

[4]Schwarz's inequality is proved in Chapter 4.

$$g_o(t_{max}) = \int_{-\infty}^{\infty} |g(\lambda)|^2 \, d\lambda = E_g \qquad (3\text{--}26)$$

which is the energy of the input signal expressed in the time domain. In other words, *the peak output signal from a matched filter,* which occurs at time t_{max}, is a voltage whose value equals *the energy contained in the input signal.*

EXAMPLE 3–1

Consider the signal $g(t) = \Pi\,[(t-1)/2]$, which is sketched in Figure 3–4a. Sketched in Figure 3–4b is the impulse response of the filter matched to this signal. The output signal is the triangular pulse with maximum value at $t = t_{max}$ sketched in Figure 3–4c. This maximum value is

$$g_o(t_{max}) = 2 \text{ (volts)}^2\text{-seconds} \qquad (3\text{--}27)$$

which is the energy in the input signal. If the input noise is white with double-sided power spectral density $N_0/2 = 1$ V^2/Hz, (3–27) is also the ratio of peak output signal squared to mean-square noise. Note that if $t_{max} < 2$ s, the filter is noncausal because its output begins before the input signal arrives.

3.2.3 Application of the Matched Filter to Binary Data Detection

3.2.3.1 General Formula for P_E.

Since the Q-function is a monotonically decreasing function of its argument, the expression for P_E for binary signaling given by (3–13) will be minimized through the choice of $H(f)$ in Figure 3–1 by maximizing $(S_2 - S_1)/2\sigma_N$ or equivalently by maximizing the square of this quantity. Letting $g_o(t) = S_2(t) - S_1(t)$ and $t_{max} = T_b$ (from now on we assume that $t_0 = 0$ for convenience) in (3–14), where $S_1(t)$ and $S_2(t)$ are the filter's response to the inputs $s_1(t)$ and $s_2(t)$, respectively, it is seen that the problem of minimizing P_E through choosing $H(f)$, which has just been pointed out is equivalent to maximizing its argument, is identical to the matched filter problem.[5] In particular, if $H(f)$ in Figure 3–1 is chosen to be

$$H_o(f) = [\mathscr{S}_2^*(f) - \mathscr{S}_1^*(f)]\exp(-j2\pi f T_b) \qquad (3\text{--}28)$$

where $\mathscr{S}_1(f)$ and $\mathscr{S}_2(f)$ are the Fourier transforms of $s_1(t)$ and $s_2(t)$ shown in Figure 3–1, the probability of error will be minimized. The impulse response of the optimum filter is

$$h_0(t) = s_2(T_b - t) - s_1(T_b - t) \qquad (3\text{--}29)$$

and the corresponding signal-to-noise ratio at the matched filter output, according to (3–19), is

$$\zeta_{max}^2 = \frac{2}{N_0} \int_0^{T_b} [s_2(t) - s_1(t)]^2 \, dt \qquad (3\text{--}30)$$

---

[5]Note that it is not being said that $s_2(t) - s_1(t)$ is the input to the receiver; this is merely an artifice to apply the matched filter results to the binary signaling problem directly.

(a) Input signal

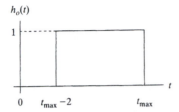

(b) Matched filter impulse response

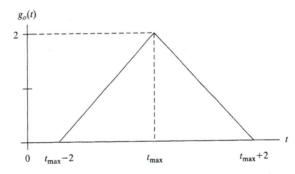

(c) Output signal and output signal-to-noise ratio for $N_0/2 = 1$ (volt)^2 /Hz

FIGURE 3–4   Illustration of a matched filter for rectangular input signal.

where the fact that the signals are zero outside the range $(0, T_b)$ has been used. If the square root of (3–30) is substituted into (3–13) for $(S_2 - S_1)/2\sigma_N$, the probability of error corresponding to the optimum receiver filter becomes

$$P_E = \frac{1}{2} \, \text{erfc} \left(\sqrt{z} \right) = Q(\sqrt{2z}) \tag{3–31}$$

where

$$z = \frac{1}{4N_0} \int_0^{T_b} [s_2(t) - s_1(t)]^2 \, dt \tag{3–32}$$

$$= \frac{1}{4N_0} \left[\int_0^{T_b} s_2^2(t)dt - 2 \int_0^{T_b} s_1(t)\, s_2(t)\, dt + \int_0^{T_b} s_1^2(t)\, dt \right]$$

$$= \frac{1}{4N_0} \left[E_1 + E_2 - 2 \int_0^{T_b} s_1(t)\, s_2(t)\, dt \right]$$

Note that P_E depends on the dissimilarity of $s_1(t)$ and $s_2(t)$ through their correlation in addition to their individual energies, denoted as E_1 and E_2. Several examples will make this clear.

3.2.3.2 Antipodal Baseband Signaling.

Suppose that $s_1(t) = -A$ and $s_2(t) = A$ for $0 \le t \le T_b$. Then $s_2(t) - s_1(t) = 2A$ and (3–32) becomes

$$z = \frac{1}{4N_0} \int_0^{T_b} (2A)^2\, dt$$

$$= \frac{A^2 T_b}{N_0} = \frac{E_b}{N_0}$$

(3–33)

where E_b is the energy in either $s_1(t)$ or $s_2(t)$, which is often referred to as the *bit energy*. Consequently, $P_E = P_b$ for this case, where we now use P_b to denote bit error probability, (3–31) becomes

$$P_b = \frac{1}{2} \operatorname{erfc}\left(\sqrt{\frac{E_b}{N_0}} \right) = Q\left(\sqrt{\frac{2E_b}{N_0}} \right)$$

(3–34)

A handy approximation to (3–34) for large values of E_b/N_0 is obtained by using the asymptotic expression

$$Q(u) \cong \frac{\exp(-u^2/2)}{\sqrt{2\pi u}}, u \gg 1$$

which is within 10% of the true value of $Q(u)$ for $u \ge 3$.

3.2.3.3 Baseband Orthogonal Signaling.

Consider next the case where the two possible baseband signals are

$$s_1(t) = \begin{cases} A, 0 \le t \le T_b/2 \\ 0, \text{ otherwise} \end{cases}$$

and

$$s_2(t) = \begin{cases} A & T_b/2 \le t \le T_b \\ 0, & \text{otherwise} \end{cases}$$

Noting that $[s_2(t) - s_1(t)]^2 = A^2$, $0 \le t \le T_b$, the expression for z given by (3–32) becomes

$$z = \frac{1}{4N_0} \int_0^{T_b} A^2 \, dt = \frac{A^2 T_b}{4N_0} = \frac{E_b}{2N_0} \tag{3–35}$$

where the "bit energy" is now $A^2 T_b / 2$ because each symbol is nonzero for half the bit period. Thus P_b for orthogonal baseband signaling is given by

$$P_b = \frac{1}{2} \operatorname{erfc}\left(\sqrt{\frac{E_b}{2N_0}}\right) = Q\left(\sqrt{\frac{E_b}{N_0}}\right) \tag{3–36}$$

Because of the difference by a factor of two in the arguments of the Q-functions between (3–34) and (3–36), it follows that the orthogonal baseband signaling case requires twice the signal-to-noise ratio, E_b/N_0, of antipodal baseband signaling to give the same bit error probability. In Chapter 4, it will be seen that this is a consequence of the "distance" between signals in the orthogonal case being less than that for the antipodal case.

3.2.3.4 Baseband On-Off Signaling.   Now suppose the two possible transmitted signals are $s_2(t) = A$ and $s_1(t) = 0$ for $0 \le t \le T_b$. Using these in (3–32) we get

$$z = \frac{1}{4N_0} \int_0^{T_b} A^2 \, dt = \frac{A^2 T_b}{4N_0} \tag{3–37}$$

It is important to note that a signal is being transmitted only half the time, on the average, assuming that $s_1(t)$ and $s_2(t)$ are equally likely. Thus the *average* bit energy is

$$E_b = \frac{1}{2} A^2 T_b + \frac{1}{2} (0) = \frac{A^2 T_b}{2} \tag{3–38}$$

Using this in (3–37) and then substituting into (3–31), we obtain the same result for the bit error probability as given by (3–36).

Consequently, baseband on-off signaling requires twice as much average signal energy as antipodal baseband signaling to produce the same P_b, which is the same result as for orthogonal baseband signaling. Results for P_b plotted versus E_b/N_0 are shown in Figure 3–5 for the three signaling schemes.

EXAMPLE 3–2

Find E_b/N_0 in decibels to give a P_b of (a) 10^{-4}, (b) 10^{-5}, (c) 10^{-6} for (i) baseband antipodal and (ii) orthogonal and on-off signaling.

Solution: Using (3–34) and (3–36) and iterative solution on a calculator or a computer mathematics package such as MATLAB[6] gives the results shown in the table below. Note that the difference between the values given in columns 2 and 3 is 3.01 dB or a factor of 2.

---

[6]MATLAB has a built-in subprogram called erfc(u), but no subprogram for $Q(u)$.

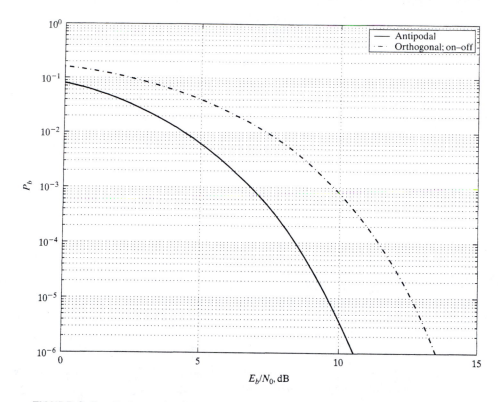

FIGURE 3–5 P_b for antipodal, orthogonal, and on-off baseband signaling versus E_b/N_0.

P_b	E_b/N_0 for antipodal, dB	E_b/N_0 for othogonal and on-off, dB
10^{-4}	8.43	11.44
10^{-5}	9.61	12.62
10^{-6}	10.54	13.55

EXAMPLE 3–3

Assume that antipodal, orthogonal, and on-off signaling are to be compared for communication through a channel that adds noise with single-sided power spectral density $N_0 = 10^{-11}$ watts/Hz. Find the amplitude, A, of the received signal that gives $P_b = 10^{-6}$ for the following data rates:

(a)   1 kilobit per second (kbps), (b) 10 kbps, (c) 100 kbps, (d) 1 Mbps.

Solution: From Example 3–2, we have $E_b/N_0 = 10.54$ dB $= 11.32$ to give $P_b = 10^{-6}$ for antipodal baseband and twice this, or 22.64, for orthogonal and on-off baseband. From (3–33), we have

$$\frac{A^2 T_b}{N_0} = \left(\frac{E_b}{N_0}\right)_{req'd} = 11.32$$

or, for antipodal baseband,

$$A = \sqrt{N_0 \left(\frac{E_b}{N_0}\right)_{req'd} R_b} = \sqrt{(10^{-11})(11.32)R_b}$$

where $R_b = 1/T_b$ is the data rate in bits per second. For $R_b = 1$ kbps $= 1000$ bps, we obtain $A = 3.3645 \times 10^{-4}$ volts. For $R_b = 10$ kbps, the result is $\sqrt{10}$ times this, and so on, which gives the results in the table below:

R_b, kbps	A, mV for antipodal	A, mV for orthogonal
1	0.336	0.476
10	1.064	1.505
100	3.365	4.758
1000	10.640	15.047

For orthogonal and on-off signaling, all results are $\sqrt{2}$ times those for antipodal signaling.

EXAMPLE 3–4

Find main lobe bandwidths for baseband antipodal, orthogonal, and on-off signaling for a data rate of R_b bits per second.

Solution: A single bit for antipodal and on-off signaling has a voltage spectrum given by

$$\Pi\left(\frac{t}{T_b}\right) \leftrightarrow T_b \operatorname{sinc}(fT_b)$$

where sinc $u = (\sin \pi u)/(\pi u)$, which has its main lobe contained between $-1 \le u \le 1$. For orthogonal signaling, the pulses are half this width and the voltage spectrum is twice as wide. Thus, we get the following single-sided bandwidths (note that the bandwidth is really infinite in all cases but, for all practical purposes, can be limited to the results here):

Antipodal and on-off: $B = R_b$ hertz

Orthogonal: $B = 2R_b$ hertz

EXAMPLE 3–5

Digital data is to be transmitted through a channel with $N_0 = 10^{-8}$ W/Hz. The channel bandwidth is 1 MHz. Consider baseband antipodal, orthogonal, and on-off signaling. (a) What is the maximum data rate that can be supported by the channel for each scheme? (b) Find the received signal power required to give $P_b = 10^{-6}$ at the data rates found in part (a).

Solution: (a) From Example 3–4, baseband antipodal and on-off signaling both require a bandwidth of $B = R_b$ Hz, so that $R_b = 1$ Mbps. For baseband orthogonal, $B = 2R_b$ so that 500 kbps can be supported.

(b) To give $P_b = 10^{-6}$, we require $E_b/N_0 = 10.54$ dB $= 11.32$ for baseband antipodal while, for orthogonal and on-off signaling, $E_b/N_0 = 13.55$ dB $= 22.65$. For baseband antipodal signaling $E_b/N_0 = A^2 T_b/N_0 = A^2/N_0 R_b$ or $P = A^2 = N_0 R_b (E_b/N_0)_{req'd}$ so that $P = (10^{-8})(10^6)(11.32) = 0.1132$ watts. For baseband on-off signaling, $P = (10^{-8})(10^6)(22.65) = 0.2265$ watts . Finally, for orthogonal signaling, $P = (10^{-8})(500,000)(22.65) = 0.1132$ watts.

3.2.4   Correlator Realization of Matched Filter Receivers

According to (3–29) and the superposition integral, the optimum receiver performs the operations depicted in Figure 3–6a. The output signal from the matched filter is

$$v(t) = y(t) * h_0(t) = \int_0^{T_b} [s_2(T_b - \lambda) - s_1(T_b - \lambda)] y(t - \lambda) d\lambda$$

or

$$v(T_b) = \int_0^{T_b} [s_2(\alpha) - s_1(\alpha)] y(\alpha) d\alpha \qquad (3\text{--}39)$$

where the change of variables $\alpha = T_b - \lambda$ has been made. Consequently, the matched filter receiver structure shown in Figure 3–6a is equivalent to the multiplier integrator structure shown in Figure 3–6b. Such a realization is referred to as a *correlation receiver*.

Various levels of *synchronization* are necessary in a receiver. In this case, only synchronization of the symbol interval is required at the receiver in order to properly line up the bits for the integration in the correlation operation. Even if a matched filter implementation is used, synchronization is still required to sample the output of the matched filter at the optimum time instant. In the next chapter, where we consider carrier modulation systems, a second level of synchronization may be required to properly align the reference

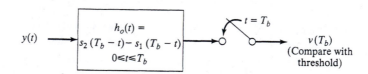

(a) Matched filter implementation

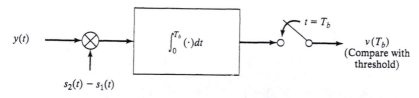

(b) Correlator implementation

FIGURE 3–6   Correlator and matched filter receiver implementations for binary data detection.

carrier at the receiver with the carrier of the incoming signal. For noncoherent modulation systems, this level of synchronization is not required. Yet a third level of synchronization, referred to as *frame synchronization,* is required in many applications where the data are grouped into blocks called *frames.* This is usually accomplished by inserting a frame synchronization code within a data block and detecting the position of this code. All of these will be discussed in Chapter 5.

3.3   SIGNALING THROUGH BANDLIMITED CHANNELS

An assumption implicit in the analysis of the data transmission schemes that we have considered so far is that the bandwidth is unconstrained. Any filtering carried out in the transmitter, channel, or receiver will result in degradation in system performance because symbols will be smeared into each other (called intersymbol interference or ISI) as a result of the filtering. In this section, special signal designs and filter functions that avoid ISI are discussed.

3.3.1   System Model

The communications system to be considered is modeled as shown in Figure 3–7. It consists of a source that emits binary symbols $a_k = +1$ or $a_k = -1$ during the kth signaling interval $(k - 1)T_b \leq t \leq kT_b$. The signal at the source output is represented for all time as

$$x_s(t) = \sum_{k=-\infty}^{\infty} a_k \delta(t - kT_b) \tag{3–40}$$

where $\delta(t)$ is the unit impulse function. The next subsystem is a transmitter filter with lowpass frequency response function $H_T(f)$ or impulse response $h_T(t) = \mathcal{F}^{-1}[H_T(f)]$. The transmitted signal is then given by

$$x_t(t) = \sum_{k=-\infty}^{\infty} a_k \delta(t - kT_b) * h_T(t) = \sum_{k=-\infty}^{\infty} a_k h_T(t - kT_b) \tag{3–41}$$

where the asterisk denotes convolution.

The channel introduces additional filtering, which is imposed by a filter with a frequency response function $H_C(f)$ and an impulse response $h_C(t) = \mathcal{F}^{-1}[H_C(f)]$ and additive Gaussian noise represented by $n(t)$ having power spectral density $G_n(f)$. Thus the channel output, or receiver input, is given by

$$y(t) = x(t) + n(t) \tag{3–42}$$

where

$$x(t) = x_t(t) * h_C(t) \tag{3–43}$$

is the channel filter output.

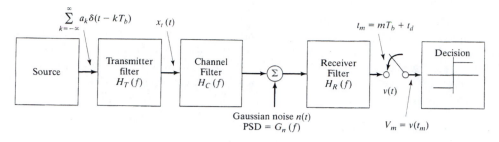

FIGURE 3–7 Idealized model for signaling through a bandlimited channel.

The receiver consists of a filter with frequency response function $H_R(f)$ and impulse response of $h_R(t)$, a sampler, and a threshold comparator. The comparison threshold can be set at 0 because of the symmetry of the data and noise amplitude distributions about 0.

The output of the receiver filter, denoted by $v(t)$, is given by

$$v(t) = y(t)*h_R(t) = \sum_{k=-\infty}^{\infty} Aa_k p_r(t - t_d - kT_b) + n_0(t), A > 0 \qquad (3\text{–}44)$$

where A is a scale factor chosen such that $p_r(0) = 1$, $n_0(t)$ is the noise component at the receiver filter output, and $p_r(t - t_d)$ is the pulse shape at the receiver filter output, which is delayed by an amount t_d relative to the epoch of $h_T(t)$ due to filtering. In terms of filter impulse responses, $n_0(t)$ and $p_r(t - t_d)$ may be written as

$$n_0(t) = n(t)*h_R(t)$$

$$Ap_r(t - t_d) = h_T(t)*h_C(t)*h_R(t) \qquad (3\text{–}45)$$

The maximum of $p_r(t - t_d)$ is assumed to occur at $t = t_d$. Thus samples should be taken at times

$$t_m = mT_b + t_d \qquad (3\text{–}46)$$

in order to sample at the peak of each received pulse. The samples at the output of the receiver filter are written as

$$V_m = v(t_m) = Aa_m p_r(0) + \sum_{\substack{k=-\infty \\ k \neq m}}^{\infty} Aa_k p_r[(m-k)T_b + t_d] + N_m \qquad (3\text{–}47)$$

$$m = 0, \pm1, \pm2, \cdots$$

where

$$N_m = n_0(t_m) = n(t)*h_R(t)\big|_{t=t_m} \qquad (3\text{–}48)$$

are the noise samples at time t_m at the receiver filter output. Because $n(t)$ is Gaussian and the receiver filter is a linear system, the noise samples are Gaussian. Furthermore, it will be assumed that $G_n(f)|H_R(f)|^2$ is sufficiently wideband so that any two separate noise samples, say, N_k and N_m, $k \neq m$, are uncorrelated and therefore independent (if this isn't the case, additional filtering can be done by what is called a "whitening filter" designed so that its output noise samples are uncorrelated).

Equation (3–47) consists of a desired signal term, $Aa_m p_r(0)$, an undesired signal term which is the second term, and the noise term, N_m. The undesired signal term is referred to as *intersymbol interference (ISI)* because it originates from received signal pulses that precede and follow the desired signal pulse. Figure 3–8, which shows a typical sequence of received pulses and their sum, illustrates the effect of the ISI component on detection of the desired symbol. Both the ISI and noise components cause errors in the detection process.

3.3.2   Designing for Zero ISI: Nyquist's Pulse-Shaping Criterion

Since the channel is assumed time invariant, the goal is to choose $H_T(f)$ and $H_R(f)$ to minimize the combined effects of ISI and noise on the decision process. The effects of ISI can be completely negated if it is possible to obtain a received pulse shape, $p_r(t)$, with the property

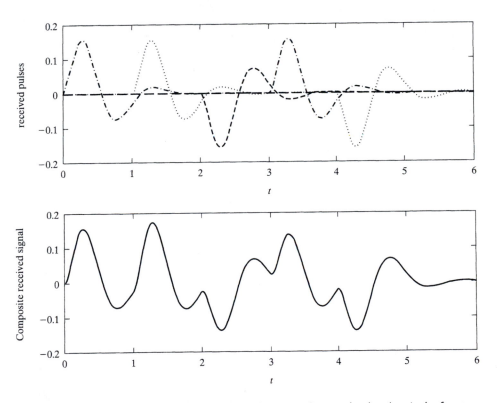

FIGURE 3–8   Typical received pulses and composite received pulse train for a bandlimited digital communication system ($T_b = 1$ s).

$$p_r(nT_b) = \begin{cases} 1, n = 0 \\ 0, n \neq 0 \end{cases}$$

This condition guarantees zero ISI. The following theorem, referred to as *Nyquist's pulse-shaping criterion,* gives a condition on the Fourier transform of $p_r(t)$, which results in a pulse shape having the zero-ISI property stated above.

THEOREM: *If $P_r(f) = \mathcal{F}[p_r(t)]$ satisfies the condition*

$$\sum_{k=-\infty}^{\infty} P_r\left(f + \frac{k}{T_b}\right) = T_b, \quad |f| \leq \frac{1}{2T_b} \tag{3-49}$$

then

$$p_r(nT_b) = \begin{cases} 1, & n = 0 \\ 0, & n \neq 0 \end{cases} \tag{3-50}$$

Proof: Break the inverse Fourier transform integral for $p_r(t)$ up into contiguous intervals of length $1/T_b$ hertz. This results in the summation

$$p_r(nT_b) = \sum_{k=-\infty}^{\infty} \int_{(2k-1)/2T_b}^{(2k+1)/2T_b} P_r(f) \exp(j2\pi fnT_b)\, df \tag{3-51}$$

By the change of variables $u = f - k/T_b$, this becomes

$$
\begin{aligned}
p_r(nT_b) &= \sum_{k=-\infty}^{\infty} \int_{-1/2T_b}^{1/2T_b} P_r\left(u + \frac{k}{T_b}\right) \exp(j2\pi\, nT_b u)\, du \\
&= \int_{-1/2T_b}^{1/2T_b} \left[\sum_{k=-\infty}^{\infty} P_r\left(u + \frac{k}{T_b}\right)\right] \exp(j2\pi\, nT_b u)\, du
\end{aligned}
\tag{3-52}
$$

where the order of integration and summation have been reversed to obtain the last expression. But the term in brackets inside the integral is T_b by the hypothesis of the theorem. Therefore,

$$
\begin{aligned}
p_r(nT_b) &= T_b \int_{-1/2T_b}^{1/2T_b} \exp(j2\pi\, nT_b u)\, du \\
&= \operatorname{sinc}(n) = \begin{cases} 1, n = 0 \\ 0, n \neq 0 \end{cases}
\end{aligned}
\tag{3-53}
$$

This completes the proof of the theorem.

Note that the condition (3–49) does not uniquely specify $P_r(f)$. Two important considerations in selecting $P_r(f)$ are that $p_r(t)$ has a fast rate of decay with a small magnitude near the sample values for $n \neq 0$ and that shaping filters for producing the desired $P_r(f)$ be possible to realize or to closely approximate. A family of spectra that satisfy the Nyquist pulse-shaping criterion is the *raised cosine family,* which is defined by

$$P_{RC}(f) = \begin{cases} T_b, & 0 \leq |f| \leq \dfrac{1-\beta}{2T_b} \\ \dfrac{T_b}{2}\left\{1 + \cos\left[\dfrac{\pi T_b}{\beta}\left(|f| - \dfrac{1-\beta}{2T_b}\right)\right]\right\}, & \dfrac{1-\beta}{2T_b} \leq |f| \leq \dfrac{1+\beta}{2T_b} \\ 0, & |f| > \dfrac{1+\beta}{2T_b} \end{cases} \quad (3\text{--}54)$$

The spectra given by (3–54) are illustrated in Figure 3–9a for several values of the parameter β. Note that the bandwidth of $P_{RC}(f)$ lies between $1/(2T_b)$ and $1/T_b$ hertz depending on the value of β. It should be clear from Figure 3–9a that $P_{RC}(f)$ satisfies the Nyquist pulse-shaping criterion: What is missing from the top half of the raised cosine for $T_b f < 0.5$ is exactly compensated by the excess for $T_b f > 0.5$. The inverse Fourier transform of $P_{RC}(f)$ can be shown to be

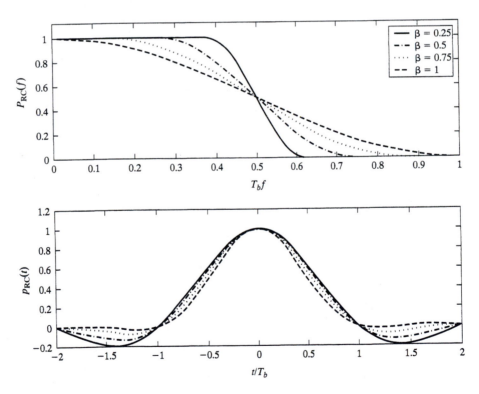

FIGURE 3–9   Raised-cosine spectra (a) and corresponding pulses (b).

$$p_{RC}(t) = \frac{\cos(\pi\beta t/T_b)}{1 - (2\beta t/T_b)^2} \operatorname{sinc}(t/T_b) \tag{3-55}$$

which is graphed in Figure 3–9b for several values of β. Note that larger bandwidths for $P_{RC}(f)$ result in pulse shapes that decay faster, which is to be expected.

3.3.3 Optimum Transmit and Receive Filters

The spectrum of the received pulse, which is the Fourier transform of (3–45), is

$$AP_r(f)\exp(-j2\pi ft_d) = H_T(f)\, H_C(f)\, H_R(f) \tag{3-56}$$

If the zero-ISI condition is required, $P_r(f)$ must satisfy (3–49), which provides a constraint between the frequency response functions of the transmitter and receiver filters for a fixed channel frequency response function, $H_C(f)$. An additional requirement, which places a constraint on $H_T(f)$ and $H_R(f)$, is that they be chosen so that the probability of making a decision error at the receiver is minimized. If the zero-ISI constraint is satisfied, (3–47) reduces to

$$V_m = Aa_m + N_m \tag{3-57}$$

If $a_m = +1$ and $a_m = -1$ occur with equal probability, it follows that the probability of error is

$$P_b = P(V_m > 0 \mid a_m = -1) = P(N_m > A) \tag{3-58}$$

Since $n(t)$ is Gaussian with zero mean and power spectral density $G_n(f)$, it follows that

$$E(N_m) = 0$$

$$\operatorname{var}(N_m) \equiv \sigma^2 = \int_{-\infty}^{\infty} G_n(f)|H_R(f)|^2\, df \tag{3-59}$$

Therefore, (3–58) may be written as

$$P_b = \int_A^{\infty} \frac{\exp(-u^2/2\sigma^2)}{\sqrt{2\pi\sigma^2}} = Q\left(\frac{A}{\sigma}\right) \tag{3-60}$$

Because the Q-function is a monotonically decreasing function of its argument, the probability of error is minimized if its argument is maximized. Equivalently, σ^2/A^2 can be minimized. Before doing so, however, A^2 will be expressed in terms of the transmitted energy per symbol, E_T. Since the kth transmitted pulse is $a_k h(t - kT_b)$, its energy is

$$E_T = E[a_k^2]\int_{-\infty}^{\infty} h_T^2(t - kT_b)\, dt = \int_{-\infty}^{\infty} |H_T(f)|^2\, df \tag{3-61}$$

which results from using Parseval's theorem and the fact that $E[a_k^2] = 1$. From (3–56), it follows that this energy can be written as

$$E_T = A^2 \int_{-\infty}^{\infty} \frac{|P_r(f)|^2}{|H_C(f)|^2|H_R(f)|^2} \, df \tag{3-62}$$

Solving for A^2 and using (3–59), σ^2/A^2 becomes

$$\frac{\sigma^2}{A^2} = \frac{1}{E_T} \int_{-\infty}^{\infty} G_n(f)|H_R(f)|^2 \, df \int_{-\infty}^{\infty} \frac{|P_r(f)|^2}{|H_C(f)|^2 \, |H_R(f)|^2} \, df \tag{3-63}$$

which is to be minimized through appropriate choice of $H_R(f)$. This minimization can be accomplished through application of Schwarz's inequality, given by (3–22), with

$$|X(f)| = G_n^{1/2}(f)|H_R(f)| \tag{3-64}$$

and

$$|Y(f)| = \frac{|P_r(f)|}{|H_C(f)| \, |H_R(f)|}$$

Schwarz's inequality then assumes the form

$$\int_{-\infty}^{\infty} G_n(f)|H_R(f)|^2 \, df \int_{-\infty}^{\infty} \frac{|P_r(f)|^2}{|H_C(f)|^2 \, |H_R(f)|^2} \, df \geq \left[\int_{-\infty}^{\infty} \frac{G_n^{1/2}(f)|P_r(f)|}{|H_C(f)|} \, df \right]^2 \tag{3-65}$$

with equality if, and only if, $|X(f)| = \alpha^2|Y(f)|$ or if

$$|H_R(f)| = \frac{\alpha|P_r(f)|^{1/2}}{G_n^{1/4}(f)|H_C(f)|^{1/2}} \tag{3-66}$$

where α is an arbitrary constant. That is, the minimum given by the right-hand side of (3–65) is achieved if the magnitude of the receiver frequency response function is given by (3–66). From (3–56) it follows that the optimum transmitter frequency response function magnitude is

$$|H_T(f)| = \frac{(A/\alpha)|P_r(f)|^{1/2} \, G_n^{1/4}(f)}{|H_C(f)|^{1/2}} \tag{3-67}$$

Note that any appropriate phase response function can be used with $|H_R(f)|$ and $|H_T(f)|$.

Using the minimum value for σ/A (maximum value for A/σ) in (3–60), the probability of error minimized through appropriate choice of $H_T(f)$ and $H_R(f)$ is

$$P_{b,\min} = Q\left\{ \sqrt{E_T} \left[\int_{-\infty}^{\infty} \frac{G_n^{1/2}(f)|P_r(f)|}{|H_C(f)|} \, df \right]^{-1} \right\} \tag{3-68}$$

A special case of interest occurs when the noise has power spectral density

$$G_n(f) = \frac{N_0}{2} \, |H_C(f)|^2 \tag{3-69}$$

where $N_0/2$ is a constant. This would result if white noise were added prior to the channel filter. From (3–66) and (3–67), the optimum receiver and transmitter frequency response-function magnitudes are

$$|H_R(f)| = \frac{\eta|P_r(f)|^{1/2}}{G_n^{1/2}(f)} = \eta_1 \frac{|P_r(f)|^{1/2}}{|H_C(f)|} \tag{3-70}$$

and

$$|H_T(f)| = \eta_2|P_r(f)|^{1/2} \tag{3-71}$$

respectively, where the ηs are arbitrary constants. Because $p_r(0) = 1$, it follows that $\int_{-\infty}^{\infty} P_r(f)\, df = 1$. Therefore, for cases where $P_r(f)$ is real and greater than or equal to 0 for all f, the minimum probability of error for this special case becomes

$$P_{b,\min} = Q\left(\sqrt{\frac{2E_T}{N_0}}\right) \tag{3-72}$$

This is identical to the error probability for matched filter detection of binary signals in AWGN.

Note that $|H_T(f)| \propto \sqrt{|P_r(f)|}$ where one possibility for $P_r(f)$ is the raised cosine spectrum shown in Figure 3–9a. This gives rise to the term "square-root raised cosine" commonly encountered in the literature on bandwidth constrained modems.

EXAMPLE 3-6

If $|H_C(f)| = $ constant, and the channel noise is white, (3–70) and (3–71) together with (3–54) give the square-root raised cosine spectrum. It can be shown that the pulse shape corresponding to this spectrum is given by [2]

$$p_{\text{srrc}}(t) = 2\beta\, \frac{\cos[(1+\beta)\pi t/T_s] + (4\beta t/T_s)^{-1}\sin[(1-\beta)\pi t/T_s]}{\pi\sqrt{T_s}[1 - (4\beta t/T_s)^2]} \tag{3-73}$$

Since this pulse shape is infinite in extent, its implementation requires time truncation. The truncated pulse has a spectrum with nonzero sidelobes. The shorter the truncation, the higher the sidelobes. Typically, the square-root raised cosine pulse shape is formed digitally. Figure 3–10 shows the spectrum of a sampled square-root raised cosine pulse (four samples per symbol) and its spectrum for a truncation of four symbol intervals. The pulse spectrum is computed using the fast Fourier transform.

EXAMPLE 3-7

Consider a binary communication system that transmits at a data rate of 9600 bits/s. The channel has a frequency response function

$$H_C(f) = \frac{1}{1 + jf/4800} \tag{3-74}$$

and the noise is white with a double-sided power spectral density $N_0/2 = 10^{-12}$ W/Hz. Assume that a received pulse with raised cosine spectrum given by (3–54) with $1/T_b = 9600$ Hz and $\beta = 1$ is desired. Find the magnitudes of the transmit- and receive-filter frequency response functions that give zero ISI and optimum detection. Also find the value of A^2/σ^2 and the transmitted signal energy required to give $P_{b,\min} = 10^{-6}$.

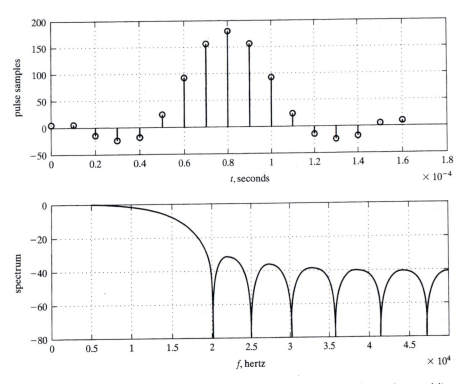

FIGURE 3–10   Time-limited sample-data square-root raised cosine pulse and its spectrum ($\beta = 0.5$).

Solution: From (3–66) and (3–67) with $G_n(f) = 10^{-12}$, the magnitude of the transmit- and receive-filter frequency response functions are

$$|H_R(f)| = |H_T(f)| = \begin{cases} \left[1 + \left(\dfrac{f}{4800}\right)^2\right]^{1/4} \cos\left(\dfrac{\pi f}{19{,}200}\right), & 0 \le |f| \le 9600 \text{ Hz} \\ 0, & \text{otherwise} \end{cases} \quad (3\text{--}75)$$

where the arbitrary constants have been chösen to make the frequency responses unity at zero frequency. To maintain an error probability of 10^{-6} or less requires that

$$Q\left(\frac{A}{\sigma}\right) \le 10^{-6}$$

or that $A/\sigma \ge 4.75$, which can be obtained by using a table for the Q-function. In the argument of (3–68), the factor

$$F = \int_{-\infty}^{\infty} \frac{P_r(f)}{|H_C(f)|}\, df = \frac{1}{9600} \int_0^{9600} \left(1 + \cos\frac{\pi f}{9600}\right)\left[1 + \left(\frac{f}{4800}\right)^2\right]^{1/2} df$$

is required. By the change of variables $u = f/9600$, this integral can be written as

$$F = \int_0^1 [1 + \cos(\pi u)] \left[1 + (2u)^2\right]^{1/2} du \cong 1.21$$

which is obtained through numerical integration. Since $G_n(f) = N_0/2 = 10^{-12}$ W/Hz, the argument of the Q-function in (3–68) is

$$\frac{1}{1.21} \sqrt{\frac{2E_T}{N_0}} = 0.83 \sqrt{\frac{2E_T}{N_0}} = \frac{A}{\sigma}$$

This differs by a factor of 0.83 from the case of matched filter detection of binary antipodal signals in white noise; that is, the finite-bandwidth channel imposes a degradation of $-20 \log_{10} 0.83 = 1.62$ dB over the infinite-bandwidth case.

Using $A/\sigma = 4.75$ and $N_0/2 = 10^{-12}$ W/Hz as given, the required signal energy is

$$E_T = \left(1.21 \frac{A}{\sigma}\right)^2 \frac{N_0}{2} = (1.21)^2 (4.75)^2 (10^{-12}) = 3.3 \times 10^{-11} \text{ J}$$

The average power is the energy divided by the symbol duration since the symbol energy is independent of which symbol is transmitted. The resulting power is

$$P_T = \frac{E_T}{T_b} = 9600 (3.3 \times 10^{-11}) = 0.317 \ \mu W = -35 \text{ dBm}$$

3.3.4 Shaped Transmit Signal Spectra

If the channel frequency response has a small magnitude for certain ranges of frequencies, it is useful to shape the transmitted signal spectrum to match the channel response; that is, where the channel response is low, the transmitted signal spectrum should be correspondingly low. This avoids the problem of having to design receiver filters with unreasonably high gains in those regions where the channel frequency response is low [see (3–70)].

The spectrum of the transmitted signal depends on both the transmitted pulse shape [transmitter filter impulse response in (3–41) and Figure 3–7] and the statistical properties of the transmitted symbols [the a_ks in (3–41) and Figure 3–7]. To investigate the effect of the latter, the power spectrum for a pulse train whose symbols are interdependent will be developed and applied to several specific cases. [7]

Consider a transmitted signal of the form

$$x_t(t) = \sum_{n=0}^{N-1} b_n x(t - nT_b) \tag{3–76}$$

[7] These examples are part of the broader subject of *line codes*. The following book, which may be somewhat difficult to acquire, includes a very extensive bibliography to the subject: N. D. Alexandru and G. Morgenstern, *Digital Line Codes and Spectral Shaping*, MATRIX ROM Publishing Co., Bucharest, Romania, 1998 (ISBN 973-9340-44-7).

where $b_0, b_1, b_2, \ldots, b_{N-1}$ are constants and $x(t)$ is of the form

$$x(t) = \sum_{k=-\infty}^{\infty} a_k h_T(t - kT_b) \qquad (3\text{--}77)$$

in which the a_ks are independent, identically distributed random variables. The power spectral density of $x(t)$ can be shown to be

$$S_x(f) = \frac{1}{T_b} E[a_k^2]|H_T(f)|^2 \qquad (3\text{--}78)$$

where $E[\cdot]$ denotes the expectation operator and $H_T(f)$ is the Fourier transform of $h(t)$.

The power spectral density of $x_t(t)$ is desired. It can be found by expressing the autocorrelation function of $x_t(t)$ in terms of the autocorrelation function of $x(t)$ and Fourier transforming it to obtain the power spectral density. Using the definition of the autocorrelation function and (3–76) for $x_t(t)$, it follows that its autocorrelation function is

$$\begin{aligned}
R_{x_t}(\tau) &= E[x_t(t)\, x_t(t + \tau)] \\
&= E\left[\sum_{n=0}^{N-1}\sum_{m=0}^{N-1} b_n b_m x(t - nT_b)x(t + \tau - mT_b)\right] \\
&= \sum_{n=0}^{N-1}\sum_{m=0}^{N-1} b_n b_m E[x(t - nT_b)x(t + \tau - mT_b)] \\
&= \sum_{n=0}^{N-1}\sum_{m=0}^{N-1} b_n b_m R_x[\tau - (m - n)T_b]
\end{aligned} \qquad (3\text{--}79)$$

The Fourier transform of (3–79) gives the power spectral density of $x_t(t)$, which is

$$S_{x_t}(f) = \sum_{n=0}^{N-1}\sum_{m=0}^{N-1} b_n b_m S_x(f)\exp[-j2\pi(m - n)f T_b] \qquad (3\text{--}80)$$

where the frequency translation theorem of Fourier transforms has been used. The application of (3–80) will now be illustrated by an example.

EXAMPLE 3–8   DICODE PULSE TRAIN

Assume that the a_ks in (3–77) are +1 for a logic 1 transmitted and −1 for a logic 0 transmitted. The transmitted pulse sequence is formed by taking the difference between $x(t)$ and $x(t - T_b)$, which is referred to as a *dicode pulse train*. Thus $b_0 = -b_1 = 1$ and $b_2 = b_3 = \ldots = 0$. From (3–80), the power spectral density of the transmitted signal becomes

$$\begin{aligned}
S_{x_t}(f) &= \sum_{n=0}^{1}\sum_{m=0}^{1} b_n b_m S_x(f)\exp[-j\,2\pi(n - m)f T_b] \\
&= [1 - \exp(-j\,2\pi f T_b) - \exp(j\,2\pi f T_b) + 1]S_x(f) \\
&= 4\sin^2(\pi f T_b)S_x(f) \\
&= \frac{4}{T_b}\sin^2(\pi f T_b)|H_T(f)|^2
\end{aligned} \qquad (3\text{--}81)$$

The presence of $\sin^2 \pi f T_b$ in (3–81) guarantees that the power spectrum of the transmitted signal is zero at $f = 0$. Therefore, dicode transmission would be a useful scheme to employ for channels with poor low-frequency response.

Other schemes could be employed for which the transmitted symbol stream is derived from more than two successive source bits. The dependency between bits thereby introduced amounts to the use of a *finite impulse response (FIR) filter.*

3.3.5 Duobinary Signaling

The baseband binary systems considered so far in this section require a transmission bandwidth of at least $1/(2T_b)$ hertz in order to transmit one symbol each T_b seconds, and a bandwidth of exactly $1/(2T_b)$ hertz implies the use of ideal, rectangular filters at the transmitter and receiver. In order to avoid the use of rectangular filters and yet require a transmission bandwidth of only $1/(2T_b)$ hertz, *partial response signaling* can be employed. Such signaling schemes, which utilize *controlled amounts* of ISI, have their origins in the early 1960s when *duobinary signaling* was invented by Adam Lender.[8] The concept of partial response signaling will be illustrated here with a brief introduction to duobinary signaling.

Duobinary signaling uses signals giving possible output samples from the receive filter of

$$v(t_m) = V_m = A(a_m + a_{m-1}) + N_m \tag{3–82}$$

[see (3–47)]. A suitable received pulse spectrum is

$$P_r(f) = \begin{cases} 2T_b \cos(\pi f T_b), & |f| \le \dfrac{1}{2T_b} \\ 0, & \text{otherwise} \end{cases} \tag{3–83}$$

which corresponds to the time response

$$p_r(t) = \frac{4 \cos(\pi t/T_b)}{\pi(1 - 4t^2/T_b^2)} \tag{3–84}$$

Depending on the values of the mth and $(m-1)$st input bits, the first term of (3–82) becomes

$$A(a_m + a_{m-1}) = \begin{cases} 2A, & \text{if } a_m = a_{m-1} = 1 \\ 0, & \text{if } a_m = -a_{m-1} \\ -2A, & \text{if } a_m = a_{m-1} = -1 \end{cases} \tag{3–85}$$

To uniquely determine the source bit in the mth signaling interval, even if an error is made on the $(m-1)$th bit, the mth source data bit, denoted by b_m, is *precoded* according to the rule

---

[8]The original work on duobinary signaling is reported in [3]. A survey article on correlative coding techniques is provided in [4].

$$d_m = b_m \oplus d_{m-1} \qquad (3\text{–}86)$$

where $\oplus$ stands for modulo-2 addition and the d_ms are the encoded bits. This rule is called *differential encoding*. Using this encoding rule, it is seen that $d_m = d_{m-1}$ if the mth input bit is 0 and $d_m = \bar{d}_{m-1}$, where the overbar denotes complement, if $b_m = 1$. The sign on the amplitude, a_m, of the mth transmitted pulse is then either $+1$ or -1 according to $b_m = 1$ or 0, respectively. It therefore follows that with no noise

$$|V_m| = \begin{cases} 2A, & \text{if } b_m = 0 \\ 0, & \text{if } b_m = 1 \end{cases} \qquad (3\text{–}87)$$

Consequently, the source data can be detected by comparing $|v(t)|$ with a suitably chosen threshold. If it exceeds this threshold, the decision $b_m = 0$ is made; if the threshold is not exceeded, the decision $b_m = 1$ is made. Thus, the following sampler output values are assumed:

$$V_m = \begin{cases} \pm 2A + N_m, & \text{if } b_m = 0 \\ N_m, & \text{if } b_m = 1 \end{cases} \qquad (3\text{–}88)$$

If $b_m = 0$ and $b_m = 1$ are equiprobable, the output levels $\pm 2A$ each occur with probability ¼ and the output level 0 occurs with probability ½ assuming no noise. If thresholds are set at $\pm A$, errors occur as follows:

$$\text{If } b_m = 0,\ 2A + N_m < A \text{ or } N_m < -A \qquad (3\text{–}89)$$

$$-2A + N_m > -A \text{ or } N_m > A$$

$$\text{If } b_m = 1,\ N_m > A \text{ or } N_m < -A \text{ (i.e., } |N_m| > A)$$

Therefore, the average probability of error is

$$P_b = \frac{1}{4} P(N_m < -A) + \frac{1}{2} P(|N_m| > A) + \frac{1}{4} P(N_m > A) \qquad (3\text{–}90)$$

But N_m is a zero-mean Gaussian random variable with variance σ^2. Thus (3–90) can be written as

$$P_b = \frac{1}{4} \int_{-\infty}^{-A} \frac{\exp(-u^2/2\sigma^2)}{\sqrt{2\pi\sigma^2}} du + \frac{1}{2} \left[\int_A^\infty \frac{\exp(-u^2/2\sigma^2)}{\sqrt{2\pi\sigma^2}} du + \int_{-\infty}^{-A} \frac{\exp(-u^2/2\sigma^2)}{\sqrt{2\pi\sigma^2}} du \right] \qquad (3\text{–}91)$$

$$+ \frac{1}{4} \int_A^\infty \frac{\exp(-u^2/2\sigma^2)}{\sqrt{2\pi\sigma^2}} du$$

Because of symmetry of the Gaussian probability density function, this may be written in terms of the *Q*-function as

$$P_b = \frac{3}{2} Q\left(\frac{A}{\sigma}\right) \qquad (3\text{–}92)$$

The probability of error can again be minimized through choosing the transmit and receive filter frequency response functions to maximize A^2/σ^2 subject to the received pulse response satisfying (3–84). The resulting frequency response functions can be shown to be given by (3–66) and (3–67).

To compare duobinary signaling with direct baseband binary signaling, consider the ratios $(A^2/\sigma^2)_{max}$ for both cases for an ideal channel $[H_C(f) = 1]$ and AWGN. For direct binary signaling, this ratio is [see (3–72)]

$$\left(\frac{A}{\sigma}\right)^2_{max, \, binary} = \frac{2E_T}{N_0} \tag{3–93}$$

For the duobinary case, it is [see (3–68) with $H_C(f) = $ constant and $G_n = N_0/2$]

$$\left(\frac{A}{\sigma}\right)^2_{max, \, duobinary} = \frac{2E_T}{N_0}\left[\int_{-\infty}^{\infty}|P_r(f)|df\right]^{-2} \tag{3–94}$$

Therefore, the argument of the Q-function expression for the error probability of duobinary differs from that of direct binary by the factor

$$F = \left[\int_{-\infty}^{\infty}|P_r(f)|df\right]^2 = \left[2T_b\int_{-1/2T_b}^{1/2T_b}\cos(\pi fT_b)df\right]^2 = \left(\frac{4}{\pi}\right)^2 \tag{3–95}$$

If the factor of 3/2 multiplying the Q-function for duobinary is ignored, the factor F amounts to a degradation in signal-to-noise ratio of

$$D = 20\log_{10}\frac{4}{\pi} = 2.1 \text{ dB}$$

of duobinary over direct binary. That is, to achieve the same error probability, the transmitter power for duobinary must be 2.1 dB greater than that for direct binary, assuming ideal channel filtering and AWGN. This is the sacrifice paid for the smaller bandwidth required by duobinary signaling.

3.4   EQUALIZATION IN DIGITAL DATA TRANSMISSION SYSTEMS[9]

3.4.1   Introduction

In Section 3–3 it was shown how proper design of the transmitter and receiver filters of a pulse-amplitude-modulated communication system (modem) would simultaneously guarantee zero ISI and maximize the signal-to-noise ratio at the sampling time, thereby minimizing the probability of error. The filter design equations were given by (3–66) and

---

[9]For an easy-to-read overview of equalization, see [5]. A multitude of other treatments on equalization are available with [6] and [7–10] recommended as examples. Two recent articles which summarize known results and provide several new results are [11, 12]. A recent introductory treatment on fractionally spaced equalizers is [13].

(3–67). In some instances it may be difficult to realize filters with these frequency responses. In other cases, the channel may be unknown or the modem may be required to transmit data through several different channels, depending on the circuit obtained at dial-up. Another case occurs in cellular radio, where buildings and geographical features result in several transmission paths between transmitter and receiver. Yet another case occurs when the channel is slowly time varying, such as a line-of-sight microwave relay link in which multipath propagation takes place due to temperature variations of the atmosphere with altitude. In all these cases, a filter with *adjustable* frequency response would be useful to employ at the receiver. Through channel measurements, the detection filter frequency response (or, equivalently, impulse response) could be adjusted to give an overall filter response at the receiver that improves modem performance over that obtainable with fixed filters. This adjustable filter is referred to as an *equalization filter,* or simply equalizer. Equalizers may be either *preset* or *adaptive.* The parameters of a preset equalizer are adjusted by making measurements of the channel impulse response and solving a set of equations for the parameters using these measurements. An adaptive equalizer is automatically adjusted by periodically sending a known signal through the channel and allowing the equalizer to adjust its own parameters in response to this known signal (in benign channel conditions, an equalizer may be designed to adapt without a training signal).

3.4.2 Zero-Forcing Equalizers

To illustrate the basic idea of equalization, consider the block diagram of Figure 3–11. This is a simplified version of Figure 3–7 with the channel and fixed receiver filters combined and the noise excluded for the moment. An equalization filter follows the channel filter giving an overall system frequency response from transmitter filter input to equalizer output of

$$H_o(f) = H_T(f)\, H_C(f) H_E(f) \tag{3–96}$$

The overall impulse response is the inverse Fourier transform of (3–96). Assume that the output of the equalizer is sampled each T_b seconds. Zero ISI results if Nyquist's first criterion is satisfied, that is, if

$$\sum_{k=-\infty}^{\infty} H_o\left(f + \frac{k}{T_b}\right) = \text{constant}, \quad |f| \le \frac{1}{2T_b} \tag{3–97}$$

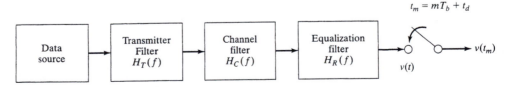

FIGURE 3–11 Simplified block diagram of a pulse-amplitude-modulated communication system with equalization filter.

which follows from (3–49). The zero-ISI property (3–50) then follows for $h_o(t)$. From (3–96) and (3–97) it follows that an ideal zero-ISI equalizer is simply an *inverse filter*, which has a frequency response that is the inverse of the frequency response of the transmitter and channel cascaded and folded about the sampling frequency, $1/T_b$. This inverse-filter equalizer is often approximated by a finite-impulse response filter or *transversal filter* as illustrated in Figure 3–12. Its impulse response is (ignoring a constant delay)

$$h_E(t) = \sum_{n=-N}^{N} C_n \delta(t - nT_b) \tag{3–98}$$

from which it follows, using the time delay theorem of Fourier transforms, that its frequency response is

$$H_E(f) = \sum_{n=-N}^{N} C_n \exp(-j2\pi n f T_b) \tag{3–99}$$

One problem with a transversal filter equalizer, with coefficients chosen to approximate the zero-ISI condition, is that it excessively enhances the channel noise at frequencies where the folded channel frequency response has high attenuation (recall that the equalizer attempts to make the overall frequency response—transmitter, channel, receiver—flat).

Because there are only $2N + 1$ unknown coefficients in (3–98) or (3–99) it follows that only a finite number of interfering symbol samples can be nulled or forced to 0. The equations for solving for the coefficients are easily found by noting that the equalizer pulse response, $p_{eq}(t)$, due to the channel output pulse response, $p_C(t)$, is

$$p_{eq}(t) = \sum_{n=-N}^{N} C_n p_C(t - nT_b) \tag{3–100}$$

The zero-ISI condition, when applied to (3–100), can hold for only $2N + 1$ sample times since only $2N + 1$ unknown constants are available for adjustment. Setting $t = mT_b + t_d$, $m = 0, \pm1, \pm2, \ldots, \pm N$ in (3–100), these conditions are

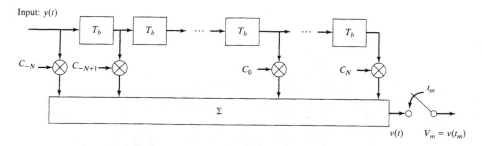

FIGURE 3–12 Transversal filter equalizer.

$$p_{eq}(mT_b + t_d) = \sum_{n=-N}^{N} C_n p_C[(m-n)T_b + t_d]$$

(3-101)

$$= \begin{cases} 1, m = 0 \\ 0, m = \pm 1, \pm 2, \cdots, \pm N \end{cases}$$

where $t = t_d$ is the sampling time giving $p_{eq}(t)$ maximum. In matrix form these equations become

$$\mathbf{P}_{eq} = \mathbf{P}_C \mathbf{C}$$

(3-102)

where $\mathbf{P}_{eq}$ and $\mathbf{C}$ are vectors or column matrices given by

$$\mathbf{P}_{eq} = \begin{bmatrix} 0 \\ \vdots \\ 0 \\ 1 \\ 0 \\ \vdots \\ 0 \end{bmatrix} \begin{matrix} \left.\begin{matrix} \\ \\ \end{matrix}\right\} N \text{ zeros} \\ \\ \left.\begin{matrix} \\ \\ \end{matrix}\right\} N \text{ zeros} \end{matrix} \qquad \mathbf{C} = \begin{bmatrix} C_{-N} \\ C_{-N+1} \\ \vdots \\ C_0 \\ C_1 \\ \vdots \\ C_N \end{bmatrix}$$

(3-103)

respectively, and $\mathbf{P}_C$ is the $(2N+1) \times (2N+1)$ matrix of channel responses of the form

$$\mathbf{P}_C = \begin{bmatrix} p_C(t_d) & p_C(-T_b + t_d) & \cdots & p_C(-2NT_b + t_d) \\ p_C(T_b + t_d) & p_C(t_d) & \cdots & p_C[(-2N+1)T_b + t_d] \\ p_C(2T_b + t_d) & p_C(T_b + t_d) & \cdots & p_C[(-2N+2)T_b + t_d] \\ \vdots & \vdots & \ddots & \vdots \\ p_C(2NT_b + t_d) & p_C[(2N-1)T_b + t_d] & \cdots & p_C(t_d) \end{bmatrix}$$

(3-104)

Thus the $4N + 1$ sample values of the channel pulse response taken at T_b-second intervals can be used to determine the $2N + 1$ unknown coefficients $C_{-N}, C_{-N+1}, \ldots, C_0, \ldots, C_N$ by solving (3-102). Exactly N zeros will be forced at the sampling instants either side of the main-pulse response. Because all components of the vector $\mathbf{P}_{eq}$ are zeros except for the center one, it follows that the optimum coefficient vector, $\mathbf{C}_o$, is the center column of $\mathbf{P}_C^{-1}$.

EXAMPLE 3-9

Consider the channel pulse response shown in Figure 3–13a. Determine the coefficients of a five-tap transversal filter equalizer that will force two 0s on either side of the main pulse response. Compute the sample values out to $\pm 3T_b$.

Solution: The sample values for the channel response are [illustrated in Figure 3–13(a)]

$$\begin{matrix} p_C(-5T_b + t_d) = 0.01 & p_C(-4T_b + t_d) = -0.02 & p_C(-3T_b + t_d) = 0.05 \\ p_C(-2T_b + t_d) = -0.1 & p_C(-T_b + t_d) = 0.2 & p_C(t_d) = 1 \\ p_C(T_b + t_d) = 0.15 & p_C(2T_b + t_d) = -0.15 & p_C(3T_b + t_d) = 0.05 \\ p_C(4T_b + t_d) = -0.02 & p_C(5T_b + t_d) = 0.005 \end{matrix}$$

(3-105)

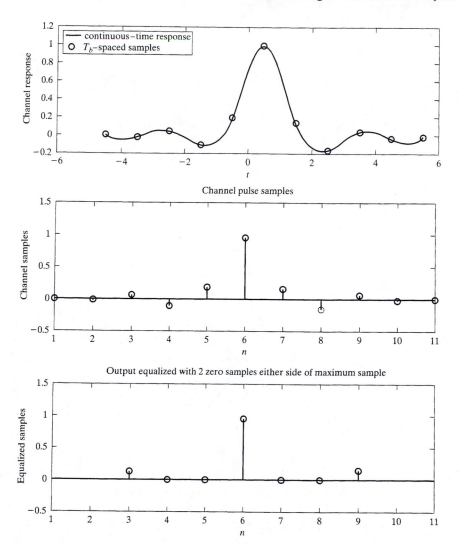

FIGURE 3–13 Channel pulse response for Example 3–10 with $t_d = 0.5$ and $T_b = 1$ s (a); samples for computing zero-forcing equalizer coefficients (b); equalized samples for five-tap equalizer (c).

Figure 3–13(b) illustrates the samples versus sample number. The channel response matrix is

$$\mathbf{P}_C = \begin{bmatrix} 1.0 & 0.2 & -0.1 & 0.05 & -0.02 \\ 0.15 & 1.0 & 0.2 & -0.1 & 0.05 \\ -0.15 & 0.15 & 1.0 & 0.2 & -0.1 \\ 0.05 & -0.15 & 0.15 & 1.0 & 0.2 \\ -0.02 & 0.05 & -0.15 & 0.15 & 1.0 \end{bmatrix} \qquad (3\text{–}106)$$

The inverse of this matrix, by numerical methods, is found to be

$$\mathbf{P}_C^{-1} = \begin{bmatrix} 1.0774 & -0.2682 & 0.1932 & -0.1314 & 0.0806 \\ -0.2266 & 1.1272 & -0.2983 & 0.2034 & -0.1314 \\ 0.2326 & -0.2737 & 1.1517 & -0.2983 & 0.1932 \\ -0.1405 & 0.2516 & -0.2737 & 1.1272 & -0.2682 \\ 0.0888 & -0.1405 & 0.2326 & -0.2266 & 1.0774 \end{bmatrix} \qquad (3\text{--}107)$$

The optimum (zero-forcing) coefficient vector is the center column of $\mathbf{P}_C^{-1}$. Therefore,

$$C_{-2} = 0.1932; \quad C_{-1} = -0.2983; \quad C_0 = 1.1517; \quad C_1 = -0.2737; \quad C_2 = 0.2326$$

The sample values of the equalized pulse response, from (3–101), are

$$p_{eq}(m) = \sum_{n=-N}^{N} C_n p_C(m - n) \qquad (3\text{--}108)$$

where, again, only the sample indices are used as the arguments for simplicity. For example,

$$p_{eq}(0) = (0.1932)(-0.15) + (-0.2983)(0.15) + (1.1517)(1) \qquad (3\text{--}109)$$
$$+ (-0.2737)(0.2) + (0.2326)(-0.1) = 1.0$$

which checks with the desired value of unity. Similarly, it can be verified that $p_{eq}(-2) = p_{eq}(-1) = p_{eq}(1) = p_{eq}(2) = 0$. Values of $p_{eq}(n)$ for $n < -2$ or $n > 2$ are not zero. For example,

$$p_{eq}(3) = (0.1932)(0.005) + (-0.2983)(-0.02) + (1.1517)(0.05) \qquad (3\text{--}110)$$
$$+ (-0.2737)(-0.15) + (0.2326)(0.15) = 0.1405$$

and

$$p_{eq}(-3) = (0.1932)(0.2) + (-0.2983)(-0.1) + (1.1517)(0.05) \qquad (3\text{--}111)$$
$$+ (-0.2737)(-0.02) + (0.2326)(0.01) = 0.1339$$

The equalizer output samples are shown in Figure 3–13(c).

The zero-forcing equations (3–102) do not account for the effects of noise. In addition, a finite-length transversal filter equalizer can minimize worst-case ISI only if the peak distortion (i.e., the magnitude of the difference between the channel output and desired signal) is sufficiently small. A type of equalizer that partially avoids these problems is the minimum-mean-square error (MMSE) equalizer. In such an equalizer, the coefficients are chosen to minimize the mean-square error, which consists of the sum of the squares of all the ISI terms plus the noise power at the equalizer output. The MMSE equalizer therefore maximizes the signal-to-distortion ratio at its output within the constraints of the equalizer length and delay.

3.4.3   Minimum Mean-Square Error Equalization

Suppose that the desired output from the transversal filter equalizer of Figure 3–12 is $d(t)$ (in the context of data transmission, this is the data, a sequence of ± 1-valued pulses each of duration T_b seconds). The filter tap weights are chosen so that the mean-square error

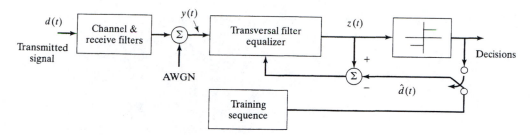

FIGURE 3–14 Definitions of waveforms pertinent to the MMSE equalizer analysis (adaptation circuit shown for future reference).

between desired output and its actual output is minimized. Since the actual output includes noise, we denote it as $z(t)$ to distinguish it from the pulse response of the transversal filter. Figure 3–14 defines these waveforms. The MMSE criterion at the equalizer filter output may be expressed as

$$\varepsilon = E\{[z(t) - d(t)]^2\} = \text{minimum} \tag{3–112}$$

For a transversal filter input denoted by $y(t)$, which includes AWGN, the filter output is

$$z(t) = \sum_{n=-N}^{N} C_n y(t - nT_b) \tag{3–113}$$

The mean-square error (3–112) is a concave function of the tap weights, so a set of sufficient conditions for minimizing the mean-square error is

$$\frac{\partial \varepsilon}{\partial C_m} = 0 = 2E\left\{[z(t) - d(t)]\frac{\partial z(t)}{\partial C_m}\right\}, \quad m = 0, \pm1, \pm2, \cdots, \pm N \tag{3–114}$$

Substitution of (3–113) into (3–114) and differentiation results in the set of conditions

$$E\{[z(t) - d(t)]y(t - mT_b)\} = 0, \quad m = 0, \pm1, \pm2, \cdots, \pm N, \tag{3–115}$$

that is, the error between output and desired signal and the received data are statistically orthogonal (known as the orthogonality condition). Taking the expectation of each term in (3–115) yields

$$R_{yz}(mT_b) = R_{yd}(mT_b), \quad m = 0, \pm1, \pm2, \cdots, \pm N \tag{3–116}$$

where

$$R_{yz}(mT_b) = E[y(t)z(t + mT_b)] \text{ and } R_{yd}(mT_b) = E[y(t)d(t + mT_b)] \tag{3–117}$$

are the cross-correlation functions of the received signal with the transversal filter output and with the desired output signal (data), respectively.

If we substitute (3–113) for $z(t)$ into (3–116), interchange the order of summation, and taking the expectation, the conditions for the optimum MMSE transversal filter weights become the matrix equation[10]

$$\mathbf{R}_{yy}\,\mathbf{C}_o = \mathbf{R}_{yd} \text{ or } \mathbf{C}_o = \mathbf{R}_{yy}^{-1}\mathbf{R}_{yd} \tag{3–118}$$

where

$$\mathbf{R}_{yy} = \begin{bmatrix} R_{yy}(0) & R_{yy}(T_b) & \cdots & R_{yy}(2NT_b) \\ R_{yy}(T_b) & R_{yy}(0) & \cdots & R_{yy}((2N-1)T_b) \\ \vdots & \vdots & \ddots & \vdots \\ R_{yy}(2NT_b) & R_{yy}((2N-1)T_b) & \cdots & R_{yy}(0) \end{bmatrix} \tag{3–119}$$

(note that since the autocorrelation function is even, negative arguments are unnecessary) and

$$\mathbf{R}_{yd} = \begin{bmatrix} R_{yd}(-NT_b) \\ R_{yd}(-(N-1)T_b) \\ \vdots \\ R_{yd}(NT_b) \end{bmatrix} \tag{3–120}$$

By substitution of (3–118) with (3–113) into (3–112), it can be shown that the MMSE is [14]

$$\varepsilon_{\min} = E[d^2(t)] - \mathbf{R}_{yd}^T\mathbf{R}_{yy}\,\mathbf{R}_{yd} \tag{3–121}$$

The optimum coefficient vector, $\mathbf{C}_o$, is defined by (3–118). Note the similarity to the zero-forcing equalizer case. The only difference is that correlation function samples appear in the equations for the MMSE equalizer, whereas pulse sample values appear in the equations for the zero-forcing equalizer.

As an interesting example illustrating MMSE equalization, we find the optimum tap weights for minimizing the distortion at the output of a simple two-path multipath channel. It is emphasized that the weights for the optimum MMSE equalizer are not usually found by solving (3–118). Instead, an adaptive tap weight adjustment algorithm, several possibilities of which are discussed shortly, is typically used.

EXAMPLE 3–10 _____

(a) Consider the design of an MMSE equalizer for a multipath channel whose output is of the form

$$y(t) = Ad(t) + bAd(t - T_m) + n(t) \tag{3–122}$$

where the second term is a multipath component and the third term is additive Gaussian noise. Assume that the data $d(t)$ is a random binary sequence with autocorrelation function $R_{dd}(\tau) = \Lambda(\tau/T_b)$, where T_b is the symbol period. Let the noise have lowpass RC-filtered

---

[10]These are known as the Wiener-Hopf equations [14].

spectrum with 3 dB cutoff frequency $f_3 = 1/T_b$. Let the tap spacing be $T_m = T_b$. Express the matrix $\mathbf{R}_{yy}$ in terms of $E_b/N_0 = A^2 T_b/N_0$, where N_0 is the single-sided power spectral density of the noise into the lowpass RC filter that produces the noise at the equalizer input. **(b)** Obtain the numerical values for the tap weights for a three-tap MMSE equalizer for $E_b/N_0 = 10$ dB and for $b = 0.1$. Assume that the data is available for obtaining $R_{yd}(nT_b)$.

Solution: **(a)** To calculate the members of $\mathbf{R}_{yy}$, consider

$$R_{yy}(\lambda) \equiv E[y(t)\,y(t+\lambda)] \tag{3-123}$$

$$= E\{[Ad(t) + bAd(t-T_b) + n(t)][Ad(t+\lambda) + bAd(t+\lambda-T_b) + n(t+\lambda)]\}$$

$$= (1+b^2)A^2 R_{dd}(\lambda) + R_{nn}(\lambda) + bA^2[R_{dd}(\lambda - T_b) + R_{dd}(\lambda + T_b)]$$

where

$$R_{dd}(\lambda) = E\{d(t)\,d(t+\lambda)\} = \Lambda\left(\frac{\lambda}{T_b}\right) \tag{3-124}$$

and

$$R_{nn}(\lambda) = \mathscr{F}^{-1}\left[\frac{N_0/2}{1 + (f/f_3)^2}\right] = \frac{\pi N_0}{2T_b}\exp\left(-\frac{2\pi|\lambda|}{T_b}\right), f_3 = \frac{1}{T_b} \tag{3-125}$$

Evaluating $R_{yy}(k)$ for $\lambda = 0, \pm T_b$, and $\pm 2T_b$, we find the matrix $\mathbf{R}_{yy}$ to be

$$\mathbf{R}_{yy} = \frac{N_0}{T_b}\begin{bmatrix} (1+b^2)\dfrac{E_b}{N_0} + \dfrac{\pi}{2} & b\dfrac{E_b}{N_0} + \dfrac{\pi}{2}\exp(-2\pi) & \dfrac{\pi}{2}\exp(-4\pi) \\[2mm] b\dfrac{E_b}{N_0} + \dfrac{\pi}{2}\exp(-2\pi) & (1+b^2)\dfrac{E_b}{N_0} + \dfrac{\pi}{2} & b\dfrac{E_b}{N_0} + \dfrac{\pi}{2}\exp(-2\pi) \\[2mm] \dfrac{\pi}{2}\exp(-4\pi) & b\dfrac{E_b}{N_0} + \dfrac{\pi}{2}\exp(-2\pi) & (1+b^2)\dfrac{E_b}{N_0} + \dfrac{\pi}{2} \end{bmatrix} \tag{3-126}$$

To find $\mathbf{R}_{yd}$ we need

$$R_{yd}(\lambda) = E[y(t)\,d(t+\lambda)]$$

$$= E\{[Ad(t) + bAd(t-T_b) + n(t)]d(t+\lambda)\} \tag{3-127}$$

$$= AR_{dd}(\lambda) + bAR_{dd}(\lambda + T_b)$$

Thus

$$\mathbf{R}_{yd} = \begin{bmatrix} R_{yd}(-T_b) \\ R_{yd}(0) \\ R_{yd}(T_b) \end{bmatrix} = \begin{bmatrix} bA \\ A \\ 0 \end{bmatrix} \tag{3-128}$$

The matrix equation for the optimum weights can be written with all matrix elements in dimensionless form by defining new weights as $a_i = AC_i$, $i = -1, 0, 1$. The resulting matrix equation is

$$\begin{bmatrix} (1+b^2)\dfrac{E_b}{N_0} + \dfrac{\pi}{2} & b\dfrac{E_b}{N_0} + \dfrac{\pi}{2}\exp(-2\pi) & \dfrac{\pi}{2}\exp(-4\pi) \\[2ex] b\dfrac{E_b}{N_0} + \dfrac{\pi}{2}\exp(-2\pi) & (1+b^2)\dfrac{E_b}{N_0} + \dfrac{\pi}{2} & b\dfrac{E_b}{N_0} + \dfrac{\pi}{2}\exp(-2\pi) \\[2ex] \dfrac{\pi}{2}\exp(-4\pi) & b\dfrac{E_b}{N_0} + \dfrac{\pi}{2}\exp(-2\pi) & (1+b^2)\dfrac{E_b}{N_0} + \dfrac{\pi}{2} \end{bmatrix} \begin{bmatrix} a_{-1} \\[1ex] a_0 \\[1ex] a_1 \end{bmatrix} \qquad (3\text{--}129)$$

$$= \begin{bmatrix} \dfrac{bE_b}{N_0} \\[2ex] \dfrac{E_b}{N_0} \\[2ex] 0 \end{bmatrix}$$

(b)   Using $E_b/N_0 = 10$ dB and $b = 0.1$ in the matrix equation results in

$$\begin{bmatrix} 11.671 & 1.003 & 5.5\times10^{-6} \\ 1.003 & 11.671 & 1.003 \\ 5.5\times10^{-6} & 1.003 & 11.671 \end{bmatrix} \begin{bmatrix} a_{-1} \\ a_0 \\ a_1 \end{bmatrix} = \begin{bmatrix} 1 \\ 10 \\ 0 \end{bmatrix} \qquad (3\text{--}130)$$

Inversion of the correlation matrix yields

$$\begin{bmatrix} a_{-1} \\ a_0 \\ a_1 \end{bmatrix} = \begin{bmatrix} 0.0863 & -0.0075 & 0.0006 \\ -0.0075 & 0.0863 & -0.0075 \\ 0.0006 & -0.0075 & 0.0863 \end{bmatrix} \begin{bmatrix} 1 \\ 10 \\ 0 \end{bmatrix} \qquad (3\text{--}131)$$

Matrix multiplication gives the tap weights as

$$\begin{bmatrix} a_{-1} \\ a_0 \\ a_1 \end{bmatrix} = \begin{bmatrix} 0.0116 \\ 0.8622 \\ -0.0741 \end{bmatrix} \qquad (3\text{--}132)$$

3.4.4   Adaptive Weight Adjustment[11]

Setting the delay-line tap coefficients of the zero-forcing and MMSE equalizers involves the solution of a set of simultaneous equations. In the use of the zero-forcing equalizer, adjustment of the tap coefficients involves measuring the channel filter output at T_b-second spaced sampling times in response to a test pulse and solving for the tap gains from (3–102). In the case of the MMSE equalizer the matrix equation to be evaluated is (3–118). Solution of these equations requires the channel response matrix (3–104) or the correlation matrices (3–119) and (3–120), which may be difficult or impossible to determine.

Considerations such as these motivate the use of *automatic* tap coefficient adjustment algorithms. These automatic systems can utilize preset algorithms, wherein spe-

---

[11]A good reference dealing with adaptive algorithms is [14].

cial sequences of pulses are used prior to data transmission or between gaps in the data transmission, and *adaptive* algorithms, which carry out the adjustment of the coefficients continuously during data transmission.

For the zero-forcing equalizer, (3–102) can be solved iteratively for the coefficient vector **C**. Let the **C**-matrix at the kth iteration be $\mathbf{C}^{(k)}$. The error in the solution to (3–102) is

$$\mathbf{E}^{(k)} = \mathbf{P}_C\mathbf{C}^{(k)} - \mathbf{P}_{eq} \tag{3–133}$$

where $\mathbf{E}^{(k)}$ is a vector with $2N + 1$ components each of which represent the error in a component of $\mathbf{C}^{(k)}$. Each component of $\mathbf{C}^{(k)}$ can be adjusted in accordance with the error in it. If α is a small positive constant, an appropriate adjustment algorithm for the jth component of $\mathbf{C}^{(k)}$ is

$$C_m^{(k+1)} = C_m^{(k)} - \alpha\, y\,(t - mT_b)\, \text{sgn}\, (E_m^{(k)}) \tag{3–134}$$

The iteration process is continued until $C_m^{(k+1)}$ and $C_m^{(k)}$ differ by some suitably small increment. The coefficient found by this iterative method can be shown to converge to the true values under fairly broad restrictions.

For the MMSE equalizer, iterative solution for the coefficients is possible because the mean-square error is a quadratic function of the tap gain coefficients. For example, for a two-delay equalizer (two coefficients), the error surface is a paraboloid or bowl-shaped surface. If the coefficients are adjusted so that travel along the surface is in a direction opposite to the gradient (slope), with respect to the tap gains, of the parabolic mean-square-error surface, the mean-square error will be minimized. Of course, it is possible that the step size for each adjustment is chosen too large so that the error oscillates about the minimum or goes off to infinity. These two possibilities are illustrated in Figure 3–15, which shows contours of the mean-square error surface for a two-coefficient case.

The mean-square-error gradient algorithm for the mth coefficient is [15]

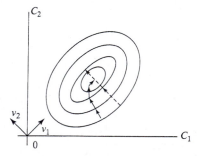

FIGURE 3–15 Illustration of a two-coefficient mean-square error surface for a MMSE equalizer. Possible coefficient adjustment trajectories are also shown: Solid is a case that converges and dashed is a case that does not converge due to the step size being too large. The coordinate directions v_1 and v_2 are aligned with the axes of the error ellipses.

$$C_m^{(k+1)} = C_m^{(k)} - \frac{\beta}{2} \frac{\partial}{\partial C_m^{(k)}} E\left[(\varepsilon^{(k)})^2\right] \tag{3-135}$$

where $E[(\varepsilon^{(k)})^2]$ is the mean-square error, defined in (3–112), and the superscript k denotes the kth step of the adjustment process. From (3–114) and following, the gradient estimate with respect to the mth coefficient is

$$\frac{\partial E\left[(\varepsilon^{(k)})^2\right]}{\partial C_m^{(k)}} = 2E\left\{\left[\sum_{n=-N}^{N} C_n^{(k)} y(t - nT_b) - d(t)\right] y(t - mT_b)\right\} \tag{3-136}$$

$$= 2\left[\sum_{n=-N}^{N} C_n^{(k)} R_{yy}[(n - m)T_b] - R_{yd}(-nT_b)\right]$$

Thus, the adjustment algorithm for the mth coefficient is

$$C_m^{(k+1)} = C_m^{(k)} - \beta\left\{\sum_{n=-N}^{N} [C_n^{(k)} R_{yy}[(n - m)T_b] - R_{yd}(-nT_b)]\right\} \tag{3-137}$$

The adjustment algorithms for *all* coefficients may be written in matrix form as

$$\mathbf{C}^{(k+1)} = \mathbf{C}^{(k)} - \beta\left[\mathbf{R}_{yy}\mathbf{C}^{(k)} - \mathbf{R}_{yd}\right] \tag{3-138}$$

$$= (\mathbf{I} - \beta\mathbf{R}_{yy})\mathbf{C}^{(k)} + \beta\mathbf{R}_{yd}$$

which is referred to as the mean-square error gradient (MSEG) algorithm.

Consideration of the convergence of the algorithm (3–138) is facilitated by transformation to a set of coordinates such that the errors in the coordinate directions are uncorrelated. This is accomplished by diagonalization of the correlation matrix $\mathbf{R}_{yy}$. It is well known from linear algebra that such a diagonalization process proceeds by finding the eigenvalues and eigenvectors of the matrix in question. The eigenvectors and eigenvalues are defined, respectively, as vectors $\mathbf{v}_i$ (i.e., column matrices) and numbers λ_i satisfying

$$\mathbf{R}_{yy}\mathbf{v}_i = \lambda_i \mathbf{v} \text{ or } (\mathbf{R}_{yy} - \lambda_i\mathbf{I})\mathbf{v}_i = \mathbf{0}, \, i = 1, 2, \cdots, \text{ order of } \mathbf{R}_{yy} \tag{3-139}$$

where $\mathbf{I}$ is the identity matrix with 1s along its main diagonal and 0s elsewhere. In the case of the correlation matrix $\mathbf{R}_{yy}$, which is $(2N + 1) \times (2N + 1)$, there will be $2N + 1$ eigenvalues (some of which may be repeated) and eigenvectors. Furthermore, all eigenvalues for a correlation matrix are greater than 0 (i.e., a correlation matrix is positive definite). The matrix $\mathbf{V}$ with columns made up of the eigenvectors transforms the correlation matrix to a diagonal matrix, $\mathbf{\Lambda}$, with main diagonal elements equal to the eigenvalues and all other elements equal to zero through the transformation

$$\mathbf{V}^t \mathbf{R}_{yy} \mathbf{V} = \begin{bmatrix} \lambda_1 & 0 & \cdots & 0 \\ 0 & \lambda_2 & \cdots & 0 \\ \vdots & \vdots & \ddots & \vdots \\ 0 & 0 & \cdots & \lambda_{2N+1} \end{bmatrix} \tag{3-140}$$

where the superscript t denotes transpose. Usually it is the case that the eigenvectors are normalized so that $VV^T = V^TV = I$. From (3–140) and normalization of V, it also follows that $V\Lambda^T = R_{yy}$ where the superscript T indicates transpose.

It can be shown [14] that the adaptive coefficient adjustment algorithm (3–138) converges if the step size parameter β is bounded by

$$0 < \beta < 2/\lambda_{max} \qquad (3–141)$$

where λ_{max} is the largest eigenvalue. The different eigenvalues and eigenvectors define what are known as modes of convergence of the algorithm, with the slowest converging mode corresponding to the largest value of $|1 - \beta\lambda_i|$. By plotting $|1 - \beta\lambda_i|$ versus β, it may be shown that [15] the optimum value of β that gives the fastest convergence is given by

$$\beta_{opt} = \frac{2}{\lambda_{min} + \lambda_{max}} \qquad (3–142)$$

For β_{opt} the modes corresponding to the minimum and maximum eigenvalues converge at the same rate.

EXAMPLE 3–11

Find the eigenvalues and eigenvectors corresponding to the correlation matrix of Example 3–10 for the values of parameters given therein. Find the range of β for convergence of the tap-weight coefficient algorithm and the value of β for fastest convergence. For the latter value of β, give the adaptive coefficient adjustment equations.

Solution: The correlation matrix, repeated below for convenience, is

$$R_{yy} = \begin{bmatrix} 11.671 & 1.003 & 5.5 \times 10^{-6} \\ 1.003 & 11.671 & 1.003 \\ 5.5 \times 10^{-6} & 1.003 & 11.671 \end{bmatrix}$$

Using numerical techniques, the eigenvalues and eigenvector matrix are found to be

$$\lambda_1 = 10.252; \lambda_2 = 11.671; \lambda_3 = 13.089$$

and

$$V = \begin{bmatrix} 0.5 & -0.707 & 0.5 \\ -0.707 & 0.5 & 0.707 \\ 0.5 & 0.707 & 0.5 \end{bmatrix}$$

respectively. Though straightforward calculations, it can be shown that (3–140) holds. Application of (3–141) results in

$$0 < \beta < 0.1528$$

for convergence and use of (3–142) gives

$$\beta_{opt} = 0.0857$$

For the optimum value of β, the coefficient adjustment algorithm is given by

$$\mathbf{C}^{(k+1)} = (\mathbf{I} - \beta_{opt}\mathbf{R}_{yy})\mathbf{C}^{(k)} + \beta_{opt}\,\mathbf{R}_{yd}$$

$$= \left(\begin{bmatrix} 1 & 0 & 0 \\ 0 & 1 & 0 \\ 0 & 0 & 1 \end{bmatrix} - 0.0857 \begin{bmatrix} 11.671 & 1.003 & 5.5 \times 10^{-6} \\ 1.003 & 11.671 & 1.003 \\ 5.5 \times 10^{-6} & 1.003 & 11.671 \end{bmatrix}\right)\mathbf{C}^{(k)} + 0.0857 \begin{bmatrix} 1 \\ 10 \\ 0 \end{bmatrix}$$

$$= \begin{bmatrix} 0 & -0.086 & 0 \\ -0.086 & 0 & -0.086 \\ 0 & -0.086 & 0 \end{bmatrix} \mathbf{C}^{(k)} + \begin{bmatrix} 0.0857 \\ 0.857 \\ 0 \end{bmatrix}$$

It is often the case that the channel is unknown or varies with time. In such cases, $\mathbf{R}_{yy}$ and $\mathbf{R}_{yd}$ must be estimated. The simplest estimate is to use (3–136) without the expectation, which results in

$$C_m^{(k+1)} = C_m^{(k)} - \beta y(t - mT_b)[z^{(k)}(t) - d(t)], \quad m = 0, \pm 1, \cdots \pm N \qquad (3\text{–}143)$$

where β is the coefficient adjustment parameter. Because of the random approximation used for the gradient, this is a type of *stochastic gradient* algorithm, also called the least-mean-square (LMS) algorithm [14, 15, 16]. Note that $z(t)$ implicitly depends on $C_m^{(k)}$ through (3–113). Stability and convergence analysis of the LMS algorithm is more difficult than the MSEG algorithm considered above. As with the MSEG algorithm, convergence can be guaranteed if the condition (3–141) holds. However, by its very purpose for use, it is most likely the case that the correlation matrix and, hence, the eigenvalues are unknown if the LMS algorithm is used. A more generally applicable condition for fixing β in the case of the LMS algorithm when applied to transversal filter structures is [14, 15]

$$0 < \beta < \frac{2}{\text{tap-input power}} < \frac{2}{T} \qquad (3\text{–}144)$$

which is derived by using the trace, T (i.e., sum of the diagonal elements) of $\mathbf{R}_{yy}$ as a conservative estimate for the top-input power.

The mean-squared error has an excess component in addition to (3–121) due to the stochastic nature of the coefficient adjustment algorithm. It can be shown to be less than the minimum mean-squared error in the limit of the coefficients approaching their final values if [14]

$$\sum_{\text{all eigenvalues}} \frac{2\lambda_i}{2 - \beta\lambda_i} < 1 \qquad (3\text{–}145)$$

EXAMPLE 3–12

Assuming that an LMS algorithm is used for the coefficient adjustment of the equalizer of Example 3–11, find the range of β for convergence based on (3–144).

Solution: Calculation of the trace of $\mathbf{R}_{yy}$ based on (3–130) gives a value of $T = 35.01$ and

$$0 < \beta < 0.0571$$

3.4.5 Other Equalizer Structures

The equalizer structures discussed so far employ a transversal filter that is a linear system. Nonlinear equalizer structures may provide better performance under many circumstances (reference [5] gives a good introductory discussion of this area).

  A simple nonlinear equalizer is the *decision feedback equalizer (DFE)*, which uses feedback of decisions on symbols already received to cancel the interference from symbols which have already been detected [6]. A typical DFE structure is shown in Figure 3–16. The basic idea is that, assuming past decisions are correct, the ISI contributed by these symbols can be canceled exactly by subtracting appropriately weighted past symbol values from the equalizer output. This is the purpose of the delay line with weights b_1, b_2, ... , b_M shown in Figure 3–16. The forward transversal filter, with weights c_0, c_1, ... , c_{N-1}, then need compensate for ISI over a smaller portion of the ISI-contaminated received signal. Both the feedback and feedforward coefficients can be adjusted simultaneously to minimize mean-square error.

  Given the same number of overall coefficients, it cannot be said, in general, whether a DFE outperforms a linear, transversal filter equalizer or not. The performance of each

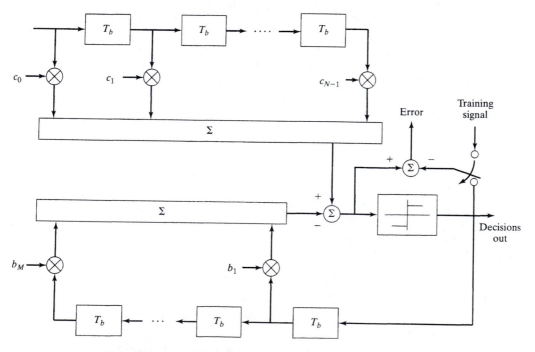

FIGURE 3–16   Decision-feedback equalizer (see [5] and [6]).

equalizer is influenced by the particular channel characteristics, but the DFE can compensate for amplitude distortion without as much noise enhancement as a linear equalizer. When a decision error occurs in a DFE, its output reflects this error during the next few symbols because of the feedback delay line. Fortunately, the errors due to a feedback error occur in short bursts that degrade performance only slightly; the error propagation in a DFE is not catastrophic.

One problem with the DFE is startup. An approach to startup is to open the feedback loop and let the equalizer initialize as a linear equalizer with adaptive weight adjustment.

Another way to compensate for the effects of memory in a digital communication channel is a Viterbi algorithm (VA) sequence estimator [17]. The VA is described in Chapter 7.

3.4.6   Equalizer Performance

Much has been published on equalizer performance, both the equalizer performance itself with a given set of tap weights and adaptation of tap weights. We briefly discuss the former in this subsection.

Many of the results appearing in the literature deal with mean-square error at the equalizer output (or a related signal-to-noise ratio). Reference [6] provides a good treatment of this approach, and [11, 12] summarize several known results. Using bounding techniques, certain approximations to the probability of error can be related to the output mean-square error or signal-to-noise ratio; these are derived and summarized in [11] with numerical examples provided in [12]. References [11, 12] are broader in scope than equalization in that diversity is included in the formulation given in these references. In considering the relative mean-square errors for linear (transversal filter) and decision feedback equalizers, [11] derives the following chain of inequalities:

$$\text{MSE}_{mf} \le \text{MSE}_{od} \le \text{MSE}_o \tag{3-146}$$

where MSE_o, MSE_{od}, and MSE_{mf} are the mean-square errors of the linear equalizer, decision feedback equalizer, and optimum detector with no intersymbol interference (called the matched filter bound), respectively. In addition, [11] provides expressions for computing each of these mean-square errors (as does [6] and other references). If zero forcing tap weights are used and very long equalizers are assumed, the mean-square error is solely due to output noise, and these expressions for the linear and decision feedback equalizers are, respectively,

$$\text{MSE}_o = \frac{T_b}{2\pi} \int_{-\pi/T_b}^{\pi/T_b} \frac{N_0}{S(\omega)} \, d\omega \tag{3-147}$$

and

$$\text{MSE}_{od} = \exp\left\{ -\frac{T_b}{2\pi} \int_{-\pi/T_b}^{\pi/T_b} \ln\left[\frac{S(\omega)}{N_0} \right] d\omega \right\} \tag{3-148}$$

T_b and N_0 are the bit interval and single-sided noise power spectral density, respectively, as before and

$$S(\omega) = \sum_{\text{all } \ell} r(\ell) e^{j\omega T_b \ell} \tag{3–149}$$

is the Fourier transform of the autocorrelation function of the channel output pulse-shape, $p(t)$, given by

$$r(\ell) = \int_{-\infty}^{\infty} p(\lambda)\, p^*(\lambda + \ell T_b)\, d\lambda \tag{3–150}$$

If zero forcing is not used, (3–147) and (3–148) are slightly more complicated [11]. In the zero-forcing case, since the output noise is Gaussian, the probability of error, conditioned on any random channel parameters, is bounded by

$$P_E \le \exp\left(-\frac{1}{\text{MSE}}\right) \tag{3–151}$$

Numerical bound results for several channel models and signaling techniques are plotted in [12].

Actual estimates for the probability of error must be done by simulation or measurement. We close this subsection with examples of decision feedback equalizer performance shown in Figure 3–17 for two different channel unit pulse responses (sample values given above the figure). Simulation is necessary in the case of decision feedback equalizer performance characterization due to the nonlinear nature of the feedback structure.

A current area receiving much attention is blind system identification and estimation [18].

3.5   A DIGITAL COMMUNICATION SYSTEM SIMULATION EXAMPLE

In this section, we consider a simple digital communication system simulation. Instead of using an optimum correlation or matched filter detector for a data sequence represented by antipodal rectangular pulses, the receiver consists of a Butterworth filter with the output sampled at bit intervals and the resulting samples compared with a threshold of zero. Because of the transient response of the filter, intersymbol interference exists between adjacent samples. The idea is to sample at the optimum delay past the beginning of a given pulse so that this intersymbol interference is minimized. The simulation program steps through a range of delays (which is an input at the beginning of the program) and plots the bit error probability versus delay for a given E_b/N_0 (also in input as is the order of the filter and its bandwidth). The MATLAB simulation program is given below followed by a typical simulation with a plot of the output.

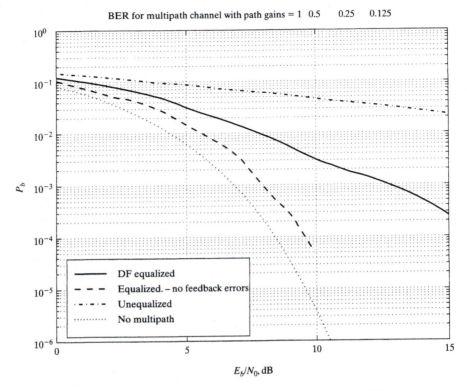

FIGURE 3–17   Decision feedback equalizer performance for two different channels (no forward transversal filter; backward tap weights match channel impulse response).

EXAMPLE 3–13 SIMULATION EXAMPLE

```
%Example 3-13
%
Eb_N0_dB = input('Enter Eb/N0 in dB ');
samp_bit = input('Enter number of samples per bit used in simulation ');
n_order = input('Enter order of Butterworth detection filter ');
BWT_bit = input('Enter filter bandwidth normalized by bit rate ');
delay_min = input('Enter beginning delay,s,for lining up data & output;
>=del_t; < 2*Tbit ');
delay_max = input('Enter ending delay, s, for lining up data and output ');
N_bits = input('Enter total number of bits in simulation ')
s = sign(rand(1,N_bits)-.5);    % Generate sequence of random polarities
L_s = length(s);
data = 0.5*(s+1);               % Logical data is sequence of 1s and 0s
Eb_N0 = 10^(Eb_N0_dB/10);       % Convert desired Eb/N0 from dB to ratio
T_bit = 1;                      % Arbitrarily take bit time as 1 second
BW = BWT_bit/T_bit;             % Compute filter bandwidth from BW*T_bit
```

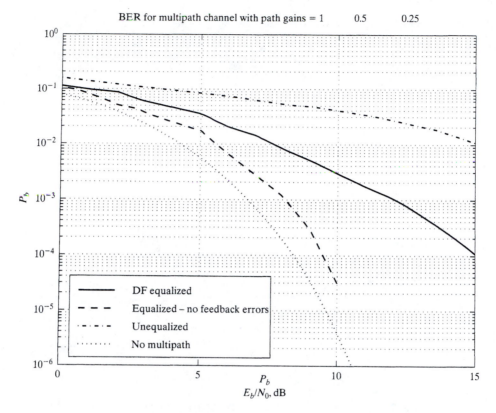

FIGURE 3–17 *Continued*

```
[num,den] = butter(n_order,2*BW*pi,'s');  % Obtain filter num/den
                                             coefficients
Eb = T_bit;                    % Bit energy is T_bit, assuming amplitude = 1
N0 = Eb/Eb_N0;                 % Compute noise spectral density from Eb/N0
del_t = T_bit/samp_bit ,       % Compute sampling interval
sigma_n = sqrt(N0/(2*del_t));  % Compute variance of noise samples
t=0:del_t:L_s*T_bit-del_t;     % Set up time axis
sig = [];
for l = 1:N_bits               % Each symbol is really samp_bit samples
    sig = [sig hold_in(s(l), samp_bit)];   % hold_in:user-defined function
end
delay = [];                    % Make sure various arrays are empty
Perror = [];
bits_out = [];
y_det = [];
dd_stop=fix((delay_max-delay_min)/del_t)+1 % Number of delay steps
noise=sigma_n*randn(size(sig)); % Form sequence of Gaussian noise samples
```

```
y=(lsim(num,den,sig+noise,t))'; % Filter signal plus noise through the
                               chosen filter
n_count = [];
for dd = 1:dd_stop  % Step through sampling delays to determine min. Perror
    delay(dd) = fix(delay_min/del_t) + (dd-1);
% detect is a user-defined function to sample filter output at T-bit intervals
%and estimate output bits, depending on whether given sample > 0 or not
 bits_out = detect(y, N_bits, samp_bit, delay(dd));
 error_array = abs(bits_out-data);   %Error array element = error
 for m=1:5 error_array(m) = 0;            % Don't count errors in 1st 5 bits
                                      due to transients

end
SS = sum(error_array);           % Total number of errors
n_count(dd) = SS;
Perror(dd) = SS/(L_s-5);         % Ratio of errors to total bits in block
end
disp(delay*del_t)
disp(Perror)
format short
[PP KK] = min(Perror);
MM = -fix(-log10(PP))-1;
d0 = delay(KK)*del_t;
display('Error counts:')  % Display the no. of errors counted for each case
display(n_count)
display('min. Perror and delay at which it occurs; Tbit = 1')
display(PP)
display(d0)                         % Display minimum Perror and delay at which
                                     it occurred
%     Plot estimate of bit error probability versus sampling delay
semilogy(delay*del_t,Perror),xlabel('sample delay/T_b_i_t'),ylabel
('P_b'),...
    axis([delay_min delay_max 10^MM 1]),...
    text(d0+.01,.9*PP,['Min. Pe; delay = ',num2str(PP),', ',num2str(d0)]),...
      title(['BER versus delay; Eb/N0 = ',num2str(Eb_N0_dB),' dB; filter
      order =',num2str(n_order),'; filter BW*T_b_i_t = ',num2str(BWT_bit)])
print c:\dig_comm\pscrp_fl\ex3_12 -deps %print curve to ps file

%   hold_in(input, k) function holds an input sample for k samples
%
function output = hold_in(in,k)
output = [];
L=length(in);
b = ones(k,1)*in;
output = reshape(b,1,L*k);

%   detect(y, N, samp_bit, samp_delay): detector for antipodal
%   signaling; y is input data vector; N is number of bits; samp_bit
%   is no. samples per bit; samp_delay is delay from beginning of bit
%   of sample used to make decision
%
function bits_out = detect(y, N, samp_bit , samp_delay)
bits_out = [];
```

```
if samp_delay > samp_bit
    for n = 1:N-1
        if y((n-1)*samp_bit+samp_delay) > 0
            bits_out(n) = 1;
        elseif y((n-1)*samp_bit+samp_delay) < 0
            bits_out(n) = 0;
        end
    end
    bits_out = [bits_out 0];
else
    for n = 1:N
        if y((n-1)*samp_bit+samp_delay) > 0
            bits_out(n) = 1;
        elseif y((n-1)*samp_bit+samp_delay) < 0
            bits_out(n) = 0;
        end
    end
end
```

The command window input for a typical run is given below. Figure 3–18 shows the results.

EDU» ex3_12
Enter Eb/N0 in dB 7
Enter number of samples per bit used in simulation 5
Enter order of Butterworth detection filter 2
Enter filter bandwidth normalized by bit rate .7
Enter beginning delay,s,for lining up data & output; >=del_t; < 2*Tbit .2
Enter ending delay, s, for lining up data and output 1.6
Enter total number of bits in simulation 1600

Error counts:
  830   757   224   22   8   2   75   606

It is important to know the confidence that can be associated with simulated data points. The computation of confidence intervals for Monte Carlo estimation of the bit error probability is dealt with in [19], where a number of approaches to computing the $100\alpha\%$ confidence intervals of the Monte Carlo simulated bit error probability estimates is given. One approximation makes use of the fact that, due to the Central Limit Theorem, the relative frequency approximation for a given bit error probability tends to a Gaussian random variable for N, the number of simulated bits, large. If the number of errors counted for a given case is denoted as r, the approximate upper and lower boundaries of the confidence interval for this data point, u_c and l_c, are found from the equations

$$\int_{-\infty}^{r/N} \frac{1}{\sqrt{2\pi[u_c(1-u_c)/N]}} \exp\left[-\frac{(y-u_c)^2}{2[u_c(1-u_c)/N]}\right] dy = \frac{1-\alpha}{2}$$

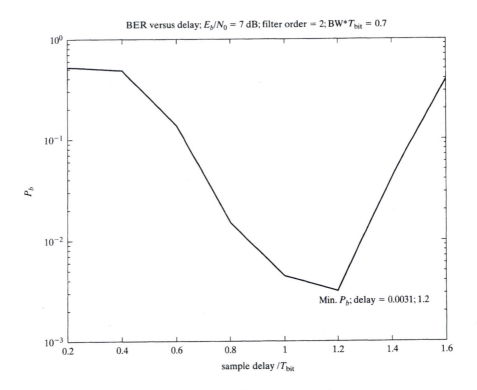

BER versus delay; $E_b/N_0 = 7$ dB; filter order $= 2$; BW*$T_{bit} = 0.7$

Min. P_b; delay $= 0.0031$; 1.2

sample delay /T_{bit}

FIGURE 3–18   Output of the simulation program of Example 3–14.

and $\displaystyle\int_{r/N}^{\infty} \frac{1}{\sqrt{2\pi[l_c\,(1 - l_c)/N]}}\, \exp\left[-\frac{(y - l_c)^2}{2[l_c\,(1 - l_c)/N]} \right] dy = \frac{1 - \alpha}{2}$

These may be solved in closed form to yield

$$u_c = \left(\frac{2r + d^2}{2N + 2d^2} \right) + \left(\frac{d}{2N + 2d^2} \sqrt{\frac{4rN + Nd^2 - 4r^2}{N}} \right)$$

$$\text{and } l_c = \left(\frac{2r + d^2}{2N + 2d^2} \right) - \left(\frac{d}{2N + 2d^2} \sqrt{\frac{4rN + Nd^2 - 4r^2}{N}} \right) \qquad (3\text{–}152)$$

$$\text{where } \int_{d}^{\infty} \frac{\exp(-y^2/2)}{\sqrt{2\pi}}\, dy = \frac{1 - \alpha}{2}$$

For example, if we evaluate (3–152) for a delay of $1.2T_b$ (the minimum error probability simulated) at a confidence level of 80% using $N = 1600$ and $r = 5$, we get $d = 1.2817$, $u_c = 0.0036 + 0.0019 = 0.0055$, and $l_c = 0.0036 - 0.0019 = 0.0017$. This tells us that the actual error probability is not greater than 0.0055 or less than 0.0017 with a confidence of 80%.

3.6   NOISE EFFECTS IN PULSE CODE MODULATION

In Section 2.6.5, the use of pulse code modulation (PCM) for transmission of analog signals was briefly discussed. In this section, we resume this discussion and give a simplified derivation of the noise performance of PCM. In PCM, distortion can arise in two main ways. The first is quantization error that was discussed in Section 2.6.5 and that we consider further here. The second is a result of bit errors that occur from transmission of the PCM data through a noisy channel, and we consider this source of error in this section also. The third way is through saturation of the A-to-D (analog-to-digital) converter, which means that the amplitude of the signal exceeds the maximum range that can be represented by the A-to-D converter. This is a complex issue, and the reader is referred to Sklar [20] for further discussion. Another way that error can enter a PCM system is through clock jitter, where the clock necessary for the reconstruction process at the receiver is not in perfect synchronism with the transmitter clock. This is a difficult problem, and we do not consider it here.

The simplified analysis given here follows closely that given in [19]. Let $x(t)$ be a lowpass signal of bandwidth W. After sampling at a rate $f_s > 2W$ and quantizing, the ith quantized signal sample can be represented as

$$x_q(t_i) = x(t_i) + \varepsilon_q(t_i) \tag{3-153}$$

where $x(t_i)$ represents the true sample value of the analog signal and $\varepsilon(t_i)$ is the error due to quantizing. Suppose that the quantizer is of the midtread type as illustrated in Figure 3–19a. Then from the quantizing error plot of Figure 3–19b, is clear that the quantizing error is bounded by

$$-\frac{\Delta}{2} \le \varepsilon_q(t_i) \le \frac{\Delta}{2} \tag{3-154}$$

We assume that $\varepsilon_q(t_i)$ is uniformly distributed throughout the interval $(-\Delta/2, \Delta/2)$ so that the mean-square error due to quantizing is

$$\overline{\varepsilon_q^2} = \frac{1}{\Delta} \int_{-\Delta/2}^{\Delta/2} \varepsilon^2 \, d\varepsilon = \frac{\Delta^2}{12} \tag{3-155}$$

The signal-to-noise ratio due to quantizing is defined as

$$(\text{SNR})_Q = \frac{\overline{x^2(t_i)}}{\overline{\varepsilon_q^2(t_i)}} = 12\frac{\overline{x^2(t_i)}}{\Delta^2} \tag{3-156}$$

If $x(t_i)$ is uniformly distributed throughout the quantizer range of $\pm\frac{1}{2}q\Delta$, where q is the number of quantization levels, then

$$\overline{x^2(t_i)} = \frac{1}{q\Delta} \int_{-q\Delta/2}^{q\Delta/2} x^2 \, dx = \frac{(q\Delta)^2}{12} \tag{3-157}$$

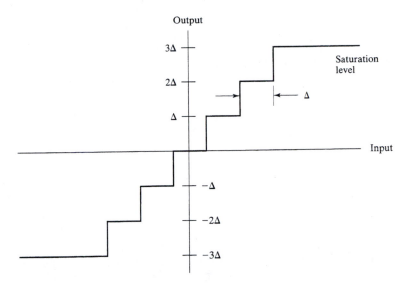

(a) Quantizer input-output characteristic

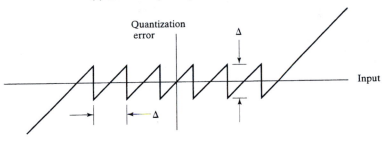

(b) Quantization error

FIGURE 3–19 Midtread type of quantizer with its quantization error characteristic.

and the signal-to-noise ratio due to quantizing error becomes

$$(\text{SNR})_Q = q^2 = 2^{2n} \tag{3–158}$$

where it is assumed that $q = 2^n$ (i.e., n bits are used to represent each sample). Equation (3–158) is a well-known result. When expressed in decibels, it becomes

$$10\log_{10}(\text{SNR})_Q = 20n \log_{10} 2 = 6.02n \tag{3–159}$$

That is, each additional bit used in quantizing amounts to roughly 6 dB more in signal-to-quantization-noise ratio.

   To put the foregoing result in terms of bandwidth, we note that at a minimum sampling rate of $2W$ samples per second the maximum time between samples is $T_{s,\,max} = 1/(2W)$. Thus each bit can have a maximum duration of

$$T_{b,\max} = \frac{T_{s,\max}}{n} = \frac{1}{2nW} \tag{3-160}$$

The bandwidth required to transmit a bit through a communication channel is proportional to $T_{b,\max}^{-1}$. Therefore, the required transmission bandwidth is

$$B_{T,\min} = \frac{k}{T_{b,\max}} = 2kWn \text{ Hz} \tag{3-161}$$

where k is the proportionality constant. That is, $(SNR)_Q$ is improved through adding bits, but the cost is increased transmission bandwidth.

Consider now the second error source—that due to channel errors. Assume that a binary communication system with error probability P_b is used to transmit the n bits representing a signal sample through the channel. The probability of a sample being received in error is

$$P_w = 1 - (1 - P_b)^n \tag{3-162}$$

However, the mean-square error due to channel errors depends on the particular bit of a sample word is in error. For the least significant bit, the error is bounded by

$$-\frac{\Delta}{2} \le \varepsilon_w \le \frac{\Delta}{2} \quad \text{(LSB)} \tag{3-163}$$

while for the most significant bit the error is

$$-\frac{q\Delta}{2} \le \varepsilon_w \le \frac{q\Delta}{2} \quad \text{(MSB)} \tag{3-164}$$

We assume that ϵ_w is uniformly distributed throughout the range (3–164), which gives a mean-square error due to channel errors of

$$\overline{\varepsilon_w^2} = (q\Delta)^2/12 \tag{3-165}$$

The total mean-square error at the receiver output is

$$\overline{\varepsilon^2} = \overline{\varepsilon_q^2}(1 - P_w) + \overline{\varepsilon_w^2} P_w \tag{3-166}$$

The signal-to-noise ratio at the D-A (digital-to-analog) converter output is

$$SNR = \frac{(q\Delta)^2/12}{\Delta^2(1 - P_w)/12 + (q\Delta)^2 P_w/12} = [1 + (2^{-2n} - 1)(1 - P_b)^n]^{-1} \tag{3-167}$$

where $q = 2^n$ has been substituted along with (3–155) and (3–165).

Now P_b is dependent on E_b/N_0. To consider an easy case, we substitute the expression for binary antipodal signaling given by (3–34). Thus the signal-to-noise ratio at the receiver is

$$SNR = \left\{1 + (2^{-2n} - 1)\left[1 - Q\left(\sqrt{\frac{2E_b}{N_0}}\right)\right]^n\right\}^{-1} \tag{3-168}$$

This is plotted in Figure 3–20 for several values of *n*. Note that a threshold exists for each curve below which the signal-to-noise ratio falls off rapidly due to channel-induced errors and above which the mean-square error due to channel errors is essentially 0. The performance could be improved further by decreasing the quantizing error via companding. An alternative to companding is to use nonuniform quantization intervals, with smaller ones at small input signal levels and larger ones at high signal levels. Note that the distribution of the input samples in an important consideration in quantizer performance and compander design.

It is important to review once again why one would employ digital transmission of analog data. First, we note that the error can be made almost independent of the channel noise through proper design. Repeaters can be placed at frequent enough intervals in the channel to provide an error probability that essentially makes the channel-induced error 0. Second, we can easily trade off bandwidth for less quantization noise as pointed out with respect to (3–161).

Finally, representation of analog messages in digital format makes it easy to put several signals through the same channel by time division multiplexing (TDM). These messages can be interlaced on a bit-by-bit format or they can be interlaced on a word-by-

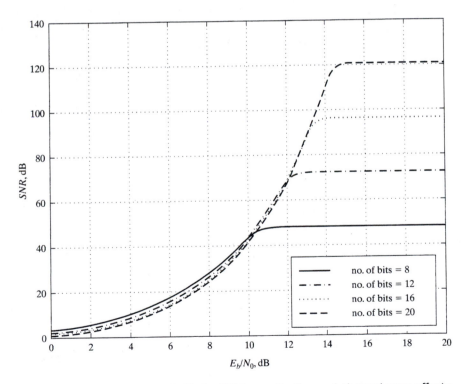

FIGURE 3–20   SNR versus E_b/N_0 for PCM; quantization and channel error effects included.

word basis. For example, the T1 carrier system for TDM telephone transmission in the United States consists of 24 channels, each channel consisting of 8-bit words representing samples taken at 8 kHz rates (one sample per 125 μsec) from each telephone conversation [20]. Thus, in each frame there are 192 bits representing telephone conversations plus 1 bit added for frame synchronization. If b_{ij} represents the jth bit in the ith channel and f represents the framing bit, the frame sequence is as follows:

$$f\, b_{11} b_{12} b_{13} b_{14} b_{15} b_{16} b_{17} b_{18} b_{21} b_{22} b_{23} b_{24} b_{25} b_{26} b_{27} b_{28} b_{31} b_{32} b_{33} b_{34} \cdots b_{24,8}$$

Each bit is (125 μseconds)/(193 bits/frame) = 0.6477 microseconds (μs) in duration and is represented in bipolar format (see Chapter 5) so that no DC component exists on the line. The framing bit for the even-numbered frames follows the sequence 001110, and for the odd-numbered frames, it follows the sequence 101010. This allows the signaling information, which consists of the eighth bit of each of the 24 channels on every sixth frame, to be identified. The data rate corresponding to a 0.6477 μs bit time is 1.5444 Mbits/s, requiring a minimum channel bandwidth of 1.544 MHz. This is about a factor of 11 more than would be required if the voice messages were stacked up in contiguous frequency bands (i.e., frequency division multiplexing, or FDM). Yet, with a TDM system it is easy to intermix analog messages and digital data, which makes it more attractive than FDM. With the advent of optical fiber channels, the bandwidth question becomes even more moot.

There are many more interesting aspects of representing analog sources in digital format. One is the question of idle noise. This is noise that arises due to quantization when no signal is present at the quantizer input. A similar problem occurs if a signal that is constant or varies very little is present at the quantizer input. A cure for this is to add a small amount of random noise to the signal before quantizing. This is called *dithering* and provides a small random error at the output of the quantizer rather than a constant large error (smaller than $\Delta/2$, of course). In effect the "bad" constant error at the quantizer output has been replaced by "good" random error. For further discussion, the reader is referred to Sklar [20].

3.7 SUMMARY

1. The simplest case of data transmission system analysis was considered in this chapter. The assumptions that make it so include the following: (a) additive, white Gaussian noise is the only perturbing factor; (b) the signal set is known exactly at the receiver, including shape and arrival time; and (c) the channel is linear. Nevertheless, several practical systems in use fit this model.
2. For the ideal model outlined under point 1, the resulting receiver hypothesized consists of a linear filter whose output is sampled at the end of each signaling interval, and these samples are compared with a threshold. The filter is optimized by choosing its frequency response function such that the peak signal-to-rms-noise ratio is maximized at its output at the sampling time. Such a filter is known as a matched filter because its impulse response is the time reverse of the signal shape.

3. Three basic binary signaling schemes, characterized in terms of probability of error versus signal energy-to-noise-spectral-density ratio, E_b/N_0, are *antipodal, orthogonal,* and *on-off signaling.* Antipodal performs the best with orthogonal and on-off performing 3 dB worse. A convenient number to remember is that antipodal signaling requires $E_b/N_0 = 10.54$ dB to give a probability of bit error of 10^{-6}.

4. The combination of optimum filtering at the transmitter and receiver was investigated to combat the effects of channel filtering. Filter frequency responses were found that provide an intersymbol-interference-free pulse out of the detection filter, thereby combating the detrimental effects of channel filtering.

5. Spectra of transmitted pulse trains can be shaped by introducing controlled memory between the pulses. An example of such shaping is the dicode pulse train.

6. Duobinary signaling can be used to avoid the use of rectangular-passband transmission filters and limit the transmitted signal band width to $R/2$ where R is the data rate in bits per second. A loss in E_b/N_0 over antipodal signaling is imposed.

7. Equalization filters provide a means for undoing the adverse effects of channel filtering. Two means for setting the tap weights were examined: zero forcing and minimum-mean-square error. Adaptive techniques can be used to adjust the tap weights if the channel characteristics are unknown or if they change slowly with time.

8. The use of PCM for transmission of analog messages was considered in a simple case. At high channel signal-to-noise ratios, the received signal-to-quantization noise ratio is dependent only on the number of quantization levels, or bits transmitted. The more bits, or correspondingly the higher transmission bandwidth, the higher the received signal-to-noise ratio. At lower signal-to-noise ratios a threshold effect sets in due to channel errors.

REFERENCES

[1] M. K. Simon, "A New Twist on the Marcum Q-Function and its Application," *IEEE Commun. Letters*, Vol. 2, pp. 39–41, Feb. 1998.

[2] G. L. Stuber, *Principles of Mobile Communication* (Boston: Kluwer, 1996).

[3] A. Lender, "The Duobinary Technique for High Speed Data Transmission," *IEEE Trans. Commun. Electron.*, Vol. 82, pp. 214–218, May 1963.

[4] S. Pasupathy, "Correlative Coding—A Bandwidth Efficient Signaling Scheme," *IEEE Commun. Magazine*, Vol. 15, pp. 4–11, July 1977.

[5] S. Qureshi, "Adaptive Equalization," *IEEE Commun. Magazine*, Vol. 20, pp. 9–16, Mar. 1982.

[6] J. G. Proakis, *Digital Communications*, 3rd ed. (New York: McGraw-Hill, 1995).

[7] M. Simon, S. Hinedi, and W. Lindsey, *Digital Communication Techniques: Signal Design and Detection* (Upper Saddle River, NJ: Prentice Hall, 1995).

[8] H. Meyr, M. Moeneclaey, and S. Fechtel, *Digital Communication Receivers* (New York: John Wiley, 1997).

[9] R. Blahut, *Digital Transmission of Information* (Reading, MA: Addison Wesley, 1990).

[10] J. Proakis, "Channel Equalization," in *The Communications Handbook* (Boca Raton, FL: CRC Press, 1997).

[11] P. Balaban and J. Salz, "Optimum Diversity Combining and Equalization in Digital Data Transmission with Applications to Cellular Mobile Radio—Part I: Theoretical Considerations," *IEEE Trans. Commun.*, Vol. 40, pp. 885–894, May 1992.

[12] P. Balaban and J. Salz, "Optimum Diversity Combining and Equalization in Digital Data Transmission with Applications to Cellular Mobile Radio—Part II: Numerical Results," *IEEE Trans. Commun.*, Vol. 40, pp. 895–907, May 1992.

[13] J. Treichler, I. Fijalkow, and C. Johnson, Jr., "Fractionally Spaced Equalizers," *IEEE Signal Proc. Magazine*, Vol. 13, pp. 65–81, May 1996.

[14] S. Haykin, *Adaptive Filter Theory*, 3rd ed. (Upper Saddle River, NJ: Prentice Hall, 1996).

[15] E. A. Lee and D. G. Messerschmitt, *Digital Communication* (Boston: Kluwer Academic Publishers, 1988).

[16] B. Widrow and S. D. Stearns, *Adaptive Signal Processing* (Upper Saddle River, NJ: Prentice Hall, 1985).

[17] G. Forney, Jr., "Maximum-Likelihood Sequence Estimation of Digital Sequences in the Presence of Intersymbol Interference," *IEEE Trans. on Inf. Theory*, Vol. IT-18, pp. 363–378, May 1972.

[18] *Proc. IEEE*, Special Issue on Blind System Identification and Estimation, Vol. 86, Oct. 1998.

[19] K. Kosbar and T. Chang, "Interval Estimation and Monte Carlo Simulation of Digital Communication Systems," *MILCOM '92 Conference Record*, pp. 3.3.1–3.3.5, Nov. 1992.

[20] B. Sklar, *Digital Communications: Fundamentals and Applications* (Upper Saddle River, NJ: Prentice Hall, 1988).

PROBLEMS

3–1. Substitute (3–6) and (3–7) into (3–8) and (3–9), respectively, and this result into (3–10). Differentiate with respect to V_T, set the result equal to zero, and derive (3–11). Hint: Leibnitz's rule for differentiation of an integral is

$$\frac{dI}{dx} = \frac{d}{dx} \int_{A(x)}^{B(x)} F(u,x)\,du$$

$$= F[B(x),x]\frac{dB(x)}{dx} - F[A(x),x]\frac{dA(x)}{dx} + \int_{A(x)}^{B(x)} \frac{\partial F(u,x)}{\partial x}\,du$$

3–2. Obtain (3–13) for the special case where $p = q = \frac{1}{2}$ and V_T is given by (3–12).

3–3. **(a)** Find the matched filter impulse response and peak output signal squared to output noise variance of the filter for the following impulse responses. Assume $N_0/2 = 1$ (A, B, C, and D are constants)

    (i) $g(t) = A\Lambda\,(t-1)$

    (ii) $g(t) = B\Pi\left(\dfrac{t-2}{4}\right)$

    (iii) $g(t) = C\Lambda\,(t)u\,(t)$

    (iv) $g(t) = D[u(t) - 2u(t-1) + 2u(t-2) - u(t-3)]$ where $u(t)$ is the unit step.

  (b) Obtain the transfer function of the matched filter in each case.

3–4. Verify (3–21) or (3–22) as the case may be for the following:

(a) $\mathbf{A} = 3\mathbf{i} + 2\mathbf{j} + \mathbf{k}$; $\mathbf{B} = 5\mathbf{i} + 7\mathbf{j} + 2\mathbf{k}$

(b) $X(f) = \Pi\left(\dfrac{f}{2B}\right)$; $Y(f) = \Lambda\left(\dfrac{f}{B}\right)$

3–5. Write a MATLAB program to compute and plot the curves of Figure 3–5. That is plot the bit error probability versus E_b/N_0 curves for binary antipodal and orthogonal signaling.

3–6. (a) Given that the bandwidth of a baseband square pulse of the form $\Pi(t/T_b)$ is approximately $1/T_b$ (from 0 frequency to the first null of the sinc-function signal spectrum), compare the bandwidths required of antipodal and orthogonal baseband signaling.

(b) Suppose a channel bandwidth of 5 kHz is available. Based on your results in (a), what is the maximum data rate possible through the channel using (i) antipodal and (ii) orthogonal baseband signaling?

(c) What are the relative powers required to obtain a certain bit error probability at a given data rate for the system of (b) (i.e., twice as much for which one?)

(d) Based on your conclusions above, why do you suppose that orthogonal signaling might be the signaling of choice in some situations?

3–7. Repeat Example 3–5, but for $P_b = 10^{-5}$. How do the answers change if the bandwidth is halved?

3–8. (a) Modify the factor F found in Example 3–7 so that it applies to any roll-off factor β.

(b) Using numerical integration, compute the degradation (i.e., $10 \log_{10} F$ as a function of β.

3–9. Show that trapezoidal spectrum, as illustrated below, satisfies Nyquist's pulse shaping criterion. Find the corresponding pulse shape function and show that zeros do indeed appear at the proper time sample values.

3–10. Redo the derivation of Section 3.3.3 for the case where the transmitter pulses are not ideal impulses but, rather, have a shape $p_t(t)$ with $\int_{-\infty}^{\infty}|p_t(t)|^2\,dt < \infty$. In particular, obtain equations to replace (3–66), (3–67), and (3–68).

3–11. Redo Example 3–8 for the case where $b_0 = 1$ and $b_1 = -0.5$.

3–12. Find the optimum transmitting and receive filters assuming a raised cosine spectrum with $\beta = 0.25$, a channel magnitude-squared transfer function of $|H_c(f)|^2 = 1/(1 + (f/f_c)^2)$, and a white noise spectral density $G_n(f) = N_0/2$. Plot for the following cases:

(a) $f_c = \dfrac{1}{4T_b}$;

(b) $f_c = \dfrac{1}{2T_b}$;

(c) $f_c = \dfrac{1}{T_b}$.

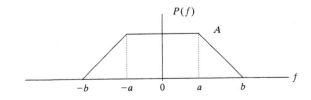

3–13. The samples of a single pulse at the output of a certain channel are 0.02, –0.10, 0.2, –0.2, 1.0, –0.1 0.1, 0.05, and –0.01, where the spacing is the symbol duration.

    (a) Find the coefficients of a three-tap transversal filter equalizer (zero-forcing) that will provide one zero either side of the main pulse response.

    (b) What are the sample values of the equalizer output at ±2 and ±3 sampling times away from the maximum?

3–14. **(a)** Go through the steps in obtaining the matrix (3–126). Write a MATLAB program to evaluate it for various parameter values and solve (3–118). Make your program general for any N.

    (b) For $E_b/N_0 = 7$ dB find the equalizer coefficients.

    (c) For $E_b/N_0 = 7$ dB find the eigenvalues of $\mathbf{R}_{yy}$. What is the range on β for convergence of the adaptive equalizer weights?

3–15. Evaluate (3–147) and (3–148) for $p(t) = \sqrt{\dfrac{2E}{\tau_0}}\exp\left(-t/\tau_0\right)u(t)$ where $u(t)$ is the unit step. Use numerical techniques. Truncate (3–149) at three terms and five terms to determine the dependence on number of terms in the sum.

3–16. Write a MATLAB simulation program to estimate the bit probability of error for a zero-forcing equalizer. Use a tapped-delay line model for the channel. It is suggested that it incorporate Prob. 3–17.

3–17. Write a MATLAB program to reproduce the curves of Fig. 3–17. Incorporate Problem 3–16.

3–18. Rewrite the simulation of Example 3–14 so that the data are processed in contiguous blocks rather than large arrays of length N_bits. This will prevent swapping between RAM and the hard disk for excessively large numbers of bits simulated. Also see if you can come up with a way to avoid the use of for loops in the main program and subprogram detect (·).

3–19. Write a computer program to evaluate the confidence interval bounds as expressed by (3–152). Determine confidence intervals for the data points shown in Figure 3–18.

3–20. Derive the relationship $Q(x) = (1/\pi)\int_0^{\pi/2}\exp[-x^2/(2\sin^2\phi)]d\phi$ (Hint: See the paper by M. Alouini & A. Goldsmith, *IEEE Trans. Commun.*, vol. 47, pp. 1324–1334, Sept. 1999, App. A).

3–21. Redo the curves of Figure 3–20 for binary orthogonal signaling.

4

Signal–Space Methods
in Digital Data Transmission

4.1 INTRODUCTION

Basic techniques for the transmission of digital data through communication channels are introduced in this chapter. Attention is focused on a simplified model for the digital data transmission problem, which includes the following features:

1. For the most part, one shot modulation schemes, where the decisions are based only on the current symbol, are considered. This means that the signals can be resolved into orthogonal basis sets, and the transmitted signal expressed as

$$x_c(t) = \text{Re}\left[A \sum_{k=1}^{K} S_k \phi_k(t) \exp(j2\pi f_0 t) \right] \tag{4–1}$$

   where A is the amplitude, f_0 is the carrier frequency in hertz, and $\phi_k(t)$ is a set of orthonormal functions.
2. The noise introduced by the channel is modeled as additive, white, and Gaussian (AWGN) with two-sided power spectral density $N_0/2$, for $-\infty < f < \infty$.
3. The frequency of the received carrier is known exactly at the receiver. The phase of the received carrier may be known (coherent system) or random, but non-time-varying within a data symbol (noncoherent system).
4. The epochs of the symbols (bits) in the message sequence are known at the receiver.

Departures of practical digital communications systems from the idealized situation summarized above result in degradation from the performance of an ideal system. Some examples of departures from the ideal situation are the following:

1. Knowledge of the phase and/or frequency of the received carrier is imperfect at the receiver.
2. The timing derived at the receiver for the epochs of the digital data symbols is imperfect.
3. The noise may not be white.
4. The channel may introduce band limiting of the transmitted signal.

5. The noise may not be Gaussian, additive, or either.
6. Nonlinearities may be present in the channel either before or after introduction of the noise, or both.

In this chapter consideration is given to digital transmission systems that are, in general, nonbinary (or M-ary). A feature of the analysis techniques used in this chapter is that signal-space methods are used to give a geometric portrayal of the M-ary digital signaling problem. This allows a geometric interpretation of why various systems perform as they do. The receiver is assumed to be optimized according to a principle called the Bayes' criterion, which is designed to minimize a cost function, in this case the probability of making a decision error. Such receiver designs utilize parallel banks of correlation detectors followed by a decision-making operation that ultimately guesses the received signal to be the one that is closest in Euclidean distance to the possible transmitted signal in signal space. Because the minimum-distance receiver minimizes the probability of error cost function it is called a *minimum probability of error receiver.*

The communication system model that will be employed in this chapter is illustrated in Figure 4–1. A memoryless message source emits a sequence of messages $\{\ldots,$ $m_{-1}, m_0, m_1, \ldots, m_k, \ldots\}$ in time at rate R_m messages per second chosen from a finite-source alphabet $A = \{0, 1, 2, \ldots, q - 1\}$. For example, if $A = \{0, 1, 2\}$, a possible message sequence is $\{\ldots 2011022102 \ldots\}$. By *memoryless* it is meant that a source output, say, m_j, at a particular time is independent of all preceding and succeeding source outputs. The next operation in the block diagram of Figure 4–1 is to associate each possible block of J message symbols with one of M possible transmitted waveforms, $\{s_i(t): i = 1, 2, \ldots,$ $M\}$. For a q-symbol alphabet, it is therefore required that $q^J = M$ (it is assumed that

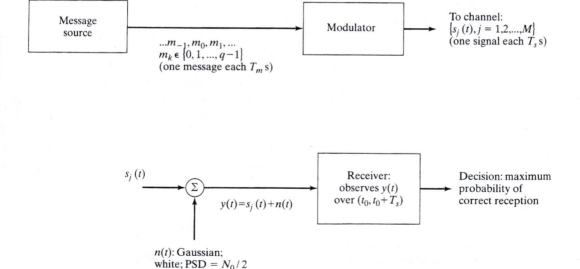

FIGURE 4–1   Block diagram of a digital communication system.

$q \leq M$). For example, with the binary alphabet, A = {0, 1}, all possible combinations of three-symbol messages can be associated with an eight-waveform modulator output according to the following table ($q = 2$, $J = 3$, and $M = 8$):

> 0 0 0: $s_1(t)$
> 0 0 1: $s_2(t)$
> 0 1 0: $s_3(t)$
> . . .
> 1 1 1: $s_8(t)$

The signals, each assumed to be of duration T_s, are sent through the channel in accordance with the message sequence emitted from the source. To avoid storing messages or having gaps in the transmitted signal sequence, the modulator signal duration T_s, must be related to the interval between messages, T_m, by

$$T_s = JT_m \text{ or } R_m = JR_s \tag{4-2}$$

where R_m and R_s are the message and symbol rates, respectively. Note that each $s_i(t)$ at the output of the modulator represents $\log_2 M$ bits. The *symbol rate* R_s and *bit rate* R_b through the channel are therefore related by

$$R_b = (\log_2 M)R_s \tag{4-3}$$

where R_b is in bits per second (bps) and R_s is in symbols per second. The channel is considered ideal in that it is infinite bandwidth and adds white Gaussian noise of two-sided power spectral density $N_0/2$ W/Hz to the transmitted signal. *Memory* may be introduced in some cases into the message sequence by encoding it before the modulation step is carried out. The effects of encoding will be considered in Chapters 6 through 8.

In order to make a decision, the receiver observes the received signal plus noise over a T_s-second interval,[1] which is assumed to be synchronized with the received signal sequence. It then processes these data so that its probability of estimating the signal correctly, given the received signal plus noise waveform, is maximized. Such a receiver, referred to as a maximum *a posteriori (MAP) receiver,* also minimizes the probability of error averaged over all possible received signals.

A general approach for finding the appropriate receiver structure is to resolve the received signal plus noise, hereafter referred to as the data, into a generalized vector space of dimension $K \leq M$. Although it may appear that this approach is unnecessary for simpler cases, the vector-space viewpoint can be made to fit virtually any signaling scheme of interest. In addition, it provides powerful insight into the relative performance of various signaling schemes. Finally, it also suggests two ways to implement the optimum receiver for a given signaling scheme (one is called the correlator implementation and the other is

---

[1]In some cases it is useful to observe the signal over a longer period than T_s. This possibility is considered in Chapter 7 where coded modulation is discussed.

known as matched filter realization). In the next section, therefore, the MAP criterion is expanded upon further and expressed in terms of generalized vector-space notation.

The end objective of this chapter is to be able to compare M-ary digital data transmission systems on the basis of power and bandwidth efficiency. It will be recalled from Chapter 1 that power efficiency refers to a modulation scheme's ability to convey information at a low error probability for a given signal-to-noise ratio, and its bandwidth efficiency refers to the information (usually measured in bits per second) conveyed per unit of bandwidth.

4.2 OPTIMUM RECEIVER PRINCIPLES IN TERMS OF VECTOR SPACES

4.2.1 Maximum a Posteriori Detectors

It is well known from statistical decision theory that a Bayes receiver, which is one that minimizes the average cost of making a decision, is implemented by means of the likelihood ratio test [1]. In the case of two alternative hypotheses, H_1 and H_2, this test is of the form

$$\Lambda(Z) = \frac{f_Z(Z \mid H_2)}{f_Z(Z \mid H_1)} \underset{H_1}{\overset{H_2}{\underset{<}{>}}} \frac{(C_{21} - C_{11})p_1}{(C_{12} - C_{22})p_2} \equiv \Lambda_0 \qquad (4\text{–}4)$$

where

$f_Z(Z \mid H_i)$ = probability density function on the data given that H_i was true
Z $\quad$ = data on which the decision is based
C_{ij} $\quad$ = cost of deciding hypothes is H_i when H_j was in actuality true
p_i $\quad$ = a priori probability that hypothesis H_i is true ($p_2 = 1 - p_1$)

The performance of a Bayes test is characterized by the average cost of making a decision. This average cost can be expressed in terms of two probabilities,

$$\begin{aligned} P_M &= P(\text{say } H_1 \text{ true} \mid H_2 \text{ really true}) \\ P_F &= P(\text{say } H_2 \text{ true} \mid H_1 \text{ really true}) \end{aligned} \qquad (4\text{–}5)$$

These probabilities are often referred to as the probabilities of a miss, P_M, and a false alarm, P_F, respectively. Their names are reminiscent of the application of decision theory to the field of radar detection beginning in World War II. In terms of P_M and P_F, the minimum average cost per decision is

$$C_{av} = p_1 C_{21} + p_2 C_{22} + p_2 (C_{12} - C_{22})P_M - p_1(C_{21} - C_{11})(1 - P_F) \qquad (4\text{–}6)$$

The special cost assignment

$C_{11} = C_{22} = 0$ (right decisions cost zero)
$C_{12} = C_{21}$ $\quad$ (either type of wrong decision is equally costly)

reduces the Bayes test to[2]

$$\frac{f_Z(Z \mid H_2)}{f_Z(Z \mid H_1)} \underset{H_1}{\overset{H_2}{\underset{<}{>}}} \frac{p_1}{p_2} \equiv \frac{P(H_1)}{P(H_2)} \tag{4–7}$$

where the notation $P(H_i)$ is used to emphasize that $p_i = P(H_i)$ is the *a priori* (i.e., before an observation) probability of H_i. This can be manipulated, using Bayes' rule, to

$$P(H_2 \mid Z) \underset{H_1}{\overset{H_2}{\underset{<}{>}}} P(H_1 \mid Z) \tag{4–8}$$

where $P(H_i \mid Z)$ is the probability of hypothesis H_i being true given the data Z. Because this modified test amounts to choosing the hypothesis corresponding to the largest *a posteriori* (i.e., after an observation) probability, $P(H_i \mid Z)$, it is referred to as a *maximum a posteriori test (MAP)* or *detector*. The average cost of a decision for a MAP detector, with $C_{12} = C_{21} = 1$, is given by

$$P_E = P_M P(H_2) + P_F P(H_1) \tag{4–9}$$

which is a minimum by virtue of the MAP test being a Bayes test. In other words, a MAP detector minimizes the average probability of making an error.

The MAP hypothesis test generalizes easily to multiple observations and multiple hypotheses. If the observed data are composed of K observations $\mathbf{Z} = (Z_1, Z_2, \ldots, Z_K)$ and M hypotheses, the M *a posteriori* probabilities,

$$P(H_i \mid Z_1, Z_2, \ldots, Z_K), \quad i = 1, 2, \ldots, M \tag{4–10}$$

are found and the hypothesis, H_j, corresponding to the largest probability is chosen as being true.

EXAMPLE 4–1

Consider the hypothesis-testing problem

$$\begin{aligned} H_1 &: Z = A + N \\ H_2 &: Z = -A + N \end{aligned} \tag{4–11}$$

with $P(H_1) = p$, $P(H_2) = 1 - p$, and N is a Gaussian random variable with zero mean and variance σ^2. Since $f_Z(Z) = f_Z(Z|H_1)P(H_1) + f_Z(Z|H_2)P(H_2)$ is independent of H_1 and H_2, we may express the MAP test as[3]

---

[2]A derivation of this test and the associated minimum cost can be found in [1], Chapter 9.

[3]Uppercase Z is used here because a test on the *observed data* is being formulated.

$$f_Z(Z \mid H_2) \, P(H_2) \underset{H_1}{\overset{H_2}{\underset{<}{\overset{>}{\,}}}} f_Z(Z \mid H_1) \, P(H_1) \tag{4-12}$$

Given H_1, Z is a Gaussian random variable of mean A and variance σ^2. Given H_2, Z is a Gaussian random variable of mean $-A$ and variance σ^2. Therefore,

$$f_Z(Z \mid H_1) = \frac{\exp\left[-(Z-A)^2/2\sigma^2\right]}{\sqrt{2\pi\sigma^2}}$$
$$f_Z(Z \mid H_2) = \frac{\exp\left[-(Z+A)^2/2\sigma^2\right]}{\sqrt{2\pi\sigma^2}} \tag{4-13}$$

The MAP test reduces to

$$(1-p)\exp\left[-\frac{(Z+A)^2}{2\sigma^2}\right] \underset{H_1}{\overset{H_2}{\underset{<}{\overset{>}{\,}}}} p\exp\left[-\frac{(Z-A)^2}{2\sigma^2}\right]$$

or, upon simplification,

$$Z \underset{H_1}{\overset{H_2}{\underset{<}{\overset{>}{\,}}}} \frac{\sigma^2}{2A}\ln\frac{1-p}{p} \tag{4-14}$$

If $p = \frac{1}{2}$, the test is "decide $+A$ if $Z > 0$ and $-A$ if $Z < 0$." If $p \neq \frac{1}{2}$ the test is biased in favor of the most probable hypothesis. If $p = \frac{1}{2}$, the probability of error, by (4–9), is

$$P_E = P_M = P_F = P(Z > 0 \mid H_2 \text{ true})$$
$$= \int_0^\infty \frac{\exp\left[-(z+A)^2/2\sigma^2\right]}{\sqrt{2\pi\sigma^2}}\,dz \tag{4-15}$$
$$= \int_{A/\sigma}^\infty \frac{\exp(-u^2/2)}{\sqrt{2\pi}}\,du = Q\left(\frac{A}{\sigma}\right)$$

where[4]

$$Q(u) = \int_u^\infty \frac{\exp(-t^2/2)}{\sqrt{2\pi}}\,dt \tag{4-16}$$

It is noted that the probability of error decreases monotonically with increasing A/σ.

---

[4]A handy proper integral representation of the Q-function is $Q(x) = (1/\pi)\int_0^{\pi/2}\exp(-x^2/(2\sin^2\theta))d\theta$, $x \geq 0$ (see M. K. Simon, "A New Twist on the Marcum Q-Function and Its Application," *IEEE Commun. Letters*, Vol. 2, pp. 39–41, Feb. 1998, for reference to the original publication of this result as well as a more general relation to be used later.

4.2.2   Vector-Space Representation of Signals [2]

4.2.2.1 *K*-Dimensional Signal–Space Representation of the Received Waveform.   The MAP criterion expressed by (4–8) is based on a finite number, K, of data samples. On the other hand, the observed signal plus noise, $z(t) = s_i(t) + n(t)$, $t_0 \le t \le t_0 + T_s$, in a digital communication system is a function of a continuous time variable that must be reduced to K numbers in order to apply the MAP criterion. This can be accomplished in various ways, but because the noise is white and Gaussian, an approach to the optimum receiver will be used here that is intuitively pleasing.

A K-dimensional generalized vector space is defined by the orthonormal basis function set $\phi_1(t), \phi_2(t), \ldots, \phi_K(t)$, where

$$\int_{t_0}^{t_0+T_s} \phi_i(t)\phi_j^*(t)\, dt = \begin{cases} 1, i = j \\ 0, i \neq j \end{cases} \tag{4–17}$$

In (4–17), the $\phi_i(t)$s may be complex and the asterisk denotes the complex conjugate. A method for choosing this basis set will be described shortly. The received signal plus noise, when resolved into this vector space, has components

$$Z_k = S_{ik} + N_k, \quad k = 1, 2, \cdots, K \tag{4–18}$$

for each $i = 1, 2, \ldots, M$, where

$$S_{ik} = \int_{t_0}^{t_0+T_s} s_i(t)\, \phi_k^*(t)\, dt$$

$$N_k = \int_{t_0}^{t_0+T_s} n(t)\, \phi_k^*(t)\, dt \tag{4–19}$$

The method of choosing the set $\{\phi_i(t), i = 1, 2, \ldots, K\}$ guarantees that any of the possible transmitted signals can be expressed as[5]

$$s_i(t) = \sum_{k=1}^{K} S_{ik}\phi_k(t), \quad t_0 \le t \le t_0 + T_s, K \le M \tag{4–20}$$

The noise, however, must be viewed as composed of two components, which are

$$n(t) = n_r(t) + n_p(t) \tag{4–21}$$

where

$$n_r(t) = \sum_{k=1}^{K} N_k\, \phi_k(t)$$

$$n_p(t) = n(t) - n_r(t) \tag{4–22}$$

Since $n(t)$ is a Gaussian process, the N_ks are Gaussian random variables.

----

[5]A representation of a continuous-time signal in the form of (4–20) is sometimes referred to as a generalized Fourier series.

The subscript r in $n_r(t)$ stands for "relevant," for this noise component is the only one relevant to making the decision as to which signal was sent. The subscript p in $n_p(t)$ denotes that it is statistically orthogonal[6] or "perpendicular" to $n_r(t)$ (this proof is left to the problems). Since $n(t)$ is Gaussian, so are $n_p(t)$ and $n_r(t)$ and, therefore, they are statistically independent random processes. Because $n_r(t)$ is independent of $n_p(t)$, $n_p(t)$ may be ignored in making the decision as to which signal was sent. Thus, in terms of making a decision, it is sufficient to consider

$$z(t) = \sum_{k=1}^{K} Z_k \phi_k(t) = \sum_{k=1}^{K} (S_{ik} + N_k) \phi_k(t) \qquad (4\text{–}23)$$

or, equivalently, the vector with components $(Z_1, Z_2, \ldots, Z_K)$. This is illustrated graphically in Figure 4–2 for $K = 3$. [The total received signal plus noise will be denoted as $y(t)$. We convey the fact that (4–23) excludes $n_p(t)$ by using $z(t)$.]

It follows that if any possible transmitted signal can be expressed in the form (4–20), the problem of representing the received waveform $z(t)$ in a generalized K-dimensional vector space, with components given by (4–18), for use in the *a posteriori* probabilities (4–8) is solved. In some cases, the choice of an appropriate set $\{\phi_k(t)\}$ may be obvious. For less obvious cases, a constructive technique, referred to as the Gram-Schmidt procedure, is given in the sequel.

4.2.2.2 Scalar Product. It is convenient first to generalize the notions of the dot product of two vectors and the magnitude of a vector to signals. The former is referred to as the *scalar product*, denoted as (u, v), and for two signals $u(t)$ and $v(t)$ for our purposes is defined as

$$(u,v) = \int_{t_0}^{t_0 + T_s} u(t) v^*(t) \, dt \qquad (4\text{–}24)$$

More generally, the scalar product is a (complex) scalar-valued function of two signals, $u(t)$ and $v(t)$, with the properties

 1. $(u, v) = (v, u)^*$.
 2. $(\alpha u, v) = \alpha(u, v)$ where α is a scalar (complex in general).
 3. $(u + v, w) = (u, w) + (v, w)$.
 4. $(u, u) \geq 0$ with equality if and only if $u \equiv 0$.

The concept of magnitude of a vector is generalized by the definition of the *norm*, $\|u\|$, of a signal, $u(t)$, which is defined in terms of the scalar product as

$$\|u\| = \sqrt{(u,u)} \qquad (4\text{–}25)$$

More generally, the norm is a nonnegative real number satisfying the properties

---

[6]Statistically orthogonal means that $n_p(t)$ and $n_r(t)$ are uncorrelated. Since they are also Gaussian, being uncorrelated means that they are also statistically independent.

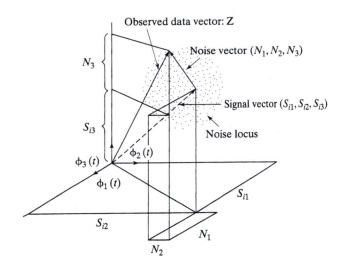

FIGURE 4–2   Signal-space representation of the received signal plus noise in a digital communication system.

1. $\|u\| = 0$ if and only if $u(t) = 0$.
2. $\|u + v\| \leq \|u\| + \|v\|$ (triangle inequality).
3. $\|\alpha u\| = |\alpha| \, \|u\|$, where α is a scalar.

Note that $\|u\|^2 = \int_{t_0}^{t_0+T_s} |u(t)|^2 \, dt$ is the energy contained in $u(t)$ if (4–24) is used as the definition of the scalar product.

The construction of orthonormal basis function sets is considered next.

4.2.2.3 Gram-Schmidt Procedure.   Given a finite set of signals $s_1(t)$, $s_2(t)$, . . . $s_M(t)$ defined on some interval $(t_0, t_0 + T_s)$, an orthonormal basis function set may be constructed according to the following algorithm:

1. Set $v_1(t) = s_1(t)$ and define

$$\phi_1(t) = \frac{v_1(t)}{\|v_1\|} \tag{4-26}$$

2. Set $v_2(t) = s_2(t) - (s_2, \phi_1) \, \phi_1$ and let

$$\phi_2(t) = \frac{v_2(t)}{\|v_2\|} \tag{4-27}$$

3. Set $v_3(t) = s_3(t) - (s_3, \phi_2) \, \phi_2 - (s_3, \phi_1) \, \phi_1$ and let

$$\phi_3(t) = \frac{v_3(t)}{\|v_3\|} \tag{4-28}$$

4. Continue until all $s_i(t)$s have been used. If one or more of the steps above yield $v_j(t)$s for which $\|v_j(t)\| = 0$, omit these from consideration so that a set of $K \leq M$ orthonormal functions is obtained.

EXAMPLE 4–2

Consider the signals

$$s_1(t) = A \cos (2\pi f_0 t), \quad 0 \leq t \leq T_s$$

$$\text{and} \quad s_2(t) = A \sin (2\pi f_0 t), \quad 0 \leq t \leq T_s$$

$$(4\text{-}29)$$

where $f_o = m/T_s$, m an integer. Find an orthonormal basis set for this signal set.

Solution: Let $v_1(t) = A \cos (2\pi f_0 t)$. Then

$$\|v_1(t)\|^2 = (v_1, v_1) = \int_0^{T_s} A^2 \cos^2 (2\pi f_0 t) \, dt$$

$$= \frac{A^2}{2} \int_0^{T_s} [1 + \cos (4\pi f_0 t)] \, dt \qquad (4\text{-}30)$$

$$= \frac{A^2 T_s}{2}$$

Therefore,

$$\phi_1(t) = \frac{v_1}{\|v_1\|} = \sqrt{\frac{2}{T_s}} \cos(2\pi f_0 t), \quad 0 \leq t \leq T_s \qquad (4\text{-}31)$$

Next, let

$$v_2(t) = s_2(t) - (s_2, \phi_1)\phi_1$$

$$\text{where} \quad (s_2, \phi_1) = \int_0^{T_s} (A \sin 2\pi f_0 t) \sqrt{\frac{2}{T_s}} \cos 2\pi f_0 t \, dt$$

$$= A \sqrt{\frac{2}{T_s}} \int_0^{T_s} \frac{1}{2} \sin 4\pi f_0 t \, dt = 0 \qquad (4\text{-}32)$$

Therefore, $v_2(t) = A \sin 2\pi f_0 t$, $0 \leq t \leq T_s$. As with $v_1(t)$, $\|v_2(t)\|^2 = A^2 T_s/2$, so that

$$\phi_2(t) = \sqrt{\frac{2}{T_s}} \sin 2\pi f_0 t, \quad 0 \leq t \leq T_s \qquad (4\text{-}33)$$

With this procedure, an orthonormal basis set is obtained that can be used to express any possible finite-member transmitted signal set in the form (4–20).[7]

Using the procedure just described and the definitions of scalar product and norm given by (4–24) and (4–25), one may prove several interesting and useful properties about generalized vector-space representations. Before proceeding with the detection of signals in noise, two such properties will be considered.

4.2.2.4 Schwarz's Inequality.

Schwarz's inequality is a very useful relationship for use in the optimization of detection systems. We now provide a proof of it based on signal space notation. It can be stated as follows:

If x(t) and y(t) are signals, then

$$|(x, y)| \leq \|x\| \|y\| \tag{4–34}$$

with equality if and only if x(t) or y(t) are identically 0 or x(t) = αy(t), where α is a scalar (possibly complex).

Proof: *Consider* $\|x + \alpha y\|^2$, *which is a nonnegative quantity for arbitrary α. Using the definition of the norm, we have*

$$\|x + \alpha y\|^2 = (x + \alpha y, x + \alpha y)$$
$$= \|x\|^2 + \alpha^*(x, y) + \alpha(x, y)^* + |\alpha|^2 \|y\|^2 \tag{4–35}$$

Since α is arbitrary, we may choose it as

$$\alpha = -\frac{(x, y)}{\|y\|^2} \tag{4–36}$$

which gives

$$\|x + \alpha y\|^2 = \|x\|^2 - \frac{|(x, y)|^2}{\|y\|^2} \geq 0 \tag{4–37}$$

or

$$|(x, y)| \leq \|x\| \|y\| \tag{4–38}$$

Furthermore, equality holds only if $\|x + \alpha y\| = 0$, *i.e., if* $x = -\alpha y$, *or if one or both of the signals is identically zero.*

---

[7]Another way of looking at this problem is that the basis functions are to be chosen such that

$$s_1(t) = S_{11}\phi_1(t)$$
$$s_2(t) = S_{21}\phi_1(t) + S_{22}\phi_2(t)$$

where the S_{ij}s are constants. The first equation is used to find $\phi_1(t)$, the second to find $\phi_2(t)$, and so on.

4.2.2.5 Parseval's Theorem. *In terms of their generalized Fourier series components, the inner product of two signals is given by*

$$(x, y) = \sum_{k=1}^{K} X_k Y_k^* \tag{4-39}$$

with the special case

$$\|x\|^2 = \sum_{k=1}^{K} |X_k|^2 \tag{4-40}$$

Proof: *Represent x(t) and y(t) in terms of their generalized Fourier series, which are*

$$x(t) = \sum_{m=1}^{K} X_m \phi_m(t)$$

$$\text{and} \quad y(t) = \sum_{n=1}^{K} Y_n \phi_n(t) \tag{4-41}$$

where $X_m = (x, \phi_m)$ and $Y_n = (y, \phi_n)$. Using the properties of the inner product, we have

$$
\begin{aligned}
(x, y) &= (\Sigma_m X_m \phi_m, \Sigma_n Y_n \phi_n) \\
&= \Sigma_m X_m(\phi_m, \Sigma_n Y_n \phi_n) \\
&= \Sigma_m X_m(\Sigma_n Y_n \phi_n, \phi_m)^* \\
&= \Sigma_m X_m[\Sigma_n Y_n^*(\phi_n, \phi_m)^*] \\
&= \sum_{m=1}^{K} X_m Y_m^* = \int_{t_0}^{t_0 + T_s} x(t) y^*(t) \, dt
\end{aligned} \tag{4-42}
$$

which follows because $(\phi_n, \phi_m) = \delta_{nm}$, where δ_{nm}, called the Kronecker delta, is 1 for $n = m$ and 0 for $n \neq m$.

EXAMPLE 4–3

Express the M-ary phase-shift-keyed signal set

$$s_i(t) = A \cos \left[2\pi \left(f_0 t + \frac{(i - 1)}{M} \right) \right], i = 1, 2, \cdots, M; 0 \leq t \leq T_s \tag{4-43}$$

in terms of a suitable orthonormal basis set. Assume that $f_0 T_s$ is an integer.

Solution: Rather than use the Gram-Schmidt procedure, note, using a trigonometric identity, that

$$s_i(t) = A \cos \left(\frac{2\pi(i - 1)}{M} \right) \cos (2\pi f_0 t) - A \sin \left(\frac{2\pi(i - 1)}{M} \right) \sin (2\pi f_0 t) \tag{4-44}$$

Therefore, $B \cos (2\pi f_0 t)$ and $B \sin (2\pi f_0 t)$, $0 \leq t \leq T_s$, form an appropriate basis set, where B is a constant of normalization. To normalize these functions, compute

$$\int_0^{T_s} B^2 \cos^2 (2\pi f_0 t)\, dt = \int_0^{T_s} B^2 \sin^2 (2\pi\, f_0 t)\, dt = \frac{B^2 T_s}{2} = 1 \tag{4-45}$$

$$\text{or} \quad B = \sqrt{\frac{2}{T_s}}$$

and the orthonormal functions are

$$\phi_1(t) = \sqrt{\frac{2}{T_s}} \cos(2\pi f_0 t), \quad 0 \le t \le T_s \tag{4-46}$$

$$\text{and} \quad \phi_2(t) = \sqrt{\frac{2}{T_s}} \sin(2\pi f_0 t), \quad 0 \le t \le T_s$$

as in Example 4–2. A plot of the signal set constellation for this signal set is provided in Figure 4–3 for two values of M, where the coordinates of the ith point are

$$\sqrt{E_s} \cos \left[\frac{2\pi(i-1)}{M} \right], \quad -\sqrt{E_s} \sin \left[\frac{2\pi(i-1)}{M} \right] \tag{4-47}$$

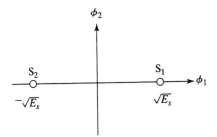

(a) Binary

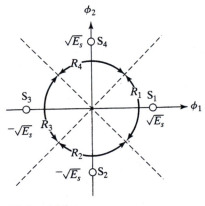

(b) Quadriphase

FIGURE 4–3 Signal constellations for *M*-ary phase-shift-keyed modulation.

For example, with $M = 2$ (called binary phase-shift keying or BPSK), the signal coordinates are

$$\mathbf{S}_1 = (\sqrt{E_s}, 0) \text{ and } \mathbf{S}_2 = (-\sqrt{E_s}, 0)$$

while for $M = 4$, they are

$$\mathbf{S}_1 = (\sqrt{E_s}, 0), \mathbf{S}_2 = (0, -\sqrt{E_s}), \mathbf{S}_3 = (-\sqrt{E_s}, 0), \mathbf{S}_4 = (0, \sqrt{E_s})$$

where $E_s = A^2 T_s/2$ is the energy of the signal.

4.2.3 MAP Detectors in Terms of Signal Spaces

In Section 4.2.2 it has been shown how the received signal plus noise in a digital communication system can be resolved into a generalized vector space of dimension $K \leq M$, where M is the number of possible signals transmitted. While the noise cannot, in general, be fully represented in this vector space, the unrepresentable component is irrelevant to deciding which signal was transmitted. The computation of the signal–space coordinates of the received data, according to (4–23), is accomplished by the parallel bank of multiplier–integrators shown in Figure 4–4a. Each multiplier–integrator combination is referred to as a *correlator,* and the overall receiver structure is called a *correlation receiver.* The kth correlator can also be replaced by a linear time-invariant filter with impulse response

$$h_k(t) = \phi_k^*(T_s - t), \quad 0 \leq t \leq T_s \tag{4–48}$$

which follows since the filter output is

$$z_k(t) = h_k(t) * z(t)$$
$$= \int_0^{T_s} \phi_k^*(T_s - t + \lambda)z(\lambda)d\lambda \tag{4–49}$$

or

$$z_k(T_s) = \int_0^{T_s} \phi_k^*(\lambda)z(\lambda)d\lambda \tag{4–50}$$

This is identical to the kth correlator output *at time* T_s. The receiver structure utilizing filters with impulse responses (4–48) in each arm is called a *matched filter* receiver, since the kth arm is matched to the kth term in the orthonormal series expansion of the receiver. This receiver is illustrated in Figure 4–4b.

It remains to determine what operation should be performed on the correlator outputs in Figure 4–4 in order to implement the MAP criterion. According to (4–10), the MAP, or minimum probability of error, receiver computes the a posteriori probabilities $P(H_i | Z_1, Z_2, \ldots, Z_K)$, $i = 1, 2, \ldots, M$, and estimates the transmitted signal to have been the one corresponding to the largest probability. Using Bayes' rule, each a posteriori probability may be rewritten as

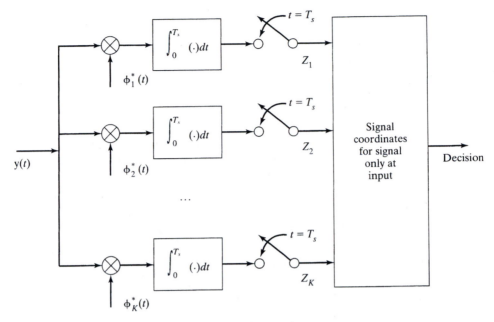

(a) Correlator implementation

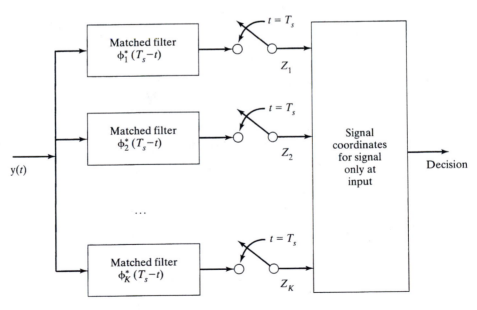

(b) Matched filter implementation

FIGURE 4–4   Block diagrams of implementations for computing signal-space co-ordinates of the received signal plus noise.

$$P(H_i \mid Z_1, Z_2, \cdots, Z_K) = \frac{f_Z(Z_1, Z_2, \cdots, Z_K \mid H_i) P(H_i)}{f_Z(Z_1, Z_2, \cdots, Z_K)} \tag{4-51}$$

$$= C \, P(H_i) f_Z(Z_1, Z_2, \cdots, Z_K \mid H_i)$$

where $f_Z(Z_1, Z_2, \ldots, Z_k)$ is the joint probability density function (pdf) of the signal space coordinates of $z(t)$. Since this joint pdf is independent of the particular signal transmitted, its inverse is replaced by a constant C.

An expression will now be obtained for $f_Z(Z_1, Z_2, \ldots, Z_K \mid H_i)$, the conditional joint pdf of the received data vector given signal $s_i(t)$ was sent. According to (4–18) and (4–19), the kth coordinate, Z_k, is a Gaussian random variable because it is obtained as a linear operation on the Gaussian noise $n(t)$. Given that $s_i(t)$ was transmitted, the mean of Z_k is just $S_{ik} = (s_i, \phi_k)$, which is the projection of $s_i(t)$ onto the $\phi_k(t)$ coordinate axis. The variance of Z_k, given $s_i(t)$ was transmitted, is simply the variance of the kth noise component, N_k. In fact, it is convenient to compute

$$\overline{N_k N_l} = \text{cov}\{Z_k, Z_l \mid H_i\}$$

$$= E\left\{ \int_{t_0}^{t_0 + T_s} n(t)\phi_k(t)dt \int_{t_0}^{t_0 + T_s} n(\lambda)\phi_l^*(\lambda)d\lambda \right\}$$

$$= \int_{t_0}^{t_0 + T_s} \int_{t_0}^{t_0 + T_s} E\{n(t)n(\lambda)\}\phi_k(t)\phi_l^*(\lambda)dt\, d\lambda \tag{4-52}$$

$$= \frac{N_0}{2} \int_{t_0}^{t_0 + T_s} \phi_k(t)\phi_l^*(t)dt$$

$$= \frac{N_0}{2} \delta_{kl}$$

which follows because $E\{n(t)n(\lambda)\} = (N_0/2)\,\delta(t - \lambda)$. This result shows that the K random variables $Z_1, Z_2, \ldots, Z_K$, which are the coordinates of the received data vector given that $s_i(t)$ was transmitted, are independent since they are Gaussian random variables with 0 conditional covariances. The mean of the kth one, given that $s_i(t)$ was transmitted, is S_{ik} and its variance, from (4–52), is $N_0/2$. Thus the joint conditional pdf of the data vector $\mathbf{Z} = (Z_1, Z_2, \ldots, Z_K)$ given that $s_i(t)$ was transmitted (hypothesis H_i) is

$$f_Z(Z_1, Z_2, \cdots, Z_K \mid H_i) = \prod_{k=1}^{K} \frac{\exp[-\mid Z_k - S_{ik} \mid^2 / N_0]}{\sqrt{\pi N_0}}$$

$$= \frac{\exp\left[-\sum_{k=1}^{K} \mid Z_k - S_{ik} \mid^2 / N_0 \right]}{(\pi N_0)^{K/2}} \tag{4-53}$$

$$= \frac{\exp\left(-\|\mathbf{Z} - \mathbf{S}_i\|^2 / N_0\right)}{(\pi N_0)^{K/2}}$$

where

$$\mathbf{Z} \Leftrightarrow z(t) = \sum_{k=1}^{K} Z_k \phi_k(t), \quad t_0 \leq t \leq t_0 + T_s$$

(4–54)

$$\mathbf{S}_i \Leftrightarrow s_i(t) = \sum_{k=1}^{K} S_{ik} \phi_k(t), \quad t_0 \leq t \leq t_0 + T_s$$

In the last equation of (4–53), the compact representation involving the norm as expressed in (4–40) has been used. The decision rule, then, is to maximize (4–53) multiplied by $P(H_i)$. By taking the natural logarithm of $f_Z(Z_1, Z_2, \ldots, Z_K | H_i) P(H_i)$, this is equivalent to minimizing (constants may be ignored)

$$\|\mathbf{Z} - \mathbf{S}_i\|^2 - N_0 \ln P(H_i)$$

If all signals are a priori equally probable, this decision rule becomes

$$\text{minimize } \|\mathbf{Z} - \mathbf{S}_i\|^2 = \sum_{k=1}^{K} |Z_k - S_{ik}|^2 = \int_{t_0}^{t_0 + T_s} |z(t) - s_i(t)|^2 \, dt \qquad (4\text{–}55)$$

which is the distance between the received data vector and the kth signal vector in the transmitted signal constellation. The decision rule (4–55) defines decision regions in the K-dimensional signal space such that if the received data vector $\mathbf{Z}$ falls within the ith region, R_i, the decision is made that signal $s_i(t)$ was transmitted. The decision regions for the signal set of Example 4–3 with $M = 4$ are illustrated in Figure 4–3b.

4.2.4   Performance Calculations for MAP Receivers

As discussed previously, the MAP decision strategy minimizes the average probability of error. The probability of error can be calculated as

$$P_s(\varepsilon) = 1 - P_s(C) = 1 - \sum_{k=1}^{K} P(H_k) P(C|H_k) \qquad (4\text{–}56)$$

where the subscript s denotes the probability of a *symbol error* (sometimes referred to as a *word error*). The probabilities $P_s(C)$ and $P(C|H_k)$ denote, respectively, the probability of correct reception averaged over all possible transmitted signals and the probability of correct reception given the hypothesis, H_k, that the kth signal was transmitted. The latter is just the probability that the data vector $\mathbf{Z}$ falls within the kth decision region, R_k, given that $s_k(t)$ really was transmitted. In terms of the joint pdf (4–53), $P(C | H_k)$ is given by

$$P(C | H_k) = \int_{R_k} \frac{\exp\left(-\|\mathbf{Z} - \mathbf{S}_k\|^2 / N_0\right)}{(\pi N_0)^{K/2}} \, d\mathbf{Z} \qquad (4\text{–}57)$$

The following observations are useful in the computation of $P(C|H_k)$:[8]

---

[8]For a more detailed discussion, see [2, Chap. 4].

1. Rotation and translation of the coordinate system defined by the orthonormal set $\{\phi_i(t)\}$ do not affect the computation of $P(C|H_k)$. (Average or peak signal energy for a given probability of correct reception, however, will be affected in general.) That this is the case is demonstrated by considering the data vector components $Z_k = S_{ik} + N_k$. Since the N_ks are equal-variance, uncorrelated, Gaussian random variables, the equal-probability contours surrounding each possible transmitted signal point are hyperspheres, which means that rotation or translation of the coordinate system will not affect the integral over R_i of the joint pdf $f_Z(\mathbf{z} \mid H_k)$.

2. The peak and average energies required to achieve a given probability of error can be minimized through appropriate translation of the coordinate system. An example involving peak energy is shown in Figure 4–5. The average energy, defined by

$$\overline{E}_s = \sum_{k=1}^{M} P(H_k)E_k = \sum_{k=1}^{M} P(H_k)\|\mathbf{S}_k\|^2 \tag{4–58}$$

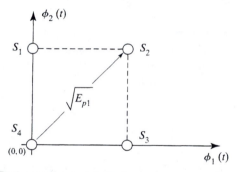

(a) Peak energy not minimized

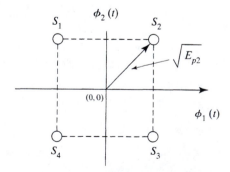

(b) Peak energy minimized

FIGURE 4–5   Minimizing peak energy, E_p, through translation of the signal-space coordinates.

can be minimized by subtracting a constant vector **a** from each signal point such that

$$\sum_{k=1}^{M} P(H_k)\|\mathbf{S}_k - \mathbf{a}\|^2 = \text{minimum} \tag{4–59}$$

which results in

$$\mathbf{a} = \sum_{k=1}^{M} P(H_k)\mathbf{S}_k \tag{4–60}$$

The proof of this is left to the problems.

EXAMPLE 4–4

Consider the signal constellation of three signal points lying on the vertices of an equilateral triangle with vertex locations $(0, 0)$, $(2, 0)$, and $(1, \sqrt{3})$ (i.e., the base lies on the x-axis from $x = 0$ to $x = 2$). Assume that the signals are equally probable. Find **a** according to (4–60) such that the average energy is minimized.

Solution: According to (4–60), **a** is given by $\mathbf{a} = (1/3)[(0, 0) + (1, \sqrt{3}) + (2, 0)] = (1, 1/\sqrt{3})$. Subtracting this from each signal point, we obtain the new signal point locations as $(-1, -1/\sqrt{3})$, $(0, \sqrt{3} - 1/\sqrt{3})$, and $(1, -1/\sqrt{3})$. As a check, we compute the distance between the latter two vertices. It is given by

$$l = \sqrt{(0 - 1)^2 + \left(\sqrt{3} - \frac{1}{\sqrt{3}} + \frac{1}{\sqrt{3}}\right)^2} = \sqrt{1 + 3} = 2$$

The average energy of the original configuration is

$$E_{\text{original}} = \frac{1}{3}(0 + 4 + 1 + 3) = \frac{8}{3} \text{ J}$$

The average energy of the new configuration is

$$E_{\text{new}} = \frac{1}{3}\left[1 + \frac{1}{3} + 0 + \left(\sqrt{3} - \frac{1}{\sqrt{3}}\right)^2 + 1 + \frac{1}{3}\right] = \frac{4}{3} \text{ J}$$

which is smaller by a factor of 2 than the energy of the original configuration.

3. Noise, N_k, disturbing the kth coordinate is independent of noise in all other coordinates because the covariances of the noise components on the coordinates is zero as shown by (4–52). Since the noise components are Gaussian, their covariances being 0 also means that they are statistically independent. Therefore, a decision may be made on the kth coordinate *independently* of any other coordinate.
4. Given a completely symmetric signal set (i.e., one for which any relabeling of the signal points can be undone by rotation, translation, or inversion of axes), the error probability is independent of the actual source statistics. An example is provided by the signal set of Figure 4–3. This will be demonstrated later.

The *union bound* often provides a tight upper bound for cases where the error probability is difficult or impossible to compute exactly. It is derived by noting that an error occurs in a digital communication system if, and only if, the received data vector $\mathbf{Z}$ is closer to at least one other signal point $\mathbf{S}_l$, $l \neq k$, than it is to $\mathbf{S}_k$, which is assumed to be the correct signal point. Therefore, given H_k, the probability of error can be written as

$$P_s(\varepsilon \mid H_k) = P\left(\bigcup_{\substack{i=1 \\ i \neq k}}^{M} \varepsilon_{ik}\right) \tag{4-61}$$

where ε_{ik} is the event that a decision is made in favor of $\mathbf{S}_i$ when $\mathbf{S}_k$, which is assumed to be the correct signal point, was really sent and $\cup$ denotes the union of these events. But by the axiom of probability that

$$P(A \cup B) \leq P(A) + P(B)$$

the probability of (4–61) is bounded by

$$P_s(\varepsilon \mid H_k) \leq \sum_{\substack{i=1 \\ i \neq k}}^{M} P(\mathbf{S}_i, \mathbf{S}_k) \tag{4-62}$$

where $P(\mathbf{S}_i, \mathbf{S}_k) = P(\varepsilon_{ik})$ is the probability of error for a hypothetical communication system that uses the two signals $\mathbf{S}_i$ and $\mathbf{S}_k$ to communicate one of two equally likely messages. Quite often, one probability in the sum dominates the sum. For an AWGN channel,

$$P(\mathbf{S}_i, \mathbf{S}_k) = Q\left(\frac{\|\mathbf{S}_i - \mathbf{S}_k\|}{\sqrt{2N_0}}\right) \tag{4-63}$$

where $Q(u)$ is the Q-function, defined by (4–16).[9]

The proof of (4–63) follows by using property 3 and choosing a coordinate direction along the vector connecting $\mathbf{S}_k$ and $\mathbf{S}_i$. Let $d = \|\mathbf{S}_i - \mathbf{S}_k\|$. Call the noise component along this coordinate direction N_1. It has mean 0 and variance $N_0/2$. Therefore, the probability of error for this signal pair is

$$
\begin{aligned}
P(\mathbf{S}_i, \mathbf{S}_k) &= P(\varepsilon \mid \mathbf{S}_i) = P(\varepsilon \mid \mathbf{S}_k) = P(N_1 > d/2) \\
&= \int_{d/2}^{\infty} \frac{\exp\left[-\dfrac{u^2}{2(N_0/2)}\right]}{\sqrt{2\pi\,(N_0/2)}}\, du \\
&= \int_{d/\sqrt{2N_0}}^{\infty} \frac{\exp(-v^2/2)}{\sqrt{2\pi}}\, dv \\
&= Q\left(\frac{d}{\sqrt{2N_0}}\right)
\end{aligned}
\tag{4-64}
$$

which is the same as (4–63).

---

[9]See [3, pp. 931 ff]. A summary of useful approximations and a brief table of values is given in Appendix E for the Q-function.

4.3   PERFORMANCE ANALYSIS OF COHERENT DIGITAL SIGNALING SCHEMES

In this section and the following two, various types of digital modulation methods will be described and characterized in terms of symbol and bit error probabilities. The latter characterization is convenient when comparing one scheme with another. The various schemes considered can be categorized as either coherent, for which a phase-coherent carrier reference at the receiver is required, or noncoherent (Section 4.4), for which no phase-coherent reference is required.

4.3.1   Coherent Binary Systems

The use of signal–space ideas in the analysis of digital communication systems will be illustrated by first considering binary signaling schemes. Let the signaling interval under consideration be $(0, T_b)$ and assume that

$$\int_0^{T_b} |s_1(t)|^2 \, dt = \int_0^{T_b} |s_2(t)|^2 \, dt = E_b \tag{4–65}$$

where the subscript b is a reminder that this is a binary case. From (4–64), the average probability of bit error is

$$P_b(\varepsilon) = Q\left(\frac{d}{\sqrt{2N_0}}\right) \tag{4–66}$$

where the Q-function has been defined previously. The distance-squared, d^2, can be evaluated as

$$d^2 = \|\mathbf{S}_1 - \mathbf{S}_2\|^2 = \|\mathbf{S}_1\|^2 + \|\mathbf{S}_2\|^2 - 2(\mathbf{S}_1, \mathbf{S}_2) = 2E_b\,(1 - \rho) \tag{4–67}$$

where

$$\rho = \frac{1}{E_b} \int_0^{T_b} s_1(t)s_2(t)dt \tag{4–68}$$

is the correlation coefficient between $s_1(t)$ and $s_2(t)$. We specialize (4–67) to two specific cases, called binary phase-shift keying (BPSK) and binary frequency-shift keying (BFSK).

EXAMPLE 4–5 _____

BPSK is defined as having the signal set

$$s_1(t) = \sqrt{\frac{2E_b}{T_b}} \cos 2\pi f_0 t, \quad 0 \leq t \leq T_b \tag{4–69}$$

$$\text{and } s_2(t) = -\sqrt{\frac{2E_b}{T_b}} \cos 2\pi f_0 t, \quad 0 \leq t \leq T_b$$

where $f_0 T_b$ is an integer (actually, $f_0 T_b \gg 1$ suffices). The correlation coefficient can be calculated as $\rho = -1$, so that $d^2 = 4E_b$. Therefore, the bit error probability is

$$P_b(\varepsilon) = Q\left(\sqrt{\frac{2E_b}{N_0}} \right) \quad \text{(BPSK)} \tag{4-70}$$

EXAMPLE 4–6

Coherent BFSK is defined by the signal set

$$s_1(t) = \sqrt{\frac{2E_b}{T_b}} \cos 2\pi \left(f_0 + \frac{\Delta f}{2} \right) t, \quad 0 \le t \le T_b$$

$$\text{and} \quad s_2(t) = \sqrt{\frac{2E_b}{T_b}} \cos 2\pi \left(f_0 - \frac{\Delta f}{2} \right) t, \quad 0 \le t \le T_b \tag{4-71}$$

where, as for BPSK, $f_0 T_b$ is assumed to be an integer for mathematical convenience (again, $f_0 T_b \gg 1$ suffices). The correlation coefficient is given by

$$\begin{aligned}
\rho &= \frac{1}{T_b} \int_0^{T_b} (\cos 4\pi f_0 t + \cos 2\pi \Delta f t) dt \\
&= \frac{\sin 2\pi \Delta f T_b}{2\pi \Delta f T_b} \equiv \text{sinc}\,(2\Delta f T_b)
\end{aligned} \tag{4-72}$$

If $2\Delta f T_b$ is an integer, the sinc function is 0 so that the correlation coefficient is 0, and the bit error probability becomes

$$P_b(\varepsilon) = Q\left(\sqrt{\frac{E_b}{N_0}} \right) \quad \text{(BFSK)} \tag{4-73}$$

Because of the factor of 2 multiplying E_b in (4–70) as compared with the argument of (4–73), it is seen that BFSK requires 3 dB more energy than BPSK to achieve the same bit error probability. The frequency separation Δf could have been chosen to minimize ρ, in which case the performance of BFSK would have been closer to BPSK. This is left to a problem. With $\rho = \rho_{\min} = -0.216$, the difference between the case $\rho = 0$ and $\rho = \rho_{\min}$ is about 0.85 dB in E_b/N_0.

4.3.2 Coherent *M*-ary Orthogonal Signaling Schemes

The signal set $\{s_i(t)\colon i = 1, 2, \ldots, M\}, 0 \le t \le T_s$ with

$$\int_0^{T_s} s_i(t) s_j(t) dt = E_s \delta_{ij}, \quad i, j = 1, 2, \cdots, M \tag{4-74}$$

is referred to an *orthogonal scheme* because the correlation coefficient of differing signals is zero. An example is M-ary FSK for which the signal set is illustrated in Figure 4–6 for $M = 3$. The subscript s on T_s and E_s (4–74) is a reminder that, in general, we are dealing with more than two symbols per T_s-second signaling interval. Because the signals em-

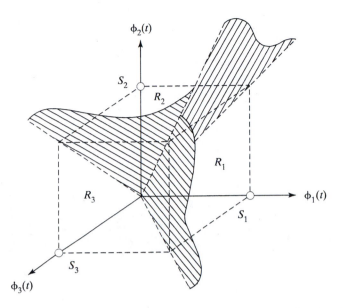

FIGURE 4–6   The signal space and its optimum partitioning for 3-ary FSK.

ployed in this scheme are orthogonal and equal energy, a suitable orthonormal basis set is defined by

$$\phi_j(t) = \frac{s_j(t)}{\sqrt{E_s}}, \quad 0 \le t \le T_s, j = 1, 2, \cdots, M \tag{4–75}$$

The signal–space coordinates of the ith signal are therefore given by

$$S_{ij} = \sqrt{E_s}\, \delta_{ij}, \quad i, j = 1, 2, \cdots, M \tag{4–76}$$

The decision rule (4–55) states that

$$d_i^2 = \|\mathbf{Z} - \mathbf{S}_i\|^2 = \sum_{k=1}^{M} (Z_k - S_{ik})^2, \quad i = 1, 2, \cdots, M \tag{4–77}$$

where Z_k is the kth coordinate of the data vector, is to be minimized through appropriate choice of $s_i(t)$. This results in the optimum partitioning of the signal space as shown in Figure 4–6 for $M = 3$. We may simplify the decision strategy still further, however, as will now be shown.

The norm of the difference between $\mathbf{Z}$ and $\mathbf{S}_i$ may be expanded as

$$\|\mathbf{Z} - \mathbf{S}_i\|^2 = \|\mathbf{Z}\|^2 - 2(\mathbf{Z}, \mathbf{S}_i) + \|\mathbf{S}_i\|^2 \tag{4–78}$$

Since $\|\mathbf{Z}\|^2$ and $\|\mathbf{S}_i\|^2 = E_s$ are independent of the particular signal chosen, (4–78) may be minimized by maximizing $(\mathbf{Z}, \mathbf{S}_i)$, which can be expressed as

$$(\mathbf{Z}, \mathbf{S}_i) = \int_0^{T_s} z(t)s_i(t)dt \tag{4-79}$$

by virtue of the definition of the scalar product (4–25) and the fact that the signals are real. Thus the decision strategy to be used on the basis of the correlator outputs of Figure 4–4 is to choose the largest output as corresponding to the transmitted signal.

The probability of symbol error, P_s, can be obtained by considering the probability of correct reception, $P_s(C \mid i)$, given that $s_i(t)$ was transmitted. In the light of the decision rule discussed earlier, this probability can be expressed as

$$P_s(C \mid i) = P(\text{all } Z_j < Z_i, j \neq i) \tag{4-80}$$

Given that $s_i(t)$ was sent, $z(t) = s_i(t) + n(t)$, so that (4–80) can be expressed as

$$P_s(C \mid i) = P(\text{all } N_j < \sqrt{E_s} + N_i, j \neq i) \tag{4-81}$$

where

$$N_j = \int_0^{T_s} n(t)\phi_j(t)dt \tag{4-82}$$

is a Gaussian random variable with zero mean and variance $N_0/2$. Since the N_js are independent Gaussian random variables, (4–81) can be expressed as

$$P_s(C \mid i) = \overline{\prod_{\substack{j=1 \\ j \neq i}}^{M} P(N_j < \sqrt{E_s} + N_i)} \tag{4-83}$$

where the overbar denotes an average over N_i. Because the pdfs of all the N_js are identical, the product in (4–83) can be written as

$$\prod_{\substack{j=1 \\ j \neq i}}^{M} P(N_j < \sqrt{E_s} + N_i) = \left[\int_{-\infty}^{\sqrt{E_s}+y} \frac{\exp(-u^2/N_0)}{\sqrt{\pi N_0}} \, du \right]^{M-1} \tag{4-84}$$

where $y = N_i$ will serve as a dummy variable of integration. Averaging with respect to N_i gives

$$P_s(C \mid i) = 1 - P_s(\varepsilon \mid i)$$

$$= \int_{-\infty}^{\infty} \frac{\exp(-v^2/2)}{\sqrt{2\pi}} \left[\int_{-\infty}^{\sqrt{2E_s/N_0}+v} \frac{\exp(-x^2/2)}{\sqrt{2\pi}} \, dx \right]^{M-1} dy \tag{4-85}$$

where the substitutions $x^2 = 2u^2/N_0$ and $v = \sqrt{2/N_0}\,u$ have been used. Since $P_s(C \mid i)$ is independent of i, the average probability of symbol error, P_s, is in fact $1 - P_s(C \mid i)$. Unfortionately, (4–85) cannot be expressed in closed form, but must be integrated numerically.[10]

The union bounding technique can be applied to obtain a tight bound for P_s for large E_b/N_0. Choosing any two signals $\mathbf{S}_i$ and $\mathbf{S}_k$, we have

$$\|\mathbf{S}_i - \mathbf{S}_k\|^2 = \|\mathbf{S}_i\|^2 - 2(\mathbf{S}_i, \mathbf{S}_k) + \|\mathbf{S}_k\|^2 \tag{4–86}$$

$$= 2E_s, \quad \text{all } i \neq k$$

so that (4–63) becomes

$$P(\mathbf{S}_i, \mathbf{S}_k) = Q\left(\sqrt{\frac{E_s}{N_0}}\right) \tag{4–87}$$

independently of the two signals selected. Therefore, the union bound (4–63) for orthogonal signals becomes

$$P_s \leq (M - 1)Q\left(\sqrt{\frac{E_s}{N_0}}\right) \tag{4–88}$$

The union bound and the exact result for P_s are compared in Figure 4–7. Also shown is the limit of P_s as $M \to \infty$. Note that *error-free* transmission can be achieved in the limit as $M \to \infty$ as long as $E_s/(N_0 \log_2 M) > \ln 2 = -1.59$ dB (compare this with the asymptote as $R/W \to -\infty$ in Figure 1–4). The signal-to-noise ratio $E_b/N_0 \equiv E_s/(N_0 \log_2 M)$ is the average *energy per bit-to-noise power spectral density ratio* because $\log_2 M$ bits of data are transmitted per M-ary symbol.

EXAMPLE 4–7

Two examples of coherent M-ary orthogonal signaling schemes are provided in this example. The first signal set is referred to as coherent, M-ary frequency-shift keying and consists of waveforms of the form

$$s_i(t) = \sqrt{\frac{2E_s}{T_s}} \cos 2\pi \left[f_0 + (i - 1)\,\Delta f\right]t, 0 \leq t \leq T_s; i = 1, 2, \cdots, M \tag{4–89}$$

where $f_0 T_s$ is taken as an integer for convenience and $(\Delta f)_{\min} = 1/(2T_s)$ is the minimum frequency spacing such that adjacent signals are orthogonal.

The second example consists of time-displaced square pulses of the form

$$s_i(t) = \sqrt{\frac{E_s}{\tau}} \prod \left[\frac{t - (i - 1/2)\tau}{\tau}\right], \tau = T_s/M; i = 1, 2, \cdots, M \tag{4–90}$$

Note that the energy of each signal in both signal sets is E_s and the average power is E_s/T_s.

---

[10]See [4] for a numerical tabulation of values for P_s.

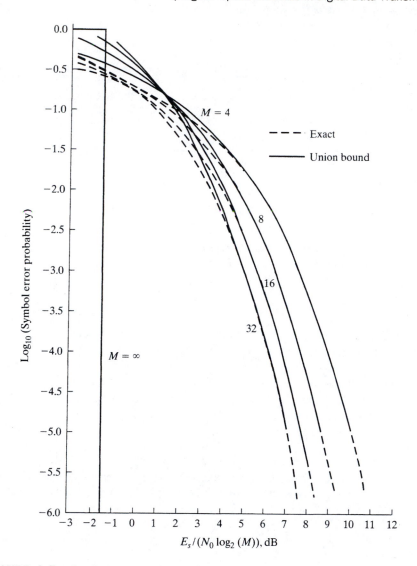

FIGURE 4–7 Symbol error probability for M-ary orthogonal signaling; both the exact results, using numerical integration, and the upper bound, using the union bound, are shown.

4.3.3 *M*-ary Phase-Shift Keying

Consider a signal set of the form

$$s_i(t) = A\cos\left[2\pi\left(f_0 t + \frac{i-1}{M}\right)\right], i = 1, 2, \cdots, M; 0 \le t \le T_s \qquad (4\text{--}91)$$

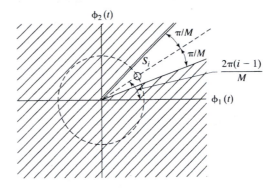

(a) Decision region (unshaded) for ith transmitted phase

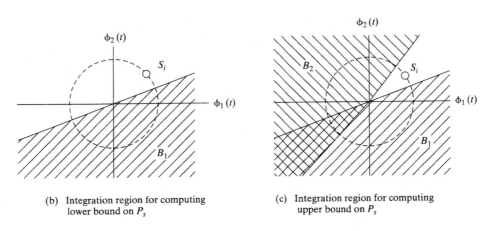

(b) Integration region for computing
     lower bound on P_s

(c) Integration region for computing
     upper bound on P_s

FIGURE 4–8   Signal–space diagrams for M-ary PSK.

which is the same signal set considered in Example 4–3. Two orthogonal functions were shown to suffice in that example. The ith signal point with its decision region is shown in Figure 4–8a. The coordinates of the received data given $s_i(t)$ was transmitted is

$$Z_1 = \sqrt{E_s} \cos \frac{2\pi(i-1)}{M} + N_1 \text{ and } Z_2 = -\sqrt{E_s} \sin \frac{2\pi(i-1)}{M} + N_2 \quad (4\text{–}92)$$

where N_1 and N_2 are Gaussian random variables of zero mean and variance $N_0/2$. The probability of error, P_s, is impossible to compute in closed form for this signal set except for $M = 2$ and $M = 4$. However, a lower bound for P_s can be computed by noting from Figure 4–8b that[11]

---

[11]This expression is clearly exact for $M = 2$, so the lower bound is exactly the symbol (bit) error probability for BPSK.

$$P_s \geq P(\mathbf{Z} \epsilon B_1) \tag{4-93}$$

because the area included in B_1 is less than that included in $\overline{R}_i$, the complement of the ith decision region, unless $M = 2$, in which case they are equal. An upper bound is obtained by noting that $\overline{R}_i$ is exceeded by the sum of the areas in B_1 and B_2 as illustrated in Figure 4–8c. That is,

$$P_s \leq P(\mathbf{Z} \epsilon B_1) + P(\mathbf{Z} \epsilon B_2) \tag{4-94}$$

But both probabilities on the right-hand side of (4–94) are equal due to the rotational symmetry of the signal set and of the noise distribution. One can easily compute $P(\mathbf{Z} \epsilon B_1)$, for example, by considering the noise to be resolved into components $N_\perp$ and $N_\parallel$, which are perpendicular and parallel, respectively, to the boundary of B_1. Only $N_\perp$ is needed, since only it can cause $\mathbf{Z}$ to be in B_1. This noise component has variance $N_0/2$. Therefore, since $\sqrt{E_s} \sin(\pi/M)$ is the distance to the boundary of B_1,

$$P(\mathbf{Z} \epsilon B_1) = P\left(N_\perp > \sqrt{E_s} \sin \frac{\pi}{M} \right)$$

$$= \int_{\sqrt{E_s} \sin(\pi/M)}^{\infty} \frac{\exp(-u^2/N_0)}{\sqrt{\pi N_o}} = Q\left(\sqrt{\frac{2E_s}{N_0}} \sin \frac{\pi}{M} \right) \tag{4-95}$$

and $P_s(\varepsilon)$ is bounded by

$$Q\left(\sqrt{\frac{2E_s}{N_0}} \sin \frac{\pi}{M} \right) \leq P_s < 2Q\left(\sqrt{\frac{2E_s}{N_0}} \sin \frac{\pi}{M} \right) \tag{4-96}$$

The upper bound becomes very tight for M fixed as E_s/N_0 becomes large. The lower bound is the exact result for $M = 2$.

The exact expression for $P_s(\varepsilon)$ is given by (see [4], pp. 228 ff.)

$$P_s = \frac{M-1}{M} - \frac{1}{2} \mathrm{erf}\left(\sqrt{\frac{E_s}{N_0}} \sin \frac{\pi}{M} \right)$$

$$- \frac{1}{\sqrt{\pi}} \int_0^{\sqrt{E_s/N_0} \sin(\pi/M)} \exp(-y^2) \mathrm{erf}\left(y \cot \frac{\pi}{M} \right) dy \tag{4-97}$$

which must be integrated numerically except for $M = 2$ and 4.

A handy proper integral representation for the symbol error probability is provided by the formula[12]

$$P_{\mathrm{MPSK}} = \frac{1}{\pi} \int_0^{\pi(1-1/M)} \exp\left[-\frac{(E_s/N_0) \sin^2(\pi/M)}{\sin^2 \phi} \right] d\phi \tag{4-98}$$

---

[12]See R. F. Pawula, "A New Formula for MDPSK Symbol Error Probability," *IEEE Commun. Letters*, Vol. 2, pp. 271–272, Oct. 1998 [5].

The upper bound of P_s for M-ary PSK versus $E_b/N_0 \equiv E_s/(N_0 \log_2 M)$ is shown in Figure 4–9. From the bounding technique, it should be clear that the upper bound closely approximates the actual result, particularly for M large.

4.3.4   Quadrature–Amplitude Modulation

Several schemes that give improved bandwidth efficiency at the expense of error probability performance are possible by combining amplitude- and phase-shift keying. One example is M-ary quadrature amplitude-shift modulation (M-QAM) in which the signaling waveforms are given by

$$s_i(t) = \sqrt{\frac{2}{T_s}}\,(A_i \cos 2\pi f_0 t + B_i \sin 2\pi f_0 t), \quad 0 \le t \le T_s \qquad (4\text{–}99)$$

where A_i and B_i take on the amplitudes

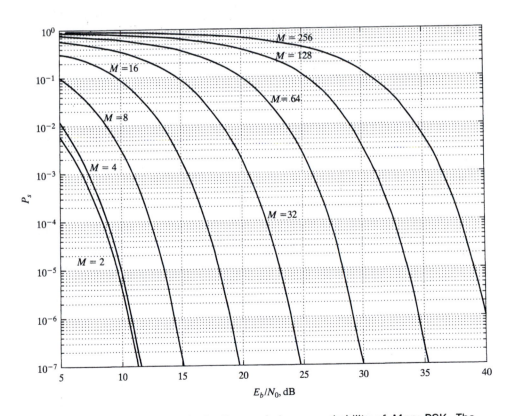

FIGURE 4–9 Upper bounds for the symbol error probability of M-ary PSK. The upper bound is very close to the actual error probability for M reasonably large.

$$A_i, B_i = \pm a, \pm 3a, \cdots, \pm(\sqrt{M} - 1)a \tag{4-100}$$

in which a is a parameter. Computation of the average energy of (4–99) over $(0, T_s)$, assuming all amplitudes equally likely, results in the following expression for a in terms of the average signal energy per symbol, E_s, and M (this is left to the problems):

$$a = \sqrt{\frac{3E_s}{2(M - 1)}} \tag{4-101}$$

The constellation of signal points is shown in Figure 4–10 for $M = 16$ together with the optimum signal–space partitioning to give minimum error probability in AWGN. We compute the probability of symbol error for the case $M = 16$ first and generalize it to the case of $M = 4^n$, where n is an integer, later. (Clearly, we require $M = 4^n = 2^{2n}$ in order to have a square array of signal points, although nonsquare arrays are used in practice to get odd powers of 2.)

In Figure 4–10, a binary representation has been associated with each point by labeling the I and Q locations according to a Gray code with the first two digits denoting I and the second two Q. This guarantees that a single bit error occurs if a nearest-neighbor symbol error occurs. Computation of the bit error probability is thereby simplified as to be discussed later.

The demodulation and detection can be accomplished with the quadrature coherent demodulator arrangement shown in Figure 4–11. From Figure 4–10 it follows that there are three types of errors as follows:

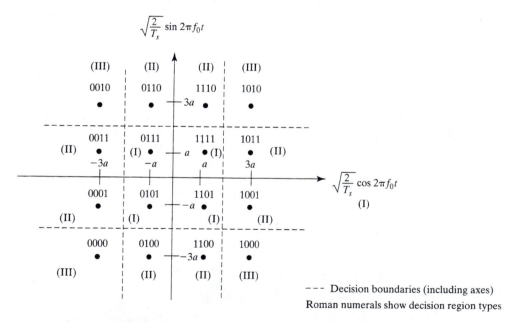

FIGURE 4–10   Signal constellation and decision regions for 16-ary QAM.

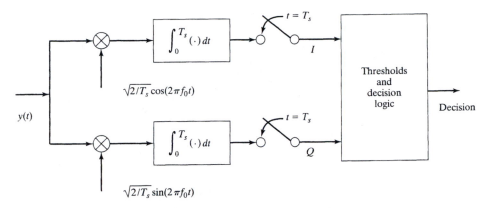

FIGURE 4–11 Detector structure for 16-ary QAM.

Type I: Signal points 0111, 0101, 1101, 1111. The decision region for determining the probability of *correct reception* for these signals is illustrated in Figure 4–12a.

Type II: Signal points 0001, 0011, 0110, 1110, 1011, 1001, 1100, 0100. The decision region for determining the correct probability of reception for these signal points is illustrated in Figure 4–12b.

Type III: Signal points 0000, 0010, 1010, 1000. The decision region for determining the probability of correct reception for these signal points is illustrated in Figure 4–12c.

Given these conditional probabilities of correct reception, denoted by $P(C \mid I)$, $P(C \mid II)$, and $P(C \mid III)$, the average probability of symbol error for $M = 16$ is

$$P_s(\varepsilon) = 1 - \left[\frac{4}{16} P(C|I) + \frac{8}{16} P(C|II) + \frac{4}{16} P(C|III) \right] \qquad (4\text{–}102)$$

Using techniques that are by now standard, it can be shown that the inphase and quadrature noise components from the integrator outputs are zero-mean Gaussian with variances

$$\operatorname{var}(N_I) = \operatorname{var}(N_Q) = \frac{N_0}{2} \qquad (4\text{–}103)$$

and are uncorrelated [this is a repeat of (4–52)]. For the type I decision regions,

$$P(C|I) = \left[\int_{-a}^{a} \frac{\exp(-u^2/N_0)}{\sqrt{\pi N_o}} \, du \right]^2$$

$$= \left[1 - 2Q\left(\sqrt{\frac{2a^2}{N_0}} \right) \right]^2 \qquad (4\text{–}104)$$

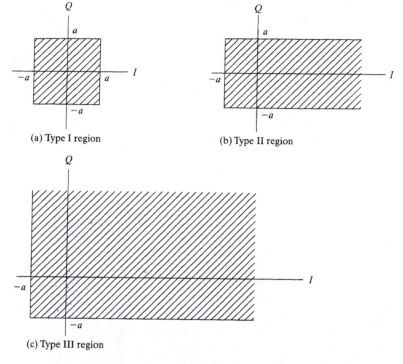

(a) Type I region   (b) Type II region

(c) Type III region

FIGURE 4–12   Type I, II, and III decision regions for 16-QAM.

where $Q(\cdot)$ is the Q-function defined previously. For the type II decision regions,

$$P(C|\text{II}) = \int_{-a}^{a} \frac{\exp(-u^2/N_0)}{\sqrt{\pi N_0}}\, du \int_{-a}^{\infty} \frac{\exp(-u^2/N_0)}{\sqrt{\pi N_0}}\, du$$

$$= \left[1 - 2Q\left(\sqrt{\frac{2a^2}{N_0}}\right)\right]\left[1 - Q\left(\sqrt{\frac{2a^2}{N_0}}\right)\right]$$

(4–105)

For the type III decision regions,

$$P(C|\text{III}) = \left[\int_{-a}^{\infty} \frac{\exp(-u^2/N_0)}{\sqrt{\pi N_0}}\, du\right]^2$$

$$= \left[1 - Q\left(\sqrt{\frac{2a^2}{N_0}}\right)\right]^2$$

(4–106)

The average probability of error can be found as a function of E_s/N_0 by using (4–101), (4–104), (4–105), and (4–106) in conjunction with (4–102).

To generalize this result to the case of $M = 4^n$, n an integer, we note that for this general case there will be $(\sqrt{M} - 2)^2$ type I decision regions, $4(\sqrt{M} - 2)$ type II decision regions, and 4 type III decision regions. The probability of correct reception given a type I, II, or III region is still given by (4–104), (4–105), or (4–106), respectively. The average probability of symbol error is then

$$P_s = 1 - \frac{1}{M}[(\sqrt{M} - 2)^2 \, P(C|\text{I}) + 4(\sqrt{M} - 2) \, P(C|\text{II}) + 4P(C|\text{III})] \quad (4\text{–}107)$$

where a is related to E_s by (4–101). Figure 4–13 shows P_s for M-ary QAM versus E_s/N_0 for several values of M.

If E_s/N_0 is large in (4–107), we may neglect the square of the Q-function in comparison with the Q-function itself. If like terms are collected and the Q-function squared terms are dropped, the result is

$$P_s \approx 4\left(1 - \frac{1}{\sqrt{M}}\right)Q\left(\sqrt{\frac{2a^2}{N_0}}\right) \approx 4Q\left(\sqrt{\frac{2a^2}{N_0}}\right), \, M, a \gg 0 \qquad (4\text{–}108)$$

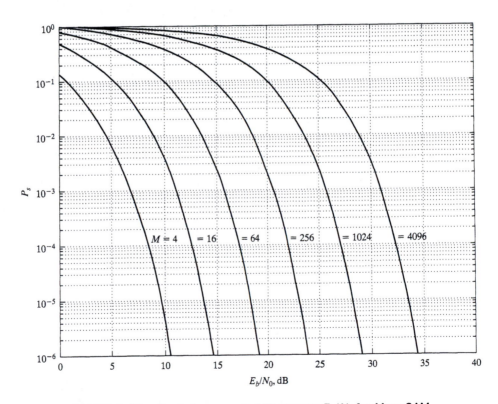

FIGURE 4–13 Symbol error probability versus E_b/N_0 for M-ary QAM.

This is exactly the result obtained if the union bound, (4–62), is applied to QAM since, for the interior of the signal–space diagram, each signaling point has four neighbors and each of them is distance $2a$ from the signal point of interest.

The limit of the symbol error probability (4–107) can be shown to be $1 - 1/M$ as $a \to 0$. This is as it should be since, with all noise, the receiver must randomly guess which symbol was sent. Since a given symbol is sent with probability $1/M$, the receiver will guess right with probability $1/M$, which means that the symbol error probability will be $1 - 1/M$ with noise only at the receiver input.

4.4 SIGNALING SCHEMES NOT REQUIRING COHERENT REFERENCES AT THE RECEIVER

In this section we consider the error probability performance of two modulation schemes that do not require coherent references at the receiver to demodulate the signal. The first to be considered is noncoherent frequency-shift keying (NFSK) and the second is differentially coherent phase-shift keying (DPSK). It will be shown that noncoherent schemes perform worse in terms of error probability for a given signal-to-noise ratio than do their coherent counterparts. Nevertheless, there are several situations where noncoherent schemes may be employed instead of a coherent signaling method. Among these are:

1. The channel may not allow the use of a coherent signaling scheme due to phase perturbations.
2. Phase-ambiguity resolution at the receiver for establishing a locally coherent reference can be avoided with schemes such as NFSK and DPSK.
3. In certain types of spread-spectrum systems, to be discussed later, the carrier frequency is hopped at regular intervals, which results in an unknown carrier phase angle being generated at each hop by the frequency synthesizer providing the carrier. Therefore, a signaling scheme is required that allows each hopped portion to be detected and used collectively to determine the data transmitted.
4. The receiver may be much simpler since the carrier reference required in a coherent system need not be generated.

4.4.1 Noncoherent Frequency-Shift Keying (NFSK)

In an NFSK system the received data during the kth signaling interval is of the form

$$z(t) = \sqrt{\frac{2E_s}{T_s}} \cos\left(2\pi f_i t + \alpha\right) + n(t), 0 \le t \le T_s, i = 1, 2, \cdots, M \quad (4\text{--}109)$$

where α is the unknown phase that is modeled as a uniformly distributed random variable in the interval $[0, 2\pi)$ and f_i is the frequency in hertz of the ith possible transmitted signal. The symbol energy, E_s, symbol duration, T_s, and noise, $n(t)$, are as defined previously. The frequency separation between adjacent signals is assumed to be sufficient to guarantee that the signals are uncorrelated (the noise components are also uncorrelated because the input noise is white). This signal set can be resolved into a $2M$-dimensional signal space spanned by the basis set

$$
\left.\begin{aligned}
\phi_{xi}(t) &= \sqrt{\frac{2}{T_s}}\cos 2\pi f_i t \\[2mm]
\phi_{yi}(t) &= \sqrt{\frac{2}{T_s}}\sin 2\pi f_i t
\end{aligned}\right\},\ 0 \le t \le T_s,\ i = 1, 2, \cdots, M \qquad (4\text{--}110)
$$

Given that $s_i(t)$ was sent, the coordinates of the received data vector, denoted as $\mathbf{Z} = (X_1, Y_1, X_2, Y_2, \ldots X_M, Y_M)$, are

$$
X_j = (\phi_{xj}, z) = \begin{cases} N_{xj}, & j \ne i \\ \sqrt{E_s}\cos\alpha + N_{xi}, & i = j \end{cases} \qquad (4\text{--}111)
$$

and

$$
Y_j = (\phi_{yj}, z) = \begin{cases} N_{yj}, & j \ne i \\ -\sqrt{E_s}\sin\alpha + N_{yi}, & i = j \end{cases} \qquad (4\text{--}112)
$$

where $j = 1, 2, \ldots, M$. The noise components, N_{xj} and N_{yj}, are uncorrelated and have variances $N_0/2$ as for the coherent FSK case. Given that $s_i(t)$ was transmitted, a correct reception is made if

$$
\sqrt{X_j^2 + Y_j^2} < \sqrt{X_i^2 + Y_i^2}, \quad \text{all } j \ne i \qquad (4\text{--}113)
$$

Evaluation of the probability of symbol error requires the pdf of the random variable $R_j = \sqrt{X_j^2 + Y_j^2}$. For $j = i$ and given α, X_j is a Gaussian random variable with mean $\sqrt{E_s}\cos\alpha$ and variance $N_0/2$. Similarly, for $j = i$, Y_j is a Gaussian random variable with mean $-\sqrt{E_s}\sin\alpha$ and variance $N_0/2$. (For $j \ne i$, both have zero means.) Furthermore, they are independent, so that their joint pdf is

$$
f_{X_j Y_j}(x, y|\alpha) = \frac{1}{\pi N_0}\exp\left\{-\frac{1}{N_0}\left[(x - \sqrt{E_s}\cos\alpha)^2 + (y + \sqrt{E_s}\sin\alpha)^2\right]\right\} \qquad (4\text{--}114)
$$

The joint pdf of X_j and Y_j unconditional on α is obtained by averaging over α, which was assumed to be uniformly distributed in $[0, 2\pi)$. A change in variables to the polar coordinates r and ϕ defined by

$$
\left.\begin{aligned}
x &= \sqrt{\frac{N_0}{2}}\,r\sin\phi \\[2mm]
y &= \sqrt{\frac{N_0}{2}}\,r\cos\phi
\end{aligned}\right\} r > 0, 0 < \phi \le 2\pi \qquad (4\text{--}115)
$$

results in the joint pdf

$$
f_{R_j \Phi_j}(r,\phi) = \frac{r}{2\pi}\exp\left[-\frac{1}{2}\left(r^2 + \frac{2E_s}{N_0}\right)\right]I_0\left(r\sqrt{\frac{2E_s}{N_0}}\right) \qquad (4\text{--}116)
$$

$$
j = i, r > 0, 0 \le \phi < 2\pi
$$

where $I_0(\cdot)$ is the modified Bessel function of the first kind and order zero. The joint pdf on r alone is obtained by integration over ϕ. It is simply (4–116) without the 2π in the denominator and is recognized as a Ricean pdf. If $j \neq i$, the pdf of R_j can be obtained by setting $E_s = 0$; the resulting pdf is Rayleigh.

In terms of the random variables R_j, $j = 1, 2, \ldots, M$, the detection criterion, given that $s_i(t)$ was transmitted, is

$$R_j < R_i, \text{ all } j \neq i \tag{4–117}$$

Since the R_js are statistically independent random variables, the probability of the compound event, given R_i, is

$$P(R_j < R_i, \text{ all } j \neq i \mid R_i) = \prod_{\substack{j=1 \\ j \neq i}}^{M} P(R_j < R_i \mid R_i) \tag{4–118}$$

But

$$P(R_j < R_i \mid R_i) = \int_0^{R_i} r \exp(-r^2/2)dr = 1 - \exp(-R_i^2/2) \tag{4–119}$$

The probability of correct reception, given $s_i(t)$ sent, is (4–118) averaged over R_i; recall that R_i has a Ricean pdf, which is 2π times (4–116). Using (4–119) in (4–118), the result for this average probability of correct reception is

$$P_s(C \mid s_i \text{ sent}) = \int_0^\infty [1 - \exp(-r^2/2)]^{M-1} r \exp[-(r^2 + 2E_s/N_0)/2] I_0\left(\sqrt{\frac{2E_s}{N_0}}\right) dr \tag{4–120}$$

Now, by the binomial theorem,

$$[1 - \exp(-r^2/2)]^{M-1} = \sum_{k=0}^{M-1} \binom{M-1}{k}(-1)^k \exp(-kr^2/2) \tag{4–121}$$

This series can be substituted into (4–120), the order of summation and integration reversed, and the integral

$$\int_0^\infty x \exp(-ax^2) I_0(bx)dx = \frac{1}{2a}\exp(b^2/4a) \tag{4–122}$$

used to produce the result

$$P_s(C \mid s_i) = \exp(-E_s/N_0)\sum_{k=0}^{M-1} \binom{M-1}{k}\frac{(-1)^k}{k+1}\exp\left[\frac{E_s}{N_0(k+1)}\right] \tag{4–123}$$

Since this result is independent of i, the probability of symbol error is

$$P_s = 1 - P_s(C \mid s_i) = \sum_{k=1}^{M-1} \binom{M-1}{k}\frac{(-1)^{k+1}}{k+1}\exp\left[-\frac{k}{(k+1)}\frac{E_s}{N_0}\right] \tag{4–124}$$

For $M = 2$, (4–124) reduces to

$$P_b = \frac{1}{2} \exp\left(-\frac{E_b}{2N_0}\right) \tag{4–125}$$

which can be shown by other means to be the result for noncoherent binary FSK (see [1], p. 490).

It is interesting to compare M-ary noncoherent FSK with a system that, corresponding to each M-ary signal, sends $n = \log_2 M$ bits independently through the channel by means of a binary noncoherent FSK system. The error probability for an n-bit "word" of such a system is

$$P_w(\varepsilon) = 1 - [1 - P_b]^n \tag{4–126}$$

where P_b is given by (4–125). This result is compared in Figure 4–14 along with (4–124) as a function of $E_b/N_0 = E_s/nN_0$ Note that the performance of the n-bit word system becomes worse relative to NFSK as n increases due to the hard decisions on each bit, whereas the M-ary NFSK system makes decisions on each symbol, each of which carries n bits.

4.4.2   Differential Phase-Shift Keying (DPSK)

In differentially coherent detection of a PSK-modulated signal, the phase of the current symbol is compared with the phase of the preceding symbol (or, possibly, symbols) in order to make a decision. This presupposes that (1) the unknown relative phase shift of the received signal due to the channel characteristics is constant over at least two symbol periods, and (2) a known relationship exists between two successive symbol phases that depends on the input data sequence.

It is easiest to illustrate the latter condition with the binary case, where this relationship between successive symbol phases is provided by differentially encoding the data from the information source. Suppose that the nth data bit from the source is denoted by D_n, which may be either 0 or 1 and that the nth bit of differentially encoded data is denoted C_n (either a 0 or 1). The operation used to produce the differentially encoded data sequence $\{C_n\}$ is

$$C_n = D_n \oplus C_{n-1} \tag{4–127}$$

where $\oplus$ denotes the exclusive-OR operation (XOR), or a binary add without carry.

The *decoding* operation is performed by forming the sequence $\{\hat{D}_n\}$ with members given by

$$\hat{D}_n = C_n \oplus C_{n-1} \tag{4–128}$$

However, when a differentially encoded data sequence is used to phase-shift key a carrier, which is referred to as DPSK, the detection operation can be implemented by comparing the present symbol with the immediately preceding symbol as shown in the block diagrams of Figure 4–15. In addition to the simplicity of differentially coherent detection of DPSK, an additional advantage accrues from the fact that the result of differentially de-

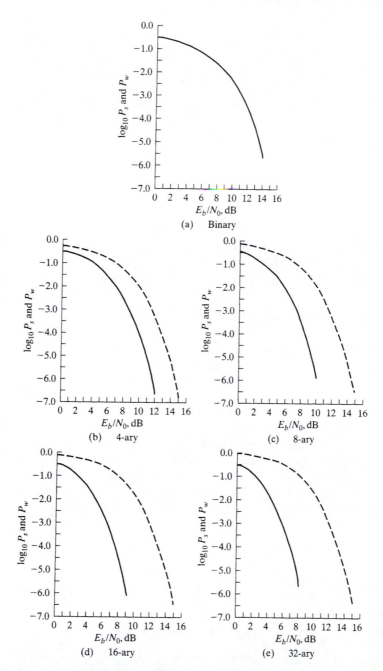

FIGURE 4–14 Comparison of symbol error probability for a noncoherent *M*-ary FSK system (solid) with the word error probability of an *n*-bit noncoherent binary system (dashed).

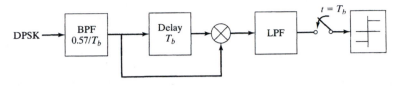

(a) IF sampling detector

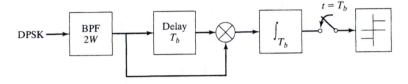

(a) IF integrate-and-dump detector

FIGURE 4–15 Suboptimum detectors for binary DPSK (see [6] for an analysis of these two types of detectors and a comparison of their performances with the optimum detector).

tecting a DPSK signal *or its inversion* results in the same output data sequence. This is illustrated in the following example.

EXAMPLE 4–8

The data sequence 10111001010 can be differentially encoded by assuming an initial reference bit of $C_{-1} = 1$ and carrying out the operation (4–127) on the successive data bits. The results are

$$\{D_n\}:\ \ 10111001010$$
$$\{C_n\}:\ 100101110011$$

This sequence is decoded using (4–128). The resulting operations are

$$\{C_n\}:\ 100101110011$$
$$\{C_{n-1}\}:\ 100101110011$$
$$\{\hat{D}_n\}:\ \ 10111001010$$

If the differentially encoded data sequence $\{C_n\}$ is accidentally inverted, the correct data sequence is still decoded, assuming that no errors are made, as follows:

$$\{\overline{C}_n\}:\ \ 011010001100$$
$$\{\overline{C}_{n-1}\}:\ 011010001100$$
$$\{D_n\}:\ \ \ 10111001010$$

Thus differential encoding and decoding can be used to solve the phase-ambiguity problem in generation of a coherent local reference in BPSK transmission.

It is emphasized that differential encoding/decoding of BPSK to solve the phase-ambiguity problem differs from DPSK. The latter makes use of the built-in phase relationship between symbols provided by differential encoding so that a detector such as illustrated in Figure 4–15 can be used. On the other hand, the probability of error for any modulation scheme (coherent PSK, say) that utilizes differential encoding and decoding of the data to resolve phase ambiguities in the detection process is given by

$$P_{DE}(\varepsilon) = 2P_b[1 - P_b] \tag{4-129}$$

where P_b is the raw bit error probability of the channel. This follows because an error occurs with differential encoding/decoding when the reference bit or the current bit from the demodulator/detector are in error, *but not both*. Note that for P_b small, the resultant error probability is essentially twice that of the channel error probability. This amounts to an SNR degradation of about 0.3 dB for small error probabilities.

To generalize the concept of differential PSK to the case of *M*-ary PSK, we suppose that the transmitted carrier phase angle at symbol time $n - 1$ is α_{n-1} and that it is desired to transmit symbol $\beta_n = \Phi$ at time n, where β_n takes on any of the values given by

$$\beta_n = \frac{(2l - 1)\pi}{M}, \, l \le M, \text{ modulo } 2\pi \tag{4-130}$$

The *transmitted phase* at time n is then

$$\alpha_n = \alpha_{n-1} + \Phi \tag{4-131}$$

Suppose that the phases received corresponding to α_{n-1} and α_n are $\theta_{n-1} = \alpha_{n-1} + \gamma$ and $\theta_n = \alpha_n + \gamma$, respectively, where γ is the unknown phase shift introduced by the channel. A correct decision is made at the receiver when the *received phase difference* $\theta = \theta_n - \theta_{n-1}$ is such that

$$\Phi - \frac{\pi}{M} < \theta \le \Phi + \frac{\pi}{M} \tag{4-132}$$

The receiver structure of Figure 4–16 can be used to compute the phase differences required for the decision rule (4–132). The decision rule (4–132) is identical to that used for coherent *M*-ary PSK except now the *phase differences* between successive symbols are used. That is, the decision procedure is to find which $2\pi/M$ wedge around each possible transmitted phase that a received phase difference falls into, as illustrated in Figure 4–17.

Assuming independent additive noise samples on successive phases, the pdf, $p(\theta)$, of the phase difference θ in (4–132) can be shown to be [4, p. 252] the convolution of the following pdf with itself:

$$f(\theta) = \frac{1}{2\pi}\left[1 + \sqrt{\frac{4\pi E_s}{N_0}} \cos\theta \exp\left(\frac{E_s}{N_0} \cos^2\theta\right) Q\left(\sqrt{\frac{2E_s}{N_0}} \cos\theta\right)\right], \quad -\pi < \theta \le \pi \tag{4-133}$$

The probability distribution function corresponding to $P(\theta)$ is, by definition, given by

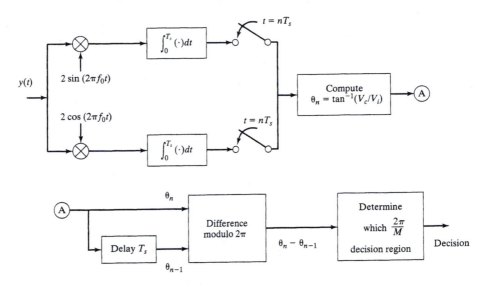

FIGURE 4–16   Block diagram of an *M*-ary differentially coherent PSK receiver.

$$P(\theta) = \int_{-\pi}^{\theta} p(u)du, \quad |\theta| \le \pi \tag{4–134}$$

which cannot be evaluated in closed form. The probability of symbol error given that phase ϕ was transmitted, from (4–132) or Figure 4–17, can be written as

$$P_s(\varepsilon|\phi) = P\left(\theta > \phi + \frac{\pi}{M} \text{ or } \theta \le \phi - \frac{\pi}{M} \right)$$

$$= 2P\left(\theta > \phi + \frac{\pi}{M} \right) \tag{4–135}$$

$$= 2\left[1 - P\left(\frac{\pi}{M} \right) \right]$$

where $P(\pi/M)$ is the phase distribution function (4–134) with $\theta = \pi/M$. This can be expressed in closed form only for $M = 2$. Since (4–135) is independent of ϕ, this is also the probability of error averaged over all possible transmitted phases.

It can be shown that the following bounds apply for (4–135) [7]:

$$\max(P_1, P_2) \le P_s(\varepsilon|\phi) \le P_1 + P_2$$

where

$$P_1 = P[\sin(\theta - \phi + \pi/M) < 0] \tag{4–136}$$

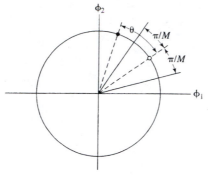

(a)   Error made

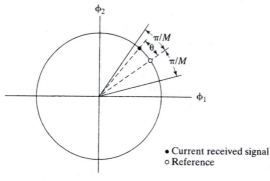

       • Current received signal
       ○ Reference

(b)   Correct decision made

FIGURE 4–17   Decision space for received phase differences in differentially co-herent detection of *M*-ary PSK.

and

$$P_2 = P[\sin(\theta - \phi - \pi/M) > 0] \qquad (4\text{–}137)$$

Because of the symmetry of the signal constellation and the rotational symmetry of the noise random variables, it follows that $P_1 = P_2$ and

$$P_1 \leq P_s \leq 2P_1 \qquad (4\text{–}138)$$

Prabhu [7] has shown that the probability P_1 can be expressed as

$$P_1 = \frac{1}{2}\sin(\pi/M)\int_{(E_s/N_0)}^{\infty}\exp(-y)I_0[y\cos(\pi/M)]dy \qquad (4\text{–}139)$$

where $I_0(u)$ is the modified Bessel function of the first kind and order zero. For $M = 2$, (4–139) reduces to

$$P_1 = P_b = \frac{1}{2} \exp\left(-\frac{E_b}{N_0}\right) \tag{4–140}$$

which is the correct result for binary DPSK.

Tight upper and lower bounds based on (4–140) were derived by Prabhu [7], but Pawula [8] has given an asymptotic expression for the symbol error probability of M-ary DPSK that is handier. It is

$$P_{s,\text{ asymp}} = 2\sqrt{\frac{1 + \cos(\pi/M)}{2\cos(\pi/M)}} \, Q\left(\sqrt{\log_2 M\left[1 - \cos\left(\frac{\pi}{M}\right)\right]\frac{2E_b}{N_0}}\right) \tag{4–141}$$

He also gave tight bounds for the symbol error probability in terms of this expression, which is

$$P_{s,\text{asymp}} < P_s < 1.03 P_{s,\text{asymp}} \tag{4–142}$$

Pawula [5] has also provided an exact expression in terms of a proper integral, which is easily integrated numerically and is given by

$$P_{s,\text{MDPSK}} = \frac{1}{\pi} \int_0^{\pi(1 - 1/M)} \exp\left[-\frac{(E_s/N_0)\sin^2(\pi/M)}{1 + \cos(\pi/M)\cos\phi}\right] d\phi \tag{4–143}$$

Results for the symbol error probability versus E_s/N_0 are shown in Figure 4–18 for several values of M and compared with similar results for M-ary PSK.

4.5   COMPARISON OF DIGITAL MODULATION SYSTEMS

From the preceding developments it is clear that the communications engineer has a wide choice of digital modulations from which to choose. Factors such as ease of implementation and effect of hardware and channel imperfections are certainly of importance in making a selection. Even before consideration of such factors, however, it is of fundamental importance to know how modulation schemes compare in terms of power and bandwidth efficiencies as mentioned in Chapter 1. To do so, two things are necessary in order to place all systems on an equivalent basis in terms of (1) power efficiency and (2) bandwidth efficiency. For example, consider power efficiency. In comparing an octal signaling scheme (such as 8-PSK) with a binary scheme, the binary scheme would be required to transmit symbols at three times the rate of the octal system since each symbol in the octal system conveys one of eight possibilities (3 bits per symbol). Considering power efficiency, if the octal system had a symbol error probability of, say, 10^{-6} for a certain E_b/N_0 and the binary system required a larger E_b/N_0 to give $P_s = 1 - (1 - P_b)^3 = 10^{-6}$, then the choice would be in favor of the octal system. Considering spectrum efficiency, if the octal

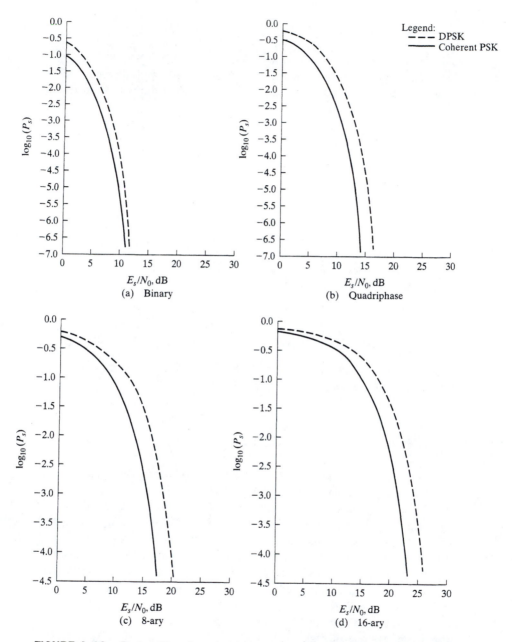

FIGURE 4–18   Probability of symbol error versus E_s/N_0 for M-ary DPSK (dashed) compared with that for coherent M-ary PSK (solid).

system required less bandwidth than the binary system while transmitting at the same bit rate, then the choice would also be in favor of the octal system. One would have to decide if the particular application favored a *power efficient* scheme or a *bandwidth efficient* scheme.

In the foregoing discussion, it is suggested that the two schemes are being compared on a symbol-by-symbol basis. This is fine as long as attention is focused only on the two systems initially chosen. However, suppose it is now desired to consider a 16-PSK system. All calculations would have to be redone. Rather than be faced with this, it is obviously be better to compare systems on the basis of *equivalent bit error probability*. This is the subject of the next section. Following this will be a consideration of the bandwidth efficiencies of the various modulation schemes considered in this chapter in terms of bits per second per hertz of bandwidth.

4.5.1   Bit Error Probabilities from Symbol Error Probabilities

To compute an equivalent bit error probability, or *bit error rate (BER)*, from a symbol error probability, two approaches may be taken depending on the structure of the signal space and the mapping of the signal space points into equivalent bit sequences.

In the first case, we assume that in going from one signal point to an adjacent signal point, only one bit in the binary word representing the signal point changes. Such is the case, for example, with M-ary PSK if a *Gray code* is used to identify the signal points, or in the case of QAM as shown with the mapping in Figure 4–10. Since the probability of mistaking an adjacent signal point for the actual signal point is a more probable error than is that of mistaking it for a nonadjacent signal point, assuming P_s is small, it follows that the most probable number of bit errors for each symbol error is one. Since there are $\log_2 M$ bits represented by each symbol in an M-ary system, it follows that the bit error probability is related to the symbol error probability for systems where the above assumptions hold by

$$P_b = \frac{P_s}{\log_2 M} \tag{4–144}$$

In the second case, it is assumed that all symbol errors are equally likely, such as would be the case for M-ary FSK, for example. If this is the case, then each symbol is in error in an M-ary system with probability $P_s/(M-1)$. Let $n = \log_2 M$ be the number of bits represented by each symbol. For a given symbol error, suppose that k bits are in error. There are $\binom{n}{k}$ ways that this can happen, which results in the ratio of the average number of bit errors per n-bit symbol error to number of bits per symbol being given by

$$P_b = \frac{1}{n} \sum_{k=1}^{n} k \binom{n}{k} \frac{P_s}{M-1} = \frac{2^{n-1}}{M-1} P_s = \frac{M}{2(M-1)} P_s \tag{4–145}$$

Note that as M becomes large, this result approaches $P_s/2$.

4.5.2 Bandwidth Efficiencies of *M*-ary Digital Communication Systems

In this subsection, we consider the bandwidth efficiencies in terms of bits per second per hertz (bps/Hz) of bandwidth of various digital modulation schemes. For an *M*-ary digital communication system, the *bit rate, R_b,* is given in terms of the *symbol rate, R_s,* as

$$R_b = (\log_2 M)R_s \tag{4–146}$$

First, consider an *M*-ary PSK system. The modulated signal spectrum for such a system has a null-to-null bandwidth for the mainlobe of $2R_s$ Hz, but in terms of *bit rate,* its null-to-null bandwidth is

$$B_{\text{MPSK}} = \frac{2R_b}{\log_2 M} \text{ Hz} \tag{4–147}$$

For MQAM and *M*-ary DPSK, the same result is obtained.

For coherent *M*-ary FSK, consider the minimum spacing between frequency "tones" of $\Delta f = 1/(2T_s) = R_s/2$. For *M* tones, the total frequency extent is $(M-1)R_s/2$. On each end, we allow another R_s Hz to get to the null on either end of the spectrum for a total bandwidth of[13]

$$2R_s + \frac{(M-1)R_s}{2} = \frac{(M+3)R_s}{2}$$

or

$$B_{\text{coh.FSK}} = \frac{M+3}{2\log_2 M} R_b \text{ Hz} \tag{4–148}$$

NFSK is similar except that the tones are spaced by $2R_s$.

The *bandwidth efficiencies* in bits/s/Hz of the various modulation schemes considered in this chapter are summarized in Table 4–1.

TABLE 4–1   Bandwidth Efficiencies for Various Modulation Schemes

Modulation Scheme	Bandwidth Efficiency (bps/Hz)
M-ary PSK, DPSK, QAM	$0.5\log_2 M$
MFSK; coherent	$\dfrac{2\log_2 M}{M+3}$
MFSK; noncoherent	$\dfrac{\log_2 M}{2M}$

[13]This is a grossly simplified treatment of the bandwidth for FSK. Actual bandwidth calculations for FSK are much more complex than given here. See (4–203) for an equation giving the spectrum for continuous-phase FSK.

4.6 COMPARISON OF *M*-ARY DIGITAL MODULATION SCHEMES ON POWER AND BANDWIDTH-EQUIVALENT BASES

4.6.1 Coherent Digital Modulation Schemes

On the basis of the discussion given in Section 4.5, we are now in a position to compare *M*-ary modulation schemes on an equivalent basis. Figures 4–19, 4–20, and 4–21 show the BER performance versus E_b/N_0 for coherent *M*-ary FSK, PSK, and QAM schemes. For Figure 4–19, (4–145) was used in conjunction with (4–88) to obtain upper bounds for the BER. For Figure 4–20, (4–144) was used along with (4–96) to obtain upper bounds for the BER, and for Figure 4–21, (4–144) was used in conjunction with (4–107) to obtain bounds for the bit error probability. In comparing these figures it is seen that in terms of bit error probability performance, *M*-ary FSK is best followed by QAM, with *M*-ary PSK performing the worst for large *M*. That is, *M*-ary FSK is the most power efficient modulation scheme, and *M*-ary PSK is the worst if $M > 4$. The reason for this is clear when one considers the signal spaces for each. *M*-ary FSK has an *M*-dimensional signal space, while QAM and PSK have two-dimensional signal spaces. Furthermore, the signal points

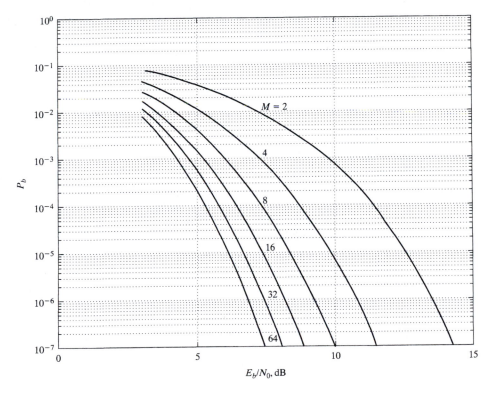

FIGURE 4–19   Bit error rate performance versus E_b/N_0 for coherent *M*-ary FSK.

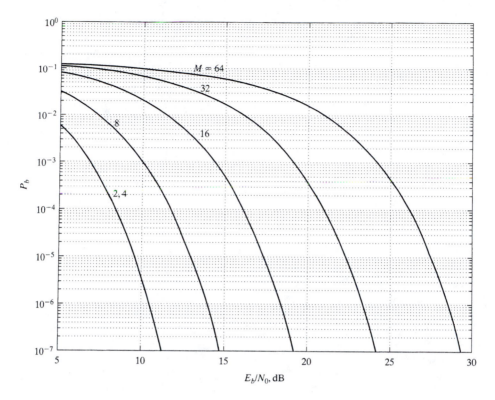

FIGURE 4–20   Bit error probabilities versus E_b/N_0 for M-ary PSK.

for PSK are constrained to lie on a circle of radius $\sqrt{E_s}$, while each signal point for FSK lies on a single coordinate axis at a distance $\sqrt{E_s}$ from the origin. Thus, as M is increased, the signal points become crowded together more so for PSK than for FSK (the exception to this observation is in going from $M = 2$ to $M = 4$, and in these cases PSK outperforms FSK) with the result that errors are more likely for the former than for the latter. For QAM the signal points are distributed at the crossing points of a grid in two-dimensional signal space rather than being constrained to lie on a circle as with PSK.

Comparing modulation schemes on the basis of power (i.e., the E_b/N_0 required for a given BER) tells only half the story, however. The other half is told by bandwidth efficiency or the bps/Hz achieved. Table 4–2 gives the values of E_b/N_0 required for $P_b = 10^{-6}$ along with the bandwidth efficiency for the various schemes discussed earlier. It is seen that the better power efficiency of M-ary FSK is obtained at the expense of bandwidth efficiency. This should not be surprising since each additional signal used in M-ary FSK adds a dimension to the signal space whereas the signal space is always two-dimensional for M-ary PSK (except for $M = 2$, of course). Therefore, the bandwidth increases with M linearly for MFSK with the number of signal points and stays constant for MPSK and MQAM.

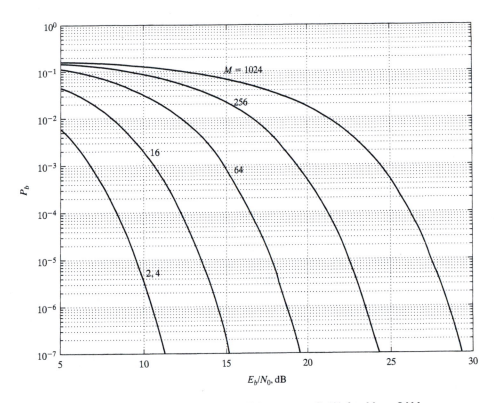

FIGURE 4–21   Bit error probabilities versus E_b/N_0 for *M*-ary QAM.

Bit error probabilities are not shown for low values of E_b/N_0 in Figures 4–19 through 4–21 because the approximation that we are accounting only for the single bit error to a closest-neighbor symbol breaks down at large probabilities of error. For the low E_b/N_0 regime, the probability of mistaking a signal point further away than closest neighbors for the correct one has non-negligible probability.

It is of interest to compare these modulation schemes with the ideal case shown in Figure 1–4 based on Shannon capacity. This ideal curve is repeated in Figure 4–22, and the points given in Table 4–2 are superimposed. There is considerable room for improvement, no matter which modulation scheme we consider. Improvement by coding is the subject of Chapters 6 and 7.

4.6.2   Noncoherent Digital Modulation Schemes

Bit error rates for noncoherent *M*-ary FSK (NFSK) and DPSK are shown versus E_b/N_0 in Figures 4–23 and 4–24, respectively. The story here is similar to that of the coherent cases. The growing dimensionality of NFSK signal space with *M* means the power efficiency of NFSK improves with increasing *M*, whereas the constant dimensionality of the

TABLE 4–2 Power and Bandwidth Efficiencies for M-ary, Coherent FSK, PSK, and QASK

Modulation Scheme		E_b/N_0 for BER = 10^{-6}	Bandwidth Efficiency Bits/s/Hz
PSK:	$M = 2$	10.5	0.5
	$M = 4$	10.5	1.0
	$M = 8$	14.0	1.5
	$M = 16$	18.5	2.0
	$M = 32$	23.4	2.5
	$M = 64$	28.5	3.0
	$M = 128$	33.8	3.5
	$M = 256$	39.2	4.0
QAM:	$M = 4$	10.5	1.0
	$M = 16$	15.0	2.0
	$M = 64$	18.5	3.0
	$M = 256$	24.0	4.0
	$M = 1024$	28.0	5.0
	$M = 4096$	33.5	6.0
FSK:	$M = 2$	13.5	0.40
	$M = 4$	10.8	0.57
	$M = 8$	9.3	0.55
	$M = 16$	8.2	0.42
	$M = 32$	7.5	0.29
	$M = 64$	6.9	0.18
	$M = 128$	6.4	0.11
	$M = 256$	6.0	0.06

DPSK signal space gives worse power efficiency with increasing M. Finally, we compare CFSK (coherent FSK) and NFSK. Table 4–3 gives the required E_b/N_0 for a BER of 10^{-6} along with the bandwidth efficiencies versus M. The results show that a small price is paid in using NFSK instead of CFSK; the advantage of NFSK over CFSK is that a coherent reference at the receiver is not required.

4.7 SOME COMMONLY USED MODULATION SCHEMES

In this section, we discuss some special digital modulation schemes that have found wide use in several application areas. In some instances, they are special cases of the modulation schemes that we have considered already. Examples of these include quadrature phase-shift keying (QPSK), offset quadrature phase-shift keying (OQPSK), and minimum-shift keying (MSK). Others fit within a given category, but have features especially built in for certain applications. Examples here are Gaussian MSK (used in the pan-

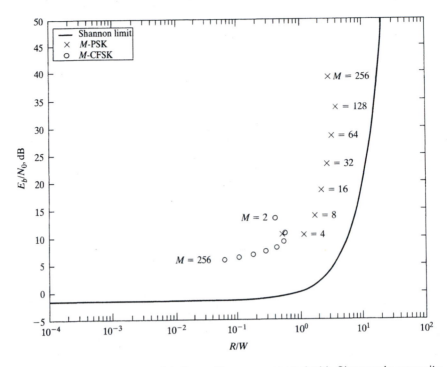

FIGURE 4–22   Various modulation schemes compared with Shannon's capacity boundary.

European second-generation digital cellular radio system) and $\pi/4$–differential QPSK (used in the U.S. second-generation digital cellular system).

4.7.1 Quadrature-Multiplexed Signaling Schemes

In this section, several signaling schemes are considered that can be viewed as resulting from impressing two different data streams on two carriers of the same frequency in phase quadrature and therefore are put under the general heading of quadrature-multiplexed signaling schemes. They are QPSK, OQPSK, and MSK as mentioned above.

4.7.1.1 Quadrature Multiplexing.   Consider two data-bearing signals, $m_1(t)$ and $m_2(t)$, which are to be modulated onto carriers of the same frequency. If the carriers are in *phase quadrature*, $m_1(t)$ and $m_2(t)$ may be separated at the receiver by sine and cosine reference waveforms as seen by the generalized analysis given previously (the sine and cosine references form an orthonormal basis set). That is, the transmitted signal is

$$x_c(t) = A_1 m_1(t) \cos\left(2\pi f_0 t + \alpha\right) - A_2 m_2(t) \sin\left(2\pi f_0 t + \alpha\right) \quad (4\text{–}149)$$

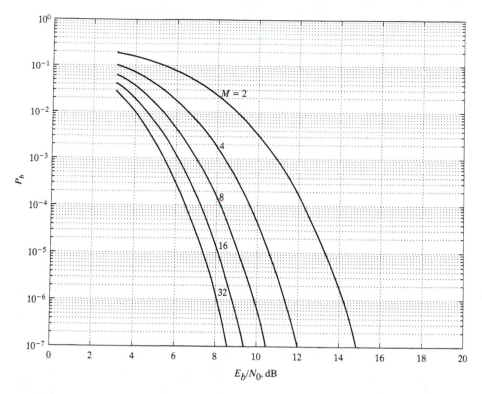

FIGURE 4–23   Bit error probability versus E_b/N_0 for noncoherent M-ary FSK.

where α is a constant phase shift which can be chosen as 0 for convenience. The block diagrams of the modulator and demodulator for such a scheme are shown in Figure 4–25.

If $m_1(t)$ and $m_2(t)$ are binary digital signals with amplitudes ± 1 that may change sign at time intervals spaced by T_s seconds, $x_c(t)$ can be written as

$$x_c(t) = A \cos \left[2\pi f_0 t + \theta(t) \right]$$

$$\text{where } \theta(t) = \tan^{-1} \left[\frac{A_2 m_2(t)}{A_1 m_1(t)} \right] \text{ and } A = \sqrt{A_1^2 + A_2^2} \tag{4-150}$$

The possible signal phasors corresponding to (4–150) are shown in Figure 4–26 for $m_1(t)$ and $m_2(t)$ binary valued. It is seen that $x_c(t)$ is, in effect, a constant-amplitude, digitally phase-modulated signal whose phase deviation takes on the values

$$\tan^{-1}\left(\frac{A_2}{A_1}\right), \tan^{-1}\left(\frac{A_2}{A_1}\right) + \pi, -\tan^{-1}\left(\frac{A_2}{A_1}\right), -\tan^{-1}\left(\frac{A_2}{A_1}\right) + \pi \tag{4-151}$$

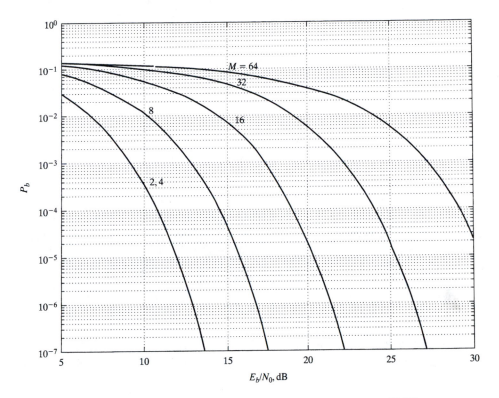

FIGURE 4–24   Bit error probability versus E_b/N_0 for M-ary DPSK.

4.7.1.2 Quadrature and Offset-Quadrature Phase-Shift Keying.   If $A_1 = A_2 = A/\sqrt{2}$ and $m_1(t)$ and $m_2(t)$ have the instants aligned when their signs can change, the resulting modulated signal is called *quadrature phase-shift keying* (QPSK). If $A_1 = A_2$, but the time instants when $m_1(t)$ can change sign are offset by $T_s/2$ seconds from the time instants when $m_1(t)$ can change sign, the resulting phase modulated signal is referred to as

TABLE 4–3   Perfomances of Noncoherent and Coherent FSK Compared

Number of symbols per signaling interval, M	E_b/N_0 in dB for $P_b = 10^{-6}$		Bandwidth Efficiency (bits/s/Hz)	
	Noncoherent	Coherent	Noncoherent	Coherent
2	14.2	13.6	0.25	0.40
4	11.4	10.8	0.25	0.57
8	9.9	9.3	0.19	0.55
16	8.8	8.2	0.13	0.42

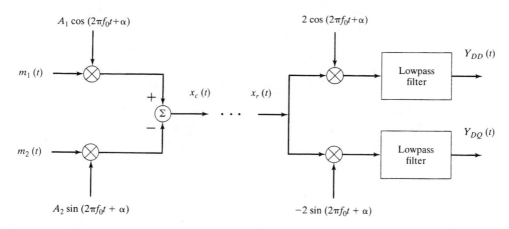

FIGURE 4–25 Block diagram of a quadrature-multiplexed communication system.

offset QPSK (OQPSK) or *staggered QPSK*. QPSK can change phase by 0, ± 90, or 180 degrees at the switching times for $m_1(t)$ and $m_2(t)$, whereas the phase shifts for OQPSK are limited to 0 or ± 90 degrees since either $m_1(t)$ or $m_2(t)$ can change sign at a given switching instant, but not both. Signal space diagrams for QPSK and OQPSK are compared in Figure 4–27, which illustrates the different phase shifts and phase transitions possible.

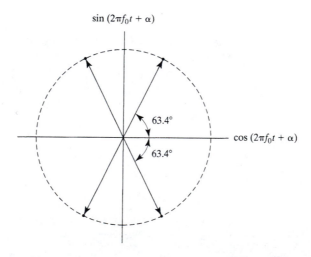

FIGURE 4–26 Phasor diagram for a quadrature-multiplexed signal where m_1 and m_2 are constant-amplitude binary signals ($A_1 = 1$ and $A_2 = 2$ assumed for purposes of illustration).

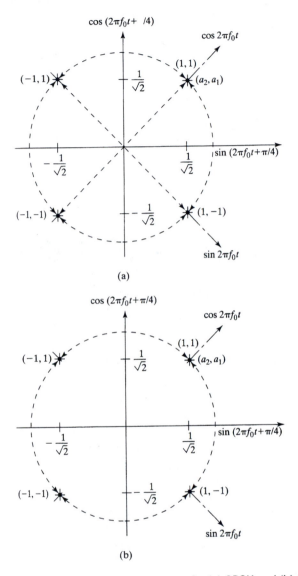

(a)

(b)

FIGURE 4–27   Signal-space (phasor) diagrams for (a) QPSK and (b) OQPSK showing possible phase transitions for each ($\alpha = \pi/4$).

The power spectra of QPSK and OQPSK are identical. However, experiments have shown that the envelope of OQPSK tends to remain more nearly constant when the waveform is filtered (this is shown by simulation in Chapter 5). Thus it is preferable over QPSK when used in applications where significant band limiting of the signal is performed.

4.7.1.3 Minimum-Shift Keying. Another choice of $m_1(t)$ and $m_2(t)$ that allows (4–149) to be expressed in constant-envelope form is

$$m_1(t) = a_1(t)\cos 2\pi f_1 t$$

$$\text{and} \quad m_2(t) = a_2(t) \sin 2\pi f_2 t \qquad (4\text{–}152)$$

with $A_1 = A_2$, where $a_1(t)$ and $a_2(t)$ are ± 1 binary-valued signals whose signs may change each T_s seconds with the switching times for $a_2(t)$ offset from those of $a_2(t)$ by $T_s/2$ seconds. The result for $x_c(t)$ is then of the form (4–150) with $A_1 = A_2 = A$, and

$$\theta(t) = \tan^{-1}\left[\frac{a_2(t)}{a_1(t)} \tan 2\pi f_1 t\right] \qquad (4\text{–}153)$$

$$= \pm 2\pi f_1 t + u_k$$

where the sign on the first term in (4–153) is minus if the signs of a_1 and a_2 are the same, and plus if they are opposite. The angle $u_k = 0$ or π modulo-2π corresponding to $a_1 = 1$ or -1, respectively. Thus, for this case, (4–150) becomes

$$x_c(t) = A\cos[2\pi(f_0 \pm f_1)t + u_k] \qquad (4\text{–}154)$$

Note that the sign in front of f_1 may change at intervals of $T_b = T_s/2$ seconds since a_1 and a_2 are staggered.

With $f_1 = 1/(2T_s) = 1/(4T_b)$ and a_1 staggered $T_b = T_s/2$ seconds relative to a_2, the phase of $x_c(t)$ is continuous, and the resulting waveform is referred to as a *minimum-shift-keyed (MSK) signal*. Its name arises from the fact that $\Delta f = 2f_1 = 1/(2T_b)$ is the minimum frequency spacing for the two signals represented by (4–154) to be coherently orthogonal (i.e., the integral of the product of the two possible transmitted signals over a T_b-second interval is zero). Waveforms for MSK are illustrated in Figure 4–28.[14]

The *peak-to-peak frequency deviation* of an angle-modulated signal can be defined as the difference between its maximum and minimum instantaneous frequencies. Thus MSK can be viewed as an FM-modulated waveform with peak-to-peak frequency deviation $1/(2T_b)$. Alternatively, it can be viewed as an OQPSK signal for which sinusoidal pulse shapes are employed for the binary message waveforms.[15]

4.7.1.4 Performance of Digital Quadrature Modulation Systems. The optimum demodulators for QPSK, OQPSK, and MSK have two correlators. For QPSK and OQPSK, the correlation signals at the receiver are

---

[14]The type of MSK described here is MSK Type I. MSK Type II modulation results if the weighting is always a positive half-cosinusoid or half-sinusoid. See S. Pasupathy, *IEEE Commun. Mag.*, Vol. 17, pp. 14–22, July 1979.

[15]In neither MSK Type I or Type II is there a one-to-one correspondence between the data bits of the serial bit stream and the instantaneous frequency of the transmitted signal. A modulation format for which this is the case is *fast-frequency shift keying* (FFSK) wherein the input bit stream is differentially encoded before performing MSK Type I modulation.

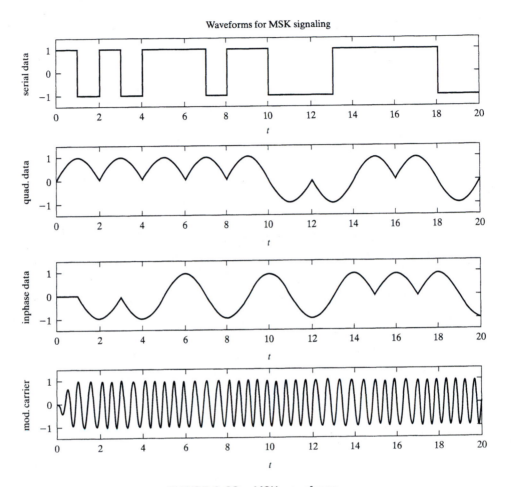

FIGURE 4–28   MSK waveforms.

$$\left.\begin{array}{l}\phi_1(t) = \sqrt{\dfrac{2}{T_s}}\cos 2\pi f_0 t \\[3mm] \phi_2(t) = \sqrt{\dfrac{2}{T_s}}\sin 2\pi f_0 t\end{array}\right\},\, 0 \le t \le T_s \qquad (4\text{–}155)$$

For MSK, they are

$$\left.\begin{array}{l}\phi_1(t) = \dfrac{2}{\sqrt{T_s}}\cos\left(\dfrac{t}{2T_s}\right)\cos 2\pi f_0 t \\[3mm] \phi_2(t) = \dfrac{2}{\sqrt{T_s}}\sin\left(\dfrac{t}{2T_s}\right)\sin 2\pi f_0 t\end{array}\right\},\, 0 \le t \le T_s \qquad (4\text{–}156)$$

In the case of QPSK, OQPSK, and MSK, the same result is obtained for the symbol error probability. By tracing the signal and noise components through the receiver block diagram, it follows that the probability of symbol error is given by

$$P_s = 2P_1 - P_1^2$$

$$\text{where} \quad P_1 = Q\left(\sqrt{\frac{E_s}{N_0}}\right) = Q\left(\sqrt{\frac{2E_b}{N_0}}\right) \tag{4-157}$$

where E_s and E_b are the symbol and bit energies, respectively.

EXAMPLE 4–9

Two data streams, $d_1(t)$ and $d_2(t)$, are to be transmitted using unbalanced QPSK, where the data rate for $d_1(t)$ is 10 kbps and that for $d_2(t)$ is 1 Mbps.

(a)   Relate A_1 and A_2 such that both bit sequences have equal energies per bit.

(b)   With A_1 and A_2 so related, find the possible phase shifts for the carrier, where $d_1(t)$ and $d_2(t)$ take on all possible combinations of $+1$ and -1.

Solution: **(a)**   To have equal energies on the quadrature bit streams, we must have

$$A_1^2 T_{b1} = A_2^2 T_{b2}$$

$$\text{or} \quad A_2 = A_1\sqrt{\frac{T_{b1}}{T_{b2}}} = A_1\sqrt{\frac{R_{b2}}{R_{b1}}}$$

Using the given data rates, this becomes

$$A_2 = 10A_1$$

(b)   From (4–150)

$$\theta(t) = \tan^{-1}\left(\frac{A_2 d_2}{A_1 d_1}\right) = \tan^{-1}\left(\frac{10\,\text{sgn}(d_2)}{\text{sgn}(d_1)}\right)$$

where sgn(u) designates the sign of u and the two-argument arctangent is used. This results in Table 4–4.

TABLE 4–4   Excess Phases for a Quadrature Multiplexed Example

d_1	d_2	θ, degrees
1	1	84.3
1	−1	−84.3
−1	1	95.7
−1	−1	−95.7

EXAMPLE 4–10

For Example 4–8, what are the values of A_1 and A_2 such that each channel of a QPSK system maintains a bit error probability of $P_b = 10^{-6}$ if $N_0 = 10^{-10}$ W/Hz?

Solution: The per channel error probability is

$$P_{bi} = Q\left(\sqrt{\frac{2E_{bi}}{N_0}}\right), i = 1, 2$$

A table of Q-function values can be used to show that

$$\left(\frac{E_b}{N_0}\right)_{req'd} = 10.54 \text{ dB} = 11.32$$

gives a bit error probability of 10^{-6}. Since, for each quadrature channel, we have

$$\frac{E_{bi}}{N_0} = \frac{A_i^2 T_{bi}}{2N_0}, i = 1, 2$$

it follows that

$$A_i = \sqrt{2N_0\left(\frac{E_b}{N_0}\right)_{req'd} R_{bi}}$$

For channel 1, with $R_{b1} = 10$ kbps,

$$A_1 = \sqrt{2(10^{-10})(11.32)(10^4)} = 4.76 \text{ mV}$$

and for channel 2, with $R_{b2} = 1$ Mbps,

$$A_2 = \sqrt{2(10^{-10})(11.32)(10^6)} = 47.6 \text{ mV}$$

EXAMPLE 4–11

A 1 Mbps bit stream is to be transmitted using QPSK. Even- and odd-indexed bits are associated with $d_1(t)$ and $d_2(t)$, respectively.

(a) What is the symbol rate?

(b) What is the required channel bandwidth if only the main lobe of the signal spectrum is to be passed?

(c) What is the symbol error probability if the carrier power is 4 mW and $N_0 = 10^{-9}$ W/Hz?

Solution:

(a) Since every other bit is assigned to $d_i(t)$, $i = 1, 2$, it follows that the symbol rate is half the bit rate or 500 kilosymbols per second.

(b) The QPSK spectrum has main lobe bandwidth of $2/T_s = 2R_s$, where T_s is the symbol duration and R_s is the symbol rate. Since the symbol rate is 500 kilosymbols per second, the required bandwidth is 1 MHz.

(c) For QPSK, the probability of symbol error is given by (4–157). If the term P_1^2 is neglected (it is small compared with the first term), we have

$$P_s \approx 2Q\left(\sqrt{\frac{A^2 T_s}{N_0}}\right) = 2Q\left(\sqrt{\frac{(4 \times 10^{-3}\,\text{W})(5 \times 10^5)^{-1}\,\text{s}}{10^{-9}\,\text{W/Hz}}}\right)$$

$$= 2Q(\sqrt{8}) = 2 \times 2.37 \times 10^{-3} = 4.74 \times 10^{-3}$$

4.7.2 Gaussian MSK (GMSK)

This scheme is produced by passing the bipolar bit stream through a lowpass filter with Gaussian impulse response (and therefore Gaussian transfer function) and passing this filtered bit stream into a voltage controlled oscillator (VCO). The output of the VCO is then the GMSK-modulated signal. The advantage of this modulation scheme is that it has much lower out-of-band power than ordinary MSK. Furthermore, it can be coherently detected, differentially detected, or discriminator detected.

If the incoming bits are represented by the sequence $\{a_n\}$, the modulated waveform can be expressed as [9]

$$x_c(t) = \sqrt{2P_c}\,\cos[2\pi f_0 t + \phi(t)]$$

where $\displaystyle \phi(t) = 2\pi f_d \sum_{n=-\infty}^{\infty} a_n g(t - nT_b)$ (4–158)

and $\displaystyle g(t) = \frac{1}{2}\left[\text{erf}\left(-\sqrt{\frac{2}{\ln 2}}\,\pi B T_b\left(\frac{t}{T_b} - \frac{1}{2}\right)\right) + \text{erf}\left(\sqrt{\frac{2}{\ln 2}}\,\pi B T_b\left(\frac{t}{T_b} + \frac{1}{2}\right)\right)\right]$

In (4–158) $\text{erf}(u) = 1 - \text{erfc}(u)$ is related to the Q-function.[16] The other parameters are defined as follows: P_c is the total power in the modulated signal; f_0 is the carrier frequency; f_d is the frequency deviation; B is the Gaussian filter bandwidth; T_b is the bit period; $g(t)$ is the phase pulse shape function.

Typical waveforms for GMSK are shown in Figure 4–29. The bit error probability is about 3 dB worse than BPSK for $BT_b = 0.5$ and about 4 dB worse for $BT_b = 0.2$. Murota and colleagues [9] have characterized the bandwidth occupancy through computer simulation; their results are summarized in the Table 4–5.

4.7.3 $\pi/4$–Differential QPSK

As shown in Figure 4–30, $\pi/4$–DQPSK is an eight-phase modulation scheme that it can be thought of as two quadrature modulation schemes, where a given symbol modulates one set of quadrature carriers, and the next symbol modulates another set of quadrature carriers phase shifted by $\pi/4$ radians from the first set. The quadrature channel symbols, I_k and Q_k, in a given time slot are related to those in the immediately preceding time slot by the equations

$$I_k = I_{k-1}\cos\Delta\phi_k - Q_{k-1}\sin\Delta\phi_k$$

$$Q_k = I_{k-1}\sin\Delta\phi_k + Q_{k-1}\cos\Delta\phi_k$$

(4–159)

---

[16]The relationship between the Q-function and $\text{erfc}(x)$ is $\text{erfc}(x) = 2Q(\sqrt{2}x)$.

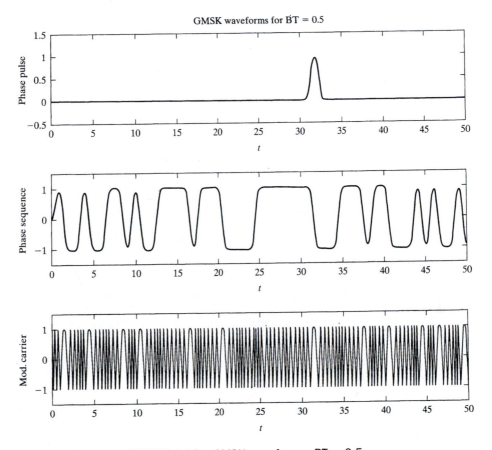

FIGURE 4–29 GMSK waveforms; $BT_b = 0.5$.

The phase difference from time slot $k - 1$ to k is determined by the quadrature-channel symbol streams, d_{1k} and d_{2k}, which are derived as the even- and odd-indexed bits of the input data to the modulator. The mapping is as given in Table 4–6.

The advantages of this modulation scheme are that the symbol transitions never go through the origin, which gives lower envelope deviation when the modulated signal is

TABLE 4–5 Occupied Bandwidth x T_b Containing a Given % Power for GMSK [9]

$BT_b \downarrow$	% Power →			
	90	**99**	**99.9**	**99.99**
0.2	0.52	0.79	0.99	1.22
0.25	0.57	0.86	1.09	1.37
0.5	0.69	1.04	1.33	2.08
MSK	0.78	1.20	2.76	6.00

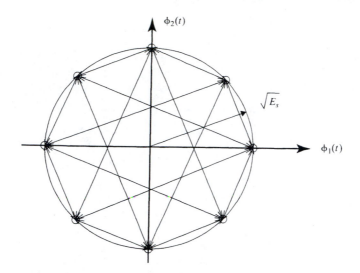

FIGURE 4–30 Signal points for $\pi/4$–DQPSK showing possible transmitted phases and the allowed transitions between them.

filtered, and there is always a transition between symbols, which means that it is easier to synchronize the demodulator.

The analytical expression for the bit error probability is more difficult to derive than those for BPSK, QPSK, etc., and will be given here without derivation [10]:

$$P_b = Q(a,b) - \frac{1}{2} I_0(ab)\exp\left[-\frac{1}{2}(a^2 + b^2) \right] \qquad (4\text{–}160)$$

where

$$a = \sqrt{2\left(1 - \frac{1}{\sqrt{2}}\right)\frac{E_b}{N_0}} \text{ and } b = \sqrt{2\left(1 + \frac{1}{\sqrt{2}}\right)\frac{E_b}{N_0}} \qquad (4\text{–}161)$$

In (4–161), $I_0(u)$ is the modified Bessel function of order 0 defined previously after (2–203) and

$$Q(a,b) = \int_b^\infty x \exp\left[-\frac{1}{2}(x^2 + a^2) \right] I_0(ax)dx \qquad (4\text{–}162)$$

TABLE 4–6   Mapping from Bits to Phase for $\pi/4$–DQPSK

Odd Bit	Even Bit	$\Delta\phi_k$
0	0	$\pi/4$
0	1	$-\pi/4$
1	0	$3\pi/4$
1	1	$-3\pi/4$

is Marcum's Q-function.

Results for the bit error probability of binary noncoherent FSK, binary DPSK, and $\pi/4$–DQPSK are shown in Figure 4–31 with the curve for BPSK given for comparison. A close approximation to the result for $\pi/4$–DQPSK derived in [11] is given by

$$P_b \approx Q\left(\sqrt{1.1716 \frac{E_b}{N_0}} \right) \qquad (4\text{--}163)$$

4.7.4   Power Spectra for Quadrature Modulation Schemes

As pointed out in Chapter 1, it is generally an objective to use the resources of bandwidth and power in a communication system as efficiently as possible. The probability of error expressions just given provide a basis for power efficiency comparisons. Rough approximations have been given previously for bandwidths of modulation schemes. In this section, we consider the computation of bandwidths for quadrature multiplexed modulation

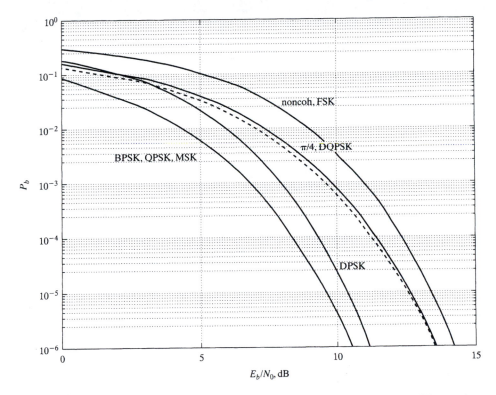

FIGURE 4–31 Bit error probabilities for noncoherent FSK, DPSK, and $\pi/4$-DQPSK with BPSK shown for comparison [dashed curve is approximation (4–163)].

schemes, which is the simplest case possible. This provides an example of a means for computing bandwidth occupancy of modulation schemes for the purpose of bandwidth efficiency comparisons.

We consider signals having complex envelopes of the form

$$z(t) = x(t) + jy(t) \tag{4-164}$$

where

$$x(t) = \sum_{k=-\infty}^{\infty} a_k p(t - kT_s + \Delta t)$$

$$\text{and} \quad y(t) = \sum_{m=-\infty}^{\infty} b_m q(t - mT_s + \Delta t) \tag{4-165}$$

in which $p(t)$ and $q(t)$ are deterministic pulse-shape functions with finite energy.

The real and imaginary parts of the complex envelope are randomly modulated pulse trains. In (4–165), $\{a_k\}$ and $\{b_m\}$ are independent, identically distributed (iid) random sequences with zero means. Each sequence member has finite mean-square value, which for the quadrature components are defined as

$$E[a_k^2] = A^2 \text{ and } E[b_m^2] = B^2 \tag{4-166}$$

respectively. The pulse shape functions, $p(t)$ and $q(t)$, have Fourier transforms $P(f)$ and $Q(f)$, and the time increment, Δt, is uniformly distributed in $(0, T_s)$ to ensure the stationarity of $z(t)$. With these assumptions, it can be shown that the power spectral density of $z(t)$ is

$$G_z(f) = \frac{A^2 |P(f)|^2 + B^2 |Q(f)|^2}{T_s} \tag{4-167}$$

It follows that the power spectrum of the real signal

$$s(t) = \text{Re}[z(t)\exp(j2\pi f_0 t + \Theta)] \tag{4-168}$$

is

$$S(f) = \frac{1}{4} G_z(f - f_0) + \frac{1}{4} G_z(f + f_0) \tag{4-169}$$

where Θ, a uniform random variable in $(0, 2\pi]$, is included to ensure stationarity of $s(t)$. This result will now be applied to compute the power spectra of BPSK, QPSK, OQPSK, and MSK.

For BPSK, the quadrature component of the envelope is identically zero and the pulse shape function is

$$p(t) = \Pi(t/T_b) \tag{4-170}$$

where T_b is the bit period. Its Fourier transform is

$$P(f) = T_b \text{ sinc } (T_b f) \tag{4-171}$$

so that the baseband spectrum for BPSK, from (4–167), is

$$G_z(f) = A^2 T_b \text{ sinc}^2 (T_b f) \tag{4-172}$$

For QPSK, $T_s = 2T_b$ and the basic pulse shapes are

$$p(t) = q(t) = \frac{1}{\sqrt{2}} \Pi\left(\frac{t}{2T_b}\right) \tag{4-173}$$

and for OQPSK they are

$$p(t) = q(t - T_b) = \frac{1}{\sqrt{2}} \Pi\left(\frac{t}{2T_b}\right) \tag{4-174}$$

Since the time shift of $q(t)$ by T_b seconds for OQPSK results in the factor $\exp(-j2\pi f T_b)$ in the Fourier transform of $q(t-T_b)$ which has magnitude one, the spectrum of OQPSK is identical to that of QPSK. Using the transform relationship

$$\frac{1}{\sqrt{2}} \Pi\left(\frac{t}{2T_b}\right) \leftrightarrow \sqrt{2} T_b \text{ sinc}(2T_b f)$$

and the fact that the quadrature components of QPSK and OQPSK have equal amplitudes, it follows that the baseband power spectrum for QPSK and OQPSK is

$$G_z(f) = 4A^2 T_b \text{sinc}^2(2T_b f) \quad \text{(QPSK and OQPSK)} \tag{4-175}$$

Finally, for MSK, the pulse shape functions are

$$p(t) = q(t - T_b) = \cos\left(\frac{\pi t}{2T_b}\right) \Pi\left(\frac{t}{2T_b}\right) \tag{4-176}$$

With $A = B$ and $T_s = 2T_b$, use of these definitions together with the transform pair

$$\cos\left(\frac{\pi t}{2T_b}\right) \Pi\left(\frac{t}{2T_b}\right) \leftrightarrow \frac{4T_b}{\pi} \frac{\cos(2\pi T_b f)}{1 - (4T_b f)^2} \tag{4-177}$$

and the time delay theorem of Fourier transforms in (4–167) results in the baseband power spectrum

$$G_z(f) = \frac{16A^2 T_b}{\pi^2} \frac{\cos^2 2\pi T_b f}{[1 - (4T_b f)^2]^2} \quad \text{(MSK)} \tag{4-178}$$

Baseband power spectra for BPSK, QPSK, OQPSK, and MSK are compared in Figure 4–32, where it is seen that the first null is at a frequency of $1/T_b$ hertz for BPSK, $1/(2T_b)$ hertz for QPSK and OQPSK, and $3/(4T_b)$ hertz for MSK. The null-to-null bandwidths for the bandpass spectra are twice these values. It will be also noted that the sidelobes for MSK fall off at a rate of 12 dB per octave, while the sidelobes for BPSK, QPSK, and OQPSK fall off at half this rate. A better comparison of bandwidth requirements for

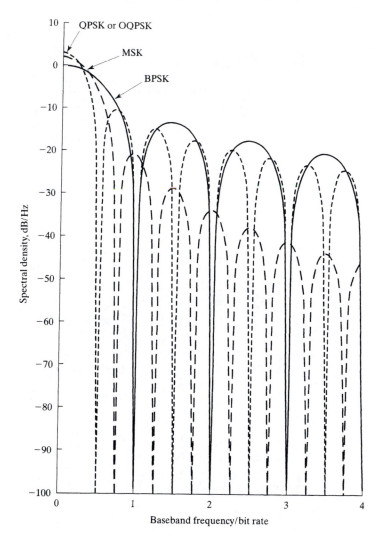

FIGURE 4–32 Baseband-equivalent power spectra of BPSK, QPSK, OQPSK, and MSK.

these modulation schemes is given in terms of fractional out-of-band power, which in terms of a signal's power spectrum, $G_z(f)$, is

$$F = \frac{\displaystyle\int_W^\infty G_z(f)df}{\displaystyle\int_0^\infty G_z(f)df} \qquad (4\text{–}179)$$

The fractional out-of-band powers of these modulation schemes are compared in Figure 4–33.

A measure of the compactness of a spectrum is the bandwidth B_{99} that contains 99% of the total power (or whatever percent that is deemed satisfactory for the application at hand). From Figure 4–33, it follows that

$$B_{99} = \begin{cases} \dfrac{1.2}{T_b}, & \text{for MSK} \\[2ex] \dfrac{7}{T_b}, & \text{for QPSK and OQPSK} \end{cases} \qquad (4\text{--}180)$$

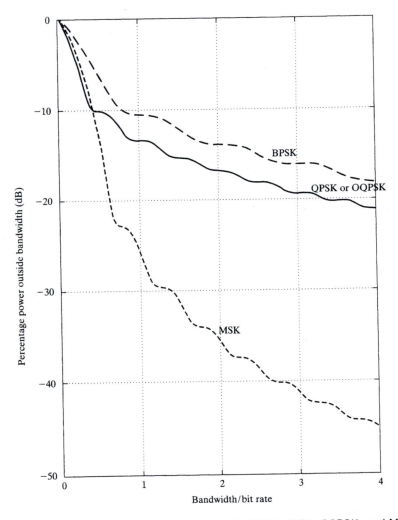

FIGURE 4–33 Fractional out-of-band power for BPSK, QPSK, OQPSK, and MSK.

Thus, while the main lobe of the MSK spectrum is broader than the main lobe of the spectrum for QPSK or OQPSK, the sidelobes decrease much more rapidly for the former than for the latter.

4.8   DESIGN EXAMPLES AND SYSTEM TRADEOFFS

In this section, we consider several design examples and discuss features of the digital modulation schemes considered in this chapter that determine the selection of a particular one for a particular task. First, we consider two examples regarding the computation of E_b/N_0 necessary for a required bit error probability performance.

EXAMPLE 4–12

Compare M-ary PSK for $M = 2, 4, 8, 16, 32$, and 64 on the basis of E_b/N_0 required for bit error probabilities of 10^{-5}, 10^{-6}, and 10^{-7}.

Solution: From previous considerations, the bit error probability for binary and quadriphase PSK is given by

$$P_b = Q\left(\sqrt{\frac{2E_b}{N_0}}\right) \tag{4-181}$$

and from (4–96), the symbol error probability for M-ary PSK is upper bounded by

$$P_s < 2\,Q\left[\sqrt{\frac{2E_s}{N_0}}\,\sin\left(\frac{\pi}{M}\right)\right] \tag{4-182}$$

where the bound is tight for $M > 4$ and moderately large signal-to-noise ratios. From (4–144) and $E_s = (\log_2 M)E_b$, we can relate the bit to symbol error probabilities and bit and symbol energies, respectively. The bound for bit error probability for $M = 8$ through 64 becomes

$$P_b < \frac{2}{\log_2 M}\,Q\left[\sqrt{2\log_2 M\,\frac{E_b}{N_0}}\,\sin\left(\frac{\pi}{M}\right)\right] \tag{4-183}$$

These equations may be implemented in MATLAB, for example, using the function **fzero**, or computed via the approximation

$$Q(u) \approx \frac{\exp(-u^2/2)}{\sqrt{2\pi}\,u}, u \gg 1. \tag{4-184}$$

The calculations may be iterated several times on a calculator to find the desired results. Results, accurate to within one decimal place in keeping with the bound used, are provided in Table 4–7 using the former method.

EXAMPLE 4–13

A channel of bandwidth 4 kHz is available; a data rate of 8 kbps is desired. If $N_0 = 10^{-9}$ W/Hz, design a modulation system that will provide this data rate at a BER of $P_b = 10^{-6}$.

TABLE 4–7   Comparison of Bit Error Probabilities for Various Modulation Schemes

Modulation Scheme	E_b/N_0 (dB) required for $P_b =$		
	10^{-5}	10^{-6}	10^{-7}
BPSK, QPSK	9.6	10.5	11.3
PSK; $M = 8$	13	14	14.8
PSK; $M = 16$	17.4	18.4	19.3
PSK; $M = 32$	22.3	23.4	24.2
PSK; $M = 64$	27.5	28.5	29.4

Solution: We need 8/4 = 2 bps/Hz. We consider M-ary PSK for achieving this. For M-ary PSK, we have

$$0.5 \log_2 M = 2$$

or $M = 16$. Using the results of Example 4–12, we have $E_b/N_0 = 18.4$ dB for 16-PSK to achieve the desired BER.

We also note that 16-QAM will work. For 16-QAM, Figure 4–13 shows that $E_b/N_0 = 15$ dB will achieve the desired BER. Clearly, 16-QAM is superior to 16-PSK in this application (16-PSK might be preferable over 16-QAM if constant amplitude due to nonlinear power amplification were an issue). In order to calculate the average carrier power, we need the average symbol energy. It is given by

$$E_s = N_0(\log_2 M)\left(\frac{E_b}{N_0}\right)_{\text{req'd}}$$

or, for 16-QAM,

$$E_s(\text{dB-joules}) = 10 \log_{10} 10^{-9} + 10 \log_{10} 4 + 15$$

$$= -90 + 6 + 15 = -69 \text{ dB-J}$$

Average energy and average carrier power are related by

$$\frac{E_s}{T_s} = P_c$$

But the symbol rate, $1/T_s = R_s$ is given by

$$R_s = \frac{R_b}{\log_2 M} = \frac{8,000}{4} = 2,000 \text{ symbols/s}$$

Hence, the average carrier power is

$$P_s(\text{dBW}) = -69 + 10 \log_{10}(2,000) = -36 \text{ dBW} = 2.51 \times 10^{-4} \text{ W}$$

In the next example, we look at various modulation schemes in a particular application from the standpoint of power and bandwidth efficiency.

EXAMPLE 4–14

(a) Give the bit rate that can be supported by a 4 kHz channel for the following modulation schemes: (1) BPSK, (2) 4-PSK, (3) 8-PSK, (4) 16-PSK, (5) 16-QAM, (6) coherent BFSK, (7) coherent 4-FSK, (8) coherent 8-FSK, (9) noncoherent BFSK, (10) noncoherent 4-FSK, and (11) noncoherent 8-FSK.

(b) If $N_0 = 10^{-8}$ W/Hz, find the carrier power required in each case to give $P_b(\varepsilon) = 10^{-6}$.

Solution: (a) Using the equations given in Table 4–1, we can solve for the data rates. For example, M-ary PSK results in the equation

$$R_b = 0.5B \log_2 M = 2000 \log_2 M$$

Coherent M-ary FSK gives the equation

$$R_b = 8000 \frac{\log_2 M}{M + 3}$$

and noncoherent M-ary FSK gives the result

$$R_b = 2000 \frac{\log_2 M}{M}$$

Using these equations, we get the results given in Table 4–8.

(b) The carrier power is

$$P_c = \frac{A^2}{2} = \frac{E_b}{T_b} = E_b R_b$$

Let z_0 be the value of E_b/N_0 required to give $P_b = 10^{-6}$ in each case. Then

$$P_c = E_b R_b = z_0 N_0 R_b$$

TABLE 4–8   Allowed Data Rates for Various Modulation Techniques.

Modulation Schemes	Data Rate, kbps
BPSK	2
4-PSK	4
8-PSK	6
16-PSK	8
16-QAM	8
Coherent BFSK	1.6
Coherent 4-FSK	2.3
Coherent 8-FSK	2.2
Noncoherent BFSK	1.0
Noncoherent 4-FSK	1.0
Noncoherent 16-FSK	0.75

TABLE 4–9   Required Powers for Various Modulations Schemes with Conditions Given in Example 4–14

Modulation Scheme	z_0, dB	R_b, dB-s^{-1}	P_c, dBW	P_c, mW
BPSK	10.5	33	−36.5	0.229
4-PSK	10.5	36	−33.5	0.457
8-PSK	13.6	37.8	−28.6	1.380
16-PSK	18.5	39	−22.5	5.623
16-QAM	14.5	39	−26.5	2.239
Coherent BFSK	13.6	32	−34.4	0.363
Coherent 4-FSK	10.8	33.6	−35.6	0.275
Coherent 8-FSK	9.0	33.4	−37.6	0.174
Noncoherent BFSK	14.2	30	−35.8	0.263
Noncoherent 4-FSK	11.2	30	−38.8	0.132
Noncoherent 8-FSK	10.0	28.3	−41.7	0.067

or

$$P_{c,dBw} = z_{0,dB} + N_{0,dB\text{-}J} + R_{b,dB\text{-}Hz}$$

$$= z_{0,dB} - 80 + R_{b,dB\text{-}Hz}$$

Using this equation and the results obtained in part (a), we get the results in Table 4–9.

Note that the bandwidth efficiency for M-ary FSK goes up with M for $M \le 4$. However, it eventually decreases with M and requires a coherent reference to be established at the receiver. Its power efficiency goes up with M. We note that the power efficiency of M-ary PSK goes down with increasing M, but its bandwidth efficiency goes up. The bandwidth efficiency of M-ary PSK is always better than that of M-ary FSK for a given value of M. This is to be expected from signal-space considerations. Note that 16-QAM appears to be a nice compromise between power and bandwidth. However, it is not a constant-envelope modulation technique and may be undesirable if nonlinear amplification is used in order to increase efficiency (such as with a traveling wave tube amplifier). Noncoherent FSK shows the same trends as coherent FSK with very little loss in power or bandwidth efficiency; since it does not require the establishment of a coherent reference at the receiver, it is usually preferable over coherent FSK.

As a final example, we consider a desired data rate and inquire into the bandwidth and power requirements to achieve a given BER.

EXAMPLE 4–15

(a)   It is desired to transmit data at R_b = 5 kbps. For the modulation schemes considered in Example 4–14, give the required channel bandwidth.

(b)   If $N_0 = 10^{-8}$ W/Hz, find the required received carrier power to give $P_b = 10^{-6}$.

Solution: (a)   From Table 4–1, we have the following formulas for the required bandwidth in terms of M and data rate:

TABLE 4–10 Bandwidths Required for Setup of Example 4–15

Modulation Scheme	Bandwidth, kHz
BPSK	10
4-PSK	5
8-PSK	3.3
16-PSK	2.5
16-QAM	2.5
Coherent BFSK	12.5
Coherent 4-FSK	8.75
Coherent 8-FSK	9.17
Noncoherent BFSK	20.0
Noncoherent 4-FSK	20.0
Noncoherent 8-FSK	26.7

$$M\text{-ary PSK, QAM: } B = \frac{2}{\log_2 M} R_b$$

$$\text{Coherent } M\text{-ary FSK: } B = \frac{M+3}{2 \log_2 M} R_b \qquad (4\text{--}185)$$

$$\text{Noncoherent } M\text{-ary FSK: } B = \frac{2M}{\log_2 M} R_b$$

Using these equations, we get the bandwidths given in Table 4–10.

(b) Using the equation developed in **(b)** of Example 4–14 gives the results of Table 4–11.

$$P_{c,dBW} = z_{0,dB} - 80 + R_{b,dB\text{-}Hz} = z_{0,dB} - 43$$

TABLE 4–11 Powers Required for Example 4–14

Modulation Scheme	P_c, dBW	P_c, mW
BPSK	−32.4	0.575
4-PSK	−32.4	0.575
8-PSK	−29.4	1.148
16-PSK	−24.5	3.550
16-QAM	−28.5	1.410
Coherent BFSK	−29.4	1.148
Coherent 4-FSK	−32.2	0.603
Coherent 8-FSK	−34.0	0.398
Noncoherent BFSK	−28.8	1.318
Noncoherent 4-FSK	−31.8	0.661
Noncoherent 8-FSK	−33.0	0.501

4.9   MULTI-*h* CONTINUOUS PHASE MODULATION

In many applications, particularly in satellite communications, modulation techniques that have constant or nearly constant envelopes versus time are required due to power amplifier considerations. In addition, good communications efficiencies in terms of low error probability for a given signal-to-noise ratio and good bandwidth efficiencies in terms of bits per second of information transmitted per hertz of bandwidth are required due to both technological and regulatory limitations.

The constant envelope requirement is easily met by employing phase and frequency modulation formats, which is one reason for the popularity of phase-shift keyed and frequency-shift-keyed modulations. For simultaneously good bandwidth and power efficiencies, QPSK, OQPSK, or MSK have been the options most often used in the past since all have identical power efficiencies under ideal AWGN conditions, all have competitive bandwidth efficiencies, and all have roughly the same complexity in terms of implementation. Shannon's capacity boundary, first given in Chapter 1 and repeated in Figure 4–22, shows that considerable room is left for improvement in terms of bandwidth and power efficiency, however. Historically, the means used for doing so has been to encode the data source output and use the encoder output to modulate the transmitted carrier. Improved power efficiency was thereby achieved at the expense of increased implementation complexity and decreased bandwidth efficiency due to the data encoder and decoder.

Another approach to this problem, referred to as *combined modulation and encoding*, where the encoding and modulation functions are combined, has been investigated. Simultaneously good power and bandwidth efficiencies can be achieved at the expense of increased complexity by means of such approaches. It is the purpose of this section to briefly describe one approach to combined modulation and encoding, referred to as *multi-h continuous-phase modulation* (CPM), and to characterize its performance. Another technique, called trellis-coded modulation, will be briefly described in Chapter 7.

In general, multi-*h* phase coding includes MSK as a special case. The optimum detection of multi-*h* CPM signals requires use of the Viterbi algorithm. A description of this algorithm is given in Chapter 7. For its application to the detection of multi-*h* CPM signals, the reader is referred to [12].

4.9.1   Description of the Multi-*h* CPM Signal Format

The general form for a multi-*h* CPM signal is

$$s(t,\boldsymbol{\alpha}) = \sqrt{\frac{2E_s}{N_0}} \cos[2\pi f_0 t + \phi(t;\boldsymbol{\alpha}) + \phi_0] \tag{4–186}$$

where E_s, T_s, and f_0 are the symbol energy, symbol duration, and carrier frequency, respectively; as before, ϕ_0 is an arbitrary carrier phase and $\phi(t, \boldsymbol{\alpha})$ is the information-carrying phase function. This *excess phase function*, as it is called, can be expressed as

$$\phi(t,\boldsymbol{\alpha}) = 2\pi \int_{-\infty}^{t} \sum_{i=-\infty}^{\infty} h_i a_i g(\tau - iT_s) d\tau, \quad -\infty < t < \infty \tag{4–187}$$

The various parameters are defined as follows

$\alpha = \{ \ldots, a_{-2}, a_{-1}, a_0, a_1, a_2, \ldots \}$ represents the data sequence. Each data sequence element can, in general, assume any one of M levels, say, $a_i = \pm 1, \pm 3, \pm 5, \ldots, \pm (M - 1)$ for any i.

$\{h_i: i = 1, 2, \ldots, K\}$ is a set of phase modulation indices that is cycled through periodically; thus $h_{i+K} = h_i$.

$g(t)$ is a *frequency pulse-shape function* that is 0 for $t < 0$ and $t > LT$, L integer, and nonzero otherwise. $L = 1$ yields a *full response signal*, while $L > 1$ yields a *partial response signal*.

It is convenient to define a *phase* pulse-shape function, $q(t)$, as

$$q(t) = \int_{-\infty}^{t} g(\tau)d\tau, \quad -\infty < t < \infty \tag{4–188}$$

with the normalization property that $q(LT_s) = 1/2$.

EXAMPLE 4–16

(a) *Continuous-phase FSK (CPFSK)* is a subclass of multi-h CPM with

(1) $h_i = h$, all i

$$(2) \quad g(t) = \begin{cases} 0, & t < 0 \\ \dfrac{1}{2T_s}, & 0 \le t \le T_s \\ 0, & t > T_s \end{cases} \tag{4–189}$$

(b) *Fast frequency-shift keying (FFSK)* is a special case of CPFSK with $h = \frac{1}{2}$. FFSK is identical to MSK with differential encoding of the quadrature data streams.

The phase pulse-shape function has a considerable effect on the asymptotic behavior of the modulated-signal power spectra. In general, it can be stated that *if the nth order derivative of the phase pulse-shape function is the lowest-order derivative that is not everywhere continuous, the power spectral envelope decays as $f^{-2(n+1)}$.* For example, the phase function of FFSK has no continuous derivatives ($n = 1$), so that its power spectrum decays as f^{-4} or at a rate of 12 dB/octave.

Another popular frequency pulse shape is *raised cosine (RC)*, for which

$$g(t) = \begin{cases} \dfrac{1}{2LT_s} \left(1 - \cos\dfrac{2\pi t}{LT_s} \right), & 0 \le t \le LT_s \\ 0, & \text{otherwise} \end{cases} \tag{4–190}$$

This form of multi-h CPM has continuous first- and second-order derivatives so that $n = 3$ in the spectral property stated earlier. Thus the power spectral envelope for RC multi-h CPM decays at a rate of 24 dB/octave.

In general, a faster roll-off rate of the sidelobes for a given multi-*h* CPM format means a wider main lobe for the power spectrum. This will be pointed out explicitly when the calculation of spectra and out-of-band power for multi-*h* CPM are discussed.

For the remainder of this section, attention is focused on full-response, rectangular frequency-pulse, multi-*h* CPM. For this special case, we can write the modulated waveform in the $(i-1)$st signaling interval as

$$s_i(t) = \sqrt{\frac{2E_s}{T_s}} \cos\left\{ 2\pi\left[f_0 t + \frac{1}{2} a_i h_i\left(\frac{t}{T_s} - i + 1 \right) \right] + \phi_i \right\}, \ (i-1)T_s \le t \le iT_s \ \ (4\text{-}191)$$

where ϕ_0 in (4-186) is 0, a rectangular frequency pulse has been assumed, and

$$\phi_i = \pi \sum_{j=-\infty}^{i-2} a_j h_j \qquad (4\text{-}192)$$

is the excess phase at a time $t = (i-1)T_s$ due to previous information digits. Note that during the *i*th signaling interval, (4-191) represents a tone displaced from the nominal carrier, f_0, by $\pm h_i/(2T_s)$ corresponding to a binary 1 or 0 for binary data $(M = 2)$; if $M > 2$, one of M tones is sent during the *i*th signaling interval. Furthermore, if

$$h_i = \frac{L_i}{q} \qquad (4\text{-}193)$$

where L_i, $i = 1, 2, \ldots, K$, and q are integers, all phase values at the transition times $t = iT_s$ are multiples of $2\pi/q$ radians. Thus a set of phase states are defined for each $t = iT_s$. This phase-state information can be used to optimally (i.e., MAP) detect the data provided:

1. The detector is synchronized to the incoming signal. There are three levels of synchronization: (a) carrier phase; (b) signal interval (baud); (c) superbaud (i.e., the sequence $h_1, h_2, \ldots h_K$).
2. The set of possible phase transitions from state to state are known.

Detection of multi-*h* CPM signals is considered more fully in a following subsection. It is instructive at this point, however, to consider a specific sequence of *h* values and plot the possible phase trajectories. Such a plot is called a *phase trellis* and is an important tool in the consideration of multi-*h* CPM properties and receiver performance.

EXAMPLE 4-17 _____

(a) Consider the *h*-sequence $\{h_1, h_2\} = \{1/4, 2/4\}$. In the *i*th signaling interval, the excess phase changes by $\pm\pi/4$ radians if $h_1 = 1/4$ is used and by $\pm\pi/2$ radians if $h_2 = 1/2$ is used. Figure 4-34a shows the development of the phase trellis assuming that the data sequence starts at time $t = 0$. The phase trajectory for the data sequence 1001110 is indicated by the heavy line.

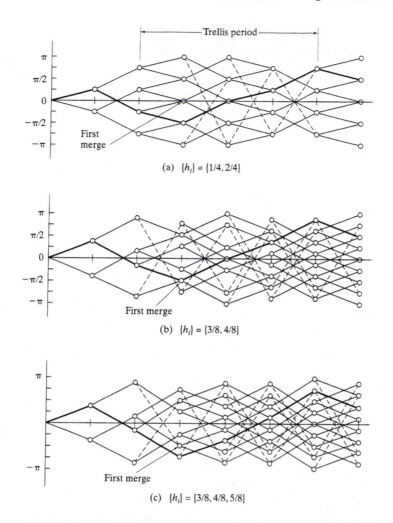

FIGURE 4–34   Excess phase trellis diagrams for various multi-h CPM signals.

(b)   Consider the h-sequence $\{3/8, 4/8\}$. Now the excess phase of the transmitted signal changes by $\pm 3\pi/8$ radians in intervals where h_1 is used and by $\pm\pi/2$ radians if h_2 is used. The development of the phase trellis is shown in Figure 4–34b.

(c)   As a final example, consider the sequence of three h-values $\{3/8, 4/8, 5/8\}$. Now the excess phase changes $\pm 3\pi/8$ radians when h_1 is used, $\pm\pi/2$ when h_2 is used, and $\pm 5\pi/8$ when h_3 is used. The development of the phase trellis is shown in Figure 4–34c.

The assumption that the h_i are rational [see (4–193)] means that the excess phase at baud-interval sampling times takes on values in a discrete set. The signal phase, as will be discussed later, may be coherently decoded in an optimal fashion by use of the Viterbi algorithm. The free distance, defined by

$$D_{min}^2 = \lim_{n \to \infty} \min_{i,j} \int_0^{nT_s} [s(t; \boldsymbol{\alpha}^{(i)}) - s(t; \boldsymbol{\alpha}^{(j)})]^2 dt \qquad (4\text{--}194)$$

where $s(t; \boldsymbol{\alpha}^{(i)})$ and $s(t; \boldsymbol{\alpha}^{(j)})$ are two signals whose phase trajectories split at $t = 0$, and re-merge some time later, is a key performance measure. Larger D_{min} is associated with better performance of the optimal detector [12].

The main factor influencing the magnitude of D_{min} is the minimum interval, C, over which the phase trajectories of signals corresponding to differing data sequences (with the same initial digit) remain *unmerged*. For binary data sequences it can be shown that the maximum value for this interval is $C = K$ only if (1) $q \geq 2^K$, and (2) no subset of $\{h_i\}$ have an integer sum. The parameter $C + 1$ is termed the *constraint length* of the code.

For the case of M-ary data, q must equal or exceed M^K and weighted sums of the h_i must not be integer valued. For example, $M = 4$ and $K = 2$ requires that $q \geq 16$ and $a_1 h_1 + a_2 h_2$ must not be integer valued for a_1 and a_2 in the set $\{0, 1, 2, 3\}$. The code $M = 3$, $K = 2$, and $\{h_i\} = \{3/16, 4/16\}$ satisfies these constraints.

EXAMPLE 4–18

(a)   The *h*-sequence $\{1/4, 2/4\}$ has $C = 2$ since $q = 4 = 2^2$ and $h_1 + h_2$ is not integer-valued.

(b)   The phase code $\{3/8, 4/8\}$ has $C = 2$ since $q = 8 \geq 2^K$ and $h_1 + h_2$ is not integer-valued.

(c)   The phase code $\{3/8, 4/8, 5/8\}$ has C less than $K = 3$ since $h_1 + h_3$ has an integer sum. From the trellis diagram of Figure 4–34c is seen that $C = 2 < K = 3$ in this case.

The second set of fundamental properties in regard to multi-*h* excess-phase trellises deal with their periods, or the minimum interval over which they repeat. For modulation-index sequences of the form $\{h_i\} = \{L_i/q\}$ where L_i and q are integers, the following can be shown:

1. If the sum $\Gamma = \sum_{i=1}^K L_i$ is *even*, the period of the trellis is $T_p = KT_s$; if this sum is *odd*, the trellis period is $T_p = 2KT_s$.
2. The number of phase states is q if Γ is even and $2q$ if Γ is odd.

The *complexity* of the optimum detector is affected by the number of phases and the periodicity of the trellis, which, as seen, is determined by the form of the h_is.

To obtain the performance of the optimum detector we can find the minimum integral-squared difference between alternative paths in the phase trellis. The probability of mistaking an incorrect path through the trellis for the correct one is then approximated by the negative exponential of this minimum integral-squared difference. The following example illustrates this.

EXAMPLE 4–19 _____

Consider the calculation of

$$d_{min}^2 = \frac{D_{min}^2}{2E_b} = \min_{\gamma_N} \left\{ 2 - \frac{1}{T_b} \int_0^{2T_b} \cos[\phi_e(\gamma_N)]dt \right\} \tag{4-195}$$

for CPFSK. The phase trellis of CPFSK is shown in Figure 4–35a. The minimum squared distance, (4–195), can be written in the form

$$d_{min}^2 = 2 - \frac{1}{T_b} \int_0^{2T_b} \cos 2\pi h[2q(t) - 2q(t - T_b)]dt \tag{4-196}$$

where

$$q(t) = \begin{cases} 0, & t \le 0 \\ \dfrac{1}{2T_b}, & 0 \le t \le 2T_b \\ \dfrac{1}{2}, & t > 2T_b \end{cases} \tag{4-197}$$

The phase difference function, $4\pi h[q(t) - q(t - T_b)]$ is shown in Figure 4–35b. From this figure it is seen that d_{min}^2 can be expressed as

$$d_{min}^2 = 2 - \frac{1}{T_b} \left\{ \int_0^{T_b} \cos \frac{2\pi ht}{T_b} dt + \int_{T_b}^{2T_b} \cos\left[2\pi h\left(\frac{2 - t}{T_b}\right)\right] dt \right\}$$

$$= 2[1 - \text{sinc}(2h)], \quad h \le 0.5 \tag{4-198}$$

where $\text{sinc}(u) = \sin(\pi u)/(\pi u)$. This result is an _upper bound_ for d_{min}^2 for all h.
Actual values for d_{min}^2 may be less than $2[1 - \text{sinc}(2h)]$ for certain ranges of h because the phase trajectories must be viewed modulo-2π.

_____

4.9.2 Calculation of Power Spectra for Multi-h CPM Signals

Because of the interdependence of the excess phase of a multi-h CPM signal between signaling intervals, the calculation of their power spectra is not as simple as for BPSK or quadrature modulation methods such as QPSK, OQPSK, or MSK. The three principal methods for obtaining power spectra of multi-h CPM signals are (1) estimation through simulation, (2) the Markov chain approach, and (3) the direct method. For a summary of these methods and several references, see the special issue of the _IEEE Transactions on Communications_ [13].

The direct approach utilizes the definition of the power spectral density of a signal, which is written as

$$G(f) = \lim_{N \to \infty} E\left[\frac{|S_{NT_s}(f)|^2}{NT_s} \right] \tag{4-199}$$

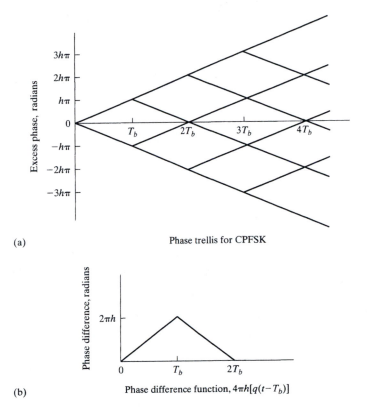

(a)   Phase trellis for CPFSK

(b)   Phase difference function, $4\pi h[q(t-T_b)]$

FIGURE 4–35   Excess phase functions for CPFSK.

where $S_{NT_s}(f)$ is the Fourier transform of an NT_s-second interval of the signal under consideration, which, for our purposes here, is given by (4–191). The expectation is taken with respect to the random data sequence and the random initial phase angle ϕ_0.

Closed-form results for the spectra of M-ary CPFSK, M-ary pulse-shaped FM, and partial-response FM signals have been obtained using the direct approach and appear in the literature. When this approach is applied to multi-h CPM signals, it is necessary to consider super-intervals of length $T' = PT_s$, where P is the period of the phase trellis (P is either K or $2K$ depending on Γ—see the discussion following Example 4–18, because the phases are not identically distributed in each signaling interval due to the memory from phase state to phase state. Thus, if a PT_s segment of an M-ary, multi-h CPM signal is considered there are M^P distinct waveforms over which the expectation in (4–199) must be carried out. For the details and equations relating to this method, the reader is referred to [13]. The one-sided lowpass power spectra of the multi-h CPM signals considered in Example 4–18 are shown in Figure 4–36a for rectangular pulse shaping and in Figure 4–36b for half-sine pulse shaping. These were obtained through a computer implementation of the direct-method computation. Figure 4–37a shows out-of-band power

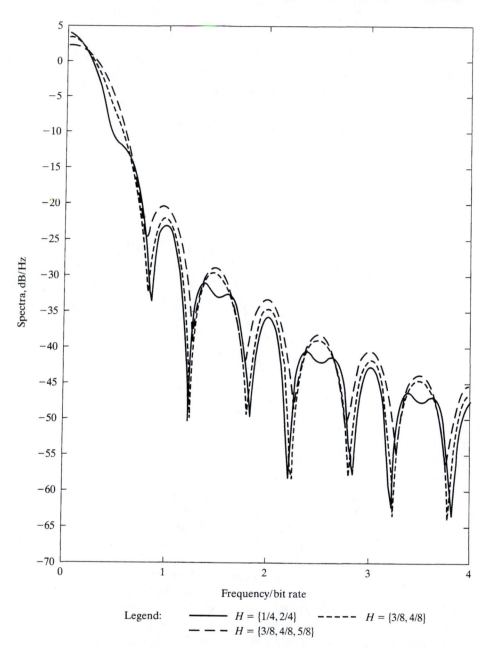

FIGURE 4–36 Spectra for the multi-h phase codes considered in Example 4–18: (a) rectangular pulse shape.

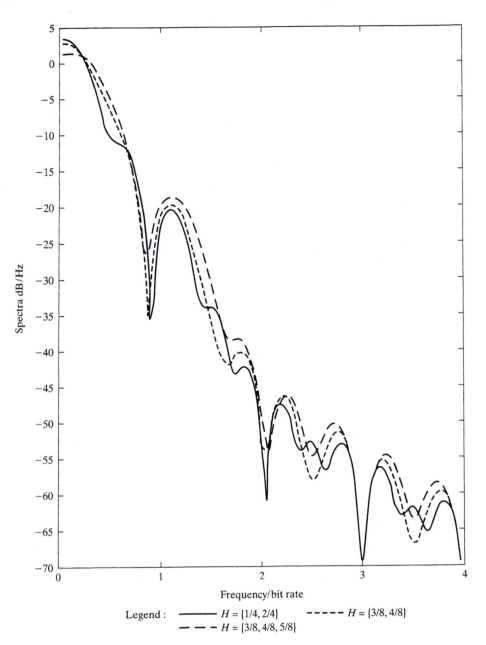

FIGURE 4–36 Spectra for the multi-*h* phase codes considered in Example 4–18: (b) half-sine pulse shape.

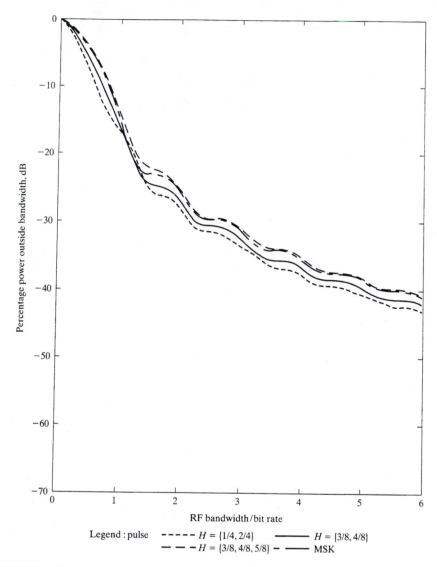

FIGURE 4–37   Out-of-band power for the multi-*h* phase codes considered in Example 4–18 : (a) rectangular pulse shape.

for these phase codes for rectangular pulse shaping and half-sine pulse shaping in Figure 4–37b. Note the faster roll-off of out-of-band power with frequency for the smoother pulse shapes.

Due to the complexity of the direct-method computations, it is beneficial to have a simpler method of obtaining rough estimates for the power spectra of multi-*h* CPM signals. Two such approximations are suggested:

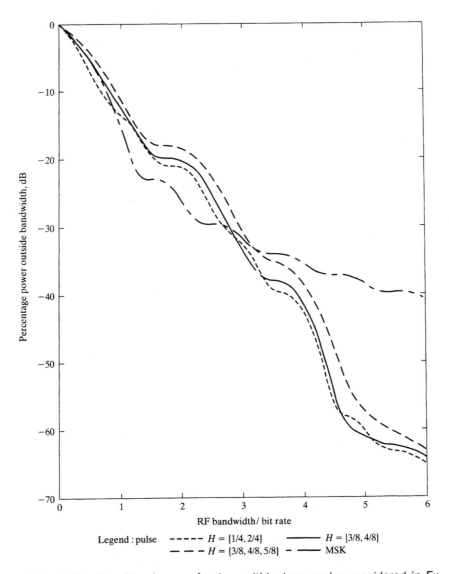

FIGURE 4–37 Out-of-band power for the multi-*h* phase codes considered in Example 4–18: (b) half-sine pulse shape.

1. The multi-*h* CPM process is visualized as spending a fraction $1/K$ of symbols at each of the K modulation indices $h_1, h_2, \ldots, h_K$. The spectrum is computed as a weighted sum of constant-*h* spectra as

$$G(f) \approx \frac{1}{K} \sum_{i=1}^{K} G_{h_i}(f) \qquad (4\text{--}200)$$

where $G_{h_i}(f)$ is the power spectrum of a constant-h signal with modulation index h_i. A closed-form expression is available for CPFSK and is given next by (4–202).

2. In the second method, the multi-h CPM signal is approximated by a constant-h signal with a modulation index that is the average over one cycle of the h_i's:

$$\bar{h} = \frac{1}{K} \sum_{i=1}^{K} h_i \tag{4–201}$$

In using either of these methods, an expression for the power spectrum of a constant-h signal is required. For CPFSK, the result is

$$G(f) = G_+(f) + G_-(f) \tag{4–202}$$

where

$$G_\pm(f) = \frac{A^2 \sin^2[\pi(f \pm f_1)T_b]\sin^2[\pi(f \pm f_2)T_b]}{2\pi^2 T_b\{1 - 2\cos[2\pi(f \pm \alpha)T_b]\cos 2\pi\beta T_b + \cos^2(2\pi\beta T_b)\}}\left[\frac{1}{f \pm f_1} - \frac{1}{f \pm f_2}\right]^2 \tag{4–203}$$

In (4–203), the following definitions are used:

T_b = bit duration;
A = signal amplitude;
f_1, f_2 = signaling frequencies in hertz (i.e., for binary CPFSK, they are $f_0 \pm h/(2T_b)$ hertz, where f_0 is the apparent carrier);

$\alpha = \frac{1}{2}(f_2 + f_1)$ and $\beta = \frac{1}{2}(f_2 - f_1)$

Examples of the use of (4–201) and (4–202) together with the approximate multi-h power spectra are left for the problems. In general, method 1 is the most accurate, with spectral computations using it being within $\pm$ 2 dB of the true spectrum for "good" multi-h codes. Good codes are defined to be those optimizing the power-bandwidth tradeoff and appear to be codes with the h-values closely grouped (e.g., {3/16, 4/16}). Method 2 indicates the correct general shape of the spectrum, but results in spectral nulls where there should be only local minima and is therefore somewhat misleading. Both methods give fairly accurate results in computing out-of-band power.

4.9.3 Synchronization Considerations for Multi-h CPM Signals[17]

Three levels of synchronization are required in the demodulation of multi-h CPM signals. These are (1) carrier phase synchronization, (2) symbol or baud timing, and (3) interval synchronization, modulo K (sometimes referred to as *superbaud timing*). One technique for acquiring such timing information is to pass the multi-h CPM signal through a qth power law device, where q is the denominator of the h-sequence. It can be shown that the spectrum of the output has discrete spectral components at the following frequencies:

---

[17]See [12]. The results of a simulation study on synchronization of multi-h is reported in [13].

(1) $\Gamma = \displaystyle\sum_{i=1}^{K} L_i$ even; $f = q f_0 + \dfrac{m-1}{KT_s}$

$$f = q f_0 + \dfrac{m}{KT_s} \tag{4-204}$$

(2) Γ odd; $f = q f_0 + \dfrac{2m \pm 1}{KT_s} \tag{4-205}$

where m is an integer. If these adjacent spectral components are extracted from the spectrum by phase-locked loops, the resulting frequencies can be mixed to produce a phase coherent signal at the superbaud clock frequency $1/KT_s$. Frequency multiplication by K then produces a clock at the symbol rate $1/T_s$.

Finally, reference frequencies at the signaling frequencies $f_0 \pm h_i/(2qT_s)$ are required. These are used to produce inphase and quadrature baseband components from the received multi-h CPM signal as illustrated in Figure 4–38. Depending on whether Γ is even or odd, frequencies are present at the qth power law device output symmetrically located about the frequency qf_0. For example, if Γ is even, two phase-locked loops may be employed with free-running frequencies, $q f_0 + m/(KT_s)$, and $q f_0 - m/(KT_s)$ to produce a frequency at $2qf_0$ when these two frequencies are mixed. Frequency division by $2q$ then produces a reference frequency of the form $A\cos(2\pi f_0 t + \pi n/q)$, where the term $\pi q/n$, n integer, represents a $2q$-fold phase ambiguity due to the frequency multiplication by the qth power device that must be resolved. A similar argument holds for Γ odd. To obtain the reference frequencies $f_0 \pm h_i/(2q T_s)$, the baud-rate clock can be frequency divided by $2q$ to obtain a reference of frequency $1/(2qT_s)$. Frequency multiplication by the appropriate h_i and mixing with f_0 then produces the frequencies $f_0 + h_i/(2qT_s)$. One remaining task must be accomplished before optimum detection of the data sequence can be carried out, and that is to resolve the multi-h signal into a vector space spanned by an orthonormal basis-vector set. Since MSK can be represented in terms of the orthogonal references

$$R_i = \cos 2\pi \left(f_0 \pm \dfrac{1}{4T_b} \right) t \tag{4-206}$$

the resolution process was accomplished easily in this case. The problem with multi-h in this regard is that the signals $\cos[2\pi(f_0 \pm h_i/2T_s)t]$, $(i-1)T_s \le t \le iT_s$, are not necessarily orthogonal for arbitrary values of h_i. Therefore, the reference signals

$$\left. \begin{aligned} R_{1i}(t) &= \phi_{1i}(t) = \sqrt{\dfrac{2}{T_s}} \cos\left[2\pi \left(f_0 + \dfrac{h_i}{2T_s} \right) t \right] \\ R_{2i}(t) &= \phi_{2i}(t) = \sqrt{\dfrac{2}{T_s}} \sin\left[2\pi \left(f_0 + \dfrac{h_i}{2T_s} \right) t \right] \\ R_{3i}(t) &= \sqrt{\dfrac{2}{T_s}} \cos\left[2\pi \left(f_0 - \dfrac{h_i}{2T_s} \right) t \right] \\ R_{3i}(t) &= \sqrt{\dfrac{2}{T_s}} \sin\left[2\pi \left(f_0 - \dfrac{h_i}{2T_s} \right) t \right] \end{aligned} \right\} \begin{aligned} & 0 \le t \le T_s \\ & i = 1, 2, \cdots, K \end{aligned} \tag{4-207}$$

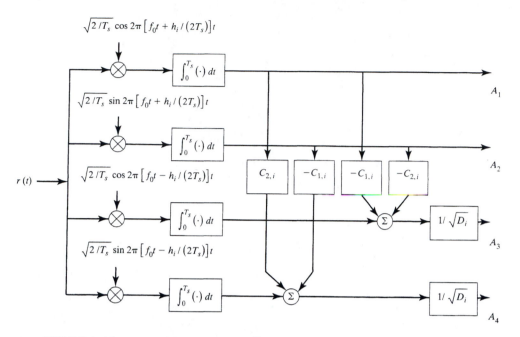

FIGURE 4–38   Resolution of multi-h CPM signals into signal-space coordinates.

are defined, and an orthogonal reference set is obtained through the Gram-Schmidt procedure.

    The preceding discussion has barely scratched the surface of the subject of band-
width and power efficient modulation. For an extensive set of papers on the subject, see
several special issues of IEEE publications [13–15] as well as the book by Anderson,
Aulin, and Sundberg [16]. TCM, to be discussed in Chapter 7, is the topic of the book
[17].

4.10   ORTHOGONAL FREQUENCY DIVISION MULTIPLEXING

4.10.1   Introduction

Orthogonal frequency-division multiplexing (OFDM), special cases of which are known
as multicarrier modulation (MCM) or discrete multitone (DMT), is a bandwidth efficient
modulation technique that is tolerant to channel disturbances such as delay spread multipath and impulse noise. Multicarrier modulation is a concept that originated in the late
1950s and early 1960s with the fielding of two modems, one the Collins Kineplex system
[18] and the other called the Kathryn modem [19]. As shown in Figure 4–39, OFDM is
implemented by serial-to-parallel converting the input bit stream and using one or more
bits to modulate each subcarrier of a synchronous, parallel sum of coherent subcarriers
spaced by the inverse of the symbol period. The reason for its resurgence, in addition to

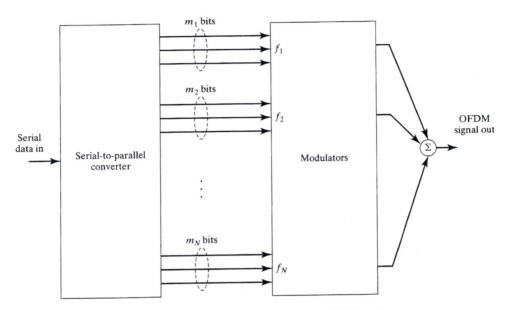

FIGURE 4–39   Block diagram of a general OFDM modulator.

being bandwidth efficient, is that it is highly flexible in terms of its adaptability to channels with nonuniform gain/noise characteristics versus frequency, its ability to combat short duration noise bursts (called impulse noise), and its robustness to multipath. The many applications of OFDM that are currently being investigated include high data-rate transmission over twisted pair lines and fiber/cable, digital terrestrial television broadcasting, high-quality digital audio broadcasting, high data-rate mobile communications, personal communications services, and simulcast broadcast.

The characteristic of OFDM that first made it popular for channels characterized by impulse noise and delay dispersion (such as nonuniform gain/phase and multipath) is its elongated symbol duration that results from the parallel transmission of several bits on the synchronous subcarriers. As long as the symbol period is long compared with the durations of these disturbances, OFDM combats them because the disturbance is small fraction of the symbol interval. As OFDM was investigated for more challenging multipath channels, it was found that it did not provide as much protection as available with serial data transmission with decision feedback equalization; with coding it is possible to achieve equivalent performance.

With a properly designed OFDM system, it appears possible to realize exceedingly good bandwidth and power efficiencies in challenging environments. These efficiencies do not come without a price, however. Because OFDM is a parallel, synchronous modulation scheme, synchronization is more challenging than for an equivalent frequency-division multiplexed (FDM) system with nonsynchronous carriers. Also, OFDM is more sensitive to channel nonlinearities, and it has a higher peak-to-rms ratio than FDM single-carrier systems. These attributes require that special attention be paid to the linearity of power amplifiers, or that special measures be taken to decrease the peak-to-rms ratio with soft limiting, and so on.

For an introduction to OFDM, two review articles are highly recommended [20, 21]. References [22–25] may be consulted for some of the original work on the development of OFDM. Finally, papers dealing with the combination of OFDM and direct-sequence spread-spectrum (DSSS) modulation are those by Kondo and Milstein [26], Sourour and Nakagawa [27], and Hara and Prasad [28].

4.10.2   The Idea Behind OFDM

As shown in Figure 4–39, the OFDM concept utilizes parsing of the input data bit stream (which may be due to a single source or several sources multiplexed) into N symbol streams, each with symbol duration t_s, and each of which in turn is used to modulate parallel, synchronous subcarriers.[18] If the modulation scheme used on the subcarriers can accommodate D bits per symbol and the subcarriers are spaced by $1/t_s$ hertz, which means they are orthogonal over the interval $(0, t_s)$, then the single-user bandwidth efficiency of the OFDM scheme is D bps/Hz and the symbol duration is $t_s = DNT_b$ seconds, where T_b is the bit duration of the input data. A typical OFDM spectrum is illustrated in Figure 4–40 for rectangular pulse shaping and separation of subcarriers by $1/t_s$.

4.10.3   Mathematical Description of DFT-Implemented OFDM

The use of the DFT, which makes for an efficient implementation of an OFDM system, was first proposed by Weinstein and Ebert in 1971 [24]. For a sufficiently large number of subcarriers, which translates directly to DFT points, it is well known that the computation of the DFT is made even more efficient with use of the fast Fourier transform (FFT). This form of OFDM implementation is summarized in this section.

Assume a symbol sequence $\{X_k\}$, which is used to modulate N simultaneously transmitted subcarriers. In the mth signaling interval, the real transmitted signal is

$$\tilde{x}_m(t) = \begin{cases} \displaystyle\sum_{k=0}^{N-1} \text{Re}[X_{(m-1)N+k}\, p[t - (m-1)T_s]\exp(j2\pi f_k t)\exp(j2\pi f_0 t)] \\ 0, \text{otherwise}, (m-1)T_s \le t \le mT_s, m = \cdots, 1, 2, 3, \cdots \end{cases} \qquad (4\text{–}208)$$

where $p(t)$ is 1 for $0 \le t \le T_s$ and 0 otherwise,

$$f_k = \frac{k}{t_s}\ \text{Hz} \qquad (4\text{–}209)$$

and

$$T_s = t_s + \Delta \qquad (4\text{–}210)$$

---

[18]T_s is reserved for another meaning later.

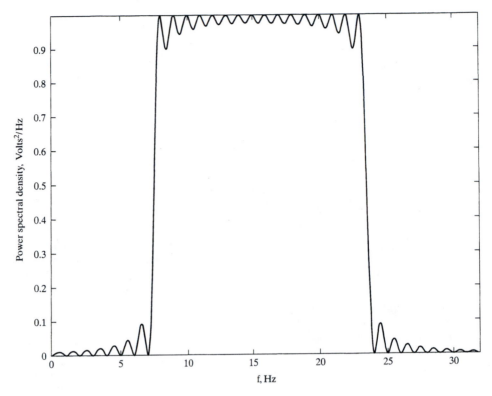

FIGURE 4–40   Spectrum for an OFDM signal (subcarrier separation of 1 Hz).

In (4–210), t_s is the duration occupied by data transmission and Δ is a guard time interval, assumed to come at the start of a new signaling period, which is used to minimize inter-symbol interference effects. It is customary to drop the real part and carrier exponential $\exp(j2\pi f_0 t)$ in (4–208) for simplicity of notation. Thus the doubly infinite duration signal can be written in complex form as

$$y(t) = \sum_{m=-\infty}^{\infty} \sum_{k=0}^{N-1} X_{(m-1)N+k}\, p\big[t - (m-1)T_s\big]\exp(j2\pi f_k t) \qquad (4\text{–}211)$$

where the tilde has been dropped to indicate the complex signal. In future discussions, we simply consider the complex baseband signal in the $m = 1$ interval, given by

$$x(t) = \sum_{k=0}^{N-1} X_k \exp(j2\pi kt/t_s),\ 0 \le t \le t_s + \Delta = T_s \qquad (4\text{–}212)$$

with the understanding that we get the real transmitted signal via (4–208).

In the interval $[0, \Delta)$ a cyclic prefix can be inserted [20] by lengthening the signaling interval to t_s:

$$x(t + t_s) = \sum_{k=0}^{N-1} X_k \exp[j2\pi k(t + t_s)/t_s]$$

(4–213)

$$= \sum_{k=0}^{N-1} X_k \exp(j2\pi kt/t_s)\exp(2\pi k) = x(t)$$

If Δ is chosen to be greater than or equal to the channel impulse response duration, the use of a cyclic prefix prevents the interfering of one signaling interval with the next since this part is dropped, as will be discussed later, before processing at the receiver. With t_s sufficiently long, the time spent sending the cyclic prefix is a negligible fraction of the total signaling interval. An additional feature of the cyclic prefix is that it maintains orthogonality between the separate subcarriers in the presence of channel filtering, since it makes the linear convolution of the channel work like a cyclic convolution (see Section 4.10.4).

The symbol stream may be considered to be formed by parsing a serial bit stream $\{d_k\}$, which may be from a single source or several time multiplexed sources. For example, if the modulation on the subcarriers is quadrature phase-shift keying (QPSK), two bits would be used to form each X_k (they would be chosen from the set $\{\pm 1 \pm j\}$), and the total number of bits used to form the subcarrier sum of (4–212) would be $2N$. In general, for a subcarrier modulation scheme using D bits per symbol, the number of bits required to modulate the subcarrier sum in the mth interval is DN. Since the subcarrier spacing is $1/t_s$ hertz, the total bandwidth occupied by the sum of N subcarriers is N/t_s hertz [allowing $1/(2t_s)$ on either end]. But $t_s = DNT_b$, where T_b is the bit period, giving a total bandwidth of

$$B_T = \frac{N}{DNT_b} = \frac{R_b}{D}$$

(4–214)

where $R_b = T_b^{-1}$ is the bit rate. Thus (4–214) gives a single-user bandwidth efficiency of

$$\frac{R_b}{B_T} = D \text{ bits/s/Hz}$$

(4–215)

(Each subcarrier may, in fact, exceed the minimum $1/t_s$ bandwidth assumed by some factor $1 + \alpha$ due to pulse shaping [23]). The signaling interval in terms of bit period is

$$T_s = DNT_b + \Delta$$

(4–216)

Thus, making the cyclic prefix duration a negligible fraction of the total signaling interval is a matter of making DN large enough.

For the moment, assume binary modulation on the subcarriers [the X_ks in (4–212) can be complex and nonbinary] and consider (4–212) with t_s replaced by NT_b in the exponent and the time variable sampled at integer increments so that $t = nT_b$. The result may be expressed as

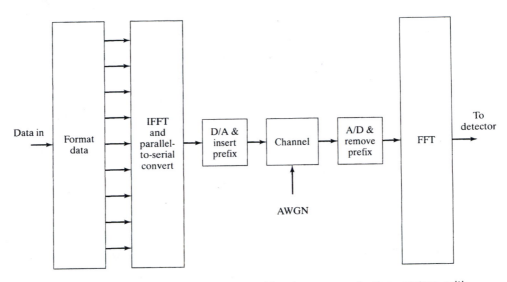

FIGURE 4–41   Block diagram of a multicarrier communication system with IFFT/FFT implementation.

$$x_n = \sum_{k=0}^{N-1} X_k \exp(j2\pi kn/N), \quad 0 \le n \le N-1 \qquad (4\text{--}217)$$

which is recognized as the inverse DFT[19] of the symbol sequence $\{X_k\}$. Thus, the DFT of the sequence $\{x_n\}$ provides the symbol stream $\{X_k\}$. It is well known that, for sufficiently large N, the DFT can be replaced by a much more computationally efficient FFT algorithm, and (4–217) with the corresponding inverse operation used at the receiver demonstrates a way to implement an OFDM modem using digital signal processing techniques as shown in Figure 4–41. The FFT/IFFT implementation used here amounts to replacing normal convolution with cyclic convolution, which requires padding (often zero padding) of the input sequence to make it equivalent to normal convolution. The padding in the case of OFDM is accomplished by the cyclic prefix.

The IFFT operation works on a successive blocks of samples that are essentially multiplied by a rectangular window. This results in $(\sin x)/x$ sidelobes in the transformed domain (it may be somewhat confusing to refer to this as the frequency domain in this case, since the IFFT is used to get there, and the output samples are D/A converted for transmission through the channel). Multiplication in one domain corresponds to convolution in the transformed domain. Convolution of the output samples with a $(\sin x)/x$ function results in relatively large sidelobes that may cause interference between

---

[19]The N-point DFT is often defined as $X_k = \sum_{n=0}^{N-1} x_n \exp(-j2\pi kn/N)$ and its inverse as $x_n = (1/N) \sum_{n=0}^{N-1} X_k \exp(j2\pi kn/N)$. The factor $1/N$ is required in front of one of the sums. Since it doesn't appear in (4–217), the definition used here assumes it to be associated with the DFT. A solution to this dilemma sometimes used is to put a factor $N^{-1/2}$ in front of both the DFT and inverse DFT. It is also often useful to note that the DFT/inverse DFT is energy preserving: $\sum_{n=0}^{N-1} |x_n|^2 = \sum_{n=0}^{N-1} |X_k|^2$.

adjacent-channel users in a multiuser application, where the separate user's clocks are most likely asynchronous. In such cases, it may be advisable to use a less abrupt window function than rectangular, such as Hamming or hanning, on the input samples.

To explicitly characterize the effect of the channel on the OFDM signal, consider (4–217) convolved with the channel impulse response function $h(t)$, which gives

$$y(t) = x(t)*h(t) + n(t) = \sum_{k=0}^{N-1} H_k X_k \exp\left(j2\pi kt/t_s\right) + n(t), \quad \Delta \leq t \leq \Delta + t_s = T_s \quad (4\text{–}218)$$

where $n(t)$ is the additive white Gaussian noise (AWGN) of Figure 4–41 and

$$H_k = A_k \exp(j\theta_k) \qquad\qquad (4\text{–}219)$$

is the baseband equivalent *frequency response* of the channel at frequency k/t_s Hz. The interval (Δ, T_s) is the time interval over which useful information is obtained since it was assumed that the maximum duration of the channel impulse response is Δ. Upon sampling the output of the channel and taking the DFT, the kth noisy output symbol is

$$Y_k = H_k X_k + N_k \qquad\qquad (4\text{–}220)$$

For a fixed channel, the H_ks would be fixed complex constants for each k. For a fading channel, they would be random variables; for example, for a Rayleigh fading channel, they would be zero-mean complex Gaussian random variables in (4–219) [A_k would be Rayleigh distributed and θ_k would be uniform in $(0, 2\pi]$.[20]

Equation (4–220) demonstrates one of the features of an OFDM modulation system, which is that the equalization necessary for a dispersive channel that is ordinarily accomplished in the time domain for a serial data transmission system is accomplished in the frequency domain via estimating the H_ks in an OFDM system. The idea of such frequency domain equalization was first published in [29]. If the objective is to only undo the channel induced distortion on the signal, the kth received subcarrier signal is multiplied by the complex constant

$$C_k = \frac{1}{H_k} \qquad\qquad (4\text{–}221)$$

It can be seen that this procedure will enhance the noise spectrum at frequencies where $|H_k|$ is small or zero. This is a well known phenomenon in zero-forcing equalizers in the case of serial data transmission to which the present case is a direct analog. If one imposes a minimum mean square error optimization criterion between the equalized received baseband signal and the true data signal, then the kth received subcarrier signal is multiplied by the complex constant

$$C_k = \frac{H_k^*}{|H_k|^2 + \sigma_n^2/\sigma_s^2} \qquad\qquad (4\text{–}222)$$

---

[20]The result in (4–220) is obtained under the assumption of negligible leakage. This will be discussed in more detail in Section 4.10.4.

where σ_n^2 and σ_s^2 are the variances of the noise component and the transmitted data signal, respectively, in (4–218). The amplitudes for the equalization coefficients can be estimated in response to known symbols or pilot tones embedded in the received signal as can their phases. In addition, the phases can be estimated differentially by employing differential encoding at the transmitter.

Sari and colleagues [21] make some observations about equalization at the output DFT of an OFDM receiver. In frequency domain equalization implemented in a serial data transmission system, there would be a inverse DFT back to the time domain after multiplication by the equalizer coefficients in the frequency domain, and decisions are based on signal energy transmitted over the entire channel bandwidth. The inverse DFT after multiplication by the constants given in (4–221) or (4–222) is not performed in the case of OFDM. Rather, the data in each DFT output is detected independently of data in the other outputs and the overall error rate is the average of the error rates in all DFT outputs. If one or more of these is in a spectral null, the error rates on them will be very poor, with the result that they will dominate the average bit error probability, thus causing a bit error rate floor. In a fixed channel this can be avoided by not using these subcarrier frequencies. In a fading channel, where the spectral nulls move about, error correction coding must be used to spread the effect of errors across all DFT outputs.

In the same vein, simulation results given in [30, 31] show that there is virtually no diversity gain with OFDM by itself in a fading channel with no coding as compared with that gained by using decision feedback equalization in serial data transmission. In order to gain the full diversity of an OFDM system, coding is necessary [32].

If coding is used with OFDM, two obvious choices present themselves [32]. One is to use a block code with block length equal to the DFT block length. The second is to use a convolutional code with the Viterbi algorithm (VA) and soft-decision detection. It is assumed also that interleaving will be employed at the transmitter with de-interleaving at the receiver to randomize errors. These are concepts that will be discussed in Chapters 6 and 7.

4.10.4 Effect of Fading on OFDM Detection

The effect of the channel on an OFDM signal was first considered in (4–218) through (4–222), where it was implicitly assumed that there was no time variation imposed by the channel on the signal envelope. Furthermore, it was assumed that errors produced by the IFFT/FFT processing were negligible. We take a more careful look at these effects now by considering two special cases with no AWGN. Specifically, these two special cases are the following:

1. A channel modeled by a time-invariant linear system with impulse response $h(t)$ and transfer function $H(f)$. In this case, the channel output in the time and frequency domains are, respectively,

$$y_1(t) = x(t)*h(t)$$
$$Y_1(f) = X(f)H(f)$$

(4–223)

2. A channel modeled as time-varying multiplicative so that the channel output in the time and frequency domains are, respectively,

$$y_2(t) = x(t)z(t)$$
$$Y_2(f) = X(f)*Z(f) \tag{4-224}$$

Recall that the discrete-time processing implied by the IFFT/FFT imposes additional errors to those imposed by the imperfect channels assumed. These include leakage, aliasing, and picket fence effects [33]. It is assumed that care has been taken in the discrete-time processing system to minimize these effects.

The discrete-time representation of (4–223) is

$$y_{1,n} = x_n*h_n \tag{4-225}$$
$$Y_{1,k} = X_k H_k, \quad 0 \leq n, k \leq M + N - 1$$

where M is the length of $\{h_n\}$. Recall that a convolution operation gives an output signal with duration that is sum of the durations of the two convolved signals and that to replace linear convolution with circular convolution (the result of a minimum FFT on both signals, taking the product of their FFTs and an inverse FFT) requires that an FFT of size equal to the sum of the lengths of the two input sequences, minus 1, be used. Recall that in addition to combating delay spread, this is another reason for the use of the guard interval in OFDM processing. Also recall the comment made in relation to windowing to cut down on sidelobe effects and minimize adjacent-channel interference.[21] The other effect that can be present in the discrete-time representations of (4–223) is leakage. This results if either of the signals in the DFT-implemented convolution operation is not periodic with period N. Estimation of the channel is an important consideration here [34].

Now consider the discrete-time processing implied by (4–224). In terms of the discrete time index, n, and the discrete frequency index, k, (4–224) becomes

$$y_{2,n} = x_n z_n$$
$$Y_{2,k} = X_k * Z_k \tag{4-226}$$

Substitute (4–217) in the first equation of (4–226) to get

$$y_{2,n} = z_n \sum_{k=1}^{N-1} X_k \exp(j2\pi kn/N), 0 \leq n \leq N - 1 \tag{4-227}$$

The receiver obtains the input to the detector by taking the DFT, so apply the DFT definition to get [recall the footnote after (4–217)]

---

[21]The comments made in regard to an FFT/IFFT operation here really should be in reference to an IFFT/FFT operation. In keeping with most of the literature on OFDM, (4–217) is viewed as an IFFT because of the sign in the exponent inside the sum. An exception is Cimini [25] who chooses his signals so that a DFT can be used to represent the transmitted signal.

$$Y_{2,m} = \frac{1}{N} \sum_{n=0}^{N-1} \left[z_n \sum_{k=1}^{N-1} X_k \exp(j2\pi kn/N) \right] \exp(-j2\pi mn/N), \; 0 \le m \le N - 1 \qquad (4\text{–}228)$$

Reverse the orders of summation and use the definition of the DFT of z_n to get the form

$$Y_{2,m} = \sum_{k=0}^{N-1} X_k Z_{m-k}, \quad 0 \le m \le N - 1 \qquad (4\text{–}229)$$

With no distortion due to the channel, this should become $Y_{2, m} = X_m$. To isolate the distortion terms, take the $k = m$ term out of the sum so that (4–229) becomes

$$Y_{2,m} = Z_0 X_m + \sum_{\substack{k=0 \\ k \ne m}}^{N-1} X_k Z_{m-k}, \quad 0 \le m \le N - 1 \qquad (4\text{–}230)$$

The first term on the right-hand side is the desired output data symbol, and the sum (second term on the right-hand side) represents intercarrier interference [also termed interchannel interference (ICI)], which is caused from the lack of orthogonality due to the multiplicative channel distortion. This interference term was first pointed out by Cimini [25].

If the Doppler spread is zero, the ICI is zero. If the Doppler spread is very low, these terms might be negligible depending on the application. Russell and Stüber [35] have analyzed the application of OFDM to HDTV where very low error rates are required and the channel is fragile due to the tremendous compression required of the video signals. In such an application, the ICI term is not negligible and must be accounted for in any analysis. The paper by Russell and Stüber considers the use of antenna diversity and trellis coded modulation (TCM) to give acceptable error probabilities for the HDTV application. Another case where these terms can be ignored is if the OFDM tones are spread wider than the minimum value of $1/t_s$.

4.10.5   Parameter Choices and Implementation Issues in OFDM

The use of OFDM in fading/multipath channels appears to reduce to a few issues. These are: (1) What is the appropriate symbol rate for combating the delay and Doppler spread? (2) How should the signal structure be designed to realize most of the diversity gain implied by the channel? (3) What are the residual losses imposed by imperfect signal design and implementation degradations?

4.10.5.1 OFDM Symbol Rate for Combating Delay Spread.   The first of these is relatively easy to answer. Based on an analysis given in Bello and Nelin [36], it follows that for communication without an equalizer, the symbol rate should satisfy the inequality

$$R_s \le \frac{1}{2\pi T_m} \qquad (4\text{–}231)$$

where T_m is the rms delay spread of the channel. Based on (4–216), this says that the minimum value for DN should be

$$\lfloor DN \rfloor_{\min} = \frac{R_b}{R_{s,\,\max}} \qquad (4\text{--}232)$$

where $\lfloor \ \ \rfloor$ means the smallest integer exceeding the quantity inside.

4.10.5.2 Realizing Diversity in OFDM. The other side of the issue is for a given transmission bandwidth, B_T, what is the maximum number of subcarriers to use? For unspread OFDM, the answer would be the maximum possible consistent with the allowed delays and Doppler spread, assuming that enough interleaving and coding can be used to realize the full diversity gain implied by the channel. With a tone spacing of $1/t_s$, the number of tones would be $B_T t_s$.

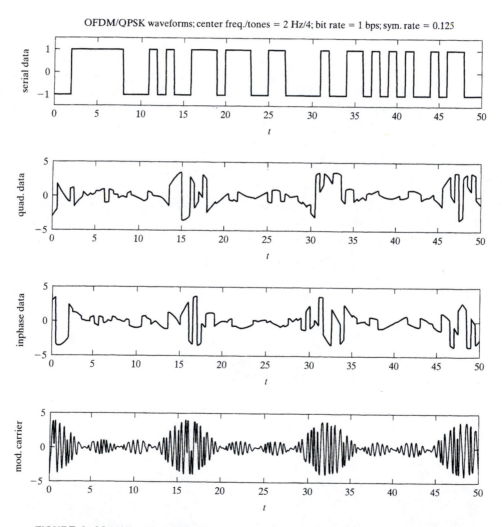

FIGURE 4–42 Waveforms for four-carrier OFDM with QPSK modulation.

4.10.5.3 Implementation Issues. A number of implementation issues are inherent in the OFDM modulation technique. One category of implementation issues emanates from the modulated signal being a coherent sum of sinusoids, which gives rise to a larger peak-to-rms ratio than for noncoherent summing as in frequency division multiplexing. Another category of issues results from the modulated signal being a comb of coherent frequencies across the transmission bandwidth that are delayed different amounts depending on the phase delay characteristics of the modem and transmission medium. An overview of these will be given in this section.

Envelope Variation. A large peak-to-envelope variation requires the use of amplifiers with large linear amplification ranges. If limiting of the signal envelope is accepted, then one is interested in degradation in modem performance that becomes more significant as limiting increases. This problem is one that has received much attention in the past in various contexts. Some references written in the context of OFDM will be summarized here. Analysis and simulation is used in O'Neill and Lopes [37] to investigate the effect on the symbol error rate of clipping the peaks of an OFDM signal. They also propose a strategy for reducing the error rate by modifying the decision regions for detection of the 16-QAM signal. The use of special block coding techniques is studied in [38] in order to decrease the peak-to-rms ratio. Distortion of the received signal by nonlinear effects is modeled as Gaussian noise in Santella and Mazzenga [39] to determine optimum nonlinear amplifier backoffs. The modulation types on the OFDM subcarriers considered were 4-PSK, 16-QAM, and 64-QAM. Predistortion of the transmitted signal is one technique that has been investigated for applications using QAM; two papers dealing with QAM are [40, 41].

Synchronization. It is important to obtain an accurate estimate of carrier frequency in OFDM systems in order to minimize degradation, particularly if, say, 16- or 64-QAM modulation is used. Frequency offset destroys the orthogonality between tones. Frequency estimates can be based on pilot signals and have typically been obtained from analysis of the signal at the output of the DFT in the receiver [42, 43]. In [44], a technique is reported that is said to avoid the drawbacks of the other schemes, including sensitivity to multipath and computational complexity. In Classen and Meyr [45] an algorithm is presented that is able to cope with offsets of the order of the frequency spacing between subcarriers. Tradeoffs are given between training symbols, computational load, degradation, and implementation effort.

Other synchronization issues are symbol timing synchronization, the effect of pulse shaping on synchronization, and the effect of spectrum overlap on synchronization.

4.10.6   Simulation of OFDM Waveforms

Figure 4–42 shows simulation results of the waveforms for four carrier OFDM with QPSK carrier modulation. Although many more carriers than four would be used in practice, these results at least give an indication of the peak-to-average ratio problem that exists with OFDM. Figure 4–43 shows spectra for four-carrier modulation for QPSK and MSK carrier modulation. This figure illustrates the importance of pulse shaping to create overall spectra with low sidelobes.

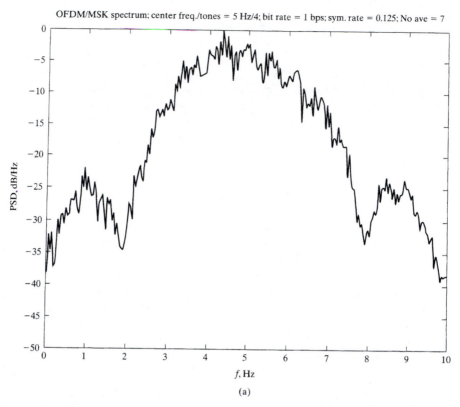

OFDM/MSK spectrum; center freq./tones = 5 Hz/4; bit rate = 1 bps; sym. rate = 0.125; No ave = 7

(a)

FIGURE 4–43   Spectra for four-carrier OFDM: **(a)** MSK modulation; **(b)** QPSK modulation.

4.11   SUMMARY

1. *M*-ary data transmission means that the transmitter may select from two or more symbols per signaling interval. The special case $M = 2$ is called a binary transmission. If the source selects from a q-symbol alphabet, then $q^J = M$, where J is an integer, assuming that $q \leq M$, to prevent gaps between symbols.

2. Assuming $M = 2^n$, n an integer, $\log_2 M$ bits are required to specify a symbol in an *M*-ary system. Thus, $\log_2 M$ bits are conveyed per symbol, or

$$R_b = (\log_2 M)R_s$$

where R_s is the symbol rate in symbols per second and R_b is the bit rate in bits per second.

3. Based on a set K of observations of the received data $\{Z_1, Z_2, \ldots, Z_K\}$, an optimum (single-shot) receiver decides as the transmitted signal (hypothesis H_i) the one that

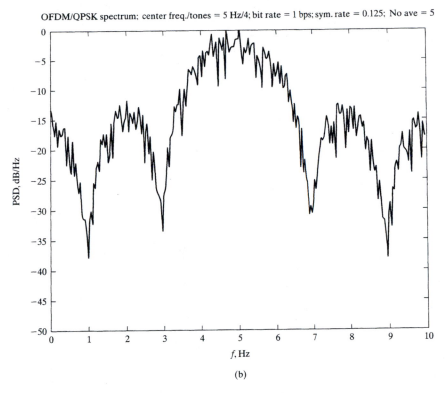

OFDM/QPSK spectrum: center freq./tones = 5 Hz/4; bit rate = 1 bps; sym. rate = 0.125; No ave = 5

(b)

FIGURE 4–43   *Continued*

corresponds to the maximum a posteriori probability, $P(H_i|Z_1,Z_2, \ldots, Z_K)$, $i = 1,2, \ldots$, M. Such a receiver, referred to as a MAP (maximum *a posteriori* receiver) corresponds to a Bayes minimum average cost decision criterion if right decisions cost zero and wrong decisions are equally costly.

4. In order to cast the continuous-time waveform problem of signal detection in white Gaussian noise into a finite number of observations, the M possible received signals, $s_1(t), s_2(t), \ldots, s_M(t)$, are used to construct an orthonormal basis set, $\{\phi_i(t), i = 1,2, \ldots, K\}$, $K \le M$, and the received signal plus noise is represented in the corresponding vector space as

$$z(t) = \sum_{k=1}^{K} (S_{ik} + N_k)\phi_k(t)$$

Each possible transmitted signal therefore is represented in terms of its coordinates $\{S_{i1}, S_{i2}, \ldots, S_{iK}\}$. The observed data coordinates equal the signal coordinates plus the noise components $\{N_1, N_2, \ldots, N_K\}$. The resulting space is referred to as the observation space.

5. The MAP criterion, under additive Gaussian noise background conditions, when put in terms of signal space, amounts to partitioning the observation space such that all observed data points closest to a given signal point are interpreted as having resulted from that signal being transmitted. This can be interpreted as the decision criterion being "Choose the closest signal point to the observed data point as corresponding to the transmitted signal." Such a decision criterion minimizes the probability of making a decision error.

6. Various useful relationships can be cast in terms of signal space terminology. These include Schwarz's inequality and Parseval's theorem.

7. A convenient bound for the probability of decision error in signal detection is the union bound. It is

$$P_s \leq \sum_{\substack{i=1 \\ i \neq k}}^{M} P(\mathbf{S}_i, \mathbf{S}_k)$$

where $P(\mathbf{S}_i, \mathbf{S}_k)$ is the probability of error for a hypothetical communication system that uses the two signals $\mathbf{S}_i$ and $\mathbf{S}_k$ to communicate one of two equally likely messages.

8. Various types of signaling schemes are cast in terms of signal space in this chapter. These include M-ary frequency-shift keying (FSK), phase-shift keying (PSK), and quadrature-amplitude modulation (QAM). All these schemes are assumed coherent; that is, a phase coherent reference is assumed available at the receiver for demodulation. Also considered are noncoherent FSK and differential PSK, the latter being the differentially coherent version of normal PSK.

9. Comparison of M-ary communication systems can be carried out on the basis of power and bandwidth efficiency. Power efficiency is measured in terms of the energy-per-bit-to-noise spectral density required to give a specified probability of bit error. Bandwidth efficiency is the data rate per hertz of bandwidth that can be supported, measured in bits per second per hertz.

10. From most power efficient to least power efficient, the coherent schemes considered in this chapter are in the following order: FSK, QAM, and PSK. This is apparent when the signal spaces for each are considered. The signal space for FSK is M-dimensional, whereas the signal spaces for PSK and QAM are both two-dimensional. Thus, as more and more signal points are considered, they become more and more crowded together for PSK and QAM, whereas they do not for FSK because of the increasing dimensionality of the signal space. Furthermore, the signal points for PSK are constrained to lie on a circle of radius equal to the square root of the symbol energy; the signal points for the type of QAM considered here are on a square-sided grid and therefore are more spread out than those for PSK for a given M. Reference [46] provides a broad perspective on digital communications. Reference [47] is a general reference on QAM.

11. The power efficiency performances of noncoherent FSK and differential PSK are only slightly worse than the corresponding performances of coherent FSK and PSK, respectively. Power efficiencies in terms of bit error probabilities were approximately computed from symbol error probabilities. Reference [48] presents a technique for obtaining bit error probabilities directly from signal space diagrams of Gray-encoded symbols.

12. Bandwidth efficiency of the various communications schemes considered are in the following order from best to worst: PSK, QAM, and DPSK; coherent FSK; noncoherent FSK. The reason can be again traced to the dimensionality of the signal spaces, which stay constant at two for the first three and increase directly with M for both types of FSK.

13. Some commonly used special cases of modulation schemes were considered. Schemes falling under the general category of quadrature multiplexed include quadrature phase-shift keying (QPSK), offset QPSK (OQPSK), and minimum-shift keying (MSK). If the former two use Gray-encoded bits to associate bits with phases, all three perform the same at moderate-to-high signal-to-noise ratios. Other popular modulation schemes briefly considered were Gaussian MSK and $\pi/4$–differential QPSK.

14. A method for computing the power spectra for quadrature multiplexed modulation schemes was presented.

15. Several design examples for M-ary modulation schemes were given to illustrate tradeoffs.

16. Simultaneous improvement of bandwidth and power efficiency can be achieved with combined modulation and coding. Two such techniques are multi-h continuous-phase modulation and trellis-coded modulation. The former was discussed in this chapter and the latter will be overviewed in Chapter 7.

17. Orthogonal frequency-division multiplexing (OFDM) is a bandwidth efficient modulation technique that is tolerant to multipath and impulse noise (this noise type is characterized by large amplitude bursts against a low level background). It is achieved by multiplexing the incoming bit stream onto a set of synchronous parallel carriers. One of its drawbacks is that it has a very poor peak-to-average power ratio, which means that any channel nonlinearities will affect its performance adversely.

REFERENCES

[1] R. E. Ziemer and W. H. Tranter, *Principles of Communications,* 4th ed. (Boston: Houghton Mifflin, 1995).

[2] J. M. Wozencraft and I. M. Jacobs, *Principles of Communication Engineering* (New York: John Wiley, 1965) (Currently available through Waveland Press, P.O. Box 400, Prospect Heights, IL 60070, ISBN 0–88133–554–1)

[3] M. Abramowitz and I. Stegun, eds., *Handbook of Mathematical Functions* (New York: Dover, 1972).

[4] W. C. Lindsey and M. K. Simon, *Telecommunications System Engineering* (Englewood Cliffs, N.J., Prentice-Hall, 1973).

[5] R. F. Pawula, "A New Formula for MDPSK Symbol Error Probability," *IEEE Commun. Letters*, Vol. 2, pp. 271–272, Oct. 1998.

[6] J. H. Park, "On Binary DPSK Reception," *IEEE Trans. Commun., Vol.* COM-26, pp. 484–486, April 1978.

[7] V. K. Prabhu, "Error Rate Performance for Differential PSK," *IEEE Trans. Commun.,* Vol. COM-30, pp. 2547–2550, December 1982.

[8] R. Pawula, "Asympotics and Error Rate Bounds for *M*-ary DPSK," *IEEE Trans. Commun.*, Vol. COM-32, pp. 93–94, January 1984.

[9] K. Morota and K. Haride, "GMSK Modulation for Digital Mobile Radio Telephony," *IEEE Trans. Commun.*, Vol. COM-29, pp. 1044–1050, July, 1981.

[10] J. G. Proakis, *Digital Communications,* 3rd ed. (New York: McGraw-Hill, 1995).

[11] C. Miller and J. Lee, "BER Expressions for Differentially Detected $\pi/4$-DQPSK Modulation," *IEEE Trans. Commun.*, Vol. 46, pp. 71–81, Jan. 1998.

[12] J. B. Anderson and D. P. Taylor, "A Bandwidth-Efficient Class of Signal Space Codes," *IEEE Trans. Inf. Theory,* Vol. IT-24, pp. 703–712, November 1978.

[13] Special Issue on Combined Modulation and Encoding, *IEEE Trans. Commun.*, Vol. COM-29, March 1981.

[14] Special Issue on Bandwidth and Power Efficient Coded Modulation, *IEEE Journal on Selected Areas in Commun.*, Vol. 7, August and December, 1989 (two parts).

[15] Special Issue on Bandwidth and Power Efficient Modulation, *IEEE Commun. Magazine,* Vol. 29, December 1991.

[16] John B. Anderson, Tor Aulin, and Carl-Erik Sunderg, *Digital Phase Modulation* (New York: Plenum, 1986).

[17] E. Biglieri, D. Divsalar, P. Mclane, and M. Simon, *Introduction to Trellis Coded Modulation with Applications* (New York: Macmillan, 1991).

[18] E. T. Doelz, T. Heald, and D. L. Martin, "Binary Data Transmission Techniques for Linear Systems," *Proc. IRE,* Vol. 45, pp. 656–661, May 1957.

[19] P. A. Bello, "Selective Fading Limitations of the Kathryn Modem and Some System Design Considerations," *IEEE Trans. Commun.*, Vol. 13, pp. 320–333, Sept. 1965.

[20] J. A. C. Bingham, "Multicarrier Modulation for Data Transmission: An Idea Whose Time Has Come," *IEEE Commun. Mag.*, Vol. 28, pp. 5–14, May 1990.

[21] H. Sari, G. Karam, and I. Jeanclaude, "Transmission Techniques for Digital Terrestrial TV Broadcasting," *IEEE Commun. Mag.*, Vol. 33, pp. 100-109, Feb. 1995.

[22] R. W. Chang, and R. A. Gibby, "A Theoretical Study of Performance of an Orthogonal Multiplexing Data Transmission Scheme," *IEEE Trans. Commun.*, Vol. COM-16, pp. 529–540, Aug. 1968.

[23] B. Hirosaki, "An Orthogonally Multiplexed QAM System Using the Discrete Fourier Transform," *IEEE Trans. Commun.*, Vol. COM-29, pp. 982–989, July 1981.

[24] S. B. Weinstein, and P. M. Ebert, "Data Transmission by Frequency-Division Multiplexing Using the Discrete Fourier Transform," *IEEE Trans. Commun.*, Vol. COM-19, pp. 628–634, Oct. 1971.

[25] L. Cimini, "Analysis and Simulation of a Digital Mobile Channel Using Orthogonal Frequency Division Multiplexing," *IEEE Trans. Commun.*, Vol. COM-33, pp. 665-675, Jul. 1985.

[26] S. Kondo, and L. Milstein, "On the Performance of Multicarrier DS CDMA Systems," *IEEE Trans. Commun.*, Vol. 44, pp. 238–246, Feb. 1996.

[27] E. Sourour, and M. Nakagawa, "Performance of Orthogonal Multi-Carrier CDMA in a Multipath Fading Channel," *IEEE Trans. Commun.*, Vol. 44, pp. 356–367, Mar. 1996.

[28] S. Hara and R. Prasad, "Overview of Multicarrier CDMA," *IEEE Commun. Mag.*, Vol. 35, pp. 126–133, Dec. 1997.

[29] T. Walzman, and M. Schwartz, "Automatic Equalization Using the Discrete Frequency Domain," *IEEE Trans. Infor. Theory*, Vol. IT-19, pp. 59–68, Jan. 1973.

[30] H. Sari, G. Karam, and I. Jeanclaude, "An Analysis of Orthogonal Frequency-Division Multiplexing for Mobile Radio Applications," *IEEE VTC Proc.*, pp. 1635–1639, June 1994.

[31] S. K. Wilson, *Digital Audio Broadcasting in a Fading and Dispersive Channel*, Ph. D. Dissertation, Electrical Engineering Department, Stanford University, Aug. 1994.

[32] H. Sari, G. Karam, and I. Jeanclaude, "Frequency-Domain Equalization of Mobile Radio Terrestrial Broadcast Channels," *IEEE Globecom Proc.*, pp. 1–5, Dec. 1994.

[33] R. Ziemer, W. Tranter, and D. Fannin, *Signals and Systems: Continuous and Discrete,* 4th ed. (Upper Saddle River, NJ: Prentice Hall, 1998).

[34] J.-J. Van de Beek, O. Edfors, M. Sandell, S. Wilson, and P. Börjesson, "On Channel Estimation in OFDM Systems," *IEEE VTC Proc.*, pp. 815–819, July 1995.

[35] M. Russell, and G. Stüber, "Interchannel Interference Analysis of OFDM in a Mobile Environment," *IEEE VTC Proc.*, pp. 820–824, July 1995.

[36] P. Bello, and B. Nelin, "The Effect of Frequency Selective Fading on the Binary Error Probabilities of Incoherent and Differentially Coherent Matched Filter Receivers," *IEEE Trans. Commun. Syst.*, Vol. CS-11, pp. 170–186, June 1963.

[37] R. O'Neill and L. Lopes, "Performance of Amplitude Limited Multitone Signals," *IEEE VTC Proc.*, pp. 1675–1679, June 1995.

[38] T. Wilkonson and A. Jones, "Minimisation of the Peak to Mean Envelope Power Ratio of Multicarrier Transmission Schemes by Block Coding," *IEEE VTC Proc.*, pp. 825–829, July 1995.

[39] G. Santella and F. Mazzenga, "A Model for Performance Evaluation in M-QAM-OFDM Schemes in Presence of Nonlinear Distortions," *IEEE VTC Proc.*, pp. 830–834, July 1995.

[40] S. Stapleton, and J. Cavers, "A New Technique for Adaptation of Linearizing Predistorters," *IEEE VTC Proc.*, pp. 753–758, June 1991.

[41] G. Karam, and H. Sari, "Improved Data Predistortion Using Intersymbol Interpolation," *IEEE ICC Proc.*, pp. 286–291, June 1989.

[42] F. Daffara and A. Chouly, "Maximum Likelihood Frequency Detectors for Othogonal Multicarrier Systems," *IEEE ICC Proc.*, pp. 766–771, May 1993.

[43] N. Philips and L. Jeanne, "System for Broadcasting and Receiving Digital Data, Receiver and Transmitter for Use in Such Systems," International Patent, Appl. No. PCT/NL92/00039, Feb. 1992.

[44] F. Daffara and O. Adami, "A New Frequency Detector for Orthogonal Multicarrier Transmission Techniques," *IEEE VTC Proc.*, pp. 804–809, July 1995.

[45] F. Classen and H. Meyr, "Frequency Synchronization Algorithms for OFDM Systems Suitable for Communication over Frequency Selectrive Fading Channels," *IEEE VTC Proc.*, pp. 1655-1659, June 1994.

[46] M. Simon, S. Hinedi, and W. Lindsey, *Digital Communication Techniques: Signal Design and Detection* (Upper Saddle River, NJ: Prentice Hall, 1995).

[47] W. T. Webb and L. Hanzo, *Modern Quadrature Amplitude Modulation* (London: Pentech Press [available through IEEE Press], 1994).

[48] J. Lu, K. Letaief, J. Chuang, and M. Liou, "M-PSK and M-QAM BER Computation Using Signal-Space Concepts," *IEEE Trans. Commun.*, Vol. 47, pp. 181–190, Feb. 1999.

PROBLEMS

4–1. A message source emitting one of q messages each $T_m = 1/R_m$ seconds, where R_m is the message rate, is used as the input to a modulator that associates a string of J messages with one of M signals (symbols) of duration $T_s = 1/R_s$ seconds, where R_s is the symbol rate. If no gaps are to exist between symbols, fill in the blanks in the following table.

q	R_m (messages/s)	M	R_s (symbols/s)
4		16	1,000
2	100,000	32	
	8,000	4	4,000
3	20,000		5,000

4–2. A message source emits messages at a rate of 1000 messages/second chosen from an alphabet of four possible messages. These are fed into a modulator that can produce one of any eight symbols each T_s seconds.
  (a) How many messages should be associated with each modulator symbol? Give a table associating each possible message sequence with each of the eight symbols.
  (b) What must the modulator symbol rate be to avoid gaps?
  (c) What is the equivalent bit rate at the modulator output?

4–3. If an M-ary communication system transmits at a rate of 10,000 symbols per second, what is the equivalent bit rate in bits per second for $M = 2$? $M = 4$? $M = 8$? $M = 16$? $M = 32$?

4–4. Consider a hypothesis-testing problem with the following conditional densities given the hypotheses H_1 and H_2, *a priori* probabilities, and costs:

$$f_Z(z|H_1) = 0.5 \exp(-|z|)$$
$$f_Z(z|H_2) = 0.1\exp(-z/10)u(z)$$
$$p_1 = 1/3; \, p_2 = 2/3$$
$$C_{11} = C_{22} = 0; \, C_{12} = C_{21} = 1$$

Obtain the following:
  (a) The likelihood ratio test based on a single sample. Simplify as much as possible.
  (b) P_m and P_F
  (c) The average cost per decision. What else can the average cost be viewed as in this particular instance?

4–5. Given the signals

$$u_1(t) = \exp(-t)u(t)$$
$$u_2(t) = \exp(-2t) \, u \, (t)$$
$$u_3(t) = \exp(-3t) \, u \, (t)$$

and the definition of scalar product (4–24) with $t_0 = 0$ and $T_s = \infty$, verify the properties of the scalar product as given below (4–24) for these signals.

4–6. Find an orthonormal basis set corresponding to the three signals given here:

$$s_1(t) = u(t) - u(t - 2)$$
$$s_2(t) = u \, (t - 1) - u \, (t - 3)$$
$$s_3(t) = u \, (t) - u \, (t - 3)$$

4–7. (a) Using the Gram-Schmidt procedure, obtain an orthonormal basis set corresponding to the signals given in Problem 4–5.
  (b) Generalize this result to N such signals, i.e., $u_n(t) = \exp(-nt)u(t)$.

4–8. Verify Schwarz's inequality for $u_1(t)$ and $u_2(t)$ given in Problem 4–5.

4–9. Show that $n_r(t)$ and $n_p(t)$, as defined by (4–22) are uncorrelated; i.e., show that $E[n_r(t)n_p(t)]$ $= 0$, and therefore $n_r(t)$ and $n_p(t)$ are statistically independent if $n(t)$ is Gaussian.

4–10. Prove that (4–60) indeed provides the vector **a** that minimizes average energy.

4–11. Assume that the signals in the following two-dimensional signal constellations are equally probable. Find the new signal coordinates in each case so that average energy is minimized. Plot the signal constellations before and after energy minimization.

    (a) $S_1 = (2, 1)$; $S_2 = (2, 4)$; $S_3 = (-3, -4)$.

    (b) $S_1 = (0, 1)$; $S_2 = (1, 3)$; $S_3 = (-5, -4)$; $S_4 = (-1, -4)$.

    (c) $S_1 = (3, 2)$; $S_2 = (1, 4)$; $S_3 = (-1, -1)$; $S_4 = (-3, -3)$.

4–12. (a) Assume that the signals in the following three-dimensional signal constellations are equally probable. Find the new signal coordinates in each case so that average energy is minimized.

    (i) $S_1 = (2, 1, 3)$; $S_2 = (1, 2, 4)$; $S_3 = (-3, -2, -4)$; $S_4 = (1, -2, 4)$.

    (ii) $S_1 = (0, 1, 0)$; $S_2 = (1, 3, 3)$; $S_3 = (-2, -5, -4)$; $S_4 = (-1, -2, -4)$.

    (b) Suppose that the probabilities are now 1/3, 1/6, 1/6, 1/3 for S_1, S_2, S_3, and S_4, respectively. Find the new energy-minimizing signal constellations now.

4–13. For the waveform set of (4–90), obtain an expression for the peak-to-average power ratio and plot as a function of M.

4–14. Using (4–144) and appropriate bounds for P_s, obtain E_b/N_0 required for achieving $P_b = 10^{-3}$ for M-ary PSK with $M = 8, 16, 32,$ and 64. (Do not use Figure 4–20.)

4–15. Using (4–144) and appropriate equations for P_s, obtain E_b/N_0 required for achieving $P_b = 10^{-3}$ for M-ary QAM for $M = 16, 64,$ and 256. (Do not use Figure 4–21.)

4–16. (a) Derive (4–101) for M-ary QAM. Hint: Make use of the identities

$$\sum_{i=1}^{m} i = \frac{m(m+1)}{2} \text{ and } \sum_{i=1}^{m} i^2 = \frac{m(m+1)(2m+1)}{6}$$

    (b) Show that (4–108) is the limiting case of (4–107) for $M \gg 0$ and $a \gg 0$.

4–17. Derive (4–104) through (4–106) for QAM.

4–18. Using (4–145) and (4–88), obtain E_b/N_0 for achieving $P_b = 10^{-5}$ for M-ary coherent FSK for $M = 8, 16, 32,$ and 64.

4–19. Using (4–145) and (4–124), obtain E_b/N_0 for achieving $P_b = 10^{-5}$ for M-ary noncoherent FSK for $M = 2, 4,$ and 8.

4–20. On the basis of null-to-null bandwidth, give the required transmission bandwidth to achieve a bit rate of 100 kbps for the following modulation schemes (see Table 4–1):

    (a) 64-QAM

    (b) 16-PSK

    (c) BPSK

    (d) 8-FSK, coherent

    (e) 8-FSK, noncoherent

    (f) 16-FSK, coherent

    (g) 16-FSK, noncoherent

    (h) 256-QAM

4-21. A channel of bandwidth 150 kHz is available. It is desired to transmit through it at a data rate of 500 kbps.
   (a) What is the required value of M for M-ary PSK, DPSK, and QAM? (Note that M should be 2^n for PSK and DPSK and 4^n for QAM where n is an integer.)
   (b) Compare the modulation schemes of part **(a)** on the basis of E_b/N_0 to give $P_b = 10^{-6}$.
   (c) Discuss the relative advantages and disadvantages of the modulation schemes considered above for this application.

4-22. On the same plot, compare the probabilities of bit error versus E_b/N_0 for 16-ary QAM, PSK, and DPSK. Use appropriate bounds as necessary.

4-23. Obtain the closed form result given by (4–140) corresponding to (4–139) for $M = 2$.

4-24. Show that $\rho_{min} = -0.216$ in Example 4–6 corresponds to the minimum probability of error versus correlation coefficient and that the difference between this minimum result and that for $\rho = 0$ is about 0.85 dB in E_b/N_0.

4-25. In a certain data transmission application, bandwidth is not an issue, but simplicity, constant envelope of the modulated signal, and a small E_b/N_0 for a desired P_b are important. Which modulation scheme(s) discussed in this chapter would you choose and why? Limit your discussion only to those considered in this chapter. Give numerical results to back up your claims where possible.

4-26. Plot a curve like Figure 4–22 with points for noncoherent FSK superimposed. Assume that $P_b = 10^{-6}$ corresponds to perfect transmission.

4-27. A channel with bandwidth of 4000 Hz is available. What data rates can be supported by the following modulation schemes?
   (a) QPSK
   (b) 16-DPSK
   (c) 32-FSK, noncoherent
   (d) 8-FSK, coherent
   (e) 64-QAM
   (f) 32-PSK

4-28. For the modulation schemes and data rates found in Problem 4–27, find the E_b/N_0 values to give (a) $P_b = 10^{-4}$; (b) $P_b = 10^{-6}$. Use bounds and/or exact formulas to get your results. Do not use the graphs.

4-29. Make up a table like Table 4–3 comparing noncoherent FSK and DPSK for several values of M.

4-30. Make up a table like Table 4–3 comparing PSK and DPSK for several values of M.

4-31. Consider *vertices-of-a-hypercube signaling*, for which the ith signal is of the form

$$s(t) = \sqrt{\frac{E_s}{N_0}} \sum_{k=1}^{n} \alpha_{ik}\phi_k(t), \quad 0 \leq t \leq T_s$$

in which the coefficients α_{ik} are permuted through the values $+1$ and -1, E_s is the signal energy, and the ϕ_ks are orthonormal. Thus $M = 2^n$, where n is an integer. For $M = 8$, $n = 3$, the signal points in signal space lie on the vertices of a cube in 3-space.
   (a) Sketch the optimum partitioning of the observation space for $M = 8$.
   (b) Show that the probability of symbol error is

$$P_s = 1 - P(C)$$

$$\text{where } P(C) = \left(1 - Q\left(\sqrt{\frac{2E_s}{nN_0}}\right)\right)^n$$

(c) Obtain P_b versus E_b/N_0 and show by plotting that it is independent of M.

(d) Obtain the bandwidth efficiency of this scheme and show that it is independent of M.

4–32. Compare the 90% power containment bandwidths of BPSK and MSK with their null-to-null bandwidths.

4–33. (a) Derive (4–167) under the assumptions that $\{a_k\}$ and $\{b_m\}$ are iid sequences in which the sequence members have zero means and Δt is uniformly distributed in $(0, T_s)$.

(b) Suitably modify (4–167) to accommodate differing symbol periods in the quadrature-channel symbol streams.

4–34. Verify the phase trellis plots of Figure 4–34.

4–35. Do the following h codes achieve the maximum possible value for constraint length?

(a) {3/16, 4/16, 5/16}

(b) {7/16, 8/16}

(c) {8/16, 9/16}

(d) {7/16, 9/16}

4–36. What are the *periods* of the multi-h codes given in Problem 4–35?

4–37. Using the idea of an average modulation index for multi-h, as expressed by (4–201), derive and calculate the approximate spectra for the multi-h phase codes {1/4, 2/4}, {3/8, 4/8}, and {3/8, 4/8, 5/8} for $f T_b = 0.5, 1, 2,$ and 3. Compare with the exact results of Figure 4–36.

4–38. Design an OFDM system for the following specifications:

Desired data rate:	100 kbps
Multipath delay spread:	1 μs
Other interference:	AWGN
Channel bandwidth:	30 kHz
Bit error probability max:	10^{-3}

Note that if the symbol duration is long enough, the multipath can be eliminated through discarding the cyclic prefix at the receiver. Thus the only other disturbance is AWGN. The overall bit error probability performance of the system is then that for each carrier. Choose a modulation technique based on the required bandwidth efficiency, and then predict the required E_b/N_0. More than one M-ary modulation scheme will work. Discuss the pros and cons of each.

4–39. Biorthogonal signals are constructed by adding to a set of orthogonal signals their negatives. Thus, let an orthogonal signal set be denoted as $s_1(t), s_2(t), \ldots, s_{M/2}(t)$; the biorthogonal set is completed by adding to these signals $-s_1(t), -s_2(t), \ldots, -s_{M/2}(t)$. The bit error probability for biorthogonal signaling is given in [46] as

$$P_b = P_{s1} + 0.5 P_{s2}$$

where

$$P_{s1} = \int_{-\infty}^{-\sqrt{E_s/N_0}} \frac{\exp(-u^2)}{\sqrt{\pi}} \{-1 + 2Q[\sqrt{2}(u + \sqrt{E_s/N_0})]\}^{M/2-1} du, M > 2$$

and

$$P_{s2} = P_s - P_{s1}$$

in which

$$P_s \leq (M - 2)Q\left(\sqrt{\frac{E_s}{N_0}}\right) + Q\left(\sqrt{\frac{2E_s}{N_0}}\right), M > 2$$

is a tight bound.

Write a MATLAB program to carry out the integrations and compare the bit error probability versus E_b/N_0 with orthogonal signaling (coherent FSK). Note that $M = 2$ is BPSK.

5

Channel Degradations
in Digital Communications

5.1 INTRODUCTION

In this chapter the effects of channel-induced degradations on the performance of communications systems are considered. These include various levels of synchronization at the receiver and degradations thereby imposed by imperfect estimates, particularly phase error. Also considered are the effects of random variations of amplitude imposed due to propagation perturbations by the channel. Typically, these are caused by multiple-path transmissions (termed multipath). Multipath transmission can be characterized by two gross parameters—delay spread and Doppler spread. The former refers to the multiple transmission paths that are manifested by the spreading of the duration of a short-pulse transmission. The latter refers to differing motion of the reflectors in the channel thus resulting in the signal components from the multiple paths having different Doppler frequency shifts that compose the received signal. It is manifested by the spreading of the spectral components of a single-frequency tone sent through the channel. Because of the superposition of multiple components of the received signal, constructive or destructive combinations give rise to a signal envelope that may vary over tremendous ranges—several tens of decibels is not uncommon.

In the final section of this chapter, various tools for digital communication system diagnosis are considered, including signal envelope plots, eye diagrams, and phasor diagrams.

We begin this chapter by considering the effects of phase perturbations in coherent communications systems.

5.2 SYNCHRONIZATION IN COMMUNICATION SYSTEMS

Referring to Figure 1–3, we see that several levels of synchronization are necessary in a complex communication system. These include generation of a carrier reference at the receiver of a coherent communication system that is phase coherent with the received carrier, generation of a clock in synchronism with the symbol sequence at the demodulator output, and possibly frame or word synchronization if the bits or symbols are grouped into blocks which must be taken together as a whole. Furthermore, if spread-spectrum modulation is employed, synchronization of the spreading code is required at the receiver.

We deal with some elementary aspects of the first three in this section. Spreading code synchronization will be dealt with in Chapter 9.

5.2.1 Carrier Synchronization

Two approaches can be taken to carrier synchronization depending on whether there is a carrier component present in the modulated signal. If a carrier component is present, a phase-lock loop circuit can be used to track it and the phase-lock loop output then used as a reference for coherent demodulation. Note that the power allocated to the carrier component is not available for data detection, but in all fairness must be considered as part of the transmitted signal power. If a carrier component is not present, as in BPSK, a nonlinear operation must be performed on the modulated signal to generate a spectral component at the carrier frequency. Several possible system block diagrams will be shown later that can be used to establish carrier-coherent references at the receiver in digital communication systems. One might consider generation of a carrier reference from the modulated signal the best course of action to take in that no power need be "wasted" in a carrier component. However, the nonlinear operation necessary to generate the carrier-coherent spectral component imposes an additional loss in the detection process and whether one approach overshadows the other is a complicated issue. We examine the first approach with respect to binary PSK briefly in this section.

Consider the block diagram of Figure 5–1. Assuming the presence of a carrier component, the received signal plus Gaussian noise at the receiver input is represented as

$$y(t) = A\sin[2\pi f_0 t + d(t)\cos^{-1} a + \theta] + n(t)$$
$$= Aa\sin(2\pi f_0 t + \theta) + Ad(t)\sqrt{1 - a^2}\cos(2\pi f_0 t + \theta) + n(t) \tag{5-1}$$

where A is the carrier amplitude

a is the modulation index

f_0 is the carrier frequency

$d(t)$ is the data which is ±1-valued in T_b-second contiguous intervals

θ is the phase deviation of the received signal due to oscillator instabilities and channel-induced perturbations

$n(t)$ is additive white Gaussian noise with two-sided power spectral density $N_0/2$

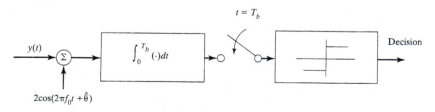

FIGURE 5–1 Correlation detector for BPSK for analyzing the effect of a carrier component and the presence of phase jitter.

The second equation of (5–1) can be derived by using the trigonometric identity for the sine of the sum of two angles and noting that $\cos(\cos^{-1}a) = a$ while $\sin(\cos^{-1}a) = \sqrt{1 - a^2}$. The second term is the modulation component with power $P_m = (1-a^2)\,P_T$ and the first one is the carrier component with power $P_c = a^2 P_T$ where P_T is the total power (see Problem 5–1). The parameter a provides a handy means for apportioning power between modulation and carrier components. This carrier component is used to facilitate the establishment of a coherent carrier reference at the receiver.

Further application of trigonometric identities shows that the product of the input signal and reference signals shown in Figure 5–1 produces

$$y_r(t) = Ad(t)\sqrt{1 - a^2}\,\cos\theta_e + Aa\sin\theta_e \tag{5–2}$$
$$+\, 2n(t)\cos(2\pi f_0 t + \hat{\theta}) + \text{double freq. term}$$

where $\theta_e = \theta - \hat{\theta}$ is the phase error, which we may model as a random process whose magnitude is small *most of the time*. The first term in (5–2) is the signal component of interest, and the second and third terms are noise components. The fourth term is eliminated by the lowpass filter assumed to follow the multiplier. Thus, we write

$$y_r(t) = Ad(t)\sqrt{1 - a^2}\,\cos\theta_e + N_{\theta_e} + n_G(t) \tag{5–3}$$

where

$$N_{\theta_e} = Aa\sin\theta_e \text{ and } n_G(t) = 2n(t)\cos(2\pi f_0 t + \hat{\theta}) \tag{5–4}$$

are the noise components due to phase jitter and Gaussian noise, respectively.

To obtain an expression for the probability of error, we first assume a fixed value for θ_e. Assuming equally likely 1s and −1s, we can find the conditional probability of error for $d(t) = -1$, for example, and this equals the average probability of error because of symmetry of the noise probability density function. The output of the integrator in Figure 5–1 for $d(t) = -1$ is

$$y_D = -A\sqrt{1 - a^2}\,T_b\cos\theta_e + N_{\theta_e}T_b + N_G \tag{5–5}$$

where

$$N_G = 2\int_0^{T_b} n(t)\cos(2\pi f_0 t + \theta)\,dt \tag{5–6}$$

is a Gaussian random variable whose mean is 0 and whose variance can be shown to be $\text{var}(N_G) = N_0 T_b$. The bit error probability, *given* θ_e, is

$$P(\varepsilon|\theta_e) = P[-A\sqrt{1 - a^2}\,T_b\cos\theta_e + N_{\theta_e}T_b + N_G > 0]$$
$$= Q\left[\sqrt{\frac{2E_b}{N_0}(1 - a^2)}\left|\cos\theta_e - \frac{a}{\sqrt{1 - a^2}}\sin\theta_e\right|\right] \tag{5–7}$$

Note that for $a = \theta_e = 0$, (5–7) reduces to the result for the probability of bit error for BPSK as it should. We also note that for a well-designed system, θ_e would normally be very small and the second term inside the absolute value is small with respect to the first term as long as $a < 1$. Normally, $a < 1$ because $a = 1$ means that the transmitted signal is pure carrier with no modulation component.

We can use (5–7) in two ways. First, it can be assumed that θ_e is a *static phase offset*, and P_b can be plotted versus E_b/N_0 with a and θ_e as parameters. This is obviously very simple to do. Under the assumption that we can neglect the second term inside the absolute value in (5–7), it follows that the *degradation* in E_b/N_0 due to both power in a carrier component and static phase error is

$$D = -10\log_{10}(1 - a^2) - 20\log_{10}(\cos\theta_e) \qquad (5\text{–}8)$$

That is, an increase of D dB in bit energy, E_b, or transmitted signal power is required to make up for the power allocated to the carrier component and the energy not realized in the detection process due to static phase offset.

EXAMPLE 5–1

Suppose that it is desired to achieve an error probability of 10^{-6} using BPSK with 10% of the total power in a carrier component ($a^2 = 0.1$) and a static phase tracking error of five degrees. How much must the value of E_b/N_0 be increased over that for a system with no power in a carrier component or tracking error to maintain the error probability at 10^{-6}?

Solution: From (5–8) the increase required in E_b/N_0 due to part of the power being allocated to a carrier component is $-10\log_{10}(1 - a^2) = -10\log_{10}(1 - 0.1) = 0.46$ dB, and the increase required due to static phase error is $-20\log_{10}\cos(5°) = 0.03$ dB. A bit error probability of 10^{-6} requires $E_b/N_0 = 10.54$ dB under ideal conditions, so the required E_b/N_0 to compensate for power allocated to a carrier component and static phase error is $10.54 + 0.46 + 0.03 = 11.03$ dB.

A second approach to characterizing a phase tracking error is to assume a statistical model for θ_e and average (5–7) with respect to the implied pdf of θ_e. As mentioned above, a simple model for this case is to assume that θ_e is Gaussian. For a first-order phase-lock loop, the phase error pdf is well approximated by [see Appendix D, (D–46) for the actual density function]

$$f_{\theta_e}(u) = \frac{\exp[-u^2/2\sigma_{\theta_e}^2]}{\sqrt{2\pi\sigma_{\theta_e}^2}}, \quad |u| \le \pi, \sigma_{\theta_e} \ll 1 \qquad (5\text{–}9)$$

This model holds for large loop signal-to-noise ratio, defined as

$$\rho = \frac{P_c}{N_0 B_L} = a^2 \frac{E_b}{N_0} \frac{R_b}{B_L} \approx \frac{1}{\sigma_{\theta_e}^2}, \quad \rho \gg 1 \qquad (5\text{–}10)$$

where $P_c = a^2 A^2/2$ is the power in the carrier component (the signal being tracked)

B_L is the equivalent noise bandwidth of the phase-lock loop in hertz

$R_b = 1/T_b$ is the data rate in bits per second

The average probability of bit error is then

$$\overline{P_b} = \int_{-\pi}^{\pi} P(\varepsilon|u)\, f_{\theta_e}(u)\, du \qquad (5\text{--}11)$$

This must be integrated numerically.

Figure 5–2 shows average bit error probability versus E_b/N_0 for fixed values of phase error variance. This might represent the case, for example, where the phase jitter is due to oscillators within the system rather than due to the effect of the additive noise on a phase tracking device such as a phase-lock loop. Note that an error floor is present in that the bit error probability curves approach an asymptote as E_b/N_0 becomes large. This is because the phase error process contributes a fixed amount of noise to the detection operation, even as the additive white Gaussian noise goes to zero ($E_b/N_0 \to \infty$).

Figure 5–3 shows average bit error probability versus E_b/N_0 for a system where the phase error variance is computed according to (5–10) using modulation index $a = 0.5$. Now there is no error floor, because in accordance with (5–10) the phase error variance

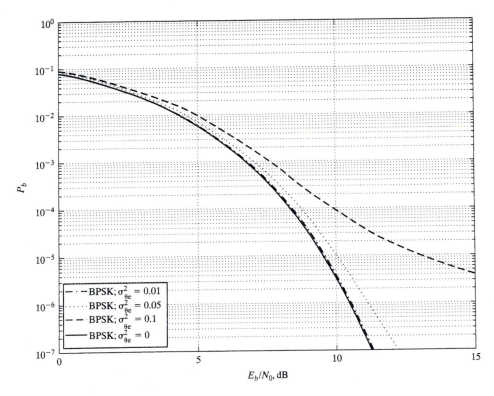

FIGURE 5–2 Average bit error probability for a BPSK system where the phase jitter has fixed value of variance.

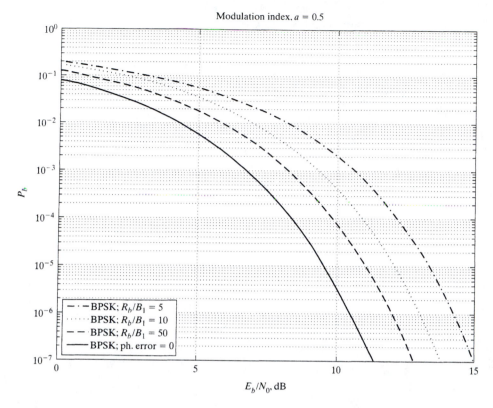

Modulation index, $a = 0.5$

FIGURE 5–3   Average bit error probability for a BPSK system where the demodulator carrier reference is modeled as being derived from a first-order phase-lock loop; modulation index = 0.5.

approaches zero as E_b/N_0 approaches infinity. Because the modulation index is 0.5, there is $-10 \log_{10}(1 - 0.25) = 1.25$ dB of degradation due to power allocated to the carrier component. Inspection of Figure 5–3 shows that this is very nearly the amount that the curve for $R_b/B_L = 50$ is to the right of the BPSK curve for zero phase error. That is, for $R_b/B_L = 50$, the effect of phase jitter is very small.

Figure 5–4 shows a similar set of curves to those shown in Figure 5–3, except that now the modulation index is 0.1 and the values of R_b/B_L are larger by a factor of 10. The degradation due to power devoted to the carrier is $-10 \log_{10}(1 - 0.01) = 0.04$ dB. The curve for the largest value of $R_b/B_L = 500$ is approximately 0.04 dB from the curve for BPSK with zero phase error.

One might ask why not make the phase-lock loop bandwidth essentially zero. The reason that this cannot be done in practice is that the oscillators in a communication system always have some phase jitter, no matter if they are the most precise available. It is this residual phase jitter that prevents the loop bandwidth from being made arbitrarily

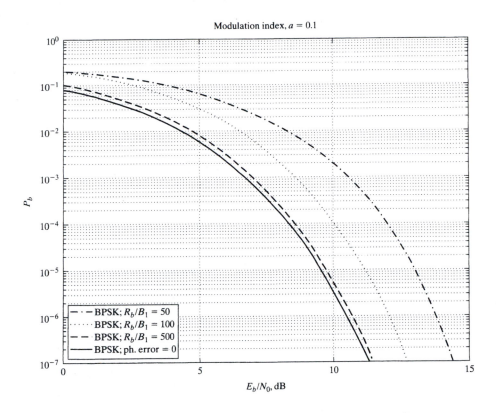

Modulation index, $a = 0.1$

E_b/N_0, dB

FIGURE 5–4 Average bit error probability for a BPSK system where the demodulator carrier reference is modeled as being derived from a first-order phase-lock loop; modulation index = 0.1.

small. In addition, the narrower the phase-lock loop bandwidth, the longer the time required for the loop to come into lock.

If a carrier component is absent, there is nothing to track in order to generate a coherent reference at the receiver. However, by passing the BPSK signal through a squarer to remove the modulation from the double frequency term at the squarer output, the frequency of the double frequency term can be tracked, and the resultant double frequency divided by 2 to provides a coherent reference. This idea also works for M-ary PSK by using an M-power device, filtering out the Mth harmonic at its output, and frequency dividing the filter output by M. This scheme is illustrated in Figure 5–5. An alternative scheme to provide a coherent reference from a BPSK-modulated signal is the Costas loop shown in Figure 5–6. That the Costas loop structure will lock onto a BPSK signal is left to the problems. In [1], the performances of BPSK communication systems using a squaring and Costas loop are compared. It shows that both perform equivalently provided that the

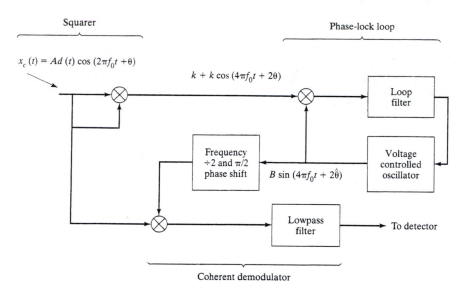

FIGURE 5–5 Squaring loop for acquiring a coherent reference from a BPSK-modulated signal.

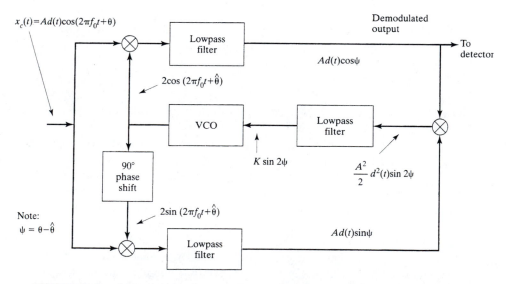

FIGURE 5–6 Costas loop for acquiring a coherent reference from a BPSK-modulated signal.

bandpass filter at the input to the squaring loop has an equivalent lowpass frequency response identical to the lowpass filters in the Costas loop arms.

One can still use (5–11) to compute the probability of error averaged over the phase-error distribution. Now, however, the phase error variance in (5–9) is given by [1, 2]

$$\sigma_{\theta_e}^2 = \frac{1}{\rho_L S_L} \tag{5–12}$$

where ρ_L is still the signal-to-noise ratio in the loop bandwidth and S_L is the *squaring loss* of the loop defined as

$$S_L = \frac{1}{1 + (\rho_L \gamma)^{-1}} \tag{5–13}$$

in which γ is the ratio of the bandwidth of the bandpass filter at the squaring loop input (or, equivalently, the double-sided bandwidth of the arm filters in the Costas loop) to the loop bandwidth, B_L.

Whether one should allocate part of the power of the transmitted signal to a carrier component to allow tracking by a phase-lock loop at the receiver, or put all the power into the modulation and use a Costas or squaring loop is an interesting trade-off whose answer depends on the system parameters. Some examples are given in the problems.

An alternative to transmitting part of the power as a continuous carrier along with the modulation component is to send a carrier burst periodically. This is typically the technique used in burst-mode communications systems such as satellite time-division multiple-access systems, in military communications systems where the data is sent in bursts for security purposes, TDMA digital cellular radios, or packet data systems such as the Internet [3, 4].

In order to obtain a carrier reference for QPSK, an extension of the squaring loop idea can be used. In the case of quadrature phase-shift keying, however, the signal must be raised to the fourth power to remove the modulation, and the phase-lock loop tracks the fourth harmonic of the desired carrier. After acquiring the fourth harmonic of the carrier, the result is frequency divided by 4 to produce the required reference. Equivalents to Costas loops are also available for tracking QPSK signals [2].

The effect of phase errors in quadrature modulation systems is somewhat more complex than in BPSK. If the modulated signal is written in complex notation as {the real signal is Re [$\tilde{x}_c(t) \exp(j2\pi f_0 t)$]}

$$\tilde{x}_c(t) = \frac{A}{\sqrt{2}} m(t)$$

$$= \frac{A}{\sqrt{2}} [m_R(t) - jm_I(t)] \tag{5–14}$$

where, $m_R(t)$ and $m_I(t)$ are the inphase and quadrature modulating signals, the coherent demodulation operation with phase error is equivalent to multiplication of (5–14) by $\exp[-(j2\pi f_0 t + \theta_e)]$. This gives quadrature-arm signals in the demodulator of the form

$$y(t) = \frac{A}{\sqrt{2}}[m_R(t) - jm_I(t)]\exp(-j\theta_e) \qquad (5\text{–}15)$$

or, in inphase-quadrature form,

$$y_R(t) = \frac{A}{\sqrt{2}}[m_R(t)\cos\theta_e - m_I(t)\sin\theta_e]$$

$$\qquad (5\text{–}16)$$

$$y_I(t) = -\frac{A}{\sqrt{2}}[m_R(t)\sin\theta_e + m_I(t)\cos\theta_e]$$

Now the data in the inphase demodulator arm affects the decisions in the quadrature arm and vice versa. For example, in QPSK, we must consider all possible combinations of symbol patterns in the inphase and quadrature arms—that is, ± 1 in the inphase arm in conjunction with ± 1 in the quadrature arm. Fortunately, the four combinations can be reduced to only two combinations because of the even symmetry about zero amplitude of the Gaussian noise. Thus, the probability of error in the inphase arm, for example, may be written as

$$P_{eR} = \frac{1}{2}P(\varepsilon|++) + \frac{1}{2}P(\varepsilon|+-) \qquad (5\text{–}17)$$

where $P(\varepsilon|++)$ denotes the probability of error given that a $+1$ was sent in the inphase portion of the signal and a $+1$ was sent in the quadrature portion of the signal, with a similar interpretation for $P(\varepsilon|+-)$. If N_I is the noise random variable at the output of the inphase detector, the former probability may be expressed as

$$P(\varepsilon|++) = P\left[\frac{A}{\sqrt{2}}(\cos\theta_e - \sin\theta_e) + N_I < 0\right]$$

$$\qquad (5\text{–}18)$$

$$= P\left(N_I < \frac{A}{\sqrt{2}}(\sin\theta_e - \cos\theta_e)\right)$$

where N_I is a zero-mean Gaussian random variable with variance $N_0 T_s$ [note that multiplication by $\exp[-j(2\pi f_0 t + \theta)]$ in the complex demodulator structure is the same as multiplying by $2\cos[2\pi f_0 t + \theta]$ and $-2\sin[2\pi f_0 t + \theta]$ in the inphase-quadrature arm structure (i.e., the real demodulator)]. Thus, the conditional probability of error (5–18) becomes

$$P(\varepsilon|++) = \int_{-\infty}^{-\frac{AT_s}{\sqrt{2}}|\sin\theta_e - \cos\theta_e|} \frac{\exp[-u^2/(2N_0 T_s)]}{\sqrt{2\pi N_0 T_s}} \, du$$

$$= \int_{-\infty}^{-\sqrt{\frac{A^2 T_s}{2N_0}}|\cos\theta_e - \sin\theta_e|} \frac{\exp(-v^2/2)}{\sqrt{2\pi}} \, dv$$

(5–19)

$$= \int_{\sqrt{\frac{A^2 T_s}{2N_0}}|\cos\theta_e - \sin\theta_e|}^{\infty} \frac{\exp(-v^2/2)}{\sqrt{2\pi}} \, dv \text{ (by eveness of the integrand)}$$

$$= Q(\sqrt{A^2 T_s/2N_0} \, |\cos\theta_e - \sin\theta_e|) = Q\left(\sqrt{\frac{E_s}{N_0}} |\cos\theta_e - \sin\theta_e|\right)$$

A similar expression holds for the quadrature arm but with the $|\cos\theta_e - \sin\theta_e|$ replaced by $|\cos\theta_e + \sin\theta_e|$. If θ_e is a random variable symmetrically distributed about 0 (e.g., Gaussian), these two probabilities give the same result when averaged over θ_e. The probability of bit error is therefore essentially the probability of error in either quadrature arm as found in Chapter 4, or

$$P_b \cong P(\varepsilon|++) = Q\left(\sqrt{\frac{2E_b}{N_0}} |\cos\theta_e - \sin\theta_e|\right)$$

(5–20)

The approximation is by virtue of the assumed Gray encoding of the quadrature data-stream bits allowing single errors to dominate. Equation (5–20) can be averaged with respect to the assumed probability density function of θ_e, probability of bit error curves plotted, and the degradation in E_b/N_0 noted by comparing the resultant curve with that for no phase error. This is left for the problems. For $\theta_e = 0$, (5–20) reduces to the result for zero phase error derived in Chapter 4.

5.2.2   Symbol Synchronization

In order to provide a clock that is in synchronism with a demodulated data stream, the ideas are basically the same as with generating a carrier reference. Shown in Figure 5–7 are various binary data formats [4]. Note that some of them have at least one transition per bit interval, such as Polar RZ. Thus, a discrete spectral component at the bit rate is present in the power spectrum of the data stream, and a phase-lock loop may be designed to track this discrete component thereby providing a clock reference. Unfortunately, data formats that have a transition per bit interval occupy wider bandwidths, in general, than do those that have no guaranteed transition.

If a data format is used that does not have a guaranteed transition each bit interval, such as nonreturn-to-zero (NRZ), a nonlinear operation must be performed on the data to generate a spectral component at the bit frequency or a multiple thereof. The delay-and-multiply circuit shown in Figure 5–8a is a popular circuit for doing this. It can be shown that for a bit stream with bit period T_b at the multiplier input, the output of the multiplier

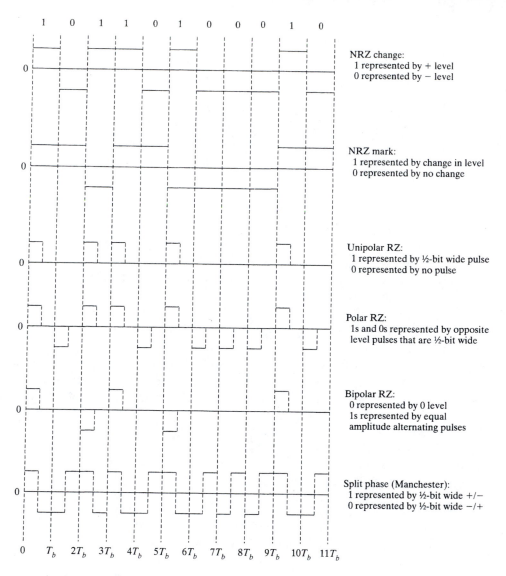

FIGURE 5–7 Abbreviated table of binary data formats. (Patterned after [4])

is periodic with period T_b and can be represented as an exponential Fourier series with coefficients [4]

$$c_n = (-1)^n \frac{|\tau|}{2T_b} \operatorname{sinc}\left(\frac{n\tau}{T_b}\right)\exp\left(-\frac{j2\pi n|\tau|}{T_b}\right) \qquad (5\text{–}21)$$

where τ is the delay. The power in the spectral component at the bit frequency is $2|c_1|^2$; it can be shown to have a maximum for a delay of $\tau = T_b/2$ (see Problem 5–6).

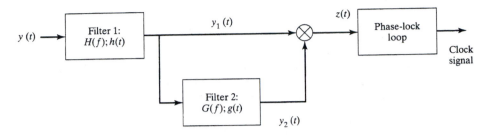

(a) Delay-multiply method

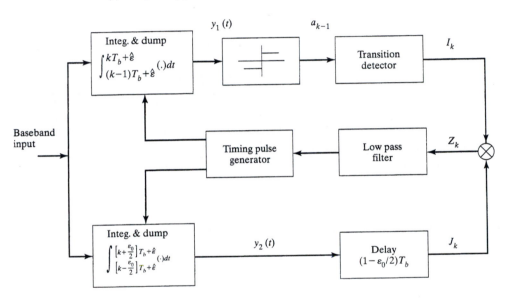

(b) Delay-lock loop method

FIGURE 5–8   Two methods for acquiring a clock from binary data.

Structures similar to the Costas loop can be designed for deriving a clock directly from a data stream. Two examples are the early-late gate synchronizer and the inphase/midphase synchronizer, also called the data transition tracking loop. A block diagram of the latter is shown in Figure 5–8b. Analysis of the characteristics of these circuits is beyond the scope of this book, and the reader is referred to the technical literature on the subject [5, 6].

5.2.3   Frame Synchronization

Frame synchronization is usually accomplished by the detection of a *unique word*, which is a known pattern of 1s and 0s that is sent in the data stream periodically, sometimes at the start of the block of data and, in some applications, in the middle. To ensure that the data itself doesn't contain the unique word pattern the process of *bit stuffing* is used. For example, if the unique word is thirteen 1s followed by a 0, the data sequence at the transmitter is examined, and if a sequence of twelve 1s occurs, a 0 is "stuffed" at the transmitter and removed at the receiver. Assume that the bit stream has been detected (i.e., consists of a 1–0 sequence). A digital correlator like the one shown in Figure 5–9 can be used to detect the position of the unique word, assumed to be N bits long, in the data stream. If the received unique word, due to bit errors, does not match the locally stored unique word in $\varepsilon + 1$ places or more it will be missed. The probability of a particular error pattern occurring obeys the binomial distribution so that the probability of a miss is given by

$$P_M = \sum_{i=\varepsilon+1}^{N} \binom{N}{i} P_E^i (1 - P_E)^{N-i} \tag{5-22}$$

where $\binom{N}{i} = N!/(i!(N - i)!)$ is the binomial coefficient and P_E is the probability that a bit is in error. A false alarm occurs if randomly occurring bits due to noise happen to match with at least ε bits in the unique word. This probability is given by

$$P_F = \frac{1}{2^N} \sum_{i=0}^{\varepsilon} \binom{N}{i} \tag{5-23}$$

Plots of the probabilities of miss and false alarm as a function of the number of bits in the unique word are shown in Figures 5–10a and 5–10b, respectively. Figure 5–10a is plotted for $P_E = 10^{-3}$.

While this treatment of synchronization is brief, it hopefully gives some appreciation for this important problem in digital communication system design and analysis. An excellent tutorial review of the subject is provided in [6].

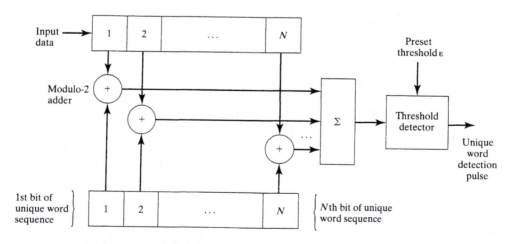

FIGURE 5–9 A digital correlator for detecting a unique word in frame synchronization.

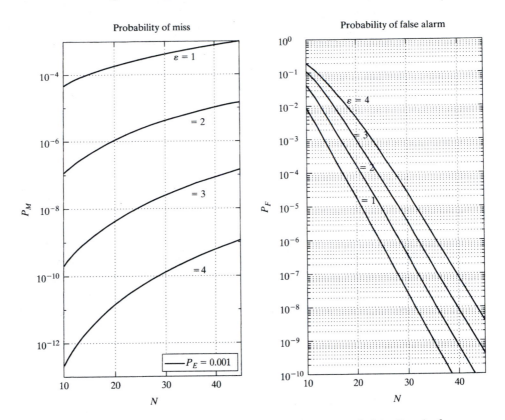

FIGURE 5-10   Performance characteristics of unique word detection in frame synchronization.

5.3   THE EFFECTS OF SLOW SIGNAL FADING IN COMMUNICATION SYSTEMS

5.3.1   Performance of Binary Modulation Schemes in Rayleigh Fading Channels

5.3.1.1 Introduction.   For many important channels the received signal strength varies randomly due to propagation conditions such as multiple transmission paths (multipath), varying refraction index, attenuation due to rain, and so on. These channels are called *fading channels*. In a fading channel a constant-amplitude sinusoidal transmitted signal is received as $R(t)\cos[2\pi f_0 t + \Theta(t)]$ where $R(t)$ and $\Theta(t)$ are random processes. It is quite often the case that a useful model for $R(t)$ is a Rayleigh random process with $\Theta(t)$ uniform in $[0, 2\pi)$. This results from modeling the received inphase and quadrature signal components as independent Gaussian random processes with zero means and equal variances (i.e., a Rayleigh envelope). It is a useful model in situations where propagation conditions within the channel can be idealized as resulting in the superposition of a large number of independent scattered components at the receiver.

5.3.1.2 Bit Error Probability Performance in Slow Rayleigh Fading.

The very simplest model for a digital communication system operating in a fading channel is where a given received bit is modeled as having a Rayleigh distributed amplitude independent of the amplitudes of all other bits. This is known as a slow Rayleigh fading model in that a given bit is assumed to be received with a fixed Rayleigh-distributed amplitude throughout the bit interval, but succeeding and following bits have Rayleigh-distributed amplitudes independent of this given bit. In keeping with the Gaussian inphase/quadrature component model mention above, the carrier phase throughout each received bit would be a particular realization of a uniform random variable in $[0, 2\pi)$. If a noncoherent signaling scheme is being used, the phase is of no consequence in the detection process. (For a differential scheme, it must be true that the phase difference between adjacent bits doesn't vary significantly. This assumption will be relaxed at the end of this section.) The thoughtful reader will notice a dichotomy here—on the one hand, constant amplitude and phase (although random) throughout the bit interval are assumed; on the other hand, amplitudes and phases from one bit to the next are assumed independent. This underscores the importance of examining a model for a given situation. Once an analysis of a particular performance criterion has been carried out, its implications should be examined carefully in the light of measured data, results of more inclusive models, or system simulation.

This simplified model is used in the following way. First, choose a particular digital modulation scheme, say noncoherent FSK. Let $Z = A^2 T_b / 2 N_0 = E_b / N_0$ be the instantaneous signal-to-noise ratio, which is a random variable under a slow fading channel model. Note that it is proportional to amplitude squared, which for a Rayleigh-distributed amplitude implies that Z has an exponential pdf. For given Z, expressions for probability of bit error for various signaling schemes are known from previous analyses.

As an example, for noncoherent FSK, the probability of bit error is $P(\epsilon|Z) = \exp(-Z/2)/2$. To find the unconditional probability of bit error, we simply average the conditional probability of error with respect to the assumed probability distribution of Z, which is exponential. For noncoherent FSK, this gives

$$\overline{P}_{b,\text{NFSK}} = \int_{-\infty}^{\infty} P(\epsilon|z) f_Z(z) \, dz$$

$$= \int_0^{\infty} \frac{1}{2} \exp(-z/2) \frac{1}{\overline{Z}} \exp(-z/\overline{Z}) dz \tag{5-24}$$

$$= \frac{1}{2 + \overline{Z}}, \text{ noncoherent binary FSK}$$

where $\overline{Z} = \overline{E}_b / N_0$ in which $\overline{E}_b$ is the average bit energy. In a similar manner it can be shown that (the derivation is left to the problems)

$$\overline{P}_{b,\,\text{DPSK}} = \frac{1}{2(1 + \overline{Z})}, \text{binary DPSK} \tag{5-25}$$

The averaging process can also be carried out for BPSK through integration by parts. If we can somehow derive a coherent carrier reference at the receiver (perhaps through transmission of a pilot tone of sufficient power), the result for BPSK is

$$\overline{P}_{b,\text{BPSK}} = \frac{1}{2}\left(1 - \sqrt{\frac{\overline{E}_b/N_0}{1 + \overline{E}_b/N_0}}\right) \tag{5-26}$$

The result for the probability of bit error of π/4-DQPSK in Rayleigh fading is given in [7] as

$$\overline{P}_{b,\pi/4\text{-DQPSK}} = \frac{1}{2}\left(1 - \frac{\overline{E}_b/N_0}{\sqrt{1/2 + 2\overline{E}_b/N_0 + (\overline{E}_b/N_0)^2}}\right) \tag{5-27}$$

These various bit error probabilities are compared as functions of $\overline{E}_b/N_0$ in Figure 5–11. Also given for comparison is the bit error probability for BPSK with no fading. Note that

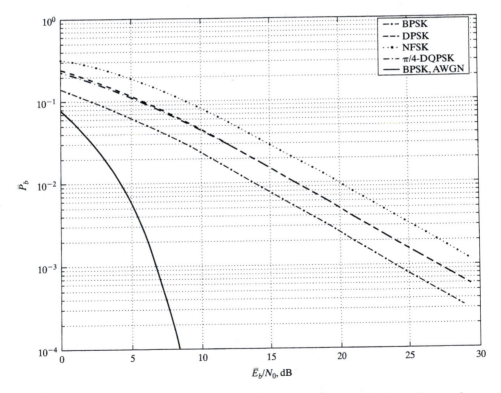

FIGURE 5–11   Bit error probabilities for various binary modulation schemes in slow Rayleigh fading with the result for BPSK in no fading for comparison.

a tremendous increase in power is required to give the same probability of bit error in Rayleigh fading as in the nonfading case. For example, to maintain a bit error probability of 10^{-3} in excess of 20 dB (i.e., 100 times) more power is required for BPSK in a slow Rayleigh fading channel than it is for nonfading conditions. For this reason, much work has been done in finding ways to combat the detrimental effects of fading. One very effective technique is diversity transmission and/or reception. This is discussed in the next subsection.

5.3.1.3 The Use of Path Diversity to Improve Performance in Fading.

The severe penalty imposed by fading on the performance of digital modulation schemes has spurred much work on finding methods to improve performance in such environments. One very effective method is to use path diversity, which makes use of a combination of several independent (or approximately so) transmission paths in the hope that not all will simultaneously experience severe fading. Another effective means for combating fading is forward error correction coding, which will be a topic of Chapters 6 and 7.

In this section, we consider only the very simplest analyses for diversity improvement in fading channels. The literature of diversity transmission is extensive and goes back to the 1950s. References [8–14] are typical of the early contributions and might be considered classic papers. The book [15], also by now a classic reference, includes many fading and diversity results and is recommended reading on the subject. A general result applying to signals with quadrature components, of which Rayleigh and Ricean fading are special cases, is succinctly treated in [16]. A generalized analysis of flat fading diversity for Rayleigh and Ricean channels based on a new Q-function representation is given in [17].

There are many ways to realize path diversity. Those mentioned and discussed in [15] are space, frequency, angle, polarization, time, and multipath. There are also several ways of combining the signals from the separate paths at the receiver. First, there is the choice of modulation scheme, which, as discussed previously, can be coherent or noncoherent. Second, the combining of the signal contributions from various paths can be categorized as predetection or postdetection, depending on whether the signals from the various paths are combined before the matched filter (or correlation) detector or after. For coherent modulation schemes, there is no difference in performance. Finally, the combining method can vary; the ways are referred to as selection, maximal-ratio, and equal-gain combining. In selection combining, the strongest path signal is selected at the receiver and the decision of a 1 or 0 is based solely on this one statistic. In maximal-ratio combining, the output signals corresponding to the various paths are first weighted according to their individual signal-to-noise ratios, co-phased to account for channel phase shifts, then summed, and the decision of a 1 or 0 based on this weighted sum. For equal-gain combining, the output signals corresponding to the various paths are simply co-phased and added without weighting and the decisions are based on this statistic. Of the three, ignoring implementation issues, maximal-ratio combining performs the best and selection combining performs the poorest. Taking implementation into account, selection combining is the easiest to implement and requires the least hardware since only one receiver channel is necessary after the selection has been made. Maximal-ratio combining is the hardest to implement (somehow, an estimate of the signal-to-noise ratio and phases in each path must be obtained) and requires the most hardware (a receiver channel is required for each path up to the point of combining).

One other point must be made before getting into performance of diversity techniques. To explain it, spatial diversity is assumed. If L transmitter antennas are used to obtain the independent paths, it is only fair that the total transmitter power is viewed as being split equally between transmission paths, and the signal-to-noise ratio in each path is then $1/L$ times the overall signal-to-noise ratio. On the other hand, if the diversity is achieved with multiple antennas at the receiver, the signal-to-noise ratio would not be divided by L since each diversity branch (antenna) receives the entire received signal power (ignoring details like differing antenna gains per branch). Thus, the results to be presented will be labeled "transmitter diversity" if each diversity path has a signal-to-noise ratio $1/L$ of the total signal-to-noise ratio; on the other hand, the term "receiver diversity" will be used if the full signal-to-noise ratio is used for each path. Results for the latter case appear rather strange at first glance because the bit error probability curves may appear better than the ideal non-diversity result for no fading.

As a first example to be analyzed in some detail, consider noncoherent FSK and equal-gain predetection combining as shown schematically in Figure 5–12. To derive the proba-

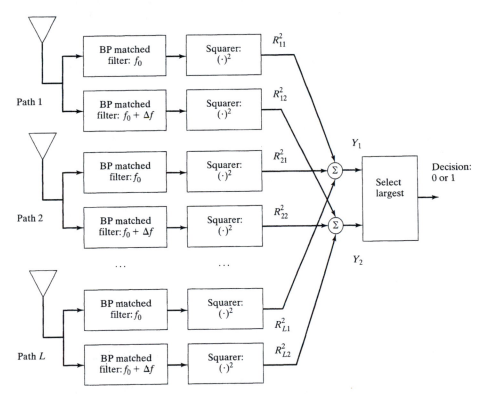

FIGURE 5–12   Diversity receiver for noncoherent FSK with equal-gain combining.

bility of error for this system, assume f_0 is transmitted (say, corresponding to a logic 0 transmitted). Let the noise, $n(t)$, be white with two-sided power spectral density $N_0/2$. Also, let $f_0 + \Delta f = f_1$ (corresponding to a logic 1 transmitted). Recall that for a slow Rayleigh fading channel, a constant amplitude sinusoid is received as $R\cos(2\pi f_0 t + \Theta)$ during each bit interval (new realization of R and Θ for each bit), where R is Rayleigh and Θ is uniform in $[0, 2\pi)$. Thus $G_c = R\cos\Theta$ and $G_s = R\sin\Theta$ are independent Gaussian random variables. Although not shown here, it follows that the bandpass matched filters can be modeled as two correlators in parallel, one where the reference signal is $\sqrt{2/T_b}\,\cos2\pi f_0 t$ and the other where the reference signal is $\sqrt{2/T_b}\,\sin2\pi f_0 t$ [or $\sqrt{2/T_b}\,\cos2\pi f_1 t$ and $\sqrt{2/T_b}\,\sin2\pi f_1 t$ for the lower branches]. The outputs of these correlators are Gaussian random variables (the inphase and quadrature signal components are Gaussian because of the fading, and the noise component is clearly Gaussian). Without going through the details, we simply state that the means of these Gaussian random variables are zero, and their variances are $E_b\sigma^2/L + N_0/2$ (frequency f_0 assumed transmitted) and $N_0/2$ (the frequency f_1 matched filter has noise alone at its input), respectively, where σ^2 is the parameter in the Rayleigh probability density function for the random envelopes and E_b is the energy per bit without fading. We have assumed transmitter diversity; if receiver diversity is assumed, the factor $1/L$ doesn't appear. Thus, Y_1 in Figure 5–12 is the sum of squares of $2L$ independent Gaussian random variables (the 2 because of the inphase and quadrature components of each matched filter) with zero means and variances $\sigma_1^2 = E_b\sigma^2/L + N_0/2$ and Y_2 is the sum of squares of $2L$ independent Gaussian random variables with zero means and variances $\sigma_2^2 = N_0/2$. This means that Y_1 and Y_2 are chi-square random variables with $2L$ degrees of freedom [see 2–202]). Their probability density functions are

$$f_{Y_1}(y_1 | f_0 \text{ transmitted}) = \frac{y_1^{L-1}\exp(-y_1^2/2\sigma_1^2)}{2^L\sigma_1^{2L}\Gamma(L)}, \; y_1 \geq 0 \tag{5-28}$$

and

$$f_{Y_2}(y_2 | f_0 \text{ transmitted}) = \frac{y_2^{L-1}\exp(-y_2^2/2\sigma_2^2)}{2^L\sigma_2^{2L}\Gamma(L)}, \; y_2 \geq 0 \tag{5-29}$$

for Y_1 and Y_2, respectively, where $\Gamma(L)$ is the gamma function, or simply $(L-1)!$ for L integer.

By symmetry, assuming equally likely 1s and 0s, the probability of bit error is

$$P_b = P(\varepsilon | f_0 \text{ sent}) = P(\varepsilon | f_1 \text{ sent})$$

$$= \int_0^\infty \left[\int_{y_1}^\infty \frac{y_2^{L-1}\exp(-y_2^2/2\sigma_2^2)}{2^L\,\sigma_2^{2L}\,\Gamma(L)}\,dy_2 \right] \frac{y_1^{L-1}\exp(-y_1^2/2\sigma_1^2)}{2^L\,\sigma_1^{2L}\,\Gamma(L)}\,dy_1 \tag{5-30}$$

Through integration by parts repeatedly, it can be demonstrated that

$$\int_x^\infty u^n \exp(-\alpha u)\,du = \exp(-\alpha x)\sum_{k=0}^n \frac{n!}{k!\alpha^{n+1-k}}x^k \tag{5-31}$$

Use of this relationship and integration term-by-term results in

$$\overline{P}_b = \frac{1}{(2 + \overline{E}_b/LN_0)^L} \sum_{k=0}^{L-1} \binom{L-1+k}{k} \left(\frac{1 + \overline{E}_b/LN_0}{2 + \overline{E}_b/LN_0}\right)^k \tag{5-32}$$

where $\overline{E}_b/N_0 = 2\sigma^2 E_b/N_0$ is the average signal-to-noise ratio (note that the expectation of a Rayleigh random variable squared is $2\sigma^2$). This is the same expression as obtained in [14, eq. (14–4–30)] by a somewhat different derivation. Iterative computation of $\overline{P}_b$ with L is facilitated by the result [18]

$$\overline{P}_b = \alpha^L \sum_{k=0}^{L-1} T_k; \quad \alpha = \left(2 + \frac{\overline{E}_b}{LN_0}\right)^{-1}; \quad T_{k+1} = \frac{L+k}{k+1}(1 - \alpha)T_k; \quad T_0 = 1 \tag{5-33}$$

For receiver diversity instead of transmitter diversity, $\overline{E}_b/LN_0$ in (5–32) is replaced by $\overline{E}_b/N_0$.

For large $\overline{E}_b/N_0$, asymptotic results for $\overline{P}_b$ in (5–32) are obtained by noting that the term in parentheses inside the sum of (5–32) approaches 1 and that $\sum_{k=0}^{L-1}\binom{L-1+k}{k} = \binom{2L-1}{L}$. Thus, (5–32) is well approximated as $\binom{2L-1}{L}[\overline{E}_b/(LN_0)]^{-L}$. Results are plotted in Figure 5–13 for both transmitter and receiver diversity for square-law combined noncoherent FSK.

Many other results are given in the literature for the performance of diversity combining receivers [16, 19]. In addition, [19] is recommended in that several known results are summarized and a novel idea is investigated called *selection 2* or *selection 3 combining* where, instead of selecting just the best single channel of L channels in a selection diversity system, the best 2 or 3 channels are selected. To give an indication of how this scheme compares with maximal-ratio and selection combining, we quote some results from [19]. For maximal-ratio combining of BPSK channels, the bit error probability is

$$\overline{P}_{b, \text{MR, BPSK}} = \frac{1}{2}\left[1 - \mu \sum_{k=0}^{L-1}\binom{2k}{k}\left(\frac{1 - \mu^2}{4}\right)^k\right], \quad \mu = \sqrt{\frac{\gamma_0}{1 + \gamma_0}} \tag{5-34}$$

where γ_0 is either $\overline{E}_b/N_0$ or $\overline{E}_b/(LN_0)$ depending on whether a receiver or transmitter diversity scheme is being considered, respectively. For selection combining and BPSK, the result is

$$\overline{P}_{b, \text{S, BPSK}} = \frac{L}{2}\left[\sum_{k=0}^{L-1}\binom{L-1}{k}(-1)^k\left(1 - \frac{1}{\sqrt{1 + (1 + k)\alpha}}\right)^k\right], \quad \alpha = \frac{1}{\gamma_0} \tag{5-35}$$

Finally, for selection 2 combining and BPSK, [19] gives the expression

$$\overline{P}_{b, \text{S, BPSK}} = \frac{L(L-1)}{2}\left\{\frac{1}{2}\left[1 - \frac{1}{\sqrt{1 + \alpha}} - \frac{\alpha}{2(1 + \alpha)\sqrt{1 + \alpha}}\right]\right.$$
$$\left. + \sum_{k=1}^{L-2}\binom{L-2}{k}(-1)^k V(k)\right\}, \quad \alpha = \frac{1}{\gamma_0}, L > 2 \tag{5-36}$$

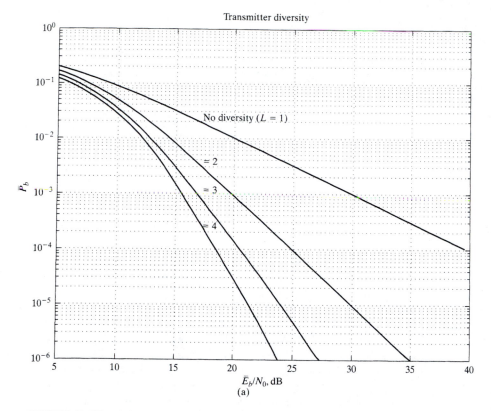

FIGURE 5–13   BER performance for square-law combined noncoherent binary FSK; (a) transmitter diversity; (b) receiver diversity.

where

$$V(k) = \frac{1}{2 + k} - \frac{1}{k\sqrt{1 + \alpha}} + \frac{2}{k(2 + k)\sqrt{1 + (2 + k)\alpha/2}} \tag{5–37}$$

Combiner performances are given in Figure 5–14 for maximal ratio and Figure 5–15 for selection combining.

Note that there is considerable loss in performance in going from maximal-ratio combining to selection diversity (about 2½ dB at $P_b = 10^{-6}$). Much of this loss is recouped (about 2 dB) with selection 2 diversity with the cost of more hardware in the receiver (two channels must be processed). Note that a crossover occurs for the curves of Figure 5–15 (a) and (b). Thus, for a given signal-to-noise ratio an optimum order of diversity exists. The crossover phenomenon occurs because selection combining is a nonlinear operation.

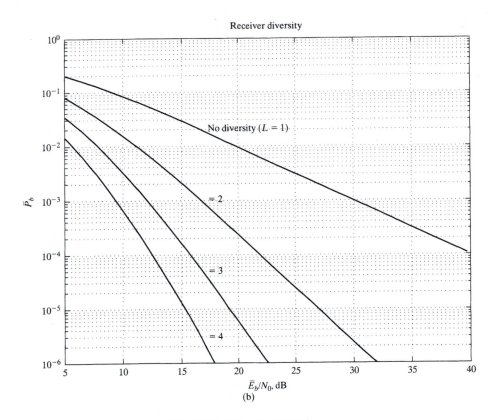

Receiver diversity

$\bar{E}_b/N_0$, dB
(b)

FIGURE 5–13   *Continued*

5.3.1.4 DPSK Performance in Moderately Fast Rayleigh Fading. It is generally a difficult problem to account for fading envelope variations from bit to bit while accounting for the correlation induced by the fading mechanism. The analysis just given is referred to as the slow fading case because it is assumed that the faded signal amplitude stays constant throughout a given bit interval. There is one case where it is fairly easy to obtain results for the moderately fast case—that is, the faded signal amplitude is, for all practical purposes, constant during a given bit interval, but the next bit interval has an amplitude that is correlated with the previous bit interval.[1] By considering the inphase and quadrature fading components of a Rayleigh fading channel, which are Gaussian, the joint probability density function for the quadrature fading components at two time instants, t and $t + \tau$, may be written down and fairly simple results for the bit error probability of a DPSK system may be derived that accounts for the correlation between signaling intervals. The results for no diversity and dual diversity are

[1]The analysis summarized here may be found in [20].

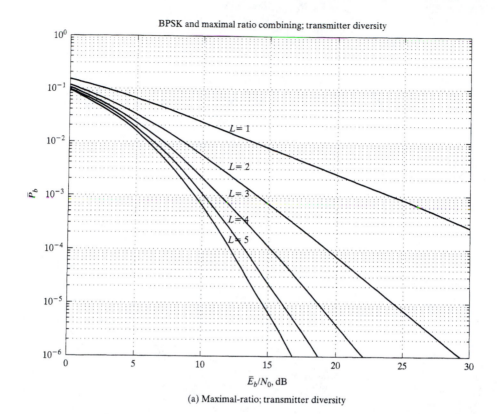

(a) Maximal-ratio; transmitter diversity

FIGURE 5–14   Performance of BPSK with maximal ratio combining.

$$\overline{P}_{b1,\,\mathrm{DPSK}} = \frac{1 + (1 - \rho)\overline{Z}}{2(1 + \overline{Z})}, \quad \overline{Z} = \frac{\overline{E}_b}{N_0} \tag{5–38}$$

and

$$\overline{P}_{b2,\,\mathrm{DPSK}} = P_{b1,\,\mathrm{DPSK}} \left[\frac{2 + (4 - \rho)\overline{Z} + (2 - \rho - \rho^2)\overline{Z}^2}{2(1 + \overline{Z})^2} \right], \overline{Z} = \frac{\overline{E}_b}{N_0} \tag{5–39}$$

respectively, where ρ is the correlation coefficient between bit intervals. Note that (5–38) reduces to (5–25) for $\rho = 1$. The general result for an arbitrary order of diversity, L, can be derived by applying the general results of [16] and, in fact, can be derived for the more general case of Ricean fading. For Rayleigh fading, a simpler approach is to apply Cauchy's integral theorem to the expression for the moment generating function given in [20]. The result is [21]

$$\overline{P}_{b,L} = \frac{1}{2^L} \left[\frac{1 + (1 - \rho)\overline{Z}}{1 + \overline{Z}} \right]^L \sum_{k=0}^{L-1} \frac{1}{2^k} \binom{L + k - 1}{k} \left[\frac{1 + (1 + \rho)\overline{Z}}{1 + \overline{Z}} \right]^k \tag{5–40}$$

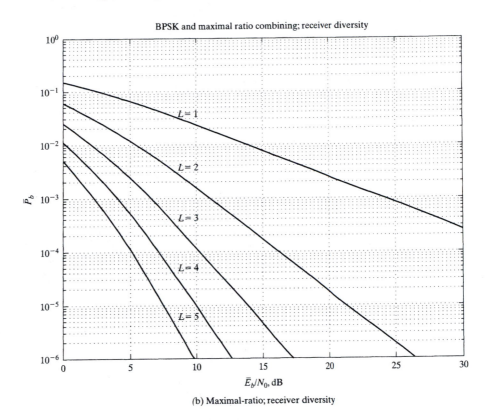

(b) Maximal-ratio; receiver diversity

FIGURE 5–14   *Continued*

where ρ is the correlation coefficient between bits and $\bar{Z} = \bar{E}_b/N_0$ as before.[2]

Results are plotted in Figure 5–16 for both the no diversity and dual diversity cases. It is seen that the lack of perfect correlation between signaling intervals results in an *error floor*, in that the bit error probability approaches a threshold as the signal-to-noise ratio gets large. Second, it is seen that the use of dual diversity is very effective in lowering this error floor.

EXAMPLE 5–2

The error floor corresponding to (5–38) is obtained by letting $\bar{Z} \to \infty$. Clearly, it is given by

$$\lim_{\bar{Z} \to \infty} \bar{P}_{b1, \text{DPSK}} = \lim_{\bar{Z} \to \infty} \left[\frac{1 + (1 - \rho)\bar{Z}}{2(1 + \bar{Z})} \right] = \frac{1 - \rho}{2}$$

An expression for general L may be obtained by taking a similar limit of (5–40).

---

[2]The generalization of the Rayleigh fading case with Doppler spread to Ricean amplitude statistics and M-ary DPSK and PSK is given in [22].

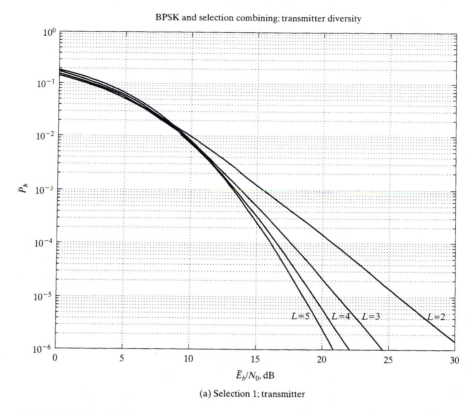

(a) Selection 1; transmitter

FIGURE 5–15   Performance of BPSK with selection 1 and selection 2 combining.

5.3.2   Performance of *M*-ary Modulation Schemes in Slow Fading

5.3.2.1 Introduction.   The performance of *M*-ary digital modulation schemes in slow fading can be analyzed similarly to the analysis used in the case of binary modulation schemes. To review, we considered the bit error probability expressions as conditioned on E_b/N_0, which was modeled as an exponentially distributed random variable (i.e., the fading was Rayleigh in amplitude), and then averaged the conditional bit error probability with respect to this exponentially distributed random variable. In this section, we do the same for the symbol error probability and then convert the averaged symbol error probability to an average bit error probability using the approximations derived in Section 4.5.1. We consider three cases in this section—*M*-ary PSK, DPSK, QAM, and noncoherent FSK—first in Rayleigh fading and then all in Ricean fading. The Rayleigh fading results are, of course, special cases of the corresponding Ricean results, but closed form expressions can be obtained for Rayleigh fading for all three modulation types considered.

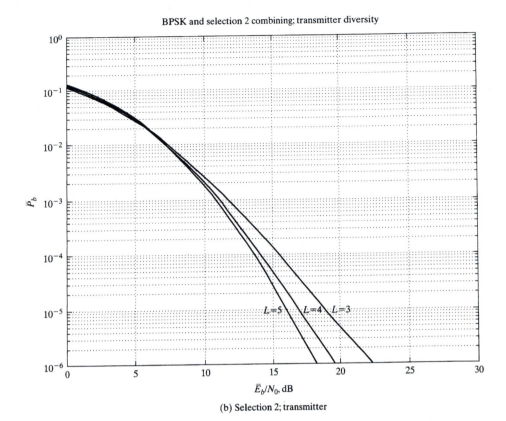

(b) Selection 2; transmitter

FIGURE 5–15   *Continued*

5.3.2.2 *M*-ary PSK and DPSK Performance in Slow Rayleigh Fading. In [23], a proper integral expression is given for the symbol error probability of both *M*-ary BPSK and DPSK. For $Z = E_s/N_0$, it is

$$P_s(Z) = \frac{1}{\pi} \int_0^{\pi(1-1/M)} \exp[-ZB(\phi)]d\phi \qquad (5\text{–}41)$$

where

$$B(\phi) = \begin{cases} \dfrac{\sin^2(\pi/M)}{\sin^2\phi}, & \text{for MPSK} \\[2ex] \dfrac{\sin^2(\pi/M)}{1+\cos(\pi/M)\cos\phi}, & \text{for MDPSK} \end{cases} \qquad (5\text{–}42)$$

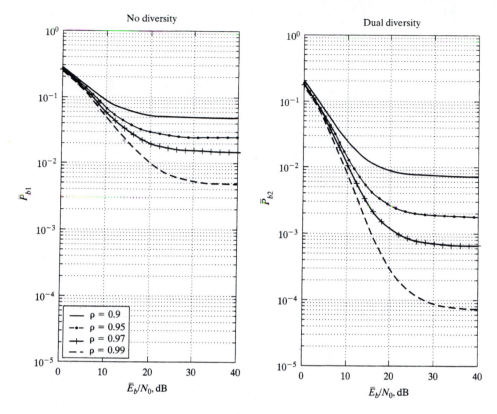

FIGURE 5–16 Effect of moderately fast fading on binary DPSK (ρ = correlation between bits); (a) no diversity; (b) dual diversity.

For Rayleigh fading, with Z exponentially distributed within a bit interval as assumed in (5–24), the expression for the average symbol error probability is

$$\overline{P}_{s,\,\text{Ray}} = \int_0^\infty \left\{ \frac{1}{\pi} \int_0^{\pi(1-1/M)} \exp[-zB\,(\phi)]d\phi \right\} \frac{1}{\overline{Z}} \exp\,(-z/\overline{Z})dz$$

$$= \frac{1}{\pi} \int_0^{\pi(1-1/M)} \left\{ \frac{1}{\overline{Z}} \int_0^\infty \exp\left[-z\left(B(\phi) + \frac{1}{\overline{Z}} \right) \right] dz \right\} d\phi$$

$$= \frac{1}{\pi} \int_0^{\pi(1-1/M)} \frac{1}{1 + \overline{Z}B(\phi)}\, d\phi, \quad \text{MPSK, MDPSK depending on } B\,(\phi) \quad (5\text{–}43)$$

which results by interchange of the orders of integration. It turns out that (5–43) can be evaluated in closed form [24] as

$$\bar{P}_{s,\text{Ray}} = \begin{cases} 1 - \dfrac{1}{M} - \dfrac{1}{\sqrt{1+\alpha}} + \dfrac{1}{\pi\sqrt{1+\alpha}} \tan^{-1}\left[\sqrt{1+\alpha}\,\tan\left(\pi/M\right)\right], \text{MPSK} \\[4mm] 1 - \dfrac{1}{M} - \dfrac{2(1-\alpha)}{\pi\sqrt{1-\beta^2}} \tan^{-1}\left[\sqrt{\dfrac{1-\beta}{1+\beta}}\,\tan\left(\dfrac{\pi(M-1)}{2M}\right)\right], \text{MDPSK} \end{cases} \tag{5-44}$$

where $\alpha = 1 \,/\, [\bar{Z}\sin^2(\pi/M)]$ for MPSK, and $\alpha = 1\,/\,[1 + \bar{Z}\sin^2(2\pi/M)]$ and $\beta = \alpha\cos(\pi/M)$ for MDPSK. It can be shown that these results reduce to the proper equations for binary signaling, that is, (5–25) and (5–26) for DPSK and BPSK, respectively.

The average bit error probabilities may be obtained by converting symbol energy to bit energy through $\bar{E}_b = \bar{E}_s/\log_2 M$ and symbol error probability to bit error probability by applying the approximation (4–144). Results for this approximate $\bar{P}_b$ versus $\bar{E}_b/N_0$ are shown in Figure 5–17 for MPSK and Figure 5–18 for MDPSK. Note that for low values of E_b/N_0 the approximation for converting symbol to bit error probabilities is most inaccurate. Also note that the results for binary and quaternary are essentially

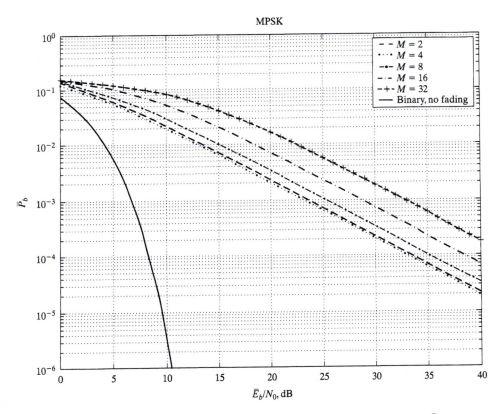

FIGURE 5–17 Bit error probabilities for MPSK in Rayleigh fading versus $\bar{E}_b/N_0$.

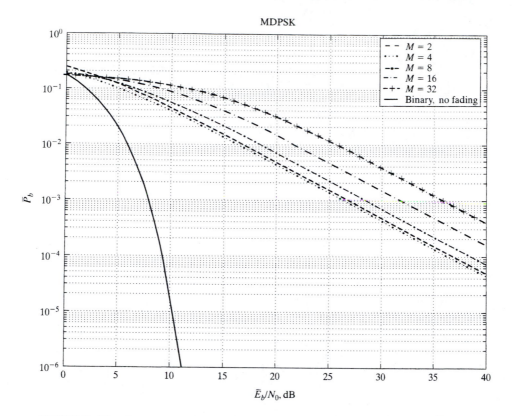

FIGURE 5–18   Bit error probabilities for MDPSK in Rayleigh fading versus $\bar{E}_b/N_0$.

the same; the slight difference again comes about because of the neglected terms in going from quaternary to binary via the approximation of dividing symbol error probabilities by $\log_2(M) = 2$. See [25] for more accurate approximations of MPSK bit error probabilities.

5.3.2.3 M-ary PSK and DPSK Performance in Slow Ricean Fading.   In the case of Ricean fading, a closed form expression for the average bit error probability is apparently not possible, although expressions are given in [16] in terms of complex transcendental functions. We derive expressions here for MPSK and MDPSK involving a single proper integral that can be readily numerically integrated.

The Ricean distribution is given by (2–221). This can be converted to the probability density function for the signal energy through the transformation $Z = R^2$ to give

$$f_Z(z) = \frac{1}{2\sigma^2} \exp\left[-\left(\frac{z}{2\sigma^2} + K\right)\right] I_0\left(\sqrt{\frac{2Kz}{\sigma^2}}\right), z \geq 0 \qquad (5\text{–}45)$$

where $K = A^2 / 2\sigma^2$ is the ratio of specular to diffuse power in the received signal. Using this to average (5–41), we obtain the double integral

$$\overline{P}_{s,\,\text{Rice}} = \int_0^\infty \left\{ \frac{1}{\pi} \int_0^{\pi(1-1/M)} \exp[-zB(\phi)]d\phi \right.$$

$$\times \left. \frac{1}{2\sigma^2} \exp\left[-\left(\frac{z}{2\sigma^2} + K \right) \right] I_0\left(\sqrt{\frac{2Kz}{\sigma^2}} \right) \right\} dz \qquad (5\text{–}46)$$

$$= \frac{\exp(-K)}{2\pi\sigma^2} \int_0^{\pi(1-1/M)} \left\{ \int_0^\infty \exp\left[-z\left(B(\phi) + \frac{1}{2\sigma^2} \right) \right] I_0\left(\sqrt{\frac{2Kz}{\sigma^2}} \right) dz \right\} d\phi$$

In the last integral of (5–46), define

$$\frac{z'}{2\sigma^2} = \left(B(\phi) + \frac{1}{2\sigma^2} \right) z \text{ and } K' = \frac{K}{1 + 2\sigma^2 B(\phi)}$$

which gives $zK = z'K'$ and therefore does not change the argument of the Bessel function of (5–46). Thus, the second integral of (5–46) becomes

$$\overline{P}_{s,\text{Rice}} = \frac{1}{\pi} \int_0^{\pi(1-1/M)} \frac{\exp(-K + K')}{1 + 2\sigma^2 B(\phi)}$$

$$\times \left\{ \int_0^\infty \frac{1}{2\sigma^2} \exp\left[-\left(\frac{z'}{2\sigma^2} + K' \right) \right] I_0\left(\sqrt{\frac{2K'z'}{\sigma^2}} \right) dz' \right\} d\phi \qquad (5\text{–}47)$$

$$= \frac{1}{\pi} \int_0^{\pi(1-1/M)} \frac{\exp(-K + K')}{1 + 2\sigma^2 A(\phi)} d\phi$$

$$= \frac{1}{\pi} \int_0^{\pi(1-1/M)} \frac{1}{1 + 2\sigma^2 B(\phi)} \exp\left[-K\frac{2\sigma^2 B(\phi)}{1 + 2\sigma^2 B(\phi)} \right] d\phi$$

where the second integral follows because the inside integral in the first line is the integral of a Ricean power probability density function and is therefore 1. The expressions for $B(\phi)$ from (5–42) may now be substituted and the remaining integration carried out numerically. A check of [17, eq. (47)] shows that (5–47) checks with previously published results for DPSK. Representative results are shown in Figure 5–19 for MPSK and in Figure 5–20 for MDPSK, where $\overline{E}_b = \overline{E}_s/\log_2 M$ has been used along with (4–144) for converting symbol to bit error probabilities.

Recall that a Ricean random process is the envelope of

$$s_2(t) = A\cos(2\pi f_0 t + \Theta) + X(t)\cos 2\pi f_0 t - Y(t)\sin 2\pi f_0 t$$

where $X(t)$ and $Y(t)$ are Gaussian random processes with zero means and variances σ^2. Since this represents the received signal in the symbol interval in Ricean fading, the aver-

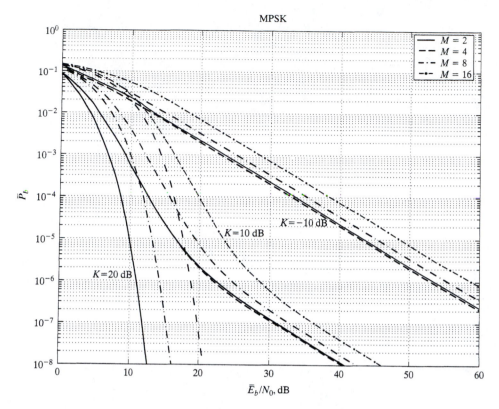

FIGURE 5–19   Bit error probabilities versus $\bar{E}_b/N_0$ for MPSK in Ricean fading.

age received signal power is $P_{\text{rec}} = A^2/2 + 2\sigma^2 = 2\sigma^2(1 + K)$ or $2\sigma^2 = P_{\text{rec}}/(1 + K)$ from which we conclude that

$$2\sigma^2 = \frac{1}{1 + K} \frac{E_s}{N_0} \qquad (5\text{--}48)$$

The results presented here correspond to those given in [26] for $M = 2$ (use single diversity in Table 3 there) as well as those presented in [27].

5.3.2.4 M-ary QAM Performance in Slow Ricean Fading.   The symbol error probability for MQAM was found in Chapter 4 to be of the form

$$P_{s,\text{QAM}} = 1 - (1 - P_{\sqrt{M}})^2 \qquad (5\text{--}49)$$

$$= 2P_{\sqrt{M}} - P^2_{\sqrt{M}}$$

where $P_{\sqrt{M}}$ is the symbol error probability of $\sqrt{M}$-ary amplitude-shift keying given by [16]

MDPSK

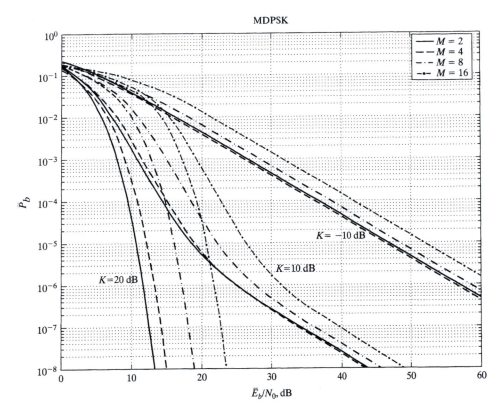

FIGURE 5–20   Bit error probabilities versus $\bar{E}_b/N_0$ for MDPSK in Ricean fading.

$$P_{\sqrt{M}} = 2\left(1 - \frac{1}{\sqrt{M}}\right)Q\left(\sqrt{\frac{3}{M-1}\frac{E_s}{N_0}}\right) \tag{5–50}$$

For large E_s / N_0, the second term in (5–49) is much smaller than the first, but we will include both terms because in [28] proper integral expressions are given for both $Q(x)$ and $Q^2(x)$ as

$$Q(x) = \frac{1}{\pi}\int_0^{\pi/2}\exp\left(-\frac{x^2}{2\sin^2\phi}\right)d\phi \quad \text{and} \quad Q^2(x) = \frac{1}{\pi}\int_0^{\pi/4}\exp\left(-\frac{x^2}{2\sin^2\phi}\right)d\phi \tag{5–51}$$

respectively. This makes the averaging process over the fading signal-to-noise ratio similar to that carried out for M-ary PSK and DPSK except we now have slightly different exponent in the error probability integral and there are two integrals instead of one. Following a series of steps similar to those used in (5–46) and (5–47), but with different limits and a different definition for $B(\phi)$, we obtain

$$\bar{P}_{s,\text{Rice}} = \frac{4}{\pi}\left(1 - \frac{1}{\sqrt{M}}\right)\int_0^{\pi/2} \frac{1}{1 + 2\sigma^2 B(\phi)} \exp\left[-K\frac{2\sigma^2 B(\phi)}{1 + 2\sigma^2 B(\phi)}\right]d\phi \tag{5-52}$$

$$- \frac{4}{\pi}\left(1 - \frac{1}{\sqrt{M}}\right)^2 \int_0^{\pi/4} \frac{1}{1 + 2\sigma^2 B(\phi)} \exp\left[-K\frac{2\sigma^2 B(\phi)}{1 + 2\sigma^2 B(\phi)}\right]d\phi, \quad \text{MQAM}$$

where K and σ^2 are defined the same as before and

$$B(\phi) = \frac{3}{2(M-1)}\frac{1}{\sin^2 \phi}, \quad \text{MQAM} \tag{5-53}$$

Bit error probability curves are produced by converting $\bar{E}_s$ to $\bar{E}_b$ and symbol error probabilities to bit error probabilities using (4–144) assuming that Gray encoding has been employed. Typical results are shown in Figure 5–21. Note that one other assumption is necessary in applying the averaging over the signal envelope in QAM. It is that some kind of adaptive estimation and adjustment algorithm is used at the receiver to vary the

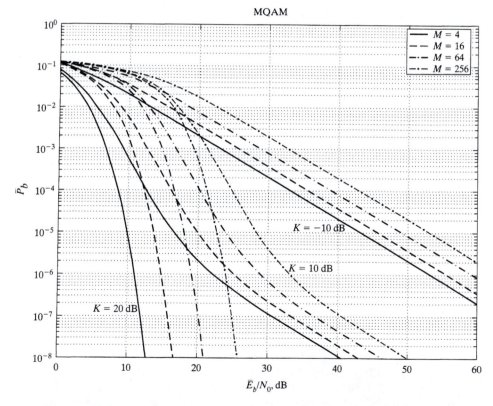

FIGURE 5–21 Bit error probabilities versus $\bar{E}_b/N_0$ in dB for MQAM in Ricean fading.

thresholds for signal detection in response to the fading. This is now necessary, whereas it was not in the case of MPSK and MDPSK, because QAM uses the amplitude (and phase) to carry the binary digits. Because of the fading, the envelope variation imposed by the channel will expand or contract the signal space plot with the result that the thresholds also must be varied in accordance with this expanding or contraction.

5.3.2.5 *M*-ary Noncoherent FSK Performance in Slow Ricean Fading.

Recall that the symbol error probability for *M*-ary noncoherent FSK is given by (4–124), wherein we now consider the symbol envelope to be a Ricean random variable (converted to energy) denoted as Z for convenience with corresponding variable of integration z. The resultant expression to be evaluated is

$$\overline{P}_{s,\text{MNFSK, Rice}} = \int_0^\infty \left\{ \sum_{k=1}^{M-1} \binom{M-1}{k} \frac{(-1)^{k+1}}{k+1} \exp\left[-\frac{k}{(k+1)} z \right] \right\}$$

$$\times \frac{1}{2\sigma^2} \exp\left[-\left(\frac{z}{2\sigma^2} + K \right) \right] I_0\left(\sqrt{\frac{2Kz}{\sigma^2}} \right) dz \qquad (5\text{--}54)$$

$$= \sum_{k=1}^{M-1} \binom{M-1}{k} \frac{(-1)^{k+1}}{k+1} \exp(-K) \int_0^\infty \frac{1}{2\sigma^2} \exp(-Cz) I_0\left(\sqrt{\frac{2Kz}{\sigma^2}} \right) dz$$

where the random variable $Z = E_s/N_0$ is represented by the dummy variable z in the integration, the orders of summation and integration have been reversed, and the constant

$$C = \frac{k}{(k+1)N_0} + \frac{1}{2\sigma^2} \qquad (5\text{--}55)$$

has been defined. Now consider the integral

$$I = \int_0^\infty \frac{1}{2\sigma^2} \exp(-Cz) I_0\left(\sqrt{\frac{2Kz}{\sigma^2}} \right) dz \qquad (5\text{--}56)$$

and define

$$\frac{z'}{2\sigma^2} = Cz \text{ and } K' = \frac{K}{2\sigma^2 C} \qquad (5\text{--}57)$$

Then $Kz = K'z'$ and the argument of the Bessel function in (5–56) doesn't change. Also, $dz = dz'/(2\sigma^2 C)$ so that (5–56) becomes

$$I = \frac{\exp(K')}{2\sigma^2 C} \int_0^\infty \frac{1}{2\sigma^2} \exp\left[-\left(\frac{z'}{2\sigma^2} + K' \right) \right] I_0\left(\sqrt{\frac{2K'z'}{\sigma^2}} \right) dz'$$

$$= \frac{\exp(K')}{2\sigma^2 C} \qquad (5\text{--}58)$$

where the integral evaluates to unity because its integrand is of the same form as (5–56) (i.e., the integral of a Ricean probability density function). As before, $P_{\text{rec}}T_s = (A^2 + 2\sigma^2)T_s$

$= 2\sigma^2(1 + K)$ or $2\sigma^2 = P_{rec}T_s/(1 + K)$ so that $2\sigma^2 = \bar{E}_s/(1 + K)$ according to (5–48). Putting (5–54), (5–57), (5–58), and (5–48) together, we obtain

$$\bar{P}_{s, \text{Rice, div}} = \sum_{k=1}^{M-1} \binom{M-1}{k} \frac{(-1)^{k+1}}{k+1} \left[1 + \frac{k}{(k+1)(K+1)} \frac{\bar{E}_s}{N_0} \right]^{-1}$$

$$\times \exp \left[-\frac{\dfrac{kK}{(k+1)(K+1)} \dfrac{\bar{E}_s}{N_0}}{1 + \dfrac{k}{(k+1)(K+1)} \dfrac{\bar{E}_s}{N_0}} \right] \tag{5–59}$$

This checks with the result given in [14, eq. (46)] and [17, eq. (47)] for $M = 2$ and [27] for M arbitrary.

Before showing results graphically for several cases, it is prudent to see if (5–59) agrees with previously derived results. To do so, we specialize it to the case of $M = 2$, which gives

$$\bar{P}_{b, \text{Rice, NFSK}} = \frac{1}{2 + \dfrac{1}{K+1} \dfrac{\bar{E}_b}{N_0}} \exp \left(-\frac{\dfrac{K}{K+1} \dfrac{\bar{E}_b}{N_0}}{2 + \dfrac{1}{K+1} \dfrac{\bar{E}_b}{N_0}} \right)$$

$$= \begin{cases} \dfrac{1}{2 + \bar{E}_b/N_0}, & K = 0 \text{ (Rayleigh fading)} \\[2ex] \dfrac{1}{2} \exp(-\bar{E}_b/2N_0), & K = \infty \text{ (no fading)} \end{cases} \tag{5–60}$$

The right-hand side limits correspond to previously derived results for binary NFSK in Rayleigh fading ($K = 0$) and in AWGN ($K = \infty$), respectively. Figure 5–22 shows the average bit error probability, as computed using (5–59), plotted versus $\bar{E}_b/N_0 = \bar{E}_s/(\log_2 M)N_0$ for $K = 0, 10, 20,$ and 30 dB. Each part of Figure 5–22 shows a different M with (a) giving binary signaling results, (b) giving 4-ary results, and so on. Note that as M increases, performance improves as it did for the nonfading case. This is because of the increasing dimensionality of the signal space with increasing M (except $M = 2$ and 4). The graphs for $K = 30$ dB are very close to the nonfading results shown in Figure 4–23, and the graphs for $K = 0$ dB are close to those for Rayleigh fading.

5.3.3 *M*-ary BPSK and DPSK Performance in Slow Fading with Diversity

5.3.3.1 Rayleigh Fading. For equal-gain combining, diversity performance results for M-ary BPSK and DPSK are easily obtained by returning to (5–41) and averaging it over Z with respect to the central chi-squared probability density function introduced in Chapter 2 given by (2–202). This follows because in equal gain combining,

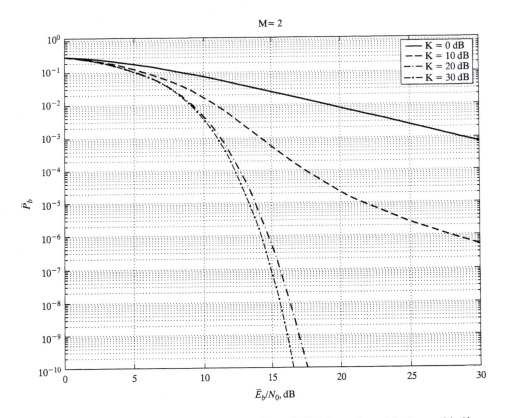

FIGURE 5–22   Bit error probabilities for M-ary NFSK for various M-values with K as a parameter.

the receiver output of each channel is added and the decision based on the sum statistic. Thus, the signal-to-noise ratio is the sum of squares of complex Gaussian random variables (inphase and quadrature components), or the sum is central chi-square of $2L$ degrees of freedom. The expression for the symbol error probability is

$$\overline{P}_{s,\,\text{Ray, EG}} = \int_0^\infty \left\{ \frac{1}{\pi} \int_0^{\pi(1-1/M)} \exp[-zB(\phi)]d\phi \right\} \frac{z^{L-1}\exp(-z/\overline{\gamma}_c)}{\overline{\gamma}_c^L\, \Gamma(L)} \, dz \qquad (5\text{–}61)$$

$$= \frac{1}{\pi\overline{\gamma}_c^L\, \Gamma(L)} \int_0^{\pi(1-1/M)} \left\{ \int_0^\infty z^{L-1} \exp\left[-z\left(B(\phi) + \frac{1}{\overline{\gamma}_c}\right)\right] dz \right\} d\phi$$

where L is the order of diversity, $\overline{\gamma}_c = \overline{E}_s/(LN_0)$ is the average symbol signal-to-noise ratio per channel, $\Gamma(L)$ is the gamma function, and $B(\phi)$ is defined in (5–42) for BPSK and DPSK. Through suitable change of variables and use of a table of integrals, the inner inte-

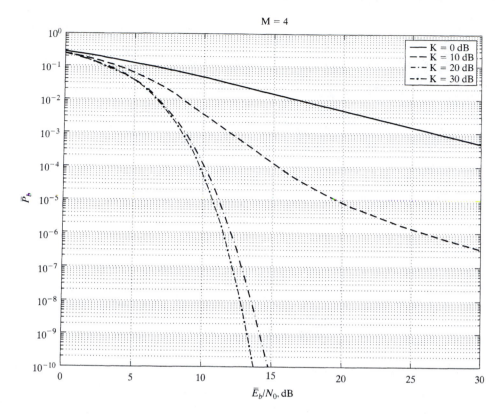

FIGURE 5–22 *Continued*

gral in (5–61) can be carried out (alternatively, through change of variables, the integrand can be expressed as another central chi-square density function) to produce the result

$$P_{s,\text{Ray, EG}} = \frac{1}{\pi} \int_0^{\pi(1 - 1/M)} \frac{d\phi}{\left[1 + \overline{\gamma}_c B(\phi)\right]^L} \tag{5–62}$$

Integration of (5–62) and use of the, by now, familiar conversions for symbol energy to bit energy and symbol error probability to bit error probability produces performance curves such as shown in Figure 5–23 for MPSK and Figure 5–24 for MDPSK. A similar procedure can be carried out for M-ary NFSK. It is left to the problems to produce the derivation and compare the relative performances of BPSK, DPSK, and NFSK. Note that the curves match with Figure 5–14a for $M = 2$ as well as those shown in [16], Figure 14–4-2, for $M = 2$.

5.3.3.2 Ricean Fading. A similar procedure can be used to find the symbol error probability with diversity and equal-gain combining for M-ary BPSK and DPSK in

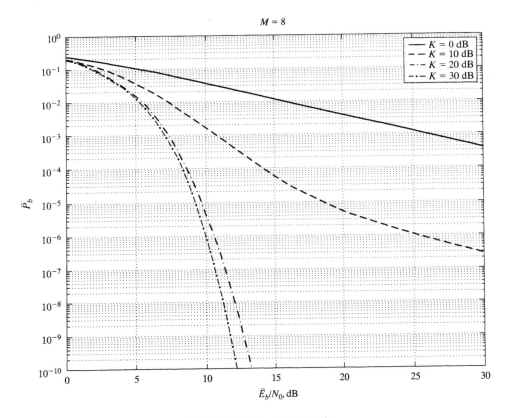

FIGURE 5–22   *Continued*

Ricean fading as was used in the previous section for Rayleigh fading, except that a noncentral chi-square density, (2–203), is used to average the symbol error probability expression, given by (5–41), rather then a central chi-square density as used in the previous section. The resulting expression for the symbol error probability is

$$
\overline{P}_{s,\text{Rice,EG}} = \int_0^\infty \left\{ \frac{1}{\pi} \int_0^{\pi(1-1/M)} \exp[-zB(\phi)]\,d\phi \right\} \frac{1}{2\sigma^2} \left(\frac{z}{A^2} \right)^{\frac{L-1}{2}}
$$

$$
\times \exp\left[-\left(K + \frac{z}{2\sigma^2} \right) \right] I_{L-1}\!\left(\sqrt{z}\,\frac{A}{\sigma^2} \right) dz
$$

$$
= \frac{e^{-K}}{\pi} \int_0^{\pi(1-1/M)} \int_0^\infty \frac{1}{2\sigma^2} \left(\frac{z}{A^2} \right)^{\frac{L-1}{2}}
$$

$$
\times \exp\left[-z\left(B(\phi) + \frac{1}{2\sigma^2} \right) \right] I_{L-1}\!\left(\sqrt{z}\,\frac{A}{\sigma^2} \right) dz\, d\phi
$$

(5–63)

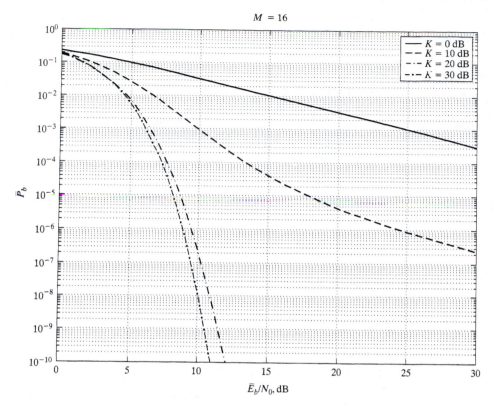

$M = 16$

FIGURE 5–22   *Continued*

where A is the specular component amplitude of the fading signal, σ^2 is the variance of the inphase (or quadrature) diffuse component of the fading signal, K is the ratio of specular to diffuse powers, $I_n(\cdot)$ is the modified Bessel function of order n, L is the order of diversity, and $B(\phi)$ is given by (5–42). In the inner integral, define the substitutions

$$z' = \frac{A^2}{A_1^2} z \text{ and } A_1 = \frac{A}{\sqrt{1 + 2\sigma^2 B(\phi)}} \tag{5–64}$$

which allows (5–63) to be written as

$$\overline{P}_{s,\text{Rice,EG}} = \frac{e^{-K}}{\pi} \int_0^{\pi(1 - 1/M)} \int_0^\infty \frac{1}{2\sigma^2} \left(\frac{z'}{1 + 2\sigma^2 B(\phi)} \right)^{\frac{L-1}{2}}$$

$$\times \exp[-z'/2\sigma^2] I_{L-1}\left(\sqrt{z'} \frac{A_1}{\sigma^2} \right) \frac{dz'}{1 + 2\sigma^2 B(\phi)} d\phi$$

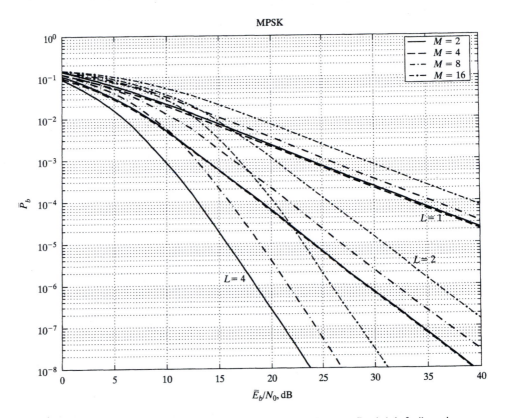

FIGURE 5-23 Probability of a bit error for M-ary MPSK over Rayleigh fading channels with diversity and equal-gain combining.

$$= \frac{1}{\pi} \int_0^{\pi(1-1/M)} \frac{\exp[(A^2 - A_1^2)/2\sigma^2]}{[1 + 2\sigma^2 B(\phi)]^L} \int_0^{\infty} \frac{1}{2\sigma^2} \left(\frac{z'}{A_1^2}\right)^{\frac{L-1}{2}}$$

$$\times \exp\left(-\frac{A_1^2 + z'}{2\sigma^2}\right) I_{L-1}\left(\sqrt{z'}\frac{A_1}{\sigma^2}\right) dz' d\phi \qquad (5\text{--}65)$$

$$= \frac{1}{\pi} \int_0^{\pi(1-1/M)} \frac{\exp\left(-K\dfrac{2\sigma^2 B(\phi)}{1 + 2\sigma^2 B(\phi)}\right)}{[1 + 2\sigma^2 B(\phi)]^L} d\phi$$

where $B(\phi)$ is given by (5–42) for MPSK and MDPSK and $2\sigma^2 = (\bar{E}_b/N_0)/[L(1 + K)]$ with the L included to reflect transmitter diversity. The inner integral in the second line above evaluates to unity since its integrand is a probability density function. The final integral in

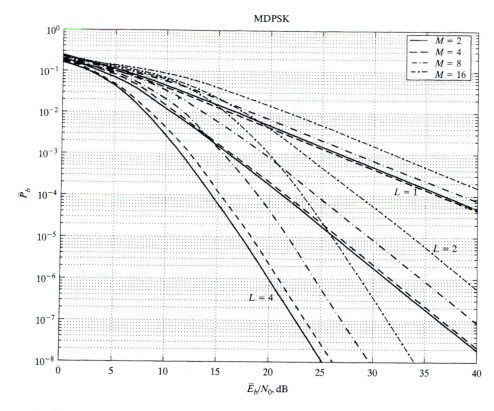

FIGURE 5–24 Probability of a bit error for *M*-ary MDPSK over Rayleigh fading channels with diversity and equal-gain combining.

(5–65) can be readily integrated numerically. Again, symbol energy is changed to bit energy and the symbol error probability converted to bit error probability as before. Typical results are shown in Figure 5–25 for DPSK and in Figure 5–26 for BPSK for $M = 4$ (same as for $M = 2$). A similar analysis can be carried out for NFSK.

EXAMPLE 5–3

From Figures 5–24 and 5–25, we note that it costs about 2 to 3 dB at a bit error probability of 10^{-4} to use DPSK as opposed to PSK in a Rayleigh fading channel depending on the order of diversity. In a channel with severe fading as modeled by Rayleigh, this seems like almost a necessity in order to avoid the near impossibility of tracking a carrier component in such channels. A similar price is paid in a Ricean channel for $K = 5$ dB (compare Figures 5–26a and 5–27a at a bit error probability of 10^{-4}). For $K = 10$ dB, the loss is something like 2 dB. The possibility of maintaining a solid phase track on a signal with $3 – 9$ ($K = 5 – 10$ dB) times the diffuse component power in a steady component is much more feasible, so it appears that one could potentially live with a factor of $1.6 – 2$ (2 to 3 dB) less transmit power if it could be

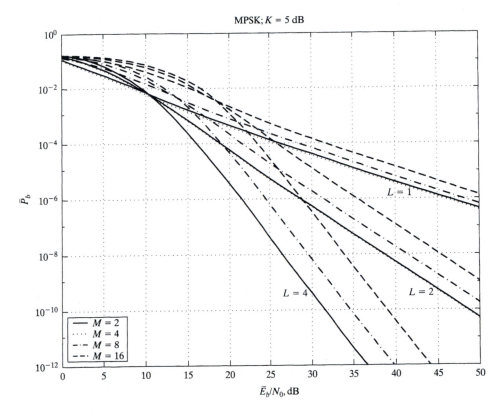

FIGURE 5–25   Bit error probabilities for *M*-ary PSK in Ricean fading with diversity and equal-gain combining for $K = 5$ dB (a) and $K = 10$ dB (b).

assumed that the Ricean model with $K = 5 - 10$ dB holds. This might be the case, for example, if small cell sizes are used in a cellular communications system (to be considered in Chapter 10). This could be the case for a number of reasons—the original cells might be split in accommodating more users or the original design may have dictated because of higher desired data rates as in third-generation systems.

5.4   DIAGNOSTIC TOOLS FOR COMMUNICATION SYSTEM DESIGN

5.4.1   Introduction

Various means can be used to diagnose the operation of digital communication systems. These include observing the envelope of the modulated signal, and viewing their phasor plots and the so-called eye diagrams over a sequence of input symbols. In this section, these are described and their usefulness in communication system design is examined.

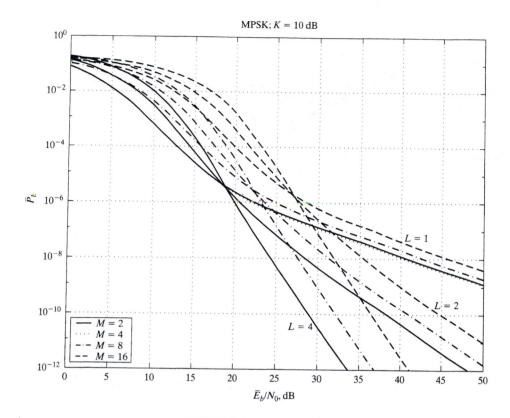

FIGURE 5–25 *Continued*

5.4.2 Eye Diagrams

An eye diagram is a convenient tool for system diagnosis. İt consists of plots of the quadrature baseband components of the demodulated signal modulo the symbol period (or more). The process of eye-diagram generation consists of laying contiguous intervals of the demodulated (but not detected) carrier that are an integer number of symbol periods in duration on top of each other. Results are shown in Figures 5–27 through 5–30 for QPSK, OQPSK, MSK, and 16-QAM, respectively, where the modulated signal is filtered by a Butterworth filter of bandwidth times bit rate given at the top of each figure.

Note that filtering partially "closes the eye." Thus, one can judge the optimum point for sampling of the demodulated signal for comparison of the samples with a threshold for detection. One can also get a rough idea of the amount of degradation imposed on the signal by filtering.

Note that in addition to controlling the spectrum by filtering, and thereby generating intersymbol interference, the spectral shaping can be achieved by shaping the pulse used

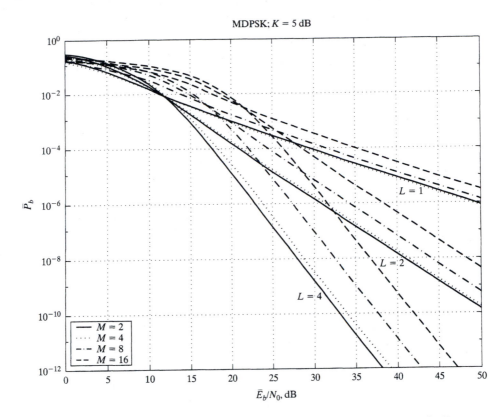

FIGURE 5–26   Bit error probabilities for *M*-ary DPSK in Ricean fading with diversity and equal-gain combining for $K = 5$ dB (a) and $K = 10$ dB (b).

to represent the symbols (i.e., the 1s and −1s) in the inphase and quadrature channels of the modulator. This results in a given pulse having 0s at symbol-spaced intervals, except at the point of desired sampling, but the resulting signal envelope for previously constant-envelope modulation techniques such as QPSK and OQPSK, is no longer constant. Note that a very special relationship must exist between the inphase and quadrature modulating waveforms in order to have a constant envelope; in particular, the sum of their squares be a constant instant by instant.

5.4.3   Envelope Functions for Digital Modulation Methods

If the constant-envelope modulation schemes discussed in Chapter 4, such as BPSK, QPSK, OQPSK, or MSK, are filtered prior to transmission or by the channel, the result will be a modulated signal with a nonconstant envelope. The reason for this can be seen

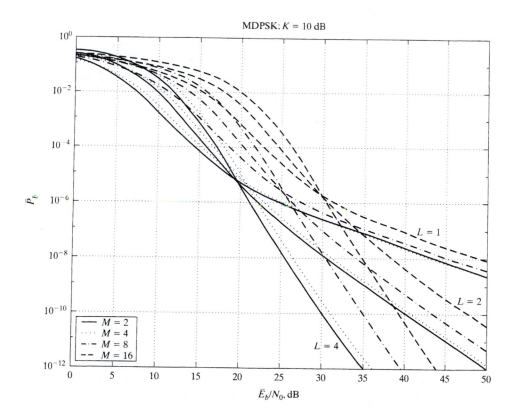

FIGURE 5–26   *Continued*

by viewing the filtering as taking place at baseband on the data streams.[3] For example, Figure 5–31 illustrates the process for BPSK. Each time the data switches sign, a transient buildup of the output takes place, which results in the modulated carrier envelope going through a null. Filtering of QPSK results in similar nulls. However, for OQPSK, only one quadrature component of the modulated carrier can go through a zero-transition at a time, so the resultant envelope of a filtered OQPSK-modulated carrier has minima that are $1/\sqrt{2}$ of the maximum amplitude at worst. MSK shows even less envelope variation due to filtering than OQPSK because of the smoother transitions.

The envelopes of filtered QPSK, OQPSK, and MSK are plotted in Figure 5–32. These were also obtained by simulation. Note that the filter bandwidth for the envelope function of BPSK, plotted in Figure 5–31, is twice that for the other three, which is only

---

[3]Recall that in Chapter 2 it was shown how the impulse response of a narrowband, bandpass filter could be represented as $h(t) = h_R(t)\cos 2\pi f_0 t - h_I(t)\sin 2\pi f_0 t = \text{Re}\,[\tilde{h}(t)\exp(j2\pi f_0 t)]$ where $h_R(t)$ and $h_I(t)$ are lowpass. Thus a bandpass filter can be represented by two lowpass filters in parallel arms where the input is mixed to zero frequency and then mixed up in frequency again.

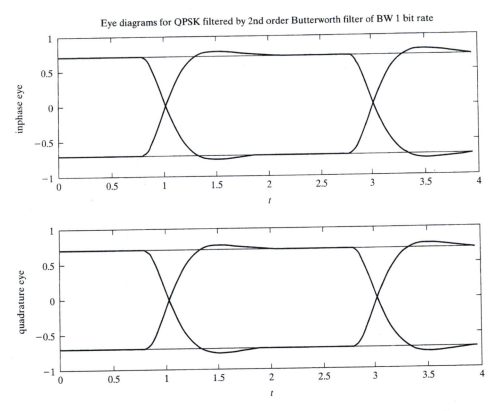

FIGURE 5–27   Eye diagram for QPSK modulation with Butterworth filtering; filter bandwidth of 1 bit rate.

fair since the symbol durations for QPSK, OQPSK, and MSK are twice the bit (symbol) duration of BPSK. Clearly BPSK and QPSK have more envelope variation than OQPSK and MSK. Also note the transient buildup shown in each figure. This results from plotting the envelope from the start of the simulation, thus showing the effects of the transient response of the filters.

5.4.4 Phasor Plots for Digital Modulation Systems

It is often helpful to visualize QPSK, OQPSK, and MSK, as well as other digital modulation systems, in terms of phasor diagrams of the inphase and quadrature modulating waveforms. These are useful in both building and troubleshooting actual hardware as well as aiding in the analytical design of digital modulation systems. In the former case, these plots would be traced as Lissajous curves on an oscilloscope screen with the vertical axis input being the data waveform in the quadrature channel, and the horizontal input being the data waveform in the inphase channel (or vice versa). In the latter case, computer sim-

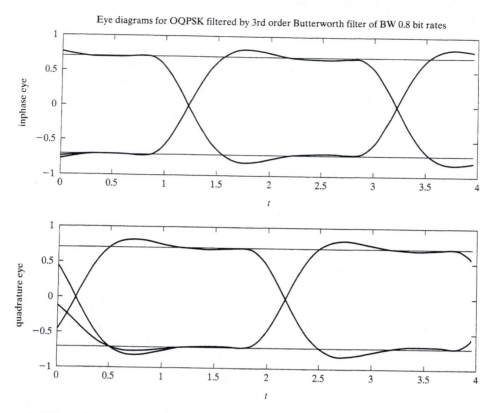

FIGURE 5–28   Eye diagram for OQPSK modulation with Butterworth filtering; filter bandwidth of 0.8 bit rates.

ulations may be used to generate the phasor diagrams. Since the inphase- and quadrature-channel signals are ±0.707-valued (assuming unit peak power) in the case of QPSK, the Lissajous curve is a square with diagonal line across the square since both ±90 and ±180 excess-phase transitions are possible. A similar statement holds for the case of OQPSK, but the diagonal lines across the square are absent since only ±90-degree excess-phase transitions are possible (the inphase- and quadrature-channel data streams are staggered by one-half symbol period). In the case of MSK, the inphase and quadrature signals are sinusoidally weighted which, ideally, produces a circle for the Lissajous curve. Only ±90-degree phase transitions are possible, so there are no diagonal transitions across the circle (only the circumference is traced in response to a random data pattern).

Of course, in the ideal case of no distortion in the system, the phasor diagrams may be easily sketched by simple reasoning. It is in the case of distortion that we resort to measurement by means of an oscilloscope in the case of actual hardware implementation, or to computer simulation for analytical design.

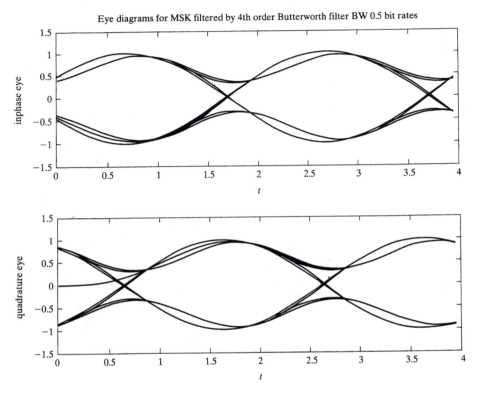

Eye diagrams for MSK filtered by 4th order Butterworth filter BW 0.5 bit rates

FIGURE 5–29   Eye diagram for MSK modulation with Butterworth filtering; filter bandwidth of 0.5 bit rates.

Figure 5–33 shows phasor diagrams, generated by computer simulation, for the case of ideal (unfiltered) QPSK, OQPSK, MSK, 16-QAM. Note that the diagrams look as expected, which provides confidence that the computer simulation is working properly. Figure 5–34 illustrates phasor diagrams for the same modulation schemes where the inphase- and quadrature-channel signals are filtered by a fourth-order Butterworth filter. This might represent bandlimiting done to limit the spectrum due to channel assignment, for example. It turns out that 16-QAM has twice the symbol duration of the other three modulation schemes considered, so the filter bandwidth used for it is half that used for the other three. Note that the filter bandwidth is expressed in terms of bit rate. Also note that the filtering causes considerable departure from the ideal, unfiltered trajectories shown in Figure 5–33.

In some cases, the filtering may represent that of a detection filter (or filters, if implemented in the inphase and quadrature channels of the receiver). In this case, one would be interested in only the samples of the Lissajous figures at instants spaced by the symbol duration. These sampling instants would, hopefully, be at maximum eye opening. In addi-

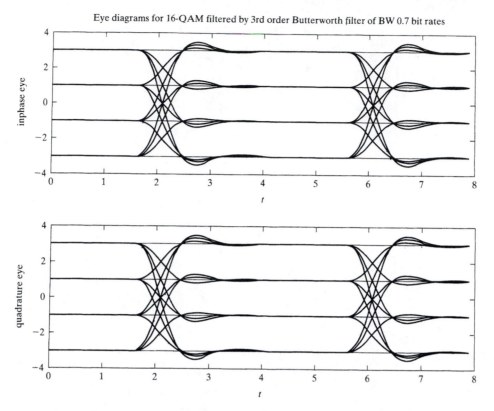

FIGURE 5–30 Eye diagram for 16-QAM modulation with Butterworth filtering; filter bandwidth of 0.7 bit rates (input signal power at filter input not normalized to unity).

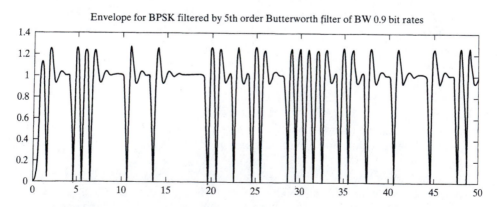

FIGURE 5–31 Envelope function for filtered BPSK obtained through simulation.

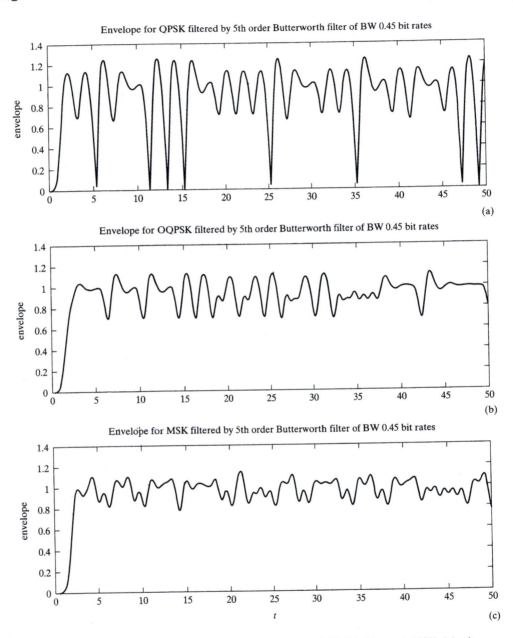

FIGURE 5–32 Envelope functions for QPSK (a), OQPSK (b), and MSK (c) obtained by simulation; bandwidths in terms of bit rates shown above figures.

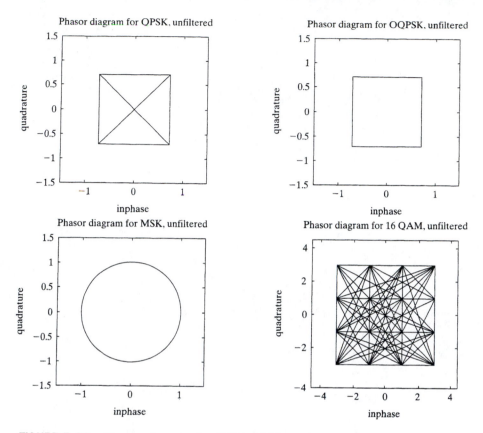

FIGURE 5–33 Phasor diagrams for QPSK, OQPSK, MSK, and 16-QAM; no filtering.

tion to filtering, other system imperfections, including nonlinearities and noise, may contribute variations in the sample locations on the inphase-quadrature plot. Thus, for a long data sequence, a cloud of sample points around each possible ideal signal location would be obtained. Such diagrams, called scatter diagrams, are also useful in system design and troubleshooting.

5.5 SUMMARY

This chapter deals with certain factors that may degrade the performance of communication systems from the ideal performance of the optimum detectors operating in AWGN that were considered in Chapter 4.

1. One important consideration for the practical implementation of a communication system is synchronization. This is necessary at the carrier, bit or symbol, and frame or data package levels.

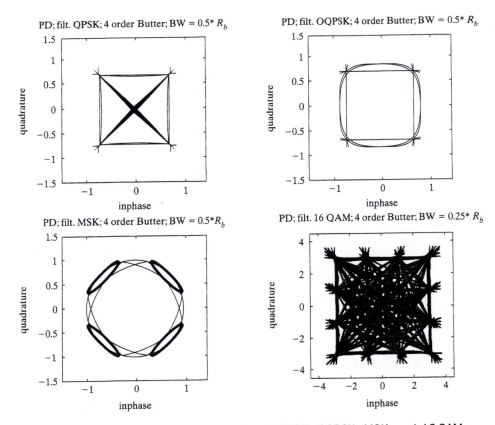

FIGURE 5–34   Phasor diagrams for filtered QPSK, OQPSK, MSK, and 16-QAM; fourth-order Butterworth filters used, with bandwidths shown at the tops of each figure.

2. Carrier synchronization is necessary for coherent communication systems. In the process of establishing a local sinusoidal reference that is in phase coherence with the received carrier, some phase error is inevitable. This degrades the bit error performance of a given modulation technique operating in an AWGN environment from the ideal performance. One simple, gross characterization of this degradation is to obtain the receiver's bit error performance for a fixed phase offset and use the difference between the signal-to-noise ratio E_b/N_0 with the phase offset and that for zero phase offset as the amount by which the E_b/N_0 must be increased to achieve the desired bit error performance. This is a worst case analysis. An average performance characterization is obtained by averaging the bit error probability, conditioned on the phase error, with respect to an appropriate phase error probability density, often approximated as Gaussian. This average bit error probability is perhaps too optimistic since, by definition, the actual bit error probability will sometimes be better than this, but sometimes will be worse than this. In actuality, it is most often the case that a design engineer must ensure that a communication system performs *no worse* than some upper bound.

3. Several possible techniques were discussed for establishing a coherent phase reference in a communication system. For *M*-ary PSK, the generic phase reference circuit is an *M*th power device, followed by a narrowband filter centered at the *M*th harmonic of the carrier, followed by a frequency divider. This technique, while very simple, has the disadvantage of requiring the generation of a carrier at *M* times the frequency of the desired carrier (actually, this would be done at some convenient and appropriately chosen intermediate frequency). Another approach to the local reference generation problem is to use a double feedback loop structure known as a Costas loop in the BPSK case. Costas loop type structures exist for non-BPSK signals as well.

4. Establishing a clock signal at the receiver in synchronism with the received data stream is necessary in order to sample at the appropriate instant and possibly initialize data detection filters (for example, an integrate-and-dump detector). Options and structures similar to the carrier acquisition devices discussed above are typically used (i.e., put the data through an even-power nonlinearity to generate a clock signal from the data is one option; using a double feedback structure called the early-late gate synchronizer is another).

5. If the data is formatted in frames, as it often is, a local frame reference must also be established. This is typically done by inserting a unique bit pattern into the data stream periodically (either at the beginning or middle of the frame) and using a correlator to detect it. A process called bit stuffing is used to avoid having the unique bit pattern appearing accidentally in the bit stream.

6. Communication systems must often operate in environments where the signal envelope fades, or varies, randomly due to perturbations in the channel (often due to multipath, or multiple transmission paths). Typically, these fades have a much longer time scale than the bit or symbol duration, while at the same time any multipath that produced the fades have relative delays much shorter than a bit duration. This gives rise to a model called slow frequency-flat fading. An often used model in such cases is to model the signal envelope as a Rayleigh distributed random variable (the power or energy is exponentially distributed), but constant in a given bit interval, independent of all other bit or symbol interval envelopes. This allows simple expressions to be derived for the bit error probability averaged over the Rayleigh fading for all common binary signaling schemes, such as BPSK, DPSK, NFSK, and so on. The degradation in E_b/N_0 at a given bit error probability from the ideal AWGN case experienced as a result of such fading is tremendous, being typically in excess of 20 dB for most common signaling techniques at bit error probabilities of 10^{-3} (that is, 100 times more power is required to ensure the same error probability as would be achieved for AWGN, *on average*).

7. Bit error probabilities for the case where the received signal envelope is undergoing slow Ricean fading can be obtained in the form of a single proper integral for most binary and *M*-ary modulation schemes. The Ricean fading model is appropriate where, in addition to diffuse or many-scatterer multipath, a direct line-of-sight path exists.

8. Diversity, or transmission/reception along many possible paths, is a scheme whereby fading may be mitigated. Diversity can be achieved many different ways, including path, polarization, and frequency. If we think of path diversity as taking place by using L transmit antennas, then the E_b/N_0 used in the error probability for a given path should be divided by L since the total power is shared among the L paths. If it is due to multiple receive antennas, than division by L is not appropriate. Diversity implementations can also be categorized by the point in the receiver at which the path outputs are combined at the receiver. If before detection, a particular diversity technique is referred to as predetection combining; if after detection, it is denoted as post-detection combining. Diversity implementations are also categorized by the manner in which the path outputs are combined at the receiver. Typical methods are maximal-ratio combining (each path output is weighted by its signal-to-noise ratio before adding), equal gain combining (path outputs are simply summed), and selection (the "best" path output is selected and the receiver's decision for that symbol interval is based only on the selected output). All other things being equal, predetection combining performs better than post-detection methods; maximal ratio performs the best, followed by equal gain, followed by selection.

9. Several diagnostic tools were illustrated by simulation. These included phasor diagrams, envelopes, and eye diagrams. Quite often, these are used in the design of a simulation program or hardware implementation to determine if the system is at least working properly insofar as these tools are able to indicate.

REFERENCES

[1] R. L. Didday and W. C. Lindsey, "Subcarrier Tracking Methods and Communication System Design," *IEEE Trans. Commun.,* Vol. COM-16, pp. 541–550, Aug. 1968.

[2] W. C. Lindsey, *Synchronization Systems in Communications and Control* (Upper Saddle River, NJ: Prentice Hall, 1972).

[3] S. Gardner, "Burst Modem Design Techniques, Part I," *Communication Systems Design,* pp. 30–37, July 1999.

[4] J. K Holmes, *Coherent Spread Spectrum Systems* (New York: John Wiley, 1982).

[5] M. K. Simon, "Nonlinear Analysis of an Absolute Value Type of an Early-Late Gate Bit Synchronizor," *IEEE Trans. Commun.,* Vol. COM-18, pp. 589–596, Oct. 1970.

[6] L. E. Franks, "Carrier and Bit Synchronization in Data Communication—A Tutorial Review," *IEEE Trans. Commun.,* Vol. COM-28, pp. 1107–1129, Aug. 1980.

[7] L. E. Miller and J. S. Lee, "BER Expressions for Differentially Detected $\pi/4$-DQPSK Modulation," *IEEE Trans. Commun.,* Vol. 46, pp. 71–81, Jan. 1998.

[8] J. N. Pierce, "Theoretical Diversity Improvement in Frequency-Shift Keying," *Proc. IRE,* Vol. 46, pp. 903–910, May 1958.

[9] J. N. Pierce and S. Stein, "Multiple Diversity with Non-Independent Fading," *Proc. IRE,* Vol. 48, pp. 89–104, Jan. 1960.

[10] D. G. Brennan, "Linear Diversity Combining Techniques," *Proc. IRE,* Vol. 47, pp. 1075–1102, Jan. 1960.

[11] G. L. Turin, "On Optimal Diversity Reception," *IRE Trans. Inform. Theory,* Vol. IT-7, pp. 154–166, July 1961.

[12] G. L. Turin, "On Optimal Diversity Reception II," *IRE Trans. Commun. Systems*, Vol. CS-12, pp. 22–31, Mar. 1962.

[13] R. Price, "Error Probabilities for the Adaptive Multichannel Reception of Binary Signals," *IRE Trans. Inform. Theory*, Vol. IT-8, pp. 305–316, Sept. 1962.

[14] W. C. Lindsey, "Error Probabilities for Ricean Fading Multichannel Reception of Binary and N-ary Signals," *IEEE Trans. Inform. Theory*, Vol. IT-10, pp. 339–350, Oct. 1964.

[15] M. Schwartz, W. R. Bennett, and S. Stein, *Communication Systems and Techniques* (New York: McGraw-Hill, 1966).

[16] J. G. Proakis, *Digital Communications*, 3rd ed. (New York: McGraw-Hill, 1995).

[17] M. K. Simon and M.-S.Alouini, "A Unified Approach to the Probability of Error for Noncoherent and Differentially Coherent Modulations over Generalized Fading Channels," *IEEE Trans. Commun.*, Vol. 46, pp. 1625–1638, Dec. 1998. See also, M. K. Simon, "A New Twist on the Marcum Q-function and Its Application," *IEEE Commun. Letters*, pp. 39–41, Feb. 1998.

[18] R. Ziemer and W. Tranter, 4th ed. *Principles of Communications: Systems, Modulation, and Noise* (New York: John Wiley, 1995).

[19] T. Eng, N. Kong, and L. B. Milstein, "Comparison of Diversity Combining Techniques for Rayleigh-Fading Channels," *IEEE Trans. Commun.*, Vol. 44, pp. 1117–1129, Sept. 1996.

[20] H. Voelcker, "Phase-Shift Keying in Fading Channels," *Proc. IEE*, Vol. 107, Part B, pp. 31–38, Jan. 1960.

[21] R. Ziemer and T. Welch, "Equal-gain combining of multichannel DPSK in Doppler-Spread Rician Fading," *IEEE Trans. on Veh. Technol.*, Vol. 49, Oct. 2000.

[22] Y. C. Chow, J. P. McGeehan, and A. R. Nix, "Simplified Error Bound Analysis for M-DPSK in Fading Channels with Diversity Reception," *IEE Proc. – Commun.*, Vol. 141, pp. 341–350, Oct. 1994.

[23] R. F. Pawula, "A New Formula for MDPSK Symbol Error Probability," *IEEE Commun. Letters*, pp. 271–272, Oct. 1998.

[24] M. R. Olsson, "New Simplified Formulas for Probability of Error for MDPSK and MPSK over Rayleigh and Rician Fading Channels with Diversity," MSEE Thesis, University of Colorado at Colorado Springs, Colorado Springs, CO, April 1999.

[25] J. Lu, B. Letaief, J. Chuang, and M. Liou, "MPSK and MQAM BER Computation Using Signal-Space Concepts," *IEEE Trans. Commun.*, Vol. 47, pp. 181–184, Feb. 1999.

[26] M. K. Simon and M.-S. Alouini, "A Unified Approach to the Performance Analysis of Digital Communication over Generalized Fading Channels," *Proc. IEEE*, Vol. 86, pp. 1860–1877, Sept. 1998.

[27] J. Sun and I. Reed, "Performance of MDPSK, MPSK, and Noncoherent MFSK in Wireless Rician Fading Channels," *IEEE Trans. Commun.*, Vol. 47, pp. 813–816, June 1999.

[28] M. K. Simon and D. Divsalar, "Some New Twists to Problems Involving the Gaussian Probability Integral," *IEEE Trans. Commun.*, Vol. 47, pp. 200–210, Feb. 1998.

PROBLEMS

5–1. Consider phase-shift keying with a carrier component that can be written as

$$x_c(t) = A\sin[2\pi f_0 t + d(t)\cos^{-1} a]$$

where $d(t)$ is binary data that is ± 1-valued in contiguous T_b-second bit intervals.

(a) Show that the ratio of powers in the carrier and modulation components is

$$\frac{P_c}{P_m} = \frac{a^2}{1 - a^2}$$

(b) Show that the powers in the modulation and carrier components, respectively, are given in terms of the total power, P_T, as

$$P_c = a^2 P_T$$

and

$$P_m = (1 - a^2)P_T$$

5–2. Write a MATLAB program to plot the curves shown in Figures 5–2 through 5–4 to compute the increase in E_b/N_0 required over the case of no phase jitter for the phase jitter variances given in Figure 5–2 at $P_E = 10^{-3}$.

5–3. Consider the squaring loop carrier acquisition circuit with the following paramters:
    Data rate – $T_b^{-1} = 10$ kbps;
    Filter bandwidth of input filter $= 20$ kHz;
    Loop bandwidth – $B_L = 500$ Hz
    Loop signal-to-noise ratio – $\rho_L = 30$ dB
(a) Find the squaring loss.
(b) Find the variance of the phase jitter.
(c) Repeat (a) and (b) but with $\rho_L = 10$ dB.

For part (c), find the corresponding E_b / N_0 and estimate the probability of error by adapting the program developed in Problem 5–2.

5–4. By deriving the signals shown in Figure 5–6, show that the Costas loop really tracks a BPSK signal. Generalize to loops for tracking QPSK.

5–5. (a) Fill in all steps in deriving (5–20).
(b) Write a MATLAB program to evaluate (5–20) for various fixed values of phase error.
(c) Generalize it to find probability of bit error averaged over a Gaussian-distributed phase error. Plot several sample curves of $\bar{P}_b$ versus $\bar{E}_b/N_0$ for various values of $\sigma_{\theta e}^2$.

5–6. Prove that $|c_1|^2$, as given by (5–21), is maximized for $\tau = T_b / 2$.

5–7. Verify the curves given in Figure 5–10 by writing a MATLAB program to plot them. If the signaling scheme is BPSK, plot Figure 5–10a for $E_b/N_0 = 5$, 7, and 9 dB. Suppose P_F no larger than 10^{-5} and P_M no larger than 10^{-6} is desired. Choose an ε and the minimum N for each of the E_b/N_0 values of 5, 7, and 9 dB to provide these performance requirements.

5–8. For $P_b = 10^{-3}$, what is the dB increase in E_b/N_0 required for DPSK, $\pi/4$-DQPSK, NFSK, and BPSK in slow Rayleigh fading over the corresponding nonfading cases.

5–9. Use integration by parts and the definition of the Q-function to derive (5–26).
Hint: Leibnitz's rule for differentiation of the Q-function integral is

$$\frac{d}{dx} Q[f(x)] = \frac{d}{dx} \int_{f(x)}^{\infty} \frac{\exp(-t^2/2)}{\sqrt{2\pi}} \, dt = -\frac{\exp[-f^2(x)/2]}{\sqrt{2\pi}} \frac{df(x)}{dx}$$

In the formula for integration by parts, let $u = Q[(2\gamma)^{1/2}]$.

5–10. Fill in the details in the derivation of (5–32).

5–11. Show that (5–32) and (5–33) are equivalent.

5–12. Plot the asymptotic result given below (5–33), namely,

$$\overline{P}_b \approx \binom{2L-1}{L}\left(\frac{E_b}{LN_0}\right)^{-L}$$

along with (5–32) on the same graph to verify that this is indeed a good approximation at large E_b/N_0.

5–13. Assume that two antennas mounted on a cellular hand-held telephone give independent signals. How much less power in a Rayleigh fading channel is required over nondiversity at $P_E = 10^{-3}$ for **(a)** NFSK with square-law combining? **(b)** BPSK with maximal-ratio combining? **(c)** BPSK with selection combining?

5–14. Reconsider Problem 5–13, but instead of receiver diversity, consider transmitter diversity.

5–15. Write a MATLAB program to plot bit error probability versus order of diversity for a given E_b/N_0 for maximal-ratio and selection combining for BPSK. By plotting particular cases, convince yourself that an optimum order of diversity exists for selection combining, but not for maximal-ratio combining.

5–16. Repeat Problem 5–15 for binary FSK and square law combining. Is there an optimum order of diversity in this case?

5–17. Write a MATLAB program to evaluate (5–40) and plot the bit error probability versus **(a)** E_b/N_0 for fixed L, and **(b)** versus L for fixed E_b/N_0. Let the correlation coefficient be a parameter in both cases.

5–18. Find a general expression for the error floor (i.e., the asymptotic value of $P_{b,L}$) exhibited in Figure 5–17. You may do this by finding the limit of (5–40) as $\overline{Z} = \overline{E}_b / N_0 \to \infty$. Plot as a function of the correlation coefficient.

5–19. Fading margin can be defined as the incremental E_b/N_0 required to provide a given desired bit error probability in a fading channel as could be achieved with the same modulation scheme as in a nonfading channel. Assume that a bit error probability of 10^{-3} is desired. Calculate (do not read off the figures) the fading margin for binary NFSK, BPSK, DPSK, and $\pi/4$–DQPSK in Rayleigh fading.

5–20. Repeat Problem 5–19 for:
   (a) 8-PSK and 16-PSK in Rayleigh fading (note that QPSK is the same as BPSK).
   (b) 8-DPSK and 16-DPSK in Rayleigh fading (note that DQPSK is the same as binary DPSK).

   You may read the required E_b/N_0 values from the appropriate curves.

5–21. Write a MATLAB program to evaluate the bit error probability for M-ary NFSK, DPSK, PSK, and QAM in Ricean fading.

5–22. Referring to Problem 5–19 for the definition of fading margin, and having done the program for Problem 5–21, evaluate the fade margin for a bit error probability of 10^{-3} for the four modulation schemes of Problem 5–21 in Ricean fading and the following K-factors with $M = 4$, 8, and 16 for NFSK, DPSK, and PSK and $M = 4$, 16, and 64 for QAM (make up a table in each case):

(a) $K = -10$ dB (note that as a check on your results, these should be fairly close to the answers found in Problem 5–19 for $M = 2$).

(b) $K = 10$ dB.

(c) $K = 0$ dB.

5–23. Show that (5–44) results by integration of (5–43).

5–24. Average (5–41) with respect to a noncentral chi-squared probability density function, thus obtaining proper integral expressions for PSK and DPSK in Ricean fading with diversity. (I.e., show all steps in deriving (5–65).) Write a MATLAB program to plot bit error probabilities versus E_b/N_0. Plot curves for some cases of interest. Does an optimum order of diversity exist for any situation?

5–25. Repeat Problem 5–24 for NFSK. Show that the result for the average bit error probability in Ricean fading is

$$\bar{P}_{s,\text{Rice,div}} = \sum_{k=1}^{M-1} \binom{M-1}{k} \frac{(-1)^{k+1}}{k+1} \left[1 + \frac{k}{(k+1)(K+1)} \frac{\bar{E}_s}{N_0} \right]^{-L}$$

$$\times \exp\left[-\frac{\dfrac{kK}{(k+1)(K+1)} \dfrac{\bar{E}_s}{N_0}}{1 + \dfrac{k}{(k+1)(K+1)} \dfrac{\bar{E}_s}{N_0}} \right]$$

Note that this is the same as (5–59), except that the factor in front of the exponent is raised to the $-L$ power instead of the -1 power. Plot a couple of cases.

5–26. Write a MATLAB program to do phasor plots like those shown in Figures 5–31 and 5–32.

5–27. Generalize the MATLAB program of Problem 5–25 to do plots of modulated signal envelope.

5–28. Generalize the MATLAB program of Problem 5–25 to plot eye diagrams.

6

Fundamentals of Information Theory and Block Coding

6.1 INTRODUCTION

In the previous chapters it has been shown that the information-bearing signal generated at the transmitter may not be correctly interpreted at the receiver due to distortion of the signal in the channel between the transmitter and receiver. This distortion may cause the matched filter detector in the receiver to make errors. A good communications system design will minimize the probability of making these errors by making wise use of the resources of power and bandwidth while simultaneously maintaining reasonable system cost (complexity). The study of information theory in this chapter will show that there are fundamental theoretical bounds relating error probability, transmitter and interference power, signal bandwidth, and system complexity. These relationships are used to evaluate the feasibility of achieving a specified system error probability performance using available resources and to gain insight into the techniques used to achieve this performance. The field of information theory began with the works of Shannon [1, 2] in the late 1940s. Since that time many researchers have extended the basic results [3–6] and have invented detailed techniques for communicating efficiently. The entire field of error control is devoted to the development of techniques to achieve the performance that Shannon proved possible. A number of important error-control techniques will be discussed in this and the next two chapters. Although the presentation in this text considers error-control and modulation theory separately, these two subjects are tied closely together. Modern research in communications considers modulation and coding as a single problem.

Study of this chapter will give the reader an understanding of what communications performance is possible given various system constraints. In addition, the study of various error-control techniques will give the reader an understanding of the underlying principles of error control and a repertoire of techniques for achieving the desired performance. The error-control techniques that will be discussed include block coding, convolutional coding, and automatic repeat request systems using error detection. (The later two are the subjects of Chapters 7 and 8, respectively). Consideration will be limited to Gaussian noise interference and, in most instances, results will be presented without proof.

Figure 6–1 is a very simplified block diagram of a communications system showing the components of interest in this chapter. The only function of the communications system is to transmit information reliably from the source to the user. The source output is a

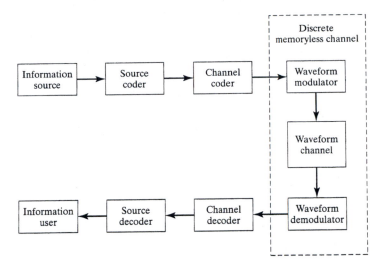

FIGURE 6–1 Communications system model.

sequence of symbols from some discrete alphabet. These symbols are processed by a source encoder that removes dependencies between symbols and assigns source codewords to symbols or groups of symbols in order to minimize the number of symbols transmitted to the users. The source coder output is input to a channel coder. The channel coder improves communications efficiency by converting source coder output sequences to a different sequence of symbols from a (possibly) different alphabet. The reasons and techniques for this conversion will be detailed later. The encoder outputs are transmitted through the discrete memoryless channel (DMC) to the channel decoder. As discussed in Chapter 1, a DMC is a useful model for the communications path between the input to the waveform modulator and the demodulator output. The DMC model includes the effects of signal distortion in the waveform channel. Using the output of the DMC, the channel decoder attempts to reconstruct the sequence originally output from the source coder. A properly designed encoder/decoder will be able to correct some of the transmission errors that occur in the DMC thus improving communications reliability. Using the channel decoder output, the source decoder constructs an estimate of the transmitted information sequence.

The subjects of information and coding theory are complex. The discussion here is brief and is intended to be introductory. The reader is referred to the text by Wozencraft and Jacobs [7] for a detailed advanced analysis of the fundamental concepts of modern communication theory including waveform design, coding, and information theory. Wozencraft and Jacobs is highly recommended reading for further study. The text by Gallager [6] is an extremely well-written treatment of information theory. Lin and Costello [8] provide a very understandable and detailed review of coding theory and applications. References [9] through [13] provide additional advanced treatments of coding and information theory for the interested reader.

6.2 BASIC CONCEPTS OF INFORMATION THEORY

The study of information theory is classically partitioned into the study of source coding and the study of channel coding. The following paragraphs continue that tradition. As illustrated in Figure 6–1, the output of the information source is input to the *source encoder.* The function of the source encoder is to reduce the average number of data bits per unit of time that must be transmitted to the user over the channel to the minimum possible. When source coding is not the subject of investigation, it will be convenient to group the source encoder with the information source and to call the result the information source. The output of the information source is input to the *channel encoder.* Channel encoding or simply "coding" is the subject of the majority of this chapter. Within this section performance bounds for both source coding and channel coding are presented from an information theoretic point of view.

6.2.1 Source Coding

There are many possible sources of information ranging from typewritten pages to video images to digitized analog voice to the binary content of a computer memory. All analog sources are assumed to have been converted to a discrete-time sequence of discrete symbols w_i from an alphabet $W = \{0, 1, 2, \ldots, q_w - 1\}$ by the process of sampling and analog-to-digital conversion. The subscript "i" in w_i is the discrete-time index. During any time interval i, w_i can be any one of the q_w distinct symbols $0, 1, 2, \ldots, q_w - 1$. The source outputs one symbol each T_m seconds (m denotes message). The symbols are *not* presumed to be output with equal probability; the probability that the source outputs a symbol $w_i = j$ is $Q_w(j)$, where $j = 0, 1, 2, \ldots, q_w - 1$. Symbols are assumed to be independent from one source output symbol to the next, that is, for different time indices. Sources whose output symbols are independent are called *memoryless sources.* The output of a source is said to possess *redundancy* if its output symbols are not equally likely or if they are not statistically independent. The number of symbols and the sampling rate required to represent an analog source is a function of the required fidelity of the information received by the user; this reasonably complex subject will not be discussed further. The interested reader is referred to the text by Viterbi and Omura [12] for a detailed treatment of source coding.

One of the important concepts of information theory is the definition of the information content of a sequence of source symbols. If the alphabet size is q_w, each symbol could be represented by $\log_2 q_w$ binary symbols $\{0, 1\}$ giving a source bit rate of[1]

$$R_m = \frac{1}{T_m} \log_2 q_w \quad \text{bits/second} \tag{6-1}$$

or

$$R'_m = \log_2 q_w \quad \text{bits/symbol}$$

[1]If q_w is not an exact power of 2, substitute the next larger power of 2 for q_w in (6–1).

Although the source output sequence could be represented by a bit stream having a rate R_m bits per second, it is usually possible to represent the sequence using a bit stream with a lower rate. The minimum possible bit rate is equal to the average information content of the sequence of symbols. The information content of each symbol is [6, 12]

$$I(j) = -\log_2 Q_w(j), \quad j = 0, 1, 2, \ldots, q_w - 1 \tag{6–2}$$

which is a function of the probability of the occurrence of that symbol. This formula says that symbols that are less likely to occur have more information content than do symbols that are more likely to occur. That this is reasonable can be seen by observing that using $I(j)$ binary digits to transmit each symbol will result in using the most bits for the least often used symbols and the least bits for the most often used symbols. In the limit where $q_w = 1$, $Q_w(1) = 1.0$ and $I(1) = 0$, indicating that the single symbol source alphabet contains no information content whatsoever. This is in agreement with intuition which says that if the symbol is known [i.e., $Q_w(1) = 1$], there is no need to transmit it to the user. The average information content of the source is $H(W)$ where

$$H(W) = -\sum_{j=0}^{q_w-1} Q_w(j) \log_2 Q_w(j) \quad \text{bits/symbol} \tag{6–3}$$

This average information content is called the *entropy* of the source. It can be shown that the entropy of a source is maximum when all symbols are equally probable. To convert these results to bits per second, the entropy should be multiplied by the source rate in symbols per second.

Associating the same number of bits with each symbol results in a bit rate equal to R_m' bits per symbol. The function of the source encoder is to reduce the average number of bits per symbol as much as possible prior to channel encoding and transmission. Associating the highly likely symbols with short codewords and the least likely symbols with long codewords accomplishes this. The best that can be done is making the length of each codeword equal to $-\log_2 Q_w(j)$, which results in an average codeword length given by Equation (6–3).

EXAMPLE 6–1

Consider a source that produces one of three possible symbols A, B, or C with respective probabilities 0.7, 0.2, and 0.1 during successive signaling intervals.

(a) Find the information one gains by being told that w_i was emitted, $w_i = A, B, C$.

(b) Find the average information, or entropy, of the source output.

(c) If 1000 symbols per second are emitted by the source, find the average information rate.

(d) What is the worst case information rate if no source coding is used?

Solution: The computations for $I(j)$ and $H(W)$ are

$$I(A) = -\log_2 (0.7) = 0.515$$

$$I(B) = -\log_2 (0.2) = 2.322$$

$$I(C) = -\log_2 (0.1) = 3.322$$

and

$$H(W) = (0.7 \times 0.515) + (0.2 \times 2.322) + (0.1 \times 3.322)$$

$$= 1.157 \quad \text{bits/symbol}$$

The average information rate is therefore 1157 bits/second. The maximum possible information rate and source entropy is achieved if the source output symbols are equally likely, giving

$$R_{max} = 1000 \log_2 3 = 1585 \quad \text{bits/second}$$

EXAMPLE 6–2 _____

An example of a source code that provides redundancy reduction is the *Morse code* in which short codewords are assigned to the most frequently occurring English letters. For example, an E is assigned the codeword DIT, while some of the more infrequently occurring letters, such as J, Q, and Y, are assigned combinations of three DAHs and a DIT. This is an example of a *variable-length* source code.

The mathematical science of information theory provides both a lower bound on the average length of a variable-length source code as well as a means for finding codes whose average length achieve or approach this lower bound. The source entropy $H(W)$ is the lower bound on the average number of bits/symbol which must be transmitted.

One method of source coding is the *Huffman procedure,* named after its inventor [14]. The Huffman procedure is most easily explained by example using a binary output alphabet. Consider a source with three output symbols *A, B,* or *C* with respective probabilities of occurrence of 0.70, 0.20, and 0.10. The entropy of this source is 1.157 bits/symbol as found in Example 6–1. The Huffman procedure for encoding this source into a variable-length binary code begins by listing the source output symbols in descending order of their probability of occurrence as on the left side of Figure 6–2. Each symbol is shown in a box with its probability of occurrence written immediately above. The least probable pair of source symbols is then combined to produce what is referred to as a reduced source. The probability of the combined symbol is the sum of the probabilities of the symbols combined to produce it. This step is illustrated in the second column of Figure 6–2, where *B* and *C* have been combined into symbol *BC,* which has probability 0.20 + 0.10 = 0.30. Lines are shown connecting the original symbols with the first reduction. Only the lines connecting symbols being combined are labeled with a "0" and a "1." The symbols of the reduced source are now reordered by descending order of their respective probabilities. The reduced source contains one less symbol than the input source. Source reductions are continued until a single combined symbol remains that has probability 1.0.

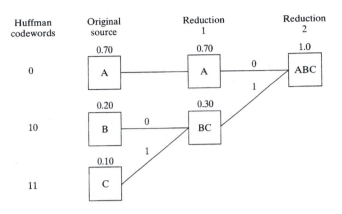

FIGURE 6–2 Huffman source coding procedure.

The output of the Huffman coder for each of the original symbols is simply the sequence of 0s and 1s found on the branches leading from the final combined symbol to the original source symbol. Again, symbols are assigned only to branches where symbols are combined. These Huffman codewords are shown in Figure 6–2. Observe that the low probability input symbols have been assigned longer codewords than the higher probability symbols. If the length of the jth codeword is denoted by ℓ_j and the probability of symbol j is $Q_w(j)$, the average codeword length is

$$L = \sum_{j=0}^{q_w - 1} \ell_j Q_w(j) \tag{6-4}$$

For the code obtained in Figure 6–2, the average codeword length is

$$L = (1 \times 0.70) + (2 \times 0.20) + (2 \times 0.10) = 1.30$$

which is larger than the minimum possible of 1.157 but considerably better than 2.00 bits per symbol required if no coding had been used.

Since the average code length is greater than the entropy of the source, one might ask if Huffman coding can achieve this lower bound on average codeword length. To achieve better results, symbols can be Huffman coded in pairs or triples rather than one at a time. If the source symbols are grouped two at a time and viewed as a new source, the resultant equivalent source is called the second extension of the actual source. Grouping three source symbols at a time results in the third extension and so on. Figure 6–3 shows the second extension of the source considered above together with the reductions necessary for obtaining the Huffman code for the extended source.

The average codeword length for the second extension of the source is 2.33 bits per extended source symbol. Since each codeword for the second extension represents two source symbols, the average number of bits per symbol is

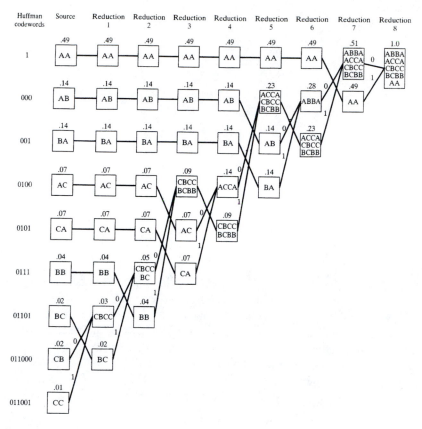

FIGURE 6–3   Huffman source coding for second extension of source.

$$L = \frac{L_2}{2} = 1.165 \quad \text{bits/source symbol}$$

This compares more favorably with the lower bound of $H(W) = 1.157$ bits/symbol than the 1.3 bits/symbol achieved by encoding one symbol at a time previously.

The average number of bits used per source symbol could be made closer to this lower bound by encoding the third extension of the source. To get a better intuitive feeling for the reduction in the number of code symbols per unit time, consider the following example.

EXAMPLE 6–3

A communication system can transmit and receive error-free binary symbols at a rate of 1250 bits/s. It is desired to send messages over this channel that are composed of sequences of three symbols A, B, C that occur with probabilities 0.7, 0.2, and 0.1, respectively. The source produces symbols at a rate of 1000 per second.

TABLE 6–1 Typical Sequence of Source Output Symbols and the Encoded Output for Three Cases

Source symbol	A	A	A	C	B	A	A	B	A	A	A	B	A	A	B	A	C	A	A	A
Fixed-length code	00	00	00	10	01	00	00	01	00	00	00	01	00	00	01	00	10	00	00	00
Huffman encoded source output	0	0	0	11	10	0	0	10	0	0	0	10	0	0	10	0	11	0	0	0
Huffman encoded output of the second extension		1		0100		001		000		1		000		1		001		0101		1

(a) Can a binary code with equal codeword lengths be used?

(b) Is it possible to use a variable-length code?

(c) Can a Huffman code for the raw source output be used?

(d) Can a Huffman code for the second extension be used?

Solution: The answer to part (a) is no, because fixed-length codewords of length 2 are required to encode the three source output symbols. The binary digit symbol rate from the encoder output will therefore be 2000 bits per second if a fixed-length code is used.

The answer to part (b) is yes, because $H(W) = 1.157$ bits/symbol, which means that the average bit rate at the output of an ideal variable-length encoder is 1157 bits per second. Since this is less than the rate at which the communications system can accept binary symbols, it is theoretically possible to design a variable-length binary code that allows the source output to be transmitted through the channel.

The answer to part (c) is no, because the Huffman coding of the raw source resulted in a bit rate of 1.3 bits per symbol or 1300 bits per second, which is beyond the channel's bit rate.

The answer to part (d) is yes, because a Huffman code for the second extension resulted in a code that required an average of 1.165 bits/source symbol. The average bit rate into the channel would therefore be 1165 bits per second, which is less than the 1250 bits per second that the communications system can support.

Note that the use of variable-length code requires a buffer to smooth the flow of binary digits from the encoder. A typical symbol pattern and bit streams using fixed-length and Huffman codes for the raw source output of the previous example and its second extension are shown in Table 6–1. The decrease in the average number of bits per symbol between the codes for the three cases is evident.

In summary, detailed consideration has been limited to discrete memoryless sources emitting one of q_w symbols each T_m seconds. In many real cases the output symbols are not equally probable, so that the information content of each symbol may be different. The information associated with a symbol $j \in W = \{0, 1, 2, \ldots, q_w - 1\}$ is $-\log_2 Q_w(j)$. The symbol sequence could be transmitted using a binary bit sequence with a rate of $(\log_2 q_w)/T_m$ bits per second. However, fewer bits per second can be used if source coding is employed. The minimum number of bits per source symbol that can be used is the entropy of the source $H(W)$. Huffman coding is one of a number of source coding strategies which achieve reduced bit rates by assigning fewer bits to the most probable symbols and more bits to less probable symbols.

6.2.2 Lempel-Ziv Procedures

In many instances a statistical description of the source sequence, for example, the probabilities of occurrence of the source symbols used in the Huffman procedure, is not *a priori* available. In this situation two options are available to the communications system designer. First, the source could be analyzed to create a statistical model after which the Huffman procedure could be used. Second, one of a number of universal source coding procedures could be used. *Universal source coding* procedures are source coding procedures that do not depend upon knowledge of a statistical model of the source. The procedures first defined by Jacob Ziv and Abraham Lempel [15,16] are widely used universal source coding procedures. In the following paragraphs one version of the 1977 Lempel-Ziv (LZ-77) encoding procedure and a modification of the 1978 Lempel-Ziv (LZ-78) procedure invented by Terry Welch [17] and denoted the Lempel-Ziv-Welch (LZW) procedure will be briefly described. Because of their effectiveness and simplicity these procedures are widely used. Specifically, the LZ-77 procedure was used in the popular personal computer hard disk drive compression products ("Stacker™" and Microsoft DOS 6.0) and the LZW procedure is used by the UNIX *compress* procedure.

The discussion of the detailed LZ-77 and LZW procedures is facilitated by the following definitions and notation. As before, the source alphabet is denoted by $\{0, 1, 2, \ldots, q - 1\}$ where q is the cardinality of the alphabet. The source output symbol at time k is denoted w_k and the source output over all time is denoted $\{w_k\}_{k=-\infty}^{\infty}$. The specific sequence to be encoded by the source coding procedure is the sequence or *string* $\{w_k\}_{k=1}^{N} \equiv \{w_1\ w_2\ w_3\ \ldots\ w_N\} \equiv W_1^N$ where N is assumed to be a very large integer. A direct symbol-by-symbol encoding of W_1^N requires $N\lceil \log_2 q \rceil$ *binary symbols* where $\lceil \log_2 q \rceil$ represents the smallest integer that is larger than $\log_2 q$. A subsequence or *substring* of this sequence beginning with symbol w_i and ending with symbol w_j, is denoted $W_i^j \equiv \{w_k\}_{k=i}^{j} \equiv \{w_i\ w_{i+1}\ w_{i+2}\ \ldots\ w_{j-1}\ w_j\}$. An arbitrary substring can be partitioned into a *prefix* $\omega \equiv W_i^{j-1}$ and the last symbol w_j of the substring, which will usually be called the *innovation symbol*. A substring is then the concatenation of the prefix and an innovation symbol denoted $\omega.w_j \equiv W_1^j$ where the "." denotes concatenation.

Consider first the **LZ-77 procedure** described in [15], which is referred to either as LZ-77 or the "sliding-window LZ algorithm." Some details of the description that follows are credited to A. Wyner and J. Ziv [18]. The string to be encoded is W_1^N. The encoder output will be a string of codewords $\{C_l\}_{l=0}^{L}$, which uniquely define W_1^N and which, hopefully, can be represented using fewer binary symbols than a direct symbol-by-symbol encoding of W_1^N. Each codeword C_l uniquely defines a substring Y_l of W_1^N. The length of the substrings Y_l varies with l; the goal of the procedure is to minimize the number of binary symbols required to represent $\{C_l\}_{l=0}^{L}$ thereby achieving the maximum compression. The Y_l are usually referred to as *phrases* of the source output. Each codeword C_l except the zeroth is the concatenation of two parameters L_l and m_l, which define the Y_l as a function of the n_w most recently encoded source output symbols. The parameter n_w, often assumed for convenience to be a power of 2, is called the *window size* of the procedure. Both the encoder and the decoder maintain a dictionary $D_1^{n_w}$ containing the n_w most recently encoded source symbols. Thus, when the phrase beginning with source symbol w_k is encoded, the dictionary contains the source symbols $W_{k-n_w}^{k-1}$. At the encoder $W_{k-n_w}^{k-1}$ is available directly from the source. At the decoder $W_{k-n_w}^{k-1}$ is the recent output of the decoding procedure. At the start of the procedure the dictionary is initialized with the first n_w symbols of W_1^N. For example, suppose that a binary alphabet is used, that $n_w = 8$, and that the first 24 symbols of W_1^N are $W_1^{24} = \{:0\ 0\ 1\ 0\ 1\ 0\ 0\ 1:0\ 0\ 0\ 0\ 1\ 1\ 0\ 1\ 1\ 0\ 1\ 1\ 0\ 0\ 0\}$.[2] The initial dictionary is $D_1^8 = \{0\ 0\ 1\ 0\ 1\ 0\ 0\ 1\}$, which is also illustrated in W_1^{24} between the symbols ":" as was done by Wyner and Ziv [18]. The procedure begins by defining the first codeword C_0 to be the initial dictionary. C_0 is thus stored (or transmitted) without source coding or compression and, for the example, $C_0 = Y_0 = \{0\ 0\ 1\ 0\ 1\ 0\ 0\ 1\}$. In general $C_0 = Y_0 = W_1^{n_w}$ and the number of bits required to store or transmit C_0 is $n_w \lceil \log_2 q \rceil$.

Next, the procedure determines C_1 by searching for the longest possible phrase Y_1 beginning with w_{n_w+1} such that a *copy* of Y_1 starting in the first n_w source symbols, that is, starting in the dictionary, and ending $L_1 \geq 1$ time units later exists. The index of the dictionary symbol where the copy of Y_1 begins is denoted p. Index $p = 1$ corresponds to the leftmost symbol in the dictionary. Define $m_1 = n_w - p$ and note $0 \leq m_1 \leq n_w - 1$. Returning to the example, $w_{n_w+1} = w_9 = 0$. The encoder tries $L_1 = 1$ and finds a copy of the phrase $Y_1 = W_9^9$ starting at $p = 1, 2, 4, 6,$ or 7 or equivalently $m_1 = 7, 6, 4, 2,$ or 1 indicated by the underscores in $W_1^N = \{:\underline{0}\ 0\ 1\ \underline{0}\ 1\ \underline{0}\ \underline{0}\ 1:0\ 0\ 0\ 0\ 1\ 1\ 0\ 1\ 1\ 0\ 1\ 1\ 0\ 0\ 0\}$. The encoder then increments L_1 so that $L_1 = 2$ and $Y_1 = W_9^{10} = \{\ 0\ 0\ \}$ and searches for a copy of Y_1 starting in the dictionary. A copy of Y_1 is found starting at $p = 1$ or 6 or equivalently $m_1 = 7$ or 2 again indicated by underlines $W_1^N = \{:\underline{0\ 0}\ 1\ 0\ 1\ \underline{0\ 0}\ 1:0\ 0\ 0\ 0\ 1\ 1\ 0\ 1\ 1\ 0\ 1\ 1\ 0\ 0\ 0\}$, L_1 is incremented again so that $L_1 = 3$ so that $Y_1 = W_9^{11} = \{000\}$ and the encoder searches for a copy of Y_1. There is no sequence $\{000\}$ beginning in the dictionary so the *previous* $Y_1 = \{00\}$ is used and the encoder output for phrase 1 is $m_1 = 2, L_1 = 2$ and $C_1 \equiv [L_1, m_1] = [2,2]$. When there is a choice for m_1, the smallest is arbitrarily selected. Having determined C_1, the encoder updates the dictionary by deleting the L_1 oldest symbols and adding the L_1 most recently encoded symbols so that $W_1^N = \{0\ 0:1\ 0\ 1\ 0\ 0\ 1\ 0\ 0:0\ 0\ 0\ 1\ 1\ 0\ 1\ 1\ 0\ 1\ 1\ 0\ 0\ 0\}$ and $D_1^8 = \{1\ 0\ 1\ 0\ 0\ 1\ 0\ 0\}$.

Next, the procedure searches for the longest possible phrase Y_2 beginning with $w_{n_w+L_1+1}$ such that a copy of Y_2 starting at $w_{n_w+L_1-m_2}$ in the updated dictionary and ending L_2 time units later exists. Trying first $Y_2 = \{w_{8+2+1}\} = \{0\}$, then trying $Y_2 = \{w_{8+2+1}\ w_{8+2+2}\} = \{0\ 0\}$, and $Y_2 = \{0\ 0\ 0\}$, and finally trying $Y_2 = \{0\ 0\ 0\ 1\}$, it is found that $Y_2 = \{0\ 0\ 0\}$ with $L_2 = 3$ and $m_2 = 0$ or 1 is the longest phrase that begins within the dictionary. Observe that Y_2 does NOT and is not required to end within the dictionary. The encoder output is $C_2 = [3, 0]$. The results for the entire encoding procedure are detailed in Table 6–2, where the last column illustrates the location of the phrase in the dictionary by underlining and the phrase itself by the overbar.

---

[2]This sequence was created by random draw from a binary alphabet where $\Pr[0] = 0.65$ and $\Pr[1] = 0.35$.

TABLE 6-2 Lempel-Ziv 77 Encoding Procedure

l	$D_1^{n_w}$	Y_l	L_l	m_l	C_l	Dictionary and phrase locations
0		{00101001}			{00101001}	
1	{00101001}	{00}	2	2	$[2,2]^3$	{:00101001:$\overline{000001}$1011011000}
2	{10100100}	{000}	3	0	[3, 0]	{00:10100100:$\overline{000}$1011011000}
3	{00100000}	{1}	1	5	[1, 5]	{00101:00$\underline{100000}$:$\overline{1}$1011011000}
4	{01000001}	{10}	2	6	[2, 6]	{001010:0$\underline{1000001}$:$\overline{10}$1011000}
5	{00000110}	{110110}	6	2	[6, 2]	{00101001:00000$\underline{110}$:$\overline{11011}$000}
6	{10110110}	{00}	2	0	[2, 0]	{00101001 000001:10110$\underline{110}$:$\overline{00}$}

Consider now the encoding of C_l into binary sequences such that successive codewords can be distinguished directly from the stored or transmitted binary encoder output sequence. This encoding begins with a comma free encoding of L_l. A *comma free* encoding is a binary encoding such that the decoder can distinguish the beginning of a new codeword directly from the binary sequence so that the decoder does not require flags, or commas, to declare the start of a new codeword. An appropriate comma free encoding is presented by Wyner and Ziv in [18]. A description of the Wyner/Ziv encoding follows. For any positive integer k define $b(k)$ to be the binary representation of k and $|b(k)| = \lceil \log_2 (k+1) \rceil$ to be the number of bits in this binary representation. Next, define a binary sequence of $k - 1$ zeros followed by a 1 by $u(k) \equiv 0^{k-1}1$. With these definitions the comma free representation of L_l is given by [18]

$$e(L_l) = \hat{e}(|b(L_l)|).b(L_l)$$

where

$$\hat{e}(p_l) = u(|b(p_l)|).b(p_l)$$

For example consider $L_5 = 6$. The binary representation $b(6) = \{110\}$ contains 3 bits. Thus, $|b(L_5)| = p_5 = 3$. The binary representation of p_5 is $b(p_5) = b(3) = \{11\}$, which contains 2 bits so that $\hat{e}(p_5) = \hat{e}(3) = u(2).b(3) = \{0111\}$ and $e(L_5) = e(6) = \{0111\}.\{110\} = \{0111110\}$. Upon receiving the sequence $\{0111110\}$, the decoder recognizes $\{01\}$ and determines that the next two bits $\{11\}$ are the binary representation of the number of bits, 3, in the binary representation of L_l. The next 3 bits $\{110\}$ are the binary representation of $L_5 = 6$. This comma free encoding works for any positive integer value of L_l. The encoding of m_l is much simpler since $0 \le m_l \le n_w - 1$ and n_w was presumed to be a power of two. Thus the encoding of m_l requires exactly $\log_2 n_w$ binary bits. Table 6-3 gives the values of L_l, m_l, and C_l for the example of Table 6-2. For this example $n_w = 8$ so that 3 bits are required to represent m_l. The complete binary sequence representing W_1^N is

{0010100101101001001101100011110101101011001111100100110100000}

---

[3]The mapping of m_l and L_l into a binary sequence will be discussed later.

TABLE 6–3 Lempel-Ziv 77 Encoding Procedure (continued)

l	L_l	$b(L_l)$	$|b(L_l)| = k$	$b(k)$	$|b(k)|$	$u(|b(k)|)$	$e(L_l)$	m_l	$b(m_l)$	C_l
0							{00101001}			{00101001}
1	2	{10}	2	{10}	2	{01}	{011010}	2	{010}	{011010010}
2	3	{11}	2	{10}	2	{01}	{011011}	0	{000}	{011011000}
3	1	{1}	1	{1}	1	{1}	{111}	5	{101}	{111101}
4	2	{10}	2	{10}	2	{01}	{011010}	6	{110}	{011010110}
5	6	{110}	3	{11}	2	{01}	{0111110}	2	{010}	{0111110010}
6	2	{10}	2	{10}	2	{01}	{011010}	0	{000}	{011010000}

Unfortunately, this example has resulted in an encoder output of 60 bits to represent the input string, which contained only 24 bits. Examples illustrating the desired compression would be much longer than 24 bits so that the dictionary could be much longer improving the chances that longer phrases could be encoded. A slight extension of the LZ-77 described in [18] would decrease the length of the encoded sequence even for short sequence lengths. The reader is referred to [18] for details of this extension.

The LZ-77 decoder receives the 60-bit sequence and has knowledge that the window size $n_w = 8$. The decoder can therefore read the first 8 received bits directly into the dictionary. Next, the decoder reads a sequence of 0s followed by the first 1 to determine the length of the encoding of p_1. In the example, the initial dictionary is followed by {01}, indicating that the following 2 bits {10} are a binary encoding of p_1, which can then be found with the result $p_1 = 2$. The decoder now knows that the binary representation of L_1 is the next 2 bits {10} so that $L_1 = 2$. Having determined L_1, the decoder knows that the following 3 bits {010} represent m_1 and, in this case, $m_1 = 2$. With knowledge of L_1 and m_1 the decoder knows that the phrase Y_1 is two symbols long and begins at position $8 - 2 = 6$. The initial dictionary is $D_1^8 = W_1^8 = \{00101001\}$, so that $Y_1 = \{w_6\, w_7\} = \{00\}$. The phrase Y_1 is appended to the dictionary and the decoder has now recovered the first ten bits of W_1^{24}, specifically, $W_1^{10} = \{00 : 10100100 : \}$. The last $n_w = 8$ symbols of W_1^{10} or W_3^{10} become the new dictionary. The next phrase is decoded similarly with the results $p_2 = 2$, $L_2 = 3$ and $m_2 = 0$, and the phrase Y_2 is three bits long beginning at symbol $8 - 0 = 8$ of the updated dictionary; thus $Y_2 = \{000\}$. The phrase Y_2 is appended to the 10 bits previously decoded to obtain $W_1^{13} = \{00101 : 00100000 : \}$. Observe that, since the encoder copy of Y_2 overlapped Y_2 itself, the decoding operation must define the first symbol of Y_2 before the second symbol can be defined. To accomplish this the following sequence of assignments are made in order: $w_{10} \rightarrow w_{11}$ followed by $w_{11} \rightarrow w_{12}$ followed by $w_{12} \rightarrow w_{13}$. Decoding continues similarly until the original sequence is completely reconstructed.

The **Lempel-Ziv-Welch procedure** [17] is a second popular version of the Lempel-Ziv family of universal source coding procedures. The LZW procedure differs from the LZ-77 procedure primarily in the manner in which the dictionary is created and used. Rather than use the previous n_w source symbols as a dictionary, the LZW procedure creates a dictionary that contains a list of previously encountered *phrases* along with an associated codeword. The initial dictionary contains only the length-one phrases correspond-ing to the source alphabet. There are thus q code-words in the initial dictionary. The en-coder examines the string of source output symbols until a phrase (i.e., string) occurs that is NOT in the dictionary. The just-identified phrase is added to the dictionary along with its associated codeword and the encoder outputs the codeword corresponding to the prefix of the just-identified phrase. The source output symbol that caused the just-identified phrase to differ from previous phrase, called the *innovation symbol,* becomes the initial symbol of the next phrase to be encoded. Assume here that codewords are positive inte-gers assigned in order. Because each new phrase is the concatenation of a previously en-countered phase and an innovation symbol, the new phrase may alternately be identified by the concatenation of the *codeword* of its prefix and the innovation symbol. The dictio-nary grows over time and will eventually exceed its allocated memory; when this over-flow occurs, the most infrequently used (or perhaps the oldest) phrases are deleted. Both the encoder and the decoder must, of course, use the same procedure for purging code-words.

As before, the sequence W_1^N will be encoded. Recall that any sequence W_i^j may be viewed as the concatenation of its prefix $\omega \equiv W_i^{j-1}$ and an innovation symbol w_j. That is $W_i^j = W_i^{j-1} . w_j$. The codeword associated with the prefix ω is denoted $C(\omega)$ and the en-coder output codeword at time l is denoted C_l. The inverse of a codeword or the phrase ω corresponding to codeword m is denoted $C^{-1}(m) = \omega$. The following is a formal descrip-tion of the encoding procedure [17].

Lempel-Ziv-Welch Encoder
Initialize the dictionary with all length-one phrases.
$k = 1; l = 0$
Read symbol w_1
$w_1 \rightarrow \omega$
10     $k + 1 \rightarrow k$
If $\{k \leq N\}$ then
        Read symbol w_k
        If $\{ \omega.w_k$ is in dictionary $\}$ then
            $\omega.w_k \rightarrow \omega$
            Go to 10
        Else
            $l + 1 \rightarrow l ; C(\omega) \rightarrow C_l$
            Add $\omega.w_k$ and its codeword to the dictionary
            $w_k \rightarrow \omega$
            Go to 10
        Endif
Else
        $C(\omega) \rightarrow C_l$
        Exit
End of procedure

EXAMPLE 6–4

Use the LZW procedure to encode the 24-bit sequence $W_1{}^{24} = \{00101101\ 100001101101100\}$. The complete encoding procedure is illustrated in Figure 6–4, which shows the 24 binary input symbols at the top, the 12 output codewords at the bottom and the dictionary at the right. The initial dictionary is the portion of the dictionary shown above the dashed line. Each phrase encountered by the encoder is shown in the middle of the figure where the first phrase encountered is at the top left and the last phrase encountered is at the bottom right. Each phrase is written above a bar that is colored black beneath the prefix of the phrase and white beneath the innovation symbol.

The encoder begins by reading the first source symbol $w_1 = 0$, which becomes the initial prefix ω, followed the second source symbol $w_2 = 0$. The phrase $\omega.w_2 = \{00\}$ is not found in the initial dictionary so it is added and assigned to codeword 3. Codeword 3 may alternately be defined as $C(\omega).w_2 = C(0).w_2 = 1.0$ where the periods indicate concatenation and are not decimal points. After adding codeword 3 to the dictionary, the encoder outputs $C(0) = 1$ as shown. Using the innovation symbol of the first phrase as the start of the prefix of the second phrase, $\omega = w_2 = 0$, the encoder reads $w_3 = 1$, creates the phrase $\omega.w_3 = \{01\}$ and searches the dictionary. The phrase $\{01\}$ is not in the dictionary so it is added as assigned to codeword 4 as illustrated and the encoder again outputs $C(0) = 1$ as shown. The encoder proceeds in this manner until the entire input sequence has been encoded. Observe the each new phrase is extended one symbol at a time until the resulting phrase cannot be found in the dictionary. At this time the newly created phrase is entered into the dictionary, the codeword of the prefix of the new phrase is output, and the procedure begins again.

The LZW decoding procedure is straightforward. The decoding of each received codeword is accomplished via an iterative procedure using the alternate representation of the codewords. Reconsidering the previous example, suppose the codeword 12 is received. The alternate representation of codeword 12 is 11.1, meaning that phrase 12 is the concatenation of the phrase represented by codeword 11 and the innovation symbol 1. Similarly, the alternate representation of codeword 11 is 6.0, meaning the phrase 11 is the concatenation of the phrase defined by codeword 6 and the innovation symbol 0. The alternate representation of codeword 6 is 4.1 so that phrase 6 is the concatenation of phrase 4 and the innovation symbol 1, and, finally, the alternate representation of codeword 4 is 1.1, meaning that phrase 4 is simply phrase 1 concatenated with 0. This iterative procedure may be written $C^{-1}(12) = C^{-1}(11).1 = C^{-1}(6).0.1 = C^{-1}(4).1.0.1 = C^{-1}(1).1.1.$ $0.1 = 0.1.1.0.1 = \{01101\}$. This process depends on the fact that the necessary phrases and their associated codewords are in the dictionary when they are needed. The decoding procedure must therefore include the timely generation of the dictionary from the received sequence of codewords.

At the commencement of the decoding procedure the decoder dictionary is initialized, just as it was in the encoder, with codewords corresponding to the source alphabet. A phrase is added to the decoder dictionary after each new codeword is received, except for the first. The first decoder input codeword always represents a single source symbol that is already in the decoder dictionary. This first received codeword C_1 also represents the *prefix* $\omega = C^{-1}(C_1)$ of the first multiple-symbol phrase entered into the encoder dictio-

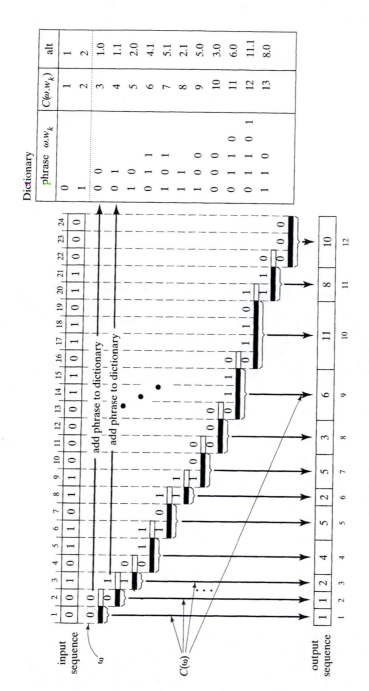

FIGURE 6–4 Lempel-Ziv-Welch encoding procedure; Example 6–4.

nary and which will be added to the decoder dictionary as soon as its innovation symbol is known. This innovation symbol will be known to the decoder as soon as the second decoder input codeword C_2 is known. The second codeword also represents a single source symbol, which is $w_2 = C^{-1}(C_2)$. Thus, after the first two decoder input codewords C_1 and C_2 are known, a new entry $\omega.w_2$ is made in the decoder dictionary. Similarly, every subsequent received codeword represents the prefix ω of a new entry into the decoder dictionary and the entry is completed when the innovation symbol is determined from the next input codeword; the innovation symbol is the first symbol of the next decoded codeword.

For example, consider the reception of the fourth codeword $C_4 = 4$ in the example above. At the time C_4 is input, the decoder dictionary contains codewords 1 through 4, since codewords 1 and 2 are the original codebook entries, codeword 3 was defined after C_1 and C_2 were processed, and codeword 4 was defined after C_2 and C_3 were processed. Similarly, when the eighth codeword is input, the decoder dictionary will contain definitions of codewords 1 through 8 and will know the prefix {10} of codeword 9. The prefix of codeword 9 was determined when the seventh codeword was decoded. The eighth codeword is $C_8 = 3$, which is decoded as $C^{-1}(3) = C^{-1}(1).0 = 0.0 = \{00\}$. The first (leftmost) symbol of {00} is the innovation symbol of codeword 9. Concatenating the known prefix {10} and the innovation symbol {0}, the ninth codeword can now be defined as {100}. The decoded eighth codeword is the prefix {00} of the tenth codeword.

The simplified decoding procedure just described works most of the time. However, it fails when certain sequences appear at the source output [17]. For certain sequences (to be defined in detail later) the decoding dictionary will not contain all of the phrases needed for decoding at the proper time.

EXAMPLE 6–5

Decode the codeword sequence $W_1^{12} = \{1, 1, 2, 4, 5, 2, 5, 3, 6, 11, 8, 10\}$. Figure 6–5 illustrates the decoding procedure. The decoder dictionary is initialized with codewords 1 and 2 for the binary source alphabet. Thus, the decoder immediately decodes $C_1 = 1$ and outputs $C^{-1}(1) = 0$. The second received symbol, $C_2 = 1$, is decoded similarly. After decoding C_2, the decoder constructs the phrase for codeword 3, by concatenating the 0 from the first codeword with the first (and only) symbol of the second codeword to obtain phrase $C^{-1}(3) = \{00\}$. Phrase 3 is then entered into the dictionary. Observe that codeword 3 can be entered into the dictionary only AFTER codewords 1 and 2 are received and decoded.

The decoder now examines $C_3 = 2$, which is a known codeword. C_3 is decoded and the decoder is now able to construct $C^{-1}(4) = \{01\}$ and further expand the dictionary. This straightforward decoding procedure continues until codeword $C_{10} = 11$ is received. Prior to receiving codeword 11 the decoder has just added codeword 10 to the dictionary. Thus, codeword 11 is received and is not yet in the dictionary. The reception of a not-yet-defined codeword occurs for specific encoder input sequences *where a codeword is used by the encoder immediately after it is defined.* Examining Figure 6–4, observe that codeword 11 is used immediately after it is defined. Fortunately, the decoder can accommodate this event since it knows precisely what caused it. Specifically, the decoder knows that the undefined phrase is the extension of the phrase it has just decoded. In the example, the decoder knows that the prefix ω of codeword phrase 11 is the just-decoded phrase {011}. Further, the decoder knows

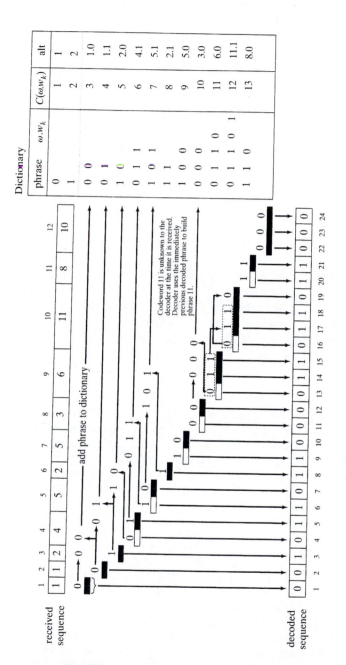

FIGURE 6–5 Lempel-Ziv-Welch decoding procedure; Example 6–5.

that the innovation symbol for phrase 11 is the first symbol {0} of the same just-decoded phrase. Concatenating {011} and {0}, the decoder creates codeword phrase 11 or $C^{-1}(11) = \{0110\}$ when can now be entered into the dictionary. The decoding of codeword 11 is illustrated by the dashed boxes and arrows in Figure 6–5.

The complete LZW decoding procedure including the accommodation of the problem discussed in the example was defined by Welch in [17]. The received sequence is denoted $\{C_1\}_1^L$. Defining temporary variables C_o, C_{old}, C_{in}, x, and y and a stack[4] that is used to properly order the output symbols, the decoding procedure is:

Lempel-Ziv-Welch Decoder
$l = 1; k = 1$
Read C_1
$C_1 \rightarrow C_o \rightarrow C_{old}$
$C^{-1}[C_o] \rightarrow X_1 \rightarrow y \rightarrow x$
100   $l + 1 \rightarrow l$
      If $\{l > L\}$ then exit
            Read C_l
            $C_l \rightarrow C_{in} \rightarrow C_o$
            If $\{C_o$ is not in dictionary$\}$ then
                Push x onto stack
                $C_{old} \rightarrow C_o$
            Endif
200   If $\{C_o$ is in dictionary AND $C_0 > A\}$ then
            $s = \omega.y = C^{-1}[C_o]$
            Push y onto stack
            $C(\omega) \rightarrow C_o$
            Go to 200
      Elseif $\{C_o$ is in dictionary AND $C_0 \le A\}$
            $k + 1 \rightarrow k$
            $C^{-1}[C_0] \rightarrow y$
            $y \rightarrow X_k$
            $y \rightarrow x$
            Pop all symbols from stack:
                  $k + 1 \rightarrow k$
                  $X_k =$ symbol removed from stack
            Add the string $C_{old}.y$ to the dictionary.
            $C_{in} \rightarrow C_{old}$
            Go to 100

---

[4]A stack is a first-in last-out buffer. For example, if the sequence c, e, f, g, r were "pushed" onto a stack, successive "pops" from the stack would result in the sequence r, g, f, e, c.

This completes the discussion of the Lempel-Ziv family of universal source coding procedures. These procedures are important since they are widely used. The performance of these procedures has been extensively analyzed in the literature [15,16, 18–22]. In this literature the reader will find detailed analyses of how well these algorithms compress the source as well as discussion of a number of variations on the procedures themselves.

6.2.3   Channel Coding and Capacity

6.2.3.1 General Considerations.   The mathematical concept of channel capacity and the associated theorems that bound transmission error probability are the most important concepts in communications. The capacity of a channel C is the number of information bits per second that can theoretically be transmitted with arbitrarily low error rate over the channel. Capacity is a function of the ratio of signal power to noise power, and a function of bandwidth. If the output of the source coder is a binary sequence with a rate R_m bits per second that is less than C, the transmission error rate can be reduced to any desired level by using forward error correction (FEC) techniques *without increasing transmitter power* above the value for which the capacity was calculated. The price paid for reducing the error rate is increased complexity and bandwidth. One strategy for reducing the error probability is block coding where source encoder outputs are collected for T seconds and processed as a block. In this time a block of $T \times R_m = k$ source bits would be collected. There are 2^k possible distinct blocks of k binary bits that could be collected in this time. These source bits are mapped into one of 2^k waveforms for transmission over the physical channel. The 2^k channel waveforms are chosen very carefully as are the associations between channel waveforms and information bit sequences. One of many means of constructing the channel waveforms is to construct a sequence of time orthogonal (i.e., nonoverlapping in time) symbols, each with duration T_s, using one of the digital modulation schemes discussed in Chapters 3 and 4. For example, the T-second waveform could be a sequence of $n = T/T_s$ BPSK symbols. Assume for now that $T_s < 1/R_m$, so that $n > k$. With this scheme there are a total of 2^n waveforms that *could* be transmitted in T seconds; 2^k of these are associated with valid messages. The selected waveform is sent over the channel to the receiver. During this transmission, noise is added to the waveform. The received signal and noise are processed by the demodulator and decoder to produce an estimate of the original k source bits. It can be shown [6] that the probability that the receiver channel decoder makes an error is bounded by

$$P_B \le \exp[-T \cdot E(R_m)] \qquad (6\text{--}5)$$

where $E(R_m)$ is called the *error exponent*. $E(R_m)$ is a function of the channel model but is independent of T. The channel model is, of course, a function of the modulation scheme used as well as the received signal-to-noise ratio. This formula says that, if $E(R_m) > 0$, then P_B can be made arbitrarily small by letting T become large. It can also be shown [6, 7] that $E(R_m)$ is, in fact, greater than zero as long as R_m is less than the channel capacity C. Figure 6–6 illustrates $E(R_m)$ as a function of R_m for a typical channel. Observe that

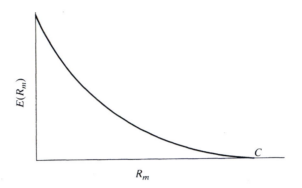

FIGURE 6–6   Error exponent for block coding for a typical channel.

$E(R_m)$ becomes very small as R_m approaches C. Increasing T to reduce the error probability increases system complexity, since as k increases, the number of channel waveforms 2^k increases exponentially.

6.2.3.2 Shannon's Capacity Formula.   Channel capacity is a function of channel characteristics such as received signal and noise powers (received signal-to-noise ratio). A number of different formulas for channel capacity are commonly used. One of these formulas, applicable only to the additive white Gaussian noise channel, is

$$C = B \cdot \log_2\left(1 + \frac{P}{N_0 B}\right) \tag{6--6}$$

where

        C = channel capacity, bits per second
        B = transmission bandwidth, hertz
        P = received signal power, watts
        N_0 = single-sided noise power spectral density, watts/hertz

An important result regarding capacity can be found by substituting $P = E_b \cdot R_m$, where E_b is the signal's energy per bit at the receiver and R_m is the transmission rate in bits per second. Normalization by the bandwidth B results in

$$\frac{C}{B} = \log_2\left[1 + \frac{E_b}{N_0}\left(\frac{R_m}{B}\right)\right] \tag{6--7}$$

Now let C equal R_m in (6–7) and plot E_b/N_0 as a function of R_m/B as shown in Figure 6–7. Setting $C = R_m$ means that the transmission rate will equal the channel capacity. The curve in Figure 6–7 represents a boundary between $(R_m/B, E_b/N_0)$ points for which arbitrarily low error probability can be achieved and those points for which arbitrarily low error probabil-

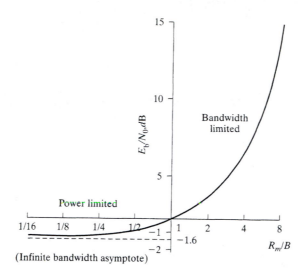

FIGURE 6–7 Power–bandwidth trade-off for error-free transmission through noisy, band-limited channels.

ity cannot be achieved. Points to the left or above the curve are points where low error probability can be achieved using coding. Thus, for any R_m/B, there exists a minimum E_b/N_0 that must be used to achieve arbitrarily low error probability by, for example, increasing the block length T for a block code. Observe that, for a fixed R_m, when B becomes very large the E_b/N_0 required approaches a lower limit of -1.6 dB. Thus, for an infinite bandwidth channel, no amount of forward error correction will yield arbitrarily low P_B if this minimum E_b/N_0 requirement is not met. Note that communication is still possible at points below the curve of Figure 6–7; however, the user will have to be content with some probability of error which cannot be further reduced without increasing transmitter power.

EXAMPLE 6–6

A communicator wishes to transmit data at a rate of 9600 bits per second over an RF channel with a bandwidth of 19.2 kHz. What E_b/N_0 is required to achieve a communications reliability of one error or less in 10^{+5} transmitted bits?

Solution: The ratio $R_m/B = 9600/19200 = 0.5$. Equation (6–7) becomes

$$9600 = 19,200 \cdot \log_2\left(1 + \frac{9600E_b}{19200N_0} \right)$$

Solving this equation for E_b/N_0 results in $E_b/N_0 = 0.828$ or -0.817 dB. If the communicator uses enough transmitter power to obtain $E_b/N_0 = -0.817$ dB or more, error correction can be used to obtain arbitrarily low error rates. Thus the required communication reliability can be achieved using $E_b/N_0 = -0.817$ dB.

6.2.3.3 Capacity of Discrete Memoryless Channels. With these general concepts in mind, consideration will now be limited to discrete memoryless channels (DMCs) with finite input alphabet $X = \{0, 1, 2, \ldots, q_x - 1\}$ and finite output alphabet $Y = \{0, 1, 2, \ldots, q_y - 1\}$. Note that there is a possible notational confusion created by numbering both channel input and output alphabets with the positive integers. At this point in the development the notation implies only that there are q_x different input symbols, with each being denoted by an integer, and q_y different output symbols, with each being denoted by an integer. The associations between these symbols is defined by the DMC transition probabilities which are the probabilities $\Pr(y \mid x)$ of a particular output symbol $y \in Y$ given a particular input symbol $x \in X$. For much of the remainder of the chapter, both the input and output alphabets will be the binary alphabets $\{0, 1\}$.

The average information content of the output of the channel is the entropy of the output defined as before by

$$H(Y) = -\sum_{y \in Y} Q_Y(y) \log_2 Q_Y(y) \quad \text{bits/symbol} \tag{6-8}$$

where $Q_Y(y)$ is the probability of occurrence of output symbol y. The entropy of the channel output given that a particular input, say, x was present is

$$H(Y \mid x) = -\sum_{y \in Y} \Pr(y \mid x) \log_2 \Pr(y \mid x) \quad \text{bits/symbol} \tag{6-9}$$

When averaged over all possible inputs $x \in X$, the conditional entropy of the output given the input $H(Y \mid X)$ is obtained

$$H(Y \mid X) = \sum_{x \in X} Q_X(x) H(Y \mid x) \quad \text{bits/symbol}$$

$$= -\sum_{x \in X} \sum_{y \in Y} Q_X(x) \Pr(y \mid x) \log_2 \Pr(y \mid x) \tag{6-10}$$

where $Q_X(x)$ is the probability of occurrence of input symbol x. In a similar fashion the conditional entropy $H(X \mid Y)$ can be defined by replacing $\Pr(y \mid x)$ by $\Pr(x \mid y)$ in this equation.

The average information or entropy of a set of symbols represents the average amount of information gained in observing the occurrence of a symbol. $H(X \mid Y)$ represents the average information known about X after observation of the channel output, averaged over all possible channel inputs and outputs. $H(X)$ represents the average information known about the input *without* knowing the channel output, also averaged over all inputs. It follows that the difference between the information known about the input before and after the observation of the output is the average amount of information conveyed through the channel.

$$I(X; Y) = H(X) - H(X \mid Y) \quad \text{bits/symbol} \tag{6-11}$$

The function $I(X; Y)$ is called the *mutual information* between the channel input and output. Thus the information conveyed through the channel is the difference between what is known about the input without communicating through the channel and what is known about the input after communicating through the channel. With the aid of Bayes' rule, it can be shown that

$$I(X; Y) = H(Y) - H(Y \mid X) \quad \text{bits/symbol} \tag{6-12}$$

and that, in either case, $I(X; Y)$ can be written as

$$I(X; Y) = \sum_{x \in X} \sum_{y \in Y} \Pr(x, y) \log_2 \frac{\Pr(x, y)}{Q_X(x) Q_Y(y)} \quad \text{bits/symbol} \tag{6-13}$$

where $\Pr(x, y) = \Pr(y \mid x) Q_X(x) = \Pr(x \mid y) Q_Y(y)$ are the joint probabilities of the event that the channel input is x and its output is y.

From (6–13) and using the theorem of total probability, it follows that the mutual information can be expressed as a function of the channel input probabilities $Q_X(x)$ for $x \in X$ and the channel transition probabilities $\Pr(y \mid x)$. For a specified channel, the transition probabilities are fixed. It is natural to ask what the maximum of $I(X; Y)$ is through proper selection of the input probabilities $Q_X(x)$. The resulting maximum is the capacity C_N of the channel [6]. Thus

$$C_N = \max I(X; Y) \tag{6-14}$$

where maximization is over all possible $Q_X(x)$. It can be shown [6, 7] that the transmission error probability is bounded by a relationship similar to (6–5) when $R'_m < C_N$, with C_N calculated using (6–14) and R'_m is the actual channel input rate in bits per channel use. The units of C_N are bits of information per channel use where a channel use is the transmission of one DMC symbol from the transmitter to the receiver.

Consider the most important DMC—the binary symmetric channel (BSC). For this channel the input and output alphabets are both $\{0, 1\}$ and the channel transition probabilities are symmetrical. Specifically, $\Pr(0 \mid 0) = \Pr(1 \mid 1) = (1 - p)$ and $\Pr(1 \mid 0) = \Pr(0 \mid 1) = p$. The transition probability or error probability is denoted p; the channel is usually described by a transition diagram such as shown in Figure 6–8. Let the probability

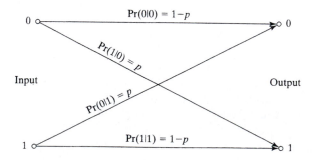

FIGURE 6–8   Binary symmetric channel transition diagram.

of the channel input symbols be $Q_X(0) = \alpha$ and $Q_X(1) = 1 - \alpha$. The mutual information is given by (6–12), which is a function of both the input symbol probabilities and the channel transition probabilities. Now calculate both terms of (6–12). Using the theorem on total probability the prior probabilities of the output symbols are

$$Q_Y(0) = \Pr(0 \mid 0)Q_X(0) + \Pr(0 \mid 1)Q_X(1)$$

$$= (1 - p)\alpha + p(1 - \alpha) \tag{6–15}$$

and

$$Q_Y(1) = \Pr(1 \mid 0)Q_X(0) + \Pr(1 \mid 1)Q_X(1)$$

$$= p\alpha + (1 - p)(1 - \alpha) \tag{6–16}$$

Using (6–8) the entropy of the channel output $H(Y)$ is

$$
\begin{aligned}
H(Y) &= -\sum_{y=0}^{1} Q_Y(y) \log_2 Q_Y(y) \\
&= -[(1 - p)\alpha + p(1 - \alpha)] \log_2 [(1 - p)\alpha + p(1 - \alpha)] \\
&\quad -[p\alpha + (1 - p)(1 - \alpha)] \log_2 [p\alpha + (1 - p)(1 - \alpha)] \\
&= \mathbf{H}[(1 - p)\alpha + p(1 - \alpha)]
\end{aligned}
\tag{6–17}
$$

where

$$\mathbf{H}(u) \equiv -(1 - u) \log_2 (1 - u) - u \log_2 u \tag{6–18}$$

is defined as the *binary entropy function*. The entropy function is defined only for $0 \leq u \leq 1.0$. The conditional entropy $H(Y \mid X)$ is calculated from (6–10):

$$
\begin{aligned}
H(Y \mid X) &= -\sum_{x=0}^{1} \sum_{y=0}^{1} Q_X(x) \Pr(y \mid x) \log_2 \Pr(y \mid x) \\
&= -\alpha[\Pr(0 \mid 0) \log_2 \Pr(0 \mid 0) + \Pr(1 \mid 0) \log_2 \Pr(1 \mid 0)] \\
&\quad -(1 - \alpha)[\Pr(0 \mid 1) \log_2 \Pr(0 \mid 1) + \Pr(1 \mid 1) \log_2 \Pr(1 \mid 1)] \\
&= -\alpha[(1 - p) \log_2 (1 - p) + p \log_2 p] \\
&\quad -(1 - \alpha)[p \log_2 p + (1 - p) \log_2 (1 - p)] \\
&= -[\alpha + 1 - \alpha][(1 - p) \log_2 (1 - p) + p \log_2 p] \\
&= \mathbf{H}(p)
\end{aligned}
\tag{6–19}
$$

Equation (6–19) is not a function of α so it may be ignored in the maximization over $Q_X(x) = \alpha$ in calculating capacity. Thus, the optimizing α can be found by finding the α

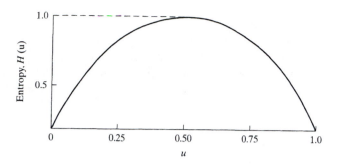

FIGURE 6-9   Binary entropy function.

which maximizes (6–17). Figure 6–9 is a plot of $\mathbf{H}(u)$ showing that the maximizing $u = \frac{1}{2}$ and $\mathbf{H}(\frac{1}{2}) = 1.0$. Thus any α which is a solution to

$$(1 - p)\alpha + p(1 - \alpha) = \tfrac{1}{2}$$

is the desired maximizing α. It is easily shown that $\alpha = \frac{1}{2}$ satisfies this equation for any transition probability p. Thus, the capacity of the BSC is

$$C_N = \mathbf{H}(\tfrac{1}{2}) - \mathbf{H}(p)$$
$$= 1 + p \log_2 p + (1 - p) \log_2 (1 - p) \tag{6-20}$$

The capacity is plotted in Figure 6–10 as a function of p. The maximum capacity is achieved when $p = 0$ or when $p = 1$, that is, when no errors are made or when errors are made on every transmission. That maximum capacity is 1.0, which says that in the best case, a single information 0 or 1 can be associated with every channel use 0 or 1. The minimum capacity is 0 and is seen when the transition probability is $p = \frac{1}{2}$. In this case no information can be transmitted over the channel and the channel is useless.

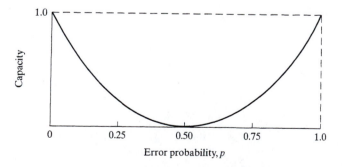

FIGURE 6-10   Channel capacity for BSC.

The capacity of the binary symmetric channel is a function of the modulation scheme used and the received E_b/N_0 since the transition probability is a function of both factors.

The most important concept to understand regarding channel capacity is, again, that error probability can be improved using error correction techniques only if the desired information transmission rate is lower than the capacity of the channel. For any binary modulation scheme, the capacity is easily calculated using (6–20). The reader is reminded that (6–20) applies only to static channels.

6.2.3.4 Computational Cutoff Rate.

Another often-used measure of the "capacity" of a channel is the *computational cutoff rate* R_0. Although the capacity C_N of the previous section is a firm theoretical limit on the number of bits per channel use, it has been demonstrated that achieving very low error probabilities at transmission rates approaching capacity requires extreme complexity. The computational cutoff rate [7], on the other hand, provides a more practical bound on the transmission rate. The bound is "more practical" in that reliable communications at rate R_0 bits per channel use can be achieved with much less system complexity than at the rate C_N bits per channel use. The cutoff rate is also a function of the modulation scheme and the received signal-to-noise ratio. It can be shown that transmission error probability is bounded by a function similar to (6–5) when $R'_m < R_0$. Thus, the error probability can be made as small as desired by increasing the number of information bits processed as a block when $R'_m < R_0$. The interested reader is referred to Wozencraft and Jacobs [7] for detailed derivations and description of the computational cutoff rate. For the binary symmetric channel with error probability p the computational cutoff rate is

$$R_0 = -\log_2[\tfrac{1}{2} + \sqrt{p(1-p)}] \qquad (6\text{–}21)$$

Observe that $R_0 \to 1$ as $p \to 0$ so that one bit of information can be reliably communicated with each channel use when $p = 0$. Both measures of capacity, C_N and R_0, can be used by the communications system engineer to assess the practicality of achieving a particular information bit error rate over a channel having constraints on bandwidth, power, or complexity. For the binary symmetric channel, Figure 6–11 illustrates the channel symbol error probability p required to communicate at a rate $R'_m = R_0$ or $R'_m = C_N$ with arbitrarily low bit error probability. This figure was generated [23] by setting $R'_m = R_0$ in Equation (6–21) and $R'_m = C_N$ in (6–20) and plotting p versus $1/R'_m$. Using Figure 6–11, if the actual channel symbol error rate were, for example, $p = 0.10$, the value of $1/R'_m$ is about 1.9 for operation at C_N or 3.1 for operation at R_0. Thus the communicator can theoretically achieve any desired error probability if the information rate is limited to $1/1.9 = 0.53$ bits per channel use. If the information rate was limited to $1/3.1 = 0.32$ bits per channel use the desired error rate could be achieved with a system with reduced complexity relative to the system operating at $R'_m = 0.53$. If, in fact, the communicator was required to transmit information at a rate of $R'_m = 1.0$ bits per channel use, the raw channel error probability of 0.1 would have to be accepted. Further, if the required information transfer

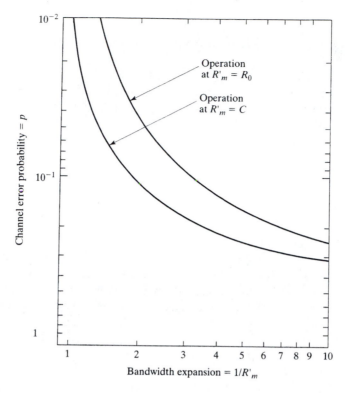

FIGURE 6-11 Coding limits for a binary symmetric channel.

rate is $0.53 < R'_m < 1.0$, error correction techniques would be useless for reducing the information bit error probability below 0.1.

Another means of using the capacity relationships is to assess the potential coding gain of a coded communication system. The *coding gain* of a system is simply the difference between the E_b/N_0 required to achieve a particular bit error probability without coding and the E_b/N_0 required to achieve the same error probability with coding. Coding gains for particular coding systems will be calculated later. The maximum possible coding gain over all possible coding techniques is a function of the desired bit error probability, the transmission rate R'_m, and the modulation strategy. For example, suppose that BPSK modulation has been selected and the desired bit error probability is $P_b = 10^{-5}$. In Chapter 4 it was shown that without coding the probability of error for BPSK is

$$P_b = Q\left(\sqrt{\frac{2E_b}{N_0}}\right) \tag{6-22}$$

so that $P_b = 10^{-5}$ is achieved with BPSK at $E_b/N_0 = 9.6$ dB. For the coded system R'_m bits of information are transmitted per channel use so that the energy per BSC symbol is $E_s = E_b R'_m$. Thus the BSC symbol error probability used to calculate C_N or R_0 is

$$p = Q\left(\sqrt{\frac{2R'_m E_b}{N_0}}\right) \tag{6-23}$$

A boundary separating values of E_b/N_0 where coding is and is not useful is obtained by setting C_N and $R_0 = R'_m$ in (6-20) and (6-21) and plotting E_b/N_0 as a function of $1/R'_m$. Figure 6-12 illustrates the result of this calculation. Suppose, somewhat arbitrarily for now, that the transmission rate must be 0.5 bits per channel use so $1/R'_m = 2$. From Figure 6-12 the E_b/N_0 required to operate at capacity C_N is 1.8 dB and to operate at R_0 is 4.65 dB. Thus, the potential coding gain is $9.6 - 1.8 = 7.8$ dB for operation near channel capacity C_N and $9.6 - 4.7 = 4.9$ dB for operation near R_0. For this rate R'_m, this modulation type, and this error rate, the communicator should never expect to achieve more than this coding gain.

Both C_N and R_0 can be calculated for many interesting channels besides the binary symmetric channel. The interested reader is referred to Odenwalder [23] for results for differential binary phase-shift keying and noncoherent M-ary frequency-shift keying.

In these discussions it has become clear that R'_m must be less than C_N or R_0 for arbitrarily reliable communications to be possible. For the binary symmetric channel this means that binary symbols are being transmitted over the channel more rapidly than binary information bits are being output from the source. Recall that the RF bandwidth re-

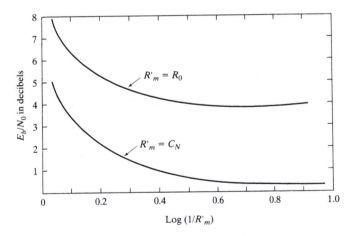

FIGURE 6-12 E_b/N_0 required to operate at $R'_m = R_0$ and $R'_m = C_N$ for a BPSK modulated signal in additive white Gaussian noise.

quired to transmit a binary symbol over the channel is proportional to the symbol rate. In an uncoded system, the symbol rate is equal to the information bit rate. Thus, a bandwidth expansion is required by a coded system. This is one of the costs of using error correction.

6.3   FUNDAMENTALS OF BLOCK CODING

The promise of information theory is that message error probability can be made to approach zero by increasing waveform complexity at a constant E_b/N_0. This promise is valid as long as the total information transmission rate is below the capacity of the channel. With the information theoretic bounds in hand, communications technologists began searching for specific techniques to reduce message error rate without increasing transmitter power or similarly to achieve the same message error probability with reduced transmitter power. Their goal was to search for waveforms which have the structure necessary to mitigate channel distortion and which can be received using a receiver with reasonable complexity. The field of coding theory is dedicated to the search for efficient methods of structuring the transmitted waveform.

When there is no possibility of feedback from the receiver to the transmitter, *forward error control* techniques are used. In this case the waveform is designed so that a specified end-to-end message (or bit) error probability limit is not exceeded at the minimum expected received E_b/N_0. When feedback from the receiver to the transmitter is possible, the receiver can tell the transmitter when a received message is too distorted to detect reliably and can request a retransmission. Techniques using feedback are called *automatic repeat request* strategies; these strategies will be discussed in Chapter 8.

Forward error control techniques include both *block coding* techniques and *convolutional coding* techniques. Both of these techniques will be discussed separately. In this section it is assumed that the source has been ideally source coded so that its output is a sequence of equally likely independent digits from the binary alphabet $\{0, 1\}$. The source output sequence is modified within the encoder to add the necessary structure for correcting transmission errors at the receiver. In most cases, the encoder input and output alphabets will be binary. In order to have the resources necessary to add structure to the transmitted signal, a binary input–output encoder's output symbol rate must be somewhat higher than its input bit rate.

The channel is assumed to be a BSC with transition probabilities $\Pr(y \mid x)$ with y and $x \in \{0,1\}$. When the channel input and output alphabets are identical, the channel is called a *hard decision channel* and the associated decoder is a *hard decision decoder*. When discussing convolutional coding in Chapter 7, the channel will be permitted to output symbols from an alphabet that is larger than the input alphabet. The larger output alphabet permits the channel to give decision reliability information to the decoder. When reliability information is output from the channel, the channel is called a *soft decision channel* and the associated decoder is a *soft decision decoder*.

6.3.1   Basic Concepts

As their name suggests, block coding techniques are those coding techniques that process information in blocks. A binary input–output *block encoder* collects blocks of k binary information symbols and maps them into blocks of n binary output symbols. The *code rate* for the block code is defined as $R = k/n$ and is equal to the rate of information transmission per channel use. That is, each time an encoder output symbol is transmitted, R bits of information are transmitted. A block of n channel uses (one encoder output block) transmits $nR = n(k/n) = k$ information bits. The information transmission rate must be lower than the channel capacity C_N if coding is expected to improve signaling reliability. For a binary input channel the capacity is at most one bit per channel use so that $R \leq C_N \leq 1.0$, and it follows that $k \leq n$.

6.3.1.1 Definition of a Block Code.   A block of k information bits will be represented by a k-vector $\mathbf{w_m} = w_{m0} \, w_{m1} \, w_{m2} \, \ldots \, w_{m(k-1)}$, where each w_{mi} is either a 0 or 1 and the subscript m identifies the particular message being considered. There are 2^k possible encoder input messages corresponding to the 2^k binary k-vectors $\mathbf{w_m}$. The probability that the source outputs the message m is denoted by $Q_M(m)$; for the binary symmetric source assumed here, all output messages are equally likely so that $Q_M(m) = 2^{-k}$ for all m. The encoder maps each unique $\mathbf{w_m}$ into a unique binary n-vector $\mathbf{x_m} = x_{m0} \, x_{m1} \, x_{m2} \, \ldots \, x_{m(n-1)}$. This mapping is one to one, meaning that no two messages are assigned to the same $\mathbf{x}$, that is, $\mathbf{x_m} \neq \mathbf{x_{m'}}$ for $m \neq m'$. An (n, k) *block code* is the set of all $\mathbf{x_m}$ along with their assignments to messages m. Each $\mathbf{x_m}$ is a *codeword* of the code. There are 2^n possible codewords and 2^k possible messages. Since $k < n$, the number of messages 2^k is less than the number of possible codewords 2^n so that not all possible n-vectors are used for codewords. In general, the fraction of all possible codewords used is $2^{k-n} = 2^{k(1-1/R)}$; observe that for a constant rate $R < 1.0$ this fraction decreases as k increases. The error correction capability of the code is due to the fact that not all possible n-vectors are used by the code. Because of this it is possible to generate codes with codewords selected so that a number of transmission errors must occur before one codeword is confused with another in the receiver.

6.3.1.2 Hamming Distance and Hamming Weight.   A typical block code is illustrated in Table 6–4. This block code collects groups of four information bits ($k = 4$) and maps them into codewords of length seven ($n = 7$). The code rate is $R = 4/7$.

Since $n = 7$, there are $2^7 = 128$ possible codewords of which only 16 have been selected for the code. Examination of the codewords of Table 6–4 will show that any two codewords differ in at least three positions. This implies that one or two transmission errors cannot transform one codeword into another codeword. In this case, the decoder is able to tell the user that transmission errors have occurred although it may not be able to correct these errors. Three transmission errors, however, can modify the transmitted codeword into a block identical to another valid codeword. In this case the decoder will not be able to detect or correct the errors. For example, if the codeword for message number 2

TABLE 6–4   Typical Block Code

Message Number	Message	Codeword
0	0000	0000000
1	1000	1101000
2	0100	0110100
3	1100	1011100
4	0010	1110010
5	1010	0011010
6	0110	1000110
7	1110	0101110
8	0001	1010001
9	1001	0111001
10	0101	1100101
11	1101	0001101
12	0011	0100011
13	1011	1001011
14	0111	0010111
15	1111	1111111

was transmitted and errors were made in positions (counting from the left) 1, 2, and 4, the received block would be identical to the codeword for message number 3. If more than three errors occur, the decoder will be able to detect errors only if the received vector is not identical to a codeword. The number of differences between a pair of codewords x_m and $x_{m'}$ is an extremely important property and is called the *Hamming distance*, denoted d_H or $d_H(x_m, x_{m'})$, between the codewords. The minimum Hamming distance between any two codewords in the code is called the *minimum distance* of the code and is denoted d_{min}. The code of Table 6–4 is one of a family of codes called *Hamming codes* after their discoverer R. W. Hamming. The minimum distance of a Hamming code is three. It will be shown later that these codes are able to correct a single transmission error in any transmitted codeword block.

The Hamming distance between a pair of codewords is equal to the number of 1s in the modulo-2 vector sum of the codewords. The modulo-2 vector sum of two codewords is the term-by-term sum of the vector components (without carry) using modulo-2 rules of addition as defined in Table 6–5 which also defines modulo-2 multiplication, which will be needed later in this chapter. Using Table 6–5 it is found that the Hamming distance between codewords 2 and 3 of the code of Table 6–4 is the number of 1s in the sum.

$$
\begin{array}{rl}
x_2 & 0\ 1\ 1\ 0\ 1\ 0\ 0 \\
+\ x_3 & 1\ 0\ 1\ 1\ 1\ 0\ 0 \\
\hline
= & 1\ 1\ 0\ 1\ 0\ 0\ 0
\end{array}
\tag{6–24}
$$

TABLE 6–5 Modulo-2 Addition and Multiplication

+	0	1		•	0	1
0	0	1		0	0	0
1	1	0		1	0	1

The number of 1s in any vector is called the *Hamming weight* of the codeword and is denoted w_H or $w_H(\mathbf{x_m})$.

6.3.1.3 Error Vectors. The codeword $\mathbf{x_m}$ is transmitted over the BSC. It is convenient to model the errors which can occur during this transmission by an error n-vector $\mathbf{e} = e_0\, e_1\, e_2\, \ldots\, e_{n-1}$. The error vector contains a 0 in every position where no transmission error occurs and a 1 in every position where an error does occur. The BSC output vector is found by calculating the modulo-2 sum of the transmitted codeword vector $\mathbf{x_m}$ and the error vector $\mathbf{e}$. For example, the error 7-vector denoting errors in positions 1, 2, and 4 of a 7-bit codeword is $\mathbf{e} = 1101000$. If the codeword corresponding to message 2 ($m = 2$) of the code of Table 6–4 were transmitted and were distorted by this error vector, the received 7-vector would be

$$
\begin{array}{ll}
\mathbf{x_2} & 0\,1\,1\,0\,1\,0\,0 \\
+\,\mathbf{e} & 1\,1\,0\,1\,0\,0\,0 \\
\hline
=\,\mathbf{y} & 1\,0\,1\,1\,1\,0\,0
\end{array}
\tag{6–25}
$$

The *received n*-vector is denoted by $\mathbf{y} = y_0\, y_1\, y_2\, \ldots\, y_{n-1}$.

The channel is assumed to be memoryless, meaning that the probability of making an error on any particular symbol is independent of what occurs on all other symbols. Further, it is assumed that the BSC transition probabilities $\Pr(y_i \mid x_i)$ are constant for all transmissions. Then

$$
\Pr[\mathbf{y} \mid \mathbf{x}] = \prod_{n'=0}^{n-1} \Pr(y_{n'} \mid x_{n'})
\tag{6–26}
$$

For the BSC denote $\Pr(1 \mid 0) = \Pr(0 \mid 1) = p$ so that $\Pr(0 \mid 0) = \Pr(1 \mid 1) = 1 - p$. Then, the probability that the BSC causes the error vector $\mathbf{e} = 1101000$ is

$$
\Pr[\mathbf{e} = 1101000] = p \times p \times (1 - p) \times p \times (1 - p)
$$
$$
\times (1 - p) \times (1 - p)
\tag{6–27}
$$

In general, the probability that the BSC causes a sequence of e' channel errors in *specific positions* in a codeword block of length n is

$$\Pr\begin{bmatrix} e' \text{ errors in} \\ \text{specific locations} \\ \text{in codeword} \end{bmatrix} = p^{e'}(1 - p)^{n-e'} \tag{6-28}$$

This result is used to find $\Pr[\mathbf{y} \mid \mathbf{x_m}]$, the probability of receiving $\mathbf{y}$ given that $\mathbf{x_m}$ was transmitted. This probability is also given by

$$\Pr(\mathbf{y} \mid \mathbf{x_m}) = p^{d_H}(1 - p)^{n-d_H} \tag{6-29}$$

where d_H is the Hamming distance between $\mathbf{x_m}$ and $\mathbf{y}$. The probability that the BSC causes e' errors without regard to the specific locations of the errors in $\mathbf{e}$ equals the number of possible sequences with e' errors times the probability of a specific sequence occurring. The number of specific sequences of length n having e' errors is given by a binomial coefficient

$$\binom{n}{e'} = \frac{n!}{e'!(n - e')!} \tag{6-30}$$

Therefore, the probability that the BSC causes *some* sequence of e' errors in a block of length n is

$$\Pr\begin{bmatrix} e' \text{ errors in} \\ \text{block of } n \end{bmatrix} = \binom{n}{e'} p^{e'}(1 - p)^{n-e'} \tag{6-31}$$

6.3.1.4 Optimum Decoding Rule.

The decoder inputs are the received vector $\mathbf{y}$, prior knowledge of the entire set of codewords $\mathbf{x_m}$ for $m = 0, \ldots, 2^k - 1$, knowledge of the source output message probabilities $Q_M(m)$, and knowledge of the channel transition probabilities $\Pr(\mathbf{y} \mid \mathbf{x_m})$. Using this information the decoder must be designed to make the best possible estimate of the transmitted codeword. The "best possible" estimate is the estimate that results in the minimum average number of bit errors delivered to the information user. The bit error probability will be denoted P_b.

First, consider the much simpler problem of choosing a decoding rule which results in the minimum probability of incorrectly estimating the transmitted codeword without regard to the number of information bit errors that a particular codeword error causes. This block decoding error probability is denoted P_B. Denote the decoder estimate of the transmitted codeword by $\hat{\mathbf{x}}$. Given that $\mathbf{y}$ was received and $\hat{\mathbf{x}} = \mathbf{x_m}$, the decoder estimate is correct if $\mathbf{x_m}$ was indeed transmitted. Therefore, P_B is minimized if the decoder chooses as its estimate $\hat{\mathbf{x}}$ the codeword that was most likely to have been transmitted. That is, choose $\hat{\mathbf{x}}$ to be that $\mathbf{x_m}$ with the largest posterior probability $\Pr[\mathbf{x_m} \mid \mathbf{y}]$. Using this rule, a decoding table can be created that identifies the decoder output $\hat{\mathbf{x}}$ for each $\mathbf{y}$. Since there are 2^n possible $\mathbf{y}$ and only 2^k codewords, many $\mathbf{y}$ will be mapped into the same $\mathbf{x_m}$ by this decoding rule. The set of all $\mathbf{y}$ for which the optimum decoder estimates $\hat{\mathbf{x}} = \mathbf{x_m}$ is called the *decision region* for $\mathbf{x_m}$. The space of all 2^n possible $\mathbf{y}$ is partitioned into 2^k non-overlapping decision regions; there is a decision region for each possible message.

In order to calculate the posterior probabilities $\Pr[\mathbf{x_m} \mid \mathbf{y}]$, Bayes' rule is used. Recall from probability theory [see (A-6)] that

$$\Pr[\mathbf{x_m} \mid \mathbf{y}] \Pr[\mathbf{y}] = \Pr[\mathbf{y} \mid \mathbf{x_m}] \Pr[\mathbf{x_m}] \tag{6-32}$$

Therefore,

$$\Pr[\mathbf{x_m} \mid \mathbf{y}] = \frac{\Pr[\mathbf{y} \mid \mathbf{x_m}] \Pr[\mathbf{x_m}]}{\Pr[\mathbf{y}]} \tag{6-33}$$

The denominator on the right side of this equation is

$$\Pr[\mathbf{y}] = \sum_{m'=0}^{2^k-1} Q_M[m'] \Pr[\mathbf{y} \mid \mathbf{x_{m'}}] \tag{6-34}$$

which is positive and independent of the message m.

Therefore, the decoding rule may be restated: Choose $\hat{\mathbf{x}}$ to be that $\mathbf{x_m}$ for which

$$\Pr[\mathbf{y} \mid \mathbf{x_m}] \Pr[\mathbf{x_m}] = \Pr[\mathbf{y} \mid \mathbf{x_m}] Q_M[m] \tag{6-35}$$

is maximum. This equation is evaluated using knowledge of the channel transition probabilities as in (6-26) and the prior probabilities for the messages.

When all message probabilities are equal, the decoding rule simplifies further to the following: Choose $\hat{\mathbf{x}}$ to be that $\mathbf{x_m}$ for which

$$\Pr[\mathbf{y} \mid \mathbf{x_m}] \tag{6-36}$$

is maximum. Observe that the concepts used to derive the optimum decoding rule are the same concepts used to derive the optimum receiver demodulator in Chapter 4. As in Chapter 4, the decoder that makes decisions without regard to the message prior probabilities is called a *maximum likelihood decoder*.

For the binary symmetric channel $\Pr[\mathbf{y} \mid \mathbf{x_m}]$ is given by (6-29). Since the logarithm is a monotone increasing function of an increasing argument, the logarithm of $\Pr[\mathbf{y} \mid \mathbf{x_m}]$ may be used in the maximum likelihood decoding rule without changing any decoder decisions. Taking the logarithm of (6-29) the decoding rule for the BSC can be stated as follows: Choose $\hat{\mathbf{x}}$ to be that $\mathbf{x_m}$ for which

$$\log\{\Pr[\mathbf{y} \mid \mathbf{x_m}]\} = d_H \log(p) + (n - d_H) \log(1 - p)$$
$$= d_H \log\left(\frac{p}{1-p}\right) + n \log(1 - p) \tag{6-37}$$

is maximum. In this equation, d_H is the Hamming distance between the received n-vector and the codeword n-vector being considered.

Since $\log[p/(1 - p)] < 0$ for $p < 0.5$, maximizing (6-37) is equivalent to minimizing d_H. Therefore, the decoding rule is a *minimum distance decoding rule*. For the BSC with $p < 0.5$ the decoder will choose as its estimate $\hat{\mathbf{x}}$ the codeword which is closest to the received vector $\mathbf{y}$ in terms of Hamming distance.

EXAMPLE 6–7

Consider the $n = 7$ and $k = 4$ Hamming code of Table 6–4. Suppose that the binary symmetric channel output is the n-tuple $\mathbf{y} = 1\ 0\ 1\ 1\ 0\ 1\ 0$. The decoder calculates the Hamming distances $d_H(\mathbf{y}, \mathbf{x}_m)$ between $\mathbf{y}$ and all possible codewords $\mathbf{x}_m$. The decoder output estimate $\hat{\mathbf{x}}$ is that $\mathbf{x}_m$ which has the minimum distance from $\mathbf{y}$. In this case that minimum distance is 1 and is message $\mathbf{x}_5 = 0011010 = \hat{\mathbf{x}}$.

The decoding rules just described achieve the minimum possible *block* decoding error probability. The minimization of block decoding error probability is assumed to also minimize decoded *bit* error probability. This will be true with proper assignment of messages to codewords. Messages are assigned such that the most probable block decoding errors cause the minimum number of bit errors. "Good" block codes all have this property.

6.3.1.5 Decoding Regions and Error Probability. The minimum distance decoder functions by finding the codeword $\mathbf{x}_m$ that is closest to the received n-vector $\mathbf{y}$. As mentioned before, conceptually this may be accomplished by partitioning the space of all possible received $\mathbf{y}$ into regions. All the $\mathbf{y}$ in any region are chosen to be closer in terms of Hamming distance to a particular $\mathbf{x}_m$ than to any other $\mathbf{x}_{m'}$. Therefore, the decoder may operate by finding the region containing the received $\mathbf{y}$ and estimating $\hat{\mathbf{x}}$ to be the $\mathbf{x}_m$ associated with that region.

Table 6–6 illustrates the partitioning of the set of all possible 7-vectors for the Hamming code of Table 6–4. The first column of Table 6–6 contains the 16 codewords of the code. The remaining columns contain all other 7-vectors. The decoding region for each codeword is the set of 7-vectors in the same row as the codeword and includes the code-

TABLE 6–6 Decoding Table for Code of Table 6–4

0000000	0000001	0000010	0000100	0001000	0010000	0100000	1000000
1101000	1101001	1101010	1101100	1100000	1111000	1001000	0101000
0110100	0110101	0110110	0110000	0111100	0100100	0010100	1110100
1011100	1011101	1011110	1011000	1010100	1001100	1111100	0011100
1110010	1110011	1110000	1110110	1111010	1100010	1010010	0110010
0011010	0011011	0011000	0011110	0010010	0001010	0111010	1011010
1000110	1000111	1000100	1000010	1001110	1010110	1100110	0000110
0101110	0101111	0101100	0101010	0100110	0111110	0001110	1101110
1010001	1010000	1010011	1010101	1011001	1000001	1110001	0010001
0111001	0111000	0111011	0111101	0110001	0101001	0011001	1111001
1100101	1100100	1100111	1100001	1101101	1110101	1000101	0100101
0001101	0001100	0001111	0001001	0000101	0011101	0101101	1001101
0100011	0100010	0100001	0100111	0101011	0110011	0000011	1100011
1001011	1001010	1001001	1001111	1000011	1011011	1101011	0001011
0010111	0010110	0010101	0010011	0011111	0000111	0110111	1010111
1111111	1111110	1111101	1111011	1110111	1101111	1011111	0111111

word as well as the 7-vectors separated from the codeword by the vertical dashed line. All 128 binary 7-vectors are represented in Table 6–6 which has 8 columns and 16 rows. The method used to construct Table 6–6 will be discussed later. It can be verified manually that any 7-vector in the decoding region for a codeword is Hamming distance 0 or 1 from the codeword. It can also be verified manually that *all* 7-vectors that are Hamming distance 0 or 1 from a codeword are in the decoding region for that codeword. The codeword itself is considered to be in the decoding region.

The block decoding error probability can be calculated once a decoding table of the form of Table 6–6 has been generated. A block decoding error will occur if a codeword $\mathbf{x_m}$ is transmitted and errors occur that cause the received n-vector $\mathbf{y}$ to be within the decoding region for a different codeword, say, $\mathbf{x_{m'}}$. Denote the decoding region for message m or codeword $\mathbf{x_m}$ by Λ_m and all n-vectors not in Λ_m by $\bar{\Lambda}_m$. When the received n-vector $\mathbf{y}$ is within Λ_m, the decoder output $\hat{\mathbf{x}} = \mathbf{x_m}$.

A decoding error occurs whenever $\mathbf{x_m}$ is transmitted and $\mathbf{y}$ is within $\bar{\Lambda}_m$. Given that message m was transmitted, the conditional block error probability P_{B_m} is given by

$$P_{B_m} = \Pr(\mathbf{y} \in \bar{\Lambda}_m \mid \mathbf{x_m})$$

$$= \sum_{\mathbf{y} \in \bar{\Lambda}_m} \Pr(\mathbf{y} \mid \mathbf{x_m}) \tag{6–38}$$

where the sum is over all n-vectors $\mathbf{y}$ that are not in the decoding region for message m. The condition on message m is removed by averaging over all messages, yielding

$$P_B = \sum_{m=0}^{2^k - 1} Q_M(m) P_{B_m} \tag{6–39}$$

EXAMPLE 6–8

For the Hamming code of Table 6–4 and the decoding Table 6–6, and for any transmitted message, a decoding error occurs whenever more than a single transmission error occurs. Therefore, P_{B_m} is independent of m and is

$$P_{B_m} = \sum_{e'=2}^{7} \Pr\begin{bmatrix} e' \text{ errors in} \\ \text{block of 7} \end{bmatrix}$$

$$= \sum_{e'=2}^{7} \binom{7}{e'} p^{e'} (1 - p)^{7 - e'}$$

The prior message probability $Q_M(m) = 2^{-k}$ for any m so that the block error probability P_B is given by

$$P_B = \sum_{m=0}^{15} \frac{1}{16} P_{B_m}$$

This relationship is relatively easy to calculate to obtain a curve of P_B as a function of the BSC crossover probability.

The relationships given relate the *block* error probability to the BSC error probability p. To complete the analysis, the block error probability P_B must be related to the decoder output *bit* error probability P_b. The number of information bit errors that occur when a block error occurs is a function of the specific decoder information output that occurs for that block error. Denote the number of bit errors that occur when transmitted message m is decoded as m' by $B(m, m')$. For example, when codeword $m = 2$ of the code of Table 6–4 is transmitted and the decoder estimates that codeword $m = 3$ was transmitted, a single bit error occurs in the fourth bit position and $B(2,3) = 1$. The probability of decoding a specific message m as another specific message m' is denoted $P_B(m, m')$. The probability $P_B(m, m')$ is the probability of receiving a vector $\mathbf{y}$ within $\Lambda_{m'}$ when $\mathbf{x_m}$ is transmitted. This probability is

$$P_B(m, m') = \sum_{\mathbf{y} \in \Lambda_{m'}} \Pr(\mathbf{y} \mid \mathbf{x_m}) \tag{6–40}$$

so that the exact bit error probability of interest is

$$P_b = \frac{1}{k} \sum_{m=0}^{2^k - 1} Q_M(m) \sum_{\substack{m'=0 \\ m' \neq m}}^{2^k - 1} B(m, m') \tag{6–41}$$

where the leading $1/k$ factor is due to the fact that k information bits are decoded with each codeword transmission. Without this term, the result would be the average number of bit errors per block. Except for the simplest of codes, the evaluation of this expression is tedious and long. For large k the calculation is not possible due to computation time bounds. For linear codes, which will be defined in the next section, this relationship can be simplified. In addition, reasonable assumptions about the decoder for linear codes will enable the generation of good upper bounds on the bit error probability.

6.3.1.6 Coding Gain. The purpose of using forward error correction is to enable improved communications efficiency in terms of the transmitter power necessary to achieve a required bit error probability. The *coding gain* of the system is the difference between the E_b/N_0 required to achieve a specified P_b without coding and the E_b/N_0 required to achieve the same P_b with coding. The coding gain is typically a function of P_b.

Calculation of coding gain is straightforward; however, care must be taken to assure that correct signal-to-noise ratio is used in the calculation of the BSC error probability for the coded case. Recall that the encoder output symbol rate is larger than its input bit rate. Therefore, the transmitted energy per encoder output symbol E_s is less than the energy per bit E_b. These two energies are related by the code rate R, specifically, $E_s = RE_b$.

Consider, for example, a system that uses binary antipodal phase-shift keying (BPSK) for which the bit error rate without FEC is given by (6–22). If the system is using FEC with a code rate R and still using BPSK, the error rate p used in the calculation of decoded bit error probability is calculated using (6–23) with $R_{m'} = R$. The calculated coding gain will be a function of technique used to calculate P_b for the coded system. In most

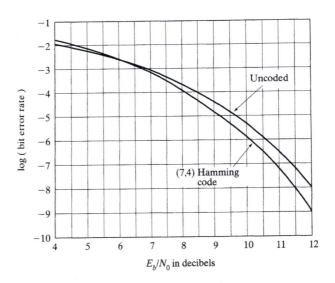

FIGURE 6–13   Bit error rate versus E_b/N_0 for the (7, 4) Hamming code.

cases bounds for P_b will be used so that the calculated coding gain will be a lower bound on the actual coding gain.

EXAMPLE 6–9

Consider a communications system that uses coherent BPSK modulation either with or without the $R = 4/7$ Hamming code of the previous three examples. Without coding the bit error probability is given by (6–22). With coding the bit error probability is calculated using (6–41) with the BSC error probability calculated using (6–23) with $R = 4/7$. The parameters necessary for the calculation of (6–41) were determined by a detailed examination of all of the codeword pairs using a digital computer. Figure 6–13 illustrates the results of this exact calculation. The coding gain is equal to the separation in decibels of the two curves of Figure 6–13. At a bit error probability of 10^{-6}, the coding gain is about 0.5 dB. The system using the $R = 4/7$ Hamming code uses 0.5 dB less transmitter power than the uncoded system to achieve the bit error probability of 10^{-6}. Observe that the separation between the two curves is not constant so that coding gain changes with signal-to-noise ratio. Finally, observe that the curves cross at an E_b/N_0 of approximately 5.75 dB indicating that the communicator is better off not using this particular error correcting code at low signal-to-noise ratios.

6.3.1.7 Summary.   An (n, k) binary block code is a one-to-one mapping of encoder input k-bit vectors (messages) to encoder output n-bit vectors (codewords). The encoder output alphabet does not have to be binary. However, in many useful cases the alphabet is binary. When the encoder output is binary, $R \leq 1.0$ and $k < n$. The total number of messages 2^k is less than the number of possible n-vectors 2^n so that a small fraction $(= 2^{k-n})$ of the possible n-vectors will be used for codewords; this fact enables the code to correct transmission errors. The 2^k codewords are selected from 2^n possibilities so that the number of differences between any codeword pair, the Hamming distance, is maximized. The assignment of messages to codewords is done so that the most likely decoding errors cause few message bit errors. The minimum Hamming distance between any two codewords in a code is the minimum distance of the code. The codewords are assumed to be transmitted over a discrete memoryless channel whose output alphabet is the same as its input alphabet (hard decision channel). The decoder uses prior knowledge of the message probabilities, the codeword set, and the channel transition probabilities along with the received n-vector (includes errors) to estimate the transmitted message. The minimum error probability decoding rule estimates the transmitted codeword to be the codeword that is closest to the received vector in terms of Hamming distance.

6.3.2 Linear Codes

The discussion of the previous section was very general in that codes were merely sets of n-vectors that were *very wisely chosen* and *very wisely assigned to message k-vectors* so that good communications performance resulted. In this section the set of code vectors are constrained to be very particular subsets of the set of all possible n-vectors. These particular subsets will have properties that facilitate both the encoding and decoding operations. In addition the properties make the prediction of the performance of the coded system easier. In order to discuss the codes of interest efficiently, an understanding of the fundamentals of modulo-2 vector arithmetic and linear vector spaces is needed.

6.3.2.1 Modulo-2 Vector Arithmetic. Consider two binary vectors $\mathbf{a} = a_0 \, a_1 \, a_2 \ldots a_{n-1}$ and $\mathbf{b} = b_0 \, b_1 \, b_2 \ldots b_{n-1}$. All components of $\mathbf{a}$ and $\mathbf{b}$ are elements of the set $\{0, 1\}$. The *modulo-2 sum,* $\mathbf{c} = \mathbf{a} + \mathbf{b}$, of these two vectors, as mentioned earlier, is the term-by-term modulo-2 sum of the vector components. Modulo-2 addition was defined in Table 6–5. Thus, $c_0 = a_0 + b_0$, $c_1 = a_1 + b_1$, and so on. The *scalar product* $\mathbf{c} = b\mathbf{a}$ of a vector $\mathbf{a}$ and a scalar element of b from the set $\{0, 1\}$ is defined to be the term-by-term modulo-2 product of the vector components and the scalar b. Modulo-2 multiplication is also defined in Table 6–5. Thus, $c_0 = b \cdot a_0$, $c_1 = b \cdot a_1$, and so on. The *dot product* $\mathbf{c} = \mathbf{a} \cdot \mathbf{b}$ is a scalar defined by

$$\mathbf{a} \cdot \mathbf{b} = (a_0 \cdot b_0) + (a_1 \cdot b_1) + (a_2 \cdot b_2) + \cdots + (a_{n-1} \cdot b_{n-1}) \tag{6–42}$$

where all additions and multiplications are performed modulo-2. If the dot product of two vectors is equal to 0, the two vectors are defined to be *orthogonal.*

Using the rules of vector arithmetic linear combinations of vectors are defined. Specifically, given any set of k binary n-vectors $\mathbf{g}_0, \mathbf{g}_1, \ldots, \mathbf{g}_{k-1}$ and any set of k binary scalars $w_0, w_1, w_2, \ldots, w_{k-1}$, the sum

$$(w_0 \cdot \mathbf{g}_0) + (w_1 \cdot \mathbf{g}_1) + (w_2 \cdot \mathbf{g}_2) + \cdots + (w_{k-1} \cdot \mathbf{g}_{k-1}) \tag{6–43}$$

is called a *linear combination* of the vectors $\mathbf{g}$. The set of k binary n-vectors is said to be *linearly independent* if there is no set of scalars $w_0, w_1, w_2, \ldots, w_{k-1}$ that are not all equal to 0 such that the linear combination is equal to $\mathbf{0} = 0\,0\,0 \ldots 0$. Otherwise, the set is defined to be *linearly dependent*.

EXAMPLE 6–10

Consider the set of four 7-vectors

$$\mathbf{g_0} = 1\,1\,0\,1\,0\,0\,0$$

$$\mathbf{g_1} = 0\,1\,1\,0\,1\,0\,0$$

$$\mathbf{g_2} = 1\,1\,1\,0\,0\,1\,0$$

$$\mathbf{g_3} = 1\,0\,1\,0\,0\,0\,1$$

There are 16 possible linear combinations of these four vectors corresponding to the 16 different binary 4-vectors $\mathbf{w} = w_0\,w_1\,w_2\,w_3$. For example, the linear combination corresponding to $\mathbf{w} = 1\,0\,1\,1$ is

$$\mathbf{x} = (1 \cdot \mathbf{g_0}) + (0 \cdot \mathbf{g_1}) + (1 \cdot \mathbf{g_2}) + (1 \cdot \mathbf{g_3})$$

$$
\begin{aligned}
= \quad & 1\,1\,0\,1\,0\,0\,0 \\
+ & 0\,0\,0\,0\,0\,0\,0 \\
+ & 1\,1\,1\,0\,0\,1\,0 \\
+ & 1\,0\,1\,0\,0\,0\,1 \\
\hline
& 1\,0\,0\,1\,0\,1\,1
\end{aligned}
$$

Although the exercise is tedious, it is straightforward to calculate all 16 linear combinations of the four vectors $\mathbf{g}$. These combinations are given in Table 6–7. Observe that there is a sin-

TABLE 6–7 Linear Combinations

w_0	w_1	w_2	w_3	**Linear Combination**
0	0	0	0	0000000
1	0	0	0	1101000
0	1	0	0	0110100
1	1	0	0	1011100
0	0	1	0	1110010
1	0	1	0	0011010
0	1	1	0	1000110
1	1	1	0	0101110
0	0	0	1	1010001
1	0	0	1	0111001
0	1	0	1	1100101
1	1	0	1	0001101
0	0	1	1	0100011
1	0	1	1	1001011
0	1	1	1	0010111
1	1	1	1	1111111

gle linear combination which is equal to the zero vector $\mathbf{0} = 0\ 0\ 0\ 0\ 0\ 0\ 0$ and that for this combination $\mathbf{w} = 0\ 0\ 0\ 0$. Therefore, the set of vectors $\mathbf{g}_0, \ldots, \mathbf{g}_3$ is linearly independent. Comparing Table 6–7 with Table 6–4, which defines the $R = 4/7$ Hamming code, it is seen that the tables are identical. Thus, the 16 possible linear combinations of the vectors $\mathbf{g}_0$ through $\mathbf{g}_3$ generate all 16 possible Hamming codewords. The particular linear combination for a codeword is defined by the binary representation of the message vector. That is, the components of the message vector w_0, w_1, w_2, w_3 define which $\mathbf{g}$s combine to form the codeword. The $R = 4/7$ Hamming code is therefore completely specified by the four vectors $\mathbf{g}_0$ through $\mathbf{g}_3$, which are called the generator vectors of the code.

6.3.2.2 Binary Linear Vector Spaces.

A *binary linear vector* space is a set of K binary n-vectors $\mathbf{x}_0, \mathbf{x}_1, \mathbf{x}_2, \ldots, \mathbf{x}_{K-1}$ that satisfy certain conditions. The following conditions must be satisfied:

1. The modulo-2 sum of any two vectors in the set is another vector in the set.
2. The modulo-2 scalar product of an element of $\{0, 1\}$ and any vector in the set is another vector in the set.
3. A distributive law is satisfied. That is, if b_1 and b_2 are scalars from the set $\{0, 1\}$ and $\mathbf{x}_1$ and $\mathbf{x}_2$ are vectors from the set, then

$$b_1 \cdot (\mathbf{x}_1 + \mathbf{x}_2) = (b_1 \cdot \mathbf{x}_1) + (b_1 \cdot \mathbf{x}_2)$$

$$(b_1 + b_2) \cdot \mathbf{x}_1 = (b_1 \cdot \mathbf{x}_1) + (b_2 \cdot \mathbf{x}_1)$$

(6–44)

4. An associative law is satisfied. That is, if b_1 and b_2 are scalars from the set $\{0, 1\}$ and $\mathbf{x}_1$ is a vector from the set, then

$$(b_1 \cdot b_2) \cdot \mathbf{x}_1 = b_1(b_2 \cdot \mathbf{x}_1)$$

(6–45)

The set of all binary n-vectors S is a vector space since all four conditions are satisfied. The first condition is satisfied since the modulo-2 sum of any two binary n-vectors is another n-vector due to the rules of vector addition and since all n-vectors are in the set. The second condition is satisfied since each component of the scalar products are binary elements so that the result is a binary n-vector. Since all binary n-vectors are in the set the scalar product is in the set. The third and fourth conditions can be similarly verified.

In all cases the binary forward error correction codes of interest in the remainder of this chapter are *subsets* of the set of all n-vectors. For example, the $R = 4/7$ Hamming code is a 16-element subset of the set of all 128 binary 7-vectors. A *subspace* of a linear vector space is a subset of the elements of the linear vector space that satisfies the four conditions given. Because the subset consists of elements of a set that is known to satisfy all four conditions, a smaller set of conditions are sufficient to define a subspace. It can be shown [8] that a subset of a linear vector space is a subspace S_{sub} of the original space if the following two conditions are satisfied.

1. The modulo-2 sum of any two vectors in the subset is also a vector in the subset.
2. The scalar product of an element b of $\{0, 1\}$ and a vector $\mathbf{x}$ in the subset is also a vector in the subset.

Consider the 16 Hamming code vectors of Table 6–4. The vector sum $\mathbf{x}_2 + \mathbf{x}_4 = \mathbf{x}_6$ is another Hamming code vector:

$$
\begin{array}{rl}
\mathbf{x}_2 & 0\ 1\ 1\ 0\ 1\ 0\ 0 \\
+\ \mathbf{x}_4 & 1\ 1\ 1\ 0\ 0\ 1\ 0 \\
\hline
=\ \mathbf{x}_6 & 1\ 0\ 0\ 0\ 1\ 1\ 0
\end{array}
$$

Although it would be tedious, all 120 possible sums of pairs of Hamming codewords could be calculated to show that any sum is another Hamming codeword. Therefore, the set of Hamming codewords is a linear subspace of the vector space of all 7-vectors.

Now consider the subset of *any* k vectors $\mathbf{g}_0, \mathbf{g}_1, \ldots, \mathbf{g}_{k-1}$ of the binary linear space of all possible n-vectors and form a larger set of $K = 2^k$ vectors $\mathbf{x}_0, \mathbf{x}_1, \mathbf{x}_2, \ldots, \mathbf{x}_{K-1}$ by forming all possible linear combinations of the k vectors. Note that if the vectors $\mathbf{g}$ are not linearly independent that all $\mathbf{x_m}$ will not be distinct. This set of K vectors $\mathbf{x_m}$ is a linear subspace of the space of all n-vectors. The linear combinations of $\mathbf{g}$ are defined by

$$
\mathbf{x_m} = (w_{m0} \cdot \mathbf{g_0}) + (w_{m1} \cdot \mathbf{g_1}) + (w_{m2} \cdot \mathbf{g_2}) + \cdots + (w_{m,k-1} \cdot \mathbf{g_{k-1}}) \tag{6–46}
$$

where $w_{m0}, w_{m1}, w_{m2}, \ldots, w_{m,k-1}$ are k elements from the set $\{0, 1\}$. In order to demonstrate that the subset is a linear subspace consider the sum of any two subset vectors $\mathbf{x_m}$ and $\mathbf{x_{m'}}$. This sum is

$$
\begin{array}{rl}
\mathbf{x_m} = & w_{m0} \cdot \mathbf{g_0} + \quad w_{m1} \cdot \mathbf{g_1} + \cdots + \quad w_{m,k-1} \cdot \mathbf{g_{k-1}} \\
\mathbf{x_{m'}} = & w_{m'0} \cdot \mathbf{g_0} + \quad w_{m'1} \cdot \mathbf{g_1} + \cdots + \quad w_{m',k-1} \cdot \mathbf{g_{k-1}} \\
\hline
= & (w_{m0} + w_{m'0}) \cdot \mathbf{g_0} + (w_{m1} + w_{m'1}) \cdot \mathbf{g_1} + \cdots + (w_{m,k-1} + w_{m',k-1}) \cdot \mathbf{g_{k-1}}
\end{array}
$$

In the result, the modulo-2 sums $(w_{m1} + w_{m'1})$ are also binary scalars so that the result is also a linear combination of the vectors $\mathbf{g}$. Therefore, since *all* linear combinations of $\mathbf{g}$ are in the set, the sum of any two vectors $\mathbf{x}$ is another vector in the set and the first condition for subspaces is met. Since $\mathbf{w} = \mathbf{0}$ defines a valid linear combination, the zero vector is in the set. The product of the scalar 0 and any vector is $0 \cdot \mathbf{x_m} = (0 \cdot x_{m0})\,(0 \cdot x_{m1}) \cdots (0 \cdot x_{m,k-1}) = 0\,0\cdots 0$, which was just shown to be in the set so the first half of the second condition is met. Finally, the product of the scalar 1 and any vector is $1 \cdot \mathbf{x_m} = (1 \cdot x_{m0})(1 \cdot x_{m1}) \cdots (1 \cdot x_{m,k-1}) = x_{m0}\, x_{m1} \cdots x_{m,k-1} = \mathbf{x_m}$, which is obviously in the set. Therefore, the second half of the second condition is met and the subset is indeed a linear subspace. Because any vector in the subspace is a linear combination of the vectors $\mathbf{g}$, the vectors $\mathbf{g}$ are said to *span* the subspace.

It has been shown that a linear vector subspace S_{sub} can be constructed by forming all linear combinations of k binary and n-vectors of a linear vector space. No conditions are placed on the k vectors except that they be members of a linear vector space. The converse of this is also true, that is, a set of k vectors $\mathbf{g}$ can always be found that can construct *any* linear subspace S_{sub}. The trivial case where the set $\mathbf{g}_0, \mathbf{g}_1, \ldots, \mathbf{g}_{k-1}$ is identical to the subspace $\mathbf{x}_0, \mathbf{x}_1, \mathbf{x}_2, \ldots, \mathbf{x}_{K-1}$ demonstrates this. The smallest set of $\mathbf{g}$s that can be found to construct a subspace is always linearly independent. To see this suppose that the set of $\mathbf{g}$s is linearly dependent and $\mathbf{g}_1 = \mathbf{g}_j + \cdots + \mathbf{g}_l$ for some combination of $\mathbf{g}$s on the right side of the equation. Any $\mathbf{x}_m$ constructed using $\mathbf{g}_1$ can also be constructed using $\mathbf{g}_j + \cdots + \mathbf{g}_l$ so that $\mathbf{g}_1$ can be discarded from the set of $\mathbf{g}$s thereby reducing the number of vectors in the set. When all linear dependencies have been eliminated, the set of $\mathbf{g}$s is linearly independent and contains the fewest possible number of elements. The set of k linearly independent vectors $\mathbf{g}_0, \mathbf{g}_1, \ldots, \mathbf{g}_{k-1}$ which span the vector subspace is called the *basis* of the subspace. The number of vectors in the basis is the *dimension* of the subspace.

Finally, consider the subset S_{null} of all n-vectors in the space S that are orthogonal to all n-vectors in S_{sub}. That is, a vector $\mathbf{y}$ in S_{null} is orthogonal to any n-vector in S_{sub} and any vector in S that is orthogonal to all $\mathbf{x}$ in S_{sub} is in S_{null}. The set S_{null} is called the *null space* of the space S_{sub}. It can be shown that the dimensionality of the null space is $n-k$ where n is the dimensionality of S and k is the dimensionality of S_{sub}. It can also be shown that the null space is a valid subspace of the space S and that S_{sub} is the null space of S_{null}.

6.3.2.3 Linear Block Codes.

A *linear block code* is defined as a block code whose codewords form a k-dimensional subspace of the linear vector space of all possible n-vectors. Applying the properties of linear spaces, it is immediately concluded that the sum of any two code vectors of a linear block code is another code vector. Also, since the sum of a code vector and itself is a valid code vector and is equal to the zero vector, the all-zero vector is a code vector in every linear block code.

EXAMPLE 6–11

Consider again the set $\mathbf{g}_0, \mathbf{g}_1, \mathbf{g}_2, \mathbf{g}_3$ of the previous example. In that example it was shown that this set is linearly independent since no linear combination except $(0 \cdot \mathbf{g}_0) + (0 \cdot \mathbf{g}_1) + (0 \cdot \mathbf{g}_2) + (0 \cdot \mathbf{g}_3)$ equals the zero vector. It was also shown that the 16 linear combinations of $\mathbf{g}$s are the 16 codewords of the Hamming code. Since all linear combinations of $\mathbf{g}$s are included in the Hamming code, the code is a linear subspace of the space of all 7-vectors. Since the $\mathbf{g}$s are independent, they are the smallest set of vectors that can be used to generate the subspace and the dimension of the subspace is 4, the number of vectors $\mathbf{g}$. Since all vectors in the subspace are generated by linear combinations of $\mathbf{g}$, the $\mathbf{g}$s span the subspace. Therefore, the Hamming code is a linear block code having dimension $k = 4$.

Since a block code forms a k-dimensional subspace of the space of all n-vectors, all code vectors can be generated by linear combinations of the k linearly independent basis vectors of the subspace. The k basis vectors are called the *generator vectors* of the code. It is convenient to use matrix arithmetic to calculate the codewords of a code. Arrange the generator vectors of a code in a column to form the *code generator matrix* $\mathbf{G}$ defined by

$$G = \begin{bmatrix} \mathbf{g_0} \\ \mathbf{g_1} \\ \vdots \\ \mathbf{g_{k-1}} \end{bmatrix} = \begin{bmatrix} g_{00} & g_{01} & \cdots & g_{0,n-1} \\ g_{10} & g_{11} & \cdots & g_{1,n-1} \\ \vdots & \vdots & & \vdots \\ g_{k-1,0} & g_{k-1,1} & \cdots & g_{k-1,n-1} \end{bmatrix} \tag{6-47}$$

Let the message vectors be defined as before by k-vectors $\mathbf{w_m} = w_{m0} \, w_{m1} \, w_{m2} \cdots w_{m,k-1}$. Then the codeword row vector $\mathbf{x_m}$ is calculated by the matrix multiplication of the row vector $\mathbf{w_m}$ and G. That is,

$$\mathbf{x_m} = \mathbf{w_m} \times G$$

$$= [w_{m0} \, w_{m1} \cdots w_{m,k-1}] \times \begin{bmatrix} g_{00} & g_{01} & \cdots & g_{0,n-1} \\ g_{10} & g_{11} & \cdots & g_{1,n-1} \\ \vdots & \vdots & & \vdots \\ g_{k-1,0} & g_{k-1,1} & \cdots & g_{k-1,n-1} \end{bmatrix} \tag{6-48}$$

From this equation it is apparent that each codeword symbol is a modulo-2 linear combination of the message symbols. The specific message symbols combined for a particular code vector symbol are defined by the generator matrix. Each code vector symbol can also be calculated using

$$x_{m,j} = \sum_{i=0}^{k-1} w_{m,i} \cdot g_{i,j} \tag{6-49}$$

where arithmetic is performed modulo-2. One of the benefits of using linear codes is that codeword generators implementing this equation are easily built.

EXAMPLE 6–12

The generator matrix for the Hamming code of the previous examples is

$$G = \begin{bmatrix} 1 & 1 & 0 & 1 & 0 & 0 & 0 \\ 0 & 1 & 1 & 0 & 1 & 0 & 0 \\ 1 & 1 & 1 & 0 & 0 & 1 & 0 \\ 1 & 0 & 1 & 0 & 0 & 0 & 1 \end{bmatrix}$$

and the codeword corresponding to the message vector $\mathbf{w} = 1\,0\,1\,1$ is

$$\mathbf{x} = \mathbf{w} \times G$$

$$= [1\,0\,1\,1] \times \begin{bmatrix} 1 & 1 & 0 & 1 & 0 & 0 & 0 \\ 0 & 1 & 1 & 0 & 1 & 0 & 0 \\ 1 & 1 & 1 & 0 & 0 & 1 & 0 \\ 1 & 0 & 1 & 0 & 0 & 0 & 1 \end{bmatrix}$$

$$= [1\,0\,0\,1\,0\,1\,1]$$

A linear code is a linear subspace of the space of all n-vectors. The null space of this subspace is also a subspace and can be represented by generator basis vectors or a generator matrix. Denote the generator matrix of the null space by $\mathbf{H}$ and the generator (basis) vectors by $\mathbf{h_0}, \mathbf{h_1}, \ldots, \mathbf{h_{n-k-1}}$. The null space generator matrix

$$\mathbf{H} = \begin{bmatrix} \mathbf{h_0} \\ \mathbf{h_1} \\ \vdots \\ \mathbf{h_{n-k-1}} \end{bmatrix} = \begin{bmatrix} h_{00} & h_{01} & \cdots & h_{0,n-1} \\ h_{10} & h_{11} & \cdots & h_{1,n-1} \\ \vdots & \vdots & & \vdots \\ h_{n-k-1,0} & h_{n-k-1,1} & \cdots & h_{n-k-1,n-1} \end{bmatrix} \tag{6-50}$$

This matrix is called the *parity check matrix* of the code defined by $\mathbf{G}$. It can be proven [10] that the dimension of the null space is $n-k$ when the dimension of the code space is k. By definition, all the vectors in the null space are orthogonal to all the vectors of the code. Since the vectors $\mathbf{h_j}$ are members of the null space, they are orthogonal to any code vector. Thus, $\mathbf{x_m} \cdot \mathbf{h_j} = 0$ for any $m = 0, \ldots, 2^k - 1$ and $j = 0, \ldots, n - k - 1$. In matrix notation

$$\mathbf{0} = \mathbf{x_m} \times \mathbf{H}^T$$

$$= \mathbf{x_m} \times \begin{bmatrix} \mathbf{h_0^T} & \mathbf{h_1^T} \cdots & \mathbf{h_{n-k-1}^T} \end{bmatrix}$$

$$= \begin{bmatrix} x_{m0} & x_{m1} & \cdots & x_{m,n-1} \end{bmatrix} \times \begin{bmatrix} h_{00} & h_{10} & \cdots & h_{n-k-1,0} \\ h_{01} & h_{11} & \cdots & h_{n-k-1,1} \\ \vdots & \vdots & & \vdots \\ h_{0,n-1} & h_{1,n-1} & \cdots & h_{n-k-1,n-1} \end{bmatrix} \tag{6-51}$$

where the superscript T denotes the matrix transpose. It is also true that any vector $\mathbf{y}$ that is not a codeword does not satisfy this relationship. Thus, a vector $\mathbf{y}$ is a codeword if and only if

$$\mathbf{0} = \mathbf{y} \times \mathbf{H}^T \tag{6-52}$$

is satisfied. A linear block code can be specified either by its generator matrix $\mathbf{G}$ or by its parity check matrix $\mathbf{H}$. Both are used in practice.

EXAMPLE 6–13

The parity check matrix for the $(7, 4)$ linear block code of the previous examples

$$\mathbf{H} = \begin{bmatrix} 1 & 0 & 0 & 1 & 0 & 1 & 1 \\ 0 & 1 & 0 & 1 & 1 & 1 & 0 \\ 0 & 0 & 1 & 0 & 1 & 1 & 1 \end{bmatrix}$$

The matrix product of the n-vector $\mathbf{y} = 1\,1\,1\,1\,0\,0\,1$ and the transpose of $\mathbf{H}$ is

$$[1\ 1\ 1\ 1\ 0\ 0\ 1] \cdot \begin{bmatrix} 1 & 0 & 0 \\ 0 & 1 & 0 \\ 0 & 0 & 1 \\ 1 & 1 & 0 \\ 0 & 1 & 1 \\ 1 & 1 & 1 \\ 1 & 0 & 1 \end{bmatrix} = [1\ 0\ 0]$$

which is not zero, indicating that **y** is not a valid codeword.

6.3.2.4 Systematic Linear Block Codes. As specified, any symbol of a code vector is a linear combination of message symbols. Thus, the message symbols themselves do not necessarily appear in the codewords. *Systematic block codes* are codes having generators of a form such that the message vector appears directly in the code vector. Systematic codes are a subset of all linear codes. The message symbols appear directly in a codeword if **G** has the form shown here:

$$\mathbf{x_m} = [x_{m0}\ x_{m1}\ \cdots\ x_{m,n-k-1}\ w_{m0}\ w_{m1}\ \cdots\ w_{m,k-1}]$$

$$= [w_{m0}\ w_{m1}\ \cdots\ w_{m,k-1}] \tag{6-53}$$

$$\times \begin{bmatrix} g_{0,0} & g_{0,1} & \cdots & g_{0,n-k-1} & 1 & 0 & 0 & \cdots & 0 \\ g_{1,0} & g_{1,1} & \cdots & g_{1,n-k-1} & 0 & 1 & 0 & \cdots & 0 \\ g_{2,0} & g_{2,1} & \cdots & g_{2,n-k-1} & 0 & 0 & 1 & \cdots & 0 \\ \vdots & \vdots & & & & & & & \vdots \\ g_{k-1,0} & g_{k-1,1} & \cdots & g_{k-1,n-k-1} & 0 & 0 & 0 & \cdots & 1 \end{bmatrix}$$

Observe that an identity matrix appears in the right side of **G.** For systematic codes the first $n-k$ code vector symbols are parity checks of the message symbols. It can be shown that a systematic code exists whose error correction performance is identical to any given linear code. Therefore, the communications system engineer may limit consideration to systematic codes without fear of overlooking a better code which is not systematic. The Hamming code of Table 6–4 is systematic with the message symbols appearing at the right in each code vector.

For systematic codes the parity check matrix **H** can be determined directly from the generator matrix. Specifically, with the generator matrix as specified, the parity check matrix is

$$\mathbf{H} = \begin{bmatrix} 1 & 0 & 0 & \cdots & 0 & g_{0,0} & g_{1,0} & \cdots & g_{k-1,0} \\ 0 & 1 & 0 & \cdots & 0 & g_{0,1} & g_{1,1} & \cdots & g_{k-1,1} \\ 0 & 0 & 1 & \cdots & 0 & g_{0,2} & g_{1,2} & \cdots & g_{k-1,2} \\ \vdots & \vdots & \vdots & & & & & & \\ 0 & 0 & 0 & \cdots & 1 & g_{0,n-k-1} & g_{1,n-k-1} & \cdots & g_{k-1,n-k-1} \end{bmatrix} \tag{6-54}$$

6.3.2.5 Distance Properties of Linear Block Codes. The distance properties of codes are key to their error correction capabilities. In good codes the Hamming distance between any two codewords is as large as possible for the codeword length n and the code rate R. For minimum distance decoders, block decoding errors are made when channel errors cause the received n-vector to be closer in Hamming distance to a codeword different than the transmitted codeword. Knowledge of the Hamming distance between all codeword pairs is necessary in order to calculate either block error or bit error probabilities.

Consider the Hamming distance $d_H(\mathbf{x}_x, \mathbf{x}_{m'})$ between any two code vectors $\mathbf{x}_m$ and $\mathbf{x}_{m'}$ of a linear block code. Suppose that third code vector $\mathbf{x}_a$ is added to both $\mathbf{x}_m$ and to $\mathbf{x}_{m'}$. The addition changes the code vector components of both $\mathbf{x}_m$ and $\mathbf{x}_{m'}$ in the same positions, specifically, the positions where $\mathbf{x}_a$ has 1s. Since both $\mathbf{x}_m$ and $\mathbf{x}_{m'}$ are changed in the same positions, the Hamming distance between the sum vectors is the same as the Hamming distance between the original vectors. That is, $d_H(\mathbf{x}_m + \mathbf{x}_a, \mathbf{x}_{m'} + \mathbf{x}_a) = d_H(\mathbf{x}_m, \mathbf{x}_{m'})$. Since $\mathbf{x}_a$ is an arbitrary code vector, let $\mathbf{x}_a = \mathbf{x}_{m'}$ so that $d_H(\mathbf{x}_m + \mathbf{x}_{m'}, \mathbf{x}_{m'} + \mathbf{x}_{m'}) = d_H(\mathbf{x}_m + \mathbf{x}_{m'}, \mathbf{0})$. Thus, the Hamming distance between any two code vectors of a linear block code is equal to the Hamming distance between the zero code vector and some code vector in the code. In fact, the distances between any particular code vector and all other code vectors is equal to the set of distances from the zero code vector to all nonzero code vectors. The minimum distance d_{min} of the block code is equal to the smallest Hamming distance between any distinct pair of code vectors. Using the linearity of the code, the minimum distance of the code is equal to the smallest distance between the zero code vector and any nonzero code vector. The minimum distance is thus the Hamming weight of the lowest weight nonzero code vector. The now familiar Hamming code of Table 6–4 has minimum distance three. Examination of Table 6–4 will show that the nonzero code vector with the minimum number of 1s has three 1s, which is consistent with the code's minimum distance.

A minimum distance decoder for a block code with a minimum distance d_{min} is able to decode correctly any transmission where $\lfloor (d_{min} - 1)/2 \rfloor \equiv t$ or fewer errors occur. In this expression the notation $\lfloor x \rfloor$ is the largest integer that is smaller than or equal to x. To prove this, consider the distances $d_H(\mathbf{x}_m, \mathbf{y})$ and $d_H(\mathbf{x}_{m'}, \mathbf{y})$, where $\mathbf{x}_m$ is the transmitted code vector, $\mathbf{y}$ is the received vector, and $\mathbf{x}_m$ and $\mathbf{x}_{m'}$, are nearest neighbors; that is, $d_H(\mathbf{x}_m, \mathbf{x}_{m'}) = d_{min}$. The decoder will decode correctly if it is impossible for $\mathbf{y}$ to be closer to $\mathbf{x}_{m'}$ than to $\mathbf{x}_m$ when t errors occur. If t transmission errors occur, $d_H(\mathbf{x}_m, \mathbf{y}) = t$ and $\mathbf{x}_m$ differs from $\mathbf{y}$ in t positions. Assume that the errors occur in the worst possible locations for decoding $\mathbf{x}_{m'}$ rather than $\mathbf{x}_m$; these positions are positions where $\mathbf{x}_m$ and $\mathbf{x}_{m'}$ differ. Every error that occurs in these positions causes $\mathbf{y}$ to be one unit closer to $\mathbf{x}_{m'}$ and one unit farther from $\mathbf{x}_m$. With t errors in these positions, $d_H(\mathbf{x}_{m'}, \mathbf{y}) = d_{min} - t$. Since $t \leq (d_{min} - 1)/2$, $d_{min} - t \geq (d_{min} + 1)/2 \geq (d_{min} - 1)/2$. Therefore, $\mathbf{y}$ is closer to $\mathbf{x}_m$ than to $\mathbf{x}_{m'}$ and correct decoding always occurs. This property will be used to obtain useful relationships for block and bit error probability. Note that, although t transmission errors can always be corrected, a minimum distance decoder can also sometimes correct error patterns having more than t errors.

6.3.2.6 Decoding Using the Standard Array. A convenient method is available for constructing the decoding regions Λ_m for linear block codes. Recall that decoding regions partition the space of all n-vectors into subsets such that all received $\mathbf{y}$ within Λ_m are most likely to have been caused by the transmission of message vector $\mathbf{x_m}$. For the binary symmetric channel with error probability < 0.5, this means that all $\mathbf{y}$ within Λ_m are closer in Hamming distance to $\mathbf{x_m}$ than to any other code vector $\mathbf{x_{m'}}$. Brute force construction of the decoding regions is accomplished by calculating the Hamming distance between each of the 2^n possible received $\mathbf{y}$ and all code vectors $\mathbf{x_m}$ and placing $\mathbf{y}$ in the appropriate region.

The construction of the decoding regions for the binary symmetric channel is greatly facilitated by using the following procedure. First, place all of the code vectors $\mathbf{x_m}$ in a row with the all-zero vector on the left. Next select an error vector $\mathbf{e_1}$ that is not identical to any codeword in the first row and place it below the all zero vector. When this procedure is completed, the error vector just selected will be a correctable error vector, meaning that, if it occurs, the received vector will be correctly decoded. Although the selection of the error vector is arbitrary, it can be shown that the ability to correct the most probable error vectors will result in the best communication system performance. Therefore, since the probability of an error vector increases with decreasing weight, the best error vector to select is the vector having the smallest weight. In all cases this first selection will be a vector with unit Hamming weight. Now add $\mathbf{e_1}$ to every nonzero code vector and place the results in a row to the right of $\mathbf{e_1}$ below the corresponding code vector. Now select another error vector $\mathbf{e_2}$ and place it below the all-zero vector. The vector $\mathbf{e_2}$ should be a vector with the lowest possible Hamming weight that does not appear in either of the first two rows. Form the sum of $\mathbf{e_2}$ and all code vectors and place the sums in a row under the corresponding code vector. Repeat this procedure until all n-vectors have been exhausted. The result is

$$
\begin{array}{ccccc}
\mathbf{x_0} & \mathbf{x_1} & \mathbf{x_2} & \cdots & \mathbf{x_{2^k-1}} \\
\mathbf{e_1 + x_0} & \mathbf{e_1 + x_1} & \mathbf{e_1 + x_2} & \cdots & \mathbf{e_1 + x_{2^k-1}} \\
\mathbf{e_2 + x_0} & \mathbf{e_2 + x_1} & \mathbf{e_2 + x_2} & \cdots & \mathbf{e_2 + x_{2^k-1}} \\
\vdots & \vdots & \vdots & & \vdots \\
\mathbf{e_{2^{n-k}-1} + x_0} & \mathbf{e_{2^{n-k}-1} + x_1} & \mathbf{e_{2^{n-k}-1} + x_2} & \cdots & \mathbf{e_{2^{n-k}-1} + x_{2^k-1}}
\end{array}
\tag{6-55}
$$

The array just constructed is called the *standard array*. It can be shown [8] that, because of the construction procedure used and because the code is linear, each n-vector in the array is distinct and that all 2^n possible n-vectors appear exactly once in the array. There are always 2^{n-k} rows in the array.

The standard array is used for decoding by defining the decoding region Λ_m to be all of the n-vectors in the column with the code vector $\mathbf{x_m}$ (including $\mathbf{x_m}$). Whenever a received vector $\mathbf{y}$ falls within the same column as $\mathbf{x_m}$, message m is decoded. Since all n-vectors appear in the array once and only once, all $\mathbf{y}$ appear in a single Λ_m (column) and are uniquely decoded. Examination of the standard array will show that, for any code vector $\mathbf{x_m}$, if the actual error pattern is any of the error vectors $\mathbf{e_j}$, the received $\mathbf{y}$ will be in the same column as x_m and will be correctly decoded. Thus, the selected error patterns are correctable. The only conditions placed on the selection of e_j is that a new selection does not appear in any of the rows above it. It can be proven that any error vectors that are *not* in the first column of the array are *not* correctable and, in fact, result in a block decoding error. For any (n, k) linear block code, standard array decoding is able to correct exactly 2^{n-k} error vectors, including the all-zero error vector.

Good communications performance is achieved by selecting correctable error vectors having the lowest weight possible of all vectors not appearing in any row already constructed. It can be proven that the decoding regions constructed from a standard array using this rule are in fact minimum distance decoding regions. Therefore, generating the standard array is a correct procedure for generating the decoding regions Λ_m for a linear block code.

Standard array decoding can be simplified by making use of the parity check matrix. Recall that any codeword of a linear code satisfies

$$0 = x_m \times H^T$$

and consider any received vector $y = x_m + e_j$. The matrix product of y and the transpose of the parity check matrix is called the *syndrome* of y and is

$$(e_j + x_m) \times H^T = e_j \times H^T + x_m \times H^T \qquad (6\text{--}56)$$

$$= e_j \times H^T + 0$$

The syndrome is a function only of the error vector e_j. It is easily shown that the syndromes of all the received vectors in a single row of the standard array are equal and further [8] that the syndromes of received vectors appearing in different rows of the array are different. Because of these facts, decoding can be accomplished using the following steps:

1. Calculate the syndrome of the received vector y.
2. Find the row in the standard array which has the same syndrome and estimate the error vector to be the error vector for that row.
3. Add the estimated error vector to the received vector to estimate the transmitted codeword.

If the actual error pattern is one of the patterns used in creating the standard array, correct decoding will occur.

EXAMPLE 6–14 _____

Table 6–8 is the standard array for the $(7, 4)$ Hamming code that has been considered in the previous examples. The first row contains all 16 codewords. The Hamming code can correct all single-error patterns. These error patterns are shown in the first column of the array. Suppose that the received vector is $y = [1\ 1\ 1\ 0\ 1\ 0\ 1]$, which is shown in the dashed box of the array. What is the decoder's estimate of the transmitted codeword?

TABLE 6–8 Standard Array for the Hamming (7, 4) Code

0000000	1101000	0110100	1011100	1110010	0011010	0101110	1000110	1010001	0111001	1100101	0001101	0100011	1001011	0010111	1111111
0000001	1101001	0110101	1011101	1110011	0011011	0101111	1000111	1010000	0111000	1100100	0001100	0100010	1001010	0010110	1111110
0000010	1101010	0110110	1011110	1110000	0011000	0101100	1000100	1010011	0111011	1100111	0001111	0100001	1001001	0010101	1111101
0000100	1101100	0110000	1011000	1110110	0011110	0101010	1000010	1010101	0111101	1100001	0001001	0100111	1001111	0010011	1111011
0001000	1100000	0111100	1010100	1111010	0010010	0100110	1001110	1011001	0110001	1101101	0000101	0101011	1000011	0011111	1110111
0010000	1111000	0100100	1001100	1100010	0001010	0111110	1010110	1000001	0101001	1110101	0011101	0110011	1011011	0000111	1101111
0100000	1001000	0010100	1111100	1010010	0111010	0001110	1100110	1110001	0011001	1000101	0101101	0000011	1101011	0110111	1011111
1000000	0101000	1110100	0011100	0110010	1011010	1101110	0000110	0010001	1111001	0100101	1001101	1100011	0001011	1010111	0111111

In this simple case where the location of the received vector is easily found in the array, the decoder estimates the transmitted codeword to be the codeword at the head of the column that contains the received vector. In this case the decoder output is $\mathbf{x} = [1\ 1\ 0\ 0\ 1\ 0\ 1]$. In more complicated cases where n is large, the decoder calculates the syndrome of the received vector and compares that syndrome with that of all correctable error patterns. The parity check matrix for the (7, 4) Hamming code is

$$\mathbf{H} = \begin{bmatrix} 1 & 0 & 0 & 1 & 0 & 1 & 1 \\ 0 & 1 & 0 & 1 & 1 & 1 & 0 \\ 0 & 0 & 1 & 0 & 1 & 1 & 1 \end{bmatrix}$$

and its transpose is

$$\mathbf{H}^T = \begin{bmatrix} 1 & 0 & 0 \\ 0 & 1 & 0 \\ 0 & 0 & 1 \\ 1 & 1 & 0 \\ 0 & 1 & 1 \\ 1 & 1 & 1 \\ 1 & 0 & 1 \end{bmatrix}$$

Prior to beginning operation, the decoder will have calculated the syndromes of all the correctable error patterns. For example, the syndrome of error pattern for $\mathbf{e} = [0\ 0\ 0\ 1\ 0\ 0\ 0]$ is

$$[0\ 0\ 0\ 1\ 0\ 0\ 0] \times \begin{bmatrix} 1 & 0 & 0 \\ 0 & 1 & 0 \\ 0 & 0 & 1 \\ 1 & 1 & 0 \\ 0 & 1 & 1 \\ 1 & 1 & 1 \\ 1 & 0 & 1 \end{bmatrix} = [1\ 1\ 0]$$

The syndromes of the other error patterns are calculated similarly. The results are

0	0	0	0	0	0	1	$\rightarrow$	1	0	1
0	0	0	0	0	1	0	$\rightarrow$	1	1	1
0	0	0	0	1	0	0	$\rightarrow$	0	1	1
0	0	0	1	0	0	0	$\rightarrow$	1	1	0
0	0	1	0	0	0	0	$\rightarrow$	0	0	1
0	1	0	0	0	0	0	$\rightarrow$	0	1	0
1	0	0	0	0	0	0	$\rightarrow$	1	0	0

After receiving $\mathbf{y}$, the decoder calculates its syndrome. The result is

$$[1\ 1\ 1\ 0\ 1\ 0\ 1] \times \begin{bmatrix} 1 & 0 & 0 \\ 0 & 1 & 0 \\ 0 & 0 & 1 \\ 1 & 1 & 0 \\ 0 & 1 & 1 \\ 1 & 1 & 1 \\ 1 & 0 & 1 \end{bmatrix} = [0\ 0\ 1]$$

This syndrome $\mathbf{s} = [0\ 0\ 1]$ is the same as the precalculated syndrome for the error pattern $\mathbf{e} = [0\ 0\ 1\ 0\ 0\ 0\ 0]$, which the decoder now estimates as the received error pattern. The transmitted codeword is the modulo-2 sum of received vector and the estimated error vector or $[1\ 1\ 1\ 0\ 1\ 0\ 1] + [0\ 0\ 1\ 0\ 0\ 0\ 0] = [1\ 1\ 0\ 0\ 1\ 0\ 1] = \mathbf{x}$. This is the same result found previously.

Since standard array decoding is able to correct all of the error vectors used in the generation of the array and no others, the block error rate P_B is

$$P_B = 1.0 - \sum_{j=0}^{2^{n-k}-1} p^{w_H(\mathbf{e}_j)}(1-p)^{n-w_H(\mathbf{e}_j)} \tag{6-57}$$

where $w_H(\mathbf{e}_j)$ is the Hamming weight of $\mathbf{e}_j$. This equation is 1 minus the probability of occurrence of any one of the correctable error vectors.

6.3.2.7 Error Probabilities for Linear Codes. Bounding techniques can be used to simplify the calculation of block error probability for linear block codes. First, reconsider the block error probability result discussed previously. The average block error probability for any code (linear or nonlinear) is the average (over all messages m) of the probability that the received vector $\mathbf{y}$ is not in the decoding region Λ_m. This error probability is

$$P_B = \sum_{m=0}^{2^k-1} Q_M(m) P_{B_m} \tag{6-58}$$

where

$$P_{B_m} = \Pr(\mathbf{y} \in \overline{\Lambda}_m \mid \mathbf{x_m}) \tag{6-59}$$

$$= \sum_{\mathbf{y} \in \overline{\Lambda}_m} \Pr(\mathbf{y} \mid \mathbf{x_m})$$

For large k and n the brute-force calculation using this relationship is difficult. To facilitate the prediction of performance of coded systems, coding theorists have applied bounding techniques to this problem.

Examine the region $\overline{\Lambda}_m$ in detail. The region $\overline{\Lambda}_m$ can be defined by

$$\overline{\Lambda}_m = \{\mathbf{y} \mid \ln[\Pr(\mathbf{y} \mid \mathbf{x_{m'}})] \geq \ln[\Pr(\mathbf{y} \mid \mathbf{x_m})] \text{ for some } m' \neq m\}$$

$$= \bigcup_{m' \neq m} [\mathbf{y} \mid \ln[\Pr(\mathbf{y} \mid \mathbf{x_{m'}})] \geq \ln[\Pr(\mathbf{y} \mid \mathbf{x_m})]\} \tag{6-60}$$

$$= \bigcup_{m' \neq m} \Lambda_{mm'}$$

where

$$\Lambda_{mm'} = \left\{ \mathbf{y} \,\middle|\, \ln\left[\frac{\Pr(\mathbf{y} \mid \mathbf{x_{m'}})}{\Pr(\mathbf{y} \mid \mathbf{x_m})}\right] \geq 0 \right\} \tag{6-61}$$

For each m and m' the region $\Lambda_{mm'}$ consists of all $\mathbf{y}$ that are more likely to be due to the transmission of $\mathbf{x_{m'}}$ than to the transmission of $\mathbf{x_m}$ without consideration of any other codewords. That is, the space of all $\mathbf{y}$ has been partitioned into two decoding regions, one for $\mathbf{x_m}$ and one for $\mathbf{x_{m'}}$. Since, for a particular m and m', all $\mathbf{y}$ are included within either $\Lambda_{mm'}$ or $\overline{\Lambda}_{mm'}$, the $\Lambda_{mm'}$ for different m and m' are not disjoint. Recall from probability theory that the probability of a union of events is less than or equal to the sum of the probabilities of the component events. Thus the block error probability can be overbounded by

$$P_{B_m} = \Pr(\mathbf{y} \in \overline{\Lambda}_m \mid \mathbf{x_m})$$

$$= \Pr\left(\mathbf{y} \in \bigcup_{m' \neq m} \Lambda_{mm'} \mid \mathbf{x_m} \right)$$

$$\leq \sum_{m \neq m'} \Pr(\mathbf{y} \in \Lambda_{mm'} \mid \mathbf{x_m}) \tag{6-62}$$

$$= \sum_{m \neq m'} P'_B(m, m')$$

where $P'_B(m, m')$ is the probability of block error under the assumption that there are only two codewords m and m' in the code.

The evaluation of $P'_B(m, m')$ is done using methods already described. Specifically, consider a code consisting of two codewords, $\mathbf{x_m}$ and $\mathbf{x_{m'}}$, separated by Hamming distance $d_H(\mathbf{x_m}, \mathbf{x_{m'}})$, and determine the probability of incorrect decoding with a minimum distance decoder. Suppose that $\mathbf{x_m}$ is transmitted. A decoding error occurs whenever transmission errors are made that cause $\mathbf{y}$ to be closer in Hamming distance to $\mathbf{x_{m'}}$ than to $\mathbf{x_m}$. Transmission errors in positions where the two codewords are identical increase the distance between $\mathbf{x_m}$ and $\mathbf{y}$ and the distance between $\mathbf{x_{m'}}$ and $\mathbf{y}$ equally and therefore have no effect on the decoding result. Thus, for d_H even, a decoding error is made whenever $(d_H/2) + 1$ or more transmission errors occur in the positions where $\mathbf{x_m}$ and $\mathbf{x_{m'}}$ differ. When only $(d_H/2)$ errors occur, $\mathbf{y}$ is equidistant from $\mathbf{x_m}$ and $\mathbf{x_{m'}}$, and a decoding error is assumed to be made one-half of the time. Thus the two-codeword error probability for d_H even is

$$P'_B(m,m') = \sum_{e=(d_H/2+1)}^{d_H} \binom{d_H}{e} p^e(1-p)^{d_H-e}, \quad d_H \text{ even}$$

$$+ \frac{1}{2} \binom{d_H}{\frac{d_H}{2}} p^{d_H/2}(1-p)^{d_H/2} \tag{6-63}$$

For d_H odd, a decoding error is made whenever $(d_H + 1)/2$ or more transmission errors occur in the positions where $\mathbf{x_m}$ and $\mathbf{x_{m'}}$ differ, and the two-codeword error probability for d_H odd is

$$P'_B(m, m') = \sum_{e=(d_H+1)/2}^{d_H} \binom{d_H}{e} p^e(1-p)^{d_H-e}, \quad d_H \text{ odd} \tag{6-64}$$

Using these relationships, the total block decoding error probability is bounded by

$$P_B \leq \sum_{m=0}^{2^k-1} Q_M(m) \sum_{\substack{m'=0 \\ m'\neq m}}^{2^k-1} P'_B(m,m') \tag{6-65}$$

The calculation of the average block error probability can be somewhat simplified through the use of upper bounds replacing (6–63) and (6–64). It can be shown [8, 12] that

$$P'_B(m, m') \leq \left[\sqrt{4p(1-p)}\right]^{d_H(m,m')} \tag{6-66}$$

where $d_H(m, m')$ is the Hamming distance between $\mathbf{x_m}$ and $\mathbf{x_{m'}}$.

Further simplification of this result is dependent on the properties of linear codes.

The specific property of importance is the fact that the set of Hamming distances $d_H(\mathbf{x_m}, \mathbf{x_{m'}})$ between a codeword $\mathbf{x_m}$ and all other codewords $\mathbf{x_{m'}}$ for $m' \neq m$, $m' = 0, \ldots,$ $2^k - 1$ is the same for all codewords $\mathbf{x_m}$. Because of this property, the second summation of the bound of (6–65) is the same for any choice of m. Therefore, the error probability is unchanged if $m = 0$ is chosen for all calculations of the second sum. Thus,

$$P_B \leq \sum_{m=0}^{2^k-1} Q_M(m) \sum_{m'=1}^{2^k-1} P'_B(0, m')$$

$$= \sum_{m'=1}^{2^k-1} P'_B(0, m') \sum_{m=0}^{2^k-1} Q_M(m) \tag{6-67}$$

$$= \sum_{m'=1}^{2^k-1} P'_B(0, m')$$

where $P'_B(0, m')$ is calculated using (6–63) and (6–64). For linear codes, therefore, the total average block error probability may be calculated by calculating only the error probability assuming that message $m = 0$ was transmitted.

In principle, the codewords for any specific code can be enumerated to determine the number of codewords that are Hamming distance d from the all-zeros codeword. The function $P_B'(0, m')$ is completely determined if the Hamming distance between $\mathbf{0}$ and $\mathbf{x_{m'}}$ is known. Therefore, the block error probability can also be expressed as a sum over values of Hamming distance

$$P_B \leq \sum_{d=d_{min}}^{n} a_d \, P_B'(d)$$

$$\leq \sum_{d=d_{min}}^{n} a_d \left[\sqrt{4p(1-p)} \right]^d$$

(6–68)

where a_d is the number of codewords that are Hamming distance d from the all-zero codeword of $P_B'(d)$ is the probability of error considering only two codewords separated by Hamming distance d. Note that $P_B'(d)$ denotes the value of $P_B'(m, m')$ for any m and m' such that $d_H(\mathbf{x_m}, \mathbf{x_{m'}}) = d$. The set of values a_d for $d = d_{min}, \ldots, n$ is called the *weight structure* of the code.

For codes with moderate k it is possible to find a_d with the aid of a digital computer. For a small set of codes a_d has been found analytically. Unfortunately, the communications systems engineer is often required to calculate P_B for codes with large k where even a fast digital computer would not be able to enumerate all codewords in a reasonable time. In these cases results can still be obtained by modifying the decoding rules somewhat and limiting consideration to systematic codes. Specifically, assume that the decoder will correct up to a maximum of M channel errors and no more. Decoders having this property are called *bounded distance decoders*. Note that a maximum likelihood decoder is guaranteed to be able to correct t channel errors but it can, in many cases, correct more than t errors. A bounded distance decoder is guaranteed to make a block decoding error whenever more than M channel errors occur. Therefore, the block error probability is simply the probability of $M + 1$ or more channel errors occurring, which is

$$P_B = \sum_{i=M+1}^{n} \binom{n}{i} p^i (1-p)^{n-1}$$

(6–69)

This result is an upper bound on P_B for a maximum likelihood decoder that is guaranteed to correct at least $M = t$ errors.

The results just discussed permit the communication system designer to predict the *block error probability* performance for any linear code. Determining the *bit error probability* requires knowledge of the number of bit errors associated with every possible block decoding error. An exact expression for bit error probability was given previously. One approach to estimating bit error probability is to use bounds that are a function of block error probability. When a block decoding error is made, a minimum of one bit error will always occur. Since k information bits are associated with each block, a single bit error corresponds to an average bit error probability of P_B/k. Thus a lower bound on bit error probability is

$$\frac{P_B}{k} \leq P_b \tag{6-70}$$

Similarly, not more than k-bit errors will occur with each block decoding error. Since k bits are decoded per block, an upper bound on bit error probability is

$$P_b \leq P_B \tag{6-71}$$

These bounds are often adequate for system design purposes.

For linear systematic block codes, improved bit error probability estimates can be made. Recall that, for a linear code, the number of codewords that are Hamming distance d from any particular codeword is the same for all codewords. Using this fact, the block error probability calculation was simplified to the calculation of the block error probability assuming that codeword $\mathbf{0}$ was transmitted. The brute-force calculation of bit error probability weights each possible block error event by the associated number of bit errors as in (6-41). Using arguments similar to those used to simplify the block error probability calculation, it can be shown that for linear systematic block codes the average bit error probability calculation simplifies to the calculation of bit error probability assuming the $\mathbf{0}$ codeword was transmitted. This simplification is possible because (1) the number of codewords Hamming distance d from any particular codeword is the same for all codewords, and (2) the number of bit errors caused by any Hamming distance d block decoding error is the same for all codewords. Consider, for example, the (7, 4) Hamming code. If message 7 was transmitted and message 13 was decoded, two bit errors would occur. The Hamming distance between the transmitted and decoded codewords is 4. There is a corresponding error event associated with the transmission of the $\mathbf{0}$ codeword. Specifically, if message 0 was transmitted and message 9 was decoded, two bit errors would occur. The Hamming distance between the transmitted and decoded codewords is 4.

The probability of information bit error P_b is calculated by assuming that message $\mathbf{0}$ is transmitted and weighting each block error event by the associated number of information bit errors. Let $B(m')$ denote the number of bit errors that occur when $m = 0$ is transmitted and m' is decoded. The average bit error probability is then bounded by extending the bound of (6-67)

$$P_b \leq \sum_{m'=1}^{2^k-1} \frac{1}{k} B(m') P_B'(0, m') \tag{6-72}$$

where $P_B'(0, m')$ is the probability of incorrectly decoding m'. Observe that $P_B'(0, m')$ is a function of the Hamming distance between $\mathbf{0}$ and $\mathbf{x_{m'}}$ and is the same for all codewords with the same Hamming distance. As before let $P_B'(d)$ denote the value of $P_B'(m, m')$ for all m and m' for which $d_H(\mathbf{x_m}, \mathbf{x_{m'}}) = d$. Let B_d denote the total number of bit errors that occur in all block error events involving codewords that are distance d from the all-zeros codeword. Equation (6-72) can be rewritten as

$$P_b < \frac{1}{k} \sum_{d=d_{\min}}^{n} B_d P_B'(d) \tag{6-73}$$

where d_{min} is the minimum distance of the code. This equation provides a good bound on bit error probability for any particular code. The values of B_d may be given or may be calculated using a computer for any particular code. For low error rates, the bit error probability is often bounded using only the first term of this equation.

The usefulness of the techniques just described are limited by the availability of values for B_d for any specific code. For moderate k, B_d can be found with a digital computer. However, for large k other techniques are used. Specifically, once again limit consideration to systematic codes and the bounded distance decoder. With a bounded distance decoder, the received vector will be changed ("corrected") in at most M positions by the decoder. Following Odenwalder [23], in the best case these changes will correct information bit errors in the information portion of the systematic codeword. In the worst case, all changes will still be in the information portion of the codeword but will change already correct information bits making them incorrect. Thus, when $i \leq M$ channel errors occur, correct decoding occurs and no bit errors occur. When $i > M$ channel errors occur, a block decoding error occurs and the maximum number of information bit errors is $\min[k, i + M]$. Clearly no more than all of the information bits can be incorrect and $i + M$ information bit errors can occur if all channel errors occur in the information portion of the codeword and M correct bits are changed by the decoder. Therefore, the bit error probability is over-bounded by

$$P_b \leq \frac{1}{k} \sum_{i=M+1}^{n} \min[k, i + M] \binom{n}{i} p^i (1 - p)^{n-i} \qquad (6\text{–}74)$$

where the $1/k$ factor is due to the fact that k information bits are decoded per block. The binomial coefficient is the usual number of ways in which i errors can occur within a block of n symbols.

Many formulas for block and bit error probability have been given in this discussion. These results are useful when used prudently by the system designer. When specific codes are discussed later, results will be calculated using a number of these methods so that the reader can begin to appreciate the conditions under which various formulas are appropriate.

6.3.3 Cyclic Codes

Recall from Section 6.3.1 that an (n, k) block code is simply a smart mapping of k information bits to n symbol codewords. The codewords and the mapping must be carefully chosen for the code to be useful with respect to improving the performance of the communication system. With no further constraints on code structure the encoding of an (n, k) block code is accomplished using table lookup. In general decoding can be accomplished using the minimum distance decoding rule also using table lookup. For large n and k, table lookup cannot be used due to the size of the required tables. In Section 6.3.2 consideration was limited to linear block codes. The linearity requirement enabled significant simplification of the encoding and decoding processes. Encoding of linear codes can be accomplished by a matrix multiplication of the information k-vector by a generator matrix **G.** Decoding of linear codes was greatly simplified using the standard array and the concept of the syndrome. In this section the encoding and decoding functions are simplified further by requiring the linear code to have additional structure. This additional structure will enable the encoder to take the form of a simple feedforward shift register. Similarly, the decoder will be a feedback shift register with some additional logic used to calculate the error vector. The subject of this section is cyclic linear codes which are a subset of all the linear codes.[5]

6.3.3.1 Definition of Cyclic Codes.   A *cyclic code* is a linear code that has, in addition to the normal properties of a linear code, the property that any cyclic shift of a codeword is also a valid codeword. Thus if $\mathbf{x} = x_0\, x_1\, x_2 \cdots x_{n-2}\, x_{n-1}$ is a codeword in a cyclic code, $\mathbf{x}' = x_{n-1}\, x_0\, x_1 x_2 \cdots x_{n-2}$ is also a codeword of the code. Applying this property repeatedly, the qth cyclic shift, denoted $\mathbf{x}^{(q)}$, of a codeword $\mathbf{x}$ is also a codeword where $\mathbf{x}^{(q)} = x_{n-q}\, x_{n-q+1} \cdots x_0 x_1 \cdots x_{n-q-1}$. Cyclic codes can be described using a generator matrix $\mathbf{G}$ or parity matrix $\mathbf{H}$; however, they are usually described using the concept of a generator polynomial. Before defining the generator polynomial, the arithmetic of polynomial multiplication and division will be reviewed.

6.3.3.2 Polynomial Arithmetic.   Let $\mathbf{w}(D) = w_0 + w_1 D + w_2 D^2 + \cdots + w_{k-1} D^{k-1}$ be a polynomial in D with each w_j from the set $\{0, 1\}$. The degree of this polynomial is the largest power of D that has a nonzero coefficient. For example, the degree of $\mathbf{w}(D) = 1 + D + D^4$ is 4. It is convenient to not show polynomial terms with zero coefficients and also to not show the multiplication by 1 explicitly. That is, write $\mathbf{w}(D) = (1 \cdot D^0) + (1 \cdot D^1) + (0 \cdot D^2) + (0 \cdot D^3) + (1 \cdot D^4)$ as $\mathbf{w}(D) = 1 + D + D^4$. This polynomial is yet another means of representing the k-bit information vector $\mathbf{w} = w_0\, w_1\, w_2 \cdots w_{k-1}$. Let $\mathbf{g}(D) = g_0 + g_1 D + g_2 D^2 + \cdots + g_{n-k} D^{n-k}$ be another polynomial. Define the polynomials $\mathbf{y}(D)$, $\mathbf{x}(D)$, and $\mathbf{e}(D)$ similarly. The modulo-2 *sum of two polynomials* $\mathbf{y}(D) = \mathbf{x}(D) + \mathbf{e}(D)$ is a polynomial $\mathbf{y}(D) = y_0 + y_1 D + y_2 D^2 + \cdots + y_t D^t$ whose coefficients are the modulo-2 sums of the coefficients of like powers of D in $\mathbf{x}(D)$ and $\mathbf{e}(D)$. That is, $y_j = x_j + e_j$. The *product of two polynomials* is a polynomial $\mathbf{x}(D) = x_0 + x_1 D + x_2 D^2 + \cdots + x_{n-1} D^{n-1}$ with coefficients given by

$$
\begin{aligned}
\mathbf{g}(D)\mathbf{w}(D) \;=\; & \left(g_{n-k} \cdot w_{k-1}\right) D^{n-1} \\
& + \left(g_{n-k} \cdot w_{k-2} + g_{n-k-1} \cdot w_{k-1}\right) D^{n-2} \\
& + \left(g_{n-k} \cdot w_{k-3} + g_{n-k-1} \cdot w_{k-2} + g_{n-k-2} \cdot w_{k-1}\right) D^{n-3} \\
& \;\;\vdots \\
& + \left(g_0 \cdot w_0\right) D^0 \\
=\; & x_{n-1} D^{n-1} + x_{n-2} D^{n-2} + \cdots + x_0 D^0
\end{aligned}
$$

$$
x_j = \sum_{i=0}^{j} w_i \cdot g_{j-i}
$$

(6–75)

---

[5]The description of cyclic codes in this section follows the description in Lin and Costello [8]. Significant additional detail can be found in this reference.

where all arithmetic is modulo-2 and coefficients outside the valid range of a polynomial are assumed equal to zero. The polynomial $\mathbf{x}(D)$ is another means of representing a code vector $\mathbf{x} = x_0 \, x_1 \, x_2 \cdots x_{n-1}$.

Equation (6–75) suggests a simple circuit that can perform polynomial multiplication. Figure 6–14 is a conceptual illustration of a circuit for calculating $\mathbf{x}(D) = \mathbf{w}(D) \cdot \mathbf{g}(D)$. Initially the shift registers of Figure 6–14 contain all 0s. The coefficients of $\mathbf{w}(D)$ are input one at a time starting with w_{k-1}. The first output on the right of the figure is $x_{n-1} = w_{k-1} \cdot g_{n-k}$. The shift register is now clocked once so that w_{k-1} is stored in register 1. The output is $x_{n-2} = (w_{k-2} \cdot g_{n-k}) + (w_{k-1} \cdot g_{n-k-1})$. The shift register is clocked a total of $n-1$ times to produce all n coefficients of $\mathbf{x}(D)$. After the kth input coefficient, 0s are input to the shift register. It will be seen later that circuits such as this greatly simplify the encoding for cyclic codes.

Next consider the quotient of the two polynomials $\mathbf{x}(D) \div \mathbf{g}(D)$. This division is performed using the normal rules of polynomial division however modulo-2 arithmetic is used everywhere. The division ends with a remainder $\rho(D)$ if $\mathbf{x}(D)$ is not divisible by $\mathbf{g}(D)$. Denoting the quotient by $\mathbf{q}(D)$

$$\mathbf{x}(D) = \mathbf{q}(D) \cdot \mathbf{g}(D) + \rho(D) \qquad (6\text{–}76)$$

The remainder $\rho(D)$ is very important in the study of cyclic codes. Modulo-2 polynomial division is most easily explained by example. Therefore consider the division of $\mathbf{x}(D) = 1 + D + D^2 + D^4 + D^5$ by $\mathbf{g}(D) = 1 + D + D^3$. This long division is

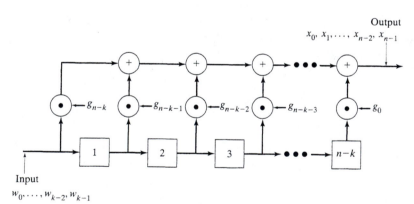

1) Input high order coefficients first

2) First output is highest order coefficient $x_{n-1} = w_{k-1} g_{n-k}$ and is present at output before first shift register clock pulse

3) Clock shift register $(n-1)$ times using zero inputs following w_0

4) $x_0 = w_0 g_0$ is present at output following $(n-1)^{\text{th}}$ clock pulse

FIGURE 6–14   Circuit for multiplying polynomials $w(D)g(D) = x(D)$. (Reproduced from Reference [8] with permission.)

$$
\begin{array}{r}
D^2 + D + 1 \leftarrow \text{Quotient}
\end{array}
$$

$$
D^3 + D + 1 \overline{\big)\, D^5 + D^4 \qquad\; + D^2 + D + 1 }
$$

$$
\underline{D^5 + \qquad D^3 + D^2}
$$

$$
D^4 + D^3 + \qquad D + 1
$$

$$
\underline{D^4 + \qquad D^2 + D}
$$

$$
D^3 + D^2 + \qquad 1
$$

$$
\underline{D^3 + \qquad D + 1}
$$

$$
D^2 + D \qquad \leftarrow \text{Remainder}
$$

Observe that the order of the terms is reversed from the order used when writing the polynomials themselves. Again, in nearly all cases the result of interest for cyclic codes is the remainder. The remainder of this division is denoted by $R_{g(D)}[x(D)] = \rho(D)$.

Although it is not obvious from this discussion, a simple circuit exists for performing polynomial division. Figure 6–15 is a conceptual illustration of a division circuit for dividing $\mathbf{x}(D)$ by $\mathbf{g}(D)$. As in polynomial multiplication, the high-order coefficients are input and output first as explained in the notes of Figure 6–15. With $\mathbf{x}$ of degree $n - 1$ and $\mathbf{g}$ of degree $n - k$ the shift register must be clocked a total $n - 1$ times to produce all coefficients of the quotient $\mathbf{q}$. A last shift is required to produce the remainder, which appears as the contents of the shift register with lowest-order coefficient on the left. Figure 6–16

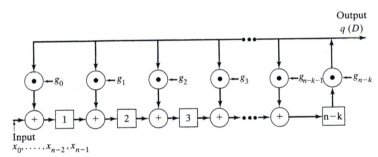

Output
$q(D)$

Input
$x_0, \ldots, x_{n-2}, x_{n-1}$

1) Input high order coefficients first

2) First output is coefficient of D^{n-1} of quotient (always equal to zero but mentioned here to associate outputs with correct power of D in quotient) and is present before first shift register clock pulse

3) First non- zero output occurs after $(n-k)^{\text{th}}$ clock pulse and is coefficient of D^{n-k} in quotient

4) Last term of quotient appears at output after $(n-1)^{\text{th}}$ clock pulse and is coefficient of D^0 in quotient

5) Shift register contains coefficients of remainder $r(D) = r_0 + r_1 D + \ldots r_{n-k-1} D^{n-k-1}$ from left to right after n^{th} clock pulse

FIGURE 6–15 Circuit for dividing $x(D)$ by $g(D)$.

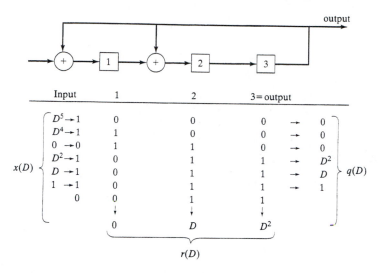

FIGURE 6.16   Circuit for dividing $x(D) = D^5 + D^4 + D^2 + D + 1$ by $g(D) = D^3 + D + 1$.

illustrates the operation of the shift register for the polynomial long division just performed.

6.3.3.3 Properties of Cyclic Codes.   Return now to the discussion of cyclic codes. For any (n, k) cyclic code all of the code vectors (code polynomials) can be represented as the product of a generator polynomial $g(D)$ having degree $r = n - k$ and a message polynomial $w(D)$ having degree $k - 1$. The product $x(D) = w(D) \cdot g(D)$ has degree $(k - 1) + (n - k) = n - 1$ as expected. There are 2^k distinct polynomials $w(D) = w_0 + w_1 D + w_2 D^2 + \cdots + w_{k-1} D^{k-1}$ corresponding to all possible binary choices for the coefficients w_j. Therefore, there are 2^k code polynomials. The codewords of a binary cyclic code are easily generated using a circuit as shown in Figure 6–14. Finding the generator polynomials for cyclic codes is beyond the scope of this discussion; however, a few useful properties of the generator polynomials are the following:

1. The generator polynomial for any cyclic code is a factor of $D^n + 1$. Thus, there will be no remainder if the long division of $D^n + 1$ by $g(D)$ is carried out. Further, any polynomial of degree $n - k$ that is a factor of $D^n + 1$ is the generator for an (n, k) cyclic code.
2. The degree of $g(D)$ is always $n - k$.
3. The qth cyclic shift of a codeword is the remainder of the division of $D^q x(D)$ by $D^n + 1$.
4. Given the generator polynomial $g(D) = g_0 + g_1 D + g_2 D^2 + \cdots + g_{n-k} D^{n-k}$ for a cyclic code, the $k \times n$ generator matrix G is

$$G = \begin{bmatrix} g_0 & g_1 & \cdot & \cdot & g_{n-k-1} & g_{n-k} & 0 & 0 & \cdot & \cdot & \cdot & 0 \\ 0 & g_0 & g_1 & \cdot & \cdot & g_{n-k-1} & g_{n-k} & 0 & 0 & \cdot & \cdot & 0 \\ 0 & 0 & g_0 & g_1 & & \cdot & g_{n-k-1} & g_{n-k} & 0 & 0 & \cdot & 0 \\ \vdots & \vdots & & & & & & & & & & \vdots \\ 0 & 0 & 0 & 0 & 0 & 0 & g_0 & g_1 & \cdot & \cdot & g_{n-k-1} & g_{n-k} \end{bmatrix} \quad (6\text{–}77)$$

5. The $(n - k) \times n$ parity check matrix for a cyclic code is

$$\begin{bmatrix} h_k & h_{k-1} & \cdot & \cdot & h_1 & h_0 & 0 & 0 & \cdot & \cdot & \cdot & 0 \\ 0 & h_k & h_{k-1} & \cdot & \cdot & h_1 & h_0 & 0 & 0 & \cdot & \cdot & 0 \\ 0 & 0 & h_k & h_{k-1} & \cdot & \cdot & h_1 & h_0 & 0 & 0 & \cdot & 0 \\ \vdots & \vdots & & & & & & & & & & \vdots \\ 0 & 0 & 0 & 0 & 0 & 0 & h_k & h_{k-1} & \cdot & \cdot & h_1 & h_0 \end{bmatrix} \quad (6\text{–}78)$$

where $h(D) = h_0 + h_1 D + h_2 D^2 + \cdots + h_k D^k$ is the result of the division of $D^n + 1$ by $g(D)$. Note that there is no remainder due to property 1. The polynomial $h(D)$ is called the *parity polynomial.*

6.3.3.4 Encoding of Cyclic Codes. Performing the multiplication of the generator polynomial by the message polynomial as described will generate all valid code polynomials; however, these polynomials will not be in systematic form. A simple procedure is described by Lin [8] that generates the code polynomials in systematic form using the polynomial division circuitry of Figure 6–15 or via manual polynomial long division. The procedure [8] is given here without proof:

Step 1. Premultiply the message $w(D)$ by D^{n-k}.
Step 2. Obtain the remainder $\rho(D)$ of the division of $D^{n-k}w(D)$ by the generator $g(D)$.
Step 3. The code polynomial is $x(D) = \rho(D) + D^{n-k}w(D)$.

6.3.3.5 Decoding of Cyclic Codes. The structure of cyclic codes enables significant simplification of the decoding process relative to noncyclic linear codes. The justification for the decoding procedure which follows can be found in many excellent references on algebraic coding [8, 10, 11]; due to the complexity of the subject, no attempt at justification will be made here.

Assume that a code polynomial $x(D)$ was transmitted and that errors were added in the channel. The errors are represented by an error polynomial $e(D) = e_0 + e_1 D + \cdots + e_{n-1}D^{n-1}$, where $e_j = 1$ indicates that an error has occurred in the jth position. The received vector is represented by a polynomial $y(D) = y_0 + y_1 D + \cdots + y_{n-1}D^{n-1} = x(D) + e(D)$. Just as was done for decoding with the standard array earlier, decoding of cyclic codes begins with the calculation of a syndrome polynomial $s(D)$. The syndrome polynomial depends only on the error polynomial; that is, the syndrome of $x_m(D) + e(D)$ is the same for all messages m. The syndrome is the remainder when the received polynomial

$y(D)$ is divided by $g(D)$; that is $s(D) = R_{g(D)}[y(D)]$. The syndrome is calculated using the circuitry of Figure 6–15. The syndrome is zero if and only if the received polynomial is identical to some code polynomial, which is the case if no errors were made or if the error polynomial is identical to some code polynomial.

The next step in the decoding process is the association of the syndrome with the most probable error polynomial. This procedure is dependent on the specific code being considered and therefore details cannot be presented here. Assume that a table is available that associates syndromes with error patterns via a table lookup. With the error polynomial determined from the syndrome, the decoding is completed by adding the estimated error polynomial to the received polynomial to determine the estimated code polynomial. In this process advantage is taken of the cyclic structure of the code. The cyclic structure enables the error estimates $e_0, e_1, \cdots, e_{n-1}$ to be made one at a time starting with e_{n-1}. The decoder operates by first estimating e_{n-1} from the initial syndrome. Then the decoder circuitry is clocked to generate another syndrome to estimate of e_{n-2} and so on through e_0. The simplification of the decoder is due to the fact that the same circuitry is used sequentially to estimate $e_{n-1}, e_{n-2}, \cdots, e_0$. As errors are detected by the decoder they are corrected in the received polynomial and at the same time the effect of the corrected error is removed from syndrome calculation circuitry. Figure 6–17 is conceptual block diagram of a decoder for a cyclic code. The received polynomial is input (highest-order term first) into a buffer register (top) and a long division circuit. Gates a, b, and d in Figure 6–17 are closed and gates c and e are open while the received sequence is being read into the de-

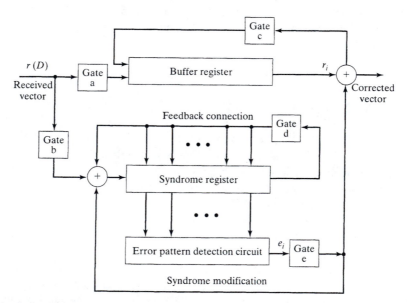

FIGURE 6.17 General cyclic code decoder with received polynomial $r(D)$ shifted into the syndrome register from the left end. (Reproduced from Reference [8] with permission.)

coder. After the received sequence is input, gates a, b and d are opened and gates c and e are closed. The long division performs the division of the received polynomial by the generator polynomial $\mathbf{g}(D)$to find the remainder $\rho(D)$, which is the first syndrome $\mathbf{s}(D)$. The syndrome is input to the "error pattern detection circuit," which will be code specific and can be quite simple. The error detection circuit outputs a 1 if it estimates that an error $e_{n-1} = 1$ has occurred in the highest-order position r_{n-1} of the received polynomial. The buffer register and the division register are simultaneously clocked to output the first decoded symbol which is corrected (if required) by the exclusive-or circuit in the upper right corner. The error estimate is simultaneously input to the division circuit to eliminate its effect on the remaining syndrome. This procedure is repeated until all n received symbols have been corrected. The complexity of the decoder for cyclic codes is proportional to the length n of the codewords. This is in contrast to the complexity of a table lookup scheme for an arbitrary block code, which must have 2^n entries (one for each possible received vector) or the complexity of a standard array decoder, which must have a table with an entry for each correctable error pattern.

6.3.4   Hamming Codes

6.3.4.1 Definition of Hamming Codes.   Hamming codes are a family of codes discovered by R. W. Hamming [4] in about 1950. The Hamming codes all have minimum distance 3 and are able to correct a single error ($t = 1$) in a block of n and to detect all double errors. Hamming codes are linear cyclic systematic codes. Hamming codes with $n = 2^j - 1$ and $k = n - j$ exist for any integer $j \geq 3$. The rate of these codes is $R = k/n = (2^j - 1 - j)/(2^j - 1)$ which approaches 1.0 as j increases. Table 6–9 is a short list of n, k, and R for the first eight Hamming codes.

The Hamming codes are always defined by their parity check matrix, which has $n - k = j$ rows and n columns. The columns consist of all possible nonzero j-component vectors. For example, the parity check matrix for the (7, 4) Hamming code which has been the subject of many of the previous examples is

TABLE 6–9   Codes Rates for Hamming Codes

j	k	n	$R = k/n$
3	4	7	0.57
4	11	15	0.73
5	26	31	0.84
6	57	63	0.90
7	120	127	0.94
8	247	255	0.97
9	502	511	0.98
10	1013	1023	0.99

TABLE 6–10 List of Code Generators for Hamming Codes

j		j	
3	$1 + D + D^3$	14	$1 + D + D^6 + D^{10} + D^{14}$
4	$1 + D + D^4$	15	$1 + D + D^{15}$
5	$1 + D^2 + D^5$	16	$1 + D + D^3 + D^{12} + D^{16}$
6	$1 + D + D^6$	17	$1 + D^3 + D^{17}$
7	$1 + D^3 + D^7$	18	$1 + D^7 + D^{18}$
8	$1 + D^2 + D^3 + D^4 + D^8$	19	$1 + D + D^2 + D^5 + D^{19}$
9	$1 + D^4 + D^9$	20	$1 + D^3 + D^{20}$
10	$1 + D^3 + D^{10}$	21	$1 + D^2 + D^{21}$
11	$1 + D^2 + D^{11}$	22	$1 + D + D^{22}$
12	$1 + D + D^4 + D^6 + D^{12}$	23	$1 + D^5 + D^{23}$
13	$1 + D + D^3 + D^4 + D^{13}$	24	$1 + D + D^2 + D^7 + D^{24}$

$$\mathbf{H} = \begin{bmatrix} 1 & 0 & 0 & 1 & 0 & 1 & 1 \\ 0 & 1 & 0 & 1 & 1 & 1 & 0 \\ 0 & 0 & 1 & 0 & 1 & 1 & 1 \end{bmatrix} \tag{6–79}$$

Observe that all nonzero 3-tuples are used as the columns of this matrix. The generator matrix for the Hamming codes is found via the relationships of (6–53) and (6–54) for linear systematic codes. The generator matrix for this code was given in a previous example. It can be shown that this definition implies that the generator polynomial $\mathbf{g}(D)$ is a member of a special class of polynomials called *primitive polynomials*. Detailed treatments of these special polynomials can be found in advanced texts [6, 8, 10, 13]. Sets of primitive polynomials[6] can be found in these references. Table 6–10 is a short list of primitive polynomials (from [8]) that can be used as generators for Hamming codes up to block length $n = 2^{24} - 1$.

6.3.4.2 Encoding of Hamming Codes.

The encoder used for the Hamming codes can take a variety of forms. If encoding speed is not critical, the encoder can be implemented in software by calculating the generator matrix multiplication directly. If speed is critical, however, other implementations are usually used. Figure 6–18 illustrates a straightforward implementation for a Hamming encoder that can be built using high-speed logic. The $(k - 1)$-bit shift register at the top of Figure 6–18 receives the information bits from the data source. After the input register is filled, the output of the modulo-2 adders are the correct codeword symbols. Each symbol is a modulo-2 sum of certain information bits defined by the generator matrix. The generator matrix can be found from the generator polynomial as was done in Section 6.3.3.3, specifically

[6]Also see Table 9–2.

$$\mathbf{G} = \begin{bmatrix} g_0 & g_1 & \cdots & g_{n-k-1} & g_{n-k} & 0 & 0 & \cdots & & 0 \\ 0 & g_0 & g_1 & \cdots & & g_{n-k-1} & g_{n-k} & 0 & 0\cdots & 0 \\ 0 & 0 & g_0 & g_1 & & \cdots & g_{n-k-1} & g_{n-k} & 00\cdots & 0 \\ \vdots & \vdots & & & & & & & \vdots & \\ 0 & 0 & 0 & 0 & & 0 & g_0 & g_1 & \cdots g_{n-k-1} & g_{n-k} \end{bmatrix} \quad (6\text{–}80)$$

The codeword symbols are strobed into the lower shift register by closing the switches below the modulo-2 adders. The codeword is then clocked out of the encoder to a modulator for transmission. The clock rates for the upper and lower shift registers are different with the lower register clock $1/R$ times the upper register clock rate. New information bits are read into the upper register at the same time that the codeword is being read out of the lower register. The encoder of Figure 6–18 can be used for any cyclic code with proper selection of the generator matrix coefficients. Observe that the complexity of this encoder is proportional to $n \times (n - k)$, which quickly becomes impractical for large block length.

Since Hamming codes are cyclic, a much simpler implementation of the encoder is possible. Recall that codewords for cyclic codes in systematic form are generated by (1) multiplying the message $\mathbf{w}(D)$ polynomial by D^{n-k}, (2) calculating the remainder $\rho(D) = R_{g(D)}[\mathbf{w}(D) \cdot D^{n-k}]$, and (3) $\mathbf{x}(D) = \rho(D) + \mathbf{w}(D) \cdot D^{n-k}$. The encoding circuit of Figure 6–19 performs exactly this calculation. This circuit is a small variation of the circuit of Figure 6–15 for dividing two polynomials. The input has been moved $n - k$ positions to the right, which implements the premultiplication of $\mathbf{w}(D)$ by D^{n-k}. Operation of the encoder begins with the switches in the positions shown. The k message bits are simultaneously input to the division circuitry and output to the user. After the last message bit is input, the shift register contains the remainder of the long division, and the positions of

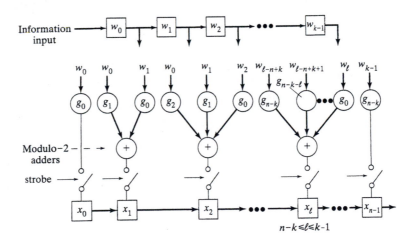

FIGURE 6–18 Hamming encoder.

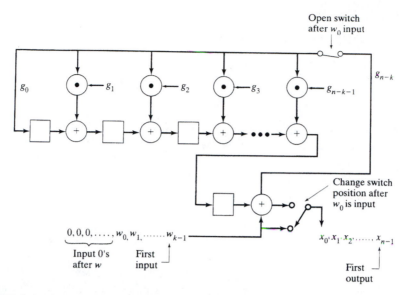

FIGURE 6–19   Feedback shift register implementation of Hamming encoder. (Reproduced from Reference [8] with permission.)

both switches are changed. The upper switch is opened and the output switch is changed to output the contents of the shift register. The shift register is clocked just enough times to output all of the parity bits to complete the encoding process. The complexity of this encoder is proportional to $n - k$, making it the clear choice of encoders for large n.

6.3.4.3 Decoding of Hamming Codes.   Decoding of Hamming codes can be accomplished using any of the techniques described previously, including table lookup, the standard array, and generalized cyclic decoder of Figure 6–17. Because of its simplicity, only the decoder of Figure 6–17 will be discussed here. It can be shown that the error pattern detection circuit of Figure 6–17 takes a particularly simple form of an $(n - k)$-input AND gate for the single error correcting Hamming codes. The decoding circuit for Hamming codes is illustrated in Figure 6–20. An error is detected (and corrected) only when the syndrome contained in the shift register is $s(D) = (0 \cdot D^0) + (0 \cdot D^1) + \cdots + (0 \cdot D^{n-k-2}) + (1 \cdot D^{n-k-1})$. The operation of the circuit is exactly as described earlier for Figure 6–17. Validation that this is the proper decoder can be found in [8]. The simplicity of this decoder is due to the algebraic structure of the code.

6.3.4.4 Performance of Hamming Codes

Block Error Probability.   The block error probability P_B of the single error correcting codes is the probability that two or more errors occur during transmission. This probability is equal to 1.0 minus the probability that 0 or 1 errors occur, which is given by (6–57):

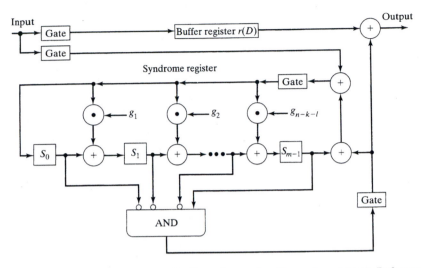

FIGURE 6–20 Decoder for cyclic Hamming code. (Reproduced from Reference [8] with permission.)

$$P_B = 1.0 - (1 - p)^n - \sum_{l=1}^{n} p(1 - p)^{n-1} \tag{6–81}$$

There is a single "error pattern" with no errors, and it occurs with probability $(1 - p)^n$, and there are $n = 2^j - 1$ error patterns with a single error that occur with probability $p(1 - p)^{n-1}$. Figure 6–21 illustrates P_B as a function of BSC crossover probability p for some of the Hamming codes of Table 6–10.

Because the Hamming decoder is able to correct all single errors and is not able to correct any other error patterns, the calculation of block error probability (6–81) was very simple. For other codes it may not be possible to derive such a simple result and the bounding techniques described earlier may have to be used. It is instructive to compare the results of the error probability bounds with the result just derived for particular codes. Consider the (7, 4) and (15, 11) Hamming codes that have $d_{min} = 3$ and can correct a single error per block of 7 or 15 symbols, respectively. An upper bound on block error probability for *any* code is simply the probability that more than $\lfloor (d_{min} - 1)/2 \rfloor = t$ errors occur. For the Hamming codes $t = 1$ and the probability that more than t errors occur is exactly the result just derived. The result is exact only for the Hamming codes and a few other codes known as "perfect codes."

Another bound on block error probability was given in (6–68):

$$P_B \leq \sum_{d=d_{min}}^{n} a_d P_B'(d) \tag{6–82a}$$

$$\leq \sum_{d=d_{min}}^{n} a_d [\sqrt{4p(1 - p)}]^d \tag{6–82b}$$

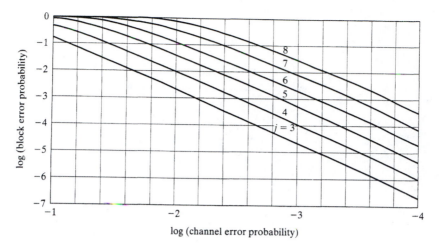

FIGURE 6–21 Block error probability for Hamming codes with $j = 3$ through 8 $(n = 2^j - 1, j \geq 3)$.

where $P_B'(d)$ is the probability of decoding the **0** codeword as another codeword that is Hamming distance d from **0**. $P_B'(d)$ is evaluated using (6–63) or (6–64). The successful use of this result requires knowledge of the weight structure of the code. Fortunately, for the Hamming codes a reasonably simple means of determining the weight structure is available. For any Hamming code the number of codewords with Hamming weight d is the coefficient of z^d in the following polynomial in z:

$$A(z) = \sum_{d=0}^{n} a_d z^d$$

$$= \frac{1}{n + 1} [(1 + z)^n + n(1 + z)^{(n-1)/2}(1 - z)^{(n+1)/2}]$$

(6–83)

For the (7, 4) Hamming code the result of the expansion is

$$A(z) = 1 + 7z^3 + 7z^4 + z^7$$

showing that there are 7 nonzero codewords with Hamming weight $= 3$, 7 with Hamming weight 4, and 1 with Hamming weight 7. This can be verified by examination of Table 6–4. For the (15, 11) code, the expansion is

$$A(z) = 1 + 35z^3 + 105z^4 + 168z^5 + 280z^6$$

$$+ 435z^7 + 435z^8 + 280z^9 + 168z^{10} + 105z^{11} + 35z^{12} + z^{15}$$

Thus, for the (15, 11) code, $a_3 = 35$, $a_4 = 105$, $a_5 = 168$, and so on. These weight structures were used in (6–82) to calculate P_B as a function of the channel error probability; the results are shown in Figure 6–22. Two different bounds were calculated using the two different formulas of (6–82). Observe that the first bound is quite accurate, whereas the second bound, while easy to calculate, is highly conservative. The differences between the bounds illustrated in Figure 6–22 are a clear indicator that care should be used when selecting a bound for communications system design. A third bound could be calculated using (6–69), which presumes a bounded distance decoder. Because the code is a "perfect code," the performance of a bounded distance decoder and the maximum likelihood decoder are the same. Thus, (6–69) yields the same result for P_B as the exact result.

Bit Error Probability.   Bit error probability can be calculated using any of the techniques described previously. Again the Hamming (7, 4) and (15, 11), codes will be considered. Bit error probability will be calculated using (6–70), (6–71), (6–73), and (6–74). Equation (6–73) is the union bound result, while (6–70) and (6–71) are upper and lower bounds which are slightly easier to calculate. Equation (6–74) is the upper bound derived assuming a bounded distance decoder. To use (6–73)

$$P_b < \frac{1}{k} \sum_{d=d_{min}}^{n} B_d P_d \tag{6–84}$$

the coefficients B_d must be found. For the (7, 4) code these can be found by inspection of the codewords in Table 6–4. There are 7 nonzero codewords with weight 3, and the total

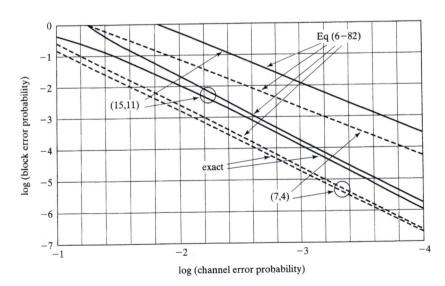

FIGURE 6–22   Comparison of block error probability bounds for (7, 4) and (15, 11) Hamming codes.

number of bit errors associated with these codewords is $B_3 = 1 + 1 + 2 + 2 + 1 + 3 + 2 = 12$. Similarly, there are 7 nonzero codewords with weight 4 and $B_4 = 2 + 1 + 3 + 2 + 2 + 3 + 3 = 16$ and $B_7 = 4$. All other $B_d = 0$. Thus, the bit error probability is bounded by

$$P_b < \frac{1}{4} \sum_{d=3}^{7} B_d P_d$$

$$= \frac{1}{4}(12P_3 + 16P_4 + 4P_7)$$

where P_d denotes $P'_B(d)$, which is calculated from (6–63) and (6–64). The values of B_d for the (15, 11) code were found by writing a short computer program that calculated each codeword in systematic form and then found the codeword weight and the number of attendant bit errors. The resulting equation for bit error probability is

$$P_b < \frac{1}{11} \sum_{d=3}^{15} B_d P_d$$

$$= \frac{1}{11}(77P_3 + 308P_4 + 616P_5 + 1232P_6$$

$$+ 2233P_7 + 2552P_8 + 1848P_9 + 1232P_{10}$$

$$+ 847P_{11} + 308P_{12} + 11P_{15})$$

Results for P_b as a function of BSC error probability p are shown in Figure 6–23 for the (7, 4) code and Figure 6–24 for the (15, 11) code. Bit error probability was also evaluated using the bounded distance decoder result (6–74). Thus, the four curves of Figures 6–23 and 6–24 are the upper bound of (6–71), the union bound of (6–73), the bounded distance decoder bound of (6–74), and the lower bound of (6–70). Examination of Figures 6–23 and 6–24 leads to the conjecture that the bounded distance result is reasonable in terms of its accuracy. This is expected since the Hamming codes are "perfect codes."

Bit error probability as a function of E_b/N_0 is plotted in Figure 6–25 for the Hamming codes with $j = 3$ to 7. BPSK signaling was assumed for Figure 6–25, and the error probability was calculated using (6–74). Comparison of exact result for the (7, 4) Hamming code presented in Figure 6–13 with the results of Figure 6–25 shows that the bound of (6–74) is quite accurate.

6.3.5 BCH Codes

6.3.5.1 Definition and Encoding for BCH Codes. Bose–Chaudhuri–Hocquenghem (BCH) codes were discovered independently by Hocquenghem [25] in 1959 and Bose and Chaudhuri [26] in 1960. These codes are among the most important block codes available since they exist for a wide range of rates, since they can achieve significant coding gain, and since the complexity of their decoders is such that they are

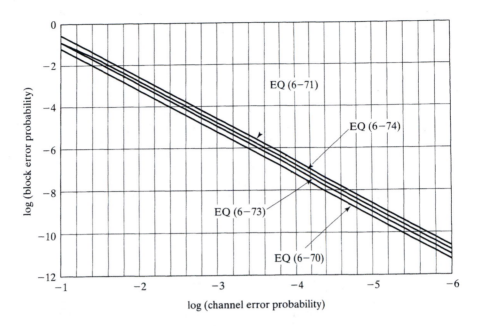

FIGURE 6–23 Bit error rate bounds for (7, 4) Hamming code.

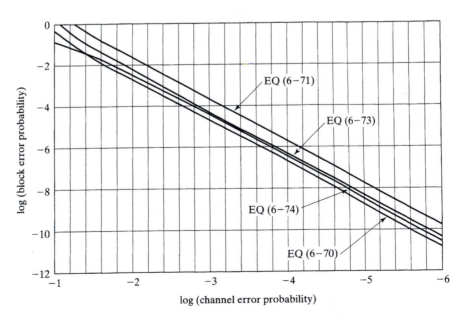

FIGURE 6–24 Bit error rate bounds for (15, 11) Hamming code.

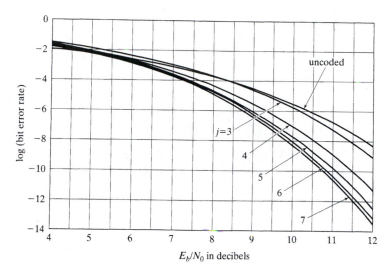

FIGURE 6–25 Bit error rate versus E_b/N_0 for Hamming codes with $j = 3$ through 7 ($n = 2^i - 1, j \geq 3$).

implementable even at high speeds. These codes have an elegant algebraic structure that is extremely interesting to study but is beyond the scope of this chapter. The reader is referred to advanced texts [6, 8, 9, 10, 11, 13] for all the theory behind the results to be presented. The BCH codes are linear cyclic codes that are always defined by their code generator polynomial. Although nonbinary BCH codes exist, discussion will be limited to the binary codes.

The block length n for BCH codes is always $n = 2^m - 1$ for $m \geq 3$, and the number of errors t that can be corrected is bounded by $t < (2^m - 1)/2$. It is also always true that $n - k \leq mt$. Specific values for t and k can be found using algebraic techniques for determining code polynomials; not all values satisfying the inequalities above are possible. Table 6–11 [8] gives all of the known values for n, k, and t for BCH codes with block lengths up to $n = 1023$. Observe that the code rate $R = k/n$ varies over a wide range and that the number of errors that can be corrected increases as the code rate decreases. The BCH code having the highest rate for any block length is a Hamming code. That is, the Hamming codes are a subset of the BCH codes. The code polynomials which generate the codes of Table 6–11 can be found in Lin and Costello [8] in their Appendix C. Another complete list of codes can be found in Peterson and Weldon [13], Table 9–1. Table 6–12 [8] is a short list of the BCH code generator polynomials for block length 63. BCH codes are applied in a variety of modern communications systems. Perhaps the best known application is in first generation cellular mobile telephony where a shortened BCH code is used for the messages that tell the mobile unit, among other things, what power and channel to use.

The BCH codes are cyclic codes so that encoding is simply accomplished using the general technique for cyclic codes discussed previously. Given the code generator $\mathbf{g}(D)$, the codewords in systematic form are found using the following steps: (1) multiply the

TABLE 6–11 List of Possible BCH Code Parameters

n	k	t	n	k	t	n	k	t
7	4	1	255	163	12	511	268	29
15	11	1		155	13		259	30
	7	2		147	14		250	31
	5	3		139	15		241	36
31	26	1		131	18		238	37
	21	2		123	19		229	38
	16	3		115	21		220	39
	11	5		107	22		211	41
	6	7		99	23		202	42
63	57	1		91	25		193	43
	51	2		87	26		184	45
	45	3		79	27		175	46
	39	4		71	29		166	47
	36	5		63	30		157	51
	30	6		55	31		148	53
	24	7		47	42		139	54
	18	10		45	43		130	55
	16	11		37	45		121	58
	10	13		29	47		112	59
	7	15		21	55		103	61
127	120	1		13	59		94	62
	113	2		9	63		85	63
	106	3	511	502	1		76	85
	99	4		493	2		67	87
	92	5		484	3		58	91
	85	6		475	4		49	93
	78	7		466	5		40	95
	71	9		457	6		31	109
	64	10		448	7		28	111
	57	11		439	8		19	119
	50	13		430	9		10	121
	43	14		421	10	1023	1013	1
	36	15		412	11		1003	2
	29	21		403	12		993	3
	22	23		394	13		983	4
	15	27		385	14		973	5
	8	31		376	15		963	6
255	247	1		367	16		953	7
	239	2		358	18		943	8
	231	3		349	19		933	9
	223	4		340	20		923	10
	215	5		331	21		913	11
	207	6		322	22		903	12

(continued)

TABLE 6–11 *Continued*

n	k	t	n	k	t	n	k	t
	199	7		313	23		893	13
	191	8		304	25		883	14
	187	9		295	26		873	15
	179	10		286	27		863	16
	171	112		277	28		858	17
1023	848	18	1023	553	52	1023	268	103
	838	19		543	53		258	106
	828	20		533	54		248	107
	818	21		523	55		238	109
	808	22		513	57		228	110
	798	23		503	58		218	111
	788	24		493	59		208	115
	778	25		483	60		203	117
	768	26		473	61		193	118
	758	27		463	62		183	119
	748	28		453	63		173	122
	738	29		443	73		163	123
	728	30		433	74		153	125
	718	31		423	75		143	126
	708	34		413	77		133	127
	698	35		403	78		123	170
	688	36		393	79		121	171
	678	37		383	82		111	173
	668	38		378	83		101	175
	658	39		368	85		91	181
	648	41		358	86		86	183
	638	42		348	87		76	187
	628	43		338	89		66	189
	618	44		328	90		56	191
	608	45		318	91		46	219
	598	46		308	93		36	223
	588	47		298	94		26	239
	578	49		288	95		16	147
	573	50		278	102		11	255
	563	51						

TABLE 6–12 Generator Polynomials of All the BCH Codes of Length 63

n	k	t	$g(D)$
63	57	1	$g_1(D) = 1 + D + D^6$
	51	2	$g_2(D) = (1 + D + D^6)(1 + D + D^2 + D^4 + D^6)$
	45	3	$g_3(D) = (1 + D + D^2 + D^5 + D^6)\, g_2(D)$
	39	4	$g_4(D) = (1 + D^3 + D^6)\, g_3(D)$
	36	5	$g_5(D) = (1 + D^2 + D^3)\, g_4(D)$
	30	6	$g_6(D) = (1 + D^2 + D^3 + D^5 + D^6)\, g_5(D)$
	24	7	$g_7(D) = (1 + D + D^3 + D^4 + D^6)\, g_6(D)$
	18	10	$g_{10}(D) = (1 + D^2 + D^4 + D^5 + D^6)\, g_7(D)$
	16	11	$g_{11}(D) = (1 + D + D^2)\, g_{10}(D)$
	10	13	$g_{13}(D) = (1 + D + D^4 + D^5 + D^6)\, g_{11}(D)$
	7	15	$g_{15}(D) = (1 + D + D^3)\, g_{13}(D)$

Source: Reproduced from Reference [8] with permission.

message polynomial $\mathbf{w}(D)$ by D^{n-k}, (2) calculate the remainder $\rho(D) = R_{g(D)}[D^{n-k}\mathbf{w}(D)]$, and (3) generate the code polynomial $\mathbf{x}(D) = \rho(D) + D^{n-k}\mathbf{w}(D)$. A simple circuit for generating the systematic codewords for Hamming codes was given in Figure 6–19. The encoder for BCH codes is the same.

6.3.5.2 Decoding of BCH Codes [27]. The foundation for all BCH decoding algorithms is the algebraic structure of the codes. The decoders are straightforward once the algebraic fundamentals are established. Decoding consists of the same three steps given previously for any cyclic code. The function of the decoder is to produce an estimate of the error polynomial that was most likely to have occurred given the received polynomial. The decoding procedure is

1. Calculate a syndrome from the received code polynomial. There are $2t$ components of the syndrome $S_1, S_2, \ldots, S_{2t}$. The syndrome of an undistorted code polynomial is zero so that it is a function only of the transmission errors and the code structure. Calculation of each component of the syndrome is done by finding the remainder of division of the received sequence by a polynomial $\phi_i(D)$, which was specified at the time of the definition of the code. The polynomial long division is accomplished using the division circuitry of Figure 6–15. The same division circuitry may sometimes be used to calculate several syndrome components. Figure 6–26 is a simple example of a BCH syndrome calculation circuit from [8]. In this figure four syndromes are calculated for a (15, 7) BCH code using two long division circuits. There are at most t different division circuits required for a t error correcting code.

2. Determine the positions of the errors in the received polynomial using a two-step procedure:

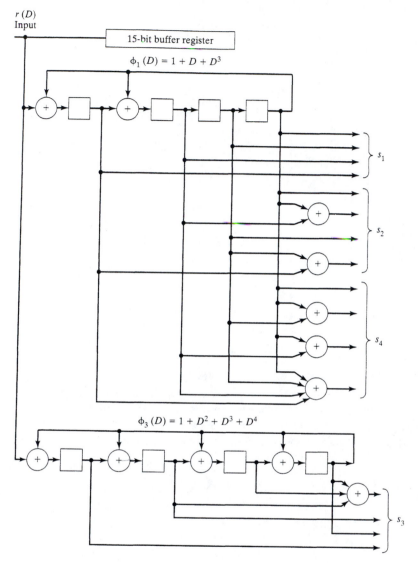

FIGURE 6–26 Syndrome computation circuit for the double error correcting (15, 7) BCH Code. (Reproduced from Reference [8] with permission.)

a. Determine an *error location polynomial* from the syndrome components found in step 1. An interactive algorithm is available [10] for finding this polynomial. This algorithm is called the Berlekamp algorithm, after its inventor. The complexity of this algorithm is proportional to $2t^2$.

b. Find the roots of the polynomial found in step 2a. These roots directly determine the locations of the errors in the received polynomial. A circuit for finding the roots and correcting errors for the (15, 7) BCH code is illustrated in Figure 6–27, which is taken from [8]. The initial shift register loads for Figure 6–27 are the coefficients of the polynomial found in step 2a. The root finding procedure that Figure 6–27 executes is called the *Chien search algorithm* [6, 28].

3. Correct the errors in the received polynomial to find the transmitted codeword and thus the transmitted information.

This brief description of a BCH decoding algorithm is intended only to communicate that, although the decoding is based on concepts beyond this text, the decoding algorithm is well defined. BCH decoders are commercially available and are widely used.

6.3.5.3 Performance of BCH Codes.

The coding gain achievable using BCH codes varies as the code parameters n and k vary. Bit error probability for BCH codes is calculated using (6–74), which is a small modification of results from [23, 29]. Equation (6–74) is an overbound on decoding bit error probability assuming a bounded distance decoder. Note that most of the known decoding algorithms for BCH codes are, in fact,

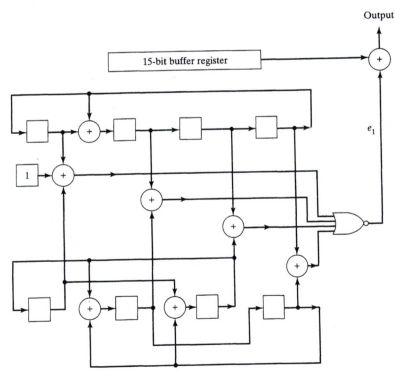

FIGURE 6–27   Chien search circuit for the double-error-correcting (15, 7) BCH code. (Reproduced from Reference [8] with permission.)

bounded distance decoders. Figures 6–28 through 6–30 illustrate bit error probability as a function of received E_b/N_0 for binary phase shift keying modulation. Figure 6–28, 6–29, and 6–30 illustrate P_b for BCH codes having code rates of approximately 1/4, 1/2, and 3/4, respectively. Observe that the best performance (lowest E_b/N_0 for a given P_b) is achieved for the rate 1/2 codes. It can be shown that very high rate ($R > 3/4$) and very low rate ($R < 1/3$) codes have less coding gain than those with rates between 1/3 and 3/4. For the rate 1/2 codes Figure 6–29 shows that coding gain is greater than 4 dB at $P_b = 10^{-5}$ for the $n = 1023$ BCH code. Observe also that in all cases the performance improves as the block length n increases. Coding gain is a function of P_b and the selected modulation scheme. Clark and Cain [9] plot P_b versus E_b/N_0 for a number of BCH codes with orthogonal signaling showing that coding gain is reduced relative to the gain for coherent BPSK illustrated here. Block error probability for BCH codes can be calculated using the bound of (6–68).

6.3.6   Reed–Solomon Codes

6.3.6.1 Definition of the Reed–Solomon Codes.   The Reed–Solomon codes are the only nonbinary codes that will be considered in this chapter. They are discussed because of their importance for use in communication systems where errors appear in bursts (rather than independent random errors), because of their importance in concatenated coding systems which will be discussed in Section 7.5.3, and because of their use in compact disc audio technology. The Reed–Solomon (RS) codes were discovered in 1960 by Reed and Solomon [30]. They are nonbinary BCH block codes

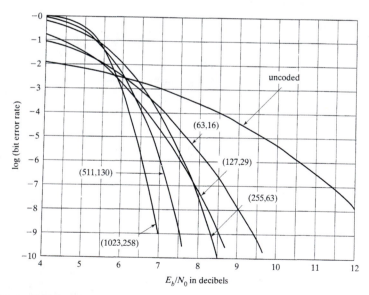

FIGURE 6–28   Bit error probability for BCH codes with $R \cong 1/4$.

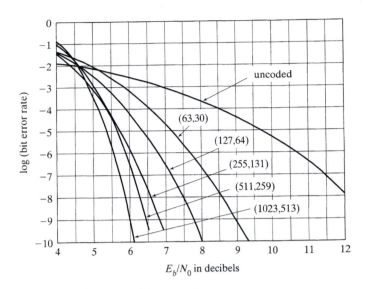

FIGURE 6–29 Bit error probability for BCH codes with $R \cong 1/2$.

that use input and output alphabets having 2^m symbols, $\{0, 1, 2, \ldots, 2^m - 1\}$. The block length of the RS codes is $n = 2^m - 1$; this block length can be extended to $n = 2^m$ or $n = 2^m + 1$ if desired. The codes are designed to correct e_0 errors within a block of n symbols. The number of parity symbols that must be used to correct e_0 errors is $n - k = n - 2e_0 = 2^m - 1 - 2e_0$. The maximum number of errors that can be corrected is a function of the minimum distance d_{min} of the code, specifically, $d_{min} = 2e_0 + 1$. The RS codes achieve the largest possible d_{min} of any linear codes with the same encoder input and output lengths. The minimum distance, and thus the error correction capability of the code, increases with block length. The Hamming distance between nonbinary codewords is defined to be the number of positions in which the codewords differ.

Reed–Solomon codes are often used on channels that are naturally nonbinary.[7] For example, an 8-FSK transmission system can be used with an $m = 3$ RS coding system. If the source and channel are naturally binary, the nonbinary alphabet can be constructed by grouping binary symbols into m-bit blocks. In this case the RS codes can be thought of as accepting $k' = k \cdot m$ information bits and mapping these k' bits into codeword blocks having length $n' = n \cdot m$ binary channel symbols. Thus the rate of the RS codes is $R = k'/n' = k/n = (2^m - 1 - 2e_0)/(2^m - 1)$. RS codes with many different block lengths and rates are known.

The codes are defined by generator polynomials or generator matrices just as the binary BCH codes are defined. For RS codes, however, the code generator polynomial has coefficients from the nonbinary alphabet $\{0, 1, 2, \ldots, 2^m - 1\}$ rather than the binary al-

[7]See T. A. Gulliver, "Matching Q-ary Reed–Solomon Codes with M-ary Modulation,: *IEEE Trans. Commun.*, Vol. 45, pp. 1349–1353, Nov. 1997 for exact relationships between decoder output probability of bit error and modulation symbol probability of error for several choices of M and Q.

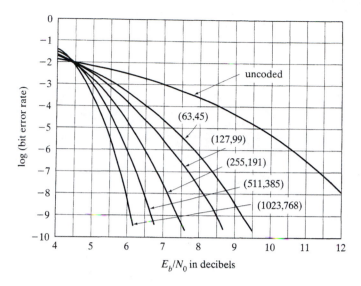

FIGURE 6–30   Bit error probability for BCH codes with $R \cong 3/4$.

phabet $\{0, 1\}$. When performing polynomial multiplication and addition, modulo-2^m arithmetic is used. A RS encoder can be implemented using a feedback shift register similar to that of Figure 6–19 but with all arithmetic performed modulo-2^m. The reader is referred to Lin and Costello [8] for the details of the modulo-2^m polynomial arithmetic necessary to generate the Reed–Solomon codes. Reference [8] also defines the method used to find the generator polynomials and provides additional references for the interested reader.

6.3.6.2 Decoding the Reed–Solomon Codes.   Reed–Solomon codes are decoded using the same concepts used to decode binary BCH codes. The decoding begins by calculating a syndrome from the received block and the known structure of the code. Next, the syndromes are used to determine an error locator polynomial which is then solved to determine the specific error estimates. The errors are then corrected in the received sequence and the information block is output. The reader is referred to Lin and Costello [8], Blahut [11], or Clark and Cain [9] for advanced discussions of RS decoding.

6.3.6.3 Performance of the Reed–Solomon Codes.   Consider an RS-coded communication system using a binary source and a naturally 2^m-ary physical link such as MFSK with $M = 2^m$. The RS code uses 2^m-ary symbols that are constructed from the binary source by grouping information bits into blocks of m. The encoder output is a sequence of 2^m-ary symbols that are transmitted to the receiver using MFSK. The performance measure of interest is the probability of decoded bit error P_b as a function of the MFSK symbol error probability p_s. It can be shown [23, 31, 32] that P_b is overbounded by

$$P_b \leq \sum_{i=e_0+1}^{2^m-1} \frac{i}{2(2^m-2)} \binom{2^m-1}{i} p_s^i (1-p_s)^{2^m-1-i} \tag{6-85}$$

For MFSK, the probability of symbol error is calculated using[8]

$$p_s = \frac{1}{M} \exp\left(-\frac{E_s}{N_0}\right) \sum_{q=2}^{M} \binom{M}{q} (-1)^q \exp\left(\frac{E_s}{qN_0}\right) \tag{6-86}$$

where $E_s/N_0 = (E_b/N_0)Rm$, since m binary bits are associated with one 2^m-ary symbol and the code rate is R.

Next, consider an RS-coded communication system using a binary source and a naturally binary physical link such as BPSK. The performance measure of interest is the probability of decoded bit error P_b as a function of the binary channel symbol error probability p. As before, (6–85) is used to calculate P_b. The probability p_s is calculated from the BPSK binary channel symbol error probability p. Specifically, p_s is equal to 1 minus the probability of transmitting an entire m-binary-symbol block without error. Thus

$$p_s = 1 - (1-p)^m \tag{6-87}$$

and

$$p = Q\left(\sqrt{\frac{2E_bR}{N_0}}\right) \tag{6-88}$$

Figure 6–31 illustrates the decoded bit error probability as a function of E_b/N_0 for RS codes with rate $\approx 1/2$ and with $m = 4, 5, 6, 7,$ and 8. Observe that the coding gain for RS codes at $P_b = 10^{-5}$ varies from about 1.5 dB for $m = 4$ to 3.4 dB for $m = 8$. The "equivalent" binary block lengths of these codes is $(2^m - 1)m$.

The Reed–Solomon codes have been used in many modern communications systems. A number of manufacturers make large-scale integrated circuits for decoding RS codes. Probably the most common use of RS codes is found in the audio recording industry where they are used in compact discs. In this application a (32, 28) shortened RS code is concatenated with a (28, 24) code [33] resulting in a $R = 3/4$ code. In addition, Reed–Solomon coding is part of a recommendation by the Consultative Committee for Space Data Systems (CCSDS) [34], which is a standards organization having NASA and the European Space Agency (and others) as members. The CCSDS recommends that an RS code be concatenated with a convolutional code. The CCSDS recommendation will be followed in the NASA space station.

6.3.7 The Golay Code

6.3.7.1 Definition of the Golay Code. The Golay code was discovered in 1949 by M. J. E. Golay [5]. The code has $n = 23$, $k = 12$, $d_{min} = 7$. It is capable of correcting three errors in a block of 23 symbols. The code's importance stems from its significant error correcting capability as well as the fact that it is one of the few known "perfect"

---

[8] Equation (6–86) can be reduced to (4–124).

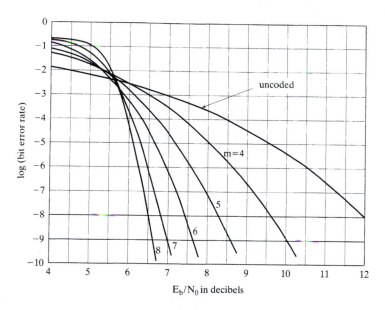

FIGURE 6–31   Bit error probability for Reed–Solomon codes with $R \cong 1/2$.

codes. A perfect code has the interesting property that all error patterns with Hamming weight t or less and no error patterns with weight greater than t are correctable using a minimum-distance maximum-likelihood decoder. The Hamming codes are also perfect codes. The Golay code is decodable using a variety of techniques. The code is a binary cyclic code whose generator polynomial is given by either

$$\mathbf{g}_1(D) = 1 + D^2 + D^4 + D^5 + D^6 + D^{10} + D^{11} \tag{6–89a}$$

or the generator polynomial

$$\mathbf{g}_2(D) = 1 + D + D^5 + D^6 + D^7 + D^9 + D^{11} \tag{6–89b}$$

The same codewords, although with different message associations, are generated by either generator. The encoding circuit for the Golay code is identical in form to the circuit for cyclic Hamming codes of Figure 6–19.

The (23, 12) Golay code is often modified by adding a parity bit making the extended (24, 12) Golay code. The extended code has $d_{min} = 8$; however, it is not a perfect code. The performance of the extended code is slightly better than the nonextended code and is easier to use since its rate is exactly 1/2. For these reasons, the extended code is often used in place of the perfect (23, 12) code.

6.3.7.2 Decoding the Golay Code. Decoding of the Golay code can be accomplished using several strategies. Of course, table lookup and standard array decoding are always conceptually possible. Since the code is cyclic, the generalized decoder of Figure 6–17 can be used. A specific implementation of the decoder which is able to correct three errors in a block of 23 bits has been found by Kasami [35] and is described in some detail in [8]. The Kasami decoder implements the error pattern detection circuit of Figure 6–17 by comparing certain sums of syndromes to fixed thresholds. Three syndrome sums are calculated to estimate error patterns.

6.3.7.3 Performance of the Golay Code.

The bit error probability for the (23, 12) Golay code is overbounded using (6–74) with $M = 3$, $n = 23$, and $k = 12$

$$P_b \leq \frac{1}{12} \sum_{i=4}^{23} \min[12, i + 3] \binom{23}{i} p^i (1 - p)^{23 - i} \qquad (6\text{–}90)$$

Figure 6–32 illustrates P_b as a function of E_b/N_0 assuming binary phase-shift keying modulation. Observe that the coding gain at $P_b = 10^{-5}$ is approximately 1.9 dB.

The weight structure for the Golay code is known and is given in [8].

$$A(z) = 1 + 253z^7 + 506z^8 + 1288z^{11} \qquad (6\text{–}91)$$
$$+ 1288z^{12} + 506z^{15} + 253z^{16} + z^{23}$$

Thus, the code has a single Hamming weight 0 codeword, 253 codewords with Hamming weight 7, 506 codewords with Hamming weight 8, and so on. Since the weight structure is known, (6–68) can be used to calculate an upper bound on block decoding error probability. The weight structure of the extended (24, 12) Golay code is also known and is [9]

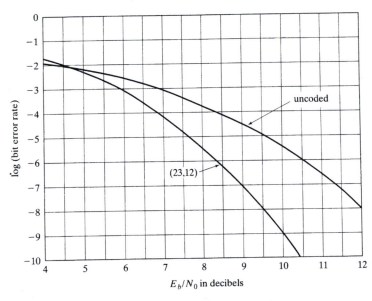

FIGURE 6–32   Bit error probability for Golay (23, 12) code.

$$A(z) = 1 + 759z^8 + 2576z^{12} + 759z^{16} + z^{24} \qquad (6\text{–}92)$$

The Golay codes have been studied extensively and have been used in modern communication systems, including recent deep space missions [36]. The formula for bit error probability can be improved upon slightly for the extended Golay code. This improvement is made possible by exact calculation of the average number of bit errors caused by a particular number of channel errors. This exact number replaces the min[12, $i + 3$] function in the formula for P_b. The reader is referred to Odenwalder [23] for the more precise expression. Results using improved formula differ from the formula used to generate Figure 6–32 only at low E_b/N_0.

6.4 CODING PERFORMANCE IN SLOW FADING CHANNELS

The purpose of error correction coding is to improve performance in channels where, for one reason or other, uncoded performance is not acceptable. As discussed in previous chapters, slow fading channels are one such example situation. To show the potential of

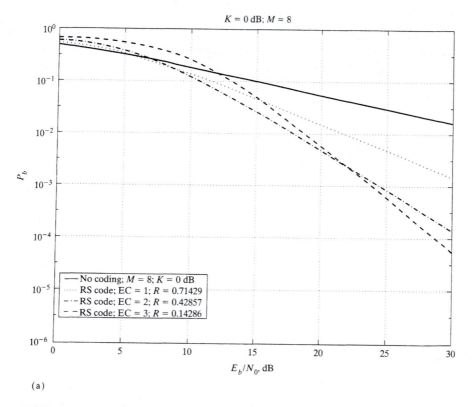

(a)

FIGURE 6–33 P_b versus E_b/N_0 of Reed–Solomon-coded, noncoherent FSK in slow Ricean fading with $K = 0$ dB. (EC = Errors corrected).

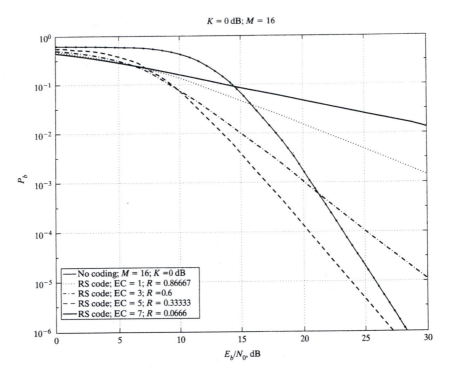

FIGURE 6–33 *Continued*

coding in such situations for improving performance, we consider Reed–Solomon code performance used in conjunction with M-ary noncoherent FSK in Ricean slow fading channels. This is a fairly easy task by using the exact expression for the symbol error probability derived in Chapter 4 for noncoherent FSK along with the bound for bit error probability performance for Reed–Solomon coding given in Section 6.3.6 as (6–85). The results to be presented in this section assume that interleaving at the transmitter and deinterleaving at the receiver are used to randomize the errors introduced in the channel. A further discussion of this technique is given in Chapter 7 (see Figure 7–25 and the accompanying discussion).

We consider two different channel conditions—a specular-to-diffuse power ratio of 0 dB, which is very nearly a Rayleigh fading channel, and a specular-to-diffuse power ratio of 10 dB, where the diffuse component is a factor of 10 below the direct received power. Figure 6–33 illustrates the former case for $M = 8$, 16, and 32, and Figure 6–34 shows the latter case for the same values of M. The code is matched to the modulation in each case in terms of code symbols and modulation symbols being equal. The parameter EC shown in the legends is the number of errors corrected, and the parameter R is the code rate. Thus, more errors corrected result in lower code rates and larger bandwidth expansion factors. Even for high code rates and few errors corrected, it is seen that

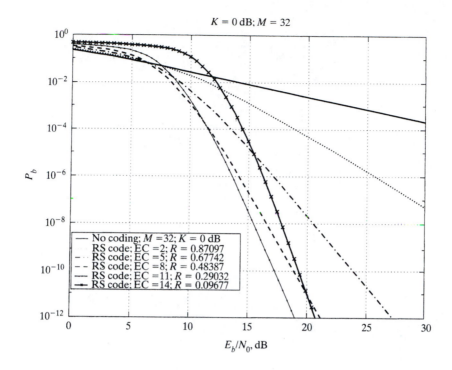

$K = 0\ \text{dB};\ M = 32$

Legend (inset):
- — No coding; $M =32;\ K = 0$ dB
- — · — RS code; EC $=2;\ R = 0.87097$
- — · · RS code; EC $=5;\ R = 0.67742$
- — — RS code; EC $=8;\ R = 0.48387$
- —— RS code; EC $=11;\ R = 0.29032$
- —×— RS code; EC $=14;\ R = 0.09677$

Axis labels: P_b (vertical), E_b/N_0, dB (horizontal)

FIGURE 6–33   *Continued*

Reed–Solomon codes are very powerful vehicles for improving performance in slow fading channels.

6.5 SUMMARY

1. The function of the communications systems engineer is to design systems making efficient use of the resources of power, bandwidth, and complexity to reliably communicate information from a source to a destination. An accepted measure of reliability is end-to-end bit error probability P_b.

2. Source coding removes signal redundancy to minimize the total number of bits per second that must be communicated.

3. Channel coding is used to correct as many channel errors as possible thereby improving reliability.

4. A discrete memoryless source represents information using a sequence of independent symbols w_0, w_1, w_2, ... from the discrete alphabet $W = \{0, 1, 2, \ldots, q_w - 1\}$. The probability that the DMS outputs symbol j during interval i is $Q_w(j)$.

5. The information content of a single DMS output symbol j is $I(j) = - \log_2 Q_w(j)$. Highly likely DMS output symbols have less information content than do less likely symbols. The entropy of the source is

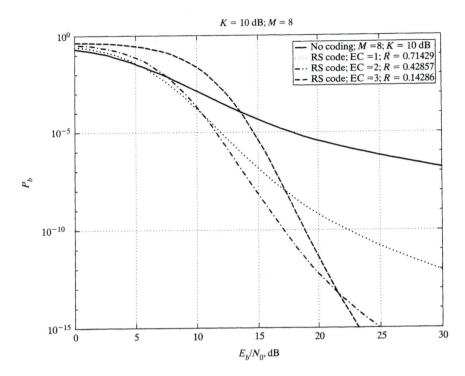

FIGURE 6–34   BEP versus E_b/N_0 of Reed–Solomon-coded, noncoherent FSK in slow Ricean fading with $K = 10$ dB.

$$H(W) = -\sum_{j=0}^{q_w-1} Q_w(j) \log_2 Q_w(j) \quad \text{bits/symbol} \tag{6-3}$$

which is the average information content of the source. The source entropy is the minimum average number of binary bits per DMS output symbol that must be transmitted over the channel. Thus, the source information cannot be communicated using fewer average bits per DMS symbol than the entropy.

6. The Huffman procedure is one intuitively satisfying method of source coding. The procedure assigns longer binary sequences to low probability DMS symbols than to higher probability symbols. DMS symbols can be Huffman coded as single symbols or in groups. Huffman coding of groups of DMS symbols produces the best results.

7. The capacity C of a channel is the number of bits per second that can theoretically be transmitted without error. Capacity is a function of the channel bandwidth and received signal-to-noise ratio. The Shannon capacity is

$$C = B \cdot \log_2\left(1 + \frac{P}{N_0 B}\right) \tag{6-6}$$

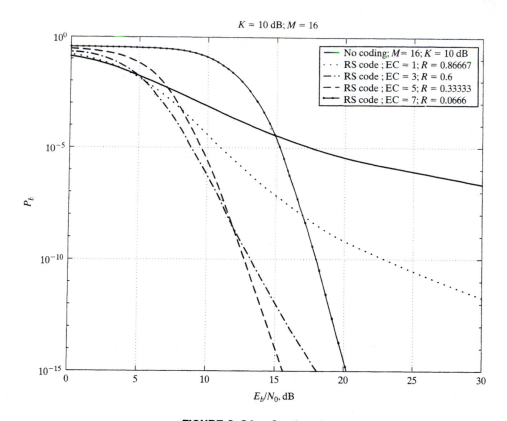

FIGURE 6–34   *Continued*

If the desired transmission rate R_m is less than C, arbitrarily low error rate can be achieved using forward error correction without increasing transmitter power. For R_m very near C, forward error correction complexity can be considerable.

8. Received E_b/N_0 must be higher than -1.6 dB for arbitrarily reliable communications to be possible. At lower E_b/N_0 no amount of coding complexity can help the communicator.

9. The capacity of a discrete memoryless channel is denoted C_N and represents the maximum number of bits of information communicated for each DMC symbol transmitted.

10. The capacity of a binary symmetric channel with error probability p is

$$C_N = 1 + p \log_2 p + (1 - p) \log_2 (1 - p) \tag{6–20}$$

11. The computational cutoff rate R_0 for a channel is another measure of capacity. It is, in fact, a practical limit on capacity that can be achieved with reasonable complexity. For the binary symmetric channel

$$R_0 = -\log_2 [\tfrac{1}{2} + \sqrt{p(1 - p)}] \tag{6–21}$$

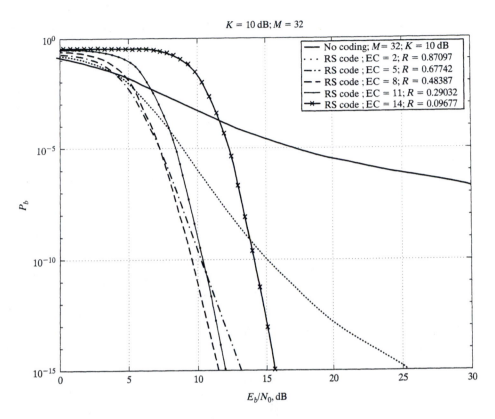

FIGURE 6–34   *Continued*

The units of R_0 are bits of information per channel use.

12. The coding gain of a forward error correction technique is the difference between E_b/N_0 required to achieve a specified bit error probability without coding and the E_b/N_0 required with coding. Coding gain is a function of the modulation technique, for example, BPSK, the coding technique, and the specified error probability.

13. A binary block code is a smart mapping of a block of k information bits called a message into a block of n binary channel symbols called a codeword. The code rate $R = k/n$ is always less than 1.0 for binary codes so that there are many more possible codewords (2^n) than possible messages (2^k).

14. The number of 1s in a binary n-vector $\mathbf{x}$ is called the Hamming weight of the vector denoted $w_H(\mathbf{x})$. The number of positions in which two binary vectors $\mathbf{x_m}$ and $\mathbf{x_{m'}}$ differ is called the Hamming distance between the vectors denoted $d_H(\mathbf{x_m}, \mathbf{x_{m'}})$. It was shown that $d_H(\mathbf{x_m}, \mathbf{x_{m'}}) = w_H(\mathbf{x_m} + \mathbf{x_{m'}})$.

15. The minimum Hamming distance between any two codewords in a code is the minimum distance of the code denoted d_{min}. The Hamming distance between codewords

makes error correction possible since a number of error must occur before codewords will be confused with one another.

16. The probability of a particular sequence of e' errors occurring in n transmissions on a BSC is

$$\Pr\left[\begin{array}{c} e' \text{ errors in} \\ \text{specific locations} \\ \text{in codeword} \end{array}\right] = p^{e'}(1 - p)^{n - e'} \tag{6–28}$$

The probability of some sequence (without regard to order) of e' errors occurring in n transmissions on a BSC is

$$\Pr\left[\begin{array}{c} e' \text{ errors in} \\ \text{block of } n \end{array}\right] = \binom{n}{e'} p^{e'}(1 - p)^{n - e'} \tag{6–31}$$

The probability of receiving n-vector $\mathbf{y}$ having transmitted codeword $\mathbf{x}$ is

$$\Pr(\mathbf{y} \mid \mathbf{x}) = p^{d_H}(1 - p)^{n - d_H} \tag{6–29}$$

17. Given prior knowledge of the code and channel, the optimum decoding rule is simply to estimate the transmitted codeword to be that codeword that was most likely to have been transmitted. For the BSC this decoding rule is equivalent to estimating the transmitted codeword to be the codeword closest to the received vector in terms of Hamming distance.

18. With the decoding rule known, decoding can be visualized as partitioning the space of all possible received n-vectors into nonoverlapping decoding regions Λ_m. Each region is associated with a unique codeword $\mathbf{x}_m$ and includes all n-vectors closer in Hamming distance to $\mathbf{x}_m$ than to any other message.

19. Given the optimum decoding regions Λ_m, a block decoding error results if $\mathbf{x}_m$ is transmitted and $\mathbf{y}$ is within $\Lambda_{m'}$ for some $m' \neq m$. The average block decoding error probability is

$$P_B = \sum_{m=0}^{2^k - 1} Q_M(m) P_{Bm} \tag{6–39}$$

where

$$P_{Bm} = \sum_{\mathbf{y} \varepsilon \overline{\Lambda}_m} \Pr(\mathbf{y} \mid \mathbf{x_m}) \tag{6–38}$$

20. Exact calculation of bit error probability requires knowledge of the number of bit errors which occur with each block decoding error. Exact bit error probability is

$$P_b = \frac{1}{k} \sum_{m=0}^{2^k - 1} Q_M(m) \sum_{\substack{m'=0 \\ m' \neq m}}^{2^k - 1} B(m, m') P_B(m, m') \tag{6–41}$$

where

$$P_B(m, m') = \sum_{\mathbf{y} \in \Lambda_{m'}} \Pr(\mathbf{y} \mid \mathbf{x_m}) \tag{6-40}$$

and $B(m, m')$ is the number of bit errors that occur when transmitted message m is decoded as message m'.

21. The modulo-2 sum of two binary n-vectors is the term-by-term modulo-2 sum of the vectors. The scalar product of a binary vector and binary scalar is the term-by-term modulo-2 product of the scalar with the vector components. The dot product of two binary vectors is

$$\mathbf{a} \cdot \mathbf{b} = (a_0 \cdot b_0) + (a_1 \cdot b_1) + (a_2 \cdot b_2) + \cdots + (a_{n-1} \cdot b_{n-1}) \tag{6-42}$$

Two vectors are orthogonal if their dot product is zero.

22. A linear combination of vectors $\mathbf{g}_i$ is

$$(w_0 \cdot \mathbf{g_0}) + (w_1 \cdot \mathbf{g_1}) + (w_2 \cdot \mathbf{g_2}) + \cdots + (w_{k-1} \cdot \mathbf{g_{k-1}}) \tag{6-43}$$

The set of vectors $\mathbf{g}_i$ is linearly independent if no set of nonzero scalars w_i exist that causes this result to be zero. Otherwise, the set is linearly dependent.

23. A binary vector space is a set of vectors satisfying (a) modulo-2 sum of any two vectors is another vector in the set, (b) scalar product of 0 or 1 and any vector is in the set, (c) there is a distributive law, and (d) there is an associative law. The set of all binary n-vectors is a vector space.

24. A subspace of a vector space is a subset of the elements of the space satisfying (a) modulo-2 sum of any two vectors in the subset is another vector in the subset, and (b) the scalar product of 0 or 1 and any vector in the set is in the set.

25. The vector set formed by calculating all possible linear combinations of any subset of a linear vector space is a subspace of the vector space. The smallest set of vectors whose linear combinations form all vectors of a space or subspace are called a basis of the space or subspace. The number of vectors in the basis is called the dimension of the space or subspace.

26. The codewords of an (n, k) binary linear block code are a k-dimensional subspace of the space of all binary n-vectors.

27. The modulo-2 sum of any two codewords of an (n, k) linear block code is another codeword in the code.

28. The all-zero n-vector is a codeword in every (n, k) linear binary block code.

29. The set of n-vectors that form the basis of an (n, k) binary linear block code are called the generator vectors of the code. The generator matrix $\mathbf{G}$ of the code is an n column by k row binary matrix whose rows are $\mathbf{g}$. Given the generator vectors $\mathbf{g}$ the codewords are calculated from

$$\mathbf{x_m} = \mathbf{w_m} \times \mathbf{G}$$

$$= \begin{bmatrix} w_{m0} & w_{m1} & \cdots & w_{m,k-1} \end{bmatrix} \times \begin{bmatrix} g_{00} & g_{01} & \cdots & g_{0,n-1} \\ g_{10} & g_{11} & \cdots & g_{1,n-1} \\ \vdots & \vdots & & \vdots \\ g_{k-1,0} & g_{k-1,1} & \cdots & g_{k-1,n-1} \end{bmatrix} \tag{6-48}$$

30. The null space of an (n, k) linear block code is an $(n, n - k)$ block code whose generator matrix is denoted **H**. The matrix **H** is called the parity check matrix for the original (n, k) block code. An n-vector **y** is a codeword of the (n, k) linear block code if and only if

$$\mathbf{0} = \mathbf{y} \times \mathbf{H}^T \qquad (6\text{--}52)$$

31. Systematic linear block codes are codes for which the message vector appears directly in each codeword. For any linear block code there is a systematic linear block code with equivalent performance. Thus, the system designer may limit consideration to systematic codes without fear of degrading system performance.

32. The generator and parity check matrices for systematic codes have the form

$$\mathbf{G} = \begin{bmatrix} g_{0,0} & g_{0,1} & \cdots & g_{0,n-k-1} & 1 & 0 & 0 & \cdots & 0 \\ g_{1,0} & g_{1,1} & \cdots & g_{1,n-k-1} & 0 & 1 & 0 & \cdots & 0 \\ g_{2,0} & g_{2,1} & \cdots & g_{2,n-k-1} & 0 & 0 & 1 & \cdots & 0 \\ \vdots & \vdots & & & & & & & \vdots \\ g_{k-1,0} & g_{k-1,1} & \cdots & g_{k-1,n-k-1} & 0 & 0 & 0 & \cdots & 1 \end{bmatrix}$$

and

$$\mathbf{H} = \begin{bmatrix} 1 & 0 & 0 & \cdots & 0 & g_{0,0} & g_{1,0} & \cdots & g_{k-1,0} \\ 0 & 1 & 0 & \cdots & 0 & g_{0,1} & g_{1,1} & \cdots & g_{k-1,1} \\ 0 & 0 & 1 & \cdots & 0 & g_{0,2} & g_{1,2} & \cdots & g_{k-1,2} \\ \vdots & \vdots & \vdots & & & & & & \\ 0 & 0 & 0 & \cdots & 1 & g_{0,n-k-1} & g_{1,n-k-1} & \cdots & g_{k-1,n-k-1} \end{bmatrix} \qquad (6\text{--}54)$$

33. The Hamming distance between any two codewords of a linear block code is equal to the Hamming distance between the all-zero codeword and some nonzero codeword in the code.

34. A minimum distance decoder for a block code with a minimum distance d_{min} is able to correctly decode any transmission where $\lfloor d_{min} - 1)/2 \rfloor \doteq t$ or fewer errors occur. In some specific cases a minimum distance decoder is able to correct more than t errors.

35. The standard array for a linear code is

$$\begin{array}{ccccc} \mathbf{x}_0 & \mathbf{x}_1 & \mathbf{x}_2 & \cdots & \mathbf{x}_{2^k-1} \\ \mathbf{e}_1 + \mathbf{x}_0 & \mathbf{e}_1 + \mathbf{x}_1 & \mathbf{e}_1 + \mathbf{x}_2 & \cdots & \mathbf{e}_1 + \mathbf{x}_{2^k-1} \\ \mathbf{e}_2 + \mathbf{x}_0 & \mathbf{e}_2 + \mathbf{x}_1 & \mathbf{e}_2 + \mathbf{x}_2 & \cdots & \mathbf{e}_2 + \mathbf{x}_{2^k-1} \\ \vdots & \vdots & \vdots & & \vdots \\ \mathbf{e}_{2^{n-k}-1} + \mathbf{x}_0 & \mathbf{e}_{2^{n-k}-1} + \mathbf{x}_1 & \mathbf{e}_{2^{n-k}-1} + \mathbf{x}_2 & \cdots & \mathbf{e}_{2^{n-k}-1} + \mathbf{x}_{2^k-1} \end{array} \qquad (6\text{--}55)$$

Codewords appear in the first row. Correctable error patterns appear in the first column. This array is used for decoding in two different manners. (a) The decoder output codeword is the codeword at the head of the column in which the received vector

y is found. (b) The syndrome vector is precalculated for each correctable error pattern. The syndrome of the received vector **y** is calculated. The decoder estimated error pattern is that error pattern having the same syndrome as the received vector.

36. The block decoding error probability for standard array decoding is

$$P_B = 1 - \sum_{j=0}^{2^{n-k}-1} p^{w_H(\mathbf{e_j})}(1-p)^{n-w_H(\mathbf{e_j})} \qquad (6\text{--}57)$$

where the sum is over all correctable error patterns.

37. The block and bit error probabilities for linear systematic codes are independent of which codeword was transmitted. Block error probability is union bounded by

$$P_B \le \sum_{d=d_{\min}}^{n} a_d P_B'(d) \qquad (6\text{--}68)$$

where a_d is the number of codewords with Hamming weight d and

$$P'_B(d) = \sum_{e=(d/2)+1}^{d} \binom{d}{e} p^e (1-p)^{d-e} \qquad (6\text{--}63)$$

$$+ \frac{1}{2} \binom{d}{d/2} p^{d/2}(1-p)^{d/2}$$

for d even and

$$P'_B(d) = \sum_{e=(d+1)/2}^{d} \binom{d}{e} p^e (1-p)^{d-e} \qquad (6\text{--}64)$$

for d odd. The bit error probability is overbounded by

$$P_b < \frac{1}{k} \sum_{d=d_{\min}}^{n} B_d P'_B(d) \qquad (6\text{--}73)$$

where B_d is the total number of bit errors associated with all block decoding error events in which a Hamming weight d codeword is decoded rather than the correct **0** codeword.

38. When detailed code parameters a_d or B_d are not available, a bounded distance decoder may be assumed and the block error probability bound is

$$P_B = \sum_{i=M+1}^{n} \binom{n}{i} p^i (1-p)^{n-i} \qquad (6\text{--}69)$$

where M is the maximum number of error corrected by the bounded distance decoder. The bit error probability bound for this same decoder is

$$P_b \le \frac{1}{k} \sum_{i=M+1}^{n} \min[k, i+M] \binom{n}{i} p^i (1-p)^{n-i} \qquad (6\text{--}74)$$

39. If the block error probability P_B for a code is known, the bit error probability P_b is bounded by

$$\frac{P_B}{k} \leq P_b \leq P_B$$

40. Modulo-2 polynomial arithmetic is the same as conventional polynomial arithmetic except that coefficients are added and multiplied using the modulo-2 rules for arithmetic. Feedback and feedforward shift registers can be used to perform both polynomial multiplication and division.

41. Cyclic codes are a subset of all linear codes. The end-around cyclic shift of any codeword of a cyclic code is another codeword in the code. Cyclic codes can be encoded and decoded using the general techniques for all linear codes; however, their structure permits simplified encoding and decoding.

42. An (n, k) cyclic code is defined by its generator polynomial $\mathbf{g}(D) = g_0 + g_1 D + g_2 D^2 + \cdots + g_{n-k} D^{n-k}$, which has degree $n - k$. The $k \times n$ generator matrix $\mathbf{G}$ is

$$\mathbf{G} = \begin{bmatrix} g_0 & g_1 & \cdots & g_{n-k-1} & g_{n-k} & 0 & 0 & \cdots & 0 \\ 0 & g_0 & g_1 & \cdots & g_{n-k-1} & g_{n-k} & 0 & 0 & \cdots & 0 \\ 0 & 0 & g_0 & g_1 & & \cdots & g_{n-k-1} & g_{n-k} & 0\,0 & \cdots & 0 \\ \vdots & \vdots & & & & & & & & \vdots \\ 0 & 0 & 0 & 0 & 0 & 0 & g_0 & g_1 & \cdots & g_{n-k-1} & g_{n-k} \end{bmatrix}$$

The $(n - k) \times n$ parity check matrix for a cyclic code is

$$\mathbf{H} = \begin{bmatrix} h_k & h_{k-1} & \cdots & \cdots & h_1 & h_0 & 0 & 0 & . & . & . & 0 \\ 0 & h_k & h_{k-1} & \cdots & \cdots & h_1 & h_0 & 0 & 0 & \cdots & \cdots & 0 \\ 0 & 0 & h_k & h_{k-1} & \cdots & \cdots & h_1 & h_0 & 0 & 0 & \cdots & 0 \\ \vdots & \vdots & & & & & & & & & \vdots \\ 0 & 0 & 0 & 0 & 0 & 0 & h_k & h_{k-1} & . & . & . & h_0 \end{bmatrix} \quad (6\text{–}78)$$

where $\mathbf{h}(D) = h_0 + h_1 D + h_2 D^2 + \cdots + h_k D^k$ is the result of the division of $D^n + 1$ by $\mathbf{g}(D)$.

43. Calculation of the code polynomials in systematic form for cyclic codes is accomplished by premultiplying the message $\mathbf{w}(D)$ by D^{n-k} and obtaining the remainder $\rho(D)$ of the division of $D^{n-k}\mathbf{w}(D)$ by the generator $\mathbf{g}(D)$; the code polynomial is $\mathbf{x}(D) = \rho(D) + D^{n-k}\mathbf{w}(D)$.

44. Decoding of cyclic codes makes use of the syndrome polynomial, which is a function of only the error polynomial and is calculated from $\mathbf{s}(D) = R_{\mathbf{g}(D)}[\mathbf{y}(D)]$. Error locations are calculated from the syndrome polynomial.

45. The parity check matrix for an (n, k) Hamming code has n columns and $n - k$ rows. The columns are all nonzero $(n - k)$-vectors. Hamming codes have $d_{\min} = 3$ and can correct all single errors. The generator polynomials $\mathbf{g}(D)$ for Hamming codes are primitive polynomials.

46. Both the encoder and decoder for Hamming codes can be implemented using shift register multiplication and division circuits.

47. The block error probability for a Hamming code with length $n = 2^j - 1$ is

$$P_B = 1.0 - (1 - p)^n - \sum_{l=1}^{2^n - 1} p(1 - p)^{n-1} \tag{6-81}$$

This result is exact since the Hamming codes are "perfect."

48. The weight structure for a code defines a_d which is the number of codewords with Hamming weight d. For the Hamming codes

$$A(z) = \sum_{d=0}^{n} a_d z^d$$
$$= \frac{1}{n+1} [(1 + z)^n + n(1 + z)^{(n-1)/2}(1 - z)^{(n+1)/2}] \tag{6-83}$$

49. BCH codes are linear cyclic codes having a wide range of code rates and error correction capability. They are defined by their generator polynomials many of which have been cataloged in advanced texts. Bit error rate performance can be estimated, assuming the bounded distance decoder results of (6–74). Decoding is accomplished using a three-step procedure that is well defined but beyond the scope of this presentation.

50. The Reed–Solomon codes are nonbinary cyclic block codes which are used in compact disc audio systems, in concatenated coding systems, and in the NASA space station. The coder input and output alphabets contain 2^m symbols which can be constructed from groups of m binary symbols if desired. These codes correct e_0 errors in a block of $n = 2^m - 1$ symbols. There are $n - k = n - 2e_0$ parity symbols and the code rate is $R = k/n$.

51. The encoder and decoders for Reed–Solomon codes is similar to the encoders and decoders for binary BCH codes except that all arithmetic is performed modulo-2^m. The bit error probability for Reed–Solomon coding is bounded above by

$$P_b \leq \sum_{i=e_0+1}^{2^m - 1} \frac{i}{2(2^m - 2)} \binom{2^m - 1}{i} p_s^i (1 - p_s)^{2^m - 1 - i} \tag{6-85}$$

where p_s is the symbol error probability for the 2^m-ary communications link. The improvement provided by Reed–Solomon codes in slow Ricean fading channels was calculated and plotted for specific cases.

52. The Golay code is one of the few known "perfect codes." The Golay code is a (23, 12) binary cyclic code. The bit error probability for the Golay code is bounded above by

$$P_b \leq \frac{1}{12} \sum_{i=4}^{23} \min[12, i + 3] \binom{23}{i} p^i (1 - p)^{23 - i} \tag{6-90}$$

where a bounded distance decoder is assumed. The weight structure for the Golay code is

$$A(z) = 1 + 253z^7 + 506z^8 + 1288z^{11}$$

$$+ 1288z^{12} + 506z^{15} + 253z^{16} + z^{23}$$

(6-91)

There is an extended (24, 12) nonperfect Golay code having slightly improved performance relative to the (23, 12) code. The weight structure for the extended code is

$$A(z) = 1 + 759z^8 + 2576z^{12} + 759z^{16} + z^{24}$$

(6-92)

REFERENCES

[1] C. E. Shannon, "A Mathematical Theory of Communication," *Bell System Technical Journal,* Vol. 27, pp. 379–423, 623–656, 1948.

[2] C. E. Shannon, "Communication in the Presence of Noise," *Proceedings of the IRE,* Vol. 37, pp. 10–21, January 1949.

[3] N. Wiener, *Extrapolation, Interpolation, and Smoothing of Stationary Time Series* (Cambridge, MA: MIT Press, 1949).

[4] R. W. Hamming, "Error Detecting and Error Correcting Codes," *Bell System Technical Journal,* April 1950.

[5] M. J. E. Golay, "Notes on Digital Coding," *Proceedings of the IRE,* Vol. 37, p. 657, June 1949.

[6] R. G. Gallager, *Information Theory and Reliable Communication* (New York: John Wiley, 1968).

[7] J. M. Wozencraft and I. M. Jacobs, *Principles of Communication Engineering* (New York: John Wiley, 1965).

[8] S. Lin and D. J. Costello, Jr., *Error Control Coding: Fundamentals and Applications* (Englewood Cliffs, NJ: Prentice-Hall, 1983).

[9] G. C. Clark and J. B. Cain, *Error-Correction Coding for Digital Communications* (New York: Plenum, 1981).

[10] E. R. Berlekamp, *Algebraic Coding Theory* (New York: McGraw-Hill, 1968).

[11] R. Bluhut, *Theory and Practice of Error Control Codes* (Reading, MA: Addisson-Wesley, 1983).

[12] A. J. Viterbi and J. K. Omura, *Principles of Digital Communication and Coding* (New York: McGraw-Hill, 1979).

[13] W. W. Peterson and E. J. Weldon, Jr., *Error-Correcting Codes* (Cambridge, MA: MIT Press, 1972).

[14] D. A. Huffman, "A Method for the Construction of Minimum Redundancy Codes," *Proceedings of the IRE,* Vol. 40, pp. 1098–1101, September, 1962.

[15] J. Ziv and A. Lempel, "A Universal Algorithm for Sequential Data Compression," *IEEE Trans. Infor. Theory,* Vol. IT-23, pp. 337–343, May 1977.

[16] J. Ziv and A. Lempel, "Compression of Individual Sequences Via Variable-Rate Coding," *IEEE Trans. Infor. Theory,* Vol. IT-24, pp. 530–536, Sept 1978.

[17] T. Welch, "A Technique for High-Performance Data Compression," *IEEE Computer,* pp. 8–19, June 1984.

[18] A. D. Wyner and J. Ziv, "The Sliding-Window Lempel-Ziv Algorithm Is Asymptotically Optimal," *Proc. IEEE*, Vol. 82, pp. 872–877, June 1984.

[19] P. E. Bender and J. K. Wolf, "New Asymptotic Bounds and Improvements on the Lempel-Ziv Data Compression Algorithm," *IEEE Trans. Infor. Theory*, Vol. 37, pp. 721–729, May 1991.

[20] A. D. Wyner and A. J. Wyner, "Improved Redundancy of a Version of the Lempel-Ziv Algorithm," *IEEE Trans. Infor. Theory*, Vol. 41, pp. 723–731, May 1995.

[21] A. J. Wyner, "The Redundancy and Distribution of the Phrase Lengths of the Fixed-Database Lempel-Ziv Algorithm," *IEEE Trans. Infor. Theory*, Vol. 43, pp. 1452–1464, Sept. 1997.

[22] A. D. Wyner, J. Ziv, and A. J. Wyner, "On the Role of Pattern Matching in Information Theory," *IEEE Trans. Infor. Theory*, Vol. 44, pp. 2045–2056, Oct. 1998.

[23] J. P. Oldenwalder, "Error Control," In *Data Communications, Networks, and Systems*, T. Bartree (ed.) (Indianapolis, IN: Howard W. Sams, 1984.)

[24] A. Papoulis, *Probability, Random Variables, and Stochastic Processes*, 2nd ed. (New York: McGraw-Hill, 1985).

[25] A. Hocquenghem, "Codes Corecteurs d'Erreurs," *Chiffres*, 1959.

[26] R. C. Bose and D. K. Ray-Chaudhuri, "On a Class of Error Correcting Binary Group Codes," *Infor. and Control*, Vol. 3, pp. 68–79, Mar. 1960.

[27] E. R. Berlekamp, "On Decoding Binary Bose-Chaudhuri-Hocquenghem Codes," *IEEE Trans. Infor. Theory*, Vol. IT-11, pp. 577–579, Oct. 1965.

[28] R. T. Chien, "Cyclic Decoding Procedure for the Bose-Chaudhuri-Hocquenghem Codes," *IEEE Trans. Infor. Theory*, Vol. IT-10, pp. 357–363, Oct. 1964.

[29] L. J. Weng, "Soft and Hard Decoding Performance Comparisons for BCH Codes, *Conf. Record: Intern. Conf. On Commun.*, pp. 25.5.1–25.5.5, June 1979.

[30] I. S. Reed and G. Solomon, "Polynomial Codes Over Certain Finite Fields," *Journ. of the Soc. For Ind. and Appl. Math.*, June 1960.

[31] M. K. Simon, J. K. Omura, R. A. Scholtz, and B. K. Levitt, *Spread Spectrum Communications* (Rockville, MD: Computer Science Press, 1985.)

[32] E. R. Berlekamp, "The Technology of Error-Correcting Codes," *Proc. IEEE*, Vol. 68, pp. 564–593, May 1980.

[33] B. Sklar, *Digital Communications, Fundamentals, and Applications* (Upper Saddle River, NJ: Prentice Hall, 1988).

[34] Consultative Committee for Space Data Systems, *Blue Book*, CCSDS 101.0B-2, 1987.

[35] T. Kasami, "A Decoding Procedure for Multiple-Error-Correcting Cyclic Codes," *IEEE Trans. Infor. Theory*, Vol. IT-10, pp. 134–138, April 1964.

[36] J. H. Yuen (ed.), *Deep Space Telecommunications Systems Engineering*, (New York: Plenum, 1983).

PROBLEMS

6–1. A discrete memoryless source outputs letters from the alphabet {0, 1, 2, 3} with probabilities {0.2, 0.4, 0.2, 0.2}.

    (a) What is the information content of each letter?

    (b) What is the average information content of the source output?

    (c) How many bits per letter is required to transmit the DMS output without source coding?

(d) Use the Huffman procedure to assign binary codewords to the letters and calculate the resultant source coder average output bit rate.

(e) Use the Huffman procedure to encode the second extension of the source and calculate the resultant source coder average output bit rate.

(f) What is the bit sequence required to communicate the DMS output symbol sequence 1, 3, 0, 1, 3, 1, 2, 0, 2, 1 using each of the three (uncoded, Huffman, and second extension Huffman) coding procedures?

6-2. A communicator must select a source code for the transmission of English text. Assume that the probability of a vowel is three times the probability of a consonant. Compare the binary channel bit rates required communicate using a fixed number of bits to represent each letter to the rate required using a variation of Morse code. Assume that Morse code DIT and DAH are transmitted using "0" and "1," respectively, and that a single "0" separates each Morse codeword.

6-3. A discrete memoryless source outputs one symbol from the alphabet {A, B, C, D, E, F, G, H} each 1.0 millisecond. The probability of occurrence for these symbols are {0.01, 0.03, 0.35, 0.02, 0.15, 0.18, 0.19, 0.07}.

(a) What is the entropy of this source?

(b) Use the Huffman procedure to assign binary codewords to all symbols.

(c) What is the average source encoded output bit rate?

(d) What is the minimum binary channel bit rate required to communicate with and without source coding?

6-4. The receiver in a communications system has a received signal power of −134 dBm, a received noise power spectral density of −164 dBm/Hz, and a bandwidth of 2000 Hz. What is the maximum rate of error-free information transfer of this system?

6-5. A BPSK channel with a symbol rate of 1000 symbols per second is available for communication of binary information. The maximum transmitter output power is used resulting in a received signal power of −134 dBm. The received noise density is −164 dBm/Hz. What is the maximum number of bits of information per second which can be transmitted over this channel without error? What is the maximum rate of error-free information transfer possible if transmitter power were permitted to increase without bound?

6-6. Given a source alphabet $\mathbf{W} = \{a,b,c\}$, use the Lempel–Ziv–Welch procedure to encode the sequence $\{a\,b\,a\,b\,c\,b\,a\,b\,a\,b\,a\,a\,a\,a\,a\,a\,a\}$. This sequence is used in the example in [17].

6-7. Use the sliding window version of the Lempel–Ziv procedure with a window size $n_w = 12$ to encode the binary sequence {0111001110101101001100001 101110000011}. Express the encoder output as a binary sequence. Decode the encoded sequence.

6-8. A Lempel–Ziv–Welch decoder knows that the source alphabet contains three symbols. Decode the received sequence {1, 2, 4, 3, 5, 8, 1, 10, 11}.

6-9. Use the sliding window Lempel–Ziv procedure to encode and then decode the following binary sequence {001010010000011010011010010110001001}. Express the codewords in the form $C_l = [m_l, L_l]$, that is, do not convert the codewords to their binary form. Use a window size $n_w = 10$.

6-10. Use the Lempel–Ziv–Welch procedure to decode the sequence {122341387699}. The source encoder alphabet is binary. What is the complete dictionary?

6–11. A binary symmetric channel with an error probability of 0.01 and rate of 9600 symbols/second is available to a communicator. The information user requires the information error rate to be better than 1 error in 10^6 received bits.

(a) Calculate the capacity C_N and cutoff rate R_0 for this channel.

(b) What is the maximum rate of information transfer to the user that can be theoretically supported and that can be supported with some confidence that the coding system will have reasonable complexity?

6–12. Calculate and plot R_0 and C_N as a function of received E_b/N_0 for a binary phase-shift keyed communication system. What is the maximum value for each of these capacity measures and why does this maximum exist?

6–13. Can communications at a rate of 2500 bps and $P_b \leq 10^{-5}$ be supported by a BSC using a symbol rate of 10,000 symbols/second that has a symbol error rate of 9 errors in 100 transmissions?

6–14. Consider an error correction code that generates codewords by simply repeating each information symbol five times.

(a) What is the code rate?

(b) How many codewords are in the code?

(c) What is the minimum distance of the code?

(d) How many channels errors would have to occur to confuse one codeword with another?

(e) What fraction of all possible codewords are used in this code?

6–15. Consider the code of Table 6–4. Calculate the number of codewords with Hamming weight $w = 0, 1, \ldots, 7$. Calculate the Hamming distance between each codeword and codeword 1111111. Compare the number of codewords with Hamming distance $w = 0, 1, \ldots, 7$ with the number of codewords with Hamming weight w from 1111111.

6–16. The codeword $\mathbf{x} = 0110100$ is transmitted and the vector $\mathbf{y} = 0010101$ is received over a BSC with error probability $p = 0.01$. What is the probability of this event? What is the error vector that caused this event?

6–17. What is the probability that three or fewer errors occur during the transmission of twelve codeword symbols over a BSC with error probability p?

6–18. Consider the code of Table 6–4. The codeword $\mathbf{x}_0 = 0000000$ is transmitted over a BSC with error probability p. What is the probability that some other valid codeword is received?

6–19. List all possible error 5-vectors with Hamming weight 2. Compare the number of 5-vectors in your list to the binomial coefficient of (6–30).

6–20. Consider again the repeat code (Problem 6–14) that generates codewords by a 5-times repetition of the information bit. List all 2^n possible received 5-vectors and partition this vector space into the optimum decoding regions. How many transmission errors must occur to cause a decoding error?

6–21. Decode the following received sequences assuming the Hamming code of Table 6–4: 1011011, 1111100, 1000110, 1100011.

6–22. Consider the code of Table 6–4. What is the probability of receiving the vector 1101111 given that all messages are equally likely and given a BSC with transmission error probability $p = 0.03$?

6–23. Suppose that a BSC was available for which $p > 0.5$. Is the minimum distance decoding rule optimum for this channel? Explain. If not, what is a better decoding rule?

6–24. Generate the optimum decoding regions for the 5-times repeat code (Problem 6–14) when the message probabilities are $Q_w(1) = 0.7$ and $Q_w(0) = 0.3$ and the BSC has transmission error probability of 0.01.

6–25. Calculate the exact bit error probability for the 5-times repeat code as a function of the BSC transmission error probability p.

6–26. A vector space is generated by forming all linear combinations of the following set of vectors:

$$\mathbf{b_0} = 1\,1\,0\,1\,0\,0\,0$$

$$\mathbf{b_1} = 0\,1\,1\,0\,1\,0\,0$$

$$\mathbf{b_2} = 0\,1\,0\,0\,0\,1\,1$$

$$\mathbf{b_3} = 1\,1\,1\,0\,0\,1\,0$$

$$\mathbf{b_4} = 1\,0\,1\,0\,0\,0\,1$$

   (a) What is the dimension of the resulting vector space?
   (b) Find a basis for the vector space.
   (c) Is the set of vectors **b** linearly independent?

6–27. Perform the vector arithmetic requested using the following vector set:

$$\mathbf{b_0} = 0\,0\,0\,0\,0\,0$$

$$\mathbf{b_1} = 0\,0\,1\,1\,1\,0$$

$$\mathbf{b_2} = 0\,1\,0\,1\,0\,1$$

$$\mathbf{b_3} = 1\,0\,0\,0\,1\,1$$

$$\mathbf{b_4} = 0\,1\,1\,0\,1\,1$$

$$\mathbf{b_5} = 1\,0\,1\,1\,0\,1$$

$$\mathbf{b_6} = 1\,1\,0\,1\,1\,0$$

$$\mathbf{b_7} = 1\,1\,1\,0\,0\,0$$

   (a) $\mathbf{b_2} + \mathbf{b_7} = ?$ **(b)** $\mathbf{b_3} + \mathbf{b_5} + \mathbf{b_7} = ?$ **(c)** $0 \cdot \mathbf{b_5} = ?$
   (d) $1 \cdot \mathbf{b_5} = ?$ **(e)** $\mathbf{b_6} \cdot \mathbf{b_2} = ?$ **(f)** $\mathbf{b_2} \cdot \mathbf{b_0} = ?$

6–28. Calculate all vectors in the linear vector space defined by the following vectors:

$$\mathbf{g_0} = 0\,0\,1\,1\,1\,0$$

$$\mathbf{g_1} = 0\,1\,0\,1\,0\,1$$

$$\mathbf{g_2} = 1\,0\,0\,0\,1\,1$$

Are the vectors **g** a basis? What is the dimension of the vector space?

6–29. A (6, 3) binary linear block code is defined by the following generator vectors:

$$\mathbf{g_0} = 0\,0\,1\,1\,1\,0$$

$$\mathbf{g_1} = 0\,1\,0\,1\,0\,1$$

$$\mathbf{g_2} = 1\,0\,0\,0\,1\,1$$

(a) What is the generator matrix **G** of the code?

(b) How many rows and columns are in the code's parity check matrix?

6–30. The parity check matrix for a linear code is

$$\mathbf{H} = \begin{bmatrix} 1 & 0 & 0 & 1 & 0 & 1 & 1 \\ 0 & 1 & 0 & 1 & 1 & 1 & 0 \\ 0 & 0 & 1 & 0 & 1 & 1 & 1 \end{bmatrix}$$

Determine whether the following vectors are codewords in the code

$$\mathbf{y_1} = 0\,0\,1\,1\,0\,0\,0$$

$$\mathbf{y_2} = 1\,0\,1\,0\,0\,0\,1$$

$$\mathbf{y_3} = 1\,1\,1\,0\,1\,0\,0$$

$$\mathbf{y_4} = 0\,1\,0\,1\,0\,1\,1$$

$$\mathbf{y_5} = 1\,1\,0\,1\,0\,0\,0$$

6–31. The generator matrix for a (6, 3) systematic binary linear block code is

$$\mathbf{G} = \begin{bmatrix} 0 & 1 & 1 & 1 & 0 & 0 \\ 1 & 0 & 1 & 0 & 1 & 0 \\ 1 & 1 & 0 & 0 & 0 & 1 \end{bmatrix}$$

(a) What is the parity check matrix for this code?

(b) Generate the standard array for this code. Note: One double error pattern will be used to complete the array.

(c) Calculate the syndrome vector for all of the correctable error patterns.

(d) Decode (i.e., find the *message* vector) the received sequence $\mathbf{y} = 101101$.

6–32. The message $\mathbf{w} = 101$ is transmitted over a communications link using ideal BPSK modulation. The system achieves $E_b/N_0 = 9.0$ dB.

(a) What is the probability of correctly receiving this message without forward error correction?

(b) What is the probability of correctly receiving this message if the (6, 3) code of Problem 6–31 is used?

6–33. Reconsider the 5-times repeat code (Problem 6–14) whose two codewords are generated by simply repeating the information symbol.

(a) Develop an exact formula for block error probability as a function of BSC error probability p assuming a minimum distance decoder.

(b) Apply the overbound of (6–68) to find block error probability as a function of BSC error probability p and compare with the result of part (a). Explain your observations.

6–34. The generator matrix for a (6, 3) systematic binary linear block code is

$$\mathbf{G} = \begin{bmatrix} 0 & 1 & 1 & 1 & 0 & 0 \\ 1 & 0 & 1 & 0 & 1 & 0 \\ 1 & 1 & 0 & 0 & 0 & 1 \end{bmatrix}$$

Assume that the communication system uses BPSK modulation.
(a) Calculate a_d and B_d for this code for $0 \le d \le n$.
(b) Calculate both bounds for P_B of (6–68) as a function of E_b/N_0 and plot your results.
(c) Calculate P_B as a function of E_b/N_0 assuming a bounded distance decoder and plot on the same graph as part (b).
(d) Calculate bit error probability P_b as a function of E_b/N_0 using both (6–73) and (6–74) and plot your results on the same graph.

6–35. Using the decoding regions for the (6, 3) code of Problem 6–34, graphically illustrate why the last result of (6–62) is an overbound rather than an exact result.

6–36. Represent the following vectors as polynomials in D:

$$\mathbf{y}_1 = 0\,0\,1\,1\,0\,0\,0$$

$$\mathbf{y}_2 = 1\,0\,1\,0\,0$$

$$\mathbf{y}_3 = 1\,1\,1\,0\,1\,0\,0\,1\,0\,1\,1\,1$$

$$\mathbf{y}_4 = 0\,1\,0\,1\,1\,1$$

$$\mathbf{y}_5 = 1\,1\,0\,1$$

6–37. Calculate the following polynomial products and illustrate the feedforward shift register that could be used to perform the calculation. Demonstrate that the shift-register functions properly by listing the contents of the shift register and its output for the first five clock cycles.
(a) $\mathbf{x}(D) = (1 + D + D^3) \cdot (1 + D^2)$
(b) $\mathbf{x}(D) = (1 + D + D^4) \cdot (D^2 + D^3 + D^4)$
(c) $\mathbf{x}(D) = (D + D^6 + D^7) \cdot (1 + D + D^9)$

6–38. Divide the polynomial $\mathbf{x}(D) = 1 + D^3$ by the polynomial $\mathbf{g}(D) = 1 + D + D^3 + D^5$ to obtain both the quotient and remainder. Illustrate the shift-register circuit that is used to perform this calculation and demonstrate its complete operation.

6–39. Show that the generator polynomial for the (15, 11) cyclic Hamming code is a factor of $D^{15} + 1$.

6–40. Consider the (7, 4) cyclic Hamming code with generator polynomial $\mathbf{g}(D) = 1 + D + D^3$. Calculate any code polynomial and its fourth cyclic shift both manually and by division of $D^4 \mathbf{x}(D)$ by $D^7 + 1$.

6–41. Find the generator and parity check matrices for the (7, 4) cyclic Hamming code in the form of (6–77) and (6–78). Generate all possible codewords from the generator matrix and compare the result with Table 6–4.

6–42. Using the three-step procedure of Section 6.3.3.4, generate the codewords for the (15, 11) Hamming code corresponding to message polynomials
(a) $\mathbf{w}(D) = 1 + D^4 + D^{10}$ and
(b) $\mathbf{w}(D) = D^3 + D^{10}$. Verify that the message polynomial appears within the code polynomial.

6–43. Illustrate the shift-register decoder for the (15, 11) Hamming code and decode the received polynomial $\mathbf{y}(D) = D^3 + D^4 + D^7 + D^9$.

6–44. Determine the parity check matrix for the (31, 26) Hamming code.

6–45. Calculate the weight structure for the (7, 4) Hamming code to verify the expansion following (6–83).

6–46. Calculate the block error probability for the (15, 11) Hamming code assuming a bounded distance decoder and compare your results to those of Figure 6–22.

6–47. Prove that, for the Hamming codes, (6–69) and (6–81) are identical.

6–48. Calculate the code polynomial corresponding to message polynomial $\mathbf{w}(D) = 1 + D^{12} + D^{21} + D^{50}$ for the (63, 51) two-error correcting BCH code.

6–49. Calculate and plot bit error probability as a function of E_b/N_0 assuming BPSK signaling for the (255, 99) 23-error correcting BCH code.

6–50. Calculate and plot the bit error probability as a function of E_s/N_0 for a Reed–Solomon code with rate $R = 1/4$ using 16–FSK modulation. How many symbol errors per codeword can be corrected by this code?

6–51. Calculate the minimum Hamming distance as a function of block length for Reed–Solomon codes with rate approximately 1/2.

6–52. Calculate the coding gain at $P_b = 10^{-5}$ for a Reed–Solomon code with rate 1/4 and $m = 5$. The physical channel is an ideal BPSK binary communications link.

6–53. Calculate and plot the block error rate for the (23, 12) Golay code using the bound of (6–68).

6–54. What fraction of all possible n-vectors is used by the Golay code?

6–55. **(a)** Calculate the (23, 12) Golay codewords for all Hamming weight 1 messages.
   (b) Compare the Hamming weight of these codewords with the weight structure given in (6–91).
   (c) Is the Hamming weight of these codewords consistent with the principles of good forward error correction code design in that the most likely error events are associated with a minimum number of bit errors?

6–56. Show that (6–86) and (4–124) are equivalent.

6–57. Write a MATLAB program to reproduce the curves shown in Figures 6–33 and 6–34.

6–58. **(i)** It is desired to communicate at 10 kbps and 10^{-5} bit error probability through a slow Ricean fading channel with $K = 0$ dB. Noncoherent MFSK with Reed–Solomon coding is to be used. Find the minimum E_b/N_0 required for the following channel bandwidths:
   (a) 100 kHz; **(b)** 150 kHz; **(c)** 250 kHz.
   (ii) Repeat for $K = 10$ dB
   You may use the graphs shown in Figures 6–33 and 6–34.
   Hint: Don't forget to include bandwidth expansion due to code rate.

7

Fundamentals of Convolutional Coding

7.1 INTRODUCTION

In this chapter a second method of forward error control called *convolutional coding* is described. The structure of a convolutional code is fundamentally different from the structure of a block code. Specifically, information sequences are not grouped into distinct blocks and encoded; rather, a continuous sequence of information bits is mapped into a continuous sequence of encoder output symbols. This mapping is highly structured, enabling a decoding method considerably different from block decoding methods to be applied. It can be argued that convolutional coding can achieve larger coding gain than can be achieved using a block code with the same complexity. Whether block coding or convolutional coding is preferable for a particular application will depend on the details of that application and the technology available at the time of the comparison. This chapter describes the fundamentals of convolutional coding and decoding and presents a method of predicting error probability performance.

7.2 BASIC CONCEPTS

Many of the basic concepts of block coding apply directly to convolutional coding. Specifically, the encoder maps sequences of source coder outputs into sequences of code symbols for transmission over a DMC. The purpose of this mapping is to improve communication efficiency by enabling the system to correct transmission errors. Convolutionally coded systems process lengthy sequences of information symbols to generate code sequences that are correspondingly lengthy. This is in contrast to block codes that process independent blocks of k information symbols at a time and use codewords containing n symbols. There is a one-to-one correspondence between information sequences and codeword sequences. The elegant structure of convolutional codes enables processing (i.e., coding and decoding) of these lengthy sequences a few symbols at a time both in the coder and the decoder. The codeword sequences will be generated in a manner that ensures that codeword sequences due to different information sequences are separated from one another in Hamming distance. This separation allows some number of transmission errors to be corrected by the decoder. The separation of codeword sequences will be made possible by using a small fraction of the possible binary channel input sequences as code-word sequences just as a small fraction, 2^{k-n}, of possible binary n-vectors were used for block code codewords. Recall that the ability of block codes to correct errors improved as block length n increased. Similarly, the performance of convolutional codes improves as a code parameter called constraint length (to be defined later) increases.

The optimum decoding rule for convolutional codes is the same as for block codes; the decoder will estimate the transmitted code sequence to be the sequence that was most likely to have been transmitted given the known code structure, channel characteristics, and received sequence. For the BSC, the most likely transmitted sequence is the sequence that is closest in Hamming distance to the received sequence. An efficient algorithm will be described for finding this closest sequence.

In the presentation of block codes, consideration was limited to hard decision decoding where the channel demodulator makes an irrevocable decision regarding the channel input symbol prior to the block decoding operation. The structure of convolutional codes enables reliability information to be easily used by the decoder. Thus, for convolutional codes the channel output will be permitted to have an alphabet larger than the input alphabet and soft decision decoding will be described.

7.2.1   Definition of Convolutional Codes

Convolutional codes are most easily described by example. Figure 7–1 illustrates a shift-register circuit that generates a rate ½ convolutional code. Input bits are clocked into the circuit from the left. After each input is received the coder output is generated by sampling and multiplexing the outputs of the two modulo-2 adders. For this code two output symbols are generated for each input bit so that the code rate is ½. Observe that a particular input bit influences the output during its own interval as well as the next two input bit intervals. A convolutional code is defined by the number of stages in the shift register, the number of outputs (i.e., the number of modulo-2 adders), and the connections between the shift register and the modulo-2 adders. The state of the encoder is defined to be the con-

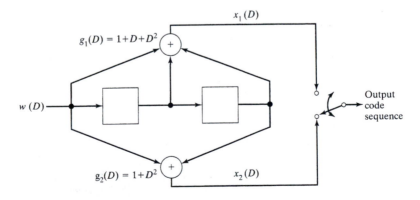

FIGURE 7–1   Rate ½ convolutional encoder.

tents of the shift register and is completely determined by the previous two information bit inputs. The encoder of Figure 7–1 has four possible states corresponding to all possible contents of the binary two-stage shift register.

Comparing Figure 6–14 with Figure 7–1 shows that the circuit of Figure 7–1 performs two different polynomial multiplications. The output of the upper modulo-2 adder is the product of the degree-2 polynomial $\mathbf{g}_1(D) = 1 + D + D^2$ and the input sequence $\mathbf{w}(D) = w_0 + w_1D + w_2D^2 + \ldots + w_jD^j + \ldots$, where $w_j \in \{0, 1\}$ represents the information bit in the jth bit time interval. The output of the lower modulo-2 adder is the product of $\mathbf{w}(D)$ and $\mathbf{g}_2(D) = 1 + D^2$. The output sequence is represented by two (in this case) semi-infinite polynomials $\mathbf{x}_1(D) = x_{10} + x_{11}D + x_{12}D^2 + \ldots + x_{1j}D^j + \ldots = \mathbf{g}_1(D)\mathbf{w}(D)$ and $\mathbf{x}_2(D) = x_{20} + x_{21}D + x_{22}D^2 + \ldots + x_{2j}D^j + \ldots = \mathbf{g}_2(D)\mathbf{w}(D)$, which are interleaved to produce the encoder output sequence. The convolutional code is completely defined by the set of *generator polynomials* $\mathbf{g}_1(D)$ and $\mathbf{g}_2(D)$. These polynomials define the length of the shift register, the connections to the modulo-2 adders, and the number of modulo-2 adders.

Convolutional codes are linear. Consider the sum of two code sequences corresponding to two distinct message polynomials $\mathbf{w}_m(D)$ and $\mathbf{w}_{m'}(D)$. These code sequences are defined by the products $\mathbf{x}_{im}(D) = \mathbf{g}_i(D)\mathbf{w}_m(D)$ and $\mathbf{x}_{im'}(D) = \mathbf{g}_i(D)\mathbf{w}_{m'}(D)$, where $i = 1, 2$. The modulo-2 sum of the two code sequences is represented by the modulo-2 sums $\mathbf{x}_{im}(D) + \mathbf{x}_{im'}(D) = \mathbf{g}_i(D)\mathbf{w}_m(D) + \mathbf{g}_i(D)\mathbf{w}_{m'}(D) = \mathbf{g}_i(D)[\mathbf{w}_m(D) + \mathbf{w}_{m'}(D)]$ for $i = 1, 2$. Since the modulo-2 sum of any two message sequences is another message sequence, and since the product of any message sequence and $\mathbf{g}_i(D)$ represents a code sequence, the sum of the two code sequences is another code sequence. Thus, the principal requirement for linearity has been satisfied. Another requirement for linearity is that the scalar product of 1 or 0 and any code sequence is a valid code sequence. That this requirement is satisfied is proven by observing that any convolutional code contains the all-zero code sequence and by considering the term-by-term multiplication of any code sequence by the binary scalars 1 or 0. The third and fourth requirements for linearity are that distributive and associative laws be satisfied. Proof that these laws are satisfied and therefore that convolutional codes are linear can be found in other texts [1].

The simple convolutional code that has just been discussed produces two output symbols for each input information bit and has code rate $R = \frac{1}{2}$. In general, convolutional codes produce n output symbols for each k input symbols and have rate $R = k/n$. Although this would appear to make convolutional codes identical to block codes, they are significantly different. Most importantly, convolutional codes have memory that causes the rule used to map the k information bits into n code symbols to be a function of past information bits. For example, the encoder of Figure 7–1 maps $k = 1$ information bit into $n = 2$ code symbols using a rule that depends on the previous two information bits. Specifically, an input 1 produces outputs 11, 00, 01, or 10 when the previous two inputs are 00, 10, 01, or 11, respectively. The state of the convolutional coder of Figure 7–1 corresponds to the previous two input bits. The number of past inputs that affect the mapping of the current k inputs into n outputs is a critical parameter of convolutional codes. This parameter affects convolutional code performance and complexity much as block length affects block code performance and complexity. The *constraint length* v of the code is one plus the number of past inputs affecting the current outputs. The code of Figure 7–1 has constraint length

$v = 3$ since the current output pair is a function of the current input plus the two previous inputs. The number of stages in the shift register is $v - 1$. Note that different definitions of constraint length can be found in the literature on convolutional coding. In all cases, however, constraint length is a measure of the memory within the encoder.

For simplicity, consideration will be limited to convolutional codes with $k = 1$ for the remainder of this chapter. The reader is referred to advanced texts such as Lin and Costello [1] for treatment of more complex codes. With this limitation, convolutional codes can be defined by a set of n generator polynomials $\{\mathbf{g}_1(D), \mathbf{g}_2(D), \ldots, \mathbf{g}_n(D)\}$, where there is one polynomial for each of n outputs. The constraint length v of the code is equal to one plus the degree of the highest-degree generator polynomial. The length of the shift register for the encoder is equal to the degree of the highest-degree generator polynomial.

Convolutional codes can be *systematic* or *nonsystematic* depending on whether the information sequence appears directly within the code sequence. For a convolutional code to be systematic, one of the code generator polynomials must equal 1 (for example, $\mathbf{g}_1(D) = 1$) so that one of the n outputs is simply the current information bit. Unlike block codes, the performance of the best systematic convolutional codes is *not* equivalent to the performance of the best nonsystematic convolutional codes. For the same code performance, a systematic code will have a longer constraint length and more complexity than the performance-equivalent nonsystematic code. For this reason, most of the convolutional codes used in practice are nonsystematic.

The convolutional code of Figure 7–1 can also be represented by a *state transition diagram* as shown in Figure 7–2. The state of the encoder (the shift-register contents) is

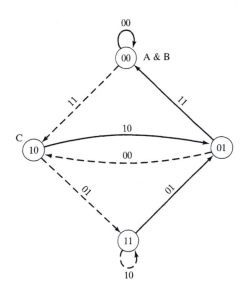

FIGURE 7–2 State transition diagram representation for rate ½ convolutional encoder.

represented by the contents of the circles. The encoder begins in state 00. If the first encoder input bit is a 0, the encoder exits state 00 on the solid branch, outputs the two code symbols found on this branch (00), and returns to state 00. If the first input bit were a 1, the encoder would exit state 00 on the dashed branch, would output the two code symbols found on this branch (11), and would enter state 10. In general, encoder inputs equal to 0 cause the encoder to move along the solid branches to the next state and to output the codeword symbols corresponding to the branch label. Encoder inputs equal to 1 cause the encoder to move along the dashed branches to the next state again outputting two codeword symbols encountered along the branch. Convolutional coders can therefore be thought of as finite state machines that change states as a function of the input sequence. The branch labels in Figure 7–2 are calculated directly from the shift register representation.

A convolutional coder can also be represented by a *trellis diagram* as illustrated in Figure 7–3 for the code of Figure 7–1. The encoder represented by Figure 7–3 has four states, which are represented by the labels within the circles of the trellis and correspond also to the states of the state transition diagram. The encoding operation starts at point *A*, which is state 00 on the far left of the trellis. If the first information bit is a 0, the encoder moves along the solid line out of state 00 arriving again at state 00 also labeled *B*. The encoder output is the symbol pair 00, which is the label on the trellis branch between the two states. If the first encoder input were a 1, the encoder would move along the dashed branch out of state 00 arriving at state 10 also labeled *C*. In this case the encoder output is 11, which is the label on the branch connecting states 00 and 10. The second encoder input causes the encoder to move to the right one more branch and to output the associated branch label. This process of moving from left to right through the trellis and outputting the branch labels continues as long as desired. Input information bits equal to 0 cause the encoder to move along the solid branches to the next state while information 1s cause the encoder to move along the dashed branches. The code sequence generated is the sequence of branch labels encountered as the coder follows the path from left to right through the trellis. A typical input and output sequence for this convolutional code is shown at the bottom of Figure 7–3. For this input sequence, the encoder follows the branches marked with arrows.

Observe that the labels on the branches leaving and entering a state do not change with time in Figure 7–3. This is characteristic of a *time-invariant convolutional code*. In general, the branch labels could vary with time and the resultant convolutional code would be a *time-varying convolutional code*. Time-varying convolutional codes will not be discussed in this chapter. In general, the branch labels on the trellis could be selected using any procedure yielding the required Hamming distance between code sequences. When there are no constraints on the procedure for assigning labels to trellis branches, the resultant code is called a *trellis code*. A trellis code is simply a trellis that defines the structure and memory of the code and an assignment of code symbols to the branches of the trellis. Trellis codes can be linear or nonlinear and can be time varying or time invariant. Convolutional codes are a subset of trellis codes where the assignment of labels to the trellis branches is constrained to follow additional rules.

The following example illustrates some of the concepts of the previous paragraphs.

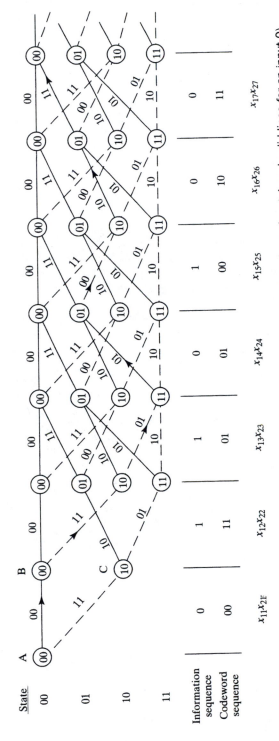

FIGURE 7–3 Trellis representation for rate ½ convolutional encoder (dashed lines for an input 1 and solid lines for an input 0).

EXAMPLE 7-1

A rate $R = \frac{1}{3}$ convolutional code is defined by the generator polynomials

$$\mathbf{g}_1(D) = 1 + D + D^2 + D^3$$

$$\mathbf{g}_2(D) = 1 + D + D^3$$

$$\mathbf{g}_3(D) = 1 + D^2 + D^3$$

Figure 7–4 illustrates the shift-register encoder for this code. Three outputs are produced for each input bit and each output is a different modulo-2 sum of the contents of the shift register and the input. The specific registers summed to produce an output are defined by the generator polynomials. None of the generators equals 1 so that the code is nonsystematic. Since all powers of D between 0 and 3 occur in the generator $\mathbf{g}_1(D)$, the first output symbol is the modulo-2 sum of the input bit and all three previous inputs stored in the shift register. The number of stages of the shift register is equal to 3, which is the degree of the largest-degree generator polynomial. The constraint length of the code is $v = 4$, which is 1 plus the degree of any of the generator polynomials. Thus, an input bit influences the output due to the next three input bits. The number of states in the trellis representation of the code is $2^{v-1} = 2^3 = 8$.

Figure 7–5 is a trellis representation of this convolutional code. For a rate $\frac{1}{3}$ code there are three binary symbols on each of the trellis branches. The trellis labels can be found using the encoder of Figure 7–4. The trellis state is the contents of the shift register of Figure 7–4, and the three components of a trellis branch label are the modulo-2 sums defined by Figure 7–4 or by the generator polynomials. Since $D^0 = 1$ is component of all three generator polynomials, the labels on the two branches leaving any trellis state are complements of one another.

Figure 7–6 is a state transition diagram representation of the convolutional code. This diagram was generated directly from the trellis diagram.

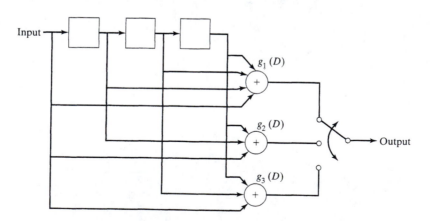

FIGURE 7-4   Rate $\frac{1}{3}$, constraint length 4 convolutional encoder.

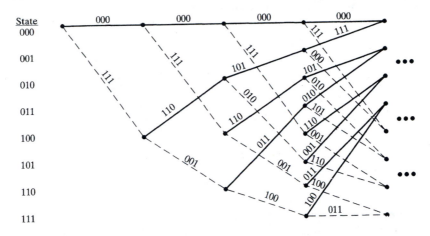

FIGURE 7–5   Trellis representation for $R = \frac{1}{3}$, constraint length 4 convolutional encoder.

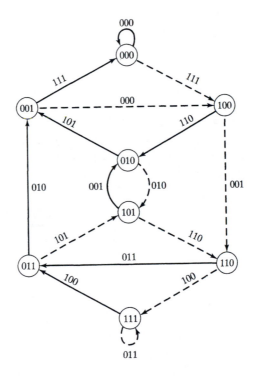

FIGURE 7–6   State transition diagram representation of rate $\frac{1}{3}$ constraint length 4 convolutional encoder.

7.2.2 Decoding Convolutional Codes

As previously stated, the decoder has knowledge of the code structure (i.e., it has a copy of the code trellis), the received sequence, and a statistical characterization (for example, the transition probabilities) of the channel. The function of the decoder is to estimate the encoder input information sequence using a rule or method that results in the minimum possible number of errors being delivered to the information user. There is a one-to-one correspondence between information sequences and code sequences. Further, any information and code sequence pair is uniquely associated with a path through the trellis. Thus, the job of the decoder may be viewed as estimating the path through the trellis that was followed by the coder.

The decoding rule for convolutional codes is developed employing the same arguments used in developing the block decoding rules. Assume that the information source is ideal so that its output symbols are equally likely and independent; thus all paths through the trellis are equally probable. It can be shown that, to achieve the minimum decoding error probability, the decoder output should be the path whose code sequence was most likely to have been input to the channel by the encoder. It is convenient at this point to denote the encoder output semi-infinite sequence corresponding to message sequence or path m by $\mathbf{x_m} = x_{m0}\,x_{m1}\,x_{m2}\ldots x_{mj}\ldots$. The DMC output sequence is denoted by $\mathbf{y} = y_0\,y_1\,y_2\ldots y_j\ldots$, and the probability of receiving the channel output $\mathbf{y}$ given that the channel input was $\mathbf{x_m}$ is

$$\Pr[\mathbf{y} \mid \mathbf{x_m}] = \prod_{n'=0}^{\infty} \Pr(y_{n'} \mid x_{mn'}) \qquad (7\text{--}1)$$

Given $\mathbf{y}$, the path most likely to have been followed through the trellis by the coder is the path whose code sequence maximizes $\Pr[\mathbf{y} \mid \mathbf{x}_m]$. The function $\Pr[\mathbf{y} \mid \mathbf{x}_m]$ is the *metric* used to compare the code sequence $\mathbf{x}_m$ and the received sequence $\mathbf{y}$. For the hard decision binary symmetric channel, maximization of this metric is equivalent to finding the path through the trellis whose code sequence is closest in Hamming distance to the received sequence. This result corresponds exactly to hard decision decoding for block codes where the decoding rule was to estimate the transmitted codeword to be the codeword that is closest in Hamming distance to the received n-vector. One method for finding this closest path is the Viterbi algorithm [2, 3], which will be discussed in detail later. For now, the decoder for the BSC can be viewed as a processor that, having the entire received sequence, searches through all trellis paths to find that single path whose code sequence is closest in Hamming distance to the received sequence.

Since the logarithm is a monotone increasing function of an increasing argument, the decoder could also use the metric $\ln[\Pr(\mathbf{y} \mid \mathbf{x}_m)]$ rather than $\Pr(\mathbf{y} \mid \mathbf{x}_m)$. In this case, the decoder would calculate $\ln[\Pr(\mathbf{y} \mid \mathbf{x}_m)]$ for all paths and would choose the path m with the largest value as the decoder output path. Taking the logarithm converts the product of (7–1) to a summation. Thus, the decoding metric is

$$\ln[\Pr(\mathbf{y} \mid \mathbf{x_m})] = \sum_{n'=1}^{\infty} \ln[\Pr(y_{n'} \mid x_{mn'})] \qquad (7\text{--}2)$$

This metric is more commonly used than the metric of (7–1) since implementing a summation in hardware is easier than implementing a product. In addition, the use of a summation permits the decoder to use *branch metrics,* which are the components of the summation of (7–2) accumulated on a particular branch of a path.

In summary, given a received sequence **y,** the maximum likelihood decoder calculates the path metric of (7–2) for every path through the trellis. The decoder output path is the path that has the largest path metric. Since there is a one-to-one correspondence between trellis paths and information sequences, estimating the trellis path is equivalent to estimating the transmitted information sequence. The Viterbi algorithm is an efficient method for finding the trellis path having the largest path metric.

EXAMPLE 7–2

Suppose (for convenience in this example) that the communicator needs to transmit a single message which is three bits long. The message is convolutionally encoded using the code defined by the trellis of Figure 7–3. In order to end the message and clear the encoder of message bits, two zeros are appended to the message. Thus, a total of five information bits are encoded by the encoder and ten code symbols are output. The code symbols are transmitted over a binary symmetric channel with crossover probability $p = 0.1$. The received sequence is 10, 01, 10, 11, 00. What is the decoder output?

The decoding trellis is illustrated in Figure 7–7. Decoding can be accomplished by calculating the path metric of (7–2) for all of the eight distinct paths through the trellis and choosing the path with the largest metric. Decoding can also be accomplished by calculating the Hamming distance between the received sequence and the path sequence for all eight paths and choosing the path with the minimum Hamming distance. Both methods will be illustrated. The eight distinct paths through the trellis are specified by their information sequences. The incremental log likelihood symbol metrics for the specified channel are

$$\ln[\Pr(0 \mid 0)] = \ln[\Pr(1 \mid 1)] = \ln(0.9) = -0.11$$

$$\ln[\Pr(1 \mid 0)] = \ln[\Pr(0 \mid 1)] = \ln(0.1) = -2.30$$

Consider the all-zero path. The code sequence on this path differs from the received sequence in five positions. Thus, the path metric is

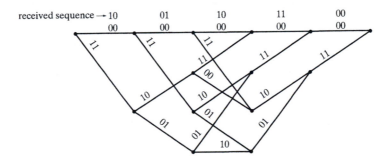

FIGURE 7–7   Decoding trellis.

$$5(-2.3) + 5(-0.11) = -12.05$$

and the Hamming distance between this path and the received sequence is five. All paths and their path metrics and Hamming distances are listed below for the received sequence: 10, 01, 10, 11, 00.

Path	Code Sequence	Path Metric	Hamming Distance
0, 0, 0, 0, 0	00, 00, 00, 00, 00	−12.05	5
0, 0, 1, 0, 0	00, 00, 11, 10, 11	−14.24	6
0, 1, 0, 0, 0	00, 11, 10, 11, 00	−5.48	2
0, 1, 1, 0, 0	00, 11, 01, 01, 11	−16.43	7
1, 0, 0, 0, 0	11, 10, 11, 00, 00	−14.24	6
1, 0, 1, 0, 0	11, 10, 00, 10, 11	−16.43	7
1, 1, 0, 0, 0	11, 01, 01, 11, 00	−7.67	3
1, 1, 1, 0, 0	11, 01, 10, 01, 11	−9.86	4

The largest path metric is −5.48, which corresponds to message sequence 0, 1, 0, 0, 0 and path sequence 00, 11, 10, 11, 00. This same path sequence is also closest in Hamming distance to the received sequence, illustrating that, for the BSC, both decoding metrics (the log likelihood function and Hamming distance) decode the same path. The decoder output is the information sequence 0, 1, 0, 0, 0.

Because of the elegant structure of the codes and the Viterbi algorithm, convolutional decoders can and do make use of channel output reliability information. This reliability information is generated by allowing the DMC to have a larger number of outputs than inputs. In the limit, the DMC output is permitted to be a continuum of values. Consider, for example, a BPSK system. The BPSK matched filter output is a real number generated by correlating the received signal with a replica of the transmitted pulse shape and integrating the result over a symbol period. For the AWGN channel, the probability density function (pdf) of the matched filter output is Gaussian as discussed in Chapter 3. To create a hard decision channel, the matched filter output space (the real number line) is partitioned into two regions. If the channel input symbols are equally likely, the boundary between regions is at zero so that matched filter outputs above zero are declared to be 1s while outputs below zero are declared to be 0s. This is illustrated in Figure 7–8, which shows the matched filter output pdf on the real number line along with the hard decision regions. To provide reliability information to the convolutional decoder, the matched filter output space can be partitioned into more than two regions. Figure 7–8 illustrates further partitioning into four or eight regions. Figure 7–9 illustrates the DMCs resulting from the partitions of Figure 7–8. When reliability information is output from the channel, the channel is called a *soft decision channel*. The transition probabilities for any of the channels of Figure 7–9 are equal to the area under the Gaussian density function between the thresholds that define the output symbol. For example, the transition probability $Pr[3 \mid 0]$ is the area shown cross-hatched in the figure. The probability of receiving a sequence **y** where

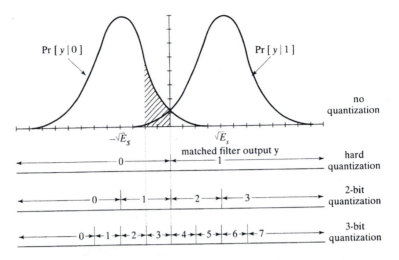

FIGURE 7–8   Soft decision demodulator thresholds.

$y_j \in \{0, 1, \dots, J-1\}$ given a channel input sequence $\mathbf{x}_m$ with $x_{mj} \in \{0, 1\}$ is still given by (7–1).

Regardless of whether the channel outputs hard or soft decisions, the decoding rule remains the same. Given the received sequence $\mathbf{y}$, the decoder output is the code sequence $\mathbf{x}_m$ (or path) that maximizes the probability $\Pr[\mathbf{y} \mid \mathbf{x}_m]$. The Viterbi algorithm can be used to find the correct path through the trellis for hard or for soft decisions.

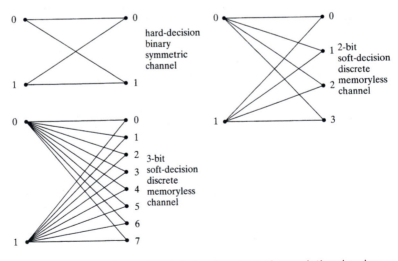

FIGURE 7–9   Channel models for decoding of convolutional codes.

7.2.3   Potential Coding Gains for Soft Decisions

In Section 6.2.3 the capacity C_N and the computational cutoff rate R_0 of hard decision channels were discussed. The capacity of a channel is the maximum number of information bits per channel use that can be transmitted with arbitrarily low error probability. That is, forward error correction can be used to decrease bit error probability to an arbitrarily low level as long as the transmission rate is below capacity. Capacity is a function of the modulation scheme and signal-to-noise ratio. For the binary symmetric channel, capacity is calculated using (6–20). The computational cutoff rate is similar to capacity with the exception that it provides a more practical bound on the number of bits of information per channel use which can be transmitted. The computational cutoff rate for the BSC is calculated using (6–21).

One of the uses of C_N and R_0 is to estimate the maximum possible coding gain that can be achieved at a given R'_m and P_b using a particular modulation format. The first step in this calculation is to determine the signal-to-noise ratio, E_b/N_0, required to set C_N or R_0 exactly equal to the selected R'_m. For a particular channel, this calculation is done by expressing the capacity as a function of E_b/N_0 and R'_m, setting the capacity equal to R'_m, and solving for E_b/N_0 as a function of R'_m. Figure 6–12 illustrates the results of this calculations for BPSK using hard decisions. For a particular R'_m the calculated value of E_b/N_0 is the minimum possible value for which arbitrarily low bit error rate can be achieved. Without coding, the selected modulation scheme requires a particular E_b/N_0 to achieve the desired P_b. The difference between the uncoded E_b/N_0 and the best possible E_b/N_0 is the maximum possible coding gain.

This same procedure is used to determine the maximum possible coding gain for soft decision channels. Consider only binary input soft decision channels. For the general binary input soft decision channel illustrated in Figure 7–10 the capacity and computational cutoff rates are given by [4]

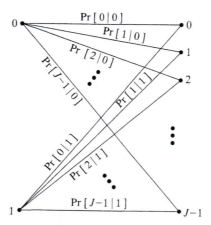

FIGURE 7–10   General binary-input soft-decision J-output discrete memoryless channel.

$$C_N = \sum_{j=0}^{J-1} \Pr[j\,|\,0] \log_2 \frac{2\,\Pr[j\,|\,0]}{\Pr[j\,|\,0] + \Pr[j\,|\,1]} \tag{7-3a}$$

and

$$R_0 = -\log_2 \frac{1}{2} \left[1 + \sum_{j=0}^{J-1} \sqrt{\Pr[j\,|\,0] \cdot \Pr[j\,|\,1]} \right] \tag{7-3b}$$

respectively.

For BPSK modulation, the transition probabilities $\Pr[j\,|\,i]$ are calculated by calculating the area under the Gaussian pdf of Figure 7–8 between the appropriate thresholds as described previously. The capacity is a function of the transition probabilities and therefore a function of the thresholds chosen for partitioning the real number line into the J output regions. The threshold selection can be optimized at a particular signal-to-noise ratio. It has been determined via simulation [4] that the thresholds shown on Figure 7–8 are close to optimum over a range of SNR. These thresholds will be used for the 2, 4, and 8 output channels.

The maximum coding gain is a function of R'_m, P_b, and the modulation format and is calculated using the same procedure used for the hard decision case. The transition probabilities are calculated as a function of E_b/N_0 and are input to (7–3). Then C_N or R_0 is set equal to R'_m in (7–3), and the equation is solved for E_b/N_0. The resultant E_b/N_0 is compared with the E_b/N_0 required to achieve P_b without coding to find the maximum possible coding gain. Figures 7–11 and 7–12 (from [4]) illustrate the results of the first part of this calculation for BPSK and operation at C_N and R_0, respectively. The curves for $J = 2$ (hard decisions) were presented previously as Figure 6–12.

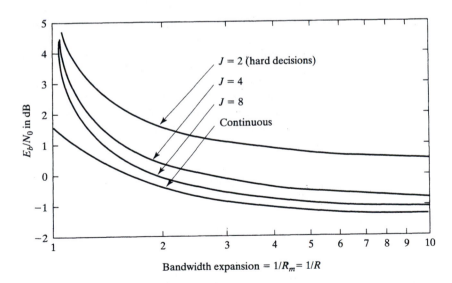

FIGURE 7–11 E_b/N_0 required to operate at $R'_m = C_N$ for a BPSK-modulated additive white Gaussian noise channel.

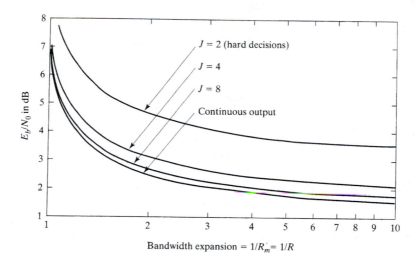

FIGURE 7-12 E_b/N_0 required to operate at $R'_m = R_0$ for a BPSK-modulated additive white Gaussian noise channel.

EXAMPLE 7-3

Find the maximum potential coding gain for a rate ½ code at a bit error probability of $P_b = 10^{-5}$ for the hard decision and $J = 8$ soft decision BPSK channel.

Solution: For operation at C_N, Figure 7–11 is used to find $E_b/N_0 = + 1.8$ dB for $J = 2$ and 0.3 dB for $J = 8$. Without coding, BPSK requires $E_b/N_0 = 9.6$ dB to achieve $P_b = 10^{-5}$. Therefore the maximum possible coding gain for $J = 2$ is $9.6 - 1.8 = 7.8$ dB and for $J = 8$ is $9.6 - 0.3 = 9.3$ dB. Observe that soft decision demodulation has provided the opportunity for 1.5 dB additional coding gain beyond that possible with hard decisions. For operation at R_0, Figure 7–12 is used to find $E_b/N_0 = 4.6$ dB for $J = 2$ and 2.7 dB for $J = 8$. Thus the maximum possible coding gains are $9.6 - 4.6 = 5.0$ dB for $J = 2$ and $9.6 - 2.7 = 6.9$ dB for $J = 8$. Soft decision demodulation has provided the opportunity for 1.9 dB additional coding gain relative to hard decision demodulation.

In the limit as $J \to \infty$ there are an infinite number of soft decision outputs. The appropriate characterization of the channel is the conditional probability density function at the matched filter output. For BPSK modulation and AWGN interference, this density function is the now familiar Gaussian density that was integrated to obtain the transition probabilities for finite J. The $J = \infty$ channel is called the *continuous output channel*. The capacities for this channel are [4].

$$C_N = \frac{1}{2} \log_2 \left(1 + 2R \frac{E_b}{N_0} \right) \tag{7-4}$$

$$R_0 = 1 - \log_2 \left[1 + \exp\left(-R \frac{E_b}{N_0} \right) \right] \qquad (7\text{--}5)$$

The maximum possible coding gain for the continuous output channel can be calculated. This maximum coding gain is only slightly greater than the maximum coding gain for the $J = 8$ output channel. Figures 7–11 and 7–12 show the E_b/N_0 required to operate at C_N or R_0 for this channel. The variable R_m' equals the number of bits per channel use and is equivalent to the code rate R. Hereafter R will be used in place of R_m'.

7.2.4   Distance Properties of Convolutional Codes

The minimum Hamming distance between any two code sequences of a convolutional code affects code performance in the same manner that d_{min} affects block code performance. Code generator polynomials are carefully selected so that distinct code sequences are separated as much as possible in Hamming distance. In addition, code sequence pairs that are separated by the minimum Hamming distance are associated with information sequence pairs that differ as little as possible. Thus, the most likely decoding errors (confusion between minimally separated code sequences) cause the fewest possible information errors. Convolutional coding theorists have chosen not to use d_{min} to represent the minimum distance between any two distinct code sequences. Rather, the *free distance*, denoted d_f, of a convolutional code is the minimum Hamming distance between two code sequences associated with trellis paths that diverge from one another at some point and remerge at some later point.

Reconsider the trellis diagram for the $R = \frac{1}{2}$ and $v = 3$ convolutional code of Figure 7–3, which is simplified and redrawn as Figure 7–13. The trellis states are shown only on the left of Figure 7–13, and all branches are solid lines. Input 0s are associated with the upper branch leaving a state, while the lower branches are associated with input 1s. Since the code is linear, the Hamming distance between any pair of code sequences corresponds to the Hamming distance between the all-zero code sequence and some nonzero code sequence. Thus for the study of distance properties it is possible to focus on the Hamming distance between the all-zero code sequence and all nonzero code sequences. In order to find the free distance of this code, the minimum Hamming weight nonzero code sequence must be found. This code sequence is the sequence of labels on some path from left to right through the trellis that diverges from the all-zero path at some point and remerges with the all-zero path at some later point. This code trellis is simple enough that this path can be found by inspection and is sequence 2 of Figure 7–13. Sequence 2 diverges from the all-zero path at node A in the diagram where an information 1 causes the coder to output code sequence pair 11 and remerges with the all-zero path at node B after three information bits have been processed. The Hamming weight of this path, and thus the free distance of the code, is five. The information sequence corresponding to this path is 100000. . . . If transmission errors cause sequence 2 to be decoded rather than the correct all-zero sequence, a single information bit error would be made in first decoded information bit. Sequence 3 of Figure 7–13 is Hamming distance 7 from the all-zero sequence,

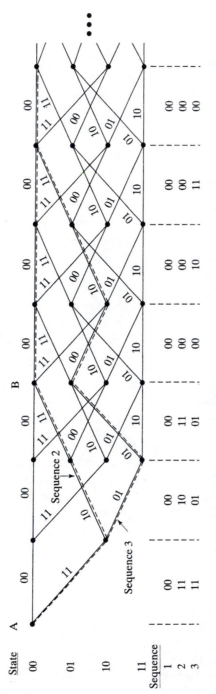

FIGURE 7–13 Simplified trellis diagram for $R = \frac{1}{2}$, $v = 3$ convolutional code.

and three information errors would occur if this sequence is decoded in place of the correct all-zero sequence. Sequence 3 is caused by information sequence 1101000. . . .

For the simple code of Figure 7–13, the free distance is reasonably easy to determine by inspection. When the code is more complex, more powerful techniques are required to determine the free distance. Free distance and other properties of the code can be found by modifying and analyzing the state transition diagram. To calculate the bit error probability performance of the code later in this chapter, a method is needed for determining the Hamming weight and the associated number of nonzero information bits for all nonzero paths through the trellis. These nonzero paths diverge once from the all-zero path and remerge once with the all-zero path at some later time.

Consider the state transition diagram representation of the rate ½ code of Figure 7–2. The spans of interest of the nonzero paths all start and end in state 00. Outside of this interval the paths are merged so that no Hamming distance is accumulated. Thus, the span of interest of a path begins when the path leaves the all-zero state and ends when the path first returns to the all-zero state. The state transition diagram is redrawn in a modified form in Figure 7–14. This modified state diagram conceptually separates the all-zero state into two states corresponding to the state from which the path of interest leaves and the state to which the path of interest returns. In addition, the loop from the state 00 to itself has been discarded since paths following this loop are outside the span of interest. The goal of the analysis is to determine the Hamming weight and the number of information is associated with all paths through the modified state transition diagram. Recognize that there are an infinite number of paths through this state diagram so that the best that can be hoped for is an enumeration of the most important paths for the subsequent analysis of bit error probability.

The branches of the modified state transition diagram are now labeled with the letters D, L, and N. The letter D raised to the power n is used to account for the number of 1s in the code symbols associated with the branch; specifically, the power of D is the number of 1s. The letter L is associated with every branch and will be used to account for the

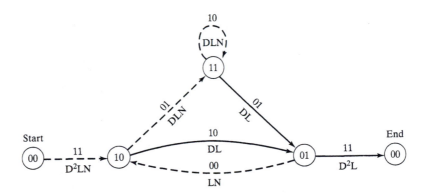

FIGURE 7–14   Modified state transition diagram for $R = ½$, $v = 3$ convolutional code.

number of branches traversed by a path. The letter N will be used to account for information 1s associated with a path; the branch label includes N only if the information bit associated with that path is a 1. To see how this accounting for code sequence 1s, information 1s, and path length works, consider the path passing through the following state sequence: 00, 10, 01, 10, 11, 01, 00. The product of the labels on this path is $D^2LN \cdot DL \cdot LN \cdot DLN \cdot DL \cdot D^2L = D^7L^6N^3$. The code sequence for this path is $\{11, 10, 00, 01, 01, 11\}$, which has seven 1s corresponding to the power of D in the path label product. The information sequence for this path is $\{1, 0, 1, 1, 0, 0)$, which has three 1s corresponding to the power of N in the path label product. The total number of branches traversed is six, corresponding to the power of L in the path label product. Thus, if it is possible to calculate a list of the path label products for all paths through the state diagram, the exponents of the parameters D, L, and N will be the desired output of the analysis.

Let S_{00s}, S_{10}, S_{01}, S_{11}, and S_{00} denote a sum of the path label products for all paths entering states 00 (start), 10, 01, 11, and 00 (end), respectively. For example, a partial list of the path label sum for state 10 is $S_{10} = D^2LN + D^2 \, LN \cdot DL \cdot LN + \cdots$. The first term accounts for the single branch from 00s to 10, and the second term accounts for the path following state sequence $\{00, 10, 01, 10\}$. The last four of these sums contain an infinite number of terms. Consider the sum S_{10}. The state 10 can only be entered from states 00 and 01. Therefore, $S_{10} = S_{00} \cdot D^2LN + S_{01} \cdot LN$. Similar equations can be written for all states:

$$S_{00s} = 1$$

$$S_{10} = S_{00s} \cdot D^2LN + S_{01} \cdot LN$$

$$S_{11} = S_{10} \cdot DLN + S_{11} \cdot DLN \qquad\qquad (7\text{--}6)$$

$$S_{01} = S_{11} \cdot DL + S_{10} \cdot DL$$

$$S_{00e} = S_{01} \cdot D^2L$$

These are five state equations in five unknowns. They can be solved for S_{00e} yielding the desired result. After some straightforward algebra, the result is

$$S_{00e} = \frac{D^5L^3N}{1 - DN(L + L^2)} \qquad\qquad (7\text{--}7)$$

Performing a long division to write this ratio as an infinite summation yields

$$S_{00e} = D^5L^3N + D^6L^4(1 + L)N^2 + D^7L^5(1 + L)^2N^3$$
$$+ D^8L^6(1 + L)^3N^4 + \cdots + D^{j+5}L^{j+3}(1 + L)^jN^{j+1} + \cdots \qquad (7\text{--}8)$$

Each term of this function corresponds to the branch label sequence for a path that diverges once and remerges once with the all-zero path. The first term, D^5L^3N, corresponds to shortest nonzero path that goes through state sequence $\{00, 10, 01, 00\}$. This path has length three corresponding to L^3, Hamming weight 5 corresponding to D^5, and information sequence Hamming weight 1 corresponding to N^1. The second and third terms, both from $D^6L^4(1 + L)N^2$, enumerate the two paths with Hamming weight 6. Both terms have information Hamming weight 2. One of the paths has length 4, while the other has length 5. The function S_{00e} is called the *generating function* of the convolution code and will be denoted $T(D, L, N)$.

The analysis technique that has just been demonstrated by example is applicable to all convolutional codes. The results of this analysis will be used in the calculation of the bit error probability performance of convolutionals code later.

7.3   THE VITERBI ALGORITHM

The Viterbi algorithm (VA) is an elegant method for performing maximum likelihood decoding of convolutional codes. The algorithm was first described mathematically by A. J. Viterbi [2] in 1967. Since that time the algorithm has been described many times by many authors; most notably, Forney [5, 6] provides a highly readable and insightful description of the algorithm and its performance.

Recall that the function of a maximum-likelihood decoder is to find the code sequence that was most likely to have been transmitted given the received channel output sequence. As discussed previously, this corresponds to finding the path through the trellis whose code sequence has the largest log-likelihood function

$$\ln[\Pr(\mathbf{y} \mid \mathbf{x_m})] = \sum_{n'=1}^{\infty} \ln[\Pr(y_{n'} \mid x_{mn'})] \tag{7-9}$$

For the BSC, maximizing this function is equivalent to finding the path through the trellis whose code sequence is closest in Hamming distance to the received sequence. The VA will be explained by example for a BSC using the Hamming distance metric.

7.3.1   Hard Decision Decoding

Consider the truncated trellis diagram of Figure 7–15a. For convenience in this explanation, the depth into the trellis is indicated above the trellis. Path segments will be denoted by the sequence of trellis states $\{S_1, S_2, S_3, \dots\}$ through which the path passes. The trellis has been truncated by clearing the encoder by inputting two known 0s as bit numbers 7 and 8. The decoder knows that the encoder is cleared at this time. The received sequence is written above the trellis.

The first decoding step is to calculate the Hamming distance between the first two received symbols and the two symbols on the trellis branches leaving state 00 at depth 0 and leading to the depth 1 states. These Hamming distances are both unity and are written above the state nodes at depth 1 as illustrated in Figure 7–15b. The decoder stores these Hamming distances and moves to depth 2 of the trellis. Now the decoder calculates the Hamming distance between the first four received symbols and the first four symbols on all four trellis paths leading to depth 2 states. The Hamming distance for the first four symbols of any path is the sum of the Hamming distance for the first two symbols and the Hamming distance accumulated in the branch leading from depth 1 to depth 2. Thus the decoder may add the

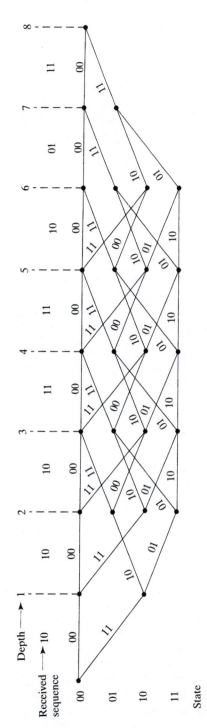

FIGURE 7–15a Truncated trellis diagram.

Hamming distances it stored in the first step to the Hamming distance accumulated in the most recent branch. For example, the Hamming distance for the path segment {00, 10, 01} is the Hamming distance written above state 10 plus 0, since no additional Hamming distance is accumulated on the branch {10, 01}. The results of these four calculations are written above the trellis states as before and are stored by the decoder.

The decoding becomes more interesting as depth 3 states are considered. There are two trellis paths leading into each of four states at depth 3. Therefore, eight path segments must be considered. The decoder calculates the accumulated Hamming distance for each path segment by adding the distance noted above the states at depth 2 to the distance accumulated in moving from depth 2 to depth 3. After performing these eight calculations, the decoder is able to discard one of the two paths leading into each state. The path discarded is the path with the higher accumulated distance at that depth. The discarded path will never again be considered by the decoder. The reason that a path segment can be discarded is that, because it has merged with another path having a lower cumulative Hamming distance, it can never be part of the path through the trellis with the lowest total Hamming distance. Consider, for example, the two paths leading into state 00 at depth 3. The path segment {00, 00, 00, 00} has accumulated Hamming distance 3 while the path segment {00, 10, 01, 00} has accumulated Hamming distance 2. Suppose that the path with the minimum total Hamming distance passed through state 00 at depth 3. Because this path has the *minimum* Hamming distance of all paths, it must include the path segment {00, 10, 01, 00} and cannot include the path segment {00, 00, 00, 00}. This discarding of one of the two paths leading into each state is the key to the efficiency of the Viterbi algorithm. Figure 7–15c illustrates the surviving path segments after the decoder has discarded half of the paths leading into depth 3 states. Observe that all paths that pass through state 00 at depth 2 have been discarded by the VA. In this and subsequent figures, the surviving paths are shown as solid lines, and the paths not yet processed by the decoder are shown as dashed lines.

The decoder now moves to depth 4 states and repeats the process. The Hamming distances for eight path segments are calculated, and the path segment with the largest Hamming distance leading into each state is discarded. The decoding process is illustrated in Figures 7–15b through 7–15h. At depth 6 note that two Hamming distance ties occur. In this case no meaningful decision can be made regarding the best path segment, and the decoder can either keep both paths leading into the state or select one arbitrarily. Both paths have been retained in Figure 7–15f. In this case both of the pairs of paths retained due to ties are discarded at depth 7. Observe that at depth 7 only two paths remain as potential decoder output paths. At depth 8 a single path is selected by the VA and decoding is complete.

Figure 7–15i illustrates the entire Viterbi decoding procedure on a single trellis. Starting with the encoding trellis, the decoder calculates Hamming distances and discards paths as just described. Rather than redraw the trellis after each step, the discarded paths are denoted by an "x" on the discarded branch leading into a state. After reaching depth 8, the decoded path is determined by reversing direction and following the branches that do not have "xs" back to depth 0.

(*text continues on page 500*)

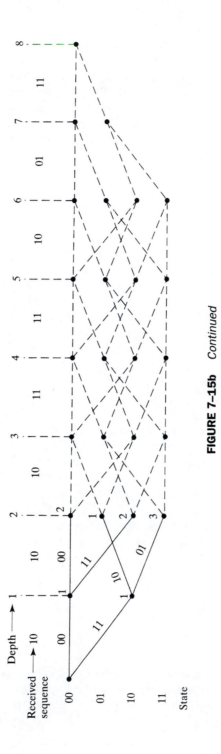

FIGURE 7–15b *Continued*

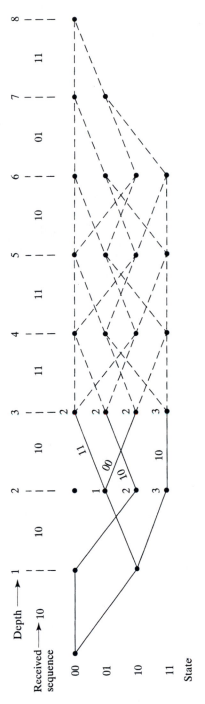

FIGURE 7-15c *Continued*

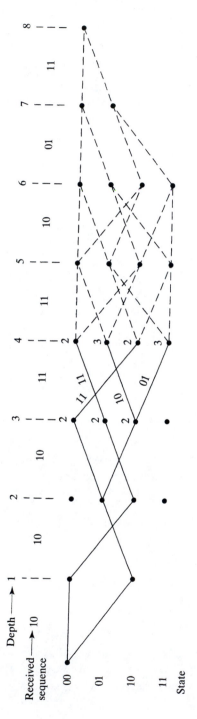

FIGURE 7–15d *Continued*

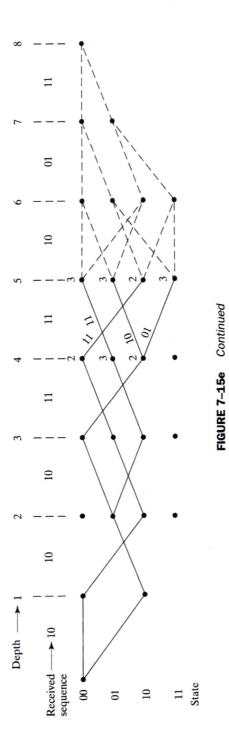

FIGURE 7–15e *Continued*

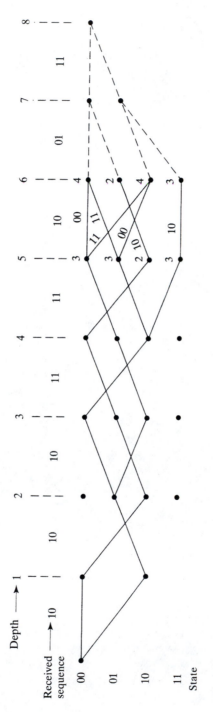

FIGURE 7-15f *Continued*

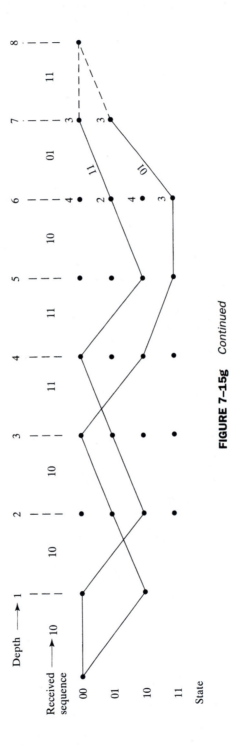

FIGURE 7–15g *Continued*

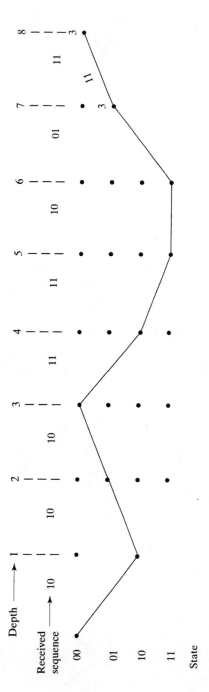

FIGURE 7–15h *Continued*

498

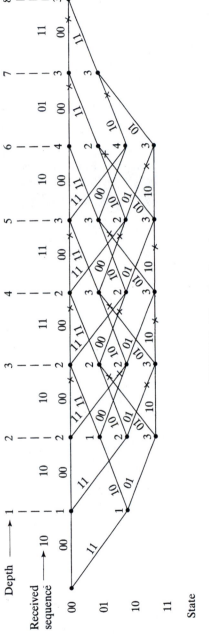

FIGURE 7–15i *Continued*

7.3.2 Soft Decision Decoding

The Viterbi algorithm described in Section 7.3.1 using the Hamming distance decoding metric works in exactly the same manner using soft-decision decoding metrics. A minor difference is that for soft-decision decoding the path with the *largest* log-likelihood metric, $\ln[\Pr(\mathbf{y} \mid \mathbf{x}_m)]$, is being found rather than the path with the *smallest* Hamming distance. Thus, discarded path segments are the segments with the smaller (rather than the larger) of the two metrics. In both cases the path most likely to have been followed by the encoder is found.

EXAMPLE 7–4

Suppose that the same truncated encoder used for the hard-decision VA description is used in a soft-decision communication system. The binary input DMC for this system is illustrated in Figure 7–16. The channel transition probabilities are shown in Figure 7–16 along with the log-likelihood metrics for all transitions. The trellis description of the encoder is illustrated in Figure 7–15a and is redrawn in Figure 7–17a, which includes the soft decision received sequence as well as all branch metrics. The branch metrics are calculated from the received sequence and the log-likelihood functions of Figure 7–16. For example, the branch metric for the branch between depth zero state 00 and depth one state 10 is

$$\ln[\Pr(3 \mid 1)] + \ln[\Pr(2 \mid 1)] = -0.22 + (-1.90) = -2.12$$

This branch metric is the number in parentheses on the branch. All branches are similarly labeled.

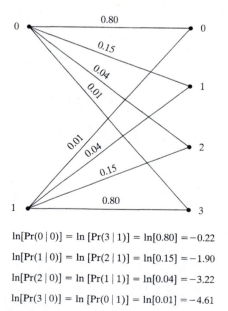

$$\ln[\Pr(0 \mid 0)] = \ln [\Pr(3 \mid 1)] = \ln[0.80] = -0.22$$
$$\ln[\Pr(1 \mid 0)] = \ln [\Pr(2 \mid 1)] = \ln[0.15] = -1.90$$
$$\ln[\Pr(2 \mid 0)] = \ln [\Pr(1 \mid 1)] = \ln[0.04] = -3.22$$
$$\ln[\Pr(3 \mid 0)] = \ln [\Pr(0 \mid 1)] = \ln[0.01] = -4.61$$

FIGURE 7–16 Binary input discrete memoryless channel.

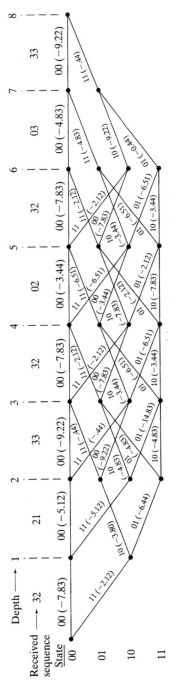

FIGURE 7-17a Soft decision Viterbi decoding branch metrics.

For clarity in the drawings, the trellis is redrawn in Figure 7–17b to show the decoding process. In this figure, the cumulative metric for the surviving path segment leading to a node is written immediately above the node. For the nodes at depth 1, the cumulative metric is exactly equal to the first branch metrics. For the nodes at depth 2, the cumulative metric is the sum of the depth 1 metric and the metric accumulated on the branch leading from depth 1 to depth 2. For example, the cumulative metric leading to state 01 at depth 2 is the metric −2.12 at depth 1 state 10 plus the branch metric −3.80 accumulated on the branch between depth 1 state 10 and depth 2 state 01.

As before, the decoding becomes more interesting at depth 3 where path segments begin to be discarded. Consider the two path segments leading into state 00 at depth 3. The cumulative metric for the path segment {00, 00, 00, 00} is (−7.83) + (−5.12) + (−9.22) = −22.17. The cumulative metric for the path segment {00, 10, 01, 00} is (−2.12) + (−3.80) + (−0.44) = −6.36. The path with the lowest metric of −22.17 is discarded by placing an "x" on that branch. The metric of the surviving path is written above state 00 at depth three. Decoding continues in this manner to the end of the trellis. After the decoder has reached depth 8, the decoder reverses direction following the surviving path to determine the correct path through the trellis. Observe that the surviving path is identical to the path found using hard-decision decoding.

Costello [1] has given the following succinct definition, valid for either hard or soft decisions, of the Viterbi algorithm. In this description, L is the total number of information bits processed by the encoder and m is the number of 0s required to clear the decoder.

THE VITERBI ALGORITHM *Step 1: Begin at depth* $j = 1$, *compute the partial metric for the single path entering each state. Store the path (the survivor) and its metric for each state.*

Step 2: Increase j *by 1. Compute the partial metric for all the paths entering a state by adding the branch metric entering that state to the metric of the connecting survivor at the preceding depth. For each state, store the path with the largest metric (the survivor), together with its metric, and eliminate all other paths.*

Step 3: If $j < L + m$, *repeat step 2. Otherwise, stop.*

The descriptions of the VA used above presume that after a finite time, the encoder is cleared with a sequence of known zero information bits. This allows the decoder to force all paths to state 00 and complete the decoding. Although this is a valid and useful decoding strategy, it is sometimes desirable to make decoding bit decisions prior to the zeroing of the encoder. The reason for this is that the number of information bits transmitted between zeroing of the encoder is usually very large (perhaps thousands of bits) requiring significant path memory. In addition, reliable bit decisions can be made well in advance of zeroing the decoder. Suppose, for example, that the encoder was never zeroed and that the number of states in the trellis is 2^{v-1}. At each depth there are 2^{v-1} surviving paths. At any depth the decoder could trace all of the surviving paths backward through the trellis for some distance. With high probability it would find that all of the 2^{v-1} surviving paths would merge into a single survivor path some distance back from the current depth. At the point where a single survivor path is observed, reliable decoding decisions can be output

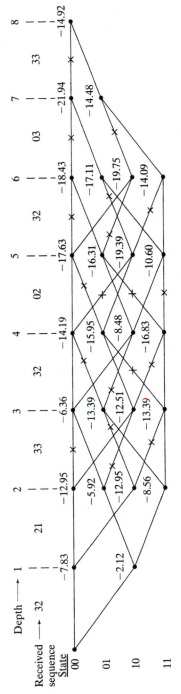

FIGURE 7–17b Soft decision Viterbi decoding cumulative path metrics.

from the decoder. The depth that must be traced backward through the trellis to the point where all paths merge is a random variable.

Rather than actually retrace through the trellis, most decoders include a fixed path memory. When that memory is filled, a decoding decision is forced at that level of the trellis. Typical decoders store all surviving paths for about five times the size of the shift register in the encoder [1, 7]. For example, the encoder of Figure 7–3 has a shift-register size of 2 bits. Thus, a practical decoder would store path segments of length $2 \times 5 = 10$ branches. With high probability all paths would have merged to a single path 10 branches back from the current decoding depth, and reliable decisions could be output.

The complexity of Viterbi decoding is directly proportional to the number of states in the trellis. The number of states grows exponentially with constraint length and decoders become impractical for large constraint length. At the time of this writing, integrated circuit Viterbi decoders are available for moderate bit rates only for constraint lengths to about $v = 9$. It will be shown later that the coding gain for these decoders can be as large as 6 dB when soft-decision decoding is used. Thus, very significant coding gains can be achieved with convolutional coding and Viterbi maximum-likelihood decoding using a single integrated circuit.

7.3.3   Decoding Error Probability

Decoding error probability for Viterbi decoding of convolutional codes is calculated using the same basic concepts used to calculate error probabilities for maximum-likelihood decoding of block codes. Error events are enumerated, their probabilities are calculated, and the results used to calculate bounds on decoding error probability. For convolutional codes with Viterbi decoding, the appropriate measure of decoding reliability is the probability that the correct path through the trellis is discarded at depth j. That is, the correct reliability measure is the probability of making an error at each opportunity for decoding error. An opportunity to discard the correct path exists each time the decoder moves one unit deeper into the trellis. This measure is comparable to the measure used for block codes where an opportunity for error exists each time a new block is decoded and the appropriate reliability measure is the block decoding error probability. Note that the probability of selecting an incorrect path over the full extent of the trellis is an inappropriate reliability measure. That is, it would not be correct to evaluate the probability that the total semi-infinite decoder output sequence is not continuously merged with the correct sequence. Over all time, the probability that the decoded path diverges from and remerges with the correct path at least once approaches unity.

Since convolutional codes are linear, overall average decoding error probability is equal to the decoding error probability calculated assuming the all-zero sequence is transmitted. For the remainder of this discussion assume, therefore, that the correct path through the trellis is the all-zero path. The decoding error probability is then the probability that a nonzero path entering state 00 at depth j of the trellis is selected as the survivor. In order to evaluate decoding error probability, all potential decoding error events at depth j are enumerated, and their error probabilities are calculated and summed. The summation is the result of a union bounding argument similar to that used for the error probability bound for block codes. The student is referred to Viterbi [3] for the details of the error probability derivation. In [3] it is shown that the decoding error probability P_E is overbounded by

$$P_E < \sum_{k=d_{\text{free}}}^{\infty} a_k P_k \tag{7-10}$$

where a_k is the number of nonzero paths with Hamming weight k that merge with the all-zero path at depth j and diverge once from the all-zero path at some previous depth, and P_k is the probability of incorrectly selecting a path with Hamming weight k. The values a_k can be found from the generating function $T(D, L, N)$ with $L = 1$ and $N = 1$. Specifically,

$$T(D, 1, 1) = \sum_{k=d_{\text{free}}}^{\infty} a_k D^k \tag{7-11}$$

The probability of incorrectly selecting a path that is Hamming distance k from the all-zero path is a function of the channel and the received signal-to-noise ratio. For the binary symmetric channel, P_k is equal to the probability that errors in the k positions where the correct and incorrect paths differ cause the received sequence to be closer in Hamming distance to the incorrect path than to the correct path. Thus, P_k is identical to the two-codeword error probability calculated using (6–63) or (6–64) depending on whether k is even or odd. Specifically,

$$P_k = \sum_{e=(k/2)+1}^{k} \binom{k}{e} p^e (1-p)^{k-e}$$

$$+ \frac{1}{2} \binom{k}{k/2} p^{k/2}(1-p)^{k/2}, \quad k \text{ even} \tag{7-12a}$$

and

$$P_k = \sum_{e=(k+1)/2}^{k} \binom{k}{e} p^e (1-p)^{k-e}, \quad k \text{ odd} \tag{7-12b}$$

For the continuous output additive white Gaussian noise channel it can be shown [8,3] that P_k is given by

$$P_k = \int_{\sqrt{2kRE_b/N_0}}^{\infty} \frac{1}{\sqrt{2\pi}} \exp\left(\frac{-x^2}{2}\right) dx$$

$$= Q\left(\sqrt{\frac{2kRE_b}{N_0}}\right) \tag{7-13}$$

For other soft-decision channels, the calculation of P_k is more complex and the student is referred to [3, 9] for details.

7.3.4   Bit Error Probability

Bit error probability is calculated using essentially the same techniques used for decoding error probability. To calculate bit error probability, each decoding error event is weighted by the number of bit errors associated with that event. Since the all-zero path is the correct path, the number of bit errors associated with a nonzero path is equal to the number of information 1s associated with that path. The generating function is used to enumerate error events along with the number of attendant bit errors. Recall that the number of information 1s on a nonzero path through the trellis is equal to the power of N in the generating function term corresponding to that path. In order to change the exponent of N into a multiplier to weight the path by the number of bit errors, the generating function is differentiated with respect to N and N is then set to unity. Consider, for example, the generating function of (7–8)

$$T(D, L, N) = D^5 L^3 N + D^6 L^4 (1 + L) N^2$$
$$+ D^7 L^5 (1 + L)^2 N^3 + D^8 L^6 (1 + L)^3 N^4 \tag{7-14}$$
$$+ \cdots + D^{j+5} L^{j+3} (1 + L)^j N^{j+1} + \cdots$$

This function enumerates all nonzero paths through the trellis of Figure 7–13. Differentiating $T(D, L, N)$ with respect to N and setting $N = 1$ and $L = 1$ (since path length does not affect the calculation) results in

$$\frac{dT(D, 1, N)}{dN}\bigg|_{N=1} = D^5 + (2 \cdot 2 \cdot D^6) + (3 \cdot 4 \cdot D^7) +$$
$$\cdots + (j + 1) \cdot 2^j \cdot D^{j+5} + \cdots \tag{7-15}$$
$$= \sum_{k=d_{free}}^{\infty} c_k D^k$$

This summation accounts for all possible nonzero paths through the trellis that merge with the all-zero path at depth j. The first term indicates that there is a single bit error associated with all nonzero paths that are Hamming distance 5 from the all-zero path. The second term indicates that there are four bit errors associated with all nonzero paths that are Hamming distance 6 from the all-zero path. These four bit errors come from two different paths, each of which is associated with two bit errors. In general, there are a total of c_k bit errors associated with all paths that are Hamming distance k from the all-zero path.

Using the generating function to weight error events by the number of bit errors, an upper bound on the bit error probability is

$$P_b < \sum_{k=d_{\text{free}}}^{\infty} c_k P_k \qquad (7\text{--}16)$$

where P_k is calculated using (7–12) for the hard-decision channel and (7–13) for the continuous output additive white Gaussian noise channel.

The results for probability of decoding error and probability of bit error are reasonably good upper bounds; they are not exact results. Computer simulations may also be used to determine error probabilities. Extensive computer simulation results are presented in a frequently referenced paper by Heller and Jacobs [10]. The simulation results of this paper show good agreement with the upper bounds for moderate to low bit error rates where the upper bounds presented herein are best. Soft and hard-decision decoding are also compared in this paper along with other interesting and practical results. Other practical results are presented in reference [4] by Odenwalder.

7.4   GOOD CONVOLUTIONAL CODES AND THEIR PERFORMANCE

Good convolutional codes are codes that result in the maximum possible coding gain in the interference environment of interest to the communications system engineer. For the additive white Gaussian noise channel, good convolutional codes, like good block codes, separate code sequences by the maximum possible Hamming distance and also associate the minimum possible number of bit errors with the most likely decoding errors. Most good convolutional codes have been found using computer search techniques. Good convolutional codes can be found in [1, 11, 12]. Tables 7–1 and 7–2 (from [4]) give the best rate-½ and rate-⅓ convolutional codes along with values of c_k for the eight most probable decoding error events. The constraint length is denoted by v in these tables so that the number of stages in the shift register of the code generator is $v - 1$ and the number of states in the state diagram or trellis is 2^{v-1}. The code generator polynomials for the codes are given in octal notation. This notation gives the connections between the encoder shift-register states and the modulo-2 adders. Consider, for example, the constraint length seven rate ½ code. The generators are (171, 133) in octal or (1111001, 1011011) in binary. This means that the connections to the first modulo-2 adder are from shift-register stages 0, 1, 2, 3, and 6 and to the second modulo-2 adder are from shift-register states 0, 2, 3, 5, and 6. This encoder is illustrated in Figure 7–18.

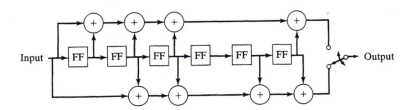

FIGURE 7–18   Rate ½ constraint length 7 convolutional encoder.

TABLE 7-1   Best Rate ½ Convolutional Codes and Their Partial Weight Structure

Constraint Length, v	Code Generators	Free Distance, d_f	d_f	d_f+1	d_f+2	d_f+3	d_f+4	d_f+5	d_f+6	d_f+7
3	(7, 5)	5	1	4	12	32	80	192	448	1024
4	(17, 15)	6	2	7	18	49	130	333	836	2069
5	(35, 23)	7	4	12	20	72	225	500	1324	3680
6	(75, 53)	8	2	36	32	62	332	701	2342	5503
7	(171, 133)	10	36	0	211	0	1404	0	11633	0
8	(371, 247)	10	2	22	60	148	340	1008	2642	6748
9	(753, 561)	12	33	0	281	0	2179	0	15035	0

Source: Reproduced from Reference [4] with permission.

508

TABLE 7-2 Best Rate ⅓ Convolutional Codes and Their Partial Weight Structure

Constraint Length, ν	Code Generators	Free Distance, d_f	c_k for $d =$							
			d_f	$d_f + 1$	$d_f + 2$	$d_f + 3$	$d_f + 4$	$d_f + 5$	$d_f + 6$	$d_f + 7$
3	(7, 7, 5)	8	3	0	15	0	58	0	201	0
4	(17, 15, 13)	10	6	0	6	0	58	0	118	0
5	(37, 33, 25)	12	12	0	12	0	56	0	320	0
6	(75, 53, 47)	13	1	8	26	20	19	62	86	204
7	(171, 145, 133)	14	1	0	20	0	53	0	184	0
8	(367, 331, 225)	16	1	0	24	0	113	0	287	0

Source: Reproduced from Reference [4] with permission.

Bit error probability P_b was calculated as a function of E_b/N_0 for all of the codes of Tables 7–1 and 7–2 using (7–16). These results are plotted in Figures 7–19 and 7–21 for hard-decision decoding and in Figures 7–20 and 7–22 for the continuous output additive white Gaussian noise channel. The modulation is assumed to be binary phase shift keying. The dashed curve on these figures is the uncoded bit error probability for BPSK. In all instances, the bit error rate performance at a fixed E_b/N_0 improves as constraint length increases. At $P_b = 10^{-5}$ the coding gain for hard-decision decoding for rate ½ codes ranges from 1.5 dB for $v = 3$ to 3.7 dB for $v = 9$. For the continuous output DMC, the comparable coding gains for rate ½ codes are 3.7 dB and 6.1 dB. These values are found directly from Figures 7–19 and 7–20 by comparing the E_b/N_0 required to achieve $P_b = 10^{-5}$ without coding to the value required with coding. For the rate ⅓ codes with hard-decision decoding, the coding gain at $P_b = 10^{-5}$ is 1.25 dB for $v = 3$ and 4.0 dB for $v = 8$. The comparable results for the continuous output channel and soft decoding are 3.6 dB and 6.25 dB.

7.5   OTHER TOPICS

Space does not permit coverage of many interesting topics related to convolutional coding. Some of these topics are briefly mentioned here along with references so that the motivated reader may investigate further.

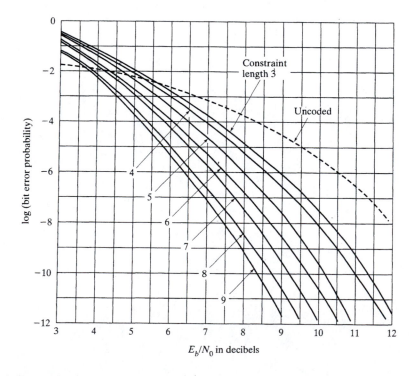

FIGURE 7–19   Bit error probability for rate ½ convolutional coding using a hard decision channel.

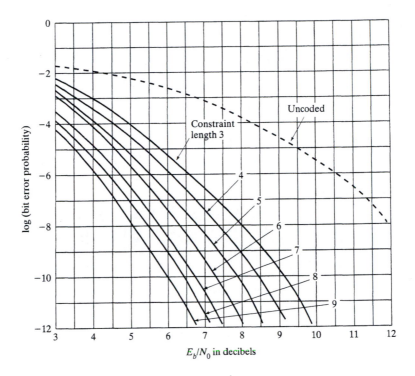

FIGURE 7–20   Bit error probability for rate ½ convolutional coding using a soft decision channel.

7.5.1   Sequential Decoding

Prior to the discovery of Viterbi decoding, convolutional codes were decoded using sequential decoding and its variants. Sequential decoding makes use of yet another representation of convolutional codes, the code "tree." Sequential decoding is not precisely maximum-likelihood decoding, although, if processing time and decoder memory is not an issue, sequential decoding can be as nearly "maximum-likelihood" as desired. The complexity of sequential decoders is independent of constraint length so that this decoding method can be used for very large constraint length convolutional codes. Sequential decoding has been used for extremely important deep space missions. The absence of further discussion of sequential decoding in this chapter is not an indication that this topic is not important. The student is referred to [1, 8] for detailed discussions of sequential decoding.

7.5.2   Threshold Decoding

Certain convolutional codes can be decoded using circuitry similar in complexity to that used in Figure 6–20 to decode Hamming codes. In order to be decoded so simply, the codes must have additional structure as defined in detail by Massey [13] and by

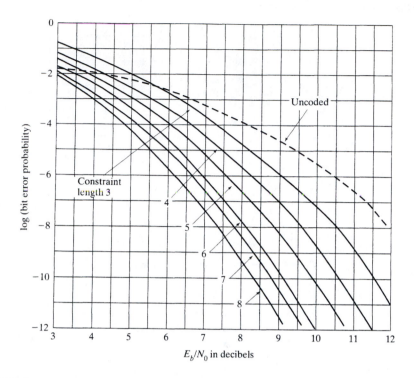

FIGURE 7–21 Bit error probability for rate ⅓ convolutional coding using a hard decision channel.

Costello [1]. The simplicity of threshold decoders makes their implementation at very high speeds possible. Although the performance of these special convolutional codes is not outstanding for the additive white Gaussian noise channel, the structure is particularly convenient for applications where interleaving is required. For channels where the interference comes in bursts, very large coding gains can be achieved using convolutional coding with threshold decoding.

7.5.3 Concatenated Reed–Solomon/Convolutional Coding

Extremely powerful error correction capability can be obtained by concatenating a Viterbi decoded convolutional code with a Reed–Solomon block code. Figure 7–23 is a block diagram of a coded communications system that uses both a convolutional and a block code. Information bits from the data source are grouped into blocks of m to create the 2^m-ary symbol alphabet used by the Reed–Solomon code. The coding system that appears first in the chain, in this case the RS code, is called the *outer code* of a concatenated code system. The RS output symbols are converted to their m-bit binary representations and input to a symbol interleaving buffer. The purpose of this buffer is to enable the spreading

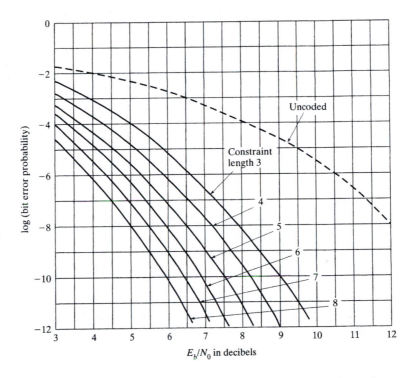

FIGURE 7-22   Bit error probability for rate ⅓ convolutional coding using a soft decision channel.

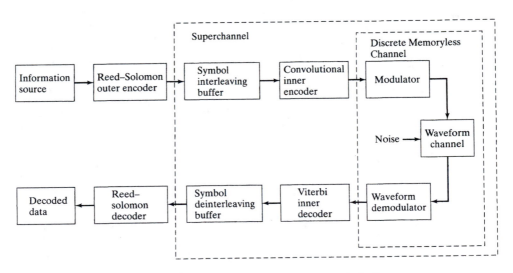

FIGURE 7-23   Concatenated coding system block diagram.

of bursts of channel symbol errors over RS codewords as uniformly as possible. The interleaver changes the order in which the RS symbols are transmitted over the channel. The symbols are put back in their original order in the deinterleaving buffer in the receiver. This process of changing the transmission order, transmitting, and reestablishing the original order causes contiguous bursts of channel errors to be spread uniformly over a number of RS codewords rather than occurring all in a single codeword. RS codes, as well as all of the other codes that have been studied, are designed to perform best when channel errors occur independently from one symbol to the next and do not occur in bursts. The reader is referred to [7, 14, 15] for additional discussions about interleaver design. For the purpose of this discussion, the interleaver/deinterleaver combination may be considered processors that take bursts of channel errors and spread these errors over some number of codewords.

The interleaver output of Figure 7–23 is input to a convolutional coder whose output is sent over the discrete memoryless channel to a Viterbi (in this case) decoder. The convolutional code and Viterbi decoder operate exactly as discussed previously; the convolutional code is called the *inner code* of the system. The output of the Viterbi decoder is an estimate of the binary sequence that was input to the encoder. The Viterbi decoder output is input to the deinterleaver. The portion of the communication system between the interleaver input and the deinterleaver output is called a *superchannel*. The superchannel includes the convolutional coding system as well as the physical channel and can be modeled as a discrete memoryless channel with attendant channel error probability. Detailed measurements and simulations of Viterbi decoder performance have shown that output errors tend to occur in bursts. It is for this reason that the interleaving scheme is required. Without the interleaver, the superchannel would not be memoryless.

The superchannel output binary symbols are grouped into blocks of m to construct the 2^m-ary symbols for input to the RS decoder. The RS decoder performs the processing required to estimate the data source sequence. The RS decoder is able to correct some of the decoding errors of the Viterbi inner decoder, thus improving communication reliability. Figure 7–24 (from [4]) illustrates the bit error probability performance of the concatenated coding system of Figure 7–23 with BPSK modulation. The convolutional code used for Figure 7–24 has $R = \frac{1}{2}$ and $v = 7$. Results are shown for a number of different RS codes with $m = 6, 7, 8,$ and 9. Observe that coding gains at $P_b = 10^{-5}$ of 7.1 dB relative to the uncoded BPSK system are possible.

Concatenated coding systems have been used by NASA on deep space missions [16]. Detailed analysis of concatenated coding systems can be found in [4, 7, 16, 17].

7.5.4 Punctured Convolutional Codes

Punctured convolutional codes, first proposed in 1979 [18], are derived from convolutional codes by puncturing or omitting encoded symbols periodically from a rate $1/n$ mother code. The decoding process uses normal Viterbi algorithm decoding for the mother code with erasure symbols (any symbol that can be recognized by the decoder as being an insertion) inserted in place of the punctured symbols. Punctured codes are used

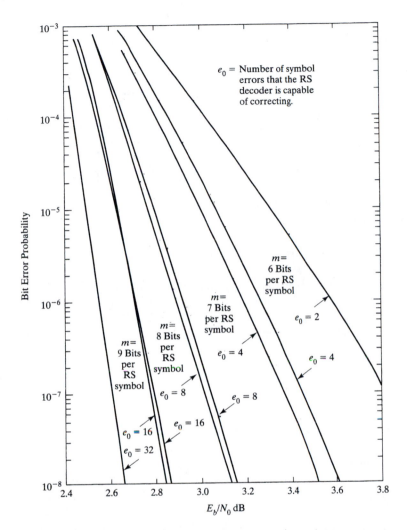

FIGURE 7–24 Summary of concatenated coding bit error probability performance with a $k = 7$, $R = \frac{1}{2}$ convolutional inner code and various RS outer codes. (Reproduced from Reference [4] with permission.)

in applications requiring a trade-off between rate and error protection and for providing variable transmission rate. The former is useful in applications such as compressed voice or video transmission where it is useful to error-protect some bits more than others. The latter is important in any application where sources with different rates are multiplexed through the same physical channel.

A family of *rate-compatible* punctured codes is derived all from the same mother code with the puncturing patterns forming a nested set; for example, if 0s represent a punctured symbol and 1s do not, the puncturing patterns 1101 1111, 1001 1111, 1001 1110 form such a nested set in that the second puncturing pattern is obtained from the first by puncturing one more symbol from the resultant first code, and the third is obtained from the second by omitting one more symbol from the resultant second code. The rates of the three codes thus generated are $4/7$, $4/6$, and $4/5$, respectively, where the denominator is the number of ones in the puncturing pattern and the numerator is the number of information bits. Rate-compatible punctured code sets allow error protection and rate to be changed at any time during transmission as long as the receiver is informed of the change in puncturing pattern. Since all codes in a rate-compatible family are derived from the same mother code, the same Viterbi algorithm structure can be used to decode any member in the family without any reconfiguration, except for the pattern of insertion of erasure symbols [19].

Lee [20] has computed the weight distribution for several "good" rate-compatible convolutional codes by taking the best known rate-$1/n$ ($3 \le n \le 13$) convolutional codes and determining rate-compatible puncturing patterns by exhaustive search for each of these mother codes by maximizing the free distances. Kim [21] has examined systematic punctured convolutional codes and shown that in almost every case these codes performed better than the best known nonsystematic codes with the same rates.

Figures 7–25 and 7–26 show bit error probability bounds computed from the weight structures given by Lee for two of the code families he found. For more explanation and the weight structures of other code families, the reader is referred to the papers by Lee and Kim.

7.5.5 Trellis-Coded Modulation

Trellis-coded modulation (TCM) is a combined coding and modulation scheme invented by Ungerboeck [22–24] in the late 1970s. It provides simultaneously both power and bandwidth efficiency by maximizing the Euclidian distance between coded/modulated signals in an efficient manner using a technique called set partitioning. Viterbi and colleagues [25] later proposed a simplified scheme using a single rate ½ convolutional code converted to the required rate-$(n-1)/n$ code by puncturing. Primarily because of its ease of implementation, its ability to provide simultaneous power and bandwidth efficiency, and its ability to provide variable error protection by changing the configuration of the code/signal structure, TCM finds extensive applications in many areas involving space, terrestrial, and guided-wave communication channels. The literature on TCM is extensive and any sampling of it would be an injustice. The reader is referred to the latest issues of the various archival communications journals. At least one book devoted entirely to TCM is available [26].

To give a simplified explanation of TCM, we consider a special case where equal-rate uncoded and TCM-coded systems are compared. The uncoded system is QPSK, which carries two bits per signaling interval. For the encoded system, we consider a rate ⅔ convolutional code used in conjunction with 8-PSK modulation, which overall also carries two bits per signaling interval.

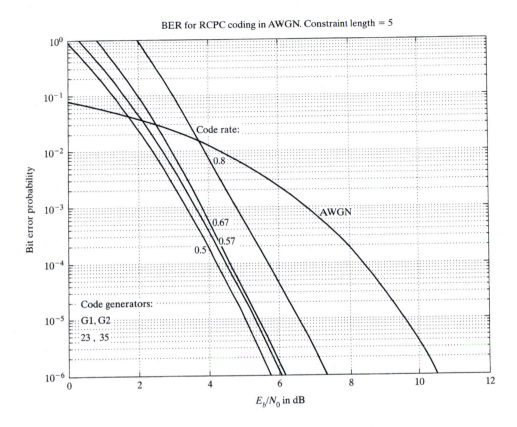

FIGURE 7–25   Bit error probability bounds for rate-compatible convolutional code family of constraint length 5.

Figure 7–27a illustrates the particular rate ⅔ convolutional encoder to be considered in this example, and Figure 7–27b shows the corresponding trellis diagram. Note that there are parallel transitions from the states at time t_i to the states at time t_{i+1} due to the uncoded bit, $d_1 = c_1$ (recall that the state of the encoder is the contents of the encoder shift register). The two parallel transitions correspond to c_1 being a 0 or a 1. That the trellis diagram corresponds to the encoder block diagram can be seen by considering any particular state of the encoder—10, say. Suppose a 1 is input. The next state is 11, and the output is then $c_2 = 1{+}1{+}0 = 0$ and $c_3 = 1{+}0 = 1$ with c_1 determined by d_1, where all arithmetic is modulo-2. If a 0 is input, then the next state is 01 and the output is $c_2 = 0{+}1{+}0 = 1$ and $c_3 = 0{+}0 = 0$ with c_1 again determined by d_1. Similarly, the other transitions and branchwords can be demonstrated in Figure 7–27b.

The three code symbols per two input bits select a signal phase using a method called *set partitioning*. The method of set partitioning for this particular example is illus-

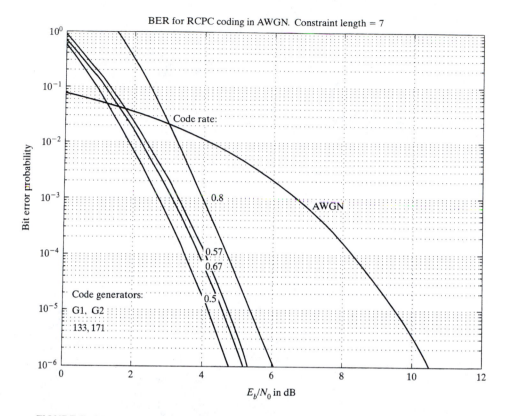

BER for RCPC coding in AWGN. Constraint length = 7

FIGURE 7–26 Bit error probability bounds for rate-compatible convolutional code family of constraint length 5.

trated in Figure 7–28. The assignment process can be viewed in terms of a trellis and proceeds according to the following rules:

1. All parallel transitions in the trellis are assigned the maximum possible Euclidian distance. Since these transitions differ by one code symbol, c_1, an error in decoding them amounts to a single bit error, which is minimized by this procedure.
2. All transitions emanating or converging into a trellis state are assigned the next to largest possible Euclidian distance.
3. All signals are used equally often.

To decode the TCM signal, the received signal plus noise in each signaling interval is correlated with each possible transition in the trellis and a trellis search is made using the Viterbi algorithm to find the path that maximally correlates with the received sequence (i.e., soft decisions are used using correlations, which also corresponds to minimum Euclidian distance).

As seen in Chapter 4, the asymptotic symbol error probability performance for any signaling method may be written in terms of the minimum distance between signal con-

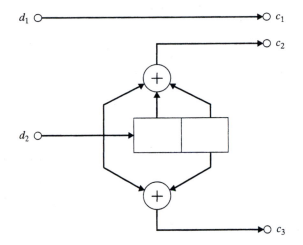

(a) Convolutional encoder

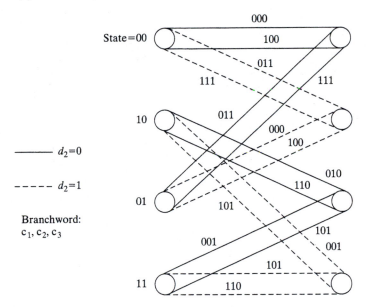

(b) Trellis diagram

FIGURE 7–27 Encoder and trellis diagram for 8-PSK TCM.

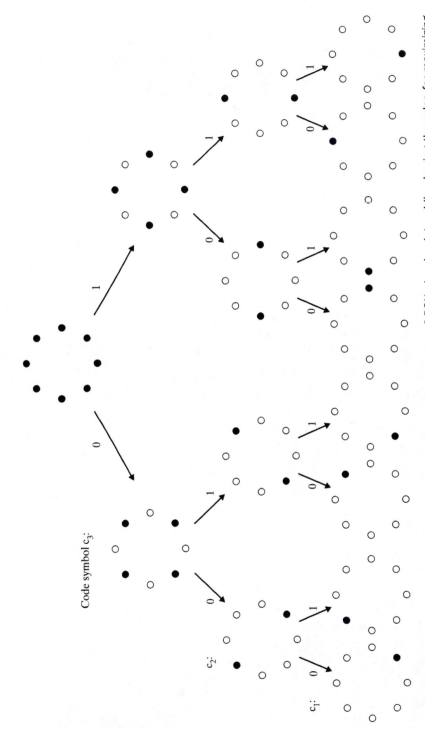

FIGURE 7-28 Set partitioning for assigning a rate ⅔ encoder output to 8-PSK signal points while obeying the rules for maximizing free distance [23].

stellation points. This idea was generalized by Ungerboeck in the case of TCM to the event error probability in terms of the free distance of the signal set. The probability of an error event in TCM is the probability that at any given time the VA makes a wrong decision among the signals associated with parallel transitions, or starts to make a sequence of wrong decisions along some path diverging by more than one transition from the correct path. It is well approximated by [23]

$$P(\text{error event}) = N_{\text{free}} Q\left(\frac{d_{\text{free}}}{\sqrt{2N_0}}\right) \tag{7-17}$$

where N_{free} denotes the number of nearest-neighbor signal sequences with distance d_{free} that diverge at any state from a given transmitted signal sequence (usually taken as the all 0s sequence) and reemerge with it after one or more transitions. The free distance is often calculated by assuming that the signal energy has been normalized to unity and that the noise spectral density accounts for this normalization.

As an example, consider the comparison of QPSK with the 8-PSK TCM example of this section. For uncoded QPSK, $d_{\text{free}} = 2^{1/2}$ and $N_{\text{free}} = 2$, because there are two adjacent signal points at distance $d_{\text{free}} = 2^{1/2}$. On the other hand, for the 4-state-coded 8-PSK example discussed here $d_{\text{free}} = 2$ and $N_{\text{free}} = 1$. Ignoring the differing factor of N_{free} in the two cases, the exponential dependence of the Q-function in (7–17) provides an asymptotic coding gain of 4-state-coded 8-PSK TCM over QPSK of $(2^2)/(2^{1/2})^2 = 2 = 3$ dB. The asymptotic results for 4-state-coded 8-PSK TCM and QPSK are compared in Figure 7–29. Simulation results given for 4-state-coded 8-PSK TCM in [23] compare favorably with the asymptotic curve at high E_s/N_0.

The assignment procedure may be generalized as follows: (1) of the m bits to be transmitted per encoder/ modulator operation, $k \leq m$ bits are expanded to $k + 1$ coded symbols via a binary rate $k/(k + 1)$ convolutional encoder; (2) the $k + 1$ coded symbols select one of 2^{k+1} subsets of a redundant 2^{m+1}-ary signal set; (3) the remaining $m - k$ coded symbols determine one of $2^{m - k}$ signals within the selected subset. Note that a variety of M-ary modulation schemes may be used, including PSK and QAM.

A final parameter that influences system performance is the number of states in the encoder. Ungerboeck published asymptotic coding gains for TCM systems employing various numbers of states. A sample of these is given in Table 7–3.

EXAMPLE 7–5 _____

Show that the second entry in Table 7–3 is correct.

Solution: This is an 8-state trellis with 8-PSK modulation assumed. The trellis showing the minimum free distance path is shown in Figure 7–30. The normalized free distance calculation (a plot of the 8-PSK phases is useful here) is

$$d_{\text{free, 8-state}} = d^2(0, 6\pi/4) + d^2(0, 7\pi/4) + d^2(0, 6\pi/4)$$

$$= (\sqrt{2})^2 + [2\sin(\pi/8)]^2 + (\sqrt{2})^2 = 4.586$$

The ratio of this to d_{free} for QPSK gives $4.586/2 = 2.293 = 3.6$ dB.

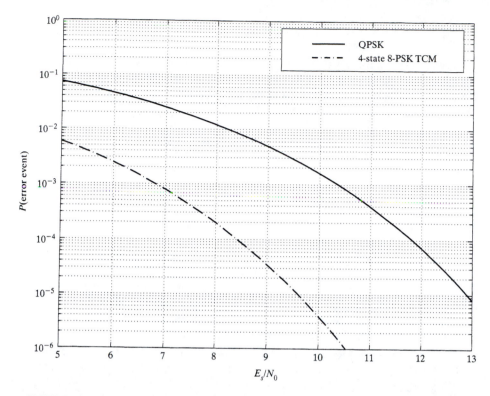

FIGURE 7–29   Comparison of asymptotic performances of QPSK and 4-state 8-PSK TCM.

As stated in the introduction, research on TCM is intense. We close with mention of some papers that deal with TCM design and analysis for fading channels [27, 28]. Recent books have appeared on the subject [29, 30], and research is being carried out on applying trellis coding to block codes [30].

7.5.6 Turbo Codes

Turbo codes came to the attention of communication theorists with the publication of a paper in 1993 at the International Communications Conference [31]. The resulting performance curves were so astounding as to be almost unbelievable in that turbo codes approach the Shannon limit closer than any other known coding technique. Later investigations by other researchers [32–38] showed that the presented results in the 1993 paper were essentially correct as presented, although one important characteristic of turbo codes was not illustrated by them. This detail was that turbo codes show a very fast fall off of bit error probability for low values of E_b/N_0, but eventually approach an error floor dependent on the encoder implementation. This will be discussed more shortly.

TABLE 7–3 Asymptotic Coding Gains for TCM Systems [24]

No. of states, 2^v	k	Asymptotic coding gain, dB	
		$G_{8PSK/OPSK}$	$G_{16PSK/8PSK}$
4	1	3.01	—
8	2	3.60	—
16	2	4.13	—
32	2	4.59	—
64	2	5.01	—
128	2	5.17	—
256	2	5.75	—
4	1	—	3.54
8	1	—	4.01
16	1	—	4.44
32	1	—	5.13
64	1	—	5.33
128	1	—	5.33
256	2	—	5.51

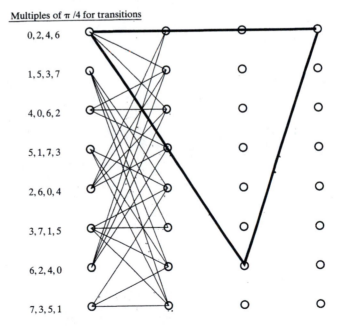

Multiples of $\pi/4$ for transitions

0, 2, 4, 6
1, 5, 3, 7
4, 0, 6, 2
5, 1, 7, 3
2, 6, 0, 4
3, 7, 1, 5
6, 2, 4, 0
7, 3, 5, 1

FIGURE 7–30 Trellis for Example 7–5 showing minimum free distance path.

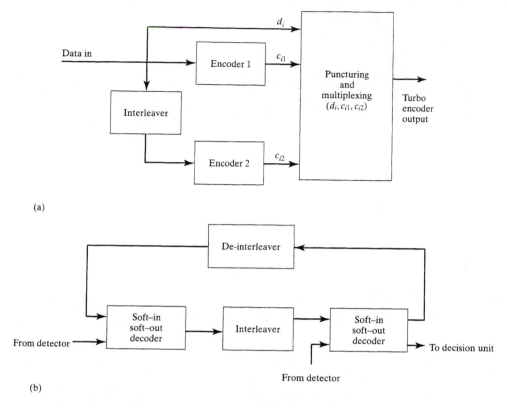

FIGURE 7–31   Block diagrams of (a) turbo encoder and (b) decoder.

Block diagrams of a typical turbo encoder and decoder are shown in Figure 7–31. As originally publicized, the turbo coding concept involved the parallel concatenation of two codes, which are typically the same code, with an interleaver between the code generators.[1] Both convolutional and block codes may be used, with [38] addressing the iterative decoding of both. Note that both encoders work with the same set of input bits, but in different sequences due to the interleaver. The type and length of interleaver influences performances with the ideal interleaver being a competely random permutation of bits. If the component codes are convolutional, it has been shown that recursive systematic convolutional codes outperform nonrecursive codes of the same complexity [34]. Typically, the overall rate is ⅓ (the systematic bit, and the outputs of the two encoders), although higher rates are possible with puncturing.

Decoding consists of the parallel concatenation of two decoders separated by an interleaver, with soft output from the second decoder fed back to improve decisions on future passes through the decoder. The decoders are soft-input soft-output Viterbi

[1]Recently, serial concatenation with interleaving has been shown to benefit from the turbo decoding mechanism [33].

algorithms for the case where the constituent codes are convolutional. The most popular algorithm for doing this is a symbol-by-symbol maximum *a posteriori* (MAP) decoder. Error probability performance improves with increasing decoding iterations and the iterative turbo decoding process seems to always converge.

The error floor effect mentioned earlier is determined by the interleaver and the free distance of the component codes. The error floor may be decreased for fixed free distance of the component codes by lengthening the interleaver length or, for fixed interleaver length, by increasing the free distance [35]. Weight spectra are provided in [34] for computing approximations to the error probability characteristics of turbo codes averaged over all possible uniform interleaver orderings for interleaver lengths of 100, 1,000, and 10,000 (as for convolutional codes, an approximation is obtained because the union bound sum is truncated to a finite number of terms). These results are shown in Figure 7–32, where a factor of ten increase in interleaver length is seen to give roughly a factor of ten lower error floor of the bit error probability. As $E_b/N_0 \to \infty$, the three curves even-

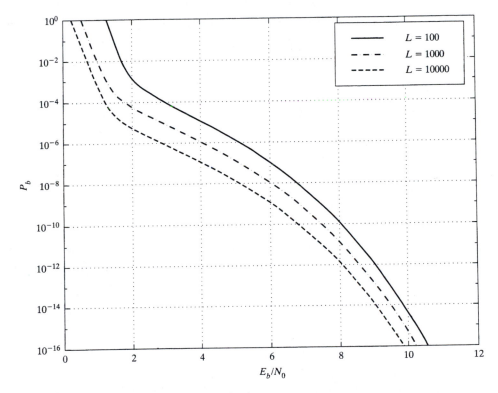

FIGURE 7–32   Average bit error probability bounds for turbo codes of interleaver lengths 100, 1,000, and 10,000 versus E_b/N_0 (averaged over all possible interleaver orderings). Constituent codes are 4-state systematic recursive convolutional codes of free distance 5; code generator is (5, 7).

tually converge. Simulation results are also given in [34]. These show the approach to the bend in the curve between low and high E_b/N_0 regimes, as the number of iterations increases, that the limiting curve is approached closer.

Turbo codes give exceedingly good performance at moderate values of bit error probability for low values of E_b/N_0. This performance depends on the number of iterations used in the decoder, which may introduce undesirable delay in some applications. The error floor may be a problem in applications where exceedingly low values of bit error probability are required, such as transfer of large data files without ARQ. It is felt by several researchers that purely random interleaving is the best, if this were possible. Turbo codes, however, appear to offer better performance than alternative coding techniques, such as convolutional codes, for interleaver lengths above a few hundred. Turbo codes are designed in [36] for low delay applications such as voice transmission, with interleaver lengths of about 200 being used. In [36] four different soft-decision decoding implementations are characterized by simulation. Simulation results show that bit error probabilities of 10^{-3} are achievable with E_b/N_0 values of about 3 to 3.5 dB for AWGN and about 4.5 dB for slow Rayleigh fading.

The area of turbo coding is currently receiving much attention for various applications. The state of the field has progressed to where books are beginning to appear on it [40].

7.5.7   Applications

Convolutional codes have been used in many modern communications systems. In particular, the National Aeronautics and Space Administration has used these codes extensively. NASA has selected standard codes for both Viterbi decoded applications and for sequential decoded applications. The codes for Viterbi decoded applications have constraint length 7 and rates ½ and ⅓, while the codes for sequential decoding have constraint length 32 and rate ½. Deep space missions often use the long constraint length code with sequential decoding. In addition, the NASA Advanced Communications Technology Satellite (ACTS) uses a constraint length 5 convolutional code which is Viterbi decoded.

Another application area of convolutional codes is cellular communications, to be discussed in Chapter 10. Trellis coding finds application in modems. Turbo codes are being considered for applications to both space and terrestrial communications. Turbo encoders and decoders have been implemented as very large scale integrated circuits [29, 34].

7.6   SUMMARY

1. Convolutional codes are fundamentally different from block codes. Whereas block codes collect k information bits and map them into blocks of n output symbols, convolutional coding processes semi-infinite sequences of information bits.
2. A convolutional code may be represented by its shift-register encoder (Figure 7–1), its state transition diagram (Figure 7–2), or its trellis diagram (Figure 7–3). In all

cases considered in this chapter, input bits are accepted one at a time and n binary output symbols are generated. The encoder output sequence may be calculated from the shift-register definition or may be found by following the path defined by the information sequence through the state diagram or trellis. Encoder output symbols are the branch labels on the transition diagram or trellis.

3. A convolutional code is defined by its generator polynomials $\mathbf{g}_i(D)$. The generator polynomials define the shift-register encoder or, equivalently, the state transition diagram or trellis diagram. The encoder output may be found by polynomial multiplication of the input polynomial $\mathbf{w}(D)$ by the code generator polynomials.

4. The constraint length of a convolutional code equals the number of input symbols that affect a particular output symbol. The constraint length equals 1 plus the degree of the highest-degree generator polynomial or 1 plus the number of stages of the shift-register encoder.

5. The state of the shift-register encoder is defined as the contents of the shift register. The states correspond to the states of state transition diagram and trellis diagram.

6. There is a one-to-one relationship between convolutional encoder input sequences, encoder output sequences, and paths through the trellis diagram or state diagram.

7. The maximum-likelihood convolutional decoder uses the code definition, the received symbol sequence, and the channel characterization to estimate the transmitted symbol sequence or, equivalently, to estimate the path followed through the trellis by the encoder. The decoder output estimate is the sequence for which

$$\ln[\Pr(\mathbf{y} \mid \mathbf{x_m})] = \sum_{n'=1}^{\infty} \ln[\Pr(y_{n'} \mid x_{mn'})] \qquad (7\text{--}2)$$

is largest. The decoder output information sequence is the sequence that generates the estimated encoder output sequence.

8. For the hard-decision BSC the maximum-likelihood decoder estimates the transmitted sequence to be the sequence that is closest in Hamming distance to the received sequence.

9. A soft-decision discrete memoryless channel is a channel with more output symbols than input symbols. The additional output symbols provide demodulation reliability information to the decoder, which can be used to improve communications efficiency.

10. A soft-decision DMC is characterized by a transition diagram illustrating the probability of receiving any channel output symbol given a particular channel input symbol. For the AWGN channel, the transition probabilities are calculated by integrating the demodulator output Gaussian probability density function between appropriate limits. In the limit, a soft-decision channel may have a continuous output.

11. The capacity in bits per channel use C_N for a soft decision discrete memoryless channel defined by its transition probabilities $\Pr[y \mid x]$ as

$$C_N = \sum_{j=0}^{J-1} \Pr[j \mid 0] \log_2 \frac{2\,\Pr[j \mid 0]}{\Pr[j \mid 0] + \Pr[j \mid 1]} \qquad (7\text{--}3)$$

The computational cutoff rate for a soft-decision channel is

$$R_0 = -\log_2 \frac{1}{2} \left[1 + \sum_{j=0}^{J-1} \sqrt{\Pr[j \mid 0] \cdot \Pr[j \mid 1]} \right] \tag{7-3}$$

12. The capacity in bits per channel use C_N for the continuous output discrete memoryless channel channel is

$$C_N = \frac{1}{2} \log_2 \left(1 + 2R \frac{E_b}{N_0} \right) \tag{7-4}$$

The computational cutoff rate R_0 for the continuous output discrete input memoryless channel is

$$R_0 = 1 - \log_2 \left[1 + \exp\left(-R \frac{E_b}{N_0} \right) \right] \tag{7-5}$$

13. The free distance of a convolutional code is denoted d_f and is the minimum Hamming distance between any two distinct paths through the code trellis. The free distance of a convolutional code is similar to the minimum distance d_{min} of a block code.

14. The generator function $T(D, L, N)$ of a convolutional code describes the Hamming weight (power of D), length (power of L), and number of information 1s (power of N) for all trellis paths that diverge from and remerge to the zero trellis state. The generator function can be found by solving a set of state equations for the modified state transition diagram.

15. The Viterbi algorithm provides a convenient means of maximum-likelihood decoding for convolutional codes. It may be used with either hard- or soft-decision demodulators. The algorithm avoids the complexity of comparing the metrics of all possible paths through the trellis by eliminating partial paths from further consideration at the first opportunity.

16. The probability that the Viterbi algorithm chooses the wrong path (i.e., eliminating the correct path) at any depth into the trellis is bounded by

$$P_E < \sum_{k=d_{free}}^{\infty} a_k P_k \tag{7-10}$$

where the a_k are calculated using the generating function

$$T(D, 1, 1) = \sum_{k=d_{free}}^{\infty} a_k D^k \tag{7-11}$$

and the error event probabilities P_k are

$$P_k = \sum_{e=(k/2)+1}^{k} \binom{k}{e} p^e (1 - p)^{k-e}$$

$$+ \frac{1}{2} \binom{k}{k/2} p^{k/2} (1 - p)^{k/2}, \qquad k \text{ even} \tag{7-12a}$$

and

$$P_k = \sum_{e=(k+1)/2}^{k} \binom{k}{e} p^e (1-p)^{k-e}, \qquad k \text{ odd} \tag{7-12b}$$

for hard-decision channels and

$$P_k = \int_{\sqrt{2kRE_b/N_0}}^{\infty} \frac{1}{\sqrt{2\pi}} \exp\left(\frac{-x^2}{2}\right) dx$$

$$= Q\left(\sqrt{\frac{2kRE_b}{N_0}}\right) \tag{7-13}$$

for the continuous output soft-decision channel.

17. The bit error probability for Viterbi decoding of convolutional codes is overbounded by

$$P_b < \sum_{k=d_{free}}^{\infty} c_k P_k \tag{7-16}$$

where P_k is calculated as in point 16 and c_k is calculated from

$$\frac{dT(D, 1, N)}{dN}\bigg|_{N=1} = \sum_{k=d_{free}}^{\infty} c_k D^k \tag{7-15}$$

18. Many good convolutional codes are known. Most have been found by computer search. A few of the best rate ½ and rate ⅓ convolutional codes are given in Tables 7–1 and 7–2. The coding gains for good convolutional codes can be as high as approximately 6 dB using soft-decision decoding.

19. Convolutional codes can also be decoded using sequential decoding. The complexity of sequential decoding is independent of constraint length so that codes with high constraint length can be decoded.

20. Concatenated convolutional and Reed–Solomon block decoding can be used where large coding gain is required. Concatenated coding systems have been used in deep space missions.

21. Puncturing of convolutional codes is a convenient technique to achieve rates between $1/n$ and 1. Rate-compatible convolutional codes derive the entire rate family from a single mother code with puncturing patterns that form a nested set. This allows the rate to be changed at will during a transmission since the same Viterbi algorithm trellis is used for decoding; the decoder only has to be informed of the new puncturing pattern when a change is made.

22. Trellis-coded modulation, invented by Ungerboeck, combines the coding and modulation operation so as to approximately maximize Euclidean distance between coded/modulated sequences. In addition to continuous-phase modulation, it provides a means to obtain simultaneous improved bandwidth and power efficiency.

23. Turbo codes achieve the closest approach to Shannon's bound of any known coding technique. They commonly use parallel concatenation of two constituent codes (serial concatenation also is used), which are most often systematic recursive convolutional codes, with random interleaving between the two constituent encoders. The decoding process is iterative and employs two soft-decision decoders with feedback of information from the second decoder to the first between iterations. Performance is highly dependent on the interleaver length, the free distance of the constituent codes, and the number of iterations used in the decoding process. Usually, iterations above ten provide little additional improvement, and interleaver lengths above a few hundred are required to give performance significantly above a convolutional code of the same complexity as the constituent codes.

REFERENCES

[1] S. Lin, and D. J. Costello, Jr., *Error Control Coding: Fundamentals and Applications* (Englewood Cliffs, NJ: Prentice-Hall, 1983).

[2] A. J. Viterbi, "Error Bounds for Convolutional Codes and an Asymptotically Optimum Decoding Algorithm," *IEEE Transactions on Information Theory*, Vol. IT-13, pp. 260–269, April 1967.

[3] A. J. Viterbi, "Convolutional Codes and Their Performance in Communication Systems," *IEEE Trans. on Commun. Tech.*, Vol. COM-19, pp. 751–772, October 1971.

[4] J. P. Odenwalder, "Error Control," in *Data Communications, Networks, and Systems*, Thomas Bartee (ed.) (Indianapolis: Howard W. Sams, 1985).

[5] G. D. Forney, "The Viterbi Algorithm," *Proceedings of the IEEE*, Vol. 61, pp. 268–278, March 1973.

[6] G. D. Forney, "Convolutional Codes II: Maximum Likelihood Decoding," *Information and Control*, Vol. 25, pp. 222–226, July 1974.

[7] G. C. Clark and J. B. Cain, *Error-Correction Coding for Digital Communications* (New York: Plenum, 1981).

[8] J. M. Wozencraft and I. M. Jacobs, *Principles of Communication Engineering* (New York: John Wiley, 1965).

[9] A. J. Viterbi and J. K. Omura, *Principles of Digital Communication and Coding* (New York: McGraw-Hill, 1979).

[10] J. A. Heller, and I. M. Jacobs, "Viterbi Decoding for Satellite and Space Communications," *IEEE Trans. on Commun. Tech.*, October 1971.

[11] J. P. Odenwalder, "Optimal Decoding of Convolutional Codes," Ph.D. dissertation, University of California, Los Angeles, 1970.

[12] K. J. Larsen, "Short Convolutional Codes with Maximum Free Distance for Rates ½, ⅓, and ¼," *IEEE Trans. on Infor. Theory*, Vol. IT-19, pp. 371–372, May 1973.

[13] J. L. Massey, *Threshold Decoding* (Cambridge, MA: MIT Press, 1963).

[14] J. B. Cain, and J. M. Geist, "Modulation, Coding, and Interleaving Tradeoffs for Spread Spectrum Systems," *Conference Record*, IEEE National Telecommunications Conference, pp. 37.2.1–37.2.6, 1981.

[15] G. D. Forney, "Burst-Correcting Codes for the Classic Bursty Channel," *IEEE Transactions on Commun. Tech.*, Vol. COM-19, pp. 772–781, October 1971.

[16] J. H. Yuen, (ed.), *Deep Space Telecommunications Systems Engineering* (New York: Plenum, 1983).

[17] G. D. Forney, *Concatenated Codes* (Cambridge, MA: MIT Press, 1967).

[18] J. B. Cain, G. C. Clark, and J. M. Geist, "Punctured convolutional codes of rate $(n-1)/n$ and simplified maximum likelihood decoding," *IEEE Trans. Inform. Theory,* Vol. IT-25, pp. 97–100, Jan. 1979.

[19] J. Hagenauer, "Rate-compatible punctured convolutional codes (RCPC codes) and their applications," *IEEE Trans. Commun.,* Vol. 36, pp. 389–400, April 1988.

[20] L. H. C. Lee, "New rate-compatible punctured convolutional codes for Viterbi decoding," *IEEE Trans. Commun.,* Vol. 42, pp. 3073–3079, Dec. 1994.

[21] M.-G. Kim, "On systematic punctured convolutional codes," *IEEE Trans. Commun.,* Vol. 45, pp. 133–139, Feb. 1997.

[22] G. Ungerboeck, "Channel coding with multilevel/phase signals," *IEEE Trans. Inform. Theory,* Vol. IT-28, pp. 55–66, Jan. 1982.

[23] G. Ungerboeck, "Trellis-coded modulation with redundant signal sets, Part I: Introduction," *IEEE Commun. Magazine,* Vol. 25, pp. 5–11, Feb. 1987.

[24] G. Ungerboeck, "Trellis-coded modulation with redundant signal sets, Part II: State of the art," *IEEE Commun. Magazine,* Vol. 25, pp. 12–21, Feb. 1987.

[25] A. J. Viterbi, J. K. Wolf, E. Zehavi, and R. Padovani, "A pragmatic approach to trellis-coded modulation," *IEEE Commun. Magazine,* Vol. 27, pp. 11–19, Jul. 1989.

[26] E. Biglieri, D. Divsalar, P. J. McLane, and M. K. Simon, *Introduction to Trellis-Coded Modulation* (New York: Macmillan, 1991.)

[27] D. Divsalar and M. K. Simon, "The Design of Trellis Coded MPSK for Fading Channels: Performance Criteria," *IEEE Trans. Commun.,* Vol. 36, pp. 1004–1011, Sept. 1988.

[28] R. G. McKay, P. J. McLane, and E. Biglieri, "Error bounds for trellis-coded MPSK on a fading mobile satellite channel," *IEEE Trans. Commun.,* Vol. 39, pp. 1750–1761, Dec. 1991.

[29] C. Schlegel, *Trellis Coding* (Piscataway, NJ: IEEE Press, 1997).

[30] S. Lin, T. Kasami, T. Fujiwara, and M. Fossorier, *Trellis and Trellis-Based Decoding Algorithms for Linear Block Codes* (Norwell, MA: Kluwer, 1998).

[31] C. Berrou, A. Glavieux, and P. Thitimajshima, "Near Shannon Limit Error-Correcting Coding and Decoding: Turbo Codes," *IEEE Inter. Commun. Conf. Record,* pp. 1064–1070, June 1993.

[32] J. Hagenauer, "The Turbo Principle: Tutorial Introduction and State of the Art," *Proc. of the Inter. Symp. on Turbo Codes & Related Topics,* pp. 111, Sept. 1997.

[33] S. Benedetto and G. Montorsi, "Serial Concatenation of Block and Convolutional Codes," *Electronic Letters,* 1996.

[34] S. Benedetto and G. Montorsi, "Unveiling Turbo Codes: Some Results on Parallel Concatenated Coding Schemes," *IEEE Trans. Inform. Theory,* Vol. IT-42, pp. 409–428, Mar. 1996.

[35] L. C. Perez, J. Seghers, and D. J. Costello, Jr., "A Distance Spectrum Interpretation of Turbo Codes," *IEEE Trans. Inform. Theory,* Vol. IT-42, pp. 1698–1709, Nov. 1996.

[36] P. Jung, "Comparison of Turbo Code Decoders Applied to Short Frame Transmission Systems," *IEEE Jour. Sel. Areas Commun.,* Vol. 14, pp. 530–537, Apr. 1996.

[37] E. K. Hall and S. G. Wilson, "Design and Performance Analysis of Turbo Codes on Rayleigh Fading Channels," *CISS Proceedings,* Mar. 1996.

[38] J. Hagenauer, E. Offer, and L. Papke, "Iterative Decoding of Binary Block and Convolutional Codes," *IEEE Trans. Inform. Theory,* Vol. IT-42, pp. 429–445, Mar. 1996.

[39] L. R. Bahl, J. Cocke, F. Jelinek, and J. Raviv, "Optimal Decoding of Linear Codes for Minimizing Symbol Error Rate, *IEEE Trans. Inform. Theory,* Vol. IT-20, pp. 284–287, Mar. 1974.

[40] C. Heegard and S. B. Wicker, *Turbo Coding* (Norwell, MA: Kluwer, 1999).

PROBLEMS

7-1. The first thirteen symbols of the input to a convolutional encoder are defined by the polynomial $w(D) = 1 + D^2 + D^3 + D^5 + D^7 + D^{11} + D^{12}$. The encoder is defined by Figure 7–1.
  (a) Find the encoder output from Figure 7–1.
  (b) Find the encoder output using the state transition diagram for the encoder.
  (c) Find the encoder output using the trellis diagram.
  (d) Find the encoder output directly from the code generator polynomials.
  (e) What is the Hamming distance between the encoder output sequence corresponding to $w(D) = 0 + 0 \cdot D + 0 \cdot D^2 + \cdots$ and the output sequence corresponding to $w(D) = 1 + 0 \cdot D + 0 \cdot D^2 + \cdots$?

7-2. The first thirteen symbols of the input to a convolutional encoder are defined by the polynomial $w(D) = 1 + D^2 + D^3 + D^5 + D^7 + D^{11} + D^{12}$. The encoder is defined by Figure 7–4.
  (a) Find the encoder output from Figure 7–4.
  (b) Find the encoder output using the state transition diagram for the encoder.
  (c) Find the encoder output using the trellis diagram.
  (d) Find the encoder output directly from the code generator polynomials.
  (e) What is the Hamming distance between the encoder output sequence corresponding to $w(D) = 0 + 0 \cdot D + 0 \cdot D^2 + \cdots$ and the output sequence corresponding to $w(D) = 1 + 0 \cdot D + 0 \cdot D^2 + \cdots$?

7-3. A convolutional code is defined by the generator polynomials

$$g_1(D) = 1 + D + D^2 + D^3 + D^4$$

$$g_2(D) = 1 + D + D^3 + D^4$$

$$g_3(D) = 1 + D^2 + D^4$$

  (a) What is the constraint length of this code?
  (b) Illustrate the shift-register encoder for this code.
  (c) How many states are in the trellis diagram for this code?
  (d) What is the encoder output sequence corresponding to the input sequence $w(D) = 1 + D + D^2 + D^5 + D^7 + D^{11}$?

7-4. Decode the received sequence $y(D) = D^3 + D^4 + D^7$ using the decoding trellis of Figure 7–7. What is the decoder output information sequence? Assume the BSC error probability $p = 0.2$.

7-5. The decoding trellis of Figure 7–7 is used with a BSC, which has an error probability $p = 0.65 > 0.50$. Decode the received sequence $y(D) = D^3 + D^4 + D^7$ using the minimum distance decoding rule as well as using the metric of Equation (7–2). Explain your results.

7-6. A binary input DMC is characterized by the transition probabilities $\Pr[0 \mid 0] = 0.8$, $\Pr[1 \mid 0] = 0.15$, $\Pr[2 \mid 0] = 0.05$, $\Pr[2 \mid 1] = 0.8$, $\Pr[1 \mid 1] = 0.15$, $\Pr[0 \mid 1] = 0.05$. Calculate C_N and R_0 for this channel.

7-7. A communicator wishes to transmit binary information with a bit error rate of better than 1 error in 10^5 transmitted bits. BPSK modulation will be used.
  (a) What E_b/N_0 is required to achieve this P_b without coding?
  (b) What is the minimum possible E_b/N_0 that could be used to achieve the desired P_b using soft decision coding with a code rate > 0.10?

(c) What is the minimum possible E_b/N_0 which could be used for the same code rate but assuring the communicator of reasonable complexity?

7–8. Calculate and plot R_0 as a function of $E_b R/N_0$ for binary input channels using BPSK modulation with

(a) hard decision output and

(b) continuous output. Why do both channels provide similar R_0 at high $E_b R/N_0$? How could R_0 be increased at high $E_b R/N_0$?

7–9. What is the free distance of the convolutional code defined in Figure 7–4?

7–10. (a) Draw the complete modified state transition diagram for the convolutional code of Figure 7–4.

(b) Write the state equations for this code.

(c) Solve the state equations to find $T(D, L, N)$.

(d) Find the free distance of the code from the generating function.

7–11. A rate ⅓ convolutional code is defined by the generator polynomials

$$g_1(D) = 1 + D$$

$$g_2(D) = 1 + D + D^2$$

$$g_3(D) = 1 + \qquad D^2$$

(a) Draw the shift-register convolutional encoder.

(b) Draw the state transition diagram.

(c) Draw the trellis diagram.

(d) Draw the modified state transition diagram.

(e) Write the state equations and solve them to find the generator function.

(f) What is the free distance of the code?

7–12. Draw the truncated trellis diagram for the code of Problem 7–11 to a depth of 8. Decode the received sequence $\mathbf{w}(D) = 1 + D + D^2 + D^8 + D^9 + D^{11} + D^{12} + D^{13} + D^{16} + D^{17}$ using the hard decision Viterbi algorithm.

7–13. Using the code of Problem 7–11 and the truncated trellis diagram of Problem 7–12 and the channel of Figure 7–16, decode the received sequence 232101013003230133111300 using soft decision Viterbi decoding.

7–14. Using the code defined by the trellis of Figure 7–15a, decode the received sequence 0111000011011110 using hard decision Viterbi decoding.

7–15. A rate ½ convolutional code is defined by the generator polynomials

$$g_1(D) = 1 + D$$

$$g_2(D) = 1$$

(a) Draw the decoding trellis to depth 8.

(b) Draw the state transition diagram.

(c) Draw the modified state transition diagram.

(d) Generate and solve the state equations and find $T(D, L, N)$.

(e) What is the free distance of this code?

(f) Is the code systematic?

(g) Decode the sequence 1101011000110111.

7–16. Develop a flow chart for implementing the Viterbi algorithm in software.

7–17. For the code of Problem 7–11, calculate and plot the overbound on bit error probability as a function of E_b/N_0 assuming BPSK modulation. Use the first seven terms of the bit error probability summations. Assume hard decision decoding. What is the coding gain at $P_b = 10^{-5}$?

7–18. Reconsider the code of Figure 7–2. Calculate and plot bit error probability as a function of E_b/N_0 assuming BPSK modulation and continuous output soft decision decoding.

7–19. **(a)** Draw the shift register encoder for the constraint length 8 rate ½ convolutional coder of Table 7–1.

      (b) What are the generator polynomials for this code?

      (c) What is the encoder output for the input information sequence $\mathbf{w}(D) = 1 + D^3 + D^7$?

7–20. **(a)** Draw the shift-register encoder for the constraint length 6 rate ⅓ convolutional coder of Table 7–2.

      (b) What are the generator polynomials for this code?

      (c) What is the encoder output for the input information sequence $\mathbf{w}(D) = 1 + D^3 + D^7$?

7–21. Write a MATLAB program to compute the bounds shown in Figures 7–24 and 7–25. Tables giving the weight spectra for the codes are given below.

Weight spectrum for (23,35) constraint length 5 code with $P = 4$ [20]

Puncturing Pattern	Code Rate	d_f	BER weight spectrum; $[c_d, d = d_f, d_f + 1, d_f + 2, \ldots]$
1111 1101	4/7	5	[1, 31, 72, 175, 1003, 2697, 8214, 27032]
1111 0101	4/6	4	[2, 0, 248, 0, 5444, 0, 101710]
1111 0100	4/5	3	[21, 137, 1344, 10854, 77549, 555111]

Weight spectrum for (133, 171) constraint length 7 code with $P = 4$ [20]

Puncturing Pattern	Code Rate	d_f	BER weight spectrum; $C_d, d = d_f, d_f + 1, d_f + 2, \ldots$
1111 1011	4/7	7	[6, 37, 1963, 581, 1771, 5833, 19557]
1111 1010	4/6	6	[6, 140, 570, 2552, 12320]
1111 1000	4/5	4	[12, 188, 1732, 15256, 15256, 121372, 945645]

7–22. Complete a table like the one below showing all possible states and inputs, coder outputs, and transmitted signal phase for the rate-⅔, 8-PSK TCM example given in the text (use Figure 7–28 to fill in the last column).

d_1	Old State	New State	c_2c_3	c_1	Enc. out	Phase
0	00	00	0	00	000	$-\pi/4$
			1		100	$3\pi/4$

7-23. **(a)** The weight spectrum for the curve for the interleaver length of 100 in Figure 7–32 is given below beginning with $m = d_{\text{free}} = 8$ and proceeding in integer steps from there:

$D_m = [0.0389\ 0.0766\ 0.1136\ 0.1508\ 0.1986\ 0.2756\ 0.4079\ 0.6292\ 1.197\ 2.359\ 4.383\ 7.599\ 12.58\ 20.46\ 33.31\ 54.65\ 91.23\ 154.9\ 265.5\ 455.6\ 779\ 1327\ 2257\ 3842\ 6556\ 11221\ 19261\ 33143]$.

The approximation for the bit error probability is

$$P_b \approx \frac{1}{2} \sum_{m=d_{\text{free}}}^{M} D_m \text{erfc}\left(\sqrt{m\frac{R_c E_b}{N_0}}\right)$$

where $R_c = \frac{1}{3}$ is the code rate and M is the maximum index used in the approximation. Plot P_b using this approximation and compare with the $L = 100$ curve in Figure 7–32. Note that your result does not match the curve given in Figure 7–32 at the lower E_b/N_0 values. This is because the authors of reference [32] extended the D_ms by doing a least-squares fit to their logarithm to extend them beyond the 28 given above. Do this using the *polyfit* function of MATLAB, extending the D_m coefficients to about 50 to see if the resulting P_b plot matches the $L = 100$ plot given in Figure 7–32 closer.

(b) Repeat part (a) for the $L = 1000$ case, the weight spectrum of which is given below:

$D_m = [0.00399\ 0.00796\ 0.01192\ 0.01586\ 0.01989\ 0.02419\ 0.02905\ 0.03485\ 0.06577\ 0.1457\ 0.2984\ 0.5472\ 0.9171\ 1.437\ 2.144\ 3.09\ 4.465\ 6.716\ 10.67\ 17.65\ 29.61\ 49.31\ 80.57\ 128.6\ 201.3\ 311.5\ 481.2\ 748.8]$.

(c) Repeat part (a) for the $L = 10,000$ case, the weight spectrum of which is given below:

$D_m = [0.0003999\ 0.0007996\ 0.0011991\ 0.0015985\ 0.0019987\ 0.00281\ 0.002402\ 0.003228\ 0.00606\ 0.0137\ 0.0285\ 0.05299\ 0.08944\ 0.1403\ 0.2082\ 0.2957\ 0.4177\ 0.6133\ 0.9577\ 1.574\ 2.646\ 4.43\ 7.267\ 11.6\ 18.04\ 27.57\ 41.88\ 63.94]$.

8

Fundamentals of Repeat
Request Systems

8.1 INTRODUCTION

In some communications systems a two-way communication link is established, thus providing a means for the receiver to tell the transmitter whether a message has been correctly received. When transmission errors occur, the receiver can ask the transmitter to repeat the message. Each message can be repeated as necessary until it is correctly received. A communication system using this strategy for error control is called an *automatic repeat request* system or *automatic repeat query* (ARQ) system. To use ARQ, the receiver must be able to detect transmission errors. Error detection requires that parity symbols be added to the information sequence. These additional symbols may be as simple as a one-bit parity check or as complex as the parity bits of a cyclic block code. More complex error detection codes permit the receiver to detect larger numbers of errors within a block. ARQ strategies can be very efficient with respect to their use of the communications resources of power and bandwidth. The reason for this is that a specific number of errors can be detected using fewer parity symbols than would be required to correct these same errors using forward error control. ARQ strategies are particularly well suited to communication networks where transmission delay is small and information occurs naturally in blocks.

In this section three common ARQ strategies will be described and analyzed. These three strategies differ with respect to their average rate of information transfer for a fixed binary channel transmission rate and transmission propagation delay. In all cases, the channel will be a binary symmetric channel with error probability p. The three ARQ strategies differ in complexity of implementation but are the same with respect to their probability of message error. The ARQ strategies will be discussed without regard to the specific coding scheme used to detect errors. The error detection code will be characterized by its rate $R = k/n$ and its probability of correctly detecting message transmission errors at the given BSC error probability. Following the description and analysis of the three ARQ strategies, the performance of specific error detection codes will be discussed.

8.2   GENERAL CONSIDERATIONS

All ARQ schemes are similar in that they all partition the information sequence into blocks, they all add parity and control symbols to these blocks prior to transmission, and they all retransmit these blocks as required until the block is estimated to be correctly received. Control symbols are used to identify the sequence number of the message and possibly (depending on the communication protocol) the source and destination address for the message. The error detection code will be designed to detect some number of transmission errors within a block but will not be able to detect all error patterns. When an undetectable error pattern occurs, the receiver believes that the message has been correctly received so retransmission is *not* requested and a message error occurs. The probability of message error, denoted P_B, is one parameter of interest to the system designer. Note that P_B is the probability of error, taking into account all possible retransmissions; transmission errors that are detected do not cause block errors and therefore do not contribute to the block error probability.

Following Lin and Costello [1], observe that three possibilities exist when a single block is transmitted. The first possibility is that no errors occur. If the transmitted block length is n and the BSC error probability is p, the probability that no errors occur is

$$P_c = (1 - p)^n \tag{8-1}$$

The second possibility is that a detectable error pattern occurs. This probability is denoted P_d and is a function of the channel and the specific error detection code used. The third possibility is that an undetectable error pattern occurs. This probability is denoted P_e and is also a function of the channel and the specific error detection code used. These three possibilities are the same for the first transmission and all subsequent retransmissions of a message. A message error occurs when an undetectable error pattern occurs on either the first transmission of a message or one of the repeat transmissions of the message. The probability of a message error on the first transmission is P_e. The probability of a message error on the second transmission is the product of the probability of a detectable error pattern on the first transmission and the probability of an undetectable error pattern on the second transmission, or $P_d P_e$. Similarly, the probability of a message error on the third transmission is $P^2_{d}P_e$, and so on. The total probability of message error P_B is the sum of the probabilities of message error on the first, second, third, . . . retransmissions. Thus

$$P_B = P_e + (P_d \cdot P_e) + (P_d^2 \cdot P_e) + (P_d^3 \cdot P_e) + \cdots$$
$$= \frac{P_e}{1 - P_d} \tag{8-2}$$

Since only three possibilities exist for a particular message transmission, the probabilities of these three possibilities must sum to 1; thus $P_c + P_d + P_e = 1.0$. Substituting this relation into the relation for P_B yields

$$P_B = \frac{P_e}{P_c + P_e} \tag{8-3}$$

which is a function of the error detection capabilities of the code but not a function of the specific ARQ strategy used. To achieve a low P_B, the code must be chosen to have a low undetectable error probability P_e.

EXAMPLE 8–1

A (7, 4) Hamming code is used for error detection in an ARQ communications system. This perfect code has $d_{min} = 3$. Referring to Table 6–4 and taking into account the linearity of the code, it is easily demonstrated that there are fifteen specific error patterns that can cause a transmitted codeword to be received as a different valid codeword. These error patterns correspond precisely to the nonzero codewords. The weight structure of the code [see (6–83)] indicates that there are seven codewords with Hamming weight 3, seven with weight 4, and one with weight 7. The probability of occurrence of one of these error patterns in a specific transmission is the probability of undetectable error and is

$$P_e = 7p^3(1 - p)^4 + 7p^4(1 - p)^3 + p^7$$

The probability of correct transmission is the probability that no error occur in seven transmissions or

$$P_c = (1 - p)^7$$

The probability of detectable error P_d is calculated from $1.0 = P_d + P_e + P_c$ and is

$$P_d = 1.0 - 7p^3(1 - p)^4 - 7p^4(1 - p)^3$$
$$- p^7 - (1 - p)^7$$

Another figure of merit of an ARQ strategy is its *throughput* η. The throughput is defined to be the number of information bits transmitted to the receiver per binary channel symbol time $T_s = 1/R_s$, where R_s is the binary channel symbol rate. Throughput is similar to code rate R for forward error correction strategies with the exception that symbols may not be output from the transmitter at every opportunity; the reason for this will be detailed later. Calculation of throughput takes into account the details of the ARQ system and will be calculated for three different ARQ systems in the next section.

A final figure of merit of an ARQ system is its complexity. Complexity includes the coding and decoding operations for error detection as well as the retransmission logic and the message buffers necessary to implement the retransmission logic.

8.3 THREE ARQ STRATEGIES

8.3.1 Stop-and-Wait ARQ

8.3.1.1 General Description. Stop-and Wait (SW) ARQ is the simplest of the three ARQ strategies. After a message is transmitted, the SWARQ transmitter simply waits for the receiver to acknowledge correct reception before transmitting the next message. The acknowledgment of correct reception is called an ACK and is returned to the transmitter if no errors occur or if an undetectable error pattern occurs. In this case the message is delivered to the information user and the next message is transmitted. If a detectable error pattern occurs during transmission, a negative acknowledgment (NAK) is returned to the transmitter and the message is retransmitted. The incorrectly received message is discarded by the receiver. During the retransmission of a message, subsequent messages from the information source are collected in a buffer in the transmitter for later transmission.

8.3.1.2 Throughput Calculation.

The length of a message block, the number of control bits added to the message, and the number of parity symbols added for error detection are all selected by the system designer to achieve the best possible communications efficiency or throughput η_{sw}. Denote the sum of the number of source output information bits and the number of control bits in a block by k. For the calculation of η_{sw}, both the source information and control bits will be considered the "message." Parity symbols are added to the k message bits to create a block of length n, which is transmitted over the channel. The error detection code rate is $R = k/n$. The minimum delay between the beginning of one message transmission and the beginning of the next message transmission is

$$T_D = T_m + 2T_d + T_c + T_a \qquad (8\text{–}4)$$

where

$\qquad T_m$ = time to transmit n channel symbols

$\qquad\quad = n/R_s$

$\qquad T_d$ = transmission delay

$\qquad T_c$ = time required for the receiver to decode the block

$\qquad T_a$ = the time required to transmit the ACK message.

For convenience, define

$$T_{dca} = 2T_d + T_c + T_a \qquad (8\text{–}5)$$

and constrain T_{dca} such that it is equal to an integer number of channel symbol times, that is $T_{dca} = n'/R_s$. Figure 8–1 illustrates both the transmitter and receiver timing relationships for a single message transmission and acknowledgment. Observe that there is a lengthy transmitter off time which occurs between the end of the transmitted message and the receipt of the acknowledgment of that same message. This off time can be long or short depending mostly on the transmission delay. Figure 8–2a illustrates a typical SWARQ message transmission sequence in which the first and second messages are transmitted without error and a detectable error pattern occurs on the transmission of the third message. The third message is therefore retransmitted and the retransmission's ACK received before the fourth message is transmitted.

   In the absence of channel errors all messages would be received correctly and the best possible throughput would be achieved for this ARQ strategy. Without errors, k information bits would be communicated each T_D seconds (or $T_D \cdot R_s$ channel symbol times) and the best possible throughput is

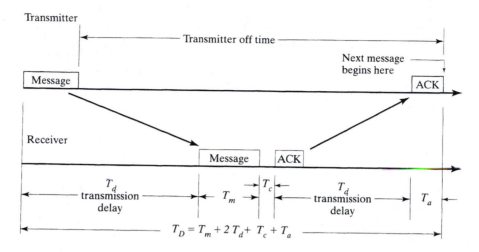

FIGURE 8–1 Stop-and-wait ARQ transmitter and receiver timing.

$$\eta_{\text{SW},0} = \frac{k}{T_D R_s}$$

$$= \frac{k}{n + n'} \tag{8–6}$$

Observe that if T_d, T_c, and T_a were all 0, the throughput would equal the code rate $R = k/n$. Observe also that the throughput decreases as the transmission delay increases since n' increases with increasing T_d.

When channel errors occur, some messages will have to be retransmitted and throughput will be reduced. Again following Lin and Costello [1], the probability that a given transmission will have to be repeated is P_d. The average number of transmissions required before a message is accepted by the receiver is

$$N_R = (1 - P_d) + 2P_d(1 - P_d) + 3P_d^2(1 - P_d) + \cdots$$

$$= (1 - P_d)(1 + 2P_d + 3P_d^2 + 4P_d^3 + \cdots) \tag{8–7}$$

$$= \frac{1}{1 - P_d}$$

Since each transmission requires T_D seconds, the average time required to transmit a message of k bits is $T_D \cdot N_R$ seconds or $T_D \cdot N_R \cdot R_s$ symbol times and the throughput is

$$\eta_{\text{SW}} = \frac{k}{T_D \cdot N_R \cdot R_s}$$

$$= \frac{k}{T_D \cdot R_s}(1 - P_d)$$

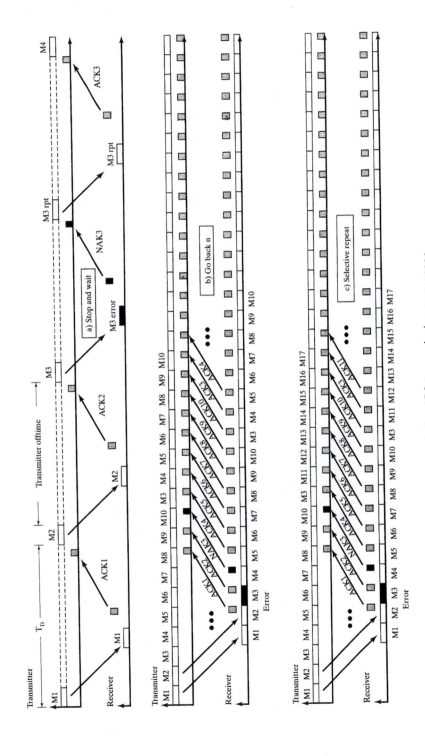

FIGURE 8-2 ARQ transmission sequences.

$$= \frac{k(1 - P_d)}{n + n'}$$

$$= \frac{\dfrac{k}{n}(1 - P_d)}{1 + \dfrac{n'}{n}} \tag{8–8}$$

This expression reduces to the previous expression when the probability of repeating a message P_d approaches zero. This analysis has presumed that no errors occur in the transmission of ACKs and NAKs from the receiver to the transmitter. In addition, the possibility of transmitter buffer overflow has been ignored. The reader is referred to the literature [1, 2, 3] for more detailed analyses.

EXAMPLE 8–2

A satellite relay communications system with a transmission delay of 280 milliseconds uses stop-and-wait ARQ. The (7, 4) Hamming code is used for error detection. The transmission rate is 75 bits per second (bps) using BPSK with $E_b/N_0 = 6.7$ dB. Assume that T_c and T_a are negligible.

(a) What is the throughput of this system in bits per channel use and in bits per second?

(b) What is the block error rate for this system?

(c) What is the block error rate and throughput for a system with the same parameters but using the code for forward error correction (i.e., non-ARQ).

Solution: The code rate is $R = 4/7 = 0.57$, which corresponds to about 2.4 dB. Thus, the BSC symbol signal-to-noise ratio E_s/N_0 is approximately $6.7 - 2.4 = 4.3$ dB. The corresponding BPSK symbol error rate is approximately $p = 10^{-2}$. The probability of detectable error P_d is calculated from the result of the pervious example and is

$$P_d = 1.0 - 7 \cdot 10^{-6}(0.99)^4 - 7 \cdot 10^{-8}(0.99)^3$$
$$- 10^{-14} - (0.99)^7$$
$$= 0.068$$

For this problem, $n = 7$. The channel symbol duration is $T_s = 1/75$ so that 280 milliseconds corresponds to 21 channel symbols; thus, $n' = 21$. Equation (8–8) for throughput is then

$$\eta_{sw} = \frac{(k/n)(1 - P_d)}{1 + n'/n}$$

$$= \frac{(4/7)(1 - 0.068)}{1 + 21/7}$$

$$= 0.133$$

This result has the units of bits per channel use. The channel symbol rate is 75 bps, so that the throughput in bits per second is $75 \times 0.133 = 9.98$ bits per second.

The block error rate for this system is calculated using (8–3) with

$$P_e = 7 \cdot 10^{-6}(0.99)^4 + 7 \cdot 10^{-8}(0.99)^3 + 10^{-14}$$

$$= 6.8 \times 10^{-6}$$

$$P_c = (0.99)^7$$

$$= 0.932$$

Therefore,

$$P_B = \frac{6.8 \times 10^{-6}}{0.932 + 6.8 \times 10^{-6}} = 7.3 \times 10^{-6}$$

The non-ARQ system throughput is simply $75 \times (4/7) = 42.9$ bps or 0.57 bits per channel use. The block error probability for the non-ARQ system is given by (6–81)

$$P_B = 1.0 - (0.99)^7 - 7 \cdot 0.01(0.99)^6 \qquad (6\text{–}81)$$

$$= 2.03 \times 10^{-3}$$

The block error probability has been considerably improved using the ARQ strategy rather than forward error correction. The price paid for this is considerably reduced (in this case) throughput.

To see how throughput η_{SW} varies with BSC symbol error rate p and with code length, make the simplifying assumption that the error detection code can detect *all* error patterns. Of course, this ideal code cannot exist except in the useless trivial case of a code having a single codeword. Nevertheless, making this assumption will provide some insight into the parameters which affect SWARQ throughput. In this case, the probability of undetectable error P_e is zero so that $P_d = 1 - P_c = 1 - (1 - p)^n$. Then the throughput becomes

$$\eta_{SW} = \left(\frac{k/n}{1 + n'/n} \right) (1 - p)^n \qquad (8\text{–}9)$$

This relationship is plotted in Figure 8–3 as a function of block length n for $n' = 512$, $R = 0.9$, and $p = 10^{-3}$, 10^{-4}, 10^{-5}, and 10^{-6}. Observe that the throughput is very low when the block length is a small fraction of the transmission delay in symbol times n'. In this case there are long delays between transmissions while the transmitter waits for the message to propagate to the receiver and the acknowledgment to return. As message length n becomes longer, the fraction of time spent waiting for transmission delays decreases and throughput increases. However, as the block length becomes longer, the probability of one or more errors in that block increases. For very long block lengths, the probability of block error dominates and throughput decreases. The optimum message length is a function of the BSC error probability as well as the propagation delay.

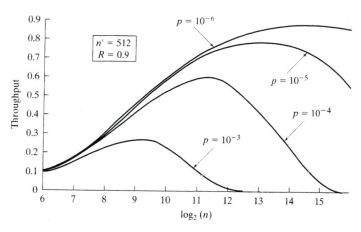

FIGURE 8–3   Efficiency of SWARQ versus block length.

Stop-and-wait is the simplest of all ARQ strategies. The transmitter SWARQ logic is very simple. Transmitter complexity is determined by the error detection encoding process and by the buffering needed to store messages output from the source that cannot be transmitted immediately due to retransmissions of previous messages. This strategy is used in modern communications systems where the transmission delays are short relative to reasonable message lengths.

8.3.2   Go-Back-N ARQ

8.3.2.1 General Description.   Go-back-N ARQ provides increased throughput relative to stop-and-wait ARQ by eliminating transmitter off time that SWARQ spent waiting for transmission delays. The off-time delays are eliminated by permitting the transmitter to transmit messages continuously until the receipt of a NAK indicating a transmission error. In the absence of errors, the transmitter would output a continuous sequence of messages M1, M2, M3, $\cdots$. When transmission errors occur and are detected by the receiver, the transmitter backs up to the incorrectly received message and retransmits that message and all subsequent messages. Figure 8–4 illustrates the transmission sequence for Go-Back-N ARQ (GBNARQ). In this figure the first two messages are transmitted without error, but an error occurs in the third message transmission. This error causes a NAK to be sent to the transmitter that arrives during the transmission of message 10. The transmitter then backs up to repeat message 3 and all subsequent messages. Observe that, in contrast to SWARQ, there is no transmitter off time. There are, however, lengthy periods when the transmitter is repeating messages that have previously been received correctly. In Figure 8–4 messages 4 through 10 were received correctly on the first transmission but are repeated nevertheless. The number of unnecessarily repeated messages is a function of the transmission delay and the channel error probability. For short transmission delays, the number of unnecessarily repeated

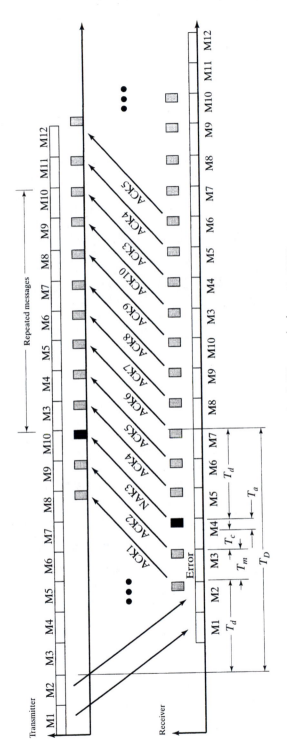

FIGURE 8–4 Go back-*N* transmission sequence.

messages will be small, and GBNARQ becomes highly efficient. No message buffering is required within the receiver for GBNARQ since all messages after an incorrectly received message are repeated. However, message buffering *is* required in the transmitter. The size of the transmitter buffer is a function of the transmission delay and the channel error probability.

8.3.2.2 Throughput Calculation. As in SWARQ, the length of the message block, the number of control bits added to the message, and the number of parity symbols added for error detection are all selected by the system designer to achieve the best possible communications efficiency or throughput η_{GBN}. Let k denote the number of bits in the message and n denote the block length for the error detection code. The code rate is $R = k/n$. The delay between messages T_m is determined only by the block length n and the channel transmission rate R_s; specifically,

$$T_m = \frac{n}{R_s} \tag{8-10}$$

In the absence of channel errors all messages would be received correctly and the best possible throughput would be achieved. In this ideal case, k information bits would be transmitted each T_m seconds or n channel symbol times and

$$\eta_{GBN,0} = \frac{k}{n} \tag{8-11}$$

Comparing $\eta_{GBN,0}$ to $\eta_{SW,0}$ observe that GBNARQ is more efficient than SWARQ in the noiseless case due to the absence of n' in the denominator of $\eta_{GBN,0}$ since GBNARQ does not require the transmitter off time.

When transmission errors occur, messages will have to be repeated and throughput will degrade. The GBNARQ strategy causes not only the retransmission of the error message but also the retransmission of all subsequent messages. The number of messages to be repeated is a function of T_d, T_c, T_m, and T_a defined previously and shown in Figure 8–4. Let

$$T_D = T_m + 2T_d + T_c + T_a \tag{8-12}$$

be the time between the beginning of a message transmission and the beginning of a retransmission of that message if required. For simplicity define $T_{dca} = 2T_d + T_c + T_a$ as before with the constraint that $T_{dca} = n'/R_s$. If a message is successfully transmitted on the first attempt, T_m seconds of channel time are used; the probability of this event is $1 - P_d$. If two transmissions are required to transmit a message successfully, $2T_m + T_{dca}$ seconds of channel time are used; the probability of this event is $P_d(1 - P_d)$. If three transmissions are required, $3T_m + 2T_{dca}$ seconds are used; the associated probability is $P_d^2(1 - P_d)$. The average amount of channel time T_{AVG} used to successfully transmit a message is

$$\begin{aligned} T_{AVG} = {} &T_m \cdot (1 - P_d) + (2T_m + T_{dca}) \cdot P_d(1 - P_d) \\ &+ (3T_m + 2T_{dca}) \cdot P_d^2(1 - P_d) + \cdots \end{aligned}$$

$$
\begin{aligned}
&= T_m[(1 - P_d) + 2P_d(1 - P_d) + 3P_d^2(1 - P_d) + \cdots] \\
&\quad + T_{\text{dca}}[P_d(1 - P_d) + 2P_d^2(1 - P_d) + 3P_d^3(1 - P_d) + \cdots] \\
&= \frac{T_m}{1 - P_d} + T_{\text{dca}}\left(\frac{P_d}{1 - P_d}\right)
\end{aligned}
\tag{8-13}
$$

Substituting to write T_m and T_{dca} in terms of the equivalent number of binary channel symbol intervals, T_{AVG} becomes

$$
\begin{aligned}
T_{\text{AVG}} &= \frac{n}{R_s(1 - P_d)} + \frac{n'P_d}{R_s(1 - P_d)} \\
&= \frac{n + n'P_d}{R_s(1 - P_d)}
\end{aligned}
\tag{8-14}
$$

Finally, the average number of channel symbol times required to transmit a single message is $T_{\text{AVG}}R_s$. Therefore, the throughput becomes

$$
\begin{aligned}
\eta_{\text{GBN}} &= \frac{k}{T_{\text{AVG}}R_s} \\
&= \frac{(k/n)(1 - P_d)}{1 + (n'/n)P_d}
\end{aligned}
\tag{8-15}
$$

Throughput varies as a function of the BSC symbol error rate p, transmission delay, and code length. In order to compare GBNARQ with SWARQ, assume again that the error detection code can detect all error patterns. Then $P_d = 1 - (1 - p)^n$ and the throughput becomes

$$
\eta_{\text{GBN}} = \frac{(k/n)(1 - p)^n}{1 + (n'/n)[1 - (1 - p)^n]}
\tag{8-16}
$$

This relationship is plotted in Figure 8–5 as a function of block length n for $n' = 512$, $R = 0.9$, and $p = 10^{-3}$, 10^{-4}, 10^{-5}, and 10^{-6}. Observe that throughput approaches the code rate R as the block length decreases. This is in contrast to SWARQ where the throughput decreases to zero as block length decreases. Comparing Figure 8–3 and 8–5, it can be seen that GBNARQ is significantly more efficient than SWARQ for small block lengths. Both SWARQ and GBNARQ transmission sequences are illustrated in Figure 8–2 using the same time scale and message error sequence. The difference in throughput of the two strategies is readily apparent from this figure. There is no optimum block length for GBNARQ as there was with SWARQ. However, the block length should not be made so long that throughput begins to degrade. The price paid for the increased throughput of GBNARQ is increased complexity in the transmitter that must maintain a buffer containing messages for possible retransmission.

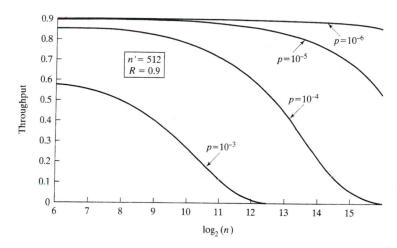

FIGURE 8–5   Throughput of GBN ARQ versus block length.

8.3.3   Selective Repeat ARQ

8.3.3.1 General Description. Further improvement in throughput of ARQ systems can be achieved by retransmitting only messages that are incorrectly received rather than the incorrect message and all subsequent messages. Selective Repeat ARQ (SRARQ) systems include the logic and message buffering necessary to reduce retransmissions to only incorrectly received messages. Figure 8–6 illustrates a typical SRARQ message sequence where the first two messages are received correctly but an error occurs in the third message. Comparing Figure 8–6 to Figure 8–4 for GBNARQ, observe that only message 3 is repeated in Figure 8–6, whereas messages 3 through 10 were repeated in Figure 8–4. The improvement in throughput is clear.

The price paid for the increased throughput of SRARQ is increased system complexity and slightly increased message overhead. Messages must be numbered in sequence, and message buffering is required in both the transmitter and receiver. Messages must be stored in the transmitter until they are acknowledged as correctly received by the receiver. The receiver must also buffer messages so that all messages can be delivered to the user in the correct order. Observe that repeated messages are out of order at the receiver; in Figure 8–6 the repeated message 3 arrives between message 10 and 11. This is in contrast to GBNARQ, where all messages are received in order at all times. Each SRARQ message is given a sequence number so that the correct order can be restored in the receiver.

Ideally, infinite buffers must be provided in both the transmitter and receiver. In practical systems the buffer size is limited thus making buffer overflow a possibility for certain message error sequences. The size of the transmitter and receiver buffers is selected as a function of the transmission delay, the message error probability, and the maximum tolerable probability of buffer overflow. If buffer overflow occurs in either the

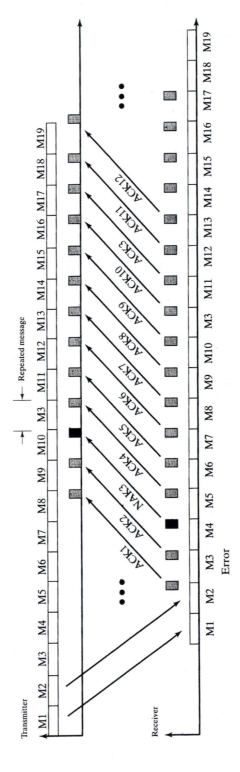

FIGURE 8-6 Selective repeat transmission sequence.

transmitter or receiver, messages are lost and system reliability degrades rapidly. The buffers must be large enough that overflow does not occur with any reasonably probable message error sequence. The reader is referred to Lin and Costello [1] for further advanced analysis of buffer sizing and overflow. Message sequence numbering is another advanced topic discussed in [1]. Sequence numbers must be reused at some time if the sequence word is finite. Since the sequence number is transmitted along with the message, throughput is increased by using the minimum possible sequence word size. Lin and Costello provide detailed analysis of these advanced topics as well as many references for further study.

8.3.3.2 Throughput Calculation.

The throughput calculation for selective repeat ARQ follows the same steps already used for SWARQ and GBNARQ. The code rate is again assumed to be $R = k/n$ and the channel transmission rate is R_s. In the absence of errors each message uses n channel symbol times and the throughput is

$$\eta_{SR,0} = \frac{k}{n} \tag{8-17}$$

The result is identical to the result for GBNARQ as expected since in both schemes messages are transmitted one after the other when no errors occur.

When transmission errors occur, messages will have to be repeated, and the throughput will degrade. As before, throughput is calculated by first calculating the average amount of channel time required to transmit a message successfully. If the message is correctly received on the first trial, the channel time used is T_m; this occurs with probability $(1 - P_d)$. If errors occur on the first transmission but not on the second, the channel time used is $2T_m$; this event occurs with probability $P_d(1 - P_d)$. The average channel time used to transmit k bits of information is

$$T_{AVG} = T_m(1 - P_d) + 2T_m P_d(1 - P_d)$$
$$+ 3T_m P_d^2(1 - P_d) + \cdots \tag{8-18}$$
$$= \frac{T_m}{1 - P_d} = \frac{n}{R_s(1 - P_d)}$$

Substituting as before for $T_m = n/R_s$ the throughput of this system is

$$\eta_{SR} = \frac{k}{T_{AVG}R_s} = \frac{k}{n}(1 - P_d) \tag{8-19}$$

Throughput varies as a function of BSC symbol error rate p and code length n. It does not vary, however, with transmission delay. To compare the three strategies assume that all error patterns are detectable so that $P_d = 1 - (1 - p)^n$ and the throughput becomes

$$\eta_{SR} = \frac{k}{n}(1 - p)^n \tag{8-20}$$

This relationship is plotted in Figure 8–7 as a function of code block length n for $R = 0.9$ and $p = 10^{-3}$, 10^{-4}, 10^{-5}, and 10^{-6}. Comparing Figures 8–3, 8–5, and 8–7, it is concluded

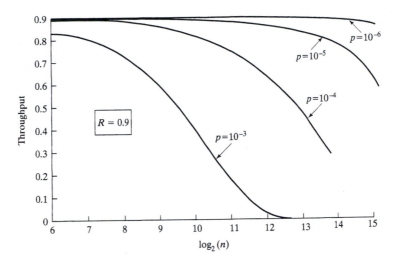

FIGURE 8–7   Throughput of SRARQ versus block length.

that selective repeat is the most efficient of the three ARQ schemes. As stated before, the price paid for this efficiency is increased complexity in both the transmitter and receiver.

In the previous paragraphs three automatic repeat request systems have been described and compared using the simplest possible analysis of reliability and throughput. Many other error control strategies are available. It is possible, for example, to switch adaptively between a selective repeat system and a go-back-N system and thereby achieve improved performance in certain cases. Further, ARQ can be combined with forward error correction to improve system performance. In this case the FEC code is used to correct a limited number of errors in order to reduce the number of repeated messages in the ARQ system. Other variations are possible and are described in the literature.

8.4   CODES FOR ERROR DETECTION

The block codes that have been discussed previously can be used for error detection in ARQ systems as well as for error correction in FEC systems. To evaluate the reliability or throughput of an ARQ system the system designer must be able to calculate two of the three probabilities P_d, P_e, and P_c. Recall that $1.0 = P_d + P_e + P_c$. The error detection properties of the most common block codes are discussed in this section; only binary linear block codes are considered.

8.4.1   General Considerations

A rate $R = k/n$ binary linear block code is a set of 2^k binary n-vectors carefully selected from the set of 2^n binary n-vectors. The code vectors are chosen to be a k-dimensional linear subspace of the n-dimensional vector space as described in Section 6.3.2.3. The linearity of the code greatly facilitates decoding and performance prediction for the code. Recall that the standard array is one method of decoding linear codes. Table 6–8 is the standard array for the (7, 4) Hamming code. The 2^k codewords form the first row of the standard array and the correctable error patterns form the first column. The remainder of the columns are the term-by-term modulo-2 sum of the codeword at the head of the column with the error pattern in the first column [recall (6–55)]. It can be shown that all n-vectors appear somewhere in the array and that no n-vector appears more than once. Decoding of a received n-vector **y** is accomplished by finding the column containing **y** and estimating the transmitted n-vector to be the code vector at the head of that column. Using this procedure all error patterns in the first column are correctable. The best code performance is achieved by selecting the error patterns of the first column to be the most probable error patterns. The most probable error patterns are those error patterns having the smallest Hamming weight.

Figure 8–8 is a conceptual illustration of a standard array for a (7, 4) linear code. In Figure 8–8 the 2^4 code vectors are denoted $\mathbf{x}_0$ through $\mathbf{x}_{15}$ and the eight correctable error patterns are denoted $\mathbf{e}_0$ through $\mathbf{e}_7$. Assume that message $\mathbf{x}_2$ was transmitted. Figure 8–8a illustrates the use of the standard array for error correction. With $\mathbf{x}_2$ transmitted, any re-

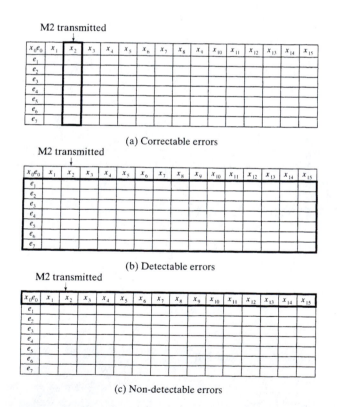

(a) Correctable errors

(b) Detectable errors

(c) Non-detectable errors

FIGURE 8–8   Standard array decoding illustrating error detection.

ceived vector in the highlighted region is due to a correctable error pattern; the decoder output estimate is the codeword at the head of the column and is correct. Figures 8–8b and c illustrate the use of the standard array for error detection. Again assume that message $\mathbf{x}_2$ is transmitted. A detectable error has occurred when the received n-vector is within the highlighted region of Figure 8–8b. In this case the decoder knows that some error has occurred since the received vector is not identical to any of the sixteen possible codewords but makes no attempt to correct that error. A message retransmission is requested. An undetectable error occurs when the received n-vector is within the highlighted region of Figure 8–8c. In this case the error pattern has caused the transmitted n-vector to be received as another valid codeword; an undetectable error pattern has occurred.

When a code is used only for error detection, all error patterns are either detectable or undetectable. The decoder makes no attempt to correct errors. The transmitted message is received correctly only if no errors occur. This event occurs with probability

$$P_c = (1 - p)^n \tag{8–21}$$

when p denotes the error probability of the BSC. An undetectable error occurs when the error pattern $\mathbf{e}$ transforms the transmitted codeword into a different but valid codeword. Suppose that codeword $\mathbf{x}_m$ is transformed into the codeword $\mathbf{x}_{m'}$, and that the Hamming distance between the two codewords is $d_H(\mathbf{x}_m, \mathbf{x}_{m'}) = d$. The Hamming weight of $\mathbf{e}$ is d and the probability of this error pattern is $p^d(1 - p)^{n-d}$. In general, the probability of a specific codeword being transformed by the channel error pattern into a different codeword Hamming distance d from the transmitted codeword is $p^d(1 - p)^{n-d}$. The specific error pattern transforming one codeword into another is the term-by-term modulo-2 sum of the two codewords. Recall that the term-by-term modulo-2 sum of any two codewords of a linear binary block code is another codeword of the code. Because of this, all undetectable error patterns are identical to codewords in the code.

Just as the error correction performance of a linear binary block code is the same for all transmitted codewords, the error detection performance can be shown to be independent of the transmitted codeword. The probability of undetectable error P_e for a code is calculated assuming that the all-zero codeword is transmitted. Then P_e is the sum of the probabilities of occurrence of all error patterns that are identical to some nonzero codeword in the code. Thus

$$P_e = \sum_{d=1}^{n} a_d p^d (1 - p)^{n-d} \tag{8–22}$$

where a_d defines the weight structure of the code. The numerical value of a_d equals the number of codewords in the code having Hamming weight d. Note that $a_d = 0$ for $d \leq d_{min} - 1$, where d_{min} is the minimum distance of the code. An error detection code with minimum distance d_{min} is capable of detecting all error patterns $\mathbf{e}$ with $d_H(\mathbf{e}) \leq d_{min} - 1$ plus any other error pattern not equal to a codeword.

The weight structure for some codes is known and for small k it can be determined via computer. For some cases it will be impossible to determine the weight structure and therefore impossible to use (8–22). In these cases it is possible to use bounding techniques to obtain results useful for systems calculations. Consider the worst case channel with error probability $p = 0.5$ for which $p^d(1 - p)^{n-d} = (\tfrac{1}{2})^n$ for all d. For any (n, k) code there are $2^k - 1$ nonzero codewords. Thus, for the worse case channel, (8–22) becomes

$$P_e = \sum_{d=1}^{n} a_d \left(\frac{1}{2}\right)^n$$

$$= \left(\frac{1}{2}\right)^n \sum_{d=1}^{n} a_d \qquad (8\text{–}23)$$

$$= \left(\frac{1}{2}\right)^n (2^k - 1)$$

$$\leq 2^{-(n-k)}$$

The student is cautioned that this result is not valid in all cases [4]. A slightly different bound is calculated by assuming that all nonzero codewords have the minimum Hamming weight $d_{\min}$. In this case

$$P_e \leq \sum_{d=1}^{n} a_d p^{d_{\min}}(1 - p)^{n-d_{\min}}$$

$$= p^{d_{\min}}(1 - p)^{n-d_{\min}} \sum_{d=1}^{n} a_d \qquad (8\text{–}24)$$

$$= p^{d_{\min}}(1 - p)^{n-d_{\min}}(2^k - 1)$$

Either of these results can be used to obtain bounds on P_e for system calculations.

In addition to being able to predict the performance of a code for error detection, the system designer must also know how to implement the error detection process. Recall that one step in most of the decoding procedures for linear block codes is the calculation of a syndrome. The syndrome of a received vector $\mathbf{y} = \mathbf{x} + \mathbf{e}$ is a function of the error pattern $\mathbf{e}$ alone and is zero for all codewords $\mathbf{x}$. The syndrome $\mathbf{s}$ of the received vector $\mathbf{y}$ is the matrix product of $\mathbf{y}$ and the transpose of the parity check matrix $\mathbf{H}$, specifically

$$\mathbf{s} = \mathbf{y} \times \mathbf{H}^T \qquad (8\text{–}25)$$

The decoder for error detection must simply calculate the syndrome of the received n-vector and determine whether it is zero. If the syndrome is zero, the received vector is identical to a codeword and either no errors have occurred or an undetectable error pattern has occurred. If the syndrome is nonzero, a detectable error pattern has occurred.

Cyclic codes can be used for error detection. In this case the syndrome is calculated via polynomial long division. Specifically, $\mathbf{s}(D) = R_{g(D)}[\mathbf{y}(D)]$, which is the remainder in the polynomial long division of received polynomial $\mathbf{y}(D)$ by the cyclic code generator polynomial $\mathbf{g}(D)$. This calculation can be performed using the circuitry illustrated in Figure 6–15. The use of the polynomial syndrome for error detection is identical to the use of the syndrome calculated by matrix multiplication. Zero syndromes are associated with correct transmissions and undetectable errors while nonzero syndromes are associated with detectable errors.

8.4.2   Hamming Codes

Recall that the Hamming codes have $d_{min} = 3$ and are therefore able to detect all error patterns with two or fewer errors. The weight structures for all Hamming codes are known

$$A(z) = \sum_{d=0}^{n} a_d z^d$$

$$= \frac{1}{n+1} [(1+z)^n + n(1+z)^{(n-1)/2}(1-z)^{(n+1)/2}]$$

(6–83)

Using this weight structure, (8–22) can be evaluated to determine P_e for any Hamming code. By combining the weight structure formula with (8–22), a general expression for P_e can be found [1]. The general formula is

$$P_e = 2^{-j}\{1 + (2^j - 1)(1 - 2p)^{2^{j-1}}\} - (1 - p)^{2^j - 1}$$

(8–26)

In this formula the parameter j specifies the particular Hamming code via the relationship $n = 2^j - 1$, where n is the codeword block length.

The probability of a correct transmission P_c is a function of only the block length n and is calculated using Equation (8–21). With P_e and P_c determined, the ARQ performance of any Hamming code can be found exactly.

Finally, the throughput performance of the (15, 11), (31, 26), and (63, 57) Hamming codes have been calculated for a selective repeat ARQ system and are compared in Figure 8–9. The block length is specified by the code, and the throughput is illustrated as a func-

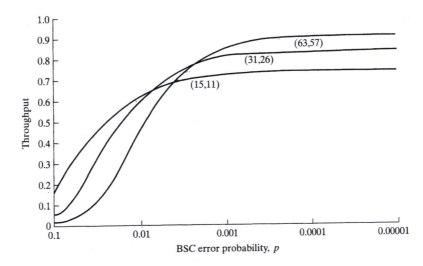

FIGURE 8–9   Throughput of Hamming codes in SRARQ system.

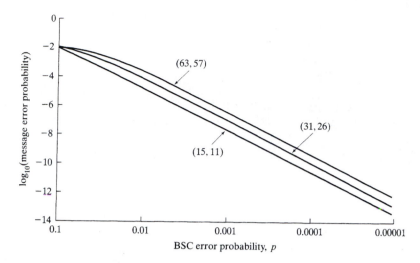

FIGURE 8–10   Message error probability of Hamming codes in SRARQ system.

tion of BSC error probability. Observe that the efficiency approaches the code rate for channel error rates of approximately 10^{-3} for each of the codes. Figure 8–10 illustrates the message error probability for the same codes and the same channel error rates as Figure 8–9. Observe that the message error probability is in the range of 10^{-7} for channel error probability of about 10^{-3}. It is concluded that good performance can be achieved in a SRARQ system using Hamming codes.

8.4.3   BCH Codes

BCH codes are also used for error detection. Unfortunately, a general formula for the weight structure for the BCH codes is not known. For double and triple error correcting primitive BCH codes the weight structure is known [1, 5] and the results can be found in [1]. The reader wishing to apply BCH codes to an error detection system is referred to Lin and Costello where a short description of the known results regarding weight structure is given along with a number of references. It has been conjectured by Lin and Costello [1] that the probability of undetected error for any primitive binary BCH code satisfies the bound $P_e \le 2^{-(n-k)}$. This result can be used to obtain ARQ performance results. The probability of correct transmission is calculated from (8–21).

8.4.4   Golay Codes

The weight structure for the two known Golay codes were given previously. For the (23, 12) Golay code the weight structure is

$$A_1(z) = 1 + 253z^7 + 506z^8 + 1288z^{11}$$

$$+ 1288z^{12} + 506z^{15} + 253z^{16} + z^{23}$$

(6-91)

Combining this result with the general formula for undetected error of (8–22) results in

$$P_e = A_1\left(\frac{p}{1-p}\right)(1-p)^{23} - 1$$

(8-27)

The weight structure of the extended (24, 12) Golay code is also known and is [6]

$$A_2(z) = 1 + 759z^8 + 2576z^{12} + 759z^{16} + z^{24}$$

(6-92)

Substituting this result in (8–22) results in

$$P_e = A_2\left(\frac{p}{1-p}\right)(1-p)^{24} - 1$$

(8-28)

As before, the probability of correct transmission for the block length n code is given by (8–21). These results for P_c and P_e can be used to calculate ARQ performance for the Golay codes.

8.5 SUMMARY

1. When a two-way communications link is available, automatic repeat request (ARQ) systems can be used to improve communications efficiency. Coding is used to *detect* errors rather than to *correct* errors. Correctly received messages are acknowledged (ACK), while incorrectly received messages are negatively acknowledged (NAK). Incorrectly received messages are repeated until they are acknowledged as correctly received. Message errors occur only when undetectable error patterns occur.

2. Three strategies for repeating messages in ARQ systems have been discussed: (a) stop-and-wait ARQ, which waits for each message to be acknowledged prior to transmitting the next message; (b) go-back-N ARQ, which transmits messages continuously but backs up to a NAKed message and repeats it and all subsequent messages; and (c) selective repeat ARQ, which continuously transmit messages and repeats only the NAKed messages.

3. Three possibilities exist for each message transmission. (a) A message is received without error with probability P_c. (b) A message is received with a detectable error pattern with probability P_d. (c) A message is received with undetectable error pattern with probability P_e.

4. The overall message error probability for all three ARQ systems considered in this chapter considering all opportunities for retransmission is P_B

$$P_B = \frac{P_e}{P_c + P_e}$$

(8-3)

Message error probability P_B is one critical parameter for ARQ system design.

5. The throughput η of an ARQ system is defined to be the number of information bits communicated to the information user per binary channel bit time $1/R_s$ or per binary channel use. Throughput is a function of the details of the ARQ protocol.

6. The throughput of stop-and-wait ARQ is

$$\eta_{SW} = \frac{(k/n)(1 - P_d)}{1 + n'/n} \tag{8-8}$$

where the error detection code rate is $R = k/n$ and n' is the time (measured in channel symbol times T_s) between the end of the message transmission and the reception of its ACK or NAK.

7. The throughput of go-back-N ARQ is

$$\eta_{GBN} = \frac{(k/n)(1 - P_d)}{1 + (n'/n)P_d} \tag{8-15}$$

8. The throughput for selective repeat ARQ is

$$\eta_{SR} = \frac{k}{n}(1 - P_d) \tag{8-19}$$

9. The codes used for error detection in ARQ systems are often the same codes used for error correction. Convolutional codes are not, however, typically used for error detection.

10. For any block error detection code the probability of a correct transmission is

$$P_c = (1 - p)^n \tag{8-21}$$

where n is the block length.

11. For any linear block error detection code the probability of undetectable error P_e is

$$P_e = \sum_{d=1}^{n} a_d p^d (1 - p)^{n-d} \tag{8-22}$$

where a_d defines the weight structure of the code.

12. For codes whose weight structure is not known, the following bounds on P_e are sometimes used for system calculations

$$P_e < 2^{-(n-k)} \tag{8-23}$$

or

$$P_e \leq p^{d_{min}}(1 - p)^{n - d_{min}}(2^k - 1) \tag{8-24}$$

13. Whether an error has occurred is estimated in an ARQ system by calculating the syndrome $\mathbf{s}$ of the received sequence $\mathbf{y}$. If the syndrome is 0, the receiver estimates that

no error has occurred. If the syndrome is nonzero the decoder estimates that an error has occurred. Of course, the syndrome of a nondetectable error pattern is 0.

14. The probability of undetectable error for the Hamming codes can be calculated exactly using

$$P_e = 2^{-j}\{1 + (2^j - 1)(1 - 2p)^{2^{j-1}}\} - (1 - p)^{2^{j}-1} \qquad (8\text{--}26)$$

15. The probability of undetectable error for the Golay codes can be calculated exactly using

$$P_e = A_1\left(\frac{p}{1-p}\right)(1-p)^{23} - 1 \qquad (8\text{--}27)$$

for the (23, 12) code or

$$P_e = A_2\left(\frac{p}{1-p}\right)(1-p)^{24} - 1 \qquad (8\text{--}28)$$

for the extended (24, 12) code.

REFERENCES

[1] S. Lin and D. J. Costello, Jr., *Error Control Coding: Fundamentals and Applications* (Englewood Cliffs, NJ: Prentice-Hall, 1983).

[2] D. Bertsekas and R. Gallagher, *Data Networks* (Englewood Cliffs, NJ: Prentice-Hall, 1987).

[3] M. Schwartz, *Telecommunication Networks: Protocols, Modeling, and Analysis* (Reading, MA: Addison Wesley Publishing Company, 1987).

[4] S. K. Leung-Yan-Cheong and M. E. Hellman, "Concerning a Bound on Undetected Error Probability," *IEEE Transactions on Information Theory*, Vol. IT-22, March 1976.

[5] T. Kasami, "Weight Distributions of Bose-Chaudhuri-Hocquenghem Codes," *Proceedings of the Conference on Combinatorial Mathematics and Its Applications* (Chapel Hill, NC: University of North Carolina Press, 1968).

[6] G. C. Clark and J. B. Cain, *Error-Correction Coding for Digital Communications* (New York: Plenum, 1981).

PROBLEMS

8–1. Calculate and plot as a function of E_b/N_0 the probability that a binary codeword with length $n = 256$ is received error-free assuming BPSK modulation and a code rate of $R = 0.9$.

8–2. The source of a stop-and-wait ARQ communications system outputs one 0.9-second message every 3 seconds. The duration of the encoder output codeword is 1 second. The delay between the end of a message transmission and the end of the receipt of its ACK or NAK is 2 seconds. The channel causes a detectable error pattern every fifth transmission but otherwise is error-free. The transmitter buffer can store twenty messages.

(a) Is the size of this buffer adequate to maintain continuous communications without buffer overflow?

(b) Calculate the throughput for this system in messages per second.

(c) Calculate the source output rate in messages per second and compare with the result of part (b).

8–3. Calculate and plot η as a function of n'/n for all three types of ARQ systems. Assume a BSC with error probability $p = 10^{-4}$, an error detection code rate $R = 0.9$, and a block length of $n = 1024$. Assume all error patterns are detectable.

8–4. A communications link uses a satellite relay with a round-trip propagation delay of 0.25 seconds. ARQ will be used. The error detection code rate is 0.9, the code block length is 1000 symbols, and a BPSK modem with a symbol rate of 10,000 symbols per second is used. The BSC error rate is $p = 10^{-4}$. What is the maximum information transfer rate in bits per second that can be supported by this system using

(a) stop-and-wait ARQ?

(b) go-back-N ARQ?

(c) selective repeat ARQ? Assume all error patterns are detectable.

8–5. A (7, 4) Hamming code is used for error detection in an ARQ communications system. Calculate P_c, P_d, and P_e for this system as a function of BSC error probability p.

8–6. A computer communication link operates using a physical link with a 4×10^6 binary transmission rate and an error probability of better than 1 error in 10^6 transmissions. The transmission delay is 1 μsec. A (1023, 1013) binary BCH code will be used for error detection. Assume that all error patterns are detectable. Calculate the maximum rate of information transfer in bits per second for

(a) stop-and-wait ARQ.

(b) go-back-N ARQ.

(c) selective repeat ARQ.

Which ARQ strategy should be selected for this system?

8–7. Calculate and plot as a function of BSC error probability p the average number of times a message is transmitted in an ARQ system using an error detection code block length of

(a) 32 symbols.

(b) 128 symbols.

(c) 1024 symbols.

Assume that all error patterns are detectable.

8–8. Consider an ARQ system. The delay between the end of a unit length message transmission and the receipt of its acknowledgment at the transmitter is four time units. Consider the first eight messages transmitted. Interference that causes detectable error patterns occurs during the following time units: 3, 7, 10, 17, 26, 27, and 37. At what time is the eighth message acknowledged as correctly received using

(a) stop-and-wait ARQ?

(b) go-back-N ARQ?

(c) selective repeat ARQ?

8–9. Calculate and plot as a function of p the probability of undetectable error for the (7, 4) Hamming code using

(a) the exact Equation (8–22).

(b) the bound of Equation (8–23).

(c) the bound of Equation (8–24).

8–10. The (23, 12) perfect Golay code is used in an ARQ communications system. BPSK modulation will be used with a symbol rate chosen so that a block of 23 symbols is transmitted in exactly 1 μsec. The propagation delay for the system is exactly 1 millisecond. Calculate and plot the system throughput as a function of E_b/N_0 for

(a) stop-and-wait ARQ.

(b) go-back-N ARQ.

(c) selective repeat ARQ.

Calculate and plot the block error probability as a function of E_b/N_0.

9

Spread-Spectrum Systems

9.1 INTRODUCTION

Many of the modulation/demodulation techniques discussed so far have been designed to communicate digital information from one place to another as efficiently as possible in a stationary additive white Gaussian noise (AWGN) environment. The transmitted signals were selected to be relatively efficient in their use of the communication resources of power and bandwidth, and the demodulators/detectors were designed to yield minimum bit error probability for the given transmitted signal in AWGN. Quantitative comparisons were made using the bandwidth and the E_b/N_0 required by the modem to achieve a specified bit error probability.

Although many real-world communication channels are accurately modeled as stationary AWGN channels, there are other important channels that do not fit this model. Consider, for example, a military communication system that might be jammed by a continuous-wave (CW) tone near the modem's center frequency or by a distorted retransmission of the modem's own signal. The interference cannot be modeled as stationary AWGN in either of these cases. Another jammer may transmit AWGN, but the jamming signal may be pulsed.

Another type of interference, which does not fit the stationary AWGN model, occurs when there are multiple propagation paths between the transmitter and receiver. The modem then interferes with itself via a delayed reception of its own signal. This phenomenon is called *multipath reception* and is a problem in line-of-sight microwave digital radios such as those used for long-haul telephone transmission and in urban mobile radio (e.g., CDMA), among other places.

This chapter is devoted to discussing a modulation and demodulation technique that can be used as an aid in mitigating the deleterious effects of the types of interference just described. This modulation and demodulation technique is called *spread spectrum* because the transmission bandwidth employed is much greater than the minimum bandwidth required to transmit the digital information. To be classified as a spread-spectrum system, the system must have the following characteristics:

1. The transmitted signal energy must occupy a bandwidth that is larger than the information bit rate (usually much larger) and is independent of the information bit rate.

2. Demodulation must be accomplished, in part, by correlation of the received signal with a replica of the signal used in the transmitter to spread the information signal.

A number of modulation techniques use a transmission bandwidth much larger than the minimum required for data transmission but are not spread-spectrum modulations. Low-rate coding, for example, results in increased transmission bandwidth but does not satisfy either of the foregoing conditions. Wideband frequency modulation also results in a large transmission bandwidth but is not spread spectrum.

Spread-spectrum techniques can be very useful in solving a wide range of communications problems. The amount of performance improvement that is achieved through the use of spread spectrum is defined as the *processing gain* of the spread-spectrum system. That is, processing gain is the difference between system performance using spread-spectrum techniques and system performance not using spread-spectrum techniques, all else being equal. Processing gain is approximately the ratio of the spread bandwidth to the information rate.

This chapter is intended to provide further motivation for the study of spread-spectrum systems and to introduce the most widely used types of spread-spectrum systems. Two important communication problems that can be partially solved using spread-spectrum techniques are described in Section 9.2. The two fundamental types of spread-spectrum systems, direct-sequence (DS) and frequency-hop (FH), are described in Section 9.3; also mentioned is hybrid spread spectrum.

Representation of spread-spectrum modulation in terms of complex envelopes is discussed in Section 9.4. As shown in Chapter 2, this is convenient for simulation purposes. The generation of spreading codes is discussed in Section 9.5, along with some of their characteristics. The process of synchronization of the spectrum spreading code at the receiver is overviewed in Section 9.6. In Section 9.7, the performance of spread-spectrum systems in various environments is summarized. Section 9.8 gives a brief overview of performance in multiple user environments and Section 9.9 gives a simplified treatment of multiuser detection. The chapter closes with a summary of several applications of spread-spectrum systems.

9.2 TWO COMMUNICATION PROBLEMS

9.2.1 Pulse-Noise Jamming

Consider a coherent binary phase-shift-keyed (BPSK) communication system which is being used in the presence of a pulse-noise jammer. A *pulse-noise jammer* transmits pulses of band-limited white Gaussian noise having total average power J referred to the receiver front end. The jammer may choose the center frequency and bandwidth of the noise to be identical to the receiver's center frequency and bandwidth. In addition, the jammer chooses its pulse duty factor ρ to cause maximum degradation to the communication link while maintaining constant average transmitted power J.

It was shown in Chapters 3 and 4 that the bit error probability of a coherent BPSK system is

$$P_b = Q\left(\sqrt{\frac{2E_b}{N_0}}\right) \tag{9-1}$$

The one-sided noise power spectral density N_0 in this expression represents receiver front end thermal noise. When transmitting, the noise jammer increases the receiver noise power spectral density from N_0 to $N_0 + N_J/\rho$, where $N_J = J/W$ is the one-sided average jammer power spectral density and W is the transmission bandwidth. The jammer transmits using duty factor ρ, so that the average bit error probability is

$$\bar{P}_b = (1 - \rho)Q\left(\sqrt{\frac{2E_b}{N_0}}\right) + \rho Q\left(\sqrt{\frac{2E_b}{N_0 + N_J/\rho}}\right) \tag{9-2}$$

The jammer, given this formula, chooses ρ to maximize $\bar{P}_b$

When a system is being designed to operate in a jamming environment, the maximum possible transmitter power is generally used and thermal noise can be safely neglected. In this case, the first term in (9-2) is negligible and $\bar{P}_b$ can be approximated by

$$\bar{P}_b \simeq \rho Q\left(\sqrt{\frac{2E_b\rho}{N_J}}\right) \tag{9-3}$$

The Q-function can be bounded (see Appendix E) by an exponential yielding

$$\bar{P}_b \leq \frac{\rho}{\sqrt{4\pi E_b\rho/N_J}}\, e^{-E_b\rho/N_J} \tag{9-4}$$

The maximum of this function over ρ can be found by taking the first derivative and setting it equal to 0. The maximizing ρ is found to be $\rho = N_J/2E_b$ and $\bar{P}_{b,\max}$ is given by

$$\bar{P}_{b,\max} \simeq \frac{1}{\sqrt{2\pi e}}\frac{1}{2E_b/N_J} \tag{9-5}$$

Of course, the duty factor must be less than or equal to unity so that (9-5) applies only when $E_b/N_J \geq 0.5$. For $E_b/N_J < 0.5$, $\bar{P}_b$ is given by (9-3) with $\rho = 1.0$. Observe that the exponential dependence of bit error probability on signal-to-noise ratio of (9-1) has been replaced by an inverse linear relationship in (9-5). Equations (9-1) and (9-5) are plotted in Figure 9-1, where it can be seen that the pulse noise jammer causes a degradation of approximately 31.5 dB at a bit error probability of 10^{-5}.

The severe degradation in system performance caused by the pulse-noise jammer can be largely eliminated by using a combination of spread-spectrum techniques and forward error correction coding with appropriate interleaving [1]. The effect of the spectrum

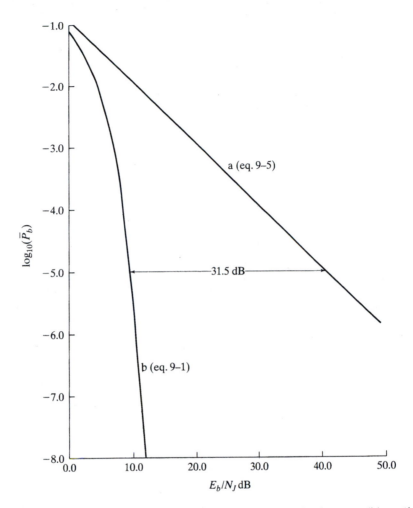

FIGURE 9–1 Bit error probability: (a) worst case pulse noise jammer; (b) continuous-noise jammer.

spreading will be to change the abscissa from E_b/N_J to $E_b K/N_J$, where K is a constant about equal to W/R, where R is the data rate of the spread-spectrum system. Error correction coding will be used to return from the inverse linear relation between error probability and signal-to-noise ratio to nearly the exponential relationship desired.

Finally, observe that in order to cause maximum degradation, the jammer must know the value of E_b/N_J at the receiver. This implies knowledge of attenuation in both the transmitter-to-receiver path and jammer-to-receiver path. This knowledge would be difficult to obtain in a tactical environment, so that the results just described are worst case. In addition, a real jammer would be limited in peak power output and would not be able to use an arbitrarily small duty factor. In spite of these limitations, the pulse jammer is a serious threat to military communications systems.

9.2.2   Low Probability of Detection

Situations exist where it is desirable that a communication link be operated without knowledge of certain parties. *Low probability of detection (LPD)* communication systems are designed to make their detection as difficult as possible by anyone but the intended receiver. This, of course, implies that the minimum signal power required to achieve a particular communications performance is used. The goal of the LPD system designer is to use a signaling scheme that results in the minimum probability of being detected within some time interval. Spread-spectrum techniques can significantly aid the system designer in achieving this goal.

Assume that the detector is using a radiometer.[1] A radiometer detects energy received in a bandwidth W by filtering to this bandwidth, squaring the output of this filter, integrating the output of the squarer for time T, and comparing the output of the integrator at time T with a threshold as illustrated in Figure 9–2. If the integrator output is above a preset threshold at time T, the signal is declared present; otherwise, the signal is declared absent. The performance of the radiometer in detecting the desired communication signal is known if the probability density function of the integrator output at time T is known. This probability density function is used to calculate the probability, P_d, of detecting the signal if it is indeed present, and probability of falsely declaring a detection when noise alone is present, P_{fa}.

Two approximations are often used for the integrator output statistics for a radiometer. One uses chi-square statistics, noncentral for the case of signal plus noise at the input and central for noise alone (see p. 112). This can further be approximated by central chi-square statistics in the signal plus noise case if suitable adjustments are made in the chi-square degrees of freedom and threshold for the detector [5]. The second approximation is useful if the time-bandwidth product, TW, of the signal is large. The resulting equations describing this situation are

$$P_d = Q\left(\frac{K_0 - TW - S}{\sqrt{TW + 2S}}\right), \quad TW \gg 1 \tag{9–6}$$

for the probability of detection, and

$$P_{fa} = Q\left(\frac{K_0 - TW}{\sqrt{TW}}\right), \quad TW \gg 1 \tag{9–7}$$

---

[1]Another type of intercept receiver is a channelized receiver with coincidence detection [2]. The idea with this type of receiver is that if the communicator changes frequency to avoid detection, a useful intercept strategy is to listen in the various frequency bands that might be used and determine the coincidence of any possible detections in these bands. It can be shown that a time-frequency hop strategy can be found to always force this interceptor to the radiometer mode.

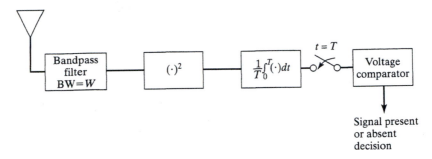

FIGURE 9–2 Energy detector or radiometer. (Reproduced from Reference [5] with permission.)

for the probability of false alarm, where S is the ratio of total signal energy to noise spectral density at the integrator *output*, E_s/N_0, in Figure 9–2, $Q(\cdot)$ is the Q-function defined in Chapter 3, and K_0 is a threshold, usually fixed, to give a certain allowable probability of false alarm. The signal-to-noise power ratio at the bandpass filter output is smaller than E_s/N_0 by the factor TW. Depending on whether the party of interest is the interceptor or the communicator, one of two strategies may be adopted:

1. If the interceptor, build the lowest noise figure receiver affordable, integrate for the longest time possible (i.e., the full communication interval if known) with the input bandpass filter set equal to the bandwidth of the signal and centered on the signal, insofar as this is possible, while accepting the highest false alarm probability tolerable.
2. If the communicator, spread the signal to the full bandwidth allowed, and communicate at the lowest power possible for the shortest duration possible.

An example will make these tradeoffs clearer.

EXAMPLE 9–1

Consider an intercept receiver performance versus TW and with the input signal-to-noise power ratio fixed at –10 dB at the output of the bandpass filter. For the purposes of this example, we assume that the signal bandwidth is fixed and that T, the integration interval, varies. This, of course, assumes that signal is present to integrate for the longest T considered. Thus, this would be the situation for an undisciplined communicator who basically communicates at will; a disciplined communicator would communicate in short bursts at randomly chosen intervals. Performance curves are shown in Figure 9–3; on the left is P_d versus TW, where it is seen that the signal may be detected with high certainty if it can be integrated long enough, and on the right is a plot of E_s/N_0 versus TW, which shows the effect of integration on increasing signal-to-noise ratio at the integrator output.

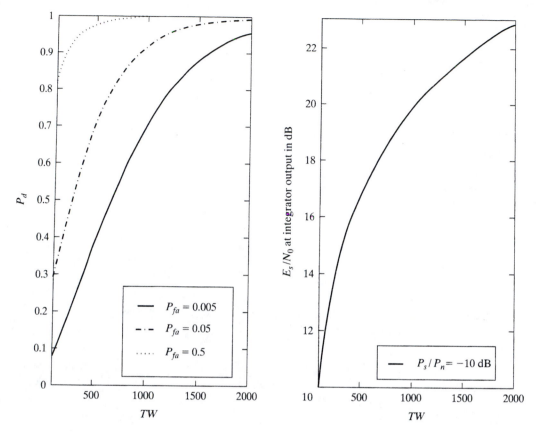

FIGURE 9–3 Probability of detection and integrator output E_s/N_0 versus *TW* for a radiometer detector for input signal-to-noise power ratio of –10 dB.

9.3 TYPES OF SPREAD-SPECTRUM SYSTEMS

A wideband spread-spectrum signal is generated from a data modulated carrier by modulating the data modulated carrier a second time using a very wideband spreading signal. The spreading modulation may be phase modulation or it may be a rapid changing of carrier frequency or it may be a combination of these and other techniques. When spectrum spreading is accomplished by phase modulation, the resultant signal is called a *direct-sequence (DS) spread-spectrum* signal. When the spectrum spreading is accomplished by rapid changing of the carrier frequency, the resultant signal is called a *frequency-hop (FH) spread-spectrum* signal. When both direct sequence and frequency hop are used, the resultant signal is called a hybrid DS-FH signal. All of these techniques will be discussed in the following paragraphs. The spreading signal is chosen to have properties that facilitate demodulation of the transmitted signal by the intended receiver and make demodulation by an unintended receiver as difficult as possible. These same properties will also make it possible for the intended receiver to discriminate between the communication signal and jamming. If the bandwidth of the spreading signal is large relative to the data bandwidth, the spread-spectrum transmission bandwidth is dominated by the spreading signal and is nearly independent of the data signal.

9.3.1   BPSK Direct-Sequence Spread Spectrum

The simplest form of DS spread spectrum employs binary phase-shift keying as the spreading modulation. It was shown earlier that ideal BPSK modulation results in instantaneous phase changes of the carrier by 180 degrees and can be mathematically represented as a multiplication of the carrier by a function $c(t)$, which takes on the values ± 1. Consider a constant-envelope data-modulated carrier having power P, radian frequency ω_0, and data phase modulation $\theta_d(t)$ given by[2]

$$s_d(t) = \sqrt{2P} \cos[\omega_0 t + \theta_d(t)] \tag{9-8}$$

This signal occupies a bandwidth typically between one-half and twice the data rate, depending on the details of the data modulation. BPSK spreading is accomplished by simply multiplying $s_d(t)$ by a function $c(t)$ representing the spreading waveform, as illustrated in Figure 9–4. The transmitted signal is

$$s_t(t) = \sqrt{2P}\, c(t) \cos[\omega_0 t + \theta_d(t)] \tag{9-9}$$

The signal of (9–9) is transmitted via a distortionless path having transmission delay T_d. The signal is received together with some type of interference and/or Gaussian noise. Demodulation is accomplished in part by remodulating with the spreading code appropriately delayed as shown in Figure 9–5. This remodulation or correlation of the received signal with the delayed spreading waveform is called *despreading* and is a critical function in all spread-spectrum systems. The signal component of the output of the despreading mixer is

$$\sqrt{2P}\, c(t - T_d)c(t - \hat{T}_d) \cos[\omega_0 t + \theta_d(t - T_d) + \phi] \tag{9-10}$$

where $\hat{T}_d$ is the receiver's best estimate of the transmission delay. Since $c(t) = \pm 1$, the product $c(t - T_d) \times c(t - \hat{T}_d)$ will be unity if $\hat{T}_d = T_d$, that is, if the spreading code at the receiver is synchronized with the spreading code at the transmitter. When correctly synchronized, the signal component of the output of the receiver despreading mixer is equal to $s_d(t)$ except for a random phase ϕ, and $s_d(t)$ can be demodulated using a conventional coherent phase demodulator.

Observe that the data modulation above does not also have to be BPSK; no restrictions have been placed on the form of $\theta_d(t)$. However, it is common to use the same type of digital phase modulation for the data and the spreading code. When BPSK is used for both modulators, one phase modulator (mixer) can be eliminated. The double-modulation

---

[2] The carrier frequency will be denoted by ω_0 rather than ω_c so that ω_c may be used for the spreading code clock frequency. For notational convenience ω_0 is used rather than f_0 which was used in previous chapters.

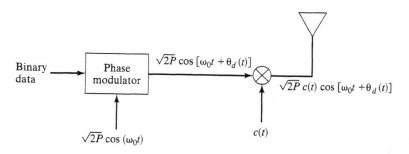

FIGURE 9–4   BPSK direct-sequence spread-spectrum transmitter. (Reproduced from Reference [5] with permission.)

process is replaced by a single modulation by the modulo-2 sum of the data and the spreading code.

Figure 9–6 illustrates the direct-sequence spreading and despreading operation when the data modulation and the spreading modulation are BPSK. In this case, the data modulation is represented by a multiplication of the carrier by $d(t)$, where $d(t)$ takes on values of ± 1. Thus

$$s_d(t) = \sqrt{2P}\, d(t) \cos \omega_0 t \tag{9–11}$$

$$s_t(t) = \sqrt{2P}\, d(t)c(t) \cos \omega_0 t \tag{9–12}$$

The data and spreading waveforms are illustrated in Figures 9–6a and b, and $s_d(t)$ and $s_t(t)$ are illustrated in Figures 9–6c and d. Figure 9–6e represents an incorrectly phased input to the receiver despreading mixer assuming zero propagation delay, and Figure 9–6f shows the output of this mixer. Observe that Figure 9–6f is not equivalent to $s_d(t)$, illustrating that the receiver must be synchronized with the transmitter. Finally, Figure 9–6g shows the despreading mixer output when the despreading code is correctly phased. In this case $c(t)s_t(t) = s_d(t)$ and the data-modulated carrier has been recovered.

It is also instructive to consider the power spectra of the signals of Figure 9–6. Recall that the two-sided power spectral density in W/Hz of a binary phase-shift-keyed carrier is given by

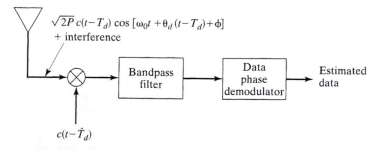

FIGURE 9–5   BPSK direct-sequence spread-spectrum receiver. (Reproduced from Reference [5] with permission.)

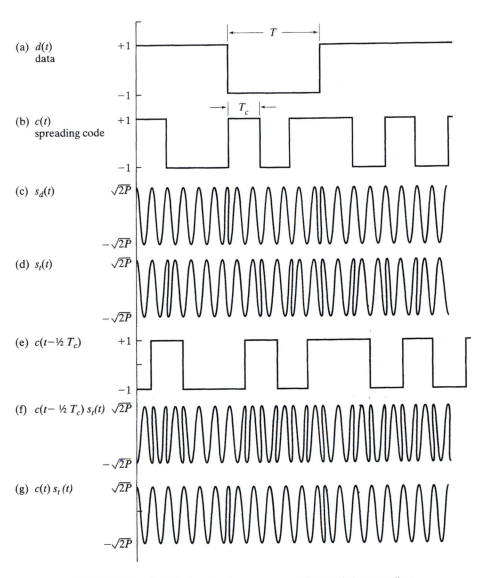

FIGURE 9–6   BPSK direct-sequence spreading and despreading.

$$s_d(f) = \tfrac{1}{2} PT\{\text{sinc}^2[(f - f_0)T] + \text{sinc}^2[(f + f_0)T]\} \qquad (9\text{–}13)$$

which is plotted in Figure 9–7. Now observe that the signal $s_t(t)$ of Figure 9–6d is also a binary phase-shift-keyed carrier and therefore has a power spectral density, which is given by (9–13) with T replaced by T_c, the duration of a spreading code symbol. The spreading code symbol duration T_c is often referred to as a spreading code *chip*. Figure 9–8 shows the power spectral density (psd) of $s_t(t)$ in the case where $T_c = T/3$. Observe

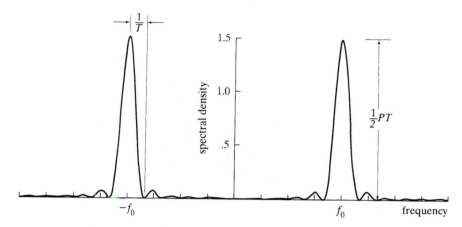

FIGURE 9–7   Power spectral density of data-modulated carrier.

that the effect of the modulation by the spreading code is to spread the bandwidth of the transmitted signal by a factor of three, and that this spreading operation reduces the level of the psd by a factor of three. In actual systems, this spreading factor is typically much larger than three.

Equation (9–13) applies only when both the data modulation and the spreading modulation are binary phase-shift keying, and when the data modulation and the spreading modulation are phase synchronous. In this case, since the data modulation is completely random, the signal $s_t(t)$ is a randomly biphase modulated signal and (9–13) applies. Consider again the case in which the data modulation is an arbitrary constant-envelope phase modulation. The data modulated carrier is represented by (9–8) and the transmitted signal is represented by (9–9). The power spectrum of the transmitted signal is

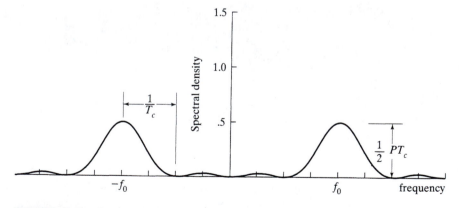

FIGURE 9–8   Power spectral density of data- and spreading code-modulated carrier.

calculated using the *Wiener–Khintchine theorem,* which states that the power spectrum and the autocorrelation function of a signal are a Fourier transform pair [3].

The data-modulated carrier is an ergodic random process, the spreading code is both deterministic and periodic, and their product, $s_t(t)$, is an ergodic random process. The signal $s_d(t)$ is independent of $c(t)$, so that the autocorrelation function $R_t(\tau)$ of the product $c(t)s_d(t)$ equals the product of the autocorrelation functions; that is,

$$R_t(\tau) = R_d(\tau)R_c(\tau) \tag{9-14}$$

Using the frequency convolution theorem of Fourier transform theory, the power spectral density of $s_t(t)$, which is the Fourier transform of $R_t(\tau)$, is

$$S_t(f) = \int_{-\infty}^{\infty} S_d(f')S_c(f - f') \, df' \tag{9-15}$$

EXAMPLE 9–2

Calculate the power spectrum of the direct-sequence spread-spectrum transmitted signal when BPSK is used for both the data modulation and the spreading modulation. Assume that the spreading code chip rate is 100 times the data rate and that the period of the spreading code is infinite.

Solution: The power spectrum of the data-modulated carrier is given by (9–13). The power spectrum of the spreading code $c(t)$ is the Fourier transform of its autocorrelation function

$$R_c(\tau) = \lim_{A \to \infty} \frac{1}{2A} \int_{-A}^{A} c(t')c(t' - \tau) \, dt' \tag{9-16}$$

When $\tau = 0$, this integral is equal to 1.0 since $c^2(t) = 1.0$. When $\tau \geq T_c$, the integral is 0 since the code has been modeled as an infinite sequence of independent random binary digits. For $0 < \tau < T_c$ the integral is equal to the fraction of the chip time for which $c(t' - T) = c(t')$, as illustrated in Figure 9–9. Therefore,

$$R_c(\tau) = \begin{cases} 1 - \dfrac{|\tau|}{T_c}, & |\tau| < T_c \\ 0, & |\tau| \geq T_c \end{cases} \tag{9-17}$$

as illustrated in Figure 9–10. The Fourier transform of this triangular waveform is easily calculated. The result is

$$S_c(f) = T_c \operatorname{sinc}^2(fT_c) = \frac{T}{100} \operatorname{sinc}^2\left(\frac{fT}{100}\right) \tag{9-18}$$

The transmitted power spectrum is then

$$\begin{aligned} S_t(f) = {} & \int_{-\infty}^{\infty} \frac{1}{2} PT \operatorname{sinc}^2[(f' - f_0)T] \frac{T}{100} \operatorname{sinc}^2\left[(f - f')\frac{T}{100}\right] df' \\ & + \int_{-\infty}^{\infty} \frac{1}{2} PT \operatorname{sinc}^2[(f' + f_0)T] \frac{T}{100} \operatorname{sinc}^2\left[(f - f')\frac{T}{100}\right] df' \end{aligned} \tag{9-19}$$

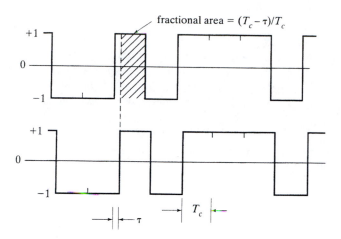

FIGURE 9–9 Calculation of autocorrelation function of an infinite sequence of random binary digits.

Because the spreading code chip rate is much larger than the data rate, the second sinc function in each integral is approximately constant over the range of significant values of the first sinc function. Thus the convolution can be approximated by

$$
\begin{aligned}
S_r(f) &\simeq \frac{PT^2}{200} \operatorname{sinc}^2\!\left[(f - f_0)\frac{T}{100}\right] \int_{-\infty}^{\infty} \operatorname{sinc}^2[(f' - f_0)T]\,df' \\
&\quad + \frac{PT^2}{200} \operatorname{sinc}^2\!\left[(f + f_0)\frac{T}{100}\right] \int_{-\infty}^{\infty} \operatorname{sinc}^2[(f' + f_0)T]\,df' \qquad (9\text{–}20) \\
&= \frac{1}{2}\frac{PT}{100}\left\{\operatorname{sinc}^2\!\left[(f - f_0)\frac{T}{100}\right] + \operatorname{sinc}^2\!\left[(f + f_0)\frac{T}{100}\right]\right\}
\end{aligned}
$$

It was claimed earlier that one of the advantages of using spread spectrum is that it will enable the receiver to reject deliberate interference or jamming. Interference rejection

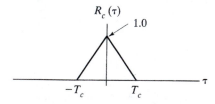

FIGURE 9–10 Autocorrelation function of an infinite sequence of random binary digits.

is accomplished by the receiver despreading mixer, which *spreads* the spectrum of the interference at the same time that the desired signal is *despread.* If the interference energy is spread over a bandwidth much larger than the data bandwidth, most of its energy will be rejected by the data matched filter.

Suppose that BPSK is used for both the data modulation and the spreading modulation and that the interference is a single tone having power J. The jammer's best strategy is to place the jamming tone directly in the center of the modem's transmission bandwidth. If no spectrum spreading were employed, the ratio of jamming power to signal power in the data bandwidth would be J/P. The power spectrum of the received signal is approximately

$$S_r(f) \simeq \tfrac{1}{2} PT_c \{ \mathrm{sinc}^2[(f - f_0)T_c] + \mathrm{sinc}^2[(f + f_0)T_c] \}$$
$$+ \tfrac{1}{2} J \{ \delta(f - f_0) + \delta(f + f_0) \} \tag{9-21}$$

and the received signal is

$$r(t) = \sqrt{2P}\, d(t - T_d) c(t - T_d) \cos(\omega_0 t + \phi)$$
$$+ \sqrt{2J} \cos(\omega_0 t + \phi') \tag{9-22}$$

Assume that the receiver despreading code is correctly phased so that the output of the despreading mixer is

$$y(t) = \sqrt{2P}\, d(t - T_d) \cos(\omega_0 t + \phi)$$
$$+ \sqrt{2J}\, c(t - \hat{T}_d) \cos(\omega_0 t + \phi') \tag{9-23}$$

The power spectrum of $y(t)$ is

$$S_y(f) = \tfrac{1}{2} PT \{ \mathrm{sinc}^2[(f - f_0)T] + \mathrm{sinc}^2[(f + f_0)T] \}$$
$$+ \tfrac{1}{2} JT_c \{ \mathrm{sinc}^2[(f - f_0)T_c] + \mathrm{sinc}^2[(f + f_0)T_c] \} \tag{9-24}$$

Observe that the data signal has been despread to the data bandwidth, while the single-tone jammer has been spread over the full transmission bandwidth of the spread-spectrum system.

The power spectra of the signals discussed earlier are illustrated in Figure 9–11. The received power spectra are shown in Figure 9–11a, and the spectra after the despreading mixer are shown in Figure 9–11b. The despreading operation in spread-spectrum receivers is followed by a filtering operation to limit the bandwidth at the input to the data demodulator to approximately the data bandwidth. The power transfer function of an ideal filter accomplishing this is shown in Figure 9–11c and the output of this filter is shown in Figure 9–11d. This ideal filter represents the noise equivalent bandwidth of an actual intermediate-frequency (IF) filter whose noise bandwidth is equal to the data rate. Nearly all of the signal power is passed by the IF filter. A large fraction of the spread jammer power, on the other hand, is rejected by this filter. The magnitude of the jammer power passed by the IF filter is

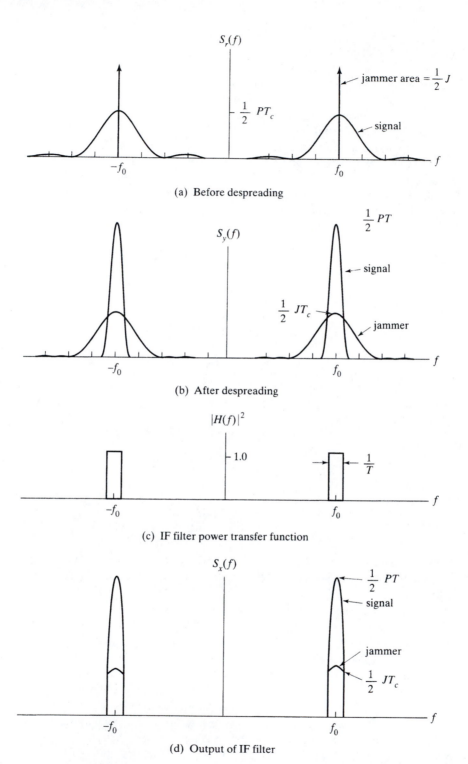

(a) Before despreading

(b) After despreading

(c) IF filter power transfer function

(d) Output of IF filter

FIGURE 9–11 Receiver power spectral densities with tone jamming.

$$J_0 = \int_{-\infty}^{\infty} S_J(f)|H(f)|^2 \, df \tag{9-25}$$

where $S_J(f)$ is the power spectrum of the jammer after the despreading mixer. If an ideal bandpass IF filter as shown in Figure 9–11c is assumed, then

$$J_0 = \int_{-f_0-1/2T}^{-f_0+1/2T} S_J(f) \, df + \int_{f_0-1/2T}^{f_0+1/2T} S_J(f) \, df$$

$$= \frac{1}{2} JT_c \int_{-f_0-1/2T}^{-f_0+1/2T} \text{sinc}^2[(f+f_0)T_c] \, df \tag{9-26}$$

$$+ \frac{1}{2} JT_c \int_{f_0-1/2T}^{f_0+1/2T} \text{sinc}^2[(f-f_0)T_c] \, df$$

For large ratios of data bandwidth to total spread bandwidth, that is, $T_c \ll T$, the sinc function is nearly constant over the range of the integration and

$$J_0 \simeq J \frac{T_c}{T} \tag{9-27}$$

Thus the jamming power at the input to the data demodulator has been reduced by a factor T_c/T over its value without the use of spread spectrum. The processing gain of this very simple spread-spectrum system is equal to the inverse of this jammer power reduction factor, or

$$G_p = \frac{T}{T_c} \tag{9-28}$$

Other equivalent definitions of processing gain are possible and are often used. Throughout this chapter a consistent definition of processing gain as an improvement factor is used. This results in different formulas for G_p, depending on the particular system being considered.

9.3.2   QPSK Direct-Sequence Spread Spectrum

Recall from Chapter 4 that it is sometimes advantageous to transmit simultaneously on two carriers that are in phase quadrature. The principal reason for doing this is to conserve spectrum, since, for the same total transmitted power, the same bit error probability is achieved using one-half the transmission bandwidth. Bandwidth efficiency is not usually of primary importance in a spread-spectrum system, but quadrature modulations are still important. The reason for this is that quadrature modulations are more difficult to detect in low probability of detection applications, and quadrature modulations are less sensitive to some types of jamming or interference.

Both the data modulation and the spreading modulation can be placed on quadrature carriers using a number of techniques. If no restriction is placed on the data phase modulator, QPSK spreading modulation can be added using the system of Figure 9–12a. Observe that the power at either output of the quadrature hybrid is one-half of the input power. The output of the QPSK modulator is[3]

$$s(t) = \sqrt{P}\, c_1(t) \cos[\omega_0 t + \theta_d(t)] + \sqrt{P}\, c_2(t) \sin[\omega_0 t + \theta_d(t)]$$
$$\triangleq a(t) + b(t) \tag{9-29}$$

where $c_1(t)$ and $c_2(t)$ are the in-phase and quadrature spreading waveforms. When written this way both spreading waveforms are assumed to take on only values of ± 1. These spreading waveforms are assumed to be chip synchronous but otherwise totally independent of one another.

The power spectrum of the QPSK spread-spectrum signal of (9–29) can be calculated by observing that both terms of this equation are identical, except for amplitude and a possible phase shift, to (9–9) for BPSK spread spectrum. Thus, since the two signals are orthogonal, the power spectrum of the sum signal equals the algebraic sum of the two power spectra. That this is true is most conveniently illustrated by calculating the autocorrelation of $s(t)$, which is

$$
\begin{aligned}
R_s(\tau) &= E[s(t)s(t + \tau)] \\
&= E[a(t)a(t + \tau)] + E[b(t)b(t + \tau)] \\
&\quad + E[a(t)b(t + \tau)] + E[b(t)a(t + \tau)] \\
&= R_a(\tau) + R_b(\tau) + E[a(t)b(t + \tau)] + E[b(t)a(t + \tau)]
\end{aligned}
\tag{9-30}
$$

If the functions $a(t)$ and $b(t)$ are orthogonal [3], the last two terms of (9–30) are equal to 0. This condition is satisfied in the present case since $c_1(t)$ and $c_2(t)$ are independent code waveforms. Since the desired power spectrum is the Fourier transform of $R_s(\tau)$, it follows that the power spectrum of a QPSK spread-spectrum signal is the sum of the power spectra of its BPSK-modulated quadrature components.

The receiver for the transmitted signal of (9–29) is shown in Figure 9–12b. In this figure the bandpass filter is centered at frequency ω_{IF} and has a bandwidth sufficiently wide to pass the data-modulated carrier with negligible distortion. Using straightforward trigonometric identities, it can be shown that the components of $x(t)$ and $y(t)$ near the intermediate frequency are given by

$$
\begin{aligned}
x(t) &= \sqrt{\frac{P}{2}}\, c_1(t - T_d)c_1(t - \hat{T}_d) \cos[\omega_{IF}t - \theta_d(t)] \\
&\quad - \sqrt{\frac{P}{2}}\, c_2(t - T_d)c_1(t - \hat{T}_d) \sin[\omega_{IF}t - \theta_d(t)]
\end{aligned}
\tag{9-31}
$$

---

[3]Another approach is to use quaternary spreading codes to be discussed in section 9.5.9.

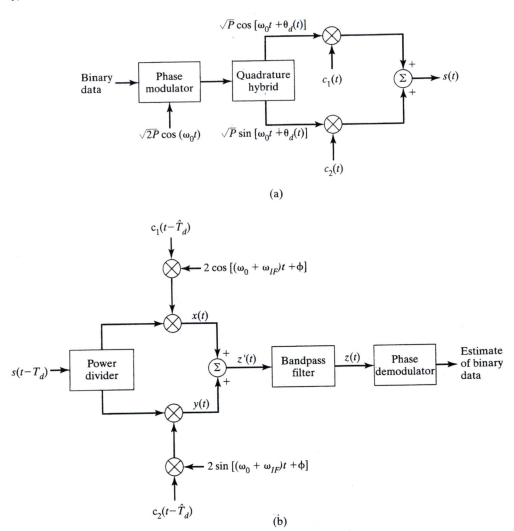

FIGURE 9–12   (a) QPSK spread-spectrum modulator with arbitrary data phase modulation; (b) QPSK spread-spectrum receiver for arbitrary data modulation. (Note: A quadrature hybrid produces two outputs in phase quadrature with each other.) (Reproduced from Reference [5] with permission.)

$$y(t) = \sqrt{\frac{P}{2}}\, c_1(t - T_d)c_2(t - \hat{T}_d)\, \sin[\omega_{IF}t - \theta_d(t)]$$

$$+ \sqrt{\frac{P}{2}}\, c_2(t - T_d)c_2(t - \hat{T}_d)\, \cos[\omega_{IF}t - \theta_d(t)]$$

(9–32)

If the receiver-generated replicas of the spreading codes are correctly phased, then

$$c_1(t - T_d)c_1(t - \hat{T}_d) = c_2(t - T_d)c_2(t - \hat{T}_d) = 1.0 \tag{9-33}$$

and the desired signals have been despread. These despread signals will pass through the bandpass filter. The undesired terms of (9–31) and (9–32) cancel, so that

$$z(t) = \sqrt{2P} \cos[\omega_{IF}t - \theta_d(t)] \tag{9-34}$$

In deriving these results, perfect receiver carrier phase tracking has been assumed. Observe in (9–34) that the data-modulated carrier has been completely recovered. That is, the QPSK spreading modulation added by the transmitter has been completely removed by the receiver despreading operation. The signal $z(t)$ is the input to a conventional phase demodulator where data is recovered. Other forms of the receiver are possible. The particular placement of the mixers and filter shown, however, is typical of an arrangement that might be found in actual hardware.

When the data modulation is binary phase-shift keying, the transmitter and receiver can be implemented as shown in Figure 9–13, where phase coherency has been assumed. The transmitted signal in this case is

$$s(t) = \sqrt{P} \, d(t) \, [c_1(t) \cos(\omega_0 t) + c_2(t) \sin(\omega_0 t)] \tag{9-35}$$

This type of modulation is called *balanced QPSK modulation* [4] since the data modulation is balanced between the in-phase and quadrature channels.

The receiver for the signal of (9–35) is shown in Figure 9–13b. The system is assumed to be coherent, so that the phase of the in-phase and quadrature local oscillators are equal to the received carrier phase. With this assumption, the difference frequency components of the mixer outputs are

$$x(t) = \sqrt{\frac{P}{2}} \, d(t - T_d)c_1(t - T_d)c_1(t - \hat{T}_d) \cos \omega_{IF}t$$

$$\tag{9-36a}$$

$$+ \sqrt{\frac{P}{2}} \, d(t - T_d)c_2(t - T_d)c_1(t - \hat{T}_d) \sin(-\omega_{IF}t)$$

$$y(t) = \sqrt{\frac{P}{2}} \, d(t - T_d)c_2(t - T_d)c_2(t - \hat{T}_d) \cos \omega_{IF}t$$

$$\tag{9-36b}$$

$$+ \sqrt{\frac{P}{2}} \, d(t - T_d)c_1(t - T_d)c_2(t - \hat{T}_d) \sin \omega_{IF}t$$

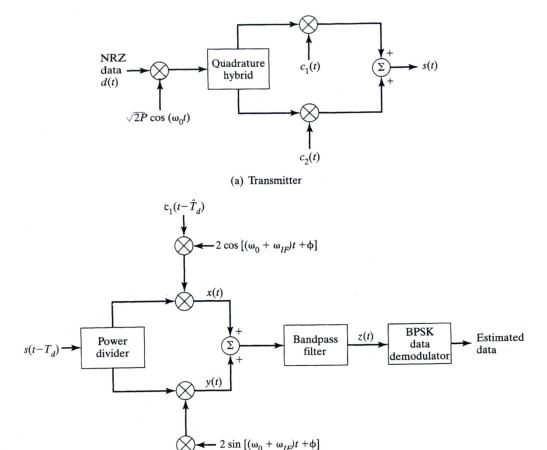

(a) Transmitter

(b) Receiver

FIGURE 9–13   Balanced QPSK direct-sequence spread-spectrum modem. (Note: A quadrature hybrid produces two outputs in phase quadrature with each other.) (Reproduced from Reference [5] with permission.)

When the receiver spreading code replica is correctly phased, the output of the bandpass filter is

$$z(t) = \sqrt{2P}\, d(t - T_d)\, \cos \omega_{\mathrm{IF}} t \tag{9–37}$$

This signal is the recovered data-modulated carrier, which is now demodulated by the BPSK data demodulator.

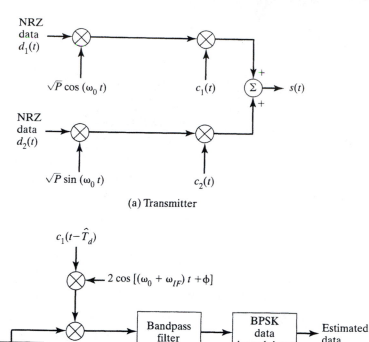

FIGURE 9–14 Dual-channel QPSK direct-sequence spread-spectrum modem: (a) transmitter; (b) receiver. (Reproduced from Reference [5] with permission.)

Another configuration for a QPSK spread-spectrum modem is shown in Figure 9–14. In this case, both the data modulation and the spreading code modulation are different for the in-phase and quadrature channels and the modulation is called [4] *dual-channel QPSK*. The transmitted waveform for dual-channel QPSK is

$$s(t) = \sqrt{P}d_1(t)c_1(t) \cos \omega_0 t + \sqrt{P}\, d_2(t)c_2(t) \sin \omega_0 t \qquad (9\text{--}38)$$

which has total power P. The receiver for this waveform is shown in Figure 9–14b and is similar in operation to the balanced QPSK modem just described. A small but important variation on the signal of (9–38) yields one of the spread-spectrum signals used for the

Tracking and Data Relay Satellite System (TDRSS). This variation is simply to permit the inphase and quadrature channels to have unequal power. Thus the transmitted signal is

$$s(t) = \sqrt{2P_I}\, d_1(t)c_1(t) \cos \omega_0 t$$
$$+ \sqrt{2P_Q}\, d_2(t)c_2(t) \sin \omega_0 t$$

(9–39)

Another variation applicable to all the QPSK spread-spectrum modems is to use offset QPSK for the spreading modulation. This variation is also employed on TDRSS.

The QPSK spread-spectrum modems discussed are the principal types of QPSK modems either currently in use or widely discussed in the literature. Other variations, especially in the details of the implementations, are possible and may be more efficient under some conditions. For example, MSK spread spectrum results by using half-sine and cosine weightings on the chips in the upper and lower arms of Figures 9–12a and 9–13a [5].

9.3.3 Noncoherent Slow-Frequency-Hop Spread Spectrum

In FH spread spectrum each carrier frequency is typically chosen from a set of 2^k frequencies that are spaced approximately the width of the data modulation spectrum apart, although neither condition is absolutely necessary. The spreading code in this case does not directly modulate the data-modulated carrier but is instead used to control the sequence of carrier frequencies. Because the transmitted signal appears as a data-modulated carrier that is hopping from one frequency to the next, this type of spread spectrum is called *frequency-hop spread spectrum (FHSS)*. In the receiver, the frequency hopping is removed by mixing (down-converting) with a local oscillator signal that is hopping synchronously with the received signal. Block diagrams of the transmitter and receiver are shown in Figure 9–15.

Because of the difficulty of building truly coherent frequency synthesizers, most frequency-hop spread-spectrum systems use either noncoherent or differentially coherent data modulation schemes. In the receiver, no effort is made to precisely recover the phase of the data-modulated carrier since it is not required by the demodulator.

A common data modulation for FH systems in M-ary frequency shift keying. Suppose, for example, that the data modulator outputs one of 2^L tones each LT seconds, where T is the duration of one information bit. Usually, these tones are spaced far enough apart so that the transmitted signals are orthogonal. This implies that the data modulator frequency spacing is at least $1/LT$ and that the data modulator output spectral width is approximately $2^L/LT$. Each T_c seconds, the data modulator output is translated to a new frequency by the frequency-hop modulator. Assume that the number of possible carrier frequencies is a power of two, specifically 2^k. When $T_c \geq LT$ the FH system is called a *slow-frequency-hop* system. The output of this spread-spectrum modulator is illustrated in Figure 9–16. In this figure the instantaneous transmitted spectrum is shown as a function of time for a system with $L = 2$ and $k = 3$. Two data bits are collected each $2T = T_s$ seconds and one of four frequencies is generated by the data modulator. This frequency is translated to one of $2^k = 8$ frequency-hop bands by the FH modulator. In this example, a new frequency-hop band is selected after each group of two symbols or four bits is transmitted.

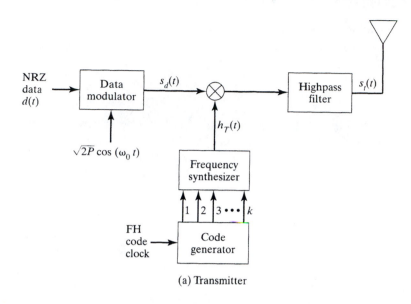

(a) Transmitter

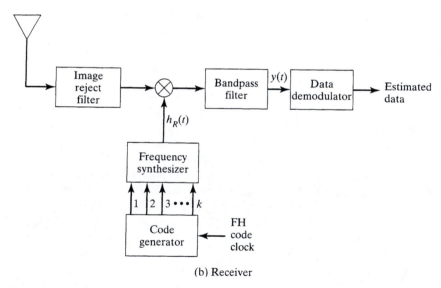

(b) Receiver

FIGURE 9–15 Frequency-hop spread-spectrum modem. (Reproduced from Reference [5] with permission.)

In the receiver, the transmitted signal is down-converted using a local oscillator that outputs the sequence of frequencies 0, $5W_d$, $6W_d$, $2W_d$, $7W_d$, ... and the output of the down-converter is a sequence of tones in the first (lowest) FH band representing the data. The down-converter output is illustrated in Figure 9–16b. In practice the local oscillator frequency is offset from the transmitted frequencies by f_{IF} so that the dehopped output is

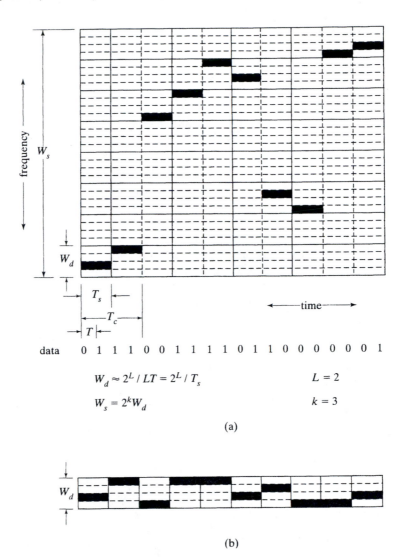

FIGURE 9–16   Pictorial representation of (a) transmitted signal for an *M*-ary FSK slow-frequency-hop spread-spectrum system; (b) receiver down-converter output. (Reproduced from Reference [5] with permission.)

at f_{IF}. This signal can be demodulated using the conventional methods for noncoherent MFSK (i.e., a bank of bandpass filters with energy detectors at their outputs).

A very preliminary estimate of the processing gain of the FH system just described can be obtained by considering a noise jammer. In the absence of frequency hopping, the jammer chooses a bandwidth W_d centered on the proper carrier frequency and forces the receiver operating signal-to-noise ratio to $E_b/N_J = E_b W_d/J$, where J is the average jammer power. When frequency hopping is added, the jammer must place noise in all 2^k frequency-hop bands in order to cause the receiver to have the same performance as before. Thus the jammer requires a total power 2^k times as large as before and the processing gain is $2^k = W_s/W_d$.

9.3.4 Noncoherent Fast-Frequency-Hop Spread Spectrum

In contrast to the slow-FH system, where the hop-frequency band changes more slowly than symbols come out of the data modulator, the hop-frequency band can change many times per symbol in a *fast-frequency-hop (FFH)* system. A significant benefit achieved when fast frequency hop is used is that frequency diversity gain is achieved on each transmitted symbol. This is particularly beneficial in a partial-band jamming environment.

A representation of the transmitted signal for a fast-frequency-hop system is illustrated in Figure 9–17. The output of the MFSK modulator is one of 2^L tones as before, but now this tone is subdivided into K chips. After each chip, the MFSK modulator output is hopped to a different frequency. Since the chip duration T_c is shorter than the data modulator output symbol duration T_s, the minimum tone spacing for orthogonal signals is now $1/T_c = K/LT$. The receiver frequency-dehopping operation functions in exactly the same way as before. The output of the down-conversion operation is shown in Figure 9–17b.

The data demodulator can operate in several different modes in a fast-frequency-hop system. One mode is to make a decision on each frequency-hop chip as it is received and to make an estimate of the data modulator output based on all K chip decisions. The decision rule could be a simple majority vote. Another mode would be to calculate the likelihood of each data modulator output symbol as a function of the total signal received over K chips and to choose the largest. A receiver that calculates the likelihood that each symbol was transmitted is optimum in the sense that minimum error probability is achieved for a given E_b/N_0. Each of these possible operating modes performs differently and has different complexity. The spread-spectrum system designer must choose the mode of operation that best solves the particular problem being considered. It will be shown later that fast frequency hop is a very useful technique in either a fading-signal environment or in a partial band-jamming environment, and its use with error correction coding is particularly convenient.

9.3.5 Hybrid Direct-Sequence/Frequency-Hop Spread Spectrum

A third method for spectrum spreading is to employ both direct-sequence and frequency-hop spreading techniques in a hybrid direct-sequence/frequency-hop system. One reason for using hybrid techniques is that some of the advantages of both types of systems are combined in a single system. Hybrid techniques are used in military spread-spectrum systems. Many methods of combining DS and FH spreading are possible. The method discussed here was selected because of its simplicity as an example of a hybrid system.

Figure 9–18 illustrates a hybrid DS/FH spread-spectrum modem that employs differential binary PSK data modulation. Because noncoherent frequency hopping is used,

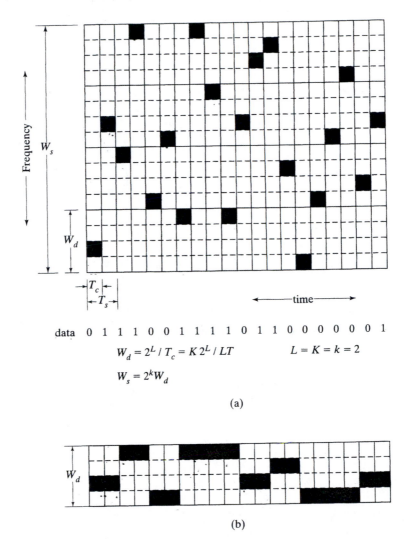

data 0 1 1 1 0 0 1 1 1 1 0 1 1 0 0 0 0 0 0 1

$$W_d = 2^L / T_c = K 2^L / LT \qquad L = K = k = 2$$

$$W_s = 2^k W_d$$

(a)

(b)

FIGURE 9–17 Pictorial representation of (a) transmitted signal for an M-ary FSK fast frequency hop spread-spectrum system; (b) receiver down-converter output. (Reproduced from Reference [5] with permission.)

the data modulation must be either noncoherent or differentially coherent. As discussed earlier, DPSK modulation requires a differential data encoding prior to carrier modulation as shown. With this encoding the sampled output of the differential demodulator is the original data sequence. In Figure 9–18a the DPSK modulated carrier is first direct sequence spread by multiplication with the DS spreading waveform $c(t)$ and then frequency hopped through up-conversion using the sequence of FH tones.

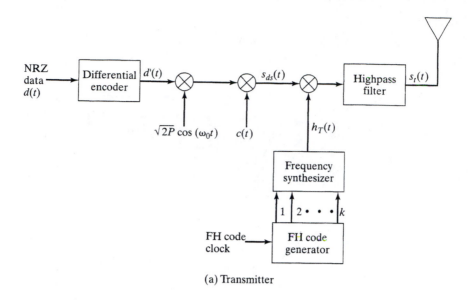

(a) Transmitter

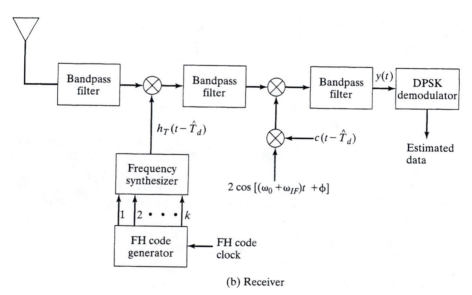

(b) Receiver

FIGURE 9–18 Hybrid direct-sequence/frequency-hop spread-spectrum modem.
(Reproduced from Reference [5] with permission.)

At the receiver, essentially the reverse set of operations takes place, as shown in Figure 9–18b. Two codes must now be acquired and tracked unless they are related to each other.

EXAMPLE 9–3

Consider the design of various types of spread spectrum systems for a channel bandwidth of 2 MHz and data rate of 20 kbps.

(a)   For DSSS with BPSK spreading and BPSK data modulation, we have approximately

$$B_{\text{chan}} \cong \frac{2}{T_c} + \frac{2}{T_b} = 2\,\text{MHz} \approx 2R_c + 0.04 \times 10^6 \text{ or } R_c = 0.98\,\text{Mchip/s}$$

(b)   For balanced QPSK DSSS, we have

$$B_{\text{chan}} \cong \frac{2}{T_c} + \frac{1}{T_b} = 2\,\text{MHz} \approx 2R_c + 0.02 \times 10^6 \text{ or } R_c = 0.99\,\text{Mchips/s}$$

(c)   For slow FHSS with noncoherent FSK data modulation, we have from (4–185) that the modulated data bandwidth on each hop is

$$B_{\text{data}} = \frac{2M}{\log_2 M} R_b$$

For $M = 2$ and 4, $B_{\text{data}} = 80$ kHz, giving

$$\text{Number of hop frequencies} = \frac{2 \times 10^6}{8 \times 10^4} = 25$$

The duration of a hop should be much longer than the inverse bandwidth of the sinusoidal burst representing a symbol, which is 0.05 ms for the binary case. Thus a hop duration of 0.5 ms or more would safely fall into the slow FHSS category.

   If the modulation is DPSK, $B_{\text{data}} = 2R_b$, giving 50 hopping frequencies. $T_b = 50$ μsec, giving a hop time of about 0.5 ms for slow FHSS (10 bits per hop). Note that for DPSK, one bit per hop will be lost due to synchronization. This could be a known bit, which cuts the data rate by 9/10 or increases the data bandwidth by 10/9, which means the number of hopping frequencies is 90 to account for synchronization on each hop.

9.4   COMPLEX-ENVELOPE REPRESENTATION OF SPREAD-SPECTRUM SYSTEMS

All of the spread-spectrum systems discussed earlier can be conveniently represented mathematically using complex-envelope notation. This common notation is useful not only as an aid in understanding the spreading/despreading process but also as an analytical and simulation tool. Recall from Section 2.3 that any bandpass signal $v(t)$ whose Fourier spectrum is centered at frequency ω_0 can be expressed as

$$v(t) = \text{Re}\left[\bar{v}(t)e^{j\omega_0 t}\right] \tag{9–40}$$

where $\tilde{v}(t)$ is the complex envelope of $v(t)$ and is a complex function of time and Re [·] is the real part of the argument. All the signal processing steps required in spread-spectrum systems (i.e., linear filtering and mixing) can be mathematically modeled as operations on the complex envelope of the signal of interest.

A generic complex envelope model of a spread-spectrum modem is illustrated in Figure 9–19. In this figure, all signals are complex functions of time, double lines present real and imaginary (in-phase and quadrature) paths, and the mixers perform complex multiplications. The actual (real) transmitted signal is $s(t) = \text{Re} \, [\tilde{s}(t)e^{j\omega_0 t}]$, where power amplification has been ignored, and $\tilde{s}(t) = \tilde{d}(t)\tilde{c}(t)$. In writing this last expression, it has been assumed that the transmitter mixing operation is also part of an up-conversion process, so that $\omega_0 = \omega_1 + \omega_2$ where ω_1 and ω_2 are the actual center frequencies at the data modulator and spreading code generator outputs.

The receiver input $\tilde{r}(t)$ is the delayed transmitter output $\tilde{s}(t - T_d)$ plus interference $\tilde{u}(t)$ plus thermal noise $\tilde{n}(t)$. In the receiver, the mixing operations are assumed to be part of the receiver down-conversion chain. Since the difference frequency components of the mixer outputs are required, the complex conjugate of the reference signal envelopes are used [6] as the mixer inputs. The first receiver mixing operation accounts for all frequency and phase differences between the received carrier (includes Doppler effects) and

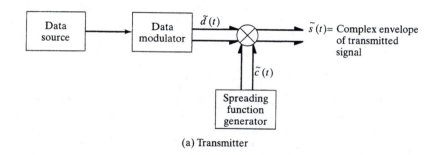

(a) Transmitter

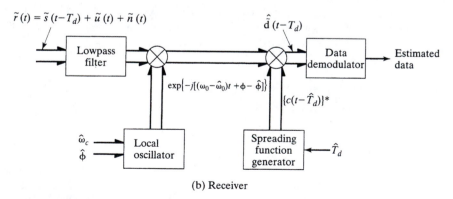

(b) Receiver

FIGURE 9–19 Generic complex-envelope model of spread-spectrum modem: (a) transmitter; (b) receiver. (Reproduced from Reference [6] with permission.)

the local reference carrier. If the system is coherent, a carrier tracking loop will force $\hat{\omega}_0 = \omega_0$ and $\hat{\phi} = \phi$ so that this complex-envelope multiplication has no effect. The second receiver mixing operation is the spread-spectrum despreading operation. In general, the input to the data demodulator is

$$
\begin{aligned}
\hat{\tilde{d}}(t - T_d) = \tilde{d}(t - T_d)\tilde{c}(t - T_d)\tilde{c}*(t - \hat{T}_d) \\
\times \exp\{-j[(\omega_0 - \hat{\omega}_0)t + \phi - \hat{\phi}]\} \\
+ \tilde{u}(t)\tilde{c}*(t - \hat{T}_d) \exp\{-j[(\omega_0 - \hat{\omega}_0)t + \phi - \hat{\phi}]\} \\
+ \tilde{n}(t)\tilde{c}*(t - \hat{T}_d) \exp\{-j[(\omega_0 - \hat{\omega}_0)t + \phi - \hat{\phi}]\}
\end{aligned}
\tag{9-41}
$$

where the input lowpass filter is assumed to have a bandwidth sufficiently wide to pass all signals without distortion.

This representation is completely general and, with proper selection of $\tilde{d}(t)$ and $\tilde{c}(t)$, can be used for any direct-sequence or frequency-hop spread-spectrum system with any type of data modulation. Table 9–1 gives the complex envelope for a number of the most common digital modulation types that can be used for either the data modulation or the spreading modulation. In this table, $p_T(t)$ and $p_{2T}(t)$ are unit pulses of duration T and $2T$ seconds, respectively. The variable T is the information bit duration when these envelopes are used for data modulation and the spreading code chip duration T_c when they are used for the spreading modulation.

EXAMPLE 9–4

Calculate the complex envelope of the data demodulator input for a fully coherent spread-spectrum modem that uses BPSK data modulation and MSK spreading modulation when the only interference is a single-tone jammer that is not at the system carrier frequency.

Solution: The complex envelope of the data modulation is

$$
\tilde{d}(t) = \sum_n d_n p_T(t - nT)
\tag{9-42}
$$

and the complex envelope of the spreading modulation is

$$
\tilde{c}(t) = \sum_m p_{T_c}(t - mT_c) \exp\left[j\left(c_m \frac{\pi t}{2T_c} + x_m\right)\right]
\tag{9-43}
$$

so that the transmitted signal is

$$
\begin{aligned}
\tilde{s}(t) &= \sqrt{2P}\, \tilde{d}(t)\tilde{c}(t) \\
&= \sqrt{2P} \sum_n \sum_m d_n p_T(t - nT) p_{T_c}(t - mT_c) \\
&\quad \times \exp\left[j\left(c_m \frac{\pi t}{2T_c} + x_m\right)\right]
\end{aligned}
\tag{9-44}
$$

TABLE 9–1   Complex Envelope of Common Digital Modulation Types

Modulation Type	Complex Envelope – $\tilde{v}(t)$
Binary phase-shift keying (BPSK)	$\tilde{v}(t) = \sum_n a_n p_T(t - nT)$ $a_n \in \{+1, -1\}$
Quaternary phase-shift keying (QPSK)	$\tilde{v}(t) = \sum_n p_{2T}(t - 2nT) \exp(j\beta_n)$ $\beta_n \in \left\{0, \dfrac{\pi}{2}, \pi, \dfrac{3\pi}{2}\right\}$
Offset quaternary phase-shift keying (OQPSK)	$\tilde{v}(t) = \sum_n p_T(t - nT) \exp(j\beta_n)$ $\beta_n = \beta_{n-1} + a_n \dfrac{\pi}{2}$ $a_n \in \{+1, 0, -1\}$
M-ary phase-shift keying (MPSK)	$\tilde{v}(t) = \sum_n p_{mT}(t - nmT) \exp(j\beta_n)$ $m = \log_2 M$ $\beta_n \in \{\beta_1, \beta_2, \cdots, \beta_m\}$
Binary frequency-shift keying (BFSK)	$\tilde{v}(t) = \sum_n p_T(t - nT) \exp[j(\omega_n t + \phi_n)]$ $\omega_n \in \{\omega_1, \omega_2\}$ $0 \le \phi_n \le 2\pi$
Minimum-shift keying (MSK)	$\tilde{v}(t) = \sum_n p_T(t - nT) \exp\left[j\left(a_n \dfrac{\pi t}{2T} + x_n\right)\right]$ $a_n \in \{+1, -1\}$ $x_n = x_{n-1} + (a_{n-1} - a_n) \dfrac{n\pi}{2}$
M-ary frequency-shift keying (MFSK)	$\tilde{v}(t) = \sum_n p_T(t - nT) \exp\{j(\omega_n t + \phi_n)\}$ $\omega_n \in \{\omega_1, \omega_2, \cdots, \omega_m\}$ $0 \le \phi_n \le 2\pi$

The transmitted signal power is P. The envelope of the jammer is

$$\tilde{u}(t) = \sqrt{2J} \exp(j \Delta\omega\, t) \tag{9–45}$$

where the offset frequency is $\Delta\omega$ and the jammer power is J.

Referring to Figure 9–19, and assuming perfect carrier tracking, the complex envelope at the input to the data demodulator is

$$\hat{\tilde{d}}(t - T_d) = \tilde{s}(t - T_d)\tilde{c}^*(t - \hat{T}_d)$$

$$+ \sqrt{2J}\, \tilde{c}^*(t - \hat{T}_d) \exp(j\Delta\omega\, t)$$

$$= \sqrt{2P} \sum_n d_n p_T(t - T_d - nT)$$

$$\times \sum_{n'} \sum_m p_{T_c}(t - T_d - n'T_c) p_{T_c}(t - \hat{T}_d - mT_c) \tag{9-46}$$

$$\times \exp\left\{ j\left[c_{n'} \frac{\pi}{2T_c}(t - T_d) + x_{n'} \right] - j\left[c_m \frac{\pi}{2T_c}(t - \hat{T}_d) + x_m \right] \right\}$$

$$+ \sqrt{2J} \sum_{m'} p_{T_c}(t - \hat{T}_d - m'T_c)$$

$$\times \exp\left\{ -j\left[c_{m'} \frac{\pi}{2T_c}(t - \hat{T}_d) + x_{m'} \right] + j\,\Delta\omega\,t \right\}$$

If perfect spreading code tracking is also assumed ($\hat{T}_d = T_d$), $x_{n'} = x_m$ then

$$\hat{\tilde{d}}(t - T_d) = \sqrt{2P} \sum_n d_n p_T(t - T_d - nT) + \sqrt{2J} \sum_{m'} p_{T_c}(t - \hat{T}_d - m'T_c)$$

$$\times \exp\left\{ -j\left[c_{m'} \frac{\pi}{2T_c}(t - \hat{T}_d) + x_{m'} \right] + j\,\Delta\omega\,t \right\} \tag{9-47}$$

and it is seen that the MSK spreading has been entirely removed from the desired signal and that the jamming tone has been MSK modulated via the despreading operation.

EXAMPLE 9–5

Calculate the complex envelope of the data demodulator input for a slow-frequency-hop spread-spectrum modem that uses differential binary PSK data modulation.

Solution: The envelope of the data modulation is the same as in Example 9–4, except that the differentially encoded data sequence is used. The envelope of the spreading modulation is

$$\tilde{c}(t) = \sum_m p_{T_c}(t - mT_c) \exp[j(\omega_m t + \phi_m)] \tag{9-48}$$

Assume that the receiver is able to track the frequency of the received signal perfectly using an AFC loop, but that no attempt is made to estimate the random phase changes associated with each frequency hop. Thus

$$\hat{\tilde{d}}(t - T_d) = \tilde{d}(t - T_d)\tilde{c}(t - T_d)\tilde{c}^*(t - \hat{T}_d) \exp[j(\phi - \hat{\phi})]$$

$$= \sqrt{2P} \sum_n d_n p_T(t - T_d - nT) \sum_m \sum_{m'} p_{T_c}(t - T_d - mT_c)$$

$$\times p_{T_c}(t - \hat{T}_d - m'T_c) \exp\{ +j[\omega_m(t - T_d) + \phi_m] \tag{9-49}$$

$$- j[\omega_{m'}(t - \hat{T}_d) + \phi_{m'}] \}$$

If perfect code tracking is assumed ($\hat{T}_d = T_d$),

$$\hat{\bar{d}}(t - T_d) = \sqrt{2P} \sum_n d_n p_T(t - T_d - nT) \sum_m p_{T_c}(t - \hat{T}_d - m T_c) \exp(j\theta_m) \quad (9\text{--}50)$$

where $\theta_m = \phi_m - \phi_{m'}$ is the difference between the transmitter and receiver frequency-hop phases.

9.5 GENERATION AND PROPERTIES OF PSEUDORANDOM SEQUENCES

The implementation of spread-spectrum systems requires the generation of periodic spreading codes at both the transmitter and receiver. Maximal-length shift-register sequences (or *m*-sequences) were introduced in Section 2.8.4. In this section, we look at two configurations for generation of such sequences. We then state several properties of *m*-sequences. Last, we look at generation of several sequences, Gold, Kasami, and Quaternary codes, with special correlation properties.

9.5.1 Definitions and Mathematical Background

It is convenient to represent a sequence of binary digits $\ldots, b_{-2}, b_{-1}, b_0, b_1, b_2, \ldots$ by a polynomial $b(D) = \cdots + b_{-2}D^{-2} + b_{-1}D^{-1} + b_0 + b_1 D + b_2 D^2 + \cdots$. The delay operator D implies simply that the binary symbol that multiplies D^j occurs during the *j*th time interval of the sequence. Because the code is periodic, $b_n = b_{N+n}$ for any n. The spreading waveform $c(t)$ derived from this spreading code is also periodic with period $T = NT_c$ and is specified by

$$c(t) = \sum_{n=-\infty}^{\infty} a_n p_{T_c}(t - nT_c) \quad (9\text{--}51)$$

where $a_n = (-1)^{b_n}$ and $p_{T_c}(t)$ is a unit pulse beginning at 0 and ending at T_c. The waveform $c(t)$ is deterministic, so that its *autocorrelation function* is defined by [7]

$$R_c(\tau) = \frac{1}{T} \int_0^T c(t)c(t + \tau) \, dt \quad (9\text{--}52)$$

Since $c(t)$ is periodic with period T, it follows that $R_c(\tau)$ is also periodic with period T. Consider two different spreading waveforms $c(t)$ and $c'(t)$. The *cross-correlation function* of these two deterministic waveforms is

$$R_{cc'}(\tau) = \frac{1}{T} \int_0^T c'(t)c(t + \tau) \, dt \quad (9\text{--}53)$$

where it has been assumed that both waveforms have the same period T. The cross-correlation function is also periodic with period T.

The variable τ in (9–52) and (9–53) can assume any value. That is, τ is not constrained to be an integral multiple of T_c. Substituting (9–51) into (9–53) yields

$$R_{cc'}(\tau) = \frac{1}{T} \sum_m \sum_n a_m a'_n \int_0^T p_{T_c}(t - mT_c) p_{T_c}(t + \tau - nT_c) \, dt \qquad (9\text{–}54)$$

The integral (9–54) is nonzero only when $p(t - mT_c)$ and $p(t + \tau - nT_c)$ overlap. The delay τ can be expressed as $\tau = kT_c + \tau_\epsilon$, where $0 \le \tau_\epsilon < T_c$. Using this substitution, the pulses overlap only for $n = k + m$ and $n = k + m + 1$, so that (9–54) becomes

$$R_{cc'}(\tau) = R_{cc'}(k, \tau_\epsilon)$$

$$= \frac{1}{N} \sum_{m=0}^{N-1} a_m a'_{k+m} \frac{1}{T_c} \int_0^{T_c - \tau_\epsilon} p_{T_c}(\lambda) p_{T_c}(\lambda + \tau_\epsilon) \, d\lambda \qquad (9\text{–}55)$$

$$+ \frac{1}{N} \sum_{m=0}^{N-1} a_m a'_{k+m+1} \frac{1}{T_c} \int_{T_c - \tau_\epsilon}^{T_c} p_{T_c}(\lambda) p_{T_c}(\lambda - T_c + \tau_\epsilon) \, d\lambda$$

where the substitution $\lambda = t - mT_c$ has also been employed. The *discrete periodic cross-correlation function* of two codes $b(D)$ and $b'(D)$ is defined by [8]

$$\theta_{bb'}(k) = \frac{1}{N} \sum_{n=0}^{N-1} a_n a'_{n+k} \qquad (9\text{–}56)$$

where $a_n = (-1)^{b_n}$. Using this definition, the cross-correlation function $R_{cc'}(\tau)$ becomes

$$R_{cc'}(\tau) = R_{cc'}(k, \tau_\epsilon)$$

$$= \left(1 - \frac{\tau_\epsilon}{T_c}\right) \theta_{bb'}(k) + \frac{\tau_\epsilon}{T_c} \theta_{bb'}(k + 1) \qquad (9\text{–}57)$$

This expression is often convenient since the theory used to analyze code sequences yields results exclusively in terms of unit delays; that is, $\theta_{bb'}(k)$ is calculated rather than $R_{cc'}(\tau)$. The discrete periodic cross-correlation function can be calculated by representing the sequences $b(D)$ and $b'(D)$ as binary vectors $\mathbf{b}$ and $\mathbf{b}'$ of length N. A delay of k time units of the original sequence is represented as a cyclic shift of k time units of the vector representation. The kth cyclic shift of $\mathbf{b}$ is represented by $\mathbf{b}(k)$. Using this notation, the function $\theta_{bb'}(k) = (N_A - N_D)/N$, where N_A is the number of places in which $\mathbf{b}(0)$ agrees and N_D the number of places in which $\mathbf{b}(0)$ disagrees with $\mathbf{b}'(k)$. Equivalently, N_A is the number of zeros and N_D the number of ones in the modulo-2 sum of $\mathbf{b}(0)$ and $\mathbf{b}(k)$. The *discrete periodic autocorrelation function* is denoted by $\theta_b(k)$ and is defined by (9–56) with $a'_n = a_n$. When the periodic autocorrelation function is used in place of the periodic cross-correlation function in (9–57), the result is the autocorrelation function

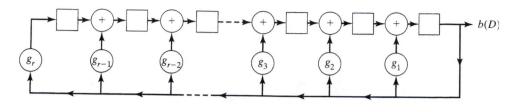

FIGURE 9–20 High-speed linear feedback shift-register generator. (Reproduced from Reference [5] with permission.)

$$R_c(\tau) = \left(1 - \frac{\tau_\epsilon}{T_c}\right)\theta_b(k) + \frac{\tau_\epsilon}{T_c}\theta_b(k+1), \quad \tau_\epsilon \le T_c \tag{9-58}$$

The calculation of $R_c(\tau)$ is important in analyzing spread-spectrum system performance.

9.5.2 *m*-Sequence Generator Configurations

Shown in Figure 9–20 is a general feedback shift-register configuration. The feedback connections are determined by the polynomial

$$g(D) = 1 + g_1D + g_2D^2 + \cdots + g_rD^r \tag{9-59a}$$

and the output is

$$b(D) = \frac{a(D)}{g(D)} \tag{9-59b}$$

where D is the unit-delay variable introduced in Chapter 7 with powers denoting multiples of delay where the g_is are from the set $\{0, 1\}$ and $a(D)$ represents the initial shift register state [5]. It can be shown that if $g(D)$ is a primitive polynomial,[4] the sequence generated by the shift register is maximal length which is deduced as follows. Each possible loading of the shift-register stages is called a state for the shift register. Since there are r stages and each one can contain a 0 or a 1, it follows that the number of states is 2^r. However, one of these states is the all-zero state. If the shift register happens to end up in this state, then it will stay in the all zero state. Thus, the maximum number of states for the feedback configuration is $2^r - 1$, which is also the maximum length of the output sequence before repeating. It can also be argued that the shift-register configuration of Figure 9–20 will never reach the all-zero state. The all-zero state would be preceded by the one where all registers except the rightmost one contain zeros. The single 1 in the rightmost register would be fed back to some other register. Since all g_is cannot be 0, the all-zero state is never reached. Thus the maximum period is $2^r - 1$. It can be significantly less than this without proper feedback connections [i.e., if $g(D)$ is not a primitive polynomial].

---

[4]$g(D)$ is a primitive polynomial if the smallest integer n for which $g(D)$ divides $D^n + 1$ is $n = 2^r - 1$.

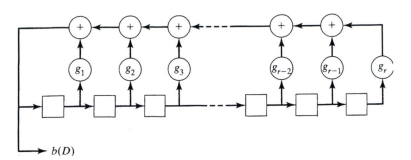

FIGURE 9–21   Linear feedback shift-register whose output satisfies the same recurrence relationship as the generator of Figure 9–20. (Reproduced from Reference [5] with permission.)

An alternative feedback configuration is shown in Figure 9–21. It can be shown to generate the same m-sequence as the configuration shown in Figure 9–20. The configuration chosen for a particular application depends on such things as the speed at which the hardware must operate and whether delayed outputs are also required. Delayed outputs for all delays up to r are available from the configuration of Figure 9–21 but not from the configuration of Figure 9–20. The configuration of Figure 9–20, however, can function at higher speeds than that of Figure 9–21 since there is less propagation delay in the feedback path.

9.5.3   Properties of *m*-Sequences

Maximal-length sequences have a number of properties that are useful in their application to spread-spectrum systems. Some of these properties are given here [8].

PROPERTY I: *A maximal-length sequence contains one more one than zero. The number of ones in the sequence is $\frac{1}{2}(N + 1)$.*

Proof: *Consider the generator of Figure 9–20, where the rightmost symbol of the shift register state is the output symbol. The shift register passes through all possible* nonzero *states. Of these states, $2^{r-1} = \frac{1}{2}(N + 1)$ have a one in the rightmost position, and $2^{r-1} - 1$ have a zero in the rightmost position. Thus there is one more one than zero in the output sequence.*

PROPERTY II: *The modulo-2 sum of an m-sequence and any phase shift of the same sequence is another phase[5] of the same m-sequence* (shift-and-add property).

Proof: *See [8]. The proof is beyond the scope of this text.*

PROPERTY III: *If a window of width r is slid along the sequence for N shifts, each r-tuple except the all-zero r-tuple will appear exactly once.*

---

[5]A phase of the sequence is any cyclic shift.

Proof: Consider the shift register generator of Figure 9–21. The sequence b(D) passes through the shift register of this generator so that the window of width r is simply the state of the shift register. Since the shift register passes through all nonzero states exactly once, all possible r-tuples, except all 0s, appear in the window exactly once.

PROPERTY IV: *The periodic autocorrelation function $\theta_b(k)$ is 2-valued and is given by*

$$\theta_b(k) = \begin{cases} 1.0, & k = lN \\ -\dfrac{1}{N}, & k \neq lN \end{cases} \tag{9–60}$$

where l is any integer and N is the sequence period.

Proof: The value of the periodic autocorrelation function $\theta_b(k)$ is $(N_A - N_D)/N$, where N_A is the number of zeros and N_D is the number of ones in the modulo-2 sum of the sequence **b** and the kth cyclic shift of **b**. For $k = lN$, the kth cyclic shift of **b** is identical to **b**, since the sequence period is N, so that the modulo-2 sum contains all zeros and $N_A = N$, $N_D = 0$, and $\theta_b(lN) = N/N = 1.0$. For $k \neq lN$, the modulo-2 sum is some phase of the original sequence by Property II. Then, by Property I, there is one more one than zero in the modulo-2 sum, so that $N_A - N_D = -1$ and $\theta_b(k) = -1/N$.

PROPERTY V: *Define a* run *as a subsequence of identical symbols within the m-sequence. The length of this subsequence is the length of the run. Then, for any m-sequence, there are*

1. *One run of 1s of length r.*
2. *One run of 0s of length r − 1.*
3. *One run of 1s and one run of 0s of length r − 2.*
4. *Two runs of 1s and two runs of 0s of length r − 3.*
5. *Four runs of 1s and four runs of 0s of length r − 4.*

$$\vdots$$

r. 2^{r-3} *runs of 1s and* 2^{r-3} *runs of 0s of length 1.*

Proof [8]: Consider the shift register of Figure 9–21. There can be no run of 1s having length $1 \geq r$ since this would require that the all-ones shift register state be followed by another all-ones state. This cannot occur since each shift-register state occurs once and only once during N cycles. Thus there is a single run of r consecutive ones, and this run is preceded by a 0 and followed by a 0.

A run of r − 1 ones must be preceded by and followed by a 0. This requires that the shift-register state, which is r − 1 1s followed by a 0, be followed immediately by the state that is a 0 followed by r − 1 1s. These two states are also passed through in the generation of the run of r 1s, where they are separated by the all-ones state. Since each state occurs only once, there can be no run of r − 1 ones. A run of r − 1 0s must be pre-

ceded by and followed by 1s. Thus the shift register must pass through the state that is a
1 followed by r − 1 0s. This state occurs only once, so there is a single run of r − 1 0s.

Now consider a run of k 1s where $1 \leq k < r - 1$. Each run of k 1s must be preceded
by and followed by a 0. Thus the shift register must pass through the state that is a 0 followed by k 1s followed by a 0, with the r − k − 2 remaining positions taking on arbitrary
values. There are 2^{r-k-2} possible ways to complete these remaining positions in the shift
register, so there are 2^{r-k-2} runs of k 1s. Similarly, there are 2^{r-k-2} runs of k 0s. The last
item (r) follows with $k = 1$.

9.5.4   Power Spectrum of *m*-Sequences

The power spectrum of the spreading waveform c(t) is frequently used in the analysis of
the performance of spread-spectrum systems. This power spectrum is easily calculated
using the Wiener–Khintchine theorem and Property IV for maximal-length spreading
waveforms. The power spectrum of c(t) is the Fourier transform of the autocorrelation
function $R_c(\tau)$, which is given by

$$R_c(\tau) = \begin{cases} \left(1 - \dfrac{|\tau|}{T_c}\right)\left(1 + \dfrac{1}{N}\right) - \dfrac{1}{N}, & |\tau| \leq T_c \\[2ex] -\dfrac{1}{N} & T_c < |\tau| \leq \dfrac{N-1}{2}T_c \end{cases} \tag{9-61}$$

Since $\theta_b(k)$ of (9–60) is periodic, $R_c(\tau)$ is also periodic with period $T = NT_c$. Thus (9–61)
defines one complete period of $R_c(\tau)$. The autocorrelation function $R_c(\tau)$ is illustrated in
Figure 9–22.

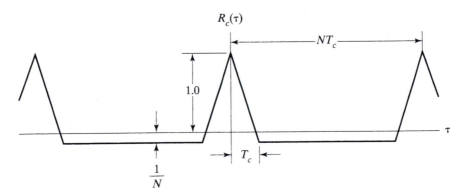

FIGURE 9–22   Autocorrelation function for a maximal-length sequence with chip
duration T_c and period NT_c.

The power spectrum is found by taking the Fourier transform of (9–61) and using (2–40). The result is

$$S_c(f) = \sum_{m=-\infty}^{\infty} P_m \delta(f - mf_0) \tag{9–62}$$

where $P_0 = 1/N^2$, $P_m = [(N + 1)/N^2] \operatorname{sinc}^2(m/N)$, $m \neq 0$, and $f_0 = 1/NT_c$. The power spectrum as a function of f is illustrated in Figure 9–23. This power spectrum consists of discrete spectral lines at all harmonics of $1/NT_c$. The envelope of the amplitudes of these lines is given by

$$[(N + 1)/N^2] \operatorname{sinc}^2(fT_c)$$

except for the dc term, which has an amplitude $1/N^2$. Note that the ordinate in Figure 9–23 is absolute and is not decibels.

Suppose that the m-sequence $c(t)$ is used to biphase modulate a sinusoidal carrier having power P and frequency f_0. The modulated carrier is

$$s(t) = \sqrt{2P} \, c(t) \cos 2\pi f_0 t \tag{9–63a}$$

The power spectrum of this modulated carrier is the convolution of the power spectrum of the carrier and the power spectrum of the spreading code. Thus

$$S_s(f) = S_c(f) * \frac{P}{2} \delta(f - f_0) + S_c(f) * \frac{P}{2} \delta(f + f_0) \tag{9–63b}$$

and the resultant power spectrum is a translation of the discrete spectrum $S_c(f)$ upward and downward by a frequency f_0. In most spread-spectrum systems the carrier is randomly modulated by data as well as the spreading code. For this reason, the transmitted spectrum is continuous and not discrete.

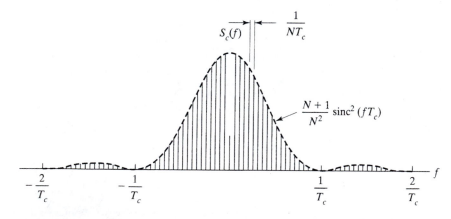

FIGURE 9–23 Power spectrum of a maximal-length sequence with chip duration T_c and period NT_c.

9.5.5 Tables of Polynomials Yielding *m*-Sequences

It is often necessary to design circuits that generate *m*-sequences having a particular number of stages. Since finding the primitive polynomials used to generate these sequences is difficult, a number of authors have generated tables of primitive polynomials for quick reference. In particular, Peterson and Weldon [9] have an extensive table of polynomials in their Appendix C.

Table 9–2 is a list of primitive polynomials of all degrees up to 40 and degrees 61 and 89. All polynomials in Table 9–2 are primitive. Each entry in brackets represents one primitive polynomial as a series of octal numbers. The octal number gives the coefficients of $g(D)$ beginning with g_0 on the right and proceeding to g_r in the last nonzero position on the left.

The entries followed by an asterisk correspond to circuit implementation with only two feedback connections. Two feedback connection implementations are very useful for high-speed applications.

EXAMPLE 9–6

The table contains the entry [367] for a degree 7 primitive polynomial. Expanding the octal entry 367 into binary form yields

3	6	7	octal
0 1 1	1 1 0	1 1 1	binary
$g_7\ g_6$	$g_5\ g_4\ g_3$	$g_2\ g_1\ g_0$	coefficient

so that

$$g(D) = 1 + D + D^2 + D^4 + D^5 + D^6 + D^7$$

The shift generator can be either the form of Figure 9–20 or 9–21.

EXAMPLE 9–7

Consider the sequence generated by the polynomial corresponding to the entry 13 of Table 9–2. The primitive polynomial is $g(D) = 1 + D + D^3$ and its reciprocal is $D^3 g(1/D) = D^3 + D^2 + 1$. Using the configuration of Figure 9–20 with an initial load of $a(D) = 1$, the output sequence for $g(D)$ is, by the polynomial long division, $1 + D + D^2 + D^4 + D^7 + \cdots$. The output corresponding to the same initial state for the reciprocal polynomial[6] is, again by long division, $1 + D^2 + D^3 + D^4 + D^7 + \cdots$.

---

[6]The reciprocal polynomial corresponding to $g(D)$ is defined by $g_r(D) = D^r g(1/D)$.

TABLE 9–2   Primitive Polynomials Having Degree $r \leq 89$

Degree	Octal Representation of Generator Polynomial (g_0 on right to g_r on left)
2	[7]*
3	[13]*
4	[23]*
5	[45]*,[75],[67]
6	[103]*,[147],[155]
7	[211]*,[217],[235],[367],[277],[325],[203]*,[313],[345]
8	[435],[551],[747],[453],[545],[537],[703],[543]
9	[1021]*,[1131],[1461],[1423],[1055],[1167],[1541],[1333], [1605],[1751],[1743],[1617],[1553],[1157]
10	[2011]*,[2415],[3771],[2157],[3515],[2773],[2033],[2443], [2461],[3023],[3543],[2745],[2431],[3177]
11	[4005]*,[4445],[4215],[4055],[6015],[7413],[4143],[4563], [4053],[5023],[5623],[4577],[6233],[6673]
12	[10123],[15647],[16533],[16047],[11015],[14127],[17673], [13565],[15341],[15053],[15621],[15321],[11417],[13505]
13	[20033],[23261],[24623],[23517],[30741],[21643],[30171], [21277],[27777],[35051],[34723],[34047],[32535],[31425]
14	[42103],[43333],[51761],[40503],[77141],[62677],[44103], [45145],[76303],[64457],[57231],[64167],[60153],[55753]
15	[100003]*,[102043],[110013],[102067],[104307],[100317], [177775] ,[103451],[110075],[102061],[114725],[103251], [100021]*,[100201]*
16	[210013],[234313],[233303],[307107],[307527],[306357],[201735], [272201],[242413],[270155],[302157],[210205],[305667],[236107]
17	[400011]*,[400017],[400431],[525251],[410117],[400731], [411335] ,[444257],[600013],[403555],[525327],[411077], [400041]*,[400101]*
18	[1000201]*,[1000247],[100224],[1002441],[1100045], [1000407] ,[1003011],[1020121],[1101005],[1000077], [1001361] ,[1001567],[1001727],[1002777]
19	[2000047],[2000641],[2001441],[2000107],[2000077], [2000157],[2000175],[2000257],[2000677],[2000737], [2001557],[2001637],[2005775],[2006677]
20	[4000011]*,[4001051],[4004515],[6000031],[4442235]
21	[10000005]*,[10040205],[10020045],[10040315],[10000635], [10103075] ,[10050335],[10002135],[17000075]
22	[20000003]*,[20001043],[22222223],[25200127],[20401207], [20430607] ,[20070217]

TABLE 9–2   *Continued*

Degree	Octal Representation of Generator Polynomial (g_0 on right to g_r on left)
23	[40000041]*,[40404041],[40000063],[40010061],[50000241],[40220151], [40006341],[40405463],[401103271],[41224445],[40435651]
24	[100000207],[125245661],[113763063]
25	[200000011]*,[200000017],[204000051],[200010031], [200402017] ,[252001251],[201014171],[204204057], [200005535] ,[200014731]
26	[400000107],[430216473],[402365755],[426225667], [510664323],[473167545],[411335571]
27	[1000000047],[1001007071],[1020024171],[1102210617],[1250025757], [1257242631],[1020560103],[1112225171],[1035530241]
28	[2000000011]*,[2104210431],[2000025051],[2020006031], [2002502115] ,[2001601071]
29	[4000000005]*,[4004004005],[4000010205],[4010000045], [4400000045],[4002200115],[4001040115],[4004204435], [4100060435] ,[4040003075],[4004064275]
30	[10,040,000,007],[10,104,264,207],[10,115,131,333],[11,362,212,703], [10,343,244,533]
31	[20,000,000,011]*,[20,000,000,017],[20,000,020,411],[21,042,104,211] [20,010,010,017] ,[20,005,000,251],[20,004,100,071],[20,202,040,217] [20,000,200,435] ,[20,060,140,231],[21,042,107,357]
32	[40,020,000,007],[40,460,216,667],[40,035,532,523],[42,003,247,143], [41,760,427,607]
33	[100,000,020,001]*,[100,020,024,001],[104,000,420,001], [100,020,224,401] ,[111,100,021,111],[100,000,031,463], [104,020,466,001] ,[100,502,430,041],[100,601,431,001]
34	[201,000,000,007],[201,472,024,107],[377,000,007,527], [225,213,433,257],[227,712,240,037],[251,132,516,577], [211,636,220,473],[200,000,140,003]
35	[400,000,000,005]*
36	[1,000,000,004,001]*
37	[2,000,000,012,005]
38	[4,000,000,000,143]
39	[10,000,000,000,021]*
40	[20,000,012,000,005]
61	[200,000,000,000,000,000,047]
89	[400,000,000,000,000,000,000,000,000,151]

Source: References [9–11].

*Entries followed by an asterisk correspond to circuit implementations with only two feedback connections.

The two output sequences are

$$g(D) \rightarrow 1\ 1\ 1\ 0\ 1\ 0\ 0, 1\ 1\ 1\ 0\ 1\ 0\ 0, \ldots$$

$$g_r(D) \rightarrow 1\ 0\ 1\ 1\ 1\ 0\ 0, 1\ 0\ 1\ 1\ 1\ 0\ 0, \ldots$$

which, except for a phase shift, are simply the reverse of one another.

9.5.6 Security of *m*-Sequences

Spread-spectrum systems are often used to protect digital transmissions from being jammed or to preclude unintended reception of the signal. Both of these objectives can only be met if the jammer or unintended receiver does not have knowledge of the spreading waveform $c(t)$. Unfortunately, when the jammer or interceptor can receive a relatively noise-free copy of the transmitted signal, the spreading code feedback connections and initial phase can be determined in a straightforward manner. For this reason, maximal length sequences are a poor choice for the spreading code when a high level of security is required.

Suppose that the unintended party has access to an uncorrupted version of the transmitted spreading code. Thus the unintended party knows the sequence $b_0, b_1, b_2, b_3, \ldots$ and would like to determine the shift register feedback connections used to generate this sequence. The party knows that an *m*-sequence is being transmitted and can easily determine the period of the sequence by measuring the received power spectrum accurately. Each symbol of the *m*-sequence must satisfy the recursion relationship of the form

$$b_i = \sum_{m=1}^{r} g_m b_{i-m} \tag{9-64}$$

which is implied by the feedback shift register of Figure 9–21, so that the unintended party can write the following series of equations:

$$b_i = b_{i-1}g_1 + b_{i-2}g_2 + \cdots + b_{i-m}g_m$$
$$b_{i+1} = b_i g_1 + b_{i-1}g_2 + \cdots + b_{i-m+1}g_m \tag{9-65}$$
$$b_{i+2} = b_{i+1}g_1 + b_i g_2 + \cdots + b_{i-m+2}g_m$$
$$\vdots$$

After m such equations have been written, the unintended party will have m equations in the m unknowns g_1 through g_m which can be solved. Massey [12] has provided an efficient technique for solving this system of equations. The purpose of the present discussion is merely to make the reader aware that algorithms exist for determining the shift register generator feedback connections so that the details of Massey's algorithm are left as a reference. The system of (9–65) can also be solved by brute force, as demonstrated in the following example.

EXAMPLE 9–8

Suppose that the sequence 0 1 1 0 0 1 0 0 is received and that the known period of the *m*-sequence is 15. Thus $m = 4$ and the set of equations to solve is

$$
\begin{align}
(1) \quad & 0 = 0 \cdot g_1 + 1 \cdot g_2 + 1 \cdot g_3 + 0 \cdot g_4 \\
(2) \quad & 1 = 0 \cdot g_1 + 0 \cdot g_2 + 1 \cdot g_3 + 1 \cdot g_4 \\
(3) \quad & 0 = 1 \cdot g_1 + 0 \cdot g_2 + 0 \cdot g_3 + 1 \cdot g_4 \\
(4) \quad & 0 = 0 \cdot g_1 + 1 \cdot g_2 + 0 \cdot g_3 + 0 \cdot g_4
\end{align}
$$

Adding (1) and (4) yields $0 = g_3$. Substituting $g_3 = 0$ into (1) yields $g_2 = 0$. Substituting $g_2 = g_3 = 0$ into (2) yields $g_4 = 1$; then substituting $g_2 = g_3 = 0$ and $g_4 = 1$ into (3) yields $g_1 = 1$. Therefore,

$$
g(D) = 1 + D + D^4
$$

Note that the number of symbols that must be received is $2m$, where m is the degree of $g(D)$ and $2m$ is much shorter than the period $N = 2^m - 1$ of the m-sequence. The assumption that the $2m$ symbols be received without error can only be made in special circumstances so that the security of m-sequences may in fact be slightly better than is implied in this discussion.

9.5.7   Gold Codes

One of the applications of spread-spectrum systems is to provide a means other than frequency-division multiple access or time-division multiple access of sharing the scarce channel resources. When channel resources are shared using spread-spectrum techniques, all users are permitted to transmit simultaneously using the same band of frequencies. Users are each assigned a different spreading code so that they can be separated in the receiver despreading process. A goal of the spread-spectrum system designer for a multiple-access system is to find a set of spreading codes or waveforms such that as many users as possible can use a band of frequencies with as little mutual interference as possible.

Recall that the receiver despreading operation is a correlation operation with the spreading code of the desired transmitter. Ideally, a received signal that has been spread using a different spreading code will not be despread and will cause minimal interference in the desired signal. The specific amount of interference from a user employing a different spreading code is related to the cross-correlation between the two spreading codes. The Gold codes introduced in this section were invented in 1967 at the Magnavox Corporation specifically for multiple-access applications of spread spectrum. Relatively large sets of Gold codes exist that have well-controlled cross-correlation properties. The treatment here is intended only to familiarize the reader with the fact that this code family exists and with some of its most fundamental properties. A considerably more thorough discussion of these codes can be found in Sarwate and Pursley [8]. This reference also provides a large bibliography for further study.

The discrete periodic cross-correlation between two spreading codes b and b' was defined in (9–56). Although the detailed correlation could be evaluated for Gold code sets, in many cases adequate information for system analysis can be obtained from the cross-correlation spectrum. The *cross-correlation spectrum* is a list of all possible values of $\theta_{bb'}(k)$ and the number of values of k that yield that particular cross-correlation. The cross-correlation spectrum is denoted by $\theta_{bb'}$. When $b = b'$, the cross-correlation spectrum becomes the *autocorrelation spectrum*. The autocorrelation spectrum for an *m*-sequence is

$$1.0 \quad \text{occurs} \quad 1 \text{ time}$$

$$-\frac{1}{N} \quad \text{occurs} \quad N - 1 \text{ times}$$

Gold sequences are formed by the modulo-2 addition of a pair of maximal-length sequences. Figure 9–24 is a conceptual block diagram for a Gold sequence generator. Each of the feedback shift registers in Figure 9–24 generates an *m*-sequence. Not every pair of *m*-sequences can be summed to form a Gold sequence. The pair must have special properties and is called a *preferred pair* of *m*-sequences. Preferred pairs of *m*-sequences have a three valued cross-correlation spectrum with cross-correlation values

$$-\frac{1}{N} t(n)$$

$$-\frac{1}{N} \tag{9–66}$$

$$\frac{1}{N}[t(n) - 2]$$

in which

$$t(n) = \begin{cases} 1 + 2^{0.5(n+1)}, & \text{for } n \text{ odd} \\ 1 + 2^{0.5(n+2)}, & \text{for } n \text{ even} \end{cases}$$

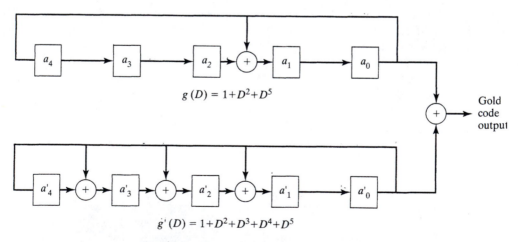

FIGURE 9–24 Typical Gold code generator.

where the code period $N = 2^n - 1$. Finding preferred pairs of m-sequences is necessary in defining sets of Gold codes [8].

Let $b(D)$ and $b'(D)$ represent a preferred pair of m-sequences having period $N = 2^n - 1$. The family of codes defined by $\{b(D), b'(D), b(D) + b'(D), b(D) + Db'(D), b(D) + D^2b'(D), \ldots, b(D) + D^{N-1}b'(D)\}$ is called the set of *Gold codes* for this preferred pair of m-sequences. In this definition, the notation $D^jb'(D)$ represents a phase shift of the m-sequence $b'(D)$ by j units. This entire family of Gold codes can be generated using a generator as illustrated in Figure 9–24. The phase shifts of the $b'(D)$ sequence are implemented through the use of different initial loads (phases) of one of the two maximal-length generators. Gold codes sets have the property that any pair of codes in the set, say, **y** and **z,** have a 3-valued cross-correlation spectrum which takes on the values defined in (9–66).

In summary, Gold codes are families of codes with well-behaved cross-correlation properties that are constructed by a modulo-2 addition of specific relative phases of a preferred pair of m-sequences. The period of any code in the family is N, which is the same as the period of the m-sequences. These codes are important since they have been selected by NASA for use on the Tracking and Data Relay Satellite System as well as the NAVSTAR Globel Positioning System. The particular set of Gold codes employed in TDRSS are defined in STDN 108 by the Goddard Space Flight Center. This brief description of Gold codes has not been rigorous and the reader is referred to Sarwate and Pursley [8] or Holmes [11] for further information on this interesting subject.

EXAMPLE 9–9

A preferred pair of m-sequences of length 31 can be shown to be (spaces for clarity only)

$$\mathbf{b} = 10101\ 11011\ 00011\ 11100\ 11010\ 01000\ 0$$

and

$$\mathbf{b'} = 10110\ 10100\ 01110\ 11111\ 00100\ 11000\ 0$$

For $n = 5$ as in this example,

$$t(n) = 1 + 2^{0.5(5+1)} = 1 + 2^3 = 9$$

and the permitted values of the cross correlation for any phase shift of **b** and **b'** are

$$-t(n)/N = -9/31;\ -1/N = -1/31;\ [t(n) - 2]/N = 7/31$$

A straightforward but tedious manual calculation of the cross-correlation spectrum of **b** and **b'** shows that for any phase shift, the three values of cross-correlation are $-9/31$, $-1/31$, and $7/31$. The thirty-three Gold codes defined by **b** and **b'** have only these cross-correlation values as well.

9.5.8   Kasami Sequences (Small Set) [8]

Let $r = 2v$, v an integer, and $d = 2^v + 1$. Let **b** be an m-sequence and let **b'** be obtained by sampling every dth member of **b** where $\mathbf{b'} \neq \mathbf{0}$. Then the Kasami sequences are **b,** $\mathbf{b + b'}, \mathbf{b + Db'}, \ldots, \mathbf{b + D^\alpha b'}$, where $\alpha = 2^v - 2$. These are 2^v sequences in the family of period $2^r - 1$ and maximum magnitude cross correlation $(1 + 2^v)/N$.

EXAMPLE 9–10

Consider the degree 4 entry in Table 9–2. It is $[2\ 3]_8 = [0\ 1\ 0\ 0\ 1\ 1]_2$. Using the maximal-length shift register configuration of Figure 9–21, we can show that the generated m-sequence is 10001 00110 10111 (spaces for clarity), where the initial load used is 0001 and the output is taken off the right side. We have $4 = 2v$, or $v = 2$ and $d = 2^2 + 1 = 5$, so $\mathbf{b'} = 101101101101101$. The four Kasami sequences in this case are

$$
\begin{array}{ll}
\mathbf{b} = & 10001\ 00110\ 10111 \\
\mathbf{b} + \mathbf{b'} = & 00111\ 11101\ 11010 \\
\mathbf{b} + D\mathbf{b'} = & 01010\ 01011\ 00001 \\
\mathbf{b} + D^2\mathbf{b'} = & 11100\ 10000\ 01100
\end{array}
$$

Checking the cross correlation of $\mathbf{b}$ with $\mathbf{b} + \mathbf{b'}$, we obtain values of $-5/15$ and $3/15$. This obeys the given bound of $(1 + 2^v)/N = 5/15$.

Note that the family of Kasami sequences is smaller than the Gold set size. There are also large and very large (also called modified Gold) sets of Kasami sequences. Sometimes it is desirable to have an even number of binary symbols in the sequences. When this is done by adding one bit to each member of the Kasami sequences, it is said to be the extended Kasami set. In the above example, this would have made the maximum cross-correlation magnitude 6/15.

9.5.9 Quaternary (Four-Phase) Sequences [13, 14]

Many modern applications of spread spectrum use phase spreading other than binary. Section 9.3 included two four-phase spread-spectrum configurations, but these used binary spreading codes in parallel inphase and quadrature channels. There is no reason, however, that multiphase spreading codes could not be used if available. Multiphase spreading codes have a more straightforward implementation and there is the possibility that the added flexibility will allow the design of larger families of sequences with good correlation properties. It appears especially important in the field of cellular radio communications to have large families of spreading sequences available for the next generation systems.

There have been many recent research results published on multiphase codes. We look at a particular set of quaternary codes in this section known as the S-series of families, labeled $S(0)$, $S(1)$, and $S(2)$ [13, 14]. The S-series of codes are multiphase codes, but we will consider only the special case of four-phase. The Gold family is included in the family $S(1)$. Before considering a particular example of this series of families, certain characteristics of them are given in Table 9–3. The following notation is used. Let $s(i, t)$ represent the distinct codes in a particular family of codes. The index i specifies the particular code in the family and t and τ are *integers* representing time; actual time is $t \times T_c$ or $\tau \times T_c$. The length N of a ⋯ 1 and the number of quaternary codes in a family is denoted M.

TABLE 9–3   Parameters for Quaternary Sequence Families Compared with Gold Codes [14]

Family	Length, N	Size, M	C_{max}	Bound on C_{max}
Gold	$2^r - 1$	$N + 2$	$[2(N+1)]^{1/2} + 1$	$\approx N^{1/2}$
$S(0)$	$2^r - 1$	$N + 2$	$(N+1)^{1/2} + 1$	$\approx N^{1/2}$
$S(1)$	$2^r - 1$	$\geq N^2 + 3N + 2$	$2(N+1)^{1/2} + 1$	$\approx(2.62N)^{1/2}$
$S(2)$	$2^r - 1$	$\geq N^3 + 4N^2 + 5N + 2$	$4(N+1)^{1/2} + 1$	$\approx(4.35N)^{1/2}$

In Table 9–3, C_{max} is defined as the maximum of the periodic correlation function of two sequences $s(i, t)$ and $s(j, t)$:

$$C_{max} = \max_{i,j,\tau}\{|c(i,j,\tau)| \,|\text{either } i \neq j \text{ or } \tau \neq 0\} \tag{9-67}$$

where

$$c(i,j,\tau) = \sum_{t=0}^{N-1} \omega_4^{s(i,\,t+\tau)-s(j,t)}, \; 1 \leq i,j, \leq M, 0 \leq \tau \leq (N-1)\,T_c \tag{9-68}$$

with $\omega_4 = \exp(j\pi/2) = j$ for four-phase sequences. For four-phase sequences, any of the $s(i, t)$s take on the values 0, 1, 2, 3.

In spread-spectrum systems, the odd correlation properties are as important or more so than the periodic (or even) correlation properties. The odd correlation properties take into account that when two sequences overlap with nonzero delay, the overlap of the second sequence into the periodic extension of the first sequence may not match up in terms of phase due to data modulation. In [14] it is shown, due to the linear cyclic nature of the S-series of codes, that the aperiodic correlation magnitudes may be expressed as

$$R(c, \tau; b) = \left|\left(\sum_{n=0}^{N-\tau-1} \omega_4^{c(nT_c)} + \omega_4^b \sum_{n=N-\tau}^{N-1} \omega_4^{c(nT_c)}\right)\right| \tag{9-69}$$

where $c(t) = s(i, t+\tau) - s(j, t)$ (note that τ is in units of T_c, the chip period) and $b = b(0) - b(T_s) \in \{0, 1, 2, 3\}$ for quaternary codes is the possible difference in data symbol value between the overlap portion of the two codes. The even periodic correlations correspond to $b = 0$.

Let

$$R_{max} = \max_{c,b,\tau} R(c, \tau; b) \tag{9-70}$$

This provides a measure of the difficulty of finding the proper synchronization of a user employing a given code in the presence of several other users employing codes in the same family. Reference [14] provides values for R_{max} obtained by computer search for the $S(0)$ family. These are given in Table 9–4. A better estimate of the extent of the correlation magnitudes may be obtained by normalizing them by the autocorrelation maxi-

TABLE 9–4   Worst-Case Correlation Magnitudes for the $S(0)$ Family [14]

r	N	R_{max}	$R_{max, norm}$
3	7	5.39	0.770
4	15	9.43	0.629
5	31	14.32	0.462
6	63	23.35	0.371
7	127	35.34	0.278
8	255	52.47	0.206
9	511	77.62	0.152

mum, which is N. These normalized values are given in the last column. Note that the longer the codes, the smaller the maximum correlation magnitude relative to the autocorrelation maximum. In cellular communications, third generation systems are anticipating the use of length 255 codes.

We close this section with the exhibit in Figure 9–25 of a circuit for generating quaternary $S(0)$ codes as given in [14]. All arithmetic is modulo-4. The $2^r + 1 = 9$ cyclically distinct sequences of length $2^r - 1 = 7$ that are generated by this circuit are obtained by loading the shift register with initial conditions and then cycling through all possible states until the initial state reappears. Cyclically distinct (i.e., no cyclic rotation is another sequence) sequences will be obtained by choosing initial loads not equal to states that have appeared previously. Table 9–5 gives the initial loads and resulting sequences.

9.5.10   Walsh Codes

The Walsh codes form an orthogonal set of length 2^n, where n is an integer. The method for constructing the set using the Hadamard array is given in Chapter 10. The Walsh codes have zero cross-correlation between codes, assuming they are perfectly synchronized. The Gold codes discussed previously obey the cross-correlation bounds given for *any* delay offset between codes.

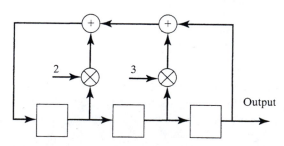

–25   Generator for quaternary sequences of length 7.

TABLE 9–5   Initial loads and sequences for
$S(0)$ family of length 7 [14]

Initial Load	Sequence
0 0 1	1 0 0 1 2 3 1
0 1 0	0 1 0 3 3 3 2
0 0 3	3 0 0 3 2 1 3
0 1 2	2 1 0 1 3 1 0
0 2 0	0 2 0 2 2 2 0
0 2 1	1 2 0 3 0 1 1
0 3 1	1 3 0 2 3 0 3
1 1 2	2 1 1 3 2 2 1
1 3 3	3 3 1 2 2 3 2

9.6   SYNCHRONIZATION IN SPREAD-SPECTRUM SYSTEMS

Spread-spectrum communications requires that the transmitter and receiver spreading waveforms be synchronized. If the two waveforms are out of synchronization by as little as one chip, insufficient signal energy will reach the receiver data demodulator for reliable data detection. The task of achieving and maintaining code synchronization is usually delegated to the receiver. There are two components of the synchronization problem. The first component is the determination of the initial code phase starting from whatever a priori information is available. This part of the problem is called *code acquisition*. The second component is the problem of maintaining code synchronization after initial acquisition. This problem is called *code tracking*.

A widely used technique for initial synchronization is to search through all potential code phases and frequencies until synchronization is achieved. Each reference phase/frequency is evaluated by attempting to despread the received signal. If the estimated code phase and frequency are correct, despreading will occur and will be sensed. If the code phase or frequency is incorrect, the received signal will not be despread, and the reference waveform will be stepped to a new phase/frequency for evaluation. This technique is called *serial search*. A simplified block diagram of such a system is shown in Figure 9–26. If the reference spreading waveform is nearly aligned, say, $\pm\frac{1}{2}$chip, with the incoming code, the received signal will be despread sufficiently so that enough signal energy will pass through the bandpass filter to cause the decision device to stop the search.

A highly efficient method of initial synchronization is to detect the received signal by passing it through a matched filter and detecting the time at which the output magnitude is maximum. The matched filter is designed to output a pulse when a particular sequence of code symbols is received. When this pulse is sensed, the receiver code generator is started using an initial condition corresponding to the received code stream, and synchronization is complete. This technique requires matched filters with extremely large time–bandwidth products. The difficulty in implementing these filters is the principal reason this synchronization technique is not more widely used.

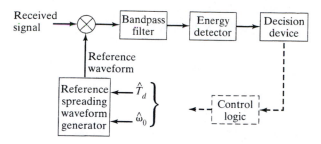

FIGURE 9–26   System used to evaluate a single spreading waveform phase and frequency.

The number of code phases and frequencies that must be evaluated to obtain initial synchronization is proportional to propagation delay uncertainty expressed in spreading code chips and the relative dynamics of the transmitter and receiver. Since the code chip duration is inversely proportional to the chip rate, synchronization time is also directly proportional to the clock rate used for the spreading code generators. Since a frequency-hop spread-spectrum system may employ a clock rate that is much lower than the transmission bandwidth, synchronization time for frequency-hop systems is typically much lower than for direct-sequence systems having the same transmission bandwidth. This factor is a principal reason why frequency hopping has been selected for some current spread-spectrum systems. Initial synchronization techniques for frequency-hop spread-spectrum systems are the same as those used for direct-sequence systems.

It can be shown [5] that for an initial uncertainty of C chips, the mean search time, assuming stepped serial search, is

$$\overline{T}_s = (C-1)T_{da}\left(\frac{2-P_d}{2P_d}\right) + \frac{T_i}{P_d} \tag{9–71}$$

where

T_i = integration time for each cell

T_{da} = $T_i + P_{fa}T_{fa}$ = average dwell time on an incorrect phase cell

P_{fa} = probability of a false alarm (i.e., indication of a correct cell when it is not)

T_{fa} = time required to reject an incorrect cell when it occurs

P_d = probability of detection when the correct cell is being evaluated

The variance of the search time can be approximated by

$$\sigma_{T_s}^2 = T_{da}^2 C^2\left(\frac{1}{12} - \frac{1}{P_d} + \frac{1}{P_d^2}\right), \quad C \gg 1; \quad P_d \simeq 1; \quad P_{fa} \ll 1 \tag{9–72}$$

One of the goals of the spread-spectrum system designer is to design a synchronization system that minimizes mean synchronization time. Equation (9–71) indicates that mean synchronization time is a function of P_d, P_{fa}, T_i, T_{fa}, and C. The designer has some degree of control over all these variables, including C. Even though the phase uncertainty region in seconds is fixed by system requirements, the region can be subdivided into any number of cells. The remaining four variables are not independent of one another, and therein lies the difficulty in the design. It can be shown that high P_d together with low P_{fa} implies large T_i. Thus there will be an optimum set of P_d, P_{fa}, T_i, T_{fa} that minimizes mean synchronization time. It is not correct to assume that minimum average synchronization time will always be achieved with $P_d \cong 1$, so that the correct phase cell is detected on the first sweep. In some cases the selection of a moderate P_d will result in a much lower T_i than a high P_d and thus result in reduced average T_s even though several sweeps of the uncertainty may be required. Analysis and design techniques for code acquisition in spread-spectrum systems are dealt with in more detail in [5].

Typically, code acquisition methods are capable of determining the received spreading code phase to within an accuracy of $\pm\frac{1}{2}$ to $\pm\frac{1}{4}$ of a chip. When the code tracking loop is closed, there may therefore be a phase error of $\pm\frac{1}{2}$ chip that the tracking loop must eliminate. This transition from the completion of the initial synchronization function to find code tracking is called *tracking loop pull-in* and is important because it affects the selection of loop bandwidth. The study of the tracking loop pull-in characteristic is a nonlinear analysis problem.

Code tracking is accomplished using phase-lock techniques very similar to those discussed in Appendix D. The principal difference between the phase-locked loops discussed there and those discussed in regard to code tracking is in the implementation of the phase discriminator. For carrier tracking, the discriminator can be as simple as a multiplier, whereas for code tracking loops, several multipliers, filters, and envelope detectors will be used. Since code tracking loops are phase-locked loops, the usual goal of an analysis of a spread-spectrum code tracking system is to develop models of the various code tracking loops which are identical to the conventional phase-locked loop model and then to draw on the vast store of phase-locked loop results.

Code tracking loops for spread-spectrum systems can be categorized in several ways. First, there are coherent and noncoherent loops. Coherent loops make use of received carrier phase information whereas noncoherent loops do not. Typical code tracking loops make use of correlation operations between the received signal and two different phases (early and late) of the receiver-generated spreading waveform. These two correlation operations can be accomplished using two independent channels or by using a single channel that is time shared. A tracking loop that makes use of two independent correlators is called a *full-time early-late tracking loop,* and a tracking loop that time shares a single correlator is called a *tau-dither early-late tracking loop.*

A baseband version of a full-time early-late tracking loop is shown in Figure 9–27. It is simplified due to the absence of modulation on the received signal. For modulated signals, the loop would include envelope detectors at the outputs of the multipliers in the delay-lock discriminator to make the early and late correlation operations dependent only on the envelope of the modulated signal. For the baseband loop shown, the difference of the two multiplier outputs, one with an early code and one with a late code relative to the incoming code, appears in Figure 9–28 for various values of delay difference Δ in chips. In the baseband case, the broadest linear characteristic about the origin is given for $\Delta = 2$

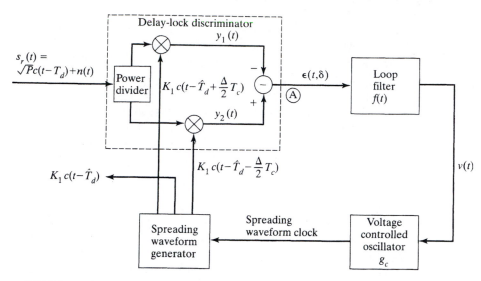

FIGURE 9-27 Conceptual block diagram: Baseband delay-lock tracking loop. (Reproduced from Reference [5] with permission.)

chips. It is important to have the widest possible linear tracking range since the phase detector output is the voltage supplied to the voltage-controlled oscillator to drive the local spreading code generator toward lock.

The tau-dither early-late tracking loop differs from the full-time early-late tracking loop in that only one correlator is used. A square-wave switching signal switches this correlator between the early and late locally generated codes. The output of the correlator is negated for the late code, and the difference between early and late correlations taken as in the full-time loop. The frequency of the square wave is low enough that transients have a chance to die out between switching instants. While there is some loss in the difference signal due to this switching, an advantage of the tau-dither loop is that the same correlator is used for both the early and late signals. This ensures that the loop tracking will not be degraded due to imbalances in the two correlation channels for the early and late reference codes.

For further details and analyses of both the noncoherent full-time and tau-dither loops, the reader is referred to [5].

9.7 PERFORMANCE OF SPREAD-SPECTRUM SYSTEMS IN JAMMING ENVIRONMENTS

9.7.1 Introduction

In this section we consider the effect of jamming on spread-spectrum communications systems. Since the only difference between a spread-spectrum system and one not using spread spectrum is the spreading and despreading of the transmitted signal, and since this

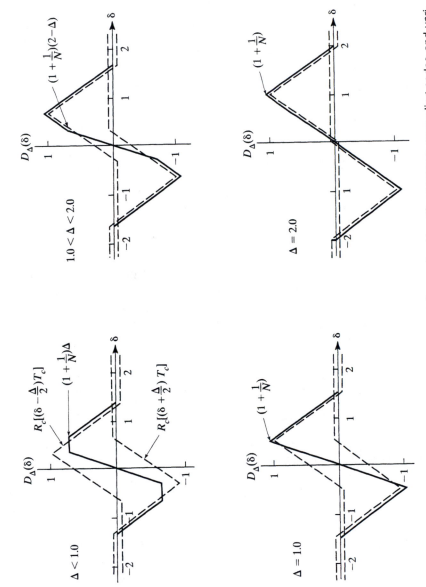

FIGURE 9–28 Delay-lock discriminator dc outputs for maximal-length sequence spreading codes and various values of Δ. (Reproduced from Reference [5] with permission.)

spreading and despreading amounts to another layer of modulation, it follows that there is no difference between the error probability performance for a spread-spectrum system and one employing a comparable digital modulation format with no spreading as long as the background noise is wideband and Gaussian, and as long as the spreading and despreading operations are perfect. That is, a DSSS system utilizing BPSK modulation will perform the same as a BPSK system without spreading in a wideband Gaussian noise environment assuming ideal synchronization. However, in a jamming environment, the spread-spectrum system will provide a margin of improvement against jamming. This margin of improvement is usually specified as the processing gain. That is, a spread-spectrum system will, under ideal conditions, reduce the effective jammer power by the processing gain. The term "ideal conditions" is used here because there are certain jamming strategies that will not allow improvement by the processing gain factor.

9.7.2 Types of Jammers

Various types of jammers are illustrated in Figure 9–29. The most benign jammer is the *barrage jammer,* which places a constant level of jamming power across all frequencies that the communication system is expected to operate in, or N_J watts/hertz across W hertz as indicated in Figure 9–29a. Since most sources are average power limited, we are interested in the total jamming power, J, which for the barrage jammer is WN_J. It is sometimes advantageous for the jammer to concentrate its power within a narrower band than the communicator's transmission bandwidth. This is illustrated in Figure 9–29 with a *partial band noise jammer* that employs a jamming bandwidth of, for example, 0.4 W hertz; this allows this jammer to increase the spectral level of the jamming power to $2.5N_J$ watts/hertz for a total power still equal to J watts. In general the partial band jammer transmits over a fraction $0 < \rho \leq 1.0$ of the band W. Yet a third type of jammer is the *single-tone jammer,* which concentrates all of its power into a single tone of J watts. This is illustrated in Figure 9.29c. Finally, spreading the jamming power out into a number of tones is sometimes useful from the jammer's standpoint. The spectrum of a *multiple-tone jammer* is illustrated in Figure 9–29d.

9.7.3 Combating Smart Jammers

It has been mentioned already that a jammer can sometimes benefit by pulsing its transmission. As pointed out in Section 9.2.1, this type of jammer is particularly effective against a DSSS system if it knows the signal-to-noise ratio of the communicator and jams accordingly. Such a jammer is called a "smart" jammer because it makes use of knowledge about the communicator to improve its effectiveness. Another type of smart jammer is the repeat jammer, which receives the communicator's transmitted signal, modifies it somehow and retransmits it. If done properly, such "spoofing"-type jammers can have devastating effects on the communicator.

Returning to the pulsed jammer, its effectiveness stems in part from being able to raise the error rate of the communicator for a short period of time, rest and then repeat the

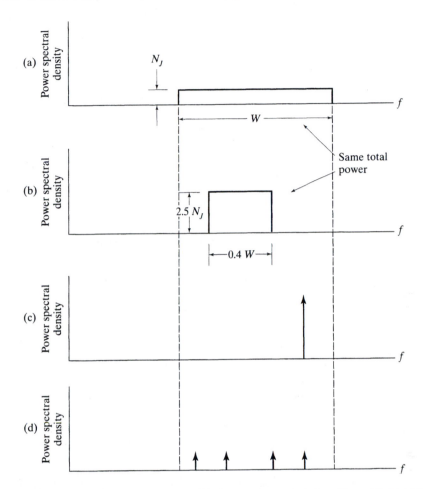

FIGURE 9–29   Typical jammer one-sided power spectral densities: (a) barrage noise jammer; (b) partial band noise jammer; (c) tone jammer; (d) multiple-tone jammer. (Reproduced from Reference [5] with permission.)

process. Because of the interspersed rests, the jammer's average transmitted power is less than it would be if it transmitted at the spectral level of the jamming pulses all the time. The communicator, on the other hand, must cope with high error bursts that, when averaged with its good periods of low error rate during off periods for the pulsed jammer, still produce a high average error rate (the effect is somewhat like a fading channel). A way for the communicator to combat this is by using coding in conjunction with interleaving and deinterleaving as shown in Figure 9–30. Since decoders work best with random errors at their inputs, the idea is to randomize the errors caused by jamming through the deinterleaving process. The combination of interleaving/deinterleaving acts as though nothing had been done to the encoded bits at all—they still come out of the deinterleaver as they

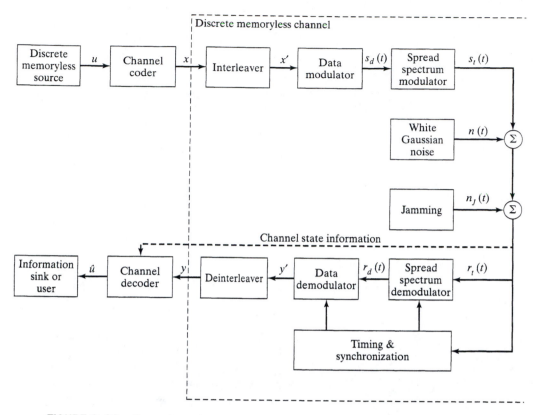

FIGURE 9–30 Spread-spectrum communication system model. (Reproduced from Reference [5] with permission.)

went into the interleaver. However, the errors that resulted from channel disturbances, in this case, jamming, are randomized at the deinterleaver output, and the decoder has random error patterns with which to work. In this fashion, it can be shown that one can gain back much that was lost in terms of error rate due to pulsed jamming [1].

9.7.4 Error Probabilities for Barrage Noise Jammers

In this subsection we give a very simple derivation that allows the error probability results for digital modulation schemes for Gaussian noise to be extended to the cases of benign jamming in spread spectrum. In the error probability expressions derived in Chapter 4, the parameter of importance was E_b/N_0. We extend this to the case of jamming by noting that N_0 in the case of Gaussian noise should be replaced by $N_0 + J/W$ in the case of jamming, where J is the jammer power and W is the bandwidth of the spread-spectrum signal that is assumed to be the bandwidth over which the jammer spreads its power (hence the name "barrage jammer").

Consider DS spread spectrum. The incoming spread spectrum signal is despread because the product of the transmitted spectrum spreading code and the locally generated code is unity under ideal synchronized conditions. If the jammer signal was wideband already (i.e., barrage), it will stay that way. Thus E_b/N_0 is replaced by

$$\frac{E_b}{N_0} \rightarrow \frac{E_b}{N_0 + J/W} = \frac{E_b/N_0}{1 + (J/P)(E_b/N_0)(R/W)}$$

$$= \frac{E_b/N_0}{1 + [(J/P)(G_p)](E_b/N_0)}$$

$$= \frac{1}{(N_0 R/P) + (J/P)(R/W)} \qquad\qquad (9\text{–}73)$$

$$= \frac{1}{(E_b/N_0)^{-1} + [(P/J)(W/R)]^{-1}}$$

where the various parameters are defined as follows:

E_b = signal energy per bit
N_0 = Gaussian noise spectral density
J = average jammer power
W = single-sided spread signal bandwidth
R = $1/T_b$ = bit rate
P = $E_b R$ = average signal power
J/P = jamming-to-signal power ratio
W/R = G_p = processing gain

The expression (9–73) can be used to replace E_b/N_0 in any of the expressions for bit error probability derived in Chapter 4 used for modulating the information signal.

This approach can also be used for narrowband jammers as an approximation as long as the effect of jamming on a DS spread-spectrum system with a particular type of data modulation *acts like Gaussian noise through the despreading operation*. This simple approach will not work for pulsed jammers and repeat jammers, however, as pointed out earlier. Note that the effect of the jamming power has been decreased by the processing gain.

Examples of spread spectrum system performance in barrage jamming are given in Figures 9–31, 9–32, and 9–33. The equations used to construct these curves are

Figure 9–31: Equation (4–70)
Figure 9–32: Equations (4–124) and (4–145) and $E_b = E_s/\log_2 M$
Figure 9–33: Equation (4–140)

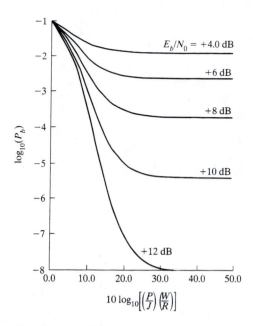

FIGURE 9–31 Performance of a coherent direct-sequence spread-spectrum system in barrage noise jamming. BPSK assumed. (Reproduced from Reference [5] with permission.)

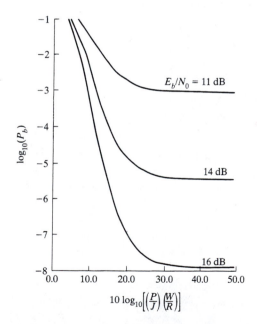

FIGURE 9–32 Performance of a FH/MFSK spread-spectrum system in barrage noise jamming. Binary NFSK assumed. (Reproduced from Reference [5] with permission.)

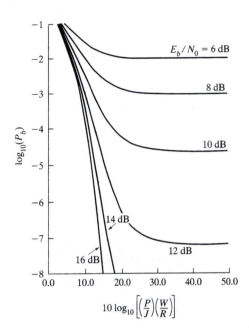

FIGURE 9–33 Performance of FH/DPSK spread-spectrum system in barrage noise jamming. Binary DPSK assumed. (Reproduced from Reference [5] with permission.)

Details are given in [5]. More accurate computations show that error probabilities obtained using this approximation for narrowband or tone jammers are somewhat pessimistic.

9.7.5 Error Probabilities for Optimized Partial Band or Pulsed Jammers

If a jammer is pulsed with duty factor ρ, we can still use the approach outlined in the previous subsection. However, we compute an average error probability where the jammer is off a fraction $(1 - \rho)$ of the time and the noise power spectral density is N_0 and where the jammer is on a fraction ρ of the time and the noise power spectral density is $N_n = N_0 + N'_J$ $= N_0 + J/(\rho W)$. Note that the average jammer power is still J. To compute the average bit error probability, we use the appropriate expression for the digital modulation scheme under consideration, call it $P_b(E_b/N_0)$, and compute

$$\overline{P}_b = (1 - \rho)P_b\left(\frac{E_b}{N_0}\right) + \rho P_b\left(\frac{E_b}{N_0 + N'_J}\right) \tag{9-74}$$

We then differentiate with respect to ρ, set the result equal to zero, and solve for $\rho = \rho_{opt}$. When ρ_{opt} is back-substituted into (9–74), we obtain the worst case $\overline{P}_b$ from the standpoint

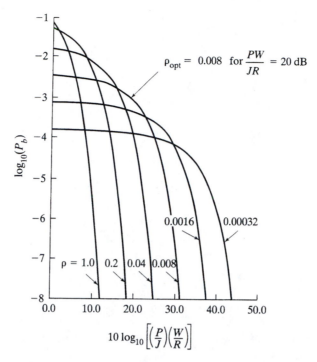

FIGURE 9–34 Performance of coherent DS spread spectrum in pulsed noise jamming. (Reproduced from Reference [5] with permission.)

of the communicator or the best case $\bar{P}_b$ from the standpoint of the jammer. For details, see [5]. Figure 9–34 shows the results of this procedure for the case of DS/BPSK with ρ as a parameter. Observe in Figure 9–34 that for any value of $(P/J)(W/R)$, there is an optimum value of ρ that maximizes the system bit error probability. The jammer has control of ρ, and the smart jammer will adjust ρ dynamically to always maximize system bit error probability.

The system performance with this worst case smart jammer for FH spread spectrum also has been calculated in [15] in the special case where the thermal noise, N_0, is negligible. The resulting curves are shown in Figure 9–35 for FH/MFSK and in Figure 9–36 for FH/DPSK. For frequency-hop systems identical performance is calculated for the pulsed-time barrage jammer and the full-time partial band jammer. In the former case ρ represents the fraction of time jammed while in the latter ρ represents the fraction of band jammed.

Comparing Figure 9–31 with Figure 9–34 shows that the jammer can be considerably more effective using pulsed jamming than using barrage jamming. This increased effectiveness is obtained by causing a large degradation to a fraction of the transmitted symbols rather than a little degradation to all symbols. The inverse linear relationship between $\bar{P}_b$ and E_b/N_J is typical of the performance of uncoded spread-spectrum communi-

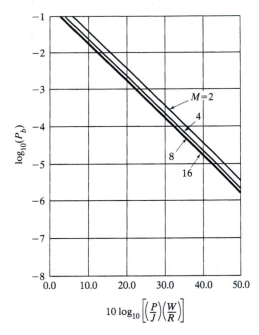

FIGURE 9–35 Performance of FH/MFSK spread spectrum in worst case partial band jamming. (Reproduced from Reference [5] with permission.)

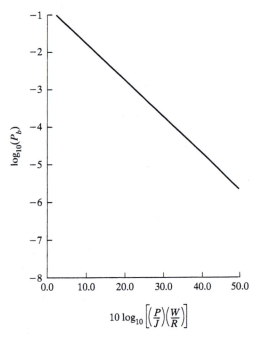

FIGURE 9–36 Performance of FH/DPSK spread spectrum in worst case partial band jamming. (Reproduced from reference [5] with permission.)

cation systems in optimized jamming. It can be shown that much of this degradation can be mitigated through the use of coding and interleaving, although we will not go into this aspect of spread-spectrum system design here [1].

9.8   PERFORMANCE IN MULTIPLE USER ENVIRONMENTS

An important application of spread spectrum systems is multiple-access communications, which means that several users may access a common channel to communicate with other users. If several users were at the same location communicating with a like number users at another common location, the terminology used would be *multiplexing* (time-division multiplexing was briefly discussed at the end of Chapter 3). Since the users are not assumed to be at a common location in the present context, the term *multiple access* is used. There are various ways to effect multiple-access communications including frequency, time, and code division multiple access.

In frequency division multiple access (FDMA), the channel resources are divided up in frequency, and each active user is assigned a subband of the frequency resource. In time division multiple access (TDMA) the communication resource is divided up in time into contiguous frames that are composed of a series of slots; each active user is assigned a sequence of slots. When all subbands or slots are assigned in FDMA and TDMA, respectively, no more users can be admitted to the system. In this sense, FDMA and TDMA are said to have hard capacity limits.

In the one remaining access system, code division multiple access (CDMA), each user is assigned a unique spreading code, and all active users transmit simultaneously over the same band of frequencies. A user who wants to receive information from a given user then correlates the sum total of all these receptions with the spreading code of the desired transmitting user and receives its transmissions, assuming that the transmitter-receiver pair are properly synchronized with each other. The performance of this strategy is related to the correlation properties of the unique spreading codes used. For example, users could be assigned Walsh codes (to be defined in Chapter 10) which are orthogonal. When orthogonal spreading codes are used, the other-user interference does not affect the post-despreading demodulation functions at all. Unfortunately, the multipath fading channels often applicable in CDMA systems distort the signal in such a manner that the orthogonality at the transmitter is degraded and other-user interference does indeed affect performance. Further, in some applications orthogonal spreading codes are not even used. In these cases performance is a function of the crosscorrelation properties of the codes as well as the channel. These partial correlations will eventually limit the total number of users that can simultaneously access the system, but the maximum number is not fixed as in the cases of FDMA and TDMA. It will depend on various system and channel parameters, such as propagation conditions. In this sense, CDMA is said to have a soft capacity limit.

Consider Figure 9–37, which shows a number of transmitting users communicating in a CDMA situation and a receiving user correlating with a given user's transmission, say user 1. We consider baseband for simplicity. Note that the summing junction in front

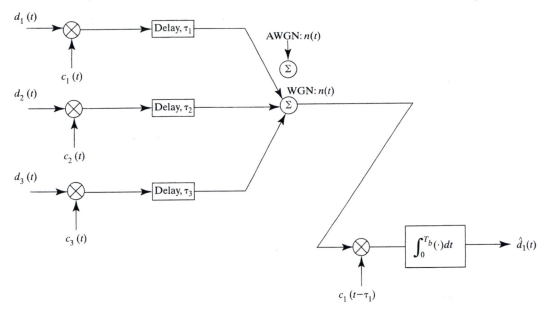

FIGURE 9–37   Block diagram for detection of user 1 in a CDMA system.

of the channel is actually part of the channel in that it represents the addition of all active users in the transmission process.

The received signal at the receiver for user 1 can be written as

$$y(t) = A_1 d_1(t - \tau_1)c_1(t - \tau_1) + \sum_{k=2}^{K} A_k d_k(t - \tau_k)c_k(t - \tau_k) + n(t) \qquad (9\text{–}75)$$

where A_k and τ_k, $k = 1, 2, \ldots K$, represent the amplitude and delay, respectively, for the kth user which are induced by the channel. As shown in Figure 9–37, $d_k(t)$ and $c_k(t)$ represent the data and code, respectively, for the kth user. Finally, $n(t)$ is Gaussian noise added by the channel (receiver front end). Assuming perfect synchronization of the local code for user 1 we can take $\tau_1 = 0$, and the output of the integrator is

$$Y = A_1 d_1(0)T_b + \sum_{k=2}^{K} A_k T_b d_k(0)\rho_{1k} + N_g \qquad (9\text{–}76)$$

where $\rho_{1k} = \dfrac{d_k(-1)}{d_k(0)} \displaystyle\int_0^{\tau_k} c_1(t)\, c_k(t + T_b - \tau_k)dt + \int_{\tau_k}^{T_b} c_1(t)c_k(t - \tau_k)dt$

The first term is the desired correlator output due to user 1, the second sum of terms is referred to as multiple access noise with ρ_{1k} being the aperiodic correlation of the receptions from user 1 and user k, and N_g is a Gaussian random variable due to integration of the Gaussian channel noise present in (9–75). Note that if an orthogonal code set were used and it were possible to maintain perfect orthogonality through the channel, the multiple access term would be 0. This is almost never the case, however, even if an orthogonal code set is used due to slight timing offsets, multipath, etc.

Several means for calculating the performance of a CDMA receiver have been published in the literature over the past couple of decades. Some papers relating to this problem are [16, 17]. We will take a fairly simplistic approach that first appeared in [18], in that the multiple access interference is assumed sufficiently well represented by an equivalent Gaussian random process. In addition, we make the usual assumption that power control is used so that all users' transmissions arrive at the receiver of user 1 with the same power. Under these conditions Pursley [18] showed that the receiver bit error probability can be approximated by

$$P_b = Q(\sqrt{SNR}) \tag{9-77}$$

where

$$SNR = \left\{ \frac{K-1}{3N} + \frac{N_0}{2E_b} \right\}^{-1} \tag{9-78}$$

in which K is the number of active users and N is the number of chips per bit, or the processing gain.

Figure 9–38 shows P_b versus E_b/N_0 for $N = 127$ and various numbers of users. It is seen that an error floor is approached for every case shown. For example, if 20 users are active and a P_b of 10^{-3} is desired, it cannot be achieved *no matter what E_b/N_0 is used*. This is one of the drawbacks of CDMA, and much research has gone into combating this problem. One of the most promising techniques currently being intensely researched is multiuser detection, where the presence of multiple users is treated as a multihypothesis detection problem. Due to the overlap of signaling intervals, multiple symbols must be detected and implementation of the true optimum receiver is computationally infeasible for moderate to large numbers of users. Various approximations to the optimum detector have been proposed and are currently being proposed. We discuss some of these approximations in the next section.

A word about accuracy of the curves shown in Figure 9–38 is in order. The Gaussian approximation is almost always optimistic, with its accuracy becoming better the more users and the larger the processing gain (Central Limit Theorem conditions are more nearly satisfied under these conditions). An extensive study of the accuracy of various approximations is given in [19].

One more effect of multiple-user communications is very important to illustrate, in particular, the near-far effect. We can illustrate it very simply by considering (9–76) for *synchronous* reception (i.e., all signaling intervals are aligned at the receiver) of two users. In this case, (9–76) takes the simplified form

$$Y = \pm A_1 T_b \pm A_2 T_b \rho_{12} + N_g \tag{9-79}$$

To find the average probability of error, we must average over the four possible sign combinations in (9–79), but these are the same in pairs (+ + gives the same result for the conditional error probability as − −, and + − gives the same result as − +). Thus, we consider

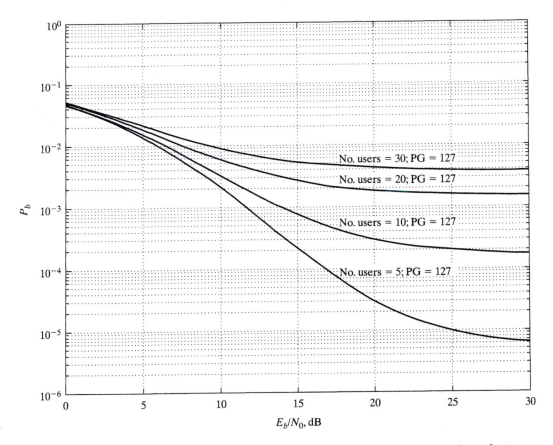

FIGURE 9–38   Bit error probability for CDMA using DSSS with the number of users as a parameter.

$$P(\epsilon|++, +-) = \Pr(A_1T_b \pm A_2T_b\rho_{12} + N_g < 0)$$

$$= \int_{-\infty}^{-(A_1\pm A_2\rho_{12})T_b} \frac{\exp(-u^2/N_0T_b)}{\sqrt{\pi N_0 T_b}}\, du \qquad (9\text{--}80)$$

$$= Q\left(\sqrt{\frac{2(1 \pm (A_2/A_1)\rho_{12})^2 E_b}{N_0}}\right)$$

The average probability of error is the average of these two cases, or

$$\overline{P}_b = \frac{1}{2} Q\left(\sqrt{\frac{2(1 + (A_2/A_1)\rho_{12})^2 E_b}{N_0}}\right) + \frac{1}{2} Q\left(\sqrt{\frac{2(1 - (A_2/A_1)\rho_{12})^2 E_b}{N_0}}\right) \qquad (9\text{--}81)$$

A plot of (9–81) is provided in Figure 9–39 for various ratios of the interfering user's signal amplitude, A_2, to the signal amplitude, A_1, of the user of interest for a specific correla-

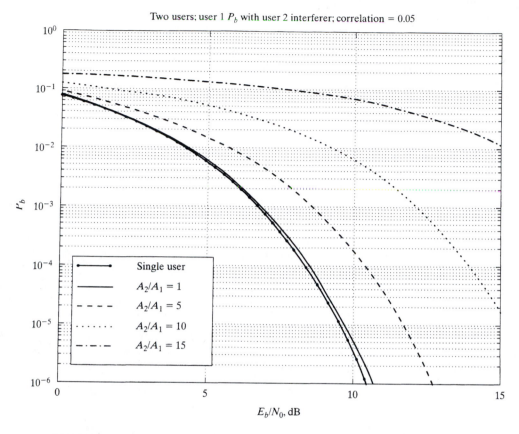

Two users; user 1 P_b with user 2 interferer; correlation = 0.05

Legend:
- ●——● Single user
- —— $A_2/A_1 = 1$
- – – – $A_2/A_1 = 5$
- ······· $A_2/A_1 = 10$
- –·–·– $A_2/A_1 = 15$

Axes: P_b (vertical), E_b/N_0, dB (horizontal)

FIGURE 9–39 Bit error probability for a user of interest in the presence of a second user, which illustrates the near-far effect.

tion $\rho_{12} = 0.05$. Not surprisingly, the probability of error curve moves to the right as A_2/A_1 increases. If $A_2/A_1 = 10$, the communication link with user 1 is virtually unusable, except for very large E_b/N_0 values. Lest the reader think that this would be an unusual situation, it would be advisable to review Section 1.4 on link power calculations to convince oneself that it would be very possible to exceed a factor of 10 due to distance differences between the user of interest and the interfering user. This is the reason for the name "near/far effect." Note also that for $\rho_{12} = 0$ (i.e., orthogonal signals) there is no near/far effect.

9.9 MULTIUSER DETECTION

Multiuser detection, which is based on the idea of treating the detection of a given transmission in the presence of other users by viewing it as a multihypothesis problem, came to the forefront of research in signal detection with the publication of a dissertation by

Verdu in 1984 [20, 21], although others had considered the concept in specific applications [22]. Verdu's solution involves a bank of matched filters followed by a Viterbi algorithm [23]. The complexity of this procedure is exponential in the number of users. Hence, much research has been done on finding computationally simpler, suboptimum algorithms for situations where the number of users is large, such as cellular radio [24, 25]. Another research area of importance to modern applications such as cellular radio is designing multiuser receivers that work well in situations where certain things are unknown such as signature sequences and received signal amplitudes [26].

The problem of multiuser detection could be attacked by considering it a multi-hypothesis decision problem. For example, consider (9–79) written for the four possible sign combinations (the notation H_1 stands for hypothesis 1, etc., each one of which is assumed to occur with *a priori* probability $\frac{1}{4}$):

$$
\begin{aligned}
&H_1\text{: } Y = (A_1 + A_2\rho_{12})T_b + N; (d_1 = 1, d_2 = 1) \\
&H_2\text{: } Y = (A_1 - A_2\rho_{12})T_b + N; (d_1 = 1, d_2 = -1) \\
&H_3\text{: } Y = (-A_1 + A_2\rho_{12})T_b + N; (d_1 = -1, d_2 = 1) \\
&H_4\text{: } Y = (-A_1 - A_2\rho_{12})T_b + N; (d_1 = -1, d_2 = -1)
\end{aligned}
\tag{9–82}
$$

If user 1 is the communicator of interest, the receiver would make minimum probability of error guesses on the four hypotheses: If H_1 or H_2, it would make the decision that user 1's transmitted bit was $d_1 = 1$; if H_3 or H_4, it would make the decision that user 1's transmitted bit was $d_1 = -1$. Clearly, receiver performance should be better by taking the multi-hypothesis approach than if the other user is treated only as interference, as was the case for the results of Figure 9–39.

Carrying this approach further, we see that for three active users the decision problem would involve $2^3 = 8$ hypotheses; for K active users it would involve 2^K hypotheses. Since this setup has assumed that all users' transmissions arrive at user 1's receiver in bit synchronism, there is no overlap from one bit interval to the next of differing users. If the receptions were not in synchronism, the decision problem would clearly involve all possible combinations of adjacent bits—in the simplest case, without multipath or other channel memory effects, a minimum of three successive bit intervals would have to be considered in order to get all possible combinations of cross interference. As mentioned above, Verdu's solution to this problem resulted in a Viterbi algorithm as the decision-making mechanism. This is still too complex in the case of $K \gg 1$ users, as would occur in cellular radio, for example, because the number of states required for the Viterbi algorithm is 2^K. For example, for the North American CDMA standard discussed in Chapter 10, a maximum of 60 users per cell is possible,* resulting in $2^{60} = 1.15 \times 10^{18}$ states if the interference from all users to a given one were taken into account. Of course, the interference from several of these users may be very weak, so it may be ignored.

To discuss some of the simplified solutions to the multiuser detection problem, we still consider the synchronous case and introduce the following notation. It is assumed

---

*The value of 60 takes only the number of available Walsh codes into account. The actual number of possible users is significantly lower.

that the first stage of the multiuser detector is a bank of correlators or matched filters. The output samples of these correlators, one for each user, forms what are termed *sufficient statistics*. The output samples of the matched filter bank at time kT_b compose the vector (column matrix) $\mathbf{y}_n$, where the vector components correspond to the matched filter outputs for the users. İt can be written as

$$\mathbf{y}_n = \mathbf{RWd}_n + \mathbf{n}_n, \, n = 1,2, \cdots, N \qquad (9\text{-}83)$$

where $\mathbf{d}_n = (K \times 1)$ data vector for time nT_b;

$\quad \mathbf{n}_n$ = Gaussian noise vector (note that its components are correlated with each other because, unlike in Chapter 4, the correlator bank is not with reference signals that are orthogonal to each other) $(K \times 1)$;

$\quad \mathbf{R} = \mathbf{cc}^T$ (superscript T denotes transpose) is the correlation matrix of the spreading codes, where $\mathbf{c}$ is the $(K \times K)$ matrix of spreading codes, one row for each user;

$\quad \mathbf{W}$ = diagonal $K \times K$ matrix of received energies for the users.

The decision process for the conventional detector, discussed for the special case of $K = 2$ in relation to the results of Figure 9–39, may be expressed in this notation as

$$\hat{\mathbf{d}}_n = \text{sign}(\mathbf{y}_n) \qquad (9\text{-}84)$$

As seen from Figure 9–39, it does not have good performance in multiuser environments, particularly in the presence of interfering users of higher power than the user of interest.

Multiplying (9–83) by $\mathbf{R}^{-1}$ we obtain

$$\mathbf{z}_n = \mathbf{R}^{-1}\mathbf{y}_n = \mathbf{Wd}_n + \mathbf{R}^{-1}\mathbf{n}_n, \, n = 1, 2, \cdots, N \qquad (9\text{-}85)$$

with corresponding decision process

$$\hat{\mathbf{d}}_n = \text{sign}(\mathbf{z}_n) \qquad (9\text{-}86)$$

Known as the decorrelating detector, it was first proposed by Schneider [22] as a means for eliminating the multiple-access interference. Its bit error probability for the ith user is

$$P_{b,i} = Q\left(\sqrt{\frac{2W_i}{N_0 R_{i,i}^{-1}}}\right) \qquad (9\text{-}87)$$

where $R_{i,i}^{-1}$ denotes the ith diagonal element of $\mathbf{R}^{-1}$.

Note that (9–86) indicates that the decorrelating detector decision process is independent of the particular user chosen, and it has been demonstrated in [27] that it is the maximum likelihood detector when the signal energies are unknown by the receiver. Because of the independence of the particular user of interest, it is the best design for the worst case, which is known as a *minimax* solution. But since it is a minimax solution, it may be too conservative, as pointed out in [28], when the signal energies are known. The $R_{i,i}^{-1}$ in the denominator of (9–87) means that the decorrelating receiver enhances the noise variance. However, a significant improvement in performance is obtained over the conventional detector provided the energies of the received signals are known. Because of the noise enhancement property of the decorrelating multiuser receiver, a minimum mean-square error solution to the multiuser problem has been proposed. Its performance is a compromise between decorrelation and noise enhancement.

In terms of the notation introduced above, the optimum detector may be expressed as [28–30]

$$\hat{\mathbf{d}}_n = \arg\left\{\max_{\mathbf{d}_n \in \{1,-1\}^K} (2\mathbf{y}_n^T \mathbf{W} \mathbf{d}_n - \mathbf{d}_n^T \mathbf{W} \mathbf{R} \mathbf{W} \mathbf{d}_n)\right\} \tag{9-88}$$

where arg $\{\cdot\}$ means the sequence $\mathbf{d}_k$ that provides the maximum. As discussed above, this detector is usually too complex to be implemented; an alternative is the multistage detector [24, 29], defined by

$$\hat{\mathbf{d}}_n = \arg\left\{\begin{matrix}\max \\ d_{n(i)} \in \{1,-1\}^K \\ x_{n(p)} = \hat{x}_n^{l-1}(p), p \neq i\end{matrix} (2\mathbf{y}_n^T \mathbf{W} \mathbf{d}_n - \mathbf{d}_n^T \mathbf{W} \mathbf{R} \mathbf{W} \mathbf{d}_n)\right\} \tag{9-89}$$

where the maximization is now performed over one user at a time and the initial stage is either a conventional detector or decorrelation detector. This considerably simplifies the problem, although detector performance is dependent on errors made in the initial stages.

Many other multiuser detectors have been discussed in the literature, and many more currently are being proposed. We will close our discussion with only these.

EXAMPLE 9–11

Compare the performances of the conventional and decorrelation detectors for the three user case where the codes used are cyclic shifts of a 7-chip PN sequence, assuming user 1 is the user of interest [30].

Solution: The receiver for user i is shown in Figure 9–40, where it is convenient to normalize the integrator output of the correlator by $1/T_b$. The receiver output may be expressed in matrix form as

$$\mathbf{y} = \begin{bmatrix} 1 & \rho_{12} & \rho_{13} \\ \rho_{12} & 1 & \rho_{23} \\ \rho_{13} & \rho_{23} & 1 \end{bmatrix} \begin{bmatrix} \sqrt{E_1/T_b} & 0 & 0 \\ 0 & \sqrt{E_2/T_b} & 0 \\ 0 & 0 & \sqrt{E_3/T_b} \end{bmatrix} \begin{bmatrix} d_1 \\ d_2 \\ d_3 \end{bmatrix} + \begin{bmatrix} n_1 \\ n_2 \\ n_3 \end{bmatrix} \tag{9-90}$$

$$= \mathbf{R} \mathbf{W} \mathbf{d} + \mathbf{n}$$

The decorrelation receiver works with the statistic

$$\mathbf{z} = \begin{bmatrix} \sqrt{E_1/T_b}\, d_1 \\ \sqrt{E_2/T_b}\, d_2 \\ \sqrt{E_3/T_b}\, d_3 \end{bmatrix} + \begin{bmatrix} 1 & \rho_{12} & \rho_{13} \\ \rho_{12} & 1 & \rho_{23} \\ \rho_{13} & \rho_{23} & 1 \end{bmatrix}^{-1} \begin{bmatrix} n_1 \\ n_2 \\ n_3 \end{bmatrix} = \mathbf{W} \mathbf{d} + \mathbf{R}^{-1}\mathbf{n} \tag{9-91}$$

The noise covariance matrix for the decorrelator receiver is

$$E[NN^T] = E[\mathbf{R}^{-1}\mathbf{n}(\mathbf{R}^{-1}\mathbf{n})^T] = E[\mathbf{R}^{-1}(\mathbf{nn})^T\mathbf{R}^{-1}]$$

$$= \mathbf{R}^{-1}E[(\mathbf{nn})]^T\mathbf{R}^{-1} = \mathbf{R}^{-1}E\left\{\frac{N_0}{2T_b}\mathbf{R}\right\}\mathbf{R}^{-1} \tag{9-92}$$

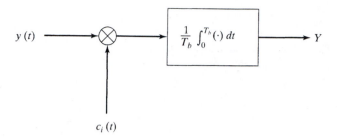

FIGURE 9–40   Correlator receiver for user i.

$$= \frac{N_0}{2T_b} \mathbf{R}^{-1}$$

which follows by using $(\mathbf{AB})^T = \mathbf{B}^T \mathbf{A}^T$ and the fact that $\mathbf{R}^{-1}$ is symmetric since $\mathbf{R}$ is symmetric. Also, we have used

$$E[n_i n_j] = \frac{1}{T_b^2} \int_0^{T_b} \int_0^{T_b} E[n_i(t)n_j(\tau)]c_i(t)c_j(\tau)dt \, d\tau$$

$$= \frac{1}{T_b^2} \int_0^{T_b} \int_0^{T_b} \frac{N_0}{2}\delta(t - \tau)c_i(t)c_j(\tau)dt \, d\tau \qquad (9\text{--}93)$$

$$= \frac{1}{T_b^2} \frac{N_0}{2} \int_0^{T_b} c_i(t)c_j(t)dt = \frac{N_0}{2T_b} \rho_{ij}$$

With the codes being cyclic shifts of the same 7-chip PN code, the various correlations are $\rho_{11} = \rho_{22} = \rho_{33} = 1$ with all correlations with unequal indices being $-1/7$. The inverse correlation matrix is

$$R^{-1} = \begin{bmatrix} 1.05 & 0.175 & 0.175 \\ 0.175 & 1.05 & 0.175 \\ 0.175 & 0.175 & 1.05 \end{bmatrix} \qquad (9\text{--}94)$$

Thus, the probability of error for the decorrelating receiver is

$$P_{b,\,\text{decorr.}} = Q\left(\sqrt{\frac{2(1.05)E_1}{N_0}} \right) \qquad (9\text{--}95)$$

The probability of error for the conventional receiver, on the other hand, is

$$P_{b,\,\text{conv.}} = \frac{1}{4} \sum_{\text{all comb'ns of sign}} Q\left(\sqrt{\frac{2(1 \pm \rho_{12}\sqrt{E_2/E_1} \pm \rho_{13}\sqrt{E_3/E_1})^2 E_1}{N_0}} \right) \qquad (9\text{--}96)$$

A comparison is given in Figure 9–41 between the conventional and decorrelating receivers in a multiuser environment, where the advantage of the multiuser detector over the conventional is clearly evident. Much more could be said about multiuser detection, but we leave the subject and refer the reader to a recent book on the subject [31].

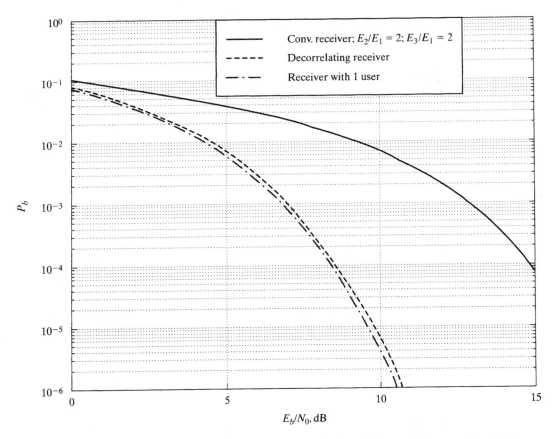

FIGURE 9–41   Comparison of the conventional and decorrelating receivers in a three-user environment.

9.10   EXAMPLES OF SPREAD-SPECTRUM SYSTEMS

Two examples of communication systems that utilize spread-spectrum modulation are briefly described in this section. All information was obtained from the unclassified literature. The application of spread spectrum to cellular radio will be discussed in Chapter 10.

9.10.1   Space Shuttle Spectrum Despreader

Communication between the NASA space shuttle and ground stations is accomplished via a number of different paths. Some of these paths are direct between the shuttle and ground and some are indirect and include the Tracking and Data Relay Satellites (TDRS) as relay stations. The TDRS System (TDRSS) is a system that includes two relay satellites in geostationary orbits about 22,300 miles above the earth's equator, giving a period of revolution of exactly one sidereal day. Thus the satellites appear to be stationary to an observer on the ground. The two TDRSS are always able to communicate with a large ground station at White Sands, New Mexico, and one of the two TDRSS is able to communicate with a low-orbiting satellite or the space shuttle most of the time. The TDRSS enables nearly continuous communication with low-orbiting satellites without an expensive network of ground stations. The space shuttle can make use of the TDRSS using either S-band or Ku-band DSSS links. The particular link discussed here is the S-band link from the TDRS to the space shuttle. The space shuttle receiver was designed and built by TRW Systems Group and detailed information is available from several sources, including [32, 33].

The space shuttle S-band forward link (TDRS to shuttle) operates at one of two carrier frequencies (2106.406 and 2287.5 MHz). The transmitted signal is a BPSK spread-spectrum signal with convolutionally coded data modulo-2 asynchronously added to the DS spreading code. The particular convolutional code used is constraint length 7, rate 1/3. The critical parameters of the S-band signal are given in Table 9–6. Observe that two data rates must be accommodated. For operation at low signal-to-noise ratios, this implies that two IF filter bandwidths must be used. A conceptual block diagram of a portion of the receiver for this application is illustrated in Figure 9–42.

Only the spread-spectrum demodulator shown in Figure 9–42 performs the spread-spectrum code acquisition and tracking functions. The received spread signal is down-converted from S-band to 31 MHz by the receiver front end (not shown) whose input is the "second IF despread output." The received IF signal is power divided and routed to three different channels. The upper channel is the acquisition channel, the middle channel is the code-tracking channel, and the lower channel is the data demodulator channel.

Consider the acquisition channel of Figure 9–42. The code acquisition strategy selected is a stepped serial search using $\frac{1}{2}$-chip steps and using fixed-integration-time energy detection. The mixer labeled "timeshare" in Figure 9–42 is the acquisition-despreading mixer. If the spreading code phase selected for evaluation by the code acquisition logic is incorrect, the output of this mixer is a wideband signal most of whose energy the bandpass filters will reject. If the phase is correct, however, the 31 MHz IF signal will be collapsed to the Manchester-coded data bandwidth and will pass through the bandpass filter. The one-sided IF bandwidths necessary to accommodate the Manchester-coded data are approximately four times the symbol rate or 384 and 864 kHz for 96 and 216 kbps, re-

TABLE 9–6   TDRS to Space Shuttle S-Band Signal Parameters [33]

Carrier Frequency	2106.406 MHz or 2287.500 MHz
Data rates	32 kbps or 72 kbps
Forward error correction	Rate-1/3, constraint length 7; convolutional code
Data modulation	BPSK Manchester
Data modulator symbol rate	96 kbps or 216 kbps
Spreading code rate	11.232 Mchips/s
Spreading code length	2047 chips
Received signal-to-noise density ratio (P/N_0)	48 dB-Hz for low data rate; 51 dB-Hz for high data rate
Code Doppler offset	±100 Hz

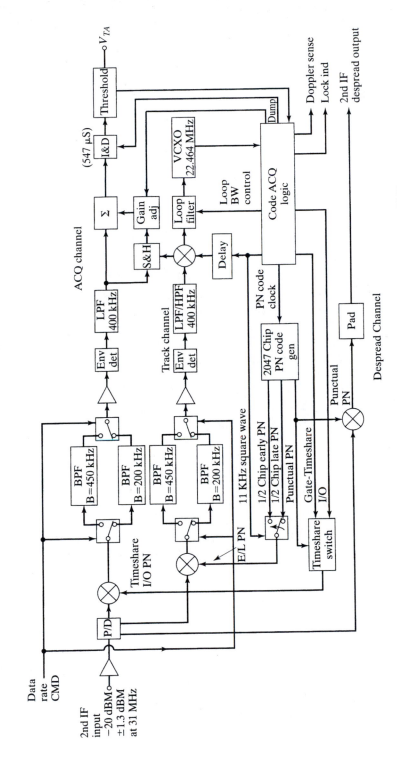

FIGURE 9-42 Space shuttle S-band spread-spectrum demodulator [32].

spectively. The bandwidths shown in Figure 9–42 are half-bandwidths or, in other words, the one-sided bandwidths of the equivalent lowpass filter. The bandwidths shown are slightly larger than one-half the values just calculated so that the despread signal will pass through the filter when Doppler offsets are present. The correctness of the spreading code phase is indicated by the presence or absence of energy at the IF filter output. The envelope detector, lowpass filter, integrate-and-dump circuitry, and the threshold detector sense this energy. The integration time is 547 microseconds.

The predetection signal-to-noise ratio is calculated at the output of the IF filter. For the wider filter (i.e., high data rate), the output signal-to-noise ratio is 51 dB-Hz − $10\log_{10}$ (900 kHz) = −8.5 dB, and for the narrowband filter, the output signal-to-noise ratio is 48 dB−Hz-$10\log_{10}$ (400 kHz) = −8 dB. Because these signal-to-noise ratios are relatively low, the energy detection time–bandwidth product must be large to achieve large detection probabilities simultaneously with low false alarm rates. For the high and low data rates the time–bandwidth products are 492 and 219, respectively. The probability density of the integrator output is accurately modeled as Gaussian at either of these time–bandwidth products.

An important feature of the acquisition strategy is the automatic gain control hardware consisting of a sample-and-hold, a gain-adjust circuit, and a summing junction. This circuitry senses and compensates for variations in energy detector input noise levels. These variations may be due to day-to-day hardware changes or other factors. A gain control feature is essential in all spread spectrum systems. Another method of accomplishing this task will be described later.

The acquisition integrator output after 547 microseconds is compared with a fixed threshold. If the output is above the threshold, the code phase is declared correct. Otherwise, the acquisition logic selects a new spreading code phase and the process repeats. After a correct detection, code tracking is attempted and the code phase is reevaluated using an integration time of 12.6 milliseconds. The long integration is used as an initial lock detector as well as a drop lock indicator. The entire acquisition strategy can be represented by the signal flow graph of Figure 9–43. The tracking loop is closed when the system enters state 2. In state 2, the integration increases to 12.6 milliseconds and a single missed detection will cause the system to reject the trial code phase. A single detection in state 2 will cause the system to enter state 3, where it can remain indefinitely. Once in state 3, five consecutive missed detections are required before the code phase is rejected. The acquisition strategy is known as a multiple-dwell strategy using two different integration times.

The middle channel of Figure 9–42 functions as the spreading code tracking discriminator. The tracking loop uses a noncoherent tau-dither early-late phase discriminator with a dither magnitude of $\pm\frac{1}{2}$ chip and a dither rate of 22 kHz accomplished by the 11 kHz square wave shown in Figure 9–42. The reference code is dithered by its early and late functions at a 22 kHz rate. The reference code is dithered by switching between early and late versions of the code. The dither discriminator energy detector is identical to the acquisition energy detector. The dither is removed and the mixer in front of the loop filter in the middle channel generates the error signal. The loop filter drives the code clock voltage-controlled oscillator, which is operating at twice the clock frequency. Observe

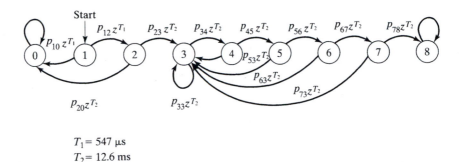

$T_1 = 547$ μs
$T_2 = 12.6$ ms

FIGURE 9–43   Acquisition signal flow diagram for the space shuttle spectrum despreader.

that the dither rate is much lower than the IF filter bandwidth. The parameters of the code-tracking loop are summarized in Table 9–7. When the code tracking loop is functioning properly, the PN code generator outputs a spreading code replica, which is precisely phase synchronous with the received spreading waveform. This punctual spreading code is used in the bottom channel of Figure 9–42 to despread the received waveform for later coherent data demodulation. This is the only function of the bottom channel.

Several other factors in the receiver design merit discussion. First, observe that the reference input to all of the despreading mixers is the spreading code directly and not the modulated carrier. The reason for using the modulated carrier reference is to avoid a potential problem with RF to IF feedthrough in nonideal mixers (see Chapter 2). Second, the code tracking loop of Figure 9–42 actually has four different loop bandwidths. The largest bandwidth is used for acquisition and the smallest for final code tracking. The step from 500 to 10 Hz is too large to maintain lock reliably during the switching transient so that two intermediate bandwidths of 135 and 37 Hz are included.

9.10.2   Global Positioning System

One of the many applications of direct-sequence spread spectrum is to ranging systems. Recall that the spread-spectrum code tracking circuitry is actually tracking the propagation delay between the transmitter and the receiver. If the transmission delay is known, the range from the transmitter to the receiver can be determined. The Global Positioning System (GPS) enables users to determine their position on or above the earth's surface by measuring their range to four to six GPS satellites whose positions are accurately known. There are 24 GPS satellites in circular orbits 12,211 miles above the earth. The orbital period of these satellites is exactly 12 hours. There are eight satellites in each of three orbits that are inclined 55 degrees with respect to the equator and are separated in longitude by 120 degrees. The mature orbital configuration is illustrated in Figure 9–44. With this configuration, a GPS user anywhere on the earth is able to receive signals from at least four satellites at any time.

TABLE 9–7   Code-Tracking Loop Parameters for the TDRS-to-Space Shuttle
S-Band Link [32]

Tracking loop type	Second order
Phase discriminator type	Noncoherent tau-dither early-late gate
Dither magnitude	$\pm\frac{1}{2}$ chip
Dither rate	22 kHz
Close-loop bandwidth (one-sided)	500 Hz for acquisition; 10 Hz for tracking

Each satellite maintains a highly accurate clock as well as data on the orbits of all 24 satellites. The clocks of all satellites are precisely synchronized through a ground station near Colorado Springs, Colorado (Schriever Air Force Base). This ground station also updates the orbital position information for all satellites using information supplied to it by a network of satellite tracking stations. For the purposes of this discussion, all satellite clocks may be considered synchronous and all satellite orbital data may be considered completely accurate. Thus each satellite knows the position of all GPS satellites at any instant in time.

Two DSSS signals, L1 and L2, are transmitted from each satellite to the ground (Figure 9–45). The L1 and L2 carrier frequencies are 1575.42 and 1227.60 MHz, respectively. Consider the L1 signal first. The spread-spectrum modulation is unbalanced QPSK and the I-channel spreading code is a Gold code of length 1023 chips. The chip rate is 1.023 MHz and the code period is 1 millisecond. A different Gold code is used for each satellite so that a ground receiver can distinguish satellites. This short spreading code is called the clear/acquisition or C/A code. The Q-channel spreading code is a very long

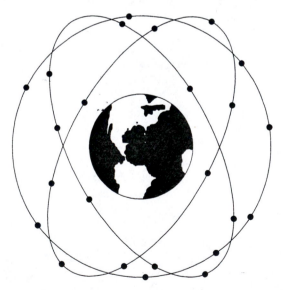

FIGURE 9–44   Operational satellite configuration of the Global Positioning System.

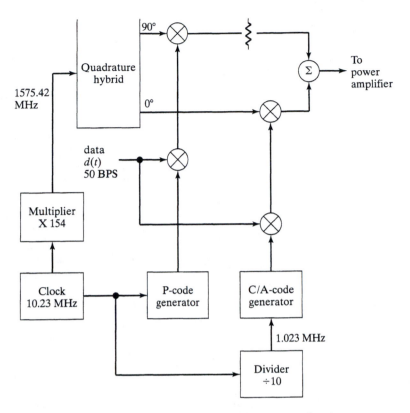

FIGURE 9–45 Generation of the GPS L1 spread-spectrum signal.

nonlinear code whose clock rate is 10.230 MHz. This code is called the precise code or P code, and its period is measured in days. Each satellite uses a different phase of the long code. The P-channel power is 3 dB less than the C/A channel power. Both the P-channel and C/A-channel signals are modulated by a 1500-bit data message that is transmitted at 50 bps and repeated cyclically. This 1500-bit message contains position information as well as data used to correct for errors in propagation time, satellite clock bias, and so on. One method of generating L1 is shown in Figure 9–45. The spread-spectrum modulation for L2 is BPSK direct sequence using the P code with a chip rate of 10.23 MHz. The data modulation is also BPSK and the data is identical to the L1 channel data. The L2 signal is intended for military users of GPS.

Suppose that the GPS user receives the L1 signal. The most sophisticated user receivers will have at least four separate channels for simultaneously demodulating the L1 signals from four different GPS satellites. The code generators for each channel will be programmed to the codes for the satellites of interest. A less complex receiver will have a single channel and will demodulate the signals from each of four satellites one after the other. In either case, the receiver first synchronizes to and tracks the C/A code. With C/A code synchronization established, carrier recovery circuits can phase lock to the C/A car-

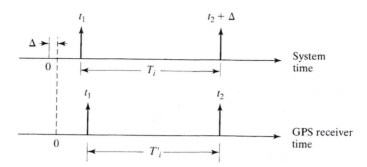

FIGURE 9–46   Time lines illustrating the relationship between system time and receiver time.

rier and data demodulation can begin. Using either information obtained from the data message or previously known data, P-code synchronization can now be accomplished.

A receiver may determine the range to a satellite using either the C/A code or the P code. Of course, the P code range information is more accurate because its chip rate is higher. Suppose that the C/A code is being used, however, to simplify this discussion. Then, after synchronization to the C/A code, the receiver records the time at which the code epoch[7] occurs. The time reference used for this measurement is the receiver's own clock, which is assumed to be offset from the system clock by Δ. The time of arrival (TOA) for the C/A code epoch from all four satellites is recorded.

The data transmitted from each satellite gives the exact position of the satellite and the system time when the code epoch event occurred. Figure 9–46 illustrates the time relationship between the system time and the receiver time. The code epoch occurred at the satellite transmitter at system time t_1. The receiver records the time of the received epoch event as t_2 (in receiver time) and calculates the propagation time $T_i' = t_2 - t_1$. Because of the error between the system and receiver clocks, T_i', is incorrect and the actual propagation time is $T_i = T_i' + \Delta$. The value of T_i' is recorded for all four satellites and is used to calculate a pseudorange $\rho_i = T_i'c$ for each. Because the satellite clocks are all synchronous, the difference between the actual range $R_i = T_ic$ and the pseudorange ρ_i is the same for all satellites. This range error is denoted by $B = c\Delta$.

The coordinate system used to calculate the user position is a rectangular system with origin at the earth's center. Let x, y, and z denote the user position and U_i, V_i, and W_i denote the position of the ith satellite in this coordinate system. Then the following set of four equations relate the pseudoranges calculated by the receiver to the user position, the satellite position, and the unknown range error:

$$
\begin{aligned}
R_1 &= \rho_1 + B = [(U_1 - x)^2 + (V_1 - y)^2 + (W_1 - z)^2]^{1/2} \\
R_2 &= \rho_2 + B = [(U_2 - x)^2 + (V_2 - y)^2 + (W_2 - z)^2]^{1/2} \\
R_3 &= \rho_3 + B = [(U_3 - x)^2 + (V_3 - y)^2 + (W_3 - z)^2]^{1/2} \\
R_4 &= \rho_4 + B = [(U_4 - x)^2 + (V_4 - y)^2 + (W_4 - z)^2]^{1/2}
\end{aligned}
\tag{9–97}
$$

[7]A code epoch is marked by any known code generator state. It is usually the all-ones state.

This is a set of four equations in four unknowns that may be solved for the user position and range error. Iterative techniques are normally used to solve these equations. The translation from the (x, y, z) coordinates to latitude, longitude, and altitude is straightforward and is discussed in [34].

This discussion of GPS is oversimplified in that many error sources are not discussed. The simplest receivers perform a calculation just as described; however, the more sophisticated receivers use more complicated algorithms. Position accuracy on the order a few meters is possible and has been demonstrated. See [35, 36] for additional information about the Global Positioning System.

9.11 SUMMARY

1. This chapter began with consideration of two communications problems for which spread-spectrum communication systems are possible solutions, in particular, combating jamming (antijam) and to hinder detection by an unintended party (low probability of detection).

2. Various types of spread spectrum systems were introduced and described in terms of waveforms, transmitter structures, and receiver structures. These included BPSK direct-sequence (DS) spread-spectrum (SS), QPSK DSSS, noncoherent slow frequency-hop (FH) SS, noncoherent fast FHSS, and hybrid DS/FHSS.

3. Complex envelope representations for SS systems were discussed. These allow convenient representation of SS systems and also facilitate simulation.

4. A discussion of the generation of spreading codes was given. For the most part, maximal-length pseudorandom sequences were considered, including generator configurations, properties, and power spectra. Other codes discussed were Kasami sequences and quaternary sequences.

5. A table of polynomials useful for designing m-sequences was given in Table 9–2.

6. It was shown that an m-sequence is insecure in that correct estimation of a number of chips equal to twice length its length plus one may be used to calculate the code generator structure.

7. Gold codes have low cross-correlation values and can be generated from proper pairs of m-sequences.

8. The synchronization of the despreading code at the receiver consists of two phases: acquisition and tracking.

9. The performance of a spread-spectrum system in AWGN is the same as a comparable (i.e., same message modulation) system using no spreading. In jamming, a spread-spectrum system can provide improvement through jamming power reduction by the processing gain. An optimized jammer, which consists of a pulsed noise source in the case of DSSS and a narrowband (tone) jammer in the case of FHSS, can drive the probability of error to be inversely dependent on E_b/N_0 rather than decreasing as a negative exponential with E_b/N_0.

10. Coding with interleaving can be used to combat the detrimental effects of a pulsed jammer in DSSS or a narrowband jammer in FHSS.

11. Performance analysis of spread spectrum communication links in multiuser environments showed that the conventional matched filter receiver experiences an error threshold at high signal-to-noise ratios. In the presence of an interfering other user of high power, a conventional spread spectrum communication link becomes virtually unusable.

12. Multiuser detectors are a promising way to recoup much of the performance loss that a conventional spread spectrum receiver experiences in a multiuser environment.

13. Two examples of systems utilizing spread spectrum were given—the space shuttle spectrum despreader and the Navstar Global Positioning System.

REFERENCES

[1] A. J. Viterbi, "Spread Spectrum Communications—Myths and Realities," *IEEE Commun. Mag.*, pp. 11–18, May 1979.

[2] R. A. Dillard, "Detectability of Spread Spectrum Signals," *IEEE Trans. on Aerosp. Electron. Syst.*, Vol. AES-15, pp. 526–537, July 1979.

[3] A. Papoulis, *Probability, Random Variables, and Stochastic Processes,* 2nd ed. (New York: McGraw-Hill, 1985).

[4] B. K. Levitt, "Effect of Modulation Format and Jamming Spectrum on Performance of Direct Sequence Spread Spectrum Systems," *Conf. Rec., IEEE Nat. Telecommun. Conf.*, pp. 3.4.1–3.4.5, Nov. 1980.

[5] R. L. Peterson, R. E. Ziemer, and D. E. Borth, *Introduction to Spread Spectrum Communications* (Upper Saddle River, NJ: Prentice Hall, 1995.)

[6] R. A. Scholtz, "The Spread Spectrum Concept," *IEEE Trans. Commun.*, Vol. COM-25, pp. 748–755, Aug. 1977.

[7] R. E. Ziemer and W. H. Tranter, *Principles of Communications: Systems, Modulation, and Noise,* 5th ed. (New York: Wiley, 1995).

[8] D. V. Sarwate and M. B. Pursley, "Cross-Correlation Properties of Pseudorandom and Related Sequences," *Proc. IEEE,* Vol. 68, pp. 593–619, May 1980.

[9] W. W. Peterson and E. J. Weldon, *Error Correction Codes* (Cambridge, MA: MIT Press, 1972).

[10] K. Metzger and R. J. Bouwens, "An Ordered Table of Primitive Polynomials over GF(2) of Degrees 2 Through 19 for Use with Linear Maximal Sequence Generators," TM107, Cooley Electronics Laboratory, Univ. of Michigan, Ann Arbor, July 1972 (AD 746876).

[11] J. K. Holmes, *Coherent Spread Spectrum Systems* (New York: Wiley-Interscience, 1982).

[12] J. L. Massey, "Shift-Register Synthesis and BCH Decoding," *IEEE Trans. Inf. Theory,* Vol. IT-15, pp. 122–127, Jan. 1969.

[13] P. V. Kumar, T. Helleseth, A. R. Calderbank, and A. R. Hammons, Jr., "Large families of quaternary sequences with low correlation," *IEEE Trans. Inf. Theory,* Vol. 42, pp. 579–592, Mar. 1996.

[14] A. R. Hammons, Jr. and P. V. Kumar, "On a recent 4-phase sequence design for CDMA," *IEICE Trans. Commun.,* Vol. E76-B, pp. 804–813, Aug. 1993.

[15] S. W. Houston, "Modulation Techniques for Communications. Part I: Tone and Noise Jamming Performance of Spread Spectrum M-ary FSK and 2, 4-ary DPSK Waveforms," *Conf. Record: NAECON,* pp. 51–88, May 1975.

[16] N. Nazari and R. E. Ziemer, "Computationally Efficient Bounds for Performance of Direct-Sequence Spread-Spectrum Multiple-Access Communications Systems in Jamming Environments," *IEEE Trans. Commun.*, vol. COM-36, pp. 577–586, May 1988.

[17] J. H. Lehnert and M. B. Pursley, "Error Probabilities for Binary Direct-Sequence Spread-Spectrum Communications with Random Signature Sequences," *IEEE Trans. Commun.*, Vol. COM-35, pp. 87–98, Mar. 1987.

[18] M. B. Pursley, "Performance Evaluation of Phase-Coded Spread-Spectrum Multiple-Access Communication," *IEEE Trans. Commun.*, Vol. COM-25, pp. 800–803, Aug. 1977.

[19] K. B. Letaief, "Efficient Evaluation of the Error Probabilities of Spread-Spectrum Multiple-Access Communications," *IEEE Trans. Commun.*, Vol. 45, pp. 139–246, Feb. 1997.

[20] S. Verdu, "Optimum Multi-User Signal Detection," Ph. D. Dissertation, Department of Electrical and Computer Engineering, University of Illinois at Urbana-Champaign. Report T-151 Coordinated Science Laboratory, Urbana, IL, Aug. 1984.

[21] S. Verdu, "Minimum Probability of Error for Asynchronous Gaussian Multiple-Access Channels," *IEEE Trans. on Infor. Theory*, Vol. IT-32, pp. 85–96, Jan. 1986.

[22] K. S. Schneider, "Optimum Detection of Code Division Multiplexed Communications," *IEEE Trans. on Aerospace and Electronic Systems*, Vol. AES-15, pp. 181–185, Jan. 1979.

[23] S. Verdu, "Recent Progress in Multiuser Detection," in M. Thoma and A. Wyner, *Lecture Notes in Control and Information Sciences*, No. 129, pp. 27–38, W. A. Porter and S. C. Kak (Eds.), *Advances in Communications and Signal Processing* (New York: Springer-Verlag, 1989.)

[24] M. Varanazi and B. Aazhang, "Multistage Detection in Asynchronous Code-Division Multiple-Access Communications," *IEEE Trans. Commun.*, Vol. 38, pp. 509–519, Apr. 1990.

[25] S. Kandala, E. Sousa, and S. Pasupathy, "Multi-User Multi-Sensor Detectors for CDMA Networks," *IEEE Trans. Commun.*, Vol. 43, pp. 946–957, Apr. 1995.

[26] M. Honig, U. Madhow, and S. Verdu, "Blind Adaptive Multiuser Detection," *IEEE Trans. on Infor. Theory*, Vol. 41, pp. 944–960, Jul. 1995.

[27] R. Lupas and S. Verdu, "Linear Multiuser Detectors for Synchronous CDMA Channels," *IEEE Trans. on Infor. Theory*, Vol. IT-35, pp. 123–136, Jan. 1989.

[28] M. K. Varanasi and B. Aazhang, "Probability of Error Comparison of Linear and Iterative Multiuser Detectors," in M. Thoma and A. Wyner, *Lecture Notes in Control and Information Sciences*, No. 129, pp. 15–26, W. A. Porter and S. C. Kak (eds.), *Advances in Communications and Signal Processing* (New York: Springer-Verlag, 1989.)

[29] A. Duel-Hallen, J. Holtzman, and Z. Zvonar, "Multiuser Detection for CDMA Systems," *IEEE Personal Commun. Mag.*, Vol. 2, pp. 45–48, April 1995.

[30] M. Juntti and J. Lilleberg, "Comparative Analysis of Conventional and Multiuser Detectors in Multisensor Receivers," *IEEE Milcom Proc*, pp. 1–6, Oct. 1997.

[31] S. Verdu, *Multiuser Detection* (Cambridge, UK: Cambridge University Press, 1998).

[32] W. K. Alem, G. K. Huth, J. K. Holmes, and S. Udalou, "Spread Spectrum Acquisition and Tracking Performance for Shuttle Communication Links," *IEEE Trans. Commun.*, Vol. COM-26, pp. 1689–1703, Nov. 1978.

[33] TRW Systems Group, "Shuttle Spectrum Despreader," Final Report, Contract NAS-9-14690, May 21, 1976.

[34] K. P. Yiu, R. Eschenback, and F. Lee, "Land Navigation with a Low Cost GPS Receiver," *Conf. Record: IEEE National Telecomm. Conf.*, pp. 55.3.1–55.3.5, Nov. 1980.

[35] B.W. Parkinson and J. J. Spilker, Jr. (Eds.), *Global Positioning System: Theory and Applications, Vols. I–III* (Washington, DC.: Amer. Inst. of Aero. and Astro., Inc., 1996).

[36] *Proc. IEEE*, Special Issue on GPS, Vol. 87, Jan. 1999.

PROBLEMS

9–1. Consider a non-spread-spectrum communication system employing differential binary PSK modulation. Suppose that this system is jammed by a narrowband noise-pulse jammer having total average power J and duty factor ρ.

    (a) Find the optimum jammer duty factor ignoring thermal noise as a function of E_b/N_J and plot bit error probability versus E_b/N_J for the optimized jammer.

    (b) Plot bit error probability versus E_b/N_J for nonoptimum jammer duty factors $\rho = 0.25$, 0.50, 0.75, and 1.0.

9–2. Consider a BPSK DSSS system using differential binary PSK data modulation. Suppose that this system is jammed by a narrowband pulse-noise jammer having a total average power J and duty factor ρ. Assume that the spreading code chip rate is 10 times the data bit rate.

    (a) Find the optimum jammer duty factor, ignoring thermal noise as a function of E_b/N_J and plot bit error probability versus E_b/N_J for the optimized jammer.

    (b) What is the processing gain of this spread-spectrum system?

    (c) Compare the optimum duty factors for Problems 9–1 and 9–2.

9–3. Consider a BPSK DSSS system with arbitrary data modulation and continuous tone jamming. Assuming that the spreading code period is infinite, plot the processing gain of the system as a function of the jamming tone center frequency relative to the system carrier frequency. Assume that the spreading code rate is 100 times the data rate.

9–4. Consider a direct-sequence BPSK spread-spectrum system that obtains its spreading code from the feedback shift-register circuit shown below. Calculate the transmitter output power spectral density for arbitrary data modulation.

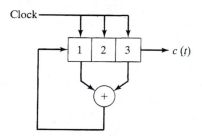

PROBLEM 9–4   Feedback shift register.

9–5. Consider a frequency-hop spread-spectrum system that uses binary FSK data modulation and 64 orthogonal frequency-hop bands. Suppose that the data rate is 1.0 Mbps and that the frequency hop rate is 10^4 hops per second. Assume that the FH synthesizer is noncoherent from hop to hop and assume any convenient carrier frequency.

    (a) Calculate the transmitter output power spectral density.

    (b) Calculate the optimum number of frequency-hop bands for a partial band-noise jammer to jam assuming that the jammer has constant total power.

9–6. Consider a frequency-hop spread-spectrum system that uses binary FSK data modulation and 64 orthogonal frequency-hop bands. Suppose that the data rate is 10 kbps and the frequency hop rate is 1.0×10^6 hops per second. Assume that the FH synthesizer is noncoherent from hop to hop and assume any convenient carrier frequency. Calculate the transmitter output power spectral density.

9–7. Consider a BPSK DSSS receiver using arbitrary data modulation having the configuration illustrated here. The received thermal noise two-sided power spectral density is $N_0/2$ watts/Hz and the noise bandwidth of the input bandpass filter is B hertz. Assuming that the spreading code chip rate is very large relative to the data rate, calculate the thermal noise spectral density at the data demodulator input for $B = 2/T_c$, $3/T_c$, and $4/T_c$. T_c is the spreading code chip duration.

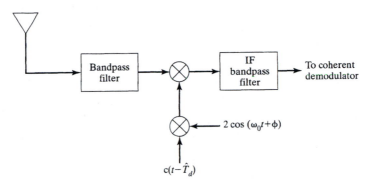

PROBLEM 9–7   Direct-sequence spread-spectrum receiver.

9–8. Consider the BPSK DSSS transmitter illustrated below. Assume that the two code generators operate synchronously and that each generates an independent sequence of random binary (± 1) symbols. Calculate the transmitted power spectral density as a function of τ, and plot results for $\tau = 0$, $T_c/4$, and $T_c/2$, where T_c is the code chip duration.

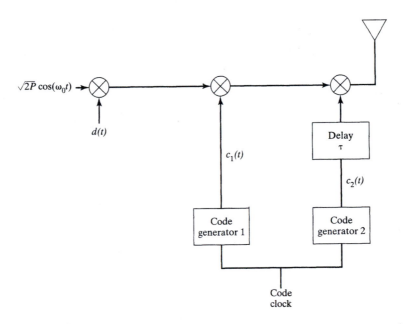

PROBLEM 9–8   Offset code direct-sequence spread-spectrum transmitter.

9–9. In Chapter 3 it was demonstrated that a filter "matched" to the signaling waveform was optimum for data detection in an AWGN environment. Show that in a BPSK direct-sequence spread-spectrum system, the receiver despreading function is part of that optimum matched filtering operation.

9–10. Consider a BPSK DSSS receiver that employs coherent BPSK data modulation as shown below. Assume that a tone jammer is used against this receiver and that the jammer knows the correct carrier phase. Assume an infinite spreading code period, a jammer power J, and a spreading code chip rate that is N times the data rate. Determine the probability density function of the integrator output at the sampling instants. Write an expression for the bit error probability as a function of the jamming, signal, and noise powers, and N.

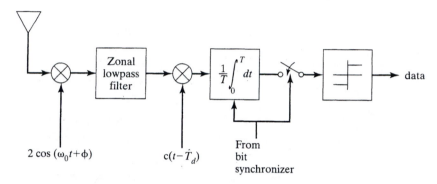

PROBLEM 9–10   Coherent BPSK spread-spectrum receiver.

9–11. Consider the feedback-shift-register configuration shown next. Determine the output of this circuit with the initial condition $a(D) = 1 + D + D^2 + D^3$.

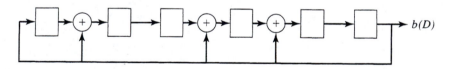

PROBLEM 9–11   Feedback shift register.

9–12. Consider the feedback-shift-register configuration shown next. Determine the output of this circuit with initial condition $a(D) = 1 + D + D^2 + D^3$ and compare with the result of Problem 9–11.

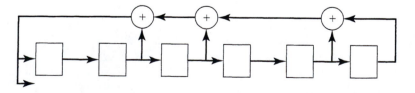

PROBLEM 9–12   Feedback shift register.

9–13. Consider the maximal-length sequence generated using the primitive polynomial $g(D) = 1 + D + D^2 + D^4 + D^5$. Demonstrate that Properties I through V for m-sequences are satisfied for this particular m-sequence.

9–14. Plot the autocorrelation function and the detailed power spectrum for the maximal-length sequence specified by $g(D) = 1 + D + D^4$ using a shift-register clock rate of 1.0 kHz.

9–15. The code of Problem 9–14 is used to BPSK modulate a 1.0 MHz carrier. Plot the power spectrum of the modulated carrier.

9–16. The code of Problem 9–14 is used to MSK modulate a 1.0 MHz carrier. Plot the power spectrum of the modulated carrier. Hint: Consider serial MSK implementations.

9–17. Two maximal-length shift register generators having periods N_1 and N_2 are run off the same clock. A third sequence is generated by modulo-2 adding the outputs of these generators. What is the period of the third output sequence?

9–18. The correlation-filter arrangement illustrated here is one part of a code tracking loop in a direct-sequence spread-spectrum modem. Suppose that the spreading code is an m-sequence having period N and that the bandpass filter is ideal and is specified by

$$H(\omega) = \begin{cases} 1.0, & |f \pm f_c| \le \dfrac{0.1}{T_c} \\ 0.0, & \text{elsewhere} \end{cases}$$

Plot the ratio of the filter output power at the carrier frequency to all other power at the filter output as a function of the code period N. All of the filter output power except that at the carrier frequency is called *code self-noise*.

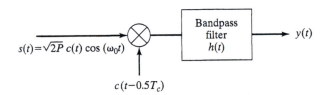

PROBLEM 9–18   Correlator illustrating spreading code self-noise.

9–19. Calculate the discrete periodic cross-correlation function for the pair of m-sequences defined by $g_1(D) = 1 + D^2 + D^5$ and $g_2(D) = 1 + D^2 + D^3 + D^4 + D^5$

9–20. Demonstrate that the Gold code of Example 9–9 achieves the permitted values of cross correlations for a Gold code of length 31. Convince yourself that it is true for $\mathbf{b} + D\mathbf{b}'$, $\mathbf{b} + D^2\mathbf{b}'$, and $\mathbf{b} + D^3\mathbf{b}'$.

9–21. Repeat Example 9–10 for the degree 6 entry in Table 9–2 with the asterisk. Write a MATLAB program to generate a m-sequence of any length as long as there are only two stages fed back. Include the generation of Kasami sequences of the allowed lengths.

9–22. (a) Show that the circuit of Figure 9–27 does indeed generate the quaternary sequences of Table 9–5.

(b) Write a MATLAB program to find the aperiodic correlations for the quaternary sequence set of Table 9–5.

9–23. Plot figures like Figures 9–32 for *M*-ary NFSK for $M = 4$ and $M = 8$.

9–24. The receiver front end illustrated in the figure below is used in a spread-spectrum communication system. At point 1, the received signal power is -116.3 dBm and the received noise single-sided noise power spectral density is -174 dBm per hertz.
   (a) Using the component gains and noise figures shown, calculate the value of E_b/N_0 at the input to the delay-lock discriminator. Assume a data rate of 10 kbps.
   (b) Assume a filter noise bandwidth of 10 MHz and calculate the signal-to-noise ratio P_s/P_N at the input to the delay-lock discriminator.

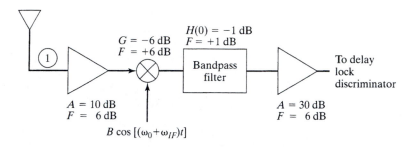

PROBLEM 9–24 Typical receiver front end.

9–25. What is the average search time and the variance of the search time for a system with an uncertainty of 10,000 half chips, an integration time per cell of 1 ms, $P_d = 0.99$, $P_{fa} = 10^{-3}$, and $T_{fa} = 10$ ms?

9–26. A communicator uses BPSK direct-sequence spreading modulation and BPSK data modulation. The DS chip rate is 10 Mchips/s, and the data rate is 75 bits per second. Calculate the ratio of barrage noise average jamming power to pulse noise average jamming power assuming that both jammers increase the communicator's average bit error probability to $P_b = 10^{-2}$. Calculate the same ratio for $P_b = 10^{-5}$.

9–27. A communicator uses FH/DPSK modulation to transmit a digital voice signal using a data rate of 32 kbps. The maximum acceptable transmission bit error probability is $P_b = 10^{-3}$. A smart partial band noise jammer has a power advantage of 30 dB over the communicator. What spread-spectrum bandwidth must be used to obtain the required bit error probability? How many different frequencies must the FH synthesizer generate?

9–28. Consider the following direct-sequence spread spectrum receiver. The receiver input is a BPSK modulated signal with BPSK spreading using chip rate $R_c = 100$ Mchips/s and data rate $R = 1$ Mbps, plus a tone jammer at frequency $f_J = f_0 + \Delta f$. What are reasonable choices for the image reject and IF bandpass filter bandwidths and center frequencies? Assume a signal-to-jammer power ratio of $10 \log (P/J) = -10$ dB. What is the received bit error probability for $\Delta f = 1.5, 5, 10,$ and 50 MHz?

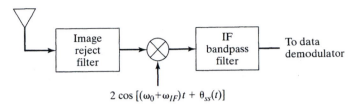

PROBLEM 9–28 Direct-sequence spread-spectrum receiver.

9–29. Consider the following frequency-hop spread-spectrum receiver. Binary FSK data modulation is used with tone spacing of 100 kHz. The data rate is 100 kbps. The FH tone spacing is 200 kHz, and there are a total of 1024 tones. Select reasonable image reject and IF bandpass filter bandwidths. The received signal is jammed by a multiple-tone jammer, and the total received signal-to-jammer power ratio is $10 \log (P/J) = -10$ dB. What is the optimal number of jamming tones? What is the optimal jammer tone spacing and tone power level? Select a frequency-hop rate. What is the received bit error probability?

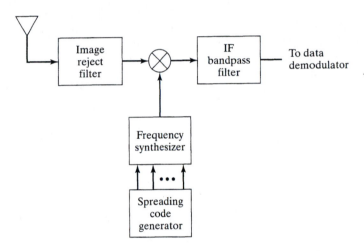

PROBLEM 9–29 Frequency-hop spread-spectrum receiver.

9–30. Given the following parameters: code length (processing gain) = 255; desired bit error probability = 10^{-4}. Using a conventional receiver, how many equal-power users can be supported at an E_b/N_0 of 20 dB.

9–31. Referring to Example 9–11, compare conventional and decorrelating detectors in AWGN for five equal power users using cyclic shifts of an $N = 15$ m-sequence for spreading codes. Write a MATLAB program to do the computations and plots.

9–32. Consider detection of four equal power users in AWGN viewed as a multiple hypothesis problem. Find the bit error probability versus E_b/N_0 and compare with the decorrelating and conventional detectors. For the latter, assume cyclic shifts of a 15-chip m-sequence for the access codes.

10

Introduction to Cellular
Radio Communications

10.1 INTRODUCTION

Cellular radio communications is one of the most challenging applications of communications technology. A goal of cellular radio is to provide reliable and cost effective voice, video, or data communications to anyone, anywhere, at any time. Achieving this goal is extremely difficult since the available spectrum is limited, user information rates are potentially high, and the propagation environment is harsh. To achieve this goal, the communications engineer must creatively apply all of the techniques discussed previously in this text along with some new concepts to be introduced in this chapter.

Cellular radio systems were developed in the United States in the 1970s by Bell Laboratories, Motorola, and other companies. At nearly the same time, similar systems were being developed in Japan and Europe. Test systems were installed in Chicago by Bell Laboratories and in Washington, DC by Motorola. These test and development systems were functional in the late 1970s and the first commercial cellphone systems went online in the United States in 1983. In Japan the first cellular system was introduced in 1979 and in Europe the first cellular system was introduced in 1981. These first-generation systems in the United States are called the Advanced Mobile Phone Service (AMPS). The growth in the number of subscribers for AMPS far exceeded predictions and by the early 1990s these systems were running out of capacity. The need for additional system capacity was correctly predicted in the mid-1980s and several major efforts were undertaken to develop capacity-enhanced systems using digital communications techniques. Some products of these efforts are the Global System for Mobile (GSM) Communications, the U.S. Digital Cellular (USDC) system, and the Code Division Multiple Access (CDMA) system. These systems are known as second-generation systems. Systems using second-generation technology were in widespread use by the mid-1990s. While AMPS is exclusively a voice communications system (with the understanding that some data transfer is possible utilizing voice-band modems), second generation systems have data transfer capability with transfer rates in the range of 10 to 15 kbps. Third-generation systems, which will have the ability to provide higher data rate services, will become available in Japan in the year 2001. It is anticipated that third-generation systems will be able to provide data rates consistent with the requirements for video teleconferencing and high-rate Internet access.

This chapter will, for the most part, be focused on the first- and second-generation cellphone systems that illustrate the application of the advanced communications concepts that are the basis for all cellular radio systems. The fundamental enabling concept for all cellular systems is the concept of frequency reuse. In order to make efficient use of the available spectrum, communications channels are used more than once in a geographic area. Thus, users will interfere with one another; this interference is controlled to simultaneously achieve high spectral efficiency and high quality service for all users. Managing the level of this interference is a significant design challenge. Frequency reuse is possible only when the users assigned to the same frequency can be separated in the receiver. This separation is possible if the received power from the desired user is large relative to the received power from the interfering user(s). In second and third generation systems the signaling waveform is designed to have special properties that facilitate separation of multiple signals at the receiver. This enables users to tolerate higher levels of interference, which in turn permits a greater degree of frequency reuse.

The chapter begins with a discussion of frequency reuse followed by an overview of the channel models applicable to cellular radio. In all cases the channel is time varying and often includes both direct and multiple reflected paths between the transmitter and receiver. These channels are called *fading multipath channels*. Reliable communications over these channels is difficult and is made more difficult by the high levels of co-channel interference designed into these systems. Next, techniques for mitigating fading multipath channels are discussed and system design techniques are described. The system design of cellphone systems includes the determination of how often a set of channels may be used while still providing every user with reliable communications. Following these general discussions, an overview of specific first and second generation cellphone systems is provided.

10.2   FREQUENCY REUSE

In order to achieve frequency reuse in cellular radio systems, a geographic area is serviced by multiple low-power base stations rather than a single high-power base station. Using the lowest possible transmit power reduces the transmission range of the base station, thus permitting channels to be reused at the closest possible distance. Consider two such low-power base station radio transceivers, denoted "A" and "B," separated by a normalized distance 2.0, and a mobile transceiver that moves from base station A towards B as illustrated in Figure 10–1. It is assumed that the base station transmit powers are equal. A reasonable but very simplified model for the signal power P_l in dBm received at the mobile from base station l is

$$P_l(d_l) = K_0 + K_1 \log_{10}(d_l/d_0), \quad \text{dBm} \tag{10--1}$$

where d_l represents the distance between base station l and the mobile, d_0 represents a reference distance where the received signal power is known to be K_0, and K_1 defines the rate of change of received power as range d_l varies. The graph of Figure 10–1 plots the received signal power at the mobile from base stations A, B, and a third base C (not illus-

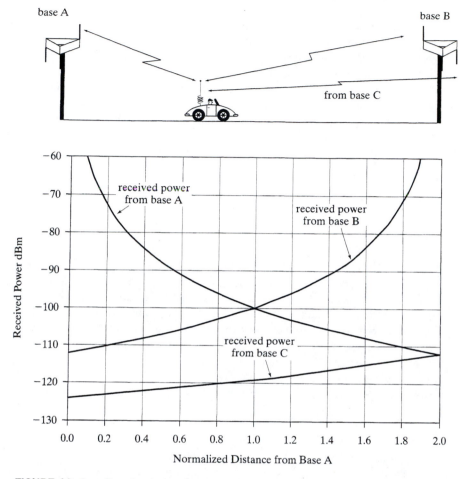

FIGURE 10–1   Received signal power at mobile from serving base station A and two interferering base stations B and C.

trated), which is located at distance 4.0, where it is assumed that $d_0 = 0.10$, $K_0 = -60$ dBm, and $K_1 = -40$. As the mobile moves from left to right, a complicated cellular call control system keeps the mobile connected to the base station that is able to provide the best service. Ignoring, for now, the details of the interference, it is reasonably assumed that the base station having the largest average received signal power at the mobile provides the best service to that mobile. For the simple path loss model implied by (10–1), the base station that the mobile receives at the highest power level is also the base station that is geographically closest to the mobile. Thus, as the mobile moves from left to right in the figure, it is served by base A from distance 0 to distance 1.0 where service is transferred to base B. For this very simple model, the call is transferred at precisely the midpoint between the base stations, which is also precisely the point where the received power from base B becomes larger than the received power from base A. Base station B serves the mobile until distance 3.0 (not shown) where service is transferred to base C. The transfer of a call from one base station to another is called *handoff* or *handover*.

The performance of the base-to-mobile communication link is a function of the signal-to-interference power ratio at the mobile. Define D to be the unnormalized distance between base stations A and B in Figure 10–1. When the mobile is distance d_A from base A, it is distance $d_B = D - d_A$ from base B. If base A and B are using the same channel, the signal power from base B becomes *co-channel interference* at the mobile and the signal-to-interference power ratio (SIR) in decibels is

$$P_A(d_A) - P_B(D - d_A) = K_0 + K_1 \log_{10}\left(\frac{d_A}{d_o}\right) - \left\{K_0 + K_1 \log_{10}\left(\frac{D - d_A}{d_o}\right)\right\} \quad \text{dB}$$

$$= -K_1 \log_{10}\left(\frac{D}{d_A} - 1\right) \quad \text{dB} \tag{10–2}$$

$$= \text{SIR}\,(d_A, D) \quad \text{dB}$$

Observe that SIR $(D/2, D) = 0$ dB, which is consistent with the fact that the received power from base A and base B are equal when the mobile is halfway between the two base stations. Recall from the analyses in the previous chapters of this text that it is difficult to achieve good system performance at a signal-to-interference ratio of 0 dB. It is even more difficult when the channel is time varying as it is here. For this reason, first-generation cellular radio systems do not use the same frequency in adjacent base stations. Rather, a different channel (or channel set) is used in the adjacent base stations and co-channel base stations are separated just enough to meet modulation interference specifications. Because base stations A and B of Figure 10–1 use different channels, the handoff at the midpoint between base stations requires a frequency change. Second-generation systems, particularly the CDMA system, have been designed to resist co-channel interference effectively, and it is possible with some of these systems to reuse a channel in the adjacent base station. Handoff is still required when channels are reused at the adjacent base stations, since it is still important to service the mobile from the base station capable of providing the best call quality.

Let R denote the largest distance a mobile is allowed to be from a base station while still being served by that base station, and let D_{co} denote the distance between a base station and the closest base station using the same frequency, that is, a co-channel base station. A mobile that is further than R from a base station would have been handed off to the adjacent base station. The worst case SIR occurs when a mobile is at the maximum range $d_A = R$ from its serving base station traveling towards the co-channel base station. That worst case SIR is found using (10–2):

$$\text{SIR}_{\min} = -K_1 \log_{10}\left(\frac{D_{co}}{R} - 1\right) \quad \text{dB} \tag{10–3}$$

The ratio D_{co}/R is often used as a figure of merit for frequency reuse plans since, noting that K_1 is negative, large D_{co}/R is associated with higher $\text{SIR}_{\min}$. If base station C were the co-channel base station in Figure 10–1, the minimum signal-to-interference ratio as the mobile journeys from A to B would be $40 \log_{10}(D_{co}/R - 1) = 40 \log_{10}(4 - 1) = 19.1$ dB.

With the concept in mind that it may not be possible to simultaneously use the same channel at adjacent base stations, consider the hexagonal grid of Figure 10–2. The entire

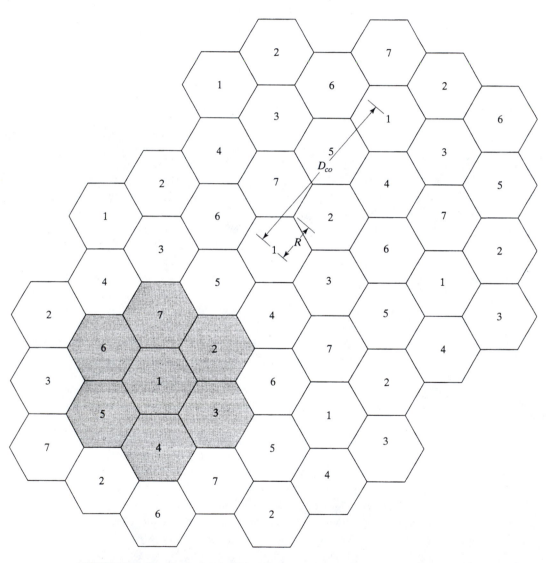

FIGURE 10–2 Hexagonal grid system representing system cells showing frequency reuse pattern of seven.

area tessellated[1] by hexagons represents the geographic area being served by the cellular radio system. Each hexagon represents the area serviced by a single base station presumed to be located at the center of the hexagon. Ideally a mobile unit that is geographically within a hexagon would be serviced by the base station at the center of the hexagon, since that base station is the geographically closest station. The hexagons are usually referred to as *cells*. The number within the hexagon represents the channel or channel set that is assigned to the base station of that cell. Observe that channels are reused in a regular pattern that results in the maximum possible geographic separation between cells using the same frequency. For this example system seven channels are reused in a regular pattern illustrated by the shaded cells and the *frequency reuse factor* is defined to be seven. Many other reuse patterns are possible.

A convenient means of describing the frequency reuse pattern of an ideal hexagonal cellular system makes use of a hexagonal grid geometry [1] as illustrated in Figure 10–3. The axes **U** and **V** of Figure 10–3 are not orthogonal; rather, they intersect with an angle of 60°. The grid spacing represents the normalized distance between adjacent base stations. Using this geometry each hexagon is centered at a point $(\mathbf{u},\mathbf{v})$ where **u** and **v** are integers and the distance from a cell center to any one of its vertices is $1/\sqrt{3}$. Many important frequency reuse patterns can be defined by this geometry using indices i and j, which define the distance along the **U** and **V** axes from a cell to the closest cell using the same channel(s). For example, the shaded cells are those which use channel set 1 of the seven-cell reuse pattern of Figure 10–2. This seven-cell pattern is defined by $i = 2$ and $j = 1$. A co-channel cell is found starting at the first cell by moving two units along the **U** axis then one unit along the **V** axis. More generally, co-channel cells are found starting at any cell and moving i units away from that cell in a straight line along any of the six possible strings of adjacent hexagons and then turning 60° to the left and moving j units along that string of hexagons. The bold arrows illustrate this concept for $i = 2$ and $j = 1$. Using this technique for locating the closest co-channel cells, it can be determined that each cell has exactly six co-channel neighbors all the same distance from the starting cell. These six cells are found by moving in the six directions corresponding to the six sides of the hexagon to find each co-channel cell. Having now determined that there are six close interfering base stations rather than just one, (10–3) must be modified to include more interfering power. Assuming that the mobile station remains at the boundary (worst case) of the cell on a radius directed toward the interfering cell, it can be seen that all of the other interfering base stations are farther away from the mobile than the base station used in the calculation of (10–3). Therefore, each of the other base stations contributes less interference than the one already considered in (10–3), and the minimum signal-to-interference ratio can be underbounded[2] by simply increasing the interference level by a factor of six (7.78 dB). Thus, equation (10–3) becomes

$$\text{SIR}_{\min} \geq -K_1 \log_{10}\left(\frac{D_{co}}{R} - 1\right) - 7.78 \quad \text{dB} \qquad (10\text{–}4)$$

---

[1]To tessellate means to arrange in a checkered or mosaic pattern.

[2]This simple analysis considers only the first ring of interfering cells and is an approximate result. Exact calculation of SIR is straightforward using hexagonal geometry and (10–1).

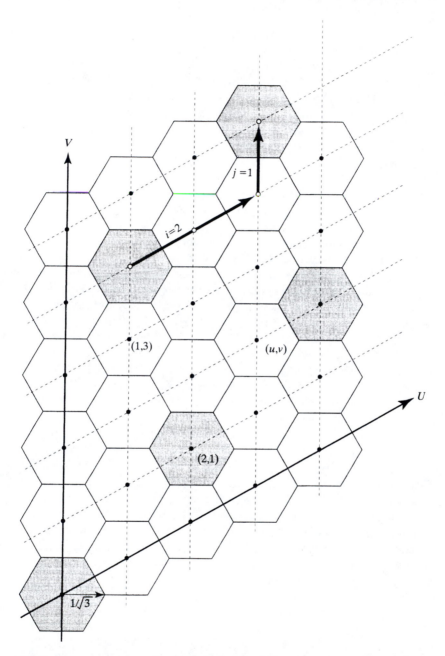

FIGURE 10–3 Hexagonal grid geometry for a seven-cell frequency reuse pattern.

It can be shown [1] that the number of cells N in the frequency reuse plan, that is, the shaded cells of Figure 10–2, is determined by i and j and is

$$N = i^2 + ij + j^2 \qquad (10\text{–}5)$$

For $i = 2$ and $j = 1$ substitution yields $N = 7$. The single-cell reuse pattern corresponds to $i = 1$ and $j = 0$. Another useful relationship derived in [1] relates N to the ratio D_{co}/R. This relationship is

$$D_{co}/R = \sqrt{3N} \qquad (10\text{–}6)$$

Spectrum efficiency is a very important figure of merit for cellular systems. Spectrum efficiency can be defined in a variety of ways. Within this text, the *spectrum efficiency for voice* η_v of a cellular system concept is equal to the number of simultaneous voice circuits that the system provides per megahertz of bandwidth per base station. This definition is oversimplified in that it does not account for the random arrivals and durations of calls and the associated blocking characteristics. The definition does take frequency reuse into account as well as the bandwidth efficiency of the link modulation and provides a meaningful means of comparing system concepts.

EXAMPLE 10–1 _____

Consider a cellular system concept utilizing a modulation scheme that requires channel spacing of 25 kHz and an $\mathrm{SIR}_{min} = 20$ dB for each voice channel. A total bandwidth of 6 MHz is available that must provide both base-to-mobile (forward link) and mobile-to-base (reverse link) communications. The total bandwidth is partitioned into $6 \times 10^6/25 \times 10^3 = 240$ channels. Half of these channels are used for the forward and half for the reverse links, resulting in 120 possible voice circuits. Assume that the variation in received signal power with range follows the relationship of (10–1) with $K_1 = -40$. With K_1 and the minimum SIR determined, (10–4) becomes

$$20 = 40 \log_{10}\left(\frac{D_{co}}{R} - 1\right) - 7.78 \quad \text{dB}$$

which can be solved for $D_{co}/R = 5.94$. With D_{co}/R known, the number of cells in the frequency reuse plan N can be determined using (10–6). The result is $D_{co}/R = 5.94 = \sqrt{3N}$, which may be solved for $N = 11.76$. Since N can only be an integer, use the next larger integer $N = 12$. The 120 voice circuits are partitioned into twelve different groups of ten circuits each. Because of co-channel interference and the 20 dB limit of the selected modulation scheme, the system is only able to use 8% of the voice circuits in each cell. The resulting spectrum efficiency is

$$\eta_v = \frac{10 \text{ circuits}}{6 \text{ MHz}} = 1.67 \text{ voice circuits per base station per MHz}$$

Now suppose that a new modulation scheme was found that provided adequate performance at $\mathrm{SIR}_{min} = 14$ dB. Solving for D_{co}/R yields $D_{co}/R = 4.5$. Then solving for N yields $N = 6.75$, which is increased to the nearest integer 7. In this case the 120 channels are partitioned into seven groups of approximately 17 channels and the spectrum efficiency is

$$\eta_v = \frac{17 \text{ circuits}}{6 \text{ MHz}} = 2.83 \text{ voice circuits per base station per MHz}$$

Observe that improving the sensitivity of the modulation scheme from 20 dB to 14 dB has resulted in an increase in spectrum efficiency of 1.69.

The discussions in this section have been intentionally very simplified in order to present the notion of frequency reuse and its relation to spectrum efficiency. A "real" cellular radio system is much, much more complex. The received signal power is not nicely behaved with location as in (10–1). Fast variations in signal power occur as signals received via multiple reflected paths reinforce one another for a short time and then cancel one another. Slower variations of the received signal power occur when the mobile passes large obstructions that shadow the mobile from a direct path to the base station. Because the propagation paths are not well behaved, handoff does not occur at the midpoint between base stations. Further, in most cases both the base station and mobile stations are power controlled making the calculation of signal-to-interference ratios dependent upon the number and location of the mobiles. Many of these more complicated issues will be discussed in the sections that follow.

10.3   CHANNEL MODELS

In previous chapters, the channel over which signals were transmitted was often assumed to be time invariant. That means simply that the attenuation between the transmitter and receiver is constant over time even though it may be a function of frequency due to the finite bandwidth of the channel. The analyses of previous chapters ignored the path attenuation since these were analyses of the performance of a modulation and (possibly) coding scheme. Thus, these analyses could be characterized in terms of the *received* signal and interference levels and were not dependent upon the details of the system level conditions which resulted in these signal and interference levels.

More complex channel models must be considered for the analysis of cellular radio systems. The mobile communications channel is both rapidly and slowly time varying and the modulation and coding strategy must be designed to mitigate these variations. Furthermore, the analysis of cellular radio systems involves more than the study of a single radio communications link. The many simultaneous communications links of a cellular radio system interfere with one another and the designer must do system studies to evaluate the performance for all users simultaneously. System studies require knowledge of the absolute path loss or attenuation between the base stations and all mobiles in the system. In the following paragraphs, three components of the channel model are identified and studied. The first component is the *path loss* between the transmitter and receiver. Path loss accounts for the very slowly decreasing received signal level as the receiver moves away from the transmitter. The second component is *log-normal shadow fading,* which is sometimes referred to just as *shadow fading.* Shadow fading models slow variations in signal attenuation as various physical obstructions are encountered in the transmitter-to-receiver path. The third component of the channel model is *multipath propagation.* Two different categories of multipath propagation will be modeled. The first category includes groups of propagation paths whose path length differences are so small that the intended receiver cannot resolve the resulting small time differences of arrival. In this case the receiver input is the phasor addition of multiple transmission paths (direct, refracted, and reflected). This phasor addition causes rapid changing of the received signal magnitude and phase referred to as *multipath fast fading*. The rate of change of this fading is a function of the speed of the mobile, the carrier frequency, and the details of the physical environment creating the direct, reflected, and refracted paths. The second category of multipath includes paths or groups of paths whose propagation path length differences are large enough that the associated propagation times can be resolved by the intended receiver. It will be shown that this second category causes the channel to be frequency selective. Understanding these components of the channel model is essential to the study of cellular radio systems.

10.3.1   Path Loss and Shadow Fading Models

As the distance between the transmitting and receiving antennas increases, the signal power available to the receiver decreases slowly even though the transmitted power may be constant. The rate at which the available signal power decreases with increasing distance is a function of many factors including, but not limited to, the transmission frequency, the height of the antennas above the surrounding terrain, the details of the changes in elevation of the terrain between the antennas, and the foliage and/or density and type of buildings between the antennas. Because path loss is affected by these factors (and others) and since the physical characteristics of most distinct propagation paths are different, there is no single path loss model applicable to all situations. Rather, there are many different models and the system designer must be careful in selecting the model applicable to the physical environment of interest. Numerous studies of path loss have been documented in the literature; specific references will be given later. In some instances these studies have resulted in simple algebraic formulas while other studies have graphed and characterized the results statistically. The path loss models discussed below are a sampling of the most often used models. The simplest path loss models have the form

$$l = C \left(\frac{d_0}{d} \right)^n$$

where l denotes path loss, C is a constant, d_0 is a known distance used for absolute calibration of the model, d is the distance from the transmitter to the receiver in the same units as d_0, and n is the *path loss exponent*. The path loss exponent is determined by the physical environment and is a critical parameter in the design of cellular systems. Typical values of path loss exponent are between 2 and 4.

Since path loss models the very slow variation in the attenuation of the transmitted signal with distance, it is understood that the faster variations of attenuation due to shadow fading and/or multipath fast fading are not included. If path loss were to be measured, the measurement strategy would have to be carefully designed so that shadow fading and multipath fast fading were averaged out of the measurement.

10.3.1.1 Free Space Path Loss. Consider first the propagation of transmitted electromagnetic energy through free space. In free space there are no obstructions that can attenuate, reflect, or refract the energy so that the energy simply radiates outward from the transmitting antenna. The relation between the transmitted and received power $P_r(d)$ in free space is governed in the far field by Friis's law [2]:

$$P_r(d) = P_t G_t G_r \left(\frac{\lambda}{4 \pi d} \right)^2 \tag{10-7}$$

where

    P_t = transmitted power in watts

    G_t = gain of the transmitting antenna in the direction of the receiver

    G_r = gain of the receiving antenna in the direction of the transmitter

    λ = carrier wavelength

    d = distance between transmitter and receiver in same units as λ

The transmitting and receiving antenna gains are a measure of how effectively these antennas focus the transmitted power in a particular direction relative to an antenna that radiates uniformly in all directions. Directional antennas are often used in cellular radio systems. When performing system studies, the system designer will often need to know the transmitter and receiver antenna gain as a function of direction.

Transmitter to receiver path loss is defined to be the ratio of received power to transmitted power for the case of omnidirectional, $G_t = G_r = 1.0$, antennas. Thus,

$$l_F = \frac{P_r(d)}{P_t} = \left(\frac{\lambda}{4\pi d} \right)^2$$

$$= \left(\frac{c}{4\pi d f} \right)^2 \tag{10-8}$$

where the subscript F denotes free space and wavelength has been expressed as a function of carrier frequency f and the speed of light c. The path loss exponent n for free-space propagation is 2. Defining *free space path attenuation* $L_F = -10.0 \log l_F$ results in

$$L_F \equiv -10\log_{10} l_F = +32.44 + 20 \log_{10} d_{km} + 20 \log_{10} f_{MHz} \quad \text{dB} \tag{10-9}$$

where d_{km} is expressed in kilometers and f_{MHz} in MHz. This formula indicates that the path attenuation increases by 20 dB per decade or 6 dB per octave with distance or carrier frequency. The increase in path attenuation with increasing carrier frequency is an important issue since there is strong motivation to select very high carrier frequencies for future generations of cellular systems. The principal motivation is that the bandwidths available at higher frequencies are larger and having a larger bandwidth facilitates data transmission at higher rates.

10.3.1.2 Flat Earth Path Loss.   Next consider the propagation of signal energy from a transmitting antenna to a receiving antenna over a perfectly reflecting plane as illustrated in Figure 10–4. In this figure h_t and h_r represent the heights of the transmitting and receiving antennas respectively and d represents the distance between the antennas. All distances, heights, and the carrier wavelength will be measured using the same units. There are two possible propagation paths between the transmitter and receiver. The first path is the line-of-sight (LOS) path illustrated by the top dashed line in the figure. The second path propagates toward the plane and is reflected towards the receiving antenna. A phasor addition of the LOS and reflected signals occurs at the receiving antenna. In analyses of this propagation scenario it is usually assumed that h_r, $h_t \ll d$ so that the lengths of the LOS path and the reflected path are nearly equal and the attenuation over the two paths is nearly the same. The power received via either the LOS or reflected paths is given by Friis's law using distance d. The phasor addition is then the addition of two approximately equal amplitude phasors with amplitude (square root of power) given by

$$|E| = \sqrt{P_t G_t G_r} \left(\frac{\lambda}{4\pi d} \right) \tag{10–10}$$

The phase difference between the two phasors is due to differences in path lengths, which are small in absolute magnitude but which are significant with respect to the carrier wavelength.

In order to calculate path loss, the magnitude of the phasor addition of the two signals will be calculated. The phasor addition requires knowledge of the carrier phase difference between the two propagation paths. Denote the distance from the base of the transmitting antenna to the reflection point by d_1 and the distance from the reflection point to the base of the receiving antenna by d_2. Denote the total length of the reflected path by d_R. Using straightforward geometry

$$d_R = \sqrt{d_1^2 + h_t^2} + \sqrt{d_2^2 + h_r^2}$$

$$= d_1\sqrt{1 + \left(\frac{h_t}{d_1} \right)^2} + d_2\sqrt{1 + \left(\frac{h_r}{d_2} \right)^2}$$

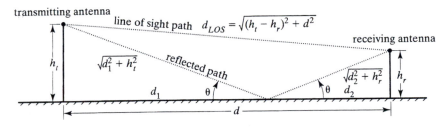

FIGURE 10–4   Model for the calculation of flat earth path loss.

and

$$d_{LOS} = \sqrt{d^2 + (h_t - h_r)^2}$$

$$= d\sqrt{1 + \left(\frac{h_t - h_r}{d}\right)^2}$$

The angles of incidence and reflection are equal so that $h_t/d_1 = h_r/d_2$. By definition $d = d_1 + d_2$. Solving these two equations for d_1 yields $d_1 = dh_t/(h_t + h_r)$ and using these relations in the equation for d_R yields

$$d_R = d_1\sqrt{1 + \left(\frac{h_t}{d_1}\right)^2} + d_2\sqrt{1 + \left(\frac{h_t}{d_1}\right)^2}$$

$$= (d_1 + d_2)\sqrt{1 + \left(\frac{h_t}{d_1}\right)^2}$$

$$= d\sqrt{1 + \left(\frac{h_t + h_r}{d}\right)^2}$$

The difference Δ in path lengths is therefore

$$\Delta = d\sqrt{1 + \left(\frac{h_t + h_r}{d}\right)^2} - d\sqrt{1 + \left(\frac{h_t - h_r}{d}\right)^2}$$

Using the formula $\sqrt{1 + x} = 1 + \frac{1}{2}x - \frac{1}{8}x^2 + \frac{1}{16}x^3 - \cdots$ and keeping only zeroth and first order terms since $h_r, h_t \ll d$ yields

$$\Delta \approx d\left\{\left[1 + \frac{1}{2}\left(\frac{h_t + h_r}{d}\right)^2\right] - \left[1 + \frac{1}{2}\left(\frac{h_t - h_r}{d}\right)^2\right]\right\}$$

$$= \frac{d}{2}\left\{\left(\frac{h_t + h_r}{d}\right)^2 - \left(\frac{h_t - h_r}{d}\right)^2\right\}$$

$$= \frac{2h_r h_t}{d}$$

Thus, the phase difference θ in radians between the two phasors is

$$\theta = \frac{2\,h_r h_t}{d} \cdot \frac{2\pi}{\lambda} \tag{10-11}$$

Before the phasor addition can be completed, the transformation of the signal as it is reflected from the plane must be considered. Detailed studies [3,4] of reflection from the earth's surface show that there exists a complex reflection coefficient ρ, which is a function of the angle of incidence, the dielectric constant of the earth, and the conductivity of the earth at the point of reflection. These studies also show that when the angle of incidence is small (i.e., near grazing angles) the reflection coefficient is very near $\rho \approx -1$. Using (10–10) for the magnitude of the $|E|$ of the phasors, the phasor sum E_Σ is

$$E_\Sigma = |E| (1 + \rho \, e^{j\theta})$$

$$= \sqrt{P_t G_t G_r} \left(\frac{\lambda}{4\pi d} \right) (1 - e^{j\theta}) \qquad (10\text{–}12)$$

$$= \sqrt{P_t G_t G_r} \left(\frac{\lambda}{4\pi d} \right) (1 - \cos\theta - j\sin\theta)$$

The magnitude of this phasor sum is calculated as follows

$$|E_\Sigma| = \sqrt{P_t G_t G_r} \left(\frac{\lambda}{4\pi d} \right) \sqrt{(1 - \cos\theta)^2 + \sin^2\theta}$$

$$= \sqrt{P_t G_t G_r} \left(\frac{\lambda}{4\pi d} \right) \sqrt{2 - 2\cos\theta}$$

$$= \sqrt{4 \, P_t G_t G_r} \left(\frac{\lambda}{4\pi d} \right) \sin\left(\frac{\theta}{2} \right)$$

Substituting (10–11) for θ yields

$$|E_\Sigma| = \sqrt{4 P_t G_t G_r} \left(\frac{\lambda}{4\pi d} \right) \sin\left(\frac{h_r h_t}{d} \cdot \frac{2\pi}{\lambda} \right)$$

For large d the sine function may be approximated using $\sin x = x - (x^3/3!) + (x^5/5!) - \ldots$ to obtain, after discarding all but the first term, the result

$$|E_\Sigma| = \sqrt{4 \, P_t G_t G_r} \left(\frac{\lambda}{4\pi d} \right) \left(\frac{h_r h_t}{d} \cdot \frac{2\pi}{\lambda} \right)$$

$$= \sqrt{4 \, P_t G_t G_r} \left(\frac{h_r h_t}{2 \, d^2} \right)$$

Finally, the received power is proportional to the square of the magnitude of the received voltage. Thus,

$$P_r = 4 \, P_t G_t G_r \left(\frac{h_r h_t}{2 \, d^2} \right)^2 \qquad (10\text{–}13)$$

Considering only omnidirectional unit gain antennas at both the transmitter and receiver, the path loss, denoted l_{PE}, is

$$l_{PE} = \frac{P_r}{P_t} = \frac{(h_r h_t)^2}{d^4} \qquad (10\text{–}14)$$

The path loss exponent n for flat earth propagation is 4. Using this relationship, the path attenuation $L_{PE} = -10 \log l_{PE}$ in decibels is

$$L_{PE} = -20 \log_{10} (h_t h_r) + 40 \log_{10} d_{km} + 120$$
$$= +120.0 - 20 \log_{10} h_t - 20 \log_{10} h_r + 40 \log_{10} d_{km} \quad \text{dB}$$
(10–15)

This relationship should be compared with (10–9) for free space propagation. Observe that, while (10–9) is a function of carrier frequency, (10–15) is independent of carrier frequency. The other important difference between (10–9) and (10–15) is the rate of change of path attenuation with distance. In (10–9) the path attenuation increased by 6 dB for each doubling of range d_{km}, whereas in (10–15) the path attenuation increases by 12 dB for each doubling of range. It will be shown later that this increased attenuation with range will permit the reuse of channels more often in a cellular radio system and is, in this sense, better. Unfortunately, the designer has little choice in the applicable channel model so it is fortunate that the rate of change of path attenuation with range experienced in actual systems is typically similar to that in (10–15). Observe that (10–15) is a function of both the transmitter and the receiver antenna heights and the system designer has control over these heights and thus has some control over the total path attenuation.

The development of the flat-earth path loss model has not taken into account some of the items which were listed earlier as having an effect on path attenuation. Nevertheless, the gross variation of path attenuation with range predicted by this model, that is, 40 dB per decade, has been approximately validated by many measurement campaigns beginning with that of W. R. Young [5] in the early 1950s and Y. Okumura and colleagues [6] in the 1960s. The items not accounted for include building type and density, foliage, and variation in terrain elevation between the two antennas. Taking these additional factors into account greatly complicates the analysis and typically the designer must resort to statistical characterizations of path attenuation based upon measurement campaigns.

10.3.1.3 Okumura/Hata Path Attenuation Model.   Recognizing the limitations and complexity of purely analytical methods for determining path attenuation for scenarios where building type and density as well as foliage and terrain variations are important, Y. Okumura, E. Ohmori, T. Kawano, and K. Fukuda performed extensive measurements of path attenuation at six different frequencies between 200 and 1920 MHz in and around Tokyo, Japan. The results of these measurements were characterized statistically and presented in the now classic paper [6]. This paper presents their measurement technique in some detail and then presents a large number of graphs that enable the reader to determine path attenuation as a function of range, carrier frequency, antenna height, the elevation variations of the terrain, and the characteristics of the buildings (if any) on the terrain.

Since Okumura's results are presented graphically, they are difficult to use in system design. This difficulty was largely eliminated by M. Hata [7], who developed a series of path attenuation formulas based upon the Okumura graphical results. These formulas are widely recognized as being accurate in the sense that comparative system studies may be based upon them and reasonably accurate results will be obtained. The formulas are not typically used as the basis for the detailed layout and design of any specific cellular system. Results are given for a number of different propagation environments. Okumura [6] has defined an *urban area* to be a built-up area with densely packed buildings. Within the classification of urban area he defines a *large city* as an area where building height averages more than 15 meters and a *medium city* as an area where average building height is approximately 5 meters. Okumura also characterizes *suburban areas* having scattered buildings, foliage, and highways and *open areas* where there are essentially no obstacles to propagation. Given these classifications, the path attenuation for an **urban area** is [7]

$$L_{H,urban} = 69.55 + 26.16 \log_{10} f_c - 13.82 \log_{10} h_b - a(h_m)$$
$$+ (44.9 - 6.55 \log_{10} h_b) \log_{10} d_{km} \quad \text{dB} \tag{10-16}$$

where, for a *medium city*

$$a(h_m) = (1.1 \log_{10} f_c - 0.7)h_m - (1.56 \log_{10} f_c - 0.8) \quad \text{dB} \tag{10-17}$$

and for a *large city*

$$a(h_m) = 8.29(\log_{10} 1.54 h_m)^2 - 1.1 \quad \text{dB} \quad \text{for } f_c \le 200\text{MHz} \tag{10-18a}$$

$$a(h_m) = 3.2(\log_{10} 11.75 h_m)^2 - 4.97 \quad \text{dB} \quad \text{for } f_c \ge 400\text{MHz} \tag{10-18b}$$

For a **suburban area** the following formula applies:

$$L_{H,sub} = L_{H,urban} - 2\left\{\log_{10}\left(\frac{f_c}{28}\right)\right\}^2 - 5.4 \quad \text{dB} \tag{10-19}$$

For an **open area** the following formula applies:

$$L_{H,open} = L_{H,urban} - 4.78(\log_{10} f_c)^2 + 18.33 \log_{10} f_c - 40.94 \quad \text{dB} \tag{10-20}$$

where f_c is the carrier frequency in MHz, h_b is the base station effective antenna height in meters, h_m is the mobile antenna height in meters, and d_{km} is the distance from the base to the mobile in kilometers. These formulas are applicable when

$$150 \le f_c \le 1500 \quad \text{MHz}$$

$$30 \le h_b \le 200 \quad \text{meters}$$

$$1 \le h_m \le 10 \quad \text{meters} \tag{10-21}$$

$$1 \le d_{km} \le 20 \quad \text{km}$$

Equations (10–16) through (10–20) illustrate that path attenuation is a function of antenna heights, carrier frequency, terrain, and the distance between the transmitter and receiver as expected. Observe that even in a clear area the path attenuation is a function of carrier frequency; this contradicts the assertion in the discussion of flat earth path loss that showed that path loss was independent of carrier frequency. The flat earth path loss calculation was not incorrect; however, it did not consider details of the propagation environment that would create the frequency dependence measured by Okumura and modeled by

Hata. The Hata formulas are valid only over the range of parameters presented in (10–21), even though the Okumura paper presents results over significantly larger ranges of parameters. The designer solving problems requiring the use of parameters outside of the range of (10–21) should work directly with the graphs presented in [6].

Although the Okumura/Hata model is based upon extensive measurements, care must be used in its application. This is due to the fact that the propagation environment in other areas, say New York in the 1990s, may be very different from the propagation environment in Tokyo in the 1960s. Nevertheless, the model illustrates the factors that influence path loss to the greatest degree.

Figure 10–5 illustrates the path attenuation in decibels calculated using the Hata formulas as well as using the flat-earth path loss model for carrier frequencies of 850 MHz and 1500 MHz and base station antenna heights of 30 and 100 meters. The Okumura/Hata path attenuation is larger than the path loss predicted by the flat earth model since obstructions to the propagation path have been taken into account in the Okumura/Hata model. Observe also that the carrier frequency has a significant impact on path loss and that the slopes of all of the path loss curves vary between approximately 32 and 40 dB per decade of range with lower slopes being associated with higher base station antenna heights.

10.3.1.4 Log-Normal Shadow Fading.

The path loss models discussed above predict the average path loss between a transmitter and receiver at the distance d_{km}. Only the Okumura/Hata model has taken propagation path obstructions such as buildings and foliage into account, and even this model has accounted for buildings and foliage only in an average sense. Thus, a series of path loss measurements taken on an arc at distance d_{km} from the transmitter would have an average near the calculated path loss value but individual measurements would vary significantly as a function of whether there were physical obstructions in the propagation path. Numerous measurement campaigns [5, 6, 8, 9] have demonstrated that transmitter-to-receiver attenuation varies significantly as a function of obstructions in the transmission path. These measurement campaigns have also demonstrated that the received power in decibels may be statistically modeled by a normal probability distribution with mean value equal to the path attenuation and a standard deviation σ in decibels, which is a function of the terrain variability and the carrier frequency. The slow variation due to physical obstructions of signal attenuation around the mean value predicted by the path attenuation model is called *log-normal shadow fading*.

Let $L(d_{km})$ denote the path attenuation in decibels and let L_s denote the total slowly varying attenuation due to the shadowing from buildings, foliage, and terrain obstructions between the transmitter and receiver. The total slowly varying attenuation is $L(d_{km}) + L_s$. The probability density $f_{L_s}(x)$ of L_s is

$$f_L(x) = \frac{1}{\sqrt{2\pi\,\sigma^2}} \exp\left(-\frac{x^2}{2\sigma^2}\right) \tag{10–22}$$

where σ is a function of the characteristics of the terrain and the buildings and/or foliage on that terrain and a function of carrier frequency. In (10–22) σ is in decibels and typical values of σ are between 6 and 12 dB.

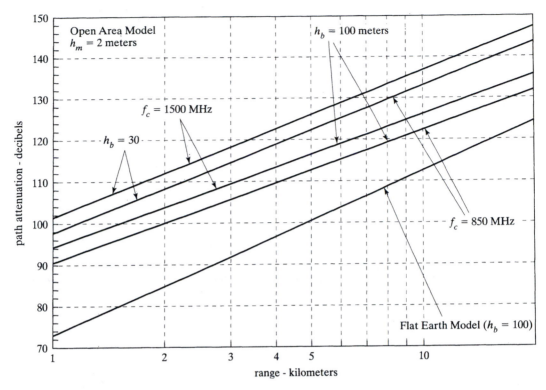

FIGURE 10–5   Okumura/Hata path attenuation versus range for base station antenna heights of 30 and 100 meters and carrier frequencies of 850 and 1500 MHz.

As a mobile moves through the cellular service area, the value of L_s changes slowly. Since L_s is due to physical obstructions in the propagation path, it is reasonable that measurements of L_s closely spaced in distance are strongly correlated. Independent measurements of L_s occur only when the distance between measurement points are far enough apart that the physical environment surrounding those points are independent. In cellular system modeling for estimating the probability that service will be available to a user, a correlation distance for shadow fading is defined. This distance is strongly a function of the terrain and therefore will be different for different systems and even different locations within a system. Typical correlation distances are between 10 and 100 meters.

10.3.2   Multipath Channel Models

In most instances there are multiple propagation paths between a cellular system base station and a mobile which is being serviced by that base station. These multiple paths are due to reflections of the signal off various physical objects that may be distant high-rise buildings or mountains or may be nearby buildings or other large physical objects. Suppose that there are N propagation paths and the delay and path loss of path n are denoted τ_n and g_n respectively. Suppose also that the transmitted and received signals, denoted $s(t)$ and $r(t)$ respectively, are narrowband and have complex envelopes $\tilde{s}(t)$ and $\tilde{r}(t)$. The received signal is the linear combination of the signals propagating over all paths

$$r(t) = \sum_{n=1}^{N} g_n \, s(t - \tau_n) \qquad (10\text{--}23a)$$

In terms of the complex envelopes

$$\mathrm{Re}\big[\tilde{r}(t)e^{j\omega_0 t}\big] = \sum_{n=1}^{N} g_n \, \mathrm{Re}\big[\tilde{s}\,(t - \tau_n)e^{j\omega_0(t - \tau_n)}\big]$$

$$= \mathrm{Re}\left[\sum_{n=1}^{N} g_n \, \tilde{s}\,(t - \tau_n)e^{j\omega_0(t - \tau_n)}\right] \qquad (10\text{--}23b)$$

$$= \mathrm{Re}\left[\sum_{n=1}^{N} g_n e^{-j\omega_0 \tau_n}\, \tilde{s}\,(t - \tau_n)e^{j\omega_0 t}\right]$$

where ω_0 denotes the carrier frequency. By inspection of (10–23b)

$$\tilde{r}\,(t) = \sum_{n=1}^{N} g_n e^{-j\omega_0 \tau_n}\, \tilde{s}\,(t - \tau_n) \qquad (10\text{--}24)$$

Equation (10–24) represents the signal received at a fixed point in the system at one instant in time. During a cellular communication the mobile is likely to be moving through the system and, as a result the multipath parameters τ_n and g_n, vary with time. As the mobile moves over a significant distance, the number N of multipath components may also change. Furthermore, the propagation environment may itself change as a result of the movement of vehicles and even slowly moving foliage. As a result, even if the transmitted signal were constant, the received signal amplitude and phase vary as a function of time.

Consider a propagation experiment in which an impulse is transmitted from a base station at time zero and in which the mobile receiver is precisely calibrated and has a bandwidth, practically speaking, large enough to receive the impulse without significant distortion. Figure 10–6 depicts the time waveform at the receiver for this experiment when done in a propagation environment in which there are $N = 6$ paths. Observe that the six paths occur in two groups of three. Figure 10–7 is a crude illustration showing how the six paths of Figure 10–6 might have been created in the physical environment. Figure 10–7 illustrates a base station in the lower right that is servicing a rapidly moving mobile in the center of the figure. The first propagation path is the line-of-sight path to the mobile. The transmitted impulse is received over this direct path with the smallest delay and attenuation of any of the six paths. This direct path is shown passing through foliage, which may result in shadow loss at the particular instant illustrated. The second path is a reflected path from the base station to a truck near the mobile and then to the mobile. The impulse propagating over this path is received shortly after the direct path but with considerably less amplitude due to the small reflection cross section of the truck. The third path is another indirect path; this path is from the base station to a group of large build-

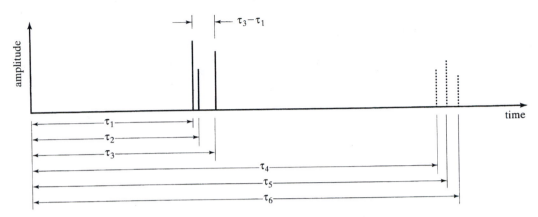

FIGURE 10–6 Time of arrival and amplitude of multipath impulses received at mobile with channel input of an impulse at time zero.

ings and then to the mobile. Paths 1 through 3 are shown using solid lines in Figure 10–7. Paths 4 through 6, illustrated as dotted lines, are all reflected paths having the common feature of being reflected off a distant mountain range. Following the reflection from the distant mountain, the paths are again a direct path to the mobile, a path reflected off the truck, and a path reflected off the urban center.

Figures 10–6 and 10–7 depict the two multipath cases of interest in this chapter and in general. Multipath signals that arrive at close to the same time may not be distinguishable by the communications receiver and thus may represent *unresolvable multipath components*. In this illustration paths 1 through 3 represent groups of (possibly) unresolvable multipaths as do paths 4 through 6. In contrast, the intended receiver is probably able to separate the paths reflected off the mountain range from those that are not since the delay differences between these paths is "large." Thus, any pair of paths consisting of one path from each group of three represent *resolvable multipaths*. Whether any pair of multipaths is resolvable is a function of the bandwidth of the intended receiver. Cellular systems of today have receive bandwidths ranging from approximately 25 kHz to 1.25 MHz.[3] Paths that are unresolvable to the narrowband systems may be resolvable in the wider bandwidth systems.

10.3.2.1 Rayleigh Fading (Unresolvable-Multipath) Models.

Unresolvable multipath components are those components whose arrival times differ from one another by less than (approximately) the duration of the impulse response of the input filter of the receiver. In this case, the filter is still responding to a received impulse when the following one arrives and, after receive filter processing, it is difficult to separate filter outputs due to different multipath components. Reconsider the channel defined by Figure 10–6 and suppose that the six multipath components have delays and amplitudes defined

---

[3]Systems under development at the time of writing of this text have bandwidths as large as 15 MHz.

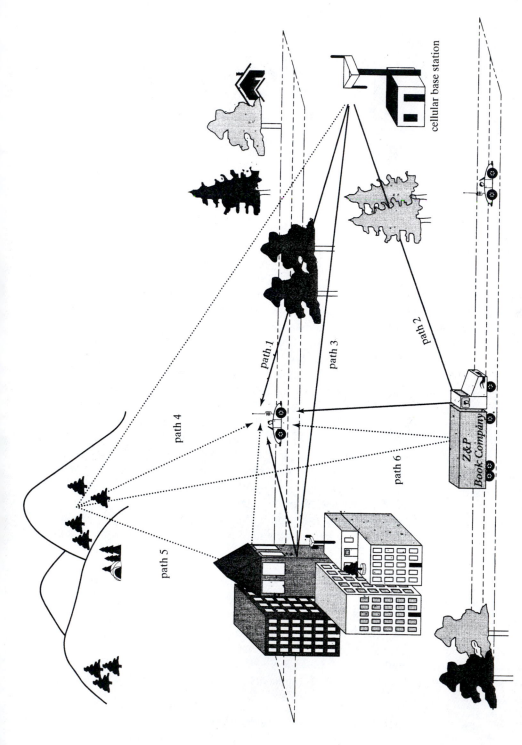

FIGURE 10–7 Typical direct and reflected propagation paths between a base station and a mobile station.

in Table 10–1. Recall that in drawing Figure 10–6 the receive filter bandwidth was assumed to be "large enough" that the impulses were received essentially without distortion. Consider now two different receive filters having bandwidths of approximately 1.25 MHz and 12.5 MHz. The specific 1.25 MHz filter, which is considered a digital filter, is defined in the specification for the IS-95 Code Division Multiple Access cellular standard. Figures 10–8a and 10–8b illustrate the real part of the response of these two filters to the channel output defined by Figure 10–6 and Table 10–1 with a single unit amplitude input impulse at time zero. Observe that the channel multipath components at τ_1, τ_2, and τ_3 have been distorted by the 1.25 MHz filter and that the three responses appear to be a single longer response, that is, the three multipath components are unresolvable after receive filtering. However, in Figure 10–8b, where the filter bandwidth has been increased by an order of magnitude to 12.5 MHz, the three channel impulses remain well defined at the filter output, that is, the multipath components are resolvable using this filter. This example illustrates that multipath resolvability is a function of the receive filter bandwidth and the time interval between multipath arrivals, not just the time interval between multipath arrivals.

Further examination of Figure 10–8 shows that the second group of three multipath components is also resolvable after wideband filtering but not resolvable after narrowband filtering. However, the two *groups* of multipath components—group 1 consisting of multipath components 1, 2, and 3 and group 2 consisting of multipath components 4, 5, and 6—are themselves resolvable with either receive filter. That is, the narrowband 1.25 MHz filter output appears as two separate responses, the first response due to multipath components 1,2 and 3 and the second due to multipath components 4, 5, and 6.

In order to analyze the performance of communication links in an unresolvable multipath environment an easy-to-use analytical model is desired. As a first step in creating this model, consider the transmission of an unmodulated sinewave to a mobile located at an arbitrary location. The sinewave propagates via multiple paths and the receiver responds to the complex envelope (or phasor) sum of the multipath signals. Figure 10–9a illustrates a frame of reference for the calculation of this phasor sum; the location of the center of the coordinate system is arbitrary and the mobile, which is possibly moving at

TABLE 10–1 Multipath Delays and Magnitude for the Channel of Figure 10–6 and the Receiver Responses of Figure 10–8

Multipath Component j	Delay in μsec	Magnitude g_j
1	0.0	0.5000
2	0.8	0.3535
3	1.6	0.3535
4	8.0	0.3535
5	8.8	0.5000
6	9.6	0.3535

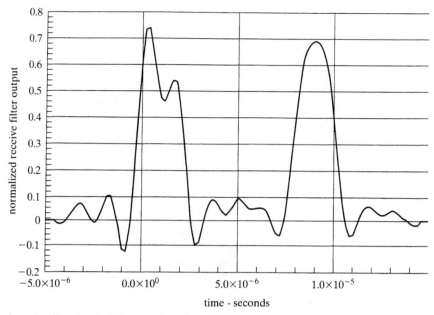

a) receive filter bandwidth approximately 1.25 MHz

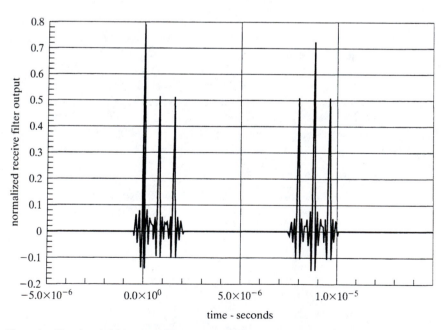

b) receive filter bandwidth approximately 12.5 MHz

FIGURE 10–8 Receive filter output in response to impulse applied at time 0 and channel of Figure 10–6.

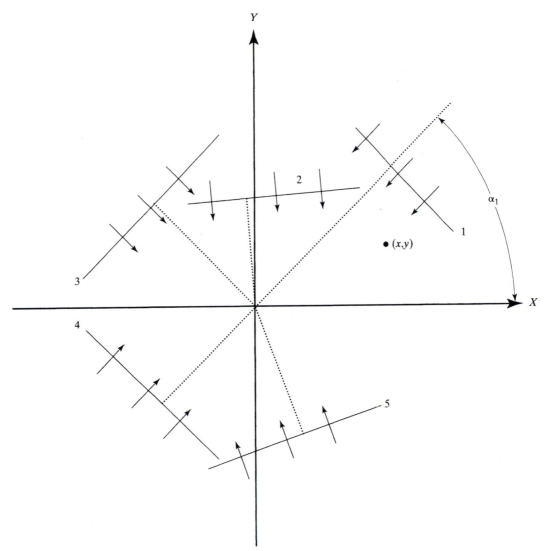

(a) Five wavefronts arriving at the mobile from five
different directions.

FIGURE 10–9   Calculation of phasor sum of wavefronts impinging on mobile at
arbitrary location.

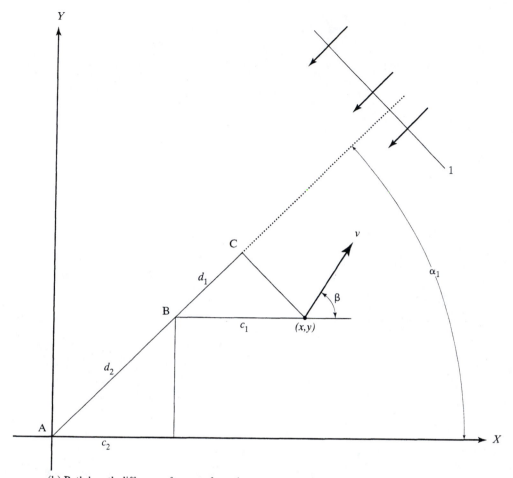

(b) Path length difference for wavefront 1.

FIGURE 10–9   *Continued*

velocity v, is at location (x,y). Five wavefronts are shown impinging on the mobile. *At the center of the coordinate system* the voltage at the antenna terminal due to wavefront n is

$$e_n(t) = E_n \cos\{\omega_0 t + \vartheta_n\} \tag{10–25}$$

or in complex envelope notation

$$\tilde{e}_n = E_n \exp\left[j\vartheta_n\right] \tag{10–26}$$

where the amplitude E_n is a function of the transmitted signal power and the path loss and shadowing and ϑ_n represents the phase shift due to the transmission delay τ_n to point $(0,0)$. The phase ϑ_n is assumed constant at the center of the coordinate system for this analysis. That is, everything about the propagation environment is assumed constant except for possible movement of the mobile. With this assumption, (10–25) is a function of time only through the sinewave oscillation of the carrier. The complex envelope (10–26) of a single multipath component is time invariant.

The complex envelope sum at the mobile location (x,y) must account for the difference in phase of all received wavefronts between point $(0,0)$ and point (x,y). Figure 10–9b illustrates the calculation of the phase difference $\phi_1(x,y)$ between point (x,y) and point $(0,0)$ for wavefront 1. Referring to the figure, the phase difference is $\phi_1(x,y) = 2\pi(d_1 + d_2)/\lambda_0$ where λ_0 represents the wavelength of the carrier. Using straightforward geometry, it can be shown that $d_1 + d_2 = y \sin \alpha_1 + x \cos \alpha_1$. An identical calculation is applicable to each wavefront. Accounting for $\phi_1(x,y)$ in (10–26), the desired complex envelope sum is

$$\tilde{e} = \sum_{n=1}^{N} E_n \exp[\,j\{\mathcal{I}_n - \phi_n(x,y)\}]$$

$$= \sum_{n=1}^{N} E_n \exp\left[j\left\{\mathcal{I}_n - \frac{2\pi}{\lambda_0}(y \sin \alpha_n + x \cos \alpha_n)\right\}\right] \tag{10–27}$$

Observe that this complex envelope sum is a function of the position of the mobile (x,y), and it is proper to write $\tilde{e}(x,y)$ to show this dependence explicitly. This dependence upon location is strong, resulting in large variations in $\tilde{e}(x,y)$ with variations in location of less than one-half the carrier wavelength. Figure 10–10 is a plot of the amplitude of (10–27) in decibels illustrating the dependence on location for a system having $N = 16$ wavefronts with $E_n = \sqrt{2}/16$ and angles α_n and $\mathcal{I}_n$ both uniform random variables over $[0,2\pi)$ radians. In this figure, location variables have been normalized to the carrier wavelength λ_0 and the normalized range of both x and y are three wavelengths. Observe that the received signal has very large variations in amplitude as the location varies over distances on the order of one carrier wavelength.

As the mobile moves with velocity v in direction β with respect to the horizontal axis in Figure 10–9b, the location $(x,y) = (x_0 + v\,t\,\cos\beta, y_0 + v\,t\,\sin\beta)$ where (x_0,y_0) is the initial location. With (x,y) now a function of (x_0,y_0), mobile velocity and direction, and time, (10–27) becomes

$$\tilde{e}(t,x_0,y_0) = \sum_{n=1}^{N} E_n \exp\left[j\left\{\mathcal{I}_n - \frac{2\pi}{\lambda_0}([y_0 + v\,t\,\sin\beta]\sin\alpha_n + [x_0 + v\,t\,\cos\beta]\cos\alpha_n)\right\}\right]$$

$$\tag{10–28}$$

This expression defines variation with time in received phasor as the mobile moves in a straight line through the location dependent variations in signal amplitude illustrated in Figure 10–10. Figure 10–11 illustrates this time variation for a mobile moving radially outward at a speed of 100 km/hour along the x-axis of Figure 10–10. The carrier frequency assumed for Figure 10–11 is 1960 MHz, and the impinging wavefronts are the same as used to generate Figure 10–10. Observe that over the short time interval shown

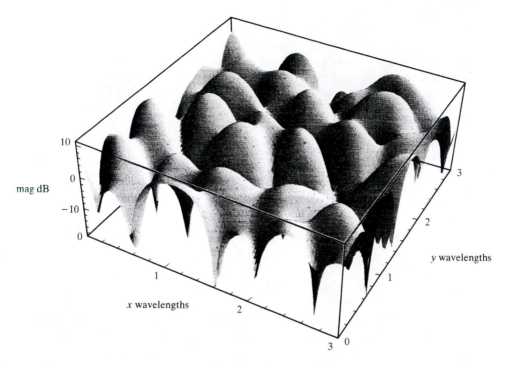

FIGURE 10–10   Multipath magnitude in dB as a function of normalized location.

(~60 ms) many large variations in received signal amplitude occur illustrating fast fading due to unresolvable multipaths. The rate of time variations of Figure 10–11 is directly proportional to mobile speed v and inversely proportional to carrier wavelength λ_0.

The time variation in signal amplitude illustrated in Figure 10–11 implies that the signal received at the mobile has nonzero bandwidth. Recall that the transmitted signal was an unmodulated and therefore zero bandwidth sinewave. The nonzero received bandwidth is due to the mobile motion. The spectral components of (10–28) can be identified by rewriting

$$\tilde{e}(t,x_0,y_0) = \sum_{n=1}^{N} E_n \exp\left[j\left\{ \mathcal{I}_n - \frac{2\pi}{\lambda_0}(y_0 \sin \alpha_n + x_0 \cos \alpha_n) \right.\right.$$

$$\left.\left. - \frac{2\pi v t}{\lambda_0}(\sin \beta \sin \alpha_n + \cos \beta \cos \alpha_n) \right\} \right]$$

$$= \sum_{n=1}^{N} E_n \exp\left[j\left\{ \mathcal{I}_n - \frac{2\pi}{\lambda_0}(y_0 \sin \alpha_n + x_0 \cos \alpha_n) - \frac{2\pi v t}{\lambda_0}\cos(\beta - \alpha_n) \right\} \right]$$

$$= \sum_{n=1}^{N} E_n \exp\left[j\left\{ \mathcal{I}_n - \frac{2\pi}{\lambda_0}(y_0 \sin \alpha_n + x_0 \cos \alpha_n) - \omega_n t \right\} \right] \qquad (10\text{–}29)$$

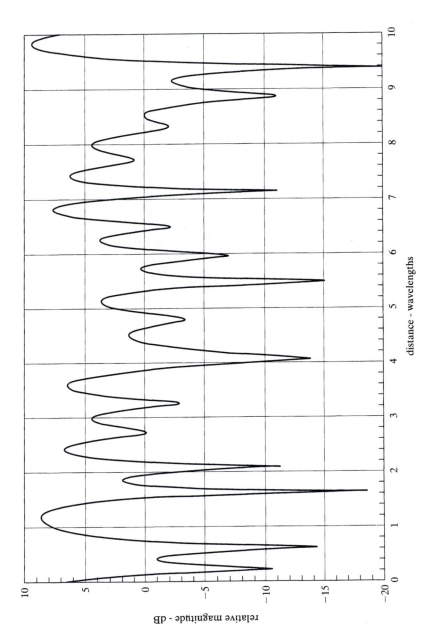

FIGURE 10–11 Magnoitude of phasor sum of 16 multipath components as a function of time and distance at mobile receiver traveling at 100 km/hr.

where

$$\omega_n \equiv \frac{2\pi\, v}{\lambda_0} \cos(\beta - \alpha_n) \tag{10-30a}$$

or equivalently

$$f_n \equiv \frac{v}{\lambda_0} \cos(\beta - \alpha_n) \tag{10-30b}$$

is the frequency offset of wavefront n. This frequency offset is the Doppler shift of wavefront n due to the component of mobile speed in the same direction that the wavefront is propagating. The linear combination of (10–29) includes N components each having a different Doppler shift and the spectrum of (10–29) is therefore spread over the range of all of these Doppler shifts. The spectrum will not necessarily be flat, although a flat spectrum is possible. The magnitude of the spectrum at a particular frequency is proportional to the magnitude of multipath component arriving from a direction yielding the Doppler shift equal to that frequency. The maximum Doppler shift is $f_M = v/\lambda_0$.

In summary, it has been shown that the unresolvable multipath environment combined with the motion of the mobile causes significant amplitude and phase modulation of a transmitted unmodulated sinewave. This modulation is called *fast fading*. The model yielding this result is a simple phasor sum of sinusoids arriving at the moving mobile with different amplitudes, phases, and Doppler shifts. Although this development has focused on a single transmitted sinewave, the model applies directly to any transmitted signal because the sum of multipath components is a linear operation.

The most widely used [9,10,11] model for unresolvable multipath is a straightforward extension of the sum of N sinewaves discussed in the previous paragraphs. Specifically, the number N is allowed to become large (approaching infinity), and it is assumed that the arrival angles α_n are uniformly distributed over $(0,2\pi]$. The received signal due to a single transmitted sinewave is therefore the sum of a very large number of sinewaves having different amplitudes, phases, and Doppler shifts. Recalling the law of large numbers, the sum of a large number of such sinewaves approaches a Gaussian random process [12,13,14] and a reasonable multipath channel model is a processor that transforms an input sinewave having power P to an output Gaussian random process having the same total power and the appropriate power spectrum. Requiring that the input and output of the channel model have the same power is done so that the multipath channel model and path loss model may be considered independently. In terms of the input and output complex envelopes, a channel input $\tilde{s}(t) = \sqrt{2P} \exp(j\phi)$ produces a channel output $\tilde{r}(t) = \sqrt{P}\, n_{fI}(t) + j\sqrt{P}\, n_{fQ}(t)$ where $n_{fI}(t)$ and $n_{fQ}(t)$ represent independent zero-mean unit-power baseband Gaussian noise processes with identical power spectra. The subscript f on $n_{fI}(t)$ and $n_{fQ}(t)$ distinguishes these processes from the thermal noise process $n_I(t)$ and $n_Q(t)$ used elsewhere in this text. Figure 10–12a illustrates the baseband channel model widely used to represent multipath fast fading. Since the model is a straightforward complex multiplier, this unresolvable-multipath fading is sometimes called *multiplicaive fading*. The delay element of Figure 10–12a represents the average

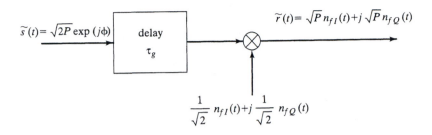

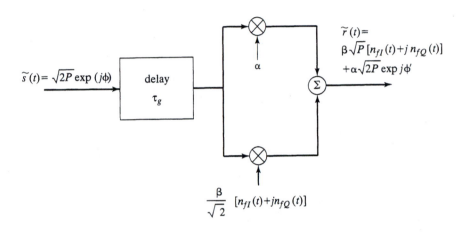

a) Rayleigh fading

b) Ricean fading

FIGURE 10–12 Complex envelope model for unresovable multipath fast fading.

delay of the group of delays being modeled by the complex multiplier. Specifically, $\tau_{gj} = \Sigma_n \gamma'_n \tau_n$ where γ'_n denotes the fraction of total power contributed by path n, the sum is over all paths contributing to the unresolvable group and the index j is used to identify a specific group of paths when more than one group is being considered. When the impulse response of the channel is such that there is a single unresolvable group of paths, the absolute delay and thus the delay element of Figure 10–12a does not affect link performance and is typically ignored.

The Gaussian random processes $n_{fI}(t)$ and $n_{fQ}(t)$ are completely characterized by their means, variances, and power spectra. Only their power spectra require further definition. Consider first the one-sided power spectrum $S_r(f)$ centered on the carrier frequency ω_0 of the received signal $r(t)$. The units of $S_r(f)$ are watts per hertz. Assume that equal power is arriving from all directions and denote the total power by P. In writing $S_r(f)$ as a continuous function of f it has been assumed that the number N of contributing wavefronts is approaching infinity. Figure 10–13 illustrates wavefronts arriving at the mobile from differential angle increment $d\alpha$ centered on angle α. Assume that the initial location of

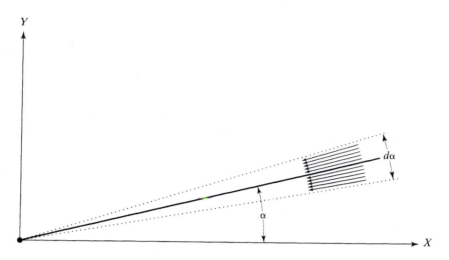

FIGURE 10–13   Wavefronts arriving from a differential angular range $d\alpha$ centered on α.

the mobile $(x_0,y_0) = (0,0)$ and the direction of movement of the mobile $\beta = 0$; identical results could be derived for nonzero β and (x_0,y_0) using slightly more involved arithmetic.
With these assumptions, the frequency of the signal received in the wavefront arriving at
angle α is $f = f_0 + f_M \cos \alpha$. Because the cosine is an even function, the frequency of the
signal in a wavefront arriving at angle $-\alpha$ is also $f = f_c + f_M \cos \alpha$. The fractional received
power due to the wavefronts of Figure 10–13 is $P \mid d\alpha \mid / 2\pi$. This fractional power plus the
fractional power from a similar angular increment centered at $-\alpha$ equal $S_r(f) \mid df \mid$ the
power in the differential frequency increment df. That is $S_r(f) \mid df \mid = P \mid d\alpha \mid / \pi$. The differential $d\alpha$ is calculated as a function of the differential df by taking the differential of
$f = f_0 + f_M \cos \alpha$. The result is

$$df = -f_M \sin \alpha \, d\alpha \tag{10–31}$$

which may be combined with $f = f_0 + f_M \cos \alpha$ to obtain

$$d\alpha = \frac{-df}{\sqrt{f_M^2 - (f - f_0)^2}} \tag{10–32}$$

Combining the results immediately above yields

$$S_r(f) \mid df \mid = \frac{P \mid d\alpha \mid}{\pi} = \frac{P \mid df \mid}{\pi \sqrt{f_M^2 - (f - f_0)^2}} \tag{10–33}$$

and

$$S_r(f) = \frac{P}{\pi \sqrt{f_M^2 - (f - f_0)^2}} \qquad \frac{\text{watts}}{\text{Hz}} \tag{10–34}$$

over the frequency range $f_0 - f_M \leq f \leq f_0 + f_M$.

Since $\tilde{r}(t) = \sqrt{P}\, n_{fI}(t) + j\sqrt{P}\, n_{jQ}(t)$ is the complex envelope of the bandpass process $r(t)$, the power spectra of the baseband Gaussian processes $n_{fI}(t)$ and $n_{fQ}(t)$ are found by translating $S_r(f)$ to baseband and dividing by P since $n_{fI}(t)$ and $n_{fQ}(t)$ were de-fined as unit power processes and the absolute power accounted for by the multiplier $\sqrt{P}$ in the expression for $\tilde{r}(t)$. Thus,

$$S_{n_{fI}}(f) = S_{n_{fQ}}(f) = \frac{1}{\pi\sqrt{f_M^2 - f^2}} \qquad (10\text{–}35)$$

Integrating (10–35) over $-f_M \leq f \leq f_M$ will show that $n_{fI}(t)$ and $n_{fQ}(t)$ have unit power as desired. Figure 10–14 is a plot of (10–35) using normalized frequency $f' = f/f_M$ as the in-dependent variable.

The spectrum defined by (10–35) has been used extensively in the analysis and simulation of the link performance in cellular radio. In simulations the functions $n_{fI}(t)$ and $n_{fQ}(t)$ are often generated by digitally filtering a spectrally white Gaussian process with a filter shaped to output a noise process with the spectrum of (10–35). While (10–35) is applicable to many propagation environments, it is not applicable universally. When the propagation environment is such that wavefronts arrive at the mobile from all direc-

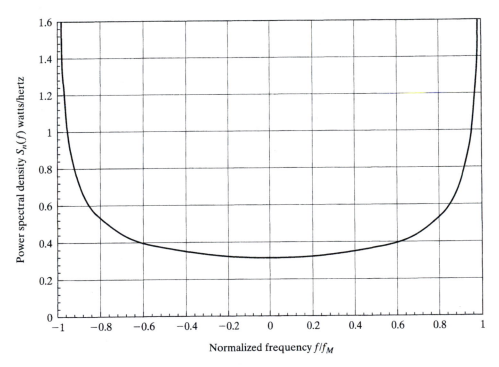

FIGURE 10–14   Power spectrum of the baseband Gaussian random processes $n_i(t)$ assuming uniformly spaced angles of arrival over $(0, 2\pi]$.

tions in both azimuth and elevation, that is, when the propagation environment is three-dimensional rather than two as in this discussion, the power spectrum is flat [4,15]. Further, in microcellular systems measurements show [16] that the distribution of angles of arrival are not uniform, resulting in power spectra very different than illustrated in Figure 10–14. The system engineer must therefore apply (10–35) with detailed knowledge that the propagation environment is consistent with the assumptions made in its derivation.

The channel model for unresolvable multipath is complete. The channel is a complex multiplier as illustrated in Figure 10–12a where the random processes $n_{fI}(t)$ and $n_{fQ}(t)$ have been completely defined in the preceding paragraphs. The theory of Gaussian random processes may now be applied to characterize the channel output further. Again, discussion is limited to the case where the channel input is an unmodulated sinewave with power P so that the channel output is a narrowband Gaussian random process. The complex envelope of the channel output is $\tilde{r}(t) = \sqrt{P}n_{fI}(t) + j\sqrt{P}n_{fQ}(t)$ which may also be expressed in the form

$$\tilde{r}(t) = r_f(t)\exp[-j\theta(t)] \tag{10–36}$$

where

$$r_f(t) = \sqrt{P} \times \sqrt{n_{fI}^2(t) + n_{fQ}^2(t)} \tag{10–37a}$$

$$\theta(t) = \tan^{-1}\left(\frac{n_{fQ}(t)}{n_{fI}(t)}\right) \tag{10–37b}$$

With $n_{fI}(t)$ and $n_{fQ}(t)$ independent zero-mean Gaussian random processes, the statistical characteristics of $r_f(t)$ and $\theta(t)$ are well known [17,18]. At any instant of time the probability density of the phase $\theta(t)$, denoted $p_\Theta(\theta)$, is uniform over $(0, 2\pi]$ and the probability density of the envelope $r_f(t)$, denoted $p_{r_f}(r)$, is Rayleigh. Thus,

$$p_\Theta(\theta) = \frac{1}{2\pi} \qquad\qquad 0 \le \theta < 2\pi \tag{10–38}$$

$$p_{r_f}(r) = \frac{r}{\sigma^2}\exp\left(-\frac{r^2}{2\sigma^2}\right) \qquad 0 \le r \tag{10–39}$$

where $\sigma^2 = P$ the total received signal power. Figure 10–15 illustrates $p_{r_f}(r)$ for $\sigma^2 = 1.0$. Using (10–39) the mean $E[r_f(t)]$ and mean square of the envelope random process $r_f(t)$ may be calculated. The results are [18]

$$E[r_f(t)] \equiv \int_0^\infty r\, p_{r_f}(r)dr = \sigma\sqrt{\frac{\pi}{2}} \tag{10–40}$$

$$E[r_f^2(t)] \equiv \int_0^\infty r^2\, p_{r_f}(r)\, dr = 2\sigma^2 \tag{10–41}$$

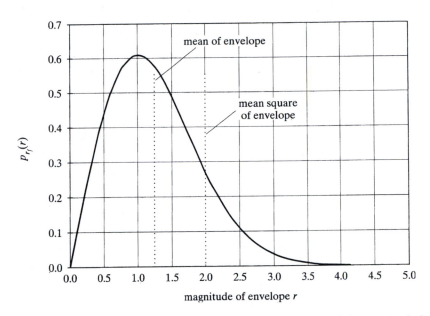

FIGURE 10–15 Probability density function for the envelope of the received signal experiencing Rayleigh fading.

Denote the instantaneous power of the received signal by $u(t)$. In terms of the complex envelope, the instantaneous power is $u(t) = P(n^2_{fI}(t) + n^2_{fQ}(t))/2$. It can be shown [18,19] via change of variables that the probability density $p_U(u)$ of $u(t)$ is exponential, specifically,

$$p_U(u) = \frac{1}{P} \exp\left(-\frac{u}{P}\right), \quad 0 \le u \tag{10–42}$$

Finally, the probability that $r_f(t) \le R$ at a particular instant in time is

$$\Pr[r_f \le R] = \int_0^R p_{r_f}(r)\, dr = 1 - \exp\left(-\frac{R^2}{2\sigma^2}\right) \equiv P_{r_f}(R) \tag{10–43}$$

EXAMPLE 10–2

It is often useful to know the probability that the instantaneous power of the received signal is more than X decibels *below* the average received power σ^2. The instantaneous power of the received faded signal is $u(t) = \frac{1}{2} r_f^2(t)$. Let R denote the magnitude of the complex envelope at the point where the power is X dB below the average, then

$$\sigma^2 \times 10^{-X/10} = \tfrac{1}{2} R^2.$$

Solving for R^2, the result is

$$R^2 = 2\sigma^2 \times 10^{-X/10}.$$

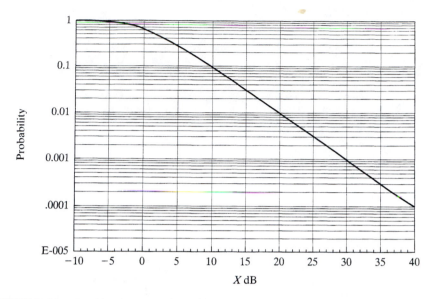

FIGURE 10–16   Probability that the envelope of a signal experiencing Rayleigh fading is X dB or more below the mean.

Substitute into (10–43) to obtain

$$\Pr[r_f \le R] = 1 - \exp\left(-\frac{2\sigma^2 \times 10^{-X/10}}{2\sigma^2}\right) = 1 - \exp(-10^{-X/10}).$$

This result is plotted in Figure 10–16. Observe that the probabilities of the instantaneous received power being 10, 20, and 30 dB below the average are approximately 10%, 1%, and 0.1% respectively.

Because the probability density of the envelope of the received signal is Rayleigh, the unresolvable-multipath fading modeled in the preceding paragraphs is called Rayleigh fading. *Rayleigh fading* occurs whenever there are many unresolvable propagation paths between the transmitter and receiver. It is not necessary that the power spectrum of the received signal be specified by (10–35) for the fading envelope to have a Rayleigh probability density.

In the analysis of communications link performance it is often useful to characterize the variations of the signal envelope with time. Characterization of the time variation of the envelope is useful, for example, in the design and analysis of a forward error control strategy for a cellular system where the time variations are used in, for example, specifying the size of the interleaver. The autocovariance function $L_{r_f}(\tau)$ of the received envelope, the level crossing rate N_R of the envelope, and the average duration of fades provide useful information and have been calculated . The results of these calculations follow. Detailed derivations may be found in [4] or [10]. The autocovariance function of the envelope $r_f(t)$ is defined by

$$L_{r_f}(\tau) \equiv E[\{r_f(t) - E[r_f(t)]\}\{r_f(t+\tau) - E[r_f(t)]\}] \qquad (10\text{–}44)$$

which is the autocorrelation function with the mean value removed [18]. For the Rayleigh fading envelope with a power spectrum given by (10–35) the autocovariance function is given *approximately* by

$$L_{r_f}(\tau) = \frac{\pi}{16} E[r_f^2] J_0^2(2\pi f_M \tau) = \frac{\pi}{8} P J_0^2(2\pi f_M \tau) \qquad (10\text{–}45)$$

where $J_0(\cdot)$ is the Bessel function of the first kind of order zero. Figure 10–17 is a plot of this function normalized to unity at $\tau = 0$ as a function of normalized delay $f_M\tau$. This function is approximate due to a step in its derivation requiring the use of the first several terms of a series expansion of a complicated function [10]. The normalized autocovariance function is a measure of the degree of correlation between samples of the received signal envelope taken τ seconds apart. As expected, the correlation between samples taken at nearly the same time, that is, $\tau \to 0$, is nearly unity. By definition $f_M\tau = v\tau/\lambda$, so Figure 10–17 also shows the correlation as a function of the normalized distance traveled by the mobile. The correlation is below 0.2 after the mobile has moved only one-quarter wavelength.

Next consider the rate N_R at which the envelope $r_f(t)$ crosses a particular level R with positive slope. With this definition the rate is the number of times per second that the envelope crosses a certain level, counting only the level crossing as the envelope in-

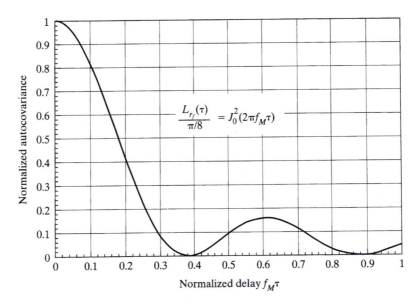

FIGURE 10–17 Normailzed autocovariance function of the envelope of a signal experiencing Rayleigh fading.

creases or comes out of a fade and not the crossing when the envelope decreases into the fade. Jakes [10] provides a detailed derivation yielding

$$N_R = \sqrt{2\pi} f_M \frac{R}{\sqrt{E[r_f^2(t)]}} \exp\left(-\frac{R^2}{E[r_f^2(t)]}\right) \qquad (10\text{–}46)$$

where the mean-square of the envelope $E[r_f^2(t)]$ was given in (10–41). The normalized level crossing rate N_R/f_M is plotted in Figure 10–18 as a function of the threshold R in decibels relative to the root mean square value of the envelope, that is, as a function of $\rho \equiv 20 \log_{10}(R/\sqrt{E[r_f^2(t)]})$ as was done in [10]. Examination of Figure 10–18 shows that very deep fades, say to levels of 30 or 40 dB below the RMS level, occur at a low rate. This is consistent with low probability of a deep fade that was deduced from the examination of the probability density function of the envelope.

The communication system designer also needs to know something about the duration of the fades being experienced by the signal. The average length of time $\bar{\tau}(R)$ the envelope spends below a threshold R has also been calculated by Jakes [10]. The result is

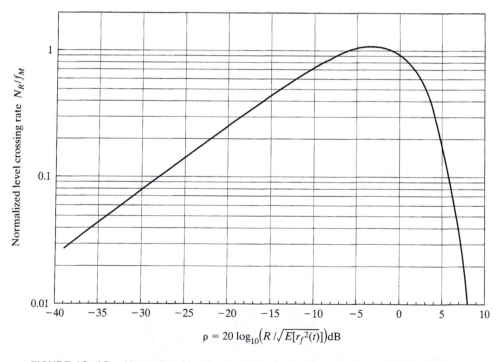

FIGURE 10–18   Normalized level crossing rate for the envelope of a signal experiencing Raleigh fading [10].

$$\bar{\tau}(R) = \frac{\exp\left(\dfrac{R^2}{E[r_f^2]}\right) - 1}{\sqrt{2\pi}\, f_M \dfrac{R}{\sqrt{E[r_f^2(t)]}}} \tag{10-47}$$

This result, normalized by the period of the maximum Doppler shift, is plotted in Figure 10–19 as a function of ρ, which was defined above.

10.3.2.2 Ricean (Unresolvable) Fading.   The derivations above relating to Rayleigh fading were based upon the assumption that the transmitted signal was received at the mobile via many independent paths and that no one of these paths was dominant. Now suppose that a single dominant path exists in addition to a group of N paths that sum to create Rayleigh fading. The Rayleigh fading linear sum is modeled exactly as above and the complex envelope of the received signal in this case is described by

$$\tilde{r}(t) = \sqrt{P_f}\, n_{fI}(t) + j\sqrt{P_f}\, n_{fQ}(t) + \sqrt{2P_0}\, \exp(j\theta_0)$$
$$= r_f(t)\, \exp[\, j\theta_f(t)\,] + \sqrt{2P_0}\, \exp(j\theta_0) \tag{10-48}$$

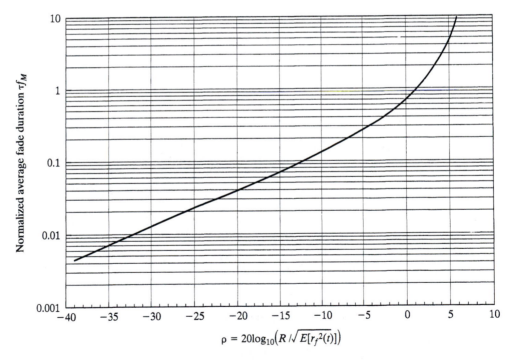

FIGURE 10–19   Normalized average duration of fades for a signal experiencing Rayleigh fading.

where the subscript f denotes the Rayleigh or diffuse fading component and the subscript 0 denotes the dominant specular received component. The total received power is denoted $P \equiv P_f + P_0$. Figure 10–12b illustrates the complex envelope model for this fading channel which is referred to as a *Ricean fading channel*. In Figure 10–12b constants $a = \sqrt{P_0/P}$ and $\beta = \sqrt{P_f/P}$ are used to relate the total power P and the specular P_0 and diffuse P_f fading channel components. The phase of the output specular component ϕ' is different from that of the input due to the delay τ_g. The complex envelope of the specular component is assumed constant over time, although neither the magnitude nor the phase may be known to the receiver. Let $r_R(t)$ and $\theta_R(t)$ denote the envelope and phase of $\tilde{r}(t)$, then

$$\tilde{r}(t) = r_R(t) \exp[j\theta_R(t)] \tag{10–49}$$

where the subscript R denotes Ricean fading. The probability densities of $r_R(t)$ and $\theta_R(t)$ are well known [4,13,14,18,19] and the results are

$$p_{r_R}(r) = \frac{r}{P_f} \exp\left(-\frac{P_0}{P_f}\right) \exp\left(-\frac{r^2}{2P_f}\right) I_0\left(\frac{r\sqrt{2P_0}}{P_f}\right), \quad r \geq 0 \tag{10–50}$$

where $I_0(\cdot)$ is the modified Bessel function of the first kind of order zero, and [18]

$$p_{\Theta_R}(\theta) = \frac{1}{2\pi} \exp\left(-\frac{P_0}{P_f}\right)$$

$$+ \left[\sqrt{\frac{P_0}{P_f}} \frac{1}{2\sqrt{\pi}} \exp\left(-\frac{P_0}{P_f} \sin^2(\theta - \theta_0)\right) \cos(\theta - \theta_0)\right] \tag{10–51}$$

$$\times \left[1 + \text{erf}\left(\sqrt{\frac{P_0}{P_f}} \cos(\theta - \theta_0)\right)\right], \quad 0 < \theta \leq 2\pi$$

where erf($\cdot$) is the error function (see Appendix E) and θ_0 is the phase of the received specular component. These densities are plotted in Figures 10–20 and 10–21 with $K_{\text{dB}} = 10\log_{10}(P_0/P_f) = 10\log_{10} K$ as a parameter and assuming $P_f = 1.0$ and $\theta_0 = \pi/4$. The parameter $K = P_0/P_f$ is widely used to define the level of the specular component in Rician distributions. Observe in Figure 10–20 that for $K_{\text{dB}} = -40$ dB the specular component is very small and the probability distribution is nearly Rayleigh (compare with Figure 10–15). As the specular component becomes larger the probability density approaches a Gaussian shape with mean becoming larger as K increases. Figure 10–21 shows that the density function of the phase is nearly flat and equal to $1/2\pi$ when $K_{\text{dB}} = -40$ dB and becomes concentrated near the phase of the specular component θ_0 as K becomes large.

The mean square of the envelope of a signal experiencing Ricean fading and the cumulative distribution that the magnitude of the envelope are known [18]. The probability $\Pr[r_R \leq R]$ that the envelope is smaller than R is

$$\Pr[r_R \leq R] = \int_0^R p_{r_R}(r)dr \tag{10–52}$$

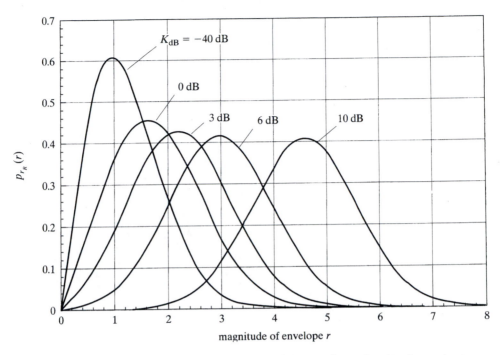

FIGURE 10–20   Probability density function of the envelope of a signal experiencing Ricean fading.

which may be written in terms of the Marcum Q-function, defined [18] as

$$Q_M(\alpha, \beta) \equiv \int_\beta^\infty z \exp\left(-\frac{z^2 + \alpha^2}{2}\right) I_0(\alpha z) dz. \qquad (10\text{--}53)$$

In terms of the Marcum Q-function the desired probability is

$$\Pr[r_R \leq R] = 1.0 - \int_R^\infty p_{r_R}(r)\, dr$$

$$= 1.0 - \int_R^\infty \frac{r}{P_f} \exp\left(-\frac{P_0}{P_f}\right) \exp\left(-\frac{r^2}{2P_f}\right) I_0\left(\frac{r\sqrt{2P_0}}{P_f}\right) dr \qquad (10\text{--}54)$$

$$= 1.0 - \int_{R/\sqrt{P_f}}^\infty z \exp\left(-\frac{z^2 + \alpha^2}{2}\right) I_0(z\,\alpha)\, dz$$

$$= 1.0 - Q_M\left(\alpha, \frac{R}{\sqrt{P_f}}\right)$$

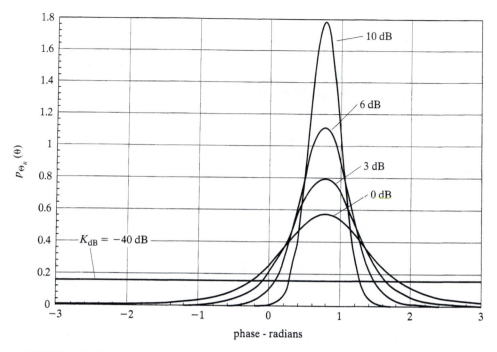

FIGURE 10–21 Probability density function for the phase of a signal experiencing Ricean fading (the phase of the specular component is $\pi/4$).

where $\alpha = \sqrt{2P_0/P_f}$ and the change of variables $z = r/\sqrt{P_f}$ has been applied. It can also be shown [18] that the mean square of the envelope of a Ricean fading signal is

$$E[r_R^2(t)] = 2(P_0 + P_f) \tag{10–55}$$

EXAMPLE 10–3

Reconsider the problem of Example 10–2. Calculate and plot the probability that the received power for a Ricean fading signal is X dB or more below the average received power. Let R denote the magnitude of the complex envelope at the point where the received power is X dB below the average. The average received power $P = P_0 + P_f$ so that $R = \sqrt{2P \times 10^{-X/10}} = \sqrt{2(P_0 + P_f) \times 10^{-X/10}}$. Substituting into (10–54) the desired probability is

$$\Pr[r_R(t) \le R] = 1.0 - Q_M\left(\sqrt{\frac{2P_0}{P_f}}, \sqrt{2\left(\frac{P_0}{P_f} + 1\right) \times 10^{-X/10}}\right).$$

This result is plotted in Figure 10–22 with K_{dB} as a parameter. For $K_{dB} = -40$ dB the result is nearly identical to the result of Figure 10–16 for Rayleigh fading. Observe that as K increases, the probability that the received signal power is a particular number of decibels

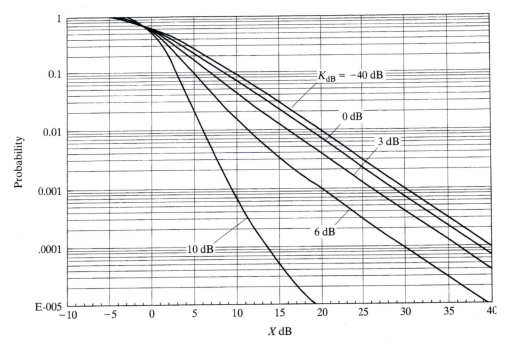

FIGURE 10–22   Probability that the envelope of a signal experiencing Ricean fading is X dB or more below the mean.

below the average decreases significantly. It is concluded that Ricean fading is less degrading to communications system performance than Rayleigh fading.

10.3.2.3 Summary.   The Rayleigh and Ricean fading models discussed above and illustrated in Figure 10–12a and 10–12b account for multipath components having closely spaced time of arrivals that cannot be resolved by the intended receiver. The first three or the last three arrivals of Figure 10–6 could be groups of such unresolvable paths. The model accounts for all of the components of a group through the amplitude and phase variations of the complex multiplier $[n_{fI}(t) + j\, n_{fQ}(t)]/\sqrt{2}$ of Figure 10–12a for Rayleigh fading or this expression plus a complex constant for Rician fading. Rayleigh fading models multipath environments in which there is no specular received component while Ricean fading models environments having a specular component. Although the discussion was lengthy, the models themselves are reasonably simple to implement in simulations. In a simulation the designer must generate two independent Gaussian random processes representing $n_{fI}(t)$ and $n_{fQ}(t)$ with the correct power spectra and perform the multiplications indicated in Figure 10–12. These Gaussian random processes can be generated by first generating a white noise source and then filtering the output of that source to create the desired spectra always being careful to maintain the correct total

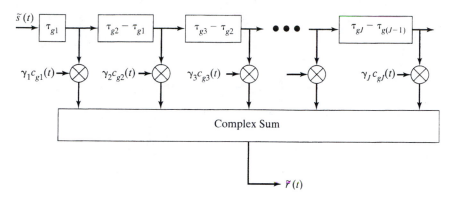

FIGURE 10–23 Tapped delay line model for resovable multipath groups for WSSUS multipath channel.

power in the waveforms. The most commonly used spectrum was defined in Figure 10–14. Other spectra are possible and correct for specific multipath environments.

10.3.2.4 Resolvable Multipath Components.

Consider next the extension of the multipath channel model to include multiple *groups* of unresolvable paths. Each group of unresolvable paths will be modeled as in Figure 10–12 by single complex multiplier (Rayleigh fading) or the sum of a complex multiplier and a constant (Ricean fading) and delay element. The index $1 \leq j \leq J$ will be used to identify a specific group. For example, the six paths of Figure 10–6 will be modeled as two groups $j = 1,2$ of three paths where each of the two groups is modeled as in Figure 10–12. Figure 10–23 is a block diagram of the model for the case where all of the groups are Rayleigh faded. The input $\tilde{s}(t)$ and the output $\tilde{r}(t)$ are the complex envelopes of the bandpass input and output waveforms. All arithmetic in the figure is complex. The delay associated with the group τ_{gj} is sum of the delay elements to the left of the multiplier. Thus, each delay element represents the differential delay between groups. While communications link performance is affected by the delays between multipliers of Figure 10–23, the affect of the first delay is only to delay the received signal by a fixed amount of time. In most instances this absolute delay is unimportant and the first delay is ignored.

This model is widely used since it accurately represents a large fraction of actual multipath environments. Each complex channel multiplier $c_{gj}(t)$ of Figure 10–23 is a complex Gaussian process with zero mean (Rayleigh) or nonzero mean (Ricean) and unit power. The real multipliers γ_j associated with each group enable the adjustment of the fraction of the total power contributed by that group. It is convenient and typical to require that $\Sigma_j \gamma_j^2 = 1.0$ so that the total received power (sum of all paths) is equal to the channel input power. With this convention the path loss and shadow fading may be considered independently from the multipath fading model. Recall that the channel multiplier of Figure 10–12 was calibrated so that the input and output powers of that figure were the same.

The model of Figure 10–23 applies to the class of wide-sense stationary uncorrelated scattering (WSSUS) channels defined by Bello [20] in his classic paper upon which much modern research in propagation modeling is based. In order for this model to apply, each of the groups $j = 1, \ldots, J$ of unresolvable multipaths must be wide-sense stationary. This means that the parameters of the Rayleigh or Ricean distribution are constant over reasonable ranges of time. Furthermore, the WSSUS model requires that each of the groups be uncorrelated. Thus, since the processes $c_{gj}(t)$ are Gaussian, the $c_{gj}(t)$ are independent for different j. The independence of the multipliers $c_{gj}(t)$ is reasonable, since groups of multipath components having significantly different delays have traveled over significantly different, and thus independent, physical paths. Most propagation environments of interest in cellular radio satisfy these requirements.

10.3.2.5 A Mathematical Model for the WSSUS Channel.

The arguments presented above were brief so that the fundamental issues affecting the gross behavior of the cellular mobile radio channel could be presented as quickly as possible. These developments were based upon a large body of literature where highly detailed and mathematically rigorous developments may be found [4,10,11,15,19–24]. The following paragraphs summarize a number of the mathematical modeling results for WSSUS fading channels. A WSSUS channel is defined as a channel that is both wide sense stationary (WSS) and exhibits uncorrelated scattering (US). A WSS channel is a channel for which the statistics of the fading process are stationary over reasonable lengths of time; all channels of interest for cellular mobile radio satisfy this requirement. A channel exhibits uncorrelated scattering (US) when the time variations in the impulse response at one delay are uncorrelated with the time variations at a different delay; most channels of interest exhibit this property. In the more detailed literature, the multipath channel is modeled as a time-varying linear filter whose complex envelope impulse response is denoted $h(\tau;t)$ where τ represents the usual delay variable and t represents time. The *time-varying impulse response* $h(\tau;t)$ defines the (complex) response of the channel at time t to an impulse applied τ seconds earlier. When $h(\tau;t)$ is nonzero for more than a single delay τ, this channel spreads the transmitted signal over time. Writing the impulse response as a function of both delay τ and time t recognizes that the channel impulse response itself can change over time. Figure 10–24 illustrates the magnitude $|h(\tau;t)|$ for a typical channel impulse response as a function of delay τ; the shape of the impulse response illustrated could be different at a later or earlier sampling (or sounding) of the channel. In the time domain the complex envelope $\tilde{r}(t)$ of the channel output is the convolution of the impulse response $h(\tau;t)$ with the complex envelope $\tilde{s}(t)$ of the channel input, that is [19,21],

$$\tilde{r}(t) = \int_{-\infty}^{\infty} h(t - \tau;t)\, \tilde{s}(\tau)\, d\tau \tag{10–56}$$

The Fourier transform of $h(\tau;t)$ with respect to the delay variable τ is the *time-varying equivalent low-pass transfer function* [19,21] of the channel

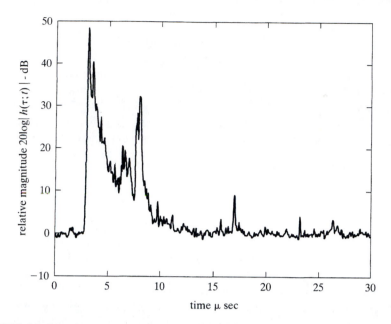

FIGURE 10–24 Measured multipath channel impulse response using receiver with 10 MHz bandwidth (Washington St., Phoenix, AZ) (plot courtesy of Insung Kang of Motorola).

$$H(f;t) = \int_{-\infty}^{\infty} h(\tau;t)\exp(-j\,2\pi f\tau)\,d\tau \tag{10-57}$$

where f represents the offset from the nominal carrier. In the frequency domain, the Fourier transform of the output $\tilde{R}(f;t)$ is the product of the Fourier transform of the input $\tilde{S}(f)$ and $H(f;t)$ and the envelope of the channel output is the inverse Fourier transform of this product,[4] that is

$$\tilde{r}(t) = \int_{-\infty}^{\infty} H(f;t)\tilde{S}(f)\exp[\,j2\pi f t\,]\,df \tag{10-58}$$

If the channel input is a sinewave, $\tilde{S}(f) = \sqrt{2P}\,\delta(f - f_0)$, the complex envelope of the channel output is

$$\tilde{r}(t) = \int_{-\infty}^{\infty} H(f;t)\{\sqrt{2P}\,\delta(f - f_0)\}\exp[\,j2\pi f t\,]\,df$$

$$= \sqrt{2P}\,H(f_0;t)\exp[\,j2\pi f_0\,t\,] \tag{10-59}$$

[4]It is assumed that the time variation of the channel is slow relative to the channel response time.

Thus, the magnitude of the time-varying transfer function represents the magnitude of the complex envelope of the channel output when channel input is an unmodulated sinewave.

The *multipath intensity profile*[5] denoted $p_d(\tau)$ of the channel is a measure of the average channel output power at delay τ in response to a channel input impulse at time zero. Mathematically [21]

$$p_d(\tau) \equiv E\left[\tfrac{1}{2} h(\tau;t) \, h^*(\tau;t)\right] \qquad (10\text{–}60)$$

where the expectation is over all sample functions $h(\tau;t)$. The right side of (10–60) contains the variable t indicating that the multipath intensity profile can change slowly with time. The multipath intensity profile can be measured directly using channel sounding techniques [9]. The delay of the channel between the impulse input instant and first output energy does not affect communications reliability and this delay is usually ignored or set to 0. For example, τ_1 in Figure 10–6 would be assumed to be 0. With the understanding that initial delay is ignored, the maximum delay for which $p_d(t) > 0$ is defined to be the *delay spread* T_m of the channel. For the channel of Figure 10–6, $T_m = \tau_6 - \tau_1$. Delay spread for typical cellular radio channels is strongly a function of the physical environment and typical values range from a few nanoseconds to tens of microseconds. Several measures of delay spread are commonly used. The *average delay spread* is denoted D and is defined by

$$D \equiv \frac{\displaystyle\int_0^\infty \tau \, p_d(\tau) \, d\tau}{\displaystyle\int_0^\infty p_d(\tau) \, d\tau} \qquad (10\text{–}61)$$

and the *root mean square delay spread* is denoted S and is defined by

$$S \equiv \sqrt{\frac{\displaystyle\int_0^\infty (\tau - D)^2 \, p_d(\tau) \, d\tau}{\displaystyle\int_0^\infty p_d(\tau) \, d\tau}}. \qquad (10\text{–}62)$$

EXAMPLE 10–4

Consider the multipath channel defined in Figure 10–6 and Table 10–1. The power associated with each multipath component is the square of the magnitude given in Table 10–1 and the multipath intensity profile is

$$p_d(\tau) = \sum_{j=1}^{6} g_j^2 \, \delta(\tau - \tau_j)$$

---

[5]Also called the *power delay profile*.

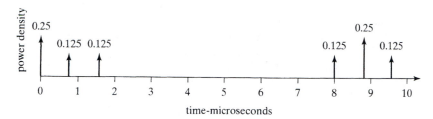

FIGURE 10–25   Multipath intensity profile for Example 10–4.

which is illustrated in Figure 10–25. Observe that the gains have been selected so that $\Sigma_{j=1}^{6} g_j^2 = 1.0$. Inserting the discrete multipath intensity into (10–61) and (10–62) yields $D = \Sigma_{j=1}^{6} \tau_j g_j^2 = 4.7$ μs. Using $D = 4.7$ μsec in (10–63) yields $S = \sqrt{\Sigma_{j=1}^{6} (\tau_j - 4.7)^2 g_j^2} = 4.14$ μsec

It can be shown [20] that a channel with $T_m > 0$ exhibits frequency selectivity in that the channel response at one carrier frequency, say f_1, may be different from the channel response at another frequency, say f_2. The degree to which the channel responses at two carrier frequencies separated by $\Delta f = |f_2 - f_1|$ are correlated is given by the *normalized spaced-frequency correlation function* [19]

$$\rho_F(\Delta f) = \frac{R_F(\Delta f)}{R_F(0)} \tag{10–63}$$

where [19–22]

$$R_F(\Delta f) = \int_{-\infty}^{\infty} P_d(\tau) \exp[-j\,2\,\pi\,\Delta f\,\tau]\,d\tau. \tag{10–64}$$

The subscript F is a reminder that frequency correlation is being considered. The normalized spaced-frequency correlation function is important in the analysis of frequency diversity transmission systems where, for example, symbols may be transmitted multiple times using different carrier frequencies in order to improve reliability. If the two carrier frequencies are separated adequately, the fading processes observed at the two frequencies are loosely correlated and the probability that both fade at the same instant is less than the probability that either one of the carriers is itself in a fade. Because of the Fourier transform relationship (10–64), channels with small delay spread require larger frequency separation to achieve a specified degree of signal decorrelation than channels with large delay spread. This relationship is sometimes [22] quantified by defining the *correlation bandwidth* B_c of the channel to be the inverse of the delay spread, that is, $B_c = 1/T_m$. The correlation bandwidth provides an indicator of the type of fading that will be experienced on the channel. Suppose that the bandwidth of the signal being transmitted is $B \ll B_c$. Then each frequency component of the transmitted signal experiences nearly the same fading, that is, all components of the transmitted signal fade together and the channel is said to be *frequency nonselective* or *flat*. In this case the channel may be modeled as in Figure 10–12 as a multiplicative fading channel.

Time variations in $h(\tau;t)$ and $H(f;t)$ are due to variations in the propagation environment itself as well as motion of the transmitter and/or the receiver; these time variations result in spreading the received signal in frequency. This spreading in frequency is due to Doppler shifting of the transmitted signal as demonstrated previously. A measure of the degree of spreading is the *Doppler power spectrum* [19] of the channel that is denoted $V_F(\lambda)$, where the variable λ represents Doppler shift or Doppler frequency. The Doppler power spectrum could be measured using a spectrum analyzer at the channel output while an unmodulated carrier is input to the channel. Figure 10–14 illustrated the Doppler power spectrum for a specific channel in which the received wavefronts arrived from all directions with nearly equal magnitude and equal probability. In all cases $V_F(\lambda)$ is nonzero only over a finite range of Doppler frequency. The range of frequency over which $V_F(\lambda)$ is nonzero is called the *Doppler spread* of the channel denoted B_D. The Doppler power spectrum is important since it provides information about the time variability of the fading process. Specifically, define the *spaced-time correlation function*

$$R_T(\Delta t) \equiv E[\tfrac{1}{2} H(f;t) H^*(f; t + \Delta t)] \tag{10–65}$$

It can be shown that $R_T(\Delta t)$ is the inverse Fourier transform of the Doppler spectrum [19], that is,

$$R_T(\Delta t) = \int_{-\infty}^{\infty} V_F(\lambda) \exp[j 2\pi\lambda\Delta t]\, d\lambda. \tag{10–66}$$

Recalling that $H(f;t)$ represents the envelope of the channel output when the channel input is an unmodulated sinewave, $R_T(\Delta t)$ then represents the correlation between samples of the fading process spaced in time by Δt. This function is important in the analysis of time diversity systems where a symbol is transmitted at two times separated adequately such that the sample of the fading process experienced by one sample is largely decorrelated with the sample of the fading process experienced by the other. Thus, the probability of both transmissions experiencing a fade is less than the probability that either experiences a fade by itself. The *normalized spaced-time correlation function* is defined by

$$\rho_T(\Delta t) = \frac{R_T(\Delta t)}{R_T(0)} \tag{10–67}$$

Correlation time is related to the bandwidth of the Doppler spectrum through the Fourier transform relationship of (10–66). Large Doppler spread is associated with short fading correlation times and small Doppler spread is associated with large fading correlation times. The correlation time of the channel, denoted T_D, is sometimes approximated by $T_D = 1/B_D$.

The purpose of this discussion is to make the reader aware that extensive research has been done on the topic of mobile radio channel modeling and to introduce the basic issues affecting cellular mobile communications. Clearly, communicating over the multipath fading channel provides a challenge requiring creative application of communication technology. The interested reader will find the seminal work by Bello [20] interesting, complete, and highly challenging. Stein [19, 21] and Proakis [22] provide excellent overviews of fading channels and are highly recommended reading.

10.4 MITIGATION TECHNIQUES FOR THE MULTIPATH FADING CHANNEL

10.4.1 Introduction

The Rayleigh and Ricean fading channels defined in Section 10.3 are some of the most difficult channels for the communications system designer. The complex gain (magnitude and phase) of these channels can vary rapidly over large ranges, making it difficult to estimate channel gain and/or phase for coherent communications and/or for calculating appropriate decoding metrics for soft-decision decoding. If the variations occur slowly enough, channel estimation is possible but, even then, the gain variations profoundly affect performance. In order to gain insight into the manner in which channel gain variations affect signaling reliability, consider a channel modeled as simple real-valued gain multiplier having only two states. Denote the voltage gains of the two channel states by β_1 and β_2 where $\beta_1 < \beta_2$ and suppose that channel gain β_1 occurs randomly with probability ρ and channel gain β_2 occurs randomly with probability $1 - \rho$. Assume that channel state changes occur infrequently so that perfect channel estimation is possible in either state. Recall that the multiplicative fading channel model derived previously was normalized so that the average (over all channel states) power gain was unity and select β_1 and β_2 such that this is also true for this two-state channel, that is,

$$\rho\,\beta_1^2 + (1 - \rho)\,\beta_2^2 = 1.0 \tag{10–68}$$

To complete the specification of the channel, require that the gain β_1 and its probability of occurrence be related in a manner analogous to the gain and probability relationships for the Rayleigh fading channel. Specifically, recall Figure 10–16, in which it was shown that a channel gain X_{dB} below the average gain occurs, approximately, with probability $\rho_{X_{dB}} = 10^{-X_{dB}/10}$ or simply $\rho_{X_{dB}} = X$ where X is the *power* gain (not in decibels) of the channel relative to the average. Using this approximate relationship, let $\beta_1^2 = \rho$ and, using (10–68), $\beta_2^2 = 1 + \rho$. Suppose that coherent BPSK (or QPSK) modulation is used over this two-state channel. Recall that, for a constant signal-to-noise ratio, bit error probability for BPSK or QPSK is given by $Q(\sqrt{2E_b/N_0})$. Since the channel is slowly varying, the *average* bit error probability at the channel output is given by

$$\overline{P}_E = \rho\,Q\left(\sqrt{\frac{2\beta_1^2\,E_b}{N_0}}\right) + (1 - \rho)\,Q\left(\sqrt{\frac{2\beta_2^2\,E_b}{N_0}}\right)$$

$$= \rho\,Q\left(\sqrt{\frac{2\rho\,E_b}{N_0}}\right) + (1 - \rho)\,Q\left(\sqrt{\frac{2(1 + \rho)\,E_b}{N_0}}\right) \tag{10–69}$$

where the first term corresponds to channel state 1 with signal-to-noise ratio $\rho\,E_b/N_0$ and the second term corresponds to channel state 2 with signal-to-noise ratio $(1 + \rho)\,E_b/N_0$.

Equation (10–69) is plotted in Figure 10–26 with ρ as a parameter. Consider one of the curves of this figure with ρ << 1.0. As E_b/N_0 increases, there are three different regions of bit error probability performance. For extremely low E_b/N_0, both ρ E_b/N_0 and $(1 + \rho)E_b/N_0$ are small and the bit error probability for either is approaching 0.5. As E_b/N_0 increases, the bit error probability corresponding to $(1 + \rho)\,E_b/N_0$ begins to decrease much more rapidly than the bit error probability corresponding to ρ E_b/N_0 and the second term becomes negligible relative to the first. For some ρ a plateau is reached where $Q(\sqrt{2\rho\, E_b/N_0})$ remains near 0.5 while $Q(\sqrt{2(1 + \rho)\, E_b/N_0})$ is negligible and the average bit error probability is dominated by the first term and is approximately ρ/2. As E_b/N_0 increases further, ρ E_b/N_0 eventually becomes large enough that the exponential decrease in bit error probability for the first term of (10–69) is observed. This figure illustrates that a channel state with very low signal-to-noise ratio can affect average bit error probability significantly even when that channel state occurs very rarely. For example, examination of the curve ρ = 0.0001 for which a channel gain of –40 dB occurs only 0.01% of the time shows that an E_b/N_0 of approximately 39 dB is required to achieve an average bit error probability of 10^{-5}. A single state channel requires $E_b/N_0 \approx 9.6$ dB to achieve the same error probability. Another extreme but illustrative case is a channel that has zero gain for a fraction ρ of time. In this case, the average bit error probability will never be lower than

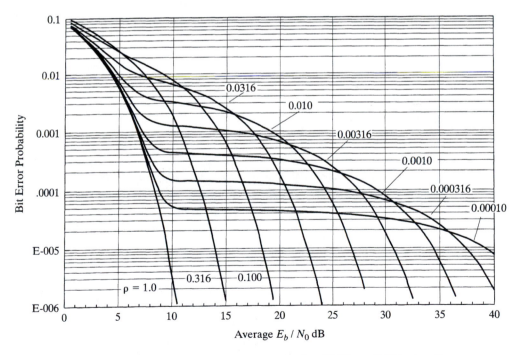

FIGURE 10–26   Average bit error probability for BPSK or QPSK signaling over two-state channel.

$\rho/2$ for any E_b/N_0. Finally, compare Figure 5–21 of Chapter 5 for Rayleigh fading with Figure 10–26 and observe that the envelope of the performance curves for the simple two-state channel model strongly resembles performance in Rayleigh fading in that the average bit error probability decreases linearly with increasing signal-to-noise ratio. When the channel is static, that is, not fading, bit error probability decreases exponentially with increasing signal-to-noise ratio in most cases.

As shown quantitativly in Chapter 5, the large variations of received signal power due to fading cost tens of decibels in the average signal power required to achieve a specified link bit error probability relative to the power required for the same bit error probability for a static nonfading channel. The large performance penalties are due to the extremely poor performance of the communications link for the short periods of time when the channel is experiencing a deep fade. Communications techniques are available to mitigate the performance degradation due to fading. In most cases these techniques involve the concept of *diversity* either at the receiver or at the transmitter or both. Second-generation cellular radio systems make extensive use of the diversity concepts, which are introduced below.

Suppose that L independent Rayleigh (or Ricean) fading channels are available between the information source and the receiver and that L transmitters and receivers are available.[6] Each of the fading channels experiences deep but infrequent and short fading events. Since the deep fading events are independent, infrequent, and short, it is unlikely that all channels will experience a deep fading event at precisely the same instant. Thus, if the same information is transmitted over more than one channel, the likelihood that the information will be correctly received is larger than if only a single channel were used. One possible receiver that could take advantage of the independence of the fading on the L channels would be a receiver that knows, via channel estimation, which path has the least attenuation at any instant in time and selects that channel for demodulation. A system based upon this technique is said to be using *selection diversity*. Another strategy for utilizing the L independent channels is to combine the outputs of the channels in a manner that improves performance. The channel outputs can be combined either before or after demodulation. When the signals are combined before demodulation, the receiver is said to be using *predetection diversity combining*. When the signals are combined after demodulation, the receiver is said to be using *post-detection diversity combining*. The diversity combining of the L signals may be coherent or noncoherent. Furthermore, the signal combining may treat all signals as equals or may weight the signals so that, for example, signals received higher signal-to-interference ratios are given more weight than those received at lower signal-to-interference ratios. The performance of various modulation schemes for the best known diversity combining techniques was analyzed in Chapter 5.

It was shown in Chapter 5 that the large performance degradations due to Rayleigh or Ricean fading can be mitigated by diversity. In the following paragraphs the most commonly employed methods of both creating diversity channels and making use of the diversity created by the physical environment are discussed. Although the analyses in Chapter 5 assumed that the diversity channels are independent, it can be shown that complete inde-

---

[6]Specific techniques for creating these L channels will be discussed later.

pendence is not required. In fact, large performance gains are achieved even when there is significant correlation between the fading processes of the diversity channels.

10.4.2   Space Diversity

More often than not multiple diversity channels are available without using multiple transmitters. Nearly independent diversity channels can be obtained with a single transmitter and multiple receivers each using a different physically separated receive antenna. In Section 10.3.2 the fading process was shown to be created by the linear sum of a large number of unresolvable multipath components. As illustrated in Figures 10–10 or 10–11 the magnitude of the fading varied as a function of mobile location and it was shown that an essentially independent sample of the fading process was experienced after the mobile had moved only a few wavelengths. Because of the dependence of the fading process on position, nearly independent fading process are observed at two receiving antennas separated by several wavelengths (or more) at any instant in time. Diversity systems that create nearly independent channels by using two or more receiving antennas separated in space are said to be using *space diversity*.

   Space diversity is used at the base stations of all cellular radio systems but is used in the mobile station of only a few systems. The very small size of many current mobile stations limits the physical separation of the receive antennas and therefore limits the performance of the space diversity system. Nevertheless, as the carrier frequencies become higher, the physical separation required becomes smaller and separations of 10 to 20 cm have been successfully used in experimental systems using 2 GHz carrier frequencies. The mobile-to-base station transmission for IS-95 CDMA, in addition to using conventional space diversity receivers at each base station, utilizes space diversity in the form of soft handoff wherein multiple geographically separated base stations receive and demodulate the transmissions of a given mobile. A form of selection diversity is used wherein an error detection code is used to determine which, if any, base station has correctly received the transmitted information. The correctly received information is then routed to the user.

   A significant advantage of space diversity for cellular systems is that the required per channel E_b/N_0 is achieved without increasing the total power transmitted in support of a communications link. Increasing the power transmitted in support of a link using, for example, multiple transmitters increases the interference experienced by other users and must be accounted for in the system design. Similarly, space diversity requires no additional bandwidth to support the link. The cost of space diversity is that two physically separated receive antennas and the associated receivers, demodulators, and synchronization and combining circuitry are required.

10.4.3   Frequency Diversity

As discussed earlier, when a multipath channel has significant differential delay spread, the channel will be frequency selective. The presence of frequency selectivity implies that transmissions using different carrier frequencies experience different fading. When the carrier frequencies are separated by more than the coherence bandwidth of the channel, the fading on the different carriers is largely independent. Thus, nearly independent diversity channels may be created using multiple transmitters having different carrier frequencies; systems using this approach are said to be using *frequency diversity*. A significant disadvantage of this approach is that multiple transmitters are required.

While frequency diversity in exactly the form described above is not used in cellular systems, frequency selectivity is exploited in some systems through the use of frequency-hop (FH) spread spectrum modulation. Systems using FH modulation periodically change the carrier frequency of a single transmitter. The frequency changes are typically slow so that a large number of symbols are transmitted during the dwell time on a particular frequency.[7] A finite set of carrier frequencies are used and the combined bandwidth of all of these carriers may be large. When the bandwidth over which the FH carrier changes is large with respect to the coherence bandwidth of the channel, the fading experienced on each frequency hop will be largely independent of the fading experienced on the previous and following hops. A simple means of exploiting the hop-to-hop independence is to repeat-code the information and interleave the encoder output symbols such that the symbols associated with a particular information bit are transmitted on different frequency hops. A more powerful means of exploiting frequency-hop diversity is to employ forward error correction coding with interleaving designed so that encoder output symbols are spread over multiple independent frequency hop dwells. Since at any instant of time only a single carrier frequency is used in these FH systems, this type of frequency diversity is actually a combination of pure frequency diversity and time diversity, defined in the following paragraph. Frequency-hop spread spectrum is a powerful technology for cellular systems. The periodic changing of the carrier frequency not only exploits frequency diversity but also has an interference averaging effect that has a strong positive impact on system capacity.

10.4.4   Time Diversity

Recall that when the mobile station is moving, the fading channel gain varies as a function of time, as illustrated in Figure 10–11. The rate of change of the channel gain is directly proportional to the mobile speed. Consider two samples of the fading process that are spaced in time. The correlation between these samples decreases as the time between them increases. If the samples are spaced widely enough in time, they are largely independent. This independence between widely spaced time samples of the fading process may be exploited to obtain nearly independent diversity channels by coding and interleaving the information bits before transmission and, of course, performing the inverse operations at the receiver. The coding process spreads the information content of a single bit over multiple encoder output symbols and the interleaving assures that the time-adjacent encoder output symbols are transmitted at times different enough that independent samples of the fading process are experienced. Time diversity using powerful error correction codes and interleaving is used in all second-generation cellular systems on both the

---

[7]Frequency-hop systems exist that hop at rates higher than the symbol rate. These systems are referred to as *fast-frequency hop* systems, which were discussed in Chapter 9.

mobile-to-base-station and base-station-to-mobile links. While forward error correction and interleaving achieve large performance gains in many cases, performance gain is limited in certain other cases. Specifically, performance is dependent upon the speed of the mobile with performance at high speeds being better than at lower speeds. Performance depends on speed since the span (length) of the interleaver is always fixed and thus there will always be a mobile speed below which the fading becomes too slow for the interleaver to be effective in adequately separating symbols in time. Below this speed, the diversity gain degrades and at very low speeds performance equals the performance of a system without diversity. The size of the interleaver cannot be made arbitrarily large since the interleaving/deinterleaving process creates delay in the communications link and this delay must be controlled. In spite of these limitations, time diversity via forward error correction and interleaving is extremely effective in cellular systems.

10.4.5 Multipath Diversity and RAKE Receivers

Consider the WSSUS resolvable multipath channel of Figure 10–23. Recall that each of the taps in this tapped delay line model is independently Rayleigh or Ricean faded via the complex multiplier $c_{gj}(t)$. Thus, the environment has created the independently fading paths needed for a diversity communications system. Unfortunately, these independently fading paths are linearly summed in space before the receiving antenna so that the communications receiver does not have the opportunity to apply a complex weighting function to the paths as required for the diversity combining schemes discussed in Chapter 5. Long before the birth of cellular systems, researchers Price and Green [27] devised a clever method for making use of the multipath diversity of the WSSUS channel. The method devised by Price and Green in 1958 makes use of direct-sequence spread-spectrum techniques (Chapter 9) to separate the signals that were added in space and then recombines those signals using the appropriate coherent or noncoherent combining method.

Consider the output $\tilde{r}(t)$ of the WSSUS channel of Figure 10–23. Using complex envelope notation, this output is

$$\tilde{r}(t) = \sum_{j=1}^{J} \gamma_j c_{gj}(t)\, \tilde{s}(t - \tau_j) \tag{10–70}$$

where γ_j are real weighting factors used in the model to permit the multipath components to have different average power and to adjust the total power gain of the channel model to 1.0, and τ_j represents the total delay for multipath component j. Although γ_j are adjusted in this model such that the total power is 1.0, their relative magnitudes are determined by the environment and not by the communications engineer. Figure 10–27 illustrates a receiver used to separate and then recombine the J multipath components of (10–70). The receiver input is the result of (10–70) plus interference, which will be presumed to be additive white Gaussian noise denoted $\tilde{n}(t)$ with one-sided power spectral density N_0. A single thermal noise process affects all received signal components. The required signal separation is accomplished using a matched filter for each of the multipath components.

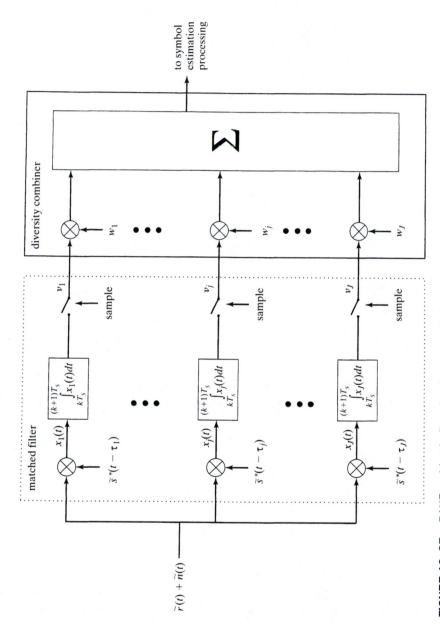

FIGURE 10–27 RAKE multipath diversity signal processing.

The correlate and integrate form of the matched filters are shown. The reference waveform $\tilde{s}^*(t - \tau_j)$ for each of the matched filters includes a delay identical to the delay of the multipath component of interest. The precise time synchronization of the reference waveform to the multipath delay is critical to the operation of this system. In the particular implementation of Figure 10–27, fully coherent matched filters are assumed implying that carrier recovery has been accomplished on all multipath components. That is, carrier recovery circuitry is required for each branch of the receiver.

The output of the integrator for the *j*th path is (assume all delays τ_j are small relative to a symbol duration T_s)

$$v_j = \int_{kT_s}^{(k+1)T_s} \tilde{s}^*(t - \tau_j) \times [\tilde{r}(t) + \tilde{n}(t)]dt$$

$$= \int_{kT_s}^{(k+1)T_s} \tilde{s}^*(t - \tau_j) \times \left[\sum_{j'=1}^{J} \gamma_{j'} c_{gj'}(t)\tilde{s}(t - \tau_{j'}) + \tilde{n}(t) \right] dt \qquad (10\text{–}71)$$

$$= \sum_{j'=1}^{J} \gamma_{j'} c_{gj'}(kT_s) \int_{kT_s}^{(k+1)T_s} \tilde{s}^*(t - \tau_j)\tilde{s}(t - \tau_{j'})dt + \int_{kT_s}^{(k+1)T_s} \tilde{s}^*(t - \tau_j)\tilde{n}(t)\, dt$$

where the complex multiplicative fading $c_{gj'}(t)$ has been assumed constant over a single symbol interval T_S and taken outside of the integral. According to (10–71), the matched filter output v_j is affected by the signal in all *J* components of the channel output and the matched filter does not appear to have accomplished its function of separating the signal paths.

Fortunately, the communication systems designer has control of the signal waveforms $\tilde{s}(t)$ and can design these waveforms such that

$$\int_{kT_s}^{(k+1)T_s} \tilde{s}^*(t - \tau_j)\tilde{s}(t - \tau_{j'})dt \ll \int_{kT_s}^{(k+1)T_s} \tilde{s}^*(t - \tau_j)\tilde{s}(t - \tau_j)dt \qquad (10\text{–}72)$$

for any $j' \neq j$. That is, the signals are designed such that their autocorrelation function over a symbol period T_s approaches 0 for delays equal to or greater than the smallest differential delay between channel multipath components. If the autocorrelation was exactly 0 for delays equal to or greater than the smallest differential delay, (10–71) would simplify to

$$v_j = \gamma_j c_{gj}(kT_s) \int_{kT_s}^{(k+1)T_s} |\tilde{s}(t - \tau_j)|^2\, dt + \int_{kT_s}^{(k+1)T_s} \tilde{s}^*(t - \tau_j)\tilde{n}(t)dt \qquad (10\text{–}73)$$

and the output v_j is affected only by multipath component *j* and the thermal noise, and signal separation would have been perfectly accomplished. One signal design that has the desired autocorrelation properties over a symbol period is a direct-sequence spread-spectrum signal (DSSS) as defined in Chapter 9. The autocorrelation function of a DSSS waveform is 1.0 for zero delay and decreases to a small value for delays greater than the chip duration. Thus, if the DSSS chip rate is larger than the inverse of the smallest differential delay of the multipath channel, and if the autocorrelation function of the spreading code over the symbol time is small for time offsets greater than the chip period, the multipath signals can be separated by the receiver. Viewing Figure 10–27 as a multipath spread-spectrum receiver, the matched filtering function may be partitioned into two components. In practical implementations, the multiplier of Figure 10–27 is the despreading multiplier, which is followed by a narrowband (information bandwidth) bandpass filter whose output is processed by a data coherent matched filter. In this practical implementation carrier recovery is accomplished after post-despread filtering. Separate carrier recovery processing is still required for each multipath channel.

It has been shown that, with the signals properly designed, the processor of Figure 10–27 is able to separate the multipath components of the received signal resulting in samples v_j affected by independent samples of the fading processes. These samples are weighted by a factor w_j and summed as in other diversity receivers. A receiver using this signal processing strategy to achieve diversity gain is called a *RAKE receiver* [27]. The output of the summation is processed by the usual symbol estimation processor. Finally, observe that the noise components of each v_j are affected by the same thermal noise $\tilde{n}(t)$ but that, prior to integration, the noise is multiplied by $\tilde{s}*(t - \tau_j)$. The delay τ_j for each channel is different and it can be shown that, because of the correlation properties of $\tilde{s}*(t - \tau_j)$ the products of the noise waveforms and $\tilde{s}*(t - \tau_j)$ are nearly uncorrelated.

Performance analyses for the RAKE receiver may be found in [21,22,27]. In the special case where all multipath channel gains γ_j are identical, the results for the maximal-ratio diversity combiner given previously apply. However, the gains γ_j are rarely the same so that more complex results are usually needed. Finally, care must be exercised when comparing RAKE receiver performance results to results for other diversity schemes. RAKE performance results are often presented as a function of the total received signal-to-noise ratio, while results for other schemes are often presented as a function of per diversity channel signal-to-noise ratio. RAKE receivers are effectively used in the CDMA second-generation cellular system and will be used in third-generation systems that employ direct-sequence spreading modulation.

10.5 SYSTEM DESIGN AND PERFORMANCE PREDICTION

10.5.1 Introduction

Communications system design for cellular systems is extremely challenging, involving much more than the design of a physical communications link using the techniques of earlier chapters. Base stations must be wisely placed throughout the geographic service area and a frequency plan developed so that a user at any location may be provided with high-quality service and so that the anticipated number of users may be simultaneously serviced. The task of base station location is critically dependent upon the propagation (path loss) environment and the anticipated geographic distribution of users. The designer, of course, must also minimize cost by using the minimum number of base stations. Once the locations of the base stations and a frequency plan are known, call control strategies are developed that include the methods for detecting and processing service requests such that the mobile is always serviced by the optimum base station. The optimum base station for servicing a mobile is the base station that, if all mobiles were serviced by their respective optimum bases, would result in all mobiles being provided with acceptable service quality and, simultaneously, the maximum system capacity. As the mobile moves, the call control procedure must continually monitor the call and execute handoff to another base station if call quality degrades and if that handoff would result in acceptable performance for the mobile and for all other users of the system. The call control process is complicated by the fact that the interference in a cellular system operating near capacity is mostly other-user interference rather than thermal receiver noise. This other-user interference is highly time varying due to the fact that users are turning on/off at random times and users are in motion and experiencing time varying path loss that is responded to by transmit power control processes.

The complexity of the design, analysis, and operation of a cellular system prohibits the development of a completely analytic theory and associated analytical design process although some aspects of the system have been successfully analyzed. More often than not, system designers rely upon complex simulations to predict performance and evaluate system design and control concepts. In some cases simulations have been developed that may be reasonably run on modern workstations. In other cases, complex simulations that include extensive detail have been developed that may require supercomputing technology to execute. A few of the most important issues in cellular system design are presented in the following paragraphs; much additional detail may be found in [1,10,25,26,28–32].

10.5.2   Performance Figures of Merit

Perhaps the most important cellular radio performance metric is system capacity or *spectrum efficiency for voice* η_v, which is defined in Section 10.1 to be the number of simultaneous voice circuits that the system provides per megahertz of bandwidth per base station. In Section 10.1 some very preliminary calculations of spectrum efficiency for voice were done, illustrating its sensitivity to the modulation efficiency and to the frequency reuse factor. Spectrum efficiency can also be defined for systems providing data services of varying rates. In this case, *spectrum efficiency for information* η_i is more appropriately defined as the total number of information bits per second per megahertz of bandwidth per base station that the system can support. Total number of bits per second is used rather than using the number of data circuits to anticipate the existence of data circuits (channels) having more than one rate and to anticipate packet data services. Because neither the physical environment nor the distribution of users is homogeneous over the service area of any real cellular system, η_v or η_i will not be the same for all base stations. Therefore, it could be correctly argued that a single value of spectrum efficiency cannot represent any real system. Nevertheless, calculations of spectrum efficiency based upon ideal homogeneous environments provide valuable information for the communications system designer. Yet another useful measure of system capacity is obtained by explicitly taking into account the actual geographic area covered by a cell and defining η'_v (η'_i) to be the number of voice circuits (bits per second) per megahertz per unit area.

When a system is initially placed into service, capacity is not an issue since there are few users. A more important issue during the early stage of system development is that a user be able to obtain reliable service at any geographic location in the service area. For economic reasons, initial system deployment will always use the minimum possible number of base stations. This is in contrast to a mature system where a large number of base stations will have been added to enable providing service to the largest possible number of users. *Cellular system coverage* is defined as the fraction of the total geographic service area in which users are provided reliable communications. Systems are typically designed with a target coverage of greater than 90%; often, 95% or 99% values are required. Coverage is not 100% due to propagation shadowing, which may cause a small number of locations to receive insufficient signal power and/or to experience insufficient signal-to-interference ratio for reliable communications. Furthermore, the specific areas of outage may change due to the continuous changing of the distribution of users. Coverage is also difficult to predict and the designer usually resorts to complex simulations for performance prediction.

Many complex processes execute simultaneously in a cellular system. These processes include dynamic power control, call initiation, handoff, and others. These processes interact with one another and the time-varying environment usually making call control imperfect. In all systems a small fraction of users will experience dropped calls due to a variety of causes. These include, for example, signaling errors resulting in incorrect or missed handoffs and temporary propagation anomalies resulting in the call being serviced by an inappropriate[8] base station. The inappropriate base station may be able to service the call until the propagation anomaly changes. At that time the inappropriate base will attempt handoff but will most likely fail since the handoff candidates are also inappropriate for the geographic location of the user. The *dropped call rate* is defined as the fraction of calls that are ended by the system prior to the time the user wishes to end the call. Dropped call rate is a widely used performance metric and is extremely difficult to predict. Developers once again resort to complex dynamic system simulations that actually model the motion of all mobiles through the environment to predict dropped call rates. Service providers, while always targeting 0% dropped calls, typically experience dropped call rates of at least a few percent.

10.5.3 Frequency Reuse

Frequency reuse, the fundamental enabling concept of cellular radio, was introduced in Section 10–2. In that discussion a perfect hexagonal cellular system and perfect omnidirectional base station antennas were assumed. A hexagonal geometry was presented and a

---

[8]An "inappropriate" base station has acceptable path attenuation to the mobile due to a propagation anomaly but is geographically distant from the mobile. When the anomalous propagation conditions change, the inappropriate base station will have unacceptably large path attenuation to the mobile.

simple formula for worst-case signal-to-interference ratio was given as a function of the reuse factor $N = i^2 + ij + j^2$ where $i,j \geq 1$ and the path loss exponent n. The reuse factor N is the number of hexagons in a contiguous group that share the available set of channels. In Figure 10–2 a reuse factor of $N = 7$ was illustrated. As presented in Section 10–2, the worst-case base-to-mobile signal-to-interference ratio for a mobile at the boundary of the cell in an ideal hexagonal system satisfies

$$\text{SIR}_{min} \geq 10n\log_{10}\left(\frac{D_{co}}{R} - 1\right) - 7.78 \quad \text{dB}$$

(10–74)

$$\geq 10n\log_{10}(\sqrt{3N} - 1) - 7.78 \quad \text{dB}$$

In this equation D_{co} is the distance from the center of the hexagon to the co-channel interfering cell nearest the mobile and R is the radius of the hexagon. The result of (10–74) is approximate as a result of simplifying the calculation of worst-case SIR by assuming all interfering base stations are equidistant from the mobile and that distance is the same as the distance to the closest interfering base station. Another simplification used in the calculation of (10–74) and was that only a single ring of co-channel interfering cells was considered. Finally, the result is approximate since thermal noise is ignored under the presumption that the system is strongly interference limited. Given these simplifications, as well as the path loss exponent and minimum acceptable signal-to-interference ratio, (10–74) is used to determine the reuse factor N. The reuse factor is the smallest integer N that satisfies (10–74) and simultaneously the relationship $N = i^2 + ij + j^2$. For example, if $n = 4$ and the minimum usable signal-to-interference ratio is 17 dB, (10–74) is solved for $N = 8.89$ and the minimum reuse factor is the smallest integer greater than 8.89 which also satisfies $N = i^2 + ij + j^2$, which is $N = 12$. Any larger N would also satisfy the SIR constraint but would result in reduced spectral efficiency.

Suppose that the radius R of the hexagons of an ideal cellular system is known and is fixed. Let N_T equal the total number of channels available to the system and assume that each channel services only one voice circuit and has bandwidth B MHz. With reuse factor N, each cell is assigned N_T/N voice channels and the spectrum efficiency is the number of voice circuits available in a single cell divided by the total bandwidth required to provide those voice circuits or

$$\eta_v = \frac{(N_T/N)}{N_T B} = \frac{1}{N B} \quad \text{voice circuits per MHz per cell.}$$

(10–75)

Thus, spectrum efficiency increases with decreasing N. Since N decreases with decreasing SIR_{min}, spectrum efficiency also increases with decreasing SIR_{min}. It is therefore important that the selected modulation technique provide acceptable reliability at the lowest possible signal-to-interference ratio. The second-generation Code Division Multiple Access (CDMA) cellular system, to be defined in detail later, accomplishes this through application of diversity, forward error correction, and spectrum spreading. The CDMA system is able to operate at a very low signal-to-interference ratio resulting in an amazing frequency reuse factor of $N = 1$.

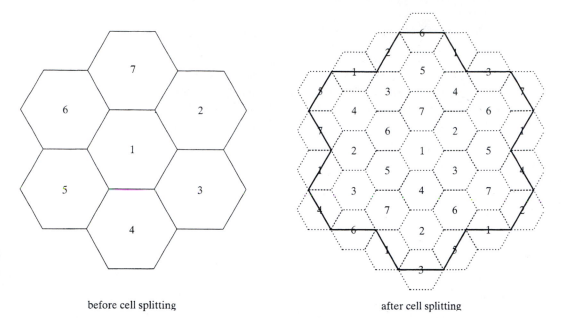

before cell splitting   after cell splitting

FIGURE 10–28   Cell splitting in an ideal homogeneous cellular system using a seven-cell repeat pattern.

An important relationship to observe from (10–74) is that, for a constant path loss exponent, the worst-case signal-to-interference ratio is *not* a function of the absolute radius of the cell. Rather, it is a function only of the ratio D_{co}/R or the reuse factor N. Thus, the radius of the cell may be reduced without affecting SIR_{min}, provided that N or, equivalently, D_{co}/R, is held constant. Thus, decreasing the cell radius, does not affect spectrum efficiency η_v as defined above. However, since the physical area covered by the cell decreases as the radius decreases, the spectrum efficiency η_v' increases rapidly as the cell radius decreases. The fact that η_v' increases with decreasing cell radius was a primary motivation for the introduction of cellular radio. The concept of *cell splitting* [1] to increase capacity is based on this principle. Cell splitting is illustrated in Figure 10–28. Before cell splitting, the service area depicted in Figure 10–28 is covered by seven cells having normalized radius $R = 1.0$. After cell splitting, approximately the same total area is covered by 37 cells with normalized radius 0.5. If the original system could provide, for example, 20 voice circuits per base station or 140 total voice circuits over the entire system, the second system would also provide 20 voice circuits per base station but the total number of voice circuits would increase to 740. A simple calculation will show that the geographic area covered after cell splitting is larger than the original area by a factor $37/28 = 1.32$. Thus η_v' has increased by a factor $(740/140) \div 1.32 = 4.0$.

Based upon the previous paragraph, it might be concluded that cellular system capacity η_v' could be increased without limit via cell splitting. This theory fails, however, for three reasons. First, eventually the base stations become so close together that line-of-sight propagation conditions exist between base stations and mobiles. When a line-of-sight path exists, the path loss exponent—which was assumed to be four in Figure 10–28—decreases to a value closer the exponent in free space, which is two. With a lower path loss exponent, a larger repeat factor will be required, thus decreasing capacity. Second, the number of physical locations for base stations greatly increases with cell splitting. Obtaining real estate for base stations is a difficult problem for service providers and cell splitting is therefore limited. Finally, as cell radius decreases, the number of handoffs required to maintain a call increases. Eventually the speed of the handoff process becomes inadequate and the signaling required for handoff becomes impractical.

Yet another means for increasing system capacity is the use of directional antennas or *sectoring* at the base station. When used for transmitting, the directional antenna focuses the transmitted power in the direction of interest and reduces the transmitted power in other directions. The overall result is that, ideally, some (not all) base stations that were causing interference in a mobile receiver, when using omnidirectional antennas, cause less interference (ideally none) with directional antennas. This reduction in interference then permits the frequency reuse pattern to be shrunk (smaller N) and capacity is increased. A similar reduction in interference results through the use of directional receive antennas at the base station. The benefit of directional antennas is illustrated in Figure 10–29. Figure 10–29a illustrates the radiation pattern for all of the co-channel cells in a system using omnidirectional antennas and a seven-cell frequency reuse pattern. Co-channel cells have been shaded for easy identification. The mobile in the center cell denoted by "M" receives its desired base-to-mobile signal from cell A and receives interference from cells B through G. In Figure 10–29b, 120° sector antennas have been applied and the radiation patterns of all of the co-channel base stations have been appropriately reduced in azimuth. Each base station uses three separate 120° antennas to cover the entire cell even though only one antenna is represented in the figure. With the sector antennas the mobile still receives the desired signal from base station A, but now the co-channel transmissions from base stations C through F are directed away from the mobile and no longer cause interference. This reduction in interference is depicted through the use of dashed arrow radiation patterns for these cells. The co-channel transmissions from base stations B and G still cause interference at the mobile. Because of the reduction in interference level, the channel reuse pattern can be shrunk, as illustrated in Figure 10–29c where a reuse factor of $N = 3$ has been used, resulting in higher system capacity. Also illustrated in Figure 10–29c is the further partitioning of the channel set into three subsets for each cell. After this partitioning there are nine subsets, denoted 1–1, 1–2, 1–3, 2–1, 2–2, 2–3, 3–1, 3–2, and 3–3. This further partitioning is required because the benefit of sectoring would be lost if the same channels were used in all three sectors. With this further partitioning all of the channels are still reused in the three-cell pattern so that spectrum efficiency is not degraded. The cost of sectoring is, of course, the more expensive directional antennas and the increased complexity of the call control processes since each sector will now be viewed as a "cell" in some respects.

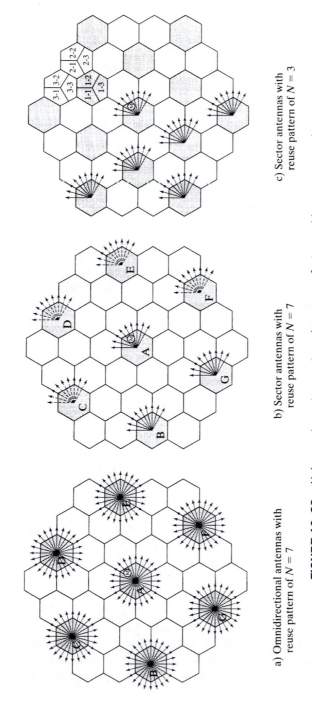

a) Omnidirectional antennas with reuse pattern of $N = 7$

b) Sector antennas with reuse pattern of $N = 7$

c) Sector antennas with reuse pattern of $N = 3$

FIGURE 10–29 Using sector antennas to reduce reuse factor and increase capacity.

10.5.4   Cells Are Never Hexagons

All of the previous discussion of system capacity, cell splitting, sectoring, and so on was based upon the notion of hexagonal cells with homogeneous path loss over the entire service area. Unfortunately, no cellular system has ever been installed that meets these requirements. In actual systems the path loss exponent varies from place to place, base stations are installed where real estate is available, which is likely not at the center of any hexagon, and physical obstructions to propagation are randomly placed. Thus, cells are very irregular and the convenience of hexagonal geometry is no longer applicable. Fortunately, the basic concepts introduced through the use of the hexagonal system layouts are correct. Cell splitting does indeed work and is used; frequency reuse patterns are roughly independent of the absolute cell radius; and sectoring works well to increase capacity. The reader is strongly cautioned, therefore, that the wonderful convenience of the hexagonal geometry *cannot* be used in actual system designs. Rather, the basic concepts must be applied carefully with results validated via computer simulation or any other system and environment specific means. On the other hand, hexagonal geometries may correctly be used for the comparison of modulation, diversity, and call control techniques, provided that the complete channel model including path loss, shadowing, and multipath are accurate statistical representations of an actual service area of interest.

10.5.5   Interference Averaging

As briefly discussed earlier, poor link performance may be experienced by a particular user due to a combination of being in a marginal geographic location and being there at a time when interference at that location is high. The system was probably designed so that the average performance over time and location meets service provider requirements. Unfortunately, a particular user at a particular place and time experiences a single sample of the system performance random process and does not experience the average performance. This is analogous to the sampling of any random process such as a Rayleigh fading process where the average of that process may result in good system performance but at particular times—for example, in deep fades—the performance may not be acceptable.

Consider the base-to-mobile link of the ideal hexagonal system and assume that power control is used to minimize the base station transmit power for each mobile. Figure 10–30 illustrates how a particular placement of mobiles may result in unacceptable interference and how interference averaging mitigates this problem. Figure 10–30a shows a nominal placement of mobiles. The user-of-interest is served by the center cell using a channel denoted f_0. The user-of-interest is located near a vertex of the cell hexagon and is experiencing large path loss. Within the center cell no other users are assigned f_0 and no co-channel interference is generated in this cell. In every other shaded co-channel reuse cell, f_0 is reused by exactly one mobile. The system is designed so that under most conditions the interference caused by co-channel reuse is acceptable; Figure 10–30a illustrates one such user placement. Mobiles using f_0 within interfering cells are at locations experiencing less than worst-case path attenuation and therefore requiring less than maximum

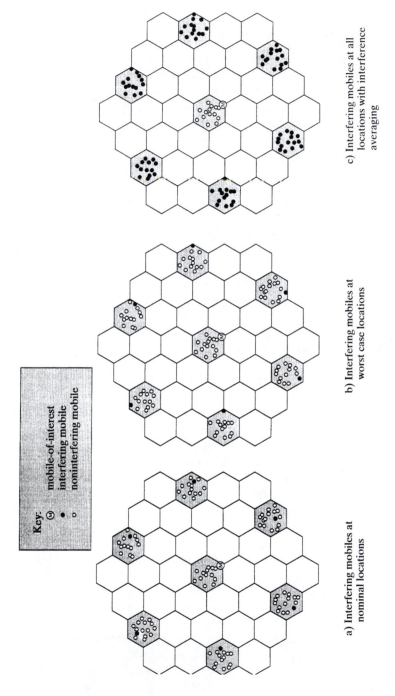

Key:
	mobile-of-interest
M (circled)	
●	interfering mobile
○	noninterfering mobile

a) Interfering mobiles at nominal locations

b) Interfering mobiles at worst case locations

c) Interfering mobiles at all locations with interference averaging

FIGURE 10–30   Nominal and worst case interference with and without interference averaging.

transmit power from their respective base stations. As a mobile moves farther from its controlling base station, path attenuation increases and the base transmit power is increased. Figure 10–30b illustrates a situation where all of the co-channel mobiles using f_0 have simultaneously moved to the boundary of their respective cells. When this occurs, all of the co-channel base stations transmit the maximum possible power on channel f_0 and co-channel interference is maximum. Under these rarely occurring conditions the base station serving the user-of-interest may not have adequate transmit power to maintain the link and the call may fail.

This problem may be mitigated by *interference averaging*. Rather than have the co-channel interference level determined by the locations of a specific small number of mobiles, advanced modulation techniques are used that result in the link performance being a function of the locations and transmit powers of all mobiles being serviced as illustrated in Figure 10–30. Two different modulation techniques achieve this interference averaging; both of these techniques use the spread-spectrum concepts of Chapter 9. The first technique is slow-frequency-hop (SFH) spread spectrum [33–36], which accomplishes this averaging by utilizing a different frequency-hop code in each interfering cell. Thus, the co-channel interference level on each frequency hop dwell is related to a different set of interfering mobiles and, over a short period, all possible sets of interfering users have influenced the link performance. The actual averaging of the influence of multiple different sets of interferers is done through the use of error correction coding and interleaving, which spans many frequency hop dwells. The second technique is direct-sequence spread spectrum as implemented in the US Interim Standard 95 (IS-95), commonly referred to as CDMA [31]. In CDMA all users are assigned a common channel but each user is assigned a distinct spreading code. All users are power controlled, and since all users are on the same channel, the interference averaging may be thought to take place in the linear addition of signals in the channel. CDMA will be discussed later in this chapter. Interference averaging is extremely powerful in combination with forward error correction and diversity. Combining all of these techniques, frequency reuse patterns having $N = 1$ are possible and are currently used in cellular radio.

10.6 ADVANCED MOBILE PHONE SERVICE

10.6.1 Introduction

The Advanced Mobile Phone Service (AMPS) was the first cellular radio service to be deployed in the United States. AMPS and its derivative NAMPS (narrowband AMPS) are *first generation cellular systems* that are deployed in every major metropolitan area of the United States. AMPS makes use of many of the principles described earlier in this chapter and book including diversity, forward error correction, frequency reuse, power control, handoff, and others. The basic concepts leading to AMPS were conceived in the late 1940s at Bell Laboratories [37] and detailed development of AMPS spanned a lengthy period between the United States Federal Communications Commission (FCC) issuance of Docket 18262 in 1968 until the first system became operational in 1983. FCC Docket

18262 made 40 MHz of spectrum available, specifically 825–845 MHz and 870–890 MHz, for the purpose of relieving a huge backlog of unsatisfied requests for mobile telephone service. Much later, the FCC allocated an additional 10 MHz of bandwidth contiguous to the first allocation. The complete definition of the AMPS air interface may be found in EIA/TIA Standard 553 [38]. AMPS technology has been enormously successful in making mobile telephony widely available.

Figure 10–31 illustrates the carrier frequency plan defined in [38] for AMPS. There are currently 832 channels, numbered 1 through 799 and 991 through 1023, available for AMPS. These channels are partitioned into an "A" band assigned to the non-wireline service providers and a "B" band assigned to the wireline service providers. This partitioning of the channels into two sets of 416 channels permits two service providers to be active in any metropolitan area. As illustrated in Figure 10–31, the lower 25 MHz of spectrum is used for the mobile-to-base links also called the *reverse links* and the upper 25 MHz of spectrum is used for the base-to-mobile links also called the *forward links*. The forward and reverse links of a specific channel number are separated by 45 MHz, making it possible to have simultaneous communications on both links using frequency division duplex (FDD). Numerically adjacent AMPS channels are separated by 30 kHz. The specific carrier frequency f_c is related to the channel number N_c by

$$
\begin{aligned}
f_c &= 0.03 N_c + 825.0 \quad \text{MHz} & 1 \le N \le 799 \\
&= 0.03 \left(N_c - 1023 \right) + 825.0 \quad \text{MHz} & 991 \le N \le 1023
\end{aligned}
\qquad (10\text{–}76)
$$

for the reverse link and the channel frequency for the forward link is 45 MHz higher.

The first AMPS systems used omnidirectional base station antennas with a frequency reuse factor of roughly 12 resulting in about 34 channels being available in each cell. Current systems are capacity limited and have gone through the cell-splitting process several times. These capacity limited systems commonly use 120° sector antennas and a frequency reuse factor of 7, resulting in about 19 channels being available in each sector of each cell. In some instances, 60° sector antennas have been used to successfully reduce the reuse factor to 3. Because the system requires information transfer for call initialization and general system management, all channels cannot be used for user voice communications. In every cell a number of channels are reserved for digital signaling.

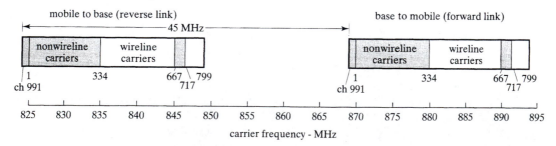

FIGURE 10–31   Carrier frequency plan for AMPS.

10.6.2   Call Setup and Control

The call setup and control procedures used in AMPS illustrate the basic processes that must be accomplished in all cellular radio systems. System management processes must include a means for the mobile station to determine that cellular service is (or is not) available and to place that mobile in a state in which calls may be routed to or from that mobile. During this process the mobile and the system authenticate that the mobile is indeed that of a valid user and determine whether the mobile is in its home service area or a foreign service area and is thus a *roamer*. Following these initial processes, a means is provided for the mobile to monitor system paging and respond if it is paged and to inform the system that it intends to originate a call.

These procedures begin when the mobile station is powered on. At this time the mobile scans all of the *dedicated control channels* for either the A or B channel set. The mobile has the channel numbers for these control channels stored in semi-permanent memory. Each cell of the system has one dedicated control channel used to communicate system identification and parameter information. The scanning is done to measure the received signal strength on each channel for the purpose of selecting the channel with the maximum strength. Having found the control channel with the largest signal strength, the mobile demodulates the digital information being transmitted, which includes the channel numbers of the paging channels for that cell along with system identification. Each cell has one or more forward link *paging channels* and associated reverse link *random access channels*. Next, the mobile scans the paging channels and tunes to the strongest to receive confirmation of the system identification, additional system parameters, and then to receive pages. Information received on the paging channels assists the mobile in registering with the system; the mobile must, of course, register so that the system is aware of the mobile's presence and can then route calls to that mobile. The registration process includes the determination that the mobile is indeed a valid customer.

After identification of the best paging channel and registration, the mobile monitors the paging channel waiting to receive pages. During this time the mobile may re-register periodically and will also scan the dedicated control channels periodically to determine whether another cell might be able to provide more reliable service. If the control channel signal power received from a different cell is significantly larger than that of the current cell the mobile retunes and re-registers in that cell. Thus, even when the mobile is idle, system control processes are active to continually monitor the location of the mobile to assure that the mobile is reliably serviced.

The process of routing a call to the mobile involves several steps. First, since the system knows location of the cell in which the mobile is active due to the registration process, the system sends a page message to the mobile from that cell and a few surrounding cells.[9] The mobile hears the page and immediately rescans the paging channels to redetermine which channel is strongest. Having determined the best paging channel the

---

[9]Some systems have recently been enhanced to enable calls to the mobile to be correctly and automatically routed even when the mobile is roaming perhaps in a distant location thousands of kilometers away from its home service area.

mobile responds to the page with a message on a random access channel associated with the paging channel. The system receives this page response and quickly sends another message to the mobile on the paging channel telling the mobile to tune to a specific traffic channel where the actual voice conversation takes place. After the mobile has retuned, the system and the mobile execute procedures to confirm that the mobile has indeed retuned correctly and is ready for voice communications.

During voice communications, scanning receivers in the base stations of the serving cell as well as a small number of surrounding cells periodically monitor the strength of the mobile signal. These measurements are used to determine whether a handoff is required. If a handoff is required, the appropriate commands are sent by the system controller to the mobile and the two base stations involved to execute a handoff. Control commands are sent to the mobile during a voice conversation using blank and burst techniques. Power measurements of the mobile signal strength at the base station are also used for mobile transmit power control. Power control processes attempt to maintain the mobile transmit power at the minimum level, which achieves reliable communications thus minimizing the interference created by that mobile.

It should be clear that call management in a cellular system is very complex, involving digital signaling on a number of dedicated channels as well as on the voice traffic channels. Received power measurements are made and compared with one another and various thresholds in an effort to continually maintain high-quality service at the mobile while simultaneously minimizing interference to other mobiles. The descriptions of the call processing procedures above are very simplified; the actual procedures are complex and many are proprietary to the equipment manufacturers. The interested reader is referred to [37,38] for additional detail.

10.6.3   Modulation and Signaling Formats

Both analog and digital modulations are utilized in AMPS. Voice communication uses narrowband frequency modulation with a maximum deviation of ± 12 kHz for both the forward and reverse links. Voice channels are typically demodulated using a noncoherent frequency discriminator. A large number of studies (e.g., [39]) indicate that narrowband FM voice transmission in Rayleigh fading requires an average received signal-to-interference ratio of approximately $+17$ dB to achieve high quality. This SIR requirement sets the minimum possible frequency reuse factors as previously discussed. Signaling for system management and call control utilizes binary frequency shift keying (BFSK) with a deviation of ± 8 kHz and a channel symbol rate of 10 kbps. The NRZ data is bi-phase (Manchester) encoded before BFSK modulation. The actual information transfer rate is considerably less than 10 kbps due to the need for significant redundancy to mitigate the fading channel. Digital communication is done both on the channels reserved in every cell solely for this purpose and using a blank-and-burst techniques on the voice traffic channels.

Digital transmission on the forward control channels (both the dedicated control channels and the paging channels) make use of both repeat coding and Bose–Chandhuri–Hacquenghem (BCH) coding to mitigate fading. A continuous 10 kbps binary symbol stream is transmitted enabling the mobile to achieve and maintain synchronization.

Figure 10–32a illustrates the message stream used on these dedicated control channels. Each message consists of one or more words, and each word is error correction coded using a (40,28,5) BCH code and then repeated five times. The BCH code is systematic so that its codewords consist of 28 information bits followed by 12 parity bits; the minimum distance of this code is 5. The 5-times repeating is interleaved with the repeats for a different message addressed to a different mobile (or mobile group) and the combined 10-codeword sequence is preceded by a synchronization preamble. The synchronization preamble is a 10-bit dotting sequence [1010101010] facilitating symbol synchronization followed by an eleven bit word synchronization sequence [11100010010]. Each of these word blocks transmits $28 \times 2 = 56$ information bits. Word blocks are transmitted periodically with a period of 46.3 msec resulting in an overall information transfer rate of approximately 1200 bps.

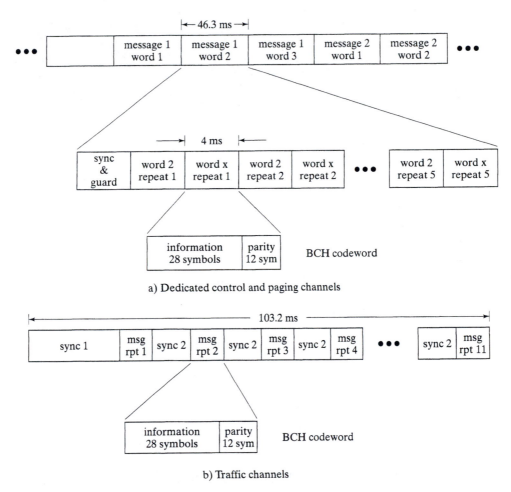

a) Dedicated control and paging channels

b) Traffic channels

FIGURE 10–32   Forward link signaling data formats for AMPS.

Digital transmission on the forward voice channels uses blank and burst techniques. That is, the analog FM voice transmission is stopped for a very short period while a digital message is sent. This signaling burst is not perceptible to the user. Symbol modulation is at 10 kbps using binary FSK. Figure 10–32b illustrates the message stream used for forward traffic channel signaling. The total burst is 103.2 ms long and includes eleven repeats of the BCH-coded message word. The BCH code is the same code used on the dedicated signaling channels. Each repeat of the BCH codeword is preceded by a synchronization preamble. The first synchronization preamble is a 101-bit dotting sequence [1010 ... 101] followed by an 11-bit synchronization word [11100010010]. All other codeword repeats are preceded by a 37-bit dotting sequence [1010 ... 101] followed by the same 11-bit synchronization word.

Reverse link digital signaling on the access channel must accommodate the fact that the information sources are asynchronous since they are in mobile stations geographically separated from one another. When a mobile transmits a message, it is therefore possible that this transmission will collide with the transmission of another mobile. The probability of this event is reduced by requiring the mobile to listen for an access-channel busy indicator transmitted by the base station on the forward signaling channel before beginning the transmission. The call control protocol accounts for the fact that the probability of collision is significant by requiring message confirmation and allowing repeated transmission attempts spaced randomly in time. The access data stream transmitted by the mobile consists of between one and five messages each repeated five times as illustrated in Figure 10–33a. The access message is preceded by a synchronization preamble, which consists of a 30-bit dotting sequence [1010 ... 10] followed by an 11-bit synchronization word and a 7-bit digital color code (see [38]). BCH coding using a (48,36,5) code that has a minimum distance of 5.

Reverse link signaling on the voice channel is similar to the forward channel. The reverse channel uses a 5-times repeat code and the (48,36,5) BCH code. There can be either one or two messages sent. The message format is illustrated in Figure 10–33b. The synchronization words are identical to those used on the forward voice channel.

10.7   GLOBAL SYSTEM FOR MOBILE COMMUNICATIONS

10.7.1   Introduction

During the early 1980s a number of similar but incompatible cellular standards were being installed in Europe. Because different countries were using incompatible systems, a European cellular customer would not be able to travel throughout the continent and receive uninterrupted cellular service using a single mobile station. European telecommunications service providers and regulatory authorities foresaw this problem and decided to begin developing a second generation cellular system that would, among other things, be the same all across Europe. The result of this decision was a development effort that lasted nearly a decade and produced the Global System for Mobile Communications (GSM™).[10] Initially called the Group Spécial Mobile, GSM uses digital signaling for

[10]"Global System for Mobile Communications" and "GSM" are trademarks of the European Telecommunications Standards Institute. "GSM" will be used hereafter as an abbreviation for "GSM™."

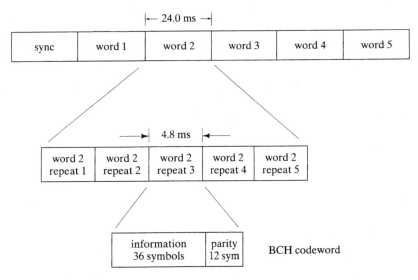

a) Random access channel

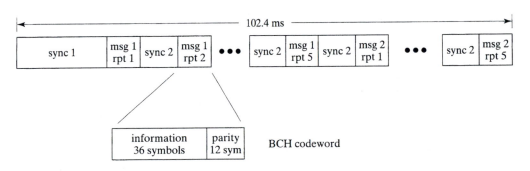

b) Traffic channels

FIGURE 10–33   Reverse link signaling data formats for AMPS.

both voice communications and for call control. The use of digital signaling enables application of all the powerful diversity and forward error correction schemes discussed earlier in this book resulting in a cellular system that has features not possible with AMPS. GSM also has an improved spectrum efficiency relative to AMPS. GSM was developed by a collaboration of university and manufacturer researchers and others beginning in December 1982. This collaboration was initially under the auspices of the Conférence Européenne des Postes et Télécommunications (CEPT) and later under the auspices of European Telecommunications Standards Institute (ETSI). The first demonstration GSM system was operational in 1991 and full systems were placed into operation during 1992.

The system continues to evolve with enhanced services continually being introduced. GSM has been widely accepted and systems based on the GSM standard are currently operational worldwide including in the United States.

The development of GSM is important not only because of the digital signaling and call control technology that was developed, but also because the developers had the vision to know that the standard should encompass the interfaces and processing in the supporting telecommunications network. Important benefits of the digital signaling itself are that the system can support a range of purely digital services such as short message service, encryption, and a range of bearer data services. Bearer data services with information rates in the range 2400 to 9600 bps with or without ARQ are supported.[11] Furthermore, the forward error correction and equalization used in GSM enables reliable communications at lower signal-to-interference ratios than AMPS which in turn results in improved system capacity. The GSM standard [40] is more than 5000 pages long providing much detail in all aspects of the system. The current specification defines operation at 900 MHz as well as at 1800 MHz. The system at 900 MHz continues to be called GSM but the system at 1800 MHz is called the Digital Cellular System 1800 (DCS1800). The GSM specification is summarized and elaborated upon in an authoritative and well-written text [41] by Michel Mouly and Marie-Bernadette Pautet available directly from the authors. Other readable and reasonably detailed descriptions of GSM may be found in [42] by Rappaport and in [43] by Hanzo and Stefanov. System details not included in the following extremely short description may be found in these references.

10.7.2   System Overview

Figure 10–34 illustrates the basic components of a GSM cellular system, which are the Mobile Switching Centre (MSC), the Base Stations (BS), and the Mobile Stations (MS). There is typically one MSC, many BS, and very many MS per system. The Base Stations are further partitioned into a Base Station Controller (BSC) and a number of Base Transceiver Stations (BTS). The function of this system, of course, is to provide both voice and data communications between mobile stations and (usually) the Public Switched Telephone Network (PSTN). The interface to the PSTN is a conventional CCITT Signaling System Number 7 (SS7) interface, which is not modified by GSM and terminates at the MSC. The MSC provides all the switching and control necessary to connect the user signal between the MS and the PSTN through the BS. The MSC is part of a larger subsystem (not illustrated) called the Network and Switching Subsystem (NSS), which includes the MSC and the databases necessary for registering and authenticating users and for keeping track of the approximate location of mobile stations. One MSC is capable of controlling many base stations distributed throughout the cellular service area. An important feature of GSM is that the system engineers carefully and precisely defined the interfaces between the various subsystems. The interface between the MSC and the BSC is called the *A interface*, the interface between the BSC and the BTS is called the *Abis interface*, and the interface between the MS and the BTS is called the *Um interface*. The Um interface is

---

[11]Development of system enhancements supporting higher data rates are ongoing at the time of this writing.

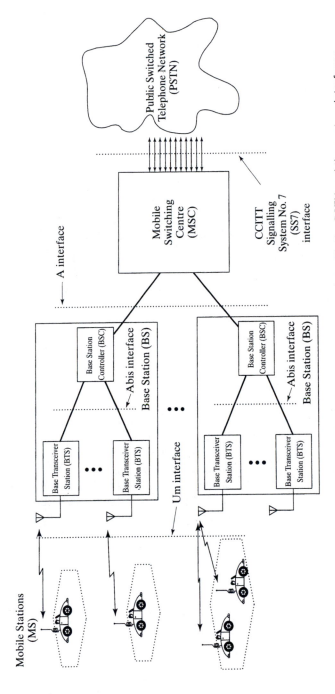

FIGURE 10–34 Architecture of the GSM system showing connection with the PSTN and the system interfaces.

the physical radio communications link that has been the subject of the majority of this book and that will be discussed in the following section.

10.7.3   Modulation and Signaling Formats

The digital modulation technique used in the GSM radio interface is GMSK, previously discussed in Chapter 4. This modulation format is very similar to conventional MSK with additional constraints on the trellis phase trajectories followed as a function of the information being transmitted. Recall that for MSK the modulator input binary symbol causes the excess phase of the transmitted signal to change linearly from its starting state to $\pm\pi/2$ over an input symbol period T. The phase change for Gaussian MSK is also $\pm\pi/2$; however, the change is not linear and requires longer than one symbol time to complete. The GMSK output phase change is defined by [41][12]:

$$\Phi\left(\frac{t}{T}\right) = \frac{\pi}{2}\left[G\left(\frac{t}{T} + \frac{1}{2}\right) - G\left(\frac{t}{T} - \frac{1}{2}\right)\right] \qquad (10\text{--}77)$$

where

$$G(x) = x\int_{-\infty}^{x} \frac{1}{\sqrt{2\pi\sigma^2}} \exp\left[-\frac{y^2}{2\sigma^2}\right]dy + \frac{\sigma}{\sqrt{2\pi}} \exp\left[-\frac{x^2}{2\sigma^2}\right]$$

and

$$\sigma = \frac{\sqrt{\ln 2}}{2\pi\, BT}$$

and BT is the product of the modulation symbol period and the bandwidth of a Gaussian filter used to control the modulation phase changes. For GSM the product $BT = 0.3$. As BT increases the excess phase trajectories approach the linear phase trajectories of MSK. Figure 10–35 illustrates the time-shifted excess phase $\Phi(t/T)$ for GMSK with $BT = 0.16$, 0.3, and 0.8 and for MSK; observe that the discontinuities in the derivative with respect to time of the excess phase that occur with MSK at $t/T = \pm 0.5$ do not occur for GMSK. This smoothing of the phase trajectory greatly reduces the relative magnitude of the sidelobes of the power spectrum of GMSK relative to MSK and is a primary reason that GMSK was selected by GSM. The power spectrum of GMSK for various BT and for MSK may be found in [44].

The GMSK modulator output is $v(t) = \sqrt{2P} \cos[\omega_0 t + \phi(t)]$ where the excess phase $\Phi(t)$ as a function of the binary input sequence $\{\ldots d_{i-1}, d_i, d_{i+1}, \ldots\}$ is [41]

$$\phi(t) = \phi_0 + \sum_i k_i\Phi(t - iT) \qquad (10\text{--}78)$$

---

[12]There is a typographical error in the expression for $G(x)$ in [41]. The expression given here is believed to be correct.

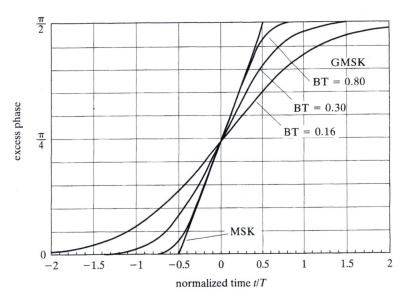

FIGURE 10–35 Excess phase for Gaussian MSK and conventional MSK.

where

$$k_i = \quad 1 \quad \text{if } d_i = d_{i-1}$$
$$= -1 \quad \text{if } d_i \neq d_{i-1}.$$

GMSK is a constant envelope modulation since the signal amplitude does not vary as a function of the transmitted information. GMSK is usually demodulated coherently. The design of the demodulator must account for the fact that the phase trajectory function (10–77) is much longer than one symbol period. Examination of Figure 10–35 shows that that for the GSM parameter selection $BT = 0.3$ a single modulator input symbol will influence the modulator output for approximately three symbol times. The demodulator accounts for this overlap by considering a sequence of symbols when making demodulator output symbol estimates, rather considering a single symbol at a time. This can be done through application of the Viterbi algorithm, previously applied to the decoding of convolutional codes, to perform maximum likelihood sequence estimation [45] on a segment of the received signal. The controlled intersymbol interference problem due to (10–77) is only a part of the GSM intersymbol interference problem. Recall that there may be severe multipath delay spread in a mobile communications system. The GSM specification document requires that signaling reliability be achieved in a two-equal-ray multipath environment with differential delay of nearly four symbol periods (16 μs). This degree of intersymbol interference forces the inclusion of an equalizer in the demodulator and, typically, this equalizer has been implemented using the Viterbi algorithm. Observing that the GMSK controlled intersymbol interference and the channel multipath are different instances of the same problem, the same Viterbi maximum-likelihood sequence estimator is usually designed to solve both problems. The performance of GMSK is discussed in [42,43,44].

The GMSK binary symbol rate used in GSM is $13 \times 10^6/48 \approx 270.8833$ kbps (period 3.69 μs) and the channel spacing is 200 kHz. The standard specifies the frequency band 935–960 MHz for the forward (base to mobile) link and 890–915 MHz for the reverse (mobile to base) link; observe that the forward link and the reverse link are spaced by 45 MHz as they were in AMPS. For DCS1800 the spacing between forward and reverse links is increased to 75 MHz. Carrier center frequencies are numbered starting at zero at frequency 890.2 MHz and going upwards. With a 200 kHz spacing there are 124 different paired (forward and reverse) carriers in the 2×25 MHz available bandwidth. GSM utilizes both time division multiple access (TDMA) and frequency division multiple access (FDMA) techniques to share resources. A user is assigned to one of the 124 carriers as in a conventional FDMA system.[13] Each carrier has capacity to support eight users and is shared using TDMA techniques. The TDMA hierarchy groups 156.25 GMSK symbols into a time slot (or burst) of length $15/26 \approx 0.577$ ms. Eight bursts are grouped to form a frame of length $120/26 \approx 4.615$ ms and each user is assigned one burst per frame on both the forward and reverse carriers. A *channel* in GSM is defined by a carrier number and a burst assignment sequence which ranges from one burst per frame (e.g., a full-rate traffic channel) on a single carrier to four bursts per 51 frames (e.g., the FCCH to be defined later). Figure 10–36 illustrates the GSM TDMA hierarchy. Two categories of channels are defined. *Dedicated channels* are channels that are assigned to a specific user for either voice or data communications for the duration of a call. *Common channels* are resources shared by all users of the system for initial access, for synchronization, for paging and page responses and for other system control functions.

A number of burst types are defined to support a variety of dedicated and common channels. For the user voice or data traffic dedicated channels, a *Normal Burst* is defined that includes 114 coded information bits, a 26-bit synchronization midamble, two bits called *stealing flags* to tell the mobile whether the burst is being used for traffic or for signaling, 6 bits called *tail bits* used to facilitate the Viterbi equalizer design, and 8.25 bits of guard time. The *Normal Burst,* illustrated in Figure 10–36, is by far the most often used burst in GSM. Three other bursts, whose functions will be described later, are defined for the common channels. The *F Burst* is the same length as the Normal Burst (148 bits + 8.25 guard) and is used for frequency synchronization. The F Burst is 148 consecutive zeros that, for GMSK, is equivalent to transmitting a single unmodulated tone. The *S Burst* is also the same length as the Normal Burst, but the number of information bits and the length of the synchronization midamble are different. The S Burst has a 64-bit midamble inserted between two 39-bit information words. Finally, the *Access Burst* is shorter than the normal burst being only 87 bits long. The Access Burst contains a 41-bit training preamble and 36 bits of information.

Consider now the logical channels created by assigning bursts of a specific type periodically to a particular function. The most important channel is the full-rate traffic chan-

---

[13]The GSM specification includes an option for frequency hopping. For simplicity this discussion presumes frequency hopping is not used.

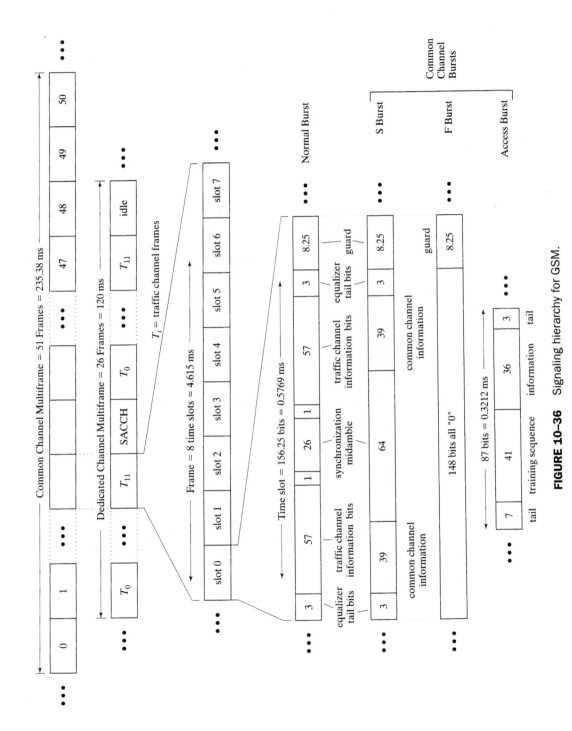

FIGURE 10–36 Signaling hierarchy for GSM.

nel which uses the Normal Burst. The full-rate traffic channel includes both the user voice or data channel and two in-band signaling channels. In order to include both user traffic and signaling a *dedicated channel multiframe* is defined. The dedicated channel multiframe, illustrated in Figure 10–36, is a sequence of twenty-six frames having length exactly 120 ms. The full-rate traffic channel utilizes one burst in each of the 26 frames. A traffic channel can be assigned to any of the eight time slots of a burst except on particular carriers designated for common channel signaling (to be discussed below) where time-slot 0 is reserved. Twenty-four of the 26 bursts are allocated to user traffic. Of the two remaining bursts, one is used to create a *Slow Associated Control CHannel (SACCH)*, which is used for nonurgent messages such as mobile assisted handoff measurements. The SACCH uses the Normal Burst structure. The 26th burst is idle. Recalling that the Normal Burst contains 114 information bits, the user information rate for the full-rate traffic channel is $(114 \times 24) \div 120$ ms = 22.8 kbps. A second control channel, the *Fast Associated Control CHannel (FACCH)*, is defined for control signaling for which the SACCH is too slow. The FACCH is created as required by stealing bursts from the user traffic channel. Recall that two bits in the Normal Burst were called stealing flags. The state of these two bits tells the receiver whether the burst information content is user data or is FACCH data.

A number of common control channels are created using the F Burst, the S Burst, and the Access Burst. These common control channels are created using time-slot 0 of every burst on certain specially designated carrier frequencies. They are most easily described by first defining the *common channel multiframe*, which is a sequence of 51 frames (235 ms.), also illustrated in Figure 10–36. Four channels are created using one burst of each of the 51 frames of the multiframe. The bursts are numbered 0 through 50. The first channel created is the *Frequency Correction Channel (FCCH)*, which uses burst numbers 0, 10, 20, 30, and 40. The FCCH uses the F Burst, which contains an unmodulated tone that is used by the mobiles to facilitate frequency synchronization. The time slot containing the FCCH is defined to be time slot 0 and all other TDMA numbering is synchronized to the FCCH. The second channel created is the *Synchronization CHannel (SCH)*, which uses burst numbers 1, 11, 21, 31, and 41, which immediately follow the FCCH bursts. The SCH uses the S Burst, which includes a long training sequence as well as system information. The SCH is the first channel demodulated by the mobile during the initial access procedure. By demodulating the SCH the mobile will be able to precisely time synchronize to the base station. The third channel created is the *Broadcast Control CHannel (BCCH)*, which, for a full-rate channel, uses the Normal Burst in frame numbers 2 through 5 of the common channel multiframe. The BCCH is used to communicate the system identity as well as much other information needed by the mobile to access the system. The last forward link common channel is the *Paging and Access Grant CHannel (PAGCH)*, which also uses the Normal Burst and 36 of the remaining 37 bursts. Time slot 0 of the last (51st) frame of the common channel multiframe is idle. As its name suggests, the PAGCH is used to page mobiles known, via registration, to be in the vicinity of the base station. These common signaling channels are illustrated conceptually in Figure 10–37. A sequence of 51 frames that make a common channel multiframe is illustrated at the top of the figure. Time slot or burst number 0 of each frame is used to create the common signaling channels. At the bottom of the figure the sequence of 51 time-slot-0 bursts

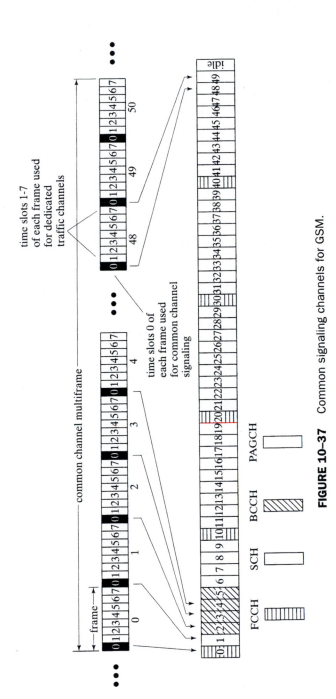

FIGURE 10–37 Common signaling channels for GSM.

are shown with shading indicating their use for the FCCH, SCH, BCCH, or PAGCH. The only reverse link common channel is the *Random Access CHannel (RACH),* which is used by the mobile to request services and to respond to pages on the PAGCH. The RACH utilizes the Access Burst.

The common signaling channels are used to control the system in much the same manner that the paging and control channels were used in AMPS. A mobile wishing to enter the system identifies and measures the signal strength on the common control channels broadcast from nearby base stations and selects the strongest. The mobile then synchronizes to that strongest base station by first correcting frequency and obtaining crude timing from the FCCH. The mobile then synchronizes to the SCH and obtains initial parameter information about the system; finally, the mobile demodulates the BCCH to obtain more detailed system information. The mobile is now in a state where it is possible to register and monitor the PAGCH for pages or to initiate calls via a random access procedure making use of the reverse link RACH.

The GSM link design makes extensive use of forward error control technology. The FEC strategy has been carefully designed in conjunction with the GSM speech coder. The speech coding technique used in GSM encodes 20 ms segments of speech into blocks of 260 bits that do not all have the same sensitivity to transmission errors. That is, the user's perception of the quality of the transmitted speech is highly affected by errors in some bits and less affected by errors in other bits. As a result, three types of speech encoder output bits are defined. Fifty of the 260 bits are highly sensitive to transmission errors and are therefore coded using both a parity check code (CRC) and a rate-½ constraint-length-5 convolutional code. A second group of 132 bits is less sensitive to transmission errors but still requires protection. This group of bits is rate-½ convolutionally encoded but is not protected by the CRC. The final group of 78 bits is the least sensitive to transmission errors and is transmitted without any error correction. The overall information rate at the speech coder output is $260/20 \times 10^{-3} = 13$ kbps. After coding, the user's transmission rate is 22.8 kbps or 456 bits per 20 ms speech segment. Interleaving is used along with forward error correction in order to achieve improved diversity needed for communications over fading channels.

10.7.4   Summary and Additional Comments

This extremely brief description of the GSM system addresses a very small fraction of the system detail. The reader interested in additional detail is directed to [41,42,43]. The GSM system is an excellent example of the application of digital communications technology in solving the very difficult cellular communications problem. A number of the key features of the system are:

- The use of *digital signaling* facilitates call control and makes the use of strong error correction codes possible. Error correction coding enables the system to operate at high interference levels corresponding to high system capacity. In addition, the use of digital signaling permits the application of encryption technology, thus prohibiting the casual eavesdropping that is possible with AMPS. The specific selection of

GMSK digital modulation enhances power amplifier efficiency since GMSK is a constant envelope modulation.

- The selection of TDMA for resource sharing permits up to eight users to share a single carrier, thereby reducing system hardware cost. The use of TDMA also facilitates call control by making it possible for the mobile to make measurements of the signal levels from nearby base stations in support of handoff decisions. Mobiles regularly report signal levels to the base station in support of a process called *Mobile Assisted HandOff (MAHO)*. Mobile assisted handoff greatly improves the efficiency of the handoff procedure.

- *Transmit power control* is wisely used to reduce the power transmitted in support of any communications to the minimum possible. Furthermore, the system design includes a *discontinuous transmission* mode in which the traffic channel power is reduced to a very low level when periods of voice inactivity are sensed.

- The system includes a *frequency-hopping* mode of operation. Frequency hopping has been shown to increase system capacity through frequency diversity when the channel is highly frequency selective and through interference averaging.

- *Burst coherent modulation* and demodulation are used with appropriate synchronization midambles, making it possible to adapt to the time varying channel on each transmission burst.

- A *Subscriber Identity Module (SIM)* has been defined for the GSM mobile unit. The SIM is a plug-in circuit module that contains information about the subscriber. This information may include the subscriber home system identification and mobile unit telephone number, subscriber billing information, a description of the services that the subscriber wishes to use, and other information relevant to the subscriber. The SIM makes it possible for the subscriber to use more than one GSM transceiver with the same user subscription detail. The GSM specification requires that a SIM card be installed in the mobile unit for the unit to have full functionality. A mobile unit without a SIM is, however, usable for emergency calling.

Many additional pages could be dedicated to GSM. The discussion ends here in order to leave space for the description of another excellent second generation system, CDMA, in the following section.

10.8   CODE DIVISION MULTIPLE ACCESS

10.8.1   Introduction

Throughout this text methods for efficient use of the electromagnetic spectrum have been discussed. Spectrum is a fundamental resource of the communication system designer and is carefully regulated by national governments. The spectrum allocated to cellular communications is valuable because of the extremely high demand for personal wireless communications and the fact that the amount of efficiently usable spectrum is limited. Recall that one of the measures of goodness of a cellular system is spectrum efficiency, which is basically the number of users that the system can support per cell or per unit area using a given amount of spectrum. The value of spectrum has motivated some of the most capable communications system designers to investigate methods of achieving higher and higher spectrum efficiency for cellular systems. The GSM system, which achieves a significant improvement in spectrum efficiency relative to AMPS, is one example of this. Code Division Multiple Access (CDMA), which achieves spectrum efficiencies superior to GSM and is described in this section, is another example.

Ignore cellular frequency reuse for a moment and consider the sharing of spectrum in a single cell. This spectrum can be shared among users in three different ways, all of which are based upon the concept of making the transmissions of one user orthogonal to the transmissions of another user so that same-cell users have minimum interference with one another. The AMPS system utilizes frequency division multiple access (FDMA) wherein the spectrum is partitioned into narrowband nonoverlapping (orthogonal) channels that are assigned to users as needed. The GSM system utilized a combination of FDMA and time division multiple access (TDMA) wherein medium bandwidth orthogonal channels capable of supporting eight users are partitioned into nonoverlapping (orthogonal) time slots. Although orthogonality between transmitted signals is most easily understood in terms of nonoverlapping frequency bands or nonoverlapping time slots, waveforms can be orthogonal that share the same frequency band at the same time. Code division multiple access is based on this principle. Consider, for example, a set of four baseband waveforms defined over $0 \le t \le 4T_c$ as:

$$w_i(t) = \sum_{j=0}^{3} (-1)^{w_{ij}} p_{T_c}(t - jT_c) \qquad i = 0, 1, 2, 3 \tag{10--79}$$

where $p_{T_c}(t)$ is the unit amplitude pulse of duration T_c and w_{ij} are specified by the matrix

$$W = \begin{bmatrix} w_{00} & w_{01} & w_{02} & w_{03} \\ w_{10} & w_{11} & w_{12} & w_{13} \\ w_{20} & w_{21} & w_{22} & w_{23} \\ w_{30} & w_{31} & w_{32} & w_{33} \end{bmatrix} = \begin{bmatrix} 0 & 0 & 0 & 0 \\ 0 & 1 & 0 & 1 \\ 0 & 0 & 1 & 1 \\ 0 & 1 & 1 & 0 \end{bmatrix}. \tag{10--80}$$

It can be easily demonstrated that the cross-correlation between any two of the waveforms $w_i(t)$ and $w_{i'}(t)$ is

$$\int_0^{4T_c} w_i(t) \times w_{i'}(t) \, dt = 0$$

for $i \ne i'$ and these waveforms are orthogonal even though they occupy the same spectrum (baseband) at the same time $0 \le t \le 4T_c$. Now suppose that the four waveforms $w_i(t)$ are used as carriers of binary information symbols d_i so that the transmitted waveforms are

$$s_i(t) = d_i \, w_i(t) \qquad 0 \le t \le 4T_c.$$

Because of the orthogonality of the carriers $w_i(t)$, all four signals $s_0(t)$, $s_1(t)$, $s_2(t)$, and $s_3(t)$ may be simultaneously transmitted without interfering with one another. The received baseband signal in this case would be

$$s(t) = s_0(t) + s_1(t) + s_2(t) + s_3(t)$$

$$= d_0 w_0(t) + d_1 w_1(t) + d_2 w_2(t) + d_3 w_3(t)$$

and the signal of interest, say, for example, user 0, is recovered by correlating this received signal with orthogonal carrier $w_0(t)$ over the period $0 \le t \le 4T_c$. Thus

$$\frac{1}{4T_c} \int_0^{4T_c} w_0(t) \times s(t) \, dt = \frac{1}{4T_c} \int_0^{4T_c} w_0(t) \big[d_0 w_0(t) + d_1 w_1(t) + d_2 w_2(t) + d_3 w_3(t) \big] \, dt$$

$$= \frac{1}{4T_c} d_0 \int_0^{4T_c} w_0(t) \, w_0(t) \, dt + \frac{1}{4T_c} d_1 \int_0^{4T_c} w_1(t) \, w_0(t) \, dt$$

$$+ \frac{1}{4T_c} d_2 \int_0^{4T_c} w_2(t) \, w_0(t) \, dt + \frac{1}{4T_c} d_3 \int_0^{4T_c} w_3(t) \, w_0(t) \, dt$$

$$= d_0$$

The other data symbols may be recovered in the same manner. This simple example illustrates the basic principle of CDMA, which is that properly coded information symbols from different users can be simultaneously transmitted in the same band and not interfere with one another. In an actual system, however, channel impairments and lack of perfect phase synchronization causes this ideal noninterference principle to be only partially realized. The coding via multiplication of the data by the orthogonal waveforms $w_i(t)$ is a particular example of direct-sequence spread-spectrum communications discussed in Chapter 9 and discussed in detail in [36]. The use of spread-spectrum as a multiple access technique has been known and used for many years and its application to cellular systems required only that the appropriate digital hardware technology be developed.

Figure 10–38 illustrates the spectrum sharing techniques used by the cellular systems discussed in this chapter. For AMPS, the left illustration shows that the frequency axis is partitioned into channels, one of which is assigned to the user for all time. The figure shows no partitioning for the code axis, indicating that codes are not used in AMPS. The middle illustration shows that GSM utilizes larger frequency channels than AMPS but that these channels are partitioned in time. Again, no partitioning is shown on the code axis, illustrating that GSM does not use code division. The right illustration, for CDMA, indicates that all frequencies are used at all times by all users and that the spectral resource is shared by assigning a different code to each user. The spectrum sharing illustrated in Figure 10–38 represents either the forward or the reverse links of the indicated systems. All of these systems also use frequency division multiplexing (FDM) to isolate the forward and reverse links.

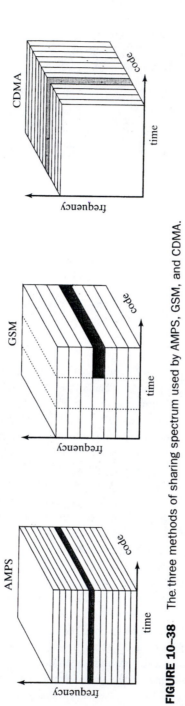

FIGURE 10–38 The three methods of sharing spectrum used by AMPS, GSM, and CDMA.

It is interesting that the application of spread-spectrum technology to cellular radio was proposed by George Cooper and Ray Nettleton of Purdue University at about the time that the AMPS trial systems were being implemented [46–49]. Their proposals were recognized and widely discussed but were not implemented because of the great momentum of the AMPS development in the late 1970s and because the digital technology required for their system was more costly than the mostly analog technology used in AMPS. Years later, Qualcomm, Inc. engineers under the technical guidance of Andrew Viterbi and Irwin Jacobs reinvestigated the application of spread spectrum to cellular radio and developed the basis for what is now known as CDMA, the specific subject of this section. Qualcomm first proposed the CDMA system publicly in June 1989. Their proposal has since evolved considerably and is now defined in a Telecommunications Industry Association (TIA) Interim Standard, specifically IS-95 [50], for use in North America. The CDMA system was designed to gradually replace AMPS in the 800 MHz frequency band. This goal is, in part, achieved by making the bandwidth required for CDMA, 1.25 MHz for a single forward or reverse link channel, exactly one-tenth of the bandwidth allocated to a single AMPS service provider. The CDMA system is most easily described by examining the forward and reverse link block diagrams. The modulation formats used for the forward and reverse links are considerably different and will be described separately.

10.8.2   Forward Link Description

Figure 10–39 is a conceptual block diagram of the CDMA forward-link base station transmitter. Five distinct signal processing paths are shown in Figure 10–39. The two paths at the top of the diagram are identical and represent the processing for user information that will be assumed to be digitally encoded voice. The ellipsis indicates that more identical paths are added as required to service additional users. The number of users that can be serviced is limited by the number of available orthogonal spreading codes (the orthogonal Walsh codes) and the effect of these additional users on system capacity to be discussed later. The CDMA voice coder outputs binary information at a maximum rate of 8600 bps. One of the important features of the CDMA system design is that the voice coder rate is variable and is reduced to as low as 800 bps when the user is not speaking. The transmit power is reduced (approximately) in proportion to the reduction in data rate resulting in less interference being created during voice pauses than during speaking intervals. Four data rates are used in the system, although only the highest is shown in Figure 10–39. To facilitate this description assume that the user data rate is fixed at 8600 bps.

Voice coder output bits are processed in 20 ms blocks of 172 symbols. These 172 binary symbols are error detection encoded using a CRC code that appends 12 bits to the information block. On the forward link the user binary CRC-coded data is further encoded for forward error control using a rate-½ constraint-length-9 convolutional code with generator polynomials (defined in Chapter 7)

$$g_1(D) = 1 + D + D^2 + D^3 + D^5 + D^7 + D^8$$
$$g_2(D) = 1 + D^2 + D^3 + D^4 + D^8$$

(10–81)

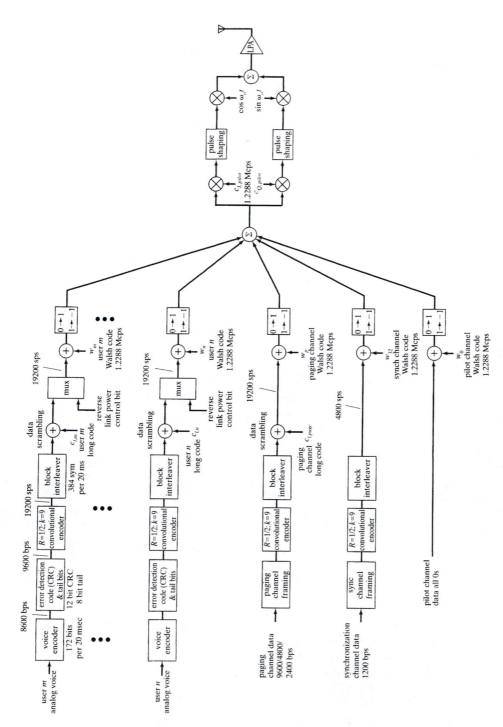

FIGURE 10–39 Code Division Multiple Access forward-link transmitter conceptual block diagram.

Figure 10–40 is a block diagram of the encoder. This code has free distance 12 and its partial weight structure is given in Table 7–1 of Chapter 7. In order to facilitate the decoding operation in the mobile, the encoder state is forced to zero at the end of each 20 ms block by appending 8 zeros, called *tail bits,* to the block. Including the CRC bits and the tail bits, the 20 ms block now contains $172 + 12 + 8 = 192$ bits and the corresponding encoder output block contains $2 \times 192 = 384$ bits. The binary symbol rate at the output of the encoder is therefore $384/20 \times 10^{-3} = 19200$ ksps. The forward-link traffic channel frame structure is illustrated in Figure 10–41. The encoder output is input to a block interleaver that accepts blocks of 384 symbols, reorders these symbols, and outputs the reordered symbols to the next processing step. The details of the block interleaver may be found in [50]. The interleaver input and output symbol rates are the same, 19200 ksps.

Following the interleaver, the information is scrambled by modulo-2 addition with a user-specific binary code of length $2^{42} - 1$. This *long code* is generated by decimating a maximal-length sequence operating at 1.2288 Mcps by sampling the generator output every 64 bits resulting in a scrambling sequence rate of $1.2288 \times 10^6/64 = 19,200$. The generator polynomial for the long code is

$$g_{long}(D) = 1 + D + D^2 + D^3 + D^5 + D^6 + D^7 + D^{10} + D^{16} + D^{17} + D^{18}$$
$$+ D^{19} + D^{21} + D^{22} + D^{25} + D^{26} + D^{27} + D^{31} + D^{33} + D^{35} + D^{42}$$

(10–82)

where the notation of Chapter 9, Figure 9–20 has been used. All traffic channels use the same long code and are distinguished by using different user-specific code phases. The period of this sequence, $2^{42} - 1$, is extremely long (tens of days) so that very many distinguishable phases are possible. User-specific phases of this code are generated by modulo-2 addition of specific code-generator shift register outputs as illustrated in Figure 10–42. It is known [36] that the modulo-2 sum of shift register outputs as in Figure 10–42 results in a code that is a phase shift of the original maximal-length sequence. The particular shift

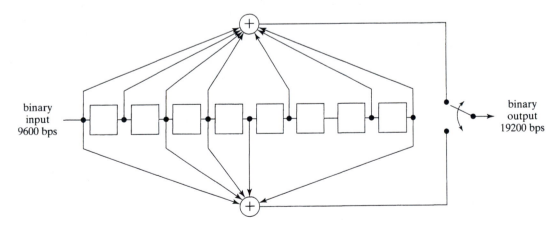

FIGURE 10–40   Rate-½ constraint-length-9 convolutional code used for CDMA forward-link traffic channels.

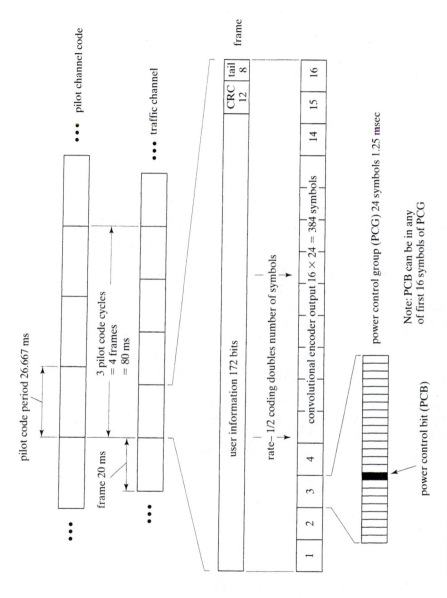

FIGURE 10—41 CDMA forward link traffic channel framing structure.

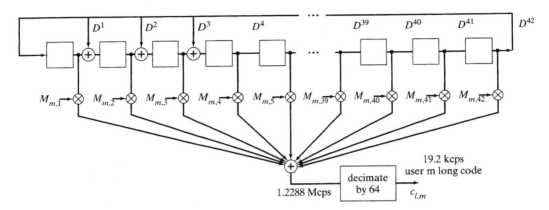

FIGURE 10–42   User-*m* long code generator.

register outputs, which are modulo-2 summed, are specified by the vector $\mathbf{M}_m = \{M_{m,1}, M_{m,2}, \ldots, M_{m,42}\}$, where the subscript m denotes the user. The resulting long scrambling code is denoted $c_{l,m}$. The vector $\mathbf{M}_m$ is defined in the standard and includes, among other items, the electronic serial number of the mobile station. In order for the user-specific phase shift to have meaning, the phase of the original (i.e., before the user-specific modulo-2 sum) code must be known. This phase is known a priori to all base stations and mobiles since the CDMA system specification requires that the long code absolute phase be synchronized to international time standards. This is accomplished by incorporating a Global Positioning System (GPS) receiver in each base station and starting the long code at a phase consistent with the system requirement that the first long code cycle begin at midnight on January 6, 1980. The absolute timing of the CDMA system is both a feature (enabling more efficient synchronization and code usage) and a problem (requiring GPS in every base station).

An important enabling feature of CDMA is that the mobile-to-base station transmissions utilize fast closed-loop power control which attempts to maintain constant received power[14] at the base station. If the mobile transmitters were not power controlled, transmissions received at the base station from nearby mobiles would be much stronger than transmissions from distant mobiles and, therefore, the nearby mobiles would cause excessive interference. This problem is called the *near-far problem* of spread-spectrum multiple-access systems, which has been well known for many years. The near-far problem is mitigated by fast closed-loop power control. Fast closed-loop power control is implemented by having the base station estimate the power received from the mobile station, comparing this power estimate with a threshold, and telling the mobile to power up or down by 1 dB to place the base station received power closer to the threshold. The power up/down message to the mobile is implemented via the insertion of a *Power Control Bit (PCB)* periodically on the forward-link transmission.

---

[14]Constant received signal-to-interference ratio may also be the goal of fast power control.

Following long code data scrambling, the symbol sequence is partitioned into 24-bit or 1.25 ms groups called *Power Control Groups (PCG)*. A single reverse-link[15] power control bit is inserted in each PCG. There are 16 power control groups and therefore 16 power control bits in each 20 ms block as illustrated in Figure 10–41. Observe that when a PCB is transmitted, an information symbol is deleted. That is, the frame structure does not accommodate the PCB by having a designated PCB bit position. The error control strategy is strong enough that the overall system functions well even with this deletion of 1 out of every 24 transmitted symbols. The power control update rate is 800 Hz, which is fast enough to partially follow the fading channel when the mobile is moving at low to moderate speeds. The performance of the fast power control loop is limited by transport delay in the loop and because fading is sometimes more rapid than can be followed with a loop having an 800 Hz update rate. The fast power control loop is part of a larger reverse link power control strategy which includes frame error rate based slow power control.

The next step in the signal processing chain is the direct-sequence spreading of the user symbol stream using the channel-specific orthogonal Walsh codes. Walsh codes [51] are sets of 2^n binary sequences, each of length 2^n, which are orthogonal to one another. A Walsh code set containing two codes of length 2 is defined by the rows of

$$W_{2^1} = \begin{bmatrix} 0 & 0 \\ 0 & 1 \end{bmatrix} \equiv \begin{bmatrix} w_0 \\ w_1 \end{bmatrix} \tag{10–83}$$

and sets of all other lengths are defined iteratively by[16]

$$W_{2^n} = \begin{bmatrix} W_{2^{n-1}} & W_{2^{n-1}} \\ W_{2^{n-1}} & \overline{W_{2^{n-1}}} \end{bmatrix} \equiv \begin{bmatrix} w_0 \\ \vdots \\ w_{2^n-1} \end{bmatrix} \tag{10–84}$$

Thus, for example,

$$W_4 = \begin{bmatrix} 0 & 0 & 0 & 0 \\ 0 & 1 & 0 & 1 \\ 0 & 0 & 1 & 1 \\ 0 & 1 & 1 & 0 \end{bmatrix} \quad \text{and} \quad W_8 = \begin{bmatrix} 0 & 0 & 0 & 0 & 0 & 0 & 0 & 0 \\ 0 & 1 & 0 & 1 & 0 & 1 & 0 & 1 \\ 0 & 0 & 1 & 1 & 0 & 0 & 1 & 1 \\ 0 & 1 & 1 & 0 & 0 & 1 & 1 & 0 \\ 0 & 0 & 0 & 0 & 1 & 1 & 1 & 1 \\ 0 & 1 & 0 & 1 & 1 & 0 & 1 & 0 \\ 0 & 0 & 1 & 1 & 1 & 1 & 0 & 0 \\ 0 & 1 & 1 & 0 & 1 & 0 & 0 & 1 \end{bmatrix}$$

[15]Although this bit is transmitted on the forward link, it is indeed the reverse link PCB since it is controlling the transmitted power on the reverse link.

[16]The notation w_0 through w_{2^n-1} is used to denote the rows of the Walsh matrix for any n. Thus $w_1 = [0\ 1]$ for W_2 and $w_1 = [0\ 1\ 0\ 1]$ for W_4. The specific Walsh code set being considered should be clear from the context.

The set W_{64}, containing 64 orthogonal codes denoted w_0 through w_{63}, is used in CDMA. One of these Walsh codes, that is, one row of W_{64}, is assigned to each user and is used as the BPSK direct-sequence spreading code. The direct-sequence chip rate is 1.2288×10^6 chips per second (cps) and the prespreading symbol rate is 19200 symbols per second (sps), so that there are exactly $1.2288 \times 10^6/19200 = 64$ spreading code chips per symbol and a complete Walsh code is used for every symbol. After Walsh spreading, the binary chip sequence alphabet is converted from $\{0,1\}$ to $\{1,-1\}$ in preparation for the linear summing of all base station transmit sequences and subsequent carrier modulation.

Although the BPSK spectrum spreading by the Walsh codes is sufficient to enable the separation of signals from a single base station, system performance, which requires separation of signals from all base stations, is improved by an additional QPSK direct-sequence spreading operation using inphase-channel and quadrature-phase channel spreading codes denoted $c_{I,pilot}$ and $c_{Q,pilot}$, respectively, as shown in Figure 10–39. These codes are extended m-sequences defined by the generator polynomials (using the notation of Chapter 9, Figure 9–21)

$$g_{I,pilot}(D) = 1 + D^2 + D^6 + D^7 + D^8 + D^{10} + D^{15}$$

$$g_{Q,pilot}(D) = 1 + D^3 + D^4 + D^5 + D^9 + D^{10} + D^{11} + D^{12} + D^{15}$$

(10–85)

These code generators are illustrated in Figure 10–43. The period of the m-sequence generators is $2^{15} - 1$; this period is extended by 1 by adding a 0 at the end of the natural sequence period. Thus the period is exactly 2^{15} chips or 512 information symbols. The code period is $2^{15}/1.2288 \times 10^6 = 26.667$ ms. and there are precisely 3 code cycles in 80 ms as illustrated in Figure 10–41. All base stations use the code generators of (10–85) and distinguish themselves by using different phases of this code. Pilot spreading code phase is referenced to the system absolute time reference. In order to make the notation here consistent with that of Chapter 9, the generators (10–85) are the reciprocals of the polynomials given in the CDMA specification. The code generators shown in Figure 10–43 are identical using either notation. Finally, the inphase and quadrature signals are filtered to control the spectral properties of the transmitted signal. The filtered signals modulate quadrature carriers which are summed, amplified and transmitted.

The forward-link information modulation is BPSK, which will be coherently demodulated in the mobile receiver. To enable coherent demodulation, the base station transmits a pilot channel, illustrated as the bottom signal processing chain in Figure 10–39. The pilot channel Walsh code spreading uses w_0, which is an all-zeros sequence. The pilot "data" is itself all-zeros so that the pilot channel input to the sum before QPSK spreading in Figure 10–39 is a constant +1. The mobile receiver can therefore recover an unmodulated pilot carrier by removing the QPSK spreading codes via the usual direct-sequence despreading operations. Received carrier phase is then recovered from this pilot and used to demodulate the other received channels.

Finally, CDMA system control requires the usual paging and system control information channels. These channels are illustrated in Figure 10–39. System timing information is transmitted to the mobile on the sync channel and system configuration messages are transmitted to the mobile on both the sync channel and the paging channel. All of the

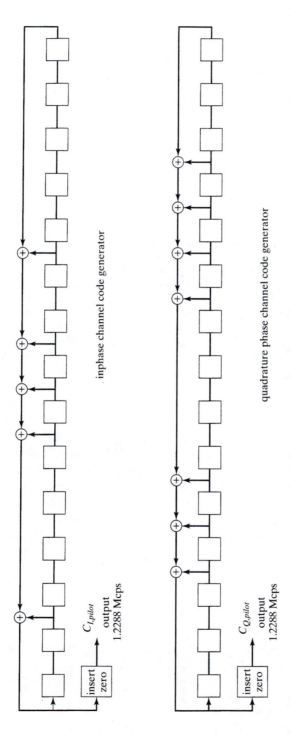

FIGURE 10–43 Pilot spreading code generators.

base station channels (multiple traffic channels, pilot channel, multiple paging channels, and the sync channel) are linearly summed prior to QPSK direct-sequence spreading as shown. Because of this linear addition, a highly linear power amplifier is required in the base station.

The transmitted signal is distorted by a fading multipath channel before arriving at the mobile receiver along with similarly modulated and faded waveforms from other base stations. The mobile receiver uses a RAKE receiver [31] to recover the maximum possible energy from the channel. The RAKE receiver coherently sums all multipath received components.[17] The receiver uses the pilot channel to estimate carrier phase for this maximal-ratio combining. The RAKE process is complicated by the fact that the multipath environment is constantly changing. Because of the dynamics of the propagation environment, the receiver must continually search for new multipath components with the goal of demodulating the strongest of these components at all times. Having estimated the transmitted symbols after the RAKE combiner, the receiver performs the inverses of the interleaving, convolutional coding, and voice coding functions to recover the user voice waveform.

10.8.3   Reverse Link Description

The mobile-to-base station modulation for CDMA is considerably different from the modulation described above. Figure 10–44 is a conceptual block diagram of the mobile transmitter. Again, assume that only voice information is transmitted. The voice encoder is identical to that of the mobile station, including its use of four different output rates used to limit the transmit output power during periods of voice silence. At its maximum rate, the voice coder outputs blocks of 172 information bits, which are CRC coded, creating 12 additional bits. As done for the forward link, 8 convolutional encoder tail bits are added to the CRC output block, resulting in a block containing 192 bits and a data rate of 9600 bps. At this point the signal processing for the forward and reverse link diverge. The convolutional encoder used in the reverse link is a rate-⅓ constraint-length-9 code with generator polynomials

$$g_1(D) = 1 + D^2 + D^3 + D^5 + D^6 + D^7 + D^8$$

$$g_2(D) = 1 + D + D^3 + D^4 + D^7 + D^8 \tag{10–86}$$

$$g_3(D) = 1 + D + D^2 + D^5 + D^8$$

The encoder is illustrated in Figure 10–45. This encoder outputs three binary symbols for each input bit so that 576 symbols are output in a 20 ms block and the output binary symbol rate is $576/20 \times 10^{-3} = 28800$ symbols per second. The convolutional encoder output block is interleaved as before; interleaver detail may be found in the speci-

---

[17]Actually the receiver demodulates and sums as many multipath components as there are up to a maximum limited by the complexity of the receiver. In some cases received multipath components exist which cannot be recovered by the receiver and signal energy is therefore lost.

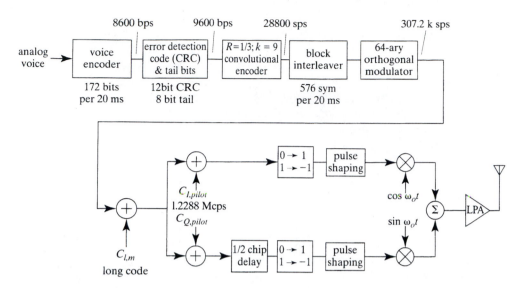

FIGURE 10–44   Code Division Multiple Access reverse-link transmitter conceptual block diagram.

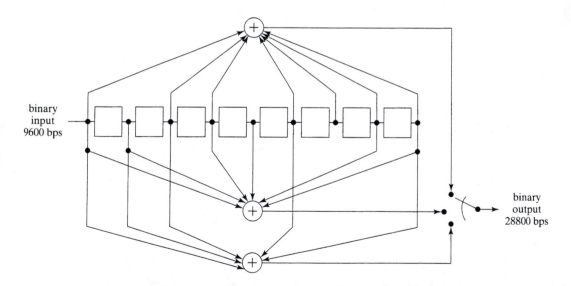

FIGURE 10–45   Rate-⅓ constraint-length-9 convolutional code used for CDMA reverse-link traffic channels.

fication. The interleaver output 576-bit block is partitioned into 16 power control groups each containing 36 binary symbols.

In contrast to the coherent BPSK modulation used on the forward link, the reverse link uses 64-ary orthogonal modulation, which may be coherently or noncoherently demodulated. At the highest level the modulator may be viewed as a functional block that accepts blocks of six binary input symbols and outputs one of $2^6 = 64$ orthogonal waveforms. Interestingly, the set of orthogonal waveforms is the Walsh set W_{64}, which was used on forward link as direct-sequence spreading codes. Each of the orthogonal waveforms denoted w_0 through w_{63} is composed of 64 binary information symbols so that the modulator outputs 64 binary symbols for each six input binary symbols. The orthogonal modulator output binary symbol rate is therefore $28000 \times 64/6 = 307.2$ ksps. In [36] Borth noted that the 64-ary modulation process is identical to encoding the symbols using a first-order Reed-Muller code [51,52]. Recognizing this relationship, Figure 10–46 illustrates a simple method of generating w_0 through w_{63}. The 6-bit block to be encoded is represented by the binary vector $u_6\, u_5\, u_4\, u_3\, u_2\, u_1$. The synchronous 5-bit binary counter is assumed initially reset to all 0s. All the counters are then synchronously clocked from a common 307.2 kHz clock. The outputs of the clock and each of the counters are weighted by one of the symbol values in the binary vector $u_6\, u_5\, u_4\, u_3\, u_2\, u_1$ and then modulo-2 summed. After 64 clock cycles the 64-bit word representing Walsh symbol $u_6\, u_5\, u_4\, u_3\, u_2\, u_1$ will have been generated. Figure 10–47 illustrates the reverse-link frame structure which has just been described.

The 307.2 kbps output of the orthogonal modulator is direct-sequence spread using a long code denoted $c_{l,m}$, which has a chip rate of 1.2288×10^6 chips per second. This is the same long code used for the forward link defined by the generator of (10–82) and illustrated in Figure 10–42 except that the code is not decimated for use in the reverse link. Each user is assigned a unique phase of this very long $2^{42} - 1$ chip code. The particular phase is a function of the electronic serial number assigned to the user. There are $1.2288 \times$

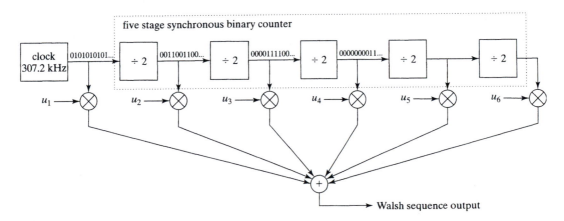

FIGURE 10–46   64-ary orthogonal sequence generator.

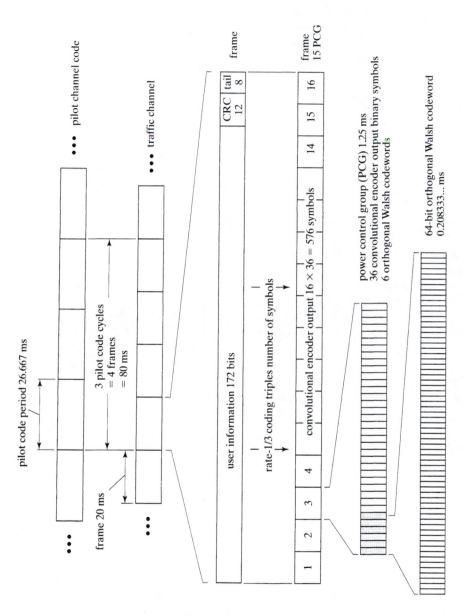

FIGURE 10–47 CDMA reverse link traffic channel framing structure.

$10^6/(307.2 \times 10^3) = 4$ spreading code chips per orthogonal modulator output symbol. The output of the long code spreader is routed to both inphase and quadrature phase direct-sequence spreading function. The inphase and quadrature phase spreading codes are defined in (10–85) and illustrated in Figure 10–43. After the final spreading operation, the inphase channel is delayed ½ chip so that the final modulation is offset-QPSK in contrast to the QPSK modulation used on the forward link. The quadrature direct-sequence spreader outputs are filtered and used to modulate quadrature carriers that are summed, amplified, and transmitted.

The transmitted signal is again distorted by a fading multipath channel before arriving at the base station receiver along with similarly modulated and faded waveforms from other mobile stations. The base station receiver removes the direct-sequence spreading modulation using conventional spread-spectrum techniques [36]. The receiver then estimates the 64-ary transmitted symbol by correlating the despread waveform with each possible orthogonal Walsh code and then selecting the largest. This correlation operation may be simplified using fast Hadamard transform [53] techniques. After estimating the transmitted Walsh sequence, the inverse operations for the interleaver, convolutional coding, and voice coding are performed to recover the user voice signal.

10.8.4   Capacity of CDMA

The most controversial issue regarding cellular CDMA is the estimation of its capacity. An early journal article by the creators of CDMA [54] claimed, under certain very specific conditions, that CDMA "offers at least an eighteenfold increase in capacity" relative to AMPS. The capacity of a CDMA system is extremely difficult to estimate and equally difficult to evaluate in an actual system due, in part, to one of the features of CDMA—that is, the capacity limit is soft. When the *soft capacity* limit is exceeded, all users experience slightly degraded signal quality, and this may be acceptable for short periods of time. This is in contrast to the hard capacity limits of AMPS where channel blocking limits the number of users that may be simultaneously serviced. The first issue that must be addressed in the calculation of CDMA capacity is the precise definition of capacity. The next issue that must be addressed is that capacity is strongly a function of the multipath propagation environment and will very likely be different in different cells. Thus, there is no single correct value for CDMA capacity. Nevertheless, the following analysis (simplified from [54]) illustrates some of the fundamental features of CDMA.

Consider the mobile-to-base or reverse link of an ideal CDMA cellular system conceptually illustrated in Figure 10–48. Assume that the same CDMA carrier frequency is reused in every sector of every cell so that interferers are potentially located anywhere in the system as illustrated in Figure 10–48a. Suppose that mobiles are distributed uniformly throughout the system and that each mobile is serviced by the base station at the center of the ideal hexagonal cell in which it is located, even though in a real system propagation anomalies would create exceptions to this.

Three types of mobiles are identified in the figure. The type-0 mobile is the test mobile whose link quality will be the focus of the capacity calculation. The test mobile is ser-

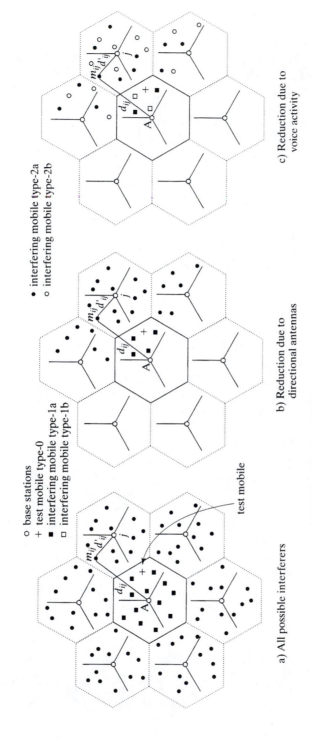

○ base stations
+ test mobile type-0
■ interfering mobile type-1a
□ interfering mobile type-1b

● interfering mobile type-2a
○ interfering mobile type-2b

test mobile

a) All possible interferers

b) Reduction due to directional antennas

c) Reduction due to voice activity

FIGURE 10–48 CDMA cellular uplink capacity calculation.

viced by and therefore power controlled by the center base station labeled "A." The reverse link is being considered so that interference to the test mobile is due to the transmissions of other mobiles that are received at base station A. Both type-1 and type-2 mobiles potentially create this interference. A type-1 mobile is an interfering mobile that is in the same cell as the test mobile and is therefore also power controlled by base station A. Type-2 mobiles are serviced by and therefore power controlled by surrounding base stations. Both type-1 and type-2 mobile categories are further partitioned into subcategories indicating whether, at a particular instant in time, a mobile is actually transmitting. As mentioned previously, one of the features of the CDMA system is that it can take advantage of voice pauses by not transmitting during these pauses thereby reducing system interference. Type-1a and type-2a mobiles are mobiles that are actually transmitting at the particular sample instant that the interference is being calculated while type-1b and type-2b mobiles are not. The probability that a particular mobile is transmitting at a given instant in time will be denoted by ρ. Studies [54,55] have shown $\rho = 3/8$ is reasonable for normal conversation.

Assume that perfect $120°$ sector antennas are used in all cells.[18] These perfect antennas reject all received energy from their back lobes and receive all energy from their front lobes without loss. The transition between the antenna front and back lobe is assumed to be a step function. With this assumption the interference to the test mobile is created only by type-1 and type-2 mobiles in the main lobe of the test mobile's serving base station antenna and two-thirds of the potential interference is eliminated. The remaining potentially interfering mobiles are illustrated in Figure 10–48b. In general, other sector antenna beamwidths are possible—for example, $60°$—and the fraction of the potentially interfering mobiles which are actually received will be denoted by g. For $120°$ and $60°$ sector antennas $g = 1/3$ and $g = 1/6$ respectively. The number of actual interfering mobiles is further reduced by voice inactivity. Figure 10–48c illustrates the actual interfering (type-1a and type-2a) and noninterfering (type-1b and type-2b) mobiles. Observe that the number of actual interferers in Figure 10–48c is greatly reduced from the number of potentially interfering mobiles in Figure 10–48a. The majority of the capacity increase of CDMA relative to AMPS is qualitatively accounted for in this figure. The reuse of carrier frequencies in every cell is an important feature of CDMA made possible, in part, by the strong error control strategy.

The following highly simplified analysis will quantify CDMA capacity.[19] Consider again all of the potentially interfering mobiles of Figure 10–48a. All mobiles are perfectly power controlled. The resulting constant average received power at the mobile's serving base station is denoted P_r, corresponding to received energy per information bit $E_b = P_r/R$. Denote the number of mobiles within each cell by N. The interference to the test mobile is from three sources: (1) receiver thermal noise with one-sided power spectral density N_0; (2) the $(N - 1)$ type-1 mobiles in the same sector as the test mobile; and (3) the N type-2

---

[18]This perfect antenna cannot, of course, be built. Nevertheless, this assumption illustrates how antenna sectorization increases system capacity.

[19]It cannot be overemphasized that simplified capacity calculations such as this cannot be used for system design. Rather, this analysis is intended only to illustrate the principles of CDMA.

mobiles in every cell that can be received by the main beam of the base station sector antenna serving the test mobile. Consider the interference caused by the type-1 interferers. Ignoring the benefit of antenna sectorization for a moment, the total interfering power I_1' from type-1 interferers is the summation over all mobiles $j = 2, N$ controlled by base A except for the test mobile

$$I_1' = \sum_{j=2}^{N} v_j P_r \qquad (10\text{-}87)$$

where v_j is a binary random variable that models voice activity and therefore takes on value $v_j = 1$ with probability ρ and value $v_j = 0$ with probability $1 - \rho$. The interference I_1' is a random variable taking on different values at different times as a function of the voice activity of specific mobiles. For simplicity, ignore this time variability and consider only its mean value, which is $\bar{I}_1' = \rho(N - 1)P_r$. The value of $\bar{I}_1'$ represents the mean interference from all type-1 interferers. Antenna sectorization reduces this mean value by approximately the factor g so that the actual mean interference from type-1 mobiles is $\bar{I}_1 = g\bar{I}_1' = g\rho(N - 1)P_r$.

Next consider the interference from type-2 mobiles. These mobiles are power controlled to surrounding base stations, so it cannot be assumed that the received power at base A from any of them equals P_r. A typical type-2 mobile, labeled m_{ij} in Figure 10–48, is distance d_{ij}' from its serving base station j and distance d_{ij} from the test mobile's serving base station A. The subscripts i and j denote ith mobile in the jth surrounding cell. It can be shown that the interference power at base station A due to mobile m_{ij} is

$$P_{ij} = P_r \left(\frac{d_{ij}'}{d_{ij}}\right)^n 10^{(\xi_{ij} - \xi_{ij}')/10} \qquad (10\text{-}88)$$

where n denotes the propagation path loss exponent and ξ_{ij} and ξ_{ij}' represent the log-normal shadow fading on the two paths. Again ignoring the benefit of antenna sectorization, the total interference power due to type-2 mobiles is then

$$I'_2 = \sum_{j=1}^{J} \sum_{i=1}^{N} v_{ij} P_r \left(\frac{d'_{ij}}{d_{ij}}\right)^n 10^{(\xi_{ij} - \xi'_{ij})/10} \qquad (10\text{-}89)$$

where the inner sum is over all interfering mobiles $i = 1, N$ in surrounding cell j. The interference I_2' is also a random variable that is a function of the specific locations of the interfering mobiles, the instantaneous values of the log-normal shadowing, and voice activity. The statistics of this random variable may be calculated using Monte-Carlo simulation techniques or, with certain assumptions, may be calculated analytically [56]. The interested reader is referred to [31,54,56–58] for detailed analysis of (10–89). For simplicity only the mean value $\bar{I}_2'$ of (10–89) is considered here. The value of $\bar{I}_2'$ is usually [31,56] presented in terms of an *other-cell interference factor f*, which is $f \equiv \bar{I}_2'/(\rho N P_r)$, the ratio of the total interference power from cells other than the test mobile serving cell to the total received power from all mobiles in the test mobile serving cell. The other-cell interference factor has been calculated under various conditions [56]; a typical value is $f = 0.44$ calculated for a path loss exponent of $n = 4$ with no log-normal shadow fading. Ignoring the benefit of directional antennas, the total type-2 mobile mean interference may then be written $\bar{I}'_2 = f\,\rho N P_r$. Taking into account directional antennas $\bar{I}_2 = f\,g\,\rho N P_r$.

Considering all interference sources then, the total average interference to the test mobile is

$$\bar{I}_{tot} = N_0 W + \bar{I}_1 + \bar{I}_2 \tag{10-90}$$

$$= N_0 W + g\rho(N-1)P_r + f g \,\rho P_r N$$

Finally, because spread-spectrum modulation is being used, assume that the interference from other users may be modeled as Gaussian noise with equivalent total power. The equivalent interference power spectral density is denoted $N_{tot} = I_{tot}/W$ and the performance of the test mobile is determined by the received energy per bit to noise power spectral density

$$\frac{E_b}{N_{tot}} = \frac{P_r(W/R)}{N_0 W + g\,\rho(N-1)\,P_r + f g \,\rho\, P_r N}$$

$$= \frac{(W/R)}{\dfrac{N_0 W}{P_r} + g\,\rho(N-1) + f g\,\rho\,N} \tag{10-91}$$

Careful examination of (10–91) will yield insight into CDMA capacity estimation. The left side of this equation is the signal-to-noise ratio required by the coding and modulation scheme in order to achieve the desired signaling reliability in the expected fading environment. For CDMA the desired signaling reliability is often assumed to correspond to a bit error probability of 10^{-3} with a corresponding signal-to-noise ratio of 7 dB [54]. Thus, the values of all of the parameters on the right side of this equation must combine to yield a signal-to-noise ratio at least as large as the target E_b/N_{tot}. The denominator contains three interference terms corresponding to thermal noise, interference from mobiles in the same cell as the test mobile, and interference from mobiles in other cells. As expected, as N increases, the interference from other mobiles (the last two terms of the denominator) increases and the received signal-to-noise ratio decreases. CDMA capacity could therefore be defined as the maximum N for which the received E_b/N_{tot} remains above its minimum acceptable value. Interestingly, however, for any N the denominator of (10–91) can be decreased by increasing the power control target P_r. Therefore, the number of users that can be supported can, up to a limit, be increased by increasing P_r. The dependency of capacity on P_r is illustrated in Figure 10–49, which is a graph of the required P_r as a function of N with all other parameters of (10–91) fixed at the values shown in the figure. Observe the gradual rise in P_r as N increases until a value of $N = 145 \equiv N_{pole}$ is reached. For $N > N_{pole}$, the target E_b/N_{tot} cannot be achieved for any P_r, and the absolute maximum capacity has been achieved. This maximum capacity is called the *pole capacity* of the CDMA system.

Equation (10–91) shows several other relationships important to CDMA. First, the numerator W/R is the usual spread-spectrum processing gain; its presence in the numerator shows that received signal-to-noise ratio increases with increasing processing gain.

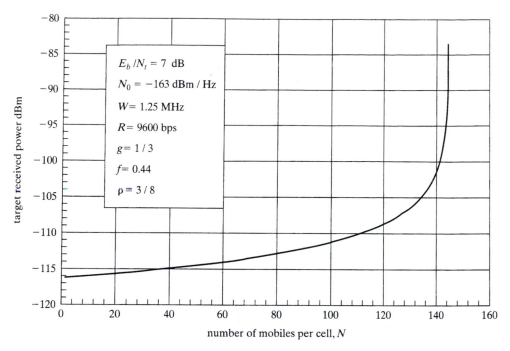

FIGURE 10–49 CDMA cellular uplink pole capacity.

Thus, increasing processing gain permits more mobiles to be served, but overall spectrum efficiency may or may not be improved depending on the manner in which processing gain was increased. Second, decreasing the sector antenna factor g reduces the denominator of (10–91) and will thus increase capacity. The factor g decreases as the beamwidth of the sector antennas decreases. Thus, capacity increases directly with decreasing sector antenna beamwidth. Third, the denominator of (10–91) decreases with decreasing voice activity probability ρ. Although the system designer cannot control ρ, it should be noted that ρ accounts for a significant amount of CDMA capacity increase. Finally, capacity will increase if the other-cell interference factor f is decreased. The factor f is determined by the physical environment and cannot therefore be easily controlled. Increasing path loss exponent is associated with decreasing other-cell interference factor.

10.8.5   Additional Comments

This brief introduction to CDMA is far from complete. Many many subtleties and additional issues are important to the detailed design of a CDMA system. A few of these issues are briefly mentioned in the following paragraphs.

- Soft handoff wherein a mobile is simultaneously connected to more than a single base station is effectively used to increase system capacity. Call control procedures including handoff and soft handoff are complex to design and are usually designed with the assistance of complex computer programs. The handoff processes make use of mobile measurements of the received pilot channel power from a short list of (hopefully) nearby base station handoff candidates.
- The very simple capacity calculation described above considered only the reverse link. Until recently researchers believed that CDMA capacity would be limited by the reverse link since noncoherent modulation was used. Many systems are now known to be forward link capacity limited thus motivating research into methods of improving the forward link.
- CDMA capacity is directly related to the extremely strong forward error correction scheme used on both the forward and reverse links. Equation (10–91) shows that capacity would increase inversely with decreasing E_b/N_0. Thus, a 3 dB decrease in the required signal-to-noise ratio would approximately double reverse link capacity.
- CDMA makes use of every possible diversity method. Time diversity is implemented in the form of coding and interleaving. Frequency diversity is implemented using the wide bandwidth spread-spectrum signaling scheme. Space diversity is used on the reverse link where multiple base station receive antennas are employed. Soft handoff is also an instance of space diversity. Multipath diversity is implemented using a RAKE receiver made possible by the spread-spectrum signaling.

In summary, CDMA is a communication system that makes use of most modern communications techniques. A detailed study of CDMA will therefore prepare the reader for the study of a wide range of related systems. Much literature on the subject of CDMA is available to the interested reader, including a text [31] by one of the inventors and numerous journal papers. CDMA is now a widely accepted technology with systems installed worldwide.

10.9   RECOMMENDED FURTHER READING

In spite of the length of this chapter, it has only addressed the most fundamental concepts related to cellular mobile radio. Much additional literature is available for the reader desiring to bring her or his level of understanding to the level required to do research in the area.

10.9.1   Cellular Concepts and Systems

The subject of cellular radio and wireless communications in general has been the subject of a number of excellent textbooks, special issues of prominent journals, and very many journal papers. The classic text *Microwave Mobile Communications* by William Jakes Jr. [10] and others published first in 1974 and since republished by the Institute of Electrical and Electronics Engineers (IEEE) was, for years, the primary quoted reference on cellular systems. Jakes details all of the principles upon which the AMPS system is based. Jakes is strongly recommended reading for the cellular systems engineer. Another excellent reference for AMPS systems technology is a special issue of the *Bell System Technical Journal* dedicated to AMPS [37] and published in January 1979. This special issue, particularly the introductory papers and the paper on modulation performance, are essential reading. Yet another early text (1982) that covers basic concepts in detail is *Mobile Communications Engineering* by William Lee [25]. Lee's book is quite detailed and is often referenced. Finally, in 1984 the IEEE published a compendium [60] on cellular systems, *Land-Mobile Communications Engineering,* which contains many important papers published prior to 1984 and therefore focused primarily on AMPS technology.

Second-generation systems as well as basic cellular concepts are discussed in great detail in the text *Mobile Radio Communications* [43], edited by Raymond Steele and authored by Steele and others. Because this text is well written and contains a very detailed description of GSM, it is recommended for those desiring focus in this area. GSM is also the subject of an entire book, *The GSM System for Mobile Communications* by Michel Mouly and Marie-Bernadette Pautet [41], published in 1992. The "GSM book," as it is often referred to, details the GSM system itself and covers general concepts only as they relate to GSM. Readers interested in CDMA systems should read *CDMA: Principles of Spread Spectrum Communication* by Andrew Viterbi [31], who is a co-inventor of the CDMA system concept. Viterbi's book provides detailed mathematical analyses of many of the fundamental principles of CDMA. Finally, second-generation systems are the subject of a special issue titled "Digital Cellular Technologies" of the *IEEE Transactions on Vehiclular Technology* in May 1991. This special issue contains excellent papers on both CDMA and GSM.

Another recommended text, *Wireless Communications: Principles and Practice* [42], written by Theodore Rappaport (1996), is an introductory text that extensively covers basic principles as well as details of AMPS, GSM, and CDMA. Rappaport also provides description of a number of systems that are not covered in this chapter due to space limitations. Specific systems covered in the Rappaport book that were not discussed here are United States Digital Cellular (USDC), which is another second-generation system, the Digital European Cordless Telephone (DECT), and the Japanese Personal Handyphone System (PHS). Finally, basic principles of cellular design and coverage are analyzed in two books, *Land-Mobile Radio System Engineering* and *Handbook of Land-Mobile Radio System Coverage,* by Garry Hess [28,29].

10.9.2 Channel Modeling and Propagation

The text by Jakes [10] begins with several significant chapters on multipath propagation and path loss that are highly recommended reading. Be aware, however, that the power spectrum of the fading processes introduced in Jakes is based upon the assumption that scatterers are uniformly spaced in azimuth; more recent research indicates that this may not always be a valid assumption. Most researchers working in mobile communications are familiar with the Jakes text. Another classic text, *Communication Systems and Techniques* by Schwartz, Bennett, and Stein [21], includes an excellent chapter written by Seymour Stein on the subject of fading channels. This chapter includes analyses of the performance of various modulation schemes in Rayleigh fading. More recently (1987), Stein has summarized important fading channel issues in the paper "Fading Channel Issues in System Engineering" [19]. This paper provides a concise overview of channel modeling as well as associated mitigation techniques. The text by Steele [43] includes a lengthy chapter by D. Greenwood and L. Hanzo on mobile radio channels. This chapter begins with a discussion of the basic concepts of complex envelope representations of signals and systems and continues through the details of time-varying channels, thereby providing a complete treatment of this subject. Rappaport's text [26] also provides several detailed chapters on mobile radio multipath and path loss models. Although not addressing mobile radio channels specifically, the classic and widely referenced text by John Proakis *Digital Communications* [22] has a chapter titled "Digital Signaling Over Fading Multipath Channels" that includes the basic fast-fading channel descriptions and continues through a discussion of diversity receivers including RAKE concepts. Finally, the subject of propagation for mobile radio is broad enough that David Parsons has dedicated the entire text, *The Mobile Radio Propagation Channel* [4], to the subject. The Parsons text is very detailed and includes discussion of much of the research that preceded its publication in 1992. All of the propagation references mentioned above are built upon the mathematical foundation by Bello in the classic 1963 paper "Characterization of Randomly Time-Variant Linear Channels" [20]. This paper is extremely detailed and mathematical and is recommended reading only after some of the more recent literature is studied. The Bello paper is included in an IEEE compendium, *Communications Channels: Characterization and Behavior,* edited by Bernard Goldberg [59]; this compendium also contains other important references on propagation. Additional important papers may be found in the February 1987 issue of *IEEE Journal on Selected Areas in Communications,* on "Fading and Multipath Channel Communications," which includes the tutorial by Stein mentioned above.

The references of the preceding paragraph address primarily the fast fading channel. Path loss has also been the subject of much research. The Jakes text [10] addresses path loss as do the texts by Steele [43], Rapapport [26], and Parsons [4]. The reader is directed to the paper "Field Strength and its Variability in UHF and VHF Land-Mobile Radio Service" by Okumura and colleagues [6] and the related paper, "Empirical Formula for Propagation Loss in Land Mobile Radio Services" by Hata [7], for comprehensive treatments of how the physical environment affects path loss. These papers are often referenced.

A currently hot area that is anticipated to provide significant increases in CDMA cellular system capacity is that of space-time coding or, the more attention-grabbing term, smart antennas. The reader is referred to a recent textbook [61] and a collection of papers to learn more about this topic [62].

10.9.3   Concluding Remarks

The basic principles of cellular mobile radio have been introduced. While understanding the principles of frequency reuse, fading multipath channels, path loss, call control, and diversity to mitigate the difficult mobile channel are all essential components of the cellular system design, much additional analysis would be required to design a complete digital cellular system. As mentioned previously, cellular communications system design is a creative and highly complex combination of nearly all modern communications, computer, and system technologies. The detailed study of cellular systems will therefore provide the reader with a broad understanding of technologies applicable to this and other interesting communications problems.

REFERENCES

[1] V. H. McDonald, "The Cellular Concept," *The Bell System Technical Journal,* Vol. 58, No. 1, January 1979.

[2] H. T. Friis, "A Note on a Simple Transmission Formula," *Proceedings of the Institute of Radio Engineers,* Vol. 34, 1946.

[3] E. C. Jordan and K. G. Balmain, *Electromagnetic Waves and Radiating Systems* (Englewood Cliffs, NJ: Prentice-Hall, Inc.,1968).

[4] D. Parsons, *The Mobile Radio Propagation Channel* (New York: John Wiley & Sons, 1992).

[5] W. R. Young, "Comparison of Mobile Radio Transmission at 150, 450, 900, and 3700 MHz," *Bell System Technical Journal,* Vol. 31, 1952.

[6] Y. Okumura, E. Ohmori, T. Kawano, and K. Fukuda, "Field Strength and Its Variability in UHF and VHF Land-Mobile Radio Service," *Review of the Tokyo Electronic Communications Laboratory,* Vol. 16, No. 9–10, 1968. (Also published in: B. Goldberg [editor], *Communications Channels: Characterization and Behavior,* New York: IEEE Press, 1976).

[7] M. Hata, "Empirical Formula for Propagation Loss in Land Mobile Radio Services," *IEEE Trans. on Vehicular Tech.,* Vol. VT-29, No 3, August, 1980.

[8] D.O. Reudink, "Comparison of Radio Transmission at X-band Frequencies in Suburban and Urban Areas," *IEEE Transactions on Antennas and Propagation,* 1972.

[9] J.D. Parsons, "Signal Strength Prediction in Build-Up Areas Part 2: Signal Variability," *IEEE Proc.,* August 1983.

[10] W. C. Jakes, Jr. [Editor], *Microwave Mobile Communications* (New York, John Wiley & Sons, 1974).

[11] R. H. Clarke, "A Statistical Theory of Mobile Radio Reception," *Bell System Technical Journal,* July 1968.

[12] W. R. Bennett, "Distribution of the Sum of Randomly Phased Components," *Quarterly of Applied Mathematics,* 1948.

[13] S. O. Rice, "Mathematical Analysis of Random Noise," *Bell System Technical Journal,* July 1944 and January 1945.

[14] S. O. Rice, "Statistical Properties of a Sine Wave Plus Random Noise," *Bell System Technical Journal,* January 1948.

[15] T. Aulin, "A Modified Model for the Fading Signal at a Mobile Radio Channel," *IEEE Trans. on Vehicular Tech.,* 1979.

[16] V. Pérez and J. Jiménez (editors), "Final Propagation Model," Report R2020/TDE/PS/DS/P/040/b1 of RACE project R2020 (CODIT), European Telecommunications Standards Institute, June 1994.

[17] W. B. Davenport Jr. and W. L. Root, *An Introduction to the Theory of Random Signals and Noise* (New York: McGraw-Hill Book Co., 1958).

[18] A. D. Whalen, *Detection of Signals in Noise* (New York: Academic Press, Inc., 1971).

[19] S. Stein, "Fading Channel Issues in System Engineering," *IEEE Journal on Selected Areas in Communications,* February 1987.

[20] P. A. Bello, "Characterization of Randomly Time-Variant Linear Channels," *IEEE Trans. on Commun. Sys.,* December 1963. (Also reprinted in: B. Goldberg [editor], *Communications Channels: Characterization and Behavior* New York: IEEE Press, 1976).

[21] M. Schwartz, W. Bennett, and S. Stein, *Communication Systems and Techniques* (New York: McGraw-Hill, 1966).

[22] J. Proakis, *Digital Communications,* 3rd Edition (New York: McGraw-Hill Book Company, 1995).

[23] W. R. Braun and U. Dersch, "A Physical Mobile Radio Channel Model," *IEEE Trans. on Vehicular Tech.,* May 1991.

[24] U. Dersch and E. Zollinger, "Physical Characteristics of Urban Micro-Cellular Propagation," *IEEE Trans. on Antennas and Propagation,* November 1994.

[25] W. C. Y. Lee, *Mobile Communications Engineering* (New York, McGraw-Hill Book Company, 1982).

[26] T. S. Rappaport, *Wireless Communications: Principles and Practice* (New York: Prentice-Hall, 1996).

[27] R. Price and P. E. Green, "A Communication Technique for Multipath Channels," *Proceedings of the IRE,* March 1958.

[28] G. C. Hess, *Handbook of Land-Mobile Radio System Coverage* (Norwood, MA, Artech House, 1998).

[29] G. C. Hess, *Land-Mobile Radio System Engineering* (Norwood, MA, Artech House, 1993).

[30] J-P Linnartz, *Narrowband Land-Mobile Radio Networks* (Norwood, MA, Artech House, 1993).

[31] A. J. Viterbi, *CDMA: Principles of Spread Spectrum Communication* (Reading, MA, Addison-Wesley, 1995).

[32] T. S. Rappaport (editor), *Cellular Radio and Personal Communications: A Book of Selected Reprints* (Piscataway, NJ: IEEE Press, 1995).

[33] P. D. Rasky, G. M. Chiasson, and D. E. Borth, "Hybrid Slow Frequency Hop CDMA-TDMA as a Solution for High-Mobility, Wide-Area Personal Communications," *Proceedings of the Fourth WINLAB workshop on Third Generation Wireless Information Networks,* East Brunswick, NJ, October 19–20, 1993.

[34] P. D. Rasky, G. M. Chiasson, and D. E. Borth, "An Experimental Slow Frequency Hopped Personal Communication System for the Proposed U.S. 1850–1990 MHz Band," *Proceedings of the Second International Conference on Universal Personal Communications,* Ottawa, Canada, October 12–15, 1993.

[35] P. D. Rasky, G. M. Chiasson, D. E. Borth and R. L. Peterson, "Slow Frequency Hop TDMA/CDMA for Macrocellular Personal Communication Systems," *IEEE Personal Commun. Mag.,* Second Quarter, 1994.

[36] R. L. Peterson, R. E. Ziemer, and D. E. Borth, *Introduction to Spread Spectrum Communications* (New York, Prentice-Hall, 1995).

[37] W. R. Young et al., "Advanced Mobile Phone Service," *Special Issue of the Bell System Technical Journal,* January 1979.

[38] EIA/TIA-553- 1989 , "Mobile Station–Land Station Compatibility Specifications," Electronic Industries Association, Washington, DC.

[39] G. A. Arredondo, J. C. Feggler, and J. I. Smith, "Voice and Data Transmission," Special Issue of the *Bell System Technical Journal,* January 1979.

[40] European Telecommunications Standards Institute, *GSM Specifications* (Sophia Antipolis, France: ETSI TC-SMG, 1991).

[41] M. Mouly and M.-B. Pautet, *The GSM System for Mobile Communications* (Palaiseau, France: 1992).

[42] T. S. Rappaport, *Wireless Communications: Principles and Practice* (Upper Saddle River, NJ: Prentice-Hall PTR, 1996).

[43] R. Steele (editor), *Mobile Radio Communications* (New York: IEEE Press, 1992).

[44] K. Murota and K. Hirade, "GMSK Modulation for Digital Mobile Radio Telephony," *IEEE Trans. on Commun.*, July 1981.

[45] G. D. Forney Jr., "Maximum Likelihood Sequence Estimation of Digital Sequences in the Presence of Intersymbol Interference," *IEEE Trans. on Information Theory*, May 1972.

[46] G. R. Cooper and R. W. Nettleton, "A Spread Spectrum Technique for High Capacity Mobile Communications," *IEEE Trans. on Vehicular Tech.*, November 1978.

[47] G. R. Cooper and R. W. Nettleton, "Spectral Efficiency in Cellular Land–Mobile Communications; A Spread Spectrum Approach," Final Report, TR-EE 78-44, Purdue University, West Lafayette, Indiana, October 31, 1978.

[48] G. R. Cooper and R. W. Nettleton, "A Spread Spectrum Technique for High Capacity Mobile Communications," *Proceedings of the 27th Vehicular Technology Conference*, March 1977.

[49] G. R. Cooper, R. W. Nettleton, and D.P.Grybos, "Cellular Land Mobile Radio: Why Spread Spectrum?" *IEEE Communications Magazine*, March 1979.

[50] TIA/EIA/IS-95 Interim Standard, *Mobile Station–Base Station Compatibility Standard for Dual Mode Wideband Spread Spectrum Cellular Systems*, Telecommunications Industry Association, Washington, DC, July 1993.

[51] F. J. MacWilliams and N. J. A. Sloane, *The Theory of Error Correcting Codes* (New York: North-Holland, 1977).

[52] W. C. Lindsey and M. K. Simon, *Telecommunications Systems Engineering* (Englewood Cliffs, NJ: Prentice-Hall, 1973).

[53] E. C. Posner, "Combinatorial Structures in Planetary Reconnaissance," in *Error Correcting Codes*, H. B. Mann, editor (New York: Wiley, 1969).

[54] K. S. Gilhousen, I. M. Jacobs, R. Padovani, A. J. Viterbi, L. A. Weaver, Jr., and C. E. Wheatley III, "On the Capacity of a Cellular CDMA System," *IEEE Trans. on Vehicular Tech.*, May 1991.

[55] P. T. Brady, "A Statistical Analysis of On-Off Patterns in Sixteen Conversations," *Bell System Technical Journal*, January 1968.

[56] A. J. Viterbi, A. M. Viterbi, and E. Zehavi, "Other-Cell Interference in Cellular Power-Controlled CDMA," *IEEE Trans. on Commun.*, February/March/April 1994.

[57] Viterbi, A. M. and A. J. Viterbi, "Erlang Capacity of a Power Controlled CDMA System," *IEEE J Selected Areas in Commun.*, August 1993.

[58] A. J. Viterbi, A. M. Viterbi, and E. Zehavi, "Performance of Power-Controlled Wideband Terrestrial Digital Communications," *IEEE Trans. on Commun.*, April 1993.

[59] B. Goldberg (editor), *Communications Channels: Characterization and Behavior* (New York: IEEE Press, 1976).

[60] D. Bodson, G. F. McClure, and S. R. McConnoughey (editors), *Land Mobile Communications Engineering* (New York: IEEE Press, 1984).

[61] J. Liberti, Jr. and T. Rappaport, *Smart Antennas for Wireless Communications* (Upper Saddle River , NJ: Prentice Hall, 1999).

[62] T. Rappaport (editor), *Smart Antennas: Adaptive Arrays, Algorithms, and Wireless Position Location* (Piscataway, NJ: IEEE Press, 1998).

PROBLEMS

10–1. Prove that the radius of a hexagon in Figure 10–3 equals $1/\sqrt{3}$ when the distance between cell centers is 1.0. Derive a formula for the area of a hexagon in terms of its radius. What is "pi" for hexagons?

10–2. Derive equations 10–5 and 10–6.

10–3. Consider a cellular system using squares to tesselate the service area rather than hexagons. Suppose that a nine-cell frequency reuse pattern is used as illustrated in Figure P10–3. Calculate the minimum signal-to-noise ratio experienced by a mobile anywhere in the system assuming that a mobile is always serviced by the geographically closest base station.

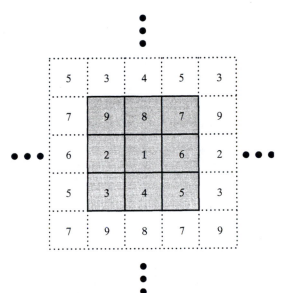

FIGURE P10–3   Nine cell square frequency reuse pattern.

10–4. Calculate the spectrum efficiency of a cellular system using a modulation scheme requiring a received signal-to-interference ratio of +7 dB and requiring 30 kHz of bandwidth for both the forward and reverse links.

10–5. Derive (10–4) from (10–3) and the fact that there are six closest co-channel interferers in an ideal hexagonal cellular system as in Figure 10–3.

10–6. Consider an ideal hexagonal grid cellular system using a carrier frequency of 850 MHz. Suppose that the base station antenna height is 30 meters and the mobile antenna height is 3 meters. Suppose also that the modulation requires a bandwidth of 25 kHz and a received signal-to-interference ratio of at least +17 dB for acceptable performance. Considering only base-to-mobile transmissions, calculate and compare the minimum frequency reuse factors

N, assuming (a) free space path loss and (b) flat-earth path loss. For the same conditions calculate and compare the spectrum efficiencies. (Of course, free space path loss formulas do not apply to this propagation environment. The purpose of the requested comparison is to illustrate that a path loss exponent larger than the free-space exponent is desirable for cellular systems.)

10–7. Consider a single base station with an antenna height of 30 meters transmitting to a mobile with an antenna height of 3 meters and using a carrier frequency of 850 MHz. Suppose that digital modulation at a bit rate $R = 9600$ bps is used and that the required received $E_b/N_0 = +7$ dB. Suppose that the thermal noise at the mobile antenna terminals is -174 dBm/Hz and that the mobile receiver noise figure is 10 dB. Assume that the base station transmit power is 1 W and calculate and compare the maximum range of the base station for (a) free-space path loss and (b) flat-earth path loss.

10–8. Calculate and plot flat-earth path attenuation as a function of range for base station antenna heights of 5, 10, 20, and 40 meters. Assume a mobile antenna height of 3 meters. What is the change in path attenuation for each doubling of base station antenna height?

10–9. In the derivation of (10–13) for flat-earth path loss is was assumed that $(2\pi h_t h_r)/(d\lambda) \ll 1.0$ so that $\sin x = x - (x^3/3!) + (x^5/5!) - \ldots$ could be approximated by its first term. Calculate and plot flat-earth path loss with and without this assumption to determine the minimum range for which (10–13) is applicable. Assume base station and mobile antenna heights of 30 and 3 meters respectively and a carrier frequency of 850 MHz.

10–10. Calculate and plot the path loss exponent for the Okumura/Hata path loss model as a function of base station antenna height.

10–11. Consider a single isolated cell of a cellular communications system in a suburban area. Calculate the base station average transmit power required to achieve a minimum received signal power at a mobile that is 6 km from that base of -107 dBm. Assume that the base station and mobile antennas are omnidirectional, that the base station antenna height is 50 meters, that the mobile antenna height is 3 meters, that the carrier frequency is 850 MHz, and that propagation is accurately modeled by the Okumura/Hata model. Ignore lognormal shadow fading.

10–12. Consider two propagation paths that are identical except that each experiences independent log-normal shadow fading. At any instant in time a receiver selects the path having the minimum path loss for communications. Calculate and plot the probability density function of the shadow fading at the output of the selector function.

10–13. A perfectly reflecting wall denoted A-B is located distance $d = 100$ meters from a base station as shown in Figure P10–12. A mobile is moving away from the base station along a line parallel to the wall at speed $v = 1.0$ meter/sec. The base station is transmitting an unmodulated unit amplitude carrier whose frequency is 850 MHz. Calculate and plot the magnitude of the envelope of the signal received at the mobile station as a function of time for $1 \leq t \leq 3$ seconds and $1001 \leq t \leq 1013$ seconds.

10–14. Demonstrate for α_1 in any quadrant that the phase difference between point (x,y) and point $(0,0)$ for wavefront 1 of the Figure 10–9b is $\phi_n(x,y) = 2\pi(y \sin \alpha_1 + x \cos \alpha_1)/\lambda_0$.

10–15. Plot the power spectrum of signal received at a mobile moving with velocity 100 km/h radially outward from a base station that is transmitting a sinewave at frequency 850 MHz. Assume that there are 36 equal-amplitude multipath components arriving at the mobile at angles $0°, 10°, 20°, \ldots, 350°$ relative to the mobile direction.

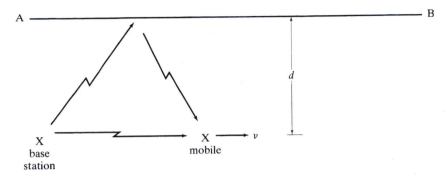

FIGURE P10–12

10–16. Derive (10–32) from (10–31) and the relation $f = f_0 + f_M \cos \alpha$.

10–17. Calculate the total power in the Gaussian random process $n_{f\,i}(t)$ used in the model for multiplicative Rayleigh fading by integrating its power spectrum $S_{n_{f\,i}}(f)$ given by (10–35).

10–18. Show that the very short term average of the instantaneous power (extend 11) $u(t)$ of a narrowband signal $s(t)$ with complex envelope $\tilde{s}(t)$ is $\frac{1}{2}|\tilde{s}(t)|^2$.

10–19. Consider a mobile communications system using ideal biorthogonal signaling [22] (see Problem 4–39) with an infinitely large signal set. This signaling design (although unrealizable because of the infinitely large signal set) achieves zero error probability for a received $E_b/N_0 \geq -1.6$ dB and an error probability of 0.5 for $E_b/N_0 < -1.6$ dB. Suppose that the mobile is moving at speed 30 km per hour and is using a carrier frequency of 1900 MHz and that the mobile is experiencing Rayleigh fading. What must the average received signal-to-noise ratio $\overline{E_b/N_0}$ be on this link in order to achieve an average link bit error probability of 10^{-3}?

10–20. Reconsider the communications system described in the previous problem and recalculate the required average received signal-to-noise ratio if, instead of Rayleigh fading, the mobile is experiencing Ricean fading with $K_{dB} = +6$.

10–21. A mobile operating at a carrier frequency of 900 MHz is experiencing Rayleigh fading. Calculate the number of fading events per second having instantaneous received power 3, 6, 10, and 20 dB lower than the average received power for vehicle speeds of 10, 30, and 100 km/hr. Calculate the average duration of these fading events.

10–22. Calculate the total received power in the Ricean faded signal defined in (10–48).

10–23. Express the instantaneous envelope $r_R(t)$ and phase $\theta_R(t)$ of the complex envelope $\tilde{r}(t)$ of a sinewave experiencing Ricean fading as a function of P_f, P_0, $n_{f\,I}$, $n_{f\,Q}$, and θ_0.

10–24. Consider a WSSUS multipath channel having three independently fading paths. Suppose that channel output power due to the second path is 3 dB lower than the power due to the first path and that the power due to the third path is 3 dB lower than the power due to the second path. Calculate γ_1, γ_2, and γ_3 of Figure 10–23.

10–25. The impulse response of a bandpass channel is defined by $h(\tau; t) = K \exp(-b\tau)\, u(\tau)$ where $u(\tau)$ is the unit step function. Calculate the equivalent low-pass transfer function, the multipath intensity profile, the average delay spread, and the RMS delay spread as a function of b.

10–26. Table P10-26 defines the multipath profile for three channels denoted A, B, and C. The relative power column of this table defines the power output of the specified WSSUS channel model tap relative to the total output power. (a) Calculate the voltage gains for all taps. (b) Plot the multipath intensity profile for each channel. (c) Calculate the delay spread, the average delay spread, and RMS delay spread for each channel. (d) Calculate the normalized spaced-frequency correlation function for each channel.

TABLE P10-26   Typical Outdoor Residential Multipath Profiles

	Channel A		Channel B		Channel C	
tap	delay (nsec)	relative power dB	delay (nsec)	relative power dB	delay (nsec)	relative power dB
1	0	−10.4	0	−5.4	0	−5.3
2	50	−7.4	250	−5.8	2450	−5.5
3	150	−4.4	1300	−7.7	13000	−4.1
4	500	−11.1	5200	−5.5	22000	−16.8
5	850	−5.6	12000	−26.2	37000	−18.5
6	1325	−20.4				
7	1750	−27.8				

10–27. Consider the two-state channel discussed in Section 10.4.1 whose bit error probability for BPSK signaling is defined by (10–69). Show that for very small ρ the average bit error probability at the plateau of the curves of Figure 10–26 is $\rho/2$.

10–28. Consider once again the two-state channel discussed in Section 10.4.1. Suppose that binary FSK modulation is used with noncoherent detection in the receiver. Calculate the average signal-to-noise ratio required to achieve an average bit error probability of 10^{-5} as a function of the probability ρ that the channel is in its poor state.

10–29. Consider a two-state channel that has gain K_{dB} for 99% of the time and gain $K_{dB} = 10$ dB for 1% of the time. Assume binary FSK signaling with noncoherent detection is used and that the receiver one-sided thermal noise power spectral density is N_o. What average received energy per bit $\overline{E}_b$ must be used to achieve an average received bit error probability of 10^{-6}? Compare this result with the required $\overline{E}_b$ for a single state channel for the same bit error probability.

10–30. Calculate and plot the probability that L independent Rayleigh fading channels will simultaneously experience a fade of 10 dB and 20 dB below their mean values as a function of L.

10–31. Consider the ideal hexagonal cellular system using omnidirectional antennas and a seven cell reuse pattern illustrated in Figure 10–29a. Ignore thermal noise. Calculate the signal-to-interference ratio experienced by a test mobile at the vertex of cell A illustrated in Figure P10-34. Assume that the co-channel interference mobiles in all co-channel reuse cells are located in the same relative vertex as the test mobile and that power control adjusts the received forward link power at all mobiles to the same value. Assume that the path loss exponent is 4. Recalculate the signal-to-interference ratio assuming that the omnidirectional antennas are replaced by ideal 120° sector antennas.

10–32. Calculate the worst case forward link signal-to-interference ratio experienced by an AMPS mobile if a single cell frequency reuse pattern were to be employed with omnidirectional base station antennas. Assume the cellular system consists of only 7 ideal hexagonal cells; ignore shadow fading; assume a path loss exponent of $n = 4$.

10–33. Derive equation (10–89).

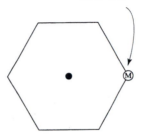

Mobile location in
all co-channel cells

FIGURE P10–34

10–34. Consider the GSM paging channels which utilize the normal burst structure of Figure 10–36. The paging channel uses a concatenated coding scheme consisting of a (224,184) Fire Code and a rate-½ constraint-length-5 convolutional code that is forced to the 0 shift register state after each Fire codeword. What is the maximum information bit rate available for paging for a single GSM carrier?

10–35. Consider the GSM synchronization channels that utilize the S-burst structure of Figure 10–36. The synchronization channel uses a concatenated coding scheme consisting of a (35,25) Cyclic Redundancy Check Code and a rate-½ constraint-length-5 convolutional code that is forced to the 0 shift register state after each CRC codeword. What is the maximum information bit rate available for synchronization for a single GSM carrier?

10–36. Demonstrate that the waveforms of (10–79) are orthogonal to one another and sketch a conceptual block diagram of the receiver that is simultaneously receiving the linear sum of four user signals each assigned a different waveform as defined in (10–79). Is the orthogonality of these waveforms maintained if the users are not time synchronized?

11

Satellite Communications

11.1 INTRODUCTION

The purpose of this chapter is to provide an overview of satellite communications—an area that has gone increasingly digital in recent years. Objectives are to consider link power budgets for typical satellite communications systems, explore possible applications of satellite communications links, and examine implications of various methods of making use of a common frequency resource. It is impossible to do this broad area justice in one chapter. Therefore, rather than a thorough coverage of satellite communications, this chapter merely provides an overview.

The concentration in this chapter is on civil satellite communications as opposed to military satellite communications. The problems and design issues are similar for both, however. Also, the area of deep space communications is not addressed. The reader is referred to reference [1] for an overview and history of this area.

11.1.1 A Brief History of Satellite Communications

Arthur C. Clarke, a British science fiction writer, is generally credited with having suggested the concept of communications by satellite in a stationary orbit in 1945 [2]. During the 1950s the engineering concept was developed further. The launch of *Sputnik I* by the Union of Soviet Socialist Republics in 1957 forced the United States to play catch-up in the space race. The first successful U.S. satellite was Score, launched on December 18, 1958. Score recorded a message sent over the uplink from one earth station and played it back to another earth station when requested [3]. The uplink and downlink frequencies were 150 and 132 MHz, respectively.

Echo I and Echo II, launched by AT&T on August 12, 1960 and January 25, 1961, respectively, were passive reflecting spheres. They had no batteries to run down, but since they acted as radar reflectors with the attendant power loss proportional to the fourth power of the path length, earth station power and antenna requirements were severe [3].

The Bell system launched the first successful broadband transponder satellites, known as Telstar I and Telstar II, in July 1962 and May 1963, respectively. They utilized an uplink frequency of 6389.58 MHz and a downlink frequency of 4169.72 MHz with a bandwidth of 50 MHz that could accommodate FM-modulated signals. The 6/4 GHz bands were thereby standardized for use by communications satellites for several years until the scarcity of spectrum in these bands forced the move to higher frequencies. Since the orbital periods of the Telstar I and II satellites were 158 and 225 minutes, respectively, access by a given earth station was limited to a fraction of the orbit, and antenna tracking of the satellite was necessary [3]. Telstar I lasted only a few weeks due to radiation damage from the newly discovered Van Allen radiation belts [4].

The Syncom satellite series provided the first successful 24-hour-period equatorial orbits (known as geostationary), and therefore 24-hour access from a given ground station was possible. Syncom I failed to be successfully injected into synchronous orbit; Syncom II and Syncom III were successfully launched by NASA in July 1963 and August 1964, respectively. The successful launch of these satellites proved the feasibility of the geostationary orbit concept.

The Communications Satellite Act of 1962 led to the establishment of the Communications Satellite Corporation in 1963 and provided the environment for the establishment of Intelsat in July 1964, an organization that now has well over 100 member nations. Intelsat's purpose was to design, develop, construct, establish, and maintain the operation of the space segment of a global commercial communications satellite system [4]. This led to a series of Intelsat satellites, the first known as Early Bird (Intelsat I), launched in April 1965 and decommissioned in January 1969. At this time full coverage of both the Atlantic and Pacific oceans was provided by two series of satellites—Intelsats II and III. Intelsat II provided 240 full duplex (or 480 half) telephone circuits and one television channel between the United States and Europe (only two simultaneous "accesses" were possible due to transponder nonlinearities). This grew to 1200 circuits in Intelsat III and 6000 circuits in Intelsat IV-A, which was launched in January 1970. Intelsat IV was the first communications satellite to be limited by bandwidth (500 MHz) rather than by power. With the launch of Intelsat V, a new stabilization concept, known as three-axis stabilization, was used. Previous Intelsat satellites were spin-stabilized (these terms will be enlarged upon shortly). Intelsat V (12,500 full duplex circuits) provided the first international use of time-division multiple access (TDMA), and Intelsat VI (40,000 circuits) provided the first international use of satellite-switched TDMA, both to be discussed later in this chapter. Intelsat VII, launched in 1992, provides another example of a capacity increasing scheme—frequency reuse by spatial and polarization separation. Its C-band spectrum (5.925–6.425 GHz up and 3.7–4.2 GHz down) is multiplied to an effective 1.5 GHz of bandwidth through fourfold spectrum reuse, and its Ku-band spectrum of 500 MHz is multiplied to about 900 MHz through twofold spectrum reuse [5]. Intelsat VII utilizes solid-state power amplifiers at C band as opposed to the more common traveling-wave tube amplifiers to provide a more nearly linear transponder and thereby mitigate intermodulation products.

The Intelsat system is known as a global civil telecommunications satellite system. Another global civil telecommunications satellite system is the USSR's Intersputnik, which utilizes satellites in 12-hour, highly elliptical orbits at 63.4-degree inclinations. Such orbits are able to more effectively provide access to the Russia's landmass than geosynchronous orbits. Other types of satellite systems are regional and domestic systems.

11.1.2 Basic Concepts and Terminology

An accessing technique used in the first satellites, known as single channel per carrier (SCPC), modulated a single message on a carrier transmitted to the satellite, whereupon the satellite translated it to another frequency and rebroadcast it after power amplification. Later satellites accepted a band of messages frequency-division multiplexed together and placed on a single carrier, frequency translated this band, and rebroadcast it after power amplification. Such satellites use a technique known as frequency-division multiple access (FDMA), to be described in more detail later, for sharing their frequency resources among several users. Since the carrier modulation often employed is FM, the overall modulation technique is denoted as FDM/FM/FDMA. The frequency translation is necessary to prevent ring-around from the transmitting antenna to the receiving antenna and thence through the satellite communications system again. Later satellite systems used time-division multiplexing to place several users on one carrier, digital modulation of some sort (quite often QPSK or OQPSK), and sharing of the satellite frequency resource through TDMA.

Another type of satellite communication system, which is referred to later in the chapter as a demod/remod system (also called regenerative), demodulates and detects the data, processes it, and remodulates the transmitted carrier for retransmission to the ground. This scheme is particularly appropriate for digital data and digitized analog signals, which can be temporarily stored, switched to other beams, and retransmitted. Indeed, this is the concept used for modern communications satellites, which typically have several receiving, and several transmitting antennas, some of which may be switched between several spot beams. The NASA Advanced Communications Technology Satellite (ACTS) is an example of a multibeam satellite that includes on-board data storage and switching [6]. ACTS includes a baseband processor mode as well as a radio frequency (RF) switch mode for switching data between beams without demodulation and subsequent remodulation.

Several low and medium earth-orbit voice messaging satellite systems have been proposed (their characteristics are summarized in Section 11.5). In May 1998, the first five of a series of 66 IRIDIUM™ satellites, an idea originated by Motorola, Inc., were launched with completion of all 66 by fall 1998. The details of the constellation and communication system are summarized in Section 11.5. The IRIDIUM constellation enables voice and paging communications from any point on the earth's surface (or 100 nmi up) to any other point using hand-held units operating in the 1.5–1.6 GHz frequency range. Since it was the first of several proposed such systems to be launched, it is singled out for mention.

In addition to the communications relay system on board a satellite, other communications systems include ranging (to provide a range measurement to the satellite), command (to receive commands from an earth station to control the satellite), and telemetry (to relay data about the satellite's condition back to the earth). A separate beacon, utilizing an antenna separate from the communications antenna, is often used for telemetry, command, and ranging. A simplified block diagram showing these various communication systems onboard a satellite is given in Figure 11–1. Early satellite transmissions took place in the UHF, L, and C bands, where these letter designations are specified in Table

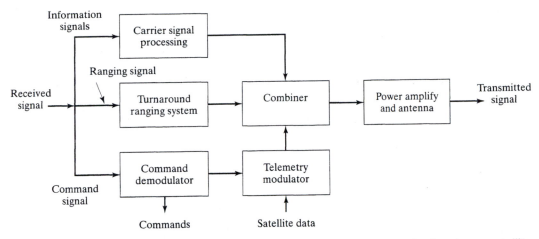

FIGURE 11-1 Illustration of the various communications systems that may be found on a satellite.

11-1. Because of the subsequent crowding of these bands, additional bands were utilized (S, X, and K bands). As mentioned, Intelsat VII uses C and Ku bands. Intelsat VII's frequency plan is shown in Figure 11-2. Transponder bandwidth allocations are 36 MHz in most instances. Military satellites typically utilize transmission bandwidths of 5, 25, 40, and 50 MHz.

Satellite communications services can be classified as fixed point (between a satellite and fixed ground station), broadcast, and mobile (e.g., communications to aircraft, ships, land vehicles, or persons). Intersatellite communications refers to communications between satellites. Both commercial and military satellite communications applications find widespread use. Military satellite systems include the Global Positioning System (or GPS) and message transmission systems such as the MILSTAR and DSCS satellites. GPS also is used extensively for civilian applications.

Early satellites were spin-stabilized, which means that the satellites were physically spun about an axis; this kept them oriented in a particular relationship to the earth due to

TABLE 11-1 Frequency Band Designations

Band Designation	Frequency (GHz)
VHF	0.3–3
L	1–2
S	2–4
C	4–8
X	8–12.4
Ku	12.4–18
K	18–26.5
Ka	26.5–40

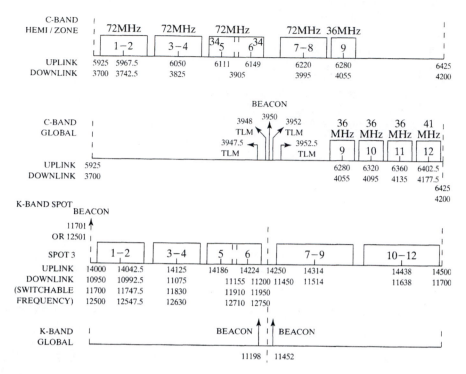

FIGURE 11-2 Frequency plan for Intelsat VII (TLM stands for telemetry). (Reproduced from Reference [5] with permission.)

the gyroscopic effect. Stabilization is necessary in order to keep the antennas and solar cells pointed in the proper directions. Because of the difficulty in despinning complex antenna systems, present-day satellites are almost all three-axis stabilized. This means that a three-axis gyroscope system is used onboard to sense deviations from the desired orientation. Control signals generated from the gyroscopic sensors are used to turn thruster jets on and off in order to maintain the desired satellite orientation. Another important control function for geosynchronous satellites is station keeping. Due to the gravitational attraction of the moon (and to a minor extent the sun) and oblateness of the earth, a geosynchronous satellite will trace out a figure-eight pattern about its subsatellite point on the equator, requiring periodic corrections to keep this motion within bounds.

11.1.3 Orbital Relationships

Figure 11-3 depicts a general satellite orbit along with associated terminology. The inclination is the angle that the plane of the satellite's orbit makes with the equatorial plane. An orbit inclined at 90 degrees is known as a polar orbit, whereas an orbit inclined at 0 degrees is referred to as an equatorial orbit. For a circular orbit of altitude h above the earth's surface, a satellite must achieve an orbital speed of [3]

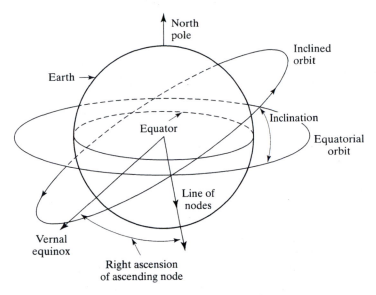

FIGURE 11–3   General orbital definitions.

$$v_s = \sqrt{\frac{g_0}{r_e + h}} \tag{11-1}$$

where $g_o = 1.4 \times 10^{16}$ ft^3/s^2 is the gravitational coefficient and r_e is the earth's radius, which is 6378 km or 3963 statute miles. The orbital period, t_s, satisfies the relationship $\dot{\theta}_s t_s = 2\pi$ radians, where $\dot{\theta}_s$ is the angular velocity in radians per second. Since $v_s = (r_e + h)\dot{\theta}_s$, it follows that

$$t_s = \frac{2\pi(r_e + h)^{3/2}}{\sqrt{g_o}} \text{ seconds}$$

$$= \frac{\pi}{1800} \frac{(r_e + h)^{3/2}}{\sqrt{g_0}} \text{ hours} \tag{11-2}$$

EXAMPLE 11–1 _____

If a satellite is in an equatorial orbit and $t_s = 24$ h, it will appear stationary over a fixed point on the earth's surface. Such a satellite is referred to as synchronous or geostationary. Setting the left side of (11–2) equal to 24 hours and substituting the values of g_o and r_e, the synchronous altitude is found to be*

$$h_{\text{sync}} = 22{,}235 \text{ stat mi}$$

$$= 35{,}784 \text{ km} \tag{11-3}$$

*Hereafter "statute miles" will simply be referred to as "miles."

Thus, the minimum round-trip time for an electromagnetic wave to propagate to the satellite and back again is

$$\tau = \frac{2 \times 35{,}784{,}000 \text{ m}}{3 \times 10^8 \text{ m/s}} = 0.239 \text{ s} \tag{11-4}$$

This delay has important implications for satellite communications. For example, the delay is noticeable on a trans-Atlantic telephone call when one person is speaking and pauses in anticipation of an answer from the other person.

Simple geometry can be used to show that the slant range between an equatorial-orbit satellite and a ground station is

$$R = \sqrt{h^2 + 2r_e(h + r_e)(1 - \cos \phi \cos \theta_l)} \tag{11-5}$$

where

h = altitude of the satellite

r_e = equatorial radius of the earth (6378 km)

θ_ℓ = longitude of the earth station relative to the subsatellite point

ϕ = latitude of the earth station

The angle of elevation (i.e., the angle between the tangent plane to the earth at the earth station and the line connecting the location points of the earth station and the satellite) is given by

$$\theta = \cos^{-1}\left(\frac{r_e + h}{R} \sqrt{1 - \cos^2 \phi \cos^2 \theta_\ell}\right) \tag{11-6}$$

The derivation of these relationships is left to the problems. The calculation of the azimuth angle to the satellite relative to the earth station is more complex and will not be given here [3].

11.1.4 Antenna Coverage

Coverage of the earth by an antenna mounted on a satellite can be hemispherical, continental, or zonal, depending on the antenna design. Antenna designs are now possible that cover several zones or spots simultaneously on the earth's surface. Such designs allow *frequency reuse* in that the same band of frequencies can be reused in separate beams, which effectively multiplies the bandwidth of the satellite transponder available for communications by the reuse factor. As pointed out in Section 1.4.2, the maximum gain for a circular aperture antenna of diameter d and aperture efficiency ρ can be calculated from

$$G_o = \rho \left(\frac{\pi d}{\lambda}\right)^2 \tag{11-7}$$

where λ is the wavelength of the radiated signal. The half-power beamwidth in radians can be approximated as

$$\phi_{3dB} = \frac{\lambda}{d\sqrt{\rho}} \tag{11-8}$$

A convenient approximation for the antenna pattern of a parabolic reflector antenna for small angles off boresight (such that the gain is within 6 dB of the maximum value) is

$$G(\phi) = \rho \left(\frac{\pi d}{\lambda} \right)^2 \exp\left[-2.76 \left(\frac{\phi}{\phi_{3dB}} \right)^2 \right] \tag{11-9}$$

EXAMPLE 11–2

Find the aperture diameter and maximum gain for a transmit frequency of 6 GHz and $\rho = 0.65$ if, from geosynchronous altitude, the following coverages are desired: (a) hemispherical; (b) a 150 mi diameter spot.

Solution: The wavelength at 6 GHz is

$$\lambda = \frac{3 \times 10^8 \text{ m/s}}{6 \times 10^9 \text{ Hz}} = 0.05 \text{ m} = 0.164 \text{ ft} \tag{11-10}$$

(a)   Geosynchronous altitude is 22,235 stat mi, and the earth's radius is 3963 mi. The angle subtended by the earth from geosynchronous altitude is approximately

$$\phi_{\text{hemis}} = \frac{2(3963)}{(22,235 + 3963)} = 0.303 \text{ rad} \tag{11-11}$$

Equating this to ϕ_{3dB} in (11–8) and solving for d, we have

$$d = \frac{0.164}{(0.303)\sqrt{0.65}} = 0.671 \text{ ft} \tag{11-12}$$

(b)   A 150 mi diameter spot on the earth's surface directly below the satellite subtends an angle of approximately

$$\phi_{150} = \frac{150}{22,235} = 6.7 \times 10^{-3} \text{ rad} \tag{11-13}$$

from geosynchronous orbit. The diameter of an antenna with this beamwidth is

$$d = \frac{0.164}{(6.7 \times 10^{-3})\sqrt{0.65}} = 30.2 \text{ ft} \tag{11-14}$$

Note that doubling the frequency to 12 GHz would halve these diameters.

11.2   ALLOCATION OF A SATELLITE TRANSMISSION RESOURCE

There are three basic methods whereby a satellite communications resource can be allocated to different users. These are (1) in frequency, using frequency-division multiple access; (2) in time, using time-division multiple access; and (3) assigning different codes to each user for spread-spectrum modulating their signals or code-division multiple access

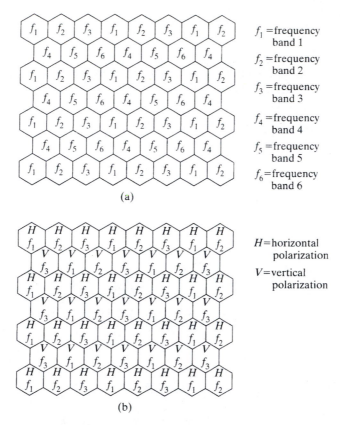

FIGURE 11–4 Frequency reuse plans for (a) single polarization antenna patterns; (b) two perpendicular (or counterrotating) polarizations.

(CDMA). Each of these methods will be described further in this section. In addition, a communications satellite can direct spot beams to different geographical locations, which allows the same band of frequencies to be reused in different spot beams. This is called frequency reuse by spatial separation. By using separate antenna polarizations, the frequency reuse factor can be doubled. Typical frequency reuse patterns are shown in Figure 11–4 for the case of a single polarization and for dual polarizations. In Figure 11–4a, for example, the same frequency band can be reused every sixth spot on the ground. The footprints of the antenna patterns on the ground are shown as hexagonal for simplicity, even though they are really circular or ellipsoidal.

11.2.1 FDMA

Figure 11–5 illustrates the idea of frequency-division multiple access (FDMA). In FDMA, signals from various users are stacked up in frequency, just as for frequency-division multiplexing. Guard bands are maintained between adjacent signal spectra to

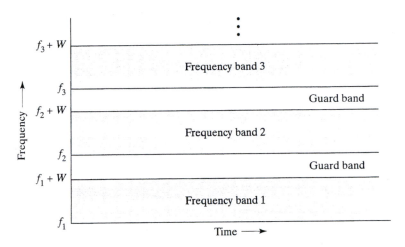

FIGURE 11–5   Scheme for dividing the communications resource by FDMA.

minimize crosstalk between channels, with a reasonable percentage of total bandwidth allowed for guard bands being 10%. The characterization of crosstalk, or adjacent channel interference, will be discussed later.

A problem with FDMA systems is intermodulation interference. This results when two or more modulated signals pass through a nonlinearity (the final power amplifier in this case) and frequency sums of the form $2f_1 - f_2$ in the case of two signals or $f_1 + f_2 - f_3$ in the case of three signals, and so on, are generated. Since f_1, f_2, and f_3 are nearly equal (within 30 MHz out of 5 GHz or more, say), these sum frequencies fall back into the transponder passband.[1] Transponder final power amplifiers may be operating in a nonlinear mode because typical amplifiers are more efficient if driven into saturation. A typical power-out versus power-in curve for a traveling-wave tube amplifier (TWTA) is shown in Figure 11–6. Characterizing the intermodulation levels for a general nonlinear amplifier is a complex problem and is beyond the scope of this book. For analytical approaches to this problem, the reader is referred to References [7, 8]. Modulation techniques that convey the information in the carrier relative phase are used for situations where transponders operate in a highly nonlinear mode. For analog transmission, FM is typically employed, while, for digital data transmission, BPSK, MSK, QPSK, and OQPSK are candidate modulation methods.

If frequency slots are assigned permanently to the users, the system is referred to as fixed assigned multiple access (FAMA). If some type of dynamic allocation scheme is used to assign frequency slots, it is referred to as a demand assigned multiple-access (DAMA) system. A DAMA system assumes that there is an auxiliary channel available to request and make the dynamic resource assignment.

---

[1]See Chapter 2.

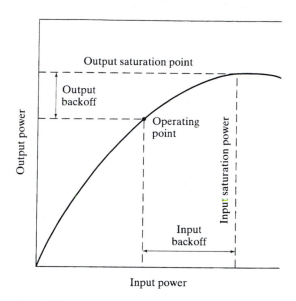

FIGURE 11–6   Typical input–output power relationship for a nonlinear repeater.

11.2.2   TDMA

In a TDMA system, the messages from various users are interlaced in time intervals called frames, as illustrated in Figure 11–7a. This is similar to time-division multiplexing. As shown in Figure 11–7b, the data from each user is conveyed in time intervals called slots. A number of slots make up a frame. Each slot is made up of a preamble plus information bits addressed to various stations as illustrated in Figure 11–7b. The functions of the preamble are to provide identification and incidental information and to allow syn-

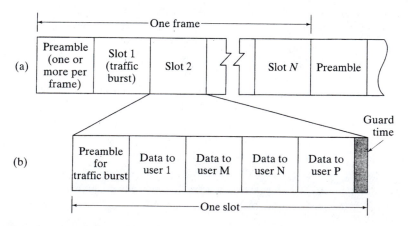

FIGURE 11–7   Scheme for dividing the communications resource by TDMA. (a) Typical layout for a frame; (b) typical layout for a slot or traffic burst.

chronization of the slot at the intended receiver. Guard times are utilized between each user's transmission to minimize crosstalk between channels.

To consider the efficiency of a TDMA system, refer to Figure 11–7b. The number of overhead bits per frame is

$$b_{OH} = N_{RB}b_{RB} + N_{TB}b_{PATB} + (N_{TB} + N_{RB})b_{GT} \qquad (11\text{--}15)$$

where

N_{RB} = number of preambles per frame (more than one may be used for redundancy)

N_{TB} = number of traffic bursts (slots) per frame

b_{RB} = number of overhead bits per reference burst

b_{PATB} = number of overhead bits per preamble in each slot

b_{GT} = number of equivalent bits in each guard time interval

The total number of bits per frame is

$$b_{TOT} = T_F R_{RF} \text{ bits} \qquad (11\text{--}16)$$

where

T_F = frame time

R_{RF} = bit rate of the radio-frequency channel

The *frame efficiency* (i.e., the percentage of bits per frame devoted to data transmission) is

$$\eta = \left(1 - \frac{b_{OH}}{b_{TOT}}\right) \times 100\% \qquad (11\text{--}17)$$

It is desirable to keep the efficiency above 90%. The number of bits per data channel (user) per frame is

$$b_{ch} = R_{ch}T_F \qquad (11\text{--}18)$$

where R_{ch} is the bit rate of each channel. Finally, the number of channels that can be accommodated per frame is

$$N_{ch/fr} = \frac{\text{total data bits/frame}}{\text{bits per channel/frame}}$$

$$= \frac{\eta R_{RF}T_F}{R_{ch}T_F} \qquad (11\text{--}19)$$

$$= \eta R_{RF}/R_{ch}$$

EXAMPLE 11–3 _____

Consider a TDMA system with the following parameters:

$$N_{RB} = 1$$

$$N_{TB} = 10$$

$$b_{RB} = 1000 \text{ bits}$$

$$b_{PATB} = 700 \text{ bits}$$

$$b_{GT} = 64 \text{ bits}$$

$$T_F = 5 \text{ milliseconds}$$

$$R_{RF} = 45 \text{ Mbps}$$

$$R_{ch} = 64 \text{ kbps}$$

From (11–15) the total number of overhead bits per frame is found to be

$$b_{OH} = 1000 + 10(800) + (10 + 1)64 = 9704 \text{ bits}$$

From (11–16), the total number of bits per frame is

$$b_{TOT} = (5 \times 10^{-3})(45 \times 10^{6}) = 2.25 \times 10^{5} \text{ bits}$$

Therefore, from (11–17), the efficiency is

$$\eta = \left(1 - \frac{9704}{2.25 \times 10^{5}}\right) \times 100 = 95.69\%$$

From (11–19), the number of channels per frame is

$$N_{ch/fr} = 0.9569 \frac{45 \times 10^{6}}{64 \times 10^{3}} = 672.8$$

Since it is impossible to have a fraction of a channel, the number of channels per frame is actually 672. Recalling that is was assumed that there are 10 slots per frame, this would be reduced to 670 for 67 channels per slot. A few iterations would be necessary to get the efficiency optimized for a certain number of channels per slot.

A question might arise as to how the distribution of overhead bits comes about in a typical situation. The following is a hypothetical allocation for these bits:

Reference burst
    Carrier and clock recovery   = 352 bits
    Unique word   = 32 bits
    Orderwire channel   = 392 bits
    Management channel   = 200 bits
    Service channel   = 24 bits
        Total for reference burst   = 1000 bits
Slot preamble
    Carrier and clock recovery   = 252 bits
    Unique word   = 32 bits
    Order wire channel   = 392 bits
    Service channel   = 24 bits
        Total for each slot preamble   = 700 bits

A brief explanation of these terms is in order. Carrier, clock, and unique word re-covery have been discussed in Section 3.6. They provide a means for synchronizing the carrier, symbol stream, and frames of the transmission. The *order wire channel* provides a means for passing instructions to and from earth stations. The *management channel* pro-vides a means for the control stations to pass management information, such as burst time plan changes, to all earth stations. The *service channel* provides a means for each earth station to send status information back to the control station [9]. Not all of these are nec-essarily employed in all frame plans. Synchronization, for example, might be done only on the reference burst preamble.

It is necessary to maintain overall network time synchronization in TDMA, unlike FDMA, since each transmitted traffic burst must arrive at the satellite in its preassigned time slot. The derivation and maintenance of this synchronization is a fairly complex problem and will not be dealt with here. However, intermodulation products are not a problem with TDMA. If, in a TDMA system, the time slots that make up each frame are preassigned to specific sources, it is referred to as FAMA; if time slots are not preas-signed, but are assigned on a dynamic basis, the technique is referred to as DAMA. DAMA schemes require some kind of network controller and a separate low-information-rate channel between each user and the controller to carry out the assignments. A DAMA TDMA system is more efficient in the face of bursty traffic than a FAMA system.

11.2.3 CDMA

In CDMA, each user is assigned a code that has minimum correlation with the codes as-signed to other users, and the transmissions of a desired user are separated from those of all other users at a given receiving site through correlation with a locally generated replica of the desired user's code. In a sense, therefore, each CDMA user utilizes the entire time-frequency plane. Two ways that the messages can be modulated with the code for a given user is through direct-sequence spread spectrum (DSSS) or frequency-hop spread spec-trum (FHSS) (see Chapter 9). The concept of CDMA using FHSS is illustrated in Figure 11–8. Although CDMA schemes can be operated with network synchronization, it is ob-viously more difficult to do this than to operate the system asynchronously. When oper-ated asynchronously, one must account for multiple-access noise, which is a manifestation of the partial correlation of a desired user's code with all other users' codes present on the system. Figure 11–9 shows probability of bit error for DSSS multiple ac-cess versus E_b/N_0 with the number of users as a parameter for the case of 511-chip Gold codes (see Chapter 9 for the definition of Gold codes).

11.3 LINK POWER BUDGET ANALYSIS

As explained in the introduction, two approaches can be taken to designing a satellite transponder. One is simply to have it accept a band of users, frequency translate this band, and redirect it to a ground station. This will be referred to as a bent-pipe relay (also called

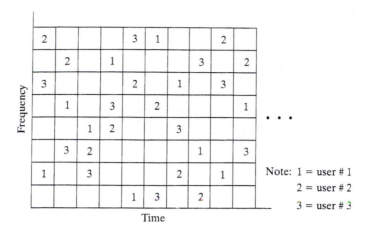

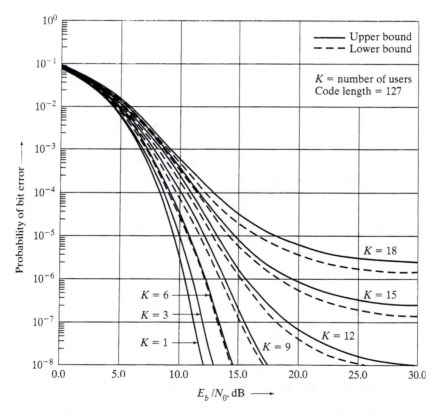

FIGURE 11–8   Illustration of the time-frequency plane for CDMA using FHSS.

FIGURE 11–9   Bit error probability versus E_b/N_0 for CDMA using DSSS with the number of users as a parameter [10]. Gold codes assumed.

nonregenerative). A second approach is to demodulate the data, redirect it to other down-link beams after perhaps temporary storage, remodulate it, and retransmit it. This will be referred to as a demod/remod, or regenerative, transponder. These two types of transponders are analyzed in this section in terms of their bit error probability characteristics. The analysis procedure follows that of Reference [11].

11.3.1 Bent-Pipe Relay

In Chapter 1, a single one-way link budget was considered for a free space propagation path. Consider now the situation depicted in Figure 11–10. A signal from a ground station is transmitted to a satellite that frequency translates it and retransmits it to the ground. Such a relay will be referred to as a "bent-pipe relay" in analogy to a bent water pipe that simply redirects the water going through it. The uplink signal is received at the satellite with power P_{us}, where the subscript "u" stands for "uplink." Noise referred to the satellite input has power P_{un}. The sum of the signal and noise is amplified by the satellite repeater to give transmitted power from the satellite of

$$P_T = G(P_{us} + P_{un}) \tag{11-20}$$

where G is the gain of the satellite repeater. The received signal power from the satellite at the receiving ground station is

$$P_{rs} = GP_{us}G_{tot} \tag{11-21}$$

where G_{tot} represents total system losses and gains on the downlink. It can be expressed as

$$G_{tot} = \frac{G_t G_r}{L_a L_p} \tag{11-22}$$

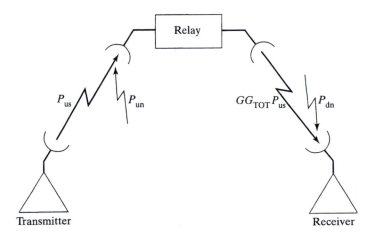

FIGURE 11–10 Definitions for computing carrier-to-noise ratio in a bent-pipe relay link. (P_{dn} includes both antenna and receive front end noise.)

where

G_t = gain of the satellite transmitter antenna

L_a = atmospheric and rain losses on the downlink

L_p = propagation or free-space loss on the downlink

G_r = gain of the ground station receive antenna

The uplink noise power transmitted by the satellite repeater and appearing at the ground station input is

$$P_{ru} = GP_{un}G_{tot} \qquad (11\text{--}23)$$

Additional noise generated by the ground station itself is added to this noise at the ground station. The ratio of P_{rs} to total noise is the received carrier-to-noise power ratio, including noise on both ground station and transponder noise contributions. It is given by

$$(\text{CNR})_r = \frac{P_{rs}}{P_{ru} + P_{dn}} \qquad (11\text{--}24)$$

Substituting previously derived expressions for each of the powers appearing on the right side of (11–24), we obtain

$$
\begin{aligned}
(\text{CNR})_r &= \frac{GG_{tot}P_{us}}{GP_{un}G_{tot} + P_{dn}} \\
&= \frac{1}{(P_{un}/P_{us}) + (P_{dn}/GG_{tot}P_{us})} \qquad (11\text{--}25) \\
&= \frac{1}{(\text{CNR})_u^{-1} + (\text{CNR})_d^{-1}}
\end{aligned}
$$

where

$(\text{CNR})_u = P_{us}/P_{un}$ = carrier-to-noise power ratio on the uplink

$(\text{CNR})_d = (GG_{tot}P_{us})/(P_{dn})$ = carrier-to-noise power ratio on the downlink

Note that the weakest of the two CNRs affects the overall carrier-to-noise power ratio the most. The overall carrier-to-noise power ratio cannot be better than the worst of two carrier-to-noise ratios that make it up. To obtain $(\text{CNR})_u$ and $(\text{CNR})_d$, we use the link power budget equations developed in Section 1.4.2.

To relate carrier-to-noise ratio to E_b/N_0 in order to calculate the error probability, we note that

$$\text{CNR} = \frac{P_c}{N_0 B_{RF}} \qquad (11\text{--}26)$$

where

P_c = average carrier power

N_0 = noise power spectral density

B_{RF} = modulated signal (radio-frequency) bandwidth

Multiplying numerator and denominator by the bit duration, T_b, we note that $P_c T_b = E_b$ is the bit energy and obtain

$$\text{CNR} = \frac{E_b}{N_0 B_{\text{RF}} T_b} \tag{11-27}$$

or, solving for E_b/N_0,

$$\frac{E_b}{N_0} = (\text{CNR}) B_{\text{RF}} T_b \tag{11-28}$$

Given a modulation scheme, we can use a suitable bandwidth criterion to determine $B_{\text{RF}} T_b$. For example, using the null-to-null bandwidth for BPSK as B_{RF}, we have $B_{\text{RF}} = 2/T_b$ or $T_b B_{\text{RF}} = 2$.

Because the CNR is related to E_b/N_0 by the constant $B_{\text{RF}} T_b$, we can write (11–25) as

$$\left(\frac{E_b}{N_0} \right)_r = \frac{1}{(E_b/N_0)_u^{-1} + (E_b/N_0)_d^{-1}} \tag{11-29}$$

where

$(E_b/N_0)_u$ = bit-energy-to-noise spectral density ratio on the uplink

$(E_b/N_0)_d$ = bit-energy-to-noise-spectral-density ratio on the downlink

EXAMPLE 11–4

Compute the relationship between $(E_b/N_0)_u$ and $(E_b/N_0)_d$ to yield a bit error probability of $P_b = 10^{-6}$ on a bent-pipe satellite relay communications link if BPSK modulation is used.

Solution: For BPSK, $(E_b/N_0)_r \simeq 10.54$ dB gives $P_b = 10^{-6}$. Thus, (11–29) becomes

$$\frac{1}{(E_b/N_0)_u^{-1} + (E_b/N_0)_d^{-1}} = 10^{1.054} \simeq 11.324 \tag{11-30}$$

This can be solved for $(E_b/N_0)_u$, say, and a table of values computed or a curve plotted. A curve is shown in Figure 11–11.

Note that the received E_b/N_0 is never better than the uplink or downlink values of E_b/N_0. For $(E_b/N_0)_u = (E_b/N_0)_d \simeq 13.55$ dB, the value of $(E_b/N_0)_r$ is 10.54. Note that as either $(E_b/N_0)_u$ or $(E_b/N_0)_d$ approaches infinity, the other energy-to-noise spectral density ratio approaches 10.54 dB.

11.3.2 Demod/Remod (Regenerative) Digital Transponder

Consider a satellite relay link where the modulation is digital and detection takes place on board the satellite with subsequent remodulation of the detected bits on the downlink carrier and subsequent demodulation and detection at the receiving ground station. This situation can be illustrated in terms of bit errors as shown in Figure 11–12.

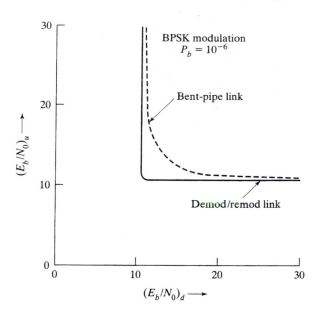

FIGURE 11-11 Trade-off between E_b/N_0 on the uplink and downlink for bent pipe and demod/remod relay links.

The channel is considered symmetrical in that errors for 1s and 0s are equally likely. It is also assumed that errors on the downlink are statistically independent of errors on the uplink, and vice versa. From Figure 11–12, it follows that the overall probability of no error given a 1 is transmitted is

$$P(C \mid 1) = q_u q_d + p_u p_d \qquad (11\text{--}31)$$

where

$q_u = 1 - p_u$ is the probability of no error on the uplink

$q_d = 1 - p_d$ is the probability of no error on the downlink

A similar expression holds for the probability of correct transmission through the channel given a 0 is transmitted, and it therefore follows that the probability of correct reception averaged over both 1s and 0s is

$$P(C) = P(C \mid 1) = P(C \mid 0) \qquad (11\text{--}32)$$

The average probability of bit error is

$$
\begin{aligned}
P_b &= 1 - P(C) \\
&= 1 - (q_u q_d + p_u p_d) \\
&= 1 - (1 - p_u)(1 - p_d) - p_u p_d \\
&= p_u + p_d - 2 p_u p_d
\end{aligned}
\qquad (11\text{--}33)
$$

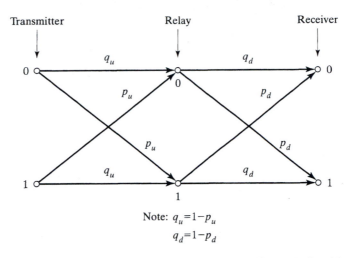

FIGURE 11–12   Uplink and downlink bit error probability relationships for a demod/remod relay link.

The following example illustrates how to calculate the uplink and downlink signal energy-to-noise-spectral-density ratios to give an overall desired P_b for a given modulation technique.

EXAMPLE 11–5 _____

Consider a demod/remod satellite communications link where BPSK is used on the uplink and the downlink. For this modulation technique

$$p_u = Q(\sqrt{2(E_b/N_0)_u}) \simeq \frac{e^{-(E_b/N_0)_u}}{2\sqrt{\pi(E_b/N_0)_u}}, \quad (E_b/N_0)_u \gtrsim 3 \qquad (11\text{--}34)$$

with a similar expression for p_d. Say we want the error probability for the overall link to be 10^{-6}. Thus, from (11–33), we have

$$10^{-6} = p_u + p_d - 2p_u p_d \qquad (11\text{--}35)$$

Solving for p_d in terms of p_u, we have

$$p_d = \frac{10^{-6} - p_u}{1 - 2p_u} \qquad (11\text{--}36)$$

A table of values of p_d can be made up versus values of p_u. The corresponding required values of $(E_b/N_0)_u$ can then be calculated from (11–34), and $(E_b/N_0)_d$ can be calculated from its counterpart for p_d.

Figure 11–11 shows $(E_b/N_0)_u$ versus $(E_b/N_0)_d$ for both the bent-pipe and demod/remod satellite relays for an overall bit error probability of 10^{-6}. Curves for other values of bit error probability for other digital modulation schemes can be obtained in a similar manner.

11.3.3   Adjacent Channel Interference

If two signals are adjacent to each other in frequency, they may interfere with one another. Let $S_{adj}(f)$ be the baseband-equivalent power spectrum of the interfering signal and assume that the desired channel is represented by a filter with frequency response $H(f)$. Then, if Δf is the spacing between channels, the interference power produced in the channel of interest by a signal in the adjacent channel is

$$P_{adj} = \int_{-\infty}^{\infty} S_{adj}(f)|H(f)|^2 \, df \tag{11-37}$$

Performing an analysis similar to the one to get $(CNR)_r$ for the bent-pipe relay, one can find the effect of adjacent channel interference on the received carrier-to-noise ratio to be

$$(CNR)_r' = \frac{1}{(CNR)_r^{-1} + (CNR)_{adj}^{-1}} \tag{11-38}$$

where

$(CNR)_r'$ = received carrier-to-noise ratio including adjacent channel interference plus thermal noise

$(CNR)_r$ = received carrier-to-interference ratio found according to (11-26)

$(CNR)_{adj}$ = carrier-to-interference ratio due to adjacent channel interference

Usually, careful spectral shaping and channel filtering will make adjacent channel interference negligible. If intermodulation interference is also present, as it could be in an FDMA system, the carrier-to-noise ratio corresponding to it would be added in (11-38) as an inverse.

A note of caution is in order: If the carrier-to-noise ratio is used to find an equivalent E_b/N_0 and this is used to find a bit error probability, we have in effect modeled the adjacent channel interference as Gaussian noise. This is a rough approximation, and accurate system characterization should rely on more careful analysis or simulation. Note that adjacent channel interference can arise in both FDMA and TDMA systems. This is obvious for FDMA, but for TDMA it will happen because transponder bands are stacked next to each other as illustrated by Figure 11-2.

EXAMPLE 11-6

Consider the calculation of adjacent channel interference for adjacent BPSK channels where the channel filtering is done with an nth-order Butterworth filter. Thus, the power spectrum of the adjacent channel signal is taken as

$$S_{adj}(f) = \tfrac{1}{2}P_c T_b \operatorname{sinc}^2[T_b(f - f_0 - \Delta f)]$$
$$+ \tfrac{1}{2}P_c T_b \operatorname{sinc}^2[T_b(f + f_0 + \Delta f)] \tag{11-39}$$

where

P_c = power of the adjacent channel signal
$T_b = 1/R_b$ = bit period of the adjacent channel signal
f_0 = carrier frequency of the desired channel signal
Δf = frequency separation between the desired and adjacent channels

The amplitude-squared response of a bandpass Butterworth filter can be approximated as

$$|H(f)|^2 = \frac{1}{1 + [(f - f_0)/f_3]^{2n}} + \frac{1}{1 + [(f + f_0)/f_3]^{2n}} \tag{11-40}$$

where f_3 is the 3 dB cutoff frequency of the channel filter and the cross term from taking the magnitude squared is assumed negligible due to the filter being narrowband. From (11–38), the ratio of power from the adjacent channel through the desired channel filter normalized by P_c (if all channels contain equal power, this is the carrier-to-adjacent-channel interference ratio) is the sum of four integrals [obtained from the product of (11–39) and (11–40)]. However, the cross terms are negligible because the channel filter is narrowband. Furthermore, the remaining two integrals are equal so that

$$\frac{P_{adj}}{P_c} = T_b \int_0^\infty \frac{\text{sinc}^2[T_b(f - f_0 - \Delta f)]}{1 + [(f - f_0)/f_3]^{2n}} \, df \tag{11-41}$$

where n is the filter order. This must be numerically integrated. It is easier to do so by making the substitution $u = T_b(f - f_0)$. The resulting integral is

$$\frac{P_{adj}}{P_c} = \int_0^\infty \frac{\text{sinc}^2(u - \Delta f/R_b)}{1 + [R_b u/f_3]^{2n}} \, du \tag{11-42}$$

If equal-power adjacent channels are present on both sides of the desired channel, this integral would be doubled. A plot of the carrier-to-adjacent-channel interference ratio is shown in Figure 11–13 for various channel separations normalized by the bit rate as a function of the number of filter poles.

11.3.4 Adjacent Satellite Interference

Another type of interference similar to adjacent channel interference is adjacent satellite interference. Satellites may be especially close in the geostationary orbit (say, within 1.5 degrees). Thus, a given earth station may intercept radiation from more than one satellite. Figure 11–14 illustrates this situation for two satellites—one at which the earth antenna is pointed and one located at an angle $\Delta\theta$ from the antenna beam center (referred to as boresight). We can find the ratio of powers from the two satellites at the earth station by using (1-26). It is

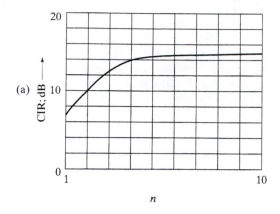

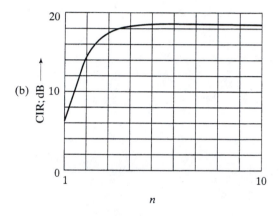

FIGURE 11–13 Carrier-to-adjacent-channel interference ratio for BPSK modulation and Butterworth channel filters: (a) $\Delta f/R_b = 2$; (b) $\Delta f/R_b = 3$. (n = number of filter poles)

$$(\text{CNR})_{\text{adj sat}} = \frac{P_R}{P_{\text{adj sat}}}$$

$$= \frac{P_{T_1} G_{T_1} G_{R_1} d_2^2}{P_{T_2} G_{T_2} G_{R_2} d_1^2} \qquad (11\text{--}43)$$

$$= \frac{(\text{EIRP})_1 \, d_2^2}{(\text{EIRP})_2 \, g(\Delta\theta) \, d_1^2}$$

where

$\quad P_{T_i} \qquad$ = power transmitted by satellite i

$\quad G_{T_i} \qquad$ = transmit antenna gain for satellite i in the direction of the earth station

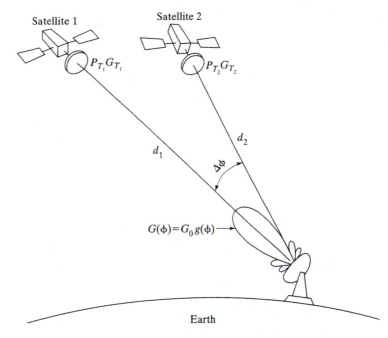

FIGURE 11–14   Illustration of geometry for analyzing adjacent satellite interference.

G_{R_i} = earth station receive antenna gain in direction of satellite i

$(\text{EIRP})_i$ = effective radiated power relative to isotropic for satellite i (assumes that transmit antennas are both pointed at ground station)

$g(\phi)$ = shape factor for receiving antenna [i.e., $G_R(\phi) = G_o g(\phi)$, and antenna boresight assumed to be aligned with desired satellite].

For example, if $(\text{EIRP})_1 = (\text{EIRP})_2$, $d_1 \simeq d_2$, and $g(\phi) = \exp[\,-2.76(\phi/\phi_{3\text{dB}})^2]$ [see (11–9)], we have

$$(\text{CNR})_{\text{adj sat}} = \exp\left[\,2.76\left(\frac{\phi}{\phi_{3\text{dB}}}\right)^2\,\right] \qquad (11\text{–}44)$$

If $\Delta\phi = 1.5\phi_{3\text{dB}}$, then

$$(\text{CNR})_{\text{adj sat}} = \exp[\,2.76 \times 2.25\,]$$

$$\simeq 500 \qquad (11\text{–}45)$$

$$= 27\ \text{dB}$$

This carrier-to-interference ratio can then be included in the overall received carrier-to-interference ratio through combining it as in (11–38).

11.3.5 Power Division in Limiting Repeaters

Another disadvantage of a nonlinear bent-pipe relay in addition to the generation of intermodulation products is that the nonlinearity favors the largest power user in terms of output power allocated to it. That is, the smallest power users are suppressed, and the larger power users are favored by the nonlinear transponder. Thus, it is important in a bent-pipe transponder that is operated in a nonlinear mode to exercise power control *at the transponder input*. This will ensure that no user gets more than its share of the output power. This is of importance in FDMA and CDMA systems. Since, in a TDMA system, only one RF carrier is present at the nonlinear amplifier input, power control is not a necessity.

Rather than carry out this power control at the transmitting ground station in the case of FDMA, a technique referred to as channelization can be implemented on the satellite. If a single TWTA amplifier is to be employed, this channelization is accomplished as shown in Figure 11–15a. If a TWTA is employed in each channel, it is implemented as shown in Figure 11–15b. Obviously, for a given TWTA size, more power can be radiated with the arrangement of Figure 11–15b at the expense of more hardware, power, and weight. Channelization allows users of approximately the same power at the satellite communications systems input to be put into a given channel, and the gain of each channel adjusted so that all carriers will have roughly the same power levels when they appear at the nonlinear amplifier input.

EXAMPLE 11–7

As an example of channelization, consider seven carriers simultaneously accessing a repeater through FDMA. The uplink and downlink signal powers for the carriers are given in Table 11–2 along with the implied gain of the repeater in each case. To have each carrier experience the appropriate gain through the repeater and keep all inputs equal, we require six channels (carriers 3 and 4 can go through the same amplifier). This would result in a total satellite transmit power of

$$P_{sat,tot} = 2000(5 \times 10^{-3}) + 3000(7 \times 10^{-3}) + 2 \times 2000(10 \times 10^{-3})$$
$$+ 2000(12 \times 10^{-3}) + 1000(15 \times 10^{-3}) + 1000(70 \times 10^{-3})$$
$$= 180 \text{ W}$$

If we are limited to a three-channel transponder, then signals might be grouped as follows: 1 and 2; 3, 4, and 5; 6 and 7. This would require amplifiers with gains of 3000, 2000, and 1000 resulting in a total satellite output power of

$$P_{sat,tot} = 3000(5 \times 10^{-3} + 7 \times 10^{-3})$$
$$+ 2000(10 \times 10^{-3} + 10 \times 10^{-3} + 12 \times 10^{-3})$$
$$+ 1000(15 \times 10^{-3} + 70 \times 10^{-3})$$
$$= 185 \text{ W}$$

This is only 5 watts more than the minimum, and all amplifiers have approximately equal power inputs.

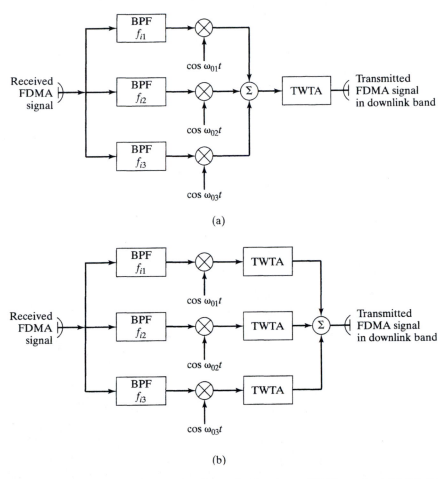

(a)

(b)

FIGURE 11–15 Two schemes for channelization in an FDMA system; (a) Single output power amplifier; (b) power amplifier in each channel.

TABLE 11–2 Powers for a Channelization Example

Carrier	Uplink Power (mW)	Downlink Power (W)	Gain
1	5	10	2000
2	7	21	3000
3	10	20	2000
4	10	20	2000
5	12	24	2000
6	15	15	1000
7	70	70	1000

11.4   EXAMPLES OF LINK POWER BUDGET CALCULATIONS

In this section, examples of link power budget calculations are given. Before considering these examples, however, some general observations are in order. First, combining (1–29) and (1–25), we obtain the following expression for the ratio of received carrier power to noise power spectral density in a free-space communications link (simply referred to as the carrier-to-noise ratio):

$$\frac{C}{N_0} = \frac{P_T G_T A_R}{4\pi d^2 L_a L_R L_i k T_s} \tag{11–46}$$

The various quantities are defined as follows:

C/N_0 = carrier-to-noise density ratio in hertz
$P_T G_T$ = equivalent isotropic radiated power (EIRP) in watts
d = range in meters
A_R = effective receive aperture in square meters $[G_R = (4\pi A_R)/\lambda^2$ by (1–24)]
T_s = system noise temperature in kelvins
k = Boltzmann's constant (6.023×10^{-23} J/K)
L_a = atmospheric losses
L_R = rain losses
L_i = incidental losses (waveguide, antenna beamshape, etc.)

The link equation is normally not used in this form, but it serves to point out that the carrier-to-noise ratio, under ideal conditions and for constant receiving aperture and transmitted EIRP, is *independent of carrier frequency*. It is sometimes thought that higher frequencies give increased receiver antenna gain (which is true), and therefore the use of smaller receiver antennas is allowed. This is misleading. In fact, the higher the carrier frequency, the greater the atmospheric and rain losses. However, for satellites in a geostationary orbit, the higher the frequency, the narrower the beamwidth, and the more able is a given receiver to discriminate against adjacent satellite interference for the same physical receiving antenna aperture. Rewriting (11–46) in terms of dB, we obtain (all terms in dB)

$$\left(\frac{C}{N_0}\right)_{dB} = \text{EIRP} + \left(\frac{G_R}{T_S}\right)_{dB} - L_S - L_a - L_R - L_i - k \quad \text{dB-Hz} \tag{11–47}$$

and, in a bandwidth of B dB-Hz, the carrier-to-noise power ratio is

$$\left(\frac{C}{N}\right)_{dB} = \left(\frac{C}{N_0}\right)_{dB} - B \quad \text{dB} \tag{11–48}$$

where

EIRP = $P_T G_T$ = equivalent isotropic radiated power in dBW
(G_R/T) = receive system figure of merit in dB/K
L_S = $20 \log_{10}(4\pi d/\lambda)$ = free-space (propagation) loss in dB

The receive system figure of merit can be calculated from the antenna gain (11–7) with the aid of the general receiver front end shown in Figure 11–16. It follows from Fiis's formula (see Appendix B) that the system effective noise temperature is (all terms are pure numbers not dB)

$$T_s = T_a + (L - 1)T_0 + LT_{LNA} + L(F - 1)T_0/G_{LNA} \quad K \qquad (11\text{--}49)$$

where

T_a = antenna temperature in kelvins, which is discussed further shortly
L = loss of the lead-in from the antenna, expressed as a ratio
T_{LNA} = equivalent noise temperature in kelvins of the low-noise amplifier
F = noise figure of the down converter expressed as a ratio
G_{LNA} = gain of the low-noise amplifier expressed as a ratio
T_0 = reference temperature (290 K)

If the gain of the RF amplifier is large, which it normally is, contributions to the system temperature by stages after the down converter are negligible.

The calculation of atmospheric losses is summarized in Appendix C as is the calculation of rain losses. The only modification to the total atmospheric losses through the zenith is multiplication by the cosecant of the elevation angle to the satellite to get slant range. For rain losses, we need the slant range to the freezing altitude which is of the order of 5 km (this simply is a recognition of the fact that frozen water imposes negligible attenuation). Thus, the attenuation due to rain can be computed from (recall that aR^b has dimensions dB/km)

$$L_R = (h_F - h_{ES}) \csc(\theta) aR^b \quad \text{dB} \qquad (11\text{--}50)$$

where a and b are coefficients given in Table C–2 and the other parameters are defined as follows:

h_F = freezing altitude in meters
h_{ES} = satellite altitude in meters
θ = elevation angle to satellite
R = rain rate in mm/hr

From the data in Appendix C, it will be seen that atmospheric and rain losses are negligible below about 5 GHz.

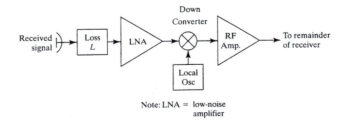

Note: LNA = low-noise amplifier

FIGURE 11–16 Receiver front end for the derivation of system noise temperature.

Rain has one more serious effect on performance of a communications link—that of raising the apparent noise temperature of the antenna due to scattering of the electromagnetic wavefronts off the rain drops. This effect can be quantified through the expression

$$T_{\text{ant}} = \frac{T_{\text{sky}} + (L_R - 1)T_0}{L_R} \tag{11–51}$$

where

L_R = loss due to rain

T_{sky} = "sky temperature," which can vary from 10 K in the night sky to 10,000 K when the sun appears within the antenna aperture

T_0 = reference temperature (290 K)

We now consider several examples using the equations developed in Section 11.3 and in this section to compute link budgets for satellite communications.

EXAMPLE 11–8

In this first example, we consider a TDMA communications link through a bent-pipe transponder with the following parameters:

$B_{\text{RF}} = 36$ MHz, $R_{\text{RF}} = T_b^{-1} = 45$ Mbps (QPSK modulation)

Degradation at ground receiver due to intersymbol interface from severe filtering = 3 dB

Desire an overall $P_b = 10^{-6}$ for transmission through the communications link (uplink cascaded with the downlink)

Uplink and downlink slant range = $d_u = d_d = 37{,}500$ km

Uplink frequency = $f_u = 14$ GHz ($\lambda_u = 0.021$ m)

Downlink frequency = $f_d = 12$ GHz ($\lambda_d = 0.025$)

Rain and atmospheric attenuation on uplink = $L_u = 7.8$ dB

Rain and atmospheric attenuation on downlink = $L_d = 4.5$ dB

Incidental attenuation on uplink and downlink = $L_i = 1.5$ dB (e.g., antenna pointing loss)

$(G/T)_{\text{sat rec}} = 3.1$ dB/K (e.g., 0.5 m physical aperture with 0.6 efficiency and $T_{\text{sat rec}} = 1644$ K)

Carrier-to-adjacent-channel-interference ratio on uplink and downlink = $(\text{CIR})_{\text{adj ch}} = 25$ dB

Carrier-to-adjacent-satellite interference ratio on downlink only = $(\text{CIR})_{\text{adj sat}} = 27$ dB

Ground station antenna physical diameter = 3 m with efficiency of 0.6

Satellite antenna physical diameter = 0.5 m with efficiency of 0.6 (we assume that the same antenna is used both on transmit and receive through the use of a diplexer which routes the transmit and receiver power in the proper directions, i.e., to the antenna or to the receiver as the case may be)

(a)   Find the required EIRP of the ground station transmitter.

(b)   Find the required transmit power of the satellite transmitter.

Solution: **(a)**   From (11–47) and (11–48),

$$(\text{EIRP})_{\text{gd stn}} = (\text{CNR})_u - (G/T)_{\text{sat rec}} \tag{11-52}$$

$$+ \; L_S + L_u + L_i + k + B_{RF} \;\; \text{dB}$$

where L_S, the free-space loss, is computed to be 207 dB from the defining relation below (11–48).

We need the total CNR for the uplink, including adjacent channel interference, which we assume affects the error probability the same as Gaussian noise (this not necessarily a good assumption, but one made for expediency). For a bit error probability of 10^{-6}, we require $E_b/N_0 = 10.54$ dB. To this is added the margin to compensate for the intersymbol-interference degradation due to the filtering of the transmitted signal. From (11–28), the overall carrier-to-noise ratio (uplink cascaded with downlink) is

$$\text{CNR}_{dB} = \left(\frac{E_b}{N_0} \right)_{dB} + 3 - (B_{RF} T_b)_{dB} \tag{11-53}$$

$$= 13.54 - 10 \log_{10}(0.8) = 14.5 \; \text{dB}$$

This must be split between the uplink and downlink in accordance with (11–25). Three candidate pairs of values are shown in Table 11–3. Since it is easier to place a larger EIRP transmitter on the ground than on the satellite, we arbitrarily choose the middle value (the design could be iterated for different pairs of values—thus, a spreadsheet layout would be convenient). The carrier-to-noise ratio on the uplink, $\text{CNR}_{u,\,tot}$, is composed of contributions due to the Gaussian noise, CNR_u, and the adjacent channel interference on the uplink, CIR_u:

$$\text{CNR}_{u,tot}^{-1} = \text{CNR}_u^{-1} + \text{CIR}_u^{-1} \tag{11-54a}$$

In other words, the CNR_u must be large enough so that $\text{CNR}_{u,\,tot}$ is 14.5 dB. Solving for CNR_u in (11–54a), we obtain

$$(\text{CNR})_u = \left[\text{CNR}_{u,\,tot}^{-1} - \text{CIR}_u^{-1} \right]^{-1} = 20.3 \; \text{dB} \tag{11-54b}$$

TABLE 11–3   Carrier-to Noise Ratio
Combinations for Uplink and Downlink

$\text{CNR}_{u,tot}$; dB	$\text{CNR}_{d,tot}$; dB
18.0	17.09
19.0	16.42
20.0	15.95

Putting the given and computed values into (11–52), we obtain

$$(\text{EIRP})_{\text{gd stn}} = 20.3 - 3.1 + 207 + 7.8 + 1.5$$

$$+ (-228.6) + 75.6 \qquad (11\text{–}55)$$

$$= 80.5 \text{ dBW}$$

where the last number in the series is the 36 MHz bandwidth expressed in dB-Hz. Using the parameters for the ground station antenna, we find from (11–7) the ground station transmit antenna gain to be

$$G_{T,\text{gd stn}} = 50.8 \text{ dB}$$

Subtracting this from the EIRP, we find the required ground transmit power to be

$$P_{T,\text{gd stn}} = 80.5 - 50.8 = 29.7 \text{ dBW} = 933.3 \text{ watts} \qquad (11\text{–}56)$$

This is the power that must be delivered to the antenna. Invariably, there are losses between the transmitting tube (most likely a TWTA) and the antenna, so the actual power output of the transmitter must be greater than this to make up for these losses.

(b) To find the transmit power of the satellite, we again combine (11–47) and (11–48) to get an equation similar to (11–52) for the downlink. Because of the slightly lower frequency on the downlink, the free-space loss turns out to be 205.6 dB as compared with 207 dB on the uplink. The (G/T) of the ground station receiver must be calculated since it isn't given. From the specifications of the ground station antenna and using (11–7), we find the receive antenna gain to be 49.3 dB. From (11–51) we find the ground station antenna temperature during rain (the worst case situation) to be

$$T_{\text{ant}} = \frac{50 + (10^{0.45} - 1)(290)}{10^{0.45}} = 204.85 \text{ K} \qquad (11\text{–}57)$$

From (11–49), we calculate the receive system noise temperature to be

$$T_s = 204.85 + (10^{0.05} - 1)(290) + 10^{0.05}(288.6)$$

$$+ \frac{10^{0.05}(10^{0.6} - 1)(290)}{10^2} \qquad (11\text{–}58)$$

$$= 573.75 \text{ K} = 27.59 \text{ dB-K}$$

where the following values have been assumed for the receiver front end:
$L \quad = 0.5 \text{ dB}$
$F_{\text{LNA}} = 3 \text{ dB}$ [therefore, $T_{\text{LNA}} = (F_{\text{LNA}} - 1)(290) = 288.6 \text{ K}$]
$F \quad = 6 \text{ dB}$
$G_{\text{LNA}} = 20 \text{ dB}$
$T_{\text{sky}} = 50 \text{ K}$

This gives

$$(G/T)_{\text{gd stn rec}} = 49.31 - 27.59 = 21.72 \text{ dB/K} \qquad (11\text{–}59)$$

The total carrier-to-noise ratio on the downlink, $\text{CNR}_{\text{d,tot}}$, is composed of contributions from the receiver noise, adjacent satellite interference, and adjacent satellite interference. Thus,

$$CNR_{d,tot}^{-1} = CNR_d^{-1} + CIR_{adj\,ch}^{-1} + CIR_{adj\,sat}^{-1} \qquad (11\text{–}60a)$$

and the downlink CNR due to receiver noise must be large enough to make the total CNR on the downlink equal to 16.42 dB [recall that we agreed to split the CNR between uplink and downlink as 19 and 16.42 dB to obtain a link CNR of 14.5 dB as specified by (11–53)]. Solving (11–60a) for CNR_d and putting in values, we obtain

$$CNR_d = \left[CNR_{d,tot}^{-1} - CIR_{adj\,ch}^{-1} - CIR_{adj\,sat}^{-1}\right]^{-1}$$

$$= \left[10^{-1.642} - 10^{-2.5} - 10^{-2.7}\right]^{-1} = 17.53 \text{ dB} \qquad (11\text{–}60b)$$

The EIRP of the downlink can now be computed as

$$(EIRP)_d = 17.53 - 21.72 + 205.56 + 4.5 + 1.5 \qquad (11\text{–}61)$$

$$+ (-228.6) + 75.56$$

$$= 54.33 \text{ dBW}$$

The satellite transmit antenna gain can be computed from (11–7) to be 33.75 dB. This results in a satellite transmit power of $54.33 - 33.75 = 20.58$ dBW = 114.3 W.

We note that a total of 18.3 dB has been allocated for losses on the uplink and downlink. Of this total, 12.3 dB is allocated for rain and atmospheric attenuation and is essentially overdesign if clear skies prevail. The question of whether additional margin could be provided from coding so that not as much power must be provided continuously is explored in the problems. For example, Chapter 7 shows that a rate-$\frac{1}{2}$ constraint-length 7 convolutional code can supply 5.8 dB of this margin at the expense of halving the data rate (note that halving the data rate above gives 3 dB).

In the next example, we examine the question of power requirements for a demod/remod satellite transponder. We will find that the power requirements are indeed less than for the bent-pipe transponder. However, the complexity of the transponder is definitely greater. The flexibility of on-board switching, in addition to the lesser power required, might make the increased cost due to the additional complexity worthwhile, however.

EXAMPLE 11–9

Rework Example 11–8 for a demod/remod transponder.

Solution: Now we need to split the carrier-to-noise ratio between uplink and downlink on the basis of (11–33). Table 11–4 gives a few values for combinations of p_u and p_d to yield an overall error probability of 10^{-6} along with the values of E_b/N_0 computed from (11–34) to give them. Note that the last term of (11–33) can be dropped because it is small. Again keeping the goal of favoring the downlink in terms of minimizing the required EIRP, we choose the last row of the table. Including the 3 dB degradation allowance for intersymbol interference on the uplink, the total uplink CNR is

$$CNR_{u,tot} = 11.31 + 3 - 10\log_{10}(0.8) = 15.28 \text{ dB} \qquad (11\text{–}62)$$

Using (11–53) we find the CNR due to satellite receiver noise only to be

$$CNR_u = (10^{-1.528} - 10^{-2.5}) = 15.77 \text{ dB} \qquad (11\text{–}63)$$

TABLE 11-4   Uplink and Downlink Error Probability Combinations

$p_u \times 10^6$	(E_b/N_0), dB	$p_d \times 10^6$	(E_b/N_0), dB
0.5	10.79	0.5	10.79
0.4	10.87	0.6	10.73
0.3	10.97	0.7	10.67
0.2	11.1	0.8	10.63
0.1	11.31	0.9	10.58

From (11–51), the ground station EIRP is

$$(EIRP)_{\text{gnd stn}} = 15.77 - 3.1 + 207 + 7.8 \tag{11-64}$$

$$+ 1.5 + (-228.6) + 75.6 = 75.97 \text{ dBW}$$

Subtracting the gain of the transmit antenna, we find the required transmit power to be

$$P_{T,\text{gnd stn}} = 75.97 - 50.8 = 25.17 \text{ dBW} = 328.85 \text{ W} \tag{11-65}$$

This compares with a ground station transmit power of 933.3 W for the case of a bent-pipe transponder. For the downlink we again include the degradation loss due to intersymbol interference as well as the conversion term between $(E_b/N_0)_d$ and $\text{CNR}_{d,\text{tot}}$ (hard decisions are made both on the uplink and the downlink), to obtain

$$\text{CNR}_{d,\text{tot}} = 10.58 + 3 - 10 \log_{10}(0.8) = 14.55 \text{ dB} \tag{11-66}$$

The CNR_d, due only to receiver noise, is

$$\text{CNR}_d = (10^{-1.455} - 10^{-2.5} - 10^{-2.7})^{-1} = 15.24 \text{ dB} \tag{11-67}$$

The EIRP for the downlink is

$$\text{EIRP}_d = 15.24 - 21.72 + 205.56 + 4.5 + 1.5 \tag{11-68}$$

$$+ (-228.6) + 75.56$$

$$= 52.04 \text{ dBW}$$

Subtracting the satellite transmit antenna gain in dB, the required satellite transmit power is found to be

$$P_{T,\text{sat}} = 52.04 - 33.75 = 18.29 \text{ dBW} = 67.5 \text{ W} \tag{11-69}$$

This compares with a satellite transmit power of 114.3 W for the bent-pipe transponder. Thus, the power requirements for both the uplink and downlink are considerably less for the demod/remod transponder than for the bent-pipe transponder, at least for the particular division of performance between the uplink and downlink considered. Of course, additional power is required for the onboard processing.

To examine the division of performance question further, consider a redesign using the middle row in Table 11–4. To obtain $p_u = 3 \times 10^{-7}$, we require

$$\text{CNR}_{u,\text{tot}} = 10.97 + 3 - 10 \log_{10}(0.8) = 14.94 \text{ dB} \tag{11-70}$$

which includes contributions due to satellite receiver noise and adjacent channel interference on the uplink. The CNR due to satellite receiver noise alone is

$$\text{CNR}_u = (10^{-1.494} - 10^{-2.5}) = 15.39 \text{ dB} \tag{11-71}$$

From (11–53), the ground station EIRP is

$$(\text{EIRP})_{\text{gnd stn}} = 15.39 - 3.1 + 207 + 7.8 + 1.5$$
$$+ (-228.6) + 75.6 \tag{11-72}$$
$$= 75.6 \text{ dBW}$$

The required transmit power is

$$P_{\text{T,gnd stn}} = 75.6 - 50.8 = 24.8 \text{ dBW} = 301.3 = \text{W} \tag{11-73}$$

For the downlink, to obtain $p_d = 7 \times 10^{-7}$, we require

$$(\text{CNR})_{d,\text{tot}} = 10.67 + 3 - 10 \log_{10}(0.8) = 14.64 \text{ dB} \tag{11-74}$$

The downlink CNR due to receiver noise alone is

$$\text{CNR}_d = (10^{-1.464} - 10^{-2.5} - 10^{-2.7})^{-1} = 15.35 \text{ dB} \tag{11-75}$$

The EIRP for the downlink is now

$$\text{EIRP}_d = 15.35 - 21.72 + 205.56 + 4.5 + 1.5$$
$$+ (-228.6) + 75.56 \tag{11-76}$$
$$= 52.15 \text{ dBW}$$

which results in a required satellite transmit power of

$$P_{\text{T,sat}} = 52.15 - 33.75 = 18.4 \text{ dBW} = 69.2 \text{ W} \tag{11-77}$$

Thus, we have *lowered* the uplink transmit power by 328.9 – 301.3 = 27.6 W for an *increase* in satellite transmit power of 69.2 – 67.5 = 1.7 W. This might appear to be a better design. However, we must keep in mind that to put power generation capability into space means extra weight and extra launch costs. Thus, any increase in required satellite transmit power should be carefully considered in light of the total mission. Since TDMA ground stations are rather complex anyway, it would probably be advisable to stay with the first design in this case. This may not be the case with FDMA or SCPC operation.

In the next and last example, we consider a link typical of ground mobile applications, for example, communication between a trucking headquarters and several over-the-road trucks or satellite-based cellular radio to be discussed in the next section. The frequency region is chosen as L band. Several different spectral regions would be required—from the base station up to the satellite, from the satellite to the base station, from a mobile unit to the satellite, and from the satellite to several mobile units. The last-mentioned links require some kind of multiple access technique, which may be FDMA, TDMA, or CDMA as discussed previously. We look at the link from a mobile unit to the satellite and the links from the satellite to several mobile users as the most critical links—the mobile unit-to-satellite link because of the limited EIRP of a mobile transmitter and the satellite-to-mobile user link because of the limited power on board the satellite and the low antenna gain of the mobile user. If a base station to satellite link is involved, this would probably be in an entirely different frequency band, and the base station could employ a directive antenna since it is in a fixed location. A mobile user, on the other hand, would probably not be able to easily steer its antenna to compensate for vehicle motion. Therefore, a low-gain broad-beamwidth antenna would be employed by the mobile user.

EXAMPLE 11–9

In this example, we will look at the trade-off between relay satellite altitude and transmit power for a ground-to-mobile-satellite link. The following parameters are assumed:

Required $E_b/N_0 = 7.93$ dB (DPSK with $P_b = 10^{-3}$)

Equal uplink and downlink E_b/N_0 values, which adds 3 dB to the required 7.93 dB

RF bandwidth accommodates main lobe of transmitted signal spectrum, or $B_{RF}T_b = 2$

Mobile unit antenna gain of 6 dB on transmit and receive

Satellite relay antenna gain of 30 dB on transmit and receive

Nominal carrier frequency of 2 GHz, or wavelength of 0.15 m

Free-space loss of $20 \log_{10}(4\pi d/\lambda) = 98.5 + 20 \log_{10}d$, d in km

Incidental losses of 3 dB on both uplink and downlink

Negligible rain or atmospheric attenuation

G/T of satellite receiver of 3 dB

G/T of mobile receiver of -12 dB

For purposes of this analysis, we leave the range, d, and data rate, R, as parameters. It is convenient to express the equation for EIRP on the uplink and downlink in the form

$$\text{EIRP} = \left(\frac{E_b}{N_0}\right)_{\text{total}} + R - \left(\frac{G}{T}\right)_{\text{rec}} + L_S + L_R + L_i + k \quad \text{dB} \qquad (11\text{–}78)$$

Inserting the given parameter values into this equation, we obtain the following equations for the uplink and downlink:

$$\text{EIRP}_u = -89.2 + 20 \log_{10} d + 10 \log_{10} R \qquad (11\text{–}79\text{a})$$

$$\text{EIRP}_d = -74.2 + 20 \log_{10} d + 10 \log_{10} R \qquad (11\text{–}79\text{b})$$

where d is the slant range in kilometers and R is the data rate in kilobits per second. Using the given values for the transmit antenna gains, the transmit powers are found to be

$$P_{T,\text{mobile}} = -95.2 + 20 \log_{10} d + 10 \log_{10} R \qquad (11\text{–}80\text{a})$$

$$P_{T,\text{sat}} = -104.2 + 20 \log_{10} d + 10 \log_{10} R \qquad (11\text{–}80\text{b})$$

We assume two different data rates, 64 kbps and 9.6 kbps. These are representative of 8-bit-per-sample PCM and speech encoded by a vocoder using differential PCM as briefly mentioned in Chapter 2. Also, we vary the slant range from 1000 to 37,500 km, the latter being representative of a geosynchronous-orbit satellite. For a repeater at 1000 km, the satellite is moving relative to the ground, and more than one repeater would be required to provide continuous coverage. Also, handover from satellite to satellite would be required. This is the trade-off required for less transmit power on both the part of the mobile unit and the satellite. Results are shown in Figure 11–17 for the EIRP and transmit power on both the uplink and

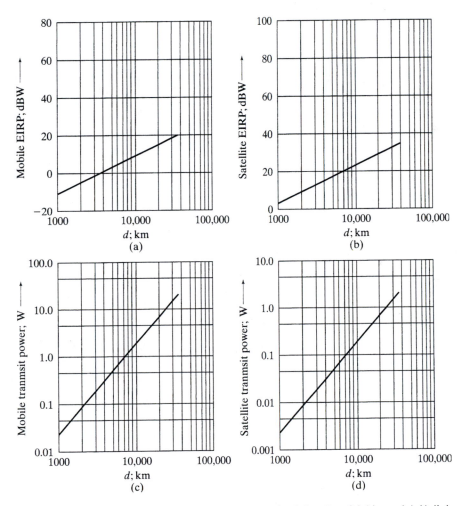

FIGURE 11–17   EIRP and transmit powers required for R = 64 kbps: (a) Uplink EIRP; (b) downlink EIRP; (c) ground station transmit power; (d) satellite transmit power.

downlink of $R = 64$ kbps and in Figure 11–18 for $R = 9.6$ kbps. Note that for a geosynchronous satellite repeater, a power of about 30 watts is required for the mobile unit using 64 kbps PCM—perhaps allowable for a truck but not for a hand-held cellular telephone. For 9.6 kbps vocoded speech, the mobile power is about 5 watts, which is more reasonable. However, we have allowed only 3 dB of incidental attenuation on the link, which is not a very large safety factor. On board the satellite, the powers *per user* are about 3.5 W and 0.5 W for PCM and vocoder operation, respectively, at geosynchronous altitude. As each user comes on the system, the satellite power must increase by these increments—for 100 users access-

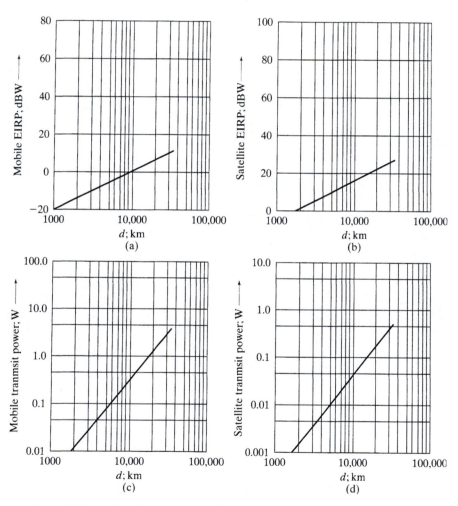

FIGURE 11–18 EIRP and transmit powers for $R = 9.6$ kbps: (a) Uplink EIRP; (b) downlink EIRP; (c) ground station transmit power; (d) satellite transmit power.

ing the satellite, these powers would be a factor of 100 greater. There is one other effect on the downlink not accounted for in this analysis. Because of the broad-beam antenna on the mobile receiver, multipath would give rise to fading and the assumed value of E_b/N_0 would be low in such a situation. Recalling (5-25) for the error probability of DPSK in Rayleigh fading, we calculate $E_b/N_0 = 27$ dB to give an error probability of 10^{-3}, which requires 19 dB more margin than we have allocated. The fading is probably not Rayleigh—Ricean would be a more appropriate model—and the required margin would be less than 19 dB, but at least a worst-case situation is provided by the assumption of Rayleigh fading. In order to provide this additional margin, it is clear that additional power could be used. Another possible solution is to use some form of diversity, including error correction coding. This is explored in the problems.

11.5   LOW- AND MEDIUM-EARTH ORBIT VOICE MESSAGING SATELLITE SYSTEMS

Several low-earth orbit (LEO) satellite systems have been proposed for voice messaging purposes. The characteristics of several of these are summarized in Table 11–5. One, IRIDIUM™, has been fully launched, and one can purchase IRIDIUM handheld phones and subscribe to the service. It is a complete worldwide messaging and paging system where each satellite is a switching center and access being possible directly from user phone to satellite and back to user phone. Alternatively, fifteen to twenty gateways are set up worldwide for access to the terrestrial phone system of a given country. Globalstar, on the other hand, depends on the terrestrial telephone system for switching, with each satellite being a bent-pipe relay. Several characteristics, it will be noted, are denoted TBD (to be determined). Whether all these systems will materialize remains to be seen. The initial subscriber response to IRIDIUM has been less than expected.[2]

It will be noted that IRIDIUM uses TDMA as the accessing method, while Globalstar will employ CDMA. One reason for the choice of TDMA is that power control of the users is not required, whereas for CDMA it is. References [12–14] deal with the issue of power control in satellite-mobile links. Due to the delays involved, power control must of necessity be open loop. For no power control error, [12] shows that, for coded CDMA with interleaving and diversity at an E_b/N_0 of 7 dB, over twenty users can be supported with a bit error probability of 10^{-4}. If the standard deviation of the power control error is 1.5 dB, this number of users drops to less than ten.

For further information on LEO voice messaging systems and other medium-earth orbit (MEO) and geosynchronous earth orbit (GEO) systems for commercial applications, the reader may consult the references [15–21]. An example is to use satellite links as a solution to the so-called "last-mile" problem—namely, to provide broadband data network access, for example, the Internet, to homes and businesses [19, 21].

---

[2]Both IRIDIUM and ICO Global have filed for Chapter 11 bankruptcy protection. At the time of publication of this book, IRIDUM service has been terminated for most users.

TABLE 11-5 Characteristics of Low- and Medium-Earth Orbit Voice Messaging Systems

Name	Company	Number of Orbital Planes	Total Satellites	Inclination Deg.	Altitude km	Spot Beams Per Satellite	Access Method	Frequencies, GHz; Feeder; Mobile User; Up/Down	Average Subscriber Unit Power; Modulation	Launch Date
Iridium	Iridium, Inc.	6	66	86.5	780	48	FDMA-TDMA demod/ remod	30/20 1.62135-1.6265	0.645 W; DQPSK	May 1998, 1st 5; full complement Fall 1998
Globalstar	Loral/ Qualcomm	6	48	52	1414	16	FDMA-CDMA bent pipe	5.1/6.9 1.61-1.62135/ 2.4835-2.49485	0.2 W PN/ QPSK;	1999
ICO-Global	ICO-Global	2	10	45	10355	163	FDMA-TDMA	5.2/6.9 1.98-2.01/ 2.17-2.2	0.625W QPSK	Early 2000
Aries	Constellation Commun., Inc.	1 equatorial 7 inclined	46	TBD	765	1	TBD	1.6/2.5	TBD	Early 2000
Ellipso	Mobile Commun. Holdings, Inc.	1 equator 2 elliptical inclined	17	116.6	8060 equatorial	61	TBD	1.610/1.611	TBD	Early 2000

11.6 SUMMARY

1. Satellites provide a large amount of capacity over wide geographic areas. The requirement for right-of-ways for relays, as with ground-based systems, is avoided with satellite systems. The initial investment cost of the satellite and ground stations is high, however.
2. The first generation communications satellites, launched in the early 1960s, frequency-division multiplexed several users together and FM modulated a carrier with the composite multiplexed signal for bent-pipe relay by the satellite.
3. Modern satellites use digital data transmission, even for analog signals such as voice. This provides tremendous flexibility, including the possibility of temporary storage on board the satellite and on-board switching between several antenna beams.
4. Methods of accessing a satellite repeater include frequency-division multiple access (FDMA), time-division multiple access (TDMA), and code-division multiple access (CDMA). In FDMA, the communications resource is partitioned in frequency; in TDMA, it is partitioned in time; and in CDMA, it is partitioned by assigning a unique code to each user that has low cross-correlation with all other users' codes.
5. Efficient power amplifiers are usually nonlinear. This generates intermodulation interference from the multiple signals passing through them. Thus, FDMA suffers from the effects of intermodulation interference in nonlinear repeaters whereas TDMA does not. However, TDMA requires network synchronization, which is not required of FDMA. In addition to the generation of intermodulation products, nonlinear repeaters have the disadvantage that the largest signal at the input gets more than its fair share of the output power. Thus, power control is necessary whenever two or more signals are present simultaneously at the input to a nonlinear transponder, such as for FDMA and CDMA.
6. In a bent-pipe relay, carrier-to-noise ratios on uplink and downlink add as inverses to give the overall inverse carrier-to-noise ratio.
7. The same rule as given in 6 holds for adjacent channel interference, adjacent satellite interference, and intermodulation interference, if these are present.
8. For a demod/remod satellite repeater the overall E_b/N_0 required to give a desired overall bit error probability is essentially that of the poorest link—that is, either uplink or downlink.
9. An emerging area of application for satellite communications is low- and medium-earth orbit systems for world-wide voice messaging, paging, and low data-rate data transmission. The characteristics of several systems are summarized in this chapter. Time will tell if this is an economically viable application area for satellites.

REFERENCES

[1] E. Posner and R. Stevens, "Deep Space Communication—Past, Present, and Future," *IEEE Communications Magazine,* Vol. 22, pp. 8–21, May 1984.
[2] Arthur C. Clarke, "Extraterrestrial Relays," *Wireless World,* Vol. 51, pp. 305–308, October 1945.

[3] T. Pratt and C. Bostian, *Satellite Communications* (New York: John Wiley & Sons, 1986).

[4] W. Pritchard, "The History and Future of Commercial Satellite Communications," *IEEE Communications Magazine,* Vol. 22, pp. 22–37, May 1984.

[5] P. Neyret, L. Dest, K. Betaharon, and W. English, "INTELSAT VII: A Flexible Spacecraft for the 1990s and Beyond," *Proc. IEEE,* Vol. 78, pp. 1057–1074, July 1990.

[6] D. L. Wright, J. R. Balombin, and P. Y. Sohn, "Advanced Communications Technology Satellite (ACTS) and Potential Systems Applications," *Proc. IEEE,* Vol. 78, pp. 1165–1175, July 1990.

[7] P. C. Jain, "Limiting of Signals in Random Noise," *IEEE Trans. Inf. Theory,* Vol. IT-10, pp. 332–340, May 1972.

[8] P. D. Shaft, "Limiting of Several Signals and Its Effect on Communication System Performance," *IEEE Trans. Commun.,* Vol. COM-13, pp. 504–511, Dec. 1965.

[9] T. Ha, *Digital Satellite Communications* (New York: McGraw-Hill, 1990).

[10] N. Nazari and R. Ziemer, "Computationally Efficient Bounds for the Performance of Direct-Sequence Spread-Spectrum Multiple-Access Communications Systems in Jamming Environments," *IEEE Trans. Commun.,* Vol. COM-36, pp. 577–587, May 1988.

[11] R. M. Gagliardi, *Satellite Communications,* 2nd ed. (New York: Van Nostrand Reinhold, 1990).

[12] A. J. Viterbi, "When Not to Spread the Spectrum—A Sequel," *IEEE Commun. Mag.,* Vol. 23, pp. 12–17, April 1985.

[13] B. Vojcic, R. Pickholtz, and L. Milstein, "Performance of DS-CDMA with Imperfect Power Control Operating Over Low Earth Orbiting Satellite Links," *IEEE Journ. Sel. Areas in Commun.,* Vol. 12, pp. 560–567, May 1994.

[14] A. Monk and L. Milstein, "Open-Loop Power Control Error in a Land Mobile Satellite System," *IEEE Journ. Sel. Areas in Commun.,* Vol. 13, pp. 205–212, Feb. 1995.

[15] J. V. Evans, "Satellite Systems for Personal Communications," *Proc. IEEE,* Vol. 86, pp. 1325–1341, July 1998.

[16] B. Miller, "Satellites Free the Mobile Phone," *IEEE Spectrum,* pp. 2635, Mar. 1998.

[17] C. Loo and J. Butterworth, "Land Mobile Satellite Channel Measurements and Modeling," *Proc. IEEE,* Vol. 86, pp. 1442–1463, July 1998.

[18] T. Logsdon, *Mobile Communication Satellites: Theory and Applications* (New York: McGraw Hill, 1995).

[19] L. Geppert and W. Sweet (Eds.), "Technology 2000 Analysis and Forecast," *IEEE Spectrum,* Jan. 2000.

[20] David D. Clark, "High-Speed Races Home," *Scientific American,* pp. 94–115, Oct. 1999.

[21] Y. Zhang, D. De Lucia, B. Ryu, and S. Dao, "Satellite Communications in the Global Internet: Issues, Pitfalls, and Potential," *Proc. INET97,* 1997 (available at http://www.isoc.org/inet97/proceedings/F5/F5_1.HTM).

PROBLEMS

11–1. Derive (11–5) and (11–6).

11–2. Show that (11–9) gives a gain of −3 dB for $\phi = \phi_{3\,dB}/2$ relative to the gain value at $\phi = 0$.

11–3. Find the altitude of a half-synchronous satellite, that is, one with a 12-hour orbit.

11–4. What is the orbital speed of a geosynchronous orbit satellite?

11–5. Derive an expression that can be used to obtain the amount of time that an equatorial-orbit satellite at altitude d will be in view from a point on the equator (i.e., the time it takes for the satellite to go from horizon to horizon). Take into account the rotation rate of the earth.

11–6. Find the periods of circular-orbit satellites at the following altitudes:
(a) 400 km (b) 800 km (c) 150 mi

11–7. (a) Find the diameter of an antenna aperture mounted on a geosynchronous satellite that will provide a 200-mile spot on the earth's surface within its 3 dB beamwidth if the operating frequency is 10 GHz and the efficiency is 0.7.
(b) Find the gain of this antenna.

11–8. Consider a satellite at altitude h. Compute the diameter d of the circle that can be illuminated if a minimum grazing angle of ϕ_g with respect to the local tangent plane is allowed at beam edge. Plot d versus h for grazing anles of 5, 10, and 15 degrees.

11–9. The antenna footprint plan of Figure 11–4a uses 6 frequency bands to obtain a separation of only 1 spot between like frequency bands. By adding only 1 more band, for a total of 7, come up with an arrangement that will provide a separation of 2 spots between like frequency bands.

11–10. Given a third-order nonlinearity with input-output characteristic

$$y(t) = x(t) + 0.1x^3(t)$$

The input is of the form

$$x(t) = A_1 \cos(2\pi f_1 t) + A_2 \cos(2\pi f_2 t) + A_3 \cos(2\pi f_3 t)$$

If $A_1 = A_2 = A_3 = 1$ and $f_1 = 1.003$ GHz, $f_2 = 1.0015$ GHz, and $f_3 = 1$ GHz show that output frequencies are present that fall back into the locality of the input frequencies.

11–11. Derive and plot curves like the one in Figure 11–11 for a bent-pipe relay if adjacent channel interference giving CIRs of 25, 30, and 35 dB are present. As in Figure 11–11, assume BPSK and an overall bit error probability of 10^{-6}.

11–12. Derive and plot a curve for a demod/remod link like the one in Figure 11–11 for BPSK modulation and a bit error probability of 10^{-5}.

11–13. Rework Problem 11–11, but for noncoherent BFSK.

11–14. Rework Problem 11–11, but for noncoherent DPSK.

11–15. Rework Problem 11–11, but include a rate-$\frac{1}{2}$ convolutional code with constraint length 7. (Requires material from Chapter 7.)

11–16. Consider two frequency-adjacent, equal-power BPSK channels each with bit rate 100 kbps. Assume a channel separation of 200 kHz. If the channels are modeled as fourth-order Butterworth filters with bandwidths of 20 kHz, find the carrier-to-adjacent-channel power ratio in this case. (Requires numerical integration.)

11–17. A satellite repeater is located at 30 degrees west longitude in geosynchronous orbit. The transmitting ground station is located at 45 degrees west longitude and 20 degrees north latitude, and the receiving ground station is located at 60 degrees west longitude and 10 degrees north latitude. The uplink and downlink frequencies are 12 GHz and 10 GHz, respectively. All antennas are 10 feet in diameter with efficiencies of 0.6.

(a) Ignoring atmospheric absorption, find a combination of uplink and downlink carrier-to-noise ratios to give a received (overall) carrier-to-noise ratio of 20 dB if the *GIT* of the satellite receiver is 4 dB and that of the ground station receiver is 7 dB.

(b) For your choice of carrier-to-noise ratios on uplink and downlink, find the transmitter power for the ground station and for the satellite.

11–18. Rework Problem 11–17, but account for atmospheric absorption on uplink and downlink. *Hint:* See Appendix C.

11–19. Rework Problem 11–17, but account for atmospheric absorption and allow enough margin for a 10 mm/hr rainstorm 5 km in vertical extent on the downlink only.

11–20. Reconsider Example 11–8 by replacing some of the 12.3 dB link attenuation allocated for rain and atmospheric attenuation by coding. Choose at least one convolutional code and one block code from Chapters 6 and 7. Account for the decreased data rate due to the code rate being less than unity.

A

Probability and Random Variables

In this appendix, basic theory regarding probability and random variables is covered. It is intended as a review for those students who may have had the material, but are somewhat rusty on it.

A.1 PROBABILITY THEORY

A.1.1 Definitions

In considering the theory of probability, as with any theory, it is convenient to introduce several definitions. Definitions that will be useful in the consideration of the theory of probability are the following:

1. *Outcome:* The end result of an experiment.
2. *Random or chance experiment:* An experiment whose outcome is not known in advance.
3. *Event:* An event A is an outcome or collection of outcomes of a random experiment.
4. *Sample space:* The sample space S of a chance experiment is the set of all possible outcomes of the chance experiment.
5. *Mutually exclusive events:* Events A and B are said to be mutually exclusive (disjoint) if they cannot occur simultaneously (contain no common outcomes).
6. *Union of events:* The union of two events A and B, denoted by $A \cup B$ (sometimes also denoted by A or B or $A + B$), is the set of all outcomes that belong to A or B, or both.
7. *Null event:* The null event, ϕ, represents an impossible outcome or impossible collection of outcomes of a chance experiment.
8. *Intersection of events:* The intersection of two events A and B, denoted by $A \cap B$ (also denoted by A and B or AB), is the set of all outcomes that belong to both A and B.
9. *Complement of an event:* B is the complement of A if it consists of all outcomes not included in A. (Notations used for the complement are A', $\bar{A}$, and A^c.)
10. *Occurrence:* Event A of a chance experiment is said to have occurred if the experiment terminates in an outcome that belongs to event A.

In probability theory, it is useful to represent events as sets in a sample space. The relationships between several events can be shown by a *Venn diagram,* which represents each event or set as an area inside a box representing *S.* Venn diagrams illustrating the definitions given are shown in Figure A–1.

A.1.2 Axioms

The whole of probability is based on three axioms. Let *A* be an event, or outcome of a chance experiment, and *P(A)* a real number called the probability of *A. P(A)* satisfies the following axioms:

(a) $P(A) \geq 0$.
(b) $P(S) = 1$, where *S* is the sample space.
(c) If $A \cap B = \phi$ (i.e., *A* and *B* are mutually exclusive), then

$$P(A \cup B) = P(A) + P(B) \tag{A-1}$$

The reasonableness of these axioms can be seen by considering the relative frequency definition of the probability of *A,* which is

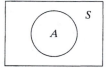

Sample space, *S,* and
Event, *A.*

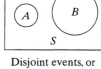

Disjoint events, or
set, *A* and *B.*

Union of two events,
or sets, *A* and *B*
(shaded).

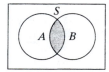

Intersection of two
events or sets, *A* and
B (shaded).

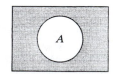

Complement of set *A* (shaded)

FIGURE A–1   Various definitions involving events in probability.

$$P(A) \triangleq \lim_{n \to \infty} \frac{n_A}{n} \qquad (A-2)$$

where n is the number of times a chance experiment is performed, and n_A the number of times event A occurs during the repeated performance of this experiment. Axiom (a) simply states that n_A and n are nonnegative; axiom (b) states that if A always occurs (i.e., is the same as S), its probability must be unity; axiom (c) says that the number of times that either of two mutually exclusive events occur in n repetitions of a chance experiment is equal to the sum of their separate occurrences.

Using only the axioms above, it is possible to show that

$$P(A \cup B) = P(A) + P(B) - P(A \cap B) \qquad (A-3)$$

where A and B are not necessarily mutually exclusive. Furthermore, if $\bar{A}$ is the *complement* of A (i.e., $A \cup \bar{A} = S$ and $A \cap \bar{A} = \emptyset$), then

$$P(\bar{A}) = 1 - P(A) \qquad (A-4)$$

A.1.3 Joint, Marginal, and Conditional Probabilities

Let A, B, C, B_1, B_2, and so on, be events. Let $P(A \mid B)$ denote the probability of event A *given* the occurrence of event B. Then the following relationships hold:

(a) $P(A \cap B) = P(A \mid B)P(B) = P(B \mid A)P(A)$ (A-5)

(b) $P(B \mid A) = \dfrac{P(A \mid B)P(B)}{P(A)}$, $P(A) \neq 0$ (Bayes' rule)   (A-6)

(c) $P(A \cap B \cap C) = P(C \mid A \cap B)P(A \cap B)$ (A-7)
$\qquad\qquad\qquad = P(C \mid A \cap B)P(B \mid A)P(A)$

    (the chain rule)

(d) $P(A) = \displaystyle\sum_{j=1}^{m} P(A \mid B_j)P(B_j)$ (A-8)

where $B_1 \cup B_2 \cup \ldots \cup B_m = S$ and $A \cap (B_1 \cup B_2 \cup \ldots \cup B_m) = A$ (i.e., mutually exclusive and exhaustive). $P(A)$ is often called a *marginal probability*.

Intuitively, if A and B are events associated with the outcomes of an experiment such that the occurrence of A does not influence the occurrence of B, they are said to be *statistically independent*. For such events, the statements

$$P(A \cap B) = P(A)P(B) \qquad (A-9a)$$

$$P(B \mid A) = P(B) \qquad (A-9b)$$

$$P(A \mid B) = P(A) \qquad (A-9c)$$

are equivalent and, in fact, any one of them defines statistical independence.

The following example illustrates some of the foregoing relationships in a communications system context.

EXAMPLE A–1

Consider the transmission of binary symbols through a communications channel. As is customary, the two possible symbols are denoted as 0 and 1. Let the probability of receiving a 0, given that a 0 was sent, $P(0r \mid 0s)$, and the probability of receiving a 1, given that a 1 was sent, $P(1r \mid 1s)$, be

$$P(0r \mid 0s) = P(1r \mid 1s) = 0.99$$

From (A–4), it follows that

$$P(1r \mid 0s) = 1 - P(0r \mid 0s) = 0.01$$

and

$$P(0r \mid 1s) = 1 - P(1r \mid 1s) = 0.01$$

respectively. These probabilities characterize the channel and would be obtained through experimental measurement or analysis. Techniques for calculating them for particular situations are discussed in Chapters 3 and 4.

In addition to these probabilities, suppose that we have determined through measurement that the probability of sending a 0 is

$$P(0s) = 0.6$$

and, therefore, from (A–4) the probability of sending a 1 is

$$P(1s) = 1 - P(0s) = 0.4$$

The probability of a 1 having been sent given a 1 was received, from (A–6), is

$$P(1s \mid 1r) = \frac{P(1r \mid 1s)P(1s)}{P(1r)}$$

To find $P(1r)$, note that

$$P(1r) = P(1r, 1s) + P(1r, 0s)$$

where

$$P(1r, 1s) = P(1r \mid 1s)P(1s) = (0.99)(0.4) = 0.396$$

$$P(1r, 0s) = P(1r \mid 0s)P(0s) = (0.01)(0.6) = 0.006$$

where a comma is used to separate joint events 1 received and 0 sent. Thus

$$P(1r) = P(1r, 1s) + P(1r, 0s)$$

$$= 0.396 + 0.006 = 0.402$$

and $Pr(1s \mid 1r)$ is found to be

$$P(1s \mid 1r) = \frac{(0.99)(0.4)}{0.402} = 0.985$$

Similarly, one could calculate $P(0s \mid 1r)$, $P(0s \mid 0r)$, and $P(1s \mid 0r)$. The necessary calculations are left to the student as an exercise.

A.2   RANDOM VARIABLES, PROBABILITY DENSITY FUNCTIONS, AND AVERAGES

A.2.1   Random Variables

A random variable is a rule, or functional relationship, that assigns a real number to each possible outcome of a chance experiment. An example of a random variable is the assignment of 1 to the occurrence of a head up and a 0 to the occurrence of a tail up when a coin is tossed. The assignment of random variables to the outcomes of chance experiments is convenient from the standpoint of analysis.

A standard notation is to denote random variables by capital letters (X, Y, etc.) and the values that they take on are denoted by the corresponding lowercase letters (x, y, etc.).

Random variables may be discrete, continuous, or mixed, depending on whether they take on a countable (discrete) or uncountable (continuous) number of values, or both.

A.2.2   Probability Distribution and Density Functions

A *probability density function*, $f_X(x)$, characterizes a continuous random variable, and is defined by the following properties:

$$f_X(x) \geq 0, \quad -\infty < x < \infty \tag{A-10}$$

$$\int_{-\infty}^{\infty} f_X(x)\, dx = 1 \tag{A-11}$$

$$P(X \leq x) = \int_{-\infty}^{x} f_X(\lambda)\, d\lambda \triangleq F_X(x) \tag{A-12}$$

The function $F_X(x)$ is called the *probabililty distribution function* of X.

From (A–12), and noting that the events $-\infty < X \leq a$ and $a < X \leq b$ are disjoint and that the union of these two events is the event $-\infty < X \leq b$, it is concluded that

$$P(a < X \leq b) = \int_{a}^{b} f_X(\lambda)\, d\lambda \tag{A-13}$$

$$= F_X(b) - F_X(a)$$

Letting $a = x$ and $b = x + \Delta x$ with Δx small, it follows that if $f_X(x)$ is continuous in $[x, x + \Delta x]$, then

$$f_X(x)\, \Delta x \simeq P(x < X \leq x + \Delta x) \tag{A-14}$$

$$= F_X(x + \Delta x) - F_X(x)$$

or, dividing by Δx and taking the limit $\Delta x \to 0$,

$$f_X(x) = \frac{dF_X(x)}{dx} \tag{A-15}$$

The distribution function, $F_X(x)$, of a continuous random variable X is a *continuous, nondecreasing* function of x with the end-point values $F_X(-\infty) = 0$ and $F_X(\infty) = 1$. The distribution function of a discrete random variable is a *nondecreasing stair step* function of x.

In a strict mathematical sense, the probability density function of a discrete random variable is undefined. If the use of delta functions is accepted, it is possible to define probability density functions for discrete random variables as well as for continuous random variables. Figure A–2 illustrates density and distribution functions for continuous and discrete random variables.

So far, probability density and distribution functions have been discussed only for single random variables. They may be defined for more than one random variable as well. For example, if X and Y are random variables, their joint probability density function, $f_{XY}(x, y)$, is a function of two variables x and y with the following properties:

$$f_{XY}(x, y) \geq 0, \quad -\infty < x, y < \infty \tag{A–16a}$$

$$\int_{-\infty}^{\infty} \int_{-\infty}^{\infty} f_{XY}(x, y)\, dx\, dy = 1 \tag{A–16b}$$

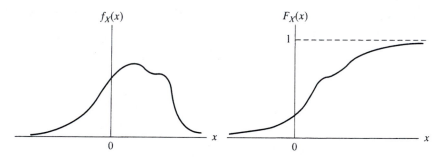

(a) Continuous random variable functions

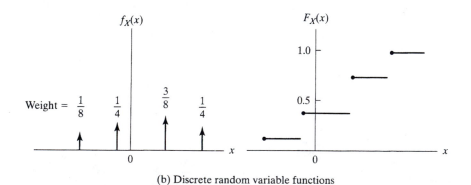

(b) Discrete random variable functions

FIGURE A–2 Probability density and distribution functions for continuous and discrete random variables.

$$P(X \leq x, Y \leq y) \triangleq F_{XY}(x, y)$$

$$= \int_{-\infty}^{x} \int_{-\infty}^{y} f_{XY}(u, v) \, du \, dv \tag{A-16c}$$

$$\int_{-\infty}^{\infty} f_{XY}(x, y) \, dy = f_X(x) \tag{A-16d}$$

$$\int_{-\infty}^{\infty} f_{XY}(x, y) \, dx = f_Y(y) \tag{A-16e}$$

where $f_X(x)$ and $f_Y(y)$ are sometimes referred to as "marginal" density functions.

Common examples of marginal and joint probability density functions are those for *Gaussian random variables*. X is Gaussian if it is described by the probability density function

$$f_X(x) = \frac{\exp[-(x - m)^2/2\sigma^2]}{\sqrt{2\pi\sigma^2}} \tag{A-17}$$

where m and σ are parameters of the density function. The *error function*, erf(x), is related to the distribution function of a Gaussian random variable, and is defined as

$$\mathrm{erf}(x) = \frac{2}{\sqrt{\pi}} \int_{0}^{x} e^{-u^2} \, du \tag{A-18}$$

The *complementary error function* is defined as $\mathrm{erfc}(x) = 1 - \mathrm{erf}(x)$. For a Gaussian random variable, it can be shown that

$$P(m - a \leq X \leq m + a) = \mathrm{erf}\left(\frac{a}{\sqrt{2}\sigma}\right) \tag{A-19}$$

where

$$m = \int_{-\infty}^{\infty} x f_X(x) \, dx \tag{A-20a}$$

$$\sigma^2 + m^2 = \int_{-\infty}^{\infty} x^2 f_X(x) \, dx \tag{A-20b}$$

Another function related to the complementary error function is the Q-function, which is defined as

$$Q(x) = \frac{1}{\sqrt{2\pi}} \int_{x}^{\infty} e^{-v^2/2} \, dv \tag{A-21}$$

By the change of variable to $u = v/\sqrt{2}$ in (A–18) it is readily shown that

$$\tfrac{1}{2}\,\mathrm{erfc}(x) = \frac{1}{\sqrt{2\pi}} \int_{\sqrt{2}x}^{\infty} e^{-v^2/2} \, dv = Q(\sqrt{2}x) \tag{A-22}$$

Appendix E provides several useful relations for $Q(x)$ as well as a table of values.

If X and Y are jointly Gaussian, they have the joint probability density function

$$f_{XY}(x, y) = \frac{\exp\left[-\dfrac{\left(\dfrac{x-m_X}{\sigma_X}\right)^2 - 2\rho\left(\dfrac{x-m_X}{\sigma_X}\right)\left(\dfrac{y-m_Y}{\sigma_Y}\right) + \left(\dfrac{y-m_Y}{\sigma_Y}\right)^2}{2(1-\rho^2)}\right]}{2\pi\sigma_X\sigma_Y\sqrt{1-\rho^2}}$$

$$(A\text{–}23)$$

It can be shown that (A–16d) and (A–16e) hold between (A–23) and (A–17). In (A–23) $m_X, m_Y, \sigma_X, \sigma_Y$, and ρ are parameters.

The *conditional probability density function* of Y given X is defined as

$$f_{Y|X}(y\,|\,x) = \frac{f_{XY}(x, y)}{f_X(x)} \qquad (A\text{–}24)$$

with a similar definition for the probability density function of X given Y.

A.2.3   Averages of Random Variables

The average of some function $g(\cdot)$ of a random variable, X, is obtained by evaluating the integral

$$E[g(X)] = \overline{g(X)} = \int_{-\infty}^{\infty} g(x)f_X(x)\,dx \qquad (A\text{–}25)$$

The average of a function of two random variables, say, $h(X, Y)$, is obtained by evaluating the double integral

$$E[h(X, Y)] = \overline{h(X, Y)} = \int_{-\infty}^{\infty}\int_{-\infty}^{\infty} h(x, y)f_{XY}(x, y)\,dx\,dy \qquad (A\text{–}26)$$

If a random variable is discrete, (A–25) and (A–26) are used with the probability density functions being sums of unit impulses $\delta(x - x_j)$ or $\delta(x - x_j)\delta(y - y_k)$ with weights equal to the probability of the particular value of X or X jointly with Y being taken on. For a discrete random variable, or set of discrete random variables, (A–25) or (A–26), as the case may be, reverts to summations. The notation $E[\cdot]$ means "expectation of" and either it or the overbar denotes a statistical average. Several of the most commonly occurring averages are the following:

$$\text{mean} = m_1 = m_X = E[X] = \int_{-\infty}^{\infty} xf_X(x)\,dx \qquad (A\text{–}27a)$$

$$\text{mean square} = m_2 = E[X^2] = \int_{-\infty}^{\infty} x^2 f_X(x)\,dx \qquad (A\text{–}27b)$$

$$\text{variance} = \sigma_X^2 = \overline{(X - \overline{X})^2} = E[\{X - E(X)\}^2] \qquad \text{(A–27c)}$$

$$\text{covariance} = \mu_{XY} = E[(X - \overline{X})(Y - \overline{Y})] \qquad \text{(A–27d)}$$

$$\text{correlation coefficient} = \rho_{XY} = \frac{\mu_{XY}}{\sigma_X \sigma_Y} \qquad \text{(A–27e)}$$

Exercise

(a) Show that the variance can be written as

$$\sigma_X^2 = m_2 - m_X^2$$

(b) Show that the covariance can be expressed as

$$\mu_{XY} = E[XY] - m_X m_Y$$

A random variable X for which $m_X = 0$ is called *zero mean*. Two random variables for which $\mu_{XY} = 0$ are said to be *uncorrelated*. If two random variables have a joint probability density function that factors, that is,

$$f_{XY}(x, y) = f_X(x) f_Y(y) \qquad \text{(A–28)}$$

they are said to be *statistically independent*. Statistically independent random variables are uncorrelated; the reverse is not necessarily true [it is for Gaussian random variables, however, since $\rho = 0$ in (A–23) means that $f_{XY}(x, y)$ factors].

Convenient theorems pertaining to averages of random variables are the following:

1. The average of a sum of random variables is equal to the sum of their respective averages. That is,

$$\overline{X_1 + X_2 + \cdots + X_N} = \overline{X}_1 + \overline{X}_2 + \cdots + \overline{X}_N \qquad \text{(A–29)}$$

2. The average of a constant is the constant itself; that is, $E[A] = A$, where A is a constant.

3. The average of a constant times a random variable is the constant times the average of the random variable; that is, $E[AX] = AE[X]$, where A is a constant.

4. The average of the product of two random variables is equal to the product of their separate averages *if they are statistically independent* (sufficient condition); that is,

$$\overline{XY} = \overline{X}\,\overline{Y}, \quad X \text{ and } Y \text{ statistically independent} \qquad \text{(A–30)}$$

A.3   CHARACTERISTIC FUNCTION AND PROBABILITY GENERATING FUNCTION

A.3.1   Characteristic Function

An extremely useful average is the *characteristic function*. For a single random variable, it is obtained by letting $g(X) = \exp(jvX)$ in (A–25), which results in the definition

$$M_X(v) = \int_{-\infty}^{\infty} f_X(x)e^{jvx}\,dx \tag{A-31}$$

For several random variables, say, $X_1, X_2, \ldots, X_N$, the *N-fold characteristic function* is given by

$$M_{X_1\cdots X_N}(v_1, v_2, \cdots, v_N) = E\left[\exp\left(j\sum_{i=1}^{N} v_i X_i\right)\right] \tag{A-32}$$

Note that setting $v_N = v_{N-1} = \cdots = v_2 = 0$ results in (A-31). Equation (A-32) can be written compactly by defining the column matrices or vectors

$$\mathbf{v} = \begin{bmatrix} v_1 \\ v_2 \\ \vdots \\ v_N \end{bmatrix} \quad \text{and} \quad \mathbf{X} = \begin{bmatrix} X_1 \\ X_2 \\ \vdots \\ X_N \end{bmatrix} \tag{A-33}$$

which results in

$$M_{\mathbf{X}}(\mathbf{v}) = E[\exp(\mathbf{v}'\mathbf{X})] \tag{A-34}$$

where the superscript t denotes transpose. The usefulness of the characteristic function is due primarily to three properties:

1. By comparing (A-31) with the definition of the Fourier transform, it is seen that the characteristic function is the Fourier transform of the probability density function of the random variable with the exception that a minus sign appears in the exponent of the normal definition of the Fourier transform. From this observation, it follows that the probability density function of a random variable can be obtained as the inverse Fourier transform of the characteristic function (accounting, of course, for the difference of sign in the exponent in the table of Fourier transforms used). Similarly, if dealing with N random variables, the Nth order joint probability density function may be obtained as the N-fold inverse Fourier transform of (A-32). Obtaining the probability density function in this fashion may be a useful approach in cases where the characteristic function is easy to obtain.[1]

2. Differentiation of (A-31) underneath the integral sign n times with respect to v and setting $v = 0$ shows that

$$E[X^n] = (-j)^n \left.\frac{d^n M_X(v)}{dv^n}\right|_{v=0} \tag{A-35}$$

A similar procedure using partial differentiation of the N-fold characteristic function (A-32) shows that

---

[1]By using the fact that the area (volume) under the probability density function is unity, one can show that (A-31) or (A-32) converge absolutely.

$$E[X_1^{n_1} X_2^{n_2} \cdots X_N^{n_N}] = (-j)^N \left. \frac{\partial^N M_X(\mathbf{v})}{\partial^{n_1} v_1\, \partial^{n_2} v_2 \cdots \partial^{n_N} v_N} \right|_{\mathbf{v}=0} \qquad (A\text{--}36)$$

where $n_1 + n_2 + \ldots + n_N = N$. Thus, the moments of a random variable or set of random variables can be obtained through differentiation of the characteristic functions.

3. Expansion of the exponentials in (A–31) or (A–32) in a power series shows that the moments of a random variable or set of random variables are the coefficients of a Taylor series expansion for the characteristic function.

These observations are useful in cases where the characteristic function of a set of random variables is easier to obtain or work with than the probability density function. The following examples develop useful relations for Gaussian random variables.

EXAMPLE A–2

The characteristic function of a Gaussian random variable, by using (A–17) in (A–31), is

$$M_X(v) = (2\pi\sigma^2)^{-1/2} \int_{-\infty}^{\infty} \exp\left[\frac{-(x-m)^2}{2\sigma^2} + jvx \right] dx$$

$$= (2\pi\sigma^2)^{-1/2} \exp(jmv - \tfrac{1}{2}\sigma^2 v^2) \int_{-\infty}^{\infty} \exp\left[-\frac{(u - j\sigma^2 v)^2}{2\sigma^2} \right] du$$

which follows by the change of variables $x = m + u$ and completing the square in the exponent. Making the change of variables $y = u - j\sigma^2 v$ and noting that $\int_{-\infty}^{\infty} (2\pi\sigma^2)^{-\frac{1}{2}} \exp(-y^2/2\sigma^2)\, dy = 1$ results in

$$M_X(v) = \exp(jmv - \tfrac{1}{2}\sigma^2 v^2) \qquad (A\text{--}37a)$$

The characteristic function of the new zero-mean Gaussian random variable $Y = X - m$ is

$$M_Y(v) = \exp(-\tfrac{1}{2}\sigma^2 v^2) = \exp[\tfrac{1}{2}\sigma^2(jv)^2] \qquad (A\text{--}37b)$$

which results simply by setting $m = 0$ in (A–37). Its moments can be obtained by repeated differentiation of $M_Y(v)$ or expansion in a power series in jv. Use of the latter approach results in

$$M_Y(v) = \sum_{n=0}^{\infty} \frac{1}{n!} \left[\frac{1}{2}\sigma^2(jv)^2 \right]^n \qquad (A\text{--}38a)$$

The nth-order moment of $Y = X - m$ is the coefficient of the term $(jv)^n/n!$ These *central moments*, as they are called, are given by

$$E[Y^{2k}] = E[(X-m)^{2k}] = \frac{(2k)!}{2^k k!} \sigma^{2k}, \quad k = 0, 1, 2, \cdots \qquad (A\text{--}38b)$$

for the even-order moments, with the odd-order moments being zero.

EXAMPLE A–3 _____

The joint probability density function of N jointly Gaussian random variables is

$$f_{\mathbf{X}}(\mathbf{x}) = (2\pi)^{-n/2}|\det \mathbf{C}|^{-1/2} \exp[-\tfrac{1}{2}(\mathbf{x} - \mathbf{m})'\mathbf{C}^{-1}(\mathbf{x} - \mathbf{m})] \qquad \text{(A–39)}$$

where $\mathbf{x}$ and $\mathbf{m}$ are column matrices defined as

$$\mathbf{x} = \begin{bmatrix} x_1 \\ x_2 \\ \vdots \\ x_N \end{bmatrix} \quad \text{and} \quad \mathbf{m} = \begin{bmatrix} m_1 \\ m_2 \\ \vdots \\ m_N \end{bmatrix} \qquad \text{(A–40)}$$

respectively, and $\mathbf{C}$ is the positive definite matrix of covariances with elements

$$C_{ij} = \frac{E[(X_i - m_i)(X_j - m_j)]}{\sigma_{X_i}\sigma_{X_j}} \qquad \text{(A–41)}$$

The joint characteristic function of the Gaussian random variables $X_1, X_2, \ldots, X_N$ is

$$M_X(\mathbf{v}) = \exp(j\mathbf{m}'\mathbf{v} - \tfrac{1}{2}\mathbf{v}'\mathbf{C}\mathbf{v}) \qquad \text{(A–42)}$$

From the power series expansion of (A–42) it follows that for any four zero-mean Gaussian random variables

$$E(X_1X_2X_3X_4) = E(X_1X_2)E(X_3X_4) + E(X_1X_3)E(X_2X_4) + E(X_1X_4)E(X_2X_3) \quad \text{(A–43)}$$

which is a rule that is sufficiently useful to commit to memory.

_____

A.3.2   Probability Generating Function

For a discrete random variable, X, taking on uniformly spaced values, a convenient tool for analyzing probability distributions is the *probability generating function*. Clearly, if a random variable takes on uniformly spaced values, it can be represented as an integer-valued random variable. Let $P(X = k) = P_k$ be the probabilities that X takes on the integer value k, and assume that $k \geq 0$.[2] The probability generating function, defined by

$$h(z) = \sum_{k=0}^{\infty} P_k z^k \qquad \text{(A–44)}$$

is recognized as the z-transform of the sequence of probabilities $\{P_k\}$ with z^{-1} replaced by z. Differentiation of (A–44) n times with respect to z and setting z in the result equal to zero shows that

$$P_n = \frac{1}{n!} \frac{d^n}{dz^n} h(z)\bigg|_{z=0} \qquad \text{(A–45)}$$

_____

[2]In what follows, negative values of k could also be accommodated, but would be slightly more complicated mathematically.

Furthermore, the derivatives of $h(z)$ at $z = 1$ result in the factorial moments so that

$$E[X(X - 1)(X - 2) \cdots (X - n + 1)] \triangleq c_n = \frac{d^n}{dz^n} h(z)\Big|_{z=1} \tag{A-46}$$

From the definition of c_n, it is seen that

$$c_1 = E[X] = m_1 \tag{A-47}$$

$$c_2 = E[X(X - 1)] = m_2 - m_1 \tag{A-48}$$

$$\sigma_X^2 = m_2 - m_1^2 = c_2 + c_1 - c_1^2 \tag{A-49}$$

The Maclaurin series expansion of $h(z)$ about $z = 1$ is

$$h(z) = \sum_{m=0}^{\infty} \frac{c_m}{m!} (z - 1)^m \tag{A-50}$$

EXAMPLE A-4

An integer-valued random variable with probabilities

$$P_k = \binom{N}{k} p^k q^{N-k}, \quad 0 \le k \le N \tag{A-51}$$

where k and N are integers and $p + q = 1$ with $p > 0$ is called a *binomial random variable*. Its probability generating function is

$$\begin{aligned}
h(z) &= \sum_{k=0}^{N} \binom{N}{k} p^k q^{N-k} z^k \\
&= \sum_{k=0}^{N} \binom{N}{k} (pz)^k q^{N-k} \\
&= (pz + q)^N \\
&= [1 + p(z - 1)]^N
\end{aligned} \tag{A-52}$$

Using the binomial theorem again, $h(z)$ can be expanded as

$$\begin{aligned}
h(z) &= \sum_{m=0}^{N} \binom{N}{m} p^m (z - 1)^m \\
&= \sum_{m=0}^{N} \frac{N! p^m (z - 1)^m}{m! (N - m)!}
\end{aligned}$$

Comparing this series with (A-50), it is seen that

$$c_m = \frac{N!}{(N - m)!} p^m \tag{A-53}$$

Therefore, the mean and variance of a binomial random variable are, from (A-47) and (A-49), given by

$$m_1 = c_1 = Np \tag{A-54a}$$

$$\sigma^2 = Np(1 - p) = Npq \tag{A-54b}$$

EXAMPLE A–5

A *Poisson random variable* is an integer-valued random variable taking on values in the range $(0, \infty)$ with probabilities

$$P_k = \frac{\lambda^k e^{-\lambda}}{k!}, \quad 0 \le k < \infty; \ \lambda > 0 \tag{A-55}$$

The probability generating function is

$$\begin{aligned}
h(z) &= \sum_{m=0}^{\infty} \frac{\lambda^k}{k!} z^k e^{-\lambda} \\
&= e^{-\lambda} e^{\lambda z} \tag{A-56} \\
&= e^{\lambda(z-1)} \\
&= \sum_{m=0}^{\infty} \frac{\lambda^m}{m!} (z - 1)^m
\end{aligned}$$

Comparing the second expansion with (A–50) shows that

$$c_m = \lambda^m \tag{A-57}$$

Therefore, the mean and variance of a Poisson random variable are given, respectively, by

$$m_1 = \lambda \tag{A-58a}$$

$$\sigma^2 = \lambda \tag{A-58b}$$

That is, the mean and variance of a Poisson random variable are equal.

A.4 TRANSFORMATIONS OF RANDOM VARIABLES

A.4.1 General Results

The transformation of a random variable or set of random variables to another random variable or set of random variables is a frequently occurring problem. Examples are the following:

1. The input at time $t = t_1$ to a nonlinear device, say, a diode, is a random variable with Gaussian probability density function. What is the probability density function of the output?
2. In shooting at a target, it is known that the errors along orthogonal axes between the bullet's impact point and the center of the target are statistically independent

Gaussian random variables. What is the probability that the distance away from the target center in any direction will be greater than some value, say, 10 cm?
3. Given the same situation as in (2), what is the joint probability density function of the impact point of the bullet being between 10 and 11 cm away from the target center and between the angles of 90 and 95 degrees?

All of these examples are cases where it is necessary to transform the distribution of one random variable, or set of random variables, to the distribution of another random variable, or set of random variables. The reasoning used to obtain the transformation rule makes use of (A–14) for single random variables, or its generalization for multiple random variables, which is

$$P(x_1 < X_1 \leq x_1 + \Delta x_1, x_2 < X_2 \leq x_2 + \Delta x_2, \cdots, x_N < X_N \leq x_N + \Delta x_N) \quad \text{(A–59)}$$

$$= f_{X_1 X_2 \cdots X_N}(x_1, x_2, \cdots, x_N) \, \Delta x_1 \, \Delta x_2 \cdots \Delta x_N$$

If a transformation of a single random variable, say,

$$Y = g(X) \quad \text{(A–60)}$$

is monotonic, the probability mass associated with the event $x < X \leq x + \Delta x$ is the same as that associated with the event $y < Y \leq y + \Delta y$. Using (A–14), this observation can be expressed as

$$f_X(x)|\Delta x| = f_Y(y)|\Delta y| \quad \text{(A–61)}$$

or in the limit as $\Delta x \to dx$ and $\Delta y \to dy$

$$f_Y(y) = f_X(x) \left| \frac{dx}{dy} \right| \Bigg|_{x = g^{-1}(y)} \quad \text{(A–62)}$$

where $g^{-1}(\cdot)$ is the inverse of $g(\cdot)$ and the absolute-value signs are necessary to ensure that $f_Y(y) > 0$. If $g(\cdot)$ is not monotonic, (A–62) generalizes to

$$f_Y(y) = \sum_{i=1}^{n} f_X(x) \left| \frac{dx}{dy} \right| \Bigg|_{x = g_i^{-1}(y)} \quad \text{(A–63)}$$

where $x = g_i^{-1}(y)$ is the ith solution to the inverse transformation. An example will make the procedure clearer.

EXAMPLE A–6

Consider a square-law device with transfer characteristic

$$Y = X^2 \quad \text{(A–64a)}$$

The input, X, is a Gaussian random variable with mean zero and variance σ^2. Use (A–63) with the two inverse functions

$$x = \sqrt{y} \quad \text{and} \quad x = -\sqrt{y} \tag{A–64b}$$

Because $Y = X^2$ is nonnegative, it follows that $f_Y(y) = 0$, $y < 0$. For both inverses, the absolute value of the derivative is

$$\left| \frac{dx}{dy} \right| = \frac{1}{2\sqrt{y}} \tag{A–65}$$

Therefore, (A–54) is

$$
\begin{aligned}
f_Y(y) &= \frac{1}{\sqrt{2\pi\sigma^2}} \left[\exp\left(\frac{-x^2}{2\sigma^2} \right) \Big|_{x=\sqrt{y}} + \exp\left(\frac{-x^2}{2\sigma^2} \right) \Big|_{x=-\sqrt{y}} \right] \frac{1}{2\sqrt{y}}, \quad y > 0 \\
&= \frac{1}{\sqrt{2\pi\sigma^2 y}} \exp\left(\frac{-y}{2\sigma^2} \right), \quad y > 0
\end{aligned}
\tag{A–66}
$$

With multiple random variables, it is easiest to assume the same number of output variables as input variables and that the transformation is one-to-one. Let such a transformation be represented by the set of equations

$$
\begin{aligned}
y_1 &= g_1(x_1, x_2, \cdots, x_N) \\
y_2 &= g_2(x_1, x_2, \cdots, x_N) \\
&\vdots \\
y_N &= g_N(x_1, x_2, \cdots, x_N)
\end{aligned}
\tag{A–67}
$$

and let the joint density functions of the input and output random variables be denoted by $f_X(x_1, x_2, \ldots, x_N)$ and $f_Y(y_1, y_2, \ldots, y_N)$, respectively. It can be shown [1] that the joint density of the output random variables is

$$f_Y(y_1, y_2, \cdots, y_N) = f_X(x_1, x_2, \cdots, x_N) \left| J\left(\begin{matrix} x_1, x_2, \cdots, x_N \\ y_1, y_2, \cdots, y_N \end{matrix} \right) \right| \tag{A–68}$$

where

$$
J\left(\begin{matrix} x_1, x_2, \cdots, x_N \\ y_1, y_2, \cdots, y_N \end{matrix} \right) =
\begin{vmatrix}
\dfrac{\partial x_1}{\partial y_1} & \dfrac{\partial x_2}{\partial y_1} & \cdots & \dfrac{\partial x_N}{\partial y_1} \\
\dfrac{\partial x_1}{\partial y_2} & \dfrac{\partial x_2}{\partial y_2} & \cdots & \dfrac{\partial x_N}{\partial y_2} \\
& & \cdots & \\
\dfrac{\partial x_1}{\partial y_N} & \dfrac{\partial x_2}{\partial y_N} & \cdots & \dfrac{\partial x_N}{\partial y_N}
\end{vmatrix}
\tag{A–69}
$$

is the Jacobian. In (A–68) the variables $x_1, x_2, \ldots, x_N$ are replaced by the inverse transformation equations

$$x_1 = g_1^{-1}(y_1, y_2, \cdots, y_N)$$

$$x_2 = g_2^{-1}(y_1, y_2, \cdots, y_N) \tag{A–70}$$

$$\vdots$$

$$x_N = g_N^{-1}(y_1, y_2, \cdots, y_N)$$

which exist by virtue of the transformation being one-to-one.

EXAMPLE A–7

Consider the transformation to polar coordinates of two statistically independent, Gaussian random variables with zero means. Thus

$$f_{\mathbf{x}}(x_1, x_2) = \frac{\exp[-(x_1^2 + x_2^2)/2\sigma^2]}{2\pi\sigma^2} \tag{A–71}$$

$$y_1 = r = \sqrt{x_1^2 + x_2^2}, \quad 0 \le r < \infty \tag{A–72a}$$

$$y_2 = \theta = \tan^{-1}\frac{x_2}{x_1}, \quad -\pi < \theta \le \pi \tag{A–72b}$$

With the restrictions placed on the ranges of r and θ, the transformation is one-to-one. It follows that

$$x_1 = r \cos \theta \tag{A–73a}$$

$$x_2 = r \sin \theta \tag{A–73b}$$

From (A–69), the Jacobian is r. The transformed probability density function is

$$f_{R\Theta}(r, \theta) = \frac{r}{2\pi\sigma^2} \exp\left(\frac{-r^2}{2\sigma^2}\right), \quad r \ge 0; \ -\pi < \theta \le \pi \tag{A–74}$$

The density over r alone is obtained by integration over θ. The result is

$$f_R(r) = \frac{r}{\sigma^2} \exp\left(\frac{-r^2}{2\sigma^2}\right), \quad r \ge 0 \tag{A–75}$$

which is known as a *Rayleigh* density.

The density function of $z = r^2$ can be found similarly to the procedure used in Example A–6. The result is

$$f_Z(z) = \frac{\exp\left(-\dfrac{z}{2\sigma^2}\right)}{2\sigma^2}, \quad z \ge 0 \tag{A–76}$$

This is known as an *exponential* probability density function.

Example A–7 illustrates a procedure that can be used to go from many-to-one random variables. Auxiliary transformations can be defined such that

$$y_1 = g_1(x_1, x_2, \cdots, x_N)$$

$$y_2 = x_2$$

$$y_3 = x_3 \qquad\qquad (A\text{-}77)$$

$$\vdots$$

$$y_N = x_N$$

The transformed density for $y_1, y_2, \ldots, y_N$ is obtained and then the unwanted variables are "integrated out."

EXAMPLE A–8

Given two independent random variables, X and Y, with density functions $f_X(x)$ and $f_Y(y)$, respectively. What is the density function of their product?

Solution: Define the random variables

$$W = X \qquad\qquad (A\text{-}78a)$$

$$Z = XY \qquad\qquad (A\text{-}78b)$$

Then the inverse transformation is

$$X = W \qquad\qquad (A\text{-}79a)$$

$$Y = \frac{Z}{W} \qquad\qquad (A\text{-}79b)$$

which is one-to-one. The Jacobian is

$$J\!\left(\frac{x, y}{w, z}\right) = \begin{vmatrix} \dfrac{\partial x}{\partial w} & \dfrac{\partial y}{\partial w} \\[2ex] \dfrac{\partial x}{\partial z} & \dfrac{\partial y}{\partial z} \end{vmatrix} = \begin{vmatrix} 1 & \dfrac{-z}{w^2} \\[2ex] 0 & \dfrac{1}{w} \end{vmatrix} = \frac{1}{w} \qquad\qquad (A\text{-}80)$$

The joint density function of W and Z is therefore

$$f_{WZ}(w, z) = f_X(x)\, f_Y(y)\, \frac{1}{|w|}\Bigg|_{\substack{x=w \\ y=z/w}} \qquad\qquad (A\text{-}81)$$

$$= f_X(w) f_Y\!\left(\frac{z}{w}\right) \frac{1}{|w|}$$

To obtain the density function of Z alone, this joint density is integrated over all values of w:

$$f_Z(z) = \int_{-\infty}^{\infty} f_X(w) f_Y\left(\frac{z}{w}\right) \frac{dw}{|w|} \tag{A–82}$$

In a similar manner it can be shown that the probability density function of $Z = X + Y$, where X and Y are independent, is

$$f_Z(z) = \int_{-\infty}^{\infty} f_X(z - u) f_Y(u)\, du \tag{A–83}$$

A.4.2 Linear Transformations of Gaussian Random Variables

If a set of jointly Gaussian random variables is transformed to a new set of random variables by a linear transformation, the resulting random variables are jointly Gaussian. To show this, consider the linear transformation

$$\mathbf{y} = \mathbf{Ax} \tag{A–84}$$

where $\mathbf{y}$ and $\mathbf{x}$ are column matrices of dimension N and $\mathbf{A}$ is a nonsingular $N \times N$ square matrix with elements $[a_{ij}]$. From (A–57), the Jacobian is

$$J\left(\begin{array}{c} x_1, x_2, \cdots, x_N \\ y_1, y_2, \cdots, y_N \end{array}\right) = \det \mathbf{A}^{-1} \tag{A–85}$$

where $\mathbf{A}^{-1}$ is the inverse matrix of $\mathbf{A}$. But $\det \mathbf{A}^{-1} = 1/\det \mathbf{A}$. Using this in (A–39) together with

$$\mathbf{x} = \mathbf{A}^{-1}\mathbf{y} \tag{A–86}$$

gives

$$f_Y(\mathbf{y}) = (2\pi)^{-N/2} |\det \mathbf{C}|^{-1/2} |\det \mathbf{A}|^{-1} \tag{A–87}$$
$$\times \exp\left[-\tfrac{1}{2}(\mathbf{A}^{-1}\mathbf{y} - \mathbf{m})^T \mathbf{C}^{-1}(\mathbf{A}^{-1}\mathbf{y} - \mathbf{m})\right]$$

Now $\det \mathbf{A} = \det \mathbf{A}^T$ and $\mathbf{A}\mathbf{A}^{-1} = \mathbf{I}$, the identity matrix, so that (A–87) can be written as

$$f_Y(\mathbf{y}) = (2\pi)^{-N/2} |\det \mathbf{ACA}^T|^{-1/2} \tag{A–88}$$
$$\times \exp\{-\tfrac{1}{2}[\mathbf{A}^{-1}(\mathbf{y} - \mathbf{Am})]^T \mathbf{C}^{-1}[\mathbf{A}^{-1}(\mathbf{y} - \mathbf{Am})]\}$$

But the rules $(\mathbf{AB})^T = \mathbf{B}^T\mathbf{A}^T$ and $(\mathbf{A}^{-1})^T = (\mathbf{A}^T)^{-1}$ allow the exponent to be written as

$$-\tfrac{1}{2}[(\mathbf{y} - \mathbf{Am})^T(\mathbf{A}^T)^{-1}\mathbf{C}^{-1}\mathbf{A}^{-1}(\mathbf{y} - \mathbf{Am})]$$

Finally, the rule $(\mathbf{AB})^{-1} = \mathbf{B}^{-1}\mathbf{A}^{-1}$ allows the exponent to be rearranged as

$$-\tfrac{1}{2}[(\mathbf{y} - \mathbf{Am})^T(\mathbf{ACA}^T)^{-1}(\mathbf{y} - \mathbf{Am})]$$

so that (A–88) becomes

$$f_Y(\mathbf{y}) = (2\pi)^{-N/2}|\det \mathbf{ACA}^T|^{-1/2}$$

$$\times \exp\{-\tfrac{1}{2}(\mathbf{y} - \mathbf{Am})^T(\mathbf{ACA}^T)^{-1}(\mathbf{y} - \mathbf{Am})\} \tag{A–89}$$

which is recognized as a joint Gaussian density for a random vector $\mathbf{Y}$ with mean vector

$$E(\mathbf{Y}) = \mathbf{Am} \tag{A–90}$$

and covariance matrix $\mathbf{ACA}^T$.

A.5   CENTRAL LIMIT THEOREM

The widespread use of Gaussian random variables as representations for signal and noise in communication systems is due in part to the relative ease with which analyses can be carried out. For example, the derivation in Section A–4 showed that the mean and covariance matrices of a linearly transformed Gaussian vector are easily obtained and that knowledge of them allows the joint density function of the transformed variables to be written down immediately using (A–39).

A second reason for the widespread use of Gaussian random variables as signal or noise models is due to the central limit theorem, which states that if $X_1, X_2, \ldots, X_N$ are N identically distributed, independent continuous random variables, all with mean m and finite variance σ^2, the random variable

$$Y = N^{-1/2} \sum_{i=1}^{N} (X_i - m) \tag{A–91}$$

approaches a zero-mean Gaussian random variable with variance σ^2 as $N \to \infty$. The conditions of independence and identically distributed may be relaxed with suitable other restrictions imposed [Papoulis].

REFERENCES

The reader is referred to any undergraduate book on probability, for example, A. Papoulis, *Probability and Statistics* (Englewood Cliffs, NJ: Prentice-Hall, 1990).

PROBLEMS

A–1. Consider two chance experiments, A and B. Experiment A can result in either of the exhaustive, mutually exclusive outcomes A_1 or A_2. Experiment B can result in any one of the exhaustive, mutually exclusive outcomes B_1, B_2, or B_3. A table listing the joint probabilities of all possible combinations of events, one from A and one from B, follows.

(a) Compute $P(A_1)$ and $P(A_2)$.
(b) Compute $P(B_1)$, $P(B_2)$, and $P(B_3)$.
(c) Compute the conditional probabilities $P(A_i \mid B_j)$, $i = 1, 2$ and $j = 1, 2, 3$.
(d) Compute the conditional probabilities $P(B_j \mid A_i)$, $j = 1, 2, 3$, and $i = 1, 2$.
(e) Are A and B statistically independent?

Table of $P(A_i, B_j)$

	B_1	B_2	B_3
A_1	0.1	0.2	0.3
A_2	0.3	0.05	0.05

A–2. The conditional probabilities $P(0r \mid 0s) = 0.8$ and $P(1r \mid 1s) = 0.9$ are obtained for a certain communications channel (see Example A–1 for an explanation of the notation). If $P(0s) = 0.4$ and $P(1s) = 0.6$, find the conditional probabilities of a 1 sent, given that a 1 was received, and a 0 sent, given that a 0 was received.

A–3. The *Rayleigh probability density function* is given by

$$f_R(r) = \begin{cases} \dfrac{r}{\sigma^2} e^{-r^2/2\sigma^2}, & 0 \le r < \infty \\ 0, & r < 0 \end{cases}$$

(a) Find the distribution function of a Rayleigh random variable.
(b) Find $P(0.1\sigma < r \le 0.2\sigma)$ for a Rayleigh random variable.
(c) Show that the mean and mean square of a Rayleigh random variable are given by $\sqrt{\pi/2}\,\sigma$ and $2\sigma^2$, respectively.
(d) Find the variance of a Rayleigh random variable.

A–4. (a) Two random variables, R and Φ, have the joint probability density function

$$f_{R\Phi}(r, \phi) = \begin{cases} \dfrac{r}{2\pi\sigma^2} \exp\left[\dfrac{-(r^2 - 2Ar\cos\phi + A^2)}{2\sigma^2}\right], & \begin{array}{l} 0 \le r < \infty; \\ -\pi < \phi \le \pi \end{array} \\ 0, & \text{otherwise} \end{cases}$$

Show that the marginal probability density function of R is

$$f_R(r) = \dfrac{r}{\sigma^2} \exp\left[\dfrac{-(A^2 + r^2)}{2\sigma^2}\right] I_0\left(\dfrac{Ar}{\sigma}\right), \quad r \ge 0$$

where $I_0(u)$, the modified Bessel function of the first kind and order zero, is given by

$$I_0(u) = \dfrac{1}{2\pi} \int_0^{2\pi} e^{u \cos\phi}\, d\phi$$

This probability density function is known as the Rice–Nakagami, or simply Ricean, density function.

(b) Show that the Ricean density function results from the transformation

$$Y = (A + N_1) \cos \Theta + N_2 \sin \Theta \equiv R \cos(\Theta + \Phi)$$

where A is a constant, Θ is uniform in $(0, 2\pi]$, and N_1 and N_2 are statistically independent Gaussian random variables with mean zero and variance σ^2.

A–5. (a) Show that m_X, m_Y, σ_X, and σ_Y in (A–23) are the means and variance of X and Y, respectively.

(b) Show that the covariance of X and Y is $\mu_{XY} = \rho\sigma_X\sigma_Y$.

A–6. Prove (A–29) and (A–30).

A–7. A random variable has probability density function

$$f_X(x) = A \exp(-b|x|), \quad b > 0$$

(a) Obtain the relationship between A and b
(b) Obtain an expression for the moments $E[X^m]$ of X.
(c) Obtain an expression for the characteristic function of X.
(d) What is the probability that $|X| \geq 1/b$?

A–8. Show that the probability density function of the sum of two independent random variables, $Z = X + Y$, is

$$f_Z(z) = \int_{-\infty}^{\infty} f_X(z - \lambda)f_Y(\lambda) \, d\lambda$$

where f_X and f_Y are the density functions of X and Y.

B

Characterization of Internally Generated Noise

Noise in a communication system can be attributed to external sources or components and subsystems making up the communication system itself. It is the purpose of this appendix to discuss briefly the characterization of internally generated noise. The internally generated noise originates from the random (Brownian) motion of charged carriers within the system components and can be categorized as flicker, shot, or thermal noise. The latter is due to the random motion of charged carriers within resistive materials and will be characterized briefly in this appendix in terms of *noise figure* or *noise temperature*. Shot noise is due to the motion of charge carriers through a junction, such as the anode of a vacuum tube or the junction between p- and n-type material of a semiconductor diode. Its name is derived from the analogy with shot falling on a metal plate. The mechanism for the generation of *flicker noise* is not well understood, but it is characterized by increasing intensity with decreasing frequency and is also referred to as $1/f$ noise.

The noise figure of a device or subsystem may be defined in either one of two ways. The first is that it is the ratio of signal-to-noise *power* ratio at the *input* of the device to the signal-to-noise ratio at its *output*. The second is that it is the ratio of *available noise power* at the *output* terminals of a device to that at its *input*. In equation form, these definitions may be expressed as

$$F = \frac{(S/N)_{in}}{(S/N)_{out}} = \frac{N_{out}}{GN_{in}} \qquad (B-1)$$

where the measurements are made at the standard temperature $T_0 = 290\ K$, and

$\quad (S/N)_{in}$ = input signal-to-noise power ratio

$\quad (S/N)_{out}$ = output signal-to-noise power ratio

$\quad N_{in}$ = available noise power at the input

$\quad N_{out}$ = available noise power at the output

$\quad G$ = system power gain

Matched conditions do not need to be specified for the case of signal-to-noise ratios since the measurement of signal and noise power is performed at the same point.

The circumstances regarding these definitions are illustrated in Figure B–1, which illustrates a device with input resistance R_i and output resistance R_o, driven by a source with internal resistance R_s, and with a load resistance R_g across its output terminals.

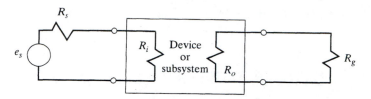

FIGURE B–1   Device or subsystem model pertaining to noise characterization.

It will be recalled that maximum power transfer takes place under *matched conditions;* that is, $R_s = R_i$ and $R_o = R_g$. By Nyquist's theorem,[1] the mean-square thermal noise voltage produced by R_s is

$$v_{rms}^2 = 4kTR_sB \quad \text{V}^2 \tag{B-2}$$

where k = Boltzmann's constant = 1.38×10^{-23} J/K, T is the temperature in kelvins, and B is the bandwidth in hertz in which the noise voltage is measured. Under matched conditions with $R_s = R_i$, half this rms voltage appears across R_s and half across R_i. The *available noise power* of the source resistance is therefore

$$P_a = \frac{(\tfrac{1}{2} v_{rms})^2}{R_s} = \frac{v_{rms}^2}{4R_s} = \frac{4kTR_sB}{4R_s} = kTB \tag{B-3}$$

which is *independent of the source resistance.* If $T = T_0 = 290$ K, which will be referred to as *standard temperature,* the available noise power per hertz of bandwidth is very nearly

$$kT_0 = 4 \times 10^{-21} \text{ W/Hz}$$

or, when expressed in decibels referenced to 1 W, the result is

$$10 \log_{10} kT_0 = -204 \text{ dBW/Hz} \tag{B-4}$$

Returning to (B–1), it is seen that the noise figure of a device can be viewed as a measure of the degradation in signal-to-noise ratio imposed by the device or subsystem under consideration, or as a measure of the increase in output noise power over input noise power due to the internal noise added by the device. According to the latter viewpoint, the noise figure can be rewritten as

$$F = \frac{kT_0BG + \Delta N}{kT_0BG} = 1 + \frac{\Delta N}{kT_0BG} \tag{B-5}$$

where G is the *available power gain* of the subsystem and ΔN is its internally generated noise power. It is important to note that T_0 is used in (B–5) to give a standardized definition for noise figure. To see how this expression generalizes for two subsystems in cascade, let G_1 and G_2 be their respective available power gains, and let ΔN_1 and ΔN_2 be their internally generated noise powers. Then the following contributions to the output noise power from the cascade may be identified:

[1]For a proof of Nyquist's theorem, see [1, pp. 7–21].

$kT_0BG_1G_2$ = available noise power at the input amplified by the cascade and appearing at the output

$\Delta N_1 G_2$ = internally generated noise of the first subsystem of the cascade, amplified by the second subsystem and appearing at the output of the cascade

ΔN_2 = internally generated noise of the second subsystem of the cascade and appearing at its output

The overall noise figure of the cascade, according to (B–5), is the total noise power appearing at its output divided by the available noise power at its input amplified by the system. Using the preceding definitions, this ratio can be written as

$$F = \frac{kT_0BG_1G_2 + \Delta N_1G_2 + \Delta N_2}{kT_0BG_1G_2}$$

$$= 1 + \frac{\Delta N_1}{kT_0BG_1} + \frac{1}{G_1}\left(1 + \frac{\Delta N_2}{kT_0BG_2} - 1\right) \tag{B–6}$$

$$= F_1 + \frac{F_2 - 1}{G_1}$$

where $F_1 = 1 + \Delta N_1/kT_0BG_1$ is the noise figure of subsystem 1 and $F_2 = 1 + \Delta N_2/kT_0BG_2$ is the noise figure of subsystem 2. The noise figure of N subsystems in cascade with noise figures $F_1, F_2, \ldots, F_N$ and available power gains $G_1, G_2, \ldots, G_N$ can be shown to be

$$F = F_1 + \frac{F_2 - 1}{G_1} + \frac{F_3 - 1}{G_1G_2} + \cdots + \frac{F_N - 1}{G_1G_2 \cdots G_{N-1}} \tag{B–7}$$

This result, known as *Friis's formula* [2], shows that it is important that the first stage in the cascade have a low noise figure and a large gain for a low overall noise figure.

Since F is dimensionless, it follows from (B–5) that the quantity $\Delta N/kBG$ has the dimensions of temperature. Accordingly, the *effective noise temperature* of a device is defined as

$$T_e = \frac{\Delta N}{kBG} \tag{B–8}$$

where ΔN is its internally generated noise power appearing at the output terminals, G is its power gain, and B is its bandwidth. This definition allows its noise figure to be written as

$$F = 1 + \frac{T_e}{T_0} \tag{B–9}$$

which, when solved for T_e, gives the effective noise temperature in terms of noise figure as

$$T_e = (F - 1)T_0 \tag{B–10}$$

For a cascade of subsystems with noise temperatures $T_1, T_2, T_3, \ldots$ and available power gains $G_1, G_2, \ldots$, the effective noise temperature of the cascade is

$$T_e = T_1 + \frac{T_2}{G_1} + \frac{T_3}{G_1 G_2} + \cdots \tag{B-11}$$

which follows by using the definition of T_e and Friis's formula.

For a receiver, it is important to include the effect of noise generated by the antenna or noise intercepted by the antenna generated by hot bodies within its field of view, such as the sun, stars, or the earth. If T_a is the antenna temperature and T_e is the effective noise temperature of the receiver excluding the antenna, the *system noise temperature, T_s,* is

$$T_s = T_a + T_e \tag{B-12}$$

which includes the effect of noise power due to the antenna and the internally generated noise of the receiver.

It is important that the first stage of any cascade of subsystems not be an attenuator, for the noise figure of an attenuator of loss factor $L = 1/G$ is simply

$$F_{\text{atten}} = L \tag{B-13}$$

if the attenuator is at standard temperature, T_0.[2]

This discussion of the characterization of internally generated noise will be closed with an example to illustrate the use of the developed relationships in characterizing the noise properties of communications systems.

EXAMPLE B–1

Crystal mixers are sometimes characterized by a *noise temperature ratio, t_r,* defined as

$$t_r = \frac{\text{actual available IF noise power}}{\text{available noise power from an equivalent resistance}}$$

$$= \frac{F_c k T_0 B G_c}{k T_0 B} = F_c G_c = \frac{F_c}{L_c} \tag{B-14}$$

where

$$F_c = \text{crystal mixer noise figure}$$

$$L_c = 1/G_c = \text{mixer conversion loss}$$

Due to flicker noise, the noise temperature ratio of a crystal mixer varies inversely with frequency from about 100 kHz down to less than 1 Hz. Above about 500 kHz, the noise temperature ratio approaches a constant value that is typically in the range 1.3 to 2.0.

Consider, first, the case where a crystal mixer with $t_r = 1.4$ and $L_c = 6$ dB is cascaded with an IF amplifier of noise figure $F_{\text{IF}} = 3$ dB. The noise figure of the cascade, using Friis's formula and the definition of t_r, is

---

[2]A derivation may be found in [3, pp. 771–772].

$$F = F_1 + \frac{F_2 - 1}{G} = L_c(t_r + F_{IF} - 1)$$

$$= 4(1.4 + 2 - 1) = 9.6 = 9.8 \text{ dB}$$

As a second part of the example, suppose that the mixer is preceded by a GaAs field-effect transistor (FET) amplifier with a noise figure of $F_0 = 2$ dB and available power gain of $G_0 = 10$ dB. The overall noise figure now becomes

$$F = F_0 + \frac{F_1 - 1}{G_0} + \frac{F_2 - 1}{G_0 G_1}$$

$$= F_0 + \frac{L_c t_r - 1}{G_0} + \frac{L_c(F_{IF} - 1)}{G_0}$$

$$= F_0 + \frac{L_c}{G_0}(t_r + F_{IF} - 1) - \frac{1}{G_0}$$

$$= 1.58 + \left(\frac{4}{10}\right)(1.4 + 1.99 - 1) - \frac{1}{10}$$

$$= 2.44$$

$$= 3.87 \text{ dB}$$

The importance of having a first stage with a moderately high gain and low noise figure is clearly evident from Example B–1.

REFERENCES

[1] A. van der Ziel, *Noise* (Englewood Cliffs, NJ: Prentice-Hall, 1954).

[2] H. F. Friis, *Proc. Inst. Radio Engs.*, Vol. 32, p. 419, 1944.

[3] R. E. Ziemer and W. H. Tranter, *Principles of Communications,* 4th ed. (Boston: MA: Houghton Mifflin, 1995).

PROBLEMS

B–1. Obtain the available power at standard temperature in a 1 MHz bandwidth for the following resistances. Express in dBW.
   (a) 1 kΩ
   (b) 10 kΩ
   (c) 1 MΩ
   (d) Two 20 kΩ resistors in parallel

B–2. *(Nyquist's Formula)* As one might suspect, the available noise power for an arbitrary network of resistors, capacitors, and inductors can be found by finding its equivalent impedance looking back into the port (terminal pair) of interest. Let this equivalent impedance be

$$Z(f) = R(f) + jX(f)$$

Then the mean-square thermal noise voltage at the port of interest is

$$v_{rms}^2 = 4kT \int_0^\infty R(f)\, df \quad V^2$$

For a purely resistive network, this simplifies to

$$v_{rms}^2 = 4kTR_{eq}B \quad V^2$$

where R_{eq} is the equivalent resistance of the network looking into the port of interest.

Using this theorem, find the mean-square noise voltage at standard temperature in a 1 MHz bandwidth of a 200 Ω resistor in series with a 1000 Ω resistor, with the series combination paralleled by 4800 Ω.

B–3. A receiver with effective noise temperature of 600 K is connected to an antenna of temperature 70 K. Show that the available noise power per hertz for this combination is −170.3 dBm.

B–4. (a) A crystal mixer with noise temperature ratio $t_r = 1.3$ and a conversion loss of $L_c = 6.5$ dB is connected to an antenna of temperature 80 K by a transmission line with a loss of $L_t = 1$ dB. The mixer output is connected to an IF amplifier with a noise figure of 5.3 dB. Find the overall effective noise temperature and the noise figure of the cascade.

(b) The mixer is now preceded by a low-noise amplifier with a gain of 12 dB and a noise figure of 1.9 dB. Everything else remains the same. Find the noise temperature and noise figure of the new arrangement.

C

Attenuation of Radio-Wave Propagation by Atmospheric Gases and Rain

The purpose of this appendix is to provide a summary of the empirical formulas for computing attenuation of radio waves by atmospheric gases and rain. As pointed out in Chapter 1, the principal gaseous constituents of the earth's atmosphere that produce significant absorption are oxygen and water vapor. The first three absorption bands due to atmospheric gases are centered at frequencies of 22.2 GHz (H_2O), 60 GHz (O_2), and 118.8 GHz (O_2). The frequency dependence of the absorption has been found to depend on an empirical line-width constant that is a function of temperature, pressure, and humidity of the atmosphere.

Based on a multiple regression analysis on a selected global sample of radiosonde profiles, a combined specific attenuation, γ_a, which includes the contributions of both oxygen and water vapor absorption, has resulted in the empirical relationship (the method that follows is based on [18] of Chapter 1)

$$\gamma_a = a + b\rho_0 - cT_0 \quad \text{dB/km} \tag{C-1}$$

where a, b, and c are empirical frequency-dependent coefficients, ρ_0 is the mean local surface water vapor concentration in g/m^3, and T_0 is the mean local surface temperature in degrees centigrade. Likewise, the *total* zenith atmospheric attenuation, A_a (i.e., looking straight up through the entire atmosphere) can be found from the empirical relationship

$$A_a = \alpha + \beta\rho_0 - \epsilon T_0 \quad \text{dB} \tag{C-2}$$

The coefficients for these two empirical expressions are listed as a function of frequency in Table C–1.

The relationship between rain rate, R (in mm/h measured at the earth's surface), and specific attenuation can be approximated by

$$\alpha_R = aR^b \quad \text{dB/km} \tag{C-3}$$

where a and b are frequency- and temperature-dependent coefficients. This expression was first obtained from empirical observations, but has since been given a theoretical basis (see, e.g., [5–18] of Chapter 1). Representative values for the parameters a and b are given in Table C–2. A typical attenuation for light rain (10 mm/hr) at 12 GHz is $\alpha_R = 0.29$ dB/km.

TABLE C–1   Coefficients for Calculation of Specific Attenuation
and Total Zenith Atmospheric Attenuation Due to Gaseous Absorption

Freq., GHz	a	b	c	α	β	ϵ
4	0.00802	0.000141	0.0000850	0.0397	0.000276	0.000176
6	0.00824	0.000300	0.0000895	0.0404	0.000651	0.000196
12	0.00898	0.00137	0.000108	0.0436	0.00318	0.000315
15	0.00953	0.00269	0.000125	0.0461	0.00634	0.000455
16	0.00976	0.00345	0.000133	0.0472	0.00821	0.000536
20	0.0125	0.0125	0.000101	0.0560	0.0346	0.00155
22	0.0181	0.0221	0.000129	0.0760	0.0783	0.00310
24	0.0162	0.0203	0.0000563	0.0691	0.0591	0.00250
30	0.0179	0.0100	0.000280	0.0850	0.0237	0.00133
35	0.0264	0.0101	0.000369	0.1230	0.0237	0.00149
41	0.0499	0.0121	0.000620	0.2370	0.0284	0.00211
45	0.0892	0.0140	0.00102	0.4260	0.0328	0.00299
50	0.267	0.0171	0.00251	1.27	0.0392	0.00572
55	3.93	0.0220	0.0158	24.5	0.0490	−0.00121
70	0.499	0.0319	0.00443	2.14	0.0732	0.0104
80	0.160	0.0391	0.00130	0.705	0.0959	0.00586
90	0.113	0.0495	0.000744	0.458	0.122	0.00574
94	0.106	0.054	0.000641	0.417	0.133	0.00594

Notes:

Dry atmosphere: 10% relative humidity, $\rho_0 = 0.001$ g/m^3
Moderate climate: 42% relative humidity, $\rho_0 = 7.5$ g/m^3
Hot-humid climate: 60% relative humidity, $\rho_0 = 18.0$ g/m^3
Coefficients at frequencies other than those given are interpolated on a logarithmic scale.

Source: Reproduced from Reference [18, p. 30] of Chapter 1 with permission.

EXAMPLE C–1 _____

(a)   Find the total specific attenuation at 12 GHz due to absorption by atmospheric gases in a moderate climate at a temperature of 20 degrees centigrade.

(b)   Assuming the a and b coefficients of (C–3) are nearly independent of temperature, find the additional specific attenuation due to steady rain at 10 mm/hr.

(c)   Repeat (a) and (b) for 20 GHz.

Solution:

(a) $\gamma_a = 0.00898 + (0.00137)(7.5) - (0.000108)(20)$

$\qquad = 0.0171$ dB/km   (C–4a)

(b) $\alpha_R = (0.0215) \times 10^{1.136}$

$\qquad = 0.294$ dB/km   (C–4b)

TABLE C–2 aR^b Coefficients for the Calculation of Rain Attenuation at 0° Centigrade; R = rain rate in mm/h

	Coefficient	
Frequency (GHz)	*a*	*b*
4	0.00147	1.016
6	0.00371	1.124
12	0.0215	1.136
15	0.0368	1.118
20	0.0719	1.097
30	0.186	1.043
40	0.362	0.972
94	1.402	0.744

Note: Coefficients at frequencies other than those given are interpolated on a logarithmic scale.

Source: Reproduced from Reference [8, p. 44] of Chapter 1 with permission.

(c) $\gamma_a = 0.0125 + (0.0125)(7.5) - (0.000101)(20)$

$\qquad = 0.1042 \text{ dB/km}$ (C–5a)

$\alpha_R = (0.0719) \times 10^{1.097}$

$\qquad = 0.899 \text{ dB/km}$ (C–5b)

EXAMPLE C–2

(a) The coefficients for total zenith attenuation at a frequency of 18 GHz are desired. Use logarithmic interpolation to find them.

(b) Use the coefficients thus obtained to find total zenith attenuation in a hot-humid climate at 32° Centigrade.

Solution: **(a)** From Table C–1, we see that values at 16 and 20 GHz bracket those at 18 GHz. For the coefficient α we have

$$\log(0.0472) = m \log(16) + b' \qquad \text{(C–6a)}$$

$$\log(0.0560) = m \log(20) + b' \qquad \text{(C–6b)}$$

Solving these for m and b' we obtain

$$m = \frac{\log(0.0472/0.0560)}{\log(16/20)} = 0.7661 \qquad \text{(C–7a)}$$

and

$$b' = \log(0.0560) - m \log(20) = -2.2485 \qquad \text{(C–7b)}$$

Therefore,

$$\log \alpha_{18\,\text{GHz}} = m \log(18) + b' = -1.2868$$

or

$$\alpha_{18\,\text{GHz}} = 0.0517 \qquad \text{(C–8a)}$$

Similarly, we find that

$$\beta_{18\,\text{GHz}} = 0.0175 \qquad \text{(C–8b)}$$

and

$$\epsilon_{18\,\text{GHz}} = 0.00094 \qquad \text{(C–8c)}$$

(b)   At 18 GHz, the total zenith attenuation is

$$A_a = 0.0517 + 0.0175(18) - 0.00094(32) \qquad \text{(C–9)}$$

$$= 0.33662 \text{ dB}$$

D

Generation of Coherent References

D.1 INTRODUCTION

The implementation and performance of several types of digital data modems were considered in Chapters 3 and 4. Generation of stable carrier and clock references is necessary at both the modulator and demodulator of a digital data communication system. In this appendix, means for generation of such reference signals are considered. Because the generation of reference signals involves the use of primary and secondary reference oscillators, the properties and statistical description of phase noise on signals produced by such reference sources will be summarized first. Phase-locked-loop structures and properties, as well as their application in establishing reference signals for carriers and clocks, are surveyed next. Finally, implementation of frequency synthesizers by the direct and phase-locked methods is described. Because of the brief treatment of these subjects, several references are recommended for further details [1–7].

D.2 DESCRIPTION OF PHASE NOISE AND ITS PROPERTIES

D.2.1 General Considerations

In order to design and characterize the behavior of systems for coherent reference generation, at least a casual understanding of the statistics of oscillator phase noise is necessary. To this end, a reference signal will be modeled as

$$r(t) = A[1 + a(t)] \cos\left[\omega_0 t + \phi(t) + \frac{\alpha t^2}{2} \right] \qquad \text{(D–1)}$$

where $\omega_0 = 2\pi f_0$ is the nominal reference frequency of interest, $\phi(t)$ is random phase jitter, and the term $\frac{1}{2}\alpha t^2$ is phase accumulation due to long-term frequency drift of the oscillator. Recalling that instantaneous frequency is the derivative with respect to time of instantaneous phase, it is seen that α is the frequency drift in radians per second. In this introductory consideration, it is assumed that the unwanted amplitude noise, $a(t)$, is negligible, although it is important to note that the amplitude fluctuations, if sufficiently large, may have a nonnegligible effect on the system operation.

The phase jitter, $\phi(t)$, in (D–1) might occur at the output of a primary reference source, as in a transmitter synthesizer, or it might represent the cumulative effects of several oscillators in a large system such as a satellite communications link. The phase jitter may include both the effects of long-term phenomena such as component aging, temperature fluctuations, and power supply variations, as well as the effects of random noise. It is customary to focus attention on the random noise effects in $\phi(t)$ and assume that any long-term effects, which result in nonstationary behavior of $\phi(t)$, can be adequately modeled in the frequency drift term, $\frac{1}{2}\alpha t^2$.

D.2.2 Phase and Frequency Noise Power Spectra

Since $\phi(t)$ is random, it is appropriate to discuss its properties in terms of statistical averages. If one is concerned with gross descriptions of phase noise effects, the standard deviation or variance of $\phi(t)$ is perhaps adequate. Assuming that $\phi(t)$ has zero mean, its variance can be obtained by integrating the phase-jitter power spectral density, $G_\phi(f)$, with units of rad^2/Hz, over all frequency. Sometimes the power spectral density of the instantaneous frequency fluctuations, $S_{\Delta f}(f)$, is used, which is related to the phase-jitter power spectral density by

$$S_{\Delta f}(f) = (2\pi f)^2 G_\phi(f) \quad (\text{rad/s})^2/\text{Hz} \tag{D–2}$$

which follows by recalling that the Fourier transform of $dx(t)/dt$ is $(j2\pi f)X(f)$. The spectra $G_\phi(f)$ and $S_{\Delta f}(f)$ are quite often plotted as single-sided (i.e., mean-square phase fluctuation is obtained by integrating over positive frequencies only) and single-sideband relative to the oscillator nominal frequency.

Typical (single-sideband) straight-line asymptote plots for $G_\phi(f)$ and $S_{\Delta f}(f)$ are shown in Figure D–1, where it is noted that the spectra consist of several regions. These regions are described as follows (f is frequency relative to the nominal carrier frequency of the oscillator):

1. Frequency flicker:

$$G_{\text{ff}}(f) = \frac{k_1}{f^3} \quad \text{rad}^2/\text{Hz} \tag{D–3}$$

   or

$$S_{\text{ff}}(f) = \frac{K_1}{f} \quad (\text{rad/s})^2/\text{Hz} \tag{D–4}$$

2. Random phase walk or white frequency noise:

$$G_{\text{wf}}(f) = \frac{k_2}{f^2} \quad \text{rad}^2/\text{Hz} \tag{D–5}$$

   or

$$S_{\text{wf}}(f) = K_2 \quad (\text{rad/s})^2/\text{Hz} \tag{D–6}$$

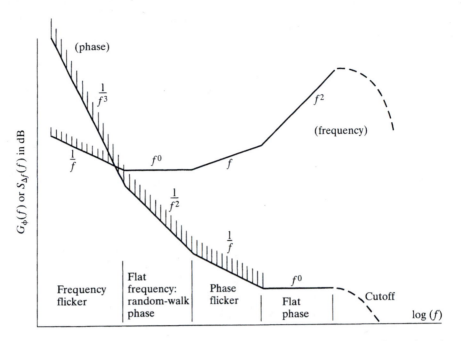

FIGURE D–1 Oscillator noise spectra; asymptotic approximations. (Reproduced from Reference [1] with permission.)

3. Phase flicker:

$$G_{pf}(f) = \frac{k_3}{f} \quad \text{rad}^2/\text{Hz} \tag{D–7}$$

or

$$S_{pf}(f) = K_3 f \quad (\text{rad/s})^2/\text{Hz} \tag{D–8}$$

4. Flat phase:

$$G_{fp}(f) = k_4 \quad \text{rad}^2/\text{Hz} \tag{D–9}$$

or

$$S_{fp}(f) = K_4 f^2 \quad (\text{rad/s})^2/\text{Hz} \tag{D–10}$$

5. Cutoff:

$$G_c(f) = S_c(f) \simeq 0 \tag{D–11}$$

In all cases, $K_i = 4\pi^2 k_i$, $i = 1, 2, 3, 4$.

From a physical standpoint, it is possible to explain the white frequency-noise and flat phase-noise portions of these spectra as being caused by the random motion of charge carriers. It is more difficult to explain the frequency-flicker and phase-flicker regions.

Flicker noise is observed as a low-frequency disturbance in nearly all active electronic devices, but an acceptable explanation of how this low-frequency noise energy is translated into radio-frequency phase or frequency fluctuations is difficult to come up with. The existence of flicker-type phase-fluctuation spectra must simply be expected on the basis of experimental measurements, several examples of which are provided in Figure D–2.

Mathematically, flicker-type spectra are difficult to work with. For example, integration of the phase fluctuation spectrum over the range of frequencies $(0, \infty)$ gives the variance of the phase fluctuations, which for spectra of the form k/f^n results in an undefined result if $n \le 1$. Empirically, a lower cutoff frequency, f_x, can be determined such that

$$\hat{\sigma}_\phi^2 = \int_{f_x}^{\infty} G_\phi(f')\, df' \ll 1 \text{ rad}^2 \tag{D–12}$$

Fluctuations with frequencies lower than f_x can be viewed as contributing to broadening of the carrier frequency and those above f_x can be viewed as modulation on this broadened carrier.

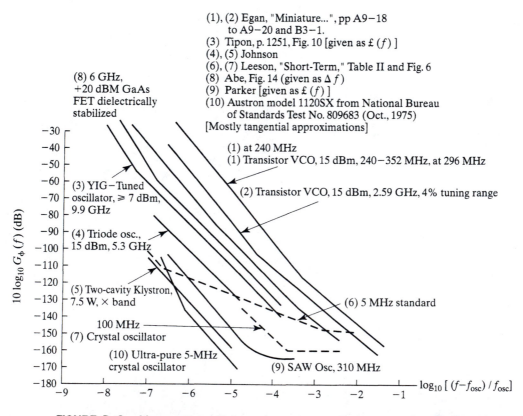

(1), (2) Egan, "Miniature...", pp A9−18
to A9−20 and B3−1.
(3) Tipon, p. 1251, Fig. 10 [given as £ (f)]
(4), (5) Johnson
(6), (7) Leeson, "Short-Term," Table II and Fig. 6
(8) Abe, Fig. 14 (given as Δ f)
(9) Parker [given as £ (f)]
(10) Austron model 1120SX from National Bureau
of Standards Test No. 809683 (Oct., 1975)
[Mostly tangential approximations]

(8) 6 GHz,
+20 dBM GaAs
FET dielectrically
stabilized

(1) at 240 MHz
(1) Transistor VCO, 15 dBm, 240−352 MHz, at 296 MHz

(2) Transistor VCO, 15 dBm, 2.59 GHz, 4% tuning range

(3) YIG−Tuned
oscillator, ≥ 7 dBm,
9.9 GHz

(4) Triode osc.,
15 dBm, 5.3 GHz

(5) Two-cavity Klystron,
7.5 W, × band

(6) 5 MHz standard

100 MHz
(7) Crystal oscillator

(10) Ultra-pure 5-MHz
crystal oscillator

(9) SAW Osc, 310 MHz

$10 \log_{10} G_\phi(f)$ (dB)

$\log_{10}[(f - f_{osc})/f_{osc}]$

FIGURE D–2 Measured oscillator noise spectra. (Reproduced from Reference [5] with permission.)

EXAMPLE D–1 _____

Consider an oscillator with the phase fluctuation spectral density shown in Figure D–3. Find k_1, k_2, k_3, and k_4 for the asymptotic approximations given by (D–3), (D–5), (D–7), and (D–9). Find f_x as defined by (D–12) such that $\hat{\sigma}_\phi^2 = 0.1$ rad^2. Replot Figure D–3 with the abscissa $\log_{10}[(f - f_0)/f_0]$ for $f_0 = 100$ MHz, where f_0 is the oscillator nominal frequency, and compare with Figure D–3.

Solution: Using the relations

$$-3 \text{ dB/octave} = -10 \text{ dB/decade} \rightarrow 10 \log_{10} f^{-1}$$

$$-6 \text{ dB/octave} = -20 \text{ dB/decade} \rightarrow 10 \log_{10} f^{-2}$$

$$-9 \text{ dB/octave} = -30 \text{ dB/decade} \rightarrow 10 \log_{10} f^{-3}$$

and a conveniently chosen set of frequencies, one obtains

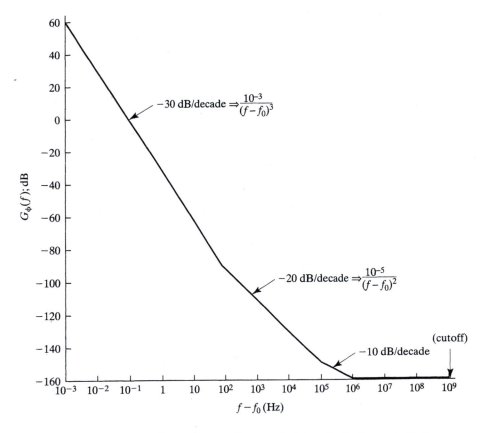

FIGURE D–3   Oscillator phase-noise spectral density for Example D–1.

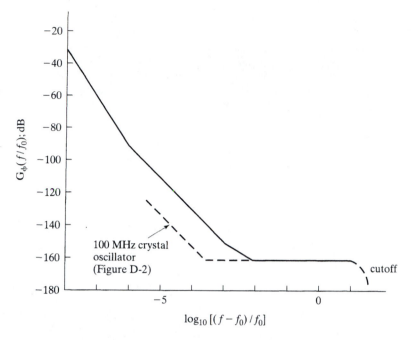

FIGURE D–4   Oscillator phase-noise spectrum of Example D–1 as a function of normalized frequency compared with spectrum of Figure D–2.

$$k_1 = 10^{-3} \quad (\text{rad-Hz})^2$$

$$k_2 = 10^{-5} \quad \text{rad}^2\text{-Hz}$$

$$k_3 = 10^{-10} \quad \text{rad}^2$$

$$k_4 = 10^{-16} \quad \text{rad}^2/\text{Hz}$$

Integration of $G_\phi(f)$ from f_x to the cutoff frequency of 10 GHz[1] results in

$$\frac{5 \times 10^{-4}}{f_x^2} + \frac{10^{-5}}{f_x} + 10^{-10} \ln f_x + 10^{-16} f_x \simeq 0.1$$

where all upper limit evaluations are neglected relative to 0.1. Since the first term on the left-hand side dominates if $f_x < 1$, it follows that

$$f_x \simeq 0.071 \text{ Hz}$$

The curve of Figure D–3, with an abscissa normalized by the nominal oscillator frequency of 100 MHz, is replotted in Figure D–4 and compared with the phase-noise spectrum of the 100 MHz crystal oscillator of Figure D–2. It is seen that the hypothetical oscillator of this example has more phase noise than the 100 MHz crystal oscillator.

---

[1]Clearly, a cutoff frequency of 10 GHz has little physical meaning compared with a center frequency of 100 MHz. It is simply a frequency beyond which the phase-noise spectrum is negligible.

D.2.3 Allan Variance

Although the phase- and frequency-noise power spectra will be used primarily in the discussion to follow, it is useful to point out the relationship of the phase-noise spectrum to frequency counter measurements of oscillator frequency variations due to noise. Define the fractional frequency stability of an oscillator as

$$\delta_j \triangleq \frac{\phi[(j+1)T] - \phi(jT)}{T\omega_0} \tag{D-13}$$

where $\phi(t_s)$ is the phase at sampling instant t_s, T is the measurement interval, and ω_0 is the nominal oscillator frequency in rad/s. A conventional frequency counter measures $\{\phi[(j+1)T] - \phi(jT)\}/2\pi$ in a T-second period. The Allan variance [7, p. 339] is defined as

$$\overline{\sigma^2(N,T)} \triangleq \overline{[1/(N-1)]\sum_{n=1}^{N} (\delta_n - \delta_{sm})^2} \tag{D-14}$$

where the overbar denotes the statistical average and δ_{sm} is the sample mean of $\{\delta_j\}$, which is

$$\delta_{sm} \triangleq \frac{1}{N}\sum_{j=1}^{N} \delta_j \tag{D-15}$$

It can be shown [5, 7] that the Allan variance is related to the frequency-noise power spectrum by

$$\overline{\sigma^2(N,T)} = \frac{N}{N-1}\int_0^\infty \frac{S_{\Delta f}(f)}{(2\pi)^2} \mathrm{sinc}^2(fT)\left(1 - \frac{\sin^2 \pi NfT}{N^2 \sin^2 \pi fT}\right) df \tag{D-16}$$

where $\mathrm{sinc}(u) = \sin(\pi u)/\pi u$. Given the phase- or frequency-noise power spectrum of an oscillator, (D–16) can be used to obtain the Allan variance. However, the reverse is not true. For further discussion of the Allan variance, see [5, Chapter 10].

D.2.4 Effect of Frequency Multipliers and Dividers on Phase-Noise Spectra

A frequency multiplier is a device whose output is a signal with instantaneous frequency that is an integer multiple of the instantaneous frequency of the signal at its input. Thus, for an input of the form

$$x(t) = A\cos[\omega_0 t + \theta(t)] \tag{D-17}$$

the output of a frequency multiplier is

$$y(t) = B\cos[n\omega_0 t + n\theta(t)] \tag{D-18}$$

where n is the multiplication factor and ω_0 is the center frequency of the signal spectrum. A similar relation can be written for a frequency divider, except that the instantaneous frequency is divided by an integer, n.

The application of this result to phase-noise power spectra means that since the phase-noise spectrum is proportional to the *square* of the instantaneous phase, the *phase-noise spectrum at the output of a frequency multiplier of multiplication factor n is n^2 times the input phase-noise spectrum.* A similar statement holds for frequency-noise spectra since instantaneous frequency is proportional to the derivative of instantaneous phase. Similarly, the phase- or frequency-noise spectra at the output of a frequency divider is $1/n^2$ times the input phase- or frequency-noise spectra, where n in the divider ratio.

D.3   PHASE-LOCKED LOOP MODELS AND CHARACTERISTICS OF OPERATION

Since phase-locked loops play important roles in establishing coherent references in digital communication systems, their properties will be described in this section.

D.3.1   Synchronized Mode: Linear Operation

The block diagram for a phase-locked loop of arbitrary order is shown in Figure D–5. It consists of a phase detector whose output is a monotonic function of the phase difference between the input signal and the reference input, a loop filter with transfer function $F(s)$, and a voltage-controlled oscillator that produces the reference signal, $e_o(t)$. The input signal is represented as

$$x_c(t) = A_c \cos(2\pi f_o t + \phi) \tag{D–19}$$

and the voltage-controlled oscillator (VCO) output, or reference signal, is represented as[2]

$$e_o(t) = -A_v \sin(2\pi f_o t + \theta) \tag{D–20}$$

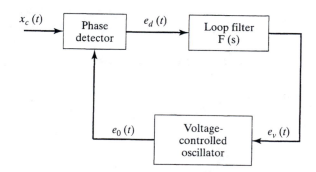

FIGURE D–5   General-order phase-locked-loop block diagram.

[2]It is initially assumed that the loop is operating in the frequency synchronized mode; that is, only the phase of the VCO must be synchronized with the input signal phase.

The frequency deviation of the VCO output is proportional to its input, $e_v(t)$; that is,

$$\frac{d\theta}{dt} = K_v e_v(t) \tag{D--21}$$

where K_v is the VCO constant in rad/s/V.

If the phase detector is assumed to be an ideal multiplier followed by a lowpass filter whose sole effect is to remove the double-frequency component at the multiplier output, the phase detector output is

$$e_d(\psi) = K_d \sin \psi \tag{D--22}$$

where

$$\psi = \phi - \theta \tag{D--23}$$

is the phase error and K_d is a proportionality constant. For the sinusoidal phase detector, $K_d = \frac{1}{2} A_c A_v K_m$, where K_m is the multiplier constant. The phase detector characteristic given by (D--22) is illustrated in Figure D--6 together with several other possible phase detector characteristics. If the phase error is small, the sinusoidal phase detector characteristic shown in Figure D--6a is linear to a good approximation. Therefore, if $|\psi| \ll 1$, all the phase detectors with characteristics shown in Figure D--6 have approximately the same effect on loop operation. If the phase error is large, all impose nonlinear effects on system operation. Such nonlinear behavior will be discussed in more detail later, but for now loop operation is assumed to be entirely within one of the linear regions with positive slope. These can be shown to be stable lock-point regions for a first-order loop which has $F(s) = 1$ by employing phase-plane arguments [7].

With the foregoing definitions and assuming operation in the linear mode, the equations describing loop operation will now be obtained. It is convenient to do so using Laplace transform notation and by considering the signal phase as the signal of interest. A loop model using Laplace transformed quantities and assuming linear operation is shown in Figure D--7. The Laplace-transformed loop equations are

$$E_d(s) = K_d[\Phi(s) - \Theta(s)] = K_d \Psi(s) \tag{D--24}$$

$$E_v(s) = F(s)E_d(s) \tag{D--25}$$

$$\Theta(s) = \frac{K_v E_v(s)}{s} \tag{D--26}$$

The following ratios of Laplace-transformed quantities, or transfer functions, relating to loop operation in the synchronized mode may be solved for, and are frequently used:

1. The closed-loop transfer function:

$$H(s) \triangleq \frac{\Theta(s)}{\Phi(s)} = \frac{K_v K_d F(s)}{s + K_v K_d F(s)} \tag{D--27}$$

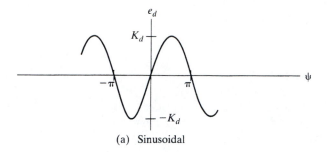

(a) Sinusoidal

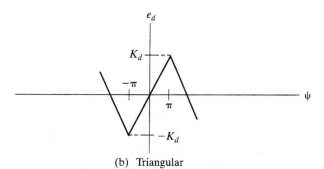

(b) Triangular

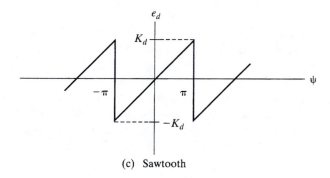

(c) Sawtooth

FIGURE D–6   Phase detector characteristics.

2. The phase error transfer function:

$$H_e(s) \triangleq \frac{\Phi(s) - \Theta(s)}{\Phi(s)} = \frac{\Psi(s)}{\Phi(s)}$$

$$= 1 - \frac{\Theta(s)}{\Phi(s)} \qquad\qquad\text{(D–28)}$$

$$= 1 - H(s) = \frac{s}{s + K_v K_d F(s)}$$

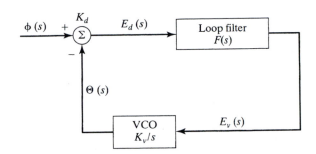

FIGURE D–7   Laplace-transformed phase-locked-loop model for operation in linear mode.

3. The VCO control-voltage/input-phase transfer function:

$$H_v(s) = \frac{E_v(s)}{\Phi(s)}$$

$$= \frac{sH(s)}{K_v} \qquad (D-29)$$

$$= \frac{K_d s F(s)}{s + K_v K_d F(s)}$$

It is convenient to write the closed-loop transfer function in terms of the open-loop transfer function, which is defined as

$$G(s) = \frac{K_v K_d F(s)}{s} \qquad (D-30)$$

Substituting (D–30) into (D–27) results in

$$H(s) = \frac{G(s)}{1 + G(s)} \qquad (D-31)$$

The open-loop dc gain is defined as

$$K = K_v K_d \qquad (D-32)$$

which is a generalization of the total effective loop gain of the first-order loop.

By appropriate choice of $F(s)$, any order closed-loop transfer function can be obtained. Consideration here will be restricted to first- and second-order loops. Various types of loop filters for second-order loops are employed. Circuit diagrams for two of these types are illustrated in Figure D–8. For second-order loops, it is customary to express the denominator of the closed-loop transfer function in terms of the damping factor, ζ, and natural frequency, ω_n, as

$$D(s) = s^2 + 2\zeta\omega_n s + \omega_n^2 \qquad (D-33)$$

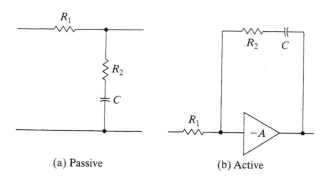

(a) Passive   (b) Active

FIGURE D–8   Second-order phase-locked-loop filters.

With these definitions, and the definition of noise equivalent bandwidth for a filter given by (2–199), the closed-loop transfer functions and noise equivalent bandwidths for the first- and second-order loops given in Table D–1 result [1, 7].

The closed-loop frequency response for a second-order loop with active filter is shown in Figure D–9 for several values of damping factor, ζ. The frequency response corresponding to its phase-error transfer function is shown in Figure D–10 for $\zeta = 0.707$. In terms of its effect on input phase, Figure D–9 shows that a phase-locked loop performs a

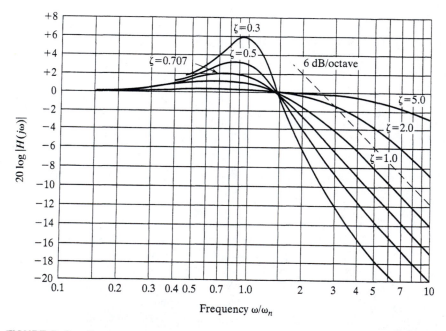

FIGURE D–9   Frequency response of a high-gain second-order loop. (Reproduced from Reference [1] with permission.)

TABLE D-1 Transfer Functions and Parameters for First- and Second-Order Phase-Locked Loops

Loop Filter, $F(s)$	Natural Frequency,* ω_n (rad/s)	Damping Factor	Closed-Loop Transfer Function, $H(s)$	Error Transfer Function, $1 - H(s)$	Single-Sided Bandwidth (Hz)
1 (first order)	K	—	$\dfrac{K}{s+K}$	$\dfrac{s}{s+K}$	$\dfrac{K}{4}$
$\dfrac{s\tau_2 + 1}{s\tau_1 + 1}$ (passive, second order)	$\sqrt{\dfrac{K}{\tau_1}}$	$\dfrac{\omega_n}{2}(\tau_2 + K^{-1})$	$\dfrac{(2\zeta\omega_n - \omega_n^2/K)s + \omega_n^2}{D(s)}$	$\dfrac{s^2 + \omega_n^2 s/K}{D(s)}$	$\dfrac{K\tau_2(1/\tau_2^2 + K/\tau_1)}{4(K + 1/\tau_2)}$ †
$\dfrac{s\tau_2 + 1}{s\tau_1}$ (active, second order)	$\sqrt{\dfrac{K}{\tau_1}}$	$\dfrac{\tau_2\omega_n}{2}$	$\dfrac{2\zeta\omega_n s + \omega_n^2}{D(s)}$	$\dfrac{s^2}{D(s)}$	$\dfrac{1}{2}\,\omega_n\left(\zeta + \dfrac{1}{4\zeta}\right)$ †
$\dfrac{1}{s\tau + 1}$ (lag, second order)	$\sqrt{\dfrac{K}{\tau}}$	$\dfrac{1}{2\sqrt{K\tau}}$	$\dfrac{\omega_n^2}{D(s)}$	$\dfrac{s^2 + 2\zeta\omega_n s}{D(s)}$	$\dfrac{K}{4}$

*$K = K_v K_d$

†For a second-order loop with $\zeta = 0.5$, $B_L = 0.5\omega_n$; with $\zeta = 1/\sqrt{2}$, $D(s) = s^2 + 2\zeta\omega_n s + \omega_n^2$ $B_L = 0.53\omega_n$. B_L is the single-sided noise bandwidth in hertz, and the dimensions of ω_n are rad/s.

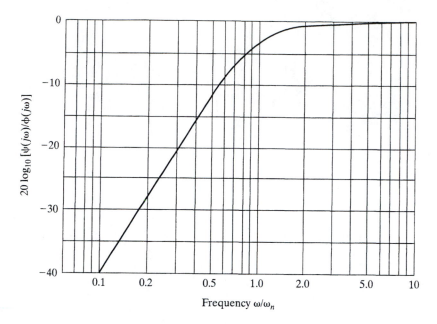

FIGURE D–10 Error response of high-gain loop, $\zeta = 0.707$. (Reproduced from Reference [1] with permission.)

lowpass filtering operation. In the application to FM demodulation, the loop bandwidth is made large in order that $\theta(t)$ closely tracks $\phi(t)$, thus making the VCO input proportional (or nearly so) to the modulating signal. This follows from the defining equation for the VCO (D–21). Conversely, when establishing a coherent reference for digital data demodulation, it is desirable to have the loop bandwidth narrow to minimize the effects of input noise to the loop on $\phi(t)$ in terms of phase jitter. The limitation on how narrow the loop bandwidth can be made is determined by the amount of phase-jitter noise on the carrier to which the loop is being locked. These points are examined further in the following sections.

D.3.2   Effects of Noise

The input to the linear phase-locked loop of Figure D–7 will now be assumed to be signal plus stationary, band-limited, Gaussian noise,

$$x_r(t) = x_c(t) + n(t) \tag{D–34}$$

where $x_c(t)$ is given by (D–19) and $n(t)$ is represented in phase/quadrature form as

$$n(t) = n_c(t) \cos 2\pi f_o t - n_s(t) \sin 2\pi f_o t \tag{D–35}$$

Using the VCO output signal representation (D–20) and the loop parameters defined previously, it can be shown that the output of an ideal multiplier-type phase detector (sinusoidal characteristic as shown in Figure D–6a) is [1]

$$e_d(t) = K_d[\sin(\phi - \theta) - n'(t)] \tag{D–36}$$

where

$$n'(t) = \frac{n_c(t)}{A_c}\cos\theta - \frac{n_s(t)}{A_c}\sin\theta \tag{D–37}$$

Thus, the noise-equivalent model for an ideal multiplier-type phase detector is as shown in Figure D–11. Furthermore, if the single-sided noise spectral density of $n(t)$ is N_0, the single-sided noise spectral density of $n'(t)$ can be shown to be

$$S_{n'}(f) = \frac{2N_0}{A_c^2}, \quad f \le \frac{B}{2} \tag{D–38}$$

If the noise bandwidth of $n(t)$ is B hertz (single-sided), the variance of the input noise is

$$\sigma_n^2 = N_0 B \tag{D–39}$$

and that of $n'(t)$, with single-sided bandwidth $B/2$, is

$$\sigma_{n'}^2 = \frac{N_0 B}{A_c^2} = \frac{\sigma_n^2}{A_c^2} \tag{D–40}$$

The only assumption made in deriving $n'(t)$ is that the VCO phase, $\theta(t)$, is very slowly varying (ideally time-invariant, but arbitrary). Linearity of the phase detector has not been imposed. Thus, since it is linearly dependent on $n_c(t)$ and $n_s(t)$, which are Gaussian, $n'(t)$ is Gaussian, assuming that θ is constant or very slowly varying.

If the input noise to the loop is sufficiently small, the $\sin(\phi - \theta)$ operation in Figure D–11 can be replaced by $(\phi - \theta)$, and the appropriate closed-loop model with noise at the input is then as shown in Figure D–12. Since the equivalent noise, $n'(t)$, is additive at the input, the variance of the VCO output phase is

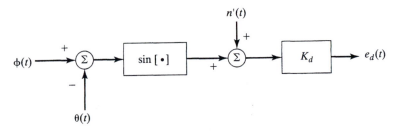

FIGURE D–11   Noise-equivalent model for sinusoidal phase detector.

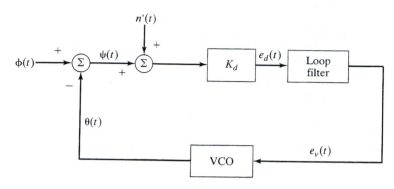

FIGURE D-12 Linear model for phase-locked loop with additive noise present at the input.

$$\sigma_\theta^2 = S_{n'}(0)B_L$$

$$= \frac{2N_0B_L}{A_c^2} \tag{D-41}$$

where B_L is the single-sided equivalent noise bandwidth of the closed loop. For the second-order loop with active filter, the ratio of equivalent noise bandwidth to natural frequency from Table D-1 is

$$\frac{B_L}{\omega_n} = \frac{\zeta + 1/(4\zeta)}{2} \tag{D-42}$$

which has a minimum value of $\frac{1}{2}$ for $\zeta = \frac{1}{2}$, giving a minimum VCO phase variance due to additive input noise of

$$\sigma_{\theta,\min}^2 = \frac{N_0\omega_n}{A_c^2} = \frac{2N_0B_L}{A_c^2} \quad \text{(second-order loop, active filter, } \zeta = \frac{1}{2}) \tag{D-43}$$

A damping factor of $\zeta = 1/\sqrt{2} = 0.707$, which is often used due to transient response considerations, gives a VCO phase variance due to noise that differs from (D-43) by only 6%.

The signal-to-noise ratio at the loop input, with noise measured in a loop bandwidth, is

$$\rho = (\text{SNR})_L = \frac{A_c^2}{2N_0B_L} \tag{D-44}$$

In terms of ρ, σ_θ^2 is given by

$$\sigma_\theta^2 = \frac{1}{\rho} \tag{D-45}$$

a result that was derived assuming operation in the linear region of the phase detector characteristic.

An exact analysis for the variance of the VCO phase due to noise has been carried out only for the first-order phase-locked loop assuming no frequency offset and no modulation on the carrier. This result is shown in Figure D–13 together with (D–43) from the linearized analysis. The method used to solve the nonlinear problem, known as the Fokker–Planck technique, gives a probability density function for the phase error of the form

$$p(\psi) = \frac{\exp(\rho \cos \psi)}{2\pi I_0(\rho)}, \quad |\psi| \le \pi \tag{D–46}$$

where $I_0(\cdot)$ is the modified Bessel function of order zero. For ρ large, it can be shown by using the asymptotic formula $I_0(\rho) \simeq \exp(\rho)/\sqrt{2\pi\rho}$ that $p(\psi)$ tends to a Gaussian density function with zero mean and variance σ_θ^2 [2]. This is called a Tikhonov pdf.

Other approximate noise analysis methods have been devised for analyzing the behavior of phase-locked loops operating into the nonlinear region. These methods deal

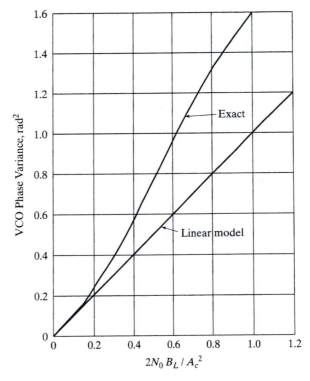

FIGURE D–13   Comparison of exact and approximate values for first-order PLL phase error variance. (Reproduced from Reference [2] with permission.)

only with second-order statistics such as variance, and do not take into account cycle slip-ping. Again, appealing to the Fokker–Planck analysis results for the first-order phase-locked loop, it has been shown [2] that the average time between cycle slips (i.e., the average time for the loop phase error to reach $\pm 2\pi$ after starting initially at 0) is given by

$$T_{av} = \frac{2\pi\rho I_0^2(\rho)}{2B_L} \tag{D-47}$$

$$\simeq \frac{\pi}{4B_L} \exp(2\rho), \quad \rho \gg 1$$

In addition, the probability distribution of the time between slips is exponential; that is,

$$P(T) = 1 - \exp\left(\frac{-T}{T_{av}}\right) \tag{D-48}$$

where T is the time to a slip given the loop started with zero error.

These results apply exactly to a first-order loop with a sinusoidal phase detector characteristic operating in additive white Gaussian noise. Exact Fokker–Planck solutions for the second-order loop have not been obtained. However, experimental measurements and approximate nonlinear analyses for the second-order loop show that the exact nonlin-ear analysis results for the first-order loop are in close agreement with the second-order loop results for $(SNR)_L > 0$ dB.

D.3.3   Phase-Locked-Loop Tracking of Oscillators with Phase Noise

The effect of oscillator phase jitter on the phase error of a second-order phase-locked loop with active filter and damping factor $\zeta = 1/\sqrt{2}$ will now be analyzed. To find the variance of the loop phase error, σ_ψ^2, due to the phase-locked loop tracking an oscillator with phase-jitter power spectral density $G_\phi(f)$, the relationship for the output noise variance of a linear system in terms of input noise spectral density and system frequency response function will be used. In the present context, however, the input noise spectral density is $G_\phi(f)$ and the system frequency response function is the loop-phase-error frequency response, $1 - \tilde{H}(f)$, where the tilde denotes $H(s)|_{s=j2\pi f}$. Thus, the loop-phase-error variance is[3]

$$\sigma_\psi^2 = \int_0^\infty G_\phi(f)|1 - \tilde{H}(f)|^2 \, df \tag{D-49}$$

where the lower limit is zero since $G_\phi(f)$ is a single-sided power spectral density. From Table D–1 it follows that

$$|1 - \tilde{H}(f)|^2 = |1 - H(s)|^2_{s=j2\pi f, \zeta=1/\sqrt{2}}$$

$$= \left|\frac{(j\pi f)^2}{(j2\pi f)^2 + 2\zeta\omega_n(j2\pi f) + \omega_n^2}\right|^2_{\zeta=1/\sqrt{2}} \tag{D-50}$$

[3]The phase-noise spectra are assumed to be single-sided and single-sideband in this appendix.

$$= \frac{(f/f_n)^4}{1 + (f/f_n)^4}$$

with $f_n \triangleq \omega_n/2\pi$. To carry out the evaluation of (D–49), $G_\phi(f)$ is represented in terms of the asymptotic expression

$$G_\phi(f) = \begin{cases} \dfrac{k_1}{f^3} + \dfrac{k_2}{f^2} + k_4, & f \le f_m \\[3mm] \dfrac{k_1}{f^3} + \dfrac{k_2}{f^2}, & f > f_m \end{cases} \tag{D–51}$$

which is based on the discussion centering on (D–3) through (D–11). The loop-phase-error variance due to phase jitter on the input signal can be written

$$\sigma_\psi^2 = \int_0^\infty \frac{f_n^{-2} k_1 x}{1 + x^4} \, dx + \int_0^\infty \frac{f_n^{-1} k_2 x^2}{1 + x^4} \, dx + \int_0^{f_m/f_n} \frac{k_1 x^4 f_n}{1 + x^4} \, dx \tag{D–52}$$

Carrying out the integration, the phase-error variance can be expressed as [7]

$$\sigma_\psi^2 = \frac{k_1 \pi^3}{\omega_n^2} + \frac{k_2 \pi^2}{\sqrt{2}\omega_n} + k_4 f_m \tag{D–53}$$

EXAMPLE D–2

Evaluate σ_ψ^2 using the values for k_1, k_2, and k_4 found in Example D–1 for a loop bandwidth of 1 Hz.

Solution: From Table D–1, if $\zeta = 1\sqrt{2}$, the loop bandwidth is

$$B_L = \frac{1}{2} \omega_n \left(\zeta + \frac{1}{4\zeta} \right) = 0.53\omega_n \tag{D–54}$$

For $B_L = 1$ Hz, $\omega_n = 1.89$ rad/s. Therefore,

$$\sigma_\psi^2 = \frac{(10^{-3})\pi^3}{(1.89)^2} + \frac{(10^{-5})\pi^2}{\sqrt{2}(1.89)} + (10^{-16})(10^9)$$

$$= 8.7 \times 10^{-3} + 3.71 \times 10^{-5} + 10^{-7} = 8.72 \times 10^{-3} \text{ rad}^2$$

or $\sigma_\psi = 0.094$ rad.

D.3.4   Phase Jitter Plus Noise Effects

From (D–41) it is seen that the VCO phase variance due to additive noise at the loop input increases linearly with B_L. For a constant input phase, this translates directly to a linear increase in phase-error variance with B_L due to noise. On the other hand, (D–53) and (D–54) show that the phase-error variance due to phase jitter on the input signal decreases

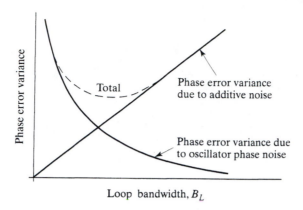

FIGURE D–14 Optimization of phase error variance.

with increasing B_L. Therefore, an optimum value of B_L exists that provides a minimum in the phase-error variance due to both additive input noise and phase jitter on the input signal. This optimum value is illustrated by Figure D–14.

EXAMPLE D–3

Find the optimum loop bandwidth (in the sense of minimum phase-error variance) for an active filter second-order loop with $\zeta = 1/\sqrt{2}$ that is tracking an oscillator with the phase-noise characteristics given in Example D–1, assuming that the loop operates in an additive noise background with

$$10 \log_{10} \left(\frac{A_c^2}{2N_0} \right) = 40 \text{ dB-Hz}$$

Solution: Total mean-square phase error, or variance, due to both phase noise and background noise from (D–41) and (D–53) is

$$\sigma_{\psi,T}^2 = \frac{2N_0 B_L}{A_c^2} + \frac{k_1 \pi^3}{\omega_n^2} + \frac{k_2 \pi^2}{\sqrt{2}\omega_n} + k_4 f_m$$

where $\omega_n = B_L/0.53 = 1.89 B_L$. Substituting previously obtained values for constants, this can be written as

$$\sigma_{\psi,T}^2 = 10^{-4} B_L + \frac{8.7 \times 10^{-3}}{B_L^2} + \frac{3.71 \times 10^{-5}}{B_L} + 10^{-7}$$

Differentiation of this with respect to B_L and setting the result equal to zero results in

$$10^{-4} - \frac{17.4 \times 10^{-3}}{B_{L,\text{opt}}^3} - \frac{3.71 \times 10^{-5}}{B_{L,\text{opt}}^2} = 0$$

or

$$B_{L,opt} \simeq 5.6 \text{ Hz}$$

For this optimum bandwidth, the total phase-error standard deviation is

$$\sigma_{\psi,T,opt} \simeq 0.03 \text{ rad}$$

Now consider a phase-locked loop with phase noise, $\theta_n(t)$, on the VCO output. It can be shown[4] that the phase-error variance due to the noisy VCO is

$$\sigma_{\psi,VCO}^2 = \int_0^\infty |1 - H(j2\pi f)|^2 \, G_{\theta_n}(f) \, df \tag{D-55}$$

where $G_{\theta n}$ is the *single-sided* power spectral density of the VCO phase noise. (Note that additive phase noise at the VCO output is no different from additive phase noise at the loop input.) Suppose that the VCO phase-noise spectral density is random phase walk with

$$G_{\theta_n}(f) = \frac{K_{VCO}}{f^2} \tag{D-56}$$

For a second-order loop with $\zeta = 1/\sqrt{2}$ and natural frequency ω_n, it follows from (D-54) that

$$\sigma_{\psi,VCO}^2 = \frac{K_{VCO}\pi^2}{\sqrt{2}\,\omega_n} = \frac{K_{VCO}\pi^2}{\sqrt{2}(1.89)B_L} \quad \left(\zeta = \frac{1}{\sqrt{2}}\right) \tag{D-57}$$

If the loop also has additive white noise present at its input, an optimum bandwidth exists, as in Example D-3, that will minimize the total phase-error variance due to VCO jitter and input noise.

One final comment needs stressing in regard to tracking an oscillator with phase jitter. If frequency multiplication or division by N is used prior to the loop, the phase noise is multiplied or divided by N and the phase-noise spectral density is multiplied or divided by N^2, respectively. This follows because the instantaneous output phase, $\theta_{out}(t)$, of a frequency multiplier is $\theta_{out}(t) = N\theta_{in}(t)$, where $\theta_{in}(t)$ is the input phase, with division by N for a divider.

D.3.5   Transient Response

The tracking error, $\psi(t)$, of the loop for various input phase functions, $\phi(t)$, can be determined by obtaining the inverse Laplace transform of

$$\psi(s) = [1 - H(s)]\phi(s) \tag{D-58}$$

---

[4]For example, see Blanchard [3]. Note that Blanchard's closed-loop VCO phase noise and instantaneous phase error due to VCO phase noise are the same.

where $1 - H(s)$ is the phase-error transfer function [see (D–28)]. Typical transient input phase functions are

1. A step, $\phi(t) = \Delta\phi\, u(t)$, for which

$$\phi_s(s) = \frac{\Delta\phi}{s} \tag{D–59}$$

2. A ramp (frequency step), $\phi(t) = \Delta\omega t u(t)$, for which

$$\phi_r(s) = \frac{\Delta\omega}{s^2} \tag{D–60}$$

3. A parabola (frequency ramp), $\phi(t) = \frac{1}{2}\Delta\dot\omega\, t^2 u(t)$, for which

$$\phi_p(s) = \frac{\Delta\dot\omega}{s^3} \tag{D–61}$$

4. A parabola in frequency, $\phi(t) = \frac{1}{6}\Delta\ddot\omega\, t^3 u(t)$, for which

$$\phi_{fp}(s) = \frac{\Delta\ddot\omega}{s^4} \tag{D–62}$$

The phase-error responses of a first-order loop to each of the first three inputs, respectively, are

$$(1)\ \psi_s(t) = \Delta\phi\, e^{-Kt} u(t) \tag{D–63}$$

$$(2)\ \psi_r(t) = \frac{\Delta\omega}{K}\left(1 - e^{-Kt}\right) u(t) \tag{D–64}$$

$$(3)\ \psi_p(t) = \frac{\Delta\dot\omega}{K^2}\left(Kt + e^{-Kt} - 1\right) u(t) \tag{D–65}$$

Note that $\psi_r(t)$ is the indefinite integral of $\psi_s(t)$ with $\Delta\phi$ replaced by $\Delta\omega$, and $\psi_p(t)$ is the indefinite integral of $\psi_r(t)$ with $\Delta\omega$ replaced by $\Delta\dot\omega$. Also note that only for the phase step is the steady-state VCO phase error zero. For the frequency step (phase ramp), the steady-state phase error is

$$\psi_{r,ss} = \frac{\Delta\omega}{K} \tag{D–66}$$

which approaches 0 as the loop gain approaches infinity. However, the loop bandwidth also goes to infinity with increasing loop gain so that phase error variance due to additive noise at the input becomes progressively larger with decreasing steady-state phase error. From (D–65), it is seen that the frequency ramp (phase parabola) results in an essentially linearly increasing phase error.

All these comments apply to the case where loop components do not saturate; that is, (D–58) is predicated under the assumption of linear loop operation. For a sinusoidal phase detector, the VCO input is really $K \sin \psi$, so that (D–66) becomes

$$\left| \frac{\Delta \omega}{K} \right| = |\sin(\psi_{r,ss})| \leq 1$$

This establishes the *hold-in range* of a first-order loop as

$$-K \leq \Delta \omega_H \leq K \quad \text{rad/s} \tag{D–67}$$

For a high-gain second-order loop, the phase-error transfer function is given by

$$1 - H(s) = \frac{s^2}{s^2 + 2\zeta\omega_n s + \omega_n^2} \tag{D–68}$$

(see Table D–1). The steady-state phase error can be found from

$$\lim_{t \to \infty} \psi(t) = \lim_{s \to 0} \{s[1 - H(s)]\phi(s)\} \tag{D–69}$$

For the phase step and phase ramp (frequency offset) inputs it is seen that the steady-state phase error for a second-order loop is zero.

The Laplace transform inversion of (D–58) in response to a frequency ramp, (D–61), and parabola in frequency, (D–62), yields, respectively, the following transient response for $\zeta < 1$ for a second-order loop:

$$\psi_p(t) = \frac{\Delta\dot{\omega}}{\omega_n^2} \{1 - e^{-\zeta\omega_n t}[\cos(\omega_n \sqrt{1 - \zeta^2}\, t)$$

$$+ \frac{\zeta}{\sqrt{1 - \zeta^2}} \sin(\omega_n \sqrt{1 - \zeta^2}\, t)]\}u(t) \quad \text{(frequency ramp)} \tag{D–70}$$

$$\psi_{fp}(t) = \frac{\Delta\ddot{\omega}}{\omega_n^3} \{\omega_n t - 2\zeta + 2\zeta e^{-\zeta\omega_n t}[\cos(\omega_n \sqrt{1 - \zeta^2}\, t)$$

$$- \frac{1 - 2\zeta^2}{2\zeta\sqrt{1 - \zeta^2}} \sin(\omega_n \sqrt{1 - \zeta^2}t)]\}u(t) \quad \text{(frequency parabola)} \tag{D–71}$$

Figure D–15 shows the transient phase error due to an input ramp in frequency, and Figure D–16 shows the transient phase error due to a parabolic frequency input. For the frequency ramp, it is seen that the steady-state phase error is

$$\psi_{ss,p} = \frac{\Delta\dot{\omega}}{\omega_n^2} \tag{D–72}$$

Again, use of a sinusoidal phase detector would have resulted in

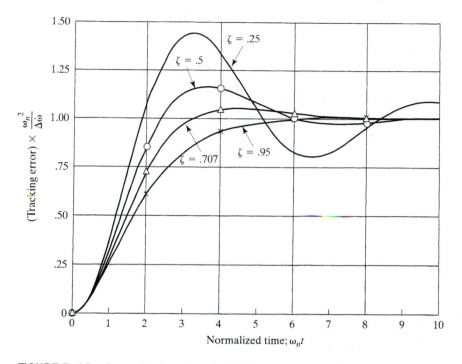

FIGURE D–15   Second-order phase-locked-loop tracking error for frequency ramp input.

$$\sin \psi_{ss,p} = \frac{\Delta \dot\omega}{\omega_n^2} \leq 1$$

which established that the *maximum permissible rate of change of input frequency to a second-order loop as*

$$\Delta \dot\omega_{max} = \omega_n^2 \, \text{rad/s}^2 = 0.53 B_L^2, \quad \zeta = \frac{1}{\sqrt{2}} \tag{D–73}$$

provided that no loop components saturate.

Theoretically, a second-order loop with infinite dc gain can never permanently lose lock. Its response to a large enough frequency offset will be a temporary loss of lock, re-sulting in cycle slipping, after which it will relock. The frequency-step limit below which the loop does *not* slip cycles is called the *pull-out frequency*. It has been established from phase-plane portraits for the second-order loop with sinusoidal phase detector that the pull-out frequency satisfies the empirical relation [1]

$$\Delta \omega_{po} = 1.8 \omega_n (\zeta + 1) \quad \text{rad/s} \tag{D–74}$$

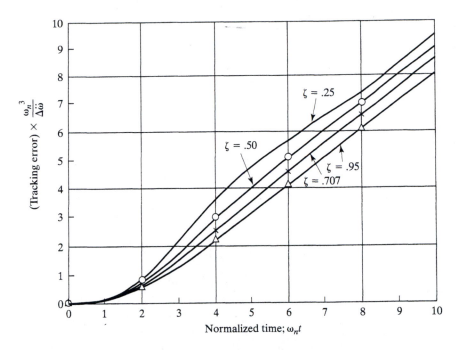

FIGURE D-16 Second-order phase-locked-loop tracking error for frequency parabola input.

D.3.6 Phase-Locked-Loop Acquisition

The initial application of a sinusoidal signal to a phase-locked loop with carrier frequency different from the quiescent frequency of the VCO results in a beat frequency at the VCO output (i.e., the loop slips cycles as illustrated in Figure D–17). The beat-frequency waveform has a nonzero average value, which tends to drive the VCO toward *frequency lock* (i.e., the VCO frequency matches that of the input carrier frequency). The dc component of the phase detector output is called the *pull-in voltage*. In a second-order loop, which includes an integrator prior to the VCO, the pull-in voltage is integrated and the loop will eventually reach frequency lock provided that saturation of a loop component does not occur first.

For a first-order loop, an integrator is not present, and the loop will acquire lock only if the frequency offset is within the *lock-in range* of the loop. The inequalities

$$-K < 2\pi(f_c - f_0) < K \tag{D-75}$$

establish the frequency offset limit of VCO quiescent frequency from input carrier frequency within which a first-order loop may acquire lock. If the magnitude of the frequency offset in rad/s exceeds K, it is impossible for a first-order loop to have a static

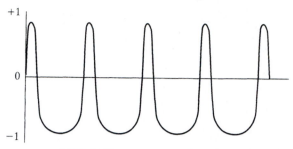

(a) Typical beat-note wave shape, first-order loop,
$\Delta\omega/K = 1.10$ (Gardner)

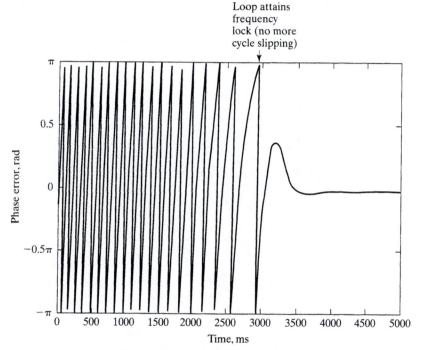

(b) Transient response of a second-order phase-locked
loop with an initial frequency offset of $\Delta f = 10$ Hz
and a Noise Bandwidth of $B_n = 5$ Hz (Spilker)

FIGURE D–17   Phase-error signals for phase-locked loops in acquisition.

phase error which will drive the VCO frequency to match the input frequency. If (D–75) is satisfied, the loop will acquire lock, but the time to lock depends on the initial phase error between the input and VCO. Figure D–18 illustrates phase error transients for a first-order phase-locked loop for an initial frequency offset of zero. It is seen that if the initial phase error is near 180 degrees, an extremely long transient can take place. This phenomenon, known as *hang-up*, is not unique to the first-order loop.

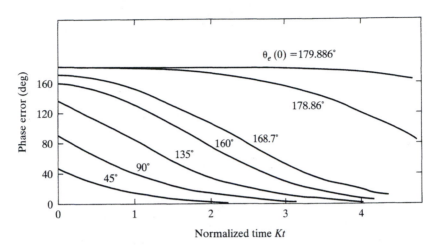

FIGURE D–18   Transient phase errors in first-order PLL. (Reproduced from Reference [1] with permission.)

Returning to the second-order loop, the duration of the initial beat frequency transient illustrated in Figure D–17b is the *pull-in time*. If $\Delta\omega - 2\pi(f_c - f_0) \gg K$, the pull-in time of a second-order loop is approximately [1]

$$T_p \simeq \frac{(\Delta\omega)^2}{2\zeta\omega_n^3} \text{ seconds} \qquad (D\text{–}76)$$

For a high-gain loop with $\zeta = 1/\sqrt{2}$, this becomes

$$T_p \simeq \frac{4(\Delta f)^2}{B_L^3} \text{ seconds} \quad \left(\zeta = \frac{1}{\sqrt{2}}\right) \qquad (D\text{–}77)$$

where $\Delta f = f_c - f_0$ hertz and B_L is the single-sided loop bandwidth in hertz. Once $\Delta\omega \leq K$, the loop ceases to skip cycles and quickly snaps into lock. The additional time required for the loop to *settle*, T_s, is approximately [7]

$$T_s \simeq \frac{1.5}{B_L} \qquad (D\text{–}78)$$

where the final phase error is 0.1 rad or less.

Because the pull-in time for a second-order loop can be exceedingly long, an *acquisition aid* is often used. This usually takes the form of a ramp applied to the VCO input or a square wave applied to the integrator input. The maximum rate of change for the VCO frequency is given by (D–71) under *noise-free* conditions. (Note that there is no difference if a frequency ramp is placed on the input or the VCO output.) With noise present, the sweep rate must be reduced. Empirical data suggest that the maximum sweep rate should be limited to[5]

---

[5]See Gardner [1, p. 81]. Note that Gardner's $(SNR)_L$ is one-half of the definition used here.

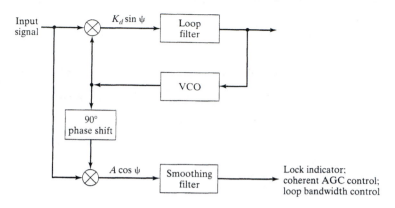

FIGURE D–19   Coherent amplitude detector.

$$\Delta\dot{\omega}_{max} = \omega_n^2[1 - (SNR)_L^{-1/2}] \tag{D–79}$$

where $(SNR)_L$ is the carrier-to-noise ratio with noise measured in a loop bandwidth. Once lock is acquired, the sweep can be removed. If injected as a square wave into the integrator of an active loop filter, the removal of the sweep does not have to be particularly rapid under normal conditions since once the loop is locked the sweep voltage is compensated by the phase detector output.

Removal of the sweep requires the use of a lock detector, which can be implemented by means of the *coherent amplitude detector* illustrated in Figure D–19. The output of such a detector, once the loop is locked, is proportional to signal amplitude at the loop input. Therefore, it can also be used to control open-loop gain, which depends on input signal amplitude. Another way to remove the effect of variations of the input signal amplitude on loop gain is to precede the loop with a limiter.

Another way in which acquisition can be speeded up is to employ a wider loop bandwidth during acquisition. This is shown by (D–77). Narrowing the loop bandwidth once acquisition has been achieved is facilitated by means of a coherent amplitude detector.

Finally, note that the settling time for a phase-locked loop is improved with the addition of noise to the loop, either as external noise or as a *dithering signal*. This is illustrated by Figure D–20 for a second-order loop. Note that an optimum value of the order of 20 dB apparently exists for loop signal-to-noise ratio to provide minimum settling time. The use of phase acquisition aids for reducing settling time has been studied with the conclusion that the phase acquisition time can be reduced for loop signal-to-noise ratios above 12 dB. Below 12 dB, no significant advantage from the acquisition aid was realized [8].

D.3.7   Effects of Transport Delay

At sufficiently high frequencies, the delay associated with the phase-locked-loop layout can effectively add additional poles to the loop transfer function. Thus, a loop designed to be a second-order loop is, in essence, a higher-than-second-order loop. Such delays may

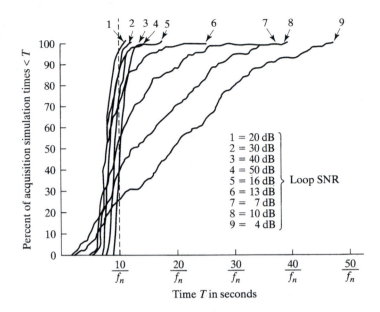

FIGURE D–20   Computer simulations of second-order phase-locked-loop acquisition time for zero-frequency offset and an initial phase error of $\epsilon_\tau = \pi$ rad. (Reproduced from Reference [9] with permission.)

cause a loop to operate in a totally different manner from the one for which it was designed. In particular, a loop designed to be second order and therefore thought to be unconditionally stable may effectively be third order or higher and therefore be only conditionally stable.

D.4   FREQUENCY SYNTHESIS

A frequency synthesizer is a device for generating several possible output frequencies from a single, highly stable reference frequency. Systems applications to communications include HF radio, frequency-division multiple-access satellite communications, and spread-spectrum communications systems. There are three main techniques used for frequency synthesizer implementation, although combinations of these may be used as well as variants of these techniques. The three methods of frequency synthesis are

1. Digital (or table lookup)
2. Direct (or mix and divide)
3. Phase-locked (or indirect)

The function of a synthesizer is described mathematically by the equation

$$f_2 = \frac{n_2 f_1}{n_1} \tag{D–80}$$

where f_1 is the reference frequency and n_1 and n_2 are integers.

Recalling that frequency multiplication of a sinusoid multiplies both the nominal frequency and the phase deviation by the multiplication factor, n_2/n_1, it is seen from (D–1) that the long-term stability of a frequency synthesizer is that of the stable reference multiplied by n_2/n_1. That is, the term $\alpha t^2/2$ in the argument of (D–1), which reflects long-term drift, is multiplied by n_2/n_1, as are the terms $\omega_0 t$ and $\phi(t)$. It is tempting at this point to say that the short-term stability, or phase noise, of the synthesized frequency is determined from $n_2 \phi(t)/n_1$. However, short-term stability depends on the manner in which the output frequencies are synthesized.

Each of the synthesis techniques listed has advantages and disadvantages. The reader is encouraged to consult more detailed discussion of synthesizer design, such as references [5, 6, 8], before embarking on any synthesizer design.

D.4.1   Digital Synthesizers

The basic idea of a digital synthesizer is illustrated by Figure D–21. With each clock pulse, which occurs at frequency f_1, the accumulator increments a phase variable, θ, by the amount $a\Delta\theta$ where a is a proportionality constant. The value of the phase variable, θ,

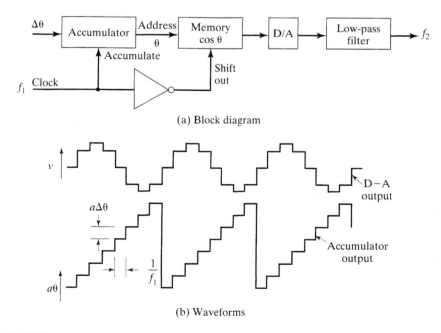

(a) Block diagram

(b) Waveforms

FIGURE D–21   Principle of operation for a digital frequency synthesizer. (Reproduced from Reference [5] with permission.)

serves as the address to a memory containing N-bit numbers proportional to $\cos\theta$, quantized to 2^N levels. The memory output is converted to an analog voltage by a digital-to-analog (D/A) converter.

The capacity of the accumulator corresponds to one complete cycle of $\cos\theta$. Let n_1 be the capacity of the accumulator and let n_2 be the increment in the accumulator value for each clock cycle. Then the number of clock cycles required to cycle the accumulator is n_1/n_2, and the frequency of the accumulator cycle, which is also the frequency of the D/A converter output, is given by (D–80). The resolution of the synthesizer is the change in frequency that occurs when n_2 changes by 1. This is

$$\Delta f = \left(\frac{n_2 + 1}{n_1} - \frac{n_2}{n_1} \right) f_1 = \frac{f_1}{n_1} \tag{D–81}$$

Because the structure of the digital synthesizer implies no fewer than two phase values for each cycle of the output, the theoretical maximum value for f_2 is $f_1/2$. However,

$$f_{2,\text{max}} = \frac{f_1}{4} \tag{D–82}$$

is more practical to allow reasonable lowpass output filters.

EXAMPLE D–4

Consider a digital synthesizer for which the capacity of the accumulator is 2^8. Obtain the following:

(a)   The clock frequency required to produce a 32 kHz resolution.

(b)   The increment in accumulator contents at each clock pulse to produce a 160 kHz output frequency.

(c)   The maximum synthesizer output frequency, $f_{2,\text{max}}$.

Solution: From (D–81) the clock frequency is

$$f_1 = n_1 \Delta f = (2^8)(2^5 \times 10^3)$$

$$= 2^{13} \text{ kHz}$$

$$= 8.192 \text{ MHz}$$

To produce $f_2 = 160$ kHz, n_2 is calculated from (D–80) to be

$$n_2 = \frac{n_1 f_2}{f_1}$$

$$= \frac{(2^8)(2^4 \times 10^4)}{2^{13} \times 10^3}$$

$$= 5$$

From (D–82) $f_{2,\text{max}} = 2^{11} \times 10^3 \text{ Hz} = 2.048 \text{ MHz}$.

Advantages of digital synthesizers are that frequencies can be changed very rapidly and that fine resolution is relatively easy to attain. A disadvantage is that the maximum synthesized frequency is limited, by the speed of the digital logic and memory. The spurious frequency components near the generated frequency depend on the quantization accuracy used to generate $\cos \theta$. Spurious sidelobe levels of -50 to -60 dB relative to the desired spectral component are possible [10].

D.4.2   Direct Synthesis

D.4.2.1 Configurations.   In the direct frequency synthesis process the desired frequency is built up by multiplication, mixing (summation or subtraction of a reference), and division of a single reference frequency. Many combinations obviously can be used to produce a desired frequency in this way. For example, 7381 kHz can be produced as the 7381th harmonic of 1 kHz or as the 7th harmonic of 1000 kHz plus the 3rd harmonic of 100 kHz plus the 8th harmonic of 10 kHz plus the first harmonic of 1 kHz.

Figure D–22 shows a direct synthesizer for producing frequencies over a 10 MHz range with a resolution of 1 Hz. The reference frequencies of 3 MHz and 27 to 36 MHz could be derived by multiplication of a 1 MHz frequency, which in turn is derived from a stable oscillator, say, of 5 MHz by division. Note that at least one input to each mixer overlaps the output frequency range. Thus, it is impossible to eliminate the mixer feed through of this frequency from the output by a fixed output filter. A more practical arrangement which avoids this problem is shown in Figure D–23.

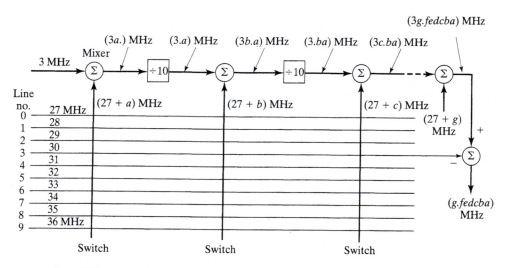

FIGURE D–22   Principle of operation for a direct frequency synthesizer. (Reproduced from Reference [5] with permission.)

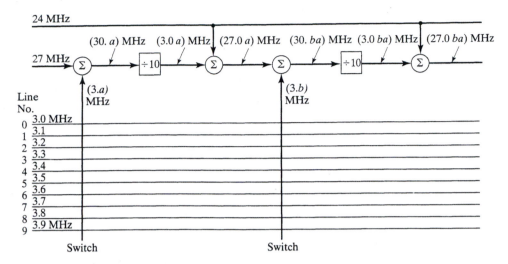

FIGURE D–23   Modified direct synthesizer that avoids mixer feedthrough problem.

EXAMPLE D–5

Synthesize the frequency 7.123456 MHz with the direct-synthesis scheme of Figure D–23.

Solution: Figure D–24 shows the mathematical construction of the desired frequency.

An advantage of direct synthesizers is that the output frequency can be changed rapidly—essentially at the speed of the switches, although some allowance must be made for delay through the system. Another advantage is that the output spectrum can be as clean as the reference oscillator spectrum with FM sidebands increased by the effective multiplication ratio from input to output. In addition, direct synthesizers can have very fine resolution. Disadvantages of direct synthesizers are that they require considerable power because of the large number of LO signals required, and they are bulky. Direct synthesizers with spurious sidelobe levels of −100 dB have been reported.

D.4.2.2 Spurious Frequency Component Generation in Direct Synthesizers. As an example of spurious frequency component generation in direct synthesizers, consider the synthesizer example of Figure D–24 and the potential spurious responses (or "spurs") in the output of the top chain of mixers and dividers.

The spurious response or spurs at a mixer output, with inputs of frequencies f_S and f_L, are defined by the relationship

$$nf_s + mf_L = f_I \tag{D–83}$$

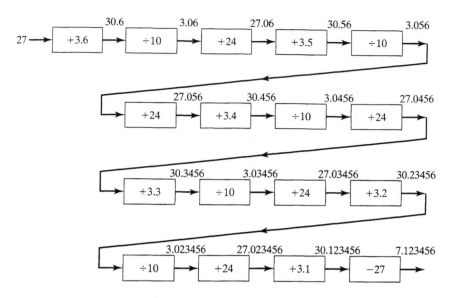

FIGURE D–24   Direct synthesis of the frequency 7.123456 MHz (all frequencies are in units of MHz).

where f_I is the mixer output frequency of interest and m and n are integers. Equation (D–83) results from the fact that no mixer is a perfect product device but, rather, is more accurately modeled as producing cross-products of integer powers of each input at its output. Only one of the resultant output frequencies, usually

$$f_{I1} = f_S + f_L \tag{D–84}$$

or

$$f_{I2} = |f_S - f_L| \tag{D–85}$$

is of interest; others are referred to as *spurs*. The condition $m = 1$, $n = 0$ identifies signal port feedthrough and $m = 0$, $n = 1$ local oscillator feedthrough. The relative amplitudes of these various spurs are a function of the particular mixer design and drive level. Further, where possible, the designer will filter out undesired spurs.

D.4.3   Phase-Locked Frequency Synthesizers

D.4.3.1 Configurations. The block diagram of a simple phase-locked synthesizer is shown in Figure D–25. The condition (D–80) is satisfied by virtue of the fact that the VCO output frequency divided by n_2 is locked to the reference frequency divided by n_1. Output frequency selection is provided by changing the divider integers, n_1 and n_2. Usually, digital counters are used to provide the desired divider integers.

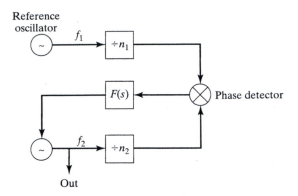

FIGURE D–25   Basic phase-locked synthesizer.

The minimum increment in output frequency is given by (D–81). The loop bandwidth must be smaller than this minimum increment in order to suppress ripple and ensure loop stability. Therefore, small increments in output frequency demand small loop bandwidths. On the other hand, output phase jitter is dominated by the VCO if loop bandwidth is small. In addition, loop acquisition time is inversely proportional to loop bandwidth [see (D–77) and (D–78)], so that small loop bandwidth implies slow switching between synthesized frequencies.

These conflicting requirements present significant challenges in the design of phase-locked synthesizers. One simple solution to this problem is illustrated in Figure D–26, where the final synthesizer output frequency is

$$f_2 = \frac{n_2 f_1}{n_1 m} \tag{D–86}$$

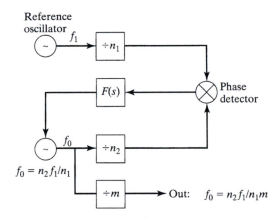

FIGURE D–26   Modified basic phase-locked synthesizer with divider at output.

so that frequency increments of

$$\Delta f = \frac{f_1}{n_1 m} \tag{D–87}$$

are obtained. However, phase comparison occurs at frequency f_1/n_1, which alleviates the loop bandwidth problem by a factor of m through operation of the dividers at the VCO output at m times the frequency required for the basic configuration of Figure D–26.

D.4.3.2 Output Phase Noise. To consider the output phase noise of a phase-locked synthesizer, the model of Figure D–27 will be used and following quantities are defined:

$G_\phi(f)$ = single-sided phase-noise power spectrum of the reference oscillator

$G_\theta(f)$ = single-sided phase-noise power spectrum of the VCO

$\dfrac{2N_0}{A_c^2}$ = equivalent single-sided power spectral level of the additive white input noise *referred to the closed loop* (see Figure D–12)

With these definitions, the phase-noise variance of the phase-locked synthesizer output is

$$\sigma_0^2 = \frac{2N_0 B_L}{A_c^2} + \left(\frac{n_2}{n_1}\right)^2 \int_0^\infty G_\phi(f)|H(f)|^2 \, df$$
$$+ \int_0^\infty G_\theta(f)|1 - H(f)|^2 \, df \tag{D–88}$$

where $H(f)$ is the closed-loop frequency response. Thus, with negligible additive noise, the output phase noise variance is the same as the VCO for small loop bandwidths and that of the reference source multiplied by $(n_2/n_1)^2$ if loop bandwidth is large.

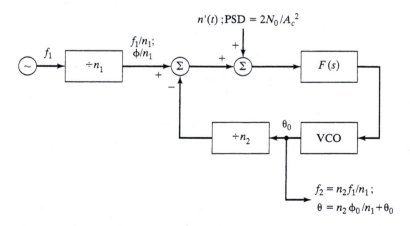

FIGURE D–27   Model for computing phase noise at output of a phase-locked synthesizer (zero subscripts on output phases denote loop filtered quantities).

D.4.3.3 Spur Generation in Indirect Synthesizers. The spur problem also exists in indirect synthesizers and is particularly troublesome in synthesizers where a large tuning range and fast acquisition are desired. The latter implies a wideband loop, although the problem can sometimes be alleviated by using preset tuning of the VCO, which permits a narrower bandwidth loop.

REFERENCES

[1] F. M. Gardner, *Phaselock Techniques,* 2nd ed. (New York: John Wiley, 1979).

[2] A. J. Viterbi, *Principles of Coherent Communication* (New York: McGraw-Hill, 1966).

[3] A. Blanchard, *Phase-Locked Loops* (New York: John Wiley, 1976).

[4] W. C. Lindsey, *Synchronization Systems in Communication and Control* (Englewood Cliffs, NJ: Prentice-Hall, 1972).

[5] W. F. Egan, *Frequency Synthesis by Phase Lock* (New York: John Wiley, 1981).

[6] V. Manassewitsch, *Frequency Synthesizers Theory and Design,* 2nd ed. (New York: John Wiley, 1981).

[7] J. J. Spilker, Jr., *Digital Communications by Satellite* (Englewood Cliffs, NJ: Prentice-Hall, 1977). Chapter 12.

[8] H. Meyr, "Phase Acquisition Statistics for Phase-Locked Loops," *IEEE Trans. Commun.,* Vol. COM-28, pp. 1365–1372, August 1980.

[9] S. L. Goldman, "Second-order Phase-Lock Loop Acquisition Time in the Presence of Narrow-band Gaussian Noise," *IEEE Trans. Commun.,* Vol. COM-21, pp. 297–300, April 1973.

[10] J. Gorski-Popiel, ed., *Frequency Synthesis: Techniques and Applications* (New York: IEEE Press, 1975).

[11] M. Abramowitz and I. Stegun, eds., *Handbook of Mathematical Functions* (New York: Dover, 1972).

The following book is not referenced in this appendix, but is a useful reference on phase-locked loops:

H. Meyr and G. Aschied, *Synchronization in Digital Communications* (New York: John Wiley, 1990).

PROBLEMS

D–1. Referring to Example D–1, find the constants describing the various asymptotes for the *frequency* fluctuation spectral density. Sketch these asymptotes as a function of frequency using a decibel scale.

D–2. For the phase-noise spectral density of Figure D–3, compute the following:
  (a) The rms phase deviation between frequencies 1 to 10^6 Hz of the nominal oscillator center frequency.
  (b) The rms frequency deviation due to phase noise for frequencies from 1 to 10^6 Hz of the carrier.

D–3. Repeat Problem D–2 with power spectra that are 10 dB lower and corner frequencies that are 100 times higher.

D–4. (a) A frequency counter measures the average frequency $\hat{f}$ of a sinusoidal source by counting the phase cycle increase in T seconds of the source output. Neglecting round-off errors and the drift term $\frac{1}{2}\alpha t^2$ in (D–1), the measurement for $\hat{f}$ can be expressed as

$$\hat{f} = \frac{\omega_0 T + \phi(T) - \phi(0)}{2\pi T}$$

where $\phi(t)$ is the phase jitter in (D–1). Let the autocorrelation function of the phase jitter be
$R_\phi(\tau)$. Show that the variance of $\hat{f}$ is

$$\text{var}(\hat{f}) = \sigma_{\hat{f}}^2 = \frac{1}{(2\pi T)^2} E\{[\phi(0) - \phi(T)]^2\}$$

$$= \frac{2}{(2\pi T)^2} [R_\phi(0) - R_\phi(T)]$$

where it is assumed that $\phi(t)$ is a zero-mean wide-sense stationary random process.
(b) If $G_\phi(f) = \mathcal{F}[R_\phi(\tau)]$ is the power spectral density of $\phi(t)$, show that

$$\sigma_{\hat{f}}^2 = 2 \int_0^\infty G_\phi(f) \frac{1 - \cos 2\pi f T}{2(\pi T)^2} df$$

(c) Verify that the result found in part (b) checks with (D–16) if $N \gg 1$.

D–5. (a) Given a phase-jitter power spectrum of the form

$$G_\phi(f) = \begin{cases} \dfrac{k}{f^2 f_1} + N_0, & f < f_1 \\[2ex] \dfrac{k}{f^3} + N_0, & f_1 < f < f_2 \\[2ex] N_0, & f_2 < f < f_3 \end{cases}$$

If $f_1 T \ll 1$ and $f_2 T \gg 1$, show that for this spectrum the frequency measurement variance $\sigma_{\hat{f}}^2$ as found in Problem D–4 is approximately

$$\sigma_{\hat{f}}^2 \approx k f_1 [\tfrac{5}{2} - \text{Ci}(2\pi f_1 T)] + [N_0 f_3 / 2(\pi T)^2][1 - \text{sinc}(2f_3 T)]$$

where $\text{Ci}(x) = \int_\infty^x [(\cos t)/t]\, dt$ is the cosine integral.
(b) The cosine integral can be expanded as

$$\text{Ci}(x) = \gamma + \ln x + \sum_{n=1}^\infty \frac{(-1)^n x^{2n}}{2n(2n)!}$$

where $\gamma = 0.577216$. Neglecting all the higher-order terms above $\ln x$ specialize the result found in part (a) to the case where $f_1 T \ll 1$. Note that $\sigma_{\hat{f}}^2$ increases slowly as f_1 decreases, eventually approaching infinity. The Allan variance, on the other hand,
remains finite.

D–6. Verify the transfer functions (D–27) through (D–29) for the linearized phase-locked loop.

D–7. Verify all the entries in Table D–1.

D–8. Show that the noise component at the output of a multiplier-type (sinusoidal characteristic) phase detector of a phase-locked loop is given by (D–37) and that its spectral density is given by (D–38).

D–9. Show that the phase-error probability density function (D–46) for a first-order phase-locked loop approaches a Gaussian density for large ρ.

D–10. (a) Verify (D–53) for the phase-error variance of a phase-locked loop tracking an oscillator with phase noise modeled by (D–51).

(b) Evaluate σ_ψ^2 for the phase-noise spectrum of Figure D–3 as a function of loop bandwidth, B_L.

D–11. Plot $B_{L,\text{opt}}$ as defined in Example D–3 as a function of $A_c^2/2N_0$. Plot the corresponding values of phase-error standard deviation.

D–12. A polynomial approximation for the modified Bessel function of order zero for $|x| \leq 3.75$ is given by [11]

$$I_0(x) = 1 + 3.5156229t^2 + 3.0899424t^4$$

$$+ 1.2067492t^6 + 0.2659732t^8$$

$$+ 0.0360768t^{10} + 0.0045813t^{12} + \epsilon$$

where $t = x/3.75$ and $|\epsilon| < 1.6 \times 10^{-7}$ [11, p. 378]). Use this approximation and the asymptotic approximation

$$I_0(x) \simeq \frac{\exp(x)}{\sqrt{2\pi x}}$$

to plot (D–46) for ρ = 0.1, 1, and 10. Compare the result for ρ = 10 with a Gaussian density with mean zero and variance 0.1.

D–13. Use the approximations given in Problem D–12 to evaluate the phase-error variance $\sigma_\psi^2 = f_{-\pi}^\pi \psi^2 p(\psi) \, d\psi$ for ρ = 0.1, 1, and 2 with the aid of a programmable calculator. Check the results obtained for ρ = 1 and 2 with Figure D–13. As ρ → 0, $\sigma_\psi^2 \to \pi^2/3$, check the result for ρ = 0.1 with this limiting result. Explain why the phase-error variance approaches $\pi^2/3$ as ρ → 0.

D–14. (a) Evaluate T_{av} as given by (D–47) for a loop bandwidth of $B_L = 20$ Hz and ρ = 0.1, 1, and 10. Comment on the meaning of the result for ρ = 10.

(b) Equation (D–47) is derived assuming a first-order loop using the Fokker–Planck equation. Experimental data have been used to obtain the empirical relation

$$B_L T_{av} = \exp(\pi\rho)$$

Compare T_{av} calculated from this equation with the results obtained in part (a).

D–15. Derive (D–70) and (D–71) for the transient response of a second-order phase-locked loop to a frequency ramp and a frequency parabola.

D–16. Consider the optimization of a second-order phase-locked loop with loop filter $F(s) = (s\tau_2 + 1)/s\tau_1$ in response to a frequency step of a specified value Δω and noise. If the integral-square phase error is to be less than or equal to some value k, what is the optimum value of ζ to minimize the phase jitter due to noise?

D–17. Given a second-order phase-locked loop with active loop filter as in Problem D–16. If its noise bandwidth is fixed, what value of damping factor will permit the largest frequency step $\Delta\omega$ without the loop being pulled out of lock, even temporarily?

D–18. A digital synthesizer that produces a maximum output frequency of $f_{2,max} = 512$ kHz with a frequency resolution of 2 kHz is desired. Compute the capacity of the accumulator and increment in accumulator value for each pulse cycle to produce the following frequencies: 6 kHz; 38 kHz; 40 kHz, 512 kHz.

D–19. **(a)** Using the symmetry of the cosine function, explain how the accumulator capacity for a digital synthesizer can be decreased from that required by (D–81) for a given clock frequency and frequency increment.

  (b) What accumulator capacity could be used in designing the synthesizer of Problem D–18 if this symmetry is employed?

D–20. Consider the digital synthesizer or Problem D–18. Sketch the output waveform for $f_2 = 512$ kHz. Compute the ratio of third harmonic to fundamental components in decibels for this waveform. What order Butterworth filter with a 3 dB cutoff frequency of 1024 kHz would suppress the third harmonic to 30 dB below the fundamental?

D–21. **(a)** Using the block diagram of Figure D–22 to show how the frequency 678.132 kHz could be synthesized. Show both a flow diagram like Figure D–24 and a diagram showing the switch closures for the frequencies 27 to 36 MHz (note that any convenient decade of frequencies separated by 1 MHZ would do).

  (b) Revise the frequency plan found in part (a) to synthesize the frequency 678.132 kHz as shown in Figure D–23. Discuss its merits over the scheme in part (a).

D–22. **(a)** Design a phase-locked-loop synthesizer to provide the maximum frequency and frequency resolution asked for in Problem D–18. Assume that $f_1 = 8.192$ MHz and that a second-order phase-locked loop with $\zeta = 1/\sqrt{2}$ is used. Use the configuration of Figure D–26. Choose a loop bandwidth that gives $T_p + T_s$ for the phase-locked loop of 1 ms or less when switching between adjacent frequencies. Make your selection of n_1 and m compatible with this bandwidth.

  (b) If

$$G_\phi(f) = \frac{10^{-3}}{f^3} + \frac{10^{-5}}{f^2}$$

and

$$G_\theta(f) = \frac{10^{-6}}{f^2}$$

compute the phase jitter on the synthesizer output.

Gaussian Probability Function[1]

The Gaussian probability density function of unit variance and zero mean is

$$Z(x) = \frac{e^{-x^2/2}}{\sqrt{2\pi}} \tag{E-1}$$

and the corresponding cumulative distribution function is

$$P(x) = \int_{-\infty}^{x} Z(t)\, dt \tag{E-2}$$

The Q-function first defined in Chapter 3 is

$$Q(x) = 1 - P(x) = \int_{x}^{\infty} Z(t)\, dt \tag{E-3}$$

An asymptotic expansion for $Q(x)$ valid for large x is

$$Q(x) = \frac{Z(x)}{x}\left[1 - \frac{1}{x^2} + \frac{1\cdot 3}{x^4} + \cdots + \frac{(-1)^n 1\cdot 3\cdots(2n-1)}{x^{2n}}\right] + R_n \tag{E-4}$$

where

$$R_n = (-1)^{n+1} 1\cdot 3\cdots(2n+1)\int_{x}^{\infty} \frac{Z(t)}{t^{2n+2}}\, dt \tag{E-5}$$

which is less in absolute value than the first neglected term. For moderate values of x, several rational approximations are available. One such approximation is

$$1 - Q(x) = P(x) = 1 - Z(x)(b_1 t + b_2 t^2 + b_3 t^3 + b_4 t^4 + b_5 t^5) + \epsilon(x)$$

$$t = \frac{1}{1 + px}$$

$$|\epsilon(x)| < 7.5 \times 10^{-8} \tag{E-6}$$

$$p = 0.2316419$$

$$b_1 = 0.319381530 \quad b_4 = -1.821255978$$

---

[1] The notation used here is that of Abramowitz and Stegun [1, pp. 931 ff.].

TABLE E–1   Abbreviated Table of Values for $Q(x)$ and $Z(x)$

x	$Q(x)$	$Z(x)$	x	$Q(x)$	$Z(x)$
0.0	0.50000	0.39894	2.2	0.01390	0.03547
0.1	0.46017	0.39695	2.3	0.01072	0.02833
0.2	0.42074	0.39104	2.4	0.00820	0.02239
0.3	0.38209	0.38138	2.5	0.00621	0.01753
0.4	0.34458	0.36827	2.6	0.00466	0.01358
0.5	0.30854	0.35206	2.7	0.00347	0.01042
0.6	0.27425	0.33322	2.8	0.00256	0.00792
0.7	0.24196	0.31225	2.9	0.00187	0.00595
0.8	0.21186	0.28969	3.0	0.00135	0.00443
0.9	0.18406	0.26608	3.1	0.00097	0.00327
1.0	0.15866	0.24197	3.2	0.00069	0.00238
1.1	0.13567	0.21785	3.3	0.00042	0.00172
1.2	0.11507	0.19419	3.4	0.00034	0.00123
1.3	0.09680	0.17137	3.5	0.00023	0.00087
1.4	0.08076	0.14973	3.6	0.00016	0.00061
1.5	0.06681	0.12952	3.7	0.00011	0.00042
1.6	0.05480	0.11092	3.8	7.24×10^{-5}	0.00029
1.7	0.04457	0.09405			
1.8	0.03593	0.07895	3.9	4.81×10^{-5}	0.00020
1.9	0.02872	0.06562			
2.0	0.02275	0.05399	4.0	3.17×10^{-5}	0.00013
2.1	0.01786	0.04398			

$$b_2 = -0.356563782 \quad b_5 = 1.330274429$$

$$b_3 = 1.781477937$$

The error function can be related to the Q-function by

$$\mathrm{erf}(x) \triangleq \frac{2}{\sqrt{\pi}} \int_0^x e^{-t^2}\, dt = 1 - 2Q(\sqrt{2}x) \tag{E–7}$$

The complementary error function can be approximated similarly to the Q-function. Note that MATLAB includes erf and erfc functions.

A short table of values for $Q(x)$ and $Z(x)$ is given in Table E–1. Extensive tables of $P(x)$, $Z(x)$ and its derivatives can be found in Abramowitz and Stegun [1].

REFERENCE

[1] M. Abramowitz and I. Stegun, *Handbook of Mathematical Functions* (New York: Dover, 1972). Originally published in 1964 as NBS Applied Mathematics Series 55.

F

Mathematical Tables

F.1   THE SINC FUNCTION

z	sinc z	sinc^2 z	z	sinc z	sinc^2 z
0.0	1.0	1.0	1.6	−0.18921	0.03580
0.1	0.98363	0.96753	1.7	−0.15148	0.02295
0.2	0.93549	0.87514	1.8	−0.10394	0.01080
0.3	0.85839	0.73684	1.9	−0.05177	0.00268
0.4	0.75683	0.57279	2.0	0	0
0.5	0.63662	0.40528	2.1	0.04684	0.00219
0.6	0.50455	0.25457	2.2	0.08504	0.00723
0.7	0.36788	0.13534	2.3	0.11196	0.01254
0.8	0.23387	0.05470	2.4	0.12614	0.01591
0.9	0.10929	0.01195	2.5	0.12732	0.01621
1.0	0	0	2.6	0.11643	0.01356
1.1	−0.08942	0.00800	2.7	0.09538	0.00910
1.2	−0.15591	0.02431	2.8	0.06682	0.00447
1.3	−0.19809	0.03924	2.9	0.03392	0.00115
1.4	−0.21624	0.04676	3.0	0	0
1.5	−0.21221	0.04503			

F.2   TRIGONOMETRIC IDENTITIES

Euler's theorem: $e^{\pm ju} = \cos u \pm j \sin u$

$\cos u = \frac{1}{2}(e^{ju} + e^{-ju})$

$\sin u = \dfrac{(e^{ju} - e^{-ju})}{2j}$

$\sin^2 u + \cos^2 u = 1$

$\cos^2 u - \sin^2 u = \cos 2u$

$2 \sin u \cos u = \sin 2u$

$\cos^2 u = \frac{1}{2}(1 + \cos 2u)$

$\sin^2 u = \frac{1}{2}(1 - \cos 2u)$

$\sin(u \pm v) = \sin u \cos v \pm \cos u \sin v$

$\cos(u \pm v) = \cos u \cos v \mp \sin u \sin v$

$\sin u \sin v = \frac{1}{2}[\cos(u - v) - \cos(u + v)]$

$\cos u \cos v = \frac{1}{2}[\cos(u - v) + \cos(u + v)]$

$\sin u \cos v = \frac{1}{2}[\sin(u - v) + \sin(u + v)]$

$$\cos^{2n} u = \frac{\left[\sum_{k=0}^{n-1} 2\binom{2n}{k}\cos 2(n-k)u + \binom{2n}{n}\right]}{2^{2n}}$$

$$\cos^{2n-1} u = \frac{\left[\sum_{k=0}^{n-1}\binom{2n-1}{k}\cos(2n-2k-1)u\right]}{2^{2n-2}}$$

$$\sin^{2n} u = \frac{\left[\sum_{k=0}^{n-1}(-1)^{n-k} 2\binom{2n}{k}\cos 2(n-k)u + \binom{2n}{n}\right]}{2^{2n}}$$

$$\sin^{2n-1} u = \frac{\left[\sum_{k=0}^{n-1}(-1)^{n+k-1}\binom{2n-1}{k}\sin(2n-2k-1)u\right]}{2^{2n-2}}$$

where

$$\binom{n}{k} = \frac{n!}{(n-k)!k!}$$

F.3   INDEFINITE INTEGRALS

$$\int \sin(ax)\,dx = -\frac{1}{a}\cos(ax)$$

$$\int \cos(ax)\,dx = \frac{1}{a}\sin(ax)$$

$$\int \sin^2(ax)\,dx = x/2 - \sin(2ax)/4a$$

$$\int \cos^2(ax)\,dx = x/2 + \sin(2ax)/4a$$

$$\int x \sin(ax)\,dx = [\sin(ax) - ax\cos(ax)]/a^2$$

$$\int x \cos(ax) \, dx = [\cos(ax) + ax \sin(ax)]/a^2$$

$$\int x^m \sin(x) \, dx = -x^m \cos(x) + m \int x^{m-1} \cos(x) \, dx$$

$$\int x^m \cos(x) \, dx = x^m \sin(x) - m \int x^{m-1} \sin(x) \, dx$$

$$\int \sin(ax) \sin(bx) \, dx = \frac{\sin(a-b)x}{2(a-b)} - \frac{\sin(a+b)x}{2(a+b)}, \quad a^2 \neq b^2$$

$$\int \sin(ax) \cos(bx) \, dx = -\left[\frac{\cos(a-b)x}{2(a-b)} + \frac{\cos(a+b)x}{2(a+b)} \right], \quad a^2 \neq b^2$$

$$\int \cos(ax) \cos(bx) \, dx = \frac{\sin(a-b)x}{2(a-b)} + \frac{\sin(a+b)x}{2(a+b)}, \quad a^2 \neq b^2$$

$$\int e^{ax} \, dx = e^{ax}/a$$

$$\int x^m e^{ax} \, dx = \frac{x^m e^{ax}}{a} - \frac{m}{a} \int x^{m-1} e^{ax} \, dx$$

$$\int e^{ax} \sin(bx) \, dx = \frac{e^{ax}}{a^2 + b^2} [a \sin(bx) - b \cos(bx)]$$

$$\int e^{ax} \cos(bx) \, dx = \frac{e^{ax}}{a^2 + b^2} [a \cos(bx) + b \sin(bx)]$$

F.4   DEFINITE INTEGRALS

$$\int_0^\infty \frac{x^{m-1}}{1+x^n} \, dx = \frac{\pi/n}{\sin(m\pi/n)}, \quad n > m > 0$$

$$\int_0^{\pi/2} \sin^n(x) \, dx = \int_0^{\pi/2} \cos^n(x) \, dx = \begin{cases} \dfrac{1 \cdot 3 \cdot 5 \cdots (n-1)}{2 \cdot 4 \cdot 6 \cdots (n)} \dfrac{\pi}{2}, & n \text{ even, } n \text{ an integer} \\[2mm] \dfrac{2 \cdot 4 \cdot 6 \cdots (n-1)}{1 \cdot 3 \cdot 5 \cdots (n)}, & n \text{ odd} \end{cases}$$

$$\int_0^\pi \sin^2(nx) \, dx = \int_0^\pi \cos^2(nx) \, dx = \pi/2, \quad n \text{ an integer}$$

$$\int_0^\pi \sin(mx) \sin(nx) \, dx = \int_0^\pi \cos(mx) \cos(nx) \, dx = 0, \quad m \neq n, m \text{ and } n \text{ integer}$$

$$\int_0^\pi \sin(mx) \cos(nx) \, dx = \begin{cases} 2m/(m^2 - n^2), & m + m \text{ odd} \\ 0, & m + n \text{ even} \end{cases}$$

$$\int_0^\infty e^{-a^2x^2} \, dx = \sqrt{\pi}/2a, \, a > 0$$

$$\int_0^\infty x^n e^{-ax} \, dx = n!/a^{n+1}, \, n \text{ an integer and } a > 0$$

$$\int_0^\infty x^{2n} e^{-ax^2} \, dx = \frac{1 \cdot 3 \cdot 5 \cdots (2n-1)}{2^{n+1} a^n} \sqrt{\frac{\pi}{a}}$$

$$\int_0^\infty e^{-ax} \cos(bx) \, dx = \frac{a}{a^2 + b^2}, \quad a > 0$$

$$\int_0^\infty e^{-ax} \sin(bx) \, dx = \frac{b}{a^2 + b^2}, \quad a > 0$$

$$\int_0^\infty e^{-a^2x^2} \cos(bx) \, dx = \frac{\sqrt{\pi}}{2a} e^{-b^2/4a^2}$$

$$\int_0^\infty x^{\alpha-1} \cos bx \, dx = \frac{\Gamma(\alpha)}{b^\alpha} \cos \tfrac{1}{2}\pi\alpha, \quad 0 < \alpha < 1, \quad b > 0$$

$$\Gamma(\alpha) \triangleq \int_0^\infty x^{\alpha-1} e^{-x} \, dx$$

$$\int_0^\infty x^{\alpha-1} \sin bx \, dx = \frac{\Gamma(\alpha)}{b^\alpha} \sin \tfrac{1}{2}\pi\alpha, \quad 0 < |\alpha| < 1, \quad b > 0$$

$$\int_0^\infty xe^{-ax^2} I_k(bx) \, dx = \frac{1}{2a} e^{b^2/4a}$$

$$\int_0^\infty \operatorname{sinc} x \, dx = \int_0^\infty \operatorname{sinc}^2 x \, dx = \tfrac{1}{2}$$

$$\int_0^\infty \frac{\cos ax}{b^2 + x^2} \, dx = \frac{\pi}{2b} e^{-ab}, \quad a > 0, \quad b > 0$$

$$\int_0^\infty \frac{x \sin ax}{b^2 + x^2} \, dx = \frac{\pi}{2} e^{-ab}, \quad a > 0, \quad b > 0$$

F.5   SERIES EXPANSIONS

$$(u + v)^n = \sum_{k=0}^n \binom{n}{k} u^{n-k} v^k$$

where

$$\binom{n}{k} = \frac{n!}{(n-k)!k!}$$

Letting $u = 1$ and $v = x$, where $|x| \ll 1$, results in the following approximations.

$$(1 + x)^n \cong 1 + nx$$

$$(1 + x)^{1/2} \cong 1 + \tfrac{1}{2}x$$

$$(1 + x)^{-n} \cong 1 - nx$$

$$\ln(1 + u) = \sum_{k=1}^{\infty} (-1)^{k+1} \frac{u^k}{k}$$

$$\log_a u = \log_e u \log_a e; \ \log_e u = \ln u = \log_a u \log_e a$$

$$e^u = \sum_{k=0}^{\infty} u^k/k! \cong 1 + u, \quad |u| \ll 1$$

$$a^u = e^{u \ln a}$$

$$\sin u = \sum_{k=0}^{\infty} (-1)^k u^{2k+1}/(2k+1)! \cong u - u^3/3!, \quad |u| \ll 1$$

$$\cos u = \sum_{k=0}^{\infty} (-1)^k u^{2k}/(2k)! \cong 1 - u^2/2!, \quad |u| \ll 1$$

$$\tan u = u + \tfrac{1}{3}u^3 + \tfrac{2}{15}u^5 + \cdots$$

$$\sin^{-1} u = u + \tfrac{1}{6}u^3 + \tfrac{3}{40}u^5 + \cdots$$

$$\tan^{-1} u = u - \tfrac{1}{3}u^3 + \tfrac{1}{5}u^5 - \cdots$$

$$\operatorname{sinc} u = 1 - (\pi u)^2/3! + (\pi u)^4/5! - \cdots$$

$$J_n(u) \cong \begin{cases} \dfrac{u^n}{2^n n!} \left[1 - \dfrac{u^2}{2^2(n+1)} + \dfrac{u^4}{2 \cdot 2^4(n+1)(n+2)} - \cdots \right], \\[4mm] \sqrt{\dfrac{2}{\pi u}} \cos\left(u - \dfrac{n\pi}{2} - \dfrac{\pi}{2} \right), \quad u \gg 1 \end{cases}$$

$$I_0(u) \cong \begin{cases} 1 + \dfrac{u^2}{2^2} + \dfrac{u^4}{2^2 4^2} + \cdots \cong e^{u^2/4}, \quad 0 \le u \ll 1 \\[4mm] \dfrac{e^u}{\sqrt{2\pi u}}, \quad u \gg 1 \end{cases}$$

$$\text{erf } u \cong \begin{cases} \dfrac{2}{\sqrt{\pi}}\left[u - \dfrac{u^3}{3} + \dfrac{u^5}{5 \cdot 2!} - \dfrac{u^7}{7 \cdot 3!} + \cdots\right] \\ 1 - \dfrac{e^{-u^2}}{u\sqrt{\pi}}\left[1 - \dfrac{1}{2u^2} + \dfrac{1 \cdot 3}{(2u^2)^2} - \dfrac{1 \cdot 3 \cdot 5}{(2u^2)^3} + \cdots\right], \quad u \gg 1 \end{cases}$$

F.6   FOURIER TRANSFORM THEOREMS

Name of Theorem	Signal	Transform
1. Superposition (a_1 and a_2 arbitrary constants)	$a_1 x_1(t) + a_2 x_2(t)$	$a_1 X_1(f) + a_2 X_2(f)$
2. Time delay	$x(t - t_0)$	$X(f)\exp(-j\,2\pi f t_0)$
3a. Scale change	$x(at)$	$\lvert a \rvert^{-1} X\left(\dfrac{f}{a}\right)$
3b. Time reversal[1]	$x(-t)$	$X(-f) = X^*(f)$
4. Duality	$X(t)$	$x(-f)$
5a. Frequency translation	$x(t)\exp(j2\pi f_0 t)$	$X(f - f_0)$
5b. Modulation	$x(t)\cos 2\pi f_0 t$	$\tfrac{1}{2}X(f - f_0) + \tfrac{1}{2}X(f + f_0)$
6. Differentiation	$\dfrac{d^n x(t)}{dt^n}$	$(j2\pi f)^n X(f)$
7. Integration	$\displaystyle\int_{-\infty}^{t} x(t')\,dt'$	$(j2\pi f)^{-1}X(f) + \tfrac{1}{2}X(0)\delta(f)$
8. Convolution	$\displaystyle\int_{-\infty}^{\infty} x_1(t - t')x_2(t')\,dt'$ $= \displaystyle\int_{-\infty}^{\infty} x_1(t')x_2(t - t')\,dt'$	$X_1(f)X_2(f)$
9. Multiplication	$x_1(t)x_2(t)$	$\displaystyle\int_{-\infty}^{\infty} X_1(f - f')X_2(f')\,df'$ $= \displaystyle\int_{-\infty}^{\infty} X_1(f')X_2(f - f')\,df'$

[1]$x(t)$ is assumed to be real in 3b.

F.7   FOURIER TRANSFORM PAIRS

Pair Number $x(t)$	$X(f)$
1. $\Pi\left(\dfrac{t}{\tau}\right)$	$\tau \operatorname{sinc}(\tau f)$
2. $2W \operatorname{sinc}(2Wt)$	$\Pi\left(\dfrac{f}{2W}\right)$
3. $\Lambda\left(\dfrac{t}{\tau}\right)$	$\tau \operatorname{sinc}^2(\tau f)$
4. $\exp(-\alpha t)u(t),\ \alpha > 0$	$\dfrac{1}{\alpha + j2\pi f}$
5. $t\exp(-\alpha t)u(t),\ \alpha > 0$	$\dfrac{1}{(\alpha + j2\pi f)^2}$
6. $\exp(-\alpha|t|),\ \alpha > 0$	$\dfrac{2\alpha}{\alpha^2 + (2\pi f)^2}$
7. $\exp(-\alpha t^2)$	$\sqrt{\dfrac{\pi}{\alpha}}\exp\left(-\dfrac{\pi^2 f^2}{\alpha}\right)$
8. $\delta(t)$	1
9. 1	$\delta(f)$
10. $\delta(t - t_0)$	$\exp(-j2\pi f t_0)$
11. $\exp(j2\pi f_0 t)$	$\delta(f - f_0)$
12. $\cos 2\pi f_0 t$	$\frac{1}{2}\delta(f - f_0) + \frac{1}{2}\delta(f + f_0)$
13. $\sin 2\pi f_0 t$	$\dfrac{1}{2j}\delta(f - f_0) - \dfrac{1}{2j}\delta(f + f_0)$
14. $u(t)$	$(j2\pi f)^{-1} + \frac{1}{2}\delta(f)$
15. $\operatorname{sgn}(t)$	$(j\pi f)^{-1}$
16. $\dfrac{1}{\pi t}$	$-j\operatorname{sgn}(f)$
17. $\hat{x}(t) = \dfrac{1}{\pi}\displaystyle\int_{-\infty}^{\infty}\dfrac{x(\lambda)}{t - \lambda}\,d\lambda$	$-j\operatorname{sgn}(f)X(f)$
18. $\displaystyle\sum_{m=-\infty}^{\infty}\delta(t - mT_s)$	$f_s\displaystyle\sum_{m=-\infty}^{\infty}\delta(f - mf_s), f_s = T_s^{-1}$

Note: $\operatorname{sinc} u = \dfrac{\sin \pi u}{\pi u}$

$\Pi(u) = \begin{cases} 1, & |u| \le 1/2 \\ 0, & \text{otherwise} \end{cases}$

$\Lambda(u) = \begin{cases} 1 - |u|, & |u| \le | \\ 0, & \text{otherwise} \end{cases}$

Author Index

Subject Index